# ROUTLEDGE HANDBOOK OF AGRICULTURAL BIODIVERSITY

The world relies on very few crop and animal species for agriculture and to supply its food needs. In recent decades, there has been increased appreciation of the risk this implies for food security and quality, especially in times of environmental change. As a result, agricultural biodiversity has moved to the top of research and policy agendas.

This Handbook presents a comprehensive overview of our current knowledge of agricultural biodiversity in a series of specially commissioned chapters. It draws on multiple disciplines including plant and animal genetics, ecology, crop and animal science, food studies and nutrition, as well as social science subjects which explore the socio-economic, cultural, institutional, legal and policy aspects of agricultural biodiversity. It focuses not only on the core requirements to deliver a sustainable agriculture and food supply, but also highlights the additional ecosystem services provided by a diverse and resilient agricultural landscape and farming practices. The book provides an indispensable reference textbook for a wide range of courses in agriculture, ecology, biodiversity conservation and environmental studies.

**Danny Hunter** is a Senior Scientist in the Healthy Diets from Sustainable Food Systems Initiative at Bioversity International, Rome, Italy, and is a member of the Healthy Food Systems node, Charles Perkins Centre, University of Sydney, Australia.

**Luigi Guarino** is currently the Director of Science at the Global Crop Diversity Trust. He has been a consultant to the Food and Agriculture Organization of the United Nations and worked for the International Plant Genetic Resources Institute (now Bioversity International), and for the Secretariat of the Pacific Community (now the Pacific Community) in the Middle East, Africa, the Caribbean, Latin America and the South Pacific.

**Charles Spillane** is the Established Professor (Chair) of Plant Science, and Head of the Plant and AgriBiosciences Research Centre (PABC) at the National University of Ireland, Galway, Ireland. Professor Spillane's Genetics and Biotechnology Lab works on both fundamental and applied research on plant and agricultural biosciences.

**Peter C. McKeown** is a Lecturer in the School of Natural Sciences, National University of Ireland, Galway, Ireland, and Coordinator of the Masters in Climate Change, Agriculture and Food Security (MSc.CCAFS).

# ROUTLEDGE HANDBOOK OF AGRICULTURAL BIODIVERSITY

*Edited by Danny Hunter, Luigi Guarino, Charles Spillane and Peter C. McKeown*

LONDON AND NEW YORK

from Routledge

First published 2017
by Routledge

2 Park Square, Milton Park, Abingdon, Oxfordshire OX14 4RN
52 Vanderbilt Avenue, New York, NY 10017

First issued in paperback 2020

*Routledge is an imprint of the Taylor & Francis Group, an informa business*



*British Library Cataloguing-in-Publication Data*
A catalogue record for this book is available from the British Library

*Library of Congress Cataloging-in-Publication Data*
Names: Hunter, Danny, editor.
Title: Routledge handbook of agricultural biodiversity / edited by Danny Hunter, Luigi Guarino, Charles Spillane and Peter McKeown.
Description: New York, NY : Routledge, 2017.
Identifiers: LCCN 2017011544 | ISBN 9780415746922 (hardback) | ISBN 9781315797359 (ebook)
Subjects: LCSH: Agrobiodiversity.
Classification: LCC S494.5.A43 R68 2017 | DDC 631.5/8—dc23
LC record available at https://lccn.loc.gov/2017011544

ISBN: 978-0-415-74692-2 (hbk)
ISBN: 978-0-367-50518-9 (pbk)

Typeset in Bembo
by Apex CoVantage, LLC

The editors pay particular tribute to the late Juliana Santilli who worked tirelessly for legal protection for the users of agricultural biodiversity and the late Bhuwon Sthapit who contributed significantly to the development of on-farm conservation and community biodiversity management. Their work has not only enriched this Handbook but also the lives of the many farmers and farming communities they supported.

# CONTENTS

# CONTRIBUTORS

**Miguel A. Altieri:** Professor, Department of Environmental Science, Policy, & Management, University of California, Berkeley, California, USA.

**Regine Andersen:** Fridtjof Nansen Institute, Lysaker, Norway.

**Simon J. Attwood:** Agroecology Scientist, Bioversity International, Rome, Italy.

**Devin M. Bartley:** Senior Fishery Resources Officer, Fisheries and Aquaculture Department, Food and Agriculture Organization of the United Nations (FAO), Rome, Italy.

**Ana Bedmar Villanueva:** Research Fellow, Bioversity International, Rome, Italy.

**Fenton Beed:** Regional Director, AVRDC-The World Vegetable Center (East and Southeast Asia), Bangkok, Thailand.

**David Boshier:** Senior Research Associate, Department of Plant Sciences, University of Oxford, Oxford, UK, and Bioversity International, Rome, Italy.

**Juan Ceballos-Müller:** Coordinator, Capacity Strengthening Programmes, ICRA, Wageningen, the Netherlands.

**Daniel Coyne:** International Institute of Tropical Agriculture (IITA), Nairobi, Kenya.

**Ian K. Dawson:** Associate Fellow, World Agroforestry Centre (ICRAF), Nairobi, Kenya.

**Walter Simon de Boef:** Senior Program Officer, Seed Systems, Access & Markets Initiative, Bill & Melinda Gates Foundation Agricultural Development Strategy, Seattle, Washington, USA.

**Fabrice DeClerck:** Senior Scientist, Agricultural Biodiversity and Ecosystem Services, Rome, Italy.

**Thomas Dubois:** Regional Director, AVRDC-The World Vegetable Center (Eastern and Southern Africa), Arusha, Tanzania.

**Ehsan Dulloo:** Programme Leader, Conservation and Availability of Genetic Resources, Bioversity International, University of Mauritius, Reduit, Mauritius.

**Ceiridwen J. Edwards:** Senior Research Fellow in Archaeogenetics, Department of Biological Sciences, School of Applied Sciences, University of Huddersfield, Queensgate, UK.

**Sunday Ekesi:** Principal Scientist and Head of Plant Health Theme, International Centre of Insect Physiology and Ecology (ICIPE), Nairobi, Kenya.

**Dag Endresen:** Senior Engineer, Global Biodiversity Information Facility (GBIF) Norway, University in Oslo Natural History Museum, Oslo, Norway.

**Johannes Engels:** Honorary Research Fellow, Bioversity International, Rome, Italy.

**John H. Fanshawe:** Senior Strategy Adviser, BirdLife International, Cambridge, UK.

**Komi K. M. Fiaboe:** Senior Scientist, Plant Health Theme, International Centre of Insect Physiology and Ecology (ICIPE), Nairobi, Kenya.

**Hannes Gaisberger:** GIS Specialist, Bioversity International, Rome, Italy.

**Barbara Gemmill-Herren:** Focal Point for the International Pollinators Initiative, 2010–2015, Food and Agriculture Organization of the United Nations (FAO), Rome, Italy.

**Paul Gepts:** Distinguished Professor, Department of Plant Sciences, University of California, Davis, California, USA.

**Alessandra Giuliani:** Post-doctoral researcher, Bern University of Applied Sciences (BFH/HAFL), Bern, Switzerland.

**Geoff M. Gurr:** Institute of Applied Ecology, Fujian Agriculture and Forestry University, Fuzhou, China and Graham Centre, Charles Sturt University, Orange, Australia.

**Michael Halewood:** Head of Policy Unit, Bioversity International, Rome, Italy.

**Matthias Halwart:** Fisheries and Aquaculture Department, Food and Agriculture Organization of the United Nations (FAO), Rome, Italy.

**Jean Hanson:** Leader, Forage Diversity Project, International Livestock Research Institute, Addis Ababa, Ethiopia.

**Robert Henry:** Director, Queensland Alliance for Agriculture and Food Innovation, University of Queensland, Brisbane St Lucia, Australia.

**Verina Ingram:** Assistant Professor FNP and Senior Researcher, Department of Environmental Sciences, Wageningen Economic Research, Wageningen, the Netherlands.

**Matthias Jaeger:** Value Chain/Market Specialist, International Center for Tropical Agriculture (CIAT), Cali, Colombia.

**Janice Jiggins:** Guest Researcher at Communication and Innovation Studies, Wageningen University Research, Wageningen, the Netherlands.

**Gudrun B. Keding:** Post-doctoral Researcher, Department für Nutzpflanzenwissenschaften, Georg August University Göttingen, Göttingen and Bioversity International, Rome, Italy.

**Katja Kehlenbeck:** Scientist, World Agroforestry Centre (ICRAF), Nairobi, Kenya.

**Gina Kennedy:** Theme Leader, Diet Diversity for Nutrition and Health, Bioversity International, Rome, Italy.

**Harriet V. Kuhnlein:** Founding Director, Centre for Indigenous Peoples' Nutrition and Environment, and School of Dietetics and Human Nutrition, McGill University, Montreal, Canada.

**Hugo Lamers:** Associate Scientist, Bioversity International, Rome, Italy.

**Marcus A. Lana:** Agricultural Engineer, Institute of Landscape Systems, Leibniz Centre for Agricultural Landscape Research (ZALF), Müncheberg, Germany.

**Kristian Le Mottee:** Junior Research Fellow, School of Environmental & Rural Science, University of New England, Armidale, Australia.

**Roger R. B. Leakey:** Professor, Agroforestry and Novel Crops Unit, Department of Marine and Tropical Biology, James Cook University, Cairns, Australia.

**Didier Lesueur:** CIRAD, UMR Eco&Sols (CIRAD-IRD-INRA-SupAgro), Senior Soil Microbiologist, Land Development Department, Office of Science for Land Development, Bangkok, Thailand, and Adjunct Associate Professor, Deakin University, School of Life and Environmental Sciences, Faculty of Science, Engineering and Built Environment, Melbourne, Australia.

**Brenda B. Lin:** Research Scientist, The Commonwealth Scientific and Industrial Research Organisation (CSIRO), Canberra, Australia.

**Judy Loo:** Science Domain Leader, Forest Genetic Resources and Restoration, Bioversity International, Rome, Italy.

**Isabel López Noriega:** Legal Specialist – Scientist, Bioversity International, Rome, Italy.

**Niels P. Louwaars:** Plantum, Netherlands Association of Seed Companies, and Law and Governance Group, Wageningen University and Research, Wageningen, the Netherlands.

**David E. MacHugh:** Associate Dean for Research, Innovation and Impact, Animal Genomics Laboratory and Conway Institute of Biomolecular and Biomedical Research, College of Health and Agricultural Sciences, University College Dublin, Dublin, Ireland.

**David A. Magee:** Post-doctoral Researcher, Animal Genomics Laboratory, College of Health and Agricultural Sciences, University College Dublin, Dublin, Ireland.

**Paul Marshall:** Centre for Biodiversity and Conservation Science, University of Queensland, Brisbane St Lucia, Australia.

**Peter J. Matthews:** Professor, Department of Social Research, Minpaku National Museum of Ethnology, Osaka, Japan.

**Wendy Lu McGill:** PhD Scholar, Plant & AgriBiosciences Research Centre, National University of Ireland, Galway, Ireland.

**Gennifer Meldrum:** Research Fellow, Nutrition and Marketing Diversity, Bioversity International, Rome, Italy.

**Patrick Mulvany:** Agriculturalist, Food Ethics Council, London, UK.

**Virginia D. Nazarea:** Director, Ethnoecology and Biodiversity Lab, Department of Anthropology, Franklin College, University of Georgia, Athens, Georgia, USA.

**Clara I. Nicholls:** Lecturer, International & Area Studies Academic Program, University of California, Berkeley, California, USA.

**Rodomiro Ortiz:** Professor of Genetics and Plant Breeding, Department of Plant Breeding, Swedish University of Agricultural Sciences (SLU), Alnarp, Sweden.

**Gloria Otieno:** Associate Expert, Genetic Resources and Food Security Policy, Bioversity International, Rome, Italy.

**Stefano Padulosi:** Senior Scientist, Integrated Conservation Methodologies and Use, Bioversity International, Rome, Italy.

**Sarah E. Park:** Managing Director, DevSci Consultancy, UK.

**Craig J. Pearson:** Dean and Professor of Agricultural Policy, Ontario Agricultural College, University of Guelph, Ontario, Canada.

**Ivette Perfecto:** George W. Pack Professor of Ecology, Natural Resources and Environment, School of Natural Resources and Environment, University of Michigan, Ann Arbor, Michigan, USA.

**David J. Perović:** Institute of Applied Ecology, Fujian Agriculture and Forestry University, Fuzhou, China.

**Prabhu L. Pingali:** Director, Tata-Cornell Agriculture and Nutrition Initiative (TCi) and Professor of Applied Economics and Management, Charles H. Dyson School of Applied Economics and Management, Cornell University, Ithaca, New York, USA.

**Srinivasan Ramasamy:** AVRDC-The World Vegetable Center, Tainan, Taiwan.

**Jessica E. Raneri:** Nutrition Research Specialist, Bioversity International, Rome, Italy, and the University of Gent, Gent, Belgium.

**Ramanatha V. Rao:** Senior Adjunct Fellow, Ashoka Trust for Research in Ecology and the Environment (ATREE), Royal Enclave Sriramapura, Bengaluru, India.

**Humberto Ríos Labrada:** Regional Coordinator Latin America, ICRA.

**Cristina Romanelli:** DPA Student, Department of Science, Technology, Engineering, and Public Policy (STEaPP), University College London, London, UK.

**Per Rudebjer:** Head *(ad interim)*, Knowledge Management and Capacity Strengthening, Bioversity International, Rome, Italy.

**Juliana Santilli** (deceased): Lawyer and Public Prosecutor in the Federal District of Brazil, Associate Researcher in Environmental Law, University of Brasília Center for Sustainable Development, and co-founding member, Instituto Socioambiental (Brazilian civil society organization).

**Pitambar Shrestha:** Program Officer, Local Initiatives for Biodiversity, Research and Development (LI-BIRD), Pokhara, Nepal.

**Bhuwon Sthapit:** Senior Scientist, Bioversity International, Rome, Italy.

**Sajal Sthapit:** Deputy Director of Programme Operations, Local Initiatives for Biodiversity, Research and Development (LI-BIRD), Pokhara, Nepal.

**Abishkar Subedi:** Senior Advisor, Genetic Resources and Seed Systems, Centre for Development Innovation, Wageningen, the Netherlands.

**Sevgan Subramanian:** Senior Scientist, Plant Health Theme, International Centre of Insect Physiology and Ecology (ICIPE), Nairobi, Kenya.

**Dan Taylor:** Director, Find Your Feet, London, UK.

**Céline Termote:** Associate Scientist, Bioversity International, Rome, Italy.

**Cristina Tirado:** UCLA Institute of the Environment and Sustainability (IoES), University of California, Los Angeles, USA.

**Irene van Loosen:** Consultant, International Center for Tropical Agriculture (CIAT), Cali, Colombia.

**Nathalie van Vliet:** Associate Researcher, Center for International Forestry Research (CIFOR), Bogor, Indonesia.

**John Vandermeer:** Asa Gray Distinguished University Professor of Ecology and Evolutionary Biology and Arthur F. Thurnau Professor, Department of Ecology and Evolutionary Biology, University of Michigan, Ann Arbor, Michigan, USA.

**Ronnie Vernooy:** Genetic Resources Policy Specialist, Bioversity International, Rome, Italy.

**Barbara Vinceti:** Scientist, Forest Genetic Resources, Bioversity International, Rome, Italy.

**David E. Williams:** Especialista Principal, Resiliencia y Gestión Integral de Riesgos en la Agricultura, Instituto Interamericano de Cooperación para la Agricultura (IICA), San José, Costa Rica.

# INTRODUCTION

## Agricultural biodiversity, the key to sustainable food systems in the 21st century

*Danny Hunter, Luigi Guarino, Charles Spillane and Peter C. McKeown*

### Introduction

Agricultural biodiversity – *the plants, animals and microorganisms that contribute to food and agriculture and whose diversity is the result of interactions between people and their environment over many millennia* – represents one of humanity's greatest resources. Yet, for the most part, we continue to underestimate its importance, let alone the important roles of agricultural biodiversity in ensuring the sustainability of agriculture and food systems. Such systems need to be sustainable if humanity is to deal with the major global challenges of the 21st century: securing universal access to sufficient, healthy, safe food for a growing human population while not destroying the planet, and doing so in a context where climate change is predicted to significantly reduce production and food supplies from major crops, especially in Africa and South Asia (Burke et al., 2009).

Despite supplying large volumes of some agricultural commodities to markets, our agriculture and food systems still fail to feed a significant part of humanity adequately in a nutritionally adequate manner (Godfray et al., 2010). Approximately 795 million people globally are considered to be 'undernourished', 2 billion people are considered 'overweight' or 'obese', while 2 billion lack the vitamins and minerals needed for optimal nutrition. Many of our current food and agricultural systems have severe negative impacts on the environment, leading to the degradation and loss of ecosystems, including the associated biodiversity and ecosystem services they provide (Whitfield et al., 2015). Both intensive and extensive agricultural systems can act as sources of pollution, act as drivers of deforestation and can contribute to climate change (Godfray et al., 2010; Pretty et al., 2010; Foley et al., 2011; Ray et al., 2013). The livelihoods, economic and social well-being provided by agricultural systems to many rural communities worldwide dictate whether farmers and their communities are forced to either hang in, step up or step out of agriculture (Dorward et al., 2009). In parallel with the need to develop more equitable food and agricultural systems, there is a need to transform the vast majority of current agriculture and food systems to more diversified, more ecologically-sound systems with reduced environmental footprints (Godfray et al., 2010; Pretty et al., 2010; Foley et al., 2011; Ray et al., 2013; Tittonell and Giller, 2013; Godfray, 2015; Whitfield et al., 2015; Global Panel on Agriculture and Food Systems for Nutrition, 2016; Haddad et al., 2016; IPES-Food, 2016; Lapena et al., 2016).

There are proposals for possible changes in the governance systems and incentivization regimes that could, in theory, support the emergence of alternative, more diversified and sustainable food systems (IPES-Food, 2016). Current agricultural and food systems are complex with strong inertia effects, including inertia effects due to concentration of power, path dependency, export orientation, expectation of cheap food, short-term and compartmentalized thinking, feed-the-world narratives and contested discourses regarding metrics of success (Vermeulen et al., 2012; Garnett, 2013; Garnett et al., 2013; Lang and Heasman 2015; Haddad et al., 2016). Improving the ways we conserve and sustainably use agricultural biodiversity in both production and consumption systems will be essential in effecting sustainability transformations.

In this Handbook, we have sought to bring together a wide range of experts in all fields relevant to addressing some of the challenges, from ensuring a robust understanding of what agricultural diversity exists, through to case studies championing its use within different forms of food production systems that aspire to be more sustainable, equitable and diversified. Many of the contributors argue that such systems have the potential to ensure greater resilience, together with healthier diets, more sustainable crop improvement and productivity and improved livelihoods, health and well-being. In this introductory section, we briefly summarize the organization of this Handbook and provide an outline of the key points that the authors of each chapter have made.

## Agricultural biodiversity and the 2030 Agenda for Sustainable Development: need for a unified community that fosters cross-sectoral approaches

Part 1, *Biological resources for agricultural biodiversity*, sets out to provide an overview of what agricultural biodiversity actually is, at every scale, and in different broad taxonomic groups. We considered whether we ought to begin with such a definition-based section, as this can give the impression that understanding agricultural biodiversity is predominantly rooted in the act of scientific cataloging, rather than also requiring a focus on the farmers (most of which are smallholders and female), indigenous peoples and other groups which manage agricultural biodiversity in the field (Doss, 2014). However, we finally concluded that one cannot sensibly discuss the context in which agricultural biodiversity is used and conserved without appreciating what the term encompasses. Notably, the concept of agricultural biodiversity is broader than may typically be appreciated, and includes wild edible species, microbes, pollinating and seed-dispersing animals, as well as the livestock, fish and crops with which it is classically associated. The understanding of agricultural biodiversity embraces a range of disciplines across both the natural and social sciences: indeed, agricultural biodiversity is managed and governed by different sectors and actors, not all of whom necessarily speak to each other or work together as effectively as they could. The situation is further complicated by the broad range of organizations, agencies and institutions, both governmental and non-governmental, that work directly on agricultural biodiversity, from the local to the global level.

Part 1 begins with considerations of crops by Robert Henry (Chapter 1), and livestock by Ceiridwen Edwards and colleagues (Chapter 2), respectively. The latter also including consideration of the processes by which genetic diversity arose via domestication using the authors' work in cattle as a case study. These chapters both emphasize that current global food production is rooted in a very narrow genetic base, especially for livestock. Forest and tree genetic resources are then considered by David Boshier and colleagues (Chapter 3), and wild plants and animals by Verina Ingram and colleagues (Chapter 4). In Chapter 5, Devin Bartley and Matthias Halwart turn to aquatic genetic resources: this chapter also considers the issue of domestication, which has occurred in some fish species such as carp (but very minimally in other aquatic species). Geoff Gurr and colleagues (Chapter 6) and Barbara Gemmill-Herren (Chapter 7) both consider the role of animals interacting with plants and livestock, either as pests, predators or parasitoids, or as pollinators, respectively. Finally, the agricultural biodiversity present in the soil is summarized by Fenton Beed and colleagues in Chapter 8.

While each chapter documents the richness of biodiversity, it is clearly evident, as we enter the beginning of the Sustainable Development Goals (SDGs) era, that the world's efforts in conserving agricultural biodiversity are falling dramatically short. The recent 13th Conference of the Parties (COP13) to the Convention on Biological Diversity held in Cancun, Mexico, in December 2016 highlighted a disappointing lack of progress on many of the Aichi Biodiversity Targets, including Target 13:

> The genetic diversity of cultivated plants and farmed and domesticated animals and of wild relatives, including other socio-economically as well as culturally valuable species, is maintained, and strategies have been developed and implemented for minimizing genetic erosion and safeguarding their genetic diversity.

The consensus of COP13 was also a general lack of progress on mainstreaming biodiversity into production systems, including agriculture, forestry and fisheries.

Why is this so? We suggest a large part of the problem is the lack of effective inter-disciplinary and cross-sectoral approaches. Society is consistently failing to recognize and realize the multiple benefits that agricultural biodiversity can bring for sustainable development. Whether it is climate change adaptation or poverty alleviation or better diets and nutrition, agricultural biodiversity can play a part, particularly when it is growing in farmers' fields as well as safeguarded in genebanks and accessible to all. Such benefits are not being realized across sectors and disciplines as they should (Lapena et al., 2016).

Does the 2030 Agenda for Sustainable Development offer an opportunity for a much better unifying narrative for agricultural biodiversity and more diversified agricultural systems? Clearly, agricultural biodiversity contributes to a number of the SDGs, but SDG2 in particular brings together agricultural biodiversity, food security, sustainable agriculture and food systems and better nutrition in a single goal. Yet it could be argued there is a need to better link targets and indicators so that SDG2 goes beyond conventional measures of yield and productivity to better promote and capture diversity and quality in agriculture and food systems and diets (Cassidy et al., 2013; Allen et al., 2014; Johnston et al., 2014). SDG2 could be a rallying point for the agricultural biodiversity community, and others, to realize the multiple benefits highlighted in the previous paragraph through consideration of more effective inter-disciplinary and cross-sectoral approaches, enabling environments and the necessary policy realignment to support dietary and livelihood transformations enabled by agricultural biodiversity.

## A shrinking gene pool: from the origins of agriculture to supermarkets

The history of agricultural biodiversity can be viewed as a series of key events, often labelled as revolutions – the Neolithic Revolution, the Columbian Exchange, the Industrial Revolution, the Green Revolution and even the more recent supermarket, health food and genomic revolutions. Each of these has had positive benefits, but they have also come at a cost, including to agricultural biodiversity (Diamond, 2005).

During the Neolithic period, humans started their transition from nomadic hunter-gatherers to sedentary farmers, which allowed the accumulation of surpluses, rapid population growth, the rise of cities and the development of civilization (Larson et al., 2014). The domestication of crop plants and livestock began 12,000 years ago in the Fertile Crescent, and it is now generally thought that far from being dramatic and sudden, the shift from hunter-gathering to settled agriculture occurred gradually over several millennia. A significant result of the domestication process was an increased reliance of humans on a much-reduced diversity of plant and animal species for their food supply and diet (Prescott-Allen and Prescott-Allen, 1990; Khoury et al., 2014). The number of plants used for food by pre-agricultural human societies is estimated to be around 7,000, but only a tiny fraction of the diversity of the plant kingdom, mostly grass and legume species, were ever domesticated. It is striking that even in the 21st century, the decision to 'choose' these handfuls of species by ancient farmers continues to dominate the world's food supply (Khoury et al., 2014).

The 'discovery' of the Americas in the 15th century boosted the inter-continental exchange of plants and animals, and was generally beneficial to the diversity of food systems and diets. The movement of exploitable plant resources was not only in the direction of the home countries, as colonial powers also took plants from one tropical region of the world to another; for example, the Portuguese took maize and cassava from America to Africa, and the Spanish took maize and sweet potatoes across the Pacific (Gepts, 2006). Freed from disease pressures, these crops, not to mention coffee and rubber, became incredibly important in their new regions (Gepts, 2012).

The Columbian Exchange was not without its downsides, however, with regards to agricultural biodiversity; often, only a few plants per species were transferred. The introduced plants had a limited genetic base that we now realize seriously constrained their exploitation (Gepts, 2012). The cultivation of a small number of susceptible potato varieties contributed to the outbreak of the pathogen *Phytophthora infestans* in Europe (Fry and Goodwin, 1997; Tyler et al., 2006; Cooke et al., 2012). This disease was to have its most devastating impact in Ireland in the mid-19th century with the Great Famine, a canonical example of the perils of over-reliance on limited crop species and varietal diversity by economically vulnerable populations with no access to alternative food supplies (Bourke, 1993; Fraser, 2003).

In developing countries, efforts to introduce modernized agriculture and agrifood models through the Green Revolution from the 1960s onward, with the aid of increased irrigation, pesticides, fertilizer and improved varieties, paved the way for huge production increases of cereals (Conway, 1998; Evenson and Gollin, 2003). These contributed to saving millions from hunger and starvation (Evenson and Gollin, 2003; Pingali, 2012), with perceptions that promotion of a limited number of high-yielding varieties contributed to the loss of landraces from farmers' fields (Smale, 1997).

Today, agriculture, food systems and diets are largely dependent on roughly a dozen plant species originally chosen and domesticated by early Neolithic farmers (Khoury et al., 2014). These crops, together with a half a dozen or so animal species, are today estimated to supply 75% of the world's food, the big three cereal staples – rice, maize and wheat – alone currently providing 60% of the world's food energy intake (Khoury et al., 2014). Within species, there has also been a significant narrowing of the diversity of varieties cultivated in farmers' fields or available in markets.

Part 2 of the Handbook, *The origins and history of agricultural biodiversity*, describes the historical development of our current, threatened agricultural biodiversity. Paul Gepts (Chapter 9) provides a detailed summary of our current understanding of the genetic changes involved in the course of crop domestication, an area where major advances have been made, albeit with many questions remaining to be addressed. The particular issues associated with the domestication of clonal crops are then considered by Peter Matthews (Chapter 10). This chapter highlights the risks of limited genetic diversity in such essential staples as cassava and banana/plantain, and the resulting threats from the spread of diseases and from climate change. David Williams (Chapter 11) and Prabhu Pingali (Chapter 12) address two of the most significant events in the history of agricultural biodiversity – the Columbian Exchange, and the Green Revolution, respectively. Finally, Part 2 concludes with two important chapters which outline the role of agroecological strategies. The first, by Miguel Altieri and colleagues (Chapter 13) considers the importance of polycultural systems while the second, by Roger Leakey (Chapter 14), focuses on the key role that trees play in agroecology.

## Why agricultural biodiversity is important: the imperative of use

Having provided an overview of the breadth of agricultural biodiversity, and the complexity of its development, Part 3, *The value of agricultural biodiversity*, turns to consider its importance: for the long-term maintenance of the agriculture matrix, for ecosystem services, for breeding programmes, as a source of novel products, for climate change resilience and for conservation (the latter a topic returned to in detail in Part 6). The authors in this section demonstrate how agricultural biodiversity is essential for sustainability and how it is the source of genetic material for current and future agricultural systems. Agricultural biodiversity has underpinned our production of food, fodder, fuel and fibre for millennia and, as the following section (Part 4) also highlights, it is essential to human health and nutrition. It is also critical for the livelihoods of many millions of smallholder farmers, and ensures the availability of ecosystem services such as natural pest and disease control, pollination and soil health. Collectively, this all contributes to options for farmers and farming systems to better manage climate and other risks.

The place of all the forms of biodiversity within the wider agricultural biome is reviewed by Ivette Perfecto and John Vandermeer (Chapter 15) using the concept of the 'agricultural matrix', which envisions landscapes as composed of natural habitat fragments embedded in a context of agriculture. They propose this as a multidimensional approach to addressing the often highlighted contradictions around biodiversity conservation, and the rights of local people to decide what to do with their land and natural resources (Clough et al., 2011; Phalan et al., 2011b; Scoones et al., 2015). They suggest that the overall conservation potential of the landscape will depend to a great degree on the nature of the agricultural matrix and that the quality of the matrix can be enhanced by the kinds of biodiverse-rich agriculture practiced by smallholder farmers using traditional or ecological frameworks.

The concept of ecosystem services, whether related specifically to agroecosystems or ecosystems more generally, was defined in the 2006 Millennium Ecosystem Assessment as benefits that people derive from ecosystems. Fabrice DeClerck shows in Chapter 16 that the use of ecosystems services as a framework has been rapidly spreading and is now considered key to documenting the importance of agrobiodiversity to human communities. He suggests that agricultural practices that are rich in biodiversity are likely to be our best opportunity for novel solutions to improve both human and environmental health. He considers that biodiversity-rich agricultural practices have the capacity to provide food and nutrition security while also providing core ecosystem services that underpin sustainable agriculture, including pollination, pest control and healthy soils.

Rodomiro Ortiz (Chapter 17), taking a different argument to that of Perfecto and Vandermeer, proposes that better land-sparing strategies will be needed to minimize the negative impacts of food production on biodiversity. He argues that this can be achieved by maximizing agricultural productivity (e.g. yield/hectare) through improved plant breeding programmes which better exploit the genetic variation in crop wild relatives, landraces or other germplasm, thereby allowing land to be set aside for nature (Phalan et al., 2011a, b; Balmford et al., 2012). This objective can also be facilitated by improved knowledge of how functional genetic diversity of crops is distributed within crop gene pools, underpinned by recent advances in rapid, low-cost genotyping and automated plant phenotyping, which allow rapid screening for desirable traits. Ortiz concludes that to fully realize this potential it will be necessary to embrace a more knowledge-led plant breeding approach to leverage agricultural biodiversity as effectively as possible.

Gennifer Meldrum and Stefano Padulosi (Chapter 18) focus on the many thousands of edible plants that have been neglected by agricultural and rural development but which have significant potential to be better exploited for the benefit of humankind. These neglected and underutilized species remain an important resource for many farming communities living in marginal areas where the Green Revolution has been less successful due to difficult growing conditions and poor access to irrigation and other inputs (Mayes et al., 2012). They argue that improving the yields, processing and marketability of these neglected crops would enhance their contribution to the food security and livelihoods of resource-poor farmers who depend on them for subsistence, as well as supporting adaptation of agriculture to climate change.

Brenda Lin (Chapter 19) describes the importance of agricultural biodiversity for ensuring resilience and food security of farming systems. Inevitably, the need for resilience is becoming ever more urgent due to the growing pressures of climate (Howden et al., 2007; Rickards and Howden, 2012). This section of the Handbook is brought to a conclusion by Simon Attwood and colleagues (Chapter 20), who demonstrate that the different approaches towards determining the value of agricultural biodiversity presented are not mutually exclusive. On the contrary, they are mutually reinforcing.

## Agricultural biodiversity, diets, nutrition and human health: a new agenda?

Part 4, *Agricultural biodiversity: human health and well-being*, addresses the topic of agricultural biodiversity for human health, nutrition and well-being, an issue that has gained in prominence in recent years. As such, it continues the theme of Part 3 by emphasizing the value of agricultural biodiversity and the wider risks to human health and well-being that arise from its loss.

In 2015, the WHO/UNEP/CBD 2015 report *Connecting Global Priorities: Biodiversity and Human Health: A State of Knowledge Review* highlighted the importance of agricultural biodiversity for food security, nutrition and human health (Romanelli et al., 2015). The Rockefeller Foundation-Lancet Commission Report on Planetary Health, *Safeguarding Human Health in the Anthropocene Epoch* (Whitmee et al., 2015), and UNEP's *Healthy Environment, Healthy People* report (UNEP, 2016), also draw attention to the links between agricultural biodiversity and ecosystems, including the essential services they provide to human health and nutrition, and the challenges posed by accelerating global change.

The topic of biodiversity and human health was the subject of a major decision (XII/21) of the CBD, at the 12th Conference of the Parties (COP12) in Korea in 2014. This includes recognition of the relevance of the cross-cutting initiative on biodiversity for food and nutrition, one of three initiatives (the other two on pollinators and soil biodiversity) which fall under the CBD's Programme of Work on Agricultural Biodiversity. Further to this, the FAO Commission on Genetic Resources for Food and Agriculture (CGRFA), at its 14th session in 2013, formally recognized the importance of agricultural biodiversity for human nutrition and diets and requested the preparation of guidelines on mainstreaming biodiversity for such purposes. The resulting *Voluntary Guidelines for Mainstreaming Biodiversity into Policies, Programmes and National and Regional Plans of Action on Nutrition* were adopted at the 15th Session of the CGRFA in 2015. The topic of agricultural biodiversity for improving diets, nutrition and human health is elaborated further in the chapters in this section.

Cristina Romanelli and Cristina Tirado (Chapter 21) provide an overview of key issues at the intersection of agrobiodiversity and human health for both policy and practice (Fanzo et al., 2013), highlighting the common drivers of agrobiodiversity loss and of poor human health outcomes. They propose sustainable pathways towards solutions, highlighting that the conservation and sustainable use of agrobiodiversity to safeguard ecosystem services is not only a promising pathway to long-term environmental and human health, but also an essential element for sustainable development. The authors argue that a focus on agrobiodiversity can not only help ameliorate the critical drivers of biodiversity loss and the incremental impacts of climate change, but in doing so it can contribute to improved health outcomes while bolstering ecosystem and human resilience. Romanelli and Tirado conclude with a call for more and better integrated and interdisciplinary approaches to exploring biodiversity and human health linkages, highlighting the rise of holistic approaches such as EcoHealth (Wilcox et al., 2004) and One Health (Zinsstag et al., 2011), which seek to connect human health with the health of other species and ecosystems. These are approaches with which the agricultural biodiversity community is now beginning to engage.

Romanelli and Tirado also highlight the importance of insect pollinators for provision of ecosystem services and their contribution to the nutritional value of our food supply, showing that without this service, large numbers of people would be vulnerable to serious nutritional deficiencies. Wendy Lu McGill and colleagues (Chapter 22) take this a step further by elaborating the nutritional benefits of the direct consumption of insects and the contributions edible insects can make to healthy and sustainable diets (Van Huis, 2013). They point out that, despite preconceived notions about eating insects being a minority activity, it is more the norm than the exception at the global scale. Edible insects provide a safe, nutritious source of micronutrients and protein for an estimated 2 billion people in Asia, sub-Saharan Africa and Latin America.

Juliana Santilli (Chapter 23) reviews how legal instruments aimed at safeguarding cultural heritage can be used to promote biodiversity-rich agricultural systems and traditional foodways (Forson and Counihan, 2013), whether tangible (agroecosystems, cultivated plants) or intangible (agricultural techniques, practices and knowledge). She singles out two particular international legal instruments, the UNESCO (1972; 2003) Convention for the Protection of the World Cultural and Natural Heritage and the Convention for the Safeguarding of the Intangible Cultural Heritage, as having multiple benefits, not only conserving and promoting agrobiodiversity and food diversity, but also many other elements of human health and well-being, especially among local and Indigenous communities, a theme taken up by the next chapter.

Indigenous peoples' food systems and cultures often demonstrate a remarkable complexity and diversity built upon many generations of nurturing and conserving a rich agricultural biodiversity heritage (Anaya 2004). Yet, Indigenous peoples, irrespective of geography, suffer higher rates of poor health compared with non-indigenous peoples, and poor diet is identified as a significant risk factor for premature death among many Indigenous groups (Stephens et al., 2005). These are themes taken up by Harriet Kuhnlein (Chapter 24), who surveys the diversity of traditional food systems of Indigenous peoples and the vast collective knowledge rooted in historical continuity within their territories. In some instances, knowledge of local food resources has been documented to include up to 390 plant and animal species, many of them uncultivated foods harvested from the wild within an ecosystem that may be only a few square kilometres in area. Yet this knowledge and the historical connection to local territories is under threat from major social, economic and environmental changes. In particular, she highlights that people's migration away from their homelands to urban areas for employment, or simply by being forced out by settlers and colonists, often sets in motion a series of events that have a serious impact on Indigenous peoples' access to their traditional food base. With this can come significant dietary change, with possible health consequences leading to chronic disease.

Jessica Raneri and Gina Kennedy (Chapter 25) then explore the possible impact pathways that can increase the availability of diverse and nutrient-dense foods for consumption by households.

They survey the significant differences in macro- and micronutrient content which exists not only among all agrobiodiversity species but also within species, highlighting that this could mean the difference between a diet being adequate or inadequate in the nutrients the body requires. Raneri and Kennedy conclude by trying to unravel the barriers to better understanding the role of biodiversity for improved diets.

## Agricultural biodiversity: the shape of things to come?

Who protects agrobiodiversity? Who *should* protect it? And by what means? Part 5, *The drivers of agricultural biodiversity*, considers these questions in light of the proliferation of policy and legal frameworks which govern key issues such as access and benefit-sharing relating to agricultural biodiversity. The section also examines how issues such as land-use planning and change, urbanization, climate change, gender, consumer-demand and seed systems can also shape agricultural biodiversity.

Juliana Santilli (Chapter 26) presents an overview of the key legal and policy frameworks within which the ownership and use of agricultural biodiversity are governed, including a focus on relevant access and benefit-sharing regulations and their impact on agricultural biodiversity under the Convention on Biological Diversity (1992) and its Nagoya Protocol (2010) and the International Treaty on Plant Genetic Resources for Food and Agriculture (2001). Issues relating to intellectual property rights and plant varieties are also considered.

Ana Bedmar Villanueva and colleagues (Chapter 27) consider the requirement for robust access and benefit-sharing policies as an essential component of any framework governing agricultural biodiversity, using the context of facilitating the exchange and use of plant genetic resources for climate change adaptation. Their chapter describes methods to identify climate change impacts and potentially adapted genetic materials, and also summarizes the progress made in selected countries to develop supportive policies.

Regine Andersen (Chapter 28) asks two key questions: Who owns agricultural biodiversity? And, what rights and responsibilities does this ownership imply? She makes use of diverse case studies, including many from the developing world, but also some based on work with Norwegian farmers.

Craig Pearson (Chapter 29) considers the links, both positive and negative, between land-use change and agricultural biodiversity. Matthias Jaeger and colleagues (Chapter 30) address the often overlooked role of consumer choice in supporting the conservation of agricultural biodiversity. Case studies from different regions of the world are presented to provide insights on the potential of market-based approaches to stimulate agrobiodiversity conservation and use while simultaneously enhancing livelihoods. In a similar vein, Chapter 31 by Walter de Boef and Abishkar Subedi considers the role that communities play in maintaining biodiversity in its entirety and how this can be better supported.

Gudrun Keding and colleagues (Chapter 32) address an aspect which will be of growing importance in the years ahead: urban agriculture as a driver of agricultural biodiversity. There are opportunities for integrating agricultural biodiversity into urban food systems and conservation schemes, but also risks related to questions of health and safety, relating to control of agricultural pests and diseases.

Janice Jiggins (Chapter 33) focuses on the gender ramifications of agricultural biodiversity conservation and use, and summarizes some lessons that have been drawn from gender research and development practice. The chapter illustrates common components of landscape-scale efforts to conserve and develop agricultural biodiversity in ways that seek to transform agricultural systems while also benefiting and empowering women.

The final chapter of this section, by Niels Louwaars (Chapter 34), considers the importance of understanding seed systems as a contributing factor to the maintenance of agrobiodiversity. It also analyses how important regulatory frameworks influence seed systems.

## The need for conservation: that which is important will not save itself!

The final section of the Handbook, Part 6, *Safeguarding agricultural biodiversity*, addresses the key question that arises from the foregoing – given that we will need agricultural biodiversity more and more and in perpetuity, how should agricultural biodiversity best be safeguarded for current and future generations? The main underlying theme is our consideration that both the *ex situ/in situ* and the conservation/use dichotomies are unhelpful and have contributed to unnecessary polarization within the field.

At a time when biodiversity is being lost in many places, as noted in Part 1, Bhuwon Sthapit and colleagues (Chapter 35) point out that there are farmers who continue to actively maintain and employ agricultural biodiversity on their farms, and who possess specialized knowledge about its characteristics and uses. They call for their recognition as 'custodian farmers' and for their current and future role in the conservation and continued evolution of agricultural biodiversity to be more systematically researched and recognized. Such a role could include the production of basic seed on behalf of community seedbanks or even private seed companies.

*Ex situ* conservation approaches are summarized by Ehsan Dulloo and colleagues (Chapter 36), including technical considerations related to long-term storage of propagules. This chapter is complemented by Ronnie Vernooy and colleagues (Chapter 37), who discuss the specific importance of community seed banks, which they describe as locally governed and managed, mostly informal, institutions whose core function is to conserve, restore, revitalize, strengthen and improve local seed systems. They also stress that many community seed banks strive to regain, maintain and increase the control of farmers and local communities over seeds and to strengthen cooperation among farmers, and between farmers and others involved in the conservation and sustainable use of agricultural biodiversity.

Chapters 38 and 39 further elaborate this theme by grounding conservation within the context of communities of 'ownership' and 'memory'. Dan Taylor (Chapter 38) revisits the notion of farmer custodianship of agricultural biodiversity and the knowledge and innovation that underpins it as an expression of farmer identity. Taylor points out that to be a farmer is a statement of practice and place that is both relational and contextual, in which seeds are embodied with cultural meaning, as well as being instrumental in food and farming outcomes. Farmers reinvent their identities in the process of seed conservation, and in the generation and selection of crop diversity. Virginia Nazarea (Chapter 39) argues that from plant exploration worldwide to conservation in genebanks the discourse of crop biodiversity conservation has been dominated by *landscapes of loss* that promote the principle of containment in cold storage, in perpetuity for humankind. By evoking *landscapes of remembrance*, she challenges this narrative, emphasizing the everyday practices and sensory memories that crops and other culturally significant plants inhabit and evoke. Nazarea argues that these compelling and enduring practices, sensations and sentiments have much relevance to the conservation of biodiversity and calls for greater examination of the interplay between *loss* and *remembrance* in biodiversity conservation.

A case study of the use of agricultural biodiversity as the basis for a participatory plant breeding program in Cuba is presented by Humberto Ríos Labrada and Juan Ceballos-Müller (Chapter 40), which highlights the re-engagement of farmers into plant breeding and crop diversity conservation as well as strengthening local innovation systems. Johannes Engels and Per Rudebjer (Chapter 41) consider the broader institutional framework and capacity needed for effective conservation and use of agrobiodiversity (again encompassing both *in situ* and *ex situ* approaches) (Spillane et al., 1999), and show how this raises two major challenges: (1) the need to operate across multiple sectors, and (2) to integrate agricultural biodiversity into research and development agendas within each sector, be it agriculture, forestry, biodiversity conservation or nutrition.

Dag Endresen (Chapter 42) provides an in-depth account of how the information generated by conservation approaches can be stored, managed and made available. This is an important issue, as there is a significant risk that accessibility of data related to conserved agrobiodiversity could become a bottleneck to its subsequent use. What happens to the records that are generated? Can farmers view them online? Can they be used by practitioners of agroecology as well as by molecular breeders?

Finally, Patrick Mulvany (Chapter 43) promotes the place of communities in ensuring sustainable use of agricultural biodiversity, in a chapter entitled, 'Biodiversity Is Given Life by Small-Scale Food Providers: Defending Agricultural Biodiversity and Ecological Food Provision in the Framework of Food Sovereignty', and which serves in some ways as a summary of the future challenges within the field. Mulvany argues that given the inter-dependencies described for agricultural biodiversity and ecological food provision developed in the framework of the food sovereignty movement (Bernstein, 2014; Jansen, 2015; McMichael, 2015), the food sovereignty movement needs to give as high a priority to defending access to, and control over, agricultural biodiversity as it does currently to defending peasant seeds.

## References


Allen, T., Prosperi, P., Cogill, B. and Flichman, G. (2014) 'Agricultural biodiversity, social–ecological systems and sustainable diets', *Proceedings of the Nutrition Society*, vol. 73, pp. 498–508.

Anaya, S. J. (2004) *Indigenous Peoples in International Law*, Oxford University Press, Oxford, UK.

Balmford, A., Green, R. and Phalan, B. (2012) 'What conservationists need to know about farming', *Proceedings of the Royal Society of London B–Biological Sciences*, vol. 279, pp. 2714–2724.

Bernstein, H. (2014) 'Food sovereignty via the "peasant way": A sceptical view', *Journal of Peasant Studies*, vol. 41, pp. 1031–1063.

Bourke, A. (1993) *'The Visitation of God?': The Potato and the Great Irish Famine*, Lilliput Press Ltd., Dublin, Ireland.

Burke, M. B., Lobell, D. B. and Guarino, L. (2009) 'Shifts in African crop climates by 2050, and the implications for crop improvement and genetic resources conservation', *Global Environmental Change*, vol. 19, pp. 317–325.

Cassidy, E. S., West, P. C., Gerber, J. S. and Foley, J. A. (2013) 'Redefining agricultural yields: From tonnes to people nourished per hectare', *Environmental Research Letters*, vol. 8, p. 034015.

Clough, Y., Barkmann, J., Juhrbandt, J., Kessler, M., Wanger, T. C., Anshary, A., Buchori, D., Cicuzza, D., Darras, K. and Putra, D. D. (2011) 'Combining high biodiversity with high yields in tropical agroforests', *Proceedings of the National Academy of Sciences USA*, vol. 108, pp. 8311–8316.

Conway, G. (1998) *The Doubly Green Revolution: Food for All in the Twenty-First Century*, Cornell University Press, Ithaca, NY, USA.

Cooke, D. E., Cano, L. M., Raffaele, S., Bain, R. A., Cooke, L. R., Etherington, G. J., Deahl, K. L., Farrer, R. A., Gilroy, E. M. and Goss, E. M. (2012) 'Genome analyses of an aggressive and invasive lineage of the Irish potato famine pathogen', *PLoS Pathogens*, vol. 8, p. e1002940.

Diamond, J. (2005) *Collapse: How Societies Choose to Fail or Succeed*, Penguin, London, UK.

Dorward, A., Anderson, S., Bernal, Y. N., Vera, E. S., Rushton, J., Pattison, J. and Paz, R. (2009) 'Hanging in, stepping up and stepping out: Livelihood aspirations and strategies of the poor', *Development in Practice*, vol. 19, pp. 240–247.

Doss, C. (2014) 'If women hold up half the sky, how much of the world's food do they produce?', pp. 69–88 in A. R. Quisumbing, R. Meinzen-Dick, T. L. Raney, A. Croppenstedt, J. A. Behrman and A. Peterman (eds.), *Gender in Agriculture*, Springer International Publishing AG, Cham, Switzerland.

Evenson, R. E. and Gollin, D. (2003) 'Assessing the impact of the Green Revolution, 1960 to 2000', *Science*, vol. 300, pp. 758–762.

Fanzo, J., Hunter, D., Borelli, T. and Mattei, F. (2013) *Diversifying Food and Diets: Using Agricultural Biodiversity to Improve Nutrition and Health*, Routledge, Abingdon, UK.

Foley, J. A., Ramankutty, N., Brauman, K. A., Cassidy, E. S., Gerber, J. S., Johnston, M., Mueller, N. D., O'Connell, C., Ray, D. K. and West, P. C. (2011) 'Solutions for a cultivated planet', *Nature*, vol. 478, pp. 337–342.

Forson, P. W. and Counihan, C. (2013) *Taking Food Public: Redefining Foodways in a Changing World*, Routledge, Abingdon, UK.

Fraser, E. D. (2003) 'Social vulnerability and ecological fragility: Building bridges between social and natural sciences using the Irish Potato Famine as a case study', *Conservation Ecology*, vol. 7, p. 9.

Fry, W. E. and Goodwin, S. B. (1997) 'Resurgence of the Irish potato famine fungus', *Bioscience*, vol. 47, pp. 363–371.

Garnett, T. (2013) 'Food sustainability: Problems, perspectives and solutions', *Proceedings of the Nutrition Society*, vol. 72, pp. 29–39.

Garnett, T., Appleby, M., Balmford, A., Bateman, I., Benton, T., Bloomer, P., Burlingame, B., Dawkins, M., Dolan, L. and Fraser, D. (2013) 'Sustainable intensification in agriculture: Premises and policies', *Science*, vol. 341, pp. 33–34.

Gepts, P. (2006) 'Plant genetic resources conservation and utilization', *Crop Science*, vol. 46, pp. 2278–2292.

Gepts, P. (2012) *Biodiversity in Agriculture: Domestication, Evolution, and Sustainability*, Cambridge University Press, Cambridge, UK.

Global Panel on Agriculture and Food Systems for Nutrition (2016) *Food Systems and Diets: Facing the Challenges of the 21st Century*, London, UK.

Godfray, H.C.J. (2015) 'The debate over sustainable intensification', *Food Security*, vol. 7 (2), pp. 199–208.

Godfray, H.C.J., Beddington, J. R., Crute, I. R., Haddad, L., Lawrence, D., Muir, J. F., Pretty, J., Robinson, S., Thomas, S. M. and Toulmin, C. (2010) 'Food security: The challenge of feeding 9 billion people', *Science*, vol. 327 (5967), pp. 812–818.

Haddad, L., Hawkes, C., Webb, P., Thomas, S., Beddington, J., Wagge, J. and Flynn, D. (2016) 'A new global research agenda for food', *Nature*, vol. 540, pp. 30–32.

Howden, S. M., Soussana, J.-F., Tubiello, F. N., Chhetri, N., Dunlop, M. and Meinke, H. (2007) 'Adapting agriculture to climate change', *Proceedings of the National Academy of Sciences USA*, vol. 104, pp. 19691–19696.

IPES-Food (2016) *From Uniformity to Diversity: A Paradigm Shift from Industrial Agriculture to Diversified Agroecological Systems*, International Panel of Experts on Sustainable Food Systems.

Jansen, K. (2015) 'The debate on food sovereignty theory: Agrarian capitalism, dispossession and agroecology', *Journal of Peasant Studies*, vol. 42, pp. 213–232.

Johnston, J. L., Fanzo, J. C. and Cogill, B. (2014) 'Understanding sustainable diets: A descriptive analysis of the determinants and processes that influence diets and their impact on health, food security, and environmental sustainability', *Advances in Nutrition*, vol. 5, pp. 418–429.

Khoury, C. K., Bjorkman, A. D., Dempewolf, H., Ramirez-Villegas, J., Guarino, L., Jarvis, A., Rieseberg, L. H. and Struik, P. C. (2014) 'Increasing homogeneity in global food supplies and the implications for food security', *Proceedings of the National Academy of Sciences USA*, vol. 111, pp. 4001–4006.

Lang, T. and Heasman, M. (2015) *Food Wars: The Global Battle for Mouths, Minds and Markets*, Routledge, Abingdon, UK.

Lapena, I., Halewood, M. and Hunter, D. (2016) 'Mainstreaming agricultural biological diversity across sectors through NBSAPs: Missing links to climate change adaptation, dietary diversity and the Plant Treaty', *Climate Change, Agriculture and Food Security (CCAFS) Info Note*, December 2016 edition, CIAT, Cali, Colombia.

Larson, G., Piperno, D. R., Allaby, R. G., Purugganan, M. D., Andersson, L., Arroyo-Kalin, M., Barton, L., Vigueira, C. C., Denham, T. and Dobney, K. (2014) 'Current perspectives and the future of domestication studies', *Proceedings of the National Academy of Sciences USA*, vol. 111, pp. 6139–6146.

Mayes, S., Massawe, F., Alderson, P., Roberts, J., Azam-Ali, S. and Hermann, M. (2012) 'The potential for underutilized crops to improve security of food production', *Journal of Experimental Botany*, vol. 63, pp. 1075–1079.

McMichael, P. (2015) 'A comment on Henry Bernstein's way with peasants, and food sovereignty', *Journal of Peasant Studies*, vol. 42, pp. 193–204.

Phalan, B., Balmford, A., Green, R. E. and Scharlemann, J. P. (2011a) 'Minimising the harm to biodiversity of producing more food globally', *Food Policy*, vol. 36, pp. S62–S71.

Phalan, B., Onial, M., Balmford, A. and Green, R. E. (2011b) 'Reconciling food production and biodiversity conservation: Land sharing and land sparing compared', *Science*, vol. 333, pp. 1289–1291.

Pingali, P. L. (2012) 'Green revolution: Impacts, limits, and the path ahead', *Proceedings of the National Academy of Sciences USA*, vol. 109, pp. 12302–12308.

Prescott-Allen, R. and Prescott-Allen, C. (1990) 'How many plants feed the world?', *Conservation Biology*, vol. 4, pp. 365–374.

Pretty, J., Sutherland, W. J., Ashby, J., Auburn, J., Baulcombe, D., Bell, M., Bentley, J., Bickersteth, S., Brown, K. and Burke, J. (2010) 'The top 100 questions of importance to the future of global agriculture', *International Journal of Agricultural Sustainability*, vol. 8, pp. 219–236.

Ray, D. K., Mueller, N. D., West, P. C. and Foley, J. A. (2013) 'Yield trends are insufficient to double global crop production by 2050', *PloS ONE*, vol. 8, p. e66428.

Rickards, L. and Howden, S. (2012) 'Transformational adaptation: Agriculture and climate change', *Crop and Pasture Science*, vol. 63, pp. 240–250.

Romanelli, C., Cooper, D., Campbell-Lendrum, D., Maiero, M., Karesh, W., Hunter, D. and Golden, C. (eds.) (2015) *Connecting Global Priorities: Biodiversity and Human Health: A State of Knowledge Review*, World Health Organistion/Secretariat of the UN Convention on Biological Diversity, Geneva, Switzerland and Montreal, Canada.

Scoones, I., Leach, M. and Newell, P. (2015) *The Politics of Green Transformations*, Routledge, Abingdon, UK.

Smale, M. (1997) 'The green revolution and wheat genetic diversity: Some unfounded assumptions', *World Development*, vol. 25, pp. 1257–1269.

Spillane, C., Engels, J., Fassil, H., Withers, L., Cooper, D. and Spillane, C. (1999) 'Strengthening national programmes for plant genetic resources for food and agriculture', pp. 1–52 in *Issues in Genetic Resources*, Vol. 8, J. Engels (ed.), Bioversity International, Maccarese, Italy.

Stephens, C., Nettleton, C., Porter, J., Willis, R. and Clark, S. (2005) 'Indigenous peoples' health: Why are they behind everyone, everywhere?', *The Lancet*, vol. 366, pp. 10–13.

Tittonell, P. and Giller, K. E. (2013) 'When yield gaps are poverty traps: The paradigm of ecological intensification in African smallholder agriculture', *Field Crops Research*, vol. 143, pp. 76–90.

Tyler, B. M., Tripathy, S., Zhang, X., Dehal, P., Jiang, R. H., Aerts, A., Arredondo, F. D., Baxter, L., Bensasson, D. and Beynon, J. L. (2006) '*Phytophthora* genome sequences uncover evolutionary origins and mechanisms of pathogenesis', *Science*, vol. 313, pp. 1261–1266.

UNESCO (1972) Convention Concerning the Protection of the World Cultural and Natural Heritage. http://whc.unesco.org/en/conventiontext/

UNESCO (2003) Text of the Convention for the Safeguarding of the Intangible Cultural Heritage. https://ich.unesco.org/en/convention

United Nations Environmental Programme (UNEP) (2016) *Healthy Environment, Healthy People*, draft report submitted to the Open-Ended CPR, UNEP, Nairobi, Kenya.

Van Huis, A. (2013) 'Potential of insects as food and feed in assuring food security', *Annual Review of Entomology*, vol. 58, pp. 563–583.

Vermeulen, S. J., Campbell, B. M. and Ingram, J. S. (2012) 'Climate change and food systems', *Annual Review of Environment and Resources*, vol. 37, pp. 195–222.

Whitfield, S., Benton, T. G., Dallimer, M., Firbank, L. G., Poppy, G. M., Sallu, S. M. and Stringer, L. C. (2015) 'Sustainability spaces for complex agri-food systems', *Food Security*, vol. 7, pp. 1291–1297.

Whitmee, S., Haines, A., Beyrer, C., Boltz, F., Capon, A. G., de Souza Dias, B. F., Ezeh, A., Frumkin, H., Gong, P. and Head, P. (2015) 'Safeguarding human health in the Anthropocene epoch: Report of The Rockefeller Foundation – Lancet Commission on planetary health', *The Lancet*, vol. 386, pp. 1973–2028.

Wilcox, B. A., Aguirre, A. A., Daszak, P., Horwitz, P., Martens, P., Parkes, M., Patz, J. A. and Waltner-Toews, D. (2004) 'EcoHealth: A transdisciplinary imperative for a sustainable future', *EcoHealth*, vol. 1, pp. 3–5.

Zinsstag, J., Schelling, E., Waltner-Toews, D. and Tanner, M. (2011) 'From "one medicine" to "one health" and systemic approaches to health and well-being', *Preventive Veterinary Medicine*, vol. 101, pp. 148–156.

# PART 1

# Biological resources for agricultural biodiversity

# 1
# PLANT GENETIC RESOURCES

*Robert Henry*

## Introduction

Plant biodiversity provides the genetic resource base for agriculture, underpinning crop and pasture selection and breeding. Molecular tools have improved understanding of the relationships between plants and provided insights into their potential use in agriculture. Agriculture utilizes a diverse group of plant species, but we rely heavily on a very small number of species for the bulk of our food. Crop wild relatives represent key genetic resources for food and agriculture. Advancing technologies allow access to genes from more diverse plants and facilitate the domestication of new species for agriculture. Plant genetic resources are found in farmers' fields, gene and seed banks and wild populations, and conservation *in situ* and *ex situ* is essential for agricultural sustainability. Productivity gains required to satisfy the growth in food demand will rely on utilization of these resources. Changing global food consumption patterns may influence the utilization of plant genetic resources. Diversification of diet with new crop options may be desirable to ensure food security and address trends towards homogenization of diets globally. Plant genetic resources may also hold the key to sources of genetic variation that can contribute to supporting healthier human populations and provide essential options in adapting agriculture to climate change.

## Global plant diversity

Plant diversity supports agriculture by providing the genetic resources from which agricultural crop and pasture species are derived. Plants are our primary source of foods, with most foods being directly derived from plants or from animals that in turn rely on plants for food. Plants are also essential for a wide range of non-food uses, being used for construction, clothing, energy and medicine. Increased productivity is required to keep pace with increased demand for agricultural products (Ray et al., 2013). This demand is driven by growth in human populations and changes in diet associated with factors such as economic development and increased awareness of food options. The amount and type of food being consumed is changing. Growing affluence results in greater consumption, and related changes in food preferences also increase pressure on food resources.

The diversity of plants can be considered at many levels. There are probably more than 300,000 species of flowering plants on earth. To utilize this diversity effectively in agriculture, we also need to understand diversity between and within species. Within species diversity is widely exploited in agriculture in the breeding of improved crop varieties. The diversity of plants at

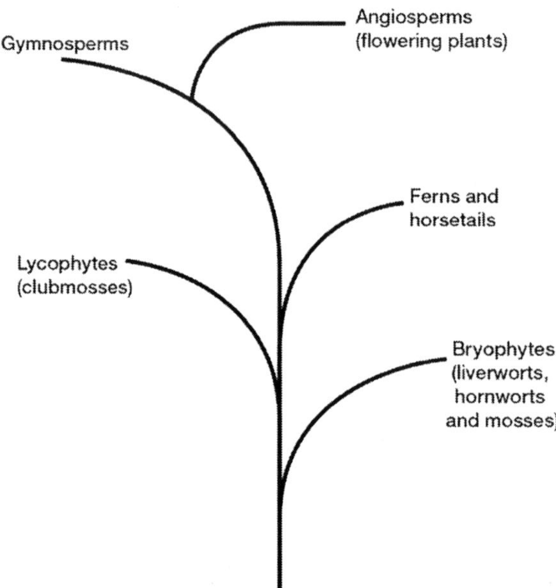


*Figure 1.1* Phylogenetic relationships between plants

*Note*: The flowering plants (angiosperms) are the main group of importance in agriculture. Some gymnosperms are also used in agriculture.

*Source*: Based on Henry (2005a).

higher taxonomic levels is also important in defining the potential to use more diverse genetic resources in the development of agricultural genotypes. Close relatives of crop plants have long been used as resource for plant breeding. Technology advances enable more distant relatives of crop plants to become options for use in crop improvement.

Plants are a very diverse group of organisms. **Figure 1.1** *Phylogenetic relationships between plants* shows the evolutionary relationships of the major groups of plants. Agriculture relies mainly on the seed plants. These can be divided into two groups: the gymnosperms and the angiosperms. The gymnosperms, such as conifers, are mainly exploited in forestry, with limited use in food production or agriculture (e.g. pine nuts). This group is unlikely to be monophyletic, that is, to all share a common ancestor (Hill, 2005). The angiosperms, or flowering plants, are the largest and most important group of plants for agriculture. Flowering plants are classified into several hundred families (Chase, 2005). Humans have found ways of using plants from many angiosperm plant families in agriculture, but we rely most heavily on species from a smaller number of families, with the most important for agriculture probably being the Poaceae, or grass family, that includes the major cereal food species and pasture grasses.

Plant species have been traditionally classified using morphological characteristics, but advances in molecular tools have provided new insights into plant diversity, allowing relationships between plants to be better understood. The relationships among the major groups of angiosperms are depicted in **Figure 1.2** *Phylogenetic relationships between flowering plants*. Most agricultural species are monocots or eudicots. Dicotyledonous plants are not monophyletic with a basal dicotyledonous group of flowering plants and a large distinct dicotyledonous group, the eudicots. The two main groups within the eudicots, the rosids and the asterids, are important in agriculture. Examples of agricultural species from these plant groups are listed in **Table 1.1** *The uses of seed plants.*

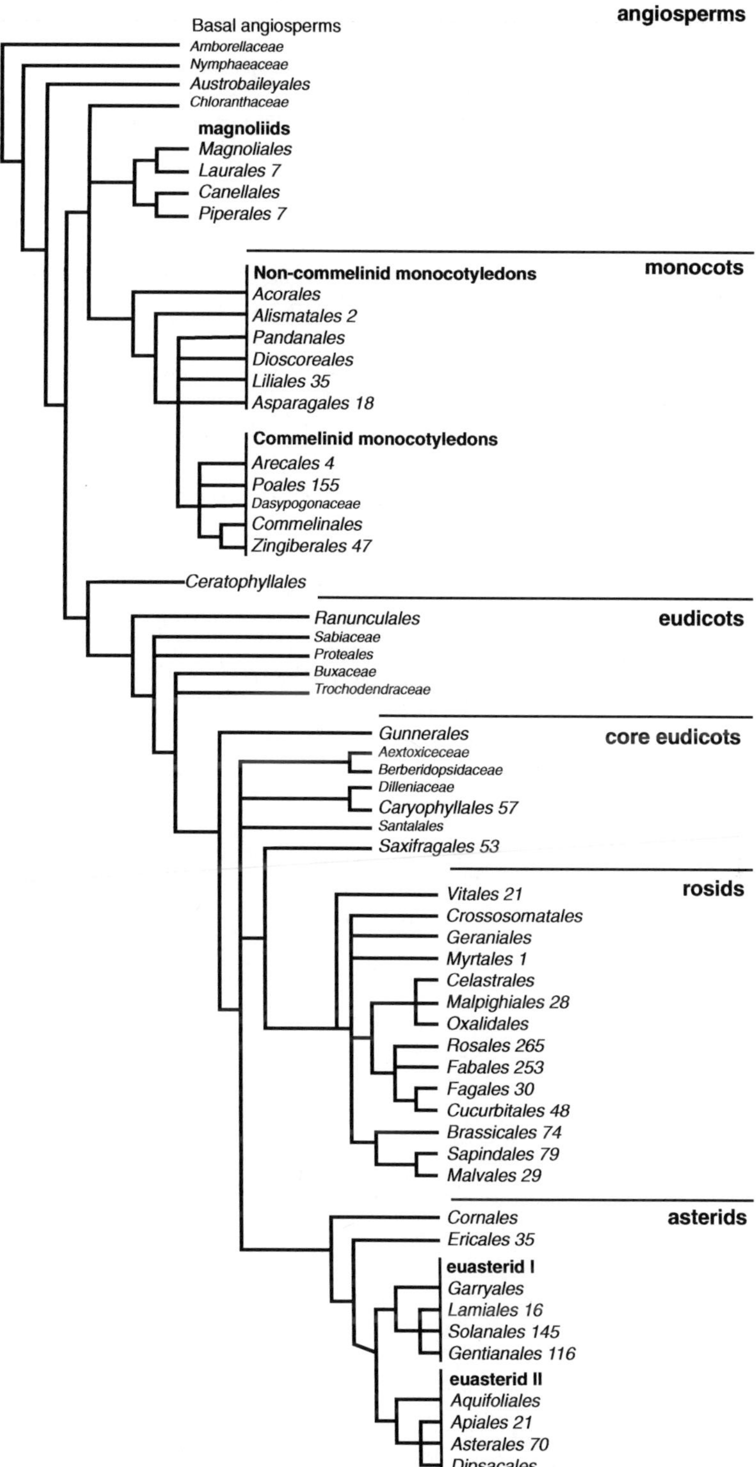


*Figure 1.2* Phylogenetic relationships between flowering plants

*Note*: The relationships between the major groups of flowering plants continue to be refined by DNA analysis, providing a guide to the most appropriate resources for use in agricultural crop improvement. This 'big picture' perspective is importance in searching for diversity that might be used in crop improvement.

*Source*: Based on Furtado et al. (2014).

*Table 1.1* The uses of seed plants

| *Plants* | *Uses* |
|---|---|
| **Gymnosperms** | Food: pine nuts, bunya nuts<br>Construction: pine |
| **Angiosperms** | |
| Amborellaceae | *Amborella* (only New Caledonia) |
| Nymphaeaceae | Ornamental: water lilies<br>Food: (seeds and rhizomes)<br>Cosmopolitan: (fresh water) |
| Austrobaileyales | One genus, two species only in Australia, no known uses |
| Chloranthaceae | Ornament: *(Chloranthus glaberi)*<br>Beverage: *(Chloranthus officinalis)*<br>Medicine: *(Hedyosmum brasiliense)* |
| Magnoliales | Food: nutmeg *(Myristica fragrans)*, custard apple *(Annona)*<br>Ornament: Magnolia<br>Construction |
| Laurales | Food: avocado *(Persea americana)* cinnamon, bay leaves<br>Ornament<br>Construction<br>Other: perfume *(Doryphora sassafras)*<br>Medicine |
| Canellales | Ornament<br>Food: white cinnamon *(Canella winterana)*<br>Medicine |
| Piperales | Food: pepper *(Piper nigrum)*<br>Beverage: kava *(Piper methysticum)*<br>Ornament<br>Medicine |
| Alismatales | Ornament<br>Food: *Sagittaria sagittifolia* (tubers) |
| Pandanales | Food: (starchy fruits)<br>Ornament: *Pandanus*<br>Other: perfume, baskets |
| Dioscoreales | Food<br>Medicine |
| Liliales | Beverage: sarsaparilla<br>Ornament: *Lilium*, *Tulipa* (tulip)<br>Medicine |
| Asparagales | Food: onions, garlic, lee, vanilla, asparagus<br>Ornament: Gladiolus, Iris, Freesia, Daffodils, Orchids<br>Medicine<br>Other: saffron *(Crocus sativus)* |
| Arecales | Food: coconuts, copra, dates, sago, palm oil<br>Fibre: coir, raffia<br>Ornament |
| Poales | Food: rice, wheat, maize, barley, sorghum, millet, sugarcane, bamboo, pineapple<br>Animal Feed: pastures<br>Ornament: lawns, water plants<br>Other: baskets, brooms, thatching |

| *Plants* | *Uses* |
|---|---|
| Dasypogonaceae | Ornament: *Xanthorrhoea*<br>Other: varnishes |
| Commelinales | Ornament: wandering Jew, water hyacinth |
| Zingiberales | Food: banana, ginger, cardamom, turmeric, arrowroot<br>Fibre: manila, hemp<br>Ornament: *Strelitzia*, Canna<br>Other: perfume |
| Ceratophyllales | Other: protects fish in fresh water |
| Ranunculales | Food: fruits<br>Ornament: *Clematis*, *Ranunculus* (buttercups)<br>Medicine: opium *(Papaver somniferum)* |
| Sabieaceae | Ornament |
| Proteales | Food: *Macadamia integrifolia*<br>Ornament: *Banksia*, *Grevillea*, *Telopea*, *Protea*, *Leucadendron*, planes<br>Construction: timber |
| Buxaceae | Ornament<br>Construction |
| Dilleniaceae | Ornament: *Hibbertia*, *Dillenia* |
| Caryophyllales | Food: Arraranthus<br>Ornament: cockscombs *(Celosia cristata)*, Ptilotus |
| Santalales | Medicine |
| Saxifragales | Food: grapes *(Vitis vinifera)*, gooseberries, currants *(Ribes)*<br>Ornament: *Hydrangeas*, *Kalanchoe*<br>Construction: timber<br>Other: perfume |
| Crossosomatales | Ornament<br>Construction<br>Medicine |
| Gereniales | Ornament: *Geranium*, *Pelargonium*<br>Construction: timber<br>Medicine<br>Other: perfume |
| Myrtales | Food: cloves *(Syzygium aromaticum)*, lilly pilly<br>Ornament: bottlebrushes, *Tibouchina*, *Fuchsias*<br>Construction: *Eucalyptus*<br>Medicine<br>Other: essential oils |
| Celastrales | Beverage: Arabia tea *(Catha edulis)*<br>Medicine<br>Other: essential oils |
| Malpighiales | Food: cassava *(Manihot glaziovii)*, passionfruit *(Passiflora)*<br>Ornament: Poinsettia *(Euphorbia)*, violets<br>Industry: castor oil *(Ricinus communis)*<br>Other: rubber *(Hevea brasiliensis)* |
| Oxalidales | Ornament: flycatcher plant *(Cephalotus follicularis)*<br>Construction: timber |

(*Continued*)

*Table 1.1* (Continued)

| *Plants* | *Uses* |
|---|---|
| Rosales | Food: fruits (apple, plum, pear, cherry, mulberries, fig, raspberries, strawberries)<br>Fibre: hemp *(Cannabis sativa)*<br>Ornament: roses<br>Beverage: hops *(Humulus lupulus)*<br>Construction: elms |
| Fabales | Food: peas, beans, groundnut (peanut), soybean<br>Animal Feed: clover, lucerne<br>Other: nitrogen fixing<br>Construction: timber<br>Ornament: *Acacia* |
| Fagales | Food: chestnut *(Castanea sativa)*, walnut, pecan<br>Construction: beeches, oaks, birches |
| Cucurbitales | Food: cucumber, pumpkin, melon<br>Ornament: Begonia |
| Brassicales | Food: oilseed rape, mustard, vegetables, (cabbage, cauliflower), papaya *(Carica papaya)*<br>Animal Feed: fodder |
| Sapindales | Food: orange, lemon, lime, mango, cashew, pistachio, lychee *(Litchi chinensis)*, maple sugar<br>Ornament: maples<br>Medicine<br>Construction: mahoganies<br>Other: perfume, posion ivy |
| Malavales | Fibre: cotton *(Gossypium)*<br>Ornament: *Hibiscus*<br>Construction<br>Other: chocolate |
| Cornales | Ornament: dogwoods |
| Ericales | Beverage: tea *(Camellia sinensis)*<br>Ornament: Camellia<br>Construction |
| Garryales | Medicine |
| Lamiales | Food: olives *(Olea europaca)* |
| Solanales | Food: potato, aubergine, tomato, pepper, sweet potato<br>Ornament: morning glory *(Ipomoea purpurea)*<br>Medicine<br>Other: tobacco |
| Gentianales | Beverage: coffee *(Coffea)*<br>Ornament: *Gentian*, oleandeas *(Nerium)*, *Gardenia*<br>Medicine: quinine *(Cinchona)* |
| Aquifoliales | Ornament: holly<br>Construction |
| Apiales | Food: carrot, celery, parley, fennel, dill<br>Medicine<br>Other: perfume |
| Asterales | Food: sunflower, lettuce, chicory, Jerusalem artichoke<br>Ornament: Dahlia, Gerbera |
| Dipsacales | Beverage: elderberry (wine)<br>Ornament: honeysuckles *(Lonicera)*<br>Medicine |

*Source*: Adapted from Henry (2005b).

The relationships between plants may be assessed by analysis of their DNA. The nuclear and maternal (chloroplast and mitochondria) genomes may show different relationships. Reticulate evolution, found in many plant groups, including agriculturally important species, allows chloroplast transfer or 'capture' between species.

The importance of the diversity of micro-organisms in the environment of plants is increasingly being revealed as an important contributor to plant performance. This genetic resource is much less well known than the plants themselves but is also important for agriculture (see also Beed et al., Chapter 8 of this Handbook).

## Diversity of species

### *Reliance on key species in agriculture*

Despite the use of many different plants by humans, a relatively small number account for a large proportion of global agricultural production and food supply (**Table 1.2** *Production of major food plants*). This concentration on a few species for most food is a key element of the vulnerability of the world food supply to the impact of climate change and the outbreak of major new plant diseases. Diversification of the food supply should contribute to greater food security. Genetic diversification may be tackled at many levels. Greater genetic diversity within major food crop species makes an important contribution to food security, but contributions from a wider range of food species would also be desirable.

### *Diversity of plants used in agriculture*

Many plants from diverse plant groups have been used to varying degrees by humans in agricultural production of food and other useful products. Many of these have only minor use in particular regions or on specific occasions. For example, some may be very important food sources in particular locations or at specific times of the year. Diversity may be found in production (on farms), in genetic resource collections (seed banks) or in wild plant populations. Changing food

*Table 1.2* Production of major food plants

| *Rank* | *Crop* | *World production (FAO) (production tons)* |
|---|---|---|
| 1 | Maize (corn) | 873 million |
| 2 | Rice | 738 million |
| 3 | Wheat | 671 million |
| 4 | Potatoes | 365 million |
| 5 | Cassava | 269 million |
| 6 | Soybeans | 241 million |
| 7 | Sweet potatoes | 108 million |
| 8 | Yams | 59.5 million |
| 9 | Sorghum | 57.0 million |
| 10 | Plantain | 37.2 million |

*Source*: From Food and Agriculture Organization of the United Nations. (2012) 'Food and Agricultural commodities production/Commodities by regions'; for further information, see FAOSTAT (http://www.fao.org/faostat/en/#home).

consumption patterns may be reducing the range of species being produced, as traditional foods are replaced by a global diet based upon a relatively small number of crops.

## *Diversity of micro-organisms important in agriculture*

The diversity of organisms at all levels is important for sustainable agricultural production. Soil microbial diversity may be critical for plant nutrition and health. Plant pathogen diversity will often dictate the need for crop plant diversity to provide the required genetic variation in plant disease resistance to support crop breeding and sustainable production. The diversity of beneficial micro-organisms may be important in determining the productivity of agricultural systems.

## Diversity within species

The diversity with domesticated crop species and their wild relatives is exploited in crop production and breeding. Clonally or vegetatively propagated species may have large populations of genetically identical individuals. Sexually propagated or seed propagated species may have varying degrees of genetic diversity within cultivated populations.

Diversity within plant species has been traditionally assessed by analysis of morphological differences. Growth rate and crop yield have been key traits assessed in crop species. Diversity in traits important to human consumers, such as appearance or taste, has been intensely selected in agriculture. Molecular tools have been widely applied in biochemical- and DNA-based assessments of diversity in crop plants. Diversity of alleles for traits of importance in agriculture is the key to selection for genetic improvement in crops. Germplasm collections in seed banks and wild populations provide an immediate source of diversity for use in crop breeding. Seed banks include very large numbers of accessions with linked data on phenotypic characteristics (see chapters in Part 6 of this Handbook). However, much of the material in seed banks remains poorly characterized, making it difficult to utilize in crop improvement. Exchange of material between collections results in an appearance of more diversity than may be present as many accession in collections may be duplicates. Further enhancement of the phenotypic data associated with seed collections and linking of genotyping data will enhance the usefulness of these collections.

The extent and nature of diversity within agricultural species varies considerably. Some species have very limited genetic variation in the domesticated gene pool. Vegetatively cultivated species can have one or a few genotypes only. Even seed propagated species may have limited genetic diversity because of their recent domestication or a genetic bottleneck in their history, such as the formation of a polyploid. Major polyploid crop plants include wheat, potato, sugarcane, coffee, peanut and cotton. A recent polyploid origin suggests in some cases that the domesticated gene pool represents the descendants of only one or a small number of plants and as result includes very little diversity. Diversity in these species may be increased by going back to the diploid progenitor species and creating new 'synthetic' polyploids that bring new diversity into the gene pool of the domesticated crop species (Anssour et al., 2009).

Phenotypic variation in traits important in agriculture and genotypic diversity may not always be closely aligned. A single gene can result in major differences in plant development and morphology in some species. In others, the plants may have very large differences in the genome at the DNA sequence level, but these are not reflected in obvious morphological differences. An understanding of these differences is important in defining the best strategies to use in the breeding of specific crop species.

Domestication for agriculture has resulted in significant loss of diversity in many parts of the genome and enrichment in regions associated with traits of importance to humans (Shi and Lai, 2015). Significant epigenetic changes may also be associated with domestication. Increased knowledge of the events associated with domestication promises to facilitate more efficient transfer of genetic diversity from wild relatives to crop species. This allows selection for essential domestication traits to be combined with selection for the trait being introduced from the wild relative.

## Crop wild relatives (CWR)

The wild relatives of crop species represent a genetic reservoir of diversity that can be used to support the continued genetic improvement of domesticated plants. The close wild relatives that can be directly interbred with the domesticated crop plants provide a critical primary gene pool for the agricultural species. More distant relatives that can be used only with greater technical intervention may represent important secondary or tertiary gene pools that can provide a much wider range of more difficult to access genetic resources.

As an example, the relationships of crop wild relatives (CWR) for rice are shown in **Figure 1.3** *The rice gene pool: relationships between a genome rice species*. Asian and African rices were separately domesticated from species that have more distantly related wild relatives in Australia, South America and Africa. DNA analysis is supporting the identification of novel crop wild relative populations for use in crop breeding (Brozynska et al., 2014). This type of analysis guides the more deliberate selection for use in plant breeding of genetic resources that are close or distant from the domesticated species and that might include different levels of useful diversity.

CWR may become more important with growing pressures of food security and the need for adaptation of agriculture to climate change. Breeding with wild germplasm can be focused on

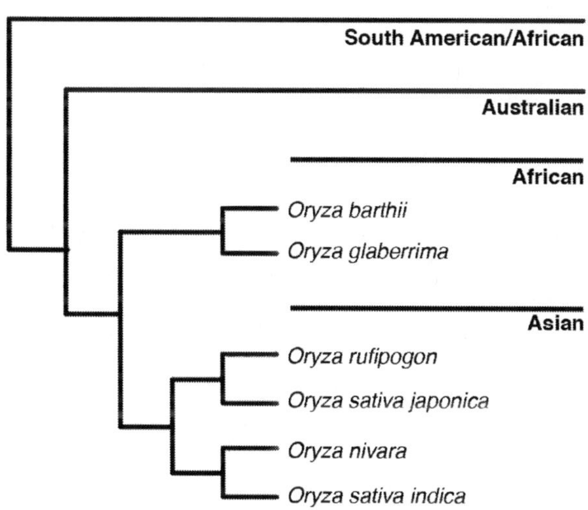


*Figure 1.3* The rice gene pool: relationships between a genome rice species

*Note*: These species are the effective gene pool (inter-fertile species) available for rice breeding. Different groups of species may be identified at different distances from the domesticated species.

*Source*: From Wambugu et al. (2015).

use of material from environments that match those that are the targets for agricultural production or are likely to have the specific pests and diseases or strains of the diseases to which resistance is required. This technique has been referred to as the 'Focused Identification of Germplasm Strategy' (FIGS; Khazaei et al., 2013). It may greatly increase the efficiency of plant breeding by more effectively identifying suitable germplasm for specific breeding applications.

Increasing understanding of the wild genetic resource from which crops were domesticated is increasing the potential for their use in crop improvement (Dillon et al., 2007). Molecular analysis of wild relatives may reveal unexpected genetic relationships that may inform and change approaches to breeding (Ochieng et al., 2008). Genomic analysis of CWR (Brozynska et al., 2015), facilitated by advances in technology, is also increasing the ease with which these resources can be accessed for crop improvement. Molecular tools support the rapid introduction of useful diversity from CWR by defining the genes or genome regions that need to be transferred into the crop (Lakew et al., 2012).

Efforts to conserve and better characterize CWR need to be prioritized to focus on key species. Some 1,667 species were recently identified as being of the highest importance (Vincent et al., 2013). This assessment was based upon both the potential and proven usefulness of the species concerned according to the literature. Collection of genotypic and phenotypic data on these CWR will provide a valuable resource for agriculture.

## New options for agriculture

The introduction of new species into agricultural production is an option for expansion of the diversity of food supply and may contribute to greater food security, as well as resilience. Humans have explored the available plant diversity over a long period of time, so we need to ask why plants that have potential for domestication have not already been domesticated. In some cases, barriers to domestication may be overcome by new technologies not available in the past. More aggressive plant selection and genetic alteration may be possible with modern plant breeding technologies.

In some cases, plants may be found only in areas where agriculture has not been practised or possible. These plants might be well suited to domestication in other environments or with the introduction of appropriate agricultural technologies. Agriculture was not apparent in some parts of the world (e.g. Australia and New Zealand) until relatively recently, but many plants with apparent potential for domestication are found in these environments. A further discussion of the domestication process is given in Part 2 of this Handbook.

Analysis of domestication has revealed the genetic changes associated with the process. Knowledge of how this has happened in the past provides a guide to approaches that might be taken to rapidly domesticate new species. For example, the domestication of the major cereal crops has relied upon a loss of shattering. Shattering is necessary in wild populations, resulting in seed being rapidly dispersed as it matures. In agriculture, a lack of shattering results in the seed being retained on the plant until harvested. Understanding this difference between the requirements for survival in the wild and in agriculture is a key to rapidly accelerating domestication. Direct selection for loss of function at the known shattering loci can result in this trait being adapted for agricultural production in a single generation (Shapter et al., 2013).

## Conservation of plant genetic resources

The conservation of genetic resources underpinning agricultural production is a key issue in ensuring food security (Henry, 2006). Biological collections provide a method for *ex situ* conservation of plant genetic resources. Seed banks, living collections and botanic gardens are key reservoirs of plant diversity for agriculture. For some species, *in vitro* conservation methods, such as cryopreservation, may be required. DNA banks may also provide a useful resource, as do databases with DNA sequence information. The value of DNA sequence information as a strategic genetic resource protecting against the impact of extinction of genes or species has increased as our ability to synthesize genes chemically advances.

Conservation of wild plant populations in their natural habitats delivers *in situ* conservation of plant genetic resources. Protected areas such as national parks and reserves are potentially important in protecting genetic resources for agriculture. Ongoing research on the distribution of CWR and the status of their conservation in the wild is needed to ensure policies for their adequate conservation are developed and implemented.

A combination of conservation *ex situ* and *in situ* is desirable to ensure adequate protection of plant diversity. Conservation *in situ* allows ongoing evolution of diversity and adaptation to changing environments. To complement this, conservation *ex situ* is important in preserving diversity that may be lost in the wild due to environmental change, and making it readily available. The management of conservation using these strategies is enhanced by the availability of molecular tools for characterization of plant genomes and analysis of diversity (Jilal et al., 2008).

Conservation of genetic resources in the fields of farmers is also important, as the diversity of domesticated populations provides resilience in crop production and allows ongoing evolution of the crop under cultivation. Effective strategies to conserve this material by ensuring ongoing cultivation are required.

## The role of data storage and management

Advances in information technology allow greater amounts of data on plant genetic resources to be collected, stored and managed. DNA sequence data have accumulated at an accelerating rate. Automation of phenotypic data collection is also increasing. These data provide key resources for agriculture and food production. Exchange of plant seeds (or other propagation material) may be slowed by quarantine or intellectual property issues. However, data on plant genetic resources can be stored and exchanged globally more rapidly, improving the efficiency of utilization of plant diversity in agriculture. Genomic sequencing of large numbers of plant accessions in collections will allow more effective international collaboration in utilization of available plant diversity. This is changing the way researchers interact with one another and with the biological materials they are working with (Rossetto and Henry, 2014). For example, whole chloroplast genome sequencing is emerging as a routine, cost effective method for plant barcoding (Li et al., 2014). This strategy is likely to extend to whole nuclear genome analysis as technology advances. Data collected in different parts of the world can be combined and analyzed collaboratively. Ultimately, complete genome sequences of all plant genetic resources stored *ex situ* anywhere in world could be globally available. Similar data on wild *(in situ)* plant genetic resources may eventually be collected, providing a platform for conservation and utilization of this resource.

## Contribution of technology to utilization of plant genetic resources

Recent advances in molecular technology have made possible the characterization of plant genetic resources by genome sequencing (Bolger et al., 2014; Wang et al., 2014). The technologies used for molecular analysis of plant diversity have advanced rapidly, with a movement from molecular markers (Henry, 2013) to DNA sequencing (Henry, 2014). The convergence of plant genotyping and plant sequencing techniques has resulted from the development of technologies that allow determination of the sequence of the entire plant genome to be obtained for a cost that is similar to the cost of analysing a genetic marker at a single locus a few years earlier. Rapid progress has thus been made in sequencing the genomes of crop plants (Michael and VanBuren, 2015). This has revealed unprecedented amounts of information about the relationships between plants and about their potential utility in agriculture (Mace et al., 2013). For example, the coffee genome revealed that caffeine has evolved separately in coffee, tea and chocolate (Denoeud et al., 2014). This increased understanding supports more rational and targeted crop improvement and domestication.

The expanding knowledge base on available genetic resources is complemented by improved technologies to select and modify the genetics of crops. These developments promise to increase the rate and breadth of utilization of plant genetic resources in agriculture. The application of genomics to seed banks (McCouch et al., 2012) is expected to result in more efficient management of collections and greatly improved utilization.

A more radical approach to adapting plant genetic resources is to use transgenic approaches to introduce new genes into the gene pool. Recent technology advances are enabling more targeted genetic modification of plants using methods such as gene editing. This allows new genetic resources to be created, complementing the approach of selecting within natural or induced (mutagenesis) variation. The lack of public acceptance of genetic manipulation in some countries has been the main factor limiting the application of these technologies. Continuing technical advances in this area will require careful communication to develop understanding and appropriate regulation of their application.

## Trends in food consumption and the role of plant genetic resources in supporting future human diets

Growing affluence in human societies is resulting in changing food consumption patterns as people eat not only more, but also different, foods. The trends will surely impact the diversity of foods produced in agricultural systems. Diets are becoming more international as global communications increase awareness of food options. This may result in an increasing homogenization of diets and the diversity of foods consumed globally (Khoury et al., 2014). The adoption of foods from other countries may expand the range of species consumed locally. However, this often involves the consumption of species that are major crops elsewhere. The result of including rice in the diets of populations that have not traditionally consumed rice does little to diversify food consumption at the global level. The net effect may be to displace regionally important minor crops and standardize diets based upon a relatively small number of species.

Plant genetic resources are key tools for keeping pace with changes in consumer food demand. Sequencing of a wild rice has revealed the likely genetic basis of lower glycemic index (Rathinasabapathi et al., 2015). Such traits may become increasingly important as consumers target food with desirable health benefits in response to increased incidence of diabetes and obesity. Modern plant breeders will need to develop plant varieties that not only allow sufficient calories and protein to be produced to feed human populations, but also foods contributing to a balanced diet that will promote health.

## Impact of climate change on plant genetic resources and diversity of agricultural production

Climate change may impact the types of crops that can be grown is some areas (Ewart et al., 2014) and result in some food production moving to new areas. Diversity of food production will be necessary to help ensure food security despite rapid change in climate (Abberton et al.,

2015). Adaptation of agriculture to climate change may be informed by the study of how wild plant populations adapt to different climatic conditions (Henry and Nevo, 2014). Adaptation to warmer climates requires adaptation not only to the higher temperatures *per se* but also to the different range of pest and disease organisms that might be encountered at higher temperatures (Fitzgerald et al., 2011). Plant biodiversity provides a rich source of genetic variation for use in adaptation of crops to climate change. CWR are a primary source of genes for use in crop adaptation to both abiotic and biotic stresses, yet many CWR and their habitats are threatened by climate change.

Agriculture needs to adapt to climate change to ensure food security, but it must also play a bigger role in climate mitigation. In a truly climate-smart agriculture, plant genetic resources will contribute to developing crop plants suitable for both adapting agriculture to climate change and contributing to climate mitigation by, for example, providing options for increased carbon capture for storage in soils or biomass.

## Conclusions

Continuous genetic improvement of agricultural crop species is necessary to protect food security. Plant diversity is an essential resource on which crop breeding depends. Ongoing efforts are required to collect, conserve, characterize and use plant diversity. Technological developments will continue to increase the ease with which these resources can be accessed for use in crop breeding. Some new species might contribute to the requirements of agriculture. However, current agricultural species are likely to remain the main options. Adapting current crop species to suit production in new or variable climates and to satisfy changing human consumer preferences will utilize available genetic resources for these species and related species.

## References

Abberton, M., Abbott, A., Batley, J., Bentley, A., Blakeney, M., Bryant, J., Cai, H., Cockram, J., Costa de Oliveira, A., Cseke, L. J., Dempewolf, H., De Pace, C., Edwards, D., Gepts, P., Greenland, A., Hall, A. E., Henry, R., Hori, K., Howe, G. T., Hughes, S., Humphreys, M., Ismail, A. M., Lightfoot, D., Marshall, A., Mayes, S., Nguyen, H. T., Ogbonnaya, F. C., Ortiz, R., Paterson, A. H., Simon, P. W., Tohme, J., Tuberosa, R., Valliyodan, B., Varshney, R., Wullschleger, S. D. and Yano, M. (2015) 'Global agricultural intensification during climate change: A role for genomics', *Plant Biotechnology Journal*, vol. 14, pp. 1095–1098.

Anssour, S., Kru, T., Sharbel, T. F., Saluz, H. P., Bonaventure, G. and Baldwin, I. T. (2009) 'Phenotypic, genetic and genomic consequences of natural and synthetic polyploidization of *Nicotiana attenuate* and *Nicotiana obtusifolia*', *Annals of Botany*, vol. 103, pp. 1207–1217.

Bolger, A., Scossa, F., Bolger, M. E., Lanz, C., Maumus, F., Tohge, T., Quesneville, H., Alseekh, S., Sorensen, I., Lichtenstein, G., Fich, E. A., Conte, M., Keller, H., Schneeberger, K., Schwacke, R., Ofner, I., Vrebalov, J., Xu, Y., Osorio, S., Aflitos, S. A., Schijlen, E., Jimenez-Gomez, J. M., Ryngajllo, M., Kimura, S., Kumar, R., Koenig, D., Headland, L. R., Maloof, J. N., Sinha, N., van Ham, R. C. H. J., Lankhorst, R. K., Mao, L., Vogel, A., Arsova, B., Panstruga, R., Fei, Z., Rose, J. K. C., Zamir, D., Carrari, F., Giovannoni, J. J., Weigel, D., Usadel, B. and Fernie, A. R. (2014) 'The genome of the stress-tolerant wild tomato species *Solanum pennellii*', *Nature Genetics*, vol. 46, pp. 1034–1038.

Brozynska, M., Omar, E. S., Furtado, A., Crayn, D., Simon, B., Ishikawa, R. and Henry, R. J. (2014) 'Chloroplast genome of novel rice germplasm identified in Northern Australia', *Tropical Plant Biology*, vol. 7, pp. 111–120.

Brozynska, M., Agnelo Furtado, A. and Henry, R. J. (2015) 'Genomics of Crop Wild Relatives: Expanding the gene pool for crop improvement', *Plant Biotechnology Journal*, vol. 14, pp. 1070–1185.

Chase, M. (2005) 'Relationships between the families of flowering plants', pp. 7–24 in R. J. Henry (ed.), *Plant Diversity & Evolution: Genotypic & Phenotypic Variation in Higher Plants*, CABI Publishing, Oxford, UK.

Denoeud, F., Carretero-Paulet, L., Dereeper, A., Droc, G., Guyot, R., Pietrella, M., Zheng, C., Alberti, A., Anthony, F., Aprea, G., Aury, J.-M., Bento, P., Bernard, M., Bocs, S., Campa, C., Cenci, A., Combes,

M.-C., Crouzillat, D., Da Silva, C., Daddiego, L., De Bellis, F., Dussert, S., Garsmeur, O., Gayraud, T., Guignon, V., Jahn, K., Jamilloux, V., Joët, T., Labadie, K., Lan, T., Leclerc, J., Lepelley, M., Leroy, T., Li, L.-T., Librado, P., Lopez, L., Muñoz, A., Noel, B., Pallavicini, A., Perrotta, G., Poncet, V., Pot, D., Priyono, Rigoreau, M., Rouard, M., Rozas, J., Tranchant-Dubreuil, C., VanBuren, R., Zhang, Q., Andrade, A. C., Argout, X., Bertrand, B., de Kochko, A., Graziosi, G., Henry, R. J., Jayarama, Ming, R., Nagai, C., Rounsley, S., Sankoff, D., Giuliano, G., Albert, V. A., Wincker, P. and Lashermes, P. (2014) 'The coffee genome provides insight into the convergent evolution of caffeine biosynthesis', *Science*, vol. 345, pp. 1181–1184.

Dillon, S. L., Shapter, F. M., Henry, R. J., Cordeiro, G., Izquierdo, L. and Lee, L. S. (2007) 'Domestication to crop improvement: Genetic resources for sorghum and saccharum (Andropogoneae)', *Annals of Botany*, vol. 100, pp. 975–989.

Ewart, F., Rotter, R. P., Bindi, M., Webber, H., Trnka, M., Kersebaum, K. C., Olsen, J. E., van Ittersum, M. K., Janssen, S., Rivington, M., Semenov, M. A., Wallach, D., Porter, J. R., Stewart, D., Verhagen, J., Gaiser, T., Palosuo, T., Nendel, C., Roggero, P. P., Bartosová, L. and Asseng, S. (2014) 'Crop modelling for integrated assessment of risk to food production from climate change', *Environmental Modelling and Software*, vol. 72, pp. 287–303.

Fitzgerald, T. L., Shapter, F. M., McDonald, S., Waters, D. L. E., Chivers, I. H., Drenth, A., Nevo, E. and Henry, R. J. (2011) 'Genome diversity in wild grasses under environmental stress', *Proceedings of the National Academy of Science USA*, vol. 108, pp. 21139–21144.

Furtado, A., Lupoi, J. S., Hoang, V. N., Healey, A., Singh, S., Simmons, B. A. and Henry, R. J. (2014) 'Modifying plants for biofuel and biomaterial production', *Plant Biotechnology Journal*, vol. 12, pp. 1246–1258.

Henry, R. J. (2005a) 'Importance of plant diversity', pp. 1–5 in R. J. Henry (ed.), *Plant Diversity & Evolution: Genotypic & Phenotypic Variation in Higher Plants*, CABI Publishing, Oxford, UK.

Henry, R. J. (2005b) 'Conserving genetic diversity in plants of environmental, social or economic importance', pp. 317–325 in R. J. Henry (ed.), *Plant Diversity & Evolution: Genotypic & Phenotypic Variation in Higher Plants*, CABI Publishing, Oxford, UK.

Henry, R. J. (ed.) (2006) *Plant Conservation Genetics*, The Haworth Press Inc., Binghamton, NY, USA.

Henry, R. J. (ed.) (2013) *Molecular Markers in Plants*, Wiley-Blackwell, Hoboken, NJ, USA.

Henry, R. J. (2014) 'Sequencing crop wild relatives to support the conservation and utilization of plant genetic resources', *Plant Genetic Resources: Characterization and Utilization*, vol. 12, pp. S9–S11.

Henry, R. J. and Nevo, E. (2014) 'Exploring natural selection to guide breeding for agriculture', *Plant Biotechnology Journal*, vol. 12, pp. 655–662.

Hill, K. (2005) 'Diversity and evolution of gymnosperms', pp. 25–44 in R. J. Henry (ed.), *Plant Diversity & Evolution: Genotypic & Phenotypic Variation in Higher Plants*, CABI Publishing, Oxford, UK.

Jilal, A., Grando, S., Henry, R. J., Lee, L. S., Rice, N., Hill, H., Baum, M. and Ceccarelli, S. (2008) 'Genetic diversity of ICARDA's worldwide barley landrace collection', *Genetic Resources and Crop Evolution*, vol. 55, pp. 1221–1230.

Khazaei, H., Street, K., Bari, A., Mackay, M. and Stoddard, F. L. (2013) 'The FIGS (Focused Identification of Germplasm Strategy) approach identifies traits related to drought adaptation in *Vicia faba* genetic resources', *PLoS ONE*, vol. 8, p. e63107.

Khoury, C. K., Bjorkman, A. D., Dempewolf, H., Ramirez-Villegas, J., Guarinof, L., Jarvis, A., Rieseberg, L. H. and Struik, P. C. (2014) 'Increasing homogeneity in global food supplies and the implications for food security', *Proceedings of the National Academy of Sciences USA*, vol. 111, pp. 4001–4006.

Lakew, B., Henry, R. J., Eglinton, J., Baum, M., Ceccarelli, S. and Grando, S. (2012) 'SSR analysis of introgression of drought tolerance from the genome of *Hordeum spontaneum* into cultivated barley (*Hordeum vulgare* ssp *vulgare*)', *Euphytica*, vol. 191, pp. 231–243.

Li, X., Yang, Y., Henry, R. J., Rossetto, M., Wang, Y. and Chen, S. (2014) 'Plant DNA barcoding: From gene to genome', *Biological Reviews*, vol. 90, pp. 157–166.

Mace, E. S., Tai, S., Gilding, E. K., Li, P., Prentis, P. J., Bian, L., Campbell, B. C., Hu, W., Innes, D. J., Han, X., Cruickshank, A., Dai, C., Frère, C., Zhang, H., Hunt, C. H., Wang, X., Shatte, T., Wang, M., Su, Z., Li, J., Lin, X., Godwin, I. D., Jordan, D. R. and Wang, J. (2013) 'Whole-genome sequencing reveals untapped genetic potential in Africa's indigenous cereal crop sorghum', *Nature Communications*, vol. 4, p. 2320.

McCouch, S. R., McNally, K. L., Wang, W. and Sackville Hamilton, R. (2012) 'Genomics of gene banks: A case study in rice', *American Journal of Botany*, vol. 99, pp. 407–423.

Michael, T. P. and VanBuren, R. (2015) 'Progress, challenges and the future of crop genomes', *Current Opinion in Plant Biology*, vol. 24, pp. 71–81.

Ochieng, J. W., Shepherd, M., Baverstock, P. R., Nikles, G., Lee, D. J., and Henry, R. J. (2008) 'Genetic variation within two sympatric spotted gum eucalypts exceeds between taxa variation', *Silvae Genetica*, vol. 57, pp. 249–256.

Rathinasabapathi, P., Natarajan Purushothaman, N., Ramprasad, V. L. R. and Parani, M. (2015) 'Whole genome sequencing and analysis of Swarna, a widely cultivated indica rice variety with low glycemic index', *Scientific Reports*, vol. 5, p. 11303.

Ray, D. K., Mueller, N. D., West, P. C. and Foley, J. A. (2013) 'Yield trends are insufficient to double global crop production by 2050', *PLoS ONE*, vol. 8, p. e66428.

Rossetto, M. and Henry, R. J. (2014) 'Escape from the laboratory: New horizons for plant genetics', *Trends in Plant Science*, vol. 19, pp. 554–555.

Shapter, F. M., Cross, M., Ablett, G., Malory, S., Chivers, I. H., King, G. J. and Henry, R. J. (2013) 'High-throughput sequencing and mutagenesis to accelerate the domestication of *Microlaena stipoides* as a new food crop', *PloS ONE*, vol. 8, p. e82641.

Shi, J. and Lai, J. (2015) 'Patterns of genomic changes with crop domestication and breeding', *Current Opinion in Plant Biology*, vol. 24, pp. 47–53.

Vincent, H., Wiersema, J., Kell, S., Fielder, H., Dobbie, S., Castañeda-Álvarez, N. P., Guarino, L., Eastwood, R., León, B. and Maxted, N. (2013) 'A prioritized crop wild relative inventory to help underpin global food security', *Biological Conservation*, vol. 167, pp. 265–275.

Wambugu, P. W., Brozynska, M., Furtado, A., Waters, D. L. and Henry, R. J. (2015) 'Relationships of wild and domesticated rice species based on whole chloroplast genome sequences', *Scientific Reports*, vol. 5, pp. 13957.

Wang, M., Yu, Y., Haberer, G., Marri, P. R., Fan, C., Goicoechea, J. L., Zuccolo, A., Song, X., Kudrna, D., Ammiraju, J. S., Cossu, R. M., Maldonado, C., Chen, J., Lee, S., Sisneros, N., de Baynast, K., Golser, W., Wissotski, M., Kim, W., Sanchez, P., Ndjiondjop, M. N., Sanni, K., Long, M., Carney, J., Panaud, O., Wicker, T., Machado, C. A., Chen, M., Mayer, K. F., Rounsley, S. and Wing, R. A. (2014) 'The genome sequence of African rice (*Oryza glaberrima*) and evidence for independent domestication', *Nature Genetics*, vol. 46, pp. 982–988.

# 2

# HOW MODERN AND ANCIENT GENOMIC ANALYSES CAN REVEAL COMPLEX DOMESTIC HISTORIES USING CATTLE AS A CASE STUDY

*Ceiridwen J. Edwards, David E. MacHugh and David A. Magee*

## Introduction

The domestication of animals was a key element in the transition of human societies from nomadic forager to sedentary agro-pastoralists (Magee et al., 2014). Zeder (2012) defined domestication as

> a sustained, multigenerational, mutualistic relationship in which humans assume some significant level of control over the reproduction and care of a plant/animal in order to secure a more predictable supply of a resource of interest and by which the plant/animal is able to increase its reproductive success over individuals not participating in this relationship, thereby enhancing the fitness of both humans and target domesticates.
> *(pp. 163–164)*

Animal domestication can be regarded as an extension of the predator-prey relationship between humans and the target species, in which humans separated a few individuals from wild populations and intervened in the life cycles of these captive individuals. This intervention would have resulted gradually in behavioural and biological changes of the target species, leading to the emergence of a completely domesticated form (Uerpmann, 1996). While it is likely that the early stages of animal domestication lacked human intentionality, subsequent stages undoubtedly involved increasing degrees of conscious and deliberate human action as the relationship between humans and their domesticates intensified. For example, human nursing behaviour may have resulted in the incorporation of young, easily manageable herbivorous wild animals, such as wild goats and sheep, into early human settlements. Although the rearing of young wild animals as pets may not have directly resulted in their domestication, successful maintenance of these animals within a few proto-Neolithic settlements could certainly have resulted in the awareness of their economic potential. The coupling of this realization with a few successive, good cereal harvests may have enabled the development of a number of small, productive domestic flocks. Once even a basic understanding of animal management had been attained, humans could (perhaps consciously) focus their attention on the domestication of larger ruminants, including wild cattle.

Intuitively, it might be expected that animal domestication would have occurred in those regions that are most productive for farming today; however, archaeological and genetic studies have shown that animal domestication occurred independently, and somewhat contemporaneously, in only a small number of areas of the world, primarily Southwest Asia (including the Near East and the Indian subcontinent), East Asia, East Africa, South America and Mesoamerica (Larson and Fuller, 2014). This contrasts with the multiple independent and contemporaneous areas of domestication for crops (Henry, Chapter 1 of this Handbook), although the asynchronous patterns seen in some species may result from the unclear distinction between '*primary*' (truly independent) and '*secondary*' (i.e. due to dispersal processes) domestication (Larson et al., 2014). Diamond (2002) noted that at the time of domestication there were 148 species of large terrestrial mammalian herbivores and omnivores available for domestication, but only 14 of these were actually domesticated. He therefore hypothesized that, of the wild animal species native to the domestication centres, only some were 'domesticable' – that is, those species that exhibited the physiological and behavioural attributes that made them amenable to domestication, including the ability to live and breed freely under diverse conditions, propensity to taming, sociability and a demonstrated usefulness to humans (Zeder, 2012; Larson and Fuller, 2014).

## Analysis of animal domestication via zooarchaeological methods

Much of what is known about the early stages of animal domestication – including *what* wild animal species were domesticated, *where* these wild animal species were domesticated and *when* these wild animal species were domesticated – has been uncovered via the scientific analysis of faunal remains and other ancient artefacts recovered from archaeological sites associated with early farming. Such studies are predicated on the ability to distinguish between wild and domestic forms; however, as many changes that occur as part of the adaptive process of domestication are morphological in nature, it is these discernable changes that allow zooarchaeologists to determine and catalogue evidence for domestication at particular sites (Clutton-Brock, 2012). Indeed, gradual changes in animal morphological markers, as documented in the archaeological record, would point towards a relationship between human societies and target species. The effects of domestication on animal morphology include the appearance of bone pathologies (e.g. due to use of the animal for draught purposes) and a decrease in overall body size due to malnutrition and physiological demands (such as the drawing of milk) within early human settlements. As well as morphological and phenotypical changes, such as shortening of the skull and reduced brain size (Zeder, 2012), temporal changes in age and sex ratios from the wild form can be used to define domestication at a site.

## Domestic animal diversity

Livestock management is an important source of livelihood for millions of people globally, particularly in the developing world (IFAD, 2010). The mammalian and avian livestock species contributing to modern agriculture and food production have been shaped by a long history of domestication and continuous breeding. Millennia of human-mediated migrations from their centres of origin to new geographic regions (e.g. due to trade or colonization), have exposed livestock species to new environments, cultures and technologies, which, when coupled with selection (both natural and artificial) and adaptation, have created the enormous variety of breeds seen today. However, of the over 50,000 known mammalian and avian species, fewer than 40 of these are considered domesticated by the Food and Agriculture Organization (FAO) of the United Nations (FAO, 2007, 2015; Ajmone-Marsan and The Globaldiv Consortium, 2010; Bruford et al., 2015; for a comparison with crop domestication rates, see Henry, Chapter 1 of this Handbook).

On a worldwide scale, the 'big five' livestock species (i.e. cattle, sheep, chickens, goats and pigs) are globally distributed and have large populations. The first three of these species display the widest distribution (cattle: ~1.5 billion animals globally; sheep: over ~1.2 billion animals; chickens: over ~21 billion animals). In contrast, goats and pigs (~1 billion animals globally for each species) are less well dispersed: goats are less numerous in the Americas, Europe and Southwest Asia than in Africa and Asia, while the majority of pigs are found in Asia with less than one-third being located in Europe and the Americas. Collectively, the 'big five species' provide the majority of the animal food products (i.e. meat and milk) consumed by humans; however, in Asia, buffalo make a major contribution to milk production, while camel milk production is significant on a regional scale in Southwest Asia. Other important uses of the big five include the production of fibres, skins, hides and pelts, particularly from sheep, cattle and goats. In the developing world, draught power, for the pulling of carts or as pack animals, is provided by cattle, horses and donkeys (FAO, 2007, 2015).

In 2007, the FAO adopted the first *Global Plan of Action for Animal Genetic Resources*, a focussed international collaboration dedicated to monitoring and recording of the world's livestock biodiversity for agriculture, rural development and food and nutrition security (FAO, 2007). FAO's *Second Report on the State of the World's Animal Genetic Resources for Food and Agriculture* provides a comprehensive update and evaluation of livestock biodiversity since the first report, drawing on new data provided by 129 countries, 15 international organizations, and four networks and regional groups, with scientific contributions from some 150 world experts (FAO, 2015). The updated *Global Databank for Animal Genetic Resources* (managed by the FAO, and which forms the basis of the *Domestic Animal Diversity Information System* [DAD-IS]) currently reports a total of 8,744 extant breeds belonging to 20 mammalian and 18 avian livestock species distributed across 182 countries (**Table 2.1** *Summary of the species included in the* Global Databank for Animal Genetic Resources). Of these, 7,718 are considered local breeds (i.e. they are found in one country only), with 510 classed as regional transboundary breeds (i.e. breeds that occur in more than one country within a single geographical region), and 546 regarded as international transboundary breeds (i.e. breeds that occur in more than one geographical region) (FAO, 2015). The 2015 report also highlights those breeds, primarily local, which are considered to be at risk, due in part to replacement by more highly productive breeds. In particular, selective breeding for highly productive types has led to growing concerns of the erosion of genetic resources of livestock species culminating in decreased genomic diversity, which could make species susceptible to as yet unforeseen future challenges. Indeed, the FAO report that 1,458 domestic mammalian and avian breeds are considered at-risk, while 647 breeds have become extinct since breed records began in

*Table 2.1* Summary of the species included in the *Global Databank for Animal Genetic Resources*

| *Category* | *Species* |
|---|---|
| Mammalian species (20) | alpaca, American bison, asses, Bactrian camels, buffalo, cattle, deer, dog, dromedaries, dromedary × Bactrian camels, goats, guinea pigs, guanaco, horses, llama, pigs, rabbit, sheep, vicuña, yak |
| Avian species (18) | chicken, cassowary, Chilean tinamous, domestic duck, domestic duck × Muscovy duck, domestic goose, emu, guinea fowl, Muscovy duck, ñandu (rhea), ostrich, partridge, peacock, pheasant, pigeons, quail, swallow, turkey |

the 1800s (FAO, 2015). As the genomic diversity of low-production breeds are considered important to the safeguarding of current or future traits of interest, as well as the future adaptation of breeds during increasing climatic change, the maintenance of these breeds is considered essential (Ajmone-Marsan and The Globaldiv Consortium, 2010; Lenstra et al., 2012).

## Genetic analyses of animal domestication

It is often posited that the domestic state is not a definitive category, but rather part of a continually evolving human-animal relationship ranging from hunting, through loose association, to the intense management of animals. The terms 'wild' and 'domestic' suggest a clear distinction between forms and transitional forms that occurred during the domestication process are not usually considered; indeed, the inherent difficulty in categorizing transitional forms as being 'wild' or 'domestic' can confound zooarchaeological studies of animal domestication. However, past population histories can be reconstructed through the examination of DNA sequence polymorphisms, with genetic information being transmitted through time from past to present populations. Past demographic events (e.g. migrations, expansions, contractions and amalgamations) and evolutionary processes (e.g. mutation, genetic drift, gene flow and natural and artificial selection) lead to altered gene frequencies, and genetic differences between populations can be indicative of their relationship since sharing a common ancestor.

In the context of animal domestication, all modern domesticates derive, with modification, from the wild animals that were incorporated into the finite genetic pool at various stages. Modern domestic populations are the endpoint of a temporal genetic continuum that stretches from the initial phases of animal domestication. The examination of the origins and ancestry of domestic animals has focussed mainly on the analysis of evolutionary neutral, non-coding regions of the nuclear genome; for example, extra-nuclear genomes (i.e. the mitochondrial genome), and nuclear genetic markers such as simple tandem repeat (STR) loci (e.g. microsatellite markers) and single nucleotide polymorphisms (SNPs). These genetic markers have been used to unravel the domestic ancestry of domesticates, with each displaying different modes of inheritance, informational content and mutation rates. More recently, pan-genomic SNP genotyping array platforms and whole genome sequencing data generated by next-generation sequencing (NGS) technologies (whereby millions of genomic DNA fragments from an individual are randomly generated, sequenced in parallel and analyzed) have allowed high-resolution analysis of genetic relationships among breeds. This has led to the identification of discrete segments of animal genomes that have been subject to the selection processes that underlie domestication.

## Domesticated cattle and their origins

Of the major five domestic species, cattle are the most economically important and, as said, number over 1,500 million on a worldwide scale, with some 800 extant cattle breeds. Cattle are an important species in all geographic areas, but especially so in Asia (with 33% of the world total) and Latin America (27%; 14% of the world's total alone is located in Brazil). Large cattle populations are also found in Africa (17% of the global population, with the highest numbers found in Ethiopia and Tanzania) and Europe and the Caucasus (9%) and North America (7%), with smaller numbers found in Southwest Asia (4%) and the Southwest Pacific (3%, with the highest numbers in Australia). Cattle breeds contribute 22% of the world's total number of recorded mammalian livestock breeds (FAO, 2015).

There are two recognized subspecies of domesticated cattle: taurine *(Bos taurus)*, which predominate in the temperate lands of Europe, Northern Asia (including Japan) and Northern and

Western Africa, and zebu or indicine *(Bos indicus)*, which are native to the Indian subcontinent, but also found in the arid and semi-arid regions of East and South Africa and the Near and Middle East (Grigson, 1978, 1980). Despite morphological differences, both domesticated taxa can freely interbreed to produce fertile offspring, presumably because they retain their original chromosome number (Melander, 1959). The two domestic cattle taxa are derived from the morphologically-similar, now-extinct, wild ox or 'aurochs' *(Bos primigenius)*. Aurochs differed distinctly in appearance to modern domesticated cattle, being much larger in size, with shoulder heights ranging up to 2 meters (Zeuner, 1963). Based on differences in fossilized horns and body shapes, archaeozoologists have segregated aurochs into three continental subspecies: Eurasian *(B. primigenius primigenius)*, North African *(B. p. opisthonomus)* and South Asian *(B. p. namadicus)* (Grigson, 1978, 1980). The earliest recorded archaeological evidence for cattle domestication comes from the early Neolithic site of Dja'de el Mughara in the Middle Euphrates Valley in Southwest Asia, where domestic *B. taurus* cattle remains date to around 10,550 calibrated years before present (cal. YBP) (Helmer et al., 2005). Zooarchaeological evidence suggests that *B. taurus* were derived from the Eurasian aurochs, *B. p. primigenius*. Conversely, zebu cattle were domesticated from *B. p. namadicus*, the South Asian aurochs (Grigson, 1980; Meadow, 1993), with domestic *B. indicus* cattle first appearing in Neolithic sites of the Indus Valley (present-day Pakistan and Northwest India) around 7,000 YBP (Allchin and Allchin, 1968; Meadow, 1996).

It is generally held that taurine cattle, along with other Near Eastern domesticates such as sheep, goats, barley and wheat, were introduced into Europe as a result of early pastoralist movements from the Near East. These animals entered Europe via two main routes: (1) a *Danubian* route, in which domestic animals first entered Greece ~9,000 cal. YBP (Reingruber and Thissen, 2009) and later followed the course of the River Danube into Southeast Europe, finally reaching the coast of Northwestern Europe ~7,150 cal. YBP (Dolukhanov et al., 2005); and (2) a more rapid maritime Mediterranean route via the Dalmatian coast, Sicily and Southern France, reaching Iberia ~7,250 cal. YBP. The Neolithic period reached Northwestern Europe ~7,150 cal. YBP, followed by Southern Scandinavia and the British Isles after 6,000 cal. YBP (Tresset and Vigne, 2007).

There have been arguments for an independent domestication of the indigenous African aurochs, *B. p. opisthonomus*, in the Eastern Sahara ~9,200 cal. YBP (Wendorf and Schild, 1994, 2001; Grigson, 2000; Marshall and Hildebrand, 2002). However, some lines of archaeological evidence suggests domestic cattle were introduced into Africa from the Near East between 9,000 and 7,000 YBP (Epstein and Mason, 1984). Although *B. indicus* cattle were thought to have entered Africa from Southwest Asia between AD 700 and 1,500, prior to and during Arab migrations (Epstein and Mason, 1984; Hourani, 1991), there is evidence from a Neolithic site in Kenya that these cattle breeds were present in East Africa at least 1,500 years earlier (Marshall, 1989). Exogenous zebu and native taurine cattle cross-bred to form populations of hybrid *sanga* cattle, the modern descendants of which are found in South and East Africa (Epstein and Mason, 1984).

## *The independent origins of* B. taurus *and* B. indicus

Early genetic investigations of modern cattle populations focussed on the analysis of mtDNA sequence variation using samples of wide geographic provenance. In particular, the clonal transmission of mitochondrial DNA (mtDNA) haplotypes from mother to daughter allows determination of discrete maternal lineages within domestic populations that may have complex genetic histories. Mitochondrial sequences that originate from different captures of a diverse wild species can maintain a phylogenetic distinction even after millennia of domestic inbreeding, which allows the resolution of pre- and post-domestic patterns of sequence diversity. These analyses

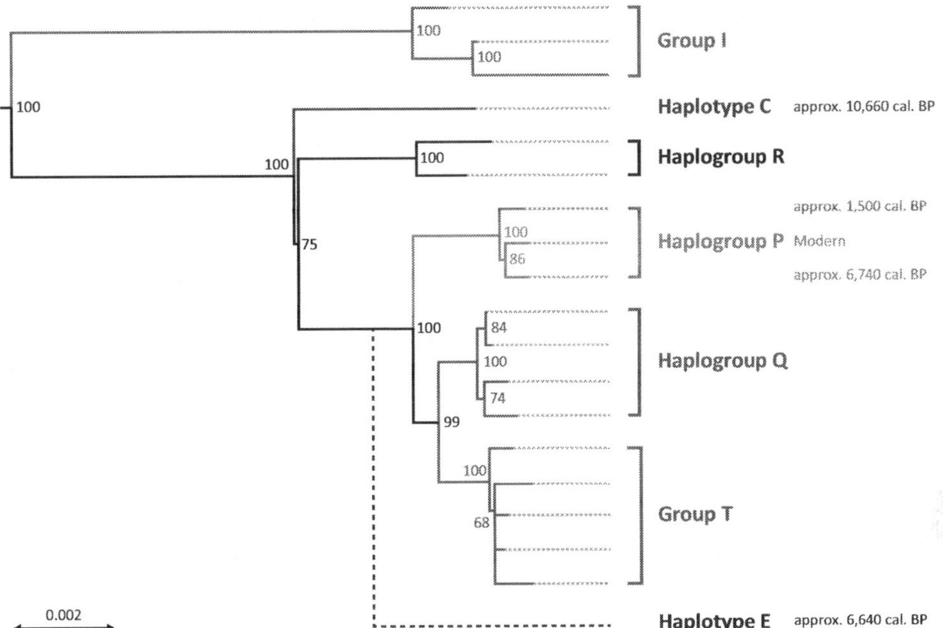


*Figure 2.1* Phylogeny of ancient and modern cattle mitogenomes (16,338 base pairs [bp])

*Note*: Modern *B. taurus* predominantly possess haplogroups from Group T (which consists of T1, T2, T3, T4 and T5), while modern *B. indicus* haplogroups from Group I (which consists of I1 and I2). Haplogroup P is the major haplogroup from the extinct Eurasian aurochs (Edwards et al., 2010; Zeyland et al., 2013), whilst haplogroup E (dashed line) refers to partial mtDNA data from a German aurochs (Edwards et al., 2007b). Haplogroups Q and R have been described in a small number of modern Italian samples (Achilli et al., 2008, 2009), whilst haplogroup C has been recently sequenced from an ancient Chinese domestic sample (Zhang et al., 2013); these data support minor local captures of wild matrilines. The tree was rooted with yak *(Bos grunniens)* sequences, and numbers indicate maximum likelihood node support after 100 bootstrap replicates.

*Source*: Modified after Zhang et al. (2013).

showed that all domestic cattle derive from either taurine or zebu wild progenitors, or are hybrids of the two types. The divergence seen between the European and African *B. taurus* and Indian *B. indicus* is indicative of a pre-domestication separation (Group T and Group I, respectively; **Figure 2.1** *Phylogeny of ancient and modern cattle mitogenomes*), dating in the order of 200,000 years (Loftus et al., 1994a, 1994b). The unambiguous distinction between the taurine and zebu mtDNA sequences has been used to locate geographical regions where historical gene flow and introgression between the two taxa have occurred post-domestication. It has been proposed that this represents a legacy of the westward introduction of zebu cattle and subsequent mating with native taurine populations in these regions (Troy et al., 2001; Edwards et al., 2007a). Similarly, the detection of taurine mtDNA sequences in the modern zebu breeds of Northern India, albeit at a low frequency, has lent support for the eastward migration of taurine cattle and mating with local zebu animals (Magee et al., 2007; Lenstra et al., 2014).

## *The complex ancestry within* B. taurus

Following Vavilov's principle (1926), the centre or origin of domestication is expected to have more ancestral biological variation, as a larger initial population of wild progenitors would have been available for capture in the domestication process. This equates to a higher genetic variation at the source, with a subsequent loss of lineages as domesticates colonize new areas. The most variation in modern-day mtDNA occurs in the Near East in Anatolian breeds, supporting the theory of a Near Eastern domestication (Troy et al., 2001; Lenstra et al., 2014; **Figure 2.2a** *Reduced median network constructed from the most variable 240bp region of the bovine mtDNA control region*). Detailed analysis of *B. taurus* mtDNA sequences has revealed a strong phylogenetic structuring throughout Eurasia and Africa. The majority of modern *B. taurus* cattle root to the taurine phylogeny through one of five distinct yet closely related haplogroups, termed T, T1, T2, T3 and T4 (Troy et al., 2001), which are spatially distributed (**Figure 2.2a**). A sixth haplotype, T5, has also been recently reported in a small number of modern Italian animals (Achilli et al., 2008, 2009). Variants T, T2 and T3 occur at appreciable frequencies in the Near East. A subset of the variation encountered in the Near East, T3 predominates across Europe, suggestive of a derived Near Eastern origin for all European cattle.

In a similar way, haplogroup T1 almost exclusively describes African diversity and is found only at low frequencies elsewhere (Troy et al., 2001; **Figure 2.2a**), and haplogroup T4 has thus far only been detected in Japanese cattle (Mannen et al., 1998). The distribution of T1 and T4 is suggestive that regional incorporation of aurochs may have formed part of the genetic history of African and East Asian-specific *B. taurus* populations. However, the difference between the major five taurine ancestral haplogroups is small, with a coalescence time around the central T haplogroup estimated at ~16,000 YBP (Troy et al., 2001; Achilli et al., 2008, 2009; Ho et al., 2008). Studies on the origins of T1 and T4 haplogroups indicate a scenario where the domestication of *B. p. primigenius* in the Near East was followed by a large population expansion and the separation of the African and East Asian haplotypes through migration and founder effects (Bradley and Magee, 2006; Bollongino and Burger, 2007; Ajmone-Marsan et al., 2010); although introgression between wild and domestic types may have occurred in regional areas such as North Africa (Bonfiglio et al., 2012).

## *The South Asian origin of* B. indicus

In a similar way to *B. taurus*, zebu mtDNA sequences fall into two major haplogroups, I1 and I2 (**Figure 2.2b**). Once again, the star-like patterns observed are due to population expansions occurring after domestication, and the estimated time-depths are congruent with zebu domestic history as determined via archaeology (Ho et al., 2008). The most likely centres of domestication for the I1 and I2 haplogroups are the Indus Valley and Northern India, respectively. There is geographic distribution across South Asia, with I1 predominating in Southeast Asia and I2 almost exclusively found within the Indian subcontinent (**Figure 2.2b**), which is most likely due to later trade routes through the region (Baig et al., 2005; Magee et al., 2007; Chen et al., 2010).

## Analyses of nuclear genetic diversity and cattle domestication

It must be emphasized that phylogenetic inference involving mtDNA is based on only one single segregating locus with an atypical mode of inheritance and unusual population dynamics. It is, therefore, not representative of genome-wide ancestry and, where possible, should be complemented with autosomal and Y-chromosomal genetic marker data. Studies of nuclear genome variation have found differences in allele frequencies between modern taurine and zebu populations, further supporting the divergent domestic origins of these two domestic types (MacHugh et al., 1997; Hanotte et al., 2002).

A)

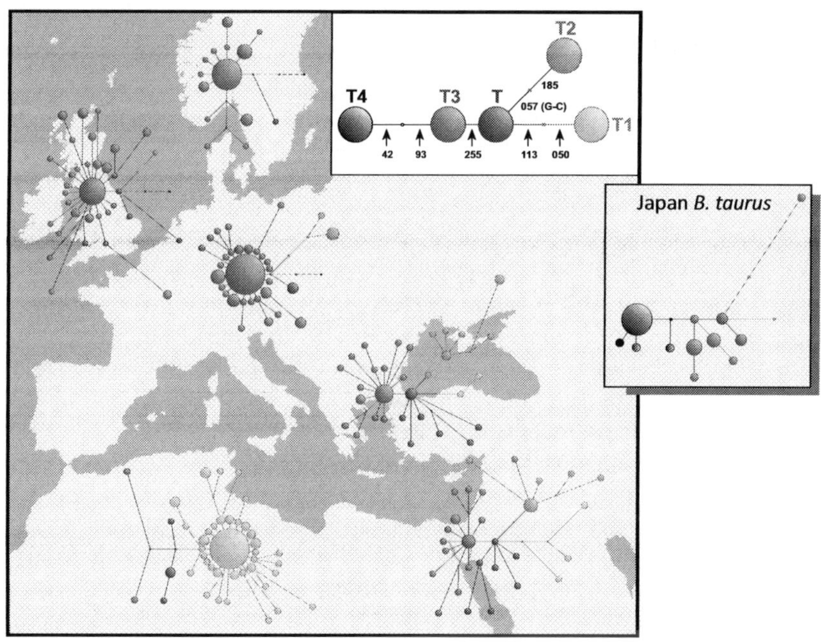


B)

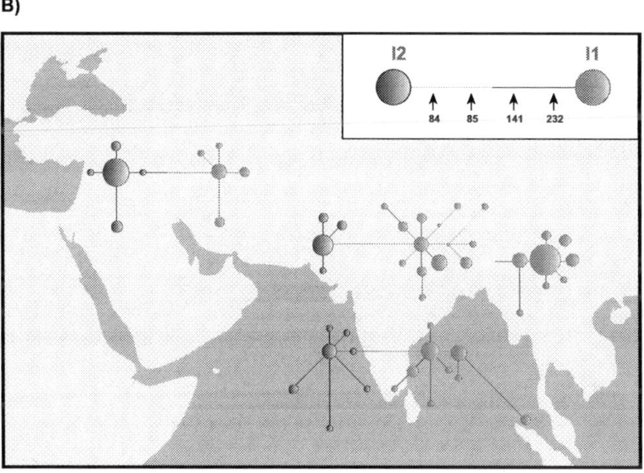


*Figure 2.2* Reduced median network constructed from the most variable 240 bp region of the bovine mtDNA control region

*Note*: (**a**) *B. taurus* and (**b**) *B. indicus* diversity comprises five taurine and two zebu major central haplogroups, respectively. Circles represent sequence haplotypes, the area being proportional to the haplotype frequency. Points are theoretical intermediate nodes introduced by the median-joining algorithm, and branches between haplotypes represent single nucleotide mutations. The positions of the nucleotide substitutions (+16,000) that distinguish each of these haplogroups are shown in the skeleton network in the upper inset in both diagrams. The networks consist of centrally-positioned, numerically-predominant and presumed ancestral haplogroups, surrounded by star-like phylogenies of haplotypes. This is consistent with past demographic expansions associated with the domestication process. (**a**) The predominant European haplogroup, T3, is a subset of the diversity encountered in the Near East, where haplogroups T, T2 and T3 are encountered at appreciable frequencies, suggesting that European taurine maternal lineages owe their ancestry to primary domestication centres proximal to the Fertile Crescent rather than to local input from wild aurochs. Both African and Far Eastern populations display two additional clusters, T1 and T4 , which are suggestive of matrilineal input from local wild aurochs. (**b**) In South Asia, zebu sequences fall into either the I1 or the I2 haplogroups.

*Source*: Modified after Magee et al. (2014).

Historical migration routes of cattle from their centres of origin have also been uncovered using nuclear markers. This is particularly evident in Africa; previous mtDNA work had shown that all modern African cattle have taurine mitochondrial genomes, whereas nuclear analysis found evidence of Indian *B. indicus* introgression (MacHugh et al., 1997; Hanotte et al., 2002; Bovine HapMap Consortium, 2009; Lenstra et al., 2014). This finding was supported by analysis of zebu-specific markers (i.e. markers that are present at high frequencies in Indian *B. indicus* populations compared with *B. taurus* populations), where a cline of zebu-derived alleles from east to west across the continent, and from north to south in West Africa, was apparent (Bradley et al., 1994; MacHugh et al., 1997; Freeman et al., 2004, 2006). This disparity between mtDNA and autosomal markers can be explained by a predominantly male-mediated introgression of zebu cattle into Africa, largely due to Arab migrations from AD 711 onward (Epstein and Mason, 1984; MacHugh et al., 1997). To date, only the trypanotolerant taurine populations of West Africa (such as the N'Dama population of Guinea) have not been subject to appreciable zebu genetic introgression (Bradley et al., 1994; MacHugh et al., 1997).

More recently, it has been possible to elucidate fine-detailed descriptions of cattle domestic history using high-resolution population genomic analyses of SNP data (Bovine HapMap Consortium, 2009; Decker et al., 2009, 2014; Gautier et al., 2010). As with mtDNA- and STR-based studies, analyses of genome-wide SNPs support the separate domestic origins of taurine and zebu cattle (**Figure 2.3** *Principal component [PC] analysis of modern* B. taurus *and* B. indicus *populations based on 44,000 autosomal SNPs*), as well as the zebu ancestry of African cattle (ranging from 0–20% in West Africa taurine populations, and from 23–74% in East, Central and South African hybrid populations; Decker et al., 2009). Decker et al. (2014) also found zebu ancestry in modern

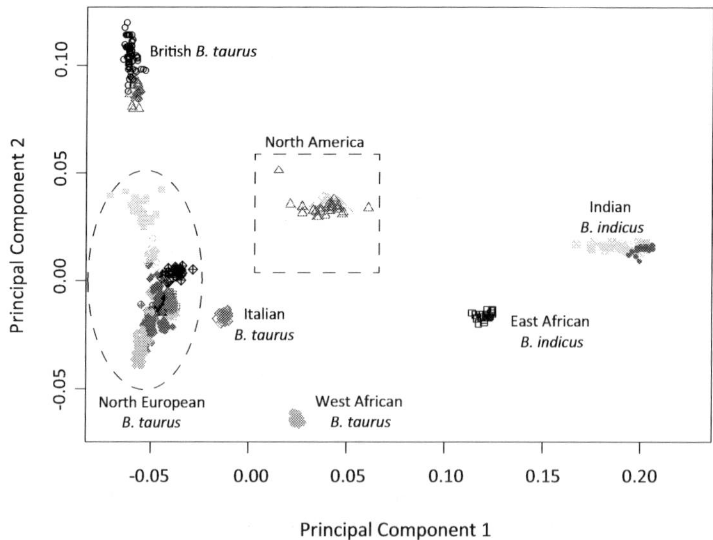


*Figure 2.3* Principal component [PC] analysis of modern *B. taurus* and *B. indicus* populations based on 44,000 autosomal SNPs (Decker et al., 2014)

*Note*: Each symbol represents a single animal. Taurine breeds are separated from zebu breeds along PC1, with admixed breeds from North America and Africa occupying intermediate positions. PC2 partitions breeds within the taurine lineage, with British taurine and West African taurine populations at the two extremes; Northern European taurine populations occupy an intermediate position along PC2.

*Source*: Modified after Magee et al. (2014).

Italian taurine breeds but not in any other European population, which may be indicative of importation from the Near East (where zebu admixture had already occurred) to Southern Europe in Roman times. Furthermore, the partial African taurine ancestry of Iberian and Italian cattle was confirmed, a legacy of historical interact1ons across the Mediterranean.

The divergence between African and European taurine cattle have been cited as support for an independent African origin of African *B. taurus* (**Figure 2.3**); however, more recent studies based on pan-genomic SNP analyses confirm that all taurine cattle share a single recent common ancestor and support the single Near Eastern domestic origin for *B. taurus* (Decker et al., 2014). Indeed, the genetic differences seen in African and Asian populations may be due to admixture with the indigenous aurochs occurring once domesticated taurine populations migrated out of the Near East into these regions (Decker et al., 2009, 2014). Indeed, even the predominance of the T1 haplogroup in Africa could be due to hybridization of T1-carrying local aurochs with early domesticates from the Near East leading to replacement of Near Eastern-derived mtDNA haplotypes (Decker et al., 2014). Purifying natural selection may have also accelerated this replacement, as the wild mtDNA haplogroup T1 may have conferred an advantage in African environments (Soares et al., 2013).

## The use of ancient DNA in cattle domestication studies

As the mitochondrial genome is present in cells at much higher copy numbers than the nuclear genome, it is ideally suited for archaeological genetic studies. The majority of ancient cattle DNA research has focussed on mtDNA variation, addressing broad questions such as the relationship of domestic cattle to the European wild aurochs (Bollongino et al., 2006; Edwards et al., 2007b; Stock et al., 2009). Mitochondrial DNA sequences from European aurochs mainly belong to the haplogroup P, although a single occurrence of a divergent haplotype, E, has also been detected (in an early Neolithic German aurochs; Edwards et al., 2007b). P is distinct to the modern European T-carrying cattle (Troy et al., 2001; Edwards et al., 2007b; **Figure 2.1**), which suggests that there was little to no introgression between domestic cattle and indigenous wild female aurochs (Troy et al., 2001; Bollongino et al., 2006; Edwards et al., 2007b). However, local domestication of aurochs within Europe cannot be completely discounted. Novel haplogroups, Q and R, have recently been sequenced from modern Italian breeds (Achilli et al., 2009; **Figure 2.1**) and, while the Q haplogroup is suggested to have been involved in the Neolithic domestication event in the Near East (Olivieri et al., 2015), reaching Italy via secondary migrations from Anatolia, R most likely entered the modern gene pool via contributions from a distinct population of aurochs (Achilli et al., 2008, 2009; Zeyland et al., 2013). Although P has not been found in any modern European cattle, it has been sequenced from a single 'Beef cattle' from Korea (reported in Achilli et al., 2008), while another haplotype, C, was found in an early Holocene assemblage from China (Zhang et al., 2013; **Figure 2.1**). Together, these results suggest minor introgression of wild matrilines into *B. taurus* populations after the arrival of domestic cattle into Europe and Asia, respectively. Evidence generated from modern and ancient DNA studies of Y-chromosomal DNA has been used to support the possibility of male-mediated introgression from the wild into domestic herds (Götherström et al., 2005), although other studies have suggested that the results can be interpreted as representing more recent farming practices rather than prehistoric herd management (Bollongino et al., 2008).

While global phylogeographic patterns of cattle mtDNA are clear, European cattle populations display little population structure (Lenstra et al., 2014). In addition, mtDNA is a single non-recombining locus, which further imposes limitations on its use for ancient DNA studies, despite the large set of available modern data. Conversely, nuclear DNA data from modern cattle provide breed-level genetic resolution, with a more distinct pattern of genetic variation across Europe (e.g. Bovine HapMap Consortium, 2009; Gautier et al., 2010; Edwards et al., 2011). It is, therefore, both desirable and practicable to extend nuclear DNA-based studies from extant populations to archaeological specimens in order to address questions of ancient population affinity. Prior to the advent of NGS technology, analysis of ancient nuclear DNA, which is present at much lower copy number than mtDNA, proved extremely difficult, and there were only a handful of studies that targeted nuclear DNA from archaeological cattle (Edwards et al., 2003; Götherström et al., 2005; Svensson et al., 2007; Telldahl et al., 2011; McGrory et al., 2012). However, with the new high-throughput DNA sequencing technologies and the recent methodological developments in ancient DNA research, whole genomes from ancient individuals are now being reconstructed, with the first ancient *Bos* genome sequence, from a British aurochs bone dated to ~ 6,750 YBP, being published in 2015 (Park et al., 2015). When compared with a large database of extant cattle genomes, population genomics analyses revealed that the British aurochs contributed significantly to the genetic makeup of modern native British and Irish cattle breeds, which challenges the picture derived from ancient and modern mtDNA data alone. It therefore appears that the boundary between early European domestic cattle populations and wild aurochs was significantly more complex than previously thought.

## The future of domestication studies

Domestication studies have been revolutionized by the recent advances in genetic technologies. NGS projects have generated annotated whole genome sequences for several key species, including those of economic importance (Larkin et al., 2012). In addition, NGS is revolutionizing palaeogenomics, opening up the possibility for investigating domestication directly through analysis of whole genomes from both wild and domestic ancient samples; for example, the first complete aurochs mtDNA genome sequence was published in 2010 (Edwards et al., 2010), followed by the generation of the first complete *B. p. primigenius* genome sequence (Park et al., 2015).

Whole genome analyses are now enabling dissection of quantitative traits in animals that have been subject to natural and artificial selection processes and, more importantly, are uncovering the identity of genes, regulatory regions and DNA sequence polymorphisms that have large phenotypic effects on economically-important production traits (Larkin et al., 2012; Qanbari et al., 2012; Ramey et al., 2013; Rothammer et al., 2013; Utsunomiya et al., 2013). Comparisons of domestic and wild genomes can answer important questions about evolutionary and domestication-related processes, and how they have shaped biological variation in animal populations through time.

## References


Achilli, A., Bonfiglio, S., Olivieri, A., Malusà, A., Pala, M., Hooshiar Kashani, B., Perego, U. A., Ajmone-Marsan, P., Liotta, L., Semino, O., Bandelt, H.-J., Ferretti, L. and Torroni, A. (2009) 'The multifaceted origin of taurine cattle reflected by the mitochondrial genome', *PLoS ONE*, vol. 4, p. e5753.

Achilli, A., Olivieri, A., Pellecchia, M., Uboldi, C., Colli, L., Al-Zahery, N., Accetturo, M., Pala, M., Hooshiar Kashani, B., Perego, U. A., Battaglia, V., Fornarino, S., Kalamati, J., Houshmand, M., Negrini, R., Semino, O., Richards, M., Macaulay, V., Ferretti, L., Bandelt, H.-J., Ajmone-Marsan, P. and Torroni, A. (2008) 'Mitochondrial genomes of extinct aurochs survive in domestic cattle', *Current Biology*, vol. 18, pp. R157–158.

Ajmone-Marsan, P., Garcia, J. F. and Lenstra, J. A. (2010) 'On the origin of cattle: How aurochs became cattle and colonized the world', *Evolutionary Anthropology*, vol. 19, pp. 148–157.

Ajmone-Marsan, P. and The Globaldiv Consortium (2010) 'A global view of livestock biodiversity and conservation – GLOBALDIV', *Animal Genetics*, vol. 41 (Suppl. 1), pp. 1–5.

Allchin, B. and Allchin, R. (1968) *The Birth of Indian Civilization: India and Pakistan before 500 B.C.*, Penguin Books, London, UK.

Baig, M., Beja-Pereira, A., Mohammad, R., Kulkarni, K., Farah, S. and Luikart, G. (2005) 'Phylogeography and origin of Indian domestic cattle', *Current Science*, vol. 89, pp. 38–40.

Bollongino, R. and Burger, J. (2007) 'Neolithic cattle domestication as seen from ancient DNA', *Proceedings of the British Academy*, vol. 144, pp. 165–187.

Bollongino, R., Edwards, C. J., Alt, K. W., Burger, J. and Bradley, D. G. (2006) 'Early history of European domestic cattle as revealed by ancient DNA', *Biology Letters*, vol. 2, pp. 155–159.

Bollongino, R., Elsner, J., Vigne, J.-D. and Burger, J. (2008) 'Y-SNPs do not indicate hybridisation between European aurochs and domestic cattle', *PLoS ONE*, vol. 3, p. e3418.

Bonfiglio, S., Ginja, C., De Gaetano, A., Achilli, A., Olivieri, A., Colli, L., Tesfaye, K., Agha, S. H., Gama, L. T., Cattonaro, F., Penedo, M. C., Ajmone-Marsan, P., Torroni, A. and Ferretti, L. (2012) 'Origin and spread of *Bos taurus*: New clues from mitochondrial genomes belonging to haplogroup T1', *PLoS ONE*, vol. 7, p. e38601.

Bovine HapMap Consortium (2009) 'Genome-wide survey of SNP variation uncovers the genetic structure of cattle breeds', *Science*, vol. 324, pp. 528–532.

Bradley, D. G., MacHugh, D. E., Loftus, R. T., Sow, R. S., Hoste, C. H. and Cunningham, E. P. (1994) 'Zebu-taurine variation in Y chromosomal DNA: A sensitive assay for genetic introgression in west African trypanotolerant cattle populations', *Animal Genetics*, vol. 25, pp. 7–12.

Bradley, D. G. and Magee, D. A. (2006) 'Genetics and the origins of domestic cattle', pp. 317–328 in M. A. Zeder, D. G. Bradley, E. Emshwiller and B. D. Smith (eds.), *Documenting Domestication: New Genetic and Archaeological Paradigms*, University of California Press, Berkeley, CA, USA.

Bruford, M. W., Ginja, C., Hoffmann, I., Joost, S., Orozco-terWengel, P., Alberto, F. J., Amaral, A. J., Barbato, M., Biscarini, F., Colli, L., Costa, M., Curik, I., Duruz, S., Ferenĉaković, M., Fischer, D., Fitak, R., Groeneveld, L. F., Hall, S. J. G., Hanotte, O., Hassan, F. U., Helsen, P., Iacolina, L., Kantanen, J., Leempoel, K., Lenstra, J. A., Ajmone-Marsan, P., Masembe, C., Megens, H.-J., Miele, M., Neuditschko, M., Nicolazzi, E. L., Pompanon, F., Roosen, J., Sevane, N., Smetko, A., Štambuk, A., Streeter, I., Stucki, S., Supakorn, C., Telo Da Gama, L., Tixier-Boichard, M., Wegmann, D. and Zhan, X. (2015) 'Prospects and challenges for the conservation of farm animal genomic resources, 2015–2025', *Frontiers in Genetics*, vol. 6, p. 314.

Chen, S., Lin, B. Z., Baig, M., Mitra, B., Lopes, R. J., Santos, A. M., Magee, D. A., Azevedo, M., Tarroso, P., Sasazaki, S., Ostrowski, S., Mahgoub, O., Chaudhuri, T. K., Zhang, Y. P., Costa, V., Royo, L. J., Goyache, F., Luikart, G., Boivin, N., Fuller, D. Q., Mannen, H., Bradley, D. G. and Beja-Pereira, A. (2010) 'Zebu cattle are an exclusive legacy of the South Asia Neolithic', *Molecular Biology and Evolution*, vol. 27, pp. 1–6.

Clutton-Brock, J. (2012) *Animals as Domesticates: A World View through History*, Michigan State University Press, East Lansing, MI, USA.

Decker, J. E., McKay, S. D., Rolf, M. M., Kim, J., Molina Alcalá, A., Sonstegard, T. S., Hanotte, O., Götherström, A., Seabury, C. M., Praharani, L., Babar, M. E., Correia de Almeida Regitano, L., Yildiz, M. A., Heaton, M. P., Liu, W. S., Lei, C. Z., Reecy, J. M., Saif-Ur-Rehman, M., Schnabel, R. D. and Taylor, J. F. (2014) 'Worldwide patterns of ancestry, divergence, and admixture in domesticated cattle', *PLoS Genetics*, vol. 10, p. e1004254.

Decker, J. E., Pires, J. C., Conant, G. C., McKay, S. D., Heaton, M. P., Chen, K., Cooper, A., Vilkki, J., Seabury, C. M., Caetano, A. R., Johnson, G. S., Brenneman, R. A., Hanotte, O., Eggert, L. S., Wiener, P., Kim, J. J., Kim, K. S., Sonstegard, T. S., Van Tassell, C. P., Neibergs, H. L., McEwan, J. C., Brauning, R., Coutinho, L. L., Babar, M. E., Wilson, G. A., McClure, M. C., Rolf, M. M., Kim, J., Schnabel, R. D. and Taylor, J. F. (2009) 'Resolving the evolution of extant and extinct ruminants with high-throughput phylogenomics', *Proceedings of the National Academy of Sciences USA*, vol. 106, pp. 18644–18649.

Diamond, J. (2002) 'Evolution, consequences and future of plant and animal domestication', *Nature*, vol. 418, pp. 700–707.

Dolukhanov, P., Shukurov, A., Gronenborn, D., Sokoloff, D., Timofeev, V. and Zaitseva, G. (2005) 'The chronology of Neolithic dispersal in Central and Eastern Europe', *Journal of Archaeological Science*, vol. 32, pp. 1441–1458.

Edwards, C. J., Baird, J. F. and MacHugh, D. E. (2007a) 'Taurine and zebu admixture in Near Eastern cattle: A comparison of mitochondrial, autosomal and Y-chromosomal data', *Animal Genetics*, vol. 38, pp. 520–524.

Edwards, C. J., Bollongino, R., Scheu, A., Chamberlain, A., Tresset, A., Vigne, J.-D., Baird, J. F., Larson, G., Ho, S. Y., Heupink, T. H., Shapiro, B., Freeman, A. R., Thomas, M. G., Arbogast, R. M., Arndt, B., Bartosiewicz, L., Benecke, N., Budja, M., Chaix, L., Choyke, A. M., Coqueugniot, E., Döhle, H. J.,

Göldner, H., Hartz, S., Helmer, D., Herzig, B., Hongo, H., Mashkour, M., Ozdogan, M., Pucher, E., Roth, G., Schade-Lindig, S., Schmölcke, U., Schulting, R. J., Stephan, E., Uerpmann, H. P., Vörös, I., Voytek, B., Bradley, D. G. and Burger, J. (2007b) 'Mitochondrial DNA analysis shows a Near Eastern Neolithic origin for domestic cattle and no indication of domestication of European aurochs', *Proceedings of the Royal Society B–Biological Sciences*, vol. 274, pp. 1377–1385.

Edwards, C. J., Connellan, J., Wallace, P. F., Park, S. D., McCormick, F. M., Olsaker, I., Eythórsdóttir, E., MacHugh, D. E., Bailey, J. F. and Bradley, D. G. (2003) 'Feasibility and utility of microsatellite markers in archaeological cattle remains from a Viking Age settlement in Dublin', *Animal Genetics*, vol. 34, pp. 410–416.

Edwards, C. J., Ginja, C., Kantanen, J., Pérez-Pardal, L., Tresset, A., Stock, F., European Cattle Genetic Diversity Consortium, Gama, L. T., Penedo, M. C., Bradley, D. G., Lenstra, J. A. and Nijman, I. J. (2011) 'Dual origins of dairy cattle farming-evidence from a comprehensive survey of European Y-chromosomal variation', *PLoS ONE*, vol. 6, p. e15922.

Edwards, C. J., Magee, D. A., Park, S. D., McGettigan, P. A., Lohan, A. J., Murphy, A., Finlay, E. K., Shapiro, B., Chamberlain, A. T., Richards, M. B., Bradley, D. G., Loftus, B. J. and MacHugh, D. E. (2010) 'A complete mitochondrial genome sequence from a mesolithic wild aurochs (*Bos primigenius*)', *PLoS ONE*, vol. 5, p. e9255.

Epstein, H. and Mason, I. L. (1984) *Evolution of Domesticated Animals*, Longman, London.

FAO (2015) *The Second Report on the State Of The World's Animal Genetics Resources for Food and Agriculture*, FAO, Rome, Italy.

Food and Agriculture Organization of the United Nations (FAO) (2007) *The State of the World's Animal Genetics Resources for Food and Agriculture*, FAO, Rome, Italy.

Freeman, A. R., Hoggart, C. J., Hanotte, O. and Bradley, D. G. (2006) 'Assessing the relative ages of admixture in the bovine hybrid zones of Africa and the Near East using X chromosome haplotype mosaicism', *Genetics*, vol. 173, pp. 1503–1510.

Freeman, A. R., Meghen, C. M., MacHugh, D. E., Loftus, R. T., Achukwi, M. D., Bado, A., Sauveroche, B. and Bradley, D. G. (2004) 'Admixture and diversity in West African cattle populations', *Molecular Ecology*, vol. 13, pp. 3477–3487.

Gautier, M., Laloe, D. and Moazami-Goudarzi, K. (2010) 'Insights into the genetic history of French cattle from dense SNP data on 47 worldwide breeds', *PLoS ONE*, vol. 5, p. e13038.

Götherström, A., Anderung, C., Hellborg, L., Elburg, R., Smith, C., Bradley, D. G. and Ellegren, H. (2005) 'Cattle domestication in the Near East was followed by hybridization with aurochs bulls in Europe', *Proceedings of the Royal Society B–Biological Sciences*, vol. 272, pp. 2345–2350.

Grigson, C. (1978) 'The craniology and relationships of four species of *Bos*. 4. The relationship between *Bos primigenius* Boj. and *Bos taurus* L. and its implications for the phylogeny of the domestic breeds', *Journal of Archaeological Sciences*, vol. 5, pp. 123–152.

Grigson, C. (1980) 'The craniology and relationships of four species of *Bos*. 5. *Bos indicus* L.', *Journal of Archaeological Sciences*, vol. 7, pp. 3–32.

Grigson, C. (2000) '*Bos africanus* (Brehm)? Notes on the archaeozoology of the native cattle of Africa', pp. 38–60 in R. M. Blench and K. C. MacDonald (eds.), *The Origins and Development of African Livestock: Archaeology, Genetics, Linguistics and Ethnography*, UCL, London, UK.

Hanotte, O., Bradley, D. G., Ochieng, J. W., Verjee, Y., Hill, E. W. and Rege, J. E. (2002) 'African pastoralism: Genetic imprints of origins and migrations', *Science*, vol. 296, pp. 336–339.

Helmer, D., Gourichon, L., Monchot, H., Peters, J. and Saña Segui, M. (2005) 'Identifying early domestic cattle from Pre-Pottery Neolithic sites on the Middle Euphrates using sexual dimorphism', pp. 86–95 in J.-D. Vigne, J. Peters and D. Helmer (eds.), *The First Steps of Animal Domestication: New Archaeozoological Approaches*, Oxbow, Oxford, UK.

Ho, S. Y., Larson, G., Edwards, C. J., Heupink, T. H., Lakin, K. E., Holland, P. W. and Shapiro, B. (2008) 'Correlating Bayesian date estimates with climatic events and domestication using a bovine case study', *Biology Letters*, vol. 4, pp. 370–374.

Hourani, A. (1991) *A History of the Arab Peoples*, Faber, London, UK.

IFAD (2010) *Rural Poverty Report 2011*, International Fund for Agricultural Development, Quintily, Rome, Italy.

Larkin, D. M., Daetwyler, H. D., Hernandez, A. G., Wright, C. L., Hetrick, L. A., Boucek, L., Bachman, S. L., Band, M. R., Akraiko, T. V., Cohen-Zinder, M., Thimmapuram, J., Macleod, I. M., Harkins, T. T., McCague, J. E., Goddard, M. E., Hayes, B. J. and Lewin, H. A. (2012) 'Whole-genome resequencing of two elite sires for the detection of haplotypes under selection in dairy cattle', *Proceedings of the National Academy of Sciences USA*, vol. 109, pp. 7693–7698.

Larson, G. and Fuller, D. Q. (2014) 'The evolution of animal domestication', *Annual Review of Ecology, Evolution, and Systematics*, vol. 45, pp. 115–136.

Larson, G., Piperno, D. R., Allaby, R. G., Purugganan, M. D., Andersson, L., Arroyo-Kalin, M., Barton, L., Climer Vigueira, C., Denham, T., Dobney, K., Doust, A. N., Gepts, P., Gilbert, M. T., Gremillion, K. J., Lucas, L., Lukens, L., Marshall, F. B., Olsen, K. M., Pires, J. C., Richerson, P. J., Rubio de Casas, R., Sanjur, O. I., Thomas, M. G. and Fuller, D. Q. (2014) 'Current perspectives and the future of domestication studies', *Proceedings of the National Academy of Sciences USA*, vol. 111, pp. 6139–6146.

Lenstra, J. A., Ajmone-Marsan, P., Beja-Pereira, A., Bollongino, R., Bradley, D. G., Colli, L., De Gaetano, A., Edwards, C. J., Felius, M., Ferretti, L., Ginja, C., Hristov, P., Kantanen, J., Liron, J. P., Magee, D. A., Negrini, R. and Radoslavov, G. A. (2014) 'Meta-analysis of mitochondrial DNA reveals several population bottlenecks during worldwide migrations of cattle', *Diversity*, vol. 6, pp. 178–187.

Lenstra, J. A., Groeneveld, L. F., Eding, H., Kantanen, J., Williams, J. L., Taberlet, P., Nicolazzi, E. L., Sölkner, J., Simianer, H., Ciani, E., Garcia, J. F., Bruford, M. W., Ajmone-Marsan, P. and Weigend, S. (2012) 'Molecular tools and analytical approaches for the characterization of farm animal genetic diversity', *Animal Genetics*, vol. 43, pp. 483–502.

Loftus, R. T., MacHugh, D. E., Bradley, D. G., Sharp, P. M. and Cunningham, P. (1994a) 'Evidence for two independent domestications of cattle', *Proceedings of the National Academy of Sciences USA*, vol. 91, pp. 2757–2761.

Loftus, R. T., MacHugh, D. E., Ngere, L. O., Balain, D. S., Badi, A. M., Bradley, D. G. and Cunningham, E. P. (1994b) 'Mitochondrial genetic variation in European, African and Indian cattle populations', *Animal Genetics*, vol. 25, pp. 265–271.

MacHugh, D. E., Shriver, M. D., Loftus, R. T., Cunningham, P. and Bradley, D. G. (1997) 'Microsatellite DNA variation and the evolution, domestication and phylogeography of taurine and zebu cattle (*Bos taurus* and *Bos indicus*)', *Genetics*, vol. 146, pp. 1071–1086.

Magee, D. A., MacHugh, D. E. and Edwards, C. J. (2014) 'Interrogation of modern and ancient genomes reveals the complex domestic history of cattle', *Animal Frontiers*, vol. 4, pp. 7–22.

Magee, D. A., Mannen, H. and Bradley, D. (2007) 'Duality in *Bos indicus* mtDNA diversity: Support for geographical complexity in zebu domestication', pp. 385–391 in M. D. Petraglia and B. Allchin (eds.), *The Evolution and History of Human Populations in South Asia: Inter-Disciplinary Studies in Archaeology, Biological Anthropology, Linguistics, and Genetics*, Springer, Dordrecht, the Netherlands.

Mannen, H., Tsuji, S., Loftus, R. T. and Bradley, D. G. (1998) 'Mitochondrial DNA variation and evolution of Japanese black cattle (*Bos taurus*)', *Genetics*, vol. 150, pp. 1169–1175.

Marshall, F. (1989) 'Rethinking the role of *Bos indicus* in Sub-Saharan Africa', *Current Anthropology*, vol. 30, pp. 235–240.

Marshall, F. and Hildebrand, E. (2002) 'Cattle before crops: The beginnings of food production in Africa', *Journal of World Prehistory*, vol. 16, pp. 99–143.

McGrory, S., Svensson, E. M., Götherström, A., Mulville, J., Powell, A. J., Collins, M. J. and O'Connor, T. P. (2012) 'A novel method for integrated age and sex determination from archaeological cattle mandibles', *Journal of Archaeological Science*, vol. 39, pp. 3324–3330.

Meadow, R. H. (1993) 'Animal domestication in the Middle East: A revised view from the Eastern Margin', pp. 295–320 in G. L. Possehl (ed.), *Harappan Civilization: A Recent Perspective*, American Institute of Indian Studies, Oxford & IBH Publishing Company, New Delhi, India.

Meadow, R. H. (1996) 'The origins and spread of pastoralism in northwestern South Asia', pp. 390–412 in D. R. Harris (ed.), *The Origins and Spread of Agriculture and Pastoralism in Eurasia*, University College London Press, London, UK.

Melander, Y. (1959) 'The mitotic chromosomes of some cavicorn mammals (*Bos-taurus* L, *Bison-bonasus* L and *Ovis-aries* L)', *Hereditas*, vol. 45, pp. 649–664.

Olivieri, A., Gandini, F., Achilli, A., Fichera, A., Rizzi, E., Bonfiglio, S., Battaglia, V., Brandini, S., De Gaetano, A., El-Beltagi, A., Lancioni, H., Agha, S., Semino, O., Ferretti, L. and Torroni, A. (2015) 'Mitogenomes from Egyptian cattle breeds: New clues on the origin of haplogroup Q and the early spread of *Bos taurus* from the Near East', *PLoS ONE*, vol. 10, p. e0141170.

Park, S. D., Magee, D. A., McGettigan, P. A., Teasdale, M. D., Edwards, C. J., Lohan, A. J., Murphy, A., Braud, M., Donoghue, M. T., Liu, Y., Chamberlain, A. T., Rue-Albrecht, K., Schroeder, S., Spillane, C., Tai, S., Bradley, D. G., Sonstegard, T. S., Loftus, B. J. and MacHugh, D. E. (2015) 'Genome sequencing of the extinct Eurasian wild aurochs, *Bos primigenius*, illuminates the phylogeography and evolution of cattle', *Genome Biology*, vol. 16, p. 234.

Qanbari, S., Strom, T. M., Haberer, G., Weigend, S., Gheyas, A. A., Turner, F., Burt, D. W., Preisinger, R., Gianola, D. and Simianer, H. (2012) 'A high resolution genome-wide scan for significant selective sweeps: An application to pooled sequence data in laying chickens', *PLoS ONE*, vol. 7, p. e49525.

Ramey, H. R., Decker, J. E., McKay, S. D., Rolf, M. M., Schnabel, R. D. and Taylor, J. F. (2013) 'Detection of selective sweeps in cattle using genome-wide SNP data', *BMC Genomics*, vol. 14, p. 382.

Reingruber, A. and Thissen, L. (2009) 'Depending on C-14 data: Chronological frameworks in the Neolithic and Chalcolithic of southeastern Europe', *Radiocarbon*, vol. 51, pp. 751–770.

Rothammer, S., Seichter, D., Forster, M. and Medugorac, I. (2013) 'A genome-wide scan for signatures of differential artificial selection in ten cattle breeds', *BMC Genomics*, vol. 14, p. 908.

Soares, P., Abrantes, D., Rito, T., Thomson, N., Radivojac, P., Li, B., Macaulay, V., Samuels, D. C. and Pereira, L. (2013) 'Evaluating purifying selection in the mitochondrial DNA of various mammalian species', *PLoS ONE*, vol. 8, p. e58993.

Stock, F., Edwards, C. J., Bollongino, R., Finlay, E. K., Burger, J. and Bradley, D. G. (2009) 'Cytochrome *b* sequences of ancient cattle and wild ox support phylogenetic complexity in the ancient and modern bovine populations', *Animal Genetics*, vol. 40, pp. 694–700.

Svensson, E. M., Anderung, C., Baubliene, J., Persson, P., Malmström, H., Smith, C., Vretemark, M., Daugnora, L. and Götherström, A. (2007) 'Tracing genetic change over time using nuclear SNPs in ancient and modern cattle', *Animal Genetics*, vol. 38, pp. 378–383.

Telldahl, Y., Svensson, E., Götherström, A. and Stora, J. (2011) 'Typing late prehistoric cows and bulls – osteology and genetics of cattle at the Eketorp ringfort on the Oland island in Sweden', *PLoS ONE*, vol. 6, p. e20748.

Tresset, A. and Vigne, J.-D. (2007) 'Substitution of species, techniques and symbols at the Mesolithic/Neolithic transition in Western Europe', pp. 189–210 in A. W. R. Whittle and V. Cummings (eds.), *Going Over: The Mesolithic-Neolithic Transition in North-West Europe*, British Academy, Oxford University Press, Oxford, UK.

Troy, C. S., MacHugh, D. E., Bailey, J. F., Magee, D. A., Loftus, R. T., Cunningham, P., Chamberlain, A. T., Sykes, B. C. and Bradley, D. G. (2001) 'Genetic evidence for Near-Eastern origins of European cattle', *Nature*, vol. 410, pp. 1088–1091.

Uerpmann, H. P. (1996) 'Animal domestication: Accident or intention?', pp. 227–237 in D. R. Harris (ed.), *The Origins and Spread of Agriculture and Pastoralism in Eurasia*, UCL Press, London, UK.

Utsunomiya, Y. T., Pérez O'Brien, A. M., Sonstegard, T. S., Van Tassell, C. P., do Carmo, A. S., Mészáros, G., Sölkner, J. and Garcia, J. F. (2013) 'Detecting loci under recent positive selection in dairy and beef cattle by combining different genome-wide scan methods', *PLoS ONE*, vol. 8, p. e64280.

Vavilov, N. (1926) *Studies on the Origin of Cultivated Plants*, Institut Botanique Appliqué et d'Amelioration des Plantes, Leningrad, USSR.

Wendorf, F. and Schild, R. (1994) 'Are the early Holocene cattle in the Eastern Saharan domestic or wild?', *Evolutionary Anthropology*, vol. 3, pp. 118–128.

Wendorf, F. and Schild, R. (2001) *Holocene Settlement of the Egyptian Sahara, Vol. 1: The Archaeology of Nabta Playa*, Kluwer Academic, New York, NY, USA.

Zeder, M. A. (2012) 'The domestication of animals', *Journal of Anthropological Research*, vol. 68, pp. 161–190.

Zeuner, A. F. E. (1963) *A History of Domesticated Animals*, Hutchinson & Co, London, UK.

Zeyland, J., Wolko, L., Bocianowski, J., Szalata, M., Słomski, R., Dzieduszycki, A. M., Ryba, M., Przystałowska, H. and Lipiński, D. (2013) 'Complete mitochondrial genome of wild aurochs (*Bos primigenius*) reconstructed from ancient DNA', *Polish Journal of Veterinary Sciences*, vol. 16, pp. 265–273.

Zhang, H., Paijmans, J. L., Chang, F., Wu, X., Chen, G., Lei, C., Yang, X., Wei, Z., Bradley, D. G., Orlando, L., O'Connor, T. and Hofreiter, M. (2013) 'Morphological and genetic evidence for early Holocene cattle management in northeastern China', *Nature Communications*, vol. 4, p. 2755.

# 3

# FOREST AND TREE GENETIC RESOURCES

*David Boshier, Judy Loo and Ian K. Dawson*

## Introduction

Trees show certain fundamental differences from agricultural crops in cultural, biological (life history, ecology, genetics) and economic terms, which result in differences in their use, management and conservation. Throughout the world, the varied cultural and religious values placed on woodlands, forests and even individual trees demonstrate their special place in the human psyche. In agricultural landscapes, many cultures retain forest patches as spirit/sacred groves which protect the burial places of ancestors as well as plants and animals, forming important but often overlooked components of a forest conservation network (Pungetti et al., 2012). Individual trees may be protected as sacred (e.g. Buddhist culture) or for aesthetic reasons (e.g. tree preservation orders in the United Kingdom). The elemental role of trees in the lives of rural people is also obvious from the many uses of tree products (e.g. construction, fencing, furniture, foods, medicines, fibres, fuels, forage). Forests and trees-outside-forests contribute to the livelihoods of more than 1.6 billion people worldwide (World Bank, 2008), with approximately 900 million people living in farm landscapes that have more than 10% tree cover, particularly in Southeast Asia, Central America and South America (Zomer et al., 2014).

The varying levels of dependency of communities on tree products and services has, however, often been poorly described or acknowledged (Byron and Arnold, 1999), although the situation has improved recently with initiatives such as the Poverty Environment Network (Angelsen et al., 2014; see also Ingram et al., Chapter 4 of this Handbook). Proper description has been hampered by the ubiquitous nature of tree products and services, and the complex inter-connections by which trees influence livelihoods (e.g. Turner et al., 2012). Poor characterization has also reflected the different sources of tree products and services, with forest and farmland sources often assessed differently by separately-operating and often little-communicating government forestry and agriculture departments (de Foresta et al., 2013). Thus, the positive roles and limitations of trees in supporting livelihoods are often neglected by policy makers, with poor targeting of development interventions related to managing trees in forests and farms (World Bank, 2008).

Recognizing the importance of trees and this lack of information, the first-ever report on the State of the World's Forest Genetic Resources (SOW-FGR) focused on the 'tree' component of forests and farmlands (FAO, 2014a). From 86 individual Country Reports (representing >85% of global forest cover), approximately 8,000 taxa of trees, shrubs, palms and bamboo were cited as useful, with 42%

used for timber and 41% for non-timber forest products (NTFPs), as discussed in Chapter 4 of this Handbook and also termed NWFPs (non-wood forest products; FAO, 2014a). In contrast to the limited number of agricultural crop species grown, the combined listings from the Country Reports indicated almost 2,300 tree, shrub, palm and bamboo species as national priorities for conservation and management, with economic value in the formal economy a major factor in prioritization. However, approximately 500 of those species were nominated as important for management at least in part for negative reasons related to their potential invasiveness (explored by Koskela et al., 2014).

The Country Reports show, however, that in the prioritization of species relatively little attention was given to the high value of tree products and services in informal economies. In most tropical regions, the most important use for NWFPs is shown as food (FAO, 2010); for example USD 90 billion worth of food and other NWFPs were estimated to be harvested annually from forests and trees in developing countries two decades ago (Pimentel et al., 1997). FAO's 2010 Global Forest Resources Assessment (GFRA) provides more recent, but lower, estimates of global value (based on 2005 figures), at USD 19 billion and 17 billion annually for NWFPs (including foods) and woodfuel removals, respectively (FAO, 2010). These values are likely to be gross underestimates, however, as many countries report only value for the 'top' few NWFP tree species of commercial importance. Tree commodity crops represent an exception to the limited information on the value of tree products, with export data compiled widely by national governments and assembled by FAO. Data from FAOSTAT for the five most important woody plant/palm commodity crops grown widely in the tropics – palm oil *(Elaeis guineensis)*, coffee (primarily *Coffea arabica*), rubber *(Hevea brasiliensis)*, cocoa *(Theobroma cacao)* and tea (primarily *Camellia sinensis*) – indicated a large export value of more than USD 80 billion in 2010, which is of the same order as total annual NWFP extractions (Dawson et al., 2014). Given the diversity of benefits from tree genetic resources, greater knowledge of these resources and the issues related to their sustainable use and conservation, both within and outside of forests, is essential.

## Threats to tree genetic resources

From the preceding section, it is evident that the loss, continued degradation and fragmentation of tree populations in forests, woodlands and agroforestry landscapes is of practical concern to rural communities worldwide. Of the 8,000 tree and other perennial plant species listed as used in the SOW-FGR Country Reports, about half were also noted as threatened. The current IUCN Red List of Threatened Species[1] lists 1,200 trees and shrubs as 'critically endangered', 1,700 as 'endangered' and another 3,700 as 'vulnerable'. Although it is generally agreed that *in situ* conservation is the first line of defence, it is only in Europe that *in situ* reserves (known as dynamic genetic conservation units) have been established systematically to conserve tree genetic resources (Lefèvre et al., 2013). On the basis of the Country Reports of the SOW-FGR, at least 1,800 tree species are conserved *ex situ* in seed banks, botanic gardens and elsewhere, with approximately 600 of these species listed as priorities for conservation and management (FAO, 2014a). Data from other sources show that the actual number of tree species stored *ex situ* is much greater, as illustrated by the more than 5,800 woody perennial species listed as available globally through seed suppliers' active collections (Dawson et al., 2013; TSSD[2]). Active collections are, however, rarely secure in the long term, while many *ex situ* collections for long-term storage suffer from limited genetic diversity due to narrow sampling, a lack of accompanying passport data (Dawson et al., 2013) and ultimately problems associated with regeneration. Better coordination is also needed between *ex situ, in situ* and *circa situm* (see **Box 3.1** *Conservation options for tree species*) conservation efforts.

This chapter considers the conservation-on-farm *(circa situm)* value of trees and how the nature and context of landscape, production system, forest/agriculture interface and socio-economic

## Box 3.1 Conservation options for tree species

- *In situ* conservation involves the conservation of flora or fauna in the location and the ecosystem (in as natural a state as possible) in which they naturally occur. Trees may be conserved under natural conditions due to their use, or that of the ecosystem in which they are found, but *in situ* conservation may also occur for other reasons such as existence value. *In situ* refers only to location rather than motivations.
- *Ex situ* conservation involves the removal of flora or fauna from the location where they naturally occur, and their conservation either in a dormant state (e.g. as tissue or seed) or in breeding populations (e.g. in seed orchards). Seed orchards may supply germplasm for planting at the same time as conserving diversity, whereas other gene banks (either planted or *in vitro*) may be inspired solely by existence value.
- *Circa situm* conservation involves the conservation of biodiversity within its native range but under conditions highly altered by human activity. Trees are often conserved *circa situm* due to their use and consequent active retention in otherwise altered landscapes. However, many other trees persist in altered ecosystems without active protection or management, due for example to their vigour or the limited resources available to farmers to remove them. *Circa situm* refers to where the conservation is carried out, rather than its motivations.
- On-farm tree management: much discussion of the importance of trees on farms has focused on their livelihood value. In this respect, on-farm tree management is clearly a form of conservation through use, although only under certain circumstances does it contribute to the conservation of biodiversity.

*Source*: Modified from Barrance et al. (2009).

and cultural values influence use and conservation options. This discussion is set against a background of how basic biological differences between tree species and annual/other crops influence levels and patterns of genetic diversity, their subsequent use and conservation. Farmland trees may play important and varied roles in the long-term viability of some native species by maintaining minimum viable populations of threatened species, facilitating gene flow between patches of native forest, conserving particular genotypes not found in reserves and acting as intermediaries and alternative host habitats for pollinators and seed dispersers (Boshier et al., 2004). It is important to recognize the complementary role that maintenance of trees on farms plays to *in situ* conservation. Underestimating the capacity of many species to persist in agroforests under current practices may lead to the misdirection of limited conservation resources towards species that are not in fact under threat. The knowledge that some tree species can be conserved through existing farming practices can free resources for the conservation of more critically threatened species needing more conventional, resource-intensive approaches.

## Trees are different from other crops in their basic biology

By its very nature, biodiversity is complex and multifaceted, incorporating ecosystems, habitats, species, populations and genes. Most natural resource planners recognize tree genetic diversity and the processes that underlie it as components of ecosystem and species stability, adaptability, conservation and use; rarely, however, is there any explicit attention to them in management planning and decision-making. As many aspects of genetic diversity are hidden ('cryptic' variation), the importance of genetic diversity is easily overlooked. The value of intraspecific variation in tree species and the importance of managing this genetic variation to support rural livelihoods, have received relatively little attention from policy makers (Dawson et al., 2009), despite the benefits to rural communities that proper consideration offers (Fisher and Gordon, 2007). Resource limitations also result in genetic information being ignored or given only minor consideration in conservation or management strategies. It is far more common for ecological, social or economic criteria, alone or in combination, to drive decisions (Graudal et al., 2014).

The primary factors that shape genetic variability within tree species are, as for other plants, breeding system, natural selection, genetic drift and gene flow (Petit and Hampe, 2006). Trees have a diverse array of breeding systems (outbreeding, mixed-mating, selfing), associated incompatibility mechanisms and sexual systems (hermaphrodite, monoecy, dioecy) that influence their reproduction and levels of genetic diversity, and hence their evolutionary trajectories, current use, prospects for future adaptation and conservation. Breeding systems not only influence genetic structure but are themselves controlled genetically and may not therefore be constant, having the flexibility to respond to changing conditions. Thus, at any moment, the genetic status of a tree population results from a combination of factors such as history, spatial distribution, flowering phenology, breeding system and patterns of both pollination and seed dispersal (Petit and Hampe, 2006). Sub-population structure, inter-population variation and gene flow all effect patterns of variation and adaptation in a tree species.

In comparison to crops, trees exhibit more extreme life history traits (i.e. long-lived, late attainment of reproductive age, overlapping generations) and experience a wider variety of stresses (natural- and human-induced) during their lives, presenting different challenges for conservation and use (Petit and Hampe, 2006). Most trees are predominantly outcrossing, maintaining high levels of genetic diversity through a range of breeding systems that allows them to cope with the various conditions they experience over their lives. Their long-lived nature results in the accumulation of mutations, both somatic and in the germline, such that trees generally carry a heavy genetic load of deleterious recessive alleles (Williams and Savolainen, 1996). Consequently, any inbreeding, and in particular selfing, may lead to reduced fertility and poorer regeneration, slower growth rates, and increased susceptibility to abiotic and biotic stresses, including pests and diseases (Griffin, 1991). For trees, there is a clear need to limit the possibility and impact of inbreeding by maintaining genetic diversity. Indeed, it may be critical in seed collections for successful on-farm planting, habitat restoration, breeding or *ex situ* conservation (e.g. Thomas et al., 2014). Despite this, there is generally a lack of recognition of the importance of genetic diversity in trees and the implications for use and conservation.

For trees, knowledge of the factors influencing the spatial scale of genetic diversity and adaptation is increasingly important for conservation (e.g. determining sampling strategies for *ex situ* collections, setting priorities for genetic reserves, understanding how to source planting material for ecological restoration), production (e.g. obtaining appropriate, productive planting material for a variety of products and services) and for ensuring future adaptability to changing environmental conditions (Alfaro et al., 2014). The development of molecular markers can facilitate answers to such questions through more direct measurements of levels and patterns of genetic variation, as well as of the spatial and temporal dynamics of mating and gene flow. For trees, such research initially focussed on species of commercial interest for timber, and consequently, most early information came from coniferous taxa of northern temperate forests (e.g. Muona, 1989; Hamrick et al., 1992). In recent decades, the balance has been partially redressed by more research on tropical trees, investigating a range of taxa representative of the diversity of ecological contexts, reproductive attributes and uses (e.g. Wickneswari et al., 2014). Genomic knowledge of forest trees lags behind that of model herbaceous species that include many of the main agricultural crops. However, for several tree species, the entire genome has been or is in the process of being sequenced (Argout et al., 2011), with novel approaches developed to link markers to important traits. Genomic or marker-assisted selection is close to being realized in some tree species, including temperate fruit trees (Muranty et al., 2015). Phenotyping and data management, however, remain considerable bottlenecks.

There is a growing understanding of the need for 'systems-oriented' approaches, as evidenced by recent studies that demonstrate the role of genetic variation in determining not only the performance of particular tree species but of entire ecosystems (Wymore et al., 2014). Such approaches can, directly or indirectly, provide insights into tree genetic structures, and actual and required effective population sizes across farm landscapes. However, for trees in agroecosystem dominated landscapes, specific challenges to increasing our understanding remain (**Box 3.2** *Challenges in characterizing tree genetic variation in agroecosystems*).

When establishing a species, the first generation of trees plays a key role in either subsequent natural regeneration or collection of seed for further planting. Low genetic diversity in the founder population may result in inbreeding and reduced fitness in future generations (McKay et al., 2005). Sampling of genetic diversity may also be smaller than is apparent purely from a census count, as overlapping generations reduce effective population size. In fragmented landscapes, reproductive dominance by a few large canopy trees (e.g. in pasture) can also reduce effective

## Box 3.2 Challenges in characterizing tree genetic variation in agroecosystems

- The large number of species involved: a large number of tree species is found on farms in a diverse array of agroforestry systems, as well as in remnant forest patches within agricultural landscapes. Farmers are interested in practical work with a wide range of species. Analysis of genetic variation in all taxa is impractical, but can studies on a subset of tree species within a particular context provide useful information for other taxa and wider ecosystems? Is the concept of 'model' species – targets for research from which general recommendations for interventions can be devised – relevant or not (Atta-Krah et al., 2004; Dawson et al., 2009)?
- Difficulties in recognizing and quantifying variation: in comparison to most crops, most forest tree species have had, until recently, little or no history of domestication. As a result, genetic variation may be difficult for farmers to evaluate in agricultural landscapes, as they are not able to recognize important 'varietal' differences in trees in the same way as they can for traditional agricultural crops. Important variation may sometimes be invisible to the naked eye (Atta-Krah et al., 2004) and 'surrogate' measures of genetic variation have not been widely explored (e.g. Jennings et al., 2001; Graudal et al., 2014). This situation particularly applies when the tree propagule is not the desired product from the tree (e.g. the eventual form and growth rate of a timber tree cannot be judged from the appearance of the seed).
- Lack of recognition of problems until too late: as trees can persist in landscapes even when they are no longer reproductively active (Janzen, 1986), problems in some species related to inbreeding, lack of seed set and regeneration may not be immediately evident. By the time problems become clear, the landscape may have been modified to such a degree that it is too late to devise practical interventions.

population size, while loss of self-incompatibility alleles may also limit regeneration in small populations. A number of studies have shown that a lack of attention to these issues can lead to genetic bottlenecks in community nurseries, in natural regeneration on farms and in restoration programmes (e.g. Kettle et al., 2014).

Unlike with annual crops, the most popular planting material for trees are nursery seedlings, partly because this enhances the success rate of planting (Godefroid et al., 2011). Consequently, the possibility of using optimal species combinations and planting materials that are both adapted to site conditions and genetically diverse is often limited by what is available in nurseries. Seed collectors and nurseries that use the seed are driven by economic and practical considerations. They may avoid some species because of a lack of appropriate protocols (e.g. to break seed dormancy, store recalcitrant seed) and often minimize the number of tree species they work with because of limited accessibility and availability of seed sources, a desire to simplify nursery management and to reduce the risk of having unsold seedlings at the end of the season. Avoidance of the vagaries of both seed and seedling availability requires tree planters to be in early communication with tree nursery managers, to allow time for seed collection and seedling production of desired species with adequate genetic diversity.

## Trees differ from crops in terms of domestication status

Although some 2,400 tree species are actively managed for their products and services, only about 700 are recorded as subject to improvement programmes, with mostly tree commodity crops (e.g. cocoa and coffee) and some timber species subject to more intensive domestication, while genetic parameters are described for only about 1% of all tree species (FAO, 2014a). The value placed on trees for food is, however, reflected in the ancient indigenous domestication of a number of tree species in regions such as Mesoamerica (Galindo-Tovar et al., 2008) and the Amazon (Clement et al., 2015). Indigenous domestication of tree species typically shows a progression from collection in the wild through management to active cultivation. In intermediate phases, tree crops tend to be managed *in situ*, whereas agricultural crops are brought onto farms. Running parallel to increases in management are increases in the movement of germplasm (very local, through regional to wide translocation), associated with progressions in commodity use and marketing (home consumption, through local marketing to regional and global marketing).

The boundaries between forest and farm settings are often in flux and can only be loosely defined. Forests that appear pristine may have been manipulated for millennia to produce 'anthropogenic forests'. In the Amazon, residual effects of pre-Columbian human management are evident as high density aggregations of useful trees such as Brazil nut *(Bertholletia excelsa)* located close to anthropogenic soils known as 'dark earths' (Clement and Junqueira, 2010). Human movement means that tree species distributions may have expanded so that divisions between natural and exotic (through planting) distributions are now unclear. As a consequence, related, but previously allopatric (isolated), species may be brought into sympatry, with the possibility of interspecific hybridization. Anderson (1954) was among the first to point to the importance of disturbed sites, such as kitchen middens and backyard gardens, as suitable habitats where otherwise isolated plant species were brought into sympatry through cultivation.

The well-documented example of the tree genus *Leucaena* shows how prevalent and influential the casual or intentional sympatry of species in cultivation can be. The genus occurs in Mexico and Central America, with some 22 species and two named hybrids, of which the seed and pods of 13 species are used for food, with eight of these species cultivated (Hughes, 1998). Given the widespread use of the seeds and pods for food, unsurprisingly most vernacular (e.g. Mixtec) names relate to species differences in pod characteristics including size, shape, colour and season of production. Fine intraspecific divisions indicative of intensive use and management are also recognized within widely cultivated and intensively used species, such as *L. esculenta*. Pre-domestication cultivation of *Leucaena* species resulted in extensive artificial sympatry and a complex series of geographically dispersed spontaneous hybrids and at least one, possibly more, polyploids (Hughes et al., 2007).

Such ancient processes are mirrored recently by a participatory approach to the domestication of wild indigenous fruit and nut trees into local cultivation in Central Africa. Communities' traditional knowledge of tree use and management is combined with scientific advances in germplasm collection, selection, propagation and market development (Leakey, 2010; see also Chapter 14 of this Handbook), with some success in promoting farm diversification and wider impacts on incomes and health (Jamnadass et al., 2011). The approach brings selected indigenous trees from local wild stands into farms, appearing to provide a good balance between farm-level productivity gains and landscape-level conservation of genetic resources (Leakey, 2010).

Some have argued that promoting tree domestication has negative impacts on the diversity of agricultural landscapes at both interspecific and intraspecific levels. At an intraspecific level, domestication by definition causes shifts and/or losses in underlying genetic diversity in the manipulated populations (Dawson et al., 2009). However, the extent and nature of changes depends on the domestication method, with some approaches more favourable for maintaining diversity. Model analysis of a participatory domestication project with *Bactris gasipaes* in Peru, for example, showed that the risk of genetic erosion in a regional context was low (Cornelius et al., 2006). The wide use of clonal propagation methods during participatory domestication could, however, cause longer-term challenges for intraspecific diversity, due to preferential or exclusive use of small numbers of clones, especially if substantial inter-village germplasm exchange occurs. Diversity losses may, however, be much greater if domestication for increased tree productivity were not to occur, as then farmers may not plant trees at all, but rather cultivate other plants that are (otherwise) more productive (Sunderland, 2011).

## The context of trees/forests on farms and in agricultural landscapes

Throughout the world, a large number of tree species are maintained and planted on farms in a range of contexts, including home gardens, fence lines, alleys, pastures and mixed with perennial or annual crops (**Table 3.1** *Examples of tree species richness in tropical agroforestry landscapes*). These different agroforestry systems reflect the various benefits sought from trees by farmers, and the suitability of different species and systems for providing them. Farming landscapes also often integrate secondary forests and forest fragments. The scale of interactions between trees and other components in agricultural landscapes is a crucial factor in determining activities and configurations for providing different products and services (Garrity, 2004). When grown on farms, tree products are often described as agroforestry tree products (AFTPs) to differentiate them from NWFPs and wood products harvested from forests (Simons and Leakey, 2004). Gradations between natural forests, anthropogenic forests and agroforests, however, mean that there is often no clear boundary between product sources, a complicating factor in estimating relative contributions of different ecosystems to livelihoods, and in devising appropriate management options for different settings (de Foresta et al., 2013). In some cases, trees are retained/planted by farmers for the products they provide on an ongoing (e.g. fruit, medicine) or one-off (e.g. large-bole timber) basis and/or for services such as soil fertility (e.g. alley cropping) and shade (e.g. shade coffee and cocoa). Trees may also be retained because they are too difficult to remove, or although they are not used by farmers they are not overly competitive, so there is no particular reason to remove them ('benign neglect'; Schroth et al., 2011).

*Table 3.1* Examples of tree species richness in tropical agroforestry landscapes (ordered by descending number of tree species identified in each study)

| *Farming system and location* | *Description of results* | *Reference* |
|---|---|---|
| 265 farm plots (each 0.5 ha) in 18 different agroecological zones, Mount Kenya, Kenya | 424 woody plant species, 306 indigenous. Mean of 17 species per plot. Eight of ten most frequent species were exotic. | Kehlenbeck et al., 2011 |
| 35 smallholders' farms (60 ha total) east of Mount Kenya, Kenya | 297 tree species, ~ ⅔ of which indigenous. Mean of 54 species per farm. Five most common species were exotic. | Lengkeek et al., 2005 |
| 5 cacao cabruca plantation plots (each 3 ha) in southern Bahia, Brazil[a] | 293 tree species, 97% indigenous. Mean of 101 species per plot. Exotic species relatively more abundant (> individuals per species) than indigenous ones. | Sambuichi and Haridasan, 2007 |
| 126 samples in range of agroecosystems, over 4 communities in southern Honduras | 241 tree and shrub species. Mean of 34.5 species per sample and 154 species per community. | Gordon et al., 2003 |
| 146 plots (each 0.063 ha) in 60 cacao agroforests from 12 villages in sub-regions of Yaoundé, Mbalmayo and Ebolowa, Cameroon | 206 mostly indigenous tree species. Mean of 21 species per agroforest. High relative abundance of non-primary forest species. | Sonwa et al., 2007 |
| 24 dairy farm pastures' (237 ha total) near Monteverde, Costa Rica | 190 tree species, 57% primary forest trees. Primary forest trees accounted for (only) 33% of all individuals. | Harvey and Haber, 2008 |
| 51 plots (each 0.1 ha) in three shade coffee cooperatives in Tacuba, El Salvador | 123 tree species identified (46 not determined). Mean of 12 to 22 species per plot, depending on cooperative. 11 species of conservation concern based on international listings. Of 58 species considered of benefit by farmers, seven of conservation concern. | Méndez et al., 2007 |
| Six forest gardens (2.68 ha in total) in two areas of West Kalimantan, Indonesia | > 120 identified tree species (precise number not given). Mean of 52 species per garden. Most species in gardens not planted; of these 'easily dispersed' and/or 'easily established' species were over-represented in gardens compared with forest. | Marjokorpi and Ruokolainen, 2003 |
| 124 plots (each 0.12 ha) in 15 shade coffee farms of three types (shade monoculture, SM; simple polyculture, SP; diverse polyculture, DP) in central Veracruz, Mexico | 107 tree species, 83 indigenous (50 primary and 33 secondary species). Mean of 11 (SM) to 29 species (DP) per farm. Three species of international conservation concern. DP farms richer in tree species than nearby forest. | López-Gómez et al., 2008 |
| 80 plots (each 0.06 ha) in 20 cacao cabruca farms in northern Espírito Santo, Brazil[a] | 105 tree species, 101 indigenous, the majority pioneer and early secondary species. Mean of 15 tree species per farm. | Rolim and Chiarello, 2004 |
| Interviews with 68 cattle ranchers and small-scale farmers in Los Santos and Rio Hato, Panama (NB, not direct farm inventory) | 99 tree species identified by farmers as used, planted or protected on their land, ¾ of which indigenous. | Garen et al., 2011 |

| *Farming system and location* | *Description of results* | *Reference* |
|---|---|---|
| 60 actively managed coffee-based agroforestry plots (of variable area) in three villages in Guinée Forestière, Guinea, West Africa | 94 species of mature trees, compared with 134 in natural forest. Mean of 59 tree species per village. A few species dominant in agroforests. Nine species in agroforests classified as vulnerable according to IUCN listings. | Correia et al., 2010 |
| 240 plots (each 0.2 ha) in coffee farms in Lampung province, Sumatra, Indonesia, outside and inside (120 plots each) Bukit Barisan Selatan National Park (BBS) | 92 identified trees species in coffee plots outside BBS, 90 in plots inside of BBS, compared with 141 in natural forest plots (with same sample area). The most abundant species in coffee plots outside and inside BBS were exotic. | Philpott et al., 2008 |
| 0.56 ha of primary forest, 21 ha cocoa agroforests, in Ondo state, Nigeria | 62 tree species in primary forest, 14 species IUCN classification. 45 tree species in agroforests, six species IUCN classification. | Oke and Odebiyi, 2007 |

a *Cabruca* – agroforestry system with cacao planted in cleared understorey within native forest

*Source*: Adapted and updated from Dawson et al. (2013).

For farmers, functional diversity is more important than high tree species diversity, such that a significant proportion of tree species diversity currently found in agricultural landscapes could probably be lost without having much effect on farm production, at least in the short- to medium-term (Kindt et al., 2006). For example, although large numbers of tree species are found in cocoa agroforests, tree species composition is distinct from, and lower in number than, that of natural forests (**Table 3.1**). Furthermore, although endangered tree species may be retained in agroforests, in many locations, there is a general transition to lower tree species diversity dominated by exotics (e.g. oil palm, mango *[Mangifera indica]*, avocado *[Persea americana]*, *Acacia* and *Eucalyptus* species) and local pioneers. Thus, although cocoa agroforests are diverse, they do not equate with primary forests. The sometimes negative attitudes of farmers towards the retention of timber and other trees in such systems may be related to factors such as tree tenure laws, the long period for trees to mature and the need for other income sources to augment farm income in the meantime and damage to perennial/annual crops that may accompany extraction.

## *Natural regeneration of tree cover may be more appropriate than planting*

In Niger, the adoption of farmer-managed natural regeneration (FMNR) of indigenous leguminous trees, such as *Faidherbia albida*, rather than their direct planting, has led to the 'regreening' of approximately 5 million hectares since 1985 (Sendzimir et al., 2011). Such practices have increased sorghum and millet yields more widely in the Sahel region of Africa, resulting in greater dietary diversity and improvements in household incomes in some locations (Place and Binam, 2013). The success of FMNR illustrates that at sites with low to intermediate levels of degradation, where soils are largely intact and there are adequate germplasm sources (e.g. mature trees or soil seed bank), natural regeneration may be the best choice for re-establishing tree cover (Chazdon, 2008). Natural regeneration can bypass some of the maladaptation risks associated with introducing germplasm and help maintain genetic integrity. However, in sites where diverse native seed sources are lacking or insufficient, seed sources suffer from genetic erosion and/or active planting is envisaged, the introduction of external planting material may either be advantageous or simply the only short-term solution. The main choice of what material to use lies in species selection, with native species generally preferred by farmers and for wider ecosystem restoration (Thomas et al., 2014). In ecosystem restoration, evidence is growing for the importance of choosing tree species that represent different functional groups based on adaptive traits (e.g. Aerts and Honnay, 2011). However, the use of native species and their selection requires more knowledge of traits associated with their reproductive biology, phenology, propagation and management. This knowledge gap for native species means that more readily available, better researched, but less well suited, exotic species are often chosen for restoration projects (Boshier et al., 2009; Newton, 2011).

An example is seen with *Leucaena salvadorensis*, where severe forest degradation in most of the species' natural distribution (seasonally dry Pacific slopes of El Salvador, Honduras, and Nicaragua between 200 and 800 masl) has left only a few small forest remnants on steep inaccessible slopes. The species is prized by local communities within its native range as a source of round timber, poles and firewood, being deliberately retained and protected by farmers around houses, in fields and within fence lines. The species is therefore more common in the landscape than the depleted state of natural forest cover would suggest. There is, however, little tradition of planting *L. salvadorensis*, which is an outcrossed diploid and produces few seed. Instead, the non-native, self-fertile and tetraploid *L. leucocephala*, which is more easily propagated, is promoted for cultivation, threatening the maintenance and local use of *L. salvadorensis*. Though the two species are similar in appearance as seedlings, *L. leucocephala* produces inferior quality wood and grows less well on degraded soils.

## *Concerns of hybridization in farm landscapes*

Hybridization of introduced species with native species is particularly prevalent in certain genera (e.g. *Leucaena*, Hughes et al., 2007; *Prosopis*, Carney et al., 2000), with obvious implications for the conservation of native gene pools. Concerns have also been raised regarding the impacts of intraspecific hybridization. Where a germplasm source is not local, planted trees are likely to have a different genetic composition, such that crossing with natural stands may lead to the dilution and loss of unique genetic diversity. Wild *Coffea arabica* stands in the few remaining fragments of Ethiopian montane forest are threatened by hybridization with introduced coffee cultivars planted on neighbouring farms (Labouisse et al., 2008; Aerts et al., 2013). Planted *Inga edulis* trees in smallholders' fields in the Peruvian Amazon were found to be different in genetic composition from neighbouring wild populations, raising concerns for natural stands if there are interactions between forest and farmland trees (Dawson et al., 2008). The 'exotic planted' *Inga* had larger fruit than local wild trees, explaining why farmers had introduced them. In such circumstances, it is necessary to understand the trade-offs between connectivity, genetic dilution and the level of return farmers receive from planting.

Although the orthodox view is that wild-cultivated interactions may be detrimental to wild stands where cultivated material is genetically very different, some scientists have argued for the mixing of populations as beneficial under scenarios of rapid anthropogenic climate change, where new combinations of alleles will facilitate rapid adaptation (Weeks et al., 2011). Research is required on the extent of outbreeding depression (breakdown of co-adapted gene complexes) in tree species that may occur from such interactions, as it remains a relatively understudied issue and there is limited evidence for it, except in the case of interspecific hybridization (Ellstrand, 2003; Edmands, 2007).

## *Low tree densities on farmland may limit conservation benefits*

Although trees and forest on farms may be important for conservation, the small size of most subsistence farms means that considering the wider scale is important in achieving potential conservation benefits. Tree species of importance from a conservation perspective are often present only at low densities in farm landscapes (Gordon et al., 2003; Dawson et al., 2013), so to bring real biodiversity benefits conservation strategies require implementation of beneficial management over a large area, and hence by large numbers of smallholders. In cocoa agroforests, for example, an emphasis on cocoa production often means that the number of cocoa plants per hectare is maximized. Consequently, cocoa agroforests although potentially rich in tree species (**Table 3.1**) typically retain lower numbers and reduced population densities of individual tree species compared with natural forest. With densities for most native tropical species of 0.05 to 0.5 trees per ha (e.g. Lengkeek et al., 2005), large areas of agroforests are required to maintain significant populations of individual species; for example, at least 10,000 ha for the lowest density species (0.05 trees/ha) to have a census population of 500 trees, while a much larger area is required for an effective population size of 500 trees. Lower tree densities may affect the reproductive capacity of individual species and levels of genetic diversity, while small forest remnants may reach a critical threshold to support forest biodiversity, due to the increased influence of surrounding land uses. Thus, the number of farmers adopting and continuing to maintain a particular production system is crucial to realizing prospective conservation benefits, and this aspect requires monitoring, given the speed with which farming practices may change.

## *The importance of production system and species characteristics in defining conservation prospects*

As is clear from the examples given in the two previous sections, the prospects for conserving tree species diversity and maintaining other associated benefits in farmland depend on the particular production system, the intensity of management, and hence the stage and complexity of agro-ecological succession attained. While, for example, shade grown coffee and cacao are generally supportive of biodiversity, the trend to monoculture seen in 'full sun' cacao and coffee, and oil palm plantations, reduces conservation value and encourages dependence by growers on single crops (e.g. Schroth et al., 2011; Ruf, 2011). However, multi-strata agroforests, such as shade cocoa and coffee, may not represent stable management systems and may change gradually or quickly towards assemblages of lower conservation value, depending on commodity price fluctuations and incentives. Similarly, although traditional rubber agroforests are compatible with habitat and biodiversity conservation, they are often under pressure for conversion to more intensive and less diverse production systems (Ekadinata and Vincent, 2011). Efforts to increase the output of such systems that depend on the rehabilitation of neglected production stands, rather than increasing the area under cultivation via deforestation, need to be promoted.

In most cases, assessments of the genetic conservation benefits of agroforestry systems also require consideration of the biology of the tree species involved. Available information suggests that the following tree species types are less likely to show genetic conservation benefits from agroforestry systems: outcrossing species that are self-compatible, slow-growing species that reproduce only when they are large (the extreme case being monocarpic species, that is, those that flower only once in their life), species with poor regeneration under human disturbance, species with highly specific pollinators or seed dispersers susceptible to disturbance, rare species with low population densities, and species with highly clumped distributions. Inevitably, such generalizations will be qualified by the range of factors that have been shown to influence genetic variation in trees.

## Tree genetic diversity and connectivity in agroecosystem landscapes

Molecular diversity studies of farmland and adjacent forest tree populations suggest that diversity in agricultural landscapes depends on the length and intensity of tree management, the degree of planting undertaken and the method of propagation. When species have been managed for millennia, bottlenecks can be observed in farmland (e.g. for the important fruit trees *Inga edulis* in the Peruvian Amazon, see Dawson et al., 2008 and *Spondias purpurea* in Mesoamerica, see Miller and Schaal, 2006). However, where management intensity is low, there may be little difference between farm and neighbouring natural populations (e.g. for the important fruit tree *Vitellaria paradoxa* in the Sahelian and Sudanian eco-zones of West Africa; Kelly et al., 2004). Overall, the limited molecular data from comparative studies suggest that although indigenous trees in farmland occasionally experience genetic bottlenecks, these are relatively minor, despite concerns connected with germplasm collection. Founder effects and impacts on production may be of more concern for exotic trees than indigenous ones (e.g. for the timber tree *Acacia mangium* introduced from Australia and Papua New Guinea into Southeast Asia; Harwood et al., 2004).

Studies of pollen-mediated gene flow between trees in forest and farmland demonstrate that pollen exchange is generally more frequent between nearby trees but transfers can occur over km in agroecosystem landscapes, even between physically isolated trees (e.g. Ward et al., 2005; Lander et al., 2011). Thus, for many tree species, populations and individuals, gene flow can be high across some fragmented landscapes with little apparent forest cover. The view of forest fragmentation as producing genetic isolation may be more of a human perception than a true reflection of actual gene flow, with the type of non-habitat (i.e. agroecosystem) between forest patches affecting patterns of insect and other animal dispersal, and hence seed and pollen dispersal (Lander et al., 2011). Thus, the focus of conservation management can move from questions such as 'How much land can be set aside?', 'How can distance be minimized between habitat patches?' and 'How can habitat bridges be created?' to measures of separation between habitat patches that incorporate variability in how easily a target organism passes through the different land-use types in the landscape (i.e. issues of permeability). Thus, farm land outside forest ceases to be just an area to pass through and is seen in terms of its own capacity to provide habitat services, as well as its ability to support or inhibit movement. The entire landscape is considered a patchwork of partial habitats of varying quality, recognizing the potential habitat services that different land uses may support, and providing a useful basis for developing landscape management strategies that integrate farm production and conservation (Lander et al., 2011).

## Conclusions

The current rate of global deforestation presents significant threats to the conservation of tree species and populations *in situ* (FAO, 2014a). With *ex situ* methods for tree conservation constrained primarily by limited representation and problems of regeneration, it seems inevitable that there will be a greater reliance on the conservation of trees *circa situm* in farm landscapes. How, then, can farmland tree species diversity be maintained or enhanced over time or at least the rate of loss reduced? How can the genetic base of farmland tree populations be ensured while supporting productivity increases that encourage farmers to plant them? How can farmland trees respond to climate change?

Although there is in some cases a growing awareness of the genetic aspect to conservation, relatively little information on conservation genetics is reaching forest scientists, managers and policy makers so that it can be translated into practice (Graudal et al., 2014). As already noted, in many cases, wider ecological, social or economic considerations may actually be the defining processes of any particular conservation strategy. The challenge for conservationists, geneticists and foresters alike, is therefore to use this information to establish the circumstances under which genetic considerations, though often unseen, may become limiting to the overall conservation goals/objectives of a particular programme. The institutional frameworks within which researchers work rarely support team-based, multidisciplinary approaches that are needed to properly assess genetic variation and then apply this knowledge through appropriately-devised management interventions. For agroforestry, the situation is acute, as 'forestry' and 'agriculture' are traditionally considered as discrete schools of research that should be treated separately, whereas aspects from both must be combined together if effective action is to be realized (Dawson et al., 2009).

The complementary benefits of different land use practices for genetic conservation must be further evaluated, recognized and promoted. There is a need to raise awareness among development professionals of the value of natural regeneration in contributing to both conservation and livelihoods. The emphasis on a limited range of tree species, often exotics, by development agencies may reduce the potential conservation (inter- and intraspecific) benefits of agroforestry systems, besides creating potential problems of invasiveness. However, there is also a need for conservation planners, more accustomed to *in situ* methods, to consider the possibility that tree populations found outside protected areas, including in farmland, have a role in biodiversity conservation (Boshier et al., 2004). This in turn requires direct involvement of development organizations in conservation, and effective interactions between them and traditional conservation organizations, to ensure both conservation and development benefits, and minimize any negative trade-offs.

A Global Plan of Action for the Conservation, Sustainable Use and Development of Forest Genetic Resources (FAO, 2014b), devised from the findings of the SOW-FGR (FAO, 2014a), identified four main action areas: (1) greater availability of information on FGR to facilitate and enable better decision making on sustainable use and management, (2) strengthening and harmonization of conservation methods to support FGR and evolutionary processes both inside and outside forests, (3) enhancing approaches to sustainably use and develop FGR to support livelihoods, and (4) developing more appropriate policies, institutions and capacity-building approaches to support successful planning in the forestry sector. Specifically there is a need to improve the availability of, and access to, information on FGR, enhance *in situ* and *ex situ* conservation and improve sustainable use and management (FAO, 2014b) of FGR. While not using the term *circa situm*, the Plan stresses the importance of tree genetic resources on-farm through strategic priority 8, 'Support and develop sustainable management and conservation of FGR on farmland' (FAO, 2014b). It is, therefore, essential to consider agricultural settings with reference to points 1 to 4.

Many of the tree species identified as priorities by the SOW-FGR, especially for local use, have received little or no research attention to their biological attributes and management options, indicating a need to associate funding with priority-setting exercises. Measures to improve smallholders' access to tree planting material and thereby enhance diversity include 'diversity fairs', training of seed collectors in appropriate germplasm sampling methods, provision of more business support to small-scale commercial tree seed and seedling enterprises to deliver germplasm sustainably and the establishment of more seed multiplication stands of key species in farmers' fields and in public lands (Dawson et al., 2009). However, some indigenous tree species of conservation concern are difficult to cultivate (López-Gómez et al., 2008) and/or are of little priority to farmers (Barrance et al., 2009). In addition, information sharing of the service and subsistence values of trees species should not be neglected, as these can be considerable and equally or more important than commercial value, depending on circumstances (Faye et al., 2011). With ratification in 2014 of the Nagoya Protocol[3] on access to genetic resources and benefit sharing, the transaction costs for sourcing tree germplasm (also materials such as leaves and bark) for research may increase, especially for trees whose natural distributions cover a large number of countries (Koskela et al., 2014). The danger is of a slowing of research when its importance in responding to climate change and other global challenges is increasing (Alfaro et al., 2014), and when new tools (e.g. genomics) could support major breakthroughs in characterization, production and adaptation (Neale and Kremer, 2011).

Forests are important sources of germplasm for ongoing and future domestication of AFTPs as well as tree commodity crops, requiring management for the characterization and maintenance of these resources (Jamnadass et al., 2011). A wider focus on indigenous trees, rather than commonly used exotics, to fulfil different production and service functions may bring conservation benefits and be more sustainable in the long term. Particular opportunities for new tree domestications were identified for Africa, where genetic diversity in a range of fruit tree species that are essentially wild has been found to be large, providing the possibility for large genetic gains under cultivation (e.g. *Allanblackia* spp., Jamnadass et al., 2010; *Sclerocarya birrea*, Thiongo and Jaenicke, 2000). Leakey et al. (2012) identified major challenges for successful tree domestication related to scaling up and out, with impact studies required to understand which domestication methods have been most effective in benefitting smallholders' incomes, food and nutritional security, and what effect different approaches have on the long-term genetic diversity of species and sustainability of production. Improved management of tree genetic resources for livelihoods requires a greater understanding of genetic processes in NTFP production and more attention to the genetic quality of tree planting material supplied to smallholders (Dawson et al., 2014).

An opportunity for understanding genetic related impacts on NTFPs may come from the growing literature on the effects of logging on timber trees, although different harvesting methods, products and growth rates mean that the ability to make generalizations may be limited. More work is also required to exploit genetic variation in wild and landrace stands of tree commodity crops to develop cultivars that perform better in more resilient and sustainable mixed-species smallholder production systems. This requires more attention to the proper valuation of tree genetic variation for breeding and production, to provide a stronger case for conservation (Geburek and Konrad, 2008).

Tree genetic resource-based responses to uncertainty in conditions related to climate change include germplasm translocation, the promotion of large effective population sizes to encourage adaptation and the use of a range of more plastic species and provenances (**Table 3.2** *Summary of smallholder constraints to tree planting*). To inform germplasm distribution strategies, new trials on indigenous trees of value to smallholders are being designed to specifically consider climate change-related traits for populations collected from different ecological zones (Alfaro et al., 2014). For such interventions to be successful, they must provide clear livelihood benefits with a focus on developing new market opportunities for local smallholders (**Table 3.2**). Current payment mechanisms for the carbon sequestration function of agroforestry trees in mitigating global environmental change are generally inefficient and further work is required if farmers are to benefit significantly (Jack et al., 2008). Even so, such payments are likely to be modest and unsustainable compared with the other products and services that trees provide (Roshetko et al., 2007). A better approach is to identify and encourage cultivation of tree species that provide both sequestration benefits and high value products.

*Table 3.2* Summary of smallholder constraints to tree planting, suggested interventions under existing challenges, and specific germplasm-based opportunities to address climate change

| *Constraint* | *Nature of constraint* | *Interventions under existing challenges* | *Specific germplasm-based opportunities under climate change* |
|---|---|---|---|
| Lack of access to high-quality germplasm | The tree germplasm currently easily available to smallholders is frequently of suboptimal performance and function; obtaining more optimal material carries high transaction costs | • Improve access to germplasm through participatory domestication, by developing local seed and seedling dealer enterprises, through enhancing local farmer-exchange networks, by establishing seed production stands<br>• Training in managing natural regeneration in farmland<br>• New introductions to farmers of more productive germplasm from elsewhere | • Link local suppliers of tree planting material with national supply programs that can facilitate germplasm translocations at larger geographic scales, nationally and internationally, to keep pace with environmental shifts. Ensure co-migrations of organisms such as pollinators and microsymbionts that are essential for tree function and production<br>• Introduce new farm management methods to enhance pollination services and maintain effective population sizes of tree species, and bring into cultivation new tree varieties that are less dependent on associations with particular animal vectors<br>• Ensure new introductions of species and provenances are flexible (plastic) in responding to extreme climate change-related weather events, but do not concentrate on a small range of 'exotic' species only |
| Absence of well-functioning markets | Market value chains are frequently biased against smallholder involvement, or are simply not present, with few opportunities for adding value through processing, and so forth | • Improve access to markets through identifying new product opportunities, by sensitizing consumers, through increasing value chain transparency, and by providing business training and credit facilities for growers and local businesses<br>• Train in simple methods for adding value during processing and introduce any necessary processing equipment | • Ensure market opportunities for climate mitigation (e.g. sequestration, biofuel production) can be met through new introductions of tree species and provenances that are productive for novel functions<br>• Ensure germplasm delivery systems are able to supply appropriate planting material of tree species that provide products able to take advantage of newly-developing markets to combat climate change health challenges (e.g. that provide medicines for disease treatment and foods to prevent malnutrition associated with climate change-related disease incidences and nutrient deficiencies)<br>• Ensure market opportunities for other local and global challenges are fully explored, so climate change-related markets don't result in narrowing of production options, over-intensification and/or tendency to monoculture that weaken resilience to environmental change |

*Source*: Adapted and updated from Dawson et al. (2009).

## Notes

The authors were supported by the CGIAR Forest Trees and Agroforestry Programme. We would like to thank the editors for their comments in reviewing this chapter.

1 IUCN Red List. www.iucnredlist.org (last accessed 23 May 2016)
2 TSSD The Tree Seed Suppliers Directory www.worldagroforestry.org/our_products/databases/tssd (last accessed 23 May 2016)
3 The Nagoya Protocol on Access and Benefit-sharing was adopted on 29 October 2010 in Nagoya, Japan, and entered into force on 12 October 2014; a full account is given in Engels and Rudebjer, Chapter 43 of this Handbook; www.cbd.int/abs/about/ (last accessed 23 May 2016),

## References

Aerts, R., Berecha, G., Gijbels, P., Hundera, K., Van Glabeke, S., Vandepitte, K., Muys, B., Roldan-Ruiz, I. and Honnay, O. (2013) 'Genetic variation and risks of introgression in the wild *Coffea arabica* gene pool in south-western Ethiopian montane rainforests', *Evolutionary Applications*, vol. 6, pp. 243–252.

Aerts, R. and Honnay, O. (2011) 'Forest restoration, biodiversity and ecosystem functioning', *BMC Ecology*, vol. 11, p. 29.

Alfaro, R. I., Fady, B., Vendramin, G. G., Dawson, I. K., Fleming, R. A., Sáenz-Romero, C., Lindig-Cisneros, R. A., Murdock, T., Vinceti, B., Navarro, C. M., Skrøppa, T., Baldinelli, G., El-Kassaby, Y. A. and Loo, J. (2014) 'The role of forest genetic resources in responding to biotic and abiotic factors in the context of anthropogenic climate change', *Forest Ecology and Management*, vol. 333, pp. 76–87.

Anderson, E. (1954) *Plants, Man and Life*, Melrose, London, UK.

Angelsen, A., Jagger, P., Babigumira, R., Belcher, B., Hogarth, N. J., Bauch, S., Borner, J., Smith-Hall, C. and Wunder, S. (2014) 'Environmental income and rural livelihoods: A global-comparative analysis', *World Development*, vol. 64, pp. S12–S28.

Argout, X., Salse, J., Aury, J.-M., Guiltinan, M. J., Droc, G., Gouzy, J., Allegre, M., Chaparro, C., Legavre, T. and Maximova, S. N. (2011) 'The genome of *Theobroma cacao*', *Nature Genetics*, vol. 43, pp. 101–109.

Atta-Krah, K., Kindt, R., Skilton, J. N. and Amaral, W. (2004) 'Managing biological and genetic diversity in tropical agroforestry', *Agroforestry Systems*, vol. 1, pp. 183–194.

Barrance, A., Schreckenberg, K. and Gordon, J. (2009) *Conservation through Use: Lessons from the Mesoamerican Dry Forest*, Overseas Development Institute, London, UK.

Boshier, D. H., Cordero, J., Detlefsen, G. and Beer, J. (2009) 'Indigenous trees for farmers: Information transfer for sustainable management in Central America and the Caribbean', pp. 397–410 in P. Joseph (ed.), *Écosystèmes forestiers des Caraïbes, Conseil Général de La Martinique*, Karthala, Martinique.

Boshier, D. H., Gordon, J. E. and Barrance, A. J. (2004) 'Prospects for *circa situm* tree conservation in Mesoamerican dry forest agro-ecosystems', pp. 210–226 in G. W. Frankie, A. Mata and S. B. Vinson (eds.), *Biodiversity Conservation in Costa Rica, Learning the Lessons in the Seasonal Dry Forest*, Berkeley, University of California Press, CA, USA.

Byron, N. and Arnold, M. (1999) 'What futures for the people of the tropical forests?', *World Development*, vol. 27 (5), pp. 789–805.

Carney, S. E., Wolf, D. E. and Rieseberg, L. H. (2000) 'Hybridisation and forest conservation', pp. 167–182 in A. Young, D. H. Boshier and T. J. Boyle (eds.), *Forest Conservation Genetics: Principles and Practice*, Commonwealth Scientific and Industrial Research organization (CSIRO) Publishing, Melbourne, Australia and CAB International, Wallingford, UK.

Chazdon, R. L. (2008) 'Beyond deforestation: Restoring forests and ecosystem services on degraded lands', *Science*, vol. 320, pp. 1458–1460.

Clement, C. R., Denevan, W. M., Heckenberger, M. J., Junqueira, A. B., Neves, E. G., Teixeira, W. G. and Woods, W. I. (2015) 'The domestication of Amazonia before European conquest', *Proceedings of the Royal Society B–Biological Sciences*, vol. 282, p. 20150813.

Clement, C. R. and Junqueira, A. B. (2010) 'Between a pristine myth and an impoverished future', *Biotropica*, vol. 42, pp. 534–536.

Cornelius, J. P., Clement, C. R., Weber, J. C., Sotelo-Montes, C., Van Leeuwen, J., Ugarte-Guerra, L. J., Ricse-Tembladera, A. and Arévalo-López, L. (2006) 'The trade off between genetic gain and conservation in a participatory improvement programme: The case of peach palm (*Bactris gasipaes* Kunth)', *Forests, Trees and Livelihoods*, vol. 16, pp. 17–34.

Correia, M., Diabaté, M., Beavogui, P., Guilavogui, K. K., Lamanda, N. and de Foresta, H. (2010) 'Conserving forest tree diversity in Guinée Forestière (Guinea, West Africa): The role of coffee-based agroforests', *Biodiversity Conservation*, vol. 19, pp. 1725–1747.

Dawson, I. K., Guariguata, M. R., Loo, J., Weber, J. C., Lengkeek, A., Bush, D., Cornelius, J., Guarino, L., Kindt, R., Orwa, C., Russell, J. and Jamnadass, R. (2013) 'What is the relevance of smallholders' agroforestry systems for conserving tropical tree species and genetic diversity in *circa situm*, *in situ* and *ex situ* settings? A review', *Biodiversity and Conservation*, vol. 22, pp. 301–324.

Dawson, I. K., Hollingsworth, P. M., Doyle, J. J., Kresovich, S., Weber, J. C., Sotelo-Montes, C., Pennington, T. D. and Pennington, R. T. (2008) 'Origin and genetic conservation of tropical trees in agroforestry systems: A case study from the Peruvian Amazon', *Conservation Genetics*, vol. 9, pp. 361–372.

Dawson, I. K., Leakey, R., Clement, C. R., Weber, J. C., Cornelius, J. P., Roshetko, J. M., Vinceti, B., Kalinganire, A., Masters, E. and Jamnadass, R. (2014) 'The management of tree genetic resources and the livelihoods of rural communities in the tropics: Non-timber forest products, smallholder agroforestry practices and tree commodity crops', *Forest Ecology and Management*, vol. 333, pp. 9–21.

Dawson, I. K., Lengkeek, A., Weber, J. C. and Jamnadass, R. (2009) 'Managing genetic variation in tropical trees: Linking knowledge with action in agroforestry ecosystems for improved conservation and enhanced livelihoods', *Biodiversity and Conservation*, vol. 18, pp. 969–986.

de Foresta, H., Somarriba, E., Temu, A., Boulanger, D., Feuilly, H. and Gauthier, M. (2013) Towards the Assessment of Trees Outside Forests, Resources Assessment Working Paper No. 183, Food and Agriculture Organization of the United Nations, Rome, Italy.

Edmands, S. (2007) 'Between a rock and a hard place: Evaluating the relative risks of inbreeding and outbreeding for conservation and management', *Molecular Ecology*, vol. 16, pp. 463–475.

Ekadinata, A. and Vincent, G. (2011) 'Rubber agroforests in a changing landscape: Analysis of land use/cover trajectories in Bungo District, Indonesia', *Forests, Trees and Livelihoods*, vol. 20, pp. 3–14.

Ellstrand, N. C. (2003) *Dangerous Liaisons? When Cultivated Plants Mate with Their Wild Relatives*, John Hopkins University Press, Baltimore, MD, USA.

FAO (2010) *Global Forest Resources Assessment 2010*, FAO Forestry Paper No. 163, FAO, Rome, Italy.

FAO (2014a) *The State of the World's Forest Genetic Resources*, Commission on Genetic Resources for Food and Agriculture, FAO, Rome, Italy.

FAO (2014b) *Global Plan of Action for the Conservation*, Sustainable Use and Development of Forest Genetic Resources, FAO, Rome, Italy.

Faye, M. D., Weber, J. C., Abasse, T. A., Boureima, M., Larwanou, M., Bationo, A. B., Diallo, B. O., Sigué, H., Dakouo, J.-M., Samaké, O. and Sonogo Diaité, D. (2011) 'Farmers' preferences for tree functions and species in the West African Sahel', *Forests, Trees and Livelihoods*, vol. 20, pp. 113–136.

Fisher, H. and Gordon, J. (2007) *Improved Australian Tree Species for Vietnam*, ACIAR Impact Assessment Series Report No. 47, The Australian Centre for International Agricultural Research, Canberra, Australia.

Galindo-Tovar, M. E., Ogata-Aguilar, N. and Arzate-Fernandez, A. M. (2008) 'Some aspects of avocado (*Persea americana* Mill.) diversity and domestication in Mesoamerica', *Genetic Resources and Crop Evolution*, vol. 55, pp. 441–450.

Garen, E. J., Saltonstall, K., Ashton, M. S., Slusser, J. L., Mathias, S. and Hall, J. S. (2011) 'The tree planting and protecting culture of cattle ranchers and small-scale agriculturalists in rural Panama: Opportunities for reforestation and land restoration', *Forest Ecology and Management*, vol. 261, pp. 1684–1695.

Garrity, D. P. (2004) 'Agroforestry and the achievement of the Millennium Development Goals', *Agroforestry Systems*, vol. 61, pp. 5–17.

Geburek, T. and Konrad, H. (2008) 'Why the conservation of forest genetic resources has not worked', *Conservation Biology*, vol. 22, pp. 267–274.

Godefroid, S., Piazza, C., Rossi, G., Buord, S., Stevens, A.-D., Aguraiuja, R., Cowell, C., Weekley, C. W., Vogg, G., Iriondo, J., Johnson, I., Dixon, B., Gordon, D., Magnanon, S., Valentin, B., Bjureke, K., Koopman, R., Vicens, M., Virevaire, M. and Vanderborght, T. (2011) 'How successful are plant species reintroductions?', *Biological Conservation*, vol. 144, pp. 672–682.

Gordon, J. E., Hawthorne, W. D., Sandoval, G. and Barrance, A. J. (2003) 'Trees and farming in the dry zone of southern Honduras II: The potential for tree diversity conservation', *Agroforestry Systems*, vol. 59, pp. 107–117.

Graudal, L., Aravanopoulos, F., Bennadji, Z., Changtragoon, S., Fady, B., Kjær, E. D., Loo, J., Ramamonjisoa, L. and Vendramin, G. G. (2014) 'Global to local genetic diversity indicators of evolutionary potential in tree species within and outside forests', *Forest Ecology and Management*, vol. 333, pp. 35–51.

Griffin, A. R. (1991) 'Effects of inbreeding on growth of forest trees and implications for management of seed supplies for plantation programmes', pp. 355–374 in K. S. Bawa and M. Hadley (eds.), *Reproductive Ecology of Tropical Forest Plants*, Vol. 7, CRC Press, Boca Raton, FL, USA.

Hamrick, J. L., Godt, M. J. W. and Sherman-Broyles, S. L. (1992) 'Factors influencing levels of genetic diversity in woody plant species', in W. T. Adams, S. H. Strauss, D. L. Copes and A. R. Griffin (eds.), *Population Genetics of Forest Trees*, Proceedings of the International Symposium on Population Genetics of Forest Trees, Corvallis, OR, USA, July 31–August 2, 1990, pp. 95–124, Springer, the Netherlands.

Harvey, C. A. and Haber, W. A. (2008) 'Remnant trees and the conservation of biodiversity in Costa Rican pastures', *Agroforestry Systems*, vol. 44, pp. 37–68.

Harwood, C. E., Thinh, H. H., Quang, T. H., Butcher, P. A. and Williams, E. R. (2004) 'The effect of inbreeding on early growth of *Acacia mangium* in Vietnam', *Silvae Genetica*, vol. 53, pp. 65–69.

Hughes, C. E. (1998) *Leucaena: A Genetic Resources Handbook*', Tropical Forestry Papers No. 37, Oxford Forestry Institute, Oxford, UK.

Hughes, C. E., Govindarajulu, R., Robertson, A., Filer, D. L., Harris, S. A. and Bailey, C. D. (2007) 'Serendipitous backyard hybridization and the origin of crops', *Proceedings of the National Academy of Sciences USA*, vol. 104, pp. 14389–14394.

Jack, B. K., Kousky, C. and Sims, K. R. (2008) 'Designing payments for ecosystem services: Lessons from previous experience with incentive-based mechanisms', *Proceedings of the National Academy of Sciences USA*, vol. 105 (28), pp. 9465–9470.

Jamnadass, R. H., Dawson, I. K., Anegbeh, P., Asaah, E., Atangana, A., Cordeiro, N., Hendrickx, H., Henneh, S., Kadu, C. A. C., Kattah, C., Misbah, M., Muchugi, A., Munjuga, M., Mwaura, L., Ndangalasi, H. J., Njau, C. S., Nyame, S. K., Ofori, D., Peprah, T., Russell, J., Rutatina, F., Sawe, C., Schmidt, L., Tchoundjeu, Z. and Simons, T. (2010) '*Allanblackia*, a new tree crop in Africa for the global food industry: Market development, smallholder cultivation and biodiversity management', *Forests, Trees and Livelihoods*, vol. 19, pp. 251–268.

Jamnadass, R. H., Dawson, I. K., Franzel, S., Leakey, R. R. B., Mithöfer, D., Akinnifesi, F. K. and Tchoundjeu, Z. (2011) 'Improving livelihoods and nutrition in sub-Saharan Africa through the promotion of indigenous and exotic fruit production in smallholders' agroforestry systems: A review', *International Forest Review*, vol. 13, pp. 338–354.

Janzen, D. H. (1986) 'Blurry catastrophes', *Oikos*, vol. 47, pp. 1–2.

Jennings, S. B., Brown, N. D., Boshier, D. H., Whitmore, T. C. and Lopes, J. do C. A. (2001) 'Ecology provides a pragmatic solution to the maintenance of genetic diversity in sustainably managed tropical rain forests', *Forest Ecology and Management*, vol. 154, pp. 1–10.

Kehlenbeck, K., Kindt, R., Sinclair, F. L., Simons, A. J. and Jamnadass, R. (2011) 'Exotic tree species displace indigenous ones on farms at intermediate altitudes around Mount Kenya', *Agroforestry Systems*, vol. 83, pp. 133–147.

Kelly, B. A., Hardy, O. J. and Bouvet, J.-M. (2004) 'Temporal and spatial genetic structure in *Vitellaria paradoxa* (shea tree) in an agroforestry system in southern Mali', *Molecular Ecology*, vol. 13, pp. 1231–1240.

Kettle, C. J., Harrison, R. and Koh, L. P. (2014) 'Future forests: Fantasy or façade? A synthesis', pp. 158–171 in C. J. Kettle and L. P. Koh (eds.), *Global Forest Fragmentation*, CABI, Wallingford, UK.

Kindt, R., Van Damme, P., Simons, A. J. and Beeckman, H. (2006) 'Planning tree species diversification in Kenya based on differences in tree species composition between farms: I. Analysis of tree uses', *Agroforestry Systems*, vol. 67, pp. 215–228.

Koskela, J., Vinceti, B., Dvorak, W., Bush, D., Dawson, I. K., Loo, J., Kjaer, E. D., Navarro, C., Padolina, C., Bordács, S., Jamnadass, R., Graudal, L. and Ramamonjisoa, L. (2014) 'Utilization and transfer of forest genetic resources: A global review', *Forest Ecology and Management*, vol. 333, pp. 22–34.

Labouisse, J., Bellachew, B., Kotecha, S. and Bertrand, B. (2008) 'Current status of coffee (*Coffea arabica* L.) genetic resources in Ethiopia: Implications for conservation', *Genetic Resources and Crop Evolution*, vol. 55, pp. 1079–1093.

Lander, T. A., Bebber, D., Choy, T. L., Harris, S. A. and Boshier, D. H. (2011) 'The Circe Principle explains how resource-rich land can waylay pollinators in fragmented landscapes', *Current Biology*, vol. 21, pp. 1302–1307.

Leakey, R. R. B. (2010) 'Agroforestry: A delivery mechanism for multi-functional agriculture', pp. 461–471 in L. R. Kellimore (ed.), *Handbook on Agroforestry: Management Practices and Environmental Impact*, Environmental Science, Engineering and Technology Series, Nova Science Publishers, Hauppauge, NY, USA.

Leakey, R. R. B., Weber, J. C., Page, T., Cornelius, J. P., Akinnifesi, F. K., Roshetko, J. M., Tchoundjeu, Z. and Jamnadass, R. (2012) 'Tree domestication in agroforestry: Progress in the second decade (2003–2012)',

pp. 145–173 in P. K. R. Nair and D. Garrity (eds.), *Agroforestry-The Future of Global Land Use, Advances in Agroforestry*, Vol. 9, Springer, the Netherlands.
Lefèvre, F., Koskela, J., Hubert, J., Kraigher, H., Longauer, R., Olrik, D. C., Schüler, S., Bozzano, M., Alizoti, P., Bakys, R. and Baldwin, C. (2013) 'Dynamic conservation of forest genetic resources in 33 European countries', *Conservation Biology*, vol. 27, pp. 373–384.
Lengkeek, A. G., Kindt, R., van der Maesen, L. J. G., Simons, A. J. and van Oijen, D. C. C. (2005) 'Tree density and germplasm source in agroforestry ecosystems in Meru, Mount Kenya', *Genetic Resources and Crop Evolution*, vol. 52, pp. 709–721.
López-Gómez, A. M., Williams-Linera, G. and Manson, R. H. (2008) 'Tree species diversity and vegetation structure in shade coffee farms in Veracruz, Mexico', *Agriculture, Ecosystems and Environment*, vol. 124, pp. 160–172.
Marjokorpi, A. and Ruokolainen, K. (2003) 'The role of traditional forest gardens in the conservation of tree species in West Kalimantan, Indonesia', *Biodiversity and Conservation*, vol. 12, pp. 799–822.
McKay, J. K., Christian, C. E., Harrison, S. and Rice, K. J. (2005) '"How local is local?": A review of practical and conceptual issues in the genetics of restoration', *Restoration Ecology*, vol. 13, pp. 432–440.
Méndez, V. E., Gliessman, S. R. and Gilbert, G. S. (2007) 'Tree biodiversity in farmer cooperatives of a shade coffee landscape in western El Salvador', *Agriculture, Ecosystems and Environment*, vol. 119, pp. 145–159.
Miller, A. J. and Schaal, B. A. (2006) 'Domestication and the distribution of genetic variation in wild and cultivated populations of the Mesoamerican fruit tree *Spondias purpurea* L. (Anacardiaceae)', *Molecular Ecology*, vol. 15, pp. 1467–1480.
Muona, O. (1989) 'Population genetics in forest tree improvement', pp. 282–298 in A. D. H. Brown, M. T. Clegg, A. L. Kahler and B. S. Weir (eds.), *Plant Population Genetics, Breeding and Resources*, Sinauer, Sunderland, MA, USA.
Muranty, H., Troggio, M., Ben Sadok, I., Al Rifai, M., Auwerkerken, A., Banchi, E., Velasco, R., Stevanato, P., van de Weg, W. E., Di Guardo, M., Kumar, S., Laurens, F. and Bink, M. A. C. M. (2015) 'Accuracy and responses of genomic selection on key traits in apple breeding', *Horticulture Research*, vol. 2, p. 15060.
Neale, D. B. and Kremer, A. (2011) 'Forest tree genomics: Growing resources and applications', *Nature Reviews Genetics*, vol. 12, pp. 111–122.
Newton, A. C. (2011) 'Synthesis: Principles and practice for forest landscape restoration', pp. 353–383 in A. C. Newton and N. Tejedor (eds.), *Principles and Practice of Forest Landscape Restoration Case Studies from the Drylands of Latin America*, Gland, Switzerland, IUCN.
Oke, D. O. and Odebiyi, K. A. (2007) 'Traditional cocoa-based agroforestry and forest species conservation in Ondo State, Nigeria', *Agriculture, Ecosystems and Environment*, vol. 122, pp. 305–311.
Petit, R. J. and Hampe, A. (2006) 'Some evolutionary consequences of being a tree', *Annual Review of Ecology, Evolution, and Systematics*, vol. 37, pp. 187–214.
Philpott, S. M., Bichier, P., Rice, R. A. and Greenberg, R. (2008) 'Biodiversity conservation, yield, and alternative products in coffee agroecosystems in Sumatra, Indonesia', *Biodiversity and Conservation*, vol. 17, pp. 1805–1820.
Pimentel, D., McNair, M., Buck, L., Pimentel, M. and Kamil, J. (1997) 'The value of forests to world food security', *Human Ecology*, vol. 25, pp. 91–120.
Place, F. and Binam, J. N. (2013) *Economic Impacts of Farmer Managed Natural Regeneration in the Sahel: End of Project Technical Report for the Free University Amsterdam and IFAD*, The World Agroforestry Centre, Nairobi, Kenya.
Pungetti, G., Oviedo, G. and Hooke, D. (eds.) (2012) *Sacred Species and Sites: Advances in Biocultural Conservation*, Cambridge University Press, Cambridge, UK.
Rolim, S. G. and Chiarello, A. G. (2004) 'Slow death of Atlantic forest trees in cocoa agroforestry in southeastern Brazil', *Biodiversity and Conservation*, vol. 13, pp. 2679–2694.
Roshetko, J. M., Lasco, R. D. and Delos Angeles, M. S. (2007) 'Smallholder agroforestry systems for carbon storage', *Mitigation and Adaptation Strategies for Global Change*, vol. 12, pp. 219–242.
Ruf, F. O. (2011) 'The myth of complex cocoa agroforests: The case of Ghana', *Human Ecology*, vol. 39, pp. 373–388.
Sambuichi, R. H. R. and Haridasan, M. (2007) 'Recovery of species richness and conservation of native Atlantic forest trees in the cacao plantations of southern Bahia in Brazil', *Biodiversity and Conservation*, vol. 16, pp. 3681–3701.
Schroth, G., Faria, D., Araujo, M., Bede, L., Van Bael, S. A., Cassano, C. R., Oliveira, L. C. and Delabie, J. H. C. (2011) 'Conservation in tropical landscape mosaics: The case of the cacao landscape of southern Bahia, Brazil', *Biodiversity and Conservation*, vol. 20, pp. 1635–1654.

Sendzimir, J., Reij, C. P. and Magnuszewski, P. (2011) 'Rebuilding resilience in the Sahel: Regreening in the Maradi and Zinder regions of Niger', *Ecology and Society*, vol. 16, p. 1.

Simons, A. J. and Leakey, R. R. B. (2004) 'Tree domestication in tropical agroforestry', *Agroforestry Systems*, vol. 61, pp. 167–181.

Sonwa, D. J., Nkongmeneck, B. A., Weise, S. F., Tchatat, M., Adesina, A. A. and Janssens, M. J. J. (2007) 'Diversity of plants in cocoa agroforests in the humid forest zone of Southern Cameroon', *Biodiversity and Conservation*, vol. 16, pp. 2385–2400.

Sunderland, T. C. H. (2011) 'Food security: Why is biodiversity important?', *International Forestry Review*, vol. 13, pp. 265–274.

Thiongo, M. K. and Jaenicke, H. (2000) 'Preliminary nutritional analysis of marula (*Sclerocarya birrea*) fruits from two Kenyan provenances', *Acta Horticulturae*, vol. 531, pp. 245–249.

Thomas, E., Jalonen, R., Loo, J., Boshier, D., Gallo, L., Cavers, S., Bordács, S., Smith, P. and Bozzano, M. (2014) 'Genetic considerations in ecosystem restoration using native tree species', *Forest Ecology and Management*, vol. 333, pp. 66–75.

Turner, W. R., Brandon, K., Brooks, T. M., Gascon, C., Gibbs, H. K., Lawrence, K. S., Mittermeier, R. A. and Selig, E. R. (2012) 'Global biodiversity conservation and the alleviation of poverty', *Bioscience*, vol. 62, pp. 85–92.

Ward, M., Dick, C. W., Gribel, R. and Lowe, A. J. (2005) 'To self, or not to self: A review of outcrossing and pollen-mediated gene flow in Neotropical trees', *Heredity*, vol. 95, pp. 246–254.

Weeks, A. R., Sgro, C. M., Young, A. G., Frankham, R., Mitchell, N. J., Miller, K. A., Byrne, M., Coates, D. J., Eldridge, M. D. B., Sunnucks, P., Breed, M. F., James, E. A. and Hoffmann, A. A. (2011) 'Assessing the benefits and risks of translocations in changing environments: A genetic perspective', *Evolutionary Applications*, vol. 4, pp. 709–725.

Wickneswari, R., Rajora, O. P., Finkeldey, R., Aravanopoulos, F., Bouvet, J.-M., Vaillancourt, R. E., Kanashiro, M., Fady, B., Tomita, M. and Vinson, C. (2014) 'Genetic effects of forest management practices: Global synthesis and perspectives', *Forest Ecology and Management*, vol. 333, pp. 52–65.

Williams, C. G. and Savolainen, O. (1996) 'Inbreeding depression in conifers: Implications for breeding strategy', *Forest Science*, vol. 42, pp. 102–117.

World Bank (2008) *Forests Sourcebook: Practical Guidance for Sustaining Forests in Development Cooperation*, World Bank, Washington, DC, USA.

Wymore, A. S., Bothwell, H. M., Compson, Z. G., Lamit, L. J., Walker, F. M., Woolbright, S. A. and Whitham, T. G. (2014) 'Community genetics applications for forest biodiversity and policy: Planning for the future', pp. 707–725 in T. Fenning (ed.), *Challenges and Opportunities for the World's Forests in the 21st Century: Forest Science*, Vol. 81, Springer Science+Business Media, New York, NY, USA.

Zomer, R. J., Trabucco, A., Coe, R., Place, F., van Noordwijk, M. and Xu, J. C. (2014) *Trees on Farms: An Update and Reanalysis of Agroforestry's Global Extent and Socio-Ecological Characteristics*, Working Paper 179, World Agroforestry Centre (ICRAF) Southeast Asia Regional Program, Bogor, Indonesia.

# 4

# WILD PLANT AND ANIMAL GENETIC RESOURCES

*Verina Ingram, Barbara Vinceti and Nathalie van Vliet*

## Introduction

Wild plant and animal resources are commonly defined as those which exist in a natural state; are not tamed, cultivated or domesticated; nor are in the care of people. A natural system (as opposed to an agricultural or human-managed system) is generally characterized by complex spatial arrangements in which different species co-exist, are genetically diverse, and consist of plants and animals of different ages and developmental stages, with offspring and seeds produced by a population in one year being the source of future generations (Alexander, 2010). Genetic resources can be defined as the heritable materials maintained within and among species that are of actual or potential economic, environmental, scientific or societal value. Genes are not consciously used, but people have taken advantage of genetic variation, by selecting plants and animals with preferred characteristics. Plant and animal genetic resources are the total genetic diversity of cultivated and domesticated species and their wild relatives, much of which may be valuable to breeders (Jackson and Ford-Lloyd, 1990).

Wild genetic resources differ from their domesticated counterparts as they reproduce independently of human control (Prescott-Allen and Prescott-Allen, 1983), as do the habitats in which they are found. The extent to which genetic resources can be considered to be wild can also be determined by their natural range, although wild populations can also result from benign introductions or deliberate reintroduction (Hemp, 2006). This wild versus cultivated dichotomy is, however, simplistic. In practice, the distinction is blurred, with resources harvested from a continuum ranging from entirely natural systems to resource enriched, reconstructed and managed systems that often appear 'wild' (Wiersum et al., 2014).

This chapter provides an introduction to the range of resources gathered from the wild and their uses, with a focus on plant and animal resources at species level, with some examples of wild tree genetic resources presented.

Covering 30% of the globe (FAO, 2015b, forests represent the predominant land cover (FAO, 2014b) and are a major source of wild genetic resources (FAO, 2015a). For this reason, examples of wild plant and animal resources from forested landscapes predominate in this chapter. Forest products provide a significant contribution to the shelter of at least 18% of the world's population and billions of people use forest products to meet their needs for food, energy and shelter. Wood energy is often the only energy source in rural areas of less developed countries, particularly by poor people, accounting for between 5% to 27% of energy supply regionally (FAO, 2015b).

Characteristics distinguishing wild resources from cultivated ones are then discussed. These include the fact that many wild species are governed as public goods or common property, raising questions about if and how they are managed, and by whom; how access to, and benefits from, these resources are arranged; and how these governance factors affect sustainable use of species and genetic diversity. The chapter illustrates how knowledge of these aspects helps to underpin the development of sustainable measures for the use and conservation of wild plant and animal resources.

## Use and dependency on wild plant and animal genetic resources

Wild resources from ecosystems around the globe have been used for millennia to meet people's basic needs for food, fuel, medicines, tools and materials, and for spiritual and cultural uses (Cunningham, 2001). As well as being the source of most crops and domesticated animals (Diamond, 2002; Zohary et al., 2012), many wild species are still used for subsistence purposes and are the source of traded commodities (Newton, 2008).

In many developing countries, subsistence farmers and rural inhabitants depend to a higher, but highly context-specific, extent on wild resources from forests, mangroves, rivers and other wildlands, for both cash and subsistence (Wunder et al., 2014). Non-timber forest products (NTFPs), which include whole and parts of plants and animals that originate from natural, modified and managed forested landscapes, particularly provide an important contribution to the livelihood of communities living inside or near forests (FAO, 2015b; Vira et al., 2015). NTFPs are used for food (e.g. berries, mushrooms, nuts, seeds, edible plants and exudates), medicinal and aromatic plants, fodder, ornamental plants, energy, materials and products, for example for cultural use.

Wild plant and animal resources in tropical and temperate climates, including both developed and developing countries, have, however, received sporadic attention in terms of quantification, valuation and mapping, due to different perceptions of their importance (Ingram, 2014; Schulp et al., 2014; see also Boshier et al., Chapter 3 of this Handbook). Many assessments focus on their direct economic value for humankind (such as economic, nutritional or functional) but miss critical supporting, regulating and cultural ecosystem services.

A global study of rural households showed that income from natural resources is higher for the poorest households and even higher when subsistence uses are considered (Angelsen et al., 2014). The study's findings challenge common thinking, as households in the highest income quintile had the highest environmental and forest incomes, indicating that wealthier people create higher pressure on natural resources, and not necessarily the poorest. Environmental income is, however, widely neglected by policy makers in poverty reduction strategies (Oksanen and Mersmann, 2003).

Along the same lines, an analysis of 8,000 households in 24 developing countries showed that 28% of income came from environmental sources, 77% of which came from natural forests (Angelsen et al., 2014). A study in Thailand (Delang, 2005) complements this global data, showing how those collecting NTFPs used less cash than people depending only on markets. The study also showed how wild food plants remain a preferred alternative to commercial food crops, being a more efficient use of time. Knowledge of species and the environment is associated with the benefits that local communities derive from wild-harvested forest products (Sheil and Salim, 2012). All too often, however, data on the source of environmental incomes and its impact on wild species do not reach policy makers.

Wild-harvested products are also sometimes preferred to cultivated products. People's perceptions of availability, preferences and consumption of forest foods in relation to other, cultivated and exotic food species can be complex, for example *Balanites aegyptiaca*, *Ziziphus spina-christi* and *Tamarindus indica* in Tanzania (Msuya et al., 2010) and *Gnetum* spp. in Cameroon (Ingram, 2014).

Assumptions concerning the dependency of rural communities on NTFPs contend that NTFPs can help to reduce poverty, promote development, buffer shocks and mitigate seasonal shortfalls in income and products used for subsistence. Only in rare cases have NTFPs been shown to create a path out of poverty, however (Kusters et al., 2006).

In many developing countries, a diversity of wild species (fish, plants, bushmeat, insects and fungi) underpin dietary diversity and good nutrition, and make an important contribution towards food security, especially in traditional 'hungry seasons' when crops are not yet ready for harvest (WHO/UNEP/CBD, 2015). For example, many wild foods are sold in Cameroonian cities, including bushmeat, fruits, vegetables, spices and insects, with an average of 25% of a household's food budget spent on wild foods (Sneyd, 2013). However, social and economic access to a diverse diet of often more nutritious foods are often priced out by imported, low cost, non-traditional staples, such as rice, alongside increasing trends towards urbanization and associated access to processed foodstuffs. Scarcity, due to seasonal availability and over-exploitation, also affects prices and dietary diversity (Sneyd, 2013). Nutritional diversity and food security are strengthened when wild foods are integrated into agro-ecological production systems managed to provide multiple benefits, combining biodiversity concerns with food production. The nutritional and livelihood benefits of diverse wild and agricultural production systems can not only help achieve food security but also be more resilient to climate induced events and other shocks (Sunderland, 2011). Wild species contribute to the agricultural biodiversity associated with dietary diversity (Johns et al., 2013; Powell et al., 2015).

Wild animal and plant genetic resources are also an important source of variation for breeding crops and livestock. They can confer characteristics of interest to domesticated species, including disease and pest resistance, higher yields, vigour and environmental adaptability. The latter is of increasing importance in relation to climate change.

## *Wild plant and fungi resources*

In the developed world, wild plant resources generally enhance, rather than form, the basis of subsistence use, although some species are the foundation for trade, such as berries and truffles. For example, at least 27 species of mushrooms and 81 species of vascular plants are known to be collected and consumed in countries throughout Europe (Schulp et al., 2014). Income, age, gender, access and cultural factors explain the current variations found in gathering wild plants in Europe. While the economic and nutritional values of wild food compose a tiny proportion of GDP and total food consumption, over 100 million European Union citizens consume wild food sourced from plants and animals. Collecting is also an appreciated recreational activity, often creating a sense of place (Schulp et al., 2014).

The use of native European medicinal and aromatic plants has a long history. International trade data from the mid-1990s indicates that at least 2,000 species are used on a commercial basis, some 1,200–1,300 of which are native to Europe. Of these, 90% are still wild collected, totalling around 20,000 to 30,000 tons per year (Lange, 1998). Wild collection is particularly prominent in Albania, Turkey, Hungary and Spain. In the European Union, medicinal and aromatic plants are cultivated on an estimated 70,000 hectares, mainly in France, Hungary and Spain. Europe imports about a quarter of annual global market imports (440,000 tons valued at USD 1.3 billion in 1996), with Germany, France, Italy, Spain and the United Kingdom among the

12 leading countries of import and Germany, Bulgaria and Poland among the 12 leading exporters (Lange, 1998). In developing countries, the historical and current medicinal and aromatic use of an estimated 50,000 species of wild plants is known, but is less well documented (Schippmann et al., 2002). Approximately 2,500 of these species are also traded. Wild species can contain unique pharmaceutical properties not easily reproduced artificially. An example are the compounds extracted from *Prunus africana* bark, which act synergistically in traditional medicine, in a way not completely understood, to cure benign prostate hyperplasia (Kadu et al., 2012). In other cases, synthetic chemicals used as an alternative to the products harvested from wild tree populations may cause additional pathologies and cannot replace natural phytochemical compounds, such as the tree *Pterocarpus erinaceus*, a West and Central African leguminose whose bark is traditionally used for its strong anti-inflammatory, analgesic and antioxidant properties (Noufou et al., 2012).

## Wild animal resources

The range of animal species gathered from the wild and their uses, with a focus on forested landscapes, is illustrated in this section.

One of the most significant and traditional uses of natural resources is that of wild animals for food. In some countries, such as Australia, hunting for subsistence use and small scale, legal trade in wild animals, mainly for food (kangaroos, wallabies, brushtail possums, short-tailed shearwaters, crocodiles and emus), co-exist. Species with large populations, such as kangaroos, wallabies, wild boars, wild goats, rabbits and foxes, are the mainstay of trade (Ramsay, 1994). Impediments to the development of this wild animal trade include public perception, parochial attitudes, administrative and legislative structures, the variable operating environment, low product values, the novelty of products, lack of information of species and markets, animal welfare issues and pest control activities that conflict with commercial harvesting. In the European Union, 38 game species are harvested and consumed, generally as part of recreational and cultural activities (Schulp et al., 2014).

In contrast, particularly in developing countries, bushmeat forms a major contribution to daily dietary needs (Nasi et al., 2008). Poor households especially can suffer from nutritional deficiencies when wildlife is removed from their diet because of their reliance on bushmeat (Golden et al., 2011). Since bushmeat is often the main source of meat available in some regions of developing countries, the loss of bushmeat species means decreases in protein, fats and important micronutrients, such as iron, in diets. The nutritional importance of bushmeat is due in part to its fat content, as fat has considerably higher energy content per unit of mass than protein and carbohydrates (Sirén and Machoa, 2008). However, bushmeat trade can also spread pathogens, increase exposure to and the transmission of zoonoses, such as from African apes to humans, and vice versa, which are linked to diseases such as HIV and Ebola (Leroy et al., 2004; Smith et al., 2012). In the Amazon and Congo Basin, a wide variety of taxa are hunted for food. In Gabon, 114 species have been recorded in hunter catches, household consumption and markets (Abernethy, 2009). In Latin America, over 200 species of mammals, around 750 bird species (including over 530 species for the pet trade), more than 60 species of reptiles and at least five amphibian species are harvested for household use and trade (Ojasti, 2000). Mammals make up the bulk of the catches both in number and biomass terms, with ungulates and rodents representing more than two-thirds of the carcasses sold in urban markets or recorded from hunter off takes in both the Congo and Amazon Basins (Nasi et al., 2011), with medium-sized species between 2 and 50 kg being the most frequently hunted and the majority of mammal species hunted not listed as threatened on the IUCN Red List of Threatened Species. Generally, hunting reduces prey populations, and continued heavy hunting pressure can cause population or species extinction

(Milner-Gulland et al., 2003). However, understanding how hunting affects animal population dynamics is essential (Weinbaum et al.,2013).

Another major use of wild animals (mostly parts of or whole) in many cultures is in traditional medicine. The Chinese, for example, have a long history of using animals to treat a variety of ailments (and pseudo-ailments) while the illegal trade in African elephant and rhino horn is largely targeted towards medicinal use in Asia (Biggs et al., 2013; Roberts, 2014). Less known and studied, though just as varied and rich, is the tradition of wild animal-based remedies in Africa and Latin America. At least 584 animal species are used in traditional medicine in Latin America (Alves and Alves, 2011). A single illness can be treated by using various animal species (e.g. In Latin America, 215 animal species are used to treat asthma and 95 for rheumatism), while many species can also be used to treat multiple illnesses, such the tegu *(Tupinambis teguixin)* and boa constrictor, used to treat 29 and 30 conditions, respectively (Alves and Alves, 2011). In all cases, however, there is a fine line between exploitation and conservation, with many parts of the trade driven by militias and cartels, so ensuring sustainable use remains a priority.

The high nutritional values of wild insects have long been known empirically around the world, and are increasingly being confirmed scientifically. For example, in Central Africa, high consumption levels of many edible insect species play an important role in diets, pharmacopeia and agriculture, at all levels of society and as a standard ingredient, particularly in children's diets (Vantomme et al., 2004; Seignonbos et al., 1996). Similarly, in southern Africa, insects such as the mopane worm – the caterpillar of the emperor moth, *Imbrasia belina* – are widely consumed by rural and urban households alike due to their high nutritional value. As a result, harvesting is increasingly changing from subsistence to commercial (Thomas, 2013). The role played by wild insects as pollinators is also critical to both wild and cultivated productive systems, as about one in three mouthfuls of food comes from insect-pollinated crops (Aizen et al., 2008). Recent declines in bee populations and threats to other insect pollinators are cause for concern in this context (UNEP, 2010).

## Issues in the governance and sustainable use of wild plant and animal resources

Two particularities distinguishing wild resources from cultivated ones are discussed: their governance and the sustainability of their exploitation, and the consequences for genetic diversity.

### *Governance*

Many wild species are governed as public goods or common property, raising questions about if and how they are managed, and by whom; and how access to, and benefits from, these resources is arranged. The sustainability of exploitation of wild resources thus depends also on their governance.

Access and rights to forests and their products have been called the elephant in the 'land rights' room (Bauer, 2015). It is essential to make sure that land rights are looked at in the context of wildlife legislation, accompanied with greatly improved support to improve access and sustainability of these resources. While wildlife conservation programs now increasingly attempt to include forest-dependent communities in their wildlife protection programs (Rodriguez-Izquierdo et al., 2010; Shackleton et al., 2010), weaknesses in hunting legislation may be an important barrier to their success (e.g. Gill et al., 2009; Shackleton et al., 2010). Among the main weaknesses are the unclear rights given to local communities. Whether recognized by statutory laws or not, rural communities often consider themselves to be the traditional owners of resources which fall within their respective domains (Laird et al., 2010; Wily, 2011). For example, in Africa, colonial administrations adapted written laws to gradually replace customary laws to promote the development of virgin lands by the government. When Central African countries started to gain independence in the early 1960s, the postcolonial land-tenure system incorporated customary land, which was considered to be vacant and unoccupied, into state land (Oyono, 2005). Customary ownership or tenure rights were replaced with user rights granted to farmers and local communities. In practice, given the scarcity of governmental resources, government laws are rarely enforced, and people are left with an ambiguity between the need to comply with legal frameworks and with what remains of their customary practices (Laird et al., 2010). While some measures have been adopted in Central African countries to devolve user rights, for example community and communal forests, such formalization and decentralization have also increased the rigidity of once relatively fluid customarily managed domains (Wily, 2011). On a global level, measures to better govern wild resources exist, summarized in **Box 4.1** *Global governance of wild species*, but also often conflict with customary or local approaches adopted on the ground.

The sustainable governance of wild genetic resources can also be complicated if there are competing claims to wild resources in a specific area. This can occur if timber extraction competes with the harvesting of NTFPs and wildlife, or if timber and NTFPs are harvested from the same species. For example, the impact of selective logging on NTFPs in three tropical cases had largely negative

## Box 4.1 Global governance of wild species

Global schemes to govern wild genetic resources intend to control or influence global processes and negotiate responses to problems affecting more than one state or region. Following are examples of such international agreements and conventions and voluntary, certification schemes:

- The 1975 **Convention on International Trade in Endangered Species of Wild Fauna and Flora (CITES)** is a voluntary, international agreement between governments which aims to ensure that international trade in wild animals and plants does not threaten their survival and contribute to species extinction. CITES accords varying degrees of protection to over 30,000 animal and plant species. Appendix I lists the most endangered species threatened with extinction, for which international trade is prohibited except for non-commercial reasons. Appendix II lists species not necessarily now threatened with extinction but that may become so unless trade is closely controlled though agreeing annual quotas. Legally binding on its Parties, it does not replace national laws but provides a framework for implementing CITES within national legislation.
- The 1993 **Convention on Biological Diversity (CBD)** aims to conserve biological diversity and the fair and equitable sharing of the benefits arising from the utilization of genetic resources, ensuring the rights of countries and communities over their biological resources are respected. Also that access to traditional knowledge occurs with the approval of such knowledge holders, who should participate equitably in the resulting benefits should this be commercialized, establishing a system for access and benefit sharing (ABS). It recognizes that access to these resources must be subject to the prior informed consent of the provider country and based on mutually agreed terms. The convention requires National Biodiversity Strategy and Action Plans to be developed by member states, which would include approaches for species used for subsistence or commercial purposes.

- The 2014 **Nagoya Protocol on Access to Genetic Resources and the Fair and Equitable Sharing of Benefits Arising from their Utilization** to the **Convention on Biological Diversity** aims at sharing the benefits arising from the utilization of genetic resources in a fair and equitable way. The Access and Benefit-sharing (ABS) Clearing-House is a platform for exchanging information on access and benefit-sharing established by Article 14 of the Protocol. It aims to enhance legal certainty and transparency on procedures for access and benefit-sharing, and monitoring the utilization of genetic resources along the value chain, including through an internationally recognized certificate of compliance. The ABS Clearing-House aims to connect users and providers of genetic resources and associated traditional knowledge.
- The **IUCN Red List of Threatened Species** aims to guide and evaluate the status of plant and animal species worldwide. Since 1994, species conservation status has been determined using a baseline and subsequent monitoring of changes. If data are available, the level of threat is categorized, ranging from 'extinct' to 'critically endangered', 'endangered', 'vulnerable', 'near threatened' and 'least concern'. A red listing can trigger conservation actions from NGOs, governments and researchers.
- The voluntary **FairWild Standard** assesses and certifies the sustainable harvest and trade of wild plants against various ecological, social and economic requirements. It aims to support efforts to ensure plants are managed, harvested and traded in a way that maintains populations in the wild and benefits rural producers. The FairWild Standard also supports the implementation of existing regulatory frameworks provided by national resource management systems and international conventions the CBD and the non-detriment findings process of CITES.
- The **International Federation of Organic Agricultural Movements (IFOAM)** sets internationally accepted basic standards for organic agriculture. **Organic wild collection** is a certification scheme with criteria to ensure the protection of the genetic diversity – for example in wild coffee populations – and the conservation of ecosystem, such as forests, authenticity. This certification scheme is applicable to wild coffee collected from unmanaged forests.
- **Forest Stewardship Council (FSC)** certification ensures that products come from well-managed forests that provide environmental, social and economic benefits. FSC certification is a way that forest owners and managers can demonstrate they are managing their forests responsibly and in the supply chain, FSC certification can provide benefits such as access to new markets. The 'Expanding FSC certification to Ecosystem Services' (ForCES) project is a multi-partner pilot for the certification of ecosystem services which addresses biodiversity.
- A **geographic indication** is a name or sign used on certain products which corresponds to a specific geographical location or origin. It can be used as a certification that the product possesses certain qualities, is made according to traditional methods or has a certain reputation, due to its geographical origin. The inherent conservation approach can safeguard species biodiversity in this geographic area.

*(Bérard and Marchenay, 2006)*

- The (IUCN and WWF) **TRAFFIC programme** aims to ensure that trade in wild plants and animals is not a threat to the conservation of nature. The long-running programme includes a wildlife trade monitoring programme, networks with monitoring and enforcement agencies worldwide and has projects to support the implementation of the CBD and CITES.

effects on NTFP availability (Rist et al., 2012). Positive impacts were limited to light-demanding tree species which respond well to canopy opening, and constitute a small proportion of species with livelihood value. Occasionally, however, multiple harvesting can be complementary (Shanley and Luz, 2003). Multiple-use landscape and forest management, taking into account timber and non-timber forest products and environmental services, is hence gaining attention as a promising approach for tropical forest conservation. Examples include the development of the ForCES certification scheme – see **Box 4.1** – and multi-objective, cross-sectoral initiatives on landscape level (see Milder et al., 2014) which address genetic diversity. Governing wild resources to provide for multiple goods and services is challenging, however – by necessity taking into account different stakeholders' views. Focusing on Brazil nuts *(Bertholletia excelsa)*, a study on multi-purpose management indicated that obstacles may include policy barriers, a lack of enforcement, high management costs associated with small financial benefits, damage from logging to Brazil nut stands and the reinvestment of forestry-derived income into livestock (Duchelle et al., 2012).

Different approaches to govern wild resources have had mixed success. Community forestry has potential to reduce over-exploitation of wild resources (Porter-Bolland et al., 2012), with community-managed forests often more resilient and experiencing lower and less variable annual deforestation than protected forests. Under specific circumstances, when external economic pressures or major environmental threats are not in place, participatory monitoring by local communities has been a successful measure in avoiding over-exploitation of NTFPs (Boissière et al., 2013). Other approaches rely on well-enforced customary rules, collective action along the value chains of wild forest products, voluntary standards and/or legislation, for example in the case of honey, woodfuel, eru (*Gnetum* spp.), bush mango (*Irvingia* spp.) and *Prunus africana* in Cameroon and Congo (Wiersum et al., 2014). Legislation has long been an approach to govern the harvest and trade of wild species. For example, in the 1990s, about 150 species of medicinal and aromatic plants in Europe were reported as threatened in at least one European country as a result of over-collection from the wild (Lange, 1998). However, alongside regulatory revisions to reflect the dynamic nature of trade, conservation requires trade monitoring, improved law enforcement, *in situ* and *ex situ* protection, improved management programmers, public awareness initiatives, enhancement of cultivation, and research into trade, and the certification of plant material from sustainable sources. Voluntary schemes, such as certification standards, can play a role in promoting innovations in sustainable trade – see **Box 4.1** – for example in maintaining wild coffee diversity in Ethiopia (Schmitt and Grote, 2006) and biodiversity in forests managed under certification schemes (van Kuijk et al., 2009).

## *Drivers of change in wild plant and animal genetic resource availability*

Wild resources worldwide are affected by a variety of factors which influence their availability and the sustainability of their extractive use. Knowledge on how different pressures affect the resource base is key to identifying management and policy measures that could help reduce negative impacts. Some important species may not be at risk of extinction as a consequence of unsustainable exploitation but specific populations, with distinct traits and valuable properties, and genetically different from other populations of the same species, may be irreversibly lost. The relative contribution of hunting wild animals and gathering wild plants, compared with other drivers such as climate change, habitat alteration (i.e. land-use changes, destruction, fragmentation) and the impact of invasive species (Wilkie et al., 2011), make it difficult to attribute causation to hunting or wild harvest alone. Globally, commercial and subsistence agriculture, logging, fuelwood collection and livestock grazing are major causes of degradation and deforestation (Kissinger et al., 2012), affecting the availability of forest resources.

Scholte (2011) described factors driving changes in wildlife populations. Underlying drivers may not themselves cause change, but indirectly act to contribute to change. Identifying drivers and, where possible, quantifying their impact, facilitates the formulation of appropriate management guidelines for extractive use of wild resources. The main drivers of change are summarized as follows:

### *Habitat loss and degradation*

Habitat destruction can be categorized as degradation, fragmentation or outright loss. Habitat loss has emerged in the 21st century as the most severe threat to biodiversity worldwide, threatening some 85% of all species classified as 'threatened' on the IUCN Red List of Threatened Species (Baillie et al., 2004).

### *Large scale extractive and production projects*

Many countries worldwide have allocated a large part of their territories to oil, mining, agriculture and extensive timber use. For example, in Central Africa selective logging is the most extensive extractive industry, with logging concessions occupying 30–45% of all tropical forests and over 70% of forests in some countries (Laporte et al., 2007). In many countries, the mineral boom has contributed to the emergence of 'growth corridors' where infrastructure upgrades will improve the competitiveness of agriculture and other economic activities (Delgado et al., 1998) which impact wildlife habitats and disturb wildlife populations (noise, pollution, etc).

### *Conflict and war*

Wars have multiple impacts on biodiversity and protected areas and livelihoods of local people dependent on natural resources. Impacts can be highly variable, and may be positive in some areas and negative in others (McNeely, 1998). Very often, war has significant negative effects directly or indirectly on threathened wildlife (Baillie et al., 2004) and their habitats (de Merode et al., 2007).

### *Human population growth*

The impacts of human population growth on wild resources are the subject of much debate. While neo-Malthusian theories place population growth in the context of a vicious circle of destruction, others suggest that such theories oversimplify environmental degradation (Sunderlin and Resosudarno, 1999; Leach and Fairhead, 2000). According to neo-Malthusian theory, population growth causes intensified pressures on natural habitats and resources to satisfy growing demand for space, housing, food and water for drinking and sanitation. However, Boserup (1996) contends that people adapt to increased population density through innovative technologies that reduce pressure on natural resources.

### *Wildlife and plant diseases*

Ecological disturbances can also influence the emergence and proliferation of plant and wildlife diseases. Each environmental change, whether occurring as a natural phenomenon or through human intervention (deforestation, changes in land use, human settlement, commercial development, road construction, water control systems, introduction of cultivated species), changes the ecological balance and context within which disease hosts or vectors and parasites breed, develop and transmit disease. The trade in wildlife provides disease transmission mechanisms (Smith et al., 2012) that can cause human and livestock disease outbreaks. Wildlife diseases can also have ecological impacts on native wildlife populations and affect the health of ecosystems. They can also severely affect local and international trade and rural livelihoods. The majority of recently emerging infectious diseases are associated with wildlife (WHO/UNEP/CBD, 2015). Recent highly publicized examples include the Ebola virus outbreak in West Africa and the avian influenza H5N1 virus outbreaks in the Middle East and Asia. Such diseases also threaten their wild species hosts. Wildlife monitoring can aid early detection and prevention of human infections (WHO/UNEP/CBD, 2015). Infection-related wild species population declines may also compromise the ecosystem services that wildlife provide. For example, White Nose Syndrome in North American bats and chytrid in amphibians may affect the pest control functions provided by these animals (WHO/UNEP/CBD, 2015). Wild plants too can act as bridges between geographically separated crops and for seasonally active infections, allowing the transmission of pathogens and contribute to the spread of plant epidemics (Dinoor, 1974). Host-pathogen interactions in wild plants and animals provide important insights concerning disease resistance and the genetic factors behind resistance.

## *Invasive species*

About 10% of invasive or 'alien' plants change the character, condition, form or nature of ecosystems over substantial areas, and can be termed 'transformers', whilst around 50% to 80% of invaders have harmful effects can be termed 'pests' and 'weeds' (Richardson et al., 2000). Human activities, especially international travel and trade, have circumvented natural barriers and oceans which have regulated the distribution of the world's biota for millions of years, leading to species invading new continents at an increasing rate (Liebhold et al., 1995). Over 120,000 non-native species of plants, animals and microbes have invaded the United States, United Kingdom, Australia, South Africa, India and Brazil. Many have led to significant economic losses in agriculture and forestry and negatively impacted ecosystem integrity, estimated to cost over USD 314 billion per year (Pimentel et al., 2001). Whilst some introduced species, like corn *(Zea mays)*, wheat (*Triticum* spp.), rice *(Oryza sativa)*, plantation forests, chicken (*Gallus* spp.) and cattle *(Bos taurus)*, are largely seen beneficial transformers, providing more than 98% of the world's food supply, some species have negative invasive impacts. For example cats *(Felis catus)*, pigs *(Sus scrofa)*, nile perch *(Lates niloticus)*, water hyacinth *(Eichhornia crassipes)* and miconia *(Miconia calvescens)* have been held responsible for the extinction of numerous wild species and lowering wild biodiversity (Lowe et al., 2000). Precise economic costs of the most ecologically damaging invasive species are generally not available (Pimentel et al., 2001).

## *Climate change*

Climate change may have diverse indirect effects on wildlife depending on the characteristics of the species (Foden et al., 2013). Similar predictions occur for wild flora. For example, forest ecosystems with low phenotypic plasticity and low genetic diversity at population level, where trees are at their adaptive limit and edge of distribution, are predicted to be more sensitive to climate changes (Loo et al., 2011). Expected impacts include mortality due to extreme climatic events and regeneration failure, increasing pest and disease attacks, changing fecundity, asynchronous timing between flowering and the availability of pollinators, increased fires, new species invasions, altered gene flow and species and population hybridization (Loo et al., 2011). Wild species with generalized and unspecialized habitat requirements are likely to be able to tolerate a greater level of climatic and ecosystem change than specialized species. However, many species rely on environmental triggers or cues for migration, breeding, egg laying, seed germination, hibernation, spring emergence and a range of other essential processes. Species dependent on interactions that are susceptible to disruption by climate change are at risk of extinction, particularly where they have high degree of specialization for the particular resource species and are unlikely to be able to switch to or substitute other species.

## *Sustainable use of wild plant and animal genetic resources*

How wild resources (and the ecosystems which provide them) are governed affects their sustainable exploitation. Sustainability is affected by supply and demand, determining how much of a wild resource is harvested, how, why and by whom. Interactions between supply and demand can determine population densities and the suitability of habitats for (different) wild and cultivated species (Green et al., 2005). Sustainability is also affected by factors such as (a) the abundance of the species from which a product originates; (b) direct anthropogenic factors such as forest degradation, as well as semi-natural ones such as climate change threats; (c) inherent species vulnerability which depends on the part(s) of the organism used; and (d) a species' tolerance to harvesting.

Worldwide, trade in timber threatens around 1,000 tree species (Rivalan et al., 2007). Regarding wood production from natural forests, there appears to be a decline in natural forest wood extraction in many nations, following a peak (around 1989) (Shearman et al., 2012; Warman, 2014). The trends observed resemble those found in non-renewable resources, as a result of many factors, primarily the limited length of the standard cutting cycles (30–40 years) that does not allow the wood volume to regenerate. Thus, an increasing move to deliberate tree cultivation in response to local or national wood shortages has been observed (Warman, 2014).

Challenges for sustainable wild collection of tree resources include determining sustainable harvest level and practices, definition of access and tenure rights, and definition of a legislative and policy framework. Many wild species are governed as public goods or common property, raising questions about how (and if!) they are managed, and by whom, and how access to, and benefits from, these resources is arranged. Tenure has a crucial role in securing sustainable use of natural resources. With regard to forests, and particularly collective forests and resources, the term 'tenure rights' is used to refer to a bundle of rights ranging from access and use rights to management, exclusion and alienation (Schlager and Ostrom, 1992). A review of more than 100 empirical cases of forest outcomes in relation to specific land tenure conditions concluded that land tenure security is associated with less deforestation, regardless of the form of tenure. In addition, state-owned protected forests tend to be associated with more positive forest outcomes than private, communal or public land (Robinson et al., 2011).

Wildlife trade threatens around a third of birds and animals and 75% of fisheries (Rivalan, 2007). 'Defaunation' is often cited as the main impact of hunting, resulting in the so-called 'empty forest' syndrome (Redford, 1992; Wilkie et al., 2011) and the 'empty savannah' syndrome (Keesing and Young, 2014). Defaunation can be defined as the local or regional population decline or species extirpation of arthropods, fish, reptile, bird or mammal species (Dirzo, 2001). Because defaunation is solely driven by human activities, it is also referred to as 'anthropocene defaunation' (Dirzo et al., 2014). Defaunation may also generate trophic cascades that alter ecological processes, leading to long-term changes in community composition and diversity loss (Dirzo et al., 2014; Muller-Landau, 2007). In many ecosystems, the larger vertebrate fauna, especially frugivorous birds, primates, ungulates and mammalian carnivores, have been extirpated or severely reduced in number. As these large animals vanish, so do their myriad, often non-redundant, ecological interactions and the processes they generate, foremost trampling, ecosystem engineering, herbivory, seed predation and dispersal (Dirzo et al., 2007). Therefore, activities such as hunting have the potential to impact not only targeted species but also the ecosystem more broadly. Examples of defaunation are numerous across the world, yet hunting does not always necessarily lead to defaunation. Species are impacted by hunting pressure to different extents. How populations respond to harvest can vary greatly depending on their social structure, reproductive strategies, dispersal patterns and intactness of habitats. Small species are typically more resilient to hunting than larger species, due to their higher reproductive rates (Cowlishaw et al., 2005). Dispersal, in particular, can have significant ramifications (both stabilizing and destabilizing) on population dynamics. Density-dependent dispersal may stabilize populations as immigration and emigration counterbalance between hunted (sink) and non-hunted (source). Junker et al. (2015) suggested that projects providing bushmeat protein alternatives and education may complement strategies to conserve chimpanzees in Liberia and possibly other countries in tropical Africa.

Many plant-based NTFPs have higher levels of exploitation than the natural carrying capacity (Kusters et al., 2006). Such exploitation has led to concerns biodiversity loss and subsequent need for conservation (Cunningham, 1991; Abensperg-Traun, 2009). The extraction of wild-harvested NTFPs tends to lead to over-exploitation and degradation of the resources with negative externalities. Although NTFPs were seen as a potentially secure and stable source of cash income, with local communities actively involved in preventing the forest degradation in the past, there is growing evidence regarding the impacts of commercializing NTFPs on exploitation and biological degradation (Peters, 1996; Ingram, 2014).

## *Measures to increase the sustainable use of wild plant and animal genetic resources*

Five major approaches, sometimes applied jointly, have led to variable degrees of success in encouraging a more sustainable governance of wild genetic resources:

1 Domestication and cultivation in farms and plantations have been the most commonly adopted approaches to fulfil multiple objectives, such as (a) subtracting species from unsustainable harvesting pressures in the wild, (b) enhancing expression of desirable traits through breeding and (c) facilitating access to the resource thanks to the proximity of planting sites. Examples of species now widely cultivated, whose genetic diversity provides a unique selling point critical to their trade and is actively promoted, include cocoa *(Theobroma cacao)* and coffee (*Coffea* spp.). However, currently, there is little evidence that cultivation has been successful in reducing pressure from wild harvested plant resources, as reviewed in Dawson et al. (2013). Furthermore, domestication determines shifts including potential losses of intraspecific diversity in the tree populations affected (Dawson et al., 2009). However, these changes depend on what methods are used, with some domestication practices leading to the maintenance of higher genetic diversity (Cornelius et al., 2006) In addition, farming can also negatively affect wild species and it is seen, for example, as the greatest extinction threat to birds (Green et al., 2005).

2 Solutions that make trade-offs between agriculture or wild nature, include environmentally-friendly farming, ecological intensification, land sparing and proactive management of trade and species, which can include initially counter-intuitive practices such as ranching and trophy hunting which can conserve specific populations (Rivalan et al., 2007; Ingram et al., 2009). The success of such approaches is often highly dependent upon local conditions.

3 Market-based approaches such as voluntary standards and certification aim to sustainably govern access and use of wild resources and their markets (Schmitt and Grote, 2006; Shanley et al., 2008; FairWild Foundation, 2010). Successes have been highly variable and context specific, depending on factors such as the costs of adoption and adherence, strictness of the standards, degree of supply and demand and consumer uptake (Potts et al., 2014).
4 Conservation in the form of customary and legal, national and international agreements that prohibit either access to areas which contain threatened wild resources, their use and/or trade has resulted in both notable successes and failures (Rodrigues et al., 2004; Porter-Bolland et al., 2012).
5 Conservation of genetic resources in the form of *in situ*, *circa situ* and *ex situ* approaches based on the characterization of intraspecific diversity and its spatial distribution. Both approaches pose some challenges. For *in situ* genetic conservation strategies to be effective, several conditions need to be in place, such as, for example, favourable policy and legislation frameworks, an appropriate characterization of the resource base through research and the establishment of genetic conservation reserves (FAO, 2014a). *Ex situ* crop collections are a way to conserve crop plant varieties and their wild varieties, and ensure genetic diversity is not lost, though this is not a viable option for all species. Several tropical tree species have recalcitrant seed, unable to survive drying and freezing. However, research has led to considerable innovation in seed storage recently, and increased tree seed longevity under drying conditions and improved storage technologies (Pritchard et al., 2014).

## The genetic consequences of exploiting wild plant resources

The wide range of goods and services provided by trees and forests is a result of, and evidence for, the genetic variability that supports their supply. Like wild species, 'wild genes' are threatened by the same pressures that drive changes in wild resources.

However, the impact of these threats is more difficult to identify and assess in wild genetic resources. Valuable gene pools of widespread species may disappear undetected, because the intraspecific diversity of these species has not been yet characterized, or because the species per se is not under threat of extinction while some populations with important, distinct characteristics may be lost. These losses can eventually lead to species extinction.

Many tree species have very large within-species diversity (Hamrick et al., 1992) but just over 1% of tree species have been subject to genetic studies and a limited number of non-planted tree species have been characterized using molecular markers (FAO, 2014a). Most of the species characterized have commercial value or significant livelihood significance. Although the number of tropical wild-harvested tree species being genetically characterized is growing, the inclusion of genetic considerations into forest management has been relatively limited (see **Box 4.2** *The genetic diversity of wild forest species*). There are also major gaps in the geographic distribution of studies, with a focus on neotropical species (Jalonen et al., 2014).

Long-term harvesting of wild plants and other kinds of disturbance at the individual and population levels can affect the genetic diversity of a species by altering individual fitness and genetic contribution. These effects can be detected through variations in genetic parameters. Knowledge about the relationships between disturbance and genetic diversity within and among populations enables us to assess the adaptive capability of plant species.

Selective logging regimes are commonly applied in tropical forest management. These practices lead to a systematic removal of the largest individuals, which often contribute to regeneration, leaving behind only residual phenotypes with less desirable qualities to contribute to regeneration (Ledig, 1992). Changes in the genetic structure of logged tree populations, have

### Box 4.2 The genetic diversity of wild forest species

Sal (*Shorea robusta* Gaertn.) is a tropical tree of high economic value and classed as endangered in Nepal due to forest clearance and range fragmentation (Pandey and Geburek, 2009). Peripheral populations have been found to be genetically less variable than central ones, although they appear to have a distinct genetic profile that makes them suited to extreme conditions (Pandey and Geburek, 2009), highlighting the value of marginal populations of tropical plants.

Actions to conserve wild fruit trees and *in situ* management of African woody species in semi-arid areas are seen as critical (Bouvet et al., 2004; Diallo et al., 2007). An example is *Sclerocarya birrea*, a multi-purpose plant in the Sahel-Sudanian savanna threatened by human pressure and climate change. An assessment of genetic diversity and spatial organization in Burkina Faso revealed a high within-species diversity and enabled the implementation of conservation initiatives (Kando et al., 2012).

The Brazil nut, *Bertholletia excelsa*, a key forest product in Brazil, Bolivia and Peru is traded for food and cosmetic use. Differences in the timing of fruiting and yields, mainly between the western and eastern Amazon led to an investigation of the genetic structure of this species across the Amazon (Sujii et al., 2015).

*Prunus africana* (Hook.f.) Kalkman is an evergreen tree found in Afromontane forests. For 40 years the bark extract has been used as the basis for treating benign prostatic hyperplasia. The international trade and over-exploitation of natural populations generated a study of the trees phylogeography, characterizing species genetic diversity in nine African countries. Insights into colonization dynamics and vegetation history enabled the identification of high priority regions for genetic diversity conservation, taking account of threats due to climatic change (Kadu et al., 2011).

To improve the understanding of the relationship between diversity in cultivated vs. wild cacao *(Theobroma cacao)*, a wide geographic sample of trees was genetically characterized (Motamayor et al., 2008). Ten genetic clusters were identified, as opposed to the two genetic groups traditionally recognized. The results provide new understanding on the diversification of Amazonian species generally, and particularly of traditional cacao cultivars.

been documented in a limited number of cases (with disputed results) in terms of changes in production volumes, timber quality and economic value (Cornelius et al., 2005), while studies on the genetic impact of harvesting NTFPs are very few in the scientific literature. Also, the duration of the application of a specific management system is a factor of high relevance (Wickneswari et al., 2014).

For NTFPs, factors such the part of a plant harvested, the breeding system and the effective population size of the plant involved need be taken into account. Destructive harvesting before maturity is generally the most severe threat. The review of Dawson et al. (2014) concludes that if the part exploited is the seed or the fruit, the effects of intensive exploitation are highest.

## Conclusions

The socio-economic benefits to humankind of such resources for the multitude of functions they provide – food, energy, medicines, materials and so forth are increasingly recognized, as is their role in ecosystem resilience. Debates on whether wild species, particularly those threatened with extinction, should be used, particularly commercially, and how to conserve them, have taken place over the last two decades (Garrison, 1994; Freese, 1998). There is a growing body of evidence supporting the need to critically examine why, when, how and where wild genetic resources are used, and by whom, in order to improve governance. Sustainable use and trade in wild genetic resources across the globe is critically important to meet a number of the Sustainable Development Goals. However, sustainable use is undermined by the continued poor and unsystematic nature of inventories of species used, of their abundance and the dependence by different peoples on their products, for both subsistence use and trade (Ingram, 2014; Schulp et al., 2014).

Five main approaches have led to variable degrees of success in encouraging a more sustainable governance of wild genetic resources: domestication and cultivation; trade-offs between agriculture and wild nature; voluntary standards and certification; customary and legal, national and international agreements prohibiting access to threatened wild resources, their use and trade; and conservation through *in situ*, *circa situ* and *ex situ* approaches. Despite some successes, the increasing number of wild species extinctions and continued habitat loss indicate that generally we are inadequately counteracting the multitude of anthropogenic threats to our valuable wild genetic resources. The picture of how many species are in danger of becoming extinct, or have become extinct without our knowing, is largely incomplete. Therefore, scaling-up and further implementing the initiatives mentioned earlier, taking account of specific ecological, economic, social-cultural contexts is imperative. Additionally, more systematic inventorying of local, traditional knowledge is needed, and improving *ex situ* collections of wild varieties and species of crops and livestock to ensure genetic diversity is not lost – guided by their risk status. Adopting new technologies such as open access, peer-checked, web-based Wikipedia-style databases could help further. It is also important to address knowledge gaps, shown in **Box 4.3** *Knowledge gaps on wild plant and animal genetic resources.*

## Box 4.3 Knowledge gaps on wild plant and animal genetic resources

- The extent to which environmental incomes depend on wild-harvested resources is not clearly documented, particularly with regard to those species that are threatened or endangered, and upon which people have a high dependence for their livelihood.
- Indicators to specifically monitor changes in genetic diversity of wild-harvested plant and animal species are currently absent from comprehensive bio-monitoring schemes. Indicators for monitoring forest genetic diversity and dynamics based on ecological and demographic surrogates of adaptive diversity and genetic markers could be adopted to identify genetic erosion processes and assess gene flow (see Graudal et al., 2014).
- Traditional and scientific knowledge of genetic diversity of the most threatened and endangered wild species is inadequate to support conservation actions.
- The geographical representativeness of *in situ* genetic conservation areas compared with the distribution range is unknown for most wild species.
- For most plant wild species, the capacity to adapt to climate change is unknown, particularly their phenotypic plasticity, the genetic adaptation, the location of areas of high adaptive potential and high conservation value (i.e. genetic diversity hotspots), the extent of standing genetic variation, the geographic distribution of future suitable habitats and dispersal rates and the current landscape fragmentation effects on their migration.

*(see Loo et al., 2011)*

## References

Abensperg-Traun, M. (2009) 'CITES, sustainable use of wild species and incentive-driven conservation in developing countries, with an emphasis on southern Africa', *Biological Conservation*, vol. 142, pp. 948–963.

Abernethy, K. and Obiang, A. M. N. (2010) *Bushmeat in Gabon*, Wildlife Department of the Ministry of Wildlife and Forests, Gabon.

Aizen, M. A., Garibaldi, L. A., Cunningham, S. A. and Klein, A. M. (2008) 'Long-term global trends in crop yield and production reveal no current pollination shortage but increasing pollinator dependency', *Current Biology*, vol. 18, pp. 1572–1575.

Alexander, H. M. (2010) 'Disease in natural plant populations, communities, and ecosystems: Insights into ecological and evolutionary processes', *Plant Disease*, vol. 94, pp. 492–503.

Alves, R. R. and Alves, H. N. (2011) 'The faunal drugstore: Animal-based remedies used in traditional medicines in Latin America', *Journal of Ethnobiology and Ethnomedicine*, vol. 7, pp. 1–43.

Angelsen, A., Jagger, P., Babigumira, R., Belcher, B., Hogarth, N., Bauch, S., Börner, J., Smith-Hall, C. and Wunder, S. (2014) 'Environmental income and rural livelihoods: A global-comparative analysis', *World Development*, vol. 64, pp. 12–28.

Baillie, J., Hilton-Taylor, C. and Stuart, S. N. (2004) *2004 IUCN Red List Of Threatened Species: A Global Species Assessment*. IUCN, Gland, Switzerland.

Bauer, J. (2015) 'Modern adverse trends which affect wildlife management efforts', pp. 1–12 in L. Pancel and M. Köhl (eds.) *Tropical Forestry Handbook*, Springer Berlin Heidelberg, Germany.

Bérard, L. and Marchenay, P. (2006) 'Local products and geographical indications: Taking account of local knowledge and biodiversity', *International Social Science Journal*, vol. 58, pp. 109–116.

Biggs, D., Courchamp, F., Martin, R. and Possingham, H. P. (2013) 'Legal trade of Africa's rhino horns', *Science*, vol. 339, pp. 1038–1039.

Boissière, M., Bastide, F., Basuki, I., Pfund, J. L. and Boucard, A. (2013) 'Can we make participatory NTFP monitoring work? Lessons learnt from the development of a multi-stakeholder system in Northern Laos', *Biodiversity and Conservation*, vol. 23, pp. 149–170.

Boserup, E. (1996) 'Development theory: An analytical framework and selected application', *Population and Development Review*, vol. 22, pp. 505–515.

Bouvet, J. M., Fontaine, C., Sanou, H. and Cardi, C. (2004) 'An analysis of the pattern of genetic variation in *Vitellaria paradoxa* using RAPD markers', *Agroforestry Systems*, vol. 60, pp. 61–69.

Cornelius, J. P., Clement, C. R., Weber, J. C., Sotelo-Montes, C., Van Leeuwen, J., Ugarte-Guerra, L. J., Ricse-Tembladera, A. and Arevalo-Lopez, L. (2006) 'The trade off between genetic gain and conservation in a participatory improvement programme: The case of peach palm (*Bactris gasipaes* Kunth)', *Forests, Trees and Livelihoods*, vol. 16, pp. 17–34.

Cornelius, J. P., Navarro, C. M., Wightman, K. E. and Ward, S. E. (2005) 'Is mahogany dysgenically selected?', *Environmental Conservation*, vol. 32, pp. 129–139.

Cowlishaw, G., Mendelson, S. and Rowcliffe, J. (2005) 'Evidence for post-depletion sustainability in a mature bushmeat market', *Journal of Applied Ecology*, vol. 42, pp. 460–468.

Cunningham, A. B. (1991) 'The herbal medicinal trade: Resource depletion and environmental management for a "hidden economy"', pp. 196–206 in E. Preston-Whyte and C. Rogerson (eds.), *South Africa's Informal Economy*, Oxford University Press, Cape Town, South Africa.

Cunningham, A. B. (2001) *Applied Ethnobotany: People, Wild Plant Use and Conservation*, Routledge, London, UK.

Dawson, I. K., Guariguata, M. R., Loo, J., Weber, J. C., Lengkeek, A., Bush, D., Cornelius, J., Guarino, L., Kindt, R., Orwa, C., Russell, J. and Jamnadass, R. (2013) 'What is the relevance of smallholders' agroforestry systems for conserving tropical tree species and genetic diversity in *circa situm*, *in situ* and *ex situ* settings? A review', *Biodiversity and Conservation*, vol. 22, pp. 301–324.

Dawson, I. K., Leakey, R., Clement, C. R., Weber, J. C., Cornelius, J. P., Roshetko, J. M., Vinceti, B., Kalinganire, A., Tchoundjeu, Z., Masters, E. and Jamnadass, R. (2014) 'The management of tree genetic resources and the livelihoods of rural communities in the tropics: Non-timber forest products, smallholder agroforestry practices and tree commodity crops', *Forest Ecology and Management*, vol. 33, pp. 9–21.

Dawson, I. K., Lengkeek, A., Weber, J. C. and Jamnadass, R. (2009) 'Managing genetic variation in tropical trees: Linking knowledge with action in agroforestry ecosystems for improved conservation and enhanced livelihoods', *Biodiversity and Conservation*, vol. 18, pp. 969–986.

Delang, C. O. (2005) 'Not just minor forest products: The economic rationale for the consumption of wild food plants by subsistence farmers', *Ecological Economics*, vol. 59, pp. 64–73.

Delgado, C. L. (ed.) (1998). *Agricultural Growth Linkages in Sub-Saharan Africa*, International Food Policy Research Institute, Washington, DC, USA.

De Merode, E., Smith, K. H., Homewood, K., Pettifor, R., Rowcliffe, M. and Cowlishaw, G. (2007) 'The impact of armed conflict on protected-area efficacy in Central Africa', *Biology Letters*, vol. 3, pp. 299–301.

Diallo, O. B., Joly, H. I., McKey, D., Hossaert-McKey, M. and Chevallier, M. H. (2007) 'Genetic diversity of *Tamarindus indica* population: Any clues on the origin from its current distribution?', *African Journal of Biotechnology*, vol. 6, pp. 853–860.

Diamond, J. (2002) 'Evolution, consequences and future of plant and animal domestication', *Nature*, vol. 418, pp. 700–707.

Dinoor, A. (1974) 'Role of wild and cultivated plants in the epidemiology of plant diseases in Israel', *Annual Review of Phytopathology*, vol. 12, pp. 413–436.

Dirzo, R. and Mendoza, O. P. (2007) 'Size-related differential seed predation in a heavily defaunated neotropical rain forest', *Biotropica*, vol. 39, pp. 355–362.

Dirzo, R., Young, H. S., Galetti, M., Ceballos, G., Isaac, N. J. B. and Collen, B. (2014) 'Defaunation in the anthropocene', *Science*, vol. 345, pp. 401–406.

Duchelle, A. E., Guariguata, M. R., Less, G., Antonio, M. and Chavez, A. (2012) 'Evaluating the opportunities and limitations to multiple use of Brazil nuts and timber in Western Amazonia', *Forest Ecology and Management*, vol. 268, pp. 39–48.

FairWild Foundation (2010) *FairWild Standard: Version 2.0*, FairWild Foundation, Weinfelden, Switzerland, 12.

FAO (2014a) *The State of the World's Forest Genetic Resources*, FAO, Rome, Italy.

FAO (2014b) *Global Land Cover Network*, www.glcn.org/databases/lc_glcshare_results_en.jsp, accessed 25 September 2015.

FAO (2015a) *Global Forest Resources Assessment 2015: How Are the World's Forests Changing?* FAO, Rome, Italy.

FAO (2015b) *State of the World's Forests 2014*, FAO, Rome, Italy.

Foden, W., Mace, G. M., Vié, J. C., Angulo, A., Butchart, S. H., DeVantier, L., Dublin, H. T., Gutsche, A., Stuart, S. and Turak, E. (2009) 'Species susceptibility to climate change impacts', pp. in J. C. Vié, C. Hilton-Taylor and S. N. Stuart (eds.) *Wildlife in a Changing World – An Analysis of the 2008 IUCN Red List of Threatened Species*, IUCN, Gland, Switzerland.

Freese, C. (1998) *Wild Species as Commodities: Managing Markets and Ecosystems for Sustainability*, Island Press, Washington, DC and Covelo, CA, USA.

Garrison, J. L. (1994) 'Convention on International Trade in Endangered Species of Wild Fauna and Flora (CITES) and the debate over sustainable use', *Pace Environmental Law Review*, vol. 12, p. 12.

Gill, R. B. (2009) 'To save a mountain lion: evolving philosophy of nature and cougars', pp. 5–16 in M. Hornocker and S. Negri (eds.) *Cougar: Ecology and Conservation*, University of Chicago Press, Chicago, IL, USA.

Golden, C. D., Fernald, L. C. H., Brashares, J. S., Rasolofoniaina, B. J. R. and Kremen, C. (2011) 'Benefits of wildlife consumption to child nutrition in a biodiversity hotspot', *Proceedings of the National Academy of Sciences USA*, vol. 108, pp. 19653–19656.

Graudal, L., Aravanopoulos, F., Bennadji, Z., Changtragoon, S., Fady, B., Kjær, E. D., Loo, J., Ramamonjisoa, L. and Vendramin, G. G. (2014) 'Global to local genetic diversity indicators of evolutionary potential in tree species within and outside forests', *Forest Ecology and Management*, vol. 333, pp. 35–51.

Green, R. E., Cornell, S. J., Scharlemann, J. P. and Balmford, A. (2005) 'Farming and the fate of wild nature', *Science*, vol. 307, pp. 550–555.

Hamrick, J. L., Godt, M. J. W. and Sherman-Broyles, S. L. (1992) 'Factors influencing levels of genetic diversity in woody plant species', *New Forests*, vol. 6, pp. 95–124.

Hemp, A. (2006) 'Vegetation of Kilimanjaro: Hidden endemics and missing bamboo', *African Journal of Ecology*, vol. 44, pp. 305–328.

Ingram, V. (2014) *Win-Wins in Forest Product Value Chains? How Governance Impacts the Sustainability of Livelihoods Based on Non-Timber Forest Products from Cameroon*, PhD Thesis, University of Amsterdam, the Netherlands.

Ingram, V., Awono, A., Schure, J. and Ndam, N. (2009) 'Guidance for a national *Prunus africana* management plan, Cameroon', Project GCP/RAF/408/EC "Mobilisation et Renforcement des Capacités des Petites et Moyennes Entreprises impliquées dans les Filières des Produits Forestiers Non Ligneux en Afrique Centrale". CIFOR. Yaoundé, Cameroun, FAO-CIFOR-SNV-World Agroforestry Center-COMIFAC-GTZ, 156.

Jackson, M. T. and Ford-Lloyd, B. V. (1990) 'Plant genetic resources: A perspective', in M. T. Jackson, B. V. Ford-Lloyd and M. L. Parry (eds.), *Climatic Change and Plant Genetic Resources*, Belhaven Press, London, UK, pp. 1–17.

Jalonen, R., Hong, L. T., Lee, S. L., Loo, J. and Snook, L. (2014) 'Integrating genetic factors into management of tropical Asian production forests: A review of current knowledge', *Forest Ecology and Management*, vol. 315, pp. 191–201.

Johns, T., Powell, B., Maundu, P. and Eyzaguirre, P. B. (2013) 'Agricultural biodiversity as a link between traditional food systems and contemporary development, social integrity and ecological health', *Journal of the Science of Food and Agriculture*, vol. 93, pp. 3433–3442.

Junker, J., Boesch, C., Mundry, R., Stephens, C., Lormie, M., Tweh, C. and Kühl, H. S. (2015) 'Education and access to fish but not economic development predict chimpanzee and mammal occurrence in West Africa', *Biological Conservation*, vol. 182, pp. 27–35.

Kadu, C. A. C., Parich, A., Schueler, S., Konrad, H., Muluvi, G. M., Eyog-Matig, O., Muchugi, A., Williams, V. L., Ramamonjisoa, L., Kapinga, C., Foahom, B., Katsvanga, C., Hafashimana, D., Cr, B. V. and Rainer Schumacher, T. G. (2012) 'Bioactive constituents in *Prunus africana*: Geographical variation throughout Africa and associations with environmental and genetic parameters', *Phytochemistry*, vol. 83, pp. 70–78.

Kadu, C. A. C., Schueler, S., Konrad, H., Muluvi, G. M., Eyog-Matig, O., Muchugi, A., Williams, V. L., Ramamonjisoa, L., Kapinga, C., Foahom, B., Katsvanga, C., Hafashimana, D., Obama, C. and Geburek, T. (2011) 'Phylogeography of the Afromontane *Prunus africana* reveals a former migration corridor between East and West African highlands', *Molecular Ecology*, vol. 20, pp. 165–178.

Kando, P. B., Bisseye, C., Nanema, R. K., Traore, E. R., Ye, H., Diallo, B. O. and Zongo, D. (2012) 'Genetic diversity of *Sclerocarya birrea* subspecies *birrea* populations in Burkina Faso detected by RAPDs', *African Journal of Biotechnology*, vol. 11, pp. 99–108.

Keesing, F. and Young, T. P. (2014) 'Cascading consequences of the loss of large mammals in an African savanna', *Bioscience*, vol. 64, pp. 487–495.

Kissinger, G., Herold, M. and De Sy, V. (2012) *Drivers of Deforestation and Forest Degradation: A Synthesis Report for REDD+ Policymakers*, Lexeme Consulting, Vancouver, Canada.

Kusters, K., Achdiawan, R., Belcher, B. and Ruiz Pérez, M. (2006) 'Balancing development and conservation? An assessment of livelihood and environmental outcomes of non-timber forest product trade in Asia, Africa, and Latin America', *Ecology and Society*, vol. 11, p. 2.

Laird, S. A. (ed.). (2010) *Biodiversity and Traditional Knowledge: Equitable Partnerships in Practice*, Earthscan for Routledge, Abingdon, UK.

Laird, S. A., McLain, R. J. and Wynberg, R. (eds.) (2010) *Wild Product Governance: Finding Policies that Work for Non-Timber Forest Products*, Earthscan for Routledge, Abingdon, UK.

Lange, D. (1998) *Europe's Medicinal and Aromatic Plants: Their Use, Trade and Conservation*, Traffic Network Report, Traffic International, Cambridge, UK.

Laporte, N. T., Stabach, J. A., Grosch, R., Lin, T. S. and Goetz, S. J. (2007) 'Expansion of industrial logging in Central Africa', *Science*, vol. 316, pp. 1451–1451.

Leach, M. and Fairhead, J. (2000) 'Challenging neo-Malthusian deforestation analyses in West Africa's dynamic forest landscapes', *Population and Development Review*, vol. 26, pp. 17–43.

Ledig, F. T. (1992) 'Human impacts on genetic diversity in forest ecosystems', *Oikos*, vol. 63, pp. 87–109.

Leroy, E. M., Rouquet, P., Formenty, P., Souquiere, S., Kilbourne, A., Froment, J-M., Bermejo, M., Smit, S., Karesh, W., Swanepoel, R., Zaki, S. R. and Rollin, P. E. (2004) 'Multiple Ebola virus transmission events and rapid decline of central African wildlife', *Science*, vol. 303, pp. 387–390.

Liebhold, A. M., MacDonald, W. L., Bergdahl, D. and Mastro, V. C. (1995) 'Invasion by exotic forest pests: A threat to forest ecosystems', *Forest Science*, vol. 41, pp. a0001–z0001.

Loo, J., Fady, B., Dawson, I., Vinceti, B. and Baldinelli, G. (2011) *Climate Change and Forest Genetic Resources: State of Knowledge, Risks and Opportunities*, Background study paper (56), Bioversity International, Maccarese, Italy.

Lowe, S., Browne, M., Boudjelas, S. and De Poorter, M. (2000) *100 of the World's Worst Invasive Alien Species: A Selection from the Global Invasive Species Database*, Invasive Species Specialist Group, Auckland, New Zealand.

McNeely, J. A. (2003) 'Biodiversity, war, and tropical forests', *Journal of Sustainable Forestry*, vol. 16, pp. 1–20.

Milder, J. C., Hart, A. K., Dobie, P., Minai, J. and Zaleski, C. (2014) 'Integrated landscape initiatives for african agriculture, development and conservation: A region-wide assessment', *World Development*, vol. 54, pp. 68–80.

Milner-Gulland, E. J., Bennette, E. L. and the SCB 2002 Annual Meeting Wild Meat Group (2003) 'Wild meat: the bigger picture', *Trends in Ecology & Evolution*, vol. 18, pp. 351–357.

Motamayor, J. C., Lachenaud, P., da Silva e Mota, J. W., Loor, R., Kuhn, D., Brown, J. S. and Schnell, R. J. (2008) 'Geographic and genetic population differentiation of the Amazonian chocolate tree (*Theobroma cacao* L.)', *PLoS ONE*, vol. 3, p. e3311.

Msuya, T. S., Kideghesho, J. R. and Mosha, T. C. E. (2010) 'Availability, preference, and consumption of indigenous forest foods in the Eastern Arc Mountains, Tanzania', *Ecology of Food and Nutrition*, vol. 49, pp. 208–227.

Muller-Landau, H. C. (2007) 'Predicting the long-term effects of hunting on plant species composition and diversity in tropical forests', *Biotropica*, vol. 39, pp. 372–384.

Nasi, R., Brown, D., Wilkie, D., Bennett, E., Tutin, C., van Tol, G. and Christophersen, T. (2008) *Conservation and Use of Wildlife-Based Resources: The Bushmeat Crisis*, Technical Series no.33. Montreal and Bogor, Secretariat of the Convention on Biological Diversity and Center for International Forestry Research (CIFOR), 50.

Nasi, R., Taber, A. and Vliet, N. V. (2011) 'Empty forests, empty stomachs? Bushmeat and livelihoods in the Congo and Amazon Basins', *International Forestry Review*, vol. 13, pp. 355–368.

Newton, A. C. (2008) 'Conservation of tree species through sustainable use: How can it be achieved in practice?', *Oryx*, vol. 42, pp. 195–205.

Noufou, O., Wamtinga, S. R., André, T., Christine, B., Marius, L., Emmanuelle, H. A. and Pierre, G. I. (2012) 'Pharmacological properties and related constituents of stem bark of *Pterocarpus erinaceus* Poir. (Fabaceae)', *Asian Pacific Journal of Tropical Medicine*, vol. 5, pp. 46–51.

Ojasti, J. (2000) *Manejo de Fauna Silvestre Neotropical*, F. Dallmeier (ed.), Smithsonian Institution, Washington D.C., USA.

Oksanen, T. and Mersmann, C. (2003) 'Forests in poverty reduction strategies — An assessment of PRSP processes in Sub-Saharan Africa', pp. 121–192 in T. Oksanen, B. Pajari and T. Tuomasjukka (eds.) *Forests in Poverty Reduction Strategies: Capturing the Potential*, EFI Proceedings No. 47.

Oyono, P. R. (2005) 'The foundations of the conflit de langage over land and forests in southern Cameroon', *African Study Monographs*, vol. 26, pp. 115–144.

Pandey, M. and Geburek, T. (2009) 'Genetic differences between continuous and disjunct populations: Some insights from sal (*Shorea robusta* Roxb.) in Nepal', *Conservation Genetics*, vol. 11, pp. 977–984.

Peters, C. M. (1996) *The Ecology and Management of Non-Timber-Forest Resources*, Technical papers, World Bank, Washington, DC, USA.

Pimentel, D., McNair, S., Janecka, J., Wightman, J., Simmonds, C., O'Connell, C., Wong, E., Russel, L., Zern, J., Aquino, T. and Tsomondo, T. (2001) 'Economic and environmental threats of alien plant, animal, and microbe invasions', *Agriculture, Ecosystems & Environment*, vol. 84, pp. 1–20.

Porter-Bolland, L., Ellis, E. A., Guariguata, M. R., Ruiz-Mallén, I., Negrete-Yankelevich, S. and Reyes-García, V. (2012) 'Community managed forests and forest protected areas: An assessment of their conservation effectiveness across the tropics', *Forest Ecology and Management*, vol. 268, pp. 6–17.

Potts, J., Lynch, M., Wilkings, A., Huppé, G., Cunningham, M. and Voora, V. (2014) 'The state of sustainability initiatives review 2014: Standards and the green economy', *International Institute for Sustainable Development (IISD) and the International Institute for Environment and Development (IIED), 332,* Winnipeg, Canada and London, UK.

Powell, B., Thilsted, S. H., Ickowitz, A., Termote, C., Sunderland, T. and Herforth, A. (2015) 'Improving diets with wild and cultivated biodiversity from across the landscape', *Food Security*, vol. 7, pp. 535–554.

Prescott-Allen, R. and Prescott-Allen, C. (1983) *Genes from the Wild: Using Wild Genetic Resources for Food and Raw Materials*, Earthscan, London, UK.

Pritchard, H. W., Moat, J. F., Ferraz, J. B. S., Marks, T. R., Camargo, J. L. C., Nadarajan, J. and Ferraz, I. D. K. (2014) 'Innovative approaches to the preservation of forest trees', *Forest Ecology and Management*, vol. 333, pp. 88–98.

Ramsay, B. J. (1994) *Commercial Use of Wild Animals in Australia*, Australian Government Publishing Service, Canberra, Australia.

Redford, K.H. (1992) 'The empty forest', *Bioscience*, vol. 42, pp. 412–422.

Richardson, D. M., Pyšek, P., Rejmánek, M., Barbour, M. G., Panetta, F. D. and West, C. J. (2000) 'Naturalization and invasion of alien plants: Concepts and definitions', *Diversity and Distributions*, vol. 6, pp. 93–107.

Rist, L., Shanley, P., Sunderland, T., Sheil, D., Ndoye, O., Liswanti, N. and Tieguhong, J. (2012) 'The impacts of selective logging on non-timber forest products of livelihood importance', *Forest Ecology and Management*, vol. 268, pp. 57–69.

Rivalan, P., Delmas, V., Angulo, E., Bull, L. S., Hall, R. J., Courchamp, F., Rosser, A. M. and Leader-Williams, N. (2007) 'Can bans stimulate wildlife trade?', *Nature*, vol. 447, pp. 529–530.

Roberts, A. M. (2014) 'Detailed look at the ivory trade and the poaching of elephants', *Quinnipiac Law Review*, vol. 33, pp. 567–580.

Robinson, B. B., Holland, M. B. and Naughton-Treves, L. (2011) 'Does secure land tenure save forests? A review of the relationship between land tenure and tropical deforestation', *Agriculture*, vol. 10, Working

Paper no 7, CGIAR Research Program on Climate Change, Agriculture and Food Security (CCAFS), Copenhagen, Denmark.

Rodrigues, A. S., Andelman, S. J., Bakarr, M. I., Boitani, L., Brooks, T. M., Cowling, R. M., Fishpool, L. D., Da Fonseca, G. A., Gaston, K. J., Hoffmann, M. and Long, J. S. (2004) 'Effectiveness of the global protected area network in representing species diversity', *Nature*, vol. 428, pp. 640–643.

Rodriguez-Izquierdo, E., Gavin, M. C. and Macedo-Bravo, M. O. (2010) 'Barriers and triggers to community participation across different stages of conservation management', *Environmental Conservation*, vol, 37, pp. 239–249.

Schippmann, U., Leaman, D. J. and Cunningham, A. (2002) 'Impact of cultivation and gathering of medicinal plants on biodiversity: Global trends and issues', Biodiversity and the Ecosystem Approach in Agriculture, Forestry and Fisheries. Satellite event on the occasion of the Ninth Regular Session of the Commission on Genetic Resources for Food and Agriculture, Rome, 12–13 October 2002. Inter-Departmental Working Group on Biological Diversity for Food and Agriculture. FAO, Rome, Italy.

Schlager, E. and Ostrom, E. (1992) 'Property-rights regimes and natural resources: A conceptual analysis', *Land Economics*, vol. 68, pp. 249–262.

Schmitt, C. and U. Grote (2006) 'Wild coffee production in Ethiopia: The role of coffee certification for forest conservation', Report project 'Conservation and use of wild populations of *Coffea arabica* in the montane rainforest of Ethiopia', Biodiversity and the ecosystem approach in agriculture, forestry and fisheries, Bonn, Germany.

Scholte, P. (2011) 'Towards understanding large mammal population declines in Africa's protected areas: A west-central African perspective', *Tropical Conservation Science*, vol. 4, pp. 1–11.

Schulp, C. J., Thuiller, W. and Verburg, P. (2014) 'Wild food in Europe: A synthesis of knowledge and data of terrestrial wild food as an ecosystem service', *Ecological Economics*, vol. 105, pp. 292–305.

Seignonbos, T. I. C., Degune, J.-P. and Aberlenc, H.-P. (1996) 'Les mofu et leurs insects', *Journale d'Agriculture Traditionale et de Bota Applique*, vol. 358, pp. 125–187.

Shackleton, C. M., Willis, T. J., Brown, K. and Polunin, N. V. C. (2010) 'Reflecting on the next generation of models for community-based natural resources management', *Environmental Conservation*, vol. 37, pp. 1–4.

Shanley, P. and Luz, L. (2003) 'The impacts of forest degradation on medicinal plant use and implications for health care in eastern Amazonia', *Bioscience*, vol. 53, pp. 573–584.

Shanley, P., Pierce, A., Laird, S. and Robinson, D. (2008) *Beyond Timber: Certification and Management of Non-Timber Forest Products*, Center for International Forestry Research (CIFOR), Bogor, Indonesia.

Shearman, P., Bryan, J. and Laurance, W. F. (2012) 'Are we approaching "peak timber" in the tropics?', *Biological Conservation*, vol. 15, pp. 17–21.

Sheil, D. and Salim, A. (2012) 'Diversity of locally useful tropical forest wild-plants as a function of species richness and informant culture', *Biodiversity & Conservation*, vol. 21, pp. 687–699.

Sirén, A. and Machoa, J. (2008) 'Fish, wildlife and human nutrition in tropical forests: a fat gap?' *Interciencia*, vol. 33, pp. 186–193.

Smith, K. M., Anthony, S. J., Switzer, W. M., Epstein, J. H., Seimon, T., Jia, H., Sanchez, M. D., Huynh, T. T., Galland, G. G., Shapiro, S. E., Sleeman, J. M., McAloose, D., Stuchin, M., Amato, G., Kolokotronis, S. O., Lipkin, W. I., Karesh, W. B., Daszak, P. and Marano, N. (2012) 'Zoonotic viruses associated with illegally imported wildlife products', *PLoS ONE*, vol. 7, p. e229505.

Sneyd, L. Q. (2013) 'Wild food, prices, diets and development: Sustainability and food security in urban Cameroon', *Sustainability*, vol. 5, pp. 4728–4759.

Sujii, P. S., Martins, K., Wadt, L. H. D. O., Azevedo, V. C. R. and Solferini, V. N. (2015) 'Genetic structure of *Bertholletia excelsa* populations from the Amazon at different spatial scales', *Conservation Genetics*, vol. 16, pp. 955–964.

Sunderland, T. C. H. (2011) 'Food security: Why is biodiversity important?', *International Forestry Review*, vol. 13, pp. 265–274.

Sunderlin, W. and Resosudarmo, I. A. P. (1999) 'The effect of population and migration on forest cover in Indonesia', *The Journal of Environment & Development*, vol. 8, pp. 152–169.

Thomas, B. (2013) 'Sustainable harvesting and trading of mopane worms *(Imbrasia belina)* in Northern Namibia: An experience from the Uukwaluudhi area', *International Journal of Environmental Studies*, vol. 70, pp. 494–502.

UNEP (2010) *Global Honey Bee Colony Disorders and Other Threats to Insect Pollinators*, United Nations Environment Programme, Nairobi, Kenya.

van Kuijk, M., Putz, F. and Zaag, R. (2009) *Effects of Forest Certification on Biodiversity*, Tropenbos International, Wageningen, the Netherlands.

Vantomme, P., Göhler, D. and N'Deckere-Ziangba, F. (2004) *Contribution of Forest Insects to Food Security and Forest Conservation: The Example of Caterpillars in Central Africa*, Wildlife Policy Briefing Number 3, ODI, 4.

Vira, B., Wildburger, C. and Mansourian, S. (eds.) (2015) *Forests, Trees and Landscapes for Food Security and Nutrition: A Global Assessment Report*, IUFRO World Series–Forests, Trees and Landscapes for Food Security and Nutrition, Collaborative Partnership on Forests, IUFRO, Vienna, Austria.

Warman, R. D. (2014) 'Global wood production from natural forests has peaked', *Biodiversity and Conservation*, vol. 28, pp. 1063–1078.

Weinbaum, K. Z., Brashares, J. S., Golden, C. D. and Getz, W. M. (2013) 'Searching for sustainability: Are assessments of wildlife harvests behind the times?' *Ecology Letters*, vol. 16, pp. 99–111.

WHO, UNEP and CBD (2015) *Connecting Global Priorities: Biodiversity and Human Health: A State of Knowledge Review*, www.cbd.int/en/health/stateofknowledge\nhttp://apps.who.int/iris/bitstream/10665/174012/1/9789241508537_eng.pdf

Wickneswari, R. W., Rajora, O. P., Finkeldey, R., Aravanopoulos, F., Bouvet, J.-M., Vaillancourt, R. E., Kanashiro, M., Fady, B., Tomita, M. and Vinson, C. (2014) 'Genetic effects of forest management practices: Global synthesis and perspectives', *Forest Ecology and Management*, vol. 333, pp. 52–65.

Wiersum, K. F., Ingram, V. J. and Ros-Tonen, M. A. F. (2014) 'Governing access to resources and markets in non-timber forest product chains', *Forest, Trees and Livelihoods*, vol. 23, pp. 6–18.

Wilkie, D. S., Bennett, E. L., Peres, C. A. and Cunningham, A. A. (2011) 'The empty forest revisited', *Annals of the New York Academy of Sciences*, vol. 1223, pp. 120–128.

Wily, L. A. (2011) *Customary Land Tenure in the Modern World. Rights to Resources in Crisis: Reviewing the Fate of Customary Tenure in Africa, Brief #1 of 5*, Rights and Resources Initiative, Washington DC, USA.

Wunder, S. (2014) 'Forests, livelihoods, and conservation: Broadening the empirical base', *World Development*, vol. 64, pp. S1–S11.

Zohary, D., Hopf, M. and Weiss, E. (2012) *Domestication of Plants in the Old World: The Origin and Spread of Domesticated Plants in Southwest Asia, Europe, and the Mediterranean Basin*, Oxford University Press, Oxford, UK.

# 5

# AQUATIC GENETIC RESOURCES

*Devin M. Bartley and Matthias Halwart*

## Introduction

Greater use of aquatic genetic resources (AqGR) and the application of genetic technologies offer many opportunities for aquaculture. These include increased production, control of reproduction, improved marketability, more accurate and effective traceability in the supply chain, better disease and parasite resistance, more efficient utilization of resources and better identification and characterization of aquatic genetic resources. These opportunities exist in both developed and developing countries. It has been stated that if all the farmed aquatic species were in a traditional selective breeding programme, the additional need for seafood in 2050 could be met with very little extra land, water, feed or other inputs (Gjedrem, 1997). This chapter briefly defines aquatic genetic resources, examines the current state of these resources in aquaculture production, describes how genetic resources help meet farmer and consumer needs, lists some of the more popular genetic technologies, highlights the aquatic animal diversity in rice fields and concludes with a summary of the opportunities and challenges regarding the use of aquatic genetic resources in aquaculture. Although the Food and Agriculture Organization of the United Nations (FAO) defines 'agricultural biodiversity' to include marine capture fisheries, this chapter will focus on aquaculture in freshwater.

Aquatic genetic resources for food and agriculture include the genetic material found in species, populations, individuals, gametes, genes and DNA of all aquatic plants and animals that provide food, products and related goods and services to humans. The world's fisheries harvest over 2,000 species from several different phyla and numerous families including fish, crustaceans, molluscs, coelenterates, echinoderms, aquatic vascular plants and algae (FAO, 2014). There is a much smaller, yet very diverse, number of aquatic species that are farmed (**Table 5.1** *Diversity of aquatic species*). Once we move inland, that is, to freshwater fisheries and aquaculture, the number of higher taxonomic groups diminishes greatly: there are no echinoderms or coelenterates harvested in freshwater, and the number of crustaceans and molluscs is much less than in the marine environment (**Figure 5.1** *Aquatic biodiversity of farmed species by environment*).

Genetic diversity can be considered at a variety of levels, including the diversity of DNA in genes, the diversity of genes in an organism, the diversity of organisms in a population, the diversity of populations in a species and the diversity of species in a community. Each level supports the level above it and helps it adapt to environmental change, inhabit new areas and continue to survive and change, that is, evolve. For example, the genetic diversity within a single rainbow trout

*Table 5.1* Diversity of aquatic species

| *Taxon* | *Wild species* | *Number of farmed species (number of families)* |
|---|---|---|
| Finfish | 31,000* | 359 (>90) |
| Molluscs | >50,000** | 103 (27) |
| Crustaceans | 47,000*** | 61 (>13) |
| Other aquatic animals | **** | 15 (>8) |
| Aquatic plants | 13,000***** | ~37 (>22) |
| Total | >150,000 | 575 |

* www.fishbase.org
** www.ucmp.berkeley.edu/taxa/inverts/mollusca/mollusca.php
*** https://en.wikipedia.org/wiki/Crustacean
**** These include echinoderms, coelenterates and tunicates too numerous to list, many of which have no potential as food and are all marine species, as well as a few amphibian and reptiles.
***** www.algebase.org; see also Guiry (2012) How many species of algae are there? *J. Phycol.* 48 (5): 1057–1063; http://link.springer.com/chapter/10.1007%2F978-1-4020-8259-7_2#page-2

*Source*: From FAO FishStatJ (2016).

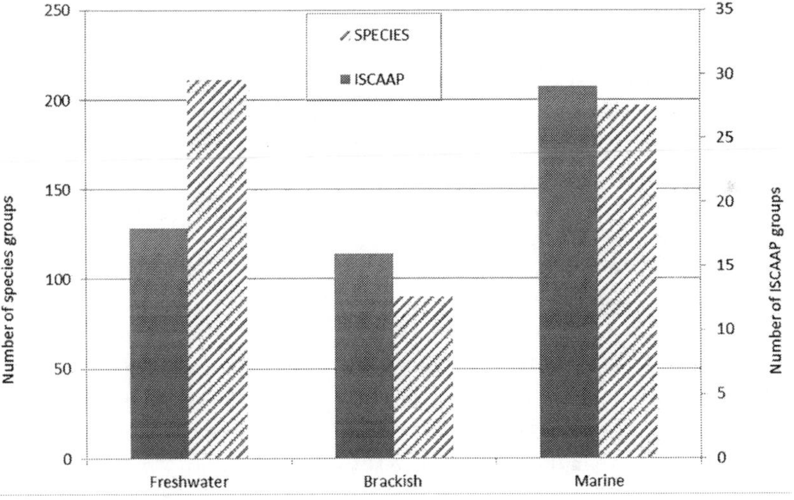


*Figure 5.1* Aquatic biodiversity of farmed species by environment

*Note*: ISCAAP is the International Standard Statistical Classification of Aquatic Animals and Plants and is used for taxonomic levels above the species level.

helps the organism survive diseases (Vallejo et al., 2010); the species genetic diversity of Pacific salmon, for example the genetically distinct runs of salmon, help the species survive glaciation and habitat degradation (Montgomery, 2000); the diversity of fish communities in tropical rivers help the community survive overfishing and 'fishing down the food web' (Welcomme, 1999). In aquaculture, the diversity helps farmers improve their product, meet consumer demands and improve production efficiency (Bakos and Gorda, 2001; ADB, 2005). Thus, genetic diversity at many levels contributes to food production and livelihoods, and helps ecosystems adapt to climate change.

## *State of farmed aquatic animals and plants at species level*

Although information on genetic diversity is useful for management and aquaculture, the state of farmed aquatic animals and plants on a global scale is available only at the species level. The Food and Agriculture Organization of the United Nations (FAO) is the specialized agency responsible for receiving information on the number of farmed aquatic species from member countries. However, this information is almost never reported below the species level. Nonetheless, the information contained in the FAO Fisheries and Aquaculture Database (www.fao.org/fishery/statistics/software/fishstatj/en) provides a good indication of the genetic diversity at species level of farmed aquatic species (**Table 5.1** *Diversity of aquatic species*).

The total production from farmed aquatic species in fresh and brackish waters was 50,865,669 in 2013. The most diverse and commonly farmed group is finfish, with more than 359 species from over 90 families. The species that account for most production from aquaculture in freshwater and brackish water in 2013 were grass carp, silver carp, common carp, Nile tilapia, white leg shrimp, bighead carp, catla, crucian carp, Rohu and milkfish. These ten species account for over 60% of aquaculture production. It is clear from the great diversity of aquatic species found in nature that there is substantial scope for increased production from aquaculture through domestication of additional species and through genetic resource management, for example selective breeding.

The aquaculture sector lags behind the crop and livestock sectors in regards to domestication, that is, managing genetic resources, for product improvement. Domestication of plants and animals started about 10,000 and 7,000 years ago, respectively. Except for common carp, *Cyprinus carpio*, that had already been domesticated in ancient China a few thousand years ago (Balon, 1974, 1995), most aquatic species have been bred in captivity only within the last two centuries (Duarte et al., 2007). The diversity of common carp forms demonstrates the changes in appearance that domestication and the management of genetic resources can produce (**Figure 5.2** *Common carp diversity*). Other aspects of domestication in aquatic species, for example disease resistance, improved growth or environmental tolerance, are not as visible.

The essential requirement for domestication is the ability to breed species under controlled conditions. Various definitions of domestication exist, and the one we have chosen here is that it can be considered to have taken place once three generations of controlled breeding have been achieved (Bilio, 2008). Of the thousands of aquatic species harvested from the world's waters, controlled breeding is possible (and profitable) for only a small percentage (Gjedrem, 1997; Duarte et al., 2007). The main constraints to domestication include problems with controlled reproduction, for example in tuna, complicated larval stages or in many crustaceans such as palinurid lobsters, and larval feeding, as occurs in many marine finfish species (Nash, 2011).

## Characterizing and harnessing aquatic genetic resources via traditional and new technologies

Genetic diversity provides the building blocks for genetic improvement and therefore increased production and profitability from aquaculture. A description of the internal mechanisms that control how genes influence an organism's appearance and behavior is beyond the scope of this chapter. However, they are influenced by a combination of an organism's genes and its environment (Kirpichnicov, 1981). For some traits such as scale pattern in carp, genes exert a major influence (Tave, 1995); for others such as growth rate, the environment often has a strong influence (Kirpichnicov, 1981). For example, if the genetic makeup is poor even the best feeds and optimized feed management will not result in better growth.

*Figure 5.2* Common carp diversity

*Note*: Common carp has been selected for body shape, colour and scale pattern for centuries. From top to bottom: Amur wild type; Szarvas selected strain 15; Polish line carp.

*Source*: Photos provided to FAO by J. Bakos, Fish Breeding Research Institute, Szarvas, Hungary (Bakos and Gorda, 2001).

The traits of most interest to aquaculturists, for example growth rate, body shape, spawning time, environmental tolerances and disease resistance, are usually controlled by a combination of genes and environment (Gjedrem and Baranski, 2009). Genes can exert a relatively stronger influence on color, for example red tilapia can be produced by inter-species hybridization or by a single gene mutation in *O. niloticus* (McAndrew et al., 1988).

The majority of farmed aquatic species are very similar to their wild relatives; that is, there are very few recognized breeds in aquaculture. This is very different from terrestrial agriculture, where millennia of selection have greatly changed the genetics and appearance of most of the crops and livestock consumed today. In agriculture, very few species contribute the majority of production; five species of livestock, the 'big five': cattle, sheep, chickens, goats and pigs account for about 90% of global meat production; sugar cane, maize, rice, wheat and potatoes compose 88% of global crop production (FAOSTAT, 2016). It is the numerous breeds of these terrestrial species that contain the genetic resources and contribute so greatly to agriculture production. The importance of breed development and intra-specific genetic diversity is currently being realized by the aquaculture industry and by the international community dealing with genetic resources for food and agriculture (**Table 5.2** *Genetic improvement strategies*).

Aquatic species have several attributes that make them amenable to genetic improvement:

- External fertilization facilitates working with gametes and collecting embryos;
- Gametes of many species are very hardy and easily handled;
- Genetic diversity is usually high;
- Fecundity is usually very high;
- Sex determination system is flexible and can be manipulated by temperature, chemicals and pressure, as well as by genes;
- Total length of adults and early life history stages is small compared with terrestrial animals thus facilitating large numbers being grown in relatively small areas; and
- Chromosomes and chromosome sets are easily manipulated.

Not all aquatic species display the previous characteristics, for example many marine species have extremely small gametes and numerous sensitive larval stages. However, a large number of freshwater species display several of these desirable characteristics. Production of tilapia (*Oreochromis* spp.), for example has been steadily increasing globally because they possess nearly all of the above traits.

A key to the greater production from terrestrial agriculture has been the selective breeding carried out by farmers over several millennia. Since ancient times, farmers kept seeds or offspring from the 'best' plants or animals to reproduce the next generation. 'Best' often meant fastest growing, but numerous other traits are influenced by genetic diversity and can therefore be improved. Aquaculture has lagged behind its terrestrial counterparts in this area. With improved breeding technology and larval rearing, aquaculturists are now taking advantage of genetic resources and technologies for improved production (**Table 5.2**).

The most common genetic technology used in aquaculture is traditional, or selective, breeding. There are refinements to simply choosing the best looking organism to breed (known as mass selection) as our ancestors did with terrestrial species. These refinements include family selection and marker assisted selection (Gjedrem and Baranski, 2009). Both of these techniques help identify good individuals for breeding whilst also preventing inbreeding. Before the selection programme starts, it is necessary to establish a base population with good levels of genetic diversity on which to select. This was done very successfully for farmed Nile tilapia through

*Table 5.2* Genetic improvement strategies

| *Genetic technologies* | *Improvement in farmed species* |
|---|---|
| *Long-term strategies* | |
| Selective breeding for: | |
| Growth rate | As high as 50% increase after ten generations in coho salmon. |
| | Gilthead sea bream mass selection gave 20% increase/generation (Hulata, 1995). |
| | Mass selection for live weight and shell length in Chilean oysters found 10–13% gain in one generation (Toro et al., 1996). |
| Body confirmation | High heritabilities in common carp, catfish and trout (Tave, 1995). |
| Physiological tolerance (stress) | Rainbow trout selected for high response showed increased levels of plasma cortisol levels (reviewed in Overli et al., 2002). |
| Disease resistance | Increased resistance to dropsy in common carp (Kirpichnicov, 1981). |
| | Increased survival after challenge test against Taura syndrome in whiteleg shrimp (Fjalestad et al., 1997). |
| Maturity and time of spawning | 60 days advance in spawning date in rainbow trout (Dunham, 1995). |
| Resistance to pollution | Tilapia progeny from lines selected for resistance to heavy metals Hg, Cd and Zn survived 3–5 times better than progeny from unexposed lines (Lourdes et al., 1995). |
| Gene transfer – usually in association with other breeding programmes | Coho salmon with a growth hormone gene and promoter from sockeye salmon grew 11 times (0–37 range) as fast as non-transgenics (Devlin et al., 1994). |
| | Atlantic salmon containing a gene encoding growth hormone from Chinook salmon grows twice as fast as selectively bred fish (Fox, 2010). |
| *Short-term strategies* | |
| Intra-specific cross-breeding | Heterotic growth seen in 55 and 22% of channel catfish and rainbow trout crosses, respectively (Dunham, 1995). |
| | Chum salmon and largemouth bass showed no heterosis. Heterosis for wild × hatchery gilthead seabream (Hulata, 1995); cross-breeds of channel catfish and common carp showed 30–60% heterosis. |
| | Increased salinity tolerance and color in tilapia (Pongthana et al., 2010). |
| Inter-specific hybridization | *Oreochromis niloticus* × *O. aureus* hybrids show a skewed male sex-ratio (Rosenstein and Hulata, 1993). |
| . | Sunshine bass hybrids (*Morone chrysops* × *Morone saxatilis*) grows faster and has better overall culture characteristics than either parental species (Smith, 1988). |
| | Walking catfish hybrids (*Clarias macrocephalus* × *C. gariepinus*) exhibit morphological features which increase consumer acceptance (Dunham, 2011). |
| Sex reversal and breeding | All male tilapia show improvements in yield of almost 60% depending on farming system and little unwanted reproduction and stunting (Beardmore et al., 2001; Lind et al., 2015). |
| | All female rainbow trout grew faster and had better flesh quality (Sheehan et al., 1999). |
| Chromosome manipulation | Improved growth and conversion efficiency in triploid rainbow trout, channel catfish, at plaice flounder hybrids; triploid Nile tilapia grew 66–90% better than diploids and showed decreased sex-dimorphism for body weight, but other studies found no advantage. Gene-environment interactions also influence performance (Dunham, 1995). |
| | Triploid Pacific oysters show 13–51% growth improvement over diploids at 8–10 months of age and better marketability due to reduced gonads (Guo et al., 1996). |
| | Polyploidization makes certain interspecific crosses viable, that is, produces sterile offspring (Wilkins et al., 1995). |

*Source*: Modified from Bartley (1998).

the GIFT Programme (Genetically Improved Farmed Tilapia) which collected tilapia from eight locations throughout its range in Africa (Ponzoni et al., 2011).

Improvements through selective breeding vary according to the trait being selected. For growth rate, gains of about 12% per generation have been achieved, although for some species the gain is much higher (Gjedrem et al., 2012). Selection for disease resistance shows similar gains for some species, but not for others (Tave, 1995; Gjedrem et al., 2012). A great advantage of selective breeding programmes is that the gains are cumulative, that is, they are a long-term strategy for increased production (**Table 5.2**).

Manipulation of chromosome-sets (polyploidization) has been accomplished for many aquatic species through thermal and chemical shocks to developing gametes and embryos. Triploid organisms, which have one extra chromosome set added, are the most common, partly because they are usually sterile and therefore able to put more energy into the growth process rather than into maturation and reproduction. Whilst chromosome-set manipulation has not been widely applied in finfish farming, the use of triploids has become an important part of the oyster farming industry. For example, triploid Pacific oysters can show up to 159% higher growth over diploid controls (Guo et al., 2009). Sterility also reduces the risk of unwanted breeding with native species, which may be of importance in biological control programmes such as the use of grass carp for vegetation control or to address the environmental impacts of fish escaping from farms (Wattendorf, 1987; Zajicek et al., 2011).

Manipulation of sex can be of advantage in species with sexual dimorphism in important traits or when reduced chance of reproduction is desired. Mono-sex male stocks have considerable commercial benefit in a number of species, most notably in male tilapia that grow faster than females and help avoid unwanted reproduction within the production system (Beardmore et al., 2001; Lind et al., 2015). However, female trout and salmon grow better than males (Sheehan et al., 1999). The sex of fish can be manipulated through hormonal treatments, for example masculization of tilapia through administering methyl testosterone in feed, and by certain interspecific hybrids, for example Nile tilapia *(O. niloticus)* crosses with *O. urolepis hornorum* and with *O. macrochir* (Wohlfarth, 1994).

In addition to producing mono-sex populations, hybridization has been effective at creating immediate improvement to farmed species through 'hybrid vigor', where the hybrid performs better than either parent and by combining desirable traits of parental species into their offspring (Bartley et al., 2001). For example African × Thai catfish *(Clarias gariepinus × C. macrocephalus)* is widely used in Thailand because it has the desirable flesh of the native catfish and the fast growth character of the African catfish (Suresh, 1991). These hybrids are fertile, however, and there are concerns about its introgression with native Thai catfish (Suresh, 1991). Similarly, the bester is a hybrid between the Beluga × sterlet sturgeon *(Huso × Acipenser ruthenus).* These hybrids are fertile, grow very well and are not anadromous. For the bester, it is important that the Beluga parent is female, as the reciprocal cross is not as desirable (Steffens et al., 1990); in other hybrid crosses, the sex of the parent influences the quality of the offspring (Bartley et al., 2001).

Transgenic fish have been produced on a research and pilot scale since the mid-1980s, with most research focused on the transfer of genes that promote better growth (Kapuscinski, 2005). The transfer of an anti-freeze protein gene from the ocean pout to Atlantic salmon produced a salmon that grows well during the cold parts of the year when non-transgenic salmon have reduced growth; the transgenic salmon therefore reaches market size much earlier (Devlin et al., 1994). Consumer resistance has prevented this fish and other transgenic fishes from entering the marketplace.[1]

Genetic engineering technology is now beginning to find application in the production of aquaculture feed to assist in reducing the industry's dependency on fishmeal and fish oil and to improve terrestrial animal- and plant-based feed ingredients. Examples include (a) genetically engineered yeast for production of important feed ingredients such as fish growth hormone and carotenoid pigments, (b) pre-processing techniques of plant material to reduce the effects of anti-nutritional factors, (c) breeding of plants with a better amino acid profile and less anti-nutritional factors, (d) converting low grade land animal by-products into high-value protein and (e) genetically modifying soybean and corn used in aquaculture feed production (Rana et al., 2009; Sissener et al., 2009; Ukibe et al., 2009).

Most breeds and strains of farmed aquatic species are not well defined either genetically or phenotypically. For livestock, the Database on Domestic Animal Diversity Information System (DAD-IS)[2] represents a global registry (FAO, 2015). Strain registries do exist in some areas, for example the registry of farmed catfish in the United States (Kincaid et al., 2000) and some specialized breeding centers document their strains of farmed fish (Bakos and Gorda, 2001). Diversity of farmed fish has been described in various scientific publications and in commercial websites (e.g. Le François et al., 2010). However, at the global level, the aquatic sector does not have a comprehensive listing of farmed aquatic diversity below the species level.

## Potential of aquatic genetic resources to contribute to increased production, food security and livelihoods

Several positive factors favor the increased use of aquatic genetic resources in aquaculture:

- There is an increasing number of aquatic species for which the life cycle has been closed and therefore would be suitable for genetic improvement and domestication;
- The field of genetics and the understanding of how genes work is advancing rapidly, while at the same time, the cost of genetic analyses is rapidly decreasing;
- There is a vast range of genetic technologies to meet specific needs in aquaculture production, from traditional breeding to genetic engineering; and
- Genetic technologies have wide application in both fisheries and aquaculture in terms of management, control, marketing and trade issues.

However, there are also limitations that must be addressed:

- There is limited application of good genetic management of broodstock resulting in genetic degradation of hatchery stocks from inbreeding depression and inadvertent hybridization;
- There is a lack of awareness of the usefulness of genetic technologies and principles in fisheries and aquaculture development and management;
- There is limited capacity to collect, analyze and interpret genetic data for genetic improvement programmes and characterization;
- The cost of developing capacity to use genetic technologies in many areas may be restrictive;
- Risk analysis, bio-security and protection of native biodiversity need to be addressed; and
- Consumer awareness and fear over certain technologies and the resulting organism need to be addressed.

Given the vast assortment of genetic diversity found in aquatic species and the untapped potential of using it in aquaculture, there is reason to be optimistic about aquaculture's ability to produce more food for a growing human population. Gjedrem et al. (2012) stated that global production from aquaculture could be doubled in the next few decades if selective breeding were applied to all farmed species. The world's demand for seafood is expected to increase by about 2% per year over the next decades, and genetic improvements from selective breeding could produce increases of about 10% per generation. Therefore, the increased demand for seafood could be met with a little additional resources just by improved management of genetic resources.

The wild relatives of all farmed aquatic species still exist in nature. This is again different from agriculture, where many wild relatives of farmed species are now extinct or extremely rare. Thus, the diversity found in the world's waters is a tremendous resource that must be protected so that it may benefit present and future populations – one case study of this diversity as it exists in rice paddy systems is presented in **Box 5.1** *Rice paddy – a wealth of traditional aquatic biodiversity that is often unappreciated* and **Figure 5.3** *Taxonomic diversity and number of species reported from rice fields.*

## Box 5.1 Rice paddy – a wealth of traditional aquatic biodiversity that is often unappreciated

There are a tremendous number of aquatic species which are caught or collected, and are extremely important to rural livelihoods, but which are seldom reported nationally or to FAO because it is very difficult to collect data on this dispersed type of fishery. One example is the aquatic biodiversity found in rice fields.

The cultivation of almost 90% of the world's rice in irrigated, rain-fed and deep-water systems (equivalent to about 134 million hectares of aquatic agroecosystems) has offered opportunities for the enhancement and culture of aquatic organisms since ancient times (Halwart and Gupta, 2004). Designs of rice fields with fish on ancient Chinese pottery from tombs of the Han Dynasty (206 BCE – 225 CE), inscriptions from a 13th century king of Thailand, and traditional sayings, such as one from Vietnam – 'rice and fish are like mother and children' – all indicate that rice and fish have been associated with prosperity and food security for millennia (Demaine and Halwart, 2001; FAO, 2014).

A wide range of aquatic organisms and rich diversity of edible species extensively used by rural people can be found in rice fields. For many rural populations, especially in South and Southeast Asia, rice and fish constitute the main components of the diet, and aquatic animals often represent the most important source of animal protein and other essential nutrients. Studies on the utilization of aquatic biodiversity from rice-based ecosystems in several countries in Asia highlight the large number of useful species, in addition to rice, found in rice fields (see **Figure 5.3**).

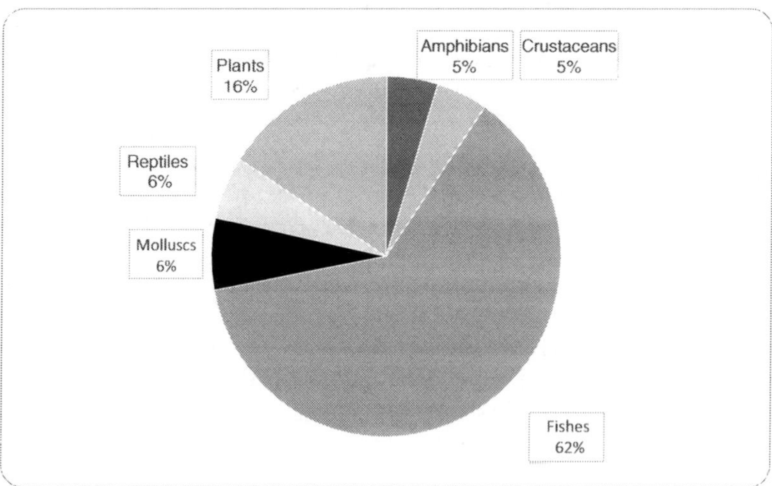


*Figure 5.3* Taxonomic diversity and number of species reported from rice fields

*Source*: From Halwart and Bartley (2005).

A recent comprehensive assessment study in three Asian countries confirmed the importance of aquatic species being gathered for food and medicine, but also as feed for livestock or used as bait, and highlighted the diversity of utilized plant species particularly in remote and hilly sites (Pedersen et al., 2014). Beyond the direct role of these aquatic species for consumption and use, they also perform important ecosystem services, for example as biological control agents of vectors and pests of both public health and agricultural significance. Fish that are specialized to feed on mosquito larvae or on particular snail species contribute to controlling malaria and schistosomiasis. Some fish species contribute to the biological control of rice pests such as apple snails, stem-borers or caseworms.

In addition, rice fields may also harbor species which are under threat of extinction. The deep-water rice ecosystem and the adjacent flooded grass- and shrub-lands near the Tonle Sap, Cambodia, are habitat for endangered bird species, among them the bengal florican. The use of some endangered species found in rice fields, for example *Ichthyophys bannanicus* (which has medicinal value) in Yunnan, is probably a blessing in the long term, since the amphibians' economic value may in fact lead to controlled cultivation, thus ultimately ensuring the survival of the species. The protection of rice fields and its aquatic biodiversity from harmful chemicals can have very positive effects, as has been shown at a Globally Important Agricultural Heritage Site in China where 'fish-friendly' rice gets a substantial price premium from the consumer. Similar positive developments can be observed in Japan and the Republic of Korea, where aquatic species provide an entry point for education and learning for school children and the public about agricultural biodiversity in general and the importance of rice fields for endangered species in particular.

## Conclusions

Aquatic species provide a rich source of biodiversity on which to base aquaculture systems and breeding programmes in many parts of the world. Aquatic species are very amenable to the application of genetic technologies ranging from simple hybridization to advance genetic engineering. Selective breeding offers the opportunity to accumulate genetic gains over many generations, but increased technical and financial resources may be needed in some areas. Although domestication is a major step in harnessing the farming potential of aquatic species, numerous species are being grown profitably by sourcing broodstock or early life history stages from the wild (Lovatelli and Holthus, 2008). As the breeding and larval rearing of aquatic species improves, many of these wild-sourced species will be domesticated.

Wild populations of aquatic species will still provide a rich source of genetic diversity for both aquaculture and capture fisheries. This diversity must be conserved. However, an ongoing study by the FAO on the state of the world's aquatic genetic diversity indicates that about 50%of the fisheries for wild relatives of farmed species are decreasing or depleted (FAO, in preparation). The world must strive to protect this natural reserve of genetic diversity and develop aquaculture with this same view. The responsible use of aquatic genetic resources and technologies will be essential in order to provide a growing human population with nutritious and affordable seafood now and in the future.

## Notes

1 At the time of publication, the first transgenic fish for consumers, an Atlantic salmon, had been approved for commercial use in the USA. www.nature.com/polopoly_fs/1.18867!/menu/main/topColumns/topLeftColumn/pdf/527417a.pdf

2 http://dad.fao.org/

## References

ADB (2005) *An Impact Evaluation of the Development of Genetically Improved Farmed Tilapia and Their Dissemination in Selected Countries*, Asian Development Bank, Bangkok, Thailand.

Bakos, J. and Gorda, S. (2001) *Genetic Resources of Common Carp at the Fish Culture Research Institute, Szarvas, Hungary*, FAO Fisheries Technical Paper 417, Food and Agriculture Organization of the United Nations (FAO), Rome, Italy.

Balon, E. K. (1974) *Domestication of the Carp,* Cyprinus carpio *L.*, Royal Ontario Museum of Life Sciences, Miscellaneous Publication, Toronto, Canada.

Balon, E. K. (1995) 'Origin and domestication of the wild carp, *Cyprinus carpio*: From Roman gourmets to the swimming flowers', *Aquaculture*, vol. 129, pp. 3–48.

Bartley, D. M. (1998) 'Genetics and breeding in aquaculture: Current status and trends', *Genetics and Breeding of Mediterranean Aquaculture Species*, Cahiers OPTIONS, vol. 68, pp. 13–30.

Bartley, D. M., Rana, K. and Immink, A. J. (2001) 'The use of inter-specific hybrids in aquaculture and fisheries', *Reviews in Fish Biology and Fisheries*, vol. 10, pp. 325–337.

Beardmore, J. A., Mair, G. C. and Lewis, R. I. (2001) 'Monosex male production in finfish as exemplified by tilapia: Applications, problems, and prospects', *Aquaculture*, vol. 197, pp. 283–301.

Bilio, M. (2008) 'Controlled reproduction and domestication in aquaculture Part IV', *Aquaculture Europe*, vol. 33, p. 3.

Demaine, H. and Halwart, M. (2001) 'An overview of rice-based small-scale aquaculture', pp. 189–197 in IIRR, IDRC, FAO, NACA, and ICLARM (eds.), *Utilizing Different Aquatic Resources for Livelihoods in Asia: A Resource Book*, IIRR, Silang, Cavite, the Philippines.

Devlin, B. H., Yesakl, T. Y., Blagl, E. A. and Donaldson, E. M. (1994) 'Extraordinary salmon growth', *Nature*, vol. 371, pp. 209–210.

Duarte, C. M., Marbà, N. and Holmer, M. (2007) 'Rapid domestication of marine species', *Science*, vol. 316, pp. 382–383.

Dunham, R. A. (1995) *The Contribution of Genetically Improved Aquatic Organisms to Global Food Security*, Thematic paper presented to the Japan/FAO International Conference on Sustainable Contribution of Fisheries to Food Security, 4–9 December, Kyoto, Japan.

Dunham, R. A. (2011) *Aquaculture and Fisheries Biotechnology: Genetic Approaches*, 2nd ed., CABI Publishing, Wallingford, UK.

FAO (2014) *State of World Fisheries and Aquaculture*, Food and Agriculture Organization of the United Nations, Rome, Italy.

FAO (2015) *The Second Report on the State of the World's Animal Genetic Resources for Food and Agriculture*, B. D. Scherf and D. Pilling (eds.) FAO Commission on Genetic Resources for Food and Agriculture Assessments, Food and Agriculture Organization of the United Nations, Rome, Italy, www.fao.org/3/a-4787e/index.html

FAO (in preparation) State of the World's Aquatic Genetic Resources for Food and Agriculture, Food and Agriculture Organization of the United Nations, Rome, Italy.

FAO FishStatJ (2016) www.fao.org/fishery/topic/18238/en, accessed 2 February 2016.

FAOSTAT (2016) http://faostat3.fao.org/home/E, accessed 2 February 2016.

Fjalestad, K. T., Gjedrem, T. Carr, W. H. and Sweeney, J. N. (1997) *Final Report: The Shrimp Breeding Program, Selective Breeding of Penaeus vannamei*, The Oceanic Institute, Waimanalo, HI, USA.

Fox, G. L. (2010) 'Transgenic salmon inches toward finish line', *Nature Biotechnology*, vol. 28, pp. 1141–1142.

Gjedrem, T. (1997) 'Selective breeding to improve aquaculture production', *World Aquaculture Society*, pp. 33–45.

Gjedrem, T. and Baranski, M. (2009) 'Selective breeding in aquaculture: An Introduction', *Reviews: Methods and Technologies in Fish Biology and Fisheries*, vol. 10, Springer, the Netherlands.

Gjedrem, T., Robinson, N. and Rye, M. (2012) 'The importance of selective breeding in aquaculture to meet future demands for animal protein: A review', *Aquaculture*, vol. 350, pp. 117–129.

Guiry M. D. (2012) 'How many species of algae are there?', *Journal of Phycology*, vol. 48, pp. 1057–1063.

Guo, X., DeBrosse, G. A. and Allen, S. K. (1996) 'All triploid oysters (Crassostrea gigas Thunberg) produced by mating tetraploids and diploids', *Aquaculture,* vol. 142, pp. 149–161.

Guo, X., Wang, Y., Xu, Z. and Yang, H. (2009) 'Chromosome set manipulation in shellfish', pp. 165–194 in G. Burnell and G. Allan (eds.), *New Technologies in Aquaculture*, CRC Press, Boca Raton, FL, USA.

Halwart, M. and Bartley, D. (eds.) (2005) *Aquatic Biodiversity in Rice-Based Ecosystems: Studies and Reports from Cambodia, China, Lao PDR and Viet Nam*, FAO, Rome, Italy, ftp://ftp.fao.org/fi/cdrom/aqbiodcd-20Jul2005/default.htm

Halwart, M., and Gupta, M. V. (2004) *Culture of Fish in Rice Fields*, FAO and WorldFish Center, FAO, Rome, Italy.

Hulata, G. (1995) 'The history and current status of aquaculture genetics in Israel', *Israeli Journal of Aquaculture-Bamidgeh*, vol. 47, pp. 142–154.

Kapuscinski, A. (2005) 'Current scientific understanding of the environmental biosafety of transgenic fish and shellfish', *Revue Scientifique et Technique-Office International Des Epizooties*, vol. 24, pp. 309–322.

Kincaid, H. L., Mengel, L. J., Gray, M. J. and Brimm, S. (2000) *National Fish Strain Registry: Catfish (NFSR-C) Operating Manual*, U.S. Geological Survey; U.S. Fish and Wildlife Service. www.sciencebase.gov/catalog/item/4f4e4b01e4b07f02db698826

Kirpichnicov, V. S. (1981) *Genetic Basis of Fish Selection*, Springer-Verlag, Berlin, Germany.

Le François, N. R., Jobling, M., Carter, C., Blier, P. U. and Savoie, A. (eds.) (2010) *Finfish Aquaculture Diversification*, CABI Publications, Wallingford, UK.

Lind, C. E., Safari, A., Agyakwah, S. K., Attipoe, F. Y. K., El-Naggar, G. O., Hamzah, A., Hulata, G., Ibrahim, N. A., Khaw, H. L., Nguyen, N. H., Maluwa, A. O., Zaid, M., Zak, T. and Ponzoni, R. W. (2015) 'Differences in sexual size dimorphism among farmed tilapia species and strains undergoing genetic improvement for body weight', *Aquaculture Reports*, vol. 1, pp. 20–27.

Lourdes, M., Cuvin-Aralar, A. and Aralar, E. V. (1995) 'Resistance to heavy metal mixture in *Oreochromis niloticus* progenies of parents chronically exposed to the same metals', *Aquaculture*, vol. 137, pp. 271–284.

Lovatelli, A. and Holthus, P. F. (2008) *Capture-Based Aquaculture: A Global Review*, FAO Fisheries Technical Paper, No. 508, FAO, Rome, Italy.

McAndrew, B. J., Roubal, F. R., Roberts, R. J., Bullock, A. M. and McEwen, I. M. (1988) 'The genetics and histology of red, blond and associated colour variants in *Oreochromis niloticus*', *Genetica*, vol. 76, pp. 127–137.

Montgomery, D. R. (2000) 'Coevolution of the Pacific salmon and Pacific Rim topography', *Geology*, vol. 28, pp. 1107–1110.

Nash, C. E. (2011) *History of Aquaculture*, Wiley-Blackwell, Hoboken, NJ, USA.

Overli, O., Pottinger, T. G, Carrick, T. R., Overli, E. and Winberg, S. (2002) 'Differences in behaviour between rainbow trout selected for high- and low-stress responsiveness', *Journal of Experimental Biology*, vol. 205, pp. 391–395.

Pedersen, O. S., Chertchai, F., Chanthavang, A., Khamvang, X. and Yoysaykham, B. (2014) 'Aquatic organisms in rice-based ecoystems in Naxaithong, Paen and Poungmanh villages, Phoukhout Districut, Xieng Khouang Province, Lao PDR', pp. 21–43 in M. Halwart, D. M. Bartley, P. B. Bueno and N. Innes Taylor (eds.), *Aquatic Biodiversity in Rice-Based Ecosystems. Studies and Reports from Indonesia, Lao PDR, and the Philippines*, FAO, Rome, Italy.

Pongthana, N., Nguyen, N. H. and Ponzoni, R. W. (2010) 'Comparative performance of four red tilapia strains and their crosses in fresh- and saline water environments', *Aquaculture*, vol. 308, pp. S109–S114.

Ponzoni, R. W., Nguyen, N. H., Khaw, H. L., Hamzah, A., Bakar, K. R. A. and Yee, H. Y. (2011) 'Genetic improvement of Nile tilapia (*Oreochromis niloticus*) with special reference to the work conducted by the WorldFish Center with the GIFT strain', *Reviews in Aquaculture*, vol. 3, pp. 27–41.

Rana, K. J., Siriwardena, S. and Hasan, M. R. (2009) *Impact of Rising Feed Ingredient Prices on Aquafeeds and Aquaculture Production*, FAO Fisheries and Aquaculture Technical Paper, No. 541, FAO, Rome, Italy.

Rosenstein, S. and Hulata, G. (1993) 'Sex reversal in the genus *Oreochromis*: Optimization of feminization protocol', *Aquaculture and Fisheries Management*, vol. 25, pp. 329–339.

Sheehan, R. J., Shasteen, S. P., Suresh, A. V., Kapuscinski, A. R. and Seeb, J. (1999) 'Better growth in all-female diploid and triploid rainbow trout', *Transactions of the American Fisheries Society*, vol. 128, pp. 491–498.

Sissener, N. H., Sanden, M., Bakke, A. M., Krogdahl, Å. and Hemre, G.-I. (2009) 'A long term trial with Atlantic salmon (*Salmo salar* L.) fed genetically modified soy; focusing general health and performance before, during and after the parr-smolt transformation', *Aquaculture*, vol. 294, pp. 108–117.

Smith, T. I. J. (1988) 'Aquaculture of striped bass and its hybrids in North America', *Aquaculture Management*, vol. 14, pp. 40–49.

Steffens, W., Jaehnichen, H. and Fredrich, F. (1990) 'Possibilities of sturgeon culture in Central Europe', *Aquaculture*, vol. 89, pp. 101–122.

Suresh, A. V. (1991) 'Culture of walking catfish in Thailand', *Journal of Aquaculture in the Tropics*, vol. 2, pp. 10–12.

Tave, D. (1995) *Selective Breeding Programmes in Medium-Sized Fish Farms*, FAO Fisheries Technical Paper 352, FAO, Rome, Italy.

Toro, J. E., Aguila, P. and Vergara, A. M. (1996) 'Spatial variation in response to selection for live weight and shell length from data on individually tagged Chilean native oysters (*Ostrea chilensis* Philippi, 1845)', *Aquaculture*, vol. 146, pp. 27–36.

Ukibe, K., Hashida, K., Yoshida, N. and Takagi, H. (2009) 'Metabolic engineering of *Saccharomyces cerevisiae* for astaxanthin production and oxidative stress tolerance', *Applied and Environmental Microbiology*, vol. 75, pp. 7205–7211.

Vallejo, R. L., Wiens, G. D., Rexroad III, C. E., Welch, T. J., Evenhuis, J. P., Leeds, T. D., Janss, L. L. G. and Palti, Y. (2010) 'Evidence of major genes affecting resistance to bacterial cold water disease in rainbow trout using Bayesian methods of segregation analysis', *Journal of Animal Science*, vol. 88, pp. 3814–3832.

Wattendorf, R. J. (1987) 'Triploid grass carp: Status and management implications', *Fisheries*, vol. 12, pp. 20–24.

Welcomme, R. L. (1999) 'A review of a model for qualitative evaluation of exploitation levels in multi-species fisheries', *Fisheries Management and Ecology*, vol. 6, pp. 1–19.

Wilkins, N. P., Gosling, E., Curatolo, A., Linnane, A., Jordan, C. and Courtney, H. P. (1995) 'Fluctuating asymmetry in Atlantic salmon, European trout and their hybrids, including triploids', *Aquaculture*, vol. 137, pp. 77–85.

Wohlfarth, G. W. (1994) 'The unexploited potential of tilapia hybrids in aquaculture', *Aquaculture and Fisheries Management*, vol. 25, pp. 781–788.

Zajicek, P., Goodwin, A. E. and Weier, T. (2011) 'Triploid grass carp: Triploid induction, sterility, reversion, and certification', *North American Journal of Fisheries Management*, vol. 31, pp. 614–618.

# 6
# PESTS, PREDATORS AND PARASITOIDS

*Geoff M. Gurr, David J. Perović and Kristian Le Mottee*

## Introduction

There is a wealth of evidence that agricultural biodiversity influences pest numbers, with diverse vegetation – either as crop mixtures or the presence of non-crop vegetation – tending to reduce pests (**Table 6.1** *Examples illustrating the diversity of crop systems and types of vegetation management that have promoted natural enemies and led to pest suppression*; Gurr et al., 2012; Lu et al., 2014; Westphal et al., 2015). A range of ecological mechanisms can account for this general trend, but the two most important are widely referred to as the 'enemies' and the 'resource concentration' hypotheses. The enemies hypothesis holds that predators and parasitoids of pests are promoted by diverse vegetation, since it may provide plant foods, such as nectar and pollen, as well as shelter and alternative prey or hosts. In contrast, the resource concentration hypothesis holds that diverse vegetation can have a direct negative effect on pests by diluting the apparent availability of suitable host plants by masking the visual or, more importantly, olfactory cues that allow pests to locate host plants. Empirical evidence suggests that both of these broad categories of ecological mechanisms are important and that both can operate simultaneously. The major focus of this chapter is on the effects of agricultural biodiversity on predators and parasitoids and – via enemies hypothesis mechanisms – on pests.

## Biological control of pests

The use of predators and parasitoids to control pests has a history dating back thousands of years. In traditional agricultural systems, in which pesticides were (and in some cases still are) absent or rare, natural enemy densities would often be adequate to provide useful levels of pest control. Early attempts to manipulate the activity of natural enemies include the marketing of ant colonies and connecting the branches of adjacent trees with bamboo poles to allow movement of non-flying predators (DeBach and Rosen, 1991).

In the 19th century, biological control involving the translocation of predators (and later, parasitoids) from country to country became popular as a means to control pests that had established in new regions, free of their usual natural enemies. This inoculative approach became known as 'classical biological control', and it remains widely practiced, though it is increasingly regulated due to previous introductions that caused unanticipated damage to non-target species or became pests in their own right (van Lenteren et al., 2006).

*Table 6.1* Examples illustrating the diversity of crop systems and types of vegetation management that have promoted natural enemies and led to pest suppression

| *Crop System* | *Vegetation management* | *Natural Enemy* | *Pest* | *Reference* |
|---|---|---|---|---|
| African maize | 'Push-pull' (molasses grass within crop to repel pest and attract parasitoids, with Napier grass borders to trap pest) | Parasitoids e.g. *Cotesia* spp. | Stemborers (Lepidoptera) e.g. *Chilo partellus* | Khan et al. (2001) |
| British wheat | Beetle bank (raised earth ridge sown to perennial grass as overwintering habitat for predators) | Staphylinid beetles and linyphiid spiders | Cereal aphids e.g. *Sitobion avenae* | Thomas et al. (1991) |
| Asian rice | Nectar plant borders | Various parasitoids and predators including tetragnathid spiders | Planthoppers, especially *Nilaparvata lugens* | Gurr et al., (2016) (see Box 6.1) |
| U.S. cotton | Cover crop of crimson clover | Predaory bugs including *Geocoris punctipes* | Lepidoptera including *Helivoverpa* spp. | Tillman et al. (2012) |

Inundative biological control, the mass-release of large numbers of cultured agents in a specific location, began to be used in the early 20th century. This form of control can provide quicker control than classical biological control when a high density of arthropods is released (van Driesche et al., 2008). Such mass-releases are most widely used in glasshouse crops where the released agents are contained. This approach is especially important in short-term crops that have a low tolerance for pests. In this situation, an inoculative release would take too long to achieve control (van Driesche et al., 2008). For example, the parasitic wasp *Eretmocerus eremicus* has been mass-released against the whitefly pest *Bemisia tabaci* in greenhouse poinsettias in northeastern United States. Whitefly populations are maintained at low levels by up to 14 weekly releases of one wasp female for each two plants (van Driesche et al., 2008).

A final form of biological control, 'conservation', has become more popular in recent decades in response to the cost and limited availability of inundative biological control and the risks of off-target effects in classical biological control. This has been encouraged by the wider interest in ecological intensification and 'wildlife friendly' agriculture that have led to agroecological schemes being introduced (Wade et al., 2008). Conservation biological control aims to conserve the predator and parasitoid species that are already present in a given location so that they have a greater impact on pests and, thereby, avoid the need for inundative or inoculative releases. Conservation biological control can involve reducing the loss of natural enemies through switching from the use of broad spectrum insecticides to more selective, target-specific chemicals. Increasingly often, however, it operates through modification of the environment, such as providing refuge habitats or food and shelter resources for the 'enemies' (van Driesche and Bellows, 1996). Thus, conservation biological control seeks to use aspects of plant diversity to promote the enemies hypothesis (see introduction, this chapter) though other benefits and ecosystem service may simultaneous result (see Boshier et al. and Leakey, Chapters 3 and 14 of this Handbook, for examples). Increased densities and activity of natural enemies can have a cascading effect on herbivores (i.e. reducing pest numbers) and plants (i.e. boosting yields; **Box 6.1** *Replacing agricultural inputs with ecosystem services*).

## Box 6.1 Replacing agricultural inputs with ecosystem services

Ecosystem services have long been replaced by high intensity agriculture characterised by reliance on chemical inputs to support monocultures that reduce biodiversity including natural enemies of pests (Matson et al., 1997). Organic agriculture is radical change for farmers and has a reputation of resulting in reduced yields and sometime income, despite the benefits (Crowder et al., 2010; Seufert et al., 2012; Ponisio et al., 2014). Multiple studies have shown that diversification can increase the density of predators and parasitoids and some studies find this reduces pest numbers, but very few have demonstrated increased crop yields (Letourneau et al., 2011).

Field studies across Thailand, China and Vietnam and repeated over four years found that adding nectar producing plants to the rice ecosystem promoted a trophic cascade (Gurr et al., 2016). In fields bordered by broad-leaf nectar producing crops such as sesame, there was enhanced parasitoid pressure which suppressed two major pest species *Nilaparvata lugens* and *Sogatella furcifera* which resulted in an 5% increase in grain yield (**Figure 6.1** *Nectar plant borders to rice fields promote biological control of pests and increase grain yields*) and allowed a 70% reduction in spraying intensity. The flowering plants used were agronomically suitable for the climate and selected in consultation with farmers, therefore increasing acceptability of the practice. This has been the first large scale, multi-country and multi-year trial that has shown locally-appropriate and inexpensive biodiversity enhancements can underpin sustainable intensification of agriculture.

The upfront cost of planting the nectar producing border crop was offset by the secondary income that these plants provided. Overall, by considering the savings from the reduced number of sprays and the higher rice yield, this practice resulted in a clear economic benefit.

*Figure 6.1* Nectar plant borders to rice fields promote biological control of pests and increase grain yields

*Source*: Photo: HV Chien.

In fact, there is scope for agricultural biodiversity to be used to support all forms of biological control, and this broad approach has been termed 'integrated biological control' (Gurr and Wratten, 1999). An example is the use of banker plants, which offer a solution to the problem of maintaining biological control agents in a crop environment at times when pests are too scarce to provide adequate food to maintain the biological control agent. A banker plant scheme utilises non-crop plants infested with herbivorous insects (that are not a pest for the host crop) to provide food and reproductive resources for parasitoids or predators (Yano, 2006). Banker plant schemes have been successfully implemented for parasitoids such as *Encarsia formosa* and *Aphidius colemani* (Yano, 2006) but there are few references to the use of predators in combination with banker plants in the literature, with the majority focusing on parasitoids. Typically, larger predator species of the Neuroptera and Coccinellidae are released curatively in a banker plant scheme rather than preventatively, with the predators on the banker plant providing additional food and reproductive resources (Yano, 2006). Pratt and Croft (2000) investigated the properties that affect banker plant systems using predatory mites to control spider mites in plant nurseries. They concluded that the success of a banker plant system is site-specific, dependent on the plants being cultured and the layout of the nursery. In a field situation, banker plants can be part of the hedgerow that surrounds an agricultural site (Pratt and Croft, 2000).

Notwithstanding the banker plant approach, it is conservation biological control that has made the greatest use of biodiversity and in which researchers have most actively sought and implemented new applications.

## Predators and parasitoids

Biological control agents have a diet range that is part of a continuum from monophagy to polyphagy, also known as specialist or generalist diets, respectively. At one end of this continuum are ultra-specialist arthropods, which select only one species to prey upon or use as a host, while at the other end of the continuum, more polyphagous arthropods exploit a range of host species. Some predatory species described in the literature as 'predators' can survive on either arthropod prey or plant-based foods, so could be considered omnivorous in addition to being described as polyphagous. Specialist predators and parasitoids, those with a narrow prey or host range, are useful in biological control because they have evolved to seek out specific targets without being distracted by the presence of alternative prey. Generalist polyphagous predators consume a wide range of insects, and suites of different generalist predators are considered to be responsible for control of native pests in native environments (Hawkins et al., 1999). Pests that are controlled by generalist natural enemies are more likely than are pests controlled by specialists to remain under effective biological control when there is a loss of diversity among natural enemies (Wilby and Thomas, 2007). However, on exotic plants hosting exotic pests in cultivated habitats, a single parasitoid has been most frequently found to give optimal levels of biological control (Hawkins et al., 1999). Reflecting this, the loss from a given system of any single species of natural enemy can lead to disruption of biological control though the impact of losing any one species can be unpredictable (Wilby and Thomas, 2007).

### *Parasitoids in biological control*

Parasitoids are common agents used against insect pests (van Driesche et al., 2008) and have been used widely in inundative releases in a variety of field and greenhouse crops over the last 40 years. Parasitoids are insects that have an immature life stage that develops either inside or attached to a single immature host, killing the host as part of its developmental cycle. Parasitoid life cycles are divided into two broad categories. Idiobionts oviposit directly into (or upon) the bodies of its host, halting development of the host. After the parasitoid eggs hatch, the larva or larvae consume the host and emerge as adult parasitoids. In contrast, ectoparasitoids do not immobilise their hosts so feeding (and associated plant damage) continue until the parasitoid immature pupates.

Hymenopteran and dipteran parasitoids have applications against a wide range of insect families, with hymenopteran species attacking pest Lepidoptera, Coleoptera, Coccoidea, Diptera, and Hemiptera, while dipteran parasitoids attack Lepidoptera, Coleoptera and Homoptera. Use of the hymenopteran *E. formosa* against greenhouse whitefly *(T. vaporariorum)* is considered a great success of greenhouse biological control after the rise of pesticide resistance in the 1970s (van Lenteren et al., 1996). In 1996, more than half of countries with greenhouse industries used *E. formosa* (van Lenteren et al., 1996). Some pest species, such as leaf mining *Lyriomyza* spp., may not have other biological control agents available. Differences in parasitoid host species can affect the larval mortality rate, the host preference of adult offspring and body size of adults, while access to supplemental food sources for adult parasitoids increases adult longevity and egg production.

## *Predators in biological control*

For arthropods, the terms 'generalist predator' and 'polyphagous predator' are used to describe a wide group of arthropods such as coccinellids, mites, carabids, staphylinids and lacewings. More specific terminologies define a predator as a generalist, rather than a specialist, if it feeds on prey in different taxonomic families. Given that a large proportion of predators collected from the field show empty guts (Greenstone, 1979), predators are often in a state of suboptimal nutrition. Generalist predators have developed behaviour to cope with prey scarcity, eating any prey items they can subdue and exploiting alternative food (non-arthropod) sources that extend survival. There may be only a small subsection of prey species that support immature development and adult reproduction by a given predator. The prey of generalist predators can be split into essential foods that facilitate reproduction and maturation of larvae and supplemental foods which maintain the predator until it can obtain essential foods. Molecular methods are increasingly being employed to study diet range of predators (Gurr and You, 2016) and can often reveal unanticipated aspects such as predators feeding on one another as well as shared species of herbivore prey (**Box 6.2** *The significance of diet studies in biological control*).

### Box 6.2 The significance of diet studies in biological control

The brown lacewing, *Micromus tasmaniae*, is native to Australia, where it is considered a polyphagous predator of significance as a natural enemy of a range of pests in crops as diverse as vineyards and vegetable crops (Samson and Blood, 1980; Hodge and Longley, 2000; Horne et al., 2001; New, 2002; Sato and Takada, 2004). The ladybird beetle *Hippodamia variegata* is a relatively recent arrival in Australia, where it is found in regions and habitats common to *M. tasmaniae*. Many Coccinellidae are known to preferentially feed on aphids (Obrycki and Kring, 1998) whilst others are generalist predators (Franzmann, 2002; Rahmani and Bandani, 2013). Relatively little is known about the likely effects of the arrival of *H. variegata* in Australia, particularly whether this will be a useful additional predator or whether it might disrupt the action of *M. tasmaniae*.

Studies on brassica farms in the central west of New South Wales showed that these species were amongst the most common predators (V. Heimoana & G. M. Gurr, unpublished data). Molecular techniques such as DNA barcoding allows for rapid and reliable species identification of prey remnants in the gut of predators by non-taxonomic researchers (Hebert et al., 2003; Furlong and Zalucki, 2010). This approach was used to investigate the extent of shared prey use for *M. tasmaniae* and *H. variegata*.

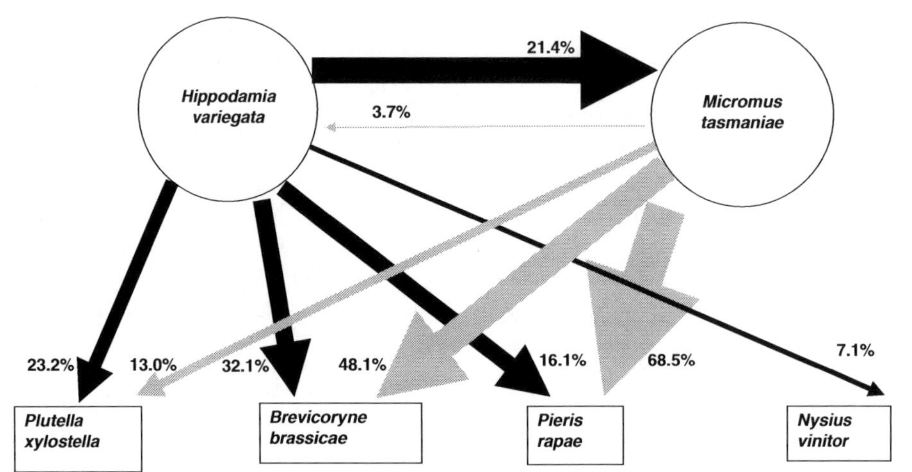


*Figure 6.2* Molecular analysis of the gut contents of generalist predators

*Note*: This can identify which species of herbivore they consume (lower section of figure) but can also reveal important interactions between predator species such as highly asymmetrical intra-guild predation (top section of figure).

*Source*: V. Heimoana & G. M. Gurr, unpublished data.

Results suggested that *H. variegata* is a generalist predator that feeds on the five prey species commonly present in in brassica crops with the cabbage aphid, *Brevicoryne brassicae*, detected most frequently (**Figure 6.2** *Molecular analysis of the gut contents of generalist predators can identify which species of herbivore they consume but can also reveal important interactions between predator species such as highly asymmetrical intra-guild predation*). In contrast, DNA of the cabbage white butterfly, *Pieris rapae*, was the prey species detected most frequently from *M. tasmaniae* whilst the Rutherglen bug, *Nysius vinitor*, was not detected from this predator. Molecular gut analysis not only revealed potentially important differences in prey range for these two generalist predators, but also detected highly asymmetrical intra-guild predation. Whilst one-third of the *H. variegata* individuals contained DNA of *M. tasmaniae*, less than 3% of *M. tasmaniae* had fed upon *H. variegata*.

## *Supplementary food sources*

Naturally occurring plant material exploitable as food for predators and parasitoids can be described as either 'direct', with sustenance coming from plants, or 'indirect', with the food source coming from plant-feeding insects. Direct food sources include nectar and pollen, extrafloral nectaries, fruits, plant sap and leaking photoassimilates. However, floral resources provide pollen and nectar only for a limited time and can sustain pest lepidopteran adults as well as biological control agents, potentially leading to increased crop damage, and these potential negatives have been important in refining the ways in which plant diversity is selected and applied in support of biological control (Baggen and Gurr, 1998). Indirect food sources such as honeydew are produced by homopteran insects such as aphids, mealybugs, scale insects and whiteflies (Jervis and Kidd, 1996). However, honeydews are discouraged in most cropping systems (Baggen and Gurr, 1998).

Supplementary foods can also be provided to the biological control agents in a way that potentially avoids the complexities of vegetation diversification. This takes the form of food sprays composed of a mixture of complex carbohydrates and protein supplements in a liquid formulation (Mensah and Khan, 1997). Food sprays have the potential to encourage immigration by natural enemies, reduce emigration away from pest containing areas, increase the reproductive capacity of biological control agents and reduce the mortality of biological control agents (Wade et al., 2008). Wade et al. (2008) reviewed the prospects of use of the food sprays and concluded that food sprays may have scope for use with other integrated pest management components including narrow spectrum insecticides, floral resources, refugia and herbivore induced plant volatiles. Despite these potential benefits, the use of food sprays has been extremely low, suggesting that performance of food sprays have been inconsistent (Wade et al., 2008). Clearly, this lack of practical uptake of food sprays reinforces the need to develop practical approaches for providing foods to predators and parasitoids using biodiversity-based strategies.

## Promoting biological control with biodiversity

A major consequence of conventional farming practices is the reduced activity of natural enemies in agricultural landscapes resulting from disturbance regimes and landscape simplification (Tscharntke et al., 2005). The conservation biological control response to this involves habitat management (Landis et al., 2000) to provide favourable conditions for the optimal performance of natural enemies, such as adequate food resources and shelter, through the modification or manipulation of habitats which are spatially and temporally favourable to natural enemies and easily integrated into production systems (Landis et al., 2000).

The Australian cotton industry's practices include habitat management and manipulation practices such as trap-cropping and growing refugia, and the latter is required of growers electing to grow genetically modified cotton varieties. Though aimed principally at affecting pest populations directly, these practices can have an indirect effect via the enemies hypothesis (Gurr et al., 2003), enhancing natural enemy populations. For example, lucerne grown as a trap crop for the pest bug *Creontiades dilutus* can act as source habitat for natural enemies (Hossain et al., 2002) and the management strategy of mowing can provide a further, 'two-way', benefit. By stopping lucerne from flowering, *C. dilutus* is more likely to remain in lucerne and not move into cotton crops; meanwhile, harvesting lucerne encourages natural enemies to migrate out of the trap crop and into cotton (Hossain et al., 2002). Unsprayed refuges grown to manage *Bt* resistance could also have a multifunctional benefit by acting as a refuge for natural enemies as well.

Habitat management techniques are generally focused at a small spatial scale using local modifications, for example intercropped strips of lucerne within cotton to provide additional habitat for natural enemies (Hossain et al., 2002), or the addition of floral strips within the crop, or in field margins, to provide additional food resources for natural enemies (Begum et al., 2006).

The efficacy of such local modifications, however, may be dependent on larger landscape-level processes (Tscharntke et al., 2005). Additions and modifications to the landscape for the benefit of natural enemies may affect taxa with small- and large-scale dispersal ability differently. Local habitat management is most likely to have a significant effect on populations of small-scale dispersers, because large-scale dispersers are able to gain resources beyond the field scale, as they experience the landscape at a greater extent (Tscharntke et al., 2005). Additionally, local modifications have been found to only significantly enhance populations of natural enemies in highly simplified landscapes (Thies and Tscharntke, 1999). This is because diversity is already high in complex landscapes, and alternative resources are already available (Tscharntke et al., 2005). So it is important that habitat manipulation practices be aimed at the appropriate spatial scale for the target taxa.

As researchers expand their perspective beyond the field-scale, and even beyond the farm-scale, it is apparent that the surrounding landscape has a strong effect on the activity of natural enemies in agricultural systems. A number of recent studies have emphasised that the wider landscape can have a significant effect on arthropod populations within crops (e.g. Schmidt and Tscharntke, 2005). A positive relationship between beneficial arthropods and non-crop areas was identified in 80% of studies reviewed by Bianchi et al. (2006). Other authors have suggested that the sometimes inconsistent relationships observed between arthropods and non-crop areas can be explained by an inappropriate spatial scale of investigations (Tscharntke et al., 2005). A number of studies have even shown that landscape-level conditions have a greater effect on natural enemies within crops than local conditions and local management practices. Östman et al. (2001), for example, observed the establishment of the bird cherry-oat aphid, *Rhopalosiphum padi*, and subsequent impact on population growth rate by their predators, was more strongly influenced by crop diversity and field margins at a landscape level than by local farming practices (organic vs. conventional). Further, Schmidt et al. (2005) identified that the species richness of spiders was enhanced in complex landscapes irrespective of farm management (organic or conventional). Finally, in cotton in the United States, Prasifka et al. (2004) found that the area of grain sorghum crops and the area of uncultivated land in the wider landscape had a stronger effect on predator numbers within cotton fields than did the presence of these same habitats adjacent to cotton fields.

Much of the recent landscape-level research has been conducted in the area around Göttingen, Germany (e.g. Schmidt et al., 2008). Researchers there have shown that within the same landscapes, in the same cropping system, different arthropod taxa respond to the same aspects of the landscape at different spatial scales. For example, Roschewitz et al. (2005) found that activity of aphid parasitoids in winter wheat increased in response to landscape complexity at a scale of 1–2 km, while aphids responded at scales beyond 3 km. Schmidt et al. (2008) showed that among different species of spiders in winter wheat, some species responded positively and others negatively to the landscape complexity, and the spatial scales of these responses ranges from 95 m to 3000 m.

Given that agriculturally important pest and natural enemy species respond to their environment at a landscape scale, conservation biological control and habitat management techniques need to be aimed at this large scale. Elements which can restore functional diversity to agroecosystems at a landscape level need to be identified and managed, in order to maximise the activity of natural enemies within agricultural landscapes. To achieve this, researchers need to identify how natural enemies utilise the landscape by understanding the following: (a) the spatial scale at which specific taxa experience the environment, (b) the resources (e.g. habitats, corridors) that they utilise and rely on and (c) how these different taxa move between available resources and into crops. With this information, landscape managers can be aware of the resources in the landscape that need to be managed or modified; the spatial scale at which management is required; and the arrangement of managed resources, relative to crops, in order to achieve better management of pests. Each of these three issues is explored in the following sections.

## 1 Identifying the spatial scale at which arthropods utilise the landscape

Identifying the spatial scale at which a species utilises the landscape is important for understanding how that species can be managed. Depending on dispersal ability, body size and trophic level, species may vary in the spatial scale at which they respond to the landscape. An approach for identifying the spatial scale at which different taxa utilise the landscape, which could be described as the *spatially specific proportional area approach*, has been widely and rapidly adopted in landscape-level studies in agricultural systems (e.g. Schmidt et al., 2008). In this approach, the proportional area of specific land uses, within various sized circular or rectangular landscape, is related to the in-crop density or activity of the arthropod taxa of interest. This technique has highlighted that different species of predators, parasitoids and hosts respond to the same landscape conditions at different spatial scales.

2 Identifying resources which natural enemies utilise within the landscape

The way that each species responds to the landscape depends on the spatial scale at which they experience the landscape as well as their specific habitat requirements. Several authors have attempted to identify the aspects of the landscape that arthropods respond to, along with the spatial scale at which they respond to these aspects, using the *spatially specific proportional area approach*. Increased landscape complexity, including increased crop (including tree) and non-crop vegetation diversity and different land uses including uncultivated land (Schmidt et al., 2005), has been identified as having a major influence on arthropod natural enemy activity at a landscape scale. Although identifying such correlations between landscape complexity and natural enemy activity does highlight the negative effects of landscape simplification, it does not give a clear message of how landscapes can be managed to improve natural enemy activity.

Some authors have used the *spatially specific proportional area approach* to identify, more specifically, the land uses that have the strongest effect on the activity of arthropods. These land uses have included specific alternative crops, for example a greater proportional area of grain sorghum in the landscape surrounding cotton was associated with greater abundance of predators in cotton crops (Prasifka et al., 2004). Further, some specific non-crop land uses, for example undisturbed woodlands and grasslands, were correlated with aphid predators in wheat (Elliott et al., 2002). Finally, pastures were positively related and horticultural areas and negatively related to predation of eggs of the moth pest *Mamestra brassicae* in Brussels sprouts (Bianchi et al., 2005).

Due to the strong correlations that exist between the proportional areas of different land uses, it is difficult to separate the effects of such strongly correlated elements using a proportional area approach. To identify, more specifically, the elements that benefit natural enemies at a landscape scale, different investigation techniques or different landscape metrics, other than proportional area, need to be investigated. One example is the cost-distance modelling to represent landscape structural-connectivity where the land uses favoured by different arthropod taxa are identified by modelling different permutations of land use preferences (Perovic et al., 2010).

3 Movement of arthropods between resources in the landscape

Identifying how conductive a landscape is for movement of arthropods between habitat patches is an important aspect for understanding how well a particular landscape will support natural enemies (Gurr et al., 2005; see also Perfecto and Vandermeer, Chapter 15 of this Handbook). Landscape conductivity is driven by two factors: (1) structural connectivity of the landscape, or how well habitats are physically connected within a landscape and (2) the species specific dispersal ability. Non-crop habitats, such as riparian areas, remnant native vegetation and shelterbelts, are important in agricultural landscapes because they can provide a buffer for disturbance and simplification associated with conventional farming practices. The ephemeral nature of crops means that in order to persist in an agricultural landscape, arthropods exist as metapopulations, moving between habitat patches within the landscape, continually falling back to alternative non-crop habitat patches and repeatedly recolonising crops.

Metapopulation theory was originally put forward by Levins (1969) as a pest management strategy; the classical theory posits that by reducing migration between habitat patches and ensuring synchronous pressure throughout the landscape, pest populations are more likely to be eradicated from landscapes. The principles of this theory are used in reverse by conservation ecology to minimise the chances of extinction for target species. The principles of metapopulation theory can also be applied in the same 'reverse' manner in conservation biological control to ensure conditions which lead to the conservation of enemy populations within a landscape. Fundamentally, this requires a number of habitat patches (large enough to support populations) to be available within the landscape, and for migration to occur between them.

Local extinctions occur regularly within crop patches due to disturbance events such as insecticide application, harvesting and ploughing. Therefore, migration between crop patches and non-crop habitat patches is essential for both recolonisation of crops during the growing season and for the persistence of natural enemy populations within the landscape. Movement between crop and non-crop resources may also be important in order for natural enemies to receive resource subsidies from non-crop habitats, such as nectar and pollen and alternate prey, which may be lacking in crop fields (Landis et al., 2000). The ability to move between these resources can therefore be the limiting factor for the persistence of a population (or metapopulation) in a cropping landscape. It is important for landscape management, then, to understand and identify which habitats may act as alternative habitats, and how different species of natural enemies move through the landscape and between these habitat patches.

## Future outlooks

A growing number of techniques are being employed by landscape ecologists to model the movement of populations throughout the landscape. Such approaches are generally adopted by conservation ecologists and could potentially be adapted to conservation biological control, as both disciplines share the common aim of conserving target animals within a particular landscape. The cost-distance approach mentioned above uses numerical 'costs' to represent the level of favourability of different land uses to dispersing animals, and can therefore be used to model the connectivity of the landscape. A second approach, which actually incorporates cost-distance, is graph theory (e.g. Saura and Pascual-Hortal, 2007), which was designed for network analysis, to identify the efficiency of information flow, but has potential in this ecological case; the larger the network (of patches), the more resilient the metapopulation of a given predator or parasitoid will be in an agricultural landscape. As these types of research methods are refined, it will help generate a more thorough understanding of the ways in which agricultural diversity, at a range of scales, affects the dynamics of pests, predators and parasitoids. Combined with further advances in molecular methods (Gurr and You, 2016), this will allow the potential power of biodiversity to be more fully harnessed to provide the ecosystem service of biological pest control.

## Acknowledgements

We thank Mrs A. C. Johnson for assistance with this chapter. GMG is supported by the Chinese Government's Thousand Talents Program; DJP was supported by the Cotton Catchment Communities Cooperative Research Centre; KLM (and the work featured in **Box 6.2**) was supported by Horticulture Australia Ltd.

## References

Baggen, L. R. and Gurr, G. M. (1998) 'The influence of food on *Copidosoma koehleri* (Hymenoptera: Encyrtidae), and the use of flowering plants as a habitat management tool to enhance biological control of potato moth, *Phthorimaea operculella* (Lepidoptera: Gelechiidae)', *Biological Control*, vol. 11, pp. 9–17.

Begum, M., Gurr, G. M., Wratten, S. D., Hedberg, P. R. and Nicol, H. I. (2006) 'Using selective food plants to maximize biological control of vineyard pests', *Journal of Applied Ecology*, vol. 43, pp. 547–554.

Bianchi, F. J., Booij, C. J. H. and Tscharntke, T. (2006) 'Sustainable pest regulation in agricultural landscapes: A review on landscape composition, biodiversity and natural pest control', *Proceedings of the Royal Society B–Biological Sciences*, vol. 273, pp. 1715–1727.

Bianchi, F. J., van Wingerden, W. K., Griffioen, A. J., van der Veen, M., ver der Straten, M. J., Wegman, R. M. A. and Meeuwsen, H. A. M. (2005) 'Landscape factors affecting the control of *Mamestra brassicae* by natural enemies in Brussels Sprout', *Agriculture Ecosystems & Environment*, vol. 107, pp. 145–150.

Crowder, D. W., Northfield, T. D., Strand, M. R. and Snyder, W. E. (2010) 'Organic agriculture promotes evenness and natural pest control', *Nature*, vol. 466, pp. 109–112.

DeBach, P. and Rosen, D. (1991) *Biological Control of Natural Enemies*, Cambridge University Press, Cambridge, UK.

Elliott, N. C., Kieckhefer, R. W. and Beck, D. A. (2002) 'Effect of aphids and the surrounding landscape on the abundance of Coccinellidae in cornfields', *Biological Control*, vol. 24, pp. 214–220.

Franzmann, B. A. (2002) '*Hippodamia variegata* (Goeze) (Coleoptera: Coccinellidae), a predacious ladybird new in Australia', *Australian Journal of Entomology*, vol. 41, pp. 375–377.

Furlong, M. J. and Zalucki, M. P. (2010) 'Exploiting predators for pest management: The need for sound ecological assessment', *Entomologia Experimentalis et Applicata*, vol. 135, pp. 225–236.

Greenstone, M. H. (1979) 'Spider feeding behaviour optimises dietary essential amino acid composition', *Nature*, vol. 282, pp. 501–503.

Gurr, G. M., Lu, Z., Zheng, X., Xu, H., Zhu, P., Chen, G., Yao, X., Cheng, J., Zhu, Z., Catindig, J. L., Villareal, S., Van Chien, H., Cuong, L. Q., Channoo, C., Chengwattana, N., Lan, L. P., Hai, L. H., Chaiwong, J., Nicol, H. I., Perovic, D. J., Wratten, S. D. and Heong, K. L. (2016) 'Multi-country evidence that crop diversification promotes ecological intensification of agriculture', *Nature Plants*, vol. 2, p. 16014.

Gurr, G. M. and Wratten, S. D. (1999) '"Integrated biological control": A proposal for enhancing success in biological control', *International Journal of Pest Management*, vol. 45, pp. 81–84.

Gurr, G. M., Wratten, S. D. and Luna, M. J. (2003) 'Multi-function agricultural biodiversity: Pest management and other benefits', *Basic and Applied Ecology*, vol. 4, pp. 107–116.

Gurr, G. M., Wratten, S. D. and Snyder, W. E. (2012) *Biodiversity and Insect Pests: Key Issues for Sustainable Management*, John Wiley & Sons, Chichester, UK.

Gurr, G. M., Wratten, S. D., Tylianakis, J., Kean, J. and Keller, M. (2005) 'Providing plant foods for natural enemies in farming systems: Balancing practicalities and theory', pp. 326–347 in F. I. Wickers, P. C. J. van Rijn and J. Bruin (eds.), *Plant-Provided Food for Carnivorous Insects: Protective Mutualism and Its Applications*, Cambridge University Press, Cambridge, UK.

Gurr, G. M. and You, M. (2016) 'Conservation biological control of pests in the molecular era: New opportunities to address old constraints', *Frontiers in Plant Science*, vol. 6, doi.org/10.3389/fpls.2015.01255

Hawkins, B. A., Mills, N. J., Jervis, M. A. and Price, P. W. (1999) 'Is the biological control of insects a natural phenomenon?', *Oikos*, vol. 86, pp. 493–506.

Hebert, P. D. N., Ratnasingham, S. and de Waard, J. R. (2003) 'Barcoding animal life: Cytochrome c oxidase subunit 1 divergences among closely related species', *Proceedings of the Royal Society of London B–Biological Sciences*, vol. 270, pp. S96–S99.

Hodge, S. and Longley, M. (2000) 'The irritant and repellent effects of organophosphates on the Tasmanian lacewing, *Micromus tasmaniae* (Neuroptera: Hemerobiidae)', *Pest Management Science*, vol. 56, pp. 916–920.

Horne, P. A, Ridland, P. M. and New, T. R. (2001) '*Micromus tasmaniae*: A key predator on aphids on field crops in Australasia?', pp. 388–394 in P. McEwen, T. R. New and A. E. Whittington (eds.), *Lacewings in the Crop Environment*, Cambridge University Press, Cambridge, UK.

Hossain, Z., Gurr, G. M., Wratten, S. D. and Raman, A. (2002) 'Habitat manipulation in lucerne *Medicago sativa*: Arthropod population dynamics in harvested and "refuge" crop strips', *Journal of Applied Ecology*, vol. 39, pp. 445–454.

Jervis, M. A. and Kidd, N. (1996) *Insect Natural Enemies*, Chapman Hall, Melbourne, Australia.

Khan, Z. R., Pickett, J. A., Wadhams, L. and Muyekho, F. (2001) 'Habitat management strategies for the control of cereal stemborers and striga in maize in Kenya', *Insect Science and Its Application*, vol. 21, pp. 375–380.

Landis, D. A., Wratten, S. D. and Gurr, G. M. (2000) 'Habitat management to conserve natural enemies of arthropod pests in agriculture', *Annual Review of Entomology*, vol. 45, pp. 175–201.

Letourneau, D. K., Armbrecht, I., Rivera, B. S., Lerma, J. M., Carmona, E. J., Daza, M. C., Escobar, S., Galindo, V., Gutierrez, C., Lopez, S. D., Mejia, J. L., Rangel, A. M. A., Rangel, J. H., Rivera, L., Saavedra,

C. A., Torres, A. M. and Trujillo, A. R. (2011) 'Does plant diversity benefit agroecosystems? A synthetic review', *Ecological Applications*, vol. 21, pp. 9–21.

Levins, R. (1969) 'Some demographic and genetic consequences of environmental heterogeneity for biological control', *Bulletin of the Entomological Society of America*, vol. 15, pp. 237–240.

Lu, Z.-X., Zhu, P.-Y., Gurr, G. M., Zheng, X.-S., Read, D. M. Y., Heong, K.-L., Yang, Y.-J. and Xu, H.-X. (2014) 'Mechanisms for flowering plants to benefit arthropod natural enemies of insect pests: Prospects for enhanced use in agriculture', *Insect Science*, vol. 21, pp. 1–12.

Matson, P. A., Parton, W. J., Power, A. G. and Swift, M. J. (1997) 'Agricultural intensification and ecosystem properties', *Science*, vol. 277, pp. 504–509.

Mensah, R. and Khan, M. (1997) 'Use of *Medicago sativa* (L.) interplantings/trap crops in the management of the green mirid, *Creontiades dilutus* (Stal) in commercial cotton in Australia', *International Journal of Pest Management*, vol. 43, pp. 197–202.

New, T. (2002) 'Prospects for extending the use of Australian lacewings in biological control', *Acta Zoologica Academiae Scientiarum Hungaricae*, vol. 48, pp. 209–216.

Obrycki, J. J. and Kring, T. J. (1998) 'Predaceous Coccinellidae in biological control', *Annual Review of Entomology*, vol. 43, pp. 295–321.

Östman, Ö., Ekbom, B. and Bengtsson, J. (2001) 'Landscape heterogeneity and farming practice influence biological control', *Basic and Applied Ecology*, vol. 2, pp. 365–371.

Perovic, D. J., Gurr, G. M., Raman, A. and Nicol, H. I. (2010) 'Effect of landscape composition and arrangement on biological control agents in a simplified agricultural system: A cost-distance approach', *Biological Control*, vol. 52, pp. 263–270.

Ponisio, L. C., M'Gonigle, L. K., Mace, K. C., Palomino, J., de Valpine, P. and Kremen, C. (2014) 'Diversification practices reduce organic to conventional yield gap', *Proceedings of the Royal Society of London B–Biological Sciences*, vol. 282, p. 20141396.

Prasifka, J. R., Heinz, K. M. and Minzenmayer, R. R. (2004) 'Relationships of landscape, prey and agronomic variables to the abundance of generalist predators in cotton (*Gossypium hirsutum*) fields', *Landscape Ecology*, vol. 19, pp. 709–717.

Pratt, P. D. and Croft, B. A. (2000) 'Banker plants: Evaluation of release strategies for predatory mites', *Journal of Environmental Horticulture*, vol. 18, pp. 211–217.

Rahmani, S. and Bandani, A. R. (2013) 'Sublethal concentrations of thiamethoxam adversely affect life table parameters of the aphid predator, *Hippodamia variegata* (Goeze) (Coleoptera: Coccinellidae)', *Crop Protection*, vol. 54, pp. 168–175.

Roschewitz, I., Hücker, M., Tscharntke, T. and Thies, C. (2005) 'The influence of landscape context and farming practices on parasitism of cereal aphids', *Agriculture Ecosystems & Environment*, vol. 108, pp. 218–227.

Samson, P. and Blood, P. (1980) 'Voracity and searching ability of *Chrysopa signata* (Neuroptera: Chrysopidae), *Micromus tasmaniae* (Neuroptera: Hemerobiidae), and *Tropiconabis capsiformis* (Hemiptera: Nabidae)', *Australian Journal of Zoology*, vol. 28, pp. 575–580.

Sato, T. and Takada, H. (2004) 'Biological studies on three *Micromus* species in Japan (Neuroptera: Hemerobiidae) to evaluate their potential as biological control agents against aphids: 1. Thermal effects on development and reproduction', *Applied Entomology and Zoology*, vol. 39, pp. 417–425.

Saura, S. and Pascual-Hortal, L. (2007) 'A new habitat availability index to integrate connectivity in landscape conservation planning: Comparison with existing indices and application to a case study', *Landscape and Urban Planning*, vol. 83, pp. 91–103.

Schellhorn, N. A., Bianchi, F. J. J. A. and Hsu, C. L. (2014) 'Movement of entomophagous arthropods in agricultural landscapes: Links to pest suppression', *Annual Review of Entomology*, vol. 59, pp. 559–581.

Schmidt, M. H., Roschewitz, I., Thies, C. and Tscharntke, T. (2005) 'Differential effects of landscape and management on diversity and density of ground-dwelling farmland spiders', *Journal of Applied Ecology*, vol. 42, pp. 281–287.

Schmidt, M. H., Thies, C., Nentwig, W. and Tscharntke, T. (2008) 'Contrasting responses of arable spiders to the landscape matrix at different spatial scales', *Journal of Biogeography*, vol. 35, pp. 157–166.

Schmidt, M. H. and Tscharntke, T. (2005) 'Landscape context of sheetweb spider (Araneae: Linyphiidae) abundance in cereal fields', *Journal of Biogeography*, vol. 32, pp. 467–473.

Seufert, V., Ramankutty, N. and Foley, J. A. (2012) 'Comparing the yields of organic and conventional agriculture', *Nature*, vol. 485, pp. 229–232.

Thies, C. and Tscharntke, T. (1999) 'Landscape structure and biological control in agroecosystems', *Science*, vol. 285, pp. 893–895.

Thomas, M. B., Wratten, S. D. and Sotherton, N. W. (1991) 'Creation of "island" habitats in farmland to manipulate populations of beneficial arthropods: Predator densities and emigration', *Journal of Applied Ecology*, vol. 28, pp. 906–917.

Tillman, P. G., Smith, H. A. and Holland, J. M. (2012) 'Cover crops and related methods for enhancing agricultural biodiversity and conservation biocontrol: Successful case studies', pp. 309–327 in G. M. Gurr, S. D. Wratten and W. E. Synder (eds.), *Biodiversity and Insect Pests*, John Wiley & Sons, Chichester, UK.

Tscharntke, T., Klein, A. M., Kruess, A., Steffan-Dewenter, I. and Thies, C. (2005) 'Landscape perspectives on agricultural intensification and biodiversity: Ecosystem service management', *Ecology Letters*, vol. 8, pp. 857–874.

van Driesche, R. G. and Bellows, T. S. (1996) *Biological Control*, Chapman Hall, Melbourne, Australia.

van Driesche, R. G., Hoddle, M. S. and Centre, T. (2008) *Control of Pests and Weeds by Natural Enemies*, Blackwell Publishing, Singapore.

van Lenteren, J. C., Bale, J., Bigler, F., Hokkanen, H. M. T. and Loomans, A. J. M. (2006) 'Assessing risks of releasing exotic biological control agents of arthropod pests', *Annual Review of Entomology*, vol. 51, pp. 609–634.

van Lenteren, J. C., van Roermund, H. J. and Sütterlin, S. (1996) 'Biological control of greenhouse whitefly *Trialeurodes vaporariorum* with the parasitoid *Encarsia formosa*: How does it work?', *Biological Control*, vol. 6, pp. 1–10.

Wade, M. R., Gurr, G. M. and Wratten, S. D. (2008) 'Ecological restoration of farmland: Progress and prospects', *Philosophical Transactions of the Royal Society B–Biological Sciences*, vol. 363, pp. 831–847.

Wade, M. R., Zalucki, M. P., Wratten, S. D. and Robinson, K. A. (2008) 'Conservation biological control of arthropods using artificial food sprays: Current status and future challenges', *Biological Control*, vol. 45, pp. 185–199.

Westphal, C., Vidal, S., Horgan, F. G., Gurr, G. M., Escalada, M., Van Chien, H., Tscharntke, T., Heong, K. L. and Settele, J. (2015) 'Promoting multiple ecosystem services with flower strips and participatory approaches in rice production landscapes', *Basic and Applied Ecology*, vol. 16, pp. 681–689.

Wilby, A. and Thomas, M. B. (2007) 'Diversity and pest management in agroecosystems: Some perspectives from ecology', pp. 269–291 in D. I. Jarvis, C. Padoch and H. D. Cooper (eds.), *Managing Biodiversity in Agricultural Ecosystems*, Columbia University Press, New York, NY, USA.

Yano, E. (2006) 'Ecological considerations for biological control of aphids in protected culture', *Population Ecology*, vol. 48, pp. 333–339.

# 7

# IMPORTANCE OF POLLINATORS IN AGRICULTURAL BIODIVERSITY

*Barbara Gemmill-Herren*

## Introduction

More than 15 years ago, in 2000, the global community registered its concern over multiple reports of declining pollinators. Through the Convention on Biological Diversity (CBD), the International Initiative for the Conservation and Sustainable Use of Pollinators (also known as the International Pollinator Initiative, or IPI) was created, adopting a plan of action two years later with four structural elements (assessment, adaptive management, capacity building and mainstreaming) to address the threats of pollinator loss.

Over this last decade and half, a parallel process has been underway with respect to perceived crises in global food systems. While recognizing the centrality of agriculture to human well-being and sustainable development, essentially every statement on the future of agriculture over at least the last decade acknowledges that a transformation is needed in the way the food is produced and how it impacts on the environment, even if and while production is increased to meet food security needs (IAASTD, 2009; Royal Society of London, 2009; Godfray et al., 2010; Foley et al., 2011). Concerns over the sustainability of agriculture and the growing ecological footprint of conventional farming systems have also substantially increased over this period. To many, particularly those in the nature conservation and biodiversity realm, agriculture looms as the major global threat: as noted in the recent Global Biodiversity Outlook 4 (CBD, 2014), agriculture is thought to be the driver for around 70% of the projected loss of terrestrial biodiversity. Policies to protect the environment are often undermined by policies that support the agriculture sector (Tanentzap et al., 2015). As agricultural production is led by consumer demand, the overall global food system is under increased scrutiny.

To what extent do these two compelling global concerns have common ground? I argue here that both the agendas and solutions for the pollination crisis, and the concerns over global agricultural sustainability, have important overlaps and synergies, and can be addressed most effectively by building on each other. I will consider here the nature of the problem, the evidence base documenting current trends in both pollination services and agricultural production, and then review current thinking on measures to conserve and manage pollinators in the context of sustainable production (for more detail, see also Gemmill-Herren, 2016).

## Pollination: contribution and crisis

### *Biodiversity and pollination*

With well over 300,000 flowering plant species dependent on pollination by animals (Ollerton et al., 2011), pollination is critical to the overall maintenance of biodiversity in many senses. Animal pollinators allow many kinds of flowering plants to co-exist in an ecosystem, rather than limiting it to the dense, lower-diversity stands of wind-pollinated plants that dominated before the flowering plants evolved. Bees, the largest group of pollinating insects, originated in the Cretaceous, roughly at the same time as the angiosperms (flowering plants), and the diversity of both groups is thought to be partly due to their co-evolution (Danforth et al., 2006). Pollination services thus shape plant communities and determine fruit and seed availability, providing tremendously important food and habitat resources for other animals.

The diversity of pollinators and pollination systems is striking. Most of the estimated 25,000 species of bees (Hymenoptera: Apidae) are effective pollinators, and together with moths, flies, wasps, beetles and butterflies, make up the majority of pollinating species. Vertebrate pollinators include bats, non-flying mammals (several species of monkey, rodents, lemur, tree squirrels, olingo and kinkajou) and birds (hummingbirds, sunbirds, honeycreepers and some parrot species). Current understanding of the pollination process shows that, while interesting specialized relationships can exist between plants and their pollinators, healthy pollination services are best ensured by an abundance and diversity of pollinators (Garibaldi et al., 2016). While bees compose over 50% of all pollinators, attention is increasingly being paid to other taxa of importance, such as flies (Rader et al., 2015).

### *Economic values and societal demands for pollination*

In agro-ecosystems, pollinators are essential for orchard, horticultural and forage production, as well as the production of seed for many root and fibre crops. About two-thirds of the crop plants that feed the world rely on pollination by insects or other animals to produce healthy fruits and seeds. Of the slightly more than 100 crop species that provide 90% of national per capita food supplies for 146 countries, 71 species are bee-pollinated (but relatively few by honeybees), and several others are pollinated by thrips, wasps, flies, beetles, moths and other insects (Klein et al., 2007). For human nutrition, the benefits of pollination include not just abundance of fruits, nuts and seeds, but also their variety and quality; the contribution of animal-pollinated foodstuffs to human nutritional diversity, vitamin sufficiency and food quality is substantial (Eilers et al., 2011). Many of the crops that are highly dependent on pollinators are also those richest in micronutrients (Chaplin-Kramer et al., 2014).

Globally, the total economic contribution of animal pollination services to the global economy had reached an estimated €153 billion even ten years ago, which at that time represented 9.5% of the value of the world agricultural production used for human food in 2005. Those crops that depend on pollination services are high-value, averaging values of €761 per ton, against €151 a ton for those crops that do not depend on animal pollination (Gallai et al., 2009). **Table 7.1** *Economic impacts of insect pollination worldwide* shows that the leading pollinator-dependent crops are vegetables and fruits, each accounting for about €50 billion each, followed by edible oil crops, stimulants (coffee, cocoa, etc.), nuts and spices. These figures do not include the contribution of pollinators to crop seed production (which can contribute significantly to seed yields), nor to pasture and forage crops. Nor do these figures include the value of pollinators to maintaining the structure and functioning of wild ecosystems: as yet these are all uncalculated.

*Table 7.1* Economic impacts of insect pollination worldwide

| *Crop category* | *Mean value/ production unit (E/ton)* | *Total production economic value (EV; 10–9E)* | *Insect pollination economic value (IPEV; 10–9E)* | *Ratio of vulnerability (IPEV/EV; %)* |
|---|---|---|---|---|
| Stimulant crops | 1,225 | 19 | 7.0 | 39.0 |
| Nuts | 1,269 | 13 | 4.2 | 31.0 |
| Fruits | 452 | 219 | 50.6 | 23.1 |
| Edible oil crops | 385 | 240 | 1.0 | 16.3 |
| Vegetables | 468 | 418 | 0.2 | 12.2 |
| Pulses | 515 | 24 | 0.0 | 4.3 |
| Spices | 1,003 | 7 | 0.0 | 2.7 |
| Cereals | 139 | 312 | 0.0 | 0.0 |
| Sugar crops | 177 | 268 | 0.0 | 0.0 |
| Roots and tubers | 137 | 98 | 0.0 | 0.0 |
| All categories | | 1,618 | 152.9 | 9.5 |

*Source*: Gallai et al. (2009).

More recent global assessments have shown trends of increasing values for the contribution of pollination, from 1993 to 2009 (Lautenbach et al., 2012). A few countries dominate these increasing trends, with China showing the largest increase in the value of pollination to agricultural output, and India, United States, Brazil, Japan and Turkey also showing large increases. Accompanying the trends of the increasing economic values of pollination are trends showing striking increases in the demand for pollination services. Analysis of Food and Agriculture Organization of the United Nations (FAO) production data has shown the following:

- Since 1961, crop yield (Mt/ha) has increased consistently at average annual growth rates of 1.5%. Temporal trends were similar between pollinator-dependent and non-dependent crops in both the developed and developing world. Over this same time, agriculture has become more pollinator dependent because of a disproportionate increase in the area cultivated with pollinator-dependent crops.

  *(Aizen et al., 2009)*

- The global population of managed honeybee hives has increased by 45% during the last half century. But, with the much more rapid (>300%) increase in the fraction of agriculture that depends on animal pollination during the last half century (**Figure 7.1** *Global pollination trends in total crop production from 1961 to 2006*), the global capacity to provide sufficient pollination services may be stressed, and more pronounced in the developing world than in the developed world.

  *(Aizen and Harder, 2009)*

- For those crops for which animal pollination is essential (i.e. 95% average yield reduction without pollinators) there was higher growth in yield and lower expansion in area than for crops with less dependence, probably reflecting the effects of explicit pollination management, such as renting hives or hand pollination.

  *(Garibaldi et al., 2009)*

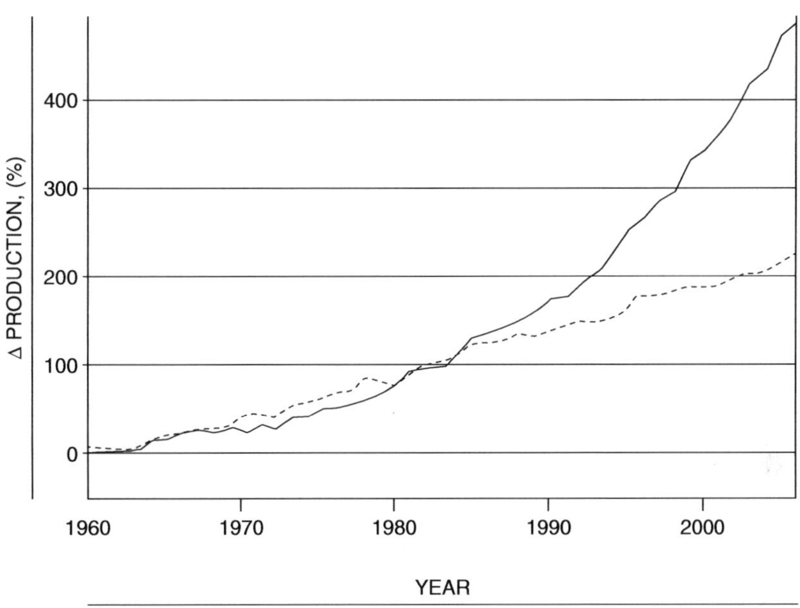


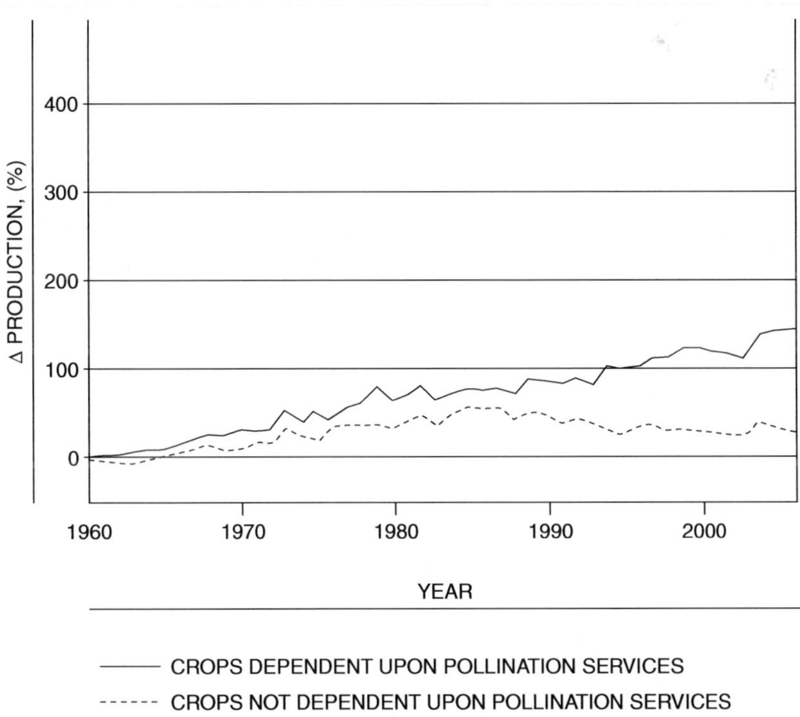


*Figure 7.1* Global pollination trends in total crop production from 1961 to 2006 (Aizen et al., 2009).

At the same time as the role of pollinators is gaining increasing attention, mounting evidence points to a serious decline in populations of wild pollinators. Globally, changes in the distributions of most pollinator taxa and pollination failures remain poorly described. To address such gaps, a special issue of the journal *Apidologie* was produced in 2009 that asked some of the world's leading experts to bring together current knowledge on the status of bees and their conservation, and factors determining bee abundance and biodiversity (Byrne and Fitzpatrick, 2009). Among the observations presented in this review were:

- The critical importance of the nine indigenous species of honeybee native to East Asia, which are extremely valuable because they are key pollinators to many crop species, and provide significant income to some of the world's poorest people. The most significant threats to local honeybee populations are deforestation and excessive hunting pressure.

  *(Oldroyd and Nanork, 2009)*

- In the Neotropics – which have a highly rich bee fauna – deforestation, agricultural intensification and the introduction and/or spread of exotic competing bee species are considered to be the main threats to most indigenous species.

  *(Freitas et al., 2009)*

- In Australia, the main threats to the native bee fauna include removal of nesting and foraging opportunities through land clearing and agriculture, the spread of exotic plant species and the consequences of climate change.

  *(Batley and Hogendoorn, 2009)*

- In Africa, the bee fauna still includes a very large number of undescribed species, making status difficult to determine.

  *(Eardley et al., 2009)*

To date, however, the strongest documented evidence of pollinator decline is only from Europe and North America and is focused on precipitous declines in bumblebees. Sixteen of Europe's 68 bumblebee species are at risk of extinction, according to a recent report from the Red List of the International Union for Conservation of Nature (IUCN, 2014; Nieto et al., 2014). The report noted, 'Of the five most important insect pollinators of European crops, three are bumblebee species. The populations of almost half of these European bumblebee species are falling and just 13% are increasing'. The assessment, the first by the Red List to look at bumblebees, identified the main threats as climate change, which is altering their habitat, and changes in agricultural land use that is causing their natural environment to disappear. Equally, in North America, the results of a three-year interdisciplinary study of changing distributions, population genetic structure and levels of pathogen infection in bumblebee populations across the United States compared current and historical distributions of eight species. It was shown that the relative abundances of four species have declined by up to 96% and that their surveyed geographic ranges have contracted by 23–87%, some within the last 20 years (Cameron et al., 2011). It was also shown that declining populations have significantly higher infection levels of the microsporidian pathogen *Nosemabombi* and lower genetic diversity compared with co-occurring populations of the stable (non-declining) species. Higher pathogen prevalence and reduced genetic diversity could thus be considered realistic predictors of these alarming patterns of decline in North America, while exact causes and effect of infections and declining genetic diversity remain uncertain.

Honeybee declines, particularly over the winter period in the United States, remain a critical concern, and merit a more in-depth treatment than is possible here (Martin, 2015). As the primary domesticated pollinator, however, concerns over domesticated bee colony disorders have contributed to an increasing focus on the role of wild pollinators in crop pollination, as discussed in the next section.

Given the significant concern over global decline in wild and managed pollinators, it is remarkable that there is no global program focused on detecting these declines. The need for such a program, or common approach that could be widely replicated across the globe, is urgent. At the time of the seminal Millennium Ecosystem Assessment ten years ago (MA, 2005) pollination was the only ecosystem service in which it was noted that its trend (declining) had only low to medium certainty. As yet, it is still not possible to report on global trends with a documentable level of certainty. Work has been underway, under the auspices of the Global Pollination Project coordinated in seven countries by the FAOs, to develop an effective and efficient approach for monitoring of pollinator population trends. A standard protocol was designed, capable of detecting at least a 10% decline in total abundance and species richness of bees over a five-year period (LeBuhn et al., 2013). In initial applications of the protocol, it has been shown to adequately deal with the high levels of variability in mobile pollinator populations, and baseline data has now been established in a number of highly diverse, developing countries. This preliminary work established the groundwork for identifying local, regional and global trends in bee species richness and total abundance and in particular to detect large scale crashes in pollinator communities.

## Pollination (as provided by biodiversity) as an agronomic input

Pollination as a factor in food production and security is little understood and appreciated, in part because it has been provided by nature at no explicit cost to human communities. It has only been over the last few decades, as farm fields have become larger, and the use of agricultural chemicals has increasingly impacted beneficial insects as well as plant pests, that it has been widely recognized that pollination is a key agricultural input. Pollination services are now considered to be at least as important as conventional inputs such as fertilizers, irrigation and pest control products. In the process of this assessment, the role of biodiversity and wild pollinators has come to the forefront.

In a wide-ranging meta-analysis published recently, the pollination of more than 40 crops in 600 fields across every populated continent was studied through a contribution of 46 scientists (Garibaldi et al., 2013). It was found that wild pollinators were twice as effective as honeybees in producing seeds and fruit on crops including oilseed rape, coffee, onions, almonds, tomatoes and strawberries. Furthermore, bringing in managed honeybee hives did not replace wild pollination when that was lost, but only supplemented the pollination that took place (**Figure 7.2** *Importance of wild pollinators in crop pollination*).

Results of meta-analysis (Garibaldi et al., 2013) indicating the relative effectiveness of wild pollinators in contrast to honeybees, for more than 40 crops across the globe. The review indicates the substantial contribution of wild insects and suggests that honeybees cannot replace the wild insects lost, as their habitat is destroyed. Authors to the study advise that relying on honeybees alone is a 'highly risky strategy' because disease can sweep through single species, as has been seen with the varroa mite, and single species cannot adapt to environmental changes nearly as well as a group of wild pollinators. Wild pollinators perform better than honeybees because they deploy a wider range of pollinating techniques, such as 'buzz' pollination – a form of pollination required by many important crops: tomatoes, chili peppers and blueberries. These crops store their pollen

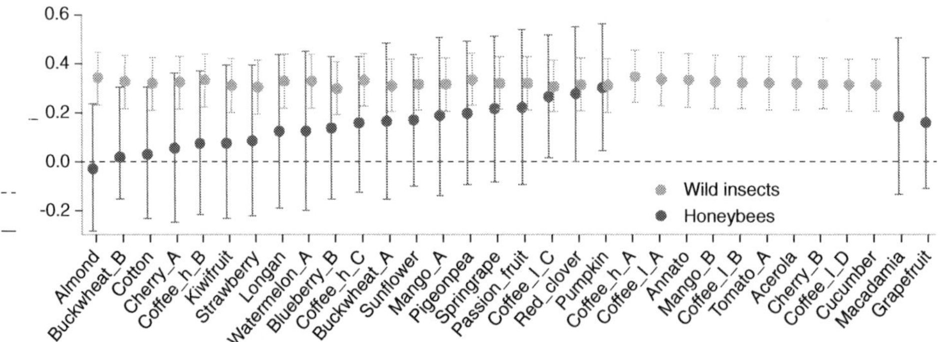


*Figure 7.2* Importance of wild pollinators in crop pollination. Results of meta-analysis of relative effectiveness of wild pollinators in contrast to honeybees (Garibaldi et al. 2013).

*Source*: ©*Science*, used with permission.

in enclosed anthers that have a small opening at the tip. A bee must land on the anther and vibrate its wings to cause a vibration (a 'buzz') at a certain frequency, upon which the pollen is shaken out of the anthers in a small puff. Only certain bees are capable of doing this, which honeybees cannot. Wild pollinators also tend to visit more plants, meaning more effective cross-pollination than honeybees, which more often carry pollen from one flower to another on the same plant.

In a newer meta-analysis (Garibaldi et al., 2016), the complete role of pollinators, including their diversity and abundance, in contributing to crop yields – not pollination alone – has been documented for the first time. Produced again under the auspices of the Global Pollination Project coordinated by the FAO, a common protocol to detect and assess levels of pollination deficit was applied to 344 fields from 33 pollinator-dependent cropping systems in small- and large-holdings in Africa, Asia and Latin America. The findings are highly significant for a greater appreciation of agricultural biodiversity: for holdings smaller than two hectares, yields could be increased by a median value of 24%, through improved pollination management resulting in higher flower-visitor density. For larger holdings, such an increase could occur only if the pollinator community visiting the crop flowers was highly diverse. Thus, the inherent propensity for small, diverse farming systems to host beneficial agricultural biodiversity that directly contributes to human livelihood is established, and also for the fact that biodiversity can compensate the negative effects of field size, under larger holdings (**Figure 7.3** *Flower-visitor density*).

For many farmers, the stability of production is as important as, if not more important than, yields. It is well known what can increase crop yields – in the form of inputs – and yield tends to increase asymptotically with such inputs, up to certain points. When yield growth declines, this can often prompt the conversion of more land to cultivation. However, as it is increasingly being understood, crop yields and their stability also depend upon the ecosystem services provided by agricultural biodiversity, such as pollination and natural pest control. A graphical model of yield-resource relations, as applied to animal pollination, predicts that incomplete and variable pollen delivery (through a loss of ecosystem services) reduces yield mean and increases the stability variability) of crops with a dependence on pollinators; the model's predictions were validated with crop production data collected by the FAO over the 1961–2008 period. Specifically, crops with greater pollinator dependence had lower mean and stability in relative yield and yield growth, despite global yield increases for most crops. Lower yield growth was compensated by increased land cultivation to enhance production of pollinator-dependent crops (Garibaldi et al., 2011). These results reveal that pollination deficits, if not managed with specific measures to maintain pollination services, hinder yield growth of pollinator-dependent crops, decreasing

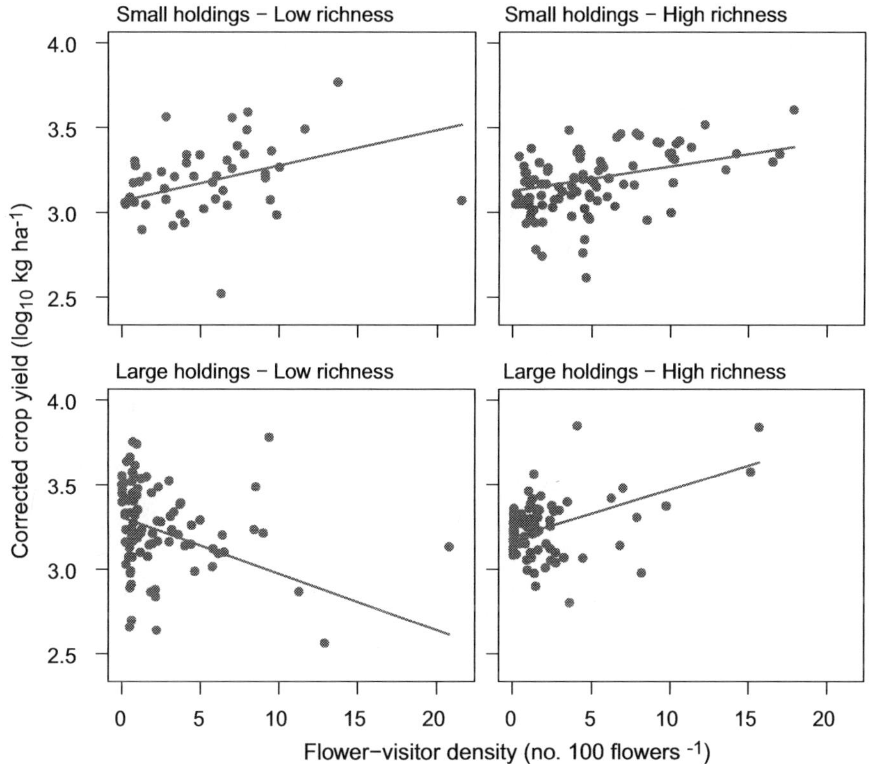


*Figure 7.3* Flower-visitor density

*Note*: Benefits of flower-visitor density to crop yield are greater for smaller (<2 ha) than for larger holdings, and when flower-visitor richness is higher; each point is a field within a crop system; yield is presented after subtracting the random intercept for each crop system; for full details, see Garibaldi et al. (2013).

*Source*: ©*Science*, used with permission.

the temporal stability of global agricultural production, while promoting compensatory land conversion to agriculture.

Pollinator abundances and diversity may have large impacts as well on yields and stability of forage crops. In Sweden, excellent data with a long-term time element was gathered on the relative abundances of bumblebee species in red clover fields during three periods (1940s, 1960s and present), and on clover seed yields since 1921. Drastic decreases were found in bumblebee community evenness, with potential consequences for level and stability of red clover seed yield. The relative abundances of two short-tongued bumblebees increased from 40% in the 1940s to entirely dominate present communities with 89%. Average seed yield declined in recent years and variation in yield doubled, suggesting that the current dependence on few species for pollination has been especially detrimental to stability in seed yield (Bommarco et al., 2011).

Pollination provides other, more subtle contributions to agricultural production. It has long been known that pollination contributes to fruit and seed quality, resulting in better-shaped and larger kiwis and apples, for example. In a blind tasting experiment in Australia, bee-pollinated tomatoes were significantly preferred over human, hand-pollinated ones, with a greater depth of flavour (Hogendoorn et al., 2010). A recent study of exclusion experiments in Germany with strawberries showed bee pollination to improve fruit quality, quantity and market value compared with wind and self-pollination. Bee-pollinated fruits were heavier, had fewer malformations and reached higher commercial grades. They had increased redness and reduced sugar and were firmer, thus improving the commercially important shelf life. Longer shelf life reduced fruit loss by at least 11% (Klatt et al., 2014).

In the almond production region of California, a lack of bees and other wild insects to pollinate almonds can reduce harvest yields more drastically than a lack of fertilizer or a failure to provide the crops with sufficient water (Klein et al., 2014). On the other hand, when almonds are adequately pollinated, the trees bear more fruit and their nutrient content changes, with increases in vitamin E (Brittain et al., 2014).

## Global food systems: crisis and contribution of ecosystem services

As suggested by the evidence presented in previous sections, agricultural production systems suffer when insufficient attention is paid to the role of ecosystem services such as pollination. The implications of this lack of recognition of ecosystem services extends far beyond pollination declines, however. If a system is defined by the *Merriam-Webster Collegiate Dictionary* as 'an organization forming a network especially for distributing something or serving a common purpose', the current global food system cannot be said to be effectively functioning. Presently, the world produces more than enough calories per day (2,700 kcal per person per day, above the required levels of 1,800–2,100 kcal per person per day). Yet nonetheless there are around 795 million people estimated to be chronically undernourished in 2012–2014, and food production levels in many regions of high food insecurity remain at the same level as they were in the 1960s (FAO, 2014). At the same time, global levels of obesity have more than doubled since 1980; in 2014, more than 1.9 billion adults, 18 years and older, were overweight. Of these, over 600 million were obese (www.who.int/mediacentre/factsheets/fs311/en/). Beyond counting calories, it is increasingly recognized that a food system must nourish, and not simply supply minimum levels of energy. Yet also over recent decades, a few major energy-dense cereals (maize, wheat and rice) and major oil crops such as soybeans have grown to dominate global diets. Food supplies worldwide have become more homogeneous and composed of processed food products, to the detriment of local, often better adapted and more nutritious food crops such as other cereals, root crops and diverse beans (Khoury et al., 2014). This is a trend that is impacting health in rapidly developing countries more quickly than projected (Kearney, 2010).

On an environmental level alone, there is cause to have considerable alarm at the level of impacts agricultural systems are imposing on the global environment. The amount of soil lost worldwide, according to the FAO, is 75 billion tons: it is estimated that soil is being lost at between 10 and 40 times the natural rate of replenishment at an estimated cost of up to $500 billion per year (Pimentel, 2006).

The current percentage of the earth's freshwater resources that are diverted to serve the agriculture sector is estimated at around 70%. More than half of the largest underground aquifers around the world are being used at rates that exceed sustainable replacement (Richey et al., 2015). One of the most wasteful trade-offs of high-input agriculture is the fate of agricultural chemicals into waterways. The application of agricultural chemicals to annual row crops is extremely 'leaky'; it is estimated that less than 15% of phosphorous applied to crops, and 40% of the nitrogen is actually absorbed by the plants; the rest remains either in soils or in waterways each year, contributing to the over 400 oceanic dead zones (Zielinski, 2014). It is a problem whose solution has remained elusive; even after 40 years of efforts by federal, state and local government in the United States, nationwide progress on controlling nutrient water pollution has not yet been achieved. Concentrations of nitrogen (N) and phosphorus (P) in streams and groundwater are 2 to 10 times higher than recommended to protect aquatic life (Dubrovsky et al., 2010).

Yet an investigation of the multiple problems of intensive high production agriculture also opens the door to understanding the role of biodiversity and ecosystem services in preventing such pollution, and the importance of 'learning from nature'. For example, the elevated nutrient levels as previously described are attributed to the historic land use change in the central United States from deep rooted, drought resistant prairies to row crop production of maize and soy. The required annual tillage and planting, the wide row crops, the amount and type of fertilizer inputs that is required by conventional production of maize, for example, means that much of the soil in maize fields has limited cover for over half of the year, and is then highly susceptible to water runoff, carrying off around 60% of the nitrogen applied (Porter et al., 2015). Solutions lie in the arena of developing agricultural production systems that mimic the ability of natural systems to maintain soil cover and sequester nutrients within the system. Indeed, studies are showing that the strategic re-integration of perennial grasses into this landscape in only 10% of row crop fields within a maize stand can reduce nitrogen in runoff water by 84% and phosphorus by 89% (Zhou et al., 2014).

The opposite side of challenges facing current agricultural systems is that in many parts of the developing world, conventional high-input agriculture has not taken – and has little chance to take – hold. In such regions, resource-poor farmers contend with issues of marginal high-risk environments, and experience poor yields just where food security is most vulnerable. The agricultural research establishment has only recently begun to focus increasingly on such sites, and to recognize that highly site-specific resource management systems are needed to sustain productivity under these conditions (Altieri, 2002).

Yet the approaches which can address both the heavy negative externalities of conventional production systems and the challenges of resource-poor farmers have a central common thread: they recognize that agriculture and food systems are biological and social systems. They can be designed to build upon and harness the forces of biodiversity and ecosystem services such that the processes that underpin agricultural production – soil fertility, natural pest control, pollination, water retention – are optimized and encouraged. Farming systems can be regenerative, building on and adding to natural capital, rather than being increasingly dependent upon external inputs that the system cannot absorb and more often than not end up as negative externalities. For example, farming practices that maintain complex food webs may have tremendous benefits for natural pest control, for pollination services, and for wild biodiversity on farms. Farming has traditionally never been a solitary operation, being carried out over millennia by communities of people. An ecosystem perspective recognizes that the regenerative aspects of agriculture occur on the level of whole farming system, at the watershed and/or landscape or community level, with the traditional knowledge and experience of farmers and empowerment of communities at its base. As such, it contributes also to building and strengthening the social capital underlying agriculture. Thus, it is critical in any formulation of the 'true costs of agriculture' to recognize that farming systems, well formulated, are capable of generating many positive externalities essential to human welfare, while minimizing the negative ones.

## Measures for conservation and management of pollination for agriculture

What does this have specifically to do with the importance of pollinators in agricultural biodiversity? With now more than 15 years of attention being applied to pollination services at the global level, in good part through the combined efforts of the IPI, there is now a strong evidence base for the importance of pollinators as an essential component of agricultural biodiversity, contributing in multiple ways to crop production. It is timely and appropriate that on the basis of the evidence provided, pollinators and pollination merit explicit conservation and management. Yet it is extremely unlikely that pollinators will be effectively conserved and protected by the farming community in isolation from harnessing the benefits of the whole suite of ecosystem services sustaining agriculture. It is in the totality of systems of agriculture that respect nature and promote the delivery of ecosystem services that measures to conserve pollinators will most effectively be employed. In the context of the IPI as coordinated by FAO, an inventory of site-specific measures to conserve and enhance pollination services to agriculture is being compiled. A few such measures are described as follows:

### *Soil management for ground-nesting bees*

The majority of the important crop pollinating bee species nest in the ground. Managing for ground-nesting bees is, therefore, a critical component of sustainable crop pollination. Management methods that induce bees to nest in soil have been extensively worked out for only a few bee species. For this reason, the most important recommendation for management is to protect existing nesting sites. Other measures include minimizing frequent, deep tilling, and avoiding flooding and other disturbances where nests may occur (Ullmann et al., 2016).

### *Promoting on-farm diversity: wildflower plantings next to crops*

Highbush blueberry was used as a model system to demonstrate the efficacy of using wildflower plantings adjacent to crop fields to increase the abundance of wild pollinators during crop bloom and enhance pollination and yield in the United States (Blaauw and Isaacs, 2014). Plantings were seeded with a mix of 15 perennial wildflower species that provided season-long bloom. The effect of these plantings was on wild bee populations: honeybees visiting blueberry flowers had similar abundance in enhanced and control fields in all four years of this study, whereas wild bee and syrphid abundance increased annually in the fields adjacent to wildflower plantings. The enhanced presence of wild bees significantly increased the percentage fruit set, berry weight and mature seeds per berry leading to higher crop yields; the associated increased revenue exceeded the cost of wildflower establishment and maintenance. More generalized guidance on promoting non-crop flowering plants in agro-ecosystems can be found in the upcoming publication (Gillespie et al., in press).

### *Shade trees and agroforestry benefits for pollinators*

While flowering strips may 'pull' pollinators into servicing adjacent crops, the temporal availability of floral resources could be critical to facilitating the persistence of key pollinators in ecosystems. Since agricultural crops are in general seasonal, the pollinator(s) on which they depend may be supported only for a short period in any given year. Hence, it is important to consider the flora available in the same location or region to understand how the pollinator populations survive in the 'off season'. In this respect, innovative systems of maintaining pollinator populations across time have been developed in the coffee and cardamom plantations of southern India. Both crops benefit from shade trees, and share common pollinators, but have relatively short blooming seasons at different times of the year. Farmers have developed managed agroforestry systems to create 'sequential blooms', planting a diversity of economically or domestically valuable trees to both provide shade and floral resources to pollinators in between the two crop blooming periods (Belavadi, in press).

## *Managing pollinator resources across landscapes and regions*

In many countries with a migratory beekeeping industry, colonies of managed honeybees are moved to farms during the pollination season. Outside the pollination season, beekeepers undertake practices that provide a honey flow, provide for colony build-up or trap swarms to replace bees that abscond or die. These practices require a good availability and accessibility of forage resources for the pollinators across wide geographic regions – that is, flowering plants supplying pollen (protein) and nectar (carbohydrates). Despite the importance of such resources to both crop and honey production, the assessment and deliberate management of these has rarely captured the attention of policymakers or landowners. The partners of the Global Pollination Project in South Africa, the South Africa National Biodiversity Institute, have undertaken the cause to raise awareness and document the seasonal and temporal importance of such resources, and the need to protect these for both wild and managed pollinators (Masehela et al., 2016).

## *Assessing pesticide risks to wild pollinators*

Increasing attention is being paid to the linkages between pesticide use and pollination services. Publications such as 'Assessing the risk of pesticides to wild pollinators' (van der Valk et al., 2013), and the companion guide on 'Pollination safety in agriculture' (Roubik, 2014) are examples of how practitioners are concerned about the issue and have requested guidance material from the FAO.

## Conclusions

The threats and risks that pollinators are facing are significant: ever greater agricultural intensification, loss of diversity in the field and amongst pollinator populations and greater levels of disturbance, including the application of external chemical inputs. Yet this worsening trend is not the only pathway to follow. Other alternative trajectories in which the negative externalities of high input, high output, high pollution agriculture are costed, and the positive externalities of ecosystem services rewarded, suggest a more sustainable alternative. This alternative trajectory is not a return to earlier, idealized eras, but rather proposes a process of transition to agro-ecological systems that are acknowledged as complex, requiring changes in practices that have the potential for greater diversification and which can be combined with an appreciation for the knowledge of farmers and for their ability to apply measures such as those described in earlier.

## References

Aizen, M. A., Garibaldi, L. A., Cunningham, S. A. and Klein, A. M. (2009) 'Long-term global trends in crop yield and production reveal no current pollination shortage but increasing pollinator dependency', *Current Biology*, vol. 18, pp. 1–4.

Aizen, M. A. and Harder, L. D. (2009) 'The global stock of domesticated honey bees is growing slower than agricultural demand for pollination', *Current Biology*, vol. 19, pp. 915–918.

Altieri, M. A. (2002) 'Agroecology: The science of natural resource management for poor farmers in marginal environments', *Agriculture, Ecosystems and Environment*, vol. 1971, pp. 1–24.

Batley, M. and Hogendoorn, K. (2009) 'Diversity and conservation status of native Australian bees', *Apidologie*, vol. 40, pp. 347–354.

Belavadi, V. V. (in press) 'Benefits of planning shade-tree cultivation to favour pollinators', in N. Azzu and B. Gemmill-Herren (eds.), *Towards Sustainable Crop Pollination*, FAO, Rome, Italy.

Blaauw, B. R. and Isaacs, R. (2014) 'Flower plantings increase wild bee abundance and the pollination services provided to a pollination-dependent crop', *Journal of Applied Ecology*, vol. 51, pp. 890–898.

Bommarco, R., Lundin, O., Smith, H. G. and Rundlof, M. (2011) 'Drastic historic shifts in bumble-bee community composition in Sweden', *Proceedings of the Royal Society B–Biological Sciences*, vol. 279, pp. 309–315.

Brittain, C., Kremen, C., Garber, A. and Klein, A.-M. (2014) 'Pollination and plant resources change the nutritional quality of almonds for human health', *PLoS ONE*, vol. 9, p. e90082.

Byrne, A. and Fitzpatrick, Ú. (2009) 'Bee conservation policy at the global, regional and national levels', *Apidologie*, vol. 40, pp. 194–210.

Cameron, S. D., Loziera, J. D., Strange, J. P., Koch, J. P., Cordesa, N., Solterd, L. F. and Griswold, T. L. (2011) 'Patterns of widespread decline in North American bumblebees', *Proceedings of the National Academy of Science USA*, vol. 108, pp. 662–667.

Chaplin-Kramer, R., Dombeck, E., Gerber, J., Knuth, K. A., Mueller, N. D., Mueller, M., Ziv, G. and Klein, A.-M. (2014) 'Global malnutrition overlaps with pollinator-dependent micro-nutrient production', *Proceedings of the Royal Society B–Biological Sciences*, vol. 281, p. 1794.

Convention on Biological Diversity (CBD) (2014) *Global Biodiversity Outlook 4*, Convention on Biological Diversity, Montréal, Canada.

Danforth, B. N., Sipes, S., Fang, J. and Brady, S. G. (2006) 'The history of early bee diversification based on five genes plus morphology', *Proceedings of the National Academy of Science USA*, vol. 103, pp. 15118–15123.

Dubrovsky, N. M., Burow, K. R., Clark, G. M., Gronberg, J. M., Hamilton, P. A., Hitt, K. J., Mueller, D. K., Munn, M. D., Nolan, B. T., Puckett, L. J., Rupert, M. G., Short, T. M., Spahr, N. E., Sprague, L. A. and Wilber, W. G. (2010) *The Quality of Our Nation's Waters: Nutrients in the Nation's Streams and Groundwater, 1992–2004*, U.S. Geological Survey Circular 1350, U.S. Geological Survey, Reston, VA, USA

Eardley, C. D., Gikungu, M. and Schwarz, M. P. (2009) 'Bee conservation in Sub-Saharan Africa and Madagascar: Diversity, status and threats', *Apidologie*, vol. 40, pp. 355–366.

Eilers, E. J., Kremen, C., Smith Greenleaf, S., Garber, A. K. and Klein, A.-M. (2011) Contribution of pollinator-mediated crops to nutrients in the human food supply', *PLoS ONE*, vol. 6, p. e21363.

FAO (2014) *The State of Food Insecurity in the World 2014*, FAO, Rome, Italy.

Foley, J. A., Ramankutty, N., Brauman, K. A., Cassidy, E. S., Gerber, J. S., Johnston, M., Mueller, N. D., O'Connell, C., Ray, D. K., West, P. C., Balzer, C., Bennett, E. M., Carpenter, S. R., Hill, J., Monfreda, C., Polasky, S., Rockström, J., Sheehan, J., Siebert, S., Tilman, D. and Zaks, D. P. (2011) 'Solutions for a cultivated planet', *Nature*, vol. 478, pp. 337–342.

Freitas, B. M., Imperatriz-Fonseca, V. L., Medina, L. M., de Matos Peixoto, A., Kleinert, L., Galetto, L., Nates-Parra, G., Javier, J. and Quezada-Euan, G. (2009) 'Diversity, threats and conservation of native bees in the Neo-tropics', *Apidologie*, vol. 40, pp. 332–346.

Gallai, N., Salles, J. M., Settele, J. and Vaissiere, B. (2009) 'Economic valuation of the vulnerability of world agriculture confronted with pollinator decline', *Ecological Economics*, vol. 68, pp. 810–821.

Garibaldi, L. A., Aizen, M. A., Cunningham, S. A. and Klein, A. M. (2009) 'Pollinator shortage and global crop yield: Looking at the whole spectrum of pollinator dependency', *Communicative and Integrative Biology*, vol. 2, pp. 37–39.

Garibaldi, L. A., Aizen, M. A., Klein, A. M., Cunningham, S. A. and Harder, L. A. (2011) 'Global growth and stability of agricultural yield decrease with pollinator dependence', *Proceedings of the National Academy of Sciences USA*, vol. 14, pp. 5909–5914.

Garibaldi, L. A., Carvalheiro, L. G., Vaissiere, B. E., Gemmill-Herren, B., Hipolito, J., Freitas, B. M., Ngo, H. T., Azzu, N., Saez, A., Astrom, J., An, J., Blochtein, B., Buchori, D., Garcia, F. J. C., Oliveira da Silva, F., Devkota, K., Ribeiro, M. d. F., Freitas, L., Gaglianone, M. C., Goss, M., Irshad, M., Kasina, M., Filho, A. J. S. P., Kiill, L. H. P., Kwapong, P., Parra, G. N., Pires, C., Pires, V., Rawal, R. S., Rizali, A., Saraiva, A. M., Veldtman, R., Viana, B. F., Witter, S. and Zhang, H. (2016) 'Mutually beneficial pollinator diversity and crop yield outcomes in small and large farms', *Science*, vol. 351, pp. 388–391.

Garibaldi, L. A., Steffan-Dewenter, I., Winfree, R., Aizen, M. A., Bommarco, R., Cunningham, S. A., Kremen, C., Carvalheiro, L. G., Harder, L. D., Afik, O., Bartomeus, I., Benjamin, F., Boreux, V., Cariveau, D., Chacoff, N. P., Dudenhöffer, J. H., Freitas, B. M., Ghazoul, J., Greenleaf, S., Hipólito, J., Holzschuh, A., Howlett, B., Isaacs, R., Javorek, S. K., Kennedy, C. M., Krewenka, K., Krishnan, S., Mandelik, Y., Mayfield, M. M., Motzke, I., Munyuli, T., Nault, B. A., Otieno, M., Petersen, J., Pisanty, G., Potts, S. G., Rader, R., Ricketts, T. H., Rundlöf, M., Seymour, C. L., Schüepp, C., Szentgyörgyi, H., Taki, H., Tscharntke, T., Vergara, C. H., Viana, B. F., Wanger, T. C., Westphal, C., Williams, N. and Klein, A. M. (2013) 'Wild pollinators enhance fruit set of crops regardless of honey bee abundance', *Science*, vol. 339, pp. 1608–1611.

Gemmill Herren, B. (ed.) (2016) *Pollination Services to Agriculture: Sustaining and Enhancing a Key Ecosystem Service*, Routledge, London and New York.

Gillespie, M. A. K., Wratten, S. and Waterhouse, B. (in press) 'Promoting non-crop flowering plants for specific insect pollinators', in N. Azzu and B. Gemmill-Herren (eds.), *Towards Sustainable Crop Pollination*, FAO, Rome, Italy.

Godfray, H. C. J., Beddington, J. R., Crute, I. R., Haddad, L., Lawrence, D., Muir, J. F., Pretty, J., Robinson, S., Thomas, S. M. and Toulmin, C. (2010) 'Food security: The challenge of feeding 9 billion people', *Science*, vol. 327, pp. 812–818.

Hogendoorn, K., Bartholomaeus, F. and Keller, M. A. (2010) 'Chemical and sensory comparison of tomatoes pollinated by bees and by a pollination wand', *Journal of Economic Entomology*, vol. 103, pp. 1286–1292.

IAASTD (2009) *Agriculture at a Crossroads, IAASTD International Assessment of Agricultural Knowledge, Science and Technology for Development: Global Report*, Island Press, Washington, DC, USA.

IUCN (2014) *Bad News for Europe's Bumblebees*, April 2, 2014. www.iucn.org/?14612/Bad-news-for-Europes-bumblebees

Kearney, J. (2010) 'Food consumption trends and drivers', *Philosophical Transactions of the Royal Society B–Biological Sciences*, vol. 365, pp. 2793–2807.

Khoury, C. K., Bjorkman, A. D., Dempewolf, H., Ramirez-Villegas, J., Guarino, L., Jarvis, A., Rieseberg, L. H. and Struik, P. C. (2014) 'Increasing homogeneity in global food supplies and the implications for food security', *Proceedings of the National Academy of Sciences USA*, vol. 111, pp. 4001–4006.

Klatt, B. K., Holzschuh, A., Westphal, C., Clough, Y., Smit, E. and Tscharntke, T. (2014) 'Bee pollination improves crop quality, shelf life and commercial value', *Proceedings of the Royal Society B–Biological Sciences*, vol. 281, p. 1775.

Klein, A.-M., Hendrix, S. D., Clough, Y., Scofield, A. and Kremen, C. (2014) 'Interacting effects of pollination, water and nutrients on fruit tree performance', *Plant Biology*, vol. 17, pp. 201–208.

Klein, A.-M., Vaissiere, B. E., Cane, J. H., Steffan, P., Dewenter, I., Cunningham, S. A., Kremen, C. and Tscharntke, T. (2007) 'Importance of pollinators in changing landscapes for world crops', *Proceedings of the Royal Society B–Biological Sciences*, vol. 274, pp. 303–313.

Lautenbach, S., Seppelt, R., Liebsher, J. and Dormann, C. F. (2012) 'Spatial and temporal trend of Global Pollination Benefit', *PLoS ONE*, vol. 7, p. 35954.

LeBuhn, G., Droege, S., Connor, E. et al. (2013) 'Detecting insect pollinator declines on regional and global scales', *Conservation Biology*, vol. 27, pp. 113–120.

MA (Millennium Ecosystem Assessment) (2005) *Ecosystems and Human Well-Being: Synthesis*, Island Press, Washington, DC, USA.

Martin, C. (2015) 'A re-examination of the pollinator crisis', *Current Biology*, vol. 25, pp. R811–R826.

Masehela, T., Poole, C. and Veldtman, R. (2016) 'Securing forage resources for indigenous managed honey bees – thoughts from South Africa', in N. Azzu and B. Gemmill-Herren (eds.), *Towards Sustainable Crop Pollination*, FAO, Rome, Italy.

Nieto, A., Roberts, S. P. M., Kemp, J., Rasmont, P., Kuhlmann, M., García Criado, M., Biesmeijer, J. C., Bogusch, P., Dathe, H. H., De la Rúa, P., De Meulemeester, T., Dehon, M., Dewul, A., Ortiz-Sánchez, F. J., Lhomme, P., Pauly, A., Potts, S. G., Praz, C., Quaranta, M., Radchenko, V. G., Scheuchl, E., Smit, J., Straka, J., Terzo, M., Tomozii, B., Window, J. and Michez, D. (2014) *European Red List of Bees*, Publication Office of the European Union, Luxembourg.

Oldroyd, B. P. and Nanork, P. (2009) 'Conservation of Asian honey bees', *Apidologie*, vol. 40, pp. 296–312.

Ollerton, J., Winfree, R. and Tarrant, S. (2011) 'How many flowering plants are pollinated by animals?', *Oikos*, vol. 120, pp. 321–326.

Pimentel, D. (2006) 'Soil erosion: A food and environmental threat', *Environment, Development and Sustainability*, vol. 8, pp. 119–137.

Porter, P. A., Mitchell, R. B. and Moore, K. J. (2015) 'Reducing hypoxia in the Gulf of Mexico: Reimagining a more resilient agricultural landscape in the Mississippi River Watershed', *Journal of Soil and Water Conservation*, vol. 70, pp. 63–68.

Rader, R., Bartomeus, I., Garibaldi, L. A., Garratt, M. P. D., Howlett, B. G., Winfree, R., Cunningham, S. A., Mayfield, M. M., Arthur, A. D., Andersson, G. K. S., Bommarco, R., Brittain, C., Carvalheiro, L. G., Chacoff, N. P., Entling, M. H., Foully, B., Freitas, B. M., Gemmill-Herren, B., Ghazoul, J., Griffin, S. R., Gross, C. L., Herbertsson, L., Herzog, F., Hipólito, J., Jaggar, S., Jauker, F., Klein, A. M., Kleijn, D., Krishnan, S., Lemos, C. Q., Lindström, S. A. M., Mandelik, Y., Monteiro, V. M., Nelson, W., Nilsson, L., Pattemore, D. E., Pereira, N. D., Pisanty, G., Potts, S. G., Reemer, M., Rundlöf, M., Sheffield, C. S., Scheper, J., Schüepp, C., Smith, H. G., Stanley, D. A., Stout, J. C., Szentgyörgyi, H., Taki, H., Vergara, C. H., Viana, B. F. and Woyciechowski, M. (2015) 'Non-bee insects are important contributors to global crop pollination', *Proceedings of the National Academy of Sciences USA*, vol. 113, pp. 146–151.

Richey, A. S., Thomas, B. F., Lo, M.-H., Famiglietti, J. S., Swenson, S. and Rodell, M. (2015) 'Uncertainty in global groundwater storage estimates in a total groundwater stress framework', *Water Resources Research*, vol. 51, pp. 5198–5216.

Roubik, D. W. (ed.) (2014) *Pollinator Safety in Agriculture*, FAO, Rome, Italy.

Royal Society of London (2009) *Reaping the Benefits: Science and the Sustainable Intensification of Global Agriculture*, Royal Society, London, UK.

Tanentzap, A. J., Lamb, A., Walker, S. and Farmer, A. (2015) 'Resolving conflicts between agriculture and the natural environment', *PLoS Biology*, vol. 13, p. 1002242.

Ullmann, K. S., Cane, J. H., Thorp, R. W. and Williams, N. M. (2016) 'Soil management for ground-nesting bees', in N. Azzu and B. Gemmill-Herren (eds.), *Towards Sustainable Crop Pollination*, FAO, Rome, Italy.

Van der Valk, H., Koomen, I., Nocelli, R., Ribeiro, M., Frietas, B., Carvalho, S., Kasina, M., Martins, D., Mutiso, M., Odhiambo, C., Kinuthia, W., Gikungu, M., Ngaruiay, P., Maina, G., Kipyap, P., Blacquière, T., van der Steen, S., Roessink, I., Wassenberg, J. and Gemmill-Herren, B. (2013) *Aspects Determining the Risk of Pesticides to Wild Bees: Risk Profiles for Focal Crops on Three Continents*, FAO, Rome, Italy.

Zhou, X., Helmers, M. J., Asbjornsen, H., Kolka, R., Tomer, M. D. and Cruse, R. M. (2014) 'Nutrient removal by prairie filter strips in agricultural landscapes', *Journal of Soil and Water Conservation*, vol. 69, pp. 54–64.

Zielinski, S. (2014) *Ocean Dead Zones Are Getting Worse Globally Due to Climate Change*, Smithsonian Institution, 10 November, www.smithsonianmag.com/science-nature/ocean-dead-zones-are-getting-worse-globally-due-climate-change-180953282/, accessed 9 June 2015.

# 8
# SOIL BIODIVERSITY

*Fenton Beed, Thomas Dubois, Daniel Coyne, Didier Lesueur and Srinivasan Ramasamy*

## Introduction

Soil is the most biologically diverse component of our global environment. Soil borne organisms directly influence ecosystem services, and hence crop-based agricultural productivity and sustainability (SP-IPM, 2012). Soil consists of beneficial organisms that confer an array of vital functions ranging from soil creation and texture, nutrient cycling, carbon sequestration, organic matter regulation and provision of natural enemies of crop pests and diseases. Conversely, soil also contains organisms that antagonize the production and quality of foods produced from crops, such as weeds, parasitic nematodes and insects, disease-causing bacteria and fungi and mycotoxin producers. Agricultural intensification, globalization, land use management, crop monocultures and the wide distribution of crop germplasm with narrow genetic diversity, creates negative selection pressures on soil biodiversity (Haddad et al., 2015; Tsiafouli et al., 2015). Climate change provides an additional selection pressure on soil borne genera, species, strains and populations by altering environmental parameters and the geographical redistribution of crops (Beed et al., 2015).

A plethora of complex interactions exists between organisms inhabiting soil, and these are exacerbated by the immense diversity of organisms present, many of which remain largely uncharacterized. This is especially true for soil microbes: of the 1 billion bacteria found in one gram of soil, fewer than 5% have been discovered and named, and for fungi, there are at least 1.5 million species with only 5% described. A typical, healthy soil contains hundreds of species of fungi and thousands of species of bacteria and Actinomycetes. It also contains a rich diversity of animals; microfauna (several species of protozoa, small nematodes, small unsegmented worms and tardigrades [eight-legged arthropods]), mesofauna (20–30 species of mites, Collembola [springtails] and dozens of species of larger nematodes) and macrofauna (several species of vertebrate animals, earthworms and millipedes and 50–100 species of insects, including ants, termites, beetles and flies). All faunal types play vital roles in different soil processes. For instance, macrofaunal insects and earthworms disrupt soil through their feeding and burrowing, and are important in mixing and redistributing organic matter and enhancing the aeration and structure of soil (Stork and Eggleton, 1992). Micro- and mesofaunas accelerate the decomposition of organic matter (from plants, animals and microbes) with the effect of increasing nutrient availability to crops (Wright et al., 1989). While more than 6,500 species of Collembola are recorded, most remain undescribed, but they are known to play a critical role in organic matter decomposition and soil microstructure formation and to be susceptible to losses in diversity (as for microbiota) as a result of acidification, nitrogen supply, climate change and intensive farming (Rusek, 1998). Oribatid mites are also extremely sensitive to soil disturbances and because of their long life span, low fecundity, slow development and low dispersion ability are of interest for bio-monitoring and as soil bio-indicators (Gulvik, 2007). The vast majority of the invertebrate species in agro-ecosystems belong to the phyla Arthropoda (especially insects), Annelida (segmented worms) and Nematoda. Ecologically, these animals are responsible for a complex web of direct and indirect interactions in foodwebs, whereby subtle changes in these interactions can dramatically modify impacts on plant productivity in agricultural systems (Cock et al., 2012).

To promote global recognition of the vast array of critical functions that soil biodiversity confers to agriculture and the well-being of our planet, the Food and Agriculture Organization of the United Nations (FAO) assigned 2015 as the International Year of Soils (**Figure 8.1** *The resilience of the food web is inextricably linked to the biodiversity within the soil*). A series of reports and awareness raising campaigns were undertaken which culminated in the publication of a report of the Status of the World's Soil Resources (FAO and ITPS, 2015). This current chapter highlights specific aspects of soil biodiversity, including microbial functions that enhance soil fertility, the impacts of agricultural practices on soil biodiversity, including a comparison of the effects of arthropod management using broad spectrum pesticides against integrated management options, and describes nematode biodiversity and its use as a soil health indicator. Finally, the evolving 'big data' research approach of combining different disciplines, analytical techniques and datasets to collectively characterize soil ecosystems is discussed (see also Endresen, Chapter 42 of this Handbook, for further perspectives on

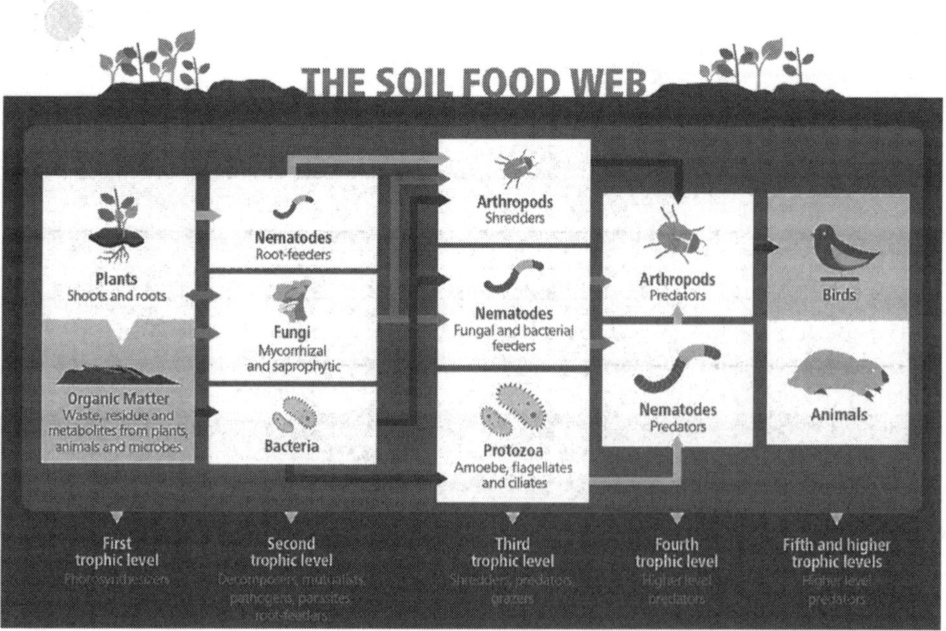


*Figure 8.1* The resilience of the food web is inextricably linked to the biodiversity within the soil

*Source*: Reproduced with permission from: Food and Agriculture Organization of the United Nations, 2015 International Year of Soil, Soils and Biodiversity www.fao.org/documents/card/en/c/43b565e7-57c2-43c6-b4f0-812091486ed3/

big data approaches), with a focus on ecosystem services and management of soil borne organisms that are pivotal to ensuring agricultural productivity and sustainability, and human health.

## What is soil?

Soil is the naturally occurring heterogeneous unconsolidated mineral and organic material at the earth's surface, and can be characterized in terms of its biological content, physical nature or chemical constituents. Soil organic matter (SOM) is largely confined to the horizons nearest the surface and is of particular importance for biological diversity, as it confers soil structure and aids retention of water, air and nutrients, and is particularly influenced by environmental conditions and land use management practices (Voroney and Heck, 2015). For instance, the utilization of cover crops with no tillage enriches SOM (and, in turn, soil biodiversity), while ploughing and other soil disturbances lead to its microbial degradation through greater exposure to oxygen.

## Microbes and soil fertility

Microorganisms contribute significantly to cycling/recycling of mineral nutrients and carbon in the soil and through their activities; nutrients can become more (through solubilization or mineralization) or less (through adsorption and immobilization) available to crops. Microbes mediate weathering of soils via exudation of organic acids and the solubilization of various forms of precipitated phosphorous (P). P-solubilizing bacteria may constitute up to 40% of the known cultivable population of soil bacteria (Chauhan et al., 2015). Nutrient availability, especially nitrogen (N), is modified by soil biota that predate bacteria and fungi, such as protozoa as well as collembola and nematodes. Basically, two main processes describe how soil microbes impact on plant productivity: (1) the transformation and mineralization by free-living microbes of natural and xenobiotic compounds and (2) direct effects on plants via microorganisms that form effective root-associations to enhance mineral nutrition of plants.

### *Free living microbes in soil*

Mineralization is the process by which soluble and insoluble organic matter is converted into inorganic forms available for plant uptake. The degradation of plant material and the development of SOM can be sequentially summarized as follows:

1. Easily degradable compounds such as soluble carbohydrates and proteins are broken down with about 50% of the carbon respired as $CO_2$, with the remainder being rapidly incorporated into new biomass.
2. Complex carbohydrates such as the plant structural polysaccharide cellulose are degraded. Bacteria of such genera as *Streptomyces*, *Pseudomonas* and *Bacillus* produce extracellular enzymes to break down this cellulose into smaller oligosaccharides composed of two or three glucose units, which are called cellobiose and cellotriose, respectively, and are readily degraded and then assimilated by plants as glucose monomers.
3. Resistant woody material – in particular, lignin – is degraded by Basidiomycete fungi and Actinomycete bacteria (e.g. *Streptomyces* spp.). However, less than 10% of the carbon in lignin is recycled into new microbial biomass.

N in soil is contained in dead organic matter and occurs as complex insoluble polymers, such as proteins, nucleic acids and chitin, which are degraded by microbial extracellular enzymes into dissolved organic N (DON). Free-living soil microorganisms either absorb DON, which can constitute a significant portion of the total soluble N pool, or it is mineralized by the microbial biomass, thereby liberating inorganic-N into the soil environment. Alternatively, after mineralization by microorganisms, plants can take up DON directly from soil in the form of amino acids (Schimel and Bennett, 2004). Terrestrial ecosystems are also occupied by N-free fixing bacteria, which can contribute to the N budget in some systems as they fix less than 3 kg of N $ha^{-1}$ $year^{-1}$.

## *Rhizosphere mediated interactions*

Bulk soil is known to have significantly less biodiversity than is found in the rhizosphere. The rhizosphere contains root carbon (C)-rich rhizo-deposits and chemical signals that selectively attract root-symbiotic microorganisms and provides substrates that drive community shifts. In other words, it means that plants select their rhizospheric microorganisms through the production of molecules by their roots. The composition of root exudates differs from one plant species to another and according to the stage of plant development, with direct effects on the associated microbial communities (Hinsinger et al., 2015). Most rhizospheric microorganisms are classified as plant growth-promoting rhizobacteria (PGPR) that enhance plant growth, alongside endophytic, associative, symbiotic or mutualistic associations (Pii et al., 2015). While only a few microorganisms, such as nodule-forming rhizobia and mycorrhizal fungi, have developed intimate symbiotic relationships with plants, they have proven to be incredibly effective with 5% to 20% (grassland and savannah) to 80% (temperate and boreal forests) of all N and up to 75% of P acquired annually by plants being provided through such relationships. Rhizobia fix atmospheric $N_2$ into ammonium-N, a function not developed by plants and similarly, mycorrhizae acquire P and potassium (K) that would otherwise be unavailable, in exchange for plant derived carbon (Perez-Montano et al., 2014). The most abundant forms of mycorrhizal fungi are the vesicular arbuscular mycorrhizal (VAM), the ectomycorrhizal (ECM) and the ericoid mycorrhizal fungi. VAM utilize the arbuscular mycorrhizal pathway to uptake soluble inorganic P, which involves unique cell types and transporters not available in the plant epidermis. VAM symbioses have been observed in a wide range of terrestrial plants (about 80%) such as pteridophytes, as well as most gymnosperms and angiosperms, including trees and shrubs. ECM form associations with tree species, dominating in northern temperate boreal and tropical forests with characteristically organic soils, and predominantly belong to Basidiomycete and Ascomycete fungi. ECM play a significant role in N acquisition in addition to P by virtue of the fact that N has been long considered as the main limiting nutrient in soil forest. However, this is changing with increasing levels of atmospheric N deposition (Smith et al., 2015). ECM are essential in N-limited communities of siliceous soils, for example heathland and macchia ecosystems as they provide amino acids to their plant partner. Both nodule-forming rhizobia and mycorrhizal fungi can co-exist to provide synergy and dual benefits for growth of, for example, certain tree legume species.

## *Negative impacts of soil biodiversity on nutrient availability*

Soil microorganisms can directly compete with plants for nutrients in the soil. Further, bacteria can reduce N availability by transforming it into more mobile forms such as nitrate (through nitrification) which is then prone to leaching (when compared with ammonium). Another microbial process that occurs under anaerobic conditions is denitrification, which is the transformation of N into gases. The impact on plant productivity is significant, and it has been estimated for tropical forests up to 50% of available N is lost through denitrification (Van Der Heijden et al., 2008). The application of synthetic inorganic fertilizer applications negatively impacts on the function of those microbes that cycle nutrients in soils. Repeated applications of inorganic fertilizer eventually lead to the reduced abundance of nutrient cycling organisms and can ultimately threaten their survival (Kamaa et al., 2011).

## Impact of agricultural practices

### *Soil biodiversity*

The importance of soil biodiversity to confer resilience to abiotic and biotic stress and the impact of different management practices on soil biodiversity has been reviewed (Brussaard et al., 2007; Cock et al., 2012). In general, high-input agriculture, particularly tilled systems with narrow crop rotation/short fallow management, led to decreased species richness and dominance of some species. In contrast, management characterized by rotations, no-tillage and organic amendments led to increased species richness and overall density. However, each agro-ecological system needs to be considered in detail and management options evaluated at both plot and landscape levels. O'Brien et al. (2016) found extreme heterogeneity in soil bacterial diversity and responses to agronomic practices at centimeter scale but that coherent patterns emerged at larger spatial scales. Thomson et al. (2015) investigated soil conditions and land use intensification effects on soil microbial communities across a range of European field sites and concluded that due to large gradients in soil variables, diversity of soil microbial communities were structured according to differences in soil conditions between the long-term observatories, more so than land use intensity. Information is lacking on the impact of the different inputs and land management on more specific groups such as the diazotrophic symbiotic bacteria, capable of fixing atmospheric nitrogen. Soybean forms nitrogen-fixing root nodules with diverse rhizobia, including a range of slow growing rhizobia referred to as bradyrhizobia, and nodulation is affected by several factors such as climate, biological, physical and chemical soil characteristics (Abaidoo et al., 2007). Herrmann et al. (2014) showed that the diversity of native rhizobia for soybean was more affected by season and residue application than by cropping system and nitrogen fertilizer application. Soil under mineral fertilization has even been shown to produce higher bradyrhizobia diversity when compared with organic fertilization (Bizarro et al., 2011). The combined effect of both organic inputs and chemical fertilizers has also been shown in other systems to enhance soil microbial diversity (Kamaa et al., 2011).

Live mulches play a significant role in enhancing soil biodiversity and in suppressing weeds, arthropod pests and plant pathogens. Lemanceau et al. (2015) showed microbial diversity was increased by cover crops (live mulch) through the enhancement of SOM. Earthworm biomass was shown to be seven times higher in maize when white clover was used as a mulch, and there were also significant increases in Collembola and microbial soil biomass (Hartwig and Ammon, 2002). A review by Kołota and Adamczewska-Sowińska (2013) revealed that onion thrips *(Thrips tabaci)* were significantly reduced on leek when grasses or white clover were deployed as mulch. Similarly, white clover as mulch suppressed cabbage aphids and moths while marigold live mulch reduced cabbage aphid and flea beetles. Tillage is also considered to be an effective way of reducing emerging pest populations, since it exposes the soil-dwelling life-stages to adverse environmental conditions, for example to kill pupae of *Heliothis* spp. However, tillage systems also remove the soil-dwelling natural predators of *Heliothis* adult moths. Conversely, Stinner and House (1990) showed that ants attacked the pre-pupae of the pest *H. zea* more frequently under no-tillage conditions than in ploughed soils. Hence, detailed studies are needed to understand the impacts of tillage on specific pests and their natural enemies across different environments and to understand how they are influenced by other land use management practices. This is because it is not just soil mediated agricultural practices that influence soil biodiversity but also above-ground practices, for example crop diversification. A four-year study replicated in China, Thailand and Vietnam showed that when nectar producing plants were cultivated as a border to rice fields, the abundance of detritivores (insects, fungi, bacteria, earthworms and nematodes) was increased (Gurr et al., 2016). Furthermore, this study reported that this form of crop diversification reduced insecticide applications by 70% and increased grain yield by 5% and profit by 7.5%.

## *Case study for arthropod pest management*

Insect and mite pests pose a significant and persistent threat to crop performance in the tropics, and the choice of method selected by farmers to mitigate these challenges impacts directly upon soil biodiversity.

### *Synthetic pesticides*

Farmers often respond through the indiscriminate application of chemical pesticides on a weekly or even daily basis, for example for control of eggplant fruit and shoot borer, whitefly, tomato fruit worm, diamondback moth and legume pod borer in South and Southeast Asia (review by Srinivasan, 2012; Schreinemachers et al., 2014). Such intensive pesticide use is highly detrimental, not only to the above-ground biodiversity, but also to the soil biodiversity and the services it confers (Chagnon et al., 2015). Adverse effects include direct toxicity, behavioral modification of organisms in the soil and altered prey-predator relationships, and studies have shown the persistence and accumulation of certain insecticides, for example neonicotinoids (Goulson, 2013). Neonicotinoids are translocated systemically and, because they persist in plant tissues, they may subsequently be incorporated into plant litter, and hence SOM. Thus, they can inhibit the ability of microbes and earthworms such as *Eiseniafetida* spp. to recycle nutrients (Pisa et al., 2015). Organochlorine and synthetic pyrethroid pesticide residues adversely affected soil microbial populations, especially for bacteria, in rice-vegetable production systems (Murugan et al., 2013). Further, pesticide applications have been shown to reduce nodulation and rhizobia populations in vegetable and grain legumes as reviewed by Kaur et al. (2015). However, flubendiamide and spinosad (a toxin derived from a soil-dwelling Actinomycete bacterium *[Saccharopolyspora spinosa]*, pesticide applications in peanut fields at recommended rates actually improved the activities of cellulase, invertase and amylase in soils (Mohiddin et al., 2015). An earlier study also confirmed that imidacloprid (a neonicotinoid) seed treatment had stimulatory effects on microbial enzyme activity for up to 60 days in peanuts (Singh and Singh, 2005). Hence, the effects of pesticides on soil microbes may vary from highly toxic to innocuous or even stimulatory, depending upon the pesticide group and dose, physical properties, and chemical and biological composition of the soil. Furthermore, microorganisms with appropriate degradative enzymes, such as bacteria *(Flavobacterium, Pseudomonas, Bacillus* and *Rhodococcus)* and fungi *(Aspergillus* and *Trichoderma)* can play an active role in degrading pesticides in the soil, for example for organophosphate, carbamate and neonicotinoid pesticides, especially under tropical conditions (Liu et al., 2011). The direct and indirect effects of indiscriminate applications of synthetic pesticides to above-ground crops on soil biodiversity cannot be underestimated, and we suggest that a greater focus is needed to generate data and to use this to sensitize policy-makers to create an enabling environment for rapid promotion of, access to, and commercialization of integrated pest management (IPM) technologies as alternatives.

### *Integrated technologies*

IPM practices that are specific to the target pest have far reduced negative impacts on soil biodiversity when compared with synthetic and broad-spectrum insecticides. An IPM strategy using sex pheromones to manage eggplant fruit and shoot borer in South Asia led to a 70% reduction in pesticide use in Bangladesh. Such a pesticide reduction allows common predators, including mantids, spiders, soil-dwelling earwigs and ants, to survive and kill the eggplant fruit borer and other pests (Alam et al., 2006). Similarly, when parasitoids, complemented by the biopesticide *Bacillus thuringiensis*, were used to control diamondback moth in brassicas, insecticide applications were reduced by 51% in Indonesia, 86% in Malaysia's highlands and 61% in the Philippines (review by Srinivasan, 2012), which in turn has significant impacts on soil biodiversity. For instance, the abundance of beneficial soil-dwelling predators (Coleoptera, Araneida, Hemiptera and Orthoptera) in the brassica IPM system in West Java, Indonesia, increased by up to 84%, and two genera of soil microorganisms (*Trichoderma* spp. and *Bacillus* spp.) that improve crop performance were also enhanced (Sastrosiswojo et al., 2001). Intercropping is an important cultural practice in IPM strategies, which not only reduces pest incidence, but also supports the build-up of natural enemy populations. When eggplant was intercropped with coriander, mint and marigold, with maize as the border crop, the diversity of natural enemies, including rove beetles (*Paederus* sp.), was increased (Sujayanand et al., 2015). Another study indicated that relay intercropping eggplant with garlic could be an ideal farming system to effectively enhance soil invertase, urease and alkaline phosphatase to improve soil nutrient content and fertility (Wang et al., 2014).

## Strategies for biological control

A key component of IPM is biological control. The soil's rich biodiversity offers the potential for the management of crop pests and diseases by promoting biological control to manipulate ecological equilibriums in favor of crop performance. The term 'biological control' encompasses several types of anthropogenic interventions to combat natural enemies: classical biological control (the introduction of natural enemies from a different geographic origin to control an exotic, invasive pest species), augmentative biological control (release of a large number of a previously mass-reared natural enemies in the environment) and conservation biological control (manipulation of the environment to increase the fitness of indigenous natural enemies without introducing them; see Chapter 6 of this Handbook by Gurr et al.). Augmentative biological control is further subdivided into inoculative (release of natural enemies that will persist in the environment by self-replication for a certain time span) and inundative (application of natural enemies for immediate action within the lifespan of the released natural enemy), with inundative biological control products often called biopesticides (Eilenberg et al., 2001). Classical biological control will not be further considered, as most applications of classical biological control relate to release of non soil borne parasitoids.

### *Augmentative biological control*

There is an evolving market for use of soil borne microbes for augmentative biological control. Worldwide, 195 strains of microbes have been registered as active ingredients of biopesticides, many originating from soils, and these have been commercialized into 780 different products. Most of these strains compose only a few species of bacteria (especially *Bacillus thuringiensis* and *Pseudomonas* spp.) and fungi (especially *Beauveria* spp., *Metarhizium* spp., *Verticillium lecanii*, *Paecilomyces* spp. and *Trichoderma* spp.). Products based on viruses are far less common, as they are more difficult to manage. However, some products based on strains of baculoviruses are available. While microbial biopesticides capture less than 1% (~ USD 400 million per year) of the worldwide pesticide market, demand is growing at a rate five times greater than that of 3% for synthetic pesticides (Beed et al., 2011b). Efficacy of inoculative biological control in soil is highly dependent on the influence of several soil biotic and abiotic factors. Simple experiments can demonstrate the direct influence of agricultural practices, such as selection of crop species and cultivars and fertilizer applications, on the relative profile and diversity of organisms in crop rhizospheres. This was demonstrated for communities of bacteria and fungi in studies using PCR-DGGE to understand factors responsible for the observed differential impact of a microbial soil borne fungal biological control agent *(Fusarium oxysporum* f.sp. *strigae)* against its host *Striga hermonthica*, a parasitic weed of cereals (Beed et al., 2007). This phenomenon is explained by direct impacts of fertilizer on microbial profiles, because plant species- and variety-specific secondary metabolites secreted as root exudates into the rhizosphere act as drivers for microbial community structures.

While interactions between introduced biocontrol agents and other soil microorganisms have typically focused on assessing effects of specific microorganisms or microbial groups on the introduced biological control agent, some studies have investigated impacts on whole communities of soil microorganisms. Bae and Knudsen (2005) found that hyphal growth and biocontrol efficacy of *Trichoderma harzianum* was significantly inhibited in soil containing higher carbon levels; microbial competition with native biota in soil favors a shift from hyphal growth to sporulation in *T. harzianum*, reducing its biological control efficacy. In general, higher levels of microbial soil biomass result in increased interactions between inoculated biological control agents and native soil biota, reducing the growth and/or efficacy of the introduced biological control agent. This can be caused by niche occupation, that is biocontrol agents occupy the same niche as naturally occurring soil microbes (Eastburn and Butler, 1988), production of volatile components by native soil biota that inhibit introduced biological control agents (Mackie and Wheatley, 1999), antibiotic production or competition for nutrients (Fravel, 1988).

The effect of inoculative biocontrol agents on native soil biota is less studied. In a laboratory study, White et al. (1994) introduced a genetically modified *Pseudomonas fluorescens* in soil to test the effect on the diversity of the indigenous microflora. Depending on soil structure and pore size, *P. fluorescens* caused a short-term reduction in the overall microbial diversity. Similarly, Gasoni et al. (2008) demonstrated that the metabolic diversity of the soil bacterial community decreased when *Trichoderma harzianum* was used to combat *F. oxysporum* f.sp. *nicotianae* in tobacco. This decrease presumably was the result of *T. harzianum* favoring growth of selected functional groups within the soil, thereby reducing soil microflora richness.

In contrast, examples are known whereby introduction of biological control agents had a positive impact on the native soil biota. Again taking biological control of *Striga hermonthica* as an example, studies surprisingly showed that when the soil borne fungal biological control agent was inundatively introduced in large populations into soil used for maize cultivation, ammonia-oxidizing Achaea responsible for nitrogen cycling and also total prokaryotic communities were promoted, thus mitigating fears that artificial increases in density of any given microbe would disrupt the function of others (Musyoki et al., 2015). Bae and Knudsen (2005) found that the addition of *T. harzianum* formulated onto alginate pellets into soil resulted in a higher population density of total bacteria compared with untreated controls; however, it may be that the pellets themselves provided nutrient sources for other soil microorganisms and *T. harzianum* merely released these nutrients from their substrate through hyphal degradation. Using the same model organisms, Bae and Knudsen (2004) found that application of *T. harzianum* added to soil to control the pathogen *Sclerotinia sclerotiorum* increased populations of the fungivorous nematode *Aphelenchoides* spp., indicating that fungivorous nematodes may be a significant biotic constraint on activity of biocontrol fungi in the field because the biological control agent is predated upon.

## Conservation biological control

Natural, undisturbed and biodiversity rich soils are often resistant to introduced biocontrol agents due to abiotic or biotic factors (Hadar et al., 1984). An alternative to introducing biological control organisms is manipulating existing, native biological control organisms through conservation biological control. Microbes in conservation biological control receive much less attention, yet their importance cannot be overestimated. Most soil microbial taxa that show biological control activity are not as yet amendable to mass production and commercialization. The order Entomophthorales solely comprises fungi that are highly specialized and important pathogens of insects, such as *Pandora neoaphidis*, an important aphid-specific fungal pathogen in temperate agro-ecosystems. However, their complex sexual reproduction does not render them suitable to artificial mass production. Equally, Microsporidia, a highly specialized group of fungi, primarily infect insect hosts but often have a complex life cycle involving multiple hosts and both asexual and sexual reproduction. However, a clear shift is noticeable from microbial biopesticide use towards use of the vast, yet untapped, potential of microbes in conservation biological control. In other words, researchers and practitioners are seeing the benefit of using cultural practices to boost conservation of naturally occurring biological control. Elucidation of their role and influence of complex interactions role is becoming possible using micro- and macro-arrays, metagenomic and proteomic evaluations (Renella et al., 2014; Mueller and Sachs, 2015). More knowledge of soil microbial biodiversity, soil ecology and complex mutual interactions will advance the management of pests and pathogens that damage our crops, and better promote soil-based conservation biological control (Beed et al., 2011b).

An example of an organism well suited for conservation biological control is *Trichoderma* spp. This commonly used biological control fungus exploits numerous strategic mechanisms to facilitate the effective control of soil borne pests and disease. These include high ecological competitive vigor to exploit available space and nutrients, the production of antifungal metabolites and antibiotics, mycoparasitism and the induction of localized or systemic plant defense responses through promotion of plant produced ethylene or terpenoid phytoalexins (Harman et al., 2004a, b). The beneficial effects of *Trichoderma* spp. extend beyond the soil ecosystem as the fungus aids in the maturation of compost for natural fertilizer production and is used to produce cellulase enzymes to improve brewing and fruit juice production, livestock and pet food digestibility, paper and pulp treatment and bioremediation through degradation of pollutants (Harman et al., 2004a; Kubicek et al., 2009).

Research into mechanisms of action of microbes for biological control is still in its infancy. For example, research into *Trichoderma* spp. has mainly focused on its biological control properties, and this has led to selection of mainly good plant rhizosphere colonizing strains as selection criterion when recovering strains from nature. However, many of these strains possess useful traits beyond biological control, and currently *Trichoderma* spp. are being used as an active ingredient in a range of agricultural products (biopesticides, bioinoculants, biofertilizers, plant strengthening agents and plant protectants) in 60 countries on virtually all groups of agricultural plants (Lorito et al., 2010). However, studies have confirmed that agricultural interventions influence *Trichoderma* spp. biodiversity. Maina et al. (2015) showed that intensified use of land in Kenya can reduce *Trichoderma* spp. occurrence and diversity, especially for irrigated fields.

Within conservation biological control, so-called 'soil conduciveness/suppressiveness' is an interesting phenomenon. Certain soils are known to be less conducive to the proliferation of certain soil borne pests and diseases, a condition termed 'soil suppressiveness'. Two types of suppressiveness have been characterized: 'general suppression', which owes its activity to the total microbial biomass in soil and is not transferable between soils, and 'specific suppression', which owes its activity to the effects of individual or select groups of microorganisms and is therefore more easily transferred. One of the best described examples of specific suppression occurs from the buildup of fluorescent *Pseudomonas* spp. in take-all (caused by *Gaeumannomyces graminis* var. *tritici*) decline soils through the production of the antifungal metabolite 2,4-diacetylphloroglucinol (Weller et al., 2002). Again, agricultural interventions can have a profound effect on soil suppressiveness. The antibiotic-producing *Trichoderma koningii* presents an especially interesting example: using ammonium sulfate as a nitrogen fertilizer, specific suppression of take-all disease was increased, yet the general level of microbial activity was decreased. The repeated application of ammonium sulfate had resulted in acidification, providing an environment highly favorable to *T. koningii*. When soils were treated with lime, both the activity of *T. koningii* and suppression of take-all were reduced (Simon and Sivasithamparam, 1989).

## Role of nematodes: antagonists, beneficial and soil health indicators

The health of a soil in terms of agricultural productivity and sustainability can be evaluated by monitoring sentinel taxa or key bioindicators, and currently nematodes are receiving particular attention to serve this role (Ferris et al., 2001; Wilson and Kakouli-Duarte, 2009). Nematodes (roundworms) are the most numerous Metazoa on earth and in soil are relatively abundant. As a virtue of their relatively short life cycle, nematodes are able to respond to environmental perturbations, food availability and recovery. They can exist either independently or as parasites of plants or animals.

Plant-pathogenic nematodes are either endoparasitic or ectoparasitic depending on their feeding mode. They may be highly polyphagous, such as *Meloidogyne* spp. (root-knot nematodes), which creates difficulties for their control, or highly host-specific, for example *Heterodera* spp. Any given crop, however, can be infected by a range of nematode profiles. Jones et al. (2013) recently classified plant-parasitic nematodes in relation to their threat to crop production, based on scientific and global economic importance, with root-knot nematodes (*Meloidogyne* spp.) regarded as the most damaging genus and arguably the single greatest biotic threat to crop production across cropping systems. By contrast, beneficial entomopathogenic nematodes (EPNs) and mollusc-parasitizing nematodes are being increasingly exploited for agricultural profit such as through their successful implementation for the control of the vine weevil *(Otiorhynchus sulcatus)* in ornamentals or field grown strawberries (Haukeland and Lola-Luz, 2010) and the grey field slug *(Deroceras reticulatum)* in vegetables (Rae et al., 2009). As with plant-parasitic nematodes, beneficial nematodes vary in terms of their host-specificity and sensitivity to climate and ecology and tend to be best adapted to the agro-ecologies from which they were recovered. They essentially belong to two families, Steinernematidae and Heterorhabditidae (Nguyen and Hunt, 2007), and vector entomopathogenic bacteria, which are the cause of host death through septicaemia, rendering nutrients accessible to nematodes. Once nutrients become depleted, nematodes depart the cadaver in search of new hosts, or survive in the soil in resting states. In less developed countries, knowledge of indigenous nematode species is at best very limited, but even cursory surveys can turn up a wealth of new findings (e.g. Kanga et al., 2012).

Nematodes are particularly well suited to soil health analyses due to their varied but critically important functions, and because of their relative ease of recovery, morphological identification and enumeration by standardized procedures (Coyne et al., 2014). A number of identity-independent indices have been developed, which are based largely on species richness and species diversity.

*Table 8.1* Colonizer-persister (c-p) value assignments for selected nematode families

| *c-p value* | *Family* |
|---|---|
| 1 | Rhabditidae, Diplogasteridae (s.l.), Panagrolaimidae, Bunonematidae |
| 2 | Cephalobidae, Plectidae, Monhysteridae, Aphelenchoididae |
| 3 | Teractocephalidae, Chromadoridae, Diptheroophoridae, Prismatolaimidae |
| 4 | Alaimidae, Mononchidae, Leptonchidae, Qudsianematidae, Dorylaimidae |
| 5 | Aporcelaimidae, Actinolaimidae, Thornenematidae, Belondiridae |

*Source*: Bongers and Bongers (1998).

Analysis of nematode communities as indicators for environmental monitoring of terrestrial communities stems from simple indices by trophic group into the use of diversity indices and the development of a maturity index (MI) – a measure of the ecological successional status, with classification of nematode families along a colonizer-persister (cp) continuum (Bongers, 1990;, Freckman and Ettema, 1993) and cp-scaling into a matrix classification of functional guilds (Bongers and Bongers, 1998; Ferris et al., 2001) (**Table 8.1** *Colonizer-persister (c-p) value assignments for selected nematode families*). While the specific objectives of a particular cropping system may influence which index to use, disagreement persists on which is optimal, although Shannon's diversity index remains the most commonly used (Neher and Darby, 2009). To increase practicality and cost efficiency, only those nematode sentinel species or taxa should be selected that are most sensitive to agro-ecological conditions of interest (Neher et al., 2004). However, Neher and Darby (2009) showed that the influence of different soil types and land use management practices on the pattern of nematode diversity was dependent on the level of resolution used; species, genus, family and trophic levels. This can be further complicated due to predation and competition from other trophic groups, such as fungi and bacteria. Progress in the development of molecular diagnostic tools has simplified such trophic diversity characterizations (Floyd et al., 2002; Zhang et al., 2014) to enable monitoring and guide remediation recommendations.

## Biodiversity and ecosystem services

The previous sections provide examples of how soil borne bacteria, archaea, fungi, arthropods and nematodes influence crop productivity and how they can be used as indicators of soil health. There are several beneficial interactions, for example symbiotic nitrogen fixing nodulating bacteria or mycohrrizhal fungi, pest control by entomopathogenic or biological control agents, and there are antagonistic effects, for example, due to organisms that cause crop disease. Furthermore, soil is the source for organisms that live as endophytes in plants, and any given plant can host hundreds. The importance of endophytes is demonstrated by plant species and their symbiotic fungi being able to collectively survive 50°C soils near geothermal vents, although neither the plants nor the fungi could tolerate soil temperatures of 40°C. This has led to the enrichment of rice with endophytes selected to tolerate climate change, that is, drought, salinity and temperature extremes (Redman et al., 2011). However, it is appreciated that getting endophytes into seeds and regulating their growth under differing environmental conditions will be problematic. There is also interest in identifying and exploiting naturally occurring and ubiquitous organisms that confer a generally conducive environment to the productivity of most crops. Progress has been made through focusing on model systems, such as *Pseudomonas* spp. and *Bacillus* spp., which have shown that *Pseudomonas* is better adapted to humid environmental conditions, whereas *Bacillus* predominates in more arid environments, but with consistently beneficial impacts to crop performance (Köberl et al., 2011; Mendes et al., 2012). There is also evidence that combinations of soil borne organisms can ensure universal crop productivity, for example soils suppressive to certain plant pathogens consist of similar sets of organisms (Mendes et al., 2013).

Other studies have focused beyond individual species and groups of organisms and on biodiversity as a whole as a measure of soil health for crop performance. There are anecdotal reports of increased biodiversity leading to increased functional redundancy (allowing previously non-prominent species to fulfill functional roles as a result of being better adapted to environmental conditions incurred due to changes in land management practices or climate). Functional redundancy is assumed to facilitate environmental integrity, provision of ecosystem services and ecosystem resilience, which in turn enhances sustainable agricultural productivity despite changes in climate (Beed et al., 2011b, 2015). The richness of microbial diversity below-ground has even been proposed as a predictor of above-ground plant diversity and productivity, based on the assumption that below-ground diversity acts as insurance for maintaining crop productivity under changing environmental conditions (Wagg et al., 2014). However, there are also studies that show no relationship between plant productivity and the diversity of soil borne organisms, and hence there is a need to more clearly define parameters – crop, soil and environment – to further elucidate whether it is increased biodiversity or specific organisms that are of the utmost importance.

The reality is that the potential is massive, and yet our knowledge remains in its infancy for two main reasons: (1) the vast complexity of soil biodiversity (e.g. up to a billion microbes residing in a single pinch or gram of soil) and (2) due to the limited characterization of soil borne biodiversity, mainly because of technical difficulties in applying analytical methods. For example, it is estimated that only 1% of total microbial diversity can be cultured outside of the soil in pure cultures under laboratory conditions and is thus amenable to characterization. However, the evolution of new methods has enabled research efforts to better characterize and potentially engineer agricultural ecosystems using 'big data' that encompasses biodiversity and functionality (Mendes et al., 2013; Renella et al., 2014; Mueller and Sachs, 2015). Methods include comparative metagenomic analysis and stable isotope probing to track plant derived carbon into microbial nucleic acids, proteomic, metabolomic and transcriptomic analyses (Berg et al., 2014). Further, engineers and computational biologists are developing better ways to manage large data sets and to merge disparate results into cohesive models to elucidate changes in the 'phytobiome'. The phytobiome consists of organisms that engage in intimate and often highly co-evolved interactions with the plant, and with one another, and with the environment (and especially the soil due to its high biodiversity), with significant consequences on crop performance, and for larger-scale ecosystem processes such as nutrient cycling and soil carbon sequestration (**Figure 8.2** *Phytiobiome: dynamic and multi-trophic interactions between plants, other organisms and the environment*). It is envisioned that characterization of the phytobiome will help to decipher the myriad of biological interactions, chemical signals and activation patterns in the rhizosphere and the influence of physical factors such as soil type, temperature, water, pH, salinity and pesticides. This information is required to understand and manage agricultural ecosystems to promote soil borne organisms beneficial to crop performance and to mitigate those that are detrimental. Crop breeding programs can select for lines that acquire and maintain naturally occurring or introduced beneficial soil borne organisms. Agronomic and land use management practices can be identified and recommended that promote interactions beneficial to sustainable crop productivity. The success of these interventions will be assessed against the

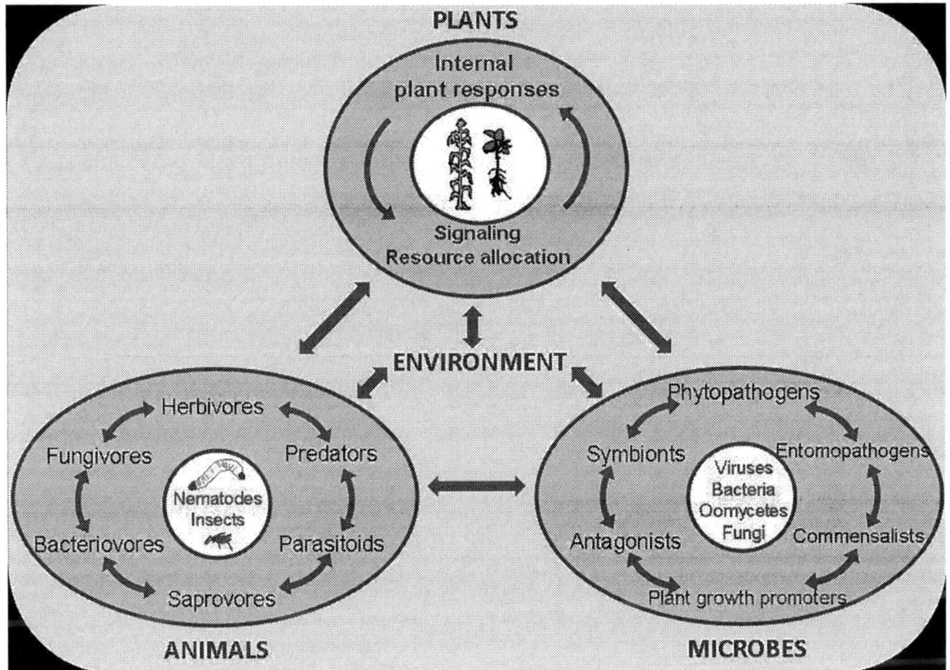


*Figure 8.2* Phytiobiome: dynamic and multi-trophic interactions between plants, other organisms and the environment

*Source*: Reproduced with permission from Gwyn A. Beattie of Phytobiomes Initiative, www.Phytobiomes.org.

background of activation patterns and induction pathways that differ between environments, crop types and species, strains and populations of soil borne organisms. In addition, true and opportunistic microbial human pathogens also inhabit the rhizosphere and can be introduced to humans through crop-based foods, so these also need to be managed in the soil and during harvest. Wall et al. (2015) reviewed links between human health and soil biodiversity and concluded that human diseases caused by soil borne pathogens were suppressed by increased soil biodiversity. Further, they stated that increased soil biodiversity resulted in the stabilization of soils and ecosystems, prevented erosion and pollution and therefore benefited human health by providing nutrients from agriculture, clean air and water. Wall et al. (2015) concluded that poor land management and climate change posed a critical threat to soil biodiversity, and hence human health.

The need for sustainable land management practices and enabling environmental policies is being promoted by the Global Soil Biodiversity Initiative (https://globalsoilbiodiversity.org) through coordination of scientific societies and global efforts to share knowledge on soil biodiversity and ecosystem services. The sustainable production of any given crop or cropping system in each environment is dependent on the functioning of specific soil borne organisms. This can be achieved through management practices to promote existing organisms and through the introduction of critically important organisms from elsewhere. This requires global databases and archived living reference collections combined with an enabling policy and technical environment to facilitate characterization, access and sharing of soil borne organisms (Beed, 2011a).

## References

Abaidoo, R. C., Keyser, H. H., Singleton, P. W., Dashiell, K. E. and Sanginga, N. (2007) 'Population size, distribution and symbiotic characteristics of indigenous *Bradyrhizobium* spp. that nodulate TGx soybean genotypes in Africa', *Applied Soil Ecology*, vol. 35, pp. 57–67.

Alam, S. N., Hossain, M. I., Rouf, F. M. A., Jhala, R. C., Patel, M. G., Rath, L. K., Sengupta, A., Baral, K., Shylesha, A. N., Satpathy, S., Shivalingaswamy, T. M., Cork, A. and Talekar, N. S. (2006) *Implementation and Promotion of an IPM Strategy for Control of Eggplant Fruit and Shoot Borer in South Asia*, Technical Bulletin No. 36. AVRDC publication number 06–672, AVRDC–The World Vegetable Center, Shanhua, Taiwan.

Bae, Y. S. and Knudsen, G. R. (2004) 'Influence of a fungus-feeding nematode on growth and biocontrol efficacy of *Trichoderma harzianum*', *Phytopathology*, vol. 91, pp. 301–306.

Bae, Y. S. and Knudsen, G. R. (2005) 'Soil microbial biomass influence on growth and biocontrol efficacy of *Trichoderma harzianum*', *Biological Control*, vol. 32, pp. 236–242.

Beed, F. (2011a) 'The impact of climate change on countries' interdependence for microbial genetic resources for agriculture', chapter 5 pp. 38–58 and 74–78, in *Background Study Paper No. 48*, Food and Agriculture Organization of the United Nations (FAO), Rome, Italy, ftp://ftp.fao.org/docrep/fao/meeting/017/ak532e.pdf

Beed, F., Benedetti, A., Cardinali, G., Chakraborty, S., Dubois, T., Garrett, K. and Halewood, M. (2011b) *Climate Change and Microorganism Genetic Resources for Food and Agriculture: State of Knowledge, Risks and Opportunities*, Background Study Paper no. 47, FAO, Rome, Italy.

Beed, F., Benedetti, A., Cardinali, G., Chakraborty, S., Dubois, T., Garrett, K. and Halewood, M. (2015) 'Micro-organism genetic resources for food and agriculture and climate change', pp. 87–101 in *Coping With Climate Change: The Roles of Genetic Resources for Food and Agriculture*, FAO, Rome, Italy.

Beed, F., Hallet, S. G., Venne, J. and Watson, A. (2007) 'Biocontrol using *Fusarium oxysporum*: A critical component of integrated *Striga* management', pp. 283–301 in G. Ejeta and J. Gressel (eds.), *Integrating New Technologies for Striga Control: Towards Ending the Witch-Hunt*, World Scientific Publishing Co. Pte Ltd, Singapore.

Berg, G., Grube, M., Schloter, M. and Smalla, K. (2014) 'Unraveling the plant microbiome, looking back and future perspectives', *Frontiers in Microbiology*, vol. 5, pp. 1–10.

Bizarro, M. J., Giongo, A., Vargas, L. K., Roesch, L. F. W., Gano, K. A., Saccol de Sá, E. L., Passaglia, P. L. M. and Selbach, P. A. (2011) 'Genetic variability of soybean bradyrhizobia populations under different soil managements', *Biology and Fertility of Soils*, vol. 47, pp. 357–362.

Bongers, T. (1990) 'The maturity index: An ecological measure of environmental disturbance based on nematode species composition', *Oecologia*, vol. 83, pp. 14–19.

Bongers, T. and Bongers, M. (1998) 'Functional diversity of nematodes', *Applied Soil Ecology*, vol. 10, pp. 239–251.

Brussaard, L., de Ruiter, P. C. and Brown, G. C. (2007) 'Soil biodiversity for agricultural sustainability', *Agriculture, Ecosystems and Environment*, vol. 121, pp. 233–244.

Chagnon, M., Kreutzweiser, D., Mitchell, E. A. D., Morrissey, C. A., Noome, D. A. and Van Der Sluijs, J. P. (2015) 'Risks of large-scale use of systemic insecticides to ecosystem functioning and services', *Environmental Science and Pollution Research*, vol. 22, pp. 119–134.

Chauhan, H., Bagyaraj, D. J., Selvakumar, G. and Sundaram, S. P. (2015) 'Novel plant growth promoting rhizobacteria: Prospects and potential', *Applied Soil Ecology*, vol. 95, pp. 38–53.

Cock, M. J. W., Biesmeijer, J. C., Cannon, R. J. C., Gerard, P. J., Gillespie, D., Jiménez, J. J., Lavelle, P. M. and Raina, S. K. (2012) 'The positive contribution of invertebrates to sustainable agriculture and food security', *CAB Reviews*, vol. 7, pp. 1–27.

Coyne, D., Nicol, J. and Claudius-Cole, A. (2014) *Practical Plant Nematology: A Field and Laboratory Guide*, International Institute of Tropical Agriculture, Ibadan, Nigeria.

Eastburn, D. M. and Butler, E. E. (1988) 'Microhabitat characterization of Trichoderma harzianum in natural soil: evaluation of factors affecting population density', *Soil Biology and Biochemistry*, vol. 20, pp. 541–545.

Eilenberg, J., Hajek, A. and Lomer, C. (2001) 'Suggestions for unifying the terminology in biological control', *Biocontrol*, vol. 4, pp. 387–400.

FAO and ITPS (Intergovernmental Technical Panel on Soils) (2015) *Status of the World's Soil Resources (SWSR): Main Report*, FAO, Rome, Italy, ffile:///D:/Documents/Library/FAO%20status%20of%20the%20World's%20Soil%20Resources%202015%20year%20of%20soils.pd

Ferris, H., Bongers, T. and De Goede, R. G. M. (2001) 'A framework for soil food web diagnostics: Extension of the nematode faunal analysis concept', *Applied Soil Ecology*, vol. 18, pp. 13–29.

Floyd, R., Abebe, E., Papert, A. and Blaxter, M. (2002) 'Molecular barcodes for soil nematode identification', *Molecular Ecology*, vol. 11, pp. 839–850.

Fravel, D. R. (1988) 'Role of antibiosis in the biocontrol of plant diseases', *Annual Review of Phytopathology*, vol. 26, pp. 75–91.

Freckman, D. W. and Ettema, C. H. (1993) 'Assessing nematode communities in agroecosystems of varying human intervention', *Agriculture, Ecosystems and Environment*, vol. 45, pp. 239–261.

Gasoni, L., Khan, N., Yokoyama, K., Chiessa, G. H. and Kobayashi, K. (2008) 'Impact of *Trichoderma harzianum* biocontrol agent on functional diversity of soil microbial community in tobacco monoculture in Argentina', *World Journal of Agricultural Sciences*, vol. 4, pp. 527–532.

Goulson, D. (2013) 'An overview of the environmental risks posed by neonicotinoid insecticides', *Journal of Applied Ecology*, vol. 50, pp. 977–987.

Gulvik, A. E. (2007) 'Mites (acari) as indicators of soil biodiversity and land use monitoring: A review', *Polish Journal of Ecology*, vol. 55, pp. 415–440.

Gurr, G. M., Lu, Z., Zheng, X., Xu, H., Zhu, P., Chen, G., Yao, X., Cheng, J., Zhu, Z., Catindig, J. L., Villareal, S., Van Chien, H., Cuong, L. Q., Channoo, C., Chengwattana, N., Lan, L. P., Hai, L. H., Chaiwong, J., Nicol, H. I., Perovic, D. J., Wratten, S. D. and Heong, K. L. (2016) 'Multi-country evidence that crop diversification promotes ecological intensification of agriculture', *Nature Plants*, vol. 2, pp. 1–4.

Hadar, Y., Harman, G. E. and Taylor, A. G. (1984) 'Evaluation of *Trichoderma koningii* and *T. harzianum* from New York soils for biological control of seed rot caused by *Pythium* spp.', *Phytopathology*, vol. 74, pp. 106–110.

Haddad, N. M., Brudvig, L. A., Clobert, J., Davies, K. F., Gonzalez, A., Holt, R. D., Lovejoy, T. E., Sexton, J. O., Austin, M. P., Collins, C. D., Cook, W. M., Damschen, E. I., Ewers, R. M., Foster, B. L., Jenkins, C. N., King, A. J., Laurance, W. F., Levey, D. J., Margules, C. R., Melbourne, B. A., Nicholls, A. O., Orrock, J. L., Song, D. X. and Townshend, J. R. (2015) 'Habitat fragmentation and its lasting impact on Earth's ecosystems', *Science Advances*, vol. 1, pp. 1–9.

Harman, G. E., Howell, C. R., Viterbo, A., Chet, I. and Lorito, M. (2004a) '*Trichoderma* species: Opportunistic, avirulent plant symbionts', *Nature Reviews*, vol. 2, pp. 43–56.

Harman, G. E., Lorito, M. and Lynch, J. M. (2004b) 'Uses of *Trichoderma* spp. to alleviate or remediate soil and water pollution', *Advances in Applied Microbiology*, vol. 56, pp. 313–330.

Hartwig, N. L. and Ammon, H. U. (2002) 'Cover crops and living mulches', *Weed Science*, vol. 50, pp. 688–699.

Haukeland, S. and Lola-Luz, T. (2010) 'Efficacy of the entomopathogenic nematodes *Steinernema kraussei* and *Heterorhabditis megidis* against the black vine weevil *Otiorhynchus sulcatus* (Coleoptera: Curculionidae) in open field grown strawberry plants', *Agricultural and Forest Entomology*, vol. 12, pp. 363–369.

Herrmann, L., Chotte, J. L., Thuita, M. and Lesueur, D. (2014) 'Effects of cropping systems, maize residues application and N fertilization on promiscuous soybean yields and diversity of native rhizobia in Central Kenya', *Pedobiologia*, vol. 57, pp. 75–85.

Hinsinger, P., Herrmann, J., Lesueur, D., Robin, A., Trap, J., Waithaisong, K. and Plassard, C. (2015) 'Impact of roots, microorganisms and microfauna on the fate of soil phosphorus in the rhizosphere', pp. 377–408 in W. C. Plaxton and H. Lambers (eds.), *Annual Plant Reviews Volume 48*, John Wiley & Sons, Chichester, UK.

Jones, J., Haegeman, A., Danchin, E. G. J., Gaur, H. S., Helder, J., Jones, M. G. K., Kikuchi, T., Manzanilla-López, R., Palomares-Rius, J. E., Wesemael, W. M. L. and Perry, R. N. (2013) 'Top 10 plant-parasitic nematodes in molecular plant pathology', *Molecular Plant Pathology*, vol. 14, pp. 946–961.

Kamaa, M., Mburu, H., Blanchart, E., Chibole, L., Chotte, J. L., Kibunja, C. and Lesueur, D. (2011) 'Effects of organic and inorganic fertilization on soil bacterial and fungal microbial diversity in the Kabete long-term trial, Kenya', *Biology and Fertility of Soils*, vol. 47, pp. 315–321.

Kanga, F. N., Waeyenberge, L., Hauser, S. and Moens, M. (2012) 'Distribution of entomopathogenic nematodes in Southern Cameroon', *Journal of Invertebrate Pathology*, vol. 109, pp. 41–51.

Kaur, H., Bhardwaj, R., Kumar, V., Sharma, A., Singh, R. and Thukral, A. K. (2015) 'Effect of pesticides on leguminous plants: An overview', pp. 91–102 in P. Ahmad (ed.), *Legumes Under Environmental Stress: Yield, Improvement and Adaptations*, John Wiley & Sons, Chichester, UK.

Köberl, M., Ramadan, E. M., Roßmann, B., Staver, C., Fürnkranz, M. and Lukesch, B. (2012) 'Using ecological knowledge and molecular tools to develop effective and safe biocontrol strategies', in *Pesticides in the Modern World: Pests Control and Pesticides Exposure and Toxicity Assessment/Book5*. www.intechopen.com/about-intech.html

Kołota, E. and Adamczewska-Sowińska, K. (2013) 'Living mulches in vegetable crops production: Perspectives and limitations (a review)', *Acta Scientiarum Polonorum, Hortorum Cultus*, vol. 12, pp. 127–142.

Kubicek, C. P., Mikus, M., Schuster, A., Schmoll, M. and Seiboth, B. (2009) 'Metabolic engineering strategies for the improvement of cellulase production by *Hypocrea jecorina*', *Biotechnology for Biofuels*, vol. 1, pp. 2–19.

Lemanceau, P., Maron, P. A., Mazurier, S., Mougel, C., Pivato, B., Plassart, P., Ranjard, L., Revellin, C., Tardy, V. and Wipf, D. (2015) 'Understanding and managing soil biodiversity: A major challenge in agroecology', *Agronomy for Sustainable Development*, vol. 35, pp. 67–81.

Liu, Z., Dai, Y., Huang, G., Gu, Y., Ni, J., Wei, H. and Yuan, S. (2011) 'Soil microbial degradation of neonicotinoid insecticides imidacloprid, acetamiprid, thiacloprid and imidaclothiz and its effects on the persistence of bioefficacy against horsebean aphid *Aphis craccivora* Koch after soil application', *Pest Management Science*, vol. 67, pp. 1245–1252.

Lorito, M., Woo, S. L., Harman, G. E. and Monte, E. (2010) 'Translational research on *Trichoderma*: From 'omics to the field', *Annual Review of Phytopathology*, vol. 48, pp. 395–417.

Mackie, A. E. and Wheatley, R. E. (1999) 'Effects and incidence of volatile organic compound interactions between soil bacterial and fungal isolates', *Soil Biology and Biochemistry*, vol. 31, pp. 375–385.

Maina, P. K., Wachira, P. M., Okoth, S. A. and Kimenju, J. W. (2015) 'Distribution and diversity of indigenous *Trichoderma* species in Machakos County, Kenya', *British Microbiology Research Journal*, vol. 9, pp. 1–15.

Mendes, R., Garbeva, P. and Raaijmakers, J. M. (2013) 'The rhizosphere microbiome: Significance of plant beneficial, plant pathogenic, and human pathogenic microorganisms', *FEMS Microbiology Reviews*, vol. 37, pp. 634–633.

Mendes, R., Kruijt, M., DeBruijn, I., Dekkers, E., VanderVoort, M. and Schneider, J. H. M. (2012) 'Deciphering the rhizosphere microbiome for disease-suppressive bacteria', *Science*, vol. 332, pp. 1097–1100.

Mohiddin, G. J., Srinivasulu, M., Meghana, D. and Rangaswamy, V. (2015) 'Influence of insecticides flubendiamide and spinosad on biological activities in tropical black and red clay soils', *3 Biotech*, vol. 5, pp. 13–21.

Mueller, U. G. and Sachs, J. L. (2015) 'Engineering microbiomes to improve plant and animal health', *Trends in Microbiology*, vol. 23, pp. 606–617.

Murugan, A. V., Swarnam, T. P. and Gnanasambandan, S. (2013) 'Status and effect of pesticide residues in soils under different land uses of Andaman Islands, India', *Environmental Monitoring and Assessment*, vol. 185, pp. 8135–8145.

Musyoki, M. K., Rasche, F., Cadisch, G., Enowashu, E., Zimmermann, J., Muema, E. K. and Beed, F. (2015) 'Promoting effect of the fungal biocontrol agent *Fusarium oxysporum* f.sp. *strigae* on abundance of nitrifying prokaryotes in a maize rhizosphere across soil types', *Biological Control*, vol. 83, pp. 37–45.

Neher, D. A. and Darby, B. J. (2009) 'General community indices that can be used for analysis of nematode assemblages', pp. 107–123 in M. J. Wilson and T. Kakouli-Duarte (eds.), *Nematodes as Environmental Bioindicators*, CAB International, Wallingford, UK.

Neher, D. A., Fiscus, D. A. and Li, F. (2004) 'Selection of sentinel taxa and biomarkers', *Nematology Monographs and Perspectives*, vol. 2, pp. 511–514, Brill Leiden-Boston.

Nguyen, K. B. and Hunt, D. J. (2007) *Entomopathogenic Nematodes: Systematics, Phylogeny and Bacterial Symbionts*, Nematology Monographs and Perspectives, Vol. 5, Brill, Leiden.

O'Brien, S. L., Gibbons, S. M., Owens, S. M., Hampton-Marcell, J., Johnston, E. R., Jastrow, J. D., Gilbert, J. A., Meyer, F. and Antonopoulos, D. A. (2016), 'Spatial scale drives patterns in soil bacterial diversity', *Environmental Microbiology*, vol. 18, pp. 2039–2051.

Perez-Montano, F., Villegas, C., Bellogin, R. A., Del Cerro, P., Espuny, M. R., Jimenez-Guerrero, I., Lopez-Baena, F. J., Ollero, F. J. and Cubo, T. (2014) 'Plant growth promotion in cereal and leguminous agricultural important plants: From microorganism capacities to crop production', *Microbiological Research*, vol. 169, pp. 325–336.

Pii, Y., Mimmo, T., Tomasi, N., Terzano, R., Cesco, S. and Crecchio, C. (2015) 'Microbial interactions in the rhizosphere: Beneficial influences of plant growth-promoting rhizobacteria on nutrient acquisition process: A review', *Biology and Fertility of Soils*, vol. 51, pp. 403–415.

Pisa, L., Amaral-Rogers, V., Belzunces, L. P., Bonmatin, J.-M., Downs, C., Goulson, D., Kreutzweiser, D., Krupke, C., Liess, M., McField, M., Morrissey, C., Noome, D. A., Settele, J., Simon-Delso, N., Stark, J., Van Der Sluijs, H., Van Dyck, H. and Wiemers, M. (2015) 'Effects of neonicotinoids and fipronil on non-target invertebrates', *Environmental Science and Pollution Research*, vol. 22, pp. 68–102.

Rae, R. G., Robertson, J. F. and Wilson, M. J. (2009) 'Optimization of biological (*Phasmarhabditis hermaphrodita*) and chemical (iron phosphate and metaldehyde) slug control', *Crop Protection*, vol. 28, pp. 765–773.

Redman, R. S., Kim, Y. O., Woodward, C. J. D. A., Greer, C., Espino, L., Doty, S. L. and Rodriguez, R. J. (2011) 'Increased fitness of rice plants to abiotic stress via habitat adapted symbiosis: A strategy for mitigating impacts of climate change', *PloS ONE*, vol. 6, pp. 1–10.

Renella, G., Ogunseitan, O., Giagnoni, L. and Arenella, M. (2014) 'Environmental proteomics: A long march in the pedosphere', *Soil Biology & Biochemistry*, 69, pp. 34–37.

Rusek, J. (1998) 'Biodiversity of Collembola and their functional role in the ecosystem', *Biodiversity & Conservation*, vol. 9, pp. 1207–1219.

Sastrosiswojo, S., Setiawati, W., Prabaningrum, L., Moekasan, T. K., Sulastrini, I., Soeriaatmadja, R. E. and Abidin, Z. (2001) *Ecological Impact of Brassica IPM Implementation in Indonesia*, Proceedings of the 4th international workshop on the management of diamondback moth and other crucifer pests, November 2001, Melbourne, Australia, pp. 381–388.

Schimel, J. P. and Bennett, J. (2004) 'Nitrogen mineralization: challenges of a changing paradigm', *Ecology*, vol. 85, pp. 591–602.

Schreinemachers, P., Srinivasan, R., Mei-Huey, W., Madhusudan, B., Ricardo, P., Sopana, Y., Vu Hong, Q. and Bui Thi Huy, H. (2014) 'Safe and sustainable management of legume pests and diseases in Thailand and Vietnam: A situational analysis', *International Journal of Tropical Insect Science*, vol. 34, pp. 88–97.

Simon, A. and Sivasithamparam, V. (1989) 'Pathogen-suppression: A case study in biological suppression of *Gaeumannomyces graminis* var. *tritici* in soil', *Soil Biology and Biochemistry*, vol. 21, pp. 331–337.

Singh, J. and Singh, D. K. (2005) 'Dehydrogenase and phosphomonoesterase activities in groundnut (*Arachishypogaea* L.) field after diazinon, imidacloprid and lindane treatments', *Chemosphere*, vol. 60, pp. 32–42.

Smith, S. E., Anderson, I. C., and Smith, F. A. (2015) 'Mycorrhizal associations and phosphorus acquisition: From cells to ecosystems', pp. 409–440 in W. C. Plaxton and H. Lambers (eds.), *Annual Plant Reviews*, Vol. 48, John Wiley &Sons, Chichester, UK.

SP-IPM (2012) *The Importance of Non-Plant Biodiversity for Crop Pest Management: Enabling Conservation and Access*, SP-IPM Secretariat, IITA, Ibadan, Nigeria.

Srinivasan, R. (2012) 'Integrating biopesticides in pest management strategies for tropical vegetable production', *Journal of Biopesticides*, vol. 5, pp. 36–45.

Stinner, B. R. and House, G. J. (1990) 'Arthropods and other invertebrates in conservation tillage agriculture', *Annual Review of Entomology*, vol. 35, pp. 299–318.

Stork, N. E. and Eggleton, P. (1992) 'Invertebrates as determinants and indicators of soil quality', *American Journal of Alternative Agriculture*, vol. 7, pp. 38–47.

Sujayanand, G. K., Sharma, R. K., Shankarganesh, K., Saha, S. and Tomar, R. S. (2015) 'Crop diversification for sustainable insect pest management in eggplant (Solanales: Solanaceae)', *Florida Entomologist*, vol. 98, pp. 305–314.

Thomson, B. C., Tisserant, E., Plassart, P., Uroz, S., Griffiths, R. I., Hannula, S. E., Buee, M., Mougel, C., Ranjard, L., Van Veen, J. A., Martin, F., Bailey, M. J. and Lemanceau, P. (2015) 'Soil conditions and land use intensification effects on soil microbial communities across a range of European field sites', *Soil Biology & Biochemistry*, vol. 88, pp. 403–413.

Tsiafouli, M. A., Thébault, E., Sgardelis, S. P., de Ruiter, P. C., van der Putten, W. H., Birkhofer, K., Hemerik, L., de Vries, F. T., Bardgett, R. D., Brady, M. V., Bjornlund, L., Jørgensen, H. B., Christensen, S., Hertefeldt, T. D., Hotes, S., Gera Hol, W. H., Frouz, J., Liiri, M., Mortimer, S. R., Setälä, H., Tzanopoulos, J., Uteseny, K., Pižl, V., Stary, J., Wolters, V. and Hedlund, K. (2015) 'Intensive agriculture reduces soil biodiversity across Europe', *Global Change Biology*, vol. 21, pp. 973–985.

Van Der Heijden, M. G. A., Bardgett, R. D. and Van Straalen, N. M. (2008) 'The unseen majority: Soil microbes as drivers of plant diversity and productivity in terrestrial ecosystems', *Ecology Letters*, vol. 11, pp. 296–310.

Voroney, R. P. and Heck, R. J. (2015) 'The soil habitat', in E. A. Paul (ed.), *Soil Microbiology, Ecology and Biochemistry*, Elsevier–Academic Press, Amsterdam, the Netherlands.

Wagg, C., Bender, S. F., Widmer, F. and van der Heijden, M. G. (2014) 'Soil biodiversity and soil community composition determine ecosystem multifunctionality', *Proceedings of the National Academy of Sciences USA*, vol. 111, pp. 5266–5270.

Wall, D. H., Nielsen, U. N. and Six, J. (2015) 'Soil biodiversity and human health', *Nature*, vol. 528, pp. 69–76.

Wang, M., Wu, C., Cheng, Z., Meng, H., Zhang, M. and Zhang, H. (2014) 'Soil chemical property changes in eggplant/garlic relay intercropping systems under continuous cropping', *PloS ONE*, vol. 9, p. e111040.

Weller, D. M., Raaijmakers, J. M., Gardener, B. B. and Thomashow, L. S. (2002) 'Microbial populations responsible for specific soil suppressiveness to plant pathogens', *Annual Review of Phytopathology*, vol. 40, pp. 309–348.

White, D., Crosbie, J., Atkinson, D. and Kilham, K. (1994) 'Effect of an introduced inoculum on soil microbial diversity', *FEMS Microbiology*, vol. 14, pp. 169–178.

Wilson, M. J. and Kakouli-Duarte, T. (2009) *Nematodes as Environmental Bioindicators*, CAB International, Wallingford, UK.

Wright, D. H., Huhta, V. and Coleman, D. C. (1989) 'Characteristics of defaunated soil: II. Effects of reinoculation and the role of the mineral component', *Pedobiologia*, vol. 33, pp. 427–435.

Zhang, Y., Cong, J., Hui Lu, H., Yang, C., Yang, Y., Zhou, J. and Li, D. (2014) 'An integrated study to analyze soil microbial community structure and metabolic potential in two forest types', *PloS ONE*, vol. 9, p. e93773.

# PART 2

# The origins and history of agricultural biodiversity

# 9

# GENETIC ASPECTS OF CROP DOMESTICATION

*Paul Gepts*

## Introduction

The use of agricultural biodiversity, and particularly crop biodiversity, is a necessary condition, almost by definition, for crop improvement. In the absence of such diversity, it would be nearly impossible to develop the wealth of cultivars on which human societies rely to obtain food, feed, fibre, and fuel. The continuous development of new cultivars requires new genes or gene combinations conferring adaptation to our changing environments, resistance to ever-evolving pathogens and pests, and tolerance to sometimes-contradictory stresses such as scarcity or excess of water. Concurrently, these same cultivars have to satisfy consumer demand, be they nutritional and organoleptic demands or industrial or technological requirements.

A central question, therefore, is to better understand the genetic diversity available to plant breeders for improvement. This diversity is not randomly or equally distributed either geographically or biologically. Geographically, the genetic diversity of specific crops is generally concentrated in centres of diversity as observed by Vavilov (1997) and largely confirmed by subsequent studies. Identifying these centres of diversity is of paramount importance for the conservation of genetic diversity, as well as its utilization. Biologically, genetic diversity is distributed over several crossability gene pools, which are not equally accessible for transfer into the domesticated gene pool of crops (Harlan and de Wet, 1971). In a similar vein, the wild progenitors of our crops are generally considered to be more diverse than the crops themselves, although exceptions to this trend have been observed. Within a genome, genetic diversity is also unequally distributed along chromosomes and is generally correlated with the level of recombination (e.g. Poland and Rife, 2012; Huang and Han, 2014).

To better understand these and other observations on the distribution and potential transfer of genetic diversity into improved cultivars, an evolutionary perspective is necessary because the distribution of diversity is the result of the evolutionary factors that have affected crop species. Darwin (1859, 1868) himself recognized the importance of using plant and animal variation under domestication as a model to study organismal evolution (for a case study of livestock domestication see Edwards et al., Chapter 2 of this Handbook). As recognized by de Candolle (1882), the domestication process is a key element in the sequence of events that have shaped the contemporary status of crop biodiversity. Nevertheless, events that took place before domestication and subsequent to it, up until our time, also play an important role in shaping crop

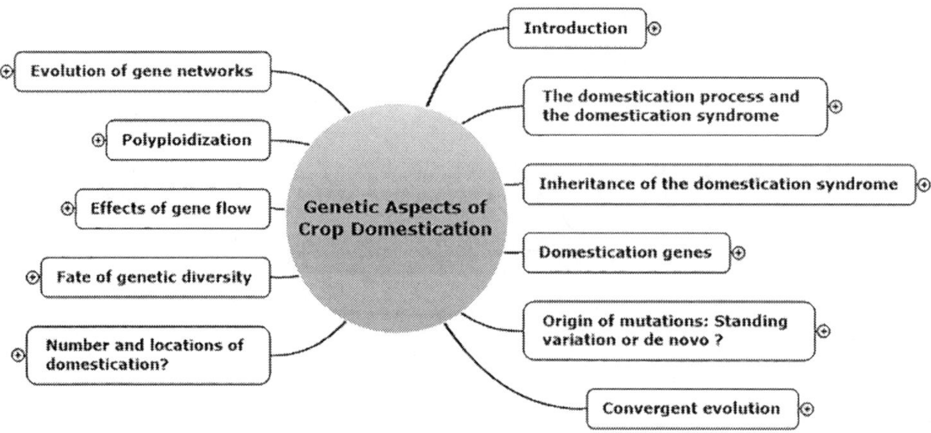


*Figure 9.1* Factors affecting crop domestication

*Note*: Domestication is a very useful experimental model to study numerous aspects of plant genetics which, in turn, offer useful guidance in genetic conservation and varietal breeding.

*Source*: Author.

biodiversity. Evolutionary trajectories are as diverse as the crops that have been subjected to domestication, from short-lived annuals to long-lived perennials, and from strictly selfing species to obligate outcrossers. Thus, understanding the distribution of genetic diversity and patterns of genetic relatedness within crop species requires phylogenetic and demographic information about their evolutionary trajectory before, during, and after domestication.

In this chapter, I will focus on a series of issues that characterize crop biodiversity and have been affected by the process of domestication, taken in a broad sense, or that, conversely, have affected domestication of individual crops (**Figure 9.1** *Factors affecting crop domestication*). It should be remembered here that, while general rules can be identified, crop evolution also displays numerous exceptions and that one should be cautious about overgeneralizing. Each section ends with a paragraph describing the consequences for conservation of crop diversity and utilization of this diversity in genetic improvement. Over the last few decades, the topic of agricultural origins in general, and domestication more specifically, has received increased attention. From being of marginal interest, these topics have now come to occupy a much more prominent position in biological research and research in general. Recent reviews on this topic include Doebley (1992), Gepts (1993, 2004, 2014a), Meyer et al. (2012), Olsen and Wendel (2013a, b), Flint-Garcia (2013), Meyer and Purugganan (2013), and Martínez-Ainsworth and Tenaillon (2016).

## The domestication process and the domestication syndrome

There are numerous definitions for the domestication process, depending on one's background, goal, and focus. For example, anthropologists, archaeologists, ecologists, or geneticists may have different views on domestication and emphasize different aspects of the process. Anthropologists might emphasize the changing relationship between humans and the natural world to reflect the transition from hunting-gathering to agriculture. Archaeobotanists might instead focus on the recovery of plant remains indicative of a change in local or global climate and subsistence patterns, whereas ecologists would emphasize the environmental framework in which domestication

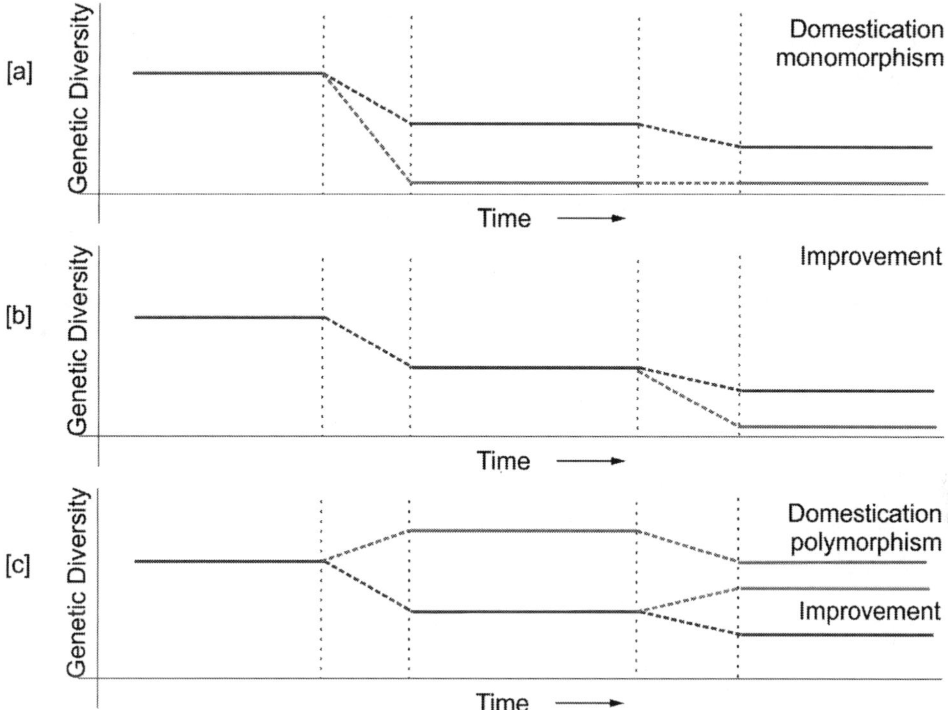


*Figure 9.2* Fate of genetic diversity during and after domestication

*Note*: Black line: neutrally evolving loci subject to genetic drift. Grey line: loci subject to selection, leading to either reduction of diversity (or even monomorphism) during the initial domestication step (a) or subsequent steps (b), or an increase of diversity (c).

*Source*: Modified from Burger et al. (2008). Used with authorization from the Botanical Society of America and the authors.

and subsequent evolution took place. As this chapter is devoted to biodiversity management, I will use a definition that is primarily genetic in nature.

I define domestication as an evolutionary process led primarily by human-driven selection, whether conscious or unconscious, leading to adaptation to human activities, including cultivation and consumption. The trajectory leading to full domestication (Gepts, 2014a; **Figure 9.2** ***Fate of genetic diversity during and after domestication***) includes the initial cultivation phase of undomesticated wild plants, the length of which is strongly debated (Allaby et al., 2008; Abbo et al., 2014), but also subsequent phases of partially or fully domesticated types, the dissemination of crops from their geographic centres of domestication to other areas of the world, and adaptation to these new cultivation areas. In the current, final phase, the process of plant breeding, mostly by selective cross-hybridization, further affects crops in ways that differ between subsistence and contemporary (intensive) agriculture.

The conditions experienced under cultivation are also quite different from the conditions in natural agro-ecosystems, so one should expect phenotypically domesticated descendants to be quite different from their wild progenitors. For example, domesticated grain plants such as cereals or grain legumes do not disperse their seeds, or at least show reduced seed dispersal, a feature that is of obvious benefit to farmers at harvest time. This trait is, however, highly deleterious in the wild and would be strongly selected against.

Different crop types tend to show the same set of traits selected during domestication, which Hammer (1984) described as the *domestication syndrome*. In grain-producing crops, the syndrome includes reduction in seed dormancy and shattering, a more compact growth habit, loss of photoperiod sensitivity, gigantism, and increase in morphological diversity of harvested parts. An additional trait found in these or other crops is a general trend from outcrossing to selfing or even vegetative reproduction, such as in tomato (Rick, 1988), grape (Picq et al., 2014) and cassava (McKey et al., 2010). Additional information about domestication syndrome traits can be found in Abbo et al. (2014), Gepts (2004, 2014b), Dempewolf et al. (2008), Meyer et al. (2012), and Olsen and Wendel (2013b).

Determining the domestication syndrome of a crop has multiple benefits. It helps identify potential selection pressures to which the crop has been subjected during its domestication trajectory. It assists archaeobotanists in identifying plant remains that show incipient domestication, for example by identifying the threshold of seed or fruit sizes that truly represent a genetic change resulting from domestication rather than merely an environmental effect, even if the latter is due to improved cultivation conditions (e.g. Smith, 1992, p. 42, for major domesticates of the North American Eastern Woodlands; Gros-Balthazard et al., 2016, for date palm). It is also the first step towards isolation of the actual genes controlling the domestication syndrome.

## Inheritance of the domestication syndrome

The inheritance of this syndrome has been investigated by several approaches. Early experiments analyzed domestication traits as individual Mendelian (i.e. qualitative) traits (Ladizinsky, 1998). The result of these studies showed that many traits, such as seed dispersal and dormancy, had a monogenic or oligogenic recessive control. With the development of the first molecular linkage maps, it became possible to conduct quantitative analyses and estimate the magnitude of the effect of loci (quantitative trait loci or QTLs) and their position on a crop's linkage map. Overall results showed that in most crops, the domestication syndrome is controlled by a limited number of major genes (consistent with Mendelian analyses), some of which tend to be loosely linked (reviewed in Gepts, 2004). The loose linkage may have facilitated the development of the domestication syndrome in the presence of gene flow between wild and domesticated types in the centres of origin (Le Thierry d'Ennequin et al., 1999).

The application of genomic approaches to the question of the inheritance of the domestication syndrome has provided a picture that appears different at first sight, and involves a much larger number of genes. For example, Hufford et al. (2012) identified some 1,200 regions of the maize genome that had been subject to selection during or after domestication. To what extent these larger numbers reflect a more powerful methodology capable of identifying diversity in a larger number of accessions, or the effect of hitchhiking or epistatic interactions, remains to be determined. A further complication is provided by the potential effect of phenotypic plasticity. Piperno et al. (2015) observed that wild maize plants (teosinte) adopted a maize-like phenotype for some traits when grown in late Pleistocene-early Holocene conditions (lower temperatures and lower atmospheric $CO_2$ contents). Thus, in maize and perhaps other crops, the first phenotypic changes linked to domestication could have taken place without actual structural DNA changes. Further research is needed to determine the potential role of phenotypic plasticity on domestication (Levis and Pfennig, 2016).

Most phenotypic variation in crosses between wild and domesticated types is accounted for by genetic segregation, suggesting that the domestication syndrome has a relatively high heritability (Gepts, 2004). The limited number of genes, their strong genetic effects (as opposed to environmental sensitivity), and their frequent linkage suggest that the marked phenotypic differences observed between wild ancestors and domesticated descendants have a simple genetic control. In turn, this simple control suggests that recovery of the domesticated phenotype in introgression experiments to introduced additional genetic diversity from the wild ancestor should generally be easy, consistent with empirical evidence that one to two backcrosses generally suffice to recover a domesticated phenotype. Nevertheless, some cases of negative linkage drag are possible, depending on the distribution of linkage disequilibrium in the genome.

## Domestication genes

The first major domestication gene isolated was the *tb1* gene of maize, the dominant allele of which conditions the single stem of domesticated maize (Wang et al., 1999). The first QTL to be cloned were also domestication genes, a fruit weight gene in tomato (Frary et al., 2000), and a flowering time gene in rice (2000). Since then, a large number of genes involved in domestication traits have been characterized (reviewed in Doebley et al., 2006; Olsen and Wendel 2013a). A general feature of these studies is that most of the genes identified are regulatory genes, which code for various classes of transcription factors. The causal mutations leading to the domestication syndrome can be located either inside or outside these genes. For example, the mutation controlling the *tb1* gene is located ~60,000 bp upstream from the *tb1* locus.

The types of mutations selected during the appearance of the domestication syndrome are very diverse (Olsen and Wendel, 2013a). Transposable elements do play an important role as previously described for the *tb1* gene. The *PvTFL1y* gene, responsible for natural variation for determinacy in common bean and possibly other *Phaseolus* species (Repinski et al., 2012), shows at least five different mutations, which lead to losses of function, including a retrotransposon insertion in the fourth exon (present in 70% of determinate types), non-synonymous substitutions, indels, a putative intron-splicing failure, and in one case the deletion of the entire locus (Kwak et al., 2012). Indeterminate varieties, whether wild or domesticated, showed only synonymous nucleotide substitutions, suggesting that variation at this locus represents *de novo* variation (see next section, 'Origin of mutations') and illustrates the importance of farmer selection in generating crop phenotypic diversity.

More generally, the *PvTFL1y* on its own illustrates the diversity of mutation types that have been identified in domestication genes, as discussed by Olsen and Wendel (2013a). This confirms predictions made by Doebley et al. (2006) that changes in developmentally complex traits will typically involve transcription factor genes, that changes in metabolic pathways will typically involve changes in structural genes within the pathway, and that changes leading to phenotypic differences among cultivars will be associated with loss-of-function mutations. However, there are many exceptions to these rules, and the classification of traits into domestication and improvement traits may not be applicable to all crops and traits.

In conclusion, understanding the molecular basis of domestication traits may help in elucidating the origin(s) of domestication of a crop, or at least the origin of the trait, that is, whether it results from standing variation or has arisen *de novo*. It also determines the genomic context of the gene involved (i.e. the region with which it is in linkage disequilibrium): this can affect the gene's introgression potential, as linkages can cause drag or induce genetic load that limits the potential usefulness of introgression.

## Origin of mutations: standing variation or *de novo* origin?

Evolution under cultivation is dependent on the availability of genetic diversity in the populations under cultivation. In turn, this diversity can appear either before or during the domestication process (Barrett and Schluter, 2008). For example, the mutation responsible for the *Tb1* mutation observed among domesticated maize may have appeared some 20,000 years ago, well before the presumed domestication event 9,000–10,000 years ago (Studer et al., 2011), and is thus part of the so-called standing variation in the teosinte gene pool.

How this mutation has persisted for such a prolonged evolutionary time among wild maize plants remains to be determined. Perhaps its phenotypic effect is not as pronounced as in the domesticated maize gene pools, which invokes the action of other genes or epigenetic effects responsible for morphological plasticity. In this scenario, the expression of the single-stem phenotype (the dominant *Tb1* allele), which is presumably less favorable than the usual branched phenotype of teosinte in natural vegetation, is tempered under natural conditions and only weakly deleterious.

One of the additional consequences of the existence of standing variation is that it may allow faster development of the domestication syndrome than variation relying on *de novo* mutations and the selection of alleles with a smaller phenotypic effect. Genomic re-sequencing can provide information that helps distinguish between mutations arising from standing variation and *de novo* mutations. Selective sweeps (the 'valleys' of low genetic diversity that surround mutations) are generally narrower for standing variations because of the longer time of existence since the original mutation event. Furthermore, recurring mutations may have happened repeatedly, and hence in different genetic backgrounds. The selective sweeps associated with standing variation also tend to be shallower (Barrett and Schluter, 2008).

Nevertheless, it is clear from observations in several organisms that adaptation arises from both standing variation and *de novo* mutations. Studies in human beings have, for example, identified mutations in both classes (e.g. Peter et al., 2012). With regard to a specific trait, lactase persistence (LP), multiple mutations with different geographic distributions are responsible for this phenotype related to dairying. The mutation prevalent in the Middle East and Europe arose from standing variation, whereas three African mutations seem to have arisen *de novo*. Another example of *de novo* variation is provided by the *PvTFL1y* locus mentioned earlier, in which the mutations leading to determinacy were found only in domesticated types; so far, none have been identified in wild beans, suggesting an exclusively *do novo* origin for this variation.

This discussion on the origins of mutations highlights an additional reason for securing the genetic diversity of wild ancestors. As highlighted in a subsequent section ('Fate of genetic diversity'), the reduction in genetic diversity during domestication and subsequent evolution provides ample justification for such conservation; however, the existence of standing variation highlights a qualitative aspect as well, namely the existence of 'cryptic genetic variation' that may be quite important in the improvement of existing domesticated gene pools but also in the domestication of new crops.

## Convergent evolution

Vavilov (discussed by Kupzow, 1975) had posited the Law of Homologous Variation, stating that closely related species and genera are characterized by similar homologous series in their genetic variability. This observation is consistent with the concept of the domestication syndrome (see also Fuller et al., 2014). This very concept suggests a phenotypic convergence, that is, that the same phenotypic traits characterize the distinction between crops and their respective wild ancestors, especially among phylogenetically more or less related crops. It is also applicable to convergent adaptation, in which different segments of the germplasm become adapted to similar conditions, as is the case for domesticated maize in highland Mexico and the Andes (Takuno et al., 2015).

The existence of phenotypic convergence raises the possibility of a parallel convergence at the molecular level, where similar phenotypes could be controlled by homologous genes. Some examples provide contradictory information on the role of homologous vs. non-homologous genes in convergent evolution. The actual importance of the role of homologous genes in convergence remains to be determined, however, because their importance may be overestimated given the emphasis given to candidate gene approaches in the isolation of domestication genes.

As an example, Takuno et al. (2015) observed that the parallel adaptations to high altitude mentioned previously involved different genes, most likely involving standing variation. Denoeud et al. (2014) observed species-specific gene family expansions and clades for N-methyl transferases (NMT) involved in caffeine biosynthesis when comparing coffee, tea, and cacao. They concluded that caffeine biosynthetic NMT activities had originated at least twice. New World cottons – *Gossypium hirsutum* and *G. barbadense* – are both allotetraploid species combining the A and D genomes (Hovav et al., 2008), resulting from independent domestications in Mexico and Peru, respectively. Following the domestication of these two species, the D genome was preferentially expressed, although with differing degrees of genome-specific bias. This shows how allopolyploidization can lead to the development of new transcriptional networks, and hence novel physiological and morphological traits. Similar observations have been made in hexaploid wheat.

An additional example is the determinacy gene, *fin*, which in common bean conditions the early appearance of a terminal reproductive meristem instead of a vegetative meristem and is responsible for the continuous production of growth modules each consisting of an internode, a trifoliolate leaf, and either an axillary branch or reproductive meristem. This trait is controlled by a single recessive allele. Multiple lines of evidence, including transformation of *Arabidopsis thaliana*, have shown that *fin* is a homolog of the *TFL1 (TERMINAL FLOWER1)* gene of *A. thaliana* (Repinski et al., 2012). In the common bean, there are three copies of this homolog; nevertheless, most, if not all, natural variation is located in one of the loci, *PvTFL1y* on chromosome Pv01. All the known mutations in this gene occurred in the Andes-domesticated common bean, with the exception of the intron-splicing failure mentioned earlier, which was observed in a few accessions from southern Mexico and Guatemala.

The determinacy trait provides an example of phenotypic convergence associated with molecular convergence in the natural variation of a crop. Furthermore, this convergence extends to other crops as well, as determinate or early flowering traits conditioned by *TFL1* homologs have been observed in other crops, both monocots and eudicots, including the *Dt1* gene in soybean (*Glycine max*; Tian et al., 2010), the *DETERMINATE* and *LATE FLOWERING* genes of pea (*Pisum sativum*; Foucher et al., 2003), the *sp (self-pruning)* gene in tomato (*Solanum lycopersicum*; Pnueli et al., 1998), *centroradialis* in snapdragon (*Antirrhinum majus*; Cremer et al., 2001) (all eudicots), and the *HvCEN* gene in the monocot barley (*Hordeum vulgare*; Comadran et al., 2012).

Common bean provides an additional example of molecular convergence involving resistance to the same disease arising independently in the same resistance gene cluster yet conferring different resistance specificities. Such is the example of anthracnose *(Colletotrichum lindemuthianum)* resistance, where the same large cluster of genes arising from multiple duplications on chromosome Pv04 confers resistance to Andean and Mesoamerican strains of the pathogen (Geffroy et al., 1999, 2000). This cluster also shows synteny in soybean (Ashfield et al., 2012). Thus, this cluster pre-existed the divergence in the *Phaseolus-Glycine* clade; multiple mutations and selections within this gene cluster have given rise to convergent resistance, yet distinct, specificities.

These contrasting observations as to the parallelism between phenotypic and molecular convergence raise the question of which factors would favour molecular convergence. Lenser and Theißen (2013) remarked that there is as yet no clear-cut answer as convergent domestications can occur at all phylogenetic levels and involve both orthologous and non-orthologous genes. Factors suggested to promote convergent molecular evolution include a nodal position in gene regulatory networks, simple pathways, minimal pleiotropic effects, selection on standing variation rather than *de novo* mutations (and hence faster response to selection during domestication), and the absence of homologous morphological structures (Lenser and Theißen, 2013).

Thus, the study of convergent evolution and whether or not it involves molecular convergence is a key to understanding the gene content underlying the phenotypic diversity that is both a necessary condition for domestication and its consequence. Further genomic analyses will allow us to further gauge the importance of molecular convergence and to apply it to crop improvement.

## Number and location of domestications

Vavilov (1997) had already observed several cases of 'vicarious domestications', namely cases of multiple domestication concerning related species in different geographic locations. Several examples exist of this pattern, including *Phaseolus* beans, *Capsicum* peppers, cotton (*Gossypium* spp.), agave (*Agave* spp.), squash (*Cucurbita* spp.), rice (*Oryza* spp.), and amaranth (*Amaranthus* spp.). In addition to providing abundant additional examples of convergent evolution, vicarious domestications suggest that the transition from hunting-gathering was less than exceptional and may even have been relatively easy. The slowness of domestication posited by some (e.g. Allaby et al., 2008) may not have been due to factors such as genetic complexity, low heritability, or the lack of a mutational store as raw material. Rather, the occurrence of vicarious domestications suggests the existence of shared factors that encouraged the transition towards agriculture, which could have included global climate change, a widespread increase of the demand for plant products, or a combination thereof. These repeated domestications also suggest that, at least in some species, domestication may be easier than in others (see also Matthews, Chapter 10 of this Handbook).

Determination of these domestication locations relies primarily on the geographic distribution of contemporary wild relatives of the crop. It is noteworthy that centres of agricultural origins and domestication are overrepresented in biodiversity hotspots (Gepts, 2008), presumably because the abundance of biotic resources, and particularly wild plant species, increases the chances of successful domestication following experimentation by the first farmers. Wild relatives in this context refer generally to the conspecific relatives of the crop, that is,those wild relatives that belong to the same biological species as the crop progeny as determined by hybridization experiments, or Gene Pool I, according to the definition of Harlan and de Wet (1971). More recent research has sought to further narrow down the actual centre of domestication, using a range of evidence, primarily molecular (DNA) comparisons between the wild ancestor and the domesticated descendant. For example, in the case of maize, the presumed centre of domestication has been narrowed down to the upper Balsas River basin in western Mexico. Earlier research using allozymes had demonstrated that *Zea mays* var. *parviglumis*, a lower altitude form of wild maize (or teosinte in Nahuatl, the Aztec language), was the closest wild relative of domesticated maize. Subsequent studies refined this finding through an analysis of simple sequence repeats (SSR; Matsuoka et al., 2002). In common bean, the presumed Mesoamerican centre of domestication has also been located in western Mexico, but in the Lerma-Santiago basin north of the Balsas basin (Kwak et al., 2009). Other Mesoamerican crops also originated in distinct areas, including pepper (*Capsicum annuum*; Kraft et al., 2014) and upland cotton (*Gossypium hirsutum*; Brubaker and Wendel, 1994).

Similar studies have shown that the *japonica* type of Asian rice *(Oryza sativa)* appears to have been domesticated in the Yangtze River basin. In some cases, genetic and archaeological data can be combined to provide mutually reinforcing information as to the origin of a crop, including maize and rice (Piperno et al., 2009; Fuller, 2011; Gross and Zhao, 2014), although in the latter case, other regions are also postulated. Other types of data can be used in a similar manner, for example for *Capsicum annuum* pepper, where genetic and archaeological data were combined with species distribution modeling and paleobiolinguistics to document a presumed origin in central or northeastern Mexico (Kraft et al., 2014).

There are several major issues associated with the search for domestication areas. First, the attempts illustrated earlier always concern individual crop species. Yet the agricultural enterprise does not focus on single species, but consists of combinations of plants (and animals) in biological, agronomic, consumption, and socio-economic complementarity. Hence, when one attempts to identify the origins of agriculture, one should consider the origins of the individual crops as a whole as well. Assembling these individual areas of origin into regions of agricultural origin compounds the uncertainties associated with each area of origin, leading to geographically enlarged areas of origin with blurred boundaries.

Vavilov (1997) identified seven major regions of agricultural origins and quantified the percentage of cultivated plants contributed by each, an endeavor which continues to the present day (Kloppenburg, 1988; Harlan, 1992; Khoury et al., 2016). Using Vavilov's designations, these regions are as follows: (1) the Tropical Centre (South China, Indochina, tropical India, and the islands of Southeastern Asia; (2) the East Asiatic Centre (Central and East China, Korea, Japan, and Taiwan); (3) the Southwest Asiatic Centre (the Caucasian and Near East Centers, as well as the Northwestern Indian Center); (4) the Mediterranean Centre; (5) the Abyssinian (Ethiopian) Centre; (6) the Central American Centre (southern North America, Mexico, northern Central America, and the West Indian islands); and (7) The Andean Centre. Clearly absent from these regions, but nevertheless important to varying degrees, are Central Asia (e.g. various vegetable and tree crops), the Sahel in Africa (e.g. drought-tolerant cereals and legumes), and lowland South America (e.g. root and tree crops). Additional centres of origin have been proposed more recently, including lowland South America (mainly the Amazon region: Clement et al., 2015; but see also McMichael et al., 2015) and Central Asia (e.g. Gladieux et al., 2008).

In many – though not all – of these centres, a similar array of complementary crops have been domesticated. Thus, ancient farmers were likely testing several plant species to domesticate not only individual crops but also to establish or domesticate characteristic agro-ecosystems. An example of such a system is the so-called 'three sisters' or *milpa* cropping system, known mainly for its three main crops – bean (*Phaseolus* spp.), maize, and squash (*Cucurbita* spp.). To what extent has the development of such an agro-ecosystem been affected by the domestication of its individual component crops and vice versa? For example, wild beans and teosinte are occasionally observed growing together (Gentry, 1969: Guerrero state; P. Gepts, pers. observ: Colima state), which could have provided the inspiration for the milpa system. Breeding research into multiple bean-maize cropping systems, however, has shown how such a system is dependent on complex genotype-maize × genotype-bean × management interactions (e.g. Francis, 1985; Davis et al., 1987; Davis and Woolley, 1993).

A second issue is the use in domestication research of contemporary wild ancestral populations and not, for obvious reasons, the wild ancestral populations that grew around the late Pleistocene to early Holocene period when domestication was initiated. Many have argued that contemporary wild populations are the 'next best thing' because they are the immediate descendants of the original populations that were domesticated. Most domestication studies have been conducted with these contemporary populations, with the added benefit that it is precisely these populations that can then be used as sources of genetic diversity in breeding (e.g. Gepts 1993, 2014a; Ross-Ibarra et al., 2007; Flint-Garcia, 2013; Martínez-Ainsworth and Tenaillon, 2016).

However, this shortcoming can also be addressed by one of several possible approaches. First, one can use ancient DNA to examine genetic or allelic changes over the course of domestication (e.g. Jones and Brown, 2000; Jaenicke-Després et al., 2003; Roullier et al., 2013; Langlie et al., 2014). This approach's main limitation is the availability of archaeobotanical remains that contain amplifiable DNA. Second, one can attempt to simulate the palaeo-environment at the transition between Pleistocene and Holocene (some 12,000–10,000 years ago) for at least some of the variables, like temperature and $CO_2$ (both lower compared with current values). A preliminary experiment has been conducted for wild maize *(Z. mays* ssp. *Parviglumis)*, which displayed traits characteristic of domesticated maize in vegetative growth, inflorescence sexuality expression, and seed ripening (Piperno et al., 2015). The authors concluded that Pleistocene phenotype and productivity could not be predicted from contemporary data. Third, the ancient distribution of the wild progenitor can be estimated from species distribution modeling and global climate models based on past data. Such an approach was used to estimate the distribution of wild pepper *(Capsicum annuum)* under the climate condition of the mid-Holocene (6000 BP). The correlation coefficient between predicted suitability for current and mid-Holocene climates was 0.92 (Kraft et al., 2014).

The third issue concerns gene flow – predominantly by pollen but also by seed – between the wild and domesticated gene pools and its effect on these gene pools. This gene flow can be quite frequent even in species that are predominantly selfing (Ellstrand, 2003) and has multiple consequences for research and conservation. For research, it causes a potential confounding effect when determining the pattern of domestication and putative domestication areas (Allaby et al., 2008; Ross-Ibarra and Gaut, 2008). One approach for identifying gene flow consists of the joint use of nuclear and cytoplasmic sequences (in the case of uniparental inheritance) to identify discordant phylogenetic patterns.

Knowing the number of domestications a plant has been subjected to and their locations is an important endeavor from a genetic conservation standpoint because each domestication may have brought a different sample of genetic diversity into the domesticated gene pool. Being able to differentiate these different samples among domesticated types guides both conservation and breeding programs. Among crop wild relatives, the contemporary descendants of the wild ancestors warrant prime attention because of their superior crossability with the crop as co-members of the primary gene pool or the same biological species. Further research is needed to fully elucidate the interactions that have been selected during the domestication of cropping systems in and outside of the different centres of agricultural origins.

## Fate of genetic diversity

One of the most generalizable features of crop domestication is the reduction in genetic diversity observed both during and after domestication and the concomitant increase in linkage disequilibrium (Olsen and Wendel, 2013a; Gepts, 2014b). Exceptions to this include some vegetatively propagated crops like apple and grape, or crops that do not tolerate inbreeding, like carrot (Iorizzo et al., 2013).

The two main reasons for this reduction in diversity are genetic drift and selection (Glémin and Bataillon, 2009). The reproductive system also plays an important role: compared with cross-pollination, self-pollination reduces effective population size which, in turn, increases the effect of genetic drift and the magnitude of linkage disequilibrium and results in larger selective sweeps. Both evolutionary factors operate at every step of the domestication process, including post-domestication dispersal and more recent plant breeding. Hence, the identification of genes selected during domestication has usually relied at least partially on detecting regions or genes with significantly reduced genetic diversity compared with those which are evolving neutrally. If one represents the crop evolution process as a simplified transition between two major stages from wild variety to landrace (domesticated) and then to bred variety (domesticated), then the reduction in diversity can occur either at the first stage (if it applies to a domestication gene *per se*) or the second stage (it applies to an 'improvement' gene) (**Figure 9.2a, b**).

Genetic drift has a genome-wide effect in reducing genetic diversity. Superimposed on the effect of drift is reduction caused by selection, which is locus-specific. Selection leads to selective sweeps, that is, areas of the genome that have reduced genetic compared with neutrally evolving areas. The size of these selective sweeps is proportional to the selection intensity and inversely proportional to the recombination level. Specific examples are the *Y1* gene for kernel color and *Tb1* for lack of branching in maize (Clark et al., 2004; Palaisa et al., 2004) and the *Waxy* gene for rice stickiness (Olsen et al., 2006). In these cases, the sweeps may be incomplete, in that they affect only certain segments of the germplasm: the yellow- vs. white-kerneled maize groups for the former and the temperate *japonicas* for the latter. Thus, it is important to capture the genetic background in which a phenotypic trait occurs through adequate characterization of neutral molecular variation, geographic origins, ecological adaptation, or a combination of these approaches.

With increased sequence capabilities, whole-genome analyses, coupled with re-sequencing of a representative sample of the wild and domesticated gene pools, it is now possible to identify selective sweeps at a genome-wide level and identify potential candidate genes for domestication and subsequent evolution (e.g. rice: Huang et al., 2012; cucumber: Qi et al., 2013; soybean: Zhou et al., 2015).

The selective sweep approach is based on the assumption that evolution leads to a reduction in diversity, regardless of the stage at which this reduction takes place (**Figure 9.2**). However, a reduction of diversity leading to a phenotypic monomorphism, such as the single stem in maize due to increased apical dominance is not necessarily the rule. As pointed out by Darwin (1859), those organs that are harvested display increased diversity in the domesticated gene pool compared with the wild gene pool. Hence, against a general background of reduced diversity, one should expect islands of increased genetic diversity corresponding to genes controlling this phenotypic diversity (**Figure 9.2c**). For example, Bellucci et al. (2014) observed that about 3% of the putatively selected expression contigs were monomorphic in their sample of wild beans but polymorphic in domesticated beans.

An example of this trend is the determinacy trait in common bean discussed previously. This trait is partially responsible for a bushy, early plant type. Kwak et al. (2012) identified at least five mutations with the same determinate phenotypic effect in the domesticated gene pool in the locus *PvTFL1y*. A duplicated locus, *PvTFL1z*, potentially also harboured an artificially induced determinacy. Furthermore, all determinacy with the exception of one, were found in the Andean domesticated gene pool. Hence, Mesoamerican farmers must have selected genes other than *PvTFL1* to obtain an early bush type: these remain to be identified. In a more general sense, identification of regions of reduced diversity but also those where diversity increases diversity should be part of the molecular characterization of germplasm diversity.

The presence of genetic redundancy and incomplete sweeps do, however, cast a note of caution for genome-wide association studies, as they could lead to negative results unless additional information regarding the distribution and structure of genetic diversity is brought into play.

The overall reduction in genetic diversity observed during domestication is the main reason for the need to conserve and utilize landraces of crops and their wild relatives, with particular emphasis on the presumed wild progenitor, which is generally conspecific with the domesticated gene pool of the crop. An in-depth knowledge of the neutral molecular, physiological, geographic, ecological, and crossability patterns of diversity is necessary, however, to fully take advantage of this diversity (Ortiz, Chapter 17 of this Handbook). Botanical exploration of the wild and landrace diversity remains essential because of the habitat loss and gene flow to which this diversity is subjected. Genome sequencing can contribute to better knowledge of the neutral molecular variation. However, without concurrent biosystematic, physiological, biochemical, and ecological information, the impact of this sequencing information remains largely inoperative (see also Endresen, Chapter 42 of this Handbook).

## Gene flow

Gene flow is a prominent but underestimated feature of crop evolution. It can take place either through seed or pollen. In the former case, genes are disseminated within or across pollination by seed movement. In the latter case, genes are spread through sexual hybridization. Even in predominantly self-pollinated crops, gene flow is a regular occurrence although at a lower frequency than in cross-pollinated crops. Over the time and spatial scales of crop evolution, however, even these rarer events do have an impact on the distribution of genetic diversity among landraces and between the wild and domesticated gene pools. An important factor affecting the magnitude of the effect of gene flow are the reproductive isolation barriers between wild and domesticated types. Harlan and de Wet (1971) pointed out that the wild progenitor and domesticated descendant belong to the primary gene pool, that is, crosses between them lead to viable and fertile progenies. Under these conditions, it is therefore no surprise to observe hybrid swarms resulting from wild × domesticated crosses (e.g. Ellstrand et al., 1999). In some cases, these hybridizations can lead to the evolution of invasive or noxious weeds or affect their allelic composition (e.g. rice: Vigueira et al., 2013; sorghum: Morrell et al., 2005).

Several cases of gene flow between domesticated populations and their respective wild populations show an asymmetric gene flow with higher levels from domesticated to wild populations than in the opposite direction (e.g. common bean: Papa and Gepts, 2003; squash: Montes-Hernandez and Eguiarte, 2002; maize: Beissinger et al., 2016). Several non-mutually exclusive causes can be invoked to account for this asymmetry, including the dominance or partial dominance of wild traits over domesticated ones, the larger pollen mass of the domesticated gene pool compared with the wild one, and the stronger potential selection on the part of the farmers against segregants with wild phenotypic traits.

Conversely, the predominant gene flow from domesticated to wild types can take place without reproductive isolation barriers and can potentially displace the genetic diversity contained in the wild gene pool if the level of migration can supersede the strength of selection for wild traits (or against domesticated traits) in areas of sympatry between wild and domesticated types. Given the uneven distribution of domestication syndrome genes across plant genomes (see 'Domestication genes'), it is also likely that the migration-selection balance varies along the chromosomes: more specifically, one can predict that at or around genes coding for domestication trait genes, selection will reduce the outcome of gene flow, whereas away from these genes displacement of wild alleles by domesticated alleles will take place more easily. Given the reduced diversity generally observed in domesticated types, a further consequence of domesticated to wild gene flow is a reduction of genetic diversity of conspecific wild relative or even their partial genetic assimilation in regions away from domestication genes.

Based on a linkage mapping of domestication syndrome genes (Koinange et al., 1996), these predictions have been verified empirically by Papa et al. (2005, 2007) using sympatric populations of wild and domesticated common bean from different regions of Mexico. Results showed that the highest levels of divergence between wild and domesticated occurred around domestication genes, whereas away from these genes divergence was significantly lower. Concurrently, the genetic diversity of regions of the wild genome not carrying domestication genes was significantly lower than those including these same genes and was comparable to diversity in syntenic regions of the domesticated gene pools. This observation suggests that gene flow *in situ* leads to genetic impoverishment of the crop ancestor, at least in sympatric regions. In a more general sense, the high frequency of gene flow leads to the existence of 'hybrid swarms', populations that are more or less stably established and consist of mixtures of wild and domesticated traits. Recently, genetically engineered sequences have been used to follow gene flow across landscapes (Bellon and Berthaud, 2004; van Heerwaarden et al., 2012) because of the uniqueness and novelty of certain transgenic sequences. These studies have demonstrated the ubiquitousness of gene flow.

Gene flow also plays a role in the domesticated gene pool, particularly for landraces among local farmers. Actions by farmers promote – directly or indirectly – gene flow by seed or pollen, the latter by hybridization of local landraces with introduced landraces of improved varieties or even local wild populations. Zizumbo Villarreal et al. (2005) showed that domesticated populations of common bean in west-central Mexico had levels of genetic diversity that were overall comparable to those of wild and weedy populations in spite of the general reduction in genetic diversity observed from wild to domesticated common bean in the Mesoamerican domestication centre. This local maintenance of genetic diversity was attributed by the authors to the actions of local farmers who tolerated wild beans and introduced improved bred varieties to the same fields in which they grew.

Further evidence for the importance of gene flow in farmers' fields comes from the process of *creolization* or '*acriollamiento*', a process by which extraneous landraces or improved varieties introduced into farmers' fields are gradually incorporated into farmers' seed stocks. Through hybridization, the introduced varieties gradually incorporate some local traits appreciated by farmers and consumers. Such creolization has been described in maize (Bellon and Risopoulos, 2001), rice (Bellon et al., 1997), and common bean (Worthington et al., 2012). The use of nuclear markers (inherited biparentally) and chloroplast markers (inherited uniparentally maternally in common bean) allowed Worthington et al. (2012) to identify an asymmetric gene flow, whereby an introduced, low-altitude ecogeographic race (adopted for market sales) was gradually being incorporated into the genetic background of the traditional, high-altitude race – but not vice versa.

In summary, gene flow is a ubiquitous phenomenon in crop plants in large part because crops and their wild ancestors belong to the same biological species. Spatial analyses of DNA variation, whether across a landscape or across genomes, have demonstrated the widespread distribution of this phenomenon, regardless of the predominant reproductive system of each crop. Gene flow plays an essential role in shaping intra- vs. interpopulation diversity and in some cases provides local adaptation to domesticates. It is responsible for the appearance of hybrid swarms in sympatric areas or even, in some crops, aggressive weeds. In other cases, however, introgression is surreptitious, as it is not revealed in the whole-plant phenotype but affects genetic diversity at the molecular level. Whether for *in situ* or *ex situ* conservation, gene flow should be taken into account, together with other biological and socio-economic variables (see Sthapit et al. and Dulloo et al., Chapters 35 and 36 of this Handbook).

## Polyploidization

Another change commonly associated with crop domestication is the occurrence of polyploidy. Whole-genome duplications (WGD) have occurred repeatedly in the evolution of higher plants (Soltis et al., 2015) and have been credited with increasing the ecological versatility and range of polyploid plants due to gene duplications and subfunctionalization following the duplication event. Polyploidization is not the only mechanism for gene duplication but its importance during and after the initial domestication process is clearly important. The most frequent natural mechanism for ploidy increase is the production of unreduced gametes, which has been described in several species, including potato and alfalfa. The specific mechanism of unreduced gametogenesis also affects the level of heterozygosity in the polyploid progeny, an important determinant of heterosis and productivity.

Domesticated plants have equally benefitted from the versatility of polyploids (Renny-Byfield and Wendel, 2014), with regard to several features important for crop plants, such as broadening of adaptation, increase in harvested organ size (gigantism), and the appearance of novel traits due to intergenic or epistatic interactions. Gigantism is a fairly common trait in domestication, although not all cases of size increases are attributable to polyploidization (e.g. squash). Nevertheless, strawberry (*Fragaria* × *ananassa*: octoploid; Liston et al., 2014), apple (*Malus* spp: triploid; Kehr, 1996), and alfalfa (*Medicago* spp: tetraploid; Rosellini et al., 2016) show increased organ (fruit) size and biomass compared with their lower ploidy relatives.

In allopolyploid plants (i.e. those that combine differentiated genomes), there is a greater change of accumulating different alleles but also an increased probability of novel epistatic interactions. The accumulation of different alleles can lead to broader adaptation as illustrated by wheat, which form a polyploid domesticated series, including a diploid (*Triticum monococcum*: genome AA), tetraploid (*T. durum*: genome AABB), and hexaploid (*T. aestivum*: genome AABBDD). Compared with tetraploid wheat, hexaploid wheat is more broadly adapted with regard to photoperiodism and vernalization, has improved tolerance or resistance against abiotic and biotic factors, and a broader range of food products (Dubcovsky and Dvorak, 2007), including leavened bread.

The tetraploid cottons *(Gossypium hirsutum* and *G. barbadense)* resulted from a monophyletic allopolyploidization event involving an Old World A genome species as maternal parent and a New World species with a D genome. Both species show a parallel single-cell, epidermal fibre phenotype. Surprisingly, most QTL for fibre quality and yield originate from the D parent, which does not produce spinnable fibres unlike the A genome parent (Jiang et al., 1998). Furthermore, the two tetraploid species have achieved their fibre phenotype through different proteomic evolutionary pathways (Hu et al., 2015).

Polyploidy is an important biological process, especially in plants, with ramifications at different levels, such as molecular and cellular biology, speciation, adaptation, and ecology. In polyploid species, it is therefore important to understand basic aspects of the polyploid nature in these species, including the mechanism(s) of origin, the parental populations or species, and the effect of polyploidization and subsequent process like diploidization on gene expression, to efficiently conserve genetic resources of polyploid species and their utilization in breeding, including re-synthesis of polyploid crops.

## Evolution of gene networks

Genomic approaches, facilitated by the development of low-cost, high-throughput sequencing techniques, provide increasingly accessible possibilities to not only sequence multiple genomes at varying levels of coverage, but also to examine the expression of such genomes. Bellucci et al. (2014) examined the changes in expression levels and co-expression networks in the Mesoamerican domestication centre of common bean. A ~60% loss of diversity was observed between wild and domesticated Mesoamerican common bean; concurrently, ~1% of genes (contigs) showed a statistically significant difference in expression levels, with the majority of them being down-regulated. The latter observation is consistent with the generally recessive, loss-of-function nature of bean domestication traits compared with those of the wild ancestor (Koinange et al., 1996). Communities of genes with correlated expression differed between wild and domesticated types; two of the domesticated gene communities were enriched in transcription factors involved in floral development, abiotic stress responses, and domestication traits. About 10% of the polymorphic gene contigs were putatively under selection during domestication; most of these were polymorphic among the ten wild types tested and monomorphic among the eight domesticated types probed. Several putatively selected contigs were homologous with genes tentatively implicated in the domestication process of other crops. A few similar approaches have been pursued in other crops, for example cotton (Rapp et al., 2010), maize (Swanson-Wagner et al., 2012), tomato (Koenig et al., 2013), tetraploid wheat (Beleggia et al., 2016) and, in the *Solanum* spp, *Phytophtora infestans* (late blight) interaction (Frades et al., 2015).

The study of expression and co-expression patterns is a very promising tool to relate genotype with phenotype in germplasm, a key goal of genetic conservation (Gepts, 2006). A note of caution, however, is appropriate in that key genes involved in domestication and adaptation in general may be masked by epistatic interactions and linkage drag. Thus, the estimates of the fraction of the genome affected by domestication are likely to be overestimates. Hitchhiking and linkage disequilibrium, especially in predominantly self-pollinated crops, are likely to increase the mutational load of domesticates (i.e. 'cost of domestication'). In contrast, these expression studies generally consider a limited number of tissues or growth stages; hence, additional studies are needed to get a more complete picture of expression changes effected during domestication. Introgression and breeding methods that promote effective recombination should be included in the normal, year-to-year workings of gene banks and breeding programs. Furthermore, the overall reduction in genetic diversity from wild to domesticated types provides a further impetus, together with the mutational load, to emphasize the conservation and utilization of crop wild ancestor, in contrast with proposals to 'prioritize' the collection of wild ancestors, for example Ramirez-Villegas et al. (2010) for common bean.

## Conclusions

The study of the domestication process and subsequent evolution provides a rich portrait of the diversity of plant genetic features. This portrait has been enhanced recently by the capabilities provided by genomics approaches and will no doubt grow further as more functional approaches are added to the structural analyses applied currently and as these studies are extended to additional crops, each with their own biological characteristics and domestication and historic contingencies.

In addition to being an experimental model for evolution studies and representing a key invention in the evolution of humanity, domestication is a key factor affecting the nature, structure, and status of a crop's genetic diversity. The famous statement of Dobzhansky (1973) – 'Nothing in biology makes sense except in the light of evolution' – is relevant here as well and applies to conservation and breeding of crops also. Nevertheless, it should be remembered that crop evolution functions in a broader context involving not only the biology of individual crop plants but also their biotic and abiotic environments and the all-important human environment. This 'domestication triangle' (Gepts, 2004), combining plant (and animal) organismal features, the environment, and the human context, makes the study of crop evolution most fascinating. It also continues to be significant for the future, as our biological resources are put under increasing stress because of relentless population increases and climate change.

## References

Abbo, S., van-Oss, R. P., Gopher, A., Saranga, Y., Ofner, I. and Peleg, Z. (2014) 'Plant domestication versus crop evolution: a conceptual framework for cereals and grain legumes', *Trends in Plant Science*, vol. 19, pp. 351–360.

Allaby, R. G., Fuller, D. Q. and Brown, T. A. (2008) 'The genetic expectations of a protracted model for the origins of domesticated crops', *Proceedings of the National Academy of Sciences of USA*, vol. 105, pp. 13982–13986.

Ashfield, T., Egan, A. N., Pfeil, B. E., Chen, N. W. G., Podicheti, R., Ratnaparkhe, M. B., Ameline-Torregrosa, C., Denny, R., Cannon, S., Doyle, J. J., Geffroy, V., Roe, B. A., Saghai Maroof, M. A., Young, N. D. and Innes, R. W. (2012) 'Evolution of a complex disease resistance gene cluster in diploid *Phaseolus* and tetraploid *Glycine*', *Plant Physiology*, vol. 159, pp. 336–354.

Barrett, R. D. H. and Schluter, D. (2008) 'Adaptation from standing genetic variation', *Trends in Ecology & Evolution*, vol. 23, pp. 38–44.

Beissinger, T. M., Wang, L., Crosby, K., Durvasula, A., Hufford, M. B. and Ross-Ibarra, J. (2016) 'Recent demography drives changes in linked selection across the maize genome', *Nature Plants*, vol. 2, p. 16084.

Beleggia, R., Rau, D., Laidò, G., Platani, C., Nigro, F., Fragasso, M., De Vita, P., Scossa, F., Fernie, A. R., Nikoloski, Z. and Papa, R. (2016) 'Evolutionary metabolomics reveals domestication-associated changes in tetraploid wheat kernels', *Molecular Biology and Evolution*, vol. 33, pp. 1740–1753.

Bellon, M. R. and Berthaud, J. (2004) 'Transgenic maize and the evolution of landrace diversity in Mexico: I importance of farmers' behavior', *Plant Physiology*, vol. 134, pp. 883–888.

Bellon, M. R., Pham, J.-L. and Jackson, M. T. (1997) 'Genetic conservation: A role for rice farmers', pp. 263–289 in N. Maxted, B. V. Ford-Lloyd and J. G. Hawkes (eds.), *Plant Genetic Conservation: The in Situ Approach*, Chapman & Hall, London, UK.

Bellon, M. R. and Risopoulos, J. (2001) 'Small-scale farmers expand the benefits of improved maize germplasm: A case study from Chiapas, Mexico', *World Development*, vol. 29, pp. 799–811.

Bellucci, E., Bitocchi, E., Ferrarini, A., Benazzo, A., Biagetti, E., Klie, S., Minio, A., Rau, D., Rodriguez, M., Panziera, A., Venturini, L., Attene, G., Albertini, E., Jackson, S. A., Nanni, L., Fernie, A. R., Nikoloski, Z., Bertorelle, G., Delledonne, M. and Papa, R. (2014) 'Decreased nucleotide and expression diversity and modified coexpression patterns characterize domestication in the common bean', *Plant Cell*, vol. 26, pp. 1901–1912.

Brubaker, C. and Wendel, J. (1994) 'Reevaluating the origin of domesticated cotton (*Gossypium hirsutum*, Malvaceae) using nuclear restriction fragment length polymorphisms (RFLPs)', *American Journal of Botany*, vol. 81, pp. 1309–1326.

Burger, J. C., Chapman, M. A. and Burke, J. M. (2008) 'Molecular insights into the evolution of crop plants', *American Journal of Botany*, vol. 95, pp. 113–122.

Clark, R. M., Linton, F., Messing, J. and Doebley, J. F. (2004) 'Pattern of diversity in the genomic region near the maize domestication gene', *tb1, Proceedings of the National Academy of Sciences USA*, vol. 101, pp. 700–707.

Clement, C. R., Denevan, W. M., Heckenberger, M. J., Junqueira, A. B., Neves, E. G., Texeira, W. G. and Woods, W. I. (2015) 'The domestication of Amazonia before European conquest', *Proceedings of the Royal Society of London B–Biological Sciences*, vol. 282, p. 20150813.

Comadran, J., Kilian, B., Russell, J., Ramsay, L., Stein, N., Ganal, M., Shaw, P., Bayer, M., Thomas, W., Marshall, D., Hedley, P., Tondelli, A., Pecchioni, N., Francia, E., Korzun, V., Walther, A. and Waugh, R. (2012) 'Natural variation in a homolog of *Antirrhinum CENTRORADIALIS* contributed to spring growth habit and environmental adaptation in cultivated barley', *Nature Genetics*, vol. 44, pp. 1388–1392.

Cremer, F., Lönnig, W.-E., Saedler, H. and Huijser, P. (2001) 'The delayed terminal flower phenotype is caused by a conditional mutation in the CENTRORADIALIS gene of snapdragon', *Plant Physiology*, vol. 126, pp. 1031–1041.

Darwin, C. (1859) *On the Origin of Species by Means of Natural Selection*, J. Murray, London, UK.

Darwin, C. (1868) *The Variation of Plants and Animals Under Domestication*, J. Murray, London, UK.

Davis, J. H. C., Roman, A. and Garcia, S. (1987) 'The effects of plant arrangement and density on intercropped beans (*Phaseolus vulgaris*) and maize II. Comparison of relay intercropping and simultaneous planting', *Field Crops Research*, vol. 16, pp. 117–128.

Davis, J. H. C. and Woolley, J. N. (1993) 'Genotypic requirement for intercropping', *Field Crops Research*, vol. 34, pp. 407–430.

de Candolle, A. (1882) *L'Origine des Plantes Cultivées (The Origin of Cultivated Plants)*, Appleton, New York, NY, USA.

Dempewolf, H., Rieseberg, L. and Cronk, Q. (2008) 'Crop domestication in the compositae: A family-wide trait assessment', *Genetic Resources and Crop Evolution*, vol. 55, pp. 1141–1157.

Denoeud, F., Carretero-Paulet, L., Dereeper, A., Droc, G., Guyot, R., Pietrella, M., Zheng, C., Alberti, A., Anthony, F., Aprea, G., Aury, J. M., Bento, P., Bernard, M., Bocs, S., Campa, C., Cenci, A., Combes, M. C., Crouzillat, D., Da Silva, C., Daddiego, L., De Bellis, F., Dussert, S., Garsmeur, O., Gayraud, T., Guignon, V., Jahn, K., Jamilloux, V., Joët, T., Labadie, K., Lan, T., Leclercq, J., Lepelley, M., Leroy, T., Li, L. T., Librado, P., Lopez, L., Muñoz, A., Noel, B., Pallavicini, A., Perrotta, G., Poncet, V., Pot, D., Priyono, Rigoreau, M., Rouard, M., Rozas, J., Tranchant-Dubreuil, C., VanBuren, R., Zhang, Q., Andrade, A. C.,

Argout, X., Bertrand, B., de Kochko, A., Graziosi, G., Henry, R. J., Jayarama, Ming, R., Nagai, C., Rounsley, S., Sankoff, D., Giuliano, G., Albert, V. A., Wincker, P. and Lashermes, P. (2014) 'The coffee genome provides insight into the convergent evolution of caffeine biosynthesis', *Science*, vol. 345, pp. 1181–1184.

Dobzhansky. T (1973) 'Nothing in biology makes sense except in the light of evolution', *The American Biology Teacher*, vol. 35, pp. 125–129.

Doebley, J. F. (1992) 'Molecular systematics and crop evolution', pp. 202–222 in P. S. Soltis, D. E. Soltis and J. J. Doyle (eds.), *Molecular Systematics of Plants*, Chapman Hall, New York, NY, USA.

Doebley, J. F., Gaut, B. S. and Smith, B. D. (2006) 'The molecular genetics of crop domestication', *Cell*, vol. 127, pp. 1309–1321.

Dubcovsky, J. and Dvorak, J. (2007) 'Genome plasticity a key factor in the success of polyploid wheat under domestication', *Science*, vol. 316, pp. 1862–1866.

Ellstrand, N. C. (2003) *Dangerous Liaisons? When Cultivated Plants Mate with Their Wild Relatives*, Johns Hopkins University Press, Baltimore, MD, USA.

Ellstrand, N. C., Prentice, H. and Hancock, J. (1999) 'Gene flow and introgression from domesticated plants into their wild relatives', *Annual Review of Ecology and Systematics*, vol. 30, pp. 539–563.

Flint-Garcia, S. A. (2013) 'Genetics and consequences of crop domestication', *Journal of Agricultural and Food Chemistry*, vol. 61, pp. 8267–8276.

Foucher, F., Morin, J., Courtiade, J., Cadioux, S., Ellis, N., Banfield, M. J. and Rameau, C. (2003) '*DETERMINATE* and *LATE FLOWERING* are two *TERMINAL FLOWER1/CENTRORADIALIS* homologs that control two distinct phases of flowering initiation and development in pea', *Plant Cell*, vol. 15, pp. 2742–2754.

Frades, I., Abreha, K. B., Proux-Wéra, E., Lankinen, Å., Andreasson, E. and Alexandersson, E. (2015) 'A novel workflow correlating RNA-seq data to *Phythophthora infestans* resistance levels in wild *Solanum* species and potato clones', *Frontiers in Plant Science*, vol. 6, p. 718.

Francis, C. A. (1985) 'Variety Development for Multiple Cropping Systems', *Critical Reviews in Plant Sciences*, vol. 3, pp. 133–168.

Frary, A., Nesbitt, T., Grandillo, S., van der Knaap, E., Cong, B., Liu, J., Meller, J., Elber, R., Alpert, K. B. and Tanksley, S. D. (2000) '*fw2.2*: A quantitative trait locus key to the evolution of tomato fruit size', *Science*, vol. 289, pp. 85–88.

Fuller, D. Q. (2011) 'Pathways to Asian civilizations: Tracing the origins and spread of rice and rice cultures', *Rice*, vol. 4, pp. 78–92.

Fuller, D. Q., Denham, T., Arroyo-Kalin, M., Lucas, L., Stevens, C. J., Qin, L., Allaby, R. G. and Purugganan, M. D. (2014) 'Convergent evolution and parallelism in plant domestication revealed by an expanding archaeological record', *Proceedings of the National Academy of Sciences USA*, vol. 111, pp. 6147–6152.

Geffroy, V., Sévignac, M., De Oliveira, J., Fouilloux, G., Skroch, P., Thoquet, P., Gepts, P., Langin, T. and Dron, M. (2000) 'Inheritance of partial resistance against *Colletotrichum lindemuthianum* in *Phaseolus vulgaris* and co-localization of QTL with genes involved in specific resistance', *Molecular Plant-Microbe Interactions*, vol. 13, pp. 287–296.

Geffroy, V., Sicard, D., de Oliveira, J., Sévignac, M., Cohen, S., Gepts, P., Neema, C., Langin, T. and Dron, M. (1999) 'Identification of an ancestral resistance gene cluster involved in the coevolution process between *Phaseolus vulgaris* and its fungal pathogen *Colletotrichum lindemuthianum*', *Molecular Plant-Microbe Interactions*, vol. 12, pp. 774–784.

Gentry, H. (1969) 'Origin of the common bean, *Phaseolus vulgaris*', *Economic Botany*, vol. 23, pp. 55–69.

Gepts, P. (1993) 'The use of molecular and biochemical markers in crop evolution studies', *Evolutionary Biology*, vol. 27, pp. 51–94.

Gepts, P. (2004) 'Domestication as a long-term selection experiment', *Plant Breeding Reviews*, vol. 24, pp. 1–44.

Gepts, P. (2006) 'Plant genetic resources conservation and utilization', *Crop Science*, vol. 46, pp. 2278–2292.

Gepts, P. (2008) 'Tropical environments, biodiversity, and the origin of crops', pp. 1–20 in P. Moore and R. Ming (eds.), *Genomics of Tropical Crop Plants*, Springer, Berlin, Germany.

Gepts, P. (2014a) 'The contribution of genetic and genomic approaches to plant domestication studies', *Current Opinion in Plant Biology*, vol. 18, pp. 51–59.

Gepts, P. (2014b) 'Domestication: Plants', pp. 474–486 in N. Van Alfen (ed.), *Encyclopedia of Agriculture and Food Systems*, Elsevier, San Diego, CA, USA.

Gladieux, P., Zhang, X. G., Afoufa-Bastien, D., Sanhueza, R. M. V., Sbaghi, M. and Le Cam, B. (2008) 'On the origin and spread of the scab disease of apple: out of central Asia', *PLoS ONE*, vol. 3, p. e1455.

Glémin, S. and Bataillon, T. (2009) 'A comparative view of the evolution of grasses under domestication', *New Phytologist*, vol. 183, pp. 273–290.

Gros-Balthazard, M., Newton, C., Ivorra, S., Pierre, M. H., Pintaud, J. C. and Terral, J. F. (2016) 'The domestication syndrome in *Phoenix dactylifera* seeds: Toward the identification of wild date palm populations', *PLoS ONE*, vol. 11, p. e0152394.

Gross, B. L. and Zhao, Z. (2014) 'Archaeological and genetic insights into the origins of domesticated rice', *Proceedings of the National Academy of Sciences USA*, vol. 111, pp. 6190–6197.

Hammer, K. (1984) 'Das domestikationssyndrom', *Die Kulturpflanze*, vol. 32, pp. 11–34.

Harlan, J. R. (1992) *Crops and Man*, American Society of Agronomy, Madison, WI, USA.

Harlan, J. R. and de Wet, J. M. J. (1971) 'Towards a rational classification of cultivated plants', *Taxon*, vol. 20, pp. 509–517.

Hovav, R., Udall, J. A., Chaudhary, B., Hovav, E., Flagel, L., Hu, G. and Wendel, J. F. (2008) 'The evolution of spinnable cotton fiber entailed prolonged development and a novel metabolism', *PLoS Genetics*, vol. 4, p. e25.

Hu, G., Koh, J., Yoo, M.-J., Chen, S., and Wendel, J. F. (2015) 'Gene-expression novelty in allopolyploid cotton: A proteomic perspective', *Genetics*, vol. 200, pp. 91–104.

Huang, X. and Han, B. (2014) 'Natural variations and genome-wide association studies in crop plants', *Annual Review of Plant Biology*, vol. 65, pp. 531–551.

Huang, X., Kurata, N., Wei, X., Wang, Z.-X., Wang, A., Zhao, Q., Zhao, Y., Liu, K., Lu, H., Li, W., Guo, Y., Lu, Y., Zhou, C., Fan, D., Weng, Q., Zhu, C., Huang, T., Zhang, L., Wang, Y., Feng, L., Furuumi, H., Kubo, T., Miyabayashi, T., Yuan, X., Xu, Q., Dong, G., Zhan, Q., Li, C., Fujiyama, A., Toyoda, A., Lu, T., Feng, Q., Qian, Q., Li, J. and Han, B. (2012) 'A map of rice genome variation reveals the origin of cultivated rice', *Nature*, vol. 490, pp. 497–501.

Hufford, M. B., Xu, X., van Heerwaarden, J., Pyhajarvi, T., Chia, J. M., Cartwright, R. A., Elshire, R. J., Glaubitz, J. C., Guill, K. E., Kaeppler, S. M., Lai, J., Morrell, P. L., Shannon, L. M., Song, C., Springer, N. M., Swanson-Wagner, R. A., Tiffin, P., Wang, J., Zhang, G., Doebley, J., McMullen, M. D., Ware, D., Buckler, E. S., Yang, S. and Ross-Ibarra, J. (2012) 'Comparative population genomics of maize domestication and improvement', *Nature Genetics*, vol. 44, pp. 808–U118.

Iorizzo, M., Senalik, D. A., Ellison, S. L., Grzebelus, D., Cavagnaro, P. F., Allender, C., Brunet, J., Spooner, D. M., Van Deynze, A. and Simon, P. W. (2013) 'Genetic structure and domestication of carrot (*Daucus carota* subsp. *sativus*) (Apiaceae)', *American Journal of Botany*, vol. 100, pp. 930–938.

Jaenicke-Després, V., Buckler, E. S., Smith, B. D., Gilbert, M. T. P., Cooper, A., Doebley, J. and Pääbo, S. (2003) 'Early allelic selection in maize as revealed by ancient DNA', *Science*, vol. 302, pp. 1206–1208.

Jiang, C.-X., Wright, R., El-Zik, K. and Paterson, A. (1998) 'Polyploid formation created unique avenues for response to selection in *Gossypium* (cotton)', *Proceedings of the National Academy of Sciences USA*, vol. 95, pp. 4419–4424.

Jones, M. and Brown, T. (2000) 'Agricultural origins: The evidence of modern and ancient DNA', *The Holocene*, vol. 10, pp. 769–776.

Kehr, A. E. (1996) 'Woody plant polyploidy', *American Nurseryman*, vol. 183, pp. 38–47.

Khoury, C. K., Achicanoy, H. A., Bjorkman, A. D., Navarro-Racines, C., Guarino, L., Flores-Palacios, X., Engels, J. M. M., Wiersema, J. H., Dempewolf, H., Sotelo, S., Ramirez-Villegas, J., Castañeda-ÁLvarez, N. P., Fowler, C., Jarvis, A., Rieseberg, L. H. and Struik, P. C. (2016) 'Origins of food crops connect countries worldwide', *Proceedings of the Royal Society of London B–Biological Sciences*, vol. 283, p. 2060792.

Kloppenburg, J. R. (1988) *First the Seed: The Political Economy of Plant Biotechnology 1492–2000*, Cambridge University Press, Cambridge, UK.

Koenig, D., Jiménez-Gómez, J. M., Kimura, S., Fulop, D., Chitwood, D. H., Headland, L. R., Kumar, R., Covington, M. F., Devisetty, U. K., Tat, A. V., Tohge, T., Bolger, A., Schneeberger, K., Ossowski, S., Lanz, C., Xiong, G., Taylor-Teeples, M., Brady, S. M., Pauly, M., Weigel, D., Usadel, B., Fernie, A. R., Peng, J., Sinha, N. R. and Maloof, J. N. (2013) 'Comparative transcriptomics reveals patterns of selection in domesticated and wild tomato', *Proceedings of the National Academy of Sciences USA*, vol. 110, pp. e2655–e2662.

Koinange, E. M. K., Singh, S. P. and Gepts, P. (1996) 'Genetic control of the domestication syndrome in common-bean', *Crop Science*, vol. 36, pp. 1037–1045.

Kraft, K. H., Brown, C. H., Nabhan, G. P., Luedeling, E., Luna Ruiz, J. de J., Coppens d'Eeckenbrugge, G., Hijmans, R. J. and Gepts, P. (2014) 'Multiple lines of evidence for the origin of domesticated chili pepper, *Capsicum annuum*, in Mexico', *Proceedings of the National Academy of Sciences USA*, vol. 111, pp. 6165–6170.

Kupzow, A. J. (1975) 'Vavilov's law of homologous series at the fiftieth anniversary of its formulation', *Economic Botany*, vol. 29, pp. 372–379.

Kwak, M., Kami, J. A. and Gepts, P. (2009) 'The putative Mesoamerican domestication center of *Phaseolus vulgaris* is located in the Lerma-Santiago basin of Mexico', *Crop Science*, vol. 49, pp. 554–563.

Kwak, M., Toro, O., Debouck, D. and Gepts, P. (2012) 'Multiple origins of the determinate growth habit in domesticated common bean (*Phaseolus vulgaris* L.)', *Annals of Botany*, vol. 110, pp. 1573–1580.

Ladizinsky, G. (1998) *Plant Evolution Under Domestication*, Kluwer, Dordrecht, the Netherlands.

Langlie, B. S., Mueller, N. G., Spengler, R. N. and Fritz, G. J. (2014) 'Agricultural origins from the ground up: Archaeological approaches to plant domestication', *American Journal of Botany*, vol. 101, pp. 1601–1617.

Lenser, T. and Theißen, G. (2013) 'Molecular mechanisms involved in convergent crop domestication', *Trends in Plant Science*, vol. 18, pp. 704–714.

Le Thierry D'Ennequin, M., Toupance, B., Robert, T., Godelle, B. and Gouyon, P. (1999) 'Plant domestication: A model for studying the selection of linkage', *Journal of Evolutionary Biology*, vol. 12, pp. 1138–1147.

Levis, N. A. and Pfennig, D. W. (2016) 'Evaluating "plasticity-first" evolution in nature: Key criteria and empirical approaches', *Trends in Ecology & Evolution*, vol. 31, pp. 563–574.

Liston, A., Cronn, R. and Ashman, T.-L. (2014) '*Fragaria*: A genus with deep historical roots and ripe for evolutionary and ecological insights', *American Journal of Botany*, vol. 101, pp. 1686–1699.

Martínez-Ainsworth, N. E. and Tenaillon, M. I. (2016) 'Superheroes and masterminds of plant domestication', *Comptes Rendus Biologies*, vol. 339, pp. 268–273.

Matsuoka, Y., Vigouroux, Y., Goodman, M. M., Sanchez, G. J., Buckler, E. and Doebley, J. (2002) 'A single domestication for maize shown by multilocus microsatellite genotyping', *Proceedings of the National Academy of Sciences USA*, vol. 99, pp. 6080–6084.

McKey, D., Elias, M., Pujol, B. and Duputié, A. (2010) 'The evolutionary ecology of clonally propagated domesticated plants', *New Phytologist*, vol. 186, pp. 318–332.

McMichael, C. H., Piperno, D. R. and Bush, M. B. (2015) 'Comment on Clement et al. 2015 "the domestication of Amazonia before European conquest"', *Proceedings of the Royal Society of London B–Biological Sciences*, vol. 282, p. 20151837.

Meyer, R. S., DuVal, A. E. and Jensen, H. R. (2012) 'Patterns and processes in crop domestication: An historical review and quantitative analysis of 203 global food crops', *New Phytologist*, vol. 196, pp. 29–48.

Meyer, R. S. and Purugganan, M. D. (2013) 'Evolution of crop species: Genetics of domestication and diversification', *Nature Review of Genetics*, vol. 14, pp. 840–852.

Miller, A. J. and Gross, B. L. (2011) 'From forest to field: Perennial fruit crop domestication', *American Journal of Botany*, vol. 98, pp. 1389–1414.

Montes-Hernandez, S. and Eguiarte, L. E. (2002) 'Genetic structure and indirect estimates of gene flow in three taxa of *Cucurbita* (Cucurbitaceae) in western Mexico', *American Journal of Botany*, vol. 89, pp. 1156–1163.

Morrell, P. L., Williams-Coplin, T. D., Lattu, A. L., Bowers, J. E., Chandler, J. M. and Paterson, A. H. (2005) 'Crop-to-weed introgression has impacted allelic composition of johnsongrass populations with and without recent exposure to cultivated sorghum', *Molecular Ecology*, vol. 14, pp. 2143–2154.

Olsen, K. M., Caicedo, A. L., Polato, N., McClung, A., McCouch, S. and Purugganan, M. D. (2006) 'Selection under domestication: Evidence for a sweep in the rice *Waxy* genomic region', *Genetics*, vol. 173, pp. 975–983.

Olsen, K. M. and Wendel, J. F. (2013a) 'A bountiful harvest: Genomic insights into crop domestication phenotypes', *Annual Review of Plant Biology*, vol. 64, pp. 47–70.

Olsen, K. M. and Wendel, J. F. (2013b) 'Crop plants as models for understanding plant adaptation and diversification', *Frontiers in Plant Science*, vol. 4, p. 290.

Palaisa, K., Morgante, M., Tingey, S. and Rafalski, A. (2004) 'Long-range patterns of diversity and linkage disequilibrium surrounding the maize *Y1* gene are indicative of an asymmetric selective sweep', *Proceedings of the National Academy of Sciences USA*, vol. 101, pp. 9885–9890.

Papa, R., Acosta, J., Delgado-Salinas, A. and Gepts, P. (2005) 'A genome-wide analysis of differentiation between wild and domesticated *Phaseolus vulgaris* from Mesoamerica', *Theoretical and Applied Genetics*, vol. 111, pp. 1147–1158.

Papa, R., Bellucci, E., Rossi, M., Leonardi, S., Rau, D., Gepts, P., Nanni, L. and Attene, G. (2007) 'Tagging the signatures of domestication in common bean (*Phaseolus vulgaris*) by means of pooled DNA samples', *Annals of Botany*, vol. 100, pp. 1039–1051.

Papa, R. and Gepts, P. (2003) 'Asymmetry of gene flow and differential geographical structure of molecular diversity in wild and domesticated common bean (*Phaseolus vulgaris* L.) from Mesoamerica', *Theoretical and Applied Genetics*, vol. 106, pp. 239–250.

Peter, B. M., Huerta-Sanchez, E. and Nielsen, R. (2012) 'Distinguishing between selective sweeps from standing variation and from a *de novo* mutation', *PLoS Genetics*, vol. 8, p. e1003011.

Picq, S., Santoni, S., Lacombe, T., Latreille, M., Weber, A., Ardisson, M., Ivorra, S., Maghradze, D., Arroyo-Garcia, R., Chatelet, P., This, P., Terral, J. F. and Bacilieri, R. (2014) 'A small XY chromosomal region explains sex determination in wild dioecious *V. vinifera* and the reversal to hermaphroditism in domesticated grapevines', *BMC Plant Biology*, vol. 14, pp. 1–17.

Piperno, D. R., Holst, I., Winter, K. and McMillan, O. (2015) 'Teosinte before domestication: Experimental study of growth and phenotypic variability in late Pleistocene and early Holocene environments', *Quaternary International*, vol. 363, pp. 65–77.

Piperno, D. R., Ranere, A. J., Holst, I., Iriarte, J. and Dickau, R. (2009) 'Starch grain and phytolith evidence for early ninth millennium B.P. maize from the Central Balsas River Valley, Mexico', *Proceedings of the National Academy of Sciences USA*, vol. 106, pp. 5019–5024.

Pnueli, L., Carmel-Goren, L., Hareven, D., Gutfinger, T., Alvarez, J., Ganal, M., Zamir, D. and Lifschitz, E. (1998) 'The *SELF-PRUNING* gene of tomato regulates vegetative to reproductive switching of sympodial meristems and is the ortholog of *CEN* and *TFL1*', *Development*, vol. 125, pp. 1979–1989.

Poland, J. A. and Rife, T. W. (2012) 'Genotyping-by-sequencing for plant breeding and genetics', *The Plant Genome*, vol. 5, pp. 92–102.

Qi, J., Liu, X., Shen, D., Miao, H., Xie, B., Li, X., Zeng, P., Wang, S., Shang, Y., Gu, X., Du, Y., Li, Y., Lin, T., Yuan, J., Yang, X., Chen, J., Chen, H., Xiong, X., Huang, K., Fei, Z., Mao, L., Tian, L., Städler, T., Renner, S. S., Kamoun, S., Lucas, W. J., Zhang, Z. and Huang, S. (2013) 'A genomic variation map provides insights into the genetic basis of cucumber domestication and diversity', *Nature Genetics*, vol. 45, pp. 1510–1515.

Ramirez-Villegas, J., Khoury, C., Jarvis, A., Debouck, D. G. and Guarino, L. (2010) 'A gap analysis methodology for collecting crop genepools: A case study with *Phaseolus* beans', *PLoS ONE*, vol. 5, p. e13497.

Rapp, R. A., Haigler, C. H., Flagel, L., Hovav, R. H., Udall, J. A. and Wendel, J. F. (2010) 'Gene expression in developing fibres of Upland cotton (*Gossypium hirsutum* L.) was massively altered by domestication', *BMC Biology*, vol. 8, pp. 1–15.

Renny-Byfield, S. and Wendel, J. F. (2014) 'Doubling down on genomes: polyploidy and crop plants', *American Journal of Botany*, vol. 101, pp. 1711–1725.

Repinski, S. L., Kwak, M. and Gepts, P. (2012) 'The common bean growth habit gene *PvTFL1y* is a functional homolog of Arabidopsis *TFL1*', *Theoretical and Applied Genetics*, vol. 124, pp. 1539–1547.

Rick, C. (1988) 'Evolution of mating systems in cultivated plants', pp. 133–147 in L. Gottlieb and S. Jain (eds.), *Plant Evolutionary Biology*, Chapman and Hall, London, UK.

Rosellini, D., Ferradini, N., Allegrucci, S., Capomaccio, S., Zago, E. D., Leonetti, P., Balech, B., Aversano, R., Carputo, D., Reale, L. and Veronesi, F. (2016) 'Sexual polyploidization in *Medicago sativa* L.: Impact on the phenotype, gene transcription, and genome methylation', *G3: Genes | Genomes | Genetics*, vol. 6, pp. 925–938.

Ross-Ibarra, J. and Gaut, B. S. (2008) 'Multiple domestications do not appear monophyletic', *Proceedings of the National Academy of Sciences USA*, vol. 105, p. E105.

Ross-Ibarra, J., Morrell, P. L. and Gaut, B. S. (2007) 'Plant domestication, a unique opportunity to identify the genetic basis of adaptation', *Proceedings of the National Academy of Sciences USA*, vol. 104, pp. 8641–8648.

Roullier, C., Benoit, L., McKey, D. B. and Lebot, V. (2013) 'Historical collections reveal patterns of diffusion of sweet potato in Oceania obscured by modern plant movements and recombination', *Proceedings of the National Academy of Sciences USA*, vol. 110, pp. 2205–2210.

Smith, B. D. (1992) *Prehistoric Plant Husbandry in Eastern North America*, Smithsonian Institution Press, Washington DC, USA.

Soltis, P. S., Marchant, D. B., Van de Peer, Y. and Soltis, D. E. (2015) 'Polyploidy and genome evolution in plants', *Current Opinion in Genetics & Development*, vol. 35, pp. 119–125.

Studer, A., Zhao, Q., Ross-Ibarra, J. and Doebley, J. (2011) 'Identification of a functional transposon insertion in the maize domestication gene *tb1*', *Nature Genetics*, vol. 43, pp. 1160–1163.

Swanson-Wagner, R., Briskine, R., Schaefer, R., Hufford, M. B., Ross-Ibarra, J., Myers, C. L., Tiffin, P. and Springer, N. M. (2012) 'Reshaping of the maize transcriptome by domestication', *Proceedings of the National Academy of Sciences USA*, vol. 109, pp. 11878–11883.

Takuno, S., Ralph, P., Swarts, K., Elshire, R. J., Glaubitz, J. C., Buckler, E. S., Hufford, M. B. and Ross-Ibarra, J. (2015) 'Independent molecular basis of convergent highland adaptation in maize', *Genetics*, vol. 200, pp. 1297–1312.

Tian, Z., Wang, X., Lee, R., Li, Y., Specht, J. E., Buckler, E. S., Hufford, M. B. and Ross-Ibarra, J. (2010) 'Artificial selection for determinate growth habit in soybean', *Proceedings of the National Academy of Sciences USA*, vol. 107, pp. 8563–8568.

van Heerwaarden, J., Del Vecchyo, D. O., Alvarez-Buylla, E. R. and Bellon, M. R. (2012) 'New genes in traditional seed systems: Diffusion, detectability and persistence of transgenes in a maize metapopulation', *PLoS ONE*, vol. 7, p. e46123.

Vavilov, N. I. (1997) *Five Continents*, International Plant Genetic Resources Institute, Rome, Italy.

Vigueira, C. C., Olsen, K. M. and Caicedo, A. L. (2013) 'The red queen in the corn: Agricultural weeds as models of rapid adaptive evolution', *Heredity*, vol. 110, pp. 303–311.

Wang, R. L., Stec, A., Hey, J., Lukens, L. and Doebley, J. (1999) 'The limits of selection during maize domestication', *Nature*, vol. 398, pp. 236–239.

Worthington, M., Soleri, D., Aragón-Cuevas, F. and Gepts, P. (2012) 'Genetic composition and spatial distribution of farmer-managed bean plantings: An example from a village in Oaxaca, Mexico', *Crop Science*, vol. 52, pp. 1721–1735.

Zhou, Z., Jiang, Y., Wang, Z., Gou, Z., Lyu, J., Li, W., Yu, Y., Shu, L., Zhao, Y., Ma, Y., Fang, C., Shen, Y., Liu, T., Li, C., Li, Q., Wu, M., Wang, M., Wu, Y., Dong, Y., Wan, W., Wang, X., Ding, Z., Gao, Y., Xiang, H., Zhu, B., Lee, S. H., Wang, W. and Tian, Z. (2015) 'Resequencing 302 wild and cultivated accessions identifies genes related to domestication and improvement in soybean', *Nature Biotechnology*, vol. 33, pp. 408–414.

Zizumbo-Villarreal, D., Colunga-García Marín, P., Payró de la Cruz, E., Delgado-Valerio, P. and Gepts, P. (2005) 'Population structure and evolutionary dynamics of wild–weedy–domesticated complexes of common bean in a Mesoamerican region', *Crop Science*, vol. 35, pp. 1073–1083.

# 10

# EVOLUTION AND DOMESTICATION OF CLONAL CROPS

*Peter J. Matthews*

## Introduction

In this chapter, examples of clonal crops are introduced in relation to methods of study, intergenerational breeding between clones, models of crop evolution and domestication, archetypes and ideotypes as targets for conscious selection, and the implications of vegetative reproduction for crop history research. Counter-examples that help us to understand clonal crop evolution and domestication are discussed as 'anti-domesticates'.

Vegetatively propagated crops vary widely in terms of evolutionary history, domestication process, plant form, utilised parts, and economic importance. Such crops (hereafter referred to as clonal crops) are present in diverse plant families and all regions of the world where plants have been domesticated. They occupy all use categories – including food, fodder, medicine, poison, living shelter, fibre, and timber – and the anatomical parts used may be vegetative (storage organs, stems, rhizomes, leaves) or floral (inflorescence, fruit, nut, or grain). Considering only the small number of globally or regionally important crops, McKey et al. (2012) noted several flowering plant families that are represented by clonally propagated crops: Araceae, Dioscoreaceae, Musaceae, Poaceae, Zingiberaceae, and other monocots; Euphorbiaceae, Moraceae, Oxalidaceae, Piperaceae, Solanaceae, and many other dicotyledonous plants. Clonal crops can also be found among the algae (Chlorophyta especially), ferns and their allies, and gymnosperms.

Most work on the domestication of grasses (Poaceae) has focused on seed propagated food crops, with the clonal crop sugarcane as a notable exception. Grivet et al. (2004) suggested that grasses involved in the domestication of sugarcane *(Saccharum officinarum)* evolved as allopatric species in Sunda *(S. spontaneum)* and Sahul *(S. robustum)* before the late Pleistocene, and subsequently became sympatric as a result of human utilisation and creation of habitats suitable for invasion by *S. spontaneum*. Widespread hybridisation among sympatric populations, from mainland Southeast Asia to New Guinea, then led to the generation of many new hybrid cultivars, distinct from earlier 'Noble' sugar-producing cultivars derived from *S. robustum* in New Guinea. Less is known about the geographical origins, domestication, and dispersal of other widespread clonal grasses such as *Arundo donax* (cane grass, giant reed) (Pilu et al., 2012) or the many edible and cane bamboos (*Bambusa*, *Phyllostachys*, and others), which are also ancient crops (Liese and Köhl, 2015).

While most clonal crops have been used for thousands of years, the domestication of new species continues (Meyer et al., 2012). In New Zealand, the flax plants *(Phormium tenax* and *P. cookianum)* were domesticated within the last thousand years as fibre crops, following the arrival of Maori ancestors from remote Oceania (Yen, 1985; Harris and Heenan, 1992). The kiwifruit species *Actinidia deliciosa* and *A. chinensis* are said to have been domesticated within the last 100 years (see 'Models of crop evolution and domestication'). The wild vegetable and medicinal plant *Houttuynia cordata* is said to have been first cultivated as a clonal crop within last several decades or years, in China and India, apparently in response to overharvesting of wild populations (Wu et al., 2006; Bhattacharyya and Sarma, 2010).

The primary significance of vegetative propagation is that it allows us to preserve selected plant types with little risk of genetic change, and expand their production whenever and wherever conditions suitable for vegetative growth prevail. When a desirable new form of a wild or cultivated plant is found (after the production of seedlings, or through somatic mutation), the new form can be multiplied without a continuing need for reselection from a breeding plant population. Zohary (2004) described the cultivars of clonal crops as 'simply clonal replications' of 'exceptional individuals' that excel in their desired qualities. The natural ecological contexts or the human modified habitats where selection takes place may strongly influence the ways that plants come to be observed, selected, and propagated. There is nothing necessarily simple about the process as a whole. Repeated selection of different clones within breeding wild or managed populations is likely to have led to very complex cycles of clonal propagation, crossing between clones of the same generation, and crossing between clones of different generations (inter-generational breeding). This is indicated by the further statement (Zohary, 2004) that cultivars of clonal crops are, 'as a rule', highly heterozygous, and that early in domestication, clonal cultivars were first selected from variable, panmictic populations, and then later from among the progeny of spontaneous and/or human-made crosses between *cultivated* × *cultivated* clones, or between *cultivated* × *wild* clones. It is thus to be expected that clonal crops have undergone ecological shifts while adapting to the disturbed, managed, and cultivated environments created by human activities, and that 'unconscious selection' (Zohary, 2004) can be just as significant for clonal crops as for seed propagated crops.

None of this excludes the possibility that for some clonal crops, domestication was instantaneous – the result of a desired type being fixed through propagation of a single clone, or a small number of clones (**Figure 10.1** *The gathering pathway*), and most likely employing obvious natural vegetative offshoots (propagules). Zohary and Hopf (1994) noted archaeological evidence for a 'first wave' of domestication of fruit crops in the Old World, and observed that the earlier crops (grape, fig, sycamore fig, pomegranate, olive, date palm) were naturally easy to propagate vegetatively by cuttings and natural offshoots. A later wave of fruit tree domesticates (including apple, pear, plum, and cherry) required the less obvious and more difficult technique of grafting, a technique that may have originated in early Chinese propagation of *Citrus* domesticates. In their survey of the history of domestication of 203 major and minor food crops, Meyer et al. (2012) confirmed two waves of domestication in perennial crop species, and link these waves to the dissemination of vegetative propagation techniques. A first wave of fruit domestication, starting 6,000 years ago (ya) and peaking around 4,000 ya, in the Old World, involved non-tree perennials and trees that can be propagated using simple techniques such as the planting of cuttings or suckers. A second wave, starting 3,000 to 2,000 ya and continuing to the present, coincided with the discovery and dissemination of scion grafting, particularly in the Mediterranean basin. An estimated 76% of all trees that are now known as clonal crops were domesticated in these two waves of domestication.

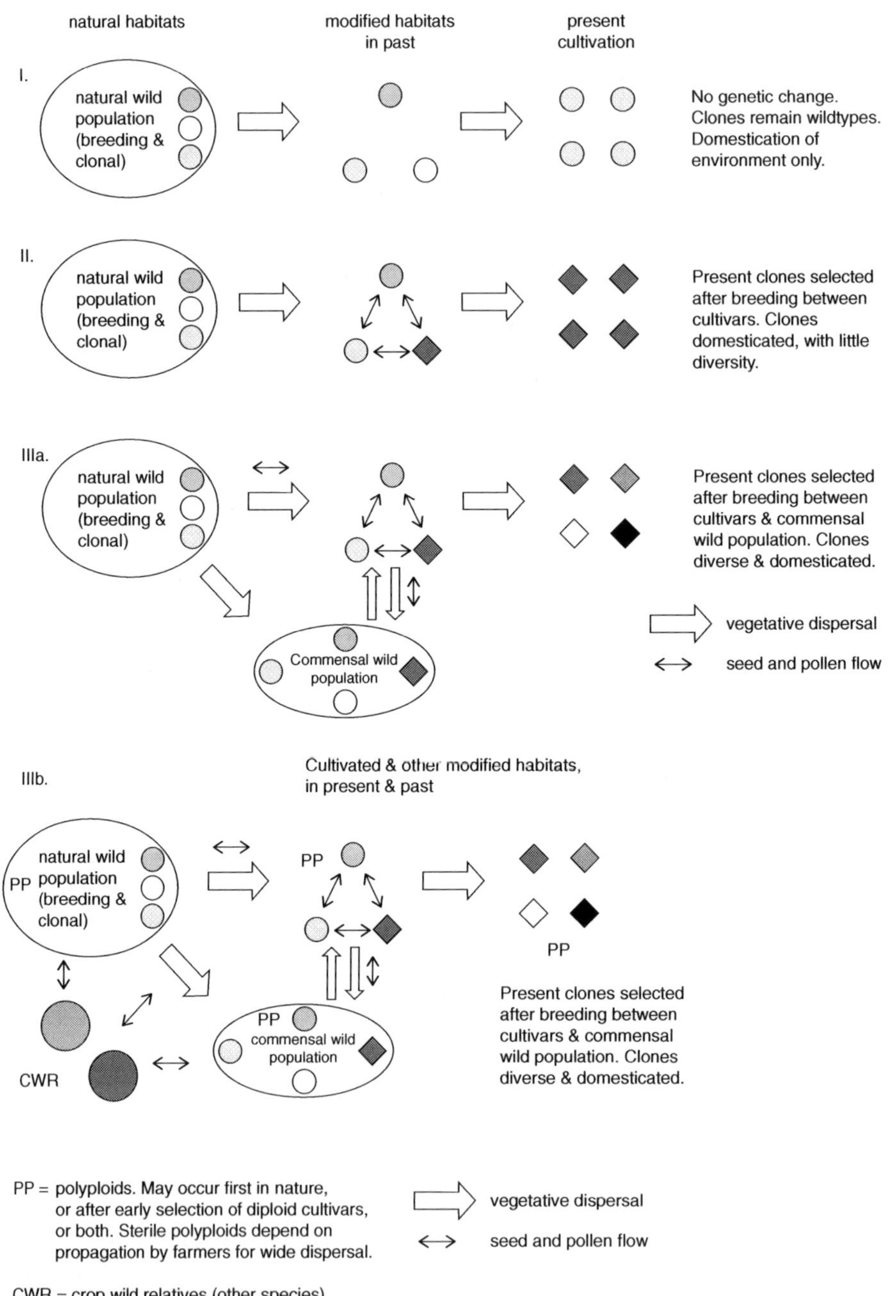


*Figure 10.1* The gathering pathway

*Note*: Circles of the same shade represent a single clonal lineage. Gathered clones may be transported and propagated by people deliberately or accidentally, and remain wildtypes with little or no genetic change. Habitat modification in the past may or may not include cultivation (soil modification). Clones transported into natural habitats (not shown), into modified but uncultivated habitats, and into cultivated habitats would all contribute to 'domestication of the environment'.

*Source*: Author.

The option of vegetative propagation is generally not exclusive; it is often possible to propagate clonal crops from seed, but most of the resulting offspring may be disappointing, unless the crop happens to 'breed true'– an unlikely scenario for clonal crops that belong to outcrossing species. Zohary (2004) noted that clonal cultivars 'do not represent true breeding races, but only clones that, as a rule, segregate widely when progeny tested,' and that 'the large majority of such segregating progeny are economically worthless' (p. 7). Nevertheless, recent studies of cassava *(Manihot esculenta)* in Central America have demonstrated that sexual reproduction, and farmer selection of volunteer seedlings found in fields, continues to contribute to variation in the crop, despite previous selection for vegetative traits that reduced flowering and increased resource allocation to stems and edible underground tubers (Olsen and Schaal, 2007). The root and leaf crop taro *(Colocasia esculenta)* is a naturally outcrossing, heterozygous species that has almost certainly undergone farmer selection of volunteer seedlings. Matthews (2014, p. 251) suggested that 'if early forms of agriculture resembled modern swiddening systems, then there were probably ample opportunities for cycles of breeding and selection' and that 'swiddening systems probably provided ideal circumstances for breeding in the history of vegetatively propagated crops such as taro'.

Meyer et al. (2012) reviewed data concerning the domestication of vegetatively propagated root crops and found that they do not exhibit significantly fewer domestication traits than annual seed crops, and that the rate of domestication (i.e. mean time to domestication from supposed first use) is no different for vegetative root crops, perennial fruit crops, and annual seed crops. The authors noted that estimates such as these are likely to be biased by the degree to which domestication traits have been characterised in different crops, and the difficulty of detecting early domestication when many domestication traits do not involve morphological changes that can be detected through archaeology.

Across taxa, vegetative propagation involves a diverse range of plant parts. Depending on where vegetative meristems are located, the parts used for propagation may not be well suited to long-term storage and long-distance transport, or may require very specific environmental conditions for optimal growth. The relative ease with which tubers of potato *(Solanum tuberosum)* can be stored and grown, compared with other root crops (**Figure 10.2** *Storability – days until decay or quality unacceptable*), may partly explain its present world dominance among root crops. (Potato has even been suggested as the first food crop that will be grown on Mars, as envisioned in the science fiction film *The Martian*).

The ease of vegetative propagation depends to a large extent on whether or not the part being used is naturally an organ of self-propagation by the plant. The potato, noted previously, is a good example of easy vegetative propagation based on a natural offshoot: the tuber, with stored starch, dormancy, and many buds for sprouting. Although the plant parts used as cuttings (for planting in a substrate) or as scion pieces for grafting (on a different plant) have specific physiological requirements that are not immediately obvious (see Goldschmidt, 2014, for example), vegetative self-propagation by many wild plants is obvious under natural conditions, and those conditions can be emulated. Vegetative propagation *per se* is thus not an 'invention', 'process', or 'device' created by humans, but deliberate and long-term use of the propagules can be regarded as an invention – a product of human thought and planning. Zohary and Hopf (1994) and Zohary (2004) noted that the planting of vegetatively propagated clones can seriously limit fruiting by species that are naturally outcrossing because of dioecy (male and female flowers on different plants) or self-incompatibility. Such limitations led to the adoption of agronomic devices to ensure fruit set (e.g. the planting of male pollen donors in orchards composed of one or more female clones) and unconscious selection for diverse mutations that overcame the limitations imposed by sex determination or self-incompatability.

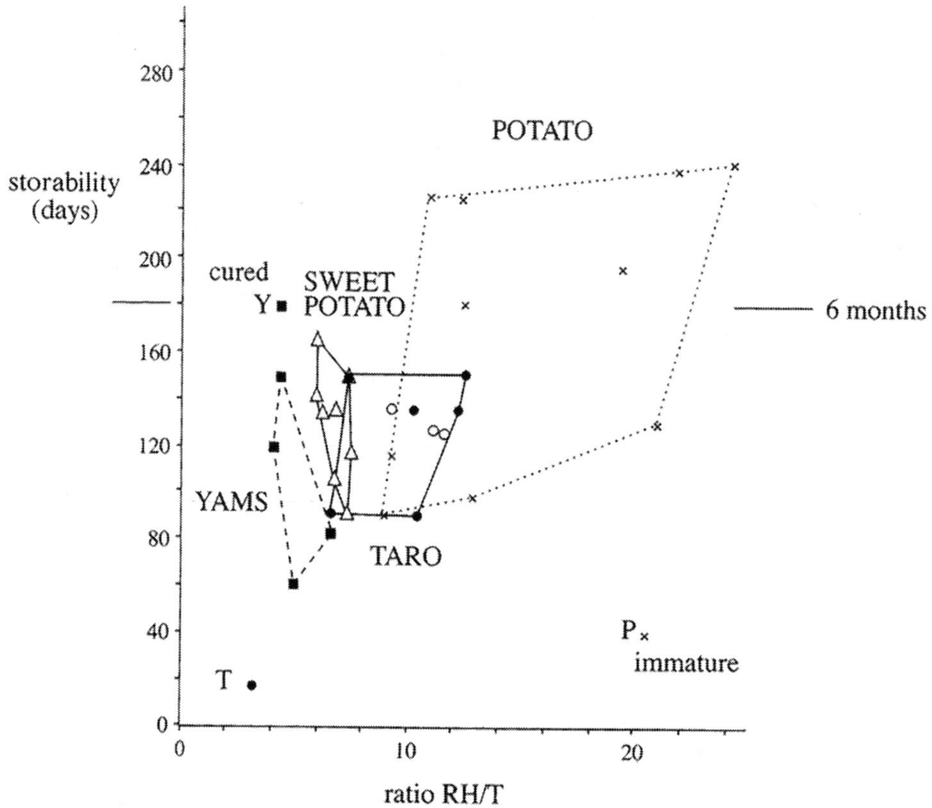


*Figure 10.2* Storability – days until decay or quality unacceptable

*Note*: Storability is shown here as a function of relative humidity over temperature (the main parameters that determine the suitability of storage conditions). Polygons have been drawn around the main clusters of storability reported for *five* common clonal root crops (yam = *Dioscorea spp*, sweet potato = *Ipomoea batatas*, taro = *Colocasia esculenta*, potato = *Solanum tuberosum*). Open circles inside the taro polygon represent yautia (*Xanthosoma* spp.). Three outlying points that are not included in polygons represent cured yam, immature potato, and taro stored at an unusually high temperature and low relative humidity.

*Source*: Matthews (2002).

Clonal crops are also closely linked to animal domestication, through the use of wild and cultivated plants as forage, the creation of open pasture habitats (**Figure 10.3** *Open pasture habitats and spread of wild taro*), the use of animals as work animals in fields and forests, the use of animals to transport goods (including plants) over thousands of years, and the creation of trails and roads (open habitats) for animal-based transport. Some large, perennial forage grasses are commonly propagated as clones (e.g. *Pennisetum purpureum*, *Panicum maximum*, *Tripsacum laxum*, *Setaria sphacelata* var. *splendida*) and other clonal herbs also serve as fodder plants (e.g. *Canna indica* var. *edulis*, *Colocasia esculenta*, *Ipomoea batatas*, *Pueraria lobata*, and *Solanum tubersosum*) (Batello et al., 2008; Woolfe, 1992; Matthews et al., 2012). The possibility of early plant domestication primarily for fodder production does not appear to have been discussed or reported, for any crop, whether propagated by seed or vegetatively.

*Figure 10.3* Open pasture habitats and spread of wild taro

*Note*: Large grazing herbivores such as cow, horse, goat, and deer do not eat the acrid stems and leaves of taro *(Colocasia esculenta)*, helping to create and maintain open wet habitats suitable for the spread of wild taro populations. Upper left, Majuli Island, Brahmaputra river, India; cows with taro in foreground. Lower left, taro on eroding bank grazed by cattle in Kopili valley, a tributary of the Brahmaputra. Upper right, horse grazing next to taro on a tributary of the Red River in Lang Son province, northern Vietnam. Lower right, shoot and stolons of wild taro floating downstream across Ba Be lake, on a tributary of the Red River in Bac Can province, northern Vietnam.

*Source*: Author.

## Methods of study

In this section, I consider methods used in biological and archaeological studies of clonal crops. Cytological methods have advanced greatly in recent decades, especially with the advent of *in situ* hybridisation methods that allow particular DNA sequences to be physically detected and mapped on chromosomes. Now it is possible to not only identify the ploidy level and the gross morphology of condensed (metaphase) chromosomes, but also to show which chromosomes in a sterile, vegetatively propagated hybrid are derived from which parent species or variety, using DNA sequences from the parent taxa to 'paint' the chromosomes in a hybrid. In sexually reproducing crops, polyploidy and hybridity require balanced and even-numbered chromosome sets so that all chromosomes can smoothly pair and separate in the offspring, and to produce normal numbers of viable seed. In contrast, clonal crops can tolerate the sterility of odd-numbered polyploids, or losses in viability resulting from unmatched chromosomes (aneuploidy) and other effects of hybridity. Increasingly it is clear that clonal crops can have complex genetic histories, and may represent hybrid species with varying degrees of compatibility with their parents. Genome sequencing and other molecular methods are now able to clarify chromosomal rearrangements and other genetic consequences expected as a result of hybridisation and hybrid speciation in plants (Hegarty and Hiscock, 2005).

McKey et al. (2012) suggests two main reasons for limited research on the evolutionary biology of clonal crops. First is a poor knowledge of the biology and ecology of their closest wild relatives, a lack that is partly due to the great diversity of plant taxa involved (as noted earlier), and second is the incomplete understanding of the reproductive ecology of the crops themselves. Because clonal crops are propagated vegetatively, sexual reproduction has often been assumed to be unimportant for such crops.

For clonal crops, the costs of maintaining living collections are also generally higher, per cultivar, than for seed crops because of the need to maintain living plants or bulky stored materials in a living condition. Keeping clonal stocks free of disease can also become expensive. Systemic transmission of some viruses, for example, may require special treatments to obtain clean planting material, and continuous monitoring of the living collection. Researchers based in agricultural institutions have often had limited access to the comparative materials needed to identify domestication traits or the source populations of cultivated plants. As molecular techniques become more powerful, the most limiting factor for research on the evolution and domestication of clonal crops may be the survival and sampling of the wild relatives and crop diversity in the field. Ecogeographic surveys are critically needed in order to establish information baselines for conservation purposes (Hunter and Heywood, 2011), and also for the design of sampling strategies for crop history research.

With clonal crops, we also have a general analytical problem because population-level estimates of genetic distance and diversity may assume that the cultivars belong to open breeding populations, just as the wild populations (more or less) do. However, the assemblages of clonal cultivars held by a particular community, or in a national collection, are not breeding populations. Deciding which mathematical methods to employ must take into account the manner in which samples were obtained. Ideally, field sampling and subsequent analyses should be aimed at testing biological and historical hypotheses that were formulated before samples were collected. Generally, most living collections of clonal crops are designed not to address historical questions, but to maximise the representation of diversity within the crop, while minimising duplication and maintenance costs. This may incidentally lead to the loss of samples of great historical significance. The geographical provenance of each sample or ramet of a single wide-ranging clone is significant for dispersal history, and the existence of closely-related but distinct clones is significant for understanding the genetic origins and antiquity of a clonal crop.

Attempts to interpret the phylogenetic history of crop species and cultivars are also limited by our knowledge and sampling of the diversity of wild populations and closely related wild taxa. The sample sets used for study generally do not include all relevant populations and taxa, and our knowledge of the existence and geographical distribution of related taxa and populations is usually incomplete. Although useful as a theoretical starting point, phylogenetic tree models may fail or be misleading if their taxonomic coverage is too poor, and if they involve populations and species with long-lived clones.

Opportunities for reticulate evolution after hybridisation may be greater in clonal than non-clonal taxa, assuming that other factors are equal. Zohary (2004) suggests that 'appreciated genotypes' of clonal crops have been maintained for long periods of time. Clones may also exist in nature for very long periods. Recombination and selection cycles are likely to be fewer for clonal crops than for seed crops, but more complex in terms of parentage or breeding pattern. The mathematical implications of inter-generational breeding and reticulate breeding patterns for diversity within a clonal crop species are discussed in the next section, 'Inter-generational breeding'. There is also no reliable way to estimate an average generation time in clonal species because of the unknown variance in lifespan between individual clones in the field. Robust theoretical and empirical approaches are therefore needed, with iterative resampling in the field to test specific theories that relate to the taxonomy, genetic relationships, geographical range, and dispersal history of each clonal crop species.

In recent years, information relevant to crop history has increased exponentially and become more accessible through advances in the archaeological, agricultural, and biological sciences. This applies especially to genome sequence information (Olsen and Wendel, 2013; see also Endresen, Chapter 42 of this Handbook). Whole genome sequencing generates vast amounts of information for which analysis and interpretation have become limiting factors. With recent improvements in microscopy, digital photography, and related methods of microanalysis, it has become easier for palaeobotanists and archaeologists to examine micro-structure in macro- and micro-remains and to examine a greater diversity of micro-fossil types (Denham et al., 2009) derived from hard and soft organs, tissues, and sub-cellular components. These advances also create new information management issues for archaeobotany.

The physical and chemical stability of plant materials depends on their density, composition, and environment, including the biotic environment (King, 1994; Lambert, 1997). Archaeobotanical studies are still largely focused on hard seeds, nutshells, and woods preserved in waterlogged conditions or in carbonised form. Most crop seeds found archaeologically are from cereals, but the seeds of vegetatively propagated crops have also been recovered. A good example is the grapevine, *Vitis vinifera* (Renfrew, 1995; McGovern, 2003). While human selection may favour certain seed types in the grapevine, or seedlessness as in some grape varieties, bananas (*Musa* spp.), figs (*Ficus* spp.) and citrus (*Citrus* spp.), selection effects on seed morphology and production are less likely for clonal crops in which fruits and seeds are rarely or never utilized (e.g. most starchy root crops, and fibre crops such as New Zealand flax, *Phormium* spp., and paper mulberry, *Broussonetia* spp.).

Scanning electron microscopy (SEM) has been used to analyse micro-structure in macro- and micro-remains of carbonised soft-tissue from vegetative organs (Hather, 1991; Harris, 2006; Oliviera, 2012). Starch is commonly distributed in seeds and vegetative storage organs, and has been widely reported on archaeological tools and in archaeological sediments (Torrence and Barton, 2006). Ancient starch may be derived from seed and clonal crops with little inherent bias, since the basic chemistry of starch is similar across different storage organs and most plant taxa. Specific or local biases in starch preservation may nevertheless arise through the particular ways in which different starchy organs are processed and decay, in particular environments. Ancient starch is of special interest for the archaeological detection of clonal, starchy root crops that lack hard tissues, but experimental research on the variability and taphonomy of starch (Barton and Matthews, 2006). Methods for analysing partially denatured, ancient starch are also needed (e.g. Horrocks et al., 2014).

When archaeological plant remains are found, it is inherently difficult to recognise them as derived from a domesticate if there is no living domesticate with comparable features, and no clear archaeological or natural sequence of previous wild forms that are different. Our ability to investigate the origins of domesticated plants through archaeology is severely constrained by a *preservation bias* that favours seeds and other hard or fibrous plant parts, and a *comparison bias* that makes it difficult to recognise domestication traits in taxa that were previously domesticated but then became extinct as cultigens (transient domesticated crops).

In principle, it should be easier to follow the archaeological appearance and disappearance of a transient seed crop than a transient clonal crop for which no hard tissues are preserved. We will never know how many plant species were once domesticated, cultivated, and then abandoned or lost in early periods of crop domestication and dispersal. Present-day domesticated crops may represent just a small fraction of plants that were, in the past, foraged, managed, cultivated, and domesticated.

Early transient crops are inherently unlikely to have left evidence of their domestication in archaeological deposits, but descendants may persist as wild populations within the natural range of the species, or as invasive or naturalised populations outside the natural range. Although it is still cultivated in mainland Southeast Asia, within its apparent natural range, the sacred lotus, *Nelumbo nucifera*, may be an example of a clonal crop that has naturalised after ancient introduction outside its natural range. It is now widespread in natural wetlands across northern Australia, and is a favoured wild food plant there. Testing this hypothesis will require palaeobotanical, archaeological, ethnobotanical, ecological, and genetic approaches in mainland Southeast Asia, island Southeast Asia, and northern Australia.

Mathematical methods for modeling and analysing population structure and interactions are also needed to study the history of clonal crops and their wild relatives. Some methods already exist for ecological and genetic research on natural and invasive populations of clonal plants, but are little discussed in the literature on clonal crops and their domestication. For mathematical models relevant to these crops, a key matter to consider will be inter-generational breeding between clones. Does this amplify the effects of inbreeding, or amplify the effects of outcrossing, in heterozygous clonal species? After introducing a tentative mathematical conjecture related to this matter, we will look at schematic models that consider, in general terms, the spread of clones and the formation of complex clonal assemblages over time and space.

## Inter-generational breeding

Although it is true that desired genotypes and phenotypes can be fixed in an instant by clonal propagation of a wild plant, such a step may be just a starting point in the domestication of a clonal crop. The first selected clone in a given location may eventually breed with (a) other ramets of the same clone, (b) ramets of the parent clones, (c) ramets of generations before the parents, (d) ramets of its own descendants already present at the location, and (e) ramets of less closely related clones that are wild or cultivated. The breeding patterns of clonal crops and their wild relatives are potentially much more complex than those of seed propagated crops because ancestral and descendant clones can, in principle, accumulate and coexist indefinitely or come into contact independently at multiple times, in multiple locations.

Mathematically the situation described previously can be conceived as leading to a cumulative, endlessly-compounding exponential increase in combinatory possibilities for parent and offspring generations. In species such as taro, in which selfing and outcrossing are both possible, this would follow, roughly, a double exponential function of the form Fn = x^(2^n) (the *double exponential function of maximum clonal diversity*; x = number of distinct clones in the starting population, each with different parental history, n = generation number). According to this function, if the starting number of genetically distinct clones at an arbitrary time zero is x = 10, then the number of distinct clones present after n = 3 generations will be in the order of 10^(2^3) = $10^8$ = 100 million, assuming that all ancestral clones continue to breed with all descendant clones, and all produce at least one descendant.

For a given number of genes and alleles in particular species, and assuming limited recombination and no ongoing mutation, the number of possible genotypes is limited. The double exponential function described previously would soon generate more possible crosses than there are possible genotypes (cross outcomes), meaning that identical or near-identical genotypes might re-occur over time. The same function applied over time, or many generations, presumably also generates more possible parental combinations than there are atoms in the universe, if it is true that the game of *go* offers such combinatory diversity in the limited space of a *go* board, with just two types (black and white) and their juxtapositions to consider. Obviously, the genetic diversity of real plants in the real world is limited by physical constraints, and the extinction of clonal lineages, but there may be situations where the combinatory possibilities in mixed clonal and sexual populations are maximised, creating genetic 'melting pots' or regions of hyper-diversity (see next section, 'Models of crop evolution and domestication').

The genetics of seed propagated plants are also very complex, especially when seeds can lie dormant for many years in a seed bank, but clonal plants can also have dormant seed banks. This has been well described in the case of cassava (McKey et al., 2012). The complexity of possible parent-offspring combinations is even further compounded when both clones and seeds are long lived. The sacred lotus is an extreme example, as its seeds can survive buried in mud for hundreds to thousands of years (Guo, 2009; Kubo et al., 2009).

## Models of crop evolution and domestication

Many models have been proposed to explain the domestication of plants and animals, in relation to different sequences of human social development, and in relation to the diverse environments in which human societies are found (Yen, 1989; Vasey, 1992; Etkin, 1994; Smith, 2001; Terrell et al., 2003; Kennedy and Clarke, 2004). Terrell et al. (2003) argued that the emphasis on domestication has led archaeology away from a more open investigation of how food and shelter were obtained from landscapes in the past. Genetic and ecological studies could contribute to this wider view of subsistence history by focusing on population history, and how useful plants or vegetation types have responded to dispersal by humans, and activities such as forest burning, land clearance, and water control. In this regard, the ever-widening field of invasion biology has much to offer (Mooney and Drake, 1986; Colautti et al., 2006; Moodley et al., 2016) even if it is mainly concerned with recent invasion history.

The dispersive and regenerative abilities of vegetative propagules are important for the invading abilities of many wild plant taxa when humans modify habitats or introduce plants to new regions. Invasive or weedy clonal plants such as *Actinidia deliciosa* (**Box 10.1** *Humans and kiwifruit: an ancient association?*), *Colocasia esculenta* (**Figure 10.3** *Open pasture habitats and spread of wild taro*), *Dioscorea* spp. (yams), *Houttuynia cordata* (**Figure 10.4** *Chameleon plant*), *Nelumbo nucifera*, *Pteridium* spp. (bracken fern), *Pueraria montana* var. *lobata* (**Figure 10.5** *Kudzu in Japan*), *Typha latifolia* (cattail), and many others (Randall, 2007) may have formed economically significant associations with habitats modified by human activity, long before agriculture appeared, and regardless of their subsequent domestication or lack of domestication. Kudzu has been used in Japan since the Jomon era (Higashi, 2000) and is still cultivated today as a starchy root crop in East Asia and Papua New Guinea. Bodner and Hymowitz (2002) concluded that although three distinct species of *Pueraria* have been cultivated, none were domesticated, possibly because of the ease of propagation by cuttings, crowns, or seed, and because there was no need to select against toxicity, spiny growths, or a deep-burying habit. They view the wildtype plant as easy to grow and relatively easy to use. Although the fibre content of kudzu tubers makes starch extraction expensive, the plant is still cultivated and valued in Japan as a source of starch for special food products (**Figure 10.5**).

## Box 10.1 Humans and kiwifruit: an ancient association?

Wild populations of edible *Actinidia* species are harvested on a large scale in China, and are mostly found in disturbed forest habitats (Ferguson and Huang, 2007). Long human occupation of eastern Eurasia makes it likely that *Actinidia* spp. were subject to various conscious and unconscious selection processes (sensu Zohary, 2004). Ancient Chinese writings suggest that 'sporadic attempts were made in the past to cultivate kiwifruit species, starting about 1200 years ago' (Zohary, 2004, p. 77). Since kiwifruit are harvested ripe or near-ripe, with mature seeds, it seems likely that humans (along with monkeys) have been intimately involved in the dispersal of edible *Actinidia* species, and early selection may have operated very loosely at a population or landscape scale, before the modern emergence of favoured clones that are now maintained as cultivars. Meyer et al. (2012) cited the history of kiwifruit *(A. deliciosa)* introduction and selection in New Zealand as an example of the less common process of domestication outside the native (or natural) range of a crop, but much remains to be learned about the natural and cultural history of *A. deliciosa* within its apparent natural range. In New Zealand, far outside the natural range, massive expansion of the kiwfruit industry has generated high 'propagule pressure' (Colautti et al., 2006), and the fast-growing, woody vine has invaded native forest and scrub, and commercial *Pinus radiata* plantations (Sullivan et al., 2007).

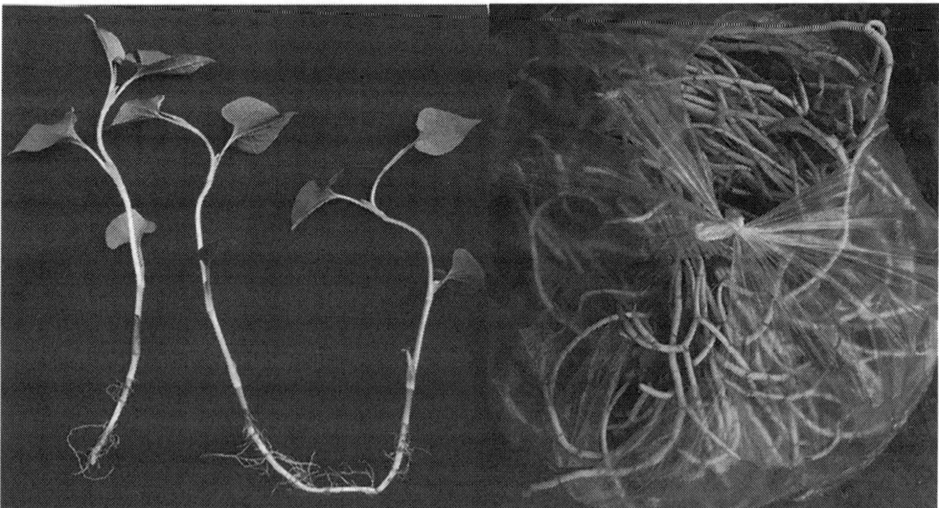

*Figure 10.4* Chameleon plant *(Houttouynia cordata)*

*Note*: Left, wild in Japan (from stream bank); right, at a restaurant in Yunnan, China. In Japan, the leaves are commonly dried for herbal tea; in India, Vietnam, and China, the leaves and stolons of wild plants are eaten as a vegetable, raw or cooked. Use of the plant is presumably very ancient, and it easily spreads in disturbed habitats, via stolons and agamic seeds (formed without fertilisation). The natural range is unknown: in regions of very recent introduction, the plant is considered a weed or potential weed. Stolon thickness is about 4 mm.

*Source*: Author.

*Figure 10.5* Kudzu *(Pueraria montana* var. *lobata)* in Japan

*Note*: Left, plant flowering in late Spring; right, noodles *(kudzu-kiri)* made with starch from the underground tubers – a traditional and expensive summer delicacy; the vine is an ancient but now minor root crop in Japan, and a modern invasive weed in North America after its introduction there to control soil erosion.

*Source*: Author.

Genetic approaches to understanding crop evolution and domestication are usually premised on a strict or limited definition of domestication as genetic modification resulting from human selection. Selection and cultivation of a clone direct from a natural wild population would not represent domestication in genetic terms (**Figure 10.1** *The gathering pathway*). In a large-scale synthesis of the global patterns of animal domestication, Larson and Fuller (2014) identified three main pathways to domestication in which wild animals may:

1 enter human habitats as commensals (the commensal pathway);
2 be first prey for hunter-gatherers (the prey pathway); or
3 be subject to directed selection in a deliberate attempt to domesticate a species (the directed pathway).

In their view, 'domestication' should refer to initial selection, from which point onward we might (in the case of plants) regard a crop as undergoing improvement or local adaptation as it spreads with humans. A particular plant species may be domesticated independently more than once, but the common distinction between 'primary' and 'secondary' domestication suggests equivalence between early and later processes that may be very different.

When domestication first happens for a given species, it may channel attention to a restricted range of diversity within the species, thus restricting the later choices. This is likely to vary case by case. Dramatic improvements that channel attention may occur during or long after initial domestication, as a result, for example, of dispersal and then hybridisation with a previously allopatric (geographically separate) species. The invasive or weedy character of many crop species, including clonal species, makes the commensal pathway to domestication appear a reasonable proposition, though distinguishing this from a process that begins with extraction from natural wild habitats (a gathering or prey pathway) may not be easy. If 'domestication of the environment' (Yen, 1985) includes both the modification of environments and active dispersal of useful plants, then the gathering and dispersal of wildtype clones (**Figure 10.1**) might trigger a process of plant invasion that greatly increases the useful productivity of an occupied landscape, especially if landscape modification and natural breeding support the invasion or naturalisation process. The possible pathways to domestication are myriad.[1] For the domestication of clonal crops, an illustrative range of models is suggested here (**Figure 10.1** *The gathering pathway*, **Figure 10.6** *Simple commensal pathway*, **Figure 10.7** *Complex commensal pathway with and without hybridisation*). The model components can be added, deleted, and rearranged to suggest further hypothetical pathways to domestication.

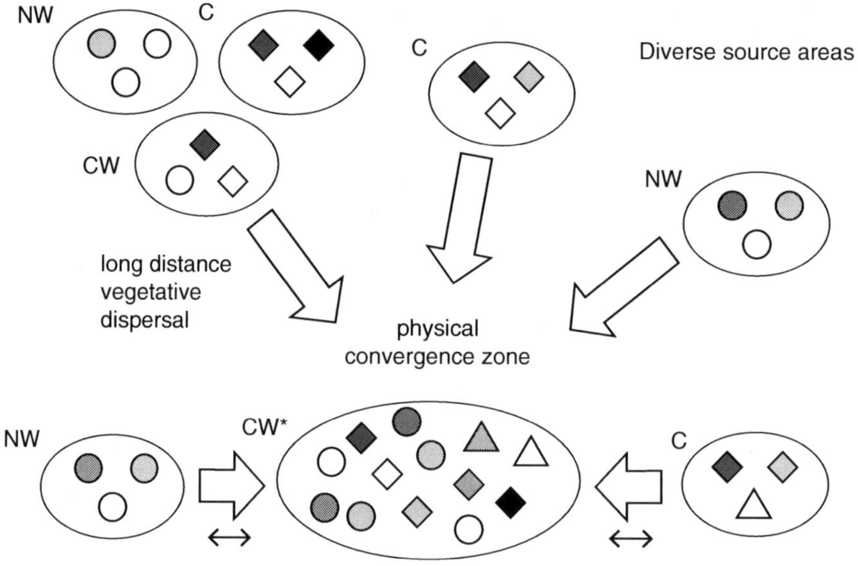


*Figure 10.6* Simple commensal pathway

*Note*. Wildtype clones (circles) are gathered from natural habitats, then undergo cycles of breeding and selection (genetic domestication) in modified habitats with commensal breeding populations. Selection leads to domesticated clones (diamonds) that are eventually cultivated. In this model, genotypes are modified, but there is little diversity, as the process depends on a limited range of clones gathered from nature.

*Source*: Author.

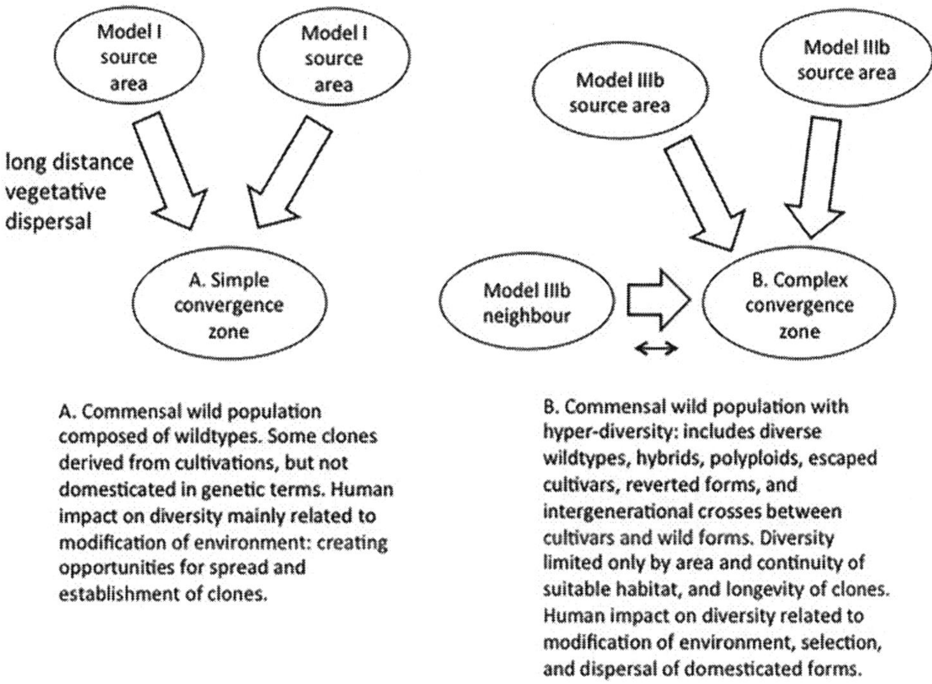


*Figure 10.7* Complex commensal pathway with and without hybridisation

*Note*: Left, without hybridisation. Commensal breeding populations in the past may have occupied diverse wild to modified habitats, providing diverse opportunities for cycles of breeding and selection, and for further improvement or adaptation after initial domestication. The present domesticated clones (diamonds) are thus more diverse than those produced in the simple commensal pathway. Right, complex commensal pathway with hybridisation. This may also involve polyploidisation (PP), the preservation of diverse production systems in modified habitats (with or without cultivation) from past to present, and interactions with crop wild relatives (CWR, including wild species and subspecies), leading to a complex genetic history from initial domestication to the present. Hybrids and polyploids may occur first in nature, or after early selection of diploid cultivars, or both. The present assemblage of domesticated clones (diamonds) is likely to be more diverse than that produced without hybridisation.

*Source*: Author.

Major commodity crops, including some clonal crops, are of great interest for historical, practical, and economic reasons, but involve a small fraction of all plants domesticated, and an even smaller fraction of all plants used in the past and present. To explore the many possible pathways to domestication requires attention to minor and major crops, to the wild relatives of crops, to our working definitions of plants and their habitats, to the full spectrum of plants between those that are completely wild and those that survive only in cultivation, and to the genetic interactions between wild and cultivated plants. Gene flow between clonal crops and their wild relatives (**Figure 10.7**) is generally poorly documented. For clonal crops that are global commodities, some information is available. Anderson and de Vicente (2010) have reviewed studies of gene flow in banana and plantain (*Musa* spp.), cassava *(Manihot esculenta)*, potato *(Solanum tuberosum)* and sweet potato *(Ipomoea batatas)*. The genetic structure of wild populations may also be altered by the spread of cultivated varieties with which they can interbreed. Crops that readily naturalise, through natural and human dispersal of vegetative plant parts, may form persistent clonal patches that interact with nearby wild relatives or cultivated populations over many plant generations.

Zohary (2004) noted that wide segregation among the sexual progeny of (heterozygous) clonal crops also means that they often regress 'towards the mean found in wild populations, showing striking resemblance to the wild forms' (p. 7). For any given wild breeding population within the likely natural range of a clonal crop species, it can be difficult to show that the population concerned represents a naturally occurring population of wildtype clones rather than a naturalising population derived from fertile clones that have reverted or regressed towards a wild mean. The task is not impossible, but requires attention to contextual information about each particular population and species, and to genetic, morphological, and ecological data from across the species range.

Identifying natural wild habitats, wildtype forms, and natural range have been the primary goals of a long-term study of the origins, domestication, and dispersal of taro *(Colocasia esculenta)* (Matthews, 1991, 2014; Matthews and Naing, 2005; Matthews et al., 2012; Matthews et al., 2015). Taro was the most widely distributed, clonal starch crop in pre-modern times, ranging across Eurasia, through Africa, and through the many islands of Oceania. Its natural range in semi-aquatic habitats may include most of mainland Southeast Asia, and within this range, simple or complex commensal pathways to domestication (**Figures 10.6, 10.7**) may have been followed more than once. In the field, it is common to observe wild taros growing near human settlements, in a great variety of disturbed habitats – along roadsides, field banks and ditches, lakesides, stream banks, and riverbanks that are grazed by cattle, goats, or horses. These large mammals avoid taro and selectively graze adjacent grasses and other herbs (**Figure 10.3**). From semi-aquatic habitats, vegetative parts of taro are commonly washed downstream, eventually resettling on bare open banks or in the vicinity of existing downstream populations. In Southeast Asia, the pre-eminence of wetland rice cultivation means that human settlement today is ubiquitous in most areas where taro is likely to spread and settle. The long-distance vegetative dispersal ability of taro in water catchments means that there is always a possibility that commensal wild populations in downstream locations are derived from upstream locations with natural wild populations, commensal wild populations, taro managed in modified habitats (without cultivation), and taro cultivations. Commensal wild populations may be located in physical convergence zones at stream and river junctions throughout a catchment area. A single, schematic example is shown in the right-hand panel of **Figure 10.7**.

The concept of a physical convergence zone can be expanded to physical locations preferentially colonised by any dispersal mechanism, and can be combined with the different models for the local interactions between wild and cultivated populations of a crop species, and crop wild relatives. If clones of different age and geographical origin persist and breed in convergence zones, and if downstream convergence zones are repeatedly colonised by clones from upstream convergence zones, then very complex patterns of genetic diversity, or *hyper-diversity*, may arise through inter-generational breeding. Gene flow from catchments into convergence zones must reflect not just the character of each species concerned, but also the biotic and abiotic conditions that channel seed, pollen, and vegetative dispersal. The resulting distribution of genetic diversity, on regional scales, may become a complex mosaic contingent on landscape history; climate history; the distribution of breeding and clonal source populations; the dispersal abilities of vegetative parts, seeds, and pollen; and the interactions between plants, animals, and humans. Humans are also active agents in the convergences that arise between crops and their wild relatives (Anderson, 1967).

To continue with the example of taro, cultivated and wild populations and closely related wild species are widespread in the mountains of South and Southeast Asia. When clones spread downstream from the tributaries of large catchments, they may eventually converge, settle, and form breeding populations in the confluences and lowland deltas of major river systems. Over thousands of years, human activities that encourage erosion and the creation of open wetland habitats may have massively increased opportunities for hyper-diversity to develop in taro. In South and Southeast Asia, the largest zones of hyper-diversity for taro may exist at the confluences and deltas of the Ganges and Brahmaputra Rivers, the Mekong, and other large rivers that originate in the Himalayan ranges. To date, the only systematic studies of diversity in wild taro populations have focused on populations scattered through the rainforest zone of Northeast Queensland, Australia, at the southern margin of the likely natural range of this species (Matthews and Terauchi, 1994; Hunt et al., 2013; Matthews, 2014), and far from the zones of hyper-diversity predicted here.

Studies of morphological diversity and genetic structure in the nearest known wild relatives of a crop are necessary starting points for tracing the genetic and geographical origins of cultivated and domesticated forms (Olsen and Schaal, 1999, 2007). So too are interpretations or models of natural range and variation (Matthews, 1991). If wild populations within the putative natural range of a plant species form genetically distinct sub-populations, then some resolution can be expected when attempting to identify the genetic and geographical origins of domesticated or cultivated forms within that species. Whether we begin with empirical data, more or less plausible models, or specific testable theories, the research process is necessarily iterative and requires repeated field exploration, sampling, analysis, and interpretation as more is learned about the diversity, distribution and utilisation of wild and cultivated populations and species. The research process must also take into account changes in our understanding of modern human behaviour and also the ability of our distant ancestors to distinguish, transport, manage, and domesticate the plants and animals around them.

## Archetypes and ideotypes: the targets of conscious selection

Over the last 2 million years of the Quaternary era (and encompassing the Pleistocene and Holocene periods), climate change has impacted not just the evolution, spread, and survival of plants and animals, but also our own species, and our near but now-extinct hominid relatives (Hewitt, 2000). While archaeological evidence points consistently to an emergence of agriculture from the late Pleistocene and early Holocene onward, our interactions with plants that are now domesticated are likely to have started much earlier (Smith, 2001; Larson and Fuller, 2014), establishing traditions and archetypic views of plants that remain salient today. It seems safe to assume that our habitat and dietary preferences have always been consciously followed, ever since our species had the technical, cultural, and intellectual means to move from one habitat and diet to another. Dietary plasticity and intellectual curiosity gave rise to the 'omnivore's dilemma' that we face as humans: how to eat safely and well, when so much can be eaten (Pollan, 2006). Although some individuals are more curious than others, most people in each society follow established food traditions when possible, making adjustments when necessary during famine, or according to economic conditions (e.g. changes in wealth). Rozin (1976) described the general tendency as *neophobia*, an aversion for the new, and noted that 'ethnic food habits in minority groups are the last vestiges of the old culture to disappear' (p. 52).

When food, textile, and other traditions develop around wild and cultivated plants, what we learn from teachers, observation, and experience allows us to recognise, use, protect, and propagate particular plants or populations that fit an *archetype* of what we want and seek: an image in the mind of what plant will serve our purpose best, or adequately. Archetypes exist for useful (or dangerous) wild plants just as they do for cultivated plants. Mithin (2006) suggested that 'natural history knowledge' is a basic cognitive realm in the human brain that allows us to perceive, classify, and remember a great variety of natural phenomena. Our ability to organise information and recognise archetypes is linked to the physiological reward system that gives us pleasure when finding something that we have been consciously searching for. Levitin (2014) believed that the human brain has been configured to acquire information about the biological world, and that we have an innate passion for naming and categorising plants. These cognitive abilities may predate our existence as modern humans *(Homo sapiens).*

In evolutionary terms, humans have been 'modern' for around 100,000 years, and have subsisted on a mixed diet of wild plant and animal foods since long before achieving 'modern' status. Wild plants and animals still play a significant economic role in modern agricultural societies (Etkin, 1994). Johns (1989) proposed a chemical-ecological model of root crop domestication: since the wild relatives of these and other crops often use biochemical defences for protection against herbivores, early foraging societies that depended on wild foods must have used only fire and other food processing techniques to greatly expand the range of plant foods that could be used. Plants can also use physical protection to resist herbivory, and traits such as fibrosity in storage tissues, and thorns on leaves, stems, or around apical shoots, and at the apex of storage organs are likely to have presented challenges for the selection and domestication of many clonal crops, including the aroid starch crop *Cyrtosperma merkusii* (stem apex protected by spines, and corm also acrid), certain species of *Dioscorea* yam (spiny stems; fibrous tubers, sometimes toxic) and the leaf-textile crop *Pandanus tectorius* (spiny leaves; edible nuts enclosed in very hard, fibrous seed cases).

To control the breeding of a seed propagated crop is difficult in mixed cultivar assemblages, and it must be increasingly difficult to keep seed stocks separate and maintain desired archetypes as the number of different cultivars increases in a single field or local assemblage. Logistically, maintaining a large but static assemblage of strongly held archetypical cultivars must be more difficult than maintaining small but dynamic assemblage of old and new cultivars that reflect loosely held archetypes and strong interest in newly found or introduced types. The logistical problems for keeping desired archetypes are not so severe with clonal crops. Sterile polyploid or hybrid clones that require vegetative propagation by farmers may be favoured in part because they cannot breed. Even if the clonal crop continues to breed, in or out of cultivation, old and new cultivars can easily be grown and stored alongside each other and the breeding population, if the cultivars are visually distinct. In the case of taro, human selection may have promoted variability in the expression of anthocyanin genes, leading to the diverse colour patterns observed in cultivars today (Matthews, 2014) and providing farmers a useful means for distinguishing archetypes with fewer visible differences in other traits of interest. Positive selection for colour variation, in clonal crops, is of course most obvious and well documented for ornamentals for which colour is the primary trait of interest. If we can apply the term archetype more broadly, the bulb propagated tulip can be regarded as an archetypical colour crop, given its prominent role in the history of ornamental plants (Pavord, 1999).

As noted previously, a third pathway to domestication is 'directed selection'. In its broadest sense, this can refer to deliberate attempts to improve a crop, through selection of plants that already display desired qualities. Less broadly, it can refer to selection aimed at creating a new form that can be imagined but does not yet exist – an *ideotype*. Using modern genetic knowledge and breeding techniques, plants can be designed according to ideotypes that are expected to be ideal for specific purposes, as proposed for potato by Donald (1968). Whether our attention is given to archetypes (existing forms of particular significance) or ideotypes (ideal forms that we wish to bring into existence), conscious selection and propagation are involved and take place in the social and cultural contexts of production, storage, processing, and utilisation.

## Vegetative reproduction and clonal crops

When a crop is described as 'vegetatively propagated', the phrase generally refers to the usual or most obvious mode of reproduction under cultivation. Even if this is the only known mode of propagation within a cultivation system, clonal crop species often have opportunities to breed and generate new varieties when the following three conditions exist:

1 The local climate (temperature, humidity, day length, and more) permits a full cycle of flowering, breeding, and seedling growth).
2 Pollen transport is successful, via insects, birds, wind, or other pollen vectors, according to the pollination system.
3 Inattention or deliberate actions by people provide opportunities for at least some individuals of a crop to grow to maturity inside the field or garden, or as commensal wild populations in less controlled, wild spaces (ruderal habitats, natural landscape remnants) in and around human habitation areas.

Under these three conditions, new cultivars may be selected as a result of both genetic mutation and recombination in the breeding cycle, and genetic mutation within vegetative lineages of the crop (somatic mutation), from one clonal generation to the next. New clonal lineages may also arise through epigenetic variation, when non-genetic changes accumulate and segregate in the cell lineages of vegetative growing points (apical and lateral meristems). As well as these intra-specific and intra-clonal processes, new cultivars or apparently new species may arise through hybridisation between a cultivated crop species and its wild relatives.

A single somatic sport or novel seedling in an otherwise homogenous field of clonal individuals may be much more obvious to a farmer than one variant among many in the heterogeneous field of a seed propagated crop. Newly found and selected variants of a seed propagated crop are more likely to be very obviously different – they would not be found otherwise. Discovery and selection in clonal crops may also be easier at the time of consumption. When seeds are consumed, they already come mixed, from multiple breeding parents. Replanting seeds from stocks kept for eating may not produce plants with the qualities found in other seeds at the time of eating.

To preserve planting stocks for different varieties in traditional farming systems, expert farmers generally select seed heads from different parents in the field, and then store the seeds separately. Genetic differences that affect consumption, and that are not linked to obvious phenotypic differences in the field, may be difficult to catch in seed crops.

In clonal root crops, when a new desirable quality is discovered while preparing, cooking, or eating a corm or tuber, the remaining kitchen supply can be converted to planting stock that will preserve the new variety. A similar process may happen with a clonal fibre crop such as bamboo: if a stalk is found with new and interesting shape or colour qualities, part of it can be used, while any unused part with a node or bud can be replanted to preserve the new variety. Exactly how and where mutation and selection take place, and how materials for planting and eating are stored and used, are significant matters for archaeological studies of domestication. Plant remains found in areas used for food storage and consumption may differ from those found in areas used to grow plants or store planting materials, and the archaeological evidence for storage *per se* may differ for different kinds of planting materials (e.g. damp pits for many root crops, or dry containers for seed crops).

Vegetative reproduction from rhizomes and stems is widespread among plants, and is the most common, obvious, and useful form of asexual reproduction for crop propagation. Some plants also reproduce asexually through apomixis, forming viable seeds without *fertilisation* or meiosis (gamete formation). In the case of *Houttyunia cordata* (**Figure 10.4**), viable pollen are not formed, and the seeds develop through apomixis. Apomixis is rarely seen in cultivated plants, but modern plant breeders are interested in using the phenomenon to propagate crops by seed while enjoying the benefit of producing a uniform selected genotype in the crop. This practical interest in apomixis has led to more exploration of its occurrence in wild species. Findings relevant to the evolution and domestication of clonal crops are that apomictic species: (a) are almost always perennial (living more than two seasons), (b) often reproduce vegetatively, through stolon production, for example, and (c) are more common in frequently-disturbed habitats and/or other environments where various barriers inhibit cross-breeding between compatible individuals, including widely-dispersed individuals in tropical rain forest (Bicknell and Koltunow, 2004).

Perhaps one of the most vexing issues in the study of crop origins is that most evidence for domestication is limited to the last 10,000 years or so, within the relatively stable but also relatively short Holocene period. Is this because agriculture could develop only under the warm and relatively stable conditions of the Holocene period, or is it because archaeological and biological evidence for domesticated plants and animals is naturally better preserved in more recent archaeological sites, and more obvious in living plant and animal populations? One way to explore crop origins deeper in time may be to study the antiquity of clonal lineages.

Most plant species living today are likely to have existed for millions of years (Hewitt, 2000), so our human ancestors could have known and used many of them for tens to hundreds of thousands of years. Our present knowledge of domesticated plants largely reflects our experience of a relatively small number of living domesticates adapted to recent, Holocene environments. Given that living species are very old, it is in principle possible that some living cultivated clones represent ancient domesticates that predate the known archaeological record of agriculture. Age estimates for natural clones of various wild plant taxa have ranged from 10,000 years BP old to as much as 1 million years (Mitton and Grant, 1996), and a molecular clock approach has been used to estimate the age of different male clones of the quaking aspen in British Columbia, Canada (Ally et al., 2010). If some clonal crops were in fact domesticated more than 10,000 years ago, and were adapted to cool Pleistocene conditions in lower latitudes or altitudes, then individual clonal lineages from that period may still survive today at higher latitudes or altitudes. This possibility can be suggested for temperate-adapted lineages of taro, which are now widespread in northeastern Asia, far north of their putative natural range in eastern Himalaya (Matthews, 2014).

If a particular cultivated clone becomes widespread, then its long-term survival chances should increase, as not all ramets will be exposed to the same threats. If clean ramets (without any attached pests and diseases) are taken to a region with no pests and diseases for that crop, the introduced ramets may avoid attack by pest and disease for a very long time. Clonal crops in the Pacific Islands, including bananas, yams, and edible aroids, may have avoided exposure to many pests and diseases for thousands of years. In recent centuries, increasingly rapid transport and crop exchange throughout the Pacific has ended an isolation that was in many ways healthy for humans and plants alike. Most clonal crops in the Pacific Islands are introduced crops with a relatively narrow genetic base, and are therefore genetically vulnerable (Lebot, 1992). For these crops, pest and disease resistance has been found, or can be expected, in regions where breeding populations have long existed, close to their natural evolutionary homelands, or hearth regions, in Southeast Asia and the western Pacific (or South America in the case of sweet potato; Roulliera et al., 2013).

In the hearth regions, continuous exposure to pests and diseases may have led to relatively frequent selection of new cultivars and turnover in clonal cultivar assemblages, assuming that:

1 new clones could be discovered, selected, and cultivated more easily because of the presence of breeding populations; and
2 new pests and diseases could more easily arise to challenge existing cultivar assemblages.

Only clones that are exceptionally resistant to pests and diseases are likely to have been long-lived in the hearth regions. If this is true, then a search for most ancient cultivated clones, or living crop elders, may require special attention to those located outside the natural geographical or ecological range of a clonal crop species.

## Anti-domesticates: relict crops, favoured natural archetypes, or just untamable?

New Zealand was one of the last large land masses reached by humans, around 1,000 years ago. Prehistorically and historically, most domesticated food plants in New Zealand have been exotic introductions, like the so-called kiwifruit (formerly 'Chinese gooseberry') (**Box 10.1**). Modern development of New Zealand native plants has been dominated by selection for ornamental cultivars, including vegetatively propagated cultivars of *Phormium* spp. (New Zealand flax), *Cordyline* spp. (cabbage tree), and *Hebe* (Harris and Heenan, 1992). For biogeographical reasons related to isolation and the absence of mammals and marsupials, the New Zealand flora contains few plants with edible underground storage organs or other edible parts that can serve as staple food sources (Partridge and Harris, 1988). Two native taxa that did become important food sources were managed but not cultivated, despite the ease with which they are vegetatively propagated: *Pteridium esculentum* (bracken fern, with starchy rhizomes) (McGlone et al., 2005), and *Cordyline australis* (cabbage tree), the latter with stem sugars that could be extracted from the fibrous trunks (Simpson, 2000). Wild populations of cattail *(Typha latifolia)* were also used, mainly as sources of leaves used for mats or thatch, but also as sources of edible starchy rhizomes and pollen (Brooker et al., 1989).

*Typha* (cattail) and *Pteridium* (bracken fern) are cosmopolitan genera with few species, and have been used in most temperate to subtropical regions of the world. These plants are easily transplanted and maintained as vegetative clones, but also have a strong ability to breed, disperse by seeds or spores, respectively, and invade open habitats created by human activities. With minor modern exceptions, they have never been domesticated, and the reason may be partly explained by the same aspects of reproduction and dispersive ability that explain their cosmopolitan distributions (Austin, 2007). In the case of *Typha*, the pollen are wind-dispersed, but not for long distances. The very numerous small seeds are attached to feathery 'wings' and can be carried by wind currents over very large distances. Isolation of a breeding population of *Typha* may be possible for short period of time, but any large area in a natural or artificial wetland is likely to be colonised by wild forms eventually, making isolation difficult to maintain. At the same time, if harvesting for fibre or food uses does not prevent breeding, and there is no strong selection pressure, a population established by vegetative propagation will easily revert to a wildtype form. There is no indication from historical and ethnographic records anywhere that cattails or bracken ferns have been subjected to deliberate or strong human selection of any kind (Austin, 2007).

In general, three explanations can be suggested for the apparent lack of domestication of widely used clonal plant species. First, they may have been cultivated and domesticated in the past, but became widely naturalised with human assistance, and no longer need to be maintained as cultigens (no examples can be offered here). Second, useful qualities of the wild plants may be appreciated so much, and the plants may be so abundant, that there has been no incentive to cultivate or domesticate them – the wild plants may be favoured natural archetypes (see kudzu, p. 179). Third, the plants may be untamable anti-domesticates, whether cultivated or not, if they are (a) naturally ubiquitous, with rapid and wide dispersal of pollen, seeds, and vegetative parts (see cattail and bracken fern, p. 187), or (b) entirely clonal in their spread, and cannot be improved by breeding and selection (see chameleon plant, p. 178).

In principle, it should be possible to domesticate fertile but clonal 'anti-domesticates' if suitable archetypes or ideotypes are first identified, and special care is taken to establish and isolate breeding populations of selected clones for further selection. With such taming, invasive clonal species have great potential for food production, biofuel production (e.g. *Arundo donax*, Pilu et al., 2012), as specialty crops for existing cottage industries based on local traditions of use, and as more easily managed versions of plants that can help reduce erosion, or restore ecological health to damaged landscapes. Such projects have inherent ecological risks also, as noted with alarm in the case of seaweeds (macro-algae) that are spreading rapidly as newly domesticated clonal crops in marine environments (Loureiro et al., 2015).

## Conclusions

The empirical foundations for developing theories about genetic history, commensal dispersal, and domestication are far from adequate for most clonal crop species, despite huge advances in the understanding of evolutionary biology, plant molecular genetics, and the molecular aspects of domestication. This is because field research and sample collection strategies have rarely been guided by questions or testable theories that address the fundamental natural and cultural history of each crop. They have been more focused on the creation of living collections that have the important tasks of maintaining crop diversity found in cultivation, and providing materials for modern plant breeding, and that are secondarily employed for historical research. As a result, the main gene pools from which modern crop development could benefit may be invisible, though standing in plain sight.

Many historically important clonal crops and potential crops are international or global in their present distribution and need to be studied on regional and inter-regional geographical scales. In general terms, natural long-distance dispersal of vegetative parts may have similar consequences for different taxa, if there is physical convergence across landscapes, and highly mixed, inter-generational breeding populations are established. In commensal wild populations of many clonal crop species, the possible existence of local or regional convergence zones with very high genetic diversity, or hyper-diversity, has not been studied.

## Acknowledgements

For research assistance and mathematical advice, I thank E. Tabuchi, National Museum of Ethnology, Japan. For long-term support for field studies in Southeast Asia, I thank K. Watanabe, Tsukuba University, Japan. For related collaboration and discussion, I thank I. Ahmed (Pakistan), C. L. Long (China), D. K. Medhi (India), V. D. Nguyen (Vietnam), E. Takei (Japan), E. M. Agoo, D. A. Madulid, and M. Medici (Philippines), and many others. For editorial support, I especially thank D. Hunter, Bioversity International, Rome. This work was supported in part by JSPS KAKENHI Grant No. 23405004, Japan.

## Note

1 A quotation from Longfellow is apropos to illustrate the meaning of 'myriad' intended here: 'The forests, with their myriad tongues, / Shouted of liberty'. The implication is that humans have never been entirely in control of domestication.

## References

Ally, D., Ritland, K. and Otto, S. P. (2010) 'Aging in a long-lived clonal tree', *PLoS Biology*, vol. 8, p. e1000454.

Anderson, E. (1967) *Plants, Man and Life*, University of California Press, Berkeley, Los Angeles, CA, USA, and London, UK.

Anderson, M. S. and de Vicente, M. C. (2010) *Gene Flow between Crops and their Wild Relatives*, Johns Hopkins University Press, Baltimore, MD, USA.

Austin, D. F. (2007) 'Sacred connections with cat-tail (*Typha*, Typhaceae): Dragons, water-serpents and reed-maces', *Ethnobotany Research & Applications*, vol. 5, pp. 273–303.

Barton, H. and Matthews, P. J. (2006) 'Taphonomy', pp. 75–94 in R. Torrence and H. Barton (eds.), *Ancient Starch Research*, Left Coast Press, Walnut Creek, CA, USA.

Batello, C., Brinkman, R., Mannetje, L.'t, Martinez, A. and Suttie, J. (2008) *Plant Genetic Resources of Forage Crops, Pasture and Rangelands*, Thematic Background Studies, Food and Agriculture Organization (FAO), Rome, Italy, www.fao.org/fileadmin/templates/agphome/documents/PGR/SoW2/thematicstudy_forage.pdf, accessed 31 May 2016.

Bhattacharyya, N. and Sarma, S. (2010) 'Assessment of availability, ecological feature, and habitat preference of the medicinal herb *Houttuynia cordata* Thunb in the Brahmaputra Valley of Assam, India', *Environmental Monitoring and Assessment*, vol. 160, pp. 277–287.

Bicknell, R. A. and Koltunow, A. M. (2004) 'Understanding apomixis: Recent advances and remaining conundrums', *Plant Cell*, vol. 16, pp. S228–S245.

Bodner, C. C. and Hymowitz, T. (2002) 'Ethnobotany of *Pueraria* species', pp. 29–58 in W. M. Keung (ed.), *The Genus Pueraria*, Taylor and Francis, New York, NY, USA.

Brooker, S. G., Cambie, R. C. and Cooper, R. V. (1989) 'Economic native plants of New Zealand', *Economic Botany*, vol. 43, pp. 79–106.

Colautti, R. I., Grigorovich, I. A. and MacIsaac, H. J. (2006) 'Propagule pressure: A null model for biological invasions', *Biological Invasions*, vol. 8, pp. 1023–1037.

Denham, T., Atchison, J., Austin, J., Bestel, S., Bowdery, D., Crowther, A., . . . Matthews, P. (2009) 'Archaeobotany in Australia and New Guinea: Practice, potential and prospects', *Australian Archaeology*, vol. 68, pp. 1–10.

Donald, C. M. (1968) 'The breeding of crop ideotypes', *Euphytica*, vol. 17, pp. 385–403.

Etkin, N. (1994) 'The cull of the wild', pp. 1–21 in N. Etkin (ed.), *Eating on the Wild Side: The Pharmacological, Ecological, and Social Implications of Using Non-cultigens*, University of Arizona Press, Tucson, AZ, USA.

Ferguson, A. R. and H.-W. Huang (2007) 'Genetic resources of kiwifruit: Domestication and breeding', *Horticultural Reviews*, vol. 33, pp. 1–121.

Goldschmidt, E. E. (2014) 'Plant grafting: New mechanisms, evolutionary implications', *Frontiers in Plant Science*, vol. 5, pp. 1–9.

Grivet, L., Daniels, C., Glaszmann, J. C. and D'Hont, A. (2004) 'A review of recent molecular genetics evidence for sugarcane evolution and domestication', *Ethnobotany Research and Applications*, vol. 2, pp. 9–17.

Guo, H. B. (2009) 'Cultivation of lotus (*Nelumbo nucifera* Gaertn. ssp. *nucifera*) and its utilization in China', *Genetic Resources and Crop Evolution*, vol. 56, pp. 323–330.

Harris, D. R. (2006) 'The interplay of ethnographic and archaeological knowledge in the study of past human subsistence in the tropics', pp. 77–95 in R. Ellen (ed.), *Ethnobiology and the Science of Humankind*, Blackwell, Malden, Oxford and London, UK.

Harris, W. and P. B. Heenan (1992) 'Domestication of the New Zealand flora: An alternative view', *New Zealand Journal of Crop and Horticultural Science*, vol. 20, pp. 257–271.

Hather, J. G. (1991) 'The identification of charred archaeological remains of vegetative parenchymatous tissues', *Journal of Archaeological Science*, vol. 18, pp. 661–675.

Hegarty, M. J., and Hiscock, S. J. (2005) 'Hybrid speciation in plants: New insights from molecular studies', *New Phytologist*, vol. 165, pp. 411–423.

Hewitt, G. (2000) 'The genetic legacy of the Quaternary ice ages,' *Nature*, vol. 405, pp. 907–913.

Higashi, K. (2000) *Pits of the Jomon Period*, Kagoshima Prefectural Archaeological Center, Kagoshima, Japan.

Horrocks, M., Nieuwoudt, M. K., Kinaston, R., Buckley, H. and Bedford, S. (2014) 'Microfossil and Fourier Transform InfraRed analyses of Lapita and post-Lapita human dental calculus from Vanuatu, Southwest Pacific', *Journal of the Royal Society of New Zealand*, vol. 44, pp. 17–33.

Hunt, H. V., Moots, H. M. and Matthews, P. J. (2013) 'Genetic data confirms field evidence for natural breeding in a wild taro population (*Colocasia esculenta*) in northern Queensland, Australia', *Genetic Resources and Crop Evolution*, vol. 60, pp. 1695–1707.

Hunter, D. and Heywood, V. (2011) *Crop Wild Relatives: A Manual of in situ Conservation*, Earthscan for Routledge, Abingdon, UK and Washington, DC, USA.

Johns, T. (1989) 'A chemical-ecological model of root and tuber domestication in the Andes', pp. 504–519 in D. R. Harris and G. C. Hillman (eds.), *Foraging and Farming: The Evolution of Plant Exploitation*, Unwin Hyman, London, UK.

Kennedy, J. and Clarke, W. (2004) *Cultivated Landscapes of the Southwest Pacific*, RMAP Working Paper No. 50. Resource Management in Asia-Pacific Program, Australian National University, Canberra, Australia.

King, F. B. (1994) 'Interpreting wild plant foods in the archaeological record', pp. 185–209 in N. Etkin (ed.), *Eating on the Wild Side: The Pharmacological, Ecological, and Social Implications of Using Non-cultigens*, University of Arizona Press, Tucson, AZ, USA.

Kubo, N., Hirai, M., Kaneko, A. and Tanaka, D. (2009) 'Classification and diversity of sacred and American *Nelumbo* species: The genetic relationships of flowering lotus cultivars in Japan using SSR markers', *Plant Genetic Resources: Characterization and Utilization*, vol. 7, pp. 260–270.

Lambert, J. B. (1997) *Traces of the Past: Unraveling the Secrets of Archaeology Through Chemistry*, Addison-Wesley, Reading, MA, USA.

Larson, G. and Fuller, D. Q. (2014) 'The evolution of animal domestication', *Annual Review of Ecology and Systematics*, vol. 45, pp. 115–136.

Lebot, V. (1992) 'Genetic vulnerability of Oceania's traditional crops', *Experimental Agriculture*, vol. 28, pp. 309–323.

Levitin, D. J. (2014) *The Organized Mind: Thinking Straight in the Age of Information Overload*, Dutton Penguin Random House, New York, NY, USA.

Liese, W. and Köhl, M. (2015) *Bamboo: The Plant and Its Uses*, Springer, the Netherlands.

Loureiro, R., Gachon, C. M. M. and Rebours, C. (2015) 'Seaweed cultivation: Potential and challenges of crop domestication at an unprecedented pace', *New Phytologist*, vol. 206, pp. 489–492.

Matthews, P. J. (1991) 'A possible tropical wildtype taro: *Colocasia esculenta* var. *aquatilis*', *Indo-Pacific Prehistory Association Bulletin*, vol. 11, pp. 69–81.

Matthews, P. J. (2002) 'Taro storage systems', pp. 135–163 in S. Yoshida and P. J. Matthews (eds.), *Vegeculture in Eastern Asia and Oceania*, The Japan Center for Area Studies, Osaka, Japan.

Matthews, P. J. (2014) *On the Trail of Taro: An Exploration of Natural and Cultural History*, National Museum of Ethnology, Osaka, Japan.

Matthews, P. J., Agoo, E. M. G., Tandang, D. N. and Madulid, D. A. (2012) Ethnobotany and ecology of wild taro (*Colocasia esculenta*) in the Philippines: Implications for domestication and dispersal', pp. 307–340 in M. Spriggs, D. Addison and P. J. Matthews (eds.), *Irrigated Taro* (Colocasia esculenta) *in the Indo-Pacific: Biological, Social and Historical Perspectives*, National Museum of Ethnology, Osaka, Japan.

Matthews, P. J. and Naing, K. W. (2005) 'Notes on the provenance and providence of wildtype taros (*Colocasia esculenta*) in Myanmar', *Bulletin of the National Museum of Ethnology*, vol. 29, pp. 587–615.

Matthews, P. J., Nguyen, V. D., Tandang, D., Agoo, E. M. and Madulid, D. A. (2015) 'Taxonomy and ethnobotany of *Colocasia esculenta* and *C. formosana* (Araceae): Implications for evolution, natural range, and domestication of taro', *Aroideana Supplement*, vol. 38E, pp. 153–176.

Matthews, P. J. and Terauchi, R. (1994) 'The genetics of agriculture: DNA variation in taro and yam', pp. 251–270 in J. G. Hather (ed.), *Tropical Archaeobotany: Applications and New Developments*, Routledge, London, UK and New York, NY, USA.

McGlone, M. S., Wilmshurst, J. M. and Leach, H. M. (2005) 'An ecological and historical review of bracken (*Pteridium esculentum*) in New Zealand, and its cultural significance', *New Zealand Journal of Ecology*, vol. 29, pp. 165–184.

McGovern, P. E. (2003) *Ancient Wine: The Search for the Origins of Viniculture*, Princeton University Press, Princeton and Oxford, USA and UK.

McKey, D. B., Elias, M., Pujol, B. and Duputié, A. (2012) 'Ecological approaches to crop domestication', pp. 377–406 in P. Gepts, T. Famula, R. Bettinger, S. B. Brush, A. B. Damania, P. E. McGuire and C. O. Qualset (eds.), *Biodiversity in Agriculture: Domestication, Evolution, and Sustainability*, Cambridge University Press, Cambridge, New York and Melbourne.

Meyer, R. S., DuVal, A. E. and Jensen, H. R. (2012) 'Patterns and processes in crop domestication: An historical review and quantitative analysis of 203 global food crops', *New Phytologist*, vol. 196, pp. 29–48.

Mithin, S. (2006) 'Ethnobiology and the evolution of the human mind', pp. 55–75 in R. Ellen (ed.), *Ethnobiology and the Science of Humankind*, Blackwell, Malden, Oxford and London, UK.

Mitton, J. B. and Grant, B. C. (1996) 'Genetic variation and the natural history of quaking aspen', *BioScience*, vol. 46, pp. 25–31.

Moodley, D., Proche, S. and Wilson, J. R. U. (2016) 'A global assessment of a large monocot family highlights the need for group-specific analyses of invasiveness', *AoB Plants*, vol. 8, p. plw009. doi: 10.1093/aobpla/plw009

Mooney, H. A. and Drake, J. A. (eds.) (1986) *Ecology of Biological Invasions of North America and Hawaii*, Springer, New York, London and Tokyo.

Oliviera, N. V. (2012) 'Recovering, analysing and identifying *Colocasia esculenta* and *Dioscorea* spp. from archaeological contexts in Timor-Leste', pp. 265–284 in M. Spriggs, D. Addison and P. J. Matthews (eds.), *Irrigated Taro* (Colocasia esculenta) *in the Indo-Pacific: Biological, Social and Historical Perspectives*, National Museum of Ethnology, Osaka, Japan.

Olsen, K. M. and Schaal, B. A. (1999) 'Evidence on the origin of cassava: Phylogeography of *Manihot esculenta*', *Proceedings of the National Academy of Sciences USA*, vol. 96, pp. 5586–5591.

Olsen, K. M. and Schaal, B. A. (2007) 'Insights on the evolution of a vegetatively propagated crop species', *Molecular Ecology*, vol. 16, pp. 2838–2840.

Olsen, K. M. and Wendel, J. F. (2013) 'A bountiful harvest: Genomic insights into crop domestication phenotypes', *Annual Review of Plant Biology*, vol. 64, pp. 47–70.

Partridge, T. R. and Harris, W. (1988) 'Use of life support species for survival purposes in New Zealand', pp. 102–107 in R. S. Paroda, P. Kapoor, R. K. Arora and B. Mal (eds.), *Life Support Plant Species: Diversity and Conservation*, National Bureau of Plant Genetic Resources, New Delhi, India.

Pavord, A. (1999) *The Tulip*, Bloomsbury, London, UK.

Pilu, R., Bucci, A., Badone, F. C. and Landoni, M. (2012) 'Giant reed (*Arundo donax* L.): A weed plant or a promising energy crop?', *African Journal of Biotechnology*, vol. 11, pp. 9163–9174.

Pollan, M. (2006) *The Omnivore's Dilemna: A Natural History of Four Meals*, Penguin Press, New York, NY, USA.

Randall, R. P. (2007) *The Introduced Flora of Australia and Its Weed Status*, CRC for Australian Weed Management, Adelaide, Australia.

Renfrew, J. M. (1995) 'Palaeoethnobotanical finds of *Vitis* from Greece', pp. 255–267 in P. E. McGovern, S. J. Fleming and S. H. Katz (eds.), *The Origins and Ancient History of Wine*, Gordon and Breach, Amsterdam, the Netherlands.

Roulliera, C., Benoit, L., McKey, D. B. and Lebot, V. (2013) 'Historical collections reveal patterns of diffusion of sweet potato in Oceania obscured by modern plant movements and recombination', *Proceedings of the National Academy of Sciences USA*, vol. 110, pp. 2205–2210.

Rozin, P. (1976) 'The selection of food by rats, humans and other animals', pp. 21–76 in J. Rosenblatt, R. A. Hinde, C. Beer and E. Shaw (eds.), *Advances in the Study of Behavior*, Vol. 6, Academic Press, New York, NY, USA.

Simpson, P. (2000) *Dancing Leaves: The Story of New Zealand's Cabbage Tree, Ti Kouka*, Canterbury University, Christchurch, New Zealand.

Smith, B. D. (2001) 'Low-level food production', *Journal of Archaeological Research*, vol. 9, pp. 1–43.

Sullivan, J. J., Mather, J. and Stahel, W. (2007) 'Control of wild kiwifruit (*Actinidia* species) in Bay of Plenty, New Zealand', *Acta Horticulturae*, vol. 753, pp. 583–590.

Terrell, J. E., Hart, J. P., Barut, S., Cellinese, N., Curet, A., Denham, T., Kusimba, C. M., Latinis, K., Oka, R., Palka, J., Pohl, M. E. D., Pope, K. O., Ryan, P., Williams, H. H. and Staller, J. E. (2003) 'Domesticated landscapes: The subsistence ecology of plant and animal domestication', *Journal of Archaeological Method and Theory*, vol. 10, pp. 323–368.

Torrence, R. and Barton, H. (2006) *Ancient Starch Research*, Left Coast Press, Walnut Creek, CA, USA.

Vasey, D. E. (1992) *An Ecological History of Agriculture, 10,000 B.C.–A.D. 10,000*, Iowa State University Press, Ames, IA, USA.

Woolfe, J. A. (1992) *Sweet Potato: An Untapped Resource*, Cambridge University Press, Cambridge, UK.

Wu, W., Zheng, Y., Li, C., Wei, Y., Yan, Z. and Yang, R. (2006) 'PCR-RFLP analysis of cpDNA and mtDNA in the genus *Houttuynia* in some areas of China', *Hereditas*, vol. 142, pp. 24–32.

Yen, D. E. (1985) 'Wild plants and domestication in Pacific Islands', pp. 315–326 in V. N. Misra and P. Bellwood (eds.), *Recent Advances in Indo-Pacific Prehistory: Proceedings of the International Symposium held at Poona, December 19–21, 1978*, Oxford and IBH Publishing Co., New Delhi, Bombay and Calcutta, India.

Yen, D. E. (1989) 'The domestication of environment', pp. 57–75 in D. R. Harris and G. C. Hillman (eds.), *Foraging and Farming: The Evolution of Plant Exploitation*, Unwin Hyman, London, UK.

Zohary, D. (2004) 'Unconscious selection and the evolution of domesticated plants', *Economic Botany*, vol. 58, pp. 5–10.

Zohary, D. and Hopf, M. (1994) *Domestication of Plants in the Old World*, Clarendon Press, Oxford, UK.

# 11
# AGRICULTURAL BIODIVERSITY AND THE COLUMBIAN EXCHANGE

*David E. Williams*

## Background

Crop plants and livestock breeds have been introduced to new lands and exchanged between human societies since prehistoric times, and this process is ongoing today. Beginning roughly 10,000 years ago, the first plant and animal species were domesticated – more or less simultaneously – by Neolithic proto-farmers in a handful of distinct and independent centres of crop origin located around the world. These 'cradles of agriculture' are now known as Vavilov centres, after the Russian botanist who first recognized and identified them (Vavilov, 1951). The advent of an agricultural economy based on those early crop and livestock species led to the establishment of large, permanent human settlements that eventually transformed those cradles of agriculture into cradles of civilization.

As farming became a successful means of human subsistence and expansion, these crop and livestock species were disseminated outward from their centres of origin to other regions, where new varieties and breeds evolved in response to their new environments. New species were also domesticated under the stewardship of different societies and cultures, adding to a growing heritage of agricultural biodiversity. Over the subsequent millennia, the diffusion, exchange and adoption of exotic crop and livestock species continued, eventually allowing many varieties and breeds to reach the most remote corners of the known world.

Yet it was not until 1492 when the landfall of the European explorer Christopher Columbus in America triggered the largest and most portentous exchange of agricultural biodiversity in history. Dubbed the 'Columbian Exchange' by the historian Alfred Crosby (1972), it initiated the sustained transfer of crops and livestock between the Old World and New World centres of domestication and diversity, and set the stage for what would become a truly global exploitation of domesticated plants and animals and a universal interdependence upon their genetic resources.

## The Columbian Exchange

It is difficult to fully assess the far-reaching impact that the Columbian Exchange had – and continues to have – on the farming practices, food consumption patterns and livelihoods of millions of people around the world. The sometimes enigmatic and often contentious consequences of this fateful turning point in human history have made it the subject of numerous previous treatments (Morrison, 1963; Crosby, 1972; Weatherford, 1988; Viola and Margolis, 1991; Hernandez-Bermejo and Leon, 1994; Sperling and Williams, 1995; Clement, 1999; Williams, 2004; Nunn and Qian, 2010, etc.).

The inter-hemispheric exchange of agriculturally important species that began in 1492 was not always rapid, nor has it been symmetrical, or even logical. In terms of the sheer number of species involved in this exchange, over 500 were transferred in either direction, with the greater proportion, roughly two-thirds, being introduced from the Old World to the Americas. The assemblage of species transferred from the Old World were domesticates originating from five Vavilov centres on three continents (Africa, Asia and Europe), in contrast to species transferred from the Americas which originated from just two centres on two continents: North America (including Mesoamerica and the Caribbean) and South America.

There were great disparities in the speed, pace and degree of adoption and dissemination of the different crops upon their introduction into the new lands, and each crop species has its own unique history in the context of the Columbian Exchange. A number of biological and cultural factors can be identified that affected, or at least help to explain, the widely variable degrees of adoption of introduced crops, including some crops that, to date, have received little or no acceptance outside their places of origin.

The absence of pests and diseases that co-evolved with the crop or breed in its area of origin is an often-cited and certainly significant biological factor that has favored dissemination and eminent success of many crops and livestock following their introduction to another continent. There is a long list of crop species (e.g. cacao, citrus, coffee, potato, peanut, soybean, sugarcane, sunflower) that have proven far more productive and more widely cultivated on continents distant from their place of origin. But pests and diseases can also move across oceans, and many eventually follow their host species abroad, re-creating the phytosanitary challenges for sustaining the initial gains in yield enjoyed earlier. Noteworthy examples of this include the potato blight *(Phytophthora infestans)* in Ireland, American maize rust *(Puccinia polyspora)* in Africa and the *Phylloxera* aphid epidemic of wine grapes around the world.

There were several limiting factors that delayed or discouraged the adoption of introduced crops. The incorporation of exotic crops into vastly different foreign agroecosystems was often an impediment to their acceptance. Monocropping of cereals and legumes was a common practice in the Old World, particularly on the Iberian Peninsula in the 15th century. The early European explorers in the New World encountered indigenous farmers engaged in mixed cropping systems involving a bewildering diversity of co-evolved cultigens inter-planted within a single field, and they were disappointed when the fields of wheat and peas they sought to establish for their own subsistence met with little success. Another important limiting factor was the dearth of associated knowledge transferred regarding their cultivation or culinary properties. Seeds and cuttings of New World plants typically arrived in Europe with virtually no accompanying information regarding their care or use.

For example, when the tomato and potato were first introduced to Europe in the 1500s, they were met with suspicion and regarded as poisonous due to their recognized relationship to the deadly nightshades of the Old World (all belong to the Solanaceae family). The tomato was cultivated only as an ornamental curiosity in Europe for nearly three centuries before ultimately finding acceptance as a foodstuff; thereafter, it was widely and enthusiastically incorporated into most local cuisines. The potato had a similarly delayed adoption in Europe, not becoming widely regarded as a foodstuff until the 18th century, when various heads of state began actively promoting its cultivation and consumption. By the early 1800s, the widespread consumption of potato is credited with fueling the pre-industrial boom that nearly doubled the population of Europe.

*Figure 11.1* Earliest known depiction of a European smoking tobacco, published by Anthony Chute, 1595

*Source*: Anthony Chute – Tabaco, Public Domain, https://commons.wikimedia.org/w/index.php?curid=14838064

In sharp contrast to the tomato and potato, another solanaceous plant, tobacco, received immediate acceptance following its introduction to Spain around 1528 (**Figure 11.1**, *Earliest known depiction of a European smoking tobacco*), and its cultivation and use in various forms (cigars, pipe, snuff, quid) spread rapidly throughout Europe, Asia and North America in subsequent decades.

## Livestock and other agricultural animals

Livestock and other agricultural animals were also involved in the Columbian Exchange. Compared with the large number of Old World livestock species and breeds, relatively few animal species were domesticated for food and agriculture in the Americas (**Table 11.1** *Livestock species involved in the Columbian Exchange*). Of those New World farm animals, only the turkey has found wide acceptance abroad. The South American guinea pig, Muscovy duck, llama and alpaca were each introduced to the Old World later and on a lesser scale, where they serve primarily as pets or specialty purpose animals (e.g., fiber). (For a more general discussion of animal domestication, see also Edwards et al., Chapter 2 of this Handbook.)

*Table 11.1* Livestock species involved in the Columbian Exchange

| | |
|---|---|
| Cattle *(Bos taurus, B. indicus)* | Turkey *(Meleagris gallopavo)* |
| Pig *(Sus scrofa domesticus)* | Cochineal *(Dactylopius coccus)* |
| Sheep *(Ovis aries)* | Muscovy duck *(Cairina moschata)* |
| Goat *(Capra aegagrus hircus)* | Guinea pig *(Cavia porcellus)* |
| Horse *(Equus ferus caballus)* | Llama *(Lama glama)* |
| Donkey *(Equus africanus asinus)* | Alpaca *(Vicugna pacos)* |
| Rabbit *(Oryctolagus cuniculus)* | |
| Chicken *(Gallus domesticus)* | |
| Duck *(Anas platyrhynchos domesticus)* | |
| Goose *(Anser domesticus)* | |
| Honeybee *(Apis mellifera)* | |

One interesting example of a New World agricultural animal is the scale insect, cochineal *(Dactylopius coccus)*, a source of carmine dye that was an important tribute item for the ancient Aztecs. Following the conquest of Mexico, cochineal was a highly prized commodity in Europe for dying textiles, including such iconic garments as the scarlet vestments of cardinals and the 'red coats' of the British military. By the early 1800s, cochineal production had become an important industry in the Canary Islands, Spain, Portugal and North Africa, where its introduction was accompanied by the *Opuntia* cacti (prickly pear, Indian fig) upon which this insect is cultivated. However, by the late 1800s, cochineal dye was almost entirely replaced by artificial dyes, and the cochineal industry collapsed, leaving feral populations of prickly pear cactus across Northern Africa and the drier parts of the Iberian Peninsula and the Mediterranean. Today, cochineal is enjoying a renaissance as a natural, non-carcinogenic colourant for foods and cosmetics; currently, Peru is the world's largest exporter.

In contrast to the relative paucity of New World livestock species, Old World breeds of horse, donkey, cattle, pig, sheep, goat, rabbit, duck, goose, chicken and honeybee were quickly adopted throughout the Americas, where they are now abundant. Curiously, neither the Dromedary nor Bactrian camels, though introduced on various occasions, found lasting acceptance as beasts of burden or transportation in the New World.

## Native crops of the Americas

The American hemisphere is a heterogeneous biogeographical setting composed of two continents, a northern and a southern, that are connected by a narrow Central American isthmus and an archipelago of Caribbean islands. The hemisphere is also characterized by imposing mountain ranges and broad highland plateaus adjoining extensive tropical lowlands, creating a complexity of ecogeographic clines that have produced an extraordinary degree of biological diversity. Two of the world centres of agricultural origins and crop domestication arose in the American tropics, one in Mesoamerica and another in the Andean region, each of which spawned a succession of increasingly stratified agrarian societies, advanced civilizations, and great empires.

To illustrate the degree of interspecific crop diversity of just one of these centres of origin, a list of 98 species cultivated in Mesoamerica at the time of the conquest is presented in **Table 11.2**

*Table 11.2* Mesoamerican cultigens at the time of European contact

| *Category* | *Species* | *Common name(s)* |
|---|---|---|
| **Cereals, pseudocereals and other grains (8)** | *Amaranthus cruentus* | Amaranth |
| | *Amaranthus hypochondriacus* | Prince's-feather |
| | *Chenopodium berlandieri* ssp. *Nuttalliae* | Huauzontle |
| | *Helianthus annuus*★ | Sunflower |
| | *Hyptis suaveolens* | Pignut |
| | *Panicum sonorum* | Mexican panicgrass |
| | *Salvia hispanica* | Chia |
| | *Zea mays*★ | Maize, corn |
| **Grain legumes (7)** | *Arachis hypogaea*★ | Peanut |
| | *Canavalia ensiformis* | Jack bean |
| | *Phaseolus acutifolius* | Tepary bean |
| | *Phaseolus coccineus*★ | Scarlet runner bean |
| | *Phaseolus dumosus* | Year-long bean |
| | *Phaseolus lunatus*★ | Lima bean |
| | *Phaseolus vulgaris*★ | Common bean |
| **Squashes and gourds (6)** | *Cucurbita argyrosperma* | Cushaw |
| | *Cucurbita ficifolia* | |
| | *Cucurbita moschata* | Squash, pumpkin |
| | *Cucurbita pepo*★ | Squash, pumpkin |
| | *Sechium edule* | |
| | *Sechium tacaco* | Tacaco |
| **Solanaceous vegetables (8)** | *Capsicum annuum*★ | Chili pepper |
| | *Capsicum chinense*★ | Yellow lantern chili |
| | *Capsicum frutescens*★ | Chili pepper |
| | *Capsicum pubescens* | Ruqutu |
| | *Jaltomata procumbens* | |
| | *Lycianthes moziniana* | Tlanochtli, nonochto |
| | *Physalis philadelphica* | Tomatillo |
| | *Solanum lycopersicum*★ | Tomato |
| **Leafy, stem and flower vegetables (9)** | *Amaranthus hybridus* | Green amaranth |
| | *Chamaedorea tepejilote* | Pacaya palm |
| | *Cnidoscolus chayamansa* | Chaya |
| | *Crotalaria longirostrata* | Chipilín |
| | *Dysphania ambrosioides* | Jesuit's tea, payqu, epazonte, Mexican tea |
| | *Fernaldia pandurata* | |
| | *Porophyllum ruderale* | |
| | *Porophyllum tagetoides* | Pepicha |
| **Roots and tubers (7)** | *Bomarea edulis* | |
| | *Dahlia coccinea* | |
| | *Dahlia pinnata* | |

| *Category* | *Species* | *Common name(s)* |
|---|---|---|
| | *Ipomoea batatas*★ | Sweet potato |
| | *Manihot esculenta*★ | Cassava |
| | *Pachyrhizus erosus* | Mexican yam bean, Mexican turnip |
| | *Xanthosoma sagittifolia* | Arrowleaf elephant ear |
| **Fiber crops (4)** | *Agave fourcroydes*★ | Agave |
| | *Agave salmeana* | Agave |
| | *Agave sisalana*★ | Sisal |
| | *Gossypium hirsutum*★ | Cotton |
| **Fruit trees (27)** | *Anacardium occidentale*★ | Cashew |
| | *Ananas comosus*★ | Pineapple |
| | *Annona cherimolia*★ | Chirimuya |
| | *Annona diversifolia* | Ilama |
| | *Annona muricata* | Guanábana |
| | *Annona purpurea* | Soncoya |
| | *Annona squamosa* | Sugar-apple |
| | *Bactris gasipaes* | |
| | *Brosimum alicastrum* | Breadnut |
| | *Byrsonima crassifolia* | |
| | *Carica papaya*★ | Papaya |
| | *Casimiroa edulis* | White sapote |
| | *Casimiroa sapota* | |
| | *Chrysophyllum cainito* | |
| | *Crataegus mexicana* | Tejocote |
| | *Diospyros nigra* | Black sapote |
| | *Manilkara zapota* | Sapodilla |
| | *Parmentiera edulis* | Guajilote |
| | *Persea americana*★ | Avocado |
| | *Pouteria campechiana* | Canisel |
| | *Pouteria sapota* | Sapote |
| | *Pouteria viridis* | Green sapote |
| | *Prunus serotina* ssp. *Capuli* | Black cherry |
| | *Psidium guajava*★ | Guava |
| | *Quararibea cordata* | |
| | *Spondias mombin* | |
| | *Spondias purpurea* | |
| **Cactaceous fruits (7)** | *Hylocereus undatus* | White-fleshed pitahaya |
| | *Nopalea cochenillifera* | |
| | *Opuntia ficus-indica*★ | Indian fig, prickly pear |
| | *Opuntia megacantha* | |
| | *Opuntia streptacantha* | |
| | *Selenicereus megalanthus* | |

(*Continued*)

*Table 11.2* (Continued)

| *Category* | *Species* | *Common name(s)* |
|---|---|---|
| | *Stenocereus queretaroensis* | |
| **Comfort plants (13)** | *Nicotiana rustica* | Wild tobacco |
| | *Nicotiana tabacum*★ | Tobacco |
| | *Theobroma cacao*★ | Cacao, chocolate |
| | *Theobroma bicolor* | |
| | *Agastachemexicana* | |
| | *Bixa orellana* | Achiote |
| | *Indigofera suffruticosa* | Guatemalan indigo |
| | *Jatropha curcas* | Jatropha (also used for biofuel) |
| | *Polianthes tuberosa* | Tuberose |
| | *Tagetes erecta* | Mexican marigold |
| | *Taxodium mucronatum* | Montezuma cypress |
| | *Tigridia pavonia* | |
| **Container crops (2)** | *Lagenaria siceraria*★ | Calabash, bottle gourd |
| | *Crescentia cuje* | |

*Note*: ★ denotes cultigens of global importance.

*Source*: Table generated by the author.

*Mesoamerican cultigens at the time of European contact.* The species marked with stars (★) are those Mesoamerican crops that have achieved global importance as a result of the Columbian Exchange. It is interesting to note that the number of globalized Mesoamerican crops represents roughly 25% of the total, while the remaining 75% of the species listed can be regarded, to varying degrees, as marginalized, neglected and/or underutilized crops. It is also important to note that this list does not reflect the amount of significant infraspecific diversity (i.e. local varieties and landraces) present within these crop species.

Characteristically, the geographic centres of agricultural origin and crop domestication as conceived by Vavilov are rich, not only in crop species and their local varieties, but also in closely related wild species, all of which together form part of the crop's gene pool (Harlan and de Wet, 1971). In many indigenous or traditional agroecosystems in the Americas, where crops are cultivated in close proximity to their sympatric wild or weedy relatives, spontaneous geneflow can occur between these taxa through introgressive hybridization (Anderson, 1952; Pickersgill, 1971). This fortuitous geneflow between wild and cultivated populations gives rise to novel combinations from which observant farmers can and do select and propagate interesting individuals, thereby contributing to the ongoing evolution of the crop and leading to the on-farm development of new, locally adapted varieties.

The genetic diversity encountered within crop species is the result of generations of both natural and human selection as the crops evolve and adapt to a range of different environmental and cultural conditions. The outcome of this dynamic process of human intervention is manifested in the rich assortment of local varieties and landraces encountered today. Local varieties are typically prized and maintained by farmers for their distinct culinary and agronomic qualities. Outstanding examples of infraspecific crop diversity can be observed in the hundreds of distinct local varieties of maize, potato, peanut and common bean, to name only a few, which after decades of sustained collecting and characterization efforts, continue to

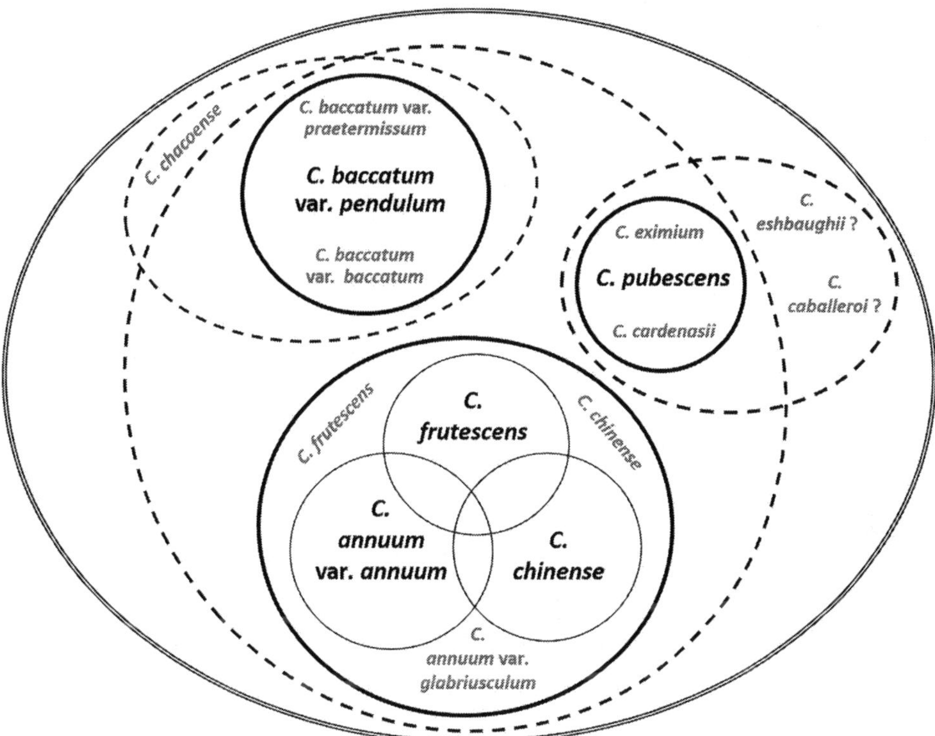


*Figure 11.2* Gene pools of domesticated Capsicum peppers

*Source*: Generated by the author based on van Zonneveld et al. (2015).

bring to light 'new' and unique varieties that were previously unknown or undocumented by science.

At the interspecific level, there are numerous instances in the Americas where two or more crop species were domesticated from within the same genus (Pickersgill, 2007). Noteworthy examples of congeneric cultigens include *Phaseolus* beans (five species), *Capsicum* peppers (five species), grain *Chenopodium* (three species), grain *Amaranthus* (four species), *Cucurbita* squashes (five species) and *Physalis* husk tomatoes (two species). These congeneric crops provide an exceptionally broad secondary gene pool from which breeders can draw and farmers may select for adaptive traits or other qualities of interest. (**Figure 11.2** *Gene pools of domesticated* Capsicum *peppers* and **Table 11.3** *Some congeneric crops from the Americas*).

## Adoption of New World crops in Europe, Africa and Asia

Numerous crops from the Americas were well received in the Old World, assuming important roles in the diets, cuisines and economic trade of their adoptive lands. In some areas, they became iconic crops closely associated with national and cultural identity. Several New World crops, such as tobacco, maize, cassava, sweet potato, common bean, squashes, red pepper and peanut, were adopted almost immediately upon their introduction to Europe and then rapidly disseminated throughout Asia and Africa. Others, for example the tomato and potato already mentioned, were at first regarded with caution – probably due to their recognized relationship to the poisonous

*Table 11.3* Some congeneric crops from the Americas.

| *Crop* | *Genus* | *No. Cultigens* |
|---|---|---|
| Agaves and magueyes | *Agave* | 10 cultigens |
| Prickly pears and nopales | *Opuntia* | >6 cultigens |
| Sapotaceous fruits | *Pouteria* | >6 cultigens |
| Annonaceous fruits | *Annona* | >5 cultigens |
| Red and green peppers | *Capsicum* | 5 cultigens |
| Squashes and gourds | *Cucurbita* | 5 cultigens |
| Common beans | *Phaseolus* | 5 cultigens |
| Potatoes | *Solanum* Sect. *Petota* | 4 cultigens |
| Grain amaranths | *Amaranthus* | 3 cultigens |
| Grain chenopods | *Chenopodium* | 3 cultigens |
| Yam beans | *Pachyrhizus* | 3 cultigens |
| Jack beans | *Canavalia* | 2 cultigens |
| Cotton | *Gossypium* | 2 cultigens |
| Tobacco | *Nicotiana* | 2 cultigens |
| Husk tomatoes | *Physalis* | 2 cultigens |
| Peach tomatoes | *Solanum* Sect. *Lasiocarpa* | 2 cultigens |

*Source*: Adapted from Pickersgill (2007).

European nightshades – and were maintained as ornamental curiosities for many years before their edible attributes were finally discovered. Still others, such as cacao and vanilla, were somewhat slower to become widely cultivated until their particular requirements for care and processing were discovered and perfected in the new lands.

During his fourth voyage to the Americas in 1502, Christopher Columbus was the first European to encounter cacao *(Theobroma cacao)*, the raw material of chocolate, while exploring the Bay Islands of Honduras. Two decades later, Bernal Diaz de Castillo (who accompanied Hernán Cortés in the conquest of Mexico) reported that the Emperor Montezuma II and members of his court consumed copious amounts of a whipped chocolate beverage that was flavored with vanilla, red peppers and other aromatic spices. Cortés introduced chocolate, in beverage form, to Spain in the mid-1500s to the delight of the Spanish royalty, and it quickly became a popular beverage of the European elite. Once the techniques for harvesting, fermenting, drying and grinding the cacao 'beans' were understood, cacao plantations were established in Spanish colonies in the West Indies, South America and the Philippines to satisfy the burgeoning demand. The world's appetite for chocolate has never stopped growing. Europeans introduced cacao to their colonies in West Africa in the 19th century, where it developed into an important export crop, eventually overtaking the major cacao producing countries in the Americas. Today, three-quarters of the world's cacao is grown in West Africa (Ivory Coast, Ghana, Nigeria, Cameroon) and Indonesia.

Together with chocolate, Hernán Cortés introduced vanilla *(Vanilla planifolia)* to Spain in the mid-1500s, after which the European demand for the spice continued to expand. In Mexico, vanilla plants are naturally pollinated by *Melipona* bees that are necessary for fruit production – a fact that enabled Mexico to monopolize vanilla production for the first 300 years following its introduction to Europe. In the early 1800s, French entrepreneurs established vanilla plants on the island of Réunion, in the Indian Ocean, but the flowers would not set fruit. When it was discovered that fruits could be produced by hand-pollinating the flowers, their cultivating was quickly expanded to Comoros and Madagascar and, by the end of the 19th century, these islands were already supplying about 80% of the global demand for vanilla. Today's largest producers are Indonesia and Madagascar, with Mexico left in a distant third place.

The introduction of New World crops to Africa brought about a striking transformation of the agricultural and dietary systems there, particularly in sub-Saharan Africa. Cassava *(Manihot esculenta)* was first introduced to West Africa in the 16th century by the Portuguese and was rapidly adopted and disseminated. Cassava became one of the most important dietary staples and subsistence crops in tropical Africa, where it is often intercropped with other New World crops such as maize, sweet potato and peanut, as well as native crops. Africa currently grows and consumes more than half of the world's cassava, with Nigeria being the largest producer.

Maize, peanut and sweet potato were also introduced to sub-Saharan Africa in the 16th century and likewise spread rapidly across the continent. Maize is currently the most important cereal crop in Africa and a staple food for millions; however, an overly heavy dietary reliance on maize in some areas has led to malnutrition and vitamin deficiency diseases such as night blindness and kwashiorkor. The peanut *(Arachis hypogaea)* was enthusiastically adopted in West Africa, becoming a staple crop there, and is widely cultivated elsewhere in sub-Saharan Africa. The sweet potato *(Ipomoea batatas)* is the third most important food crop in seven Eastern and Central African countries, outranking even cassava and maize. Sweet potato is a nutritious crop that produces good yields in areas with marginal growing conditions. International efforts are currently underway to promote the consumption of orange-fleshed varieties that are high in beta carotene (a precursor to vitamin A) to combat the aforementioned malnutrition and vitamin deficiency diseases that affect tens of millions of Africans. Already an important crop in local diets and farming systems, sweet potato production in sub-Saharan Africa is currently expanding faster than any other major crop in the region.

Another important instrument of the Columbian Exchange was the transpacific operation of Spanish galleon trade that took place for more than 250 years between the American ports of Lima and Acapulco, and Manila in the Philippines. Beginning in 1565 and lasting until 1811, the Spanish galleons (large cargo ships) made regular voyages between these colonial ports, usually once or twice per year, and were responsible for the bi-directional inter-hemispheric transfer of many crop plants. American crops introduced directly to Asia via the galleon trade included avocado, cacao, cassava, chili peppers, lima beans, pineapple, peanut, papaya, potato, sweet potato, tomato, sapodilla *(Manilkara zapota)* and yam bean *(Pachyrhizus erosus)*. Many of these crops are known in the Philippines by some derivative of their Náhuatl (Mexican) names in the Tagalog language.

Interestingly, archaeological evidence indicates that the sweet potato *(Ipomoea batatas)*, and possibly the peanut, may have been introduced to Oceania and Southeast Asia in pre-Hispanic times, probably by Polynesian and/or Chinese explorers. The richly diverse sweet potato varieties encountered in New Guinea are an integral element of ancestral agricultural systems, and primitive peanut landraces that are today nearly extinct in their land of origin are still cultivated by traditional farmers in parts of Polynesia, southern China and Madagascar.

The extraordinarily rapid adoption and dissemination of some crops such as cassava, maize, peanut, common bean and cotton in the Old World, and of apple, cocoyam, cowpea and broad bean in the New World, can be attributed, at least partially, to the pre-existence of analogue crops (see section 'Analogue crops').

## Adoption of Old World crops in the Americas

In Spain, the final decades of the 15th century were characterized by the culmination of a centuries-long military campaign to expel the Moors from the Iberian Peninsula, a monumental geopolitical feat that was ultimately achieved in 1492. Yet this historic victory for Spain's Catholic

Monarchs was only to be overshadowed in October of that very same year by an even more momentous accomplishment when their royally commissioned explorer Christopher Columbus made his first landfall in the New World.

Columbus himself was responsible for introducing the first Old World plants to the Americas during his second voyage in 1493. As part and parcel of their colonial strategy, the early European conquistadors, colonists and missionaries made a deliberate effort to introduce and quickly establish crops that were most essential to their Old World culinary habits, such as onion, garlic, lettuce, cabbage, wine grape, olive and stone fruits such as apple, peach, plum, apricot and almond, as well as forage species such as alfalfa and clover. Ironically, many of the Spanish cultivars introduced to the Americas in colonial times have since disappeared in Spain and can be found today surviving only in Latin America as relict populations conserved *in situ* in traditional indigenous communities and the orchards of some old mission churches (Hernandez-Bermejo, 2013).

Not all of the attempts to introduce European crops to the colonies were successful, at least not immediately so. Early efforts to establish wheat production in the Spanish colonies were met with failure, as the broadcast method used in Europe for planting cereals was incompatible with the indigenous polycropping methods, making it necessary to import shipments of wheat from Spain to supply the needs of the early colonists. Spanish attempts to establish commercial plantations of flax and hemp in the New World were similarly frustrated.

A characteristic element of the colonization of the Americas was the establishment of large commercial plantations, designed initially to exploit the free labor of the subjugated indigenous population. A short time later, after foreign diseases, forced relocations and mistreatment by colonial taskmasters had decimated the native population, the plantation owners began importing slave labor from Africa, which soon became a booming trade in itself. The main introduced plantation crops included sugar cane, banana, coffee and citrus, and their large-scale production represented important sources of revenue for the burgeoning colonies and their empires.

As well as relocating millions of Africans to the Americas, the transatlantic slave trade resulted in the introduction of numerous African and Asian crops in the late 1600s and 1700s, including okra, cowpea ('black-eyed pea', *Vigna unguiculata*), African rice *(Oryza glaberrima)*, millets, sorghum, sesame, yams (*Dioscorea* spp.), cocoyam *(Colocasia esculenta)* and watermelon. Several of these African crops eventually became established as 'typical' elements of many New World cuisines. In an interesting case of round-trip diffusion, the slave trade was responsible for bringing the South American peanut to North America, when it was carried from Africa as food for the slaves during their ocean voyage. The peanut had already become a widespread crop in Africa following its introduction there from Brazil by the Portuguese in the early 1600s.

## Analogue crops

To help understand the wide variation in the degree of adoption and incorporation of exotic crops introduced through the Columbian Exchange, it is useful to recognize the pre-existence of analogous crops in the two hemispheres. Analogue crops are pairs of species that were independently domesticated on separate continents, but which share important traits of appearance, management and use, and are therefore somehow recognizable to farmers and consumers upon introduction. Analogous crop pairs typically belong to the same botanical family and sometimes to the same genus, although some may be botanically unrelated yet occupy similar agroecological or culinary niches (**Table 11.4** *Some analogue crops involved in the Columbian Exchange*).

The overt similarity of introduced crops to their native analogues was often sufficient incentive for their ready adoption, but it was not always reciprocated. For example, when maize was introduced to Africa it was certainly recognized as a relative of the native sorghum and millets,

*Table 11.4* Some analogue crops involved in the Columbian Exchange

| *Some analogue crops involved in the Columbian Exchange* | | | | *Direction and extent of adoption and diffusion*[a] | |
|---|---|---|---|---|---|
| *Old World* | *New World* | *Family* | *Use* | *OW>NW* | *NW>OW* |
| *Pistacia vera* | *Anacardium occidentale* | Anacardiaceae | Nuts and fruits | 1 | 2 |
| *Mangifera indica* | *Spondias mombin, S. purpurea* | Anacardiaceae | Fruit | 3 | – |
| *Coriandrum sativum* | *Eryngium foetidum* | Apiaceae | Spice | 3 | – |
| *Colocasia* sp., *Alocasia* sp. | *Xanthosoma sagittifolium* | Araceae | Root crop | 3 | 3 |
| *Cucumis* spp., *Citrullus* sp. | *Cucurbita* spp. | Cucurbitaceae | Fruit/vegetable | 3 | 3 |
| *Dioscorea* sp. Cf. *esculenta* | *Dioscorea trifida* | Dioscoreaceae | Root crop | 3 | 1 |
| *Dioscorea* sp. Cf. *esculenta* | *Manihot esculenta* | Dioscoreaceae/ Euphorbiaceae | Root crop | 2 | 3 |
| *Vicia faba* | *Lupinus mutabilis* | Fabaceae | Pulse | 3 | – |
| *Vigna unguiculata* | *Phaseolus vulgaris* | Fabaceae | Pulse | 3 | 3 |
| *Vigna subterranea* | *Arachis hypogaea* | Fabaceae | Pulse | – | 3 |
| *Glycine max* | *Arachis hypogaea* | Fabaceae | Oilseed | (3) | 3 |
| *Juglans regia* | *Juglans nigra, J. hindsii* | Juglandaceae | Nut/rootstock | 3 | (2) |
| *Juglans regia* | *Carya illinoinensis* | Juglandaceae | Nut | 3 | 1 |
| *Gossypium herbaceum, Gossypium arboreum* | *Gossypium hirsutum, Gossypium barbadense* | Malvaceae | Fiber | – | 3 |
| *Papaver somniferum* | *Erythroxylum coca* | Papaveraceae/ Erythroxylaceae | Narcotic | 2 | – |
| *Sesamum indicum* | *Salvia hispanica, Hyptis suaveolens* | Pedaliaceae/Lamiaceae | Oilseed | 3 | (1) |

(*Continued*)

*Table 11.4* (Continued)

| *Some analogue crops involved in the Columbian Exchange* | | | | *Direction and extent of adoption and diffusion*[a] | |
|---|---|---|---|---|---|
| *Old World* | *New World* | *Family* | *Use* | *OW>NW* | *NW>OW* |
| *Piper nigrum* | *Capsicum* spp. | Piperaceae/Solanaceae | Spice | (1) | 3 |
| *Sorghum bicolor* | *Zea mays* | Poaceae | Cereal | 2 | 3 |
| *Malus domestica* | *Crataegus pubescens* | Rosaceae | Fruit | 3 | – |
| *Prunus* spp. | *Prunus serotina* subsp. *Capuli* | Rosaceae | Fruits and nuts | 3 | (1) |
| *Coffea arabica*, *C. rustica* | *Theobroma cacao* | Rubiaceae/Sterculiaceae | Beverage | (3) | (3) |
| *Atropa belladonna* | *Solanum tuberosum* | Solanaceae | Poisonous/root crop | – | (3) |
| *Atropa belladonna* | *Solanum lycopersicum* | Solanaceae | Poisonous/vegetable | – | (3) |
| *Solanum melongena* | *Solanum lycopersicum* | Solanaceae | Vegetable | (1) | (3) |
| *Vitis vinifera* | *Vitis labrusca* | Vitaceae | Fruit/rootstock | 3 | (3) |

Explanation of symbols:

- OW>NW = Old World crop adopted in the New World
- NW>OW = New World crop adopted in the Old World
- Numbers indicate degree of adoption and diffusion of crop in the new hemisphere: 1 = limited, 2 = significant, 3 = widespread, ' – ' = not adopted
- Parenthesis ( ) around numbers indicate delayed adoption or diffusion

*Source*: Adapted and updated from Williams (2004).

whose plants it strongly resembles. The same is true for the peanut, whose African analogue is the Bambara groundnut *(Vigna subterranea)*. In both cases, African farmers quickly adopted the introduced crops and their native analogues were largely displaced. Today, maize and peanut are major commercial and subsistence crops in Africa. Conversely, sorghum and other millets are presently cultivated in the Americas on a relatively small scale for fodder and birdseed, and the Bambara groundnut has found no reciprocal acceptance in the New World.

One of the primary objectives of Columbus' first voyage was to find a shorter route to the Orient in order to supply medieval Europe's avid demand for spices and condiments, especially black pepper *(Piper nigrum)*. While unsuccessful in that objective, he did encounter the analogous red peppers (*Capsicum* spp.), which quickly became one of the most widely cultivated crop genera in the world, particularly *C. annuum*. Black pepper, however, has made only limited inroads in the Americas, where it is commercially cultivated only in Brazil.

In the case of grain legumes, the American common bean *(Phaseolus)* and the Asian cowpea *(Vigna)* are perfect analogues, resembling one another so much that Linnaeus, the father of modern botanical nomenclature, originally classified them in 1753 as pertaining to the same genus *(Phaseolus)*. Today, cowpea and common bean have either replaced or are grown alongside one another throughout the world. In contrast, another pair of analogous grain legumes is the Italian lupini *(Lupinus alba)* and the Andean tarwi *(Lupinus mirabilis)*, yet neither one has found acceptance beyond their respective areas of origin. However, the presence of tarwi in the Andes certainly facilitated the early adoption of the introduced broad bean *(Vicia faba)* which largely displaced its New World analogue and became such an important element in traditional agroecosystems that, today, indigenous farmers in the Andes are surprised to learn that broad bean is in fact not a native crop.

The squashes, pumpkins and gourds (*Cucurbita* spp.) of the New World were reciprocally exchanged for the analogous melons and cucumber *(Citrullus* and *Cucumis)* of the Old World; all of which are now cultivated worldwide.

Distinct species of grapes were well known in both hemispheres before 1492, but had been domesticated only in the Old World. The European wine grape *(Vitis vinifera)* was assiduously planted throughout the New World by early colonists and missionaries. When the aphid pest *Phylloxera* began devastating vineyards around the world in the late 1800s, wild American species of *Vitis* began travelling around the world as resistant rootstocks, and are today used almost exclusively wherever commercial grapes are produced. Walnuts *(Juglans)* also have analogue species in both hemispheres, yet commercial groves of English walnut *(J. regia)* in North America are grafted onto rootstocks of the hardier American species, *Juglans hindsii*. Rosaceous fruits such as apple and cherry *(Malus* and *Prunus)* have native species on both sides of the Atlantic, but only Old World apple, apricot, peach, pear, plum and cherry have made the transoceanic trip. Although an apple-like hawthorn *(Crataegus pubescens)* and the black cherry (*Prunus serotina)* were domesticated in Mexico and the Andes in pre-Hispanic times, they remain mostly confined to their areas of origin.

The mango became a major fruit crop in the American tropics, while its New World analogues, the hog plums *(Spondias mombin* and *S. purpurea)* remain only locally important in their areas of origin. The Old World pistachio has experienced a reciprocal exchange with its New World analogue, the cashew *(Anacardium occidentale)*, whose commercial cultivation has recently expanded in India.

Different species of cotton *(Gossypium)* were domesticated in each hemisphere long before Columbus, but when the long-staple American cottons *(G. hirsutum* and *G. barbadense)* were introduced to Asia and Africa, they almost entirely displaced their short-staple Old World analogues *(G. herbaceum* and *G. arboreum)*. The botanically unrelated pair of stimulating beverage crops, coffee and cacao, were reciprocal participants in the Columbian Exchange, eventually establishing themselves as major commodity crops in their adopted hemispheres.

## Marginalization of native crops

One of the impacts of the Colombian Exchange was the marginalization of certain native crops that occurred – and continues to occur – on both sides of the Atlantic. Crop marginalization is a complex process driven by a combination of biological, cultural, economic and political factors. While precise information is often lacking for many species, the genetic erosion of native species resulting from the introduction of exotic crops can be estimated from the surviving codices, chronicles and contemporary reports that recorded the presence or relative abundance of different crops in the 15th and 16th centuries (Hernandez-Bermejo and Lora-Gonzalez, 1994; Martinez-Alfaro et al., 1994).

Based on ethnohistorical studies of early Hispano-Arabic agronomy texts and 16th-century Mexican codices such as the Florentine Codex and the Badianus Manuscript, there appear to have been some instances in which native cultigens were effectively eradicated or otherwise lost as a result of the Columbian Exchange. In most cases, it is difficult to determine exactly which or how many crop species suffered this fate, given that their ultimate demise took place anonymously hundreds of years ago. The majority of crops that suffered marginalization have thankfully survived in some form in limited geographical areas or specific cultural contexts, primarily through the efforts of generations of peasant and indigenous farmers who are themselves marginalized (National Research Council, 1989). Other 'lost' crops have persisted as relict cultigens by reverting to self-propagating, agrestic or weedy habits within or at the periphery of cultivated fields and other disturbed environments, and where they are sometimes still collected and consumed by local farmers and townspeople (Williams, 1993; Hernandez-Bermejo, 2013).

The main processes and circumstances that led to native crop marginalization include their displacement by introduced farming systems and crops; their loss of competitiveness against more productive crops; unfavorable market competition established by external economic, political and/or religious interests; and the disappearance of ethnic communities and the loss of their knowledge regarding the properties, uses and management of indigenous crops.

In the case of Spain, the significant loss of Iberian agrobiodiversity had begun in the centuries prior to the discovery of America, as a result of the prolonged conquest of the Hispano-Arabic kingdoms of Southern Spain by Christian armies. During this process, the sophisticated and diverse agricultural landscapes of Andalucía and Granada were systematically destroyed and transformed to the Castilian model, inherited from the Visigoths, of cereal monocropping and livestock husbandry. From an agrobiodiversity standpoint, this rather bleak scenario was followed closely by the introduction of exotic crops from the newly established American colonies, whose adoption served only to exacerbate the ongoing marginalization and genetic erosion of numerous Iberian crops that are now regarded as neglected or underutilized species. These include horticultural crops such as various leafy greens (e.g. chicory, golden thistle, borage, rocket, cress, watercress, sorrel, comfrey, purslane, goosefoot); savory vegetables (e.g. fennel, parsnip, salsify, horseradish); legumes (e.g. grass pea, fenugreek, vetchling, cowpea); cereals (e.g. various millets, sorghum, spelt wheat); fruit trees (e.g. citron, pistachio, lotus tree, service tree, azarole, hackberry, myrtle, fig, bergamot); and numerous spices and aromatic plants, many of which, such as coriander and rosemary, are today more frequently encountered in Latin American cooking than in modern Spanish cuisine (Hernandez-Bermejo and Lora-Gonzalez, 1994).

In the Americas, the marginalization of native crops took a different form. Native American farmers customarily employed diverse intercropping systems. They took pleasure in experimenting with new plants and were happy to include the introduced Old World crops amongst their native crops. Some of the introduced species like wheat and barley did not do as well under those mixed cropping systems as they did in Europe, and they performed no better than the native crops. As a result, the colonists began to depend more and more on native crops for their subsistence, and the resilient indigenous farming systems remained more or less intact during the colonial period.

The well-documented decimation of the native populations from disease epidemics and famine, which occurred soon after the conquest, caused serious disruption of the indigenous social, economic and religious systems, many of which entailed the use of specialized crops and varieties, some of which became lost or marginalized as a result. Moreover, there were deliberate colonial efforts to ban, for religious reasons, certain native crops, like grain amaranth and chia, which were used in making 'heathen' images. These prohibitions succeeded only in reducing their cultivation but did not eradicate them.

Livestock production and European cereal crops eventually became successful on the relatively uninhabited arid and semi-arid borderlands, where draft animals and plows were used to till the heavier, drier soils, thus recreating farms and ranches that more closely resembled those of Spain and Portugal, and causing little displacement of native crops. Native crop displacement and marginalization in the Americas became more pronounced in the 1800s due to the eventual acclimatization and evolution of adapted ecotypes of the introduced crops, enabling their commercial expansion into areas of native crop production. Nevertheless, in those areas with historically significant indigenous populations and traditions, the pre-Hispanic agricultural systems persisted and tended to incorporate the introduced Old World crops rather than being transformed by them, giving rise to a rich agricultural and culinary syncretism (Martinez-Alfaro et al., 1994).

Today, marginalized crop species are regarded as underutilized crops, reflecting not only that they previously enjoyed wider cultivation, but also that they represent unique options for future food security and valuable opportunities for agricultural development, diversification and adaptation (Williams, 2013). There have been some successful modern efforts to revive, reintroduce, repatriate and promote the use of underutilized crops. One noteworthy example is the Andean pseudocereal quinoa *(Chenopodium quinoa)*, an ancient Andean staple that suffered centuries of marginalization following the Spanish conquest of the Inca Empire. Numerous efforts in recent decades to revive this highly nutritious grain reached a high point in 2013 when FAO sponsored 'The International Year of Quinoa', a major public awareness program celebrating the virtues of the crop and promoting its cultivation and use. As a result of these efforts, quinoa has now recovered much of its former status as a gourmet food and enjoys global acceptance as a high-value, high-protein commodity crop that is sold and consumed worldwide.

Other efforts to promote, conserve and add value to underutilized crops have worked directly with indigenous communities. In one such project in northern Ecuador, activities included the characterization and documentation of local crop diversity, including the recovery of associated ancestral knowledge about the traditional management and uses for native crops. The refurbishment and enrichment of traditional dooryard gardens with native crop diversity – in some cases restoring 'lost' species and varieties with materials repatriated from genebanks – proved to be a successful means of reviving the use and promoting the *in situ* (on-farm) conservation and continued evolution of native crop species and traditional varieties (Ramirez and Williams, 2003).

## Post-exchange evolution and diversification of introduced crops

The garden strawberry is a good illustration of the further evolution of a crop species that took place following its transfer to a foreign continent, and it is also one of the few examples of a major new crop species being domesticated in historical times. Strawberries have been cultivated in the Old World since Roman times, and the pan-boreal woodland strawberry *(Fragaria vesca)* was the most widely cultivated strawberry in Europe and Central Asia up until the 18th century. The modern garden strawberry *(Fragaria ananassa)* was developed in France in the 1750s as the result of a deliberate cross between two wild *Fragaria* species brought from the Americas: *F. virginiana* from eastern North America and *F. chiloensis* from Chile. The newly developed garden strawberry produced larger and more abundant fruits than its wild relatives, and it promptly replaced *Fragaria vesca* in commercial production. Today, the garden strawberry is cultivated worldwide, with global annual production surpassing 5 million tons.

The broad bean or faba bean *(Vicia faba)* was one of the earliest Old World crops, domesticated some 8,000 years ago in the Middle East and now produced worldwide. Upon its early introduction to the Americas by the Spanish conquistadors in the 1500s, it was widely adopted by indigenous farmers. Over the past 500 years, an important secondary centre of broad bean diversity has arisen in Latin America, composed of local varieties with unique adaptive traits that developed in response to the particular abiotic, biotic and human selection pressures encountered there. Varieties tolerant to high altitude evolved in the Andes and Mexico, and the best sources of resistance to serious broad bean diseases such as chocolate spot *(Botrytis fabae)*, and faba bean rust *(Uromyces viciae-fabae)* have been identified in materials from the Andean regions of Colombia and Ecuador. Broad bean breeders around the world look to these regions as valuable sources of germplasm for these and other traits of agronomic and commercial importance.

Another example of post-exchange crop evolution is that of the Andean tree tomato *(Solanum betaceum)*. Until a few decades ago, the tree tomato was scarcely known outside its area of origin and diversity. However, in the 1990s, plant breeders in New Zealand developed improved varieties that were successfully marketed internationally as 'tamarillo'. The New Zealand varieties were subsequently reintroduced to the Andes, where they displaced the indigenous genotypes, resulting in the reduction of the overall genetic diversity of the traditional Andean landraces.

The grapefruit *(Citrus paradisi)* was first described in Barbados in 1750, where it evidently originated from a fortuitous cross between two *Citrus* species, sweet orange *(C. sinensis)* and pomelo *(C. grandis)*, which had been introduced there from Asia in the 1600s. The hybrid was brought to Florida in 1853, where it was established in groves, and by the late 1800s, a booming grapefruit industry was well underway.

Other noteworthy examples of post-Exchange diversification include the widespread use of resistant North American rootstocks for some European perennial crops such as the wine grape *(Vitis vinifera)*, whose vineyards were devastated by *Phylloxera*, and the English or Persian walnut *(Juglans regia)* to better adapt them to New World soil conditions.

## The potential of neglected, marginalized and underutilized crops

Humankind continues to rely on the agricultural legacy of our Neolithic ancestors who, thousands of years ago, successfully domesticated the same few hundred species upon which modern civilization continues to depend for its survival. Despite the enormous advances in our current understanding of genetics and genomics, coupled with the astounding recent progress in biotechnology that permits targeted genetic manipulation at the molecular level, virtually no significant new crops have been domesticated in historic times.

The story of crop species is inextricably intertwined with the history of human societies and cultures. Each crop is the product of its unique trajectory of domestication, dissemination and diversification. The two dozen or so major commodity crops have been the subject of exhaustive study and improvement to more fully exploit their genetic diversity and agronomic potential. Yet it is surprising to find that beyond those major crops, for many if not most of the other crops – and especially the 'minor', underutilized and lesser-known species – the details of their evolutionary and cultural history remain poorly understood and woefully understudied. As a result, these neglected crops possess an enormous untapped potential for improvement and increased utilization. Due to the current Green Revolution paradigm that focuses exclusively on increasing yield and expanding markets for those few commodity crops, many of the minor crops are falling into disuse, undergoing genetic erosion as their diversity becomes irretrievably lost, and in some cases are threatened with extinction.

The minor and underutilized crop species around the world represent unique and successful human achievements of plant domestication and crop diversification. Often, these minor, unimproved crop species are resistant to pests and diseases and are pre-adapted to tolerate marginal growing conditions such as poor soils, swampy or waterlogged soils, arid or semi-arid climates, high temperatures, high altitudes and frost, where they are capable of producing abundant, flavorful and nutritious food with few or no external inputs. Depending upon the particular species, underutilized crops usually possess some degree of infraspecific diversity in the form of unimproved farmer varieties or landraces, which may range in number from just a few, to a dozen, or even hundreds of named varieties, all of which represent ready opportunities for selection and crop improvement using conventional plant breeding methods.

As farmers worldwide are confronted by the challenges of a changing and unpredictable climate, it is becoming increasingly recognized that diversified production systems that include multiple crop species and varieties, such as intercropping, agroforestry and sylvo-pastoral systems, are some of the most effective means of minimizing risk, reducing vulnerability and achieving the resilience and adaptive capacity required for sustainable production and food security. Across the globe, the large number of underutilized and lesser-known crops, together with the associated cultural knowledge regarding their cultivation and use, represent vitally important options for constructing the kind of diversified production systems that will be required for farmers and farming communities to continue producing food for themselves and for urban consumers under climatic conditions that, in many regions of the world, are expected to render present farming practices less productive or unviable.

Some underutilized crops from the Americas that are obvious candidates for diversifying farming systems in arid, semi-arid, high-temperature or drought-prone regions include the following:

- The tepary bean *(Phaseolus acutifolius* var. *latifolius)* is a close relative of the common bean *(P. vulgaris)* that was long employed by Native Americans for production in regions prone to high temperatures and drought, and it is resistant to common bacterial blight disease and seed weevils. While the tepary bean has been used as a source of resistance for common bean improvement programs, only recently has the tepary itself been the object of improvement. New varieties have been released with multi-stress tolerance that offer interesting options for bean farmers in areas facing temperature and drought stress as a result of climate change.
- Cassava *(Manihot esculenta)*, is one of the most drought-tolerant crops in the world, and is capable of growing on marginal land. A huge amount of genetic diversity exists in the cassava gene pool, and scientists are working to produce improved varieties that are even more tolerant to long periods of drought.

- The so-called pseudocereals from the Andes and Mesoamerica (quinoa, cañahua, huauzontle and the grain amaranths), which all possess C4 photosynthetic pathways, which makes them far more efficient in their use of water than most plants (which have C3 metabolism). They produce highly nutritious, cereal-like grains on large seedheads, and are tolerant of drought, high altitudes and cold temperatures.
- Prickly pears (*Opuntia* spp.) and other fruit-bearing cacti such as pitayas and pitahayas (*Hylocereus*, *Stenocereus*, etc.), all of which have CAM (Crassulacean Acid Metabolism) photosynthesis, which makes them some of the most drought-tolerant and water-efficient plants on earth, enabling them to produce juicy, delicious and colourful fruits under arid conditions without irrigation and very little rainfall.
- Hog plums *(Spondias purpurea* and *S. mombin)* are the New World analogues of the South Asian mango, and produce extremely well in semi-arid environments throughout the drier parts of Mesoamerica and the Andean region.

## Interdependence, climate change and the importance of ongoing exchange of genetic resources

Since the dawn of agriculture, when domesticated crop and animal species and the practice of farming began to spread across the world from the various independent centres of origin, farmers and the societies that they fed have benefitted from new crops and livestock breeds introduced, through trade or conquest, from other centres of diversity. As farming and animal husbandry grew in importance and efficiency, societies became increasingly interested in and dependent upon exotic varieties and breeds to satisfy their needs and desires, giving rise to a growing interdependence for agricultural biodiversity. Following the Columbian Exchange, this interdependence on crop and animal genetic resources became a truly global phenomenon (Fujisaka et al., 2009).

The current threat to agricultural production posed by anthropogenic climate change underscores and exacerbates humankind's interdependence on crop and livestock diversity, and requires access to and exchange of agricultural plant and animal germplasm between countries across continents. The centres of crop origin and diversity take on new importance, not only as reservoirs of unique agricultural biodiversity, but also as sources of vital information and associated traditional knowledge about the particular properties, cultivation and uses of those plant varieties and animal breeds.

## Conclusions

The evolutionary, cultural and economic ferment brought about by the Columbian Exchange exemplifies the benefits and enormous potential of the widespread exchange and use of plant and animal genetic resources. In the middle of the 20th century, a critical juncture in agricultural research and development was reached when population growth began to outstrip food production capacity and large-scale famines were predicted in some parts of the world. This impending humanitarian disaster served as an impetus for the international community, members of which joined forces to conduct an intensive international effort of agricultural research to increase crop yields. This effort led to the so-called 'Green Revolution', with the development and dissemination of resource-intensive production systems utilizing genetically uniform high-yielding varieties of a few cereal and legume crops grown in monoculture over extensive areas. This approach proved successful in significantly increasing crop yields, and the predicted famines were averted. Green Revolution technology soon became the new paradigm for modern agriculture worldwide.

The world is fast approaching another critical juncture regarding food production and food security – perhaps the greatest challenge ever faced by humanity since the advent of agriculture. With the continued rapid growth of the global population, the widespread degradation of natural resources, and the acceleration of anthropogenic climate change, we are faced with the daunting need to increase the current global food production by 70% by the year 2050 (FAO, 2009).

While Green Revolution agriculture was and continues to be highly productive under optimum and stable growing conditions, these systems tend to require high levels of inputs and a heavy consumption of finite natural resources such as water and soil. Moreover, such systems have become highly vulnerable and increasingly unsustainable due to their ever-narrower genetic base that makes them inherently susceptible to unexpected variations in weather patterns, as well as to the shifting incidence of pests and diseases resulting from climate alteration. Commercial seed companies and the dwindling number of public sector plant breeders will be hard-pressed to keep pace with climate change by producing a steady stream of new varieties that are adapted to the unpredictable, heterogeneous and increasingly marginal growing conditions occurring around the world. As the number of commodity crop and livestock species that serve to feed the global population continues to decline, most 'modern' farming systems lack the resilience and adaptive capacity to remain productive or viable in the medium term.

The resiliency and adaptive capacity of any biological system is based on the genetic diversity within that system, and this principle applies equally to agricultural production systems (Thrupp, 1998). To achieve adaptability in modern agriculture, a transformational change to a biologically diverse model – a 'Resilience Revolution' – is required for future food systems to become adaptable, sustainable and remain productive in the face of global climate change. For this transformation in food systems to occur, the continued introduction of genetic resources from distant lands will provide the essential elements of the agricultural diversification that will be the keystone of this adaptive change. Fortunately for humankind, a rich and underutilized global legacy of agricultural biodiversity continues to exist.

## References


Anderson, E. (1952) *Plants, Man and Life*, University of California Press, Berkeley, CA, USA.

Clement, C. R. (1999) '1492 and the loss of Amazonian crop genetic resources: I. The relation between domestication and human population decline', *Economic Botany*, vol. 53, pp. 188–202.

Crosby Jr., A. W. (1972) *The Colombian Exchange: Biological and Cultural Consequences of 1492*, Greenwood Press, Westport, CT, USA.

Food and Agriculture Organization of the United Nations (FAO) (2009) *Global Agriculture Towards 2050*, United Nations Food and Agriculture Program, FAO, Rome, Italy.

Fujisaka, S., Williams, D. and Halewood, M. (eds.) (2009) *The Impact of Climate Change on Countries' Interdependence on Genetic Resources for Food and Agriculture*, Background Study Paper No. 48, 12th Regular Session of the FAO Commission on Genetic Resources for Food and Agriculture, FAO, Rome, Italy.

Harlan, J. R. and deWet, J. M. J. (1971) 'Toward a rational classification of cultivated plants', *Taxon*, vol. 20, pp. 509–517.

Hernandez-Bermejo, J. E. (2013) 'Cultivos infrautilizados en España: pasado, presente y futuro', *Ambienta*, vol. 102, pp. 38–55.

Hernandez-Bermejo, J. E. and Leon, J. (eds.) (1994) *Neglected Crops: 1492 from a Different Perspective*, FAO Plant Production and Protection Series No. 26, FAO, Rome, Italy.

Hernandez-Bermejo, J. E. and Lora-Gonzalez, A. (1994) 'Processes and causes of marginalization: The introduction of American flora in Spain', pp. 261–272 in *Neglected Crops: 1492 from a Different Perspective*, J. E. Hernández Bermejo and J. León (eds.), FAO Plant Production and Protection Series No. 26, FAO, Rome, Italy.

Martinez-Alfaro, M. A., Ortega-Paczka, R. and Cruz-Leon, A. (1994) 'Introduction of flora from the Old World and causes of crop marginalization', pp. 23–33 in J. E. Hernandez-Bermejo and J. Leon (eds.), *Neglected Crops: 1492 from a Different Perspective*, FAO Plant Production and Protection Series No. 26, FAO, Rome, Italy.

Morrison, S. E. (ed.) (1963) *Journals and Other Documents on the Life and Voyages of Christopher Columbus*, Heritage Press, New York, NY, USA.

National Research Council (1989) *Lost Crops of the Incas: Little-Known Plants of the Andes with Promise for Worldwide Cultivation*, National Academy Press, Washington DC, USA.

Nunn, N. and Qian, N. (2010) 'The Columbian exchange: A history of disease, food, and ideas', *Journal of Economic Perspectives*, vol. 24, pp. 163–188.

Pickersgill, B. (1971) 'Relationships between weedy and cultivated forms in some species of chili peppers (genus *Capsicum*)', *Evolution*, vol. 25, pp. 683–691.

Pickersgill, B. (2007) 'Domestication of plants in the Americas: Insights from Mendelian and molecular genetics', *Annals of Botany*, vol. 100, pp. 925–940.

Ramirez, M. and Williams, D. E. (2003) *Guía Agro-Culinaria de Cotacachi, Ecuador, y Alrededores*, IPGRI-Americas, Cali, Colombia.

Sperling, C. R. and Williams, D. E. (1995) 'Horticultural crop germplasm: 500 years of exchange', pp. 47–60 in R. R. Duncan (ed.), *International Germplasm Transfer – Past and Present*, CSSA Special Publication No. 23, Crop Science Society of America, Madison, WI, USA.

Thrupp, L. A. (1998) *Cultivating Diversity: Agrobiodiversity and Food Security*, World Resources Institute, Washington, DC, USA.

Van Zonneveld, M., Ramirez, M., Williams, D., Petz, M., Meckelmann, S., Avila, T., Bejarano, C., Ríos, L., Peña, K., Jäger, M., Libreros, D., Amaya, K. and Scheldeman, X. (2015) 'Screening underutilized genetic resources of *Capsicum* peppers in their primary center of diversity in Bolivia and Peru', *PLoS One*, vol. 10, p. e1371.

Vavilov, N. I. (1951) 'The origin, variation, immunity and breeding of cultivated plants' (translated by K. Starr Chester), *Chronica Botanica*, vol. 13 pp. 1–366.

Viola, H. J. and Margolis, C. (eds.) (1991) *Seeds of Change*, Smithsonian Institution Press, Washington, DC, USA.

Weatherford, J. W. (1988) *Indian Givers: How the Indians of the Americas Transformed the World*, Fawcett Columbine, New York, NY, USA.

Williams, D. E. (1993) '*Lycianthes moziniana* (Solanaceae): An underutilized Mexican food plant with "new" crop potential', *Economic Botany*, vol. 47, pp. 387–400.

Williams, D. E. (2004) 'Columbian exchange: The role of analogue crops in the adoption and dissemination of exotic cultigens', pp. 292–296 in R. M. Goodman (ed.), *Encyclopedia of Plant and Crop Science*, Marcel Dekker, Inc., New York, NY, USA and Basel, Switzerland.

Williams, D. E. (2013) 'Cultivos infrautilizados, cambio climático y un nuevo paradigma para la agricultura', *Ambienta*, vol. 102, pp. 56–65.

# 12

# THE GREEN REVOLUTION AND CROP BIODIVERSITY

*Prabhu L. Pingali*

## Introduction

The pattern of crop diversity in the fields of the developing world has changed fundamentally over the past 200 years with the intensification and commercialization of agriculture. This process accelerated with the advent of the Green Revolution (GR) in the 1960s, when public sector researchers and donors explicitly promoted the international transfer of improved seed varieties to farmers in developing countries. Since the GR, the germplasm that dominates the area planted to the major cereals has shifted from 'landraces', or the locally adapted populations that farmers have historically selected from seed they save, to 'modern varieties', or the more widely adapted seed types produced by scientific plant breeding programs and purchased by farmers.

The yield enhancing seed types enabled the intensification of agriculture in areas of the world with high population densities. Initially, they diffused through the environments best suited for their production, spreading later – and unevenly – into less favored areas (Pingali and Smale, 2001). Landraces continue to be grown in the latter and in regions with lower population densities and limited market linkages.

The developing world is at the cusp of a Green Revolution 2.0 (GR 2.0), one that extends the benefits of improved crop technologies into areas that have been by passed by the first Green Revolution and expands the set of improved crops beyond the major three staples – rice, wheat and maize (Pingali, 2012). Sub-Saharan Africa stands out as the region that has benefited the least from GR technologies, despite facing chronic food deficits for decades. The demand for intensification and hence the need for land productivity enhancing seed varieties was low at the start of the GR in the 1960s (Pingali, 2012). Also, in the decades of the 1960s and 1970s, the GR research was not focused on crops important to African smallholders, such as sorghum, millets, cassava and tropical maize (Evenson and Gollin, 2003). In the last decade, there has been a significant rise in the introduction and adoption of improved varieties of these crops (Walker and Alwang, 2015). At the same time in Asia, lower potential rice lands are witnessing the rapid spread of improved drought and flood tolerant varieties (Pandey et al., 2015).

The advent of GR 2.0 has significant implications for crop biodiversity and genetic diversity. One of the primary outcomes of the original GR was that by intensifying crop production on favorable agricultural lands it allowed significant areas of unfavorable land to be moved out of agriculture. Stevenson et al. (2013) estimated that the GR saved an estimated 18–27 million hectares from being brought into agricultural production. Would the land sparing benefits hold as the GR 2.0 spreads into more marginal production environments? Also, farming systems in the less favorable environments tend to be very diverse and are home to significant numbers of landraces of traditional food crops, such as millets. Would improved stress tolerant varieties change that system and promote monocultures as has happened in the favorable environments?

This chapter outlines some of the implications of agricultural intensification and the adoption of GR technologies on crop biodiversity and genetic diversity. The first part of the chapter describes the drivers of agricultural intensification and its consequences for land use change and crop choice. The second part of the chapter describes the spatial and temporal patterns of modern variety diffusion and examines its impact on genetic diversity across modern varieties and within varieties. The final part of the chapter presents the prospects for a Green Revolution 2.0, with a focus on areas bypassed by the original GR, and discusses its potential consequences for crop biodiversity.

## Agricultural intensification, land use change and crop diversity

Intensification of agriculture refers to the increase in output per unit of land used in production, or land productivity. Population densities, expressed as the ratio of labor to land, explain much about where and under which conditions this process has occurred (Boserup, 1981). The transition from low-yield, land-extensive cultivation systems to land-intensive, double- and triple-crop systems is profitable only in societies where the supply of uncultivated land has been exhausted. It is no accident that the modern seed-fertilizer revolution has been most successful in densely populated areas of the world, where traditional mechanisms for enhancing yields per unit area have been exhausted (Hayami and Ruttan, 1985).

Intensive cultivation will also be observed in areas with lower population densities provided that soil conditions are suitable and markets are accessible. Intensification occurs in the less densely populated areas for two reasons: (1) higher prices and elastic demand for output imply that the marginal utility of effort increases, hence farmers in the region will begin cultivating larger areas; and (2) higher returns to labor encourage migration into well-connected areas from neighboring regions with higher transport costs. Examples of regions with low population density but intensive, market-oriented production are the Central Plains of Thailand and parts of South America's Southern Cone. If the conditions described are not present, labor and other costs associated with intensive agriculture are substantially higher than its incremental economic returns. Intensification of land use and the adoption of yield-enhancing technologies have occurred in traditional as well as modern agricultural systems (Pingali and Smale, 2001).

Agricultural intensification influences the extent of crop diversity in two ways: first, through changes in land use patterns, and second, through crop choice changes. Lands that have high agricultural productivity potential, such as the irrigated and high rainfall lowlands, and lands with high soil fertility tend to become the focus of intensification efforts as population densities rise. One also witnesses the concentration of crops that are responsive to intensification pressures, that is, crops whose productivity can be enhanced through increases in input use. Hence, the choice of staple grain crops, such as rice and wheat, over millets and root crops. This change in cropping pattern preceded the Green Revolution, but the advent of high-yielding varieties certainly accelerated the process. Hence, the Green Revolution induced ubiquitous monoculture systems in the favorable production environments. The crowding out of traditional millets and pulses from the Indo-Gangetic plains of South Asia in favor of intensive rice and wheat production is a classic example of such cropping pattern changes (Pingali, 2012).

The lower productive rainfed environments, on the other hand, continue to maintain diversity of crops grown, and for individual staple grain crops, diversity in traditional varieties and landraces. Crops grown in the less favorable environments are generally lower yielding and do not respond to higher input use as compared to those grown in the more favorable environments and under higher levels of intensity. These crops, such as traditional millets and sorghum, tend to be better adapted to harsher environmental stresses, such as drought, high temperatures, or flooding, and hence are better suited to the unfavorable environments. Unlike the monoculture systems that are prevalent in the irrigated lands, the stress-prone environments tend to have multiple crops on the same field at the same time. The *Milpa* system of Mexico is a great example of inter-cropping of maize, beans and squash in order to ensure farm household food security and diet quality. Furthermore, *milpas* generate public economic value by conserving agrobiodiversity, especially that of maize landraces, which have the potential to contribute unique traits needed by plant breeders for future crop improvement (Birol et al., 2007).

## Spatial and temporal patterns of diffusion on modern varieties[1]

The change in the crop genetic landscape from predominantly traditional to largely modern patterns of genetic variation occurred over the past 200 years and at an accelerated rate since the 1960s with the advent of the Green Revolution (Pingali and Smale, 2001). Evenson and Gollin (2003) showed that adoption of modern varieties (for 11 major food crops averaged across all crops) increased rapidly during the two decades of the GR, and even more rapidly in the following decades, from 9% in 1970 to 29% in 1980, 46% in 1990 and 63% by 1998. Moreover, in many areas and in many crops, first generation modern varieties have been replaced by second and third generation modern varieties (Evenson and Gollin, 2003).

Spatial and temporal patterns in the adoption of modern varieties are largely determined by the economic factors affecting their profitability and by the performance of agricultural research institutions and seed industries (Pingali and Smale, 2001). The adoption of these varieties has been most widespread in land-scarce environments with high population densities and/or in areas well-connected to domestic and international markets, where the intensification of agriculture first began. Even in these areas, the profitability of modern variety adoption has been conditioned by the potential productivity of the land under cultivation. For instance, while modern rice and wheat varieties spread rapidly through the irrigated environments, their adoption has been less spectacular in the less favorable environments – the drought-prone and high-temperature environments for wheat, and the drought- and flood-prone environments for rice. For all three cereals, traditional landraces continue to be cultivated in the less favorable production environments across the developing world (Pingali and Heisey, 2001).

Improved varieties for crops such as sorghum, millets, pulses and cassava were not available until the 1980s (Evenson and Gollin, 2003). Hence, the limited expansion of the Green Revolution beyond the favorable irrigated lands. The limited penetration of the Green Revolution into sub-Saharan Africa up until the 1990s was partly also due to the lack of suitable improved varieties for the traditional staples, especially tropical maize, millets and cassava. The situation has changed dramatically since then. Recent evidence indicates that sub-Saharan Africa is well on its way towards adopting modern varietal technology (Walker and Alwang, 2015).

For instance, the area planted to improved cassava varieties in sub-Saharan Africa doubled from 18% in 1998 to 36% in 2009, and the area under improved maize varieties was at 57% by 2009 in West and Central Africa (Alene et al., 2015). Fuglie and Marder (2015) report that the area under improved varieties doubled from 20 to 40 million hectares between 2000 and 2010:

> This was achieved by deepening the pool of improved varieties available to farmers, both in terms of their adaptability to more environments but especially to a wider set

of crops beyond the major cereal grains, including oilseeds, legumes, roots, tubers and bananas.

*(Fuglie and Marder, 2015, p. 356)*

But sub-Saharan Africa still has improved variety diffusion rates that are significantly below those of rainfed areas in other parts of the world. The converse to this statement is, of course, that sub-Saharan Africa is still home to significant diversity in traditional varieties and landraces of food crops.

In the case of rainfed environments in South Asia, Pandey et al. (2015) indicated that the adoption of modern rice varieties, specifically targeted for those environments, increased substantially since 1998. By 2010, modern varieties occupied over 80% of the rainfed lowland rice growing area in the region, an average annual increase in adoption level in the range of 1–3% between 1998 and 2010. The rapid spread of improved varieties in the stress-prone environments raises concerns about the crowding out of crop diversity in favor of staple grain monoculture systems. A potential repeat of the Green Revolution experience witnessed in the irrigated lowlands of Asia.

## *Narrowing of crop genetic diversity?*

Crop genetic diversity broadly defined refers to the genetic variation embodied in seed and expressed when challenged by natural and human selection pressure. In applied genetics, diversity refers to the variance among alternative forms of a gene (alleles) at individual gene positions on a chromosome (loci), among several loci, among individual plants in a population or among populations (Brown et al., 1990). Diversity can be measured by accessions of seed held in gene banks, lines or populations utilized in crop-breeding programs, or varieties cultivated by farmers (cultivars). However, crop genetic diversity cannot be literally or entirely observed at any point in time; it can only be indicated with reference to a specific crop population and analytical perspective (Smale, 1997).

Whether the changes in crop varietal adoption induced by the Green Revolution have resulted in a narrowing of genetic diversity is an issue that remains largely unresolved due to conceptual and practical difficulties. Scientists disagree about what constitutes genetic narrowing or when such narrowing may have occurred. Several dimensions of diversity must be considered in this regard, including both the spatial and temporal variation between landraces and modern elite cultivars and the variation within modern cultivars (Fu, 2015).

According to Smale (1997), the adoption of modern varieties has been characterized first by a concentration on a few varieties followed by an expansion in their numbers as more varieties became available. Porceddu et al. (1988) described two major stages of genetic narrowing in wheat during modern times. The first occurred in the 19th century, when scientific plant breeding responded to the demand for new plant types. Farming systems emerged that were based on the intensive use of land and labor, livestock production, and the use of organic manure. Changes in cultivation methods favored genotypes that diverted large amounts of photosynthates into the ear and grain. Bell (1987) reported that the engineering innovations of the late 19th century led to the establishment of extensive wheat-growing areas in North America, Australia and parts of South America. In other words, mechanization of agriculture dictated uniformity in plant type.

According to Porceddu et al. (1988), a second stage of narrowing occurred in the 20th century, when genes were introduced to produce major changes in plant type. Use of the dwarfing genes Rht1 and Rht2, for example, conferred a positive genotype-by-environment interaction in which yield increases proved greater given a certain combination of soil moisture, soil fertility and weed control. Varieties carrying these dwarfing genes were developed by Norman Borlaug with the national breeding program in Mexico and later by the CIMMYT. They became known as the Green Revolution wheat or modern wheat varieties.

As the process of modernization proceeded and the offerings of scientific breeding programs expanded, the pattern of concentration declined in many European and North American countries (Lupton, 1992; Dalrymple, 1988, cited in Smale, 1997). Similarly in the early years of the GR, the dominant cultivar occupied over 80% of the wheat area in the Indian Punjab, but this share fell below 50% by 1985. By 1990, the top five bread wheat cultivars covered approximately 36% of the global wheat area planted to modern varieties (Smale, 1997).

Comparing counts of landraces and modern varieties over time may not provide a meaningful index of genetic narrowing. They also imply that even if reliable samples of the landraces originally cultivated in an area could be obtained, analyses comparing their genetic diversity might provide only part of the answer regarding genetic narrowing. While the landrace in the farmers' fields is a heterogeneous population of plants, it is derived from generations of selection by local farmers and is therefore likely to be local in adaptation (Pingali and Smale, 2001).

Evenson and Gollin's (2003) summary of the history of rice breeding suggests a process of continual expansion and narrowing of the genetic pool. Organized breeding efforts probably date earlier than AD 1000 in China. Modern efforts can be traced to the late 19th century in several parts of Asia. In temperate East Asia, the first significant advances were made by Japanese farmers and scientists when they developed relatively short-statured and fertilizer-responsive cultivars. Known as the *rono* varieties, these belonged to the *japonica* class of rice and were widely cultivated in Japan as early as the 1890s. During the Japanese occupation of Taiwan in the early part of the 20th century, Japanese scientists sought to adapt these varieties to the more tropical conditions of Taiwan. At the same time, researchers in tropical Asia were seeking more productive varieties of rice from the *indica* and *javanica* classes of rice. After World War II, the Food and Agriculture Organization of the United Nations (FAO) initiated a program to cross *indica* rice with *japonicas* as a means of increasing rice yields, culminating in the formation of IRRI and the GR varieties of rice.

To Vaughan and Chang (1992), genetic narrowing in modern rice began early in the 20th century. Development projects, population increases and forest clearing in Asia were the primary causes of the loss of wild and cultivated rice landraces. In the Mekong Delta, the replacement of traditional deep water rice by irrigated rice occurred with drainage and irrigation schemes that were introduced during the French colonial period. On the other hand, Ford-Lloyd et al. (2009) argued, based on their analysis of data of 33 years of rice landrace collections from 1962 to 1995, that they have not detected any significant reduction of actual genetic diversity of traditional rice landraces in use by farmers. They asserted that it is possible to conclude that genetic diversity in rice maintained *in situ* has continued to survive throughout South and Southeast Asia through their study period. Part of the reason for high prevalence of landraces is that modern variety use is very limited in the low productive rice lands, such as drought prone and flood prone environments. In these areas traditional rice varieties continue to be used.

Goodman (1995) reported that the major portion of the variability now found in maize developed before European contact (c. 1500), and several of the most widely grown races, including the commercially important Corn Belt dents, developed later. During the 'corn show era' in the 19th century United States, farmers exhibited their open-pollinated varieties locally and emphasis was placed on uniformity and conformity to an 'ideal type'. By the early 1950s, essentially all of the maize grown in the Corn Belt was double-cross hybrid. After the late 1950s, more and more farmers in the US Corn Belt grew single-cross rather than double-cross hybrids. Because single-cross seed must be produced on an inbred line, this type of selection contributed to a marked loss of variability in US breeding materials. To Goodman, a countervailing influence during the past 25 years has been the emphasis by public researchers on development of improved maize populations.

Not all scientists agree about what constitutes genetic narrowing or precisely when such narrowing has occurred. For instance, in contradiction with Porceddu et al. (1988), Hawkes (1983) cited the introduction of Rht1 and Rht2 genes into western wheat breeding lines as an example of how diversity has been broadened by scientific plant breeders. The Japanese line Norin 10 carried the dwarfing genes from the landrace Daruma, believed to be of Korean origin. Similarly, the efforts to increase rice yields by crossing *japonica* and *indica* classes of rice extended the gene pool accessible to rice breeders. As these examples suggest, in modern agriculture, today's broadening of the genetic pool in a plant breeding program may lead to a narrowing of the breadth of materials grown by farmers precisely because such innovations often produce varieties that are popular.

## Genetic diversity within modern varieties

Part of the concern for genetic narrowing is based on the perception that, with time, conventional plant breeding practices inevitably restrict the genetic base of modern varieties. The evidence from studies on the parentage of modern varieties of the major staples lends little support to this view (Witcombe, 1999). In an analysis of genealogies of 1,709 modern rice varieties, Evenson and Gollin (2003) found that while a variety released in the 1960s had three landraces in its pedigree, more recent releases have 25 or more. The complexity of rice pedigrees, in terms of parental combinations, geographical origin and number of ancestors, has expanded over time. A similar pattern has been shown for about 800 wheat varieties released in the developing world since the 1960s (Smale, 1997). The average number of distinct landraces found in bread wheat pedigrees grew from around 20 in the mid-1960s to about 50 in 1990.

Skovmand and de Lacy (1999) analyzed the distance among coefficients of parentage for a historical set of CIMMYT wheat varieties over the past four decades. Their results show a rate of increase in genealogical diversity that is positive, but decreases over time, with marked expansion in genealogies from 1950 to 1967 and gradual flattening through the 1990s. If progenitors were recycled and reused, the distance among them would decrease over time and the slope of the line would be negative. Kazi et al. (2013) provided evidence that bringing genes from wild relatives of wheat into breeding populations more recently has enhanced the gene pool and its utilization for managing various biotic and abiotic stresses.

Smale (2000) further points out that evidence from a number of studies does not support the pessimistic view that genetic base of modern wheat varieties is restricted and tends to decline with the introduction of modern varieties. She argues that genealogical analyses show a significant positive trend in the number of distinct landrace ancestors in the pedigrees of over a thousand varieties of spring bread wheat released in the developing world since the start of the Green Revolution in 1966.

Less evidence is available worldwide on trends in the pedigrees or ancestry of maize varieties than for rice and wheat, in part because that information is confidential in an increasingly privatized industry. Following the epidemic of corn blight in the US crop in 1970, the National Research Council (1972) concluded that the genetic base of maize in the United States was sufficiently narrow to justify concern. Duvick (1984) found that during the ten years following the 1970 epidemic, breeders had broadened their germplasm pools.

Molecular markers, like genealogies, can be used to construct indicators of the latent diversity in a set of crop populations. Using molecular markers, Donini et al. (2005) compared changes in genetic diversity between 'old' (1930s) versus 'modern' (1990s) UK bread wheat varieties and concluded that there is no objective evidence to support the assertion that modern plant breeding has reduced the genetic diversity of UK wheat. Molecular evidence for a set of CIMMYT wheat varieties indicates that genetic distance has been maintained among major parents and popular varieties over the past 30 years. Since many of the varieties of spring bread wheat grown in the developing world have a combination of CIMMYT and locally-bred materials in their ancestry (Heisey et al., 1999), these data represent a lower bound on actual genetic diversity. Furthermore, the genetic diversity that is accessible to conventional plant breeders today includes not only spring bread wheat, of course, but also wheat types with different growing habit, close relatives and wild grasses (Smith et al., 2015). Techniques of biotechnology may traverse the species barriers faced by conventional breeders (Moreta et al., 2015).

## Green Revolution 2.0 and crop biodiversity

GR 2.0 is already beginning to take place, and it is happening in low-income countries as well as in emerging economies (Pingali, 2012). Low-income countries, many of them in sub-Saharan Africa, that have been bypassed by the Green Revolution, still face chronic hunger and poverty. They continue to be plagued by the age-old constraints to enhancing productivity growth, such as the lack of technology, poor market infrastructure, appropriate institutions and an enabling policy environment (Binswanger and McCalla, 2010). Emerging economies, including much of Asia where gains from the first GR were concentrated, are well on their way towards agricultural modernization and structural transformation (Timmer, 2007). The challenge for agriculture in the emerging economies is to integrate smallholders into value chains, maintain their competitiveness and close the inter-regional income gap (Pingali, 2010).

Pingali (2012) argued that a confluence of factors has come together in recent years to generate renewed interest in agriculture and spur the early stages of GR 2.0. In the low-income countries, continued levels of food deficits and the reliance on food aid and food imports have reintroduced agriculture as an engine of growth on the policy agenda. African leaders have acknowledged the critical role of agriculture in their development process, and that lack of investment in the sector would only leave them further behind. The CAADP declaration of 2006 and resulting pledges by African Heads of State to increase agricultural investments demonstrated their commitment to improve the agriculture sector. (The Comprehensive Africa Agriculture Development Programme [CAADP] is the agricultural program of the New Partnership for Africa's Development [NEPAD], an initiative of the African Union). There is also an increasing awareness of the detrimental impacts of climate change on food security, especially for tropical agriculture systems in low-income countries (Byerlee et al., 2009).

In the emerging economies, growing private sector interest in investing in the agricultural sector has created an agricultural renaissance (Pingali, 2010). Supermarkets are spreading rapidly across urban areas in emerging economies and are encouraging national and multinational agri-business investments along the fresh produce value chains in these countries (Reardon and Minten, 2011). Consequently, staple crop monoculture systems popularized by the Green Revolution are diversifying into high value horticulture and livestock production. Despite these positive developments, inter-regional differences in productivity and poverty persist in many emerging economies. Rising demand for feed and biofuels as well as technological advances in breeding for stress tolerance could result in a revitalization of the marginal areas. The rapid rise of hybrid maize production in Eastern India is a case in point (Gulati and Dixon, 2008). Finally, at the global level, the food price crisis of 2008, sustained high prices, and more recent peaks observed in 2011 and 2012 have brought agriculture back onto the global and national agendas (FAO, 2011).

## What are the implications for crop biodiversity?

As the Green Revolution 2.0 spreads to regions that the original Green Revolution has bypassed, familiar concerns about the consequence for sustaining crop biodiversity will emerge. In order to meet the unabated rise in demand for food due to a growing population and rising incomes, the GR 2.0 would need to enhance productivity both on the favorable lands as well as the more marginal production environments. Continued focus on yield enhancing technical change is the primary mechanism for ensuring that lands will continue to be spared for non-agricultural uses, including for biodiversity conservation. Balmford et al. (2005) stated that 'Conservationists should be as concerned about future agricultural yields as they are about population growth and rising per capita consumption' (p. 1594). Agricultural R&D can help in the quest for sustainable biodiversity conservation.

Rising incomes and the consequent decline in per capita consumption of staple cereals, such as rice and wheat, provide an opportunity for moving away from monoculture systems and towards more diversified cropping systems (Pingali, 2015). This would be particularly true in the favorable production environments given their better market connectivity and irrigation and power infrastructure. However, we may see the reverse for the less favorable environments, the movement towards monoculture systems, with the advent of improved stress tolerant varieties, especially when there are only a few successful ones. Pandey et al. (2015) pointed to the spread of 'mega' varieties, in other words single varieties of rice that cover large areas in South Asia. One such variety, 'Swarna', has spread widely throughout the rainfed rice lands in India, to the extent of 30% acreage in some Eastern Indian states. The successful spread of a few rainfed varieties extend the concern about the narrowing of crop genetic diversity from the favorable environments to the unfavorable ones.

What about genetic diversity within varieties: will it rise or fall? The integration of cereal landraces into modern breeding programs could alleviate some of the risk of loss in genetic diversity within improved varieties (Smith et al., 2015). It could also lead to the incorporation of positive traits into new varieties or breeding populations for more sustainable agricultural production, in particular, their potential as sources of novel genes for disease and abiotic stress resistance, or for enhancing nutrient use efficiency and improving the nutrition quality of staple grains (Newton et al., 2010). Continued genetic improvement does not necessarily lead to loss of genetic diversity in areas where modern varieties dominate – especially when access to germplasm is relatively unrestricted and innovative plant breeding strategies may be employed. Access to diverse sources of germplasm, including landraces and wild relatives, is therefore of great importance to the success of public and private breeding programs and the supply of varieties in modern agriculture (Pingali and Smale, 2001).

What, then, is the future of landraces/traditional varieties? The coexistence of varieties and landraces of particularly crops may persist where market-based incentives exist. For example, in Asia, traditional varieties are generally of higher quality and fetch premium prices in the market. Thailand still grows low-yielding traditional rainfed varieties extensively for the export market. Basmati rice production has expanded significantly in India and Pakistan, both for domestic as well as export markets. Traditional japonica rices have risen in popularity across East Asia and are sold at a substantial premium. Quinoa, a crop native to the Andean Mountains, has become very popular in the developed world due to its nutritional qualities. Once a neglected crop, it is now receiving a lot of attention from Andean farmers as an income growth opportunity (Massawe et al., 2016). Teff from Ethiopia has been making recent inroads into developed country diets (see Massawe et al. 2016 for a review of under-utilized crops that have become or could become attractive to Western consumers due to their nutritive qualities). Market-based incentives could play a major role in reviving the prospects for under-utilized crops and ensuring their *in situ* conservation.

## Conclusions

Agricultural intensification and the adoption of modern varieties of the major staple crops led to the ubiquitous monoculture systems in the favorable production environments across the developing world. The lower productive rainfed environments, on the other hand, continue to maintain diversity of crops grown, such as traditional millets and root crops. These environments have also sustained the cultivation of landraces of rice, wheat and maize. Narrowing of crop genetic diversity in the GR areas has been averted to some extent by the replacement of the first-generation modern varieties with second- and third-generation varieties in more recent decades. The expansion in the numbers of varieties available through crop breeding programs has reduced the risk that intensive production systems would concentrate on a few dominant varieties. Modern plant breeding has also helped expand the genetic base of modern varieties by incorporating genes from landraces and wild relatives of staple grains into the breeding populations.

This chapter argues that areas that have been bypassed by the original GR are now witnessing intensification and agricultural productivity growth. This GR 2.0 is being observed in parts of sub-Saharan Africa as well as in the unfavorable environments of South Asia. Improved varieties of sorghum, millet, cassava and tropical maize are being increasingly adopted by African smallholders. In South Asia, rice varieties that are tolerant to drought, and to flooding, have made major inroads into the stress-prone environments that the original GR bypassed.

While the food security benefits of the GR 2.0 are obvious, there are significant concerns about the consequences for crop biodiversity. The spread of improved varieties of the traditional African crops could lead to the encroachment of monoculture systems in areas where multi-crop farming systems sustain diversity and landraces. In South Asia, the spread of small numbers of 'mega' varieties of rice that are stress tolerant could lead to the risk of genetic narrowing in rainfed environments where multiple landraces are cultivated today. As GR 2.0 proceeds, it would be important to learn from original GR in terms of the appropriate mechanisms to balance food security and crop biodiversity concerns.

## Note

1 This section builds on material presented in Pingali and Smale (2001).

## References

Alene, A. D., Abdoulaye, T., Rusike, J., Manyong, V. and Walker, T. S. (2015) 'The effectiveness of crop improvement programmes from the perspectives of varietal output and adoption: Cassava, cowpea, soybean and yam in sub-Saharan Africa and maize in West and Central Africa', pp. 74–122 in T. S. Walker and J. Alwang (eds.), *Crop Improvement, Adoption, and Impact of Improved Varieties in Food Crops in Sub-Saharan Africa*, CAB International, Wallingford, UK.

Balmford, A., Green, R. E. and Scharlemann, J. P. W. (2005) 'Sparing land for nature: Exploring the potential impact of changes in agricultural yield on the area needed for crop production', *Global Change Biology*, vol. 11, pp. 1594–1605.

Bell, G. D. H. (1987) 'The history of wheat cultivation', pp. 31–49 in F. G. H. Lupton (ed.), *Wheat Breeding: Its Scientific Basis*, Chapman & Hall, London, UK.

Binswanger-Mkhize, H. and McCalla., A. F. (2010) 'The changing context and prospects for agricultural and rural development in Africa', pp. 3571–3712 in P. L. Pingali and R. E. Evenson (eds.), *Handbook of Agricultural Economics* (Vol. 4, 4th ed.), Elsevier B.V., Oxford, UK.

Birol, E., Villalba, E. R. and Smale, M. (2007) 'Farmer preferences for milpa diversity and genetically modified maize in Mexico. A latent class approach', *IFPRI Discussion Paper,* International Food Policy Research Institute, Washington D.C., USA

Boserup, E. (1981) *Population and Technological Change: A Study of Long Term Change*, Chicago University Press, Chicago, IL, USA.

Brown, A. H., Clegg, M. T., Kahler, A. L. and Weir, B. S. (eds.) (1990) *Plant Population Genetics, Breeding and Genetic Resources*, Sinauer Associates, Sunderland, MA, USA.

Byerlee, D., de Janvry, A. and Sadoulet, E. (2009) 'Agriculture for development: Toward a new paradigm', *Annual Review of Resource Economics*, vol. 1, pp. 15–31.

Dalrymple, D. (1988) 'Changes in wheat varieties and yields in the United States, 1919–1984', *Agricultural History*, vol. 62, pp. 20–36.

Donini, P., Law, J., Koebner, R., Reeves, J. and Cooke, R. (2005) 'The impact of breeding on genetic diversity and erosion in bread wheat', *Plant Genetic Resources: Characteristics and Utilization*, vol. 3, pp. 391–399.

Duvick, D. N. (1984) 'Genetic diversity in major farm crops on the farm and in reserve', *Economic Botany*, vol. 38, pp. 161–178.

Evenson, R. E. and Gollin, D. (2003) 'Assessing the impact of the Green Revolution, 1960 to 2000', *Science*, vol. 300, pp. 758–762.

Food and Agriculture Organization of the United Nations (FAO) (2011) *The State of Food Insecurity in the World*, FAO, Rome, Italy.

Ford-Lloyd, B. V., Brar, D., Khush, G. S., Jackson, M. T. and Virk, P. S. (2009) 'Genetic erosion over time of rice landrace agrobiodiversity', *Plant Genetic Resources*, vol. 7, pp. 164–168.

Fu, Y-B. (2015) 'Understanding crop genetic diversity under modern plant breeding', *Theoretical and Applied Genetics*, vol. 128, pp. 2131–2142.

Goodman, M. M. (1995) 'Maize', pp. 193–202 in J. Smartt and N. W. Simmonds (eds.), *The Evolution of Crop Plants*, John Wiley and Sons, New York, NY, USA.

Gulati, A. and Dixon, J. (2008) *Maize in Asia: Changing Markets and Incentives*, Academic Foundation, New Delhi, India.

Hawkes, J. G. (1983) *The Diversity of Crop Plants*, Harvard University Press, Cambridge, MA, USA.

Hayami, Y. and Ruttan, V. W. (1985) *Agricultural Development*, John Hopkins University Press, Baltimore, MD, USA.

Heisey, P. W., Lantican, M. A. and Dubin, H. J. (1999) 'Assessing the benefits of international wheat breeding research: An overview of the global wheat impacts study', pp. 19–26 in P. L. Pingali (ed.), *CIMMYT 1998–99 World Wheat Facts and Trends: Global Wheat Research in a Changing World: Challenges and Achievements*, CIMMYT, Mexico City, Mexico.

Fuglie, K. and Marder, J. (2015) 'The diffusion and impact of improved food crop varieties in sub-Saharan Africa', pp. 338–369 in T. S. Walker and J. Alwang (eds.), *Crop Improvement, Adoption, and Impact of Improved Varieties in Food Crops in Sub-Saharan Africa*, CAB International, Wallingford, UK.

Kazi, G. A., Rasheed, A. and Mujeeb-Kazi, A. (2013) 'Biotic stress and crop improvement: A wheat focus around novel strategies', pp. 239–267 in R. K. Hakeem, P. Ahmad and M. Ozturk (eds.), *Crop Improvement: New Approaches and Modern Techniques*, Springer US, Boston, MA, USA.

Lupton, F. G. H. (1992) 'Wheat varieties cultivated in Europe', in *Changes in Varietal Distribution of Cereals in Central and Western Europe: Agroecological Atlas of Cereal Growing in Europe*, Vol. 4, Wageningen University, Wageningen, The Neatherlands.

Massawe, F., Mayes, M. and Cheng, A. (2016) 'Crop diversity: an unexploited treasure trove for food security', *Trends in Plant Science*, vol. 21, pp. 365–368.

Moreta, D. E., Mathur, P. N., van Zonneveld, M., Amaya, K., Arango, J., Selvaraj, M. G. and Dedicova, B. (2015) 'Current issues in cereal crop biodiversity', *Advances in Biochemical Engineering/Biotechnology*, vol. 147, pp. 1–35.

Newton, A. C., Akar, T., Baresel, J. P., Bebeli, P. J., Bettencourt, E., Bladenopoulos, K. V., Czembor, J. H., Fasoula, D. A., Katsiotis, A., Koutis, K., Koutsika-Sotiriou, M., Kovacs, G., Larsson, H., Pinheiro de Carvalho, M. A. A., Rubiales, D., Russell, J., Dos Santos, T. M. M. and Vaz Patto, M. C. (2010) 'Cereal landraces for sustainable agriculture: A review', *Agronomy for Sustainable Development*, vol. 30, pp. 237–269.

Pandey, S., Velasco, M. L. and Yamano, T. (2015) 'Scientific strength in rice improvement programmes, varietal outputs and adoption of improved varieties in South Asia', pp. 239–264 in T. S. Walker and J. Alwang (eds.), *Crop Improvement, Adoption, and Impact of Improved Varieties in Food Crops in Sub-Saharan Africa*, CGIAR Standing Panel on Impact Assessment (SPIA), Montpellier, France.

Pingali, P. (2010) 'Agriculture renaissance: Making "agriculture for development" work in the 21st century', *Handbook of Agricultural Economics*, vol. 4, Chapter 74, pp. 3867–3894.

Pingali, P. (2012) 'Green Revolution: Impacts, limits, and the path ahead', *Proceedings of the National Academy of Sciences USA*, vol. 109, pp. 12302–12308.

Pingali, P. (2015) 'Agricultural policy and nutrition outcomes – getting beyond the preoccupation with staple grains', *Food Security*, vol. 7, pp. 583–591.

Pingali, P. and Heisey, P. W. (2001) 'Cereal-crop productivity in developing countries: Past trends and future prospects', pp 56–82 in J. M. Alston, P. G. Pardey and M. Taylor (eds.), *Agricultural Science Policy*, IFPRI & Johns Hopkins University Press, Washington, DC, USA.

Pingali, P. and Smale, M. (2001) 'Agriculture, industrialized', pp. 85–97 in S. Levin (ed.), *Encyclopedia of Biodiversity*, Vol. 1, Academic Press, New York, NY, USA.

Porceddu, E. C., Ceoloni, D. L., Tanzarella, O. A. and Scarascia, G. T. M. (1988) 'Genetic resources and plant breeding: Problems and prospects', pp. 7–21 in *The Plant Breeding International, Cambridge Special Lecture*, Institute of Plant Science Research, Cambridge, UK.

Reardon, T. and Minten, B. (2011) 'Surprised by supermarkets: Diffusion of modern food retail in India', *Journal of Agribusiness in Developing and Emerging Economies*, vol. 1, pp. 134–161.

Skovmand, B. and DeLacy, I. (1999) 'Parentage of a historical set of CIMMYT wheats', p. 165 in *Annual Meeting Abstracts*, American Society of Agronomy, Madison, WI, USA.

Smale, M. (1997) 'The Green Revolution and wheat genetic diversity: Dome unfounded assumptions', *World Development*, vol. 25, pp. 1257–1269.

Smale, M. (2000) *Economic Incentives for Conserving Crop Genetic Diversity on Farms: Issues and Evidence.* Paper presented at the meetings of the International Agricultural Economics Association, Berlin, Germany.

Smith, S., Bubeck, D., Nelson, B., Stanek, J. and Gerke, J. (2015) 'Genetic diversity and modern plant breeding', pp. 55–88 in R. M. Ahuja and M. S. Jain (eds.), *Genetic Diversity and Erosion in Plants: Indicators and Prevention*, Springer International Publishing, Cham, Switzerland.

Stevenson, J. R., Villoria, N., Byerlee, D., Kelley, T. and Maredia, M. (2013) 'Green Revolution research saved an estimated 18 to 27 million hectares from being brought into agricultural production', *Proceedings of the National Academy of Sciences USA*, vol. 110, pp. 8363–8368.

Timmer, C. (2007) *Structural Transformation as the Pathway Out of Poverty: The Changing Role of Agriculture in Economic Development*, The AEI Press, Washington DC, USA.

Trewavas, A. J. (2001) 'The population/biodiversity paradox: Agricultural efficiency to save wilderness', *Plant Physiology*, vol. 125, pp. 174–179.

Vaughan, D. A. and Chang, T.-T. (1992) '*In situ* conservation of rice genetic resources', *Economic Botany*, vol. 46, pp. 368–383.

Walker, T. S. and Alwang, J. (eds) (2015) *Crop Improvement, Adoption, and Impact of Improved Varieties in Food Crops in Sub-Saharan Africa*, CAB International, Wallingford, UK.

Witcombe, J. R. (1999) 'Does plant breeding lead to a loss of genetic diversity?', pp. 245–272 in D. Wood and J. Lenne (eds.), *Agrobiodiversity: Characterization, Utilization and Measurement*, CAB International, Wallingford, UK.

# 13

# AGROECOLOGY

## Using functional biodiversity to design productive and resilient polycultural systems

*Miguel A. Altieri, Clara I. Nicholls and Marcus A. Lana*

### Introduction

For decades, agroecologists have contended that a key strategy in designing a sustainable and resilient agriculture is to re-incorporate biodiversity into agricultural fields and the surrounding landscapes (Altieri and Nicholls, 2004). This recommendation is based on observations and experimental evidence that support the following trends: (a) when agroecosystems are simplified, whole functional groups of species are removed, shifting the balance of the system from a desired to a less desired functional state, affecting their capacity to respond to changes and to generate ecosystem services; and (b) higher agroecosystem diversity may buffer against pest and disease problems as well as changing rainfall and temperature patterns (Folke, 2006).

In agricultural systems, the level of existing biodiversity can make the difference between the system being stressed or resilient, when confronting a biotic or abiotic perturbation. In all agroecosystems, a diversity of organisms is required for ecosystem function and to provide environmental services (Loreau et al., 2001). Diversified agroecosystems may possibly reverse downward trends in yields over the long term as a variety of crops and varieties deployed in various temporal and spatial schemes respond differently to external shocks. It is clear, however, that it is not diversity *per se* that enhances stability in agroecosystems, but rather 'functional biodiversity', a set of biota clusters that play key roles in the determination of agroecosystem processes and, through these, in the provision of ecological services, thereby reducing the need for off-farm inputs (Moonen and Barberi, 2008). In one review, Kremen and Miles (2012) found that when compared with conventional farming systems, diversified farming systems supported substantially greater biodiversity, and were associated with higher soil quality, carbon sequestration, water-holding capacity in surface soils, energy-use efficiency, and resistance and resilience to climate change. Relative to conventional monocultures, diversified farming systems also had enhanced control of weeds, diseases, and arthropod pests, and increased pollination services.

In this chapter, we focus on two well-known advantages of biodiverse cropping systems: reduction of crop vulnerability to insect pests, and to extreme climatic variability (Vandermeer et al., 1998). We also describe the ecological interactions and mechanisms at work that explain why maintaining species diversity in fields acts as a buffer against insect pests and also against uncertain weather, thus providing the foundations for plant health, crop productivity, and resiliency. As an example, we discuss the use of polycultures (intercropping of annual crops) as promising models for promoting biodiversity, conserving natural resources, sustaining yield without agrochemicals, and ensuring food security, while providing ecological services and remarkable lessons about resiliency in the face of pest pressure and continuous climatic change.

## Types and roles of biodiversity in agroecosystems

Biodiversity in agroecosystems includes the various crops, livestock, fish, weeds, arthropods, and microorganisms involved, and is affected by human management, geographical location, and climatic, edaphic, and socioeconomic factors. In general, the degree of biodiversity in agroecosystems depends on four main characteristics of the agroecosystem (Southwood and Way, 1970):

1 The type and diversity of vegetation within and around the agroecosystem;
2 The extent of the isolation of the agroecosystem from natural vegetation;
3 The permanence of the various crops within the agroecosystem; and
4 The intensity of management and the level of chemical intensification.

The biodiversity components of agroecosystems can be classified in to three groups in relation to the role they play in the functioning of cropping systems (Swift and Anderson, 1993):

1 Productive biota: crops, trees, and animals chosen by farmers that play a determining role in the diversity and complexity of the agroecosystem;
2 Resource biota: organisms that contribute to productivity through pollination, biological control, decomposition, and so forth; and
3 Destructive biota: weeds, insect pests, microbial pathogens, and so forth that reach unacceptable population levels and which farmers aim at reducing through cultural management.

Moonen and Barberi (2008) proposed another way of dividing the inhabiting biota of agroecosystems, recognizing five groups:

1 Cultivated species producing food;
2 Auxiliary species, spontaneous or introduced species which support the production process;
3 Pest species, spontaneous species damaging the production process;
4 Wild species producing goods, managed or not, which can sporadically be present within fields or hedges; and
5 Spontaneous neutral species whose presence does not affect the production services but may play other functions.

Vandermeer and Perfecto (1995) recognized that the previous classifications of biodiversity can be grouped into (a) *planned biodiversity* which includes the crops and livestock purposely included in the agroecosystem by the farmer, in various spatial/temporal arrangements; and (b) *associated biodiversity*, which includes all soil flora and fauna, herbivores, carnivores, decomposers, and so forth that colonize the agroecosystem from surrounding environments. Planned and associated biodiversity both have direct functions on the function of the ecosystem, as illustrated by the arrows connecting their boxes with the agroecosystem function box (**Figure 13.1** *The relationship between planned and associated biodiversity in determining agroecosystem function*). However, each form of biodiversity also has functions mediated through the other, illustrated by the bold arrow in the figure, which leads to indirect influences also (Vandermeer and Perfecto, 1995).

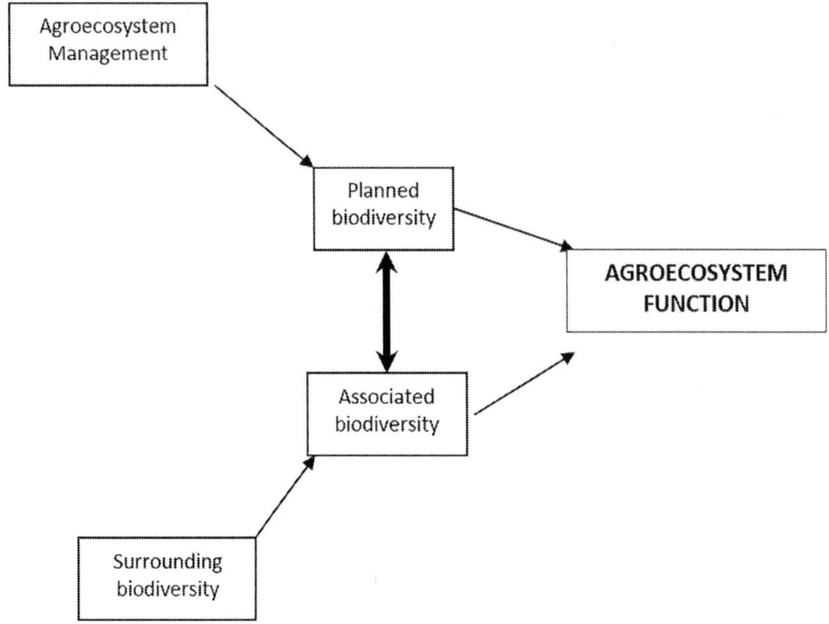


*Figure 13.1* The relationship between planned and associated biodiversity in determining agroecosystem function

*Source*: Vandermeer and Perfecto (1995).

Complementary interactions among the various biotic components can also be of a multiple nature. Some of these interactions can be used to induce positive and direct effects on the biological control of specific crop pests or on soil fertility regeneration and/or enhancement. The exploitation of these interactions in real situations involves agroecosystem design and management strategies aimed at optimizing functional biodiversity via three approaches (Hainzelin, 2013):

1. Enhancement of biodiversity above-ground, at different scales over space and time, to intensify biological cycles for nutrients and water and aiming at increasing harvested biomass production (food, fibre, energy, etc.). This strategy requires planning annual and perennial combinations with complementarity of canopy architectures and root systems among species to maximize the use of solar radiation, conservation of water, and uptake of nutrients while harboring beneficial biota.
2. Use of crop diversification in time and space to enhance natural biological control of insect pests, promote allelopathic effects to suppress weeds, and stimulate antagonists to reduce soil-borne pathogens, thus reducing losses of harvested crop biomass.
3. Stimulation of functional biodiversity below-ground via soil organic management practices, which in turn aids in amplifying biogeochemical cycles in the soil, recycling nutrients from deep profiles, and increasing beneficial microbial activity for optimal crop nutrition and health.

Thus, the optimal behavior of agroecosystems depends on the level of interactions between the various members of the functionally diverse biota, which initiates synergisms which subsidize agroecosystem processes. The key is to identify the type of biodiversity that is desirable to maintain and/or enhance in order to carry out ecological services, and then to determine the best practices that will encourage the desired biodiversity components (Altieri et al., 2015).

## Enhancing functional biodiversity in agroecosystems

Diversification occurs in many forms at the field (variety mixtures, rotations, polycultures, agroforestry, crop-livestock integration) and at the landscape level (hedgerows, forests and trees, corridors, etc.), giving farmers a wide variety of options and combinations for the implementation of this strategy (**Table 13.1** *Temporal and spatial designs of diversified farming systems and their main agroecological effects*). Emergent ecological properties develop in diversified agroecosystems that allow the system to function in ways that maintain soil fertility, crop production, and pest regulation. Most of these systems optimize the application of agroecological principles, thus increasing agroecosystem functional diversity as the foundation for soil quality, plant health, crop productivity and quality, and of system resilience (Altieri and Nicholls, 2012).

Functional diversity refers to the variety of organisms and the ecosystem services they provide for the system to continue performing and enhance its responses to environmental change and other perturbations. An agroecosystem that contains a high degree of functional diversity is usually more resilient against various types and degrees of shocks (Altieri et al., 2015). In general, there are many more species than there are functions, and thus redundancy is built into the agroecosystem. Therefore, biodiversity enhances ecosystem function because those components that appear redundant at one point in time may become important when some environmental change occurs. When change occurs, the redundancies of the system allow for continued ecosystem functioning and provisioning of ecosystem services (Cabell and Oelofse, 2012). Also, a diversity of species acts as a buffer against failure due to environmental fluctuations by enhancing the compensation capacity of the agroecosystem, because if one species fails, others can play the

*Table 13.1* Temporal and spatial designs of diversified farming systems and their main agroecological effects

**Crop rotations:** Temporal diversity in the form of cereal-legume sequences. Nutrients are conserved and provided from one season to the next, and the life cycles of insect pests, diseases, and weeds are interrupted.

**Polycultures:** Cropping systems in which two or more crop species are planted in spatial proximity result in biological complementarities that improve nutrient use efficiency and pest regulation, thus enhancing crop yield stability.

**Agroforestry systems:** Trees grown together with annual crops, in addition to modifying the microclimate, maintain and improve soil fertility, as some trees contribute to nitrogen fixation and nutrient uptake from deep soil horizons while their litter helps replenish soil nutrients, maintain organic matter, and support complex soil food webs.

**Cover crops and mulching:** The use of pure or mixed stands of grass and legumes, for example under fruit trees, can reduce erosion and provide nutrients to the soil and enhance biological control of pests. Flattening cover crop mixtures on the soil surface in conservation farming is a strategy to reduce soil erosion and lower fluctuations in soil moisture and temperature, improve soil quality, and enhance weed suppression, resulting in better crop performance.

**Crop-livestock mixtures:** High biomass output and optimal nutrient recycling can be achieved through crop-animal integration. Animal production that integrates fodder shrubs planted at high densities, intercropped with improved, highly-productive pastures and timber trees all combined in a system that can be directly grazed by livestock enhances total productivity without need of external inputs.

*Sources*: Altieri (1995) and Gliessman (1998).

same role, thus leading to more predictable aggregate community responses or ecosystem properties (Lin, 2011).

A community of organisms in an agroecosystem becomes more complex when a larger number of different kinds of plants are included, leading to more interactions among arthropods and microorganisms, components of above- and below-ground food webs. As diversity increases, so do opportunities for co-existence and beneficial interference between species that can enhance agroecosystem sustainability (van Emden and Williams, 1974). Diverse systems encourage complex food webs, which entail more potential connections and interactions among members, creating many alternative paths for energy and material flow. For this reason, a more complex community exhibits more stable production and less fluctuations in the numbers of undesirable organisms (Power and Flecker, 1996).

Apparently, a greater impact on ecosystem functioning can be achieved by increasing vegetational richness in species-poor crop systems (monocultures) with respect to species-rich systems such as polycultures. Each newly added species to a simple monoculture has a higher probability of being complementary, whereas in species-rich systems, newly added species are more likely to bring in redundant characteristics because the function is probably already fulfilled by other species. Given these considerations, agroecosystem diversification might be more successful if aimed at (a) enhancing agroecosystem resilience and stability by the presence of redundant species which gain importance following agroecosystem changes or disturbance, and (b) increasing diversity within functional groups which promote key processes (pest regulation, nutrient cycling, etc.) fundamental for agroecosystem function (Moonen and Barberi, 2008).

## Intercropping systems as models of resilience

Polycultures involve spatial diversification of cropping systems (intercropping, agroforestry systems, etc.) allowing the cultivation of two or more crops simultaneously on the same field, with or without row arrangements (Vandermeer, 1992). Intercropping systems may involve mixtures of annual crops with other annuals, annuals with perennials, or perennials with perennials. In intercropping systems, plant species are grown in close proximity so that beneficial interactions occur between them. Intercropping provides insurance against crop failure and allows lower inputs through reduced fertilizer and pesticide requirements, thus reducing production costs and minimizing environmental impacts (Vandermeer, 1992).

Intercropping is widely practiced in Latin America, Asia, and Africa by smallholders as a means of increasing crop production per unit land area, with limited capital investment and minimal risk of total crop failure. Polycultures are estimated to still provide as much as 15–20% of the world's food supply. In Latin America, farmers grow 70–90% of their beans with maize, potatoes, and other crops, whereas maize is intercropped on 60% of its growing areas in the region (Francis, 1986). Eighty-nine percent of cowpeas in Africa are intercropped and the total percentage of cropped land actually devoted to intercropping varies from a low 17% for India to a high of 94% in Malawi. In these traditional multiple cropping systems, productivity in terms of harvestable products per unit area can range from 20% to 60% higher than under sole cropping with the same level of management (Kass, 1978; Francis, 1986; Vandermeer, 1992).

### *Enhanced crop productivity*

By examining the effects of increased plant diversity on crop productivity, insect pest incidence, and resiliency to climatic extremes, we hope to illustrate how polycultural designs offer scope for developing energy-efficient, productive, pest-stable, and resilient agricultural systems.

There is an abundant literature illustrating temporal and spatial complementarity between associated crops and the magnitude of yield advantages that can be achieved in intercropping compared with sole cropping (Trenbrath, 1976). The mechanisms that result in higher productivity in diverse agroecosystems are embedded in the process of facilitation. Facilitation occurs when one crop modifies the environment in a way that benefits a second crop, for example by lowering the population of a critical herbivore, or by releasing nutrients that can be taken up by the second crop (Lithourgidis et al., 2011). Pest and pathogen incidence is generally lower in intercrops and higher total resource use efficiency results from growing together crops with different root systems and leaf morphologies. Resource capture and resource conversion efficiency and other concepts have also been suggested as mechanisms underlying yield advantages. A school of thought concerning the resource use of intercropping systems states that a combination of two contrasting species, usually a legume and a cereal, would lead to greater overall biological productivity than each species grown separately because the mixture can use resources more effectively than separate monocultures (Vandermeer, 1992). Huang et al. (2015) explored how corn-faba bean, corn-soybean, corn-chickpea, and corn-turnip intercropping affect yield output and nutrient acquisition in agricultural fields in northwest China. The authors found that intercropping increased yields in almost all instances over their monoculture counterparts. Furthermore, the intercropping systems more efficiently removed nitrogen from the soils and partially returning it via decomposing biomass, indicating increased resource use efficiency in the intercropped systems.

Zhang and Li (2003) proposed a 'competition-recovery production principle' based on several years of studies on intercropping of short-season/long-season species. They suggested that interspecific interaction increases growth, nutrient uptake, and yield of dominant species, but decreases growth and nutrient uptake of the subordinate species during the co-existence stage. After the dominant species is harvested, the subordinate species has a recovery or complementary process, so that the final yields remain unchanged or even increase compared with corresponding sole species.

## *Insect pest regulation in polycultures*

It is accepted by many entomologists that inter- (species) and intra- (genetic) specific diversity reduces crop vulnerability to insect pests. There is a large body of literature documenting that diversification of cropping systems (variety mixtures, polycultures, agroforestry systems, etc.) often leads to reduced herbivore populations (Altieri and Nicholls, 2004; Letourneau et al., 2011). Two hypotheses have been offered to explain such reductions. The *natural enemy hypothesis* predicts that there will be a greater abundance and diversity of natural enemies of pest insects in polycultures than in monocultures (Letourneau et al., 2009). Predators tend to be polyphagous and have broad habitat requirements, so they would be expected to encounter a greater array of alternative prey and microhabitats in a heterogeneous environment. Many studies suggest that the more diverse the agroecosystems and the longer this diversity remains undisturbed, the more internal links develop to promote greater insect community stability. It is clear, however, that the stability of the insect community depends not only on its trophic diversity, but also on the density-dependence nature of the trophic levels (Southwood and Way, 1970). In other words, stability will depend on the precision of the response of the third trophic (predators, parasitoids) link to an increase in the population at the herbivore level.

The *resource concentration hypothesis* is based on the fact that insect populations can be influenced directly by the concentration and spatial dispersion of their food plants. Many herbivores, particularly those with narrow host ranges, are more likely to find and remain on hosts that are growing in dense or nearly pure stands and which are thus providing concentrated resources and monotonous physical conditions (Andow, 1991).

Over the last 40 years, many studies have evaluated the effects of crop diversity on densities of herbivore pests and have tried to prove one or more of these hypotheses (see also Gurr et al., Chapter 6 of this Handbook). An early review by Risch et al. (1983) summarized 150 published studies of the effect of diversifying an agroecosystem on insect pest abundance. Some 198 total herbivore species were examined in these studies; 53% of these species were found to be less abundant in the more diversified system, 18% were more abundant in the diversified system, 9% showed no difference, and 20% showed a variable response. Andow (1991) analyzed results from 209 studies involving 287 pest species, and found that, compared with monocultures, the population of pest insects was lower in 52% of the studies (i.e. 149 species) and higher in 15% of the studies (i.e. 44 species). Of the 149 pest species with lower populations in intercrops, 60% were monophagous and 28% polyphagous. The population of natural enemies of pests was higher in the intercrop in 53% of the studies and lower in 9%. The reduction in pest numbers was almost twice for monophagous insects (53.5% of the case studies showed lowered numbers in polycultures) than for polyphagous insects (33.3%).

In a meta-analysis of 21 studies comparing pest suppression in polycultures versus monocultures, Tonhasca and Byrne (1994) found that polycultures significantly reduced pest densities by 64%. In a later meta-analysis, Letourneau et al. (2011) found a 44% increase in abundance of natural enemies (148 comparisons), a 54% increase in herbivore mortality, and a 23% reduction in crop damage on farms with species-rich vegetational diversification systems than on farms with species-poor systems. Unequivocally, earlier reviews and recent meta-analyses suggest that diversification schemes generally achieve significant positive outcomes including natural enemy enhancement, reduction of herbivore abundance, and reduction of crop damage, from a combination of bottom-up and top-down effects.

Work in Kenya by scientists at the International Centre of Insect Physiology and Ecology (ICIPE) added a new dimension by considering the chemical ecology of these systems. A habitat management system was developed to control the stem borer, using two kinds of crops that are planted together with maize: a plant that repels (pushes) borers and another that attracts (pulls) them (Khan et al., 2000). The plant chemistry responsible for stem borer control involves the release of attractive volatiles from the trap plants and repellent volatiles from the intercrops. Two of the most useful trap crops that pull in the borers' natural enemies such as the parasitic wasp *(Cotesia sesamiae)* are Napier grass and Sudan grass, both important fodder plants; these are planted in a border around the maize. Two excellent borer-repelling crops, which are planted between the rows of maize, are molasses grass, which also repels ticks, and the leguminous silverleaf *(Desmodium)*, which in addition can suppress the parasitic weed *Striga* by a factor of 40 compared with maize monocrop. *Desmodium's* N-fixing ability increases soil fertility, leading to a 15–20% increase in maize yield (Khan et al., 2000).

The push-pull strategy was adopted by more than 10,000 households in 19 districts in Kenya, five districts in Uganda, and two districts in Tanzania, helping participating farmers to increase their maize yields by an average of 20% in areas where only stem borers are present and by more than 50% in areas where both stem borers and *Striga* are problems. Participating farmers in the breadbasket of Trans Nzoia reported a 15–20% increase in maize yield. In the semi-arid Suba district, plagued by both stem borers and *Striga* a substantial increase in milk yield has occurred in the last four years, with farmers now being able to support grade cows on the fodder produced by *Desmodium* and other plants. When farmers plant maize, Napier grass and *Desmodium* together, a return of US$2.30 for every dollar invested is made, as compared with only $1.40 obtained by planting maize as a monocrop (Khan and Pickett, 2004).

Plant pathologists have also observed that mixed crop systems can decrease pathogen incidence by slowing down the rate of disease development and by modifying environmental conditions so that they are less favorable for the spread of certain pathogens (Boudreau, 2013). For soil-borne or splash-borne diseases, Hiddink et al. (2010) found that mixed cropping systems (including strip intercropping, row intercropping, relay intercropping, and intercropping of genetic variants) reduced disease in 74.5% of cases in comparison to monoculture (19.6% neutral; 5.9% negative; in a vote count of 36 studies composing 51 comparisons). Host dilution was frequently proposed as the mechanism for reducing disease incidence of both soil-borne and splash-dispersed pathogens. Other mechanisms, such as allelopathy and microbial antagonists, are thought to affect disease severity in diversified farming systems (Stone et al., 2004). Such effects lead to less crop damage and contribute to higher yields in mixed crops as compared with the corresponding monocultures.

Weed ecologists posit that many intercrops are often superior to sole crops in weed suppression, as intercrop combinations can exploit more resources than sole crops, thus suppressing the growth of weeds more effectively through greater preemptive use of resources (Poggio, 2005). Many intercropping systems still give yield advantages over sole crops without being superior in suppressing weed growth. This situation arises if intercrop yield advantages resulted from (a) increased use of resources for which competition between crops and weeds did not exist, or (b) increased resource conversion efficiency, shifts in crop biomass partitioning, microhabitat modifications, and decreased pest pressures, none of which would necessarily result in the usurpation of additional resources from weeds (Liebman and Dyck, 1993).

## *Yield stability in the midst of climatic variability*

One important reason for which intercropping is popular in the developing world is that it is more stable than monocropping, enabling farmers to produce various crops simultaneously while minimizing risks (Horwith, 1985). Data from 94 experiments on mixed cropping sorghum/pigeonpea showed that for a particular 'disaster' level, sole pigeonpea crop would fail 1 year in 5, sole sorghum crop would fail 1 year in 8, but intercropping would fail only 1 year in 36 (Willey, 1979). There are several features that make intercropping more resilient to climatic variability:

*Drought tolerance*: Polycultures exhibit greater yield stability and less productivity declines during a drought than is the case for monocultures. Natarajan and Willey (1986) examined the effect of drought on enhanced yields with polycultures by manipulating water stress on intercrops of sorghum and peanut, millet and peanut, and sorghum and millet. All the intercrops out-yielded consistently at five levels of moisture availability, ranging from 297 to 584 mm of water applied over the cropping season. Quite interestingly, the rate of over-yielding actually increased with water stress, such that the relative differences in productivity between monocultures and polycultures became more accentuated as stress increased (Natarajan and Willey, 1986).

*Enhanced soil water-holding capacity*: Polycultures are usually associated with soils richer in organic matter, which in turn are linked directly to the amount of crop residues produced by these systems and the copious amounts of compost, green manures, or cover crops used by farmers that typically practice intercropping and rotations. The positive impact of polycultural practices on soil organic matter content (Marriott and Wander, 2006) enhance the soil's moisture holding capacity, leading to higher available water for plants, which positively influences resistance and resilience of crop plants to drought conditions (Weil and Magdoff, 2004, Liu et al., 2007). Hudson (1994) showed that as soil organic matter content increased from

0.5% to 3%, available water capacity more than doubled. In long-term trials measuring the relative water-holding capacity of soils, diversified farming systems have shown a clear advantage over conventional farming systems. In the northeastern United States, five drought years occurred between 1984 and 1998, and in four of them, organic maize out-yielded conventional maize by significant margins. Organic maize yielded between 38% and 137% relative to conventional maize. The primary mechanism of the higher yield of the organic maize systems was the higher water-holding capacity of the soils in those treatments. Soils in the organic plots captured more water and retained more of it in the crop root zone than did the conventional systems (Lotter et al., 2003). In a 37-year trial, Reganold et al. (1987) found significantly higher soil organic matter levels and 42% higher surface soil moisture content in organically managed plots than in conventional plots. In a 21-year study in Switzerland, Mäder et al. (2002) reported 20% to 40% higher water-holding capacity in organically managed soils than in conventionally managed soils.

*Increased soil biological activity*: Some intercropping systems increase microbial diversity, such as vesicular arbuscular mycorrhizae (VAM; any fungus that facilitates nutrient transfer, especially phosphorus, to the associated crop). Of particular significance is the fact that plants colonized by VAM usually exhibit higher biomass and yields compared with non-mycorrhizal (NM) plants, under water stress conditions, as VAM colonization increases water-use efficiency (Li et al., 2007). There are a few reports of VAM-induced increases in drought tolerance, involving both increased dehydration avoidance and dehydration tolerance (Al-Karaki et al., 2003). However, most experiments examining mycorrhizal effects on host drought resistance have demonstrated that when VAM symbiosis improves plant drought resistance, it does so by aiding drought avoidance. Reid and Bowen (1979) noted that mycorrhizae appear to benefit the drought stressed plants primarily through direct drought avoidance (maintenance of high internal water potential). This improved drought avoidance has usually been associated with growth enhancement, probably linked to improved acquisition of P and possibly other nutrients. Putative examples of VAM promotion of drought avoidance are numerous. Relative to NM controls, VAM plants have shown higher nitrogen assimilation and better nitrogen nutrition during development of, and recovery from, drought, characterized as higher soluble proteins, amino acids, nitrogenous enzymes and tissue N (Augé, 2001).

Wheat-clover intercrops supported large earthworm populations (572 individuals $m^{-2}$ corresponding to an earthworm biomass of 203 g $m^{-2}$) primarily because the organic matter input from such systems is favorable for earthworms in terms of quantity, quality, and continuity of food supply throughout the year (Schmidt et al., 2003). Earthworms play a key role in modifying the physical structure of soils by producing new aggregates and pores, which improve water infiltration, among other things. Earthworms produce binding agents responsible for the formation of water-stable macro-aggregates, improving soil porosity and thus water circulation and storage (Blanchart et al., 1999).

*Improved water infiltration*: Improved soil quality is often indicated by increased water infiltration, which enhances movement and storage of water in the soil profile and reduces runoff. Maize-pigeonpea intercropping significantly increased rainfall infiltration in the long term due to a better soil cover with residues, more C inputs, and improved soil structure (Morris and Garrity, 1993). In Central Mozambique, intercropping maize and pigeonpea continuously for five years increased steady state rainfall infiltration from

6 mm $h^{-1}$ to 22 mm $h^{-1}$ compared with continuous maize monocropping. There was more surface water runoff (94%) on plots that were under continuous maize than on plots that were intercropped for one year (88%), or three years (68%). Infiltration characteristics in the sole maize field, and the field that was intercropped for only one year, followed an exponential decrease, whereas in the fields that had been intercropped for three to five years, the pattern followed a sigmoidal decay curve characterized by a lag-phase in decrease of infiltration (Rusinamhodzi et al., 2012).

*Enhanced water-use efficiency*: Many intercropping systems seem to improve the water-use efficiency of the crops compared with monoculture. In China, water-use efficiency in a potatoes-bean intercropping system was 13.5% greater than in monoculture (10.15 kg/$m^3$). Similar results were found for wheat-soybean by Caviglia et al. (2004) and various potato intercropping systems (Rezig et al., 2010). Morris and Garritty (1993) found that water-utilization efficiency by intercrop greatly exceeds water-utilization efficiency by sole crops, often by more than 18% and by as much as 99%. They do so by promoting the full use of soil water by plant roots, increasing water storage in the root zone, reducing inter-row evaporation, but also by controlling excessive transpiration, and by creating a special microclimate advantageous to plant growth and development. When acidity is corrected in the Brazilian semi-arid zone, Gaiser et al. (2004) found that gross water-use efficiency in a maize-cowpea intercropping system was 60% higher than the monoculture controls.

*Resistance against rainstorms*: In hillside situations, intercrops can provide significantly soil erosion protection as their complex canopies afford a better soil cover. Under heavy rains, more complex canopies and plant residues reduce the impact of raindrops that otherwise would detach soil particles and make them prone to erosion. Surface runoff is slowed by the soil cover, allowing improved moisture infiltration. Not only does above-ground growth provide soil protection, but also root systems help stabilize the soil by infiltrating the profile and holding it in place. A red clover intercrop was evaluated in terms of its ability to provide soil erosion protection and its effects on silage corn yields in Elora, Ontario (Wall et al., 1991). Soil loss was significantly lower from the silage corn intercropped with red clover system than from corn monocultures. Runoff reduction with the corn/clover system ranged from 45% to 87% and reduction of soil loss compared to the corn system ranged from 46% to 78%.

In Mesoamerican hillsides prone to heavy storms and therefore to soil degradation, there are a number of traditional intercropping systems of maize, sorghum, or cassava associated with scarlet runner bean *(Phaseolus vulgaris)*, cowpeas *(Vigna unguiculata)*, the lablab bean *(Dolichos lablab)*, rice bean *(Vigna umbellata)*, jack bean *(Canavalia ensiformis)* and, most recently, with velvet bean *(Mucuna pruriens)* (see also Williams, Chapter 11 of this Handbook). The velvet bean is particularly important because it is widely planted, reasonably tolerant to a number of stresses, fixes nitrogen, produces high levels of biomass, and is thus prolific in its leaf litter generation. These systems have spread spontaneously among tens of thousands of farmers in Mexico, Guatemala, and Honduras. In Northern Honduras, intercropping of velvet bean with maize results in 60–80% higher returns per unit of land and labour. Furthermore, continual annual rotation of velvet bean and maize can be sustained for at least 15 years at high productivity without apparent decline regardless of variability in rainfall patterns (Buckles et al., 1998).

## Conclusions

Under intercropping systems, agricultural resources, that is, land, nutrient, water, heat, and radiation, may be utilized more efficiently both in time and in space. Other processes, such as enhanced pest regulation and maintenance of soil fertility, are determined by the nature and intensity of interactions among the components of intercrops (Malézieux et al., 2009).

Assembling overlapping crop combinations in the same land thus influences abiotic components, inducing changes in soil organic matter and nutrient content and in microclimate (changes in light, temperature, and humidity). In addition, certain crop mixes enhance key functional biodiversity components (i.e. predators and parasitoids, earthworms, VAM, and other below-ground soil biodiversity) by creating more suitable habitat conditions for beneficial biota, which provide key ecological services (**Figure 13.2** *Improving agroecosystems performance through changes in biotic and abiotic conditions mediated by intercropping*). For example, introducing legumes in the mixture improves soil fertility through biological nitrogen fixation benefitting associated cereals, or one crop in the mixture provides early season alternative food sources for natural enemies of pests of the other crop in the mixture. Similarly, enhanced soil carbon and structure due to action of VAM and/or earthworms increase water storage and water use efficiency, enhancing the capacity of crop mixes to tolerate drought.

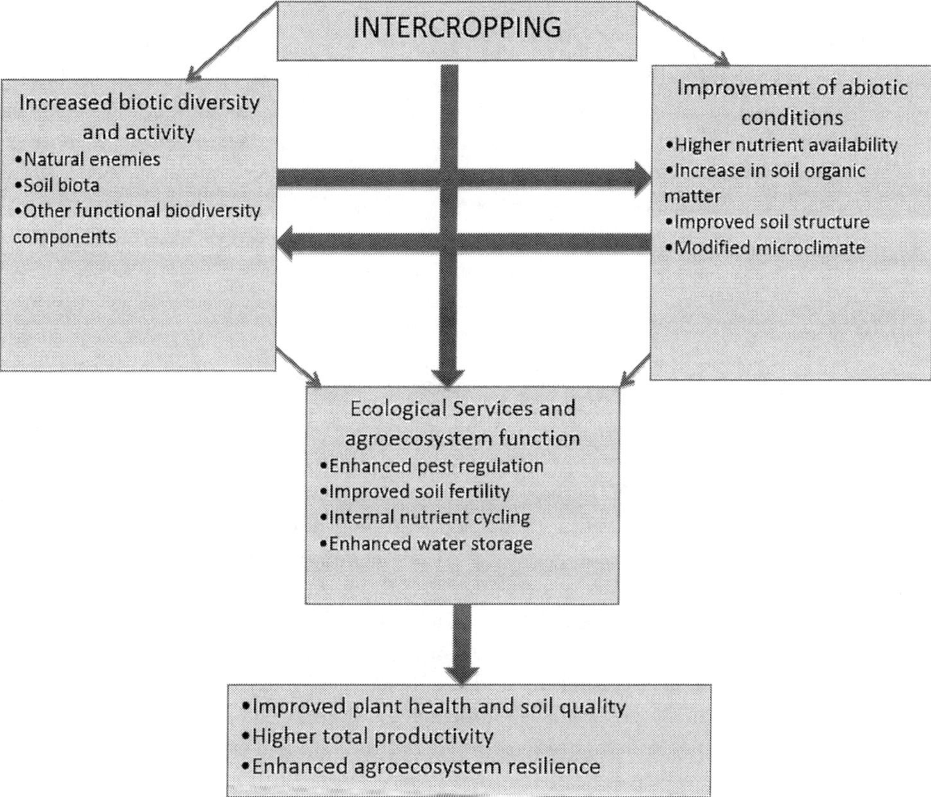


*Figure 13.2* Improving agroecosystems performance through changes in biotic and abiotic conditions mediated by intercropping

*Source*: The authors.

Intercropping is therefore an effective agroecological strategy for introducing more biodiversity into agroecosystems to increase the number and level of ecosystem services provided. Higher species richness of planned and associated biodiversity improve nutrient cycling and soil fertility; limit nutrient leaching losses; reduce the negative impacts of pests, diseases, and weeds; and enhance overall resilience of the cropping system. Further studies to improve our understanding of the ecological interactions in intercropped systems will provide the basis for designing efficient systems with potential for wider applicability both in temperate and tropical agriculture. In particular, research should focus on understanding biotic interactions that consider the effects of diversity, species composition, and food web structure on ecosystem processes and the importance of multi-trophic interactions in agroecosystems.

## References

Al-Karaki, G., McMichael, B. and Zak, J. (2003) 'Field response of wheat to arbuscular mycorrhizal fungi and drought stress', *Mycorrhiza*, vol. 14, pp. 263–269.

Altieri, M. A. (1995) *Agroecology: The Science of Sustainable Agriculture*, Westview Press, Boulder, CO, USA.

Altieri, M. A. and Nicholls, C. I. (2004) *Biodiversity and Pest Management in Agroecosystems*, Food Products Press, Binghamton, NY, USA.

Altieri, M. A. and Nicholls, C. I. (2012) 'Agroecology: Scaling up for food sovereignty and resiliency', *Sustainable Agriculture Reviews*, vol. 11, pp. 1–29.

Altieri, M. A., Nicholls, C. I., Henao, A. and Lana, M. A. (2015) 'Agroecology and the design of climate change-resilient farming systems', *Agronomy for Sustainable Development*, vol. 35, pp. 869–890.

Andow, D. (1991) 'Vegetational diversity and arthropod population response', *Annual Review of Entomology*, vol. 36, pp. 561–586.

Augé, R. M. (2001) 'Water relations, drought and vesicular-arbuscular mycorrhizal symbiosis', *Mycorrhiza*, vol. 11, pp. 3–42.

Blanchart, E., Albrecht, A., Alegre, J., Duboisset, A., Gilot, C., Pashanasi, B., Lavelle, P. and Brussaard, L. (1999) 'Effects of earthworms on soil structure and physical properties', pp. 149–171 in P. Lavelle, L. Brussaard and P. Hendrix (eds.), *Earthworm Management in Tropical Agroecosystems*, CAB International, Wallingford, UK.

Boudreau, M. A. (2013) 'Diseases in intercropping systems', *Annual Review of Phytopathology*, vol. 51, pp. 499–519.

Buckles, D., Triomphe, B. and Sain, G. (1998) *Cover Crops in Hillside Agriculture*, IDRC, Ottawa, Canada.

Cabell, J. F. and Oelofse, M. (2012) 'An indicator framework for assessing agroecosystem resilience', *Ecology and Society*, vol. 17, pp. 18–23.

Caviglia, O. P., Sadras, V. O. and Andrade, F. H. (2004) 'Intensification of agriculture in the south-eastern Pampas: I. Capture and efficiency in the use of water and radiation in double-cropped wheat-soybean', *Field Crops Research*, vol. 87, pp. 117–129.

Folke, C. (2006) 'Resilience: The emergence of a perspective for social ecological systems analyses', *Global Environmental Change*, vol. 16, pp. 253–267.

Francis, C. A. (1986) *Multiple Cropping Systems*, Macmillan, New York, NY, USA.

Gaiser, T., De Barros, I., Lange, M. and Frank, J. R. (2004) 'Water use efficiency of a maize/cowpea intercrop on a highly acidic tropical soil as affected by liming and fertilizer application', *Plant and Soil*, vol. 263, pp. 165–171.

Gliessman, S. R. (1998) *Agroecology: Ecological Process in Sustainable Agriculture*, Ann Arbor Press, MI, USA.

Hainzelin, E. (2013) *Cultivating Biodiversity to Transform Agriculture*, Springer, Dordrecht, The Netherlands.

Hiddink, G. A., Termorshuizen, A. J. and Bruggen, A. H. C. (2010) 'Mixed cropping and suppression of soilborne diseases', pp. 119–146 in E. Lichtfouse (ed.), *Genetic Engineering, Biofertilisation, Soil Quality and Organic Farming. Sustainable Agriculture Reviews*, Vol. 4, Springer Science+Business Media, Dordrecht, The Netherlands.

Horwith, B. (1985) 'A role for intercropping in modern agriculture', *Biological Sciences*, vol. 35, pp. 286–291.

Huang, C., Liu, Q. N., Stomph, T., Li, B., Liu, R., Zhang, H., Wang, C., Li, X., Zhang, C., van der Werf, W. and Zhang, F. (2015) 'Economic performance and sustainability of a novel intercropping system on the North China plain', *PLoS One*, vol. 10, p. e0135518.

Hudson, B. (1994) 'Soil organic matter and available water capacity', *Journal of Soil and Water Conservation*, vol. 49, pp. 189–194.

Kass, D. C. L. (1978) 'Polyculture cropping systems: Review and analysis', *Cornell International Agricultural Bulletin*, vol. 32, pp. 1–69.

Khan, Z. R. and Pickett, J. A. (2004) 'The "push-pull" strategy for stemborer management: A casestudy in exploiting biodiversity and chemical ecology', pp. 155–164 in G. Gurr, S. D. Waratten and M. A. Altieri (eds.), *Ecological Engineering for Pest Management: Advances in Habitat Manipulations for Arthropods*, CSIRO and CABI Publishing, Australia.

Khan, Z. R., Pickett, J. A, van den Berg, J., Wadhams, L. J. and Woodcock, C. M. (2000) 'Exploiting chemical ecology and species diversity: Stemborer and striga control for maize and sorghum in Africa', *Pest Management Science*, vol. 56, pp. 957–962.

Kremen, C. and Miles, A. (2012) 'Ecosystem services in biologically diversified versus conventional farming systems: Benefits, externalities, and trade-offs', *Ecology and Society*, vol. 17, p. 40.

Letourneau, D. K., Armbrecht, I., Salguero Rivera, B., Montoya Lerma, J., Jimenez Carmona, E., Constanza Daza, M., Escobar, S., Galindo, V., Gutierrez, C., Duque Lopez, S., Lopez Mejia, J. M., Acosta Rangel, A., Herrera Rangel, J., Rivera, L., Arturo Saavedra, C., Torres, A. M. and Reyes Trujillo, A. (2011) 'Does plant diversity benefit agroecosystems? A synthetic review', *Ecological Applications*, vol. 21, pp. 9–21.

Letourneau, D. K., Jedlicka, J. A., Bothwell, S. G. and Moreno, C. R. (2009) 'Effects of natural enemy biodiversity on the suppression of arthropod herbivores in terrestrial ecosystems', *Annual Review of Ecology, Evolution, and Systematics*, vol. 40, pp. 573–592.

Li, L., Li, M., Sun, H., Zhou, L. L., Bao, X. G., Zhang, H. G. and Zhang, F. S. (2007) 'Diversity enhances agricultural productivity via rhizosphere phosphorus facilitation on phosphorous-deficient soils', *Proceedings of the National Academy of Sciences USA*, vol. 104, pp. 11192–11196.

Liebman, M. and Dyck, E. (1993) 'Crop rotation and intercropping strategies for weed management', *Ecological Applications*, vol. 3, pp. 92–122.

Lin, B. B. (2011) 'Resilience in agriculture through crop diversification: Adaptive management for environmental change', *BioScience*, vol. 61, pp. 183–193.

Lithourgidis, A. S., Dordas, C. A., Damalas, C. A. and Vlachostergios, D. N. (2011) 'Annual intercrops: An alternative pathway for sustainable agriculture', *Australian Journal of Crop Science*, vol. 5, pp. 396–410.

Liu, B., Tu, C., Hu, S., Gumpertz, M. and Ristaino. J. B. (2007) 'Effect of organic, sustainable, and conventional management strategies in grower fields on soil physical, chemical, and biological factors and the incidence of Southern blight', *Applied Soil Ecology*, vol. 37, pp. 202–214.

Loreau, M., Naem, S., Inchausti, P., Bengtsson, J, Grime, J. P., Hooper, D. U., Huston, M. A., Taffaelli, D., Schmid, B., Tilman, D. and Wardle, D. A. (2001) 'Biodiversity and ecosystem functioning: Current knowledge and future challenges', *Science*, vol. 294, pp. 804–808.

Lotter, D., Seidel, R. and Liebhardt, W. (2003) 'The performance of organic and conventional cropping systems in an extreme climate year', *American Journal of Alternative Agriculture*, vol. 18, pp. 146–154.

Mäder, P., Fliessbach, A., Dubois, D., Gunst, L., Fried, P. and Niggli, U. (2002) 'Soil fertility and biodiversity in organic farming', *Science*, vol. 296, pp. 1694–1697.

Malézieux, C., Crozat, Y., Dupraz, C., Laurans, M., Makowski, D., Ozier-Lafontaine, H., Rapidel, B., de Tourdonnet, S. and Valantin-Morison, M. (2009) 'Mixing plant species in cropping systems: Concepts, tools and models: A review', *Sustainable Agriculture*, vol. 5, pp. 329–353.

Marriott, E. E. and Wander, M. M. (2006) 'Total and labile soil organic matter in organic and conventional farming systems', *Soil Science Society of America Journal*, vol. 70, pp. 950–959.

Moonen, A. C. and Barberi, P. (2008) 'Functional biodiversity: An agroecosystem approach', *Agriculture, Ecosystems and Environment*, vol. 127, pp. 7–21.

Morris, R. A. and Garrity, D. P. (1993) 'Resource capture and utilization in intercropping: Water', *Field Crops Research*, vol. 34, pp. 303–317.

Natarajan, M. and Willey, R. W. (1986) 'The effects of water stress on yields advantages of intercropping systems', *Field Crop Research*, vol. 13, pp. 117–131.

Poggio, S. L. (2005) 'Structure of weed communities occurring in monoculture and intercropping of field pea and barley', *Agriculture, Ecosystems and Environment*, vol. 109, pp. 48–58.

Power, A. G. and Flecker, A. S. (1996) 'The role of biodiversity in tropical managed ecosystems', pp. 173–194 in G. H. Orians, R. Dirzo, and J. H. Cushman (eds.), *Biodiversity and Ecosystem Processes in Tropical Forests*, Springer Verlag, New York, NY, USA.

Reganold, J. P., Elliott, L. F. and Unger Y. L. (1987) 'Long-term effects of organic and conventional farming on soil erosion', *Nature*, vol. 330, pp. 370–372.

Reid, C. P. P. and Bowen, G. D. (1979) 'Effect of water stress on phosphorus uptake by mycorrhizas of Pinus radiata', *New Phytologist*, vol. 83, pp. 103–107.

Rezig, M., Sahli, A., Ben Jedd, F. and Harbaoui, Y. (2010) 'Adopting intercropping system for potatoes as practice on drought mitigation under Tunisian conditions', pp. 329–334 in A. López-Francos and A. LópezFrancos (eds.), *Economics of Drought and Drought Preparedness in a Climate Change Context*. Options Méditerranéennes: Série A. Séminaires Méditerranéens; n. 95, CIHEAM/FAO/ICARDA/GDAR/CEIGRAM/MARM, Zaragoza, Spain.

Risch, S. J., Andow, D. and Altieri, M. A. (1983) 'Agroecosystem diversity and pest control: Data, tentative conclusions, and new research directions', *Environmental Entomology*, vol. 12, pp. 625–629.

Rusinamhodzi, L., Corbeels, M., Nyamangara, J. and Giller, J. E. (2012) 'Maize-grain legume intercropping is an attractive option for ecological intensification that reduces climatic risk for smallholder farmers in central Mozambique', *Field Crops Research*, vol. 136, pp. 12–22.

Schmidt, O., Clements, R. O. and Donaldson, G. (2003) 'Why do cereal-legume intercrops support large earthworm populations?', *Applied Soil Ecology*, vol. 22, pp. 181–190.

Southwood, T. R. E. and Way, M. I. (1970) 'Ecological background to pest management', pp. 6–28 in R. L. Rabb and F. E. Guthrie (eds.), *Concepts of Pest Management*, North Carolina State University, Raleigh, NC, USA.

Stone, A., Scheuerell, S., Darby, H., Magdoff, F. and Ray, R. (2004) 'Suppression of soilborne diseases in field agricultural systems: Organic matter management, cover cropping, and other cultural practices', pp. 131–177 in F. Magdoff and R. R. Weil (eds.), *Soil OrganicMatterin Sustainable Agriculture*, CRC Press, Boca Raton, FL, USA.

Swift, M. J. and Anderson, J. M. (1993) 'Biodiversity and ecosystem function in agricultural systems', pp. 15–42 in E. D. Schultze and H. Mooney (eds.), *Biodiversity and Ecosystem Function*, Springer-Verlag, Berlin, Germany.

Tonhasca Jr., A. and Byrne, D. N. (1994) 'The effects of crop diversification on herbivorous insects: A meta-analysis approach', *Ecological Entomology*, vol. 19, pp. 239–244.

Trenbath, B. R. (1976) 'Plant interactions in mixed crop communities', pp. 11–40 in R. I. Papendick, P. A. Sanchez and G. B. Triplett (eds.), *Multiple Cropping. American Society of Agronomy, Special Publications*, vol. 27.

Vandermeer, J. (1992) *The Ecology of Intercropping*, Cambridge University Press, New York, NY, USA.

Vandermeer, J. and Perfecto, I. (1995) *Breakfast of Biodiversity: The Truth About Rainforest Destruction*, Food First Books, Oakland, CA, USA.

Vandermeer, J., Van Noordwijk, M., Anderson, J., Ong, C. and Perfecto, I. (1998) 'Global change and multi-species ecosystems: Concepts and issues', *Agriculture, Ecosystems and Environment*, vol. 67, pp. 1–22.

van Emden, H. F. and Williams, G. F. (1974) 'Insect stability and diversity in agro-ecosystems', *Annual Review of Entomology*, vol. 19, pp. 455–475.

Wall, G. J., Pringle, E. A. and Sheard, R. W. (1991) 'Intercropping red clover with silage corn for soil erosion control', *Canadian Journal of Soil Science*, vol. 71, pp. 137–145.

Weil, R. R. and Magdoff, F. (2004) 'Significance of soil organic matter to soil quality and health', in F. Magdoff and R. R. Weil (eds.), *Soil Organic Matter in Sustainable Agriculture*, CRC Press, Boca Raton, FL, USA.

Willey, R. W. (1979) 'Intercropping – its importance and its research needs: I. Competition and yield advantages', *Field Crop Abstracts*, vol. 32, pp. 1–10.

Zhang, F. and Li, L. (2003) 'Using competitive and facilitative interactions in intercropping systems enhances crop productivity and nutrient-use efficiency', *Plant and Soil*, vol. 248, pp. 305–312.

# 14
# THE ROLE OF TREES IN AGROECOLOGY

*Roger R. B. Leakey*

## Introduction

In the debate about the future of agriculture, the area of consensus is that it needs to be both more sustainable and more productive (Garnett et al., 2013), and that 'business as usual' is not an option (IAASTD, 2009). This is especially important in the tropics and sub-tropics, where interactions between biophysical and socio-economic issues affect agricultural productivity due to land degradation. This is fuelled by population growth and drives farmers to become sedentary smallholders while lacking the financial resources to replenish soil fertility. This process is exacerbated by a declining resource of productive land (Leakey, 2012). The context of the problems here is important. Sedentary farmers have to survive, feed and provide for all the daily needs of their families on around 2–5 hectares of cleared land without a source of income or any emergency 'lifeline' if something goes wrong.

## Understanding the problem before seeking solutions

Current estimates are that land degradation affects 2 billion ha (38% of world cropping area), most of which is in the tropics and sub-tropics where NPK deficiencies occur on 59%, 85% and 90% of the land, respectively (Chianu et al., 2012). Soil erosion affects 83% of the global degraded area. Much of this degradation stems from the environmental mismanagement of current farming systems. However, in addition to these ecological dis-services, agroecosystems can provide many beneficial services (Garbach et al., 2014) – in other words, agriculture can be both the culprit and the cure. Lavelle et al. (2014) strongly emphasized that part of the cure is to prevent further resource degradation in by the maintenance of diverse soil cover, the incorporation of organic inputs and the reduction of pollution.

To understand the complexity of the numerous and interacting socio-economic and biophysical causal factors underlying land degradation, Leakey (2012, 2013) has added some steps to the concept that poverty drives land degradation, and that land degradation drives poverty. This is illustrated by his 'land degradation and social deprivation cycle' in which deforestation, overgrazing and unsustainable use of soils and water all lead to a loss of soil fertility and structure as well as a loss of agricultural biodiversity above- and below-ground (see Spray and

McGlothlin, 2003; Butler et al., 2007, for example). This is followed by the breakdown of ecosystem functions that regulate food chains, nutrient cycling and the incidence and severity of pests, diseases and weeds. All of these things result in lower crop yields, creating a Yield Gap (the difference between potential and actual yield) which in turn leads to hunger, malnutrition and declining livelihoods and to the next turn of the cycle. In industrialized countries, this downward cycle is held in check by the application of inorganic fertilizers, pesticides and irrigation water, all of which are expensive financially and have an environmental cost in terms of depleted natural resources, pollution and climate change. An alternative approach of using organic manures, compost and mulching is often constrained by the need for large quantities of biomass (10–40 Mg $ha^{-1}$ $yr^{-1}$).

## The agroecological approach

The agroecological alternative is to diversify the farming system and rebuild, in farmers' fields, the ecological functions driving nutrient, water and life cycles as well as the food chains. Here, trees have an important role, as they are long-lived perennials which create numerous ecological niches above- and below-ground which can be filled with organisms that restore the agroecological balance of nature (Leakey, 2014a). In the wild, this occurs as pioneer species invade a disturbed site and an ecological succession develops to maturity over many years, or decades. In agroecology, the concept is to facilitate the emergence and rapid development of this succession by wildlife-friendly interventions (Leakey, 2014a; Leaky and Prabhu, 2017).

Agroforestry starts the restoration of an agroecological succession by harnessing the capacity of leguminous plants to fix atmospheric nitrogen (Sileshi et al., 2008b, 2014) employing N-fixing technologies such as two-year improved fallows, relay cropping or 'Evergreen Agriculture', using fast-growing leguminous trees, shrubs or vines to enrich N-deficient soils through the actions of *Rhizobium* bacteria living in nodules on their roots. A study involving sixteen tree species in high density plantings like improved fallows or fodder banks, found that the rate of N-fixation could be as high as 300–650 kg N $ha^{-1}$ $yr^{-1}$. This is 3 to 12 times greater than for food or fodder legumes. A meta-analysis of research on the impact of this nitrogen enrichment indicates enhanced crop production many times greater than the 'control' (Sileshi et al., 2008a). The general experience by adopting farmers is in the order of two- to threefold increase (Sileshi et al., 2014). The combination of inorganic fertilizers and biological nitrogen can however be synergistic. Indirectly, leguminous trees can also recycle other macro- and micronutrients through uptake from their more extensive and deeper root systems and subsequent leaf litter fall and fine root turnover. By comparison with artificial fertilizers, nitrogen of tree origin is less likely to be lost to, or pollute, groundwater.

Environmentally, biological nitrogen fixation by leguminous trees and shrubs is important for soil health, as it increases the organic matter pool and so is available to other organisms (Sileshi and Mafongoya, 2006; Sileshi et al., 2008a, b) such as mycorrhizal fungi and earthworms (Lavelle et al., 2014; Garbach et al., 2014). This organic matter also improves soil structure (aggregate stability, porosity, and hydraulic conductivity), reduces soil erosion and promotes greater water infiltration. Soil organic matter content is especially important in areas where rainfall can be a limiting factor. Leguminous trees have also been shown to improve rain use efficiency (the ratio of above-ground net primary production to annual rainfall) and water-use efficiency (Sileshi et al., 2014). On the negative side, as with inorganic fertilizers, there can be $N_2O$ emissions associated with higher levels of soil nitrogen.

## Biodiversity and agroecological functions

The role of ecological processes in agricultural sustainability has been well studied and is recognized to be important for the future of global agriculture (Tscharntke et al., 2012; see also Gemmill-Herren, Chapter 7 of this Handbook). However, its application has not occurred on a scale to have impact on the global problem of land degradation. The challenge, therefore, is to demonstrate to the satisfaction of decision makers that diverse mixed cropping systems can be both productive and sustainable (Garnett et al., 2013), and hence an approach towards both ecological (Tittonell, 2014) and socially/economically sustainable intensification (Leakey and Prabhu, in prep).

Deforestation, as occurs when land is cleared for agriculture, changes the soil microflora from one associated with the forest to one associated with invading pioneers, making the establishment of trees in degraded land more difficult without mycorrhizal inoculation (Wilson et al., 1991; see also Beed et al., Chapter 8 of this Handbook). In agriculture, crops replace the invading pioneers, but as in forest plantations, trees in cropland slowly rebuild the soil inoculum.

Recognizing the role of trees in promoting ecosystem functions, Leakey (1996) described agroforestry practices as:

> *phases* in the development of a productive agroecosystem, akin to the normal dynamics of natural ecosystems . . . and the passage towards a mature agroforest of increasing ecological integrity. By the same token, with increasing scale, the integration of various agroforestry practices into the landscape is like the formation of a complex mosaic of patches in an ecosystem, each of which is composed of many niches . . . occupied by different organisms, making the system ecologically stable and biologically diverse.
>
> *(p. 6)*

In recent years, there has been a considerable increase in the number of studies examining the biological diversity associated with shade-adapted crop species such as cocoa and coffee grown in mixtures with trees, and their comparison with other farming systems (see review by Leakey, 2014a; Perfecto et al., 2014; see also Gurr et al., Chapter 6 of this Handbook). Many of these studies have found that farming systems with trees provide habitats suitable for forest-dependent species (**Table 14.1** *Assessments of biodiversity in agroforestry systems*), so maintaining levels of biodiversity considerably higher than other agricultural systems, although lower than natural forest. Thus, these tree-based farming systems are recognized as being beneficial for wildlife conservation (Schroth et al., 2004; Harvey et al., 2007; Perfecto and Vandermeer, 2008), as well as for agricultural production via the enhanced biological control of pests and weeds (Schroth et al., 2000). Depending on the tree species used, the trees can also increase the overall productivity of the farm (Leakey, 2012).

The below-ground ecosystem is very complex and poorly understood, but crucial for healthy agroecosystems. Lavelle has identified four complex assemblages of organisms with different roles and which basically differ in the size and number of individuals – from the smallest to the largest: the microflora; the micro-predators; the litter transformers; and the ecosystem engineers (Lavelle, 1996; Lavelle et al., 2014). Tillage generally disturbs the soil, killing many of the larger organisms and breaking the fungal networks, switching the soil ecosystem back to an early successional stage. On the other hand, the inclusion of trees in farming systems has been shown to promote a diverse rhizosphere that can rebuild the below-ground species assemblages as the agroecosystem matures (Wilson et al., 1991).

*Table 14.1* Assessments of biodiversity in agroforestry systems

| *Organisms* | *Country* | *Crop* |
|---|---|---|
| Phytotelmata plants and ceratopogonid pollinators | Brazil | Cocoa |
| Bat and bird | Brazil | Cocoa |
| Bat | Brazil | Cocoa |
| Ants | Brazil | Cocoa |
| Soil and litter fauna | Brazil | Cocoa |
| Sloth | Brazil | Cocoa |
| Plants | Cameroon | Cocoa |
| Soil fauna | Cameroon | Cocoa |
| Mammals | Cameroon | Cocoa |
| Birds | Costa Rica | Cocoa |
| Dung beetles, mammals, birds, bats | Costa Rica | Cocoa and banana |
| Sloth | Costa Rica | Cocoa |
| Epiphytes | Ecuador | Cocoa |
| Birds | Indonesia | Cocoa |
| Epiphytes | Indonesia | Cocoa |
| Amphibians and reptiles: ants | Indonesia | Cocoa |
| Ants | Indonesia | Cocoa |
| Rats | Indonesia | Cocoa |
| Monkey | Mexico | Cocoa |
| Birds | Mexico | Cocoa |
| Homoptera | Costa Rica | Coffee |
| Birds | Dominica | Coffee |
| Birds and seed dispersal | Ecuador | Coffee |
| Mammals | India | Coffee |
| Termites | India | Coffee |
| Soil coleoptera | Mexico | Coffee |
| Mammals | Mexico | Coffee |
| Ants | Mexico | Coffee |
| Arthropod | Mexico | Coffee |
| Birds | Mexico | Coffee |
| Birds | Mexico | Coffee |
| Ants and birds | Panama | Coffee |
| Ants | Panama | Coffee |
| Small mammals | Costa Rica and India | Coffee |
| Migratory birds | Colombia | Coffee and silvopasture |
| Collembola | Indonesia | Rubber |
| Mammals | Indonesia | Rubber, damar, durian |
| Plants | Indonesia | Rubber |
| Birds | Indonesia | Rubber, damar, durian |
| Birds, bats, butterflies, dung beetles | Nicaragua | Fallows and pastures |

*Source*: Adapted from Leakey (2014a).

Importantly, in the few studies which have looked at the effects of conserving biodiversity and the productivity of these systems, there is little, if any, evidence that including biodiversity conservation within these wildlife-friendly perennial crop agroforests has any negative effects on crop production (Clough et al., 2011). Indeed, when complex agroforests include trees that produce high-value marketable products, they become commercial fallows which can be both productive and good for the livelihoods of local communities (Leakey, 2012; Schroth et al., 2014) – a perennial and sustainable sedentary farming system. When they also include a range of food (fruit, nut and edible leaves), trees also promote dietary diversity and nutritional security (Leakey, 1999; Ingram et al., Chapter 4 of this Handbook). Maintaining the diversity through agroforestry also provides a wide range of options for adapting to changing economic, social and climatic conditions.

Unfortunately, the aforementioned focus on biodiversity conservation within productive farming systems mainly focuses on mature agroecosystems based on large trees and seldom addresses the need to understand the role of biodiversity in the pioneer stages of agroecosystem succession. One consequence of this predominant focus on mature agroecosystems as habitat for wildlife is that we still have a very poor understanding of the importance of species diversity for the control of pests, diseases and weeds in early succession agroecosystems. However, some recent research has started to fill this knowledge gap about the ecological factors affecting the phytopathology of crop productivity in agroecosystems (Cook et al., 2007; Leakey, 2014a).

Regulation processes are complex, but it is recognized that important biological synergies are a function of plant biodiversity (Altieri and Nicholls, 1999). These synergies of course vary depending on the climate (temperature and rainfall), soil types and the levels of disturbance. Numerous important factors affect the prevention of diseases, pest epidemics and weed invasions – such as the limitation of their dispersal; the density of herbivores, predators, and natural enemies and their ability to locate hosts; the distance to, and the diversity of, natural vegetation; and the management of these agroecosystems. Other sources of variation are species abundance; the density dependence of food chains and life cycles; the synchrony of life cycles; the rates of colonization, reproductive success and mortality; and species specific factors such as odours, repelling chemicals and feeding inhibitors. One conclusion from agroecological research investigating these factors has been that species composition is more important than the number of co-located species (Altieri and Nicholls, 1999). Thus, identifying the best species assemblages needs to be the focus of future research to determine ecological principles for rebuilding agroecological and nutritional functions under the very different circumstances found around the world.

## Rebuilding agroecological functions

In most tree species, mycorrhizal fungi are associated with roots of seedlings. At least in the case of ectomycorrhizal species, these fungi remain associated with young roots as the seedlings grow and radiate out away from the trees stem, allowing late stage fungi to colonize closer to the stem. In this way, a successional series of fungi develops over time. Consequently, for rapid tree establishment and land restoration, it is important to inoculate tree seedlings with early stage fungi in the tree nursery prior to planting (Wilson et al., 1991). The rapid development of these symbiotic relations is especially important on severely degraded sites where good levels of seedling survival are highly dependent on mycorrhizal inoculation with the best symbionts, although any symbiont seems to be better than none (Wilson et al., 1991). For agricultural production on severely degraded land, tree establishment is a precursor to the re-establishment of the soil inoculum. This inoculum is then beneficial to the infection and growth of associated crops. Mulch from leguminous tree species has also been found to encourage the development of soil microflora, as evidenced by increased microbial biomass and associated enzyme activity. In Zimbabwe, for example, actinomycete populations were 6 to 9 times greater when biomass of *Vachellia* and *Calliandra* species was applied to the soil surface than when incorporated into the soil (Sileshi et al., 2014).

In addition to the benefits from microbial associations, leguminous 'fertilizer' trees have also been shown to rapidly promote the return of soil fauna even in highly degraded soils. In Zambia, for example, earthworm densities were significantly increased when maize was intercropped with *Vachellia, Calliandra, Gliricidia* and *Leucaena* species compared with maize receiving inorganic fertilizer (Sileshi et al., 2014). Likewise, maize planted after Sesbania + Tephrosia and pigeon pea fallows had 2 to 3 times greater numbers of earthworms than maize alone.

Ecological knowledge about pioneer and early succession tree-based farming systems is principally based on an understanding of the regulation of pests, pathogens and weeds in a limited number of case studies. The best known case studies involve leguminous species like the shrub *Sesbania sesban* which induces 'suicide' germination of the seeds of the parasitic weed *Striga hermonthica* that lowers its infestation of cereal crops (Cook et al., 2007; Khan et al., 2007). Similarly, other legumes like *Desmodium* spp. act as a repellent to stem borers of cereals, while Napier grass *(Pennisetum purpureum)* attracts the pests away from the crops. This combination of agroecological functions has resulted in what is known as 'push-pull technology'. *Sesbania sesban* has also been reported to reduce the dispersal of maize rust, while other tree and shrub species (e.g. *Lantana camara, Melia azedarach, Azadirachta indica, Tephrosia* spp.) have been found to have insecticidal properties. However, there has been some concern that leguminous shrubs may also harbour insect herbivores. However, no evidence of herbivory was found when pure and mixed species legume fallows were examined and Tephrosia fallows had the lowest population densities of eighteen pest species (Girma et al., 2006).

Other reports of predator-prey interactions being modified by the farm diversification come from situations in which trees planted in coffee and cocoa farms provide habitat for birds, bats, spiders and ants that contribute to pest control. These on-farm interactions can be harnessed as part of an integrated pest management strategy, so reducing the need for pesticides (Dix et al., 1999).

## Maintenance of late successional or mature agroecosystems

Recently, three types of studies have reported opportunities for poor farmers to apply simple and affordable techniques to reduce pest, disease and weed problems in mature agroforestry systems by harnessing agroecological interactions. These observational studies have enumerated the interactions between certain pests and pathogens and their likely predator/parasite species (**Table 14.2** *Investigations of agroecological functions in agroforestry systems*). A recent detailed review of the effects of birds and bats on pest populations has highlighted many variables – such as season, geography and land use management – that affect their relative importance (Maas et al., 2015). Bats also play a very important role as pollinators in some fruit tree crops.

### *Shade modification*

Tree shade is important to provide an ideal growing environment for crops adapted to the forest understory. In cocoa, these shade trees can be used to control the incidence of fungal diseases like the frosty pod rot *(Moniliophthora roreri)*. Similarly, in coffee plantations, shade trees can be managed to optimize the light environment to reduce pests like coffee berry and leaf blotch *(Cercospora coffeicola)*, citrus mealy bug *(Planococcus citri)* and coffee rust *(Hemileia vastatrix)* and to

*Table 14.2* Investigations of agroecological functions in agroforestry systems

| *Organisms* | *Country* | *Crop* |
|---|---|---|
| Parasitoid wasps | Brazil | Cocoa |
| Midges | Costa Rica | Cocoa |
| Ants and beetles | Indonesia | Cocoa |
| Birds | Indonesia | Cocoa |
| Spiders | Indonesia | Cocoa |
| Birds and bats | Indonesia | Cocoa |
| Birds | Panama | Cocoa |
| *Moniliophthora* and *Phytophthora* spp. | Peru | Cocoa |
| Birds and arthropods | Costa Rica | Coffee |
| Birds | Guatemala | Coffee |
| Birds, arthropods and fungi | Jamaica | Coffee |
| Birds, ants and leaf miners | Mexico | Coffee |
| Ants and phorid flies | Mexico | Coffee |
| Birds | Mexico | Coffee |
| Birds and caterpillars | Mexico | Coffee |
| Mealy bug, coffee rust and berry blotch | Central America | Coffee |

*Source*: Adapted from Leakey (2014a).

maximize conditions for beneficial fauna and microflora, especially in the dry season. Predation of insect pests by birds is greatest when the canopy is not intensively managed, and much of the variation is explained by the species diversity. Likewise, tree diversity minimizes the risks of pest outbreaks, and shade trees have been found to provide breeding sites for beneficial insects, like the midges which are pollinators in cocoa. Consistent with these findings, the abundance of insectivorous birds has been found to be greatest when the tree canopy is dense and contains some dead vegetation, while the clearance of shade trees reduces the abundance and richness of these birds. Likewise, coffee shade and its associated herbaceous understory has been reported to provide appropriate habitat for small mammals (Caudill et al., 2014). Tscharntke et al. (2011) conclude that there is a need for better understanding of these beneficial ecology × production interactions to avoid insect pest outbreaks within a 'diversified food-and-cash crop' livelihood strategy.

## Bird exclusion

One approach to investigating the importance of bird and bat populations on pests further down the food chain is to set up exclusion experiments. One such study placed caterpillars on coffee plants with and without the exclusion of birds and confirmed that birds do reduce pest outbreaks, especially when in association with high floristic diversity. Other studies have confirmed that exclusion does generally increase the abundance of foliage-dwelling insect herbivores, with beneficial impacts on crop yield, for example by reduced leaf damage. However, there can be trade-offs between the arthropod numbers and the incidence of fungal disease (Johnson et al., 2009). A review by Maas et al., 2015) of the importance of insect predators in forests, agroforestry systems and mixed forest/farming landscapeshas confirmed the important role of birds and bats in these habitats. This review has highlighted the limited number of exclusion studies that allowed comparisons to be made between the impact of birds and bats. This has illustrated marked differences in the impacts of these two predators on pest numbers in wet and dry seasons.

## *Food chain/life cycle studies*

Agroecosystems with a well-developed canopy of shade trees have high biodiversity, a wide diversity of microclimates and ecological niches (see review by Leakey, 2014a) and fewer pest problems attributable to complex interactions between predators and their prey. For example, canopy shade reduces populations of phorid flies. This allows larger populations of the ants which control coffee berry borers. Thus, shade improves coffee production by enhancing the biological control of berry borer by ants, via the reduction of phorid fly populations. Ants also provide important ecosystem services in shaded coffee because twig-nesting ants control leaf miners. Other examples involve parasitic wasps in cocoa agroforests in which the wasp community composition was influenced by tree diversity, season, site disturbance and the scale of the cocoa planting. Conversely, canopy thinning in cocoa agroforests has led to a reduction in the richness of forest ant species, but not of beetles. Thus, these examples of contrasting canopy management interventions illustrate the differing effects of shade on different organisms and the need for better understanding of food chains and life cycles in agroecosystem functions. This is further illustrated by predatory web-building spiders. Web density relates to canopy openness and the presence of *Philidris* ants was also positively associated with orb-web density, although not with other web types. Interestingly, there also seem to be complicated interactions between sap-feeding and leaf-chewing insects and the genetic diversity of some trees (Campos-Navarrete et al., 2015).

However, in general, complex ecological relationships like these are not well understood, and there are many factors which need further study (Perfecto et al., 2014). For example, bird species vary enormously in their feeding habits (e.g. frugivores, insectivores, granivores and nectarivores) and in their preferred habitats. Thus, studies of bird populations on crop production need to take into account species from different functional groups. Nevertheless, to date, the practical importance of these studies in cocoa and coffee agroforests is that losses due to pathogens and insect attacks can be lower when the species diversity of tree canopies support beneficial agroecological interaction and functions as a result of the provision of habitat supporting pest control by insectivores (de Beenhouwer et al., 2013). So further ecological research is needed to gain a better knowledge of the ecological interactions of importance for sustainable agriculture.

## Directions for future research

To improve the management and performance of ecosystem-friendly farming systems across different spatial and temporal scales, there is a need for better understanding of the scientific principles and the ecological processes involved (Scherr et al., 2014). Aiming in this direction, Leakey (2012, 2014a) has described experimental designs involving Nelder fans and Replacement series, seeking answers to some disciplinary research questions on the health, yield and sustainability of cocoa production throughout the pioneer and mature phases of the agroecological succession – that is, from planting through to maturity (**Table 14.3** *Research questions aimed at an examination of the interactions between planned and unplanned biodiversity in cocoa agroforests*). These long-term, multidisciplinary experiments seek a better knowledge of the complex interactions between species in mixed species plantings. They examine the agroecological interactions between the 'planned-biodiversity' (the trees and crops) and the 'unplanned-biodiversity' (wildlife) in species

*Table 14.3* Research questions aimed at an examination of the interactions between planned and unplanned biodiversity in cocoa agroforests

| | |
|---|---|
| *Nelder Fan* | (1) What is the ecologically acceptable number of cocoa plants ha-1? What density of cocoa is sustainable? |
| | (2) Can an ecologically acceptable density of cocoa be made economically acceptable to farmers by diversification with other cash crops? |
| | (3) What combinations of cocoa, shade trees and other trees/shrubs can create a functioning agroecosystem that is also profitable for farmers? |
| | (4) How many trees/shrubs (the planned biodiversity) are required to create sufficient ecological niches above- and below-ground (the unplanned biodiversity) to ensure that cocoa grows well, remains healthy and produces beans on a sustainable basis? |
| | (5) Do the microclimate and biotic environment of a cocoa agroecosystem influence cocoa/chocolate quality? |
| *Replacement series* | (1) What is the effect of replacing cocoa with one to four other cash crops under upper and middle storey tree species, and what is ecologically acceptable mixture of cocoa and other cash crop plants ha-1? |
| | (2) Can a mixture of cocoa and other cash crops be made economically acceptable to farmers? |
| | (3) What combinations of cocoa, shade trees and other cash crops can create a functioning agroecosystem that is also profitable for farmers? |
| | (4) What are the impacts of different distances (with and without the physical barrier of other species) between cocoa plants on the incidence of pests and diseases? |
| | (5) What are the differences in production and in sustainability between a range of species planted as a mixed agroforest in a fifty-fifty mixture of cocoa and other cash crops (Treatment 3), and that of a monocultural mosaic? |

*Source*: Leakey (2014a).

mixtures with very different crop densities and configurations. This heterogeneity should create very different microclimates (irradiance, temperature, humidity, etc.) within the different multi-strata farming systems that will affect the colonization of the ecological niches in the ground flora and the canopy, and so influence the dynamics of the incidence and severity of pest, disease and weed organisms.

Despite numerous mentions of the importance of species richness in functional agroecosystems, it is pertinent to point out here that very few of the studies reviewed in this chapter have considered either the importance of the phases in agroecological succession or the opportunities to manipulate species richness through planting an array of crop species (the planned biodiversity). Both of these additional factors are likely to be of considerable practical importance to farmers.

Within a research agenda, Lavelle et al. (2014) has emphasized the importance of a better understanding of the below-ground agroecosystem and especially the roles of the soil biota and the need for more effective indicators of soil health (Beed et al., Chapter 8 of this Handbook). They particularly call for techniques for conserving and manipulating soil biodiversity for the provision of ecosystem services across all scales – from microbes, plant-parasite nematodes, invertebrate ecosystem engineers and pollinators to landscape-level predators and pests. In the same vein, Garbach et al. (2014) call for better mechanistic understanding of the organisms, guilds and ecological communities that provide agroecological services. They also would like to see management practices linked to ecosystem service outcomes at multiple scales.

Both Leakey's designs (2012, 2014a) embrace the idea that, in addition to shade and other environmental/ecological services, the canopy and sub-canopy trees should provide marketable products. This recognizes the fact that farmers want to increase their income and improve their livelihoods in addition to minimizing the risks of pest, disease and weed problems in commodity or food crops. Thus, income generation and livelihood enhancement has been the focus of many agroforestry projects over the last 25 years, based on strategies and techniques for the participatory domestication of indigenous trees producing food and non-food products (reviewed elsewhere: Leakey, 2012, 2014b; Boshier et al., Chapter 3 of this Handbook).

Other research outputs needed include:

- Quantitative measures of yield and ecosystem services in the same farming systems – that is, paired outcomes for yield and ecosystem services.

  *(Garbach et al., 2014)*

- Better understanding of how local agricultural decision making takes place in relation to macro-level economic and price dynamics.

  *(Scherr et al., 2014)*

- Information on how growers can manage their farms to facilitate bird- and bat-mediated suppression of insect pests (Maas et al., 2015). Information is also needed on the transferability of such recommendations across different regions and land use systems.

With regard to improving the incorporation of ecosystem services research into decision making about the sustainable use of natural resources and improvement of human well-being, Bennett et al. (2015) have identified three challenges that need to be addressed:

- How are ecosystems co-produced by social-ecological systems? As discussed earlier (see **Table 14.3**), this includes a better understanding of the role of biodiversity and other forms of heterogeneity in maintaining multiple ecosystem services?
- Who benefits from ecosystem services?
- What are the best practices for the governance of ecosystem services?

They especially highlight the need for a broad, trans-disciplinary research agenda that cuts across these challenges, and specifically:

- More integrative collaboration across social sciences and natural sciences and the humanities, as also emphasized and illustrated by Leakey (2012).
- The co-production of knowledge through research programmes designed in collaboration with decision makers and the users of ecosystem services.

## *Filling the niches below the canopy with useful plants*

The diversity of the understory habitat of tree-based farming systems has been found to enhance the abundance and species richness of small mammals to levels similar to those in adjacent forested landscapes (Caudill et al., 2014). Agroforestry often creates opportunities for useful shade-adapted species to fill shady niches and increase the benefits derived from mixed cropping systems. As most existing food crops have been selected and bred for cultivation in full sun, there are unfulfilled opportunities for plant breeders and domesticators to develop new, shade tolerant crops or crop varieties (Leakey, 2012) – such as eru *(Gnetum africanum)* in Cameroon. Likewise, these niches can be filled with socially- and commercially-important herbaceous species that meet the needs of local people for traditional foods, medicines other products. In this way, the diversification of the agroecosystem can help to meet the goals of multifunctional agriculture (Leakey, 2012).

## *Landscape and scaling issues*

With little new land for the expansion of agriculture without the loss of now scarce forest, it is clear that land rehabilitation based on agroecological restoration is an important (and indeed challenging) area for more research (Leakey, 2014a). However, perhaps the greatest challenge is posed by the need to ensure that policy makers, politicians and the public acquire the political will to scale up the practical implementation to the level needed for ecological equilibrium in agricultural landscapes.

Both agroforestry and ecoagriculture promote integrated landscape management as a means of achieving agricultural sustainability and multifunctionality. For this to be successful, Scherr et al. (2014) have highlighted the following key elements based on landscape performance criteria:

- Agreement among key stakeholders;
- Better management of the ecological, social and economic synergies and trade-offs that are found among different land and resource uses;
- The development of farming practices that contribute to multiple land use practices;
- The development of supportive markets, policies and investment; and
- The creation of collaborative processes for multi-stakeholder governance.

In practice, the achievement of scale will depend on the formation of land-use mosaics with corridors between forest patches to satisfy the needs of species from different functional groups for different habitats and natural resources in the landscape. This is important both for wildlife conservation and for the sustainable intensification of agriculture through the optimization of agroecological interactions.

We have seen earlier the importance of cocoa and coffee agroforests for the food chains of insectivorous birds. Many of these are migratory species, for which there are regional and international needs for appropriate environments. Both shade coffee and silvopastoral systems incorporating a diverse array of tree species have been found to be beneficial for the flocking activity of migratory birds, with an optimal tree cover of 25–40% (McDermott et al., 2015). Here again, there is still the need for better scientific and popular understanding. Fortunately, there is now growing information about the species composition and richness of smallholder farming systems (Nyaga et al., 2015), its causes, and its impacts on farm production and farmers livelihoods and *vice versa* (see review by Leakey, 2014a). Generally, farmers are less interested in the environment and in wildlife than in their own livelihoods; thus, it is important to explain how trees producing useful and marketable products contribute to sustainable and functional agroecosystems by creating niches above- and below-ground for the wild organisms that are vital for the completion of complex food chains and life cycles at different trophic levels.

## *The big picture: the need for agroecological benefits and income*

As mentioned in this chapter's introduction, deforestation and land degradation are now seriously affecting both agricultural crop yields in the tropics and the availability of productive land. This together with the abject poverty of many smallholders unable to purchase artificial fertilizers

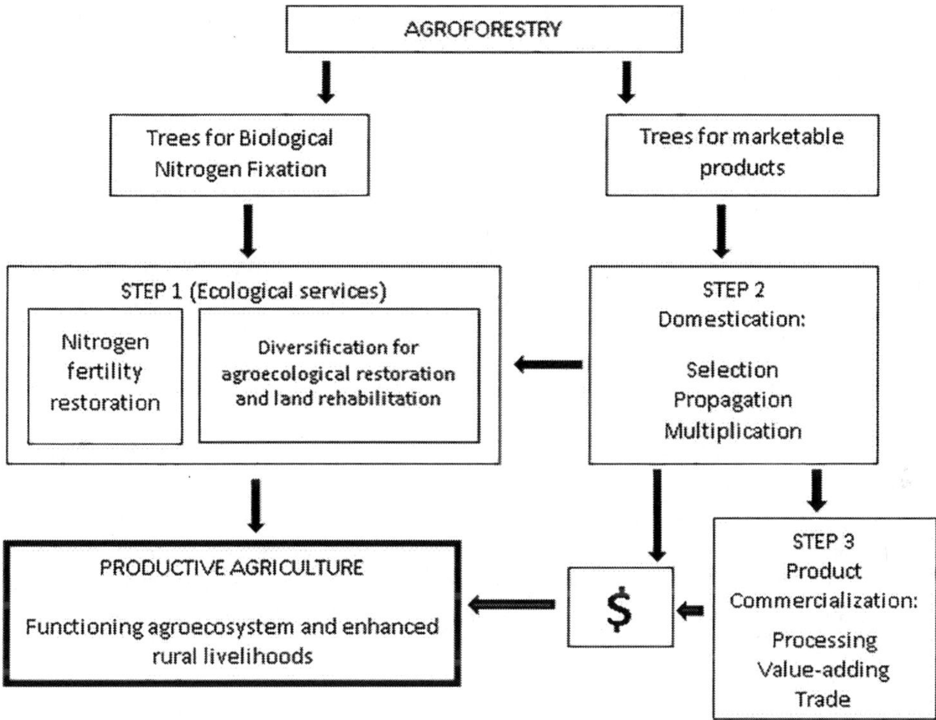


*Figure 14.1* A diagrammatic representation of the role of trees in agroecology and the development of sustainable agriculture

*Source*: Leakey (2014a).

and pesticides makes the importance of land rehabilitation by agroecosystem restoration a prime objective for rural development (Leakey, 2012). There is growing recognition that it is possible to address both food security and biodiversity enrichment simultaneously using agricultural practices that support functioning agroecosystems (Tscharntke et al., 2012). This concurs with the findings of Leakey (2012, 2013), who has proposed a generic and highly adaptable three-step agroforestry approach to resolve food and nutritional insecurity, poverty and environmental degradation (**Figure 14.1** *A diagrammatic representation of the role of trees in agroecology and the development of sustainable agriculture*) to close the Yield Gap (the difference between potential yield of a food crop and the actual yield achieved by farmers in many conventionally managed farming systems in the tropics), especially in Africa. Based on an initiative in Cameroon (Asaah et al., 2011; Degrande et al., 2012), this approach combines soil fertility enrichment using biological nitrogen fixing trees and shrubs, the diversification of the farming systems with new crops to restore agroecological functions and the participatory domestication of new indigenous tree crops using simple horticultural techniques to generate income from local tree species producing useful and marketable products for local and regional trade. In this situation, genetic diversity is additionally very important for sustainable farming systems (Gepts et al., 2012).

In this way, combining agroecological restoration with income generation, agroforestry becomes a powerful new tool to address the cycle of land degradation and social deprivation, especially when part of a participatory integrated rural development programme that provides community training in relevant skills and education (Degrande et al., 2012). The income generating component critically adds an important incentive for farmers to diversify their farming systems and thus adds value to the agroecological approach. These lessons for integrated rural development have now been drawn together as a set of 12 Principles and Premises (Leakey, 2014c) for up-scaling and wider implementation. Achieving a sustainable future for agriculture will involve more than just improving agroecological functions. Instead, it will be necessary to take a more holistic view of the problem that encompasses improved soil fertility and health; reduced risk of pests, diseases and weed outbreaks; improved crop yields; improved rural and urban livelihoods; and opportunities for economic growth. In this way, opportunities to maintain and enhance ecosystem services as part of productive agroecosystems comes from the multifunctional management of agricultural landscapes (Garbach et al., 2014).

## Conclusions

Agroecology is seen as one important approach to delivering the sustainable intensification of tropical agriculture by harnessing biodiversity to rebuild agroecological functions above-ground and below-ground. This is especially effective with regard to improving soil health and fertility and to control pest and disease problems. As described in this review, trees have a special role to play in the promotion of these ecological interactions. However, to date, in terms of our understanding of these complex interactions, research has just scratched the surface, and there is a need for much more intensive study. Trees also produce useful and marketable products; thus, tree-based agriculture offers even greater opportunities to tackle the big issues of poverty, malnutrition and hunger. In both cases, however, real impact depends on the harnessing these roles of trees on a global scale and this will depend on a change in mind-set among policy makers, development agencies and agribusiness.

## References

Altieri, M. A. and Nicholls, C. I. (1999) 'Biodiversity, ecosystem function, and insect pest management in agricultural systems', pp. 69–84 in W. W. Collins and C. O. Qualset (eds.), *Biodiversity in Agroecosystems*, CRC Press, New York, NY, USA.

Asaah, E. K., Tchoundjeu, Z., Leakey, R. R. B., Takousting, B., Njong, J. and Edang, I. (2011) 'Trees, agroforestry and multifunctional agriculture in Cameroon', *International Journal of Agricultural Sustainability*, vol. 9, pp. 110–119.

Bennett, E. M., Cramer, W., Begossi, A., Cundill, G., Díaz, S., Egoh, B. N., Geijzendorffer, I. R., Krug, C. B., Lavorel, S., Lazos, E., Lebel, L., Martín-López, B., Meyfroidt, P., Mooney, H. A., Nel, J. L., Pascual, U., Payet, K., Harguindeguy, K. P., Peterson, G. D., Prieur-Richard, A.-H., Reyers, B., Roebeling, P., Seppelt, R., Solan, M., Tschakert, P., Tscharntke, T., Turner II, B. L., Verburg, P. H., Viglizzo, E. F., White, P. C. L. and Woodward, G. (2015) 'Linking biodiversity, ecosystem services and human well-being: Three challenges for designing research for sustainability', *Current Opinion in Environmental Sustainability*, vol. 14, pp. 76–85.

Butler, S. J., Vickery, J. A. and Norris, K. (2007) 'Farmland biodiversity and the footprint of agriculture', *Science*, vol. 315, pp. 381–384.

Campos-Navarrete, M. J., Abdala-Roberts, L., Munguía-Rosas, M. A. and Parra-Tabla, V. (2015) 'Are tree species diversity and genotypic diversity effects on insect herbivores mediated by ants?', *PLoS One*, vol. 10, p. e0132671.

Caudill, S. A., DeClerck, F. J. A. and Husband, T. P. (2014) 'Connecting sustainable agriculture and wildlife conservation: Does shade coffee provide habitat for mammals?', *Agriculture, Ecosystems and Environment*, vol. 199, pp. 85–93.

Chianu, J. N., Chianu, J. N. and Mairura, F. (2012) 'Mineral fertilizer in the farming systems of Sub-Saharan Africa: A review', *Agronomy for Sustainable Development*, vol. 32, pp. 545–566.

Clough, Y., Barkmann, J., Juhrbandt, J., Kessler, M., Wanger, T. C., Anshary, A., Buchori, D., Cicuzza, D., Darras, K., Dwi Putra, D., Erasmi, S., Pitopang, R., Schmidt, C., Schulze, C. H., Seidel, D., Steffan-Dewenter,

I., Stenchly, K., Vidal, S., Weist, M., Wielgoss, A. C. and Tscharntke, T. (2011) 'Combining high biodiversity with high yields in tropical agroforests', *Proceedings of the National Academy of Sciences USA*, vol. 108, pp. 8311–8316.

Cook, S. M., Khan, Z. R. and Pickett, J. A. (2007) 'The use of "push-pull" strategies in integrated pest management', *Annual Review of Entomology*, vol. 52, pp. 375–400.

De Beenhouwer, M., Aerts, R. and Honnay, O. (2013) 'A global meta-analysis of the biodiversity and ecosystem service benefits of coffee and cacao agroforestry', *Agriculture, Ecosystems and Environment*, vol. 175, pp. 1–7.

Degrande, A., Franzel, S., Yeptiep, Y. S., Asaah, E., Tsobeng, A. and Tchoundjeu, Z. (2012) 'Effectiveness of grassroots organisations in the dissemination of agroforestry innovations', pp. 141–164 in M. L. Kaonga (ed.), *Agroforestry for Biodiversity and Ecosystem Services – Science and Practice*, InTech, Rijeka, Croatia.

Dix, M. E., Bishaw, B., Workman, S. W., Barnhart, M. R., Klopfenstein, N. B. and Dix, A. M. (1999) 'Pest management in energy- and labour-intensive agroforestry systems', pp. 131–156 in L. E. Buck, J. P. Lassoie and E. C. M. Fernandes (eds.), *Agroforestry in Sustainable Agricultural Systems*, CRC Press, Boca Raton, FL, USA.

Garbach, K., Milder, J. C., Montenegro, M., Karp, D. S. and DeClerck, F. A. J. (2014) 'Biodiversity and ecosystem services in agroecosystems', pp. 21–40 in N. van Alfen et al. (eds.), *Encyclopedia of Agriculture and Food Systems*, Vol. 2, Elsevier Publishers, San Diego, CA, USA.

Garnett, T., Appleby, M. C., Balmford, A., Bateman, I. J., Benton, T. G., Bloomer, P., Burlingame, B., Dawkins, M., Dolan, L., Fraser, D., Herrero, M., Hoffmann, I., Smith, P., Thornton, P. K., Toulmin, C., Vermeulen, S. J. and Godfray, H. C. J. (2013) 'Sustainable intensification in agriculture: Premises and policies', *Science*, vol. 341, pp. 33–34.

Gepts, P., Famula, T. R., Bettinger, R. L., Brush, S. B., Damania, A. B., McGuire, P. E. and Qualset, C. O. (2012) *Biodiversity in Agriculture: Domestication, Evolution and Sustainability*, Cambridge University Press, New York, NY, USA.

Girma, H., Rao, M. R., Day, R. and Ogol, C. K. P. O. (2006) 'Abundance of insect pests and their effects on biomass yields of single versus multi-species planted fallows', *Agroforestry Systems*, vol. 93, pp. 93–102.

Harvey, C. A. and González Villalobos, J. A. (2007) 'Agroforestry systems conserve species-rich but modified assemblages of tropical birds and bats', *Biodiversity Conservation*, vol. 16, pp. 2257–2292.

IAASTD (2009) *Agriculture at a Crossroads: Global Report*, Island Press, Washington, DC.

Johnson, M. D., Levy, N. J., Kellermann, J. L. and Robinson, D. E. (2009) 'Effects of shade and bird exclusion on arthropods and leaf damage on coffee farms in Jamaica's Blue Mountains', *Agroforestry Systems*, vol. 76, pp. 139–148.

Khan, Z. R., Midega, C. A. O., Hassanali, A., Pickett, J. A. and Wadhams, L. J. (2007) 'Assessment of different legumes for the control of *Striga hermonthica* in maize and sorghum', *Crop Science*, vol. 47, pp. 730–734.

Lavelle, P. (1996) 'Diversity of soil fauna and ecosystem function', *Biology International*, vol. 33, pp. 3–16.

Lavelle, P., Moreira, F. and Spain, A. (2014), 'Biodiversity: Conserving biodiversity in agroecosystems', pp. 41–60 in N. van Alfen et al. (eds.), *Encyclopedia of Agriculture and Food Systems*, Vol. 2, Elsevier Publishers, San Diego, CA, USA.

Leakey, R. R. B. (1996) 'Definition of agroforestry revisited', *Agroforestry Today*, vol. 8, pp. 5–7.

Leakey, R. R. B. (1999) 'Potential for novel food products from agroforestry trees', *Food Chemistry*, vol. 64, pp. 1–14.

Leakey, R. R. B. (2012) *Living with the Trees of Life: Towards the Transformation of Tropical Agriculture*, CAB International, Wallingford, UK.

Leakey, R. R. B. (2013) 'Addressing the causes of land degradation, food/nutritional insecurity and poverty: A new approach to agricultural intensification in the tropics and sub-tropics', pp. 192–198 in U. Hoffman (ed.), *Wake Up before It Is Too Late: Make Agriculture Truly Sustainable Now for Food Security in a Changing Climate, UNCTAD Trade and Environment Review 2013*, UN Publications, Geneva, Switzerland.

Leakey, R. R. B. (2014a) 'The role of trees in agroecology and sustainable agriculture in the tropics', *Annual Review of Phytopathology*, vol. 52, pp. 113–133.

Leakey, R. R. B. (2014b) 'Agroforestry – participatory domestication of trees', pp. 253–269 in N. K. van Alfen (ed.), *Encyclopedia of Agriculture and Food Systems*, vol. 2, Elsevier Publishers, San Diego, CA, USA.

Leakey, R. R. B. (2014c) *Twelve principles for better food and more food from mature perennial agroecosystems*, Proceedings of Perennial Crops for Food Security Workshop, FAO, 28th–30th August, 2013, Rome, Italy.

Leakey, R. R. B. and Prabhu, R. (2017) 'Towards sustainable intensification: An African initiative', pp. 395–416 in R. R. B. Leakey (ed.), *Multifunctional Agriculture: Scoring Sustainable Development Goals*, Elsevier Publishers, San Diego, CA, USA.

Maas, B., Karp, D. S., Bumrungsri, S., Darras, K., Gonthier, D., Huang, J. C.-C., Lindell, C. A., Maine, J. J., Mestre, L., Michel, N. L., Morrison, E. B., Perfecto, I., Philpott, S. M., Şekercioğlu, Ç. H., Silva, R. M., Taylor, P. J., Tscharntke, T., van Bael, S. A., Whelan, C. J. and Williams-Guillén, K. (2015) 'Bird and bat predation services in tropical forests and agroforestry landscapes', *Biological Reviews*, vol. 91, pp. 1081–1101.

McDermott, M. E., Rodewald, A. D. and Matthews, S. N. (2015) 'Managing tropical agroforestry for conservation of flocking migratory birds', *Agroforestry Systems*, vol. 89, pp. 383–396.

Nyaga, J., Barrios, E., Muthuri, C. W., Öborn, I., Matiru, V. and Sinclair, F. L. (2015) 'Evaluating factors influencing heterogeneity in agroforestry adoption and practices within smallholder farms in Rift Valley, Kenya', *Agriculture, Ecosystems and Environment*, vol. 212, pp. 106–118.

Perfecto, I. and Vandermeer, J. (2008) 'Biodiversity conservation and tropical agroecosystems: A new conservation paradigm', *Annals of New York Academy of Sciences*, vol. 1134, pp. 173–200.

Perfecto, I., Vandermeer, J. and Philpott, S. M. (2014) 'Complex ecological interactions in coffee agroecosystems', *Annual Review of Ecology, Evolution and Systematics*, vol. 45, pp. 137–158.

Scherr, S. J., Buck, L., Willemen, L. and Milder, J. C. (2014) 'Ecoagriculture: Integrated landscape management for people, food and nature', pp. 1–17 in N. K. van Alfen (ed.), *Encyclopedia of Agriculture and Food Systems*, Vol. 3, Elsevier Publishers, San Diego, CA, USA.

Schroth, G., da Fonseca, G. A. B., Harvey, C. A., Gascon, C., Vasconcelos, H. L. and Izac, A.-M. N. (2004) *Agroforestry and Biodiversity Conservation in Tropical Landscapes*, Island Press, Washington, DC, USA.

Schroth, G. and do Socorro Souza da Mota, M. (2014) 'Agroforestry: Complex multistrata agriculture', pp. 195–207 in N. K. van Alfen (ed.), *Encyclopedia of Agriculture and Food Systems*, Vol. 1, Elsevier Publishers, San Diego, CA, USA.

Schroth, G., Krauss, U., Gasparotto, L., Duarte Aguilar, J. A. and Vohland, K. (2000) 'Pests and diseases in agroforestry systems of the humid tropics', *Agroforestry Systems*, vol. 50, pp. 199–241.

Sileshi, G. W., Akinnifesi, F. K., Ajayi, O. C., and Place, F. (2008a) 'Meta-analysis of maize yield response to planted fallow and green manure legumes in sub-Saharan Africa', *Plants and Soil*, vol. 307, pp. 1–19.

Sileshi, G. W., Chintu, R., Mafongoya, P. L. and Akinnifesi, F. K. (2008b) 'Mixed-species legume fallows affect faunal abundance and richness and N cycling compared to single species in maize-fallow rotations', *Soil Biology and Biochemistry*, vol. 40, pp. 3065–751.

Sileshi, G. W. and Mafongoya, P. L. (2006) 'Long-term effect of legume-improved fallows on soil invertebrates and maize yield in eastern Zambia', *Agriculture Ecosystems and Environment*, vol. 115, pp. 69–78.

Sileshi, G. W., Mafongoya, P. L., Akinnifesi, F. K., Phiri, E., Chirwa, P., Beedy, T., Makumba, W., Nyamdzawo, G., Njoloma, J., Wuta, M., Nyamugafata, P. and Jiri, O. (2014) 'Agroforestry: Fertilizer trees', pp. 222–234 in N. K. van Alfen (ed.), *Encyclopedia of Agriculture and Food Systems*, Vol. 1, Elsevier Publishers, San Diego, CA, USA.

Spray, S. L. and McGlothlin, K. L. (eds.) (2003) *Loss of Biodiversity*, Rowman & Littlefield Publishers, Lanham, MD, USA.

Tittonell, P. (2014) 'Ecological intensification of agriculture – sustainable by nature', *Current Opinion in Environmental Sustainability*, vol. 8, pp. 53–61.

Tscharntke, T., Clough, Y., Bhagwat, S. A., Buchori, D., Faust, H., Hertel, D., Hölscher, D., Juhrbandt, J., Kessler, M., Perfecto, I., Scherber, C., Schroth, G., Veldkamp, E. and Wanger, T. C. (2011) 'Multifunctional shade-tree management in tropical agroforestry landscapes – a review: Multifunctional shade-tree management', *Journal of Applied Ecology*, vol. 48, p. 619.

Tscharntke, T., Clough, Y., Wanger, T. C., Jackson, L., Motzke, I., Perfecto, I., Vandermeer, J. and Whitbread, A. (2012) 'Global food security, biodiversity conservation and the future of agricultural intensification', *Biological Conservation*, vol. 151, pp. 53–59.

Wilson, J., Munro, R. C., Ingleby, K., Mason, P. A., Jefwa, J., Muthoka, P. N., Dick, J. McP. and Leakey, R. R. B. (1991) 'Agroforestry in semi-arid lands of Kenya – role of mycorrhizal inoculation and water retaining polymer', *Forest Ecology and Management*, vol. 45, pp. 153–163.

# PART 3

# The value of agricultural biodiversity

# 15
# THE QUALITY OF THE AGRICULTURAL MATRIX AND LONG-TERM CONSERVATION OF BIODIVERSITY

*Ivette Perfecto and John Vandermeer*

## Introduction

Sensible human intervention in tropical landscapes faces two contemporary problems that are at once critical and seemingly intractable. On the one hand, tropical environments face enormous pressures of biodiversity loss, deforestation, fragmentation, climate change, and others. On the other hand, historical accident has rendered the human population residing in the tropics in a general subaltern position on average. Similar to the much publicized inherent contradiction between jobs and the environment in the United States, many scholars see a contradiction between the need to manage tropical environments wisely and the needs of some of the most impoverished people on earth. Environmentalists sometimes see the masses of local people as the enemy of wise environmental policy while social advocates sometimes see environmentalists as, at best, naïve, at worst, arrogant misanthropes.

One area where this contradiction plays out with disturbingly recurrent themes is in the conservation of biodiversity, with conservationists emphasizing preservation of what they view as pristine areas and social/development activists emphasizing the rights of local people to decide what to do with their land and natural resources. Arguments that differ only in detail seem to be endlessly recycled, from the old 'single large or several small' reserves (SLOSS) debates (Diamond, 1975; Wilson and Willis, 1975), to the Forest Transition Model (Mather, 1990; Rudel et al., 2005) to the more recent Land Sparing/Sharing debate (Phalan et al., 2011), on the environmental side. Likewise on the sociopolitical side, 'old-time' Marxists worship the developmentalist dream as much as contemporary corporate capitalists, with concerns about biodiversity seen as either bourgeois prejudice or Luddite obstructionism, depending on whether the critique stems from the left or right.

Recent ecological research has produced a relatively large body of literature suggesting a new approach is in order. Whether focused on stabilizing tropical forest margins (Tscharntke et al., 2007), promoting biodiverse-rich countrysides (Daily et al., 2001), small-farm agrobiodiversity (Altieri, 2002; Jackson et al., 2007), urban/rural dynamics (Padoch et al., 2008; García-Barrios et al., 2009; Hecht, 2010), or the intersection between biodiversity conservation and food security (Chappell and LaValle, 2011; Chappell et al., 2013), this literature has focused on the intersection of what had before been treated as two distinct domains. Collectively, this new approach proposes that the biodiversity crisis will not be solved if agricultural activities are not part of the solution, and the problems of food production will become ever more severe if the ecosystem services provided by biodiversity are eroded. The approach is philosophically at the landscape level and takes seriously the structure of the whole landscape, not only the parts that are thought (or hoped) to represent unperturbed remnants of what is imagined to be the 'original' native habitat.

Although the relevant literature is large and somewhat eclectic, we feel much of it can be framed within a collection of some simple ecological principles, what has been referred to as the quality of the matrix approach (Perfecto et al., 2009; Perfecto and Vandermeer, 2010; Tscharntke et al., 2012).

## A general theoretical framework

We propose that the basic dynamics of extinction and migration can be taken as paradigmatic for the problem. The pioneering work of MacArthur and Wilson (1967) in island biogeography and that of Levins (1969) in metapopulation theory represent the ecological core upon which much has already been built, and can form a heuristic qualitative base both for collating what has already transpired in the literature and for elaborating research programs for the future.

We propose that landscapes be envisioned as a patchwork in which different patches are to different degrees sources and sinks either for biodiversity in general or for the persistence of a particular species. At the extreme, there are two qualitatively distinct patches, occupiable and unoccupiable. In the context of general species diversity, the occupiable patches are islands and the set of unoccupiable patches is the sea, or the matrix within which the islands are located. The standard theory of island biogeography applies directly. However, what changes is if the unoccupiable patches become less than completely unoccupiable, perhaps temporary sites for migration, or marginal habitat for temporary nest establishment, or degrading but not degraded patches that do not form a complete barrier to migration. Thus, the matrix replaces the sea in the island biogeography context and, most importantly, has a quality. The matrix acts as a filter, and thus can be positioned easily in the classic theory of island biogeography as a modifier of migration.

In the context of the persistence of a particular species, we also begin with occupiable and unoccupiable patches. However, in this context the occupiable patches are effectively only temporarily occupiable. They are 'propagating sinks' (Vandermeer et al., 2010) in that extinction is insured over the long term, but propagules may emanate from them to form a general migration rate. Once again, the matrix replaces the unoccupiable patches and acts as a filter to migration among the patches that are occupiable.

In either case, the important issue is the way in which the matrix acts as a filter. That filter can be relatively impervious such that migration rates are very low or even zero, or it can be very permeable such that migration rates (or simply movements of organisms between patches) are large. The management question is how to create a permeable matrix, or a high quality matrix.

## The ecological dynamics of extinctions and migrations in fragmented habitats

To explore how the dynamics of extinction and migration create a richly textured theoretical framework for thinking about the problem, we begin with a common modification of the basic Levins (1969) metapopulation model that takes into account environmental heritability (Kareiva and Wennergren, 1995; Hanski et al., 1996; Amarasekare, 1998). Suppose that only a certain fraction of the environment (h) is actually available (so, 1-h is unavailable permanently). The

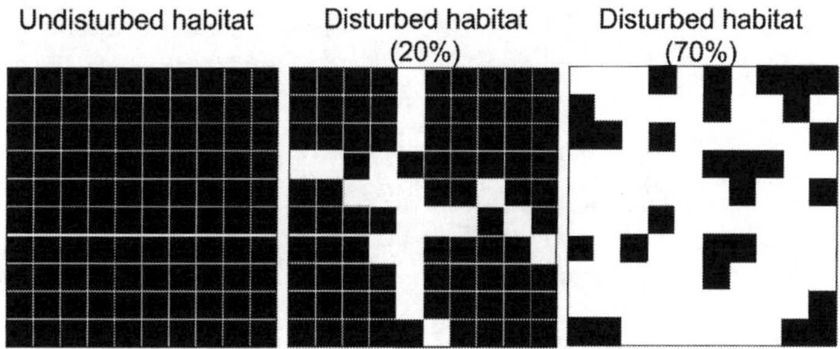


*Figure 15.1* Idealized landscape of 10 × 10 cells, with various levels of habitat 'disturbance'

*Note*: Black cells symbolize original undisturbed habitat and white cells destroyed habitats. In the case of undisturbed habitat h = 1, for the 20% destruction, h = 0.8 and for the 70% destruction, h = 0.3.

probability that an occupied habitat comes into contact with an unoccupied one becomes p(h – p), and the Levins equation becomes,

$$\frac{dp}{dt} = mp(h - p) - ep. \qquad 1$$

The basic meaning of equation 1 is illustrated diagramatically in **Figure 15.1** *Idealized landscape of 10 × 10 cells, with various levels of habitat 'disturbance'*.

This form of the model has been quite useful in clarifying the relationship of the probability of regional extinction (the extinction of the species over the entire landscape) to the amount of habitat lost. Its extension to the question of the quality of the matrix is obvious. In **Figure 15.2** *Idealized landscape of 10 × 10 cells, with various levels of habitat 'destruction'*, we illustrate this idea, a habitat that is dramatically reduced in its migratory potential (broadly speaking, the matrix quality), but with two types of habitat within the matrix (the black squares still represent the undisturbed habitat). Small arrows indicate the migratory potential of a habitat. As symbolized by the size of the arrows, the two habitat types have different migratory potentials. The overall migration coefficient is proportional to the amount of habitat type (relative number of squares of a particular shading) and the within habitat migration coefficient (relative size of the arrows).

The basic idea can be envisioned with a simple extension of the Levins model (Perfecto and Vandermeer, 2010), beginning with the modified form as presented in equation 1. Let the migration coefficient among patches of good habitat be $m_1$ and that among low quality habitat be $m_2$. Then equation 1 will be modified by making the overall migration rate proportional to the two matrix habitats, which is to say $m = m_1q_1 + m_2q_2$) to read:

$$\frac{dp}{dt} = (m_0h + m_1q_1 + m_2q_2)p(h - p) - ep \qquad 2$$

where $m_0$ is the migration rate in the original non-agricultural habitat, $m_1$ is the migration rate in the first matrix habitat and $m_2$ the migration rate in the second habitat (note that $m_0$ multiplies $h - q_1 - q_2$, which is to say, $m_0$ is the migration rate that occurs in the original habitat, the quantity of which is $h - q_1 - q_2$). To make things transparent, we look at only the case where the lowest quality

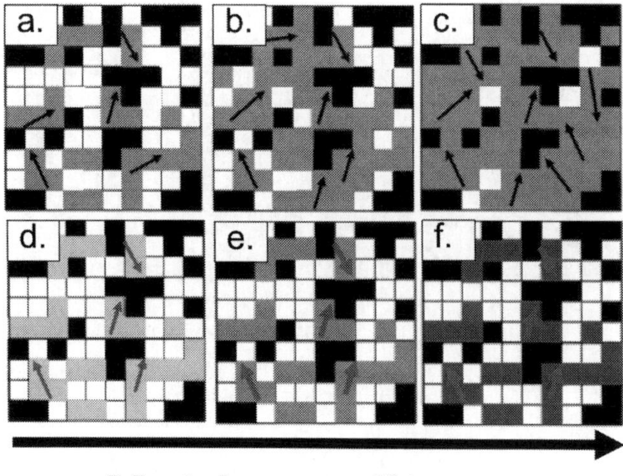


*Figure 15.2* Idealized landscape of 10 ×10 cells, with various levels of habitat 'destruction'

*Note*: Black cells symbolize original undisturbed habitat and white cells destroyed habitats, but the sub-habitats in the matrix are themselves suitable for migration, as indicated by the arrows, larger and more bold indicating higher migration, smaller and less bold illustrating lower migration. Top row of graphs indicates increasing matrix quality because the proportion of better quality patches increases. Lower row of graphs indicates increasing matrix quality because the quality of the individual patches increases.

sub-habitats in the matrix (e.g. the white squares in **Figure 15.2**) have a migration coefficient equal to zero. So, letting $q_2 = 0$, equation 2 becomes,

$$\frac{dp}{dt} = (m_0 h + m_1 q_1)p(h - p) - ep \tag{3}$$

with an equilibrium value of,

$$p^\star = h - \frac{e}{m_0 h + m_1 q_1}$$

whence, it follows that the population will persist (i.e. $p^\star > 0$) whenever,

$$h > -\frac{m_1 q_1}{2m_0} + \sqrt{\frac{m_1^2 q_1^2}{4m_0^2} + \frac{e}{m_0}} \tag{4}$$

A variety of manifestations of equation 4 are presented in **Figure 15.3** *Graphs of equation 4 illustrating the relationship between matrix quality and amount of non-native habitat.*

With this simple 'toy' model, we can then examine various scenarios of changing migration and extinction rates, as illustrated in **Figure 15.4** *Graph of equation 4 illustrating the relationship between matrix quality and amount of non-matrix (natural) habitat.* Consider, for example, the case

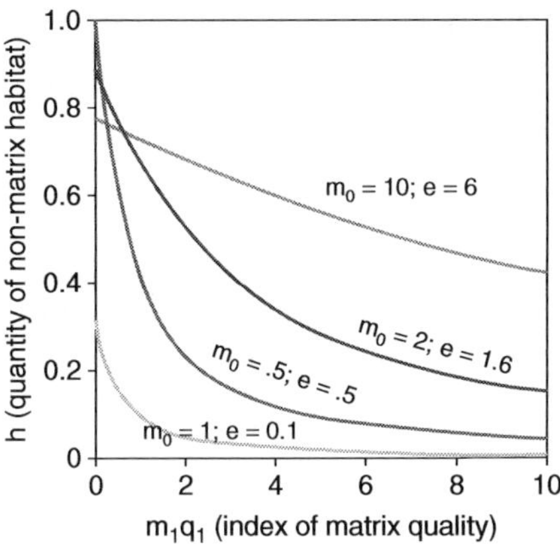


*Figure 15.3* Graphs of equation 4 illustrating the relationship between matrix quality and amount of non-native habitat, according to the dynamic metapopulation model

*Note*: The colour lines represent various forms of the function, depending on values of other parameters.

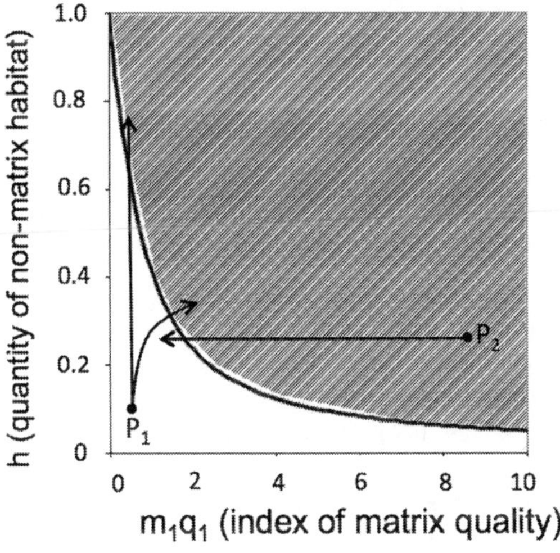


*Figure 15.4* Graph of equation 4 illustrating the relationship between matrix quality and amount of non-matrix (natural) habitat, according to the dynamic metapopulation model, illustrating two scenarios ($P_1$ and $P_2$)

*Note*: The resulting function separates the area of species survival (shaded area above the curve) from the area of species extinction (white area under the curve).

of a very low quality matrix and small amount of 'natural' habitat, illustrated as $P_1$. A strategy of trying to restore native habitat, sometimes a rather difficult prospect in and of itself, means that almost 80% of the area will have to be restored before the species in question will be saved from extinction (the vertical arrow pointing directly upward from $P_1$). An alternative strategy would be to increase the quality of the matrix while striving for restoration, leading to the scenario represented by the curved arrow. Depending on both ecological and socio-economic conditions, we expect that usually a combination of restoration and improvement of matrix quality would be the most efficient way to save this species from extinction, long term. Alternatively, consider

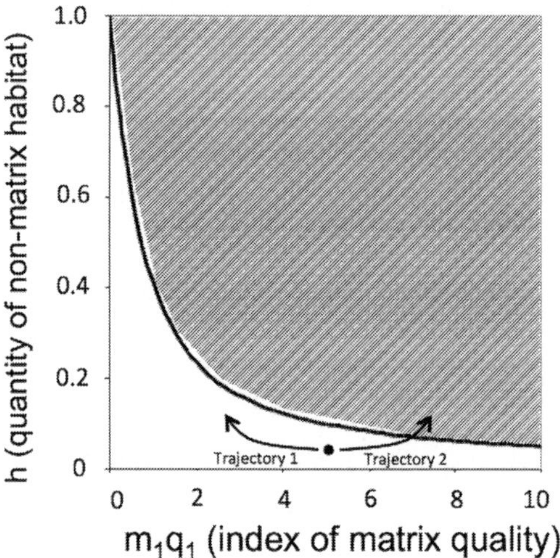


*Figure 15.5* Graph of equation 4 illustrating the relationship between matrix quality and amount of non-matrix (natural) habitat, according to the dynamic metapopulation model, illustrating a scenario in which the matrix quality is intermediate and the proportion of natural habitat in the landscape is low

*Note*: The two alternative trajectories represent two different courses of action.

point $P_2$ representing a situation of about 25% of the area in natural habitat, but with a relatively high quality matrix. While it may appear that extinction will be avoided, especially if viewed through an empirical lens that tacitly assumes constant conditions, the truth is that if the matrix quality is dynamic and decreasing, as represented by the horizontal arrow pointing to the left, the assumed 25% of the area in natural habitat will not be sufficient to waylay extinction of the species under conditions of a low quality matrix. Empirical surveys of the species, suggesting a healthy population, would thus engender a false sense of security.

A final scenario is illustrated in **Figure 15.5** *Relationship between matrix quality and non-matrix habitat when quality is intermediate and proportion of natural habitat is low.* Here we have a situation where the matrix quality is intermediate and the proportion of natural habitat in the landscape is low (5%). According to the land sparing argument, a way to improve biodiversity conservation in this situation would be to intensify agriculture, which would likely lower the quality of the matrix (by establishing monocultures, using agrochemicals, etc) so as to be able to spare land for conservation (increasing the amount of natural habitat). However, as shown in the trajectory that models this action (trajectory 1), this alternative will not take the species out of the extinction zone. On the other hand, if the quality of the matrix is improved, only a small increase in the proportion of natural habitat will take the species out of the extinction zone, as shown with trajectory 2.

## Empirical evidence of agriculture as a high quality matrix

The matrix quality model suggests that for long-term conservation, organisms must be able to move among fragments of natural habitat through what is normally an agricultural matrix. In addition, the matrix itself can serve as a habitat for biodiversity. Indeed, most terrestrial biodiversity is found outside reserve areas and within managed areas (Rouget et al., 2003; Tognelli et al., 2008; Cox and Underwood, 2011), and many species live and thrive within the agricultural landscapes (Bengtsson et al., 2005; Harvey et al., 2008; Perfecto and Vandermeer, 2008; Chazdon et al., 2009; Kleijn et al., 2009; Jha et al., 2014), including endemic and endangered species (see e.g. Goulart et al., 2013; Tisovec et al., 2014). Just as matrix quality matters for the movement of organisms between fragments of natural habitats, it also matters for the ability of organisms to establish viable populations within the matrix. For both of these reasons, a landscape dominated by industrial agriculture (large scale monocultures laden with pesticides) harbors lower levels of biodiversity than a landscape dominated by small-scale diverse agroecological farms (Benton et al., 2003; Belfrage et al., 2005; Scales and Mardsen, 2008; Geiger et al., 2010a).

The nature of a high-quality matrix seems obvious under some circumstances. For example, when the natural ecosystem is a forest, an agricultural matrix composed of agroforestry systems such as shaded coffee (Jha et al., 2014; Perfecto and Vandermeer, 2015), 'cabruca' cacao (cacao produced under an upper canopy of shade; Rice and Greenberg, 2000; Schroth and Harvey, 2007), or jungle rubber (rubber trees planted among other natural species; Michon and de Foresta, 1995) will generate a high quality matrix (Bhagwat et al., 2008). Similarly, when the natural ecosystem is a grassland, like the prairie of the Midwest in the United States, or the grasslands in Europe or the South American savannas, a high quality matrix will be composed of perennial grain polycultures (Jackson, 2002) or livestock ranches with native species (Hoogesteijn and Hoogesteijn, 2010; Magda et al., 2015).

In such cases, many of the organisms that live in such landscapes will freely move and use the agricultural matrix. Some may not even distinguish between the 'natural habitat' and the 'matrix habitat'. For example, in a study of ant diversity in the Atlantic forest of Brazil, Delabie et al. (2007) recorded little differences in the ant fauna between shaded cacao farms and native forests. Other organisms may show a preference for the native habitat (perhaps because of a lower presence of humans), but will frequently move through and use the resources within the matrix. For example, in a study comparing feeding-bouts of five frugivorous bird species in secondary forests, agroforestry home gardens and pastures in the Pontal do Paranepanema, Brazil, Goulart et al. (2011) recorded more feeding-bouts in the agroforests than in the forests in four of the species. In a study of the Andean night monkey, Guzmán et al. (2016) found that although the monkeys prefer to spend more of their time in the native forests, they used the shaded coffee farms throughout the year, particularly during the high fruit production periods. They concluded that a landscape containing shaded coffee farms mixed in with patches of natural forest (occurring usually in ravines and steep hilltops) can provide additive opportunities to increase the carrying capacity of the habitat and can become a successful conservation strategy for the monkeys. Yet, in other cases, the agroforestry system may represent an even better habitat than the forest. This is the case for the golden-headed lion tamarind in the 'cabruca' (cacao) agroforests of the Atlantic Forest of Brazil (Oliveira et al., 2011). It was found that the density of the golden-headed lion tamarind in the 'cabrucas' was the highest recorded for the species and that the adult males were significantly heavier than in the primary forest. The authors of the study attributed these differences to the high concentration of resources such as jackfruit *(Artocarpus heterophyllus)* and bromeliads in the 'cabruca' system (Oliveira et al., 2011).

More commonly, agricultural systems are not of the sort that imitates local natural vegetation. In such cases, it is more difficult to specify characteristics that lead to a high quality matrix. Nevertheless, some of those characteristics seem patently obvious. With regard to insects, landscapes that are sprayed with insecticides regularly are, by definition, hostile habitats (Brittain et al., 2010; Beketov et al., 2013). However, pesticide use has been shown to be detrimental to vertebrates as well (Relyea, 2005; Hayes et al., 2006; Bernanke and Köhler, 2009; Geiger et al., 2010b) and has been implicated in the decline of birds and amphibians in intensified agricultural landscapes (Geiger et al., 2010b). Thus, agricultural planning that avoids the use of pesticides (including herbicides) can generally be thought of as moving in the direction of a higher quality matrix.

Similarly it is well known that the use of synthetic fertilizer disturbs the soil biota considerably (Giller et al., 1997; Mäder et al., 2002), and it might be hypothesized that such an activity would promote a low quality matrix for most soil organisms. Generally speaking, agricultural activities that are usually associated with ecological agriculture, or agroecology, are likely to contribute to a higher quality matrix (Hole et al., 2005; Perfecto et al., 2009; Altieri and Toledo, 2011). Although many of the examples that we presented here come from agroforestry systems like coffee and cacao, there are also important examples in systems that are extremely important for food production like the home gardens of Indonesia, the *milpa* system in Mesoamerica, and traditional paddy rice in Asia (Perfecto et al., 2009).

One philosophy that concurs well with the idea of an agricultural matrix attaining a high quality is the idea of 'natural systems' agriculture, as alluded to earlier. Most recently associated with Wes Jackson, the idea is to plan the agroecosystem in such a way that it mimics the local natural system. The idea of natural systems agriculture has considerable historical precedent with, for example, Albert Howard (1943) explicitly stating its principles in his famous 'An Agricultural Testament', and Richard St. Barbe Baker (1970) recognizing the natural vegetation as a 'school' for learning how to properly manage ecosystems generally.

## The socio-political dynamics of creating a high quality matrix

Although it is possible to make generalized recommendations about what the structure of the agricultural matrix should be so as to result in a high quality matrix from a conservation point of view, how to get to that point, a socio-politico-economic problem, is far harder to stipulate. It is clear that farmers and farm enterprises will move in the direction of a high quality matrix when it suits their purposes, almost a tautology. But understanding those purposes and creating conditions where purposes coincide with proper practices is a more difficult issue, involving not only the technical issues of land management but also socio-political-economic issues such as land tenure and market access. The problem is multidisciplinary.

In a move towards taking on these sorts of cross-disciplinary issues, we note a common structural consistency resulting in a reticence to recognize them in the first place. If it is assumed that the 'ecology' is fixed, proposed solutions must remain within that constraint. If it is assumed that the 'economy' is fixed, proposed solutions must similarly remain within that constraint. Thus, for example, while it is clear that hunger is not strictly the result of food availability (amount of food produced) but rather is due to the fact that many people do not have the resources to obtain food (whether land to grow it or money to buy it), agronomists are rarely schooled in issues about the distribution of power. Similarly, social planners, from government officials to political activists, are rarely properly schooled in the ecological aspects of agriculture. Such balkanization of intellectual work is ultimately a barrier to the construction of high quality matrices.

In the end, prescriptions for a high quality matrix are fairly obvious – limit use of biocides (insecticides, herbicides, fungicides, etc.), employ perennials whenever possible, avoid monoculture, use the natural vegetation as a template for planning, maintain soil organic matter, etc. – in other words, agroecology. Indeed, early pioneers of agroecology, like George Washington Carver in the United States and Albert Howard and Eve Balfour in the United Kingdom, came to the same conclusions decades ago. However, it remains a challenge to get to the point where farmers have the necessary knowledge and power required for their own intellectual defense against outside pressures that degrade matrix quality (e.g. pesticide sales forces, seed monopolists, perverse subsidies). Recently, this challenge is being met by a global movement of small-scale farmers that, after a deep and prolonged political/ecological analysis, is embracing agreocology in their struggle for food sovereignty (Altieri and Toledo, 2011; Rosset and Martínez, 2012). With the application of a 'farmer-to-farmer' methodology, they are spreading agroecological farming methods in rural and urban areas throughout the world and are beginning to change the agricultural matrix (Holt-Giménez, 2006; Rosset et al., 2011). Their agenda for agroecology and food sovereignty coincide with the characteristics of the landscape that we have come to associate with a high quality matrix (Chappell et al., 2013). The largest and strongest manifestation of such a movement is 'La Via Campesina', a global peasant organization that represents about 200 million small-scale farmers from 73 countries (Desmarais, 2012; Martínez and Rosset, 2014). The movement, along with supportive academics (such as the leadership of the Latin American Scientific Society of Agroecology, SOCLA) and intellectuals within intergovernmental organizations, like Oliver De Shutter (2010), are beginning to attract the attention of governments and intergovernmental organizations, such as the FAO and the World Bank. In 2009, The International Agricultural Assessment of Knowledge, Science and Technology (IAASTD) published its report reiterating the key role of small-scale farmers and agroecological methods for reducing hunger and conserving natural resources (McIntyre, 2009). In 2014, the FAO held the first International Symposium on Agroecology for Food Security and Nutrition in Rome. This meeting was followed up by three regional meetings, one in Brazil for the Latin American and Caribbean Region and one in Senegal for the sub-Saharan African region and a multi-stakeholder consultation on agroecology held in Thailand for the Asia and Pacific region (www.fao.org/about/meetings/afns/en/?amp%3Butm_medium=weband%3Butm_campaign=featurebar). Although these are all welcome initiatives that reflect the growing awareness that 'business as usual' is not the answer, it is important not to lose perspective about the critical role that the peasant movements have played in making the real changes within the agricultural matrix.

## Conclusions

As we noted in the introduction, there is an undeniable contradiction in the collection of narratives about tropical landscapes, with alternative perspectives creating tunnel visions of solution pathways. The romance of unadulterated nature, so common in Victorian England and elsewhere, cries out for preservation of nature, in contrast to the humanistic ideal calling for transformations that would lighten the burden on the poor. The former would isolate and defend non-human nature (whatever that is), while the latter would feed the people. Our position is that such a dichotomy is false, even absurd, when examining both established principles of ecology and a plethora of empirical evidence.

Even though fragments of natural terrestrial habitat may appear to be islands, they are not nearly as isolated from one another as real islands are isolated by oceans. And the migration of organisms – animals, plants, fungi – from one fragment to another is a ubiquitous piece of ecological understanding today. Classical ecological theories, such as metapopulation or the equilibrium theory of island biogeography, make it clear that landscapes generally include the places where organisms not only temporarily live and prosper, but also continually migrate through to repopulate areas having undergone the long-term consequence of being a biological population – that is, the inevitability of local extinction. It is thus not those revered protected areas that matter so much, but rather the areas in between them, the matrix. And it is evident that some matrices are of higher quality than others (Perfecto et al., 2009), leading to the key question 'How can the quality of a matrix be enhanced?'. The answer to that question may very well be complicated and context dependent, but as an undergirding principle, it is unassailable. And even though we genuflect to the idea of context dependency, it seems to us (and many others) that a matrix consisting of insecticide-drenched monocultures with intense applications of NPK fertilizers and highly mechanized is not likely to be regarded as high quality by many organisms. In contrast, the sorts of agriculture done by small-scale producers in a more traditional or ecological framework is more likely to provide a higher quality matrix for most organisms.

The empirical evidence is enormous (see review in Perfecto and Vendermeer, 2008; Perfecto et al., 2009). It all boils down to the final conclusion that the overall landscape is crucial for long-term conservation, a fact that few professional ecologists would deny.

The final and most important question, still not completely elaborated, is how to construct that high quality matrix of small-scale agroecological farms that most agree are the best chance we have for high quality matrices and for reducing world hunger, especially in the tropics. The grassroots efforts of organizations such as 'La Via Campesina' and their program of food sovereignty seem to offer the best of current recognized alternatives.

## References


Altieri, M. A. (2002) 'Agroecology: The science of natural resource management for poor farmers in marginal environments', *Agriculture, Ecosystems and Environment*, vol. 93, pp. 1–24.

Altieri, M. A. and Toledo, V. M. (2011) 'The agroecological revolution in Latin America: Rescuing nature, ensuring food sovereignty and empowering peasants', *Journal of Peasant Studies*, vol. 38, pp. 587–612.

Amarasekare, P. (1998) 'Allele effects in metapopulation dynamics', *The American Naturalist*, vol. 152, pp. 298–302.

Beketov, M. A., Kefford, B. J., Schäfer, R. B. and Liess, M. (2013) 'Pesticides reduce regional biodiversity of stream invertebrates', *Proceedings of the National Academy of Sciences USA*, vol. 110, pp. 11039–11043.

Belfrage, K., Björklund, J. and Salomonsson, L. (2005) 'The effects of farm size and organic farming on diversity of birds, pollinators, and plants in a Swedish landscape', *AMBIO: A Journal of the Human Environment*, vol. 34, pp. 582–588.

Bengtsson, J., Ahnström, J. and Weibull, A. C. (2005) 'The effects of organic agriculture on biodiversity and abundance: A meta-analysis', *Journal of Applied Ecology*, vol. 42, pp. 261–269.

Benton, T. G., Vickery, J. A. and Wilson, J. D. (2003) 'Farmland biodiversity: Is habitat heterogeneity the key?', *Trends in Ecology and Evolution*, vol. 18, pp. 182–188.

Bernanke, J. and Köhler, H. R. (2009) 'The impact of environmental chemicals on wildlife vertebrates', *Reviews of Environmental Contamination and Toxicology*, vol. 198, pp. 1–47.

Bhagwat, S. A., Willis, K. J., Birks, H. J. B. and Whittaker, R. J. (2008) 'Agroforestry: A refuge for tropical biodiversity?', *Trends in Ecology and Evolution*, vol. 23, pp. 261–267.

Brittain, C. A., Vighi, M., Bommarco, R., Settele, J. and Potts, S. G. (2010) 'Impacts of a pesticide on pollinator species richness at different spatial scales', *Basic and Applied Ecology*, vol. 11, pp. 106–115.

Chappell, M. J. and LaValle, L. A. (2011) 'Food security and biodiversity: Can we have both? An agroecological analysis', *Agriculture and Human Values*, vol. 28, pp. 3–26.

Chappell, M. J., Wittman, H., Bacon, C. M., Ferguson, B. G., Barrios, L. G., Barrios, R. G., Jaffee, D., Lima, J., Méndez, E. V., Morales, H., Soto-Pinto, L., Vandermeer, J. and Perfecto, I. (2013) 'Food sovereignty: An alternative paradigm for poverty reduction and biodiversity conservation in Latin America', *F1000Research*, vol. 2, p. 235.

Chazdon, R. L., Harvey, C. A., Komar, O., Griffith, D. M., Ferguson, B. G., Martínez-Ramos, M., Morales, H., Nigh, R., Soto-Pinto, L., Van Breuger, M. and Philpott, S. M. (2009) 'Beyond reserves: A research agenda for conserving biodiversity in human-modified tropical landscapes', *Biotropica*, vol. 41, pp. 142–153.

Cox, R. L. and Underwood, E. C. (2011) 'The importance of conserving biodiversity outside of protected areas in Mediterranean ecosystems', *PLoS One*, vol. 6, p. e14508.

Daily, G. C., Ehrlich, P. R. and Sanchez-Azofeifa, G. A. (2001) 'Countryside biogeography: Use of human-dominated habitats by the avifauna of southern Costa Rica', *Ecological Applications*, vol. 11, pp. 1–13.

Delabie, J. H., Jahyny, B., do Nascimento, I. C., Mariano, C. S., Lacau, S., Campiolo, S., Philpott, S. M. and Leponce, M. (2007) 'Contribution of cocoa plantations to the conservation of native ants (Insecta: Hymenoptera: Formicidae) with a special emphasis on the Atlantic Forest fauna of southern Bahia, Brazil', *Biodiversity and Conservation*, vol. 16, pp. 2359–2384.

De Schutter, O. (2010) *Agroecology and the Right to Food.* United Nations, New York, NY, USA/Geneva, Switzerland.

Desmarais, A. A. (2012) *La Vía Campesina.* John Wiley and Sons, Ltd., New York, NY, USA.

Diamond, J. M. (1975) 'The island dilemma: Lessons of modern biogeographic studies for the design of natural reserves', *Biological Conservation*, vol. 7, pp. 129–146.

García-Barrios, L., Galván-Miyoshi, Y. M., Valsieso-Pérez, I. A., Masera, O. R., Bocco, G. and Vandermeer, J. (2009) 'Neotropical forest conservation, agricultural intensification, and rural out-migration: The Mexican experience', *Bioscience*, vol. 59, pp. 863–873.

Geiger, F., Bengtsson, J., Berendse, F., Weisser, W. W., Emmerson, M., Morales, M. B., Ceryngier, P., Liira, J., Tscharntke, T., Winqvist, C., Eggers, S., Bommarco, R., Pärt, T., Bretagnolle, V., Plantegenst, N., Clement, L. W., Dennis, C., Palmer, C., Oñate, J. J., Guerrero, I., Hawro, V., Aavik, T., Thies, C., Flohre, A., Hänke, S., Fischer, C., Goedhart, P. W. and Inchausti, P. (2010a) 'Persistent negative effects of pesticides on biodiversity and biological control potential on European farmland', *Basic and Applied Ecology*, vol. 11, pp. 97–105.

Geiger, F., de Snoo, G. R., Berendse, F., Guerrero, I., Morales, M. B., Oñate, J. J., Eggers, S., Pärt, T., Bommarco, M., Bengtsson, J., Clement, L. W., Weisser, W. W., Olszewski, A., Ceryngier, P., Hawro, V., Inchausti, P., Fischer, C., Flohre, A., Thies, C. and Tscharntke, T. (2010b) 'Landscape composition influences farm management effects on farmland birds in winter: A pan-European approach', *Agriculture, Ecosystems and Environment*, vol. 139, pp. 571–577.

Giller, K. E., Beare, M. H., Lavelle, P., Izac, A. M. and Swift, M. J. (1997) 'Agricultural intensification, soil biodiversity and agroecosystem function', *Applied Soil Ecology*, vol. 6, pp. 3–16.

Goulart, F. F., Salles, P. and Machado, R. B. (2013) 'How may agricultural matrix intensification affect understory birds in an Atlantic Forest landscape? A qualitative model on stochasticity and immigration', *Ecological Informatics*, vol. 18, pp. 93–106.

Goulart, F. F., Vandermeer, J., Perfecto, I. and da Matta-Machado, R. P. (2011) 'Frugivory by five bird species in agroforest home gardens of Pontal do Paranapanema, Brazil', *Agroforestry Systems*, vol. 82, pp. 239–246.

Guzmán, A., Link, A., Castillo, J. A. and Botero, J. E. (2016) 'Agroecosystems and primate conservation: Shade coffee as potential habitat for the conservation of Andean night monkeys in the northern Andes', *Agriculture, Ecosystems & Environment*, vol. 215, pp. 57–67.

Hanski, I., Moilanen, A., and Gyllenberg, M. (1996) 'Minimum viable metapopulation size', *American Naturalist*, vol. 147, pp. 527–541.

Harvey, C. A., Komar, O., Chazdon, R., Ferguson, B. G., Finegan, B., Griffith, D. M., Martinez-Ramos, M., Morales, H., Nigh, R., Soto-Pinto, L., Van Breugel, M. and Wishnie, M. (2008) 'Integrating agricultural landscapes with biodiversity conservation in the Mesoamerican hotspot', *Conservation Biology*, vol. 22, pp. 8–15.

Hayes, T. B., Case, P., Chui, S., Chung, D., Haeffele, C., Haston, K., Lee, M., Mai, V. P., Marjuoa, Y., Parker, J. and Tsui, M. (2006) 'Pesticide mixtures, endocrine disruption, and amphibian declines: Are we underestimating the impact?', *Environmental Health Perspectives*, vol. 114, p. 40.

Hecht, S. (2010) 'The new rurality: Globalization, peasants and the paradoxes of landscapes', *Land Use Policy*, vol. 27, pp. 161–169.

Hole, D. G., Perkins, A. J., Wilson, J. D., Alexander, I. H., Grice, P. V. and Evans, A. D. (2005) 'Does organic farming benefit biodiversity?', *Biological Conservation*, vol. 122, pp. 113–130.

Holt-Giménez, E. (2006) *Campesino a Campesino: Voices from Latin America's Farmer to Farmer Movement for Sustainable Agriculture*, Food First Books, Oakland CA, USA.

Hoogesteijn, A. and Hoogesteijn, R. (2010) 'Cattle ranching and biodiversity conservation as allies in South America's flooded savannas', *Great Plains Research*, vol. 20, pp. 37–50.

Howard, A. (1943) *An Agricultural Testament*. http://farmingsecrets.com/wp-content/uploads/2012/11/FS-FreeGifts-AnAgriculturalTestament.pdf

Jackson, L. E., Pascual, U. and Hodgkin, T. (2007) 'Utilizing and conserving agrobiodiversity in agricultural landscapes', *Agriculture, Ecosystems & Environment*, vol. 121, pp. 196–210.

Jackson, W. (2002) 'Natural systems agriculture: A truly radical alternative', *Agriculture, Ecosystems & Environment*, vol. 88, pp. 111–117.

Jha, S., Bacon, C. M., Philpott, S. M., Méndez, V. E., Läderach, P. and Rice, R. A. (2014) 'Shade coffee: Update on a disappearing refuge for biodiversity', *BioScience*, vol. 64, pp. 416–428.

Kareiva, P. and Wennergren, U. (1995) 'Connecting landscape patterns to ecosystem and population processes', *Nature*, vol. 373, pp. 299–302.

Kleijn, D., Kohler, F., Báldi, A., Batáry, P., Concepción, E. D., Clough, Y., Diaz, M., Gabriel, D., Holzschun, A., Knop, E., Kovács, A., Marshall, E. J. P., Tscharntke, T. and Verhulst, J. (2009) 'On the relationship between farmland biodiversity and land-use intensity in Europe', *Proceedings of the Royal Society of London B – Biological Sciences*, vol. 276, pp. 903–909.

Levins, R. (1969) 'Some demographic and genetic consequences of environmental heterogeneity for biological control', *Bulletin of the Entomological Society of America*, vol. 15, pp. 237–240.

MacArthur, R. H. and Wilson, E. O. (1967) *The Theory of Island Biogeography*, Vol. 1, Princeton University Press, Princeton, NJ, USA.

Mäder, P., Fliessbach, A., Dubois, D., Gunst, L., Fried, P. and Niggli, U. (2002) 'Soil fertility and biodiversity in organic farming', *Science*, vol. 296, pp. 1694–1697.

Magda, D., de Sainte Marie, C., Plantureux, S., Agreil, C., Amiaud, B., Mestelan, P. and Mihout, S. (2015) 'Integrating Agricultural and ecological goals into the management of species-rich grasslands: Learning from the flowering meadows competition in France', *Environmental Management*, vol. 56, pp. 1053–1064.

Martínez-Torres, M. E. and Rosset, P. M. (2014) 'Diálogo de saberes in La Vía Campesina: Food sovereignty and agroecology', *Journal of Peasant Studies*, vol. 41, pp. 979–997.

Mather, A. S. (1990) *Global Forest Resources*, Belhaven Press, London, UK.

McIntyre, B. D. (2009) *International Assessment of Agricultural Knowledge, Science and Technology for Development (IAASTD): Synthesis Report with Executive Summary: A Synthesis of the Global and Sub-Global IAASTD Reports* (No. E14–197), Global Program Review, Vol. 4, Issue 2, World Bank Group, Washington DC, USA.

Michon, G. and De Foresta, H. (1995) 'The Indonesian agro-forest model', pp. 90–106 in P. Halladay and D. A. Gilmour (eds.), *Conserving Biodiversity Outside Protected Areas: The Role of Traditional Ecosystems*, IUCN, Gland, Switzerland and Cambridge, UK.

Oliveira, L. C., Neves, L. G., Raboy, B. E. and Dietz, J. M. (2011) 'Abundance of jackfruit (*Artocarpus heterophyllus*) affects group characteristics and use of space by golden-headed lion tamarins (*Leontopithecus chrysomelas*) in cabruca agroforest', *Environmental Management*, vol. 48, pp. 248–262.

Padoch, C., Brondizio, E., Costa, S., Pinedo-Vasquez, M., Sears, R. R. and Siqueira, A. (2008) 'Urban forest and rural cities: Multi-sited households, consumption patterns, and forest resources in Amazonia', *Ecology and Society*, vol. 13, p. 2.

Perfecto, I. and Vandermeer, J. (2008) 'Biodiversity conservation in tropical agroecosystems', *Annals of the New York Academy of Sciences*, vol. 1134, pp. 173–200.

Perfecto, I. and Vandermeer, J. (2010) 'The agroecological matrix as alternative to the land-sparing/agriculture intensification model', *Proceedings of the National Academy of Sciences USA*, vol. 107, pp. 5786–5791.

Perfecto, I. and Vandermeer, J. (2015) *Coffee Agroecology: A New Approach for Understanding Agricultural Biodiversity, Ecosystem Services and Sustainable Development*, Routledge, London and New York.

Perfecto, I., Vandermeer, J. and Wright, A. (2009) *Nature's Matrix: Linking Agriculture, Conservation and Food Sovereignty*, Earthscan, London.

Phalan, B., Balmford, A., Green, R. E. and Scharlemann, J. P. (2011) 'Minimising the harm to biodiversity of producing more food globally', *Food Policy*, vol. 36, pp. S62–S71.

Relyea, R. A. (2005) 'The impact of insecticides and herbicides on the biodiversity and productivity of aquatic communities', *Ecological Applications*, vol. 15, pp. 618–627.

Rice, R. A. and Greenberg, R. (2000) 'Cacao cultivation and the conservation of biological diversity', *AMBIO: A Journal of the Human Environment*, vol. 29, pp. 167–173.

Rosset, P. M., Machin Sosa, B., Roque Jaime, A. M. and Ávila Lozano, D. R. (2011) 'The Campesino-to-Campesino agroecology movement of ANAP in Cuba: Social process methodology in the construction of sustainable peasant agriculture and food sovereignty', *The Journal of Peasant Studies*, vol. 38, pp. 161–191.

Rosset, P. M. and Martínez-Torres, M. E. (2012) 'Rural social movements and agroecology: Context, theory, and process', *Ecology and Society*, vol. 17, p. 17.

Rouget, M., Richardson, D. M. and Cowling, R. M. (2003) 'The current configuration of protected areas in the Cape Floristic Region, South Africa – reservation bias and representation of biodiversity patterns and processes', *Biological Conservation*, vol. 112, pp. 129–145.

Rudel, T. K., Coomes, O. T., Moran, E., Achard, F., Angelsen, A., Xu, J. and Lambin, E. (2005) 'Forest transitions: Towards a global understanding of land use change', *Global Environmental Change*, vol. 15, pp. 23–31.

Scales, B. R. and Marsden, S. J. (2008) 'Biodiversity in small-scale tropical agroforests: A review of species richness and abundance shifts and the factors influencing them', *Environmental Conservation*, vol. 35, pp. 160–172.

Schroth, G. and Harvey, C. A. (2007) 'Biodiversity conservation in cocoa production landscapes: An overview', *Biodiversity and Conservation*, vol. 16, pp. 2237–2244.

St. Barbe Baker, R. (1970) *My Life, My Trees*, Lutterworth Press, London, UK.

Tisovec, K. C., Cassano, C. R., Boubli, J. P. and Pardini, R. (2014) 'Mixed-species groups of marmosets and tamarins across a gradient of agroforestry intensification', *Biotropica*, vol. 46, pp. 248–255.

Tognelli, M. F., de Arellano, P. I. R. and Marquet, P. A. (2008) 'How well do the existing and proposed reserve networks represent vertebrate species in Chile?', *Diversity and Distributions*, vol. 14, pp. 148–158.

Tscharntke, T., Clough, Y., Wanger, T. C., Jackson, L., Motzke, I., Perfecto, I., Vandermeer, J. and Whitbread, A. (2012) 'Global food security, biodiversity conservation and the future of agricultural intensification', *Biological Conservation*, vol. 151, pp. 53–59.

Tscharntke, T., Leuschner, C., Zeller, M., Guhardja, E. and Bidin, A. (2007) *The Stability of Tropical Rainforest Margins, Linking Ecological, Economic and Social Constraints of Land Use and Conservation – An Introduction*, Springer, Berlin and Heidelberg, Germany.

Vandermeer, J., Perfecto, I. and Schellhorn, N. (2010) 'Propagating sinks, ephemeral sources and percolating mosaics: Conservation in landscapes', *Landscape Ecology*, vol. 25, pp. 509–518.

Wilson, E. O. and Willis, E. O. (1975) 'Applied biogeography', pp. 522–534 in M. L. Cody and J. M. Diamond (eds.), *Ecology and Evolution of Communities* Harvard University Press, Cambridge MA, USA.

# 16

# AGRICULTURAL BIODIVERSITY AND THE PROVISION OF ECOSYSTEM SERVICES

*Fabrice DeClerck*

## Introduction

Current agricultural intensification practices are the biggest threat to sustainable development and a major force behind the breaching of multiple planetary boundaries (Steffen et al., 2015b). The foods we produce from these systems struggle to nourish a growing global population where nearly 2 billion suffer from nutrient deficiencies and another 2 billion suffer from obesity.

Inasmuch as agricultural practices are important parts of the problem, they are likely to be our best bet for novel solutions to improve both human and environmental health. Increasing and improved use of agricultural biodiversity has the capacity to provide both food and nutrition security, providing the ingredients of healthy, culturally sensitive, and enjoyable meals. Mounting evidence suggests that producing food for diversified diets is often complementary with improving agriculture's sustainability record (Tilman and Clark, 2014). Agricultural biodiversity also provides the core ecosystem services that underpin sustainable agricultural intensification: pollination, pest control, and sustainably stored and sourced soil nutrients. Finally, as the planet's largest ecosystem, sustainable intensification of agricultural ecosystems has the capacity to provide multiple ecosystem services, converting agriculture from a net source to a net sink of greenhouse gases; reigning in planetary boundaries on phosphorus, nitrogen, and water; and creating a safe space for wild biodiversity.

Realizing agricultural biodiversity's potential to address these multiple global challenges, however, requires stronger interaction between business, policy, and research. Commitment from governments and leaders is necessary to support evidence and action that business-as-usual is no longer tolerable, that there is urgent need for structural change in agriculture and food systems, change that captures the true costs of agriculture and food systems (TEEBAgriFood, 2015; IPES-Food, 2016). Research must provide a better articulation of biodiversity's contribution to multiple sustainable development goals, and improved indicators and indices that facilitate impact and progress towards both environmental and human well-being targets.

## Agriculture and planetary boundaries

The first decade of the 21st century has seen a renewed emphasis on human impact on the global environment, and raised important questions regarding our vulnerability in the face of exponential changes across a multitude of biophysical, economic, and social indicators (Steffen et al., 2015a). The force of this influence is considered to be on the order of geological timescales – signifying that evidence of human activities is indelible and visible in the geological record. As such, it has been proposed that we should rename this era the Anthropocene (Steffen et al., 2007) in honour of . . . ourselves?

One of the most visible signs of our activity, obvious to anyone who has ever sat in the window seat of an airplane, or passed time on Google Earth, is the extent of our footprint on land use. Most studied have been biophysical planetary boundaries (Rockstrom et al., 2009; Steffen et al., 2015b) including (a) biochemical flows, notably N and P, (b) freshwater use, (c) land-system change, (d) biosphere integrity, (e) climate change, (f) novel entities, (g) stratospheric ozone depletion, (h) atmospheric aerosol loading, and (i) ocean acidification. The influence of agriculture on each of these boundaries is immediately evident, particularly on those boundaries that have been the most surpassed – biosphere integrity, nitrogen, and phosphorus. Agriculture contributes to between 19% and 29% of total GHG emissions (US EPA, 2011; Vermeulen et al., 2012), uses 69% of freshwater resources (AQUASTAT, 2014), and 34% of the terrestrial, ice-free surface of the planet, accounting for 31% of wild biodiversity loss (Ramankutty et al., 2008). It is the primary driver for the substantial breach of the planetary boundary for phosphorous and nitrogen (Carpenter and Bennett, 2011; Steffen et al., 2015b).

What surprises many in reviewing these planetary boundaries is the degree to which biosphere integrity is the single most surpassed boundary. Climate change dominates the global agenda, and certainly is a critical boundary; yet is still classified as 'within the zone of uncertainty (increasing risk)' by Steffen et al. (2015a), whereas biosphere integrity is classified as 'beyond zone of uncertainty (high risk)'. The means by which Steffen et al. (2015a) classified biosphere integrity is revealing. The boundary comprises two interim control variables: genetic diversity, a measure of global extinction rates, and functional diversity, estimated by the Biodiversity Intactness Index (Scholes and Biggs, 2005). These measures articulate two important dimensions of biodiversity in the global operating system. Genetic diversity represents the evolutionary information bank that ultimately determines global resilience and our option space for adaptation (**Box 16.1** *Some important definitions with an agricultural twist*). Genetic diversity is the final sum result of interactions between species over 3.7 billion years (Wilson, 2016). The second captures biodiversity's functional contribution to earth system functioning (Naeem et al., 2012) – or the functions to which biodiversity contributes in providing multiple ecosystem services (Díaz and Cabido, 2001; Flynn et al., 2009).

Both dimensions of biosphere integrity, despite continuing challenges to identify appropriate measures, emphasize biodiversity's role as the global operating system. Inasmuch as each of our personal computers has an operating system that allows us to run various programs, surf the web, check email and 'like' things on Facebook, earth's biodiversity provides a very similar role – providing essential functions that support human life. When we alter biodiversity through human activities, we fundamentally alter, for better or for worse, the functions and services biodiversity provides. There are now dedicated branches of ecology that study the relationship between biodiversity and ecosystem services (Loreau et al., 2002; Naeem et al., 2009). Similarly, in 2012, the Intergovernmental Panel on Biodiversity and Ecosystem Services (IPBES) was formed. Modeled on the Nobel Prize winning IPCC, IPBES was created to 'strengthen the science-policy interface for biodiversity and ecosystem services for the conservation and sustainable use of biodiversity, long-term human well-being and sustainable development' (Díaz et al., 2015, p. 1).

The need for such an organization comes with the recognition that the earth's biodiversity is threatened (Butchart et al., 2010), and that its loss has consequences that extend beyond the disappearance of charismatic species such as pandas and redwood trees, and which include consequences for the numerous ecosystem services provided by both wild and cultivated species

## Box 16.1 Some important definitions with an agricultural twist

**Agrobiodiversity:** The biodiversity of agricultural systems, often specifically referring to cultivated species and their wild relatives. Sometimes termed agricultural biodiversity. This can include several levels of diversity including genetic diversity, species diversity, and land use diversity which is often referred to as landscape diversity.

**Agroecological intensification:** The intensification of ecological processes in agricultural systems in order to support agricultural production and resilience.

**Agroecology:** The study of ecological principles and practices in agriculture.

**Agroecosystems:** Ecosystems that are managed by humans for the production of food, fuel, and fibre. The definition focuses on the species found in agricultural landscapes and their interaction with the environment; it does not prejudge any sustainability parameters or distinguish between types of agricultural systems, ecological or conventional.

**Biodiversity:** Biological diversity or biodiversity means the variability among living organisms from all sources including inter alia, terrestrial, marine, and other aquatic ecosystems and the ecological complexes of which they are part; this includes diversity within species, between species, and of ecosystems.

**Cultural Ecosystem Services:** The material and non-material benefits of ecosystems which include the spiritual, inspirational, educational, and recreational. While these are often some of the most challenging ecosystem services to capture, they are often the most motivating and are important drivers of ecosystem conservation.

**Ecological agriculture:** Agricultural systems that integrate agroecological principles.

**Ecosystem services:** The benefits that nature provides for humans.

**Genetic diversity:** The total number of characteristics in the genetic makeup of a species; it is distinguished from genetic variability, which describes the tendency of genetic characteristics to vary.

**Landscape diversity:** Frequently refers to the diversity of land uses in a landscape for example mosaic landscapes.

**Provisioning Ecosystem Services:** The products obtained from ecosystems such as food, fibres, medicines, water. These relate to material tangible goods.

**Regulating Ecosystem Services:** The benefits obtained from the regulation of ecosystem processes typically related to climate regulation, or the regulation of biogeochemical flows including nitrogen, phosphorus, and carbon.

**Species diversity:** The number of species in a system. In agricultural systems, this can be the number of species in a field or farming system, a farm, or a landscape. These are roughly equivalent to alpha, beta, and gamma diversity in ecology.

**Supporting Ecosystem Services:** The services necessary for the production of all other ecosystem services. In some classifications, these have been subsumed into regulating services and include such services as soil formation, nutrient cycling, and primary production.

**Sustainable intensification:** Actions to increase food production from existing farmland while minimizing pressure on the environment.

**Wild biodiversity:** Non-cultivated biodiversity.

(Naeem, 2002). It supports the Convention on Biological Diversity through the production of regional and thematic assessments of biodiversity and ecosystem services. Ecosystem services are the conditions and processes through which ecosystems, and the species that make them up, sustain and fulfill human life (Daily, 1997). There are many dimensions of ecosystem services that are increasingly garnering attention. Ecosystem services have been classified as provisioning, regulating, cultural, and supporting and while several classifications exist, we recommend considering the classification maintained by the Common International Classification of Ecosystem Services (CICES; summarized in **Box 16.1**). We also favour the conceptual framework provided by TEEB for Agriculture and Food (TEEBAgriFood, 2015), which emphasizes biodiversity's role as the source of many of the services to and from agriculture.

## The Anthropocene's largest biome: agricultural ecosystems

The term 'ecosystems' conjures images of natural systems: forests, wetlands, grasslands. However, in the strictest sense, the term simply refers to a community of organisms interacting with each other and with their environment such that energy is exchanged and system-level processes, such as the cycling of elements, emerge. As such, agroecosystems are the community of organisms found in agricultural systems and their interactions. These can be studied using the same tools and processes applied to natural ecosystems. In the Anthropocene, agroecosystems are the world largest ecosystem, covering more than 38% of the global ice-free landmass. Agroecoystems are also those systems that are most directly linked to human well-being for their capacity to provisioning ecosystem services such as food, fuel, and fibre. It may seem obvious, but by 2050, there will be 9 billion humans dependent on the services provides by agricultural ecosystems (DeClerck, 2016). What is less obvious to many is that these ecosystems do more than provide food, but that decisions we make in how we manage these ecosystems and the biodiversity they harbour determine a large suite of ecosystem services provided to, and received from, agricultural systems.

We propose that there are four critical biodiversity and agriculture interactions that merit much greater attention. We address all four in this chapter: (1) agriculture as a safe space for wild biodiversity, (2) the services that biodiversity provides to agriculture (agricultural ecosystem services), (3) the non-agricultural ecosystem services provided by biodiversity, and (4) the role of agricultural biodiversity in food system resilience.

## Getting a grip on biodiversity

Biodiversity is deceivingly simple as a term – yet it hides much complexity which can drive important assumptions and ultimately confusion (**Box 16.1**). The standard definition of biodiversity is the variety and variability of life on earth – this is often interpreted as the number of species in a determinate space, which ecologists refer to as species richness. This is distinct from ecological measures of diversity which include measures of relative abundances of species in a community (e.g. the Shannon or Simpson measures of diversity). This definition often hides four important, and all too often unspoken, nuances: what kind of diversity, what level of diversity, what measure of diversity, what use of diversity. It is common for dialogues around diversity to be imprecise about these dimensions, which can lead to important assumptions – this is particularly common when specialists discuss biodiversity with generalist audiences, leading to accusations that biodiversity and ecosystem services are opaque concepts that are not policy-ready, or even between specialists addressing different domains.

## What kind of biodiversity?

Improved use of diversity in agricultural landscapes requires specifying to which diversity we are referring. In agroecology, differentiating between managed and wild biodiversity can be useful (Karp et al., 2013). Managed diversity refers to species specifically selected by the farmer – most commonly, the crop and crop companion species (e.g. coffee as the crop species and shade trees are the companion species in coffee agroforests). Wild diversity refers to species that are naturally occurring and co-exist in agricultural lands. Agroecologists frequently study both, though those with greater agronomic background tend of focus on managed diversity, whereas those with a conservation biology background frequently focus on agroecological contributions from wild biodiversity. The term 'wild biodiversity' leaves much to be desired, however, as there are numerous wild species that interact with crop species in agricultural systems, notably pests and pathogens, but also many species that provide beneficial roles such as pollination and pest control (Ricketts et al., 2004; Karp et al., 2013; see also Gurr et al. and Gemmill-Herren, Chapters 6 and 7 of this Handbook). Many agroecological applications are designed to indirectly manage this wild biodiversity to favour the positive interactions and reduce the negative ones. Integrated pest management, for example, includes many elements of managing biodiversity to decrease crop damage. This often entails managing pest predators, thus increasing a pest control ecosystem services to reduce a crop loss ecosystem disservice. While it is relatively easy to classify and describe crop species selected by farmers at field, farm, or landscape scales, classifying wild biodiversity remains challenging with an as-of-yet undefined subset of species that interact or do not interact with cropping systems.

## What level of biodiversity?

Talk of biodiversity most often conjures images of species diversity – however, it can also refer to diversity at other levels of ecological organization: genetic, species, community, and ecosystem. Each of these levels can be measured, and can have an effect on agroecological processes – however, the mechanisms and types of services provided are often dependent on specific levels (Ostergard et al., 2009).

At the finest level, genetic diversity is an important element. Because genetic diversity is nested in higher levels, it is often implied to be the genetic diversity within a single species. In agricultural systems, there is, for example, interest in increasing the genetic diversity of monocultural cropping systems as a means of increasing field resilience to pests and diseases, or other forms of environmental abiotic stresses (Jarvis et al., 2011; Mulumba et al., 2012).

Species diversity represents the diversity of species in a defined unit of space or time. In agricultural systems, increasing species diversity refers to multi-species cropping systems. Whether these are polycultures such as agroforestry systems where species are mixed in the same field or crop rotations or where species are alternated in time. In some cases, multi-species field margins are considered to increase species diversity, even when adjacent to a monocultural crop and are managed in a way so that the species in these margins provide specific services to agricultural fields, or intercept soil, nutrients, or pests flowing from fields. In such cases, field margins can be managed with high levels of wild (and cultivated) biodiversity which play specific functions such as habitat for pollinators or for pest predators, or physical barriers or filters to sediment and nutrients.

Field and farm diversity are the next level, akin to ecological types in natural systems. This is often referred to as landscape diversity, which is somewhat of a misnomer since it refers to the diversity of land uses within a landscape. Alternatively some refer to 'mosaic' landscapes in reference to the high diversity and arrangement of alternate land uses (Perfecto and Vandermeer, Chapter 15 of this Handbook). Many benefits of diversification can be maintained even if species diversity remains low within a field, as long as the species diversity between fields remains high (akin to high beta diversity in natural systems). High field diversity typically translates into high landscape diversity – or cropping systems that have a high diversity of land uses. Mosaic landscapes can disrupt the movement of plant pests, and reduce the likelihood of large-scale pest outbreaks (Avelino et al., 2012). Integrated landscape management attempts to facilitate strategic use of landscape diversity to support multiple ecosystem services but often require community coordination, or specific institutions that enable landscape planning and targeting (DeClerck et al., 2010; Estrada-Carmona et al., 2014).

Measures of alpha, beta, and gamma diversity which are common metrics of natural systems can be used for the evaluation biodiversity in a system. The total species diversity in a landscape (gamma diversity) is determined by the mean species diversity in field or farms at a more local scale (alpha diversity) and the differentiation among those habitats (beta diversity) (Ludwig and Reynolds, 1988).

## *What measure of diversity?*

There are entire tomes written on measures of diversity into which depth we do not go here (see Ludwig and Reynolds, 1988; Naeem et al., 2009). It is important to recognize, however, that measures of diversity can simply imply the richness of the unit of measure: how many species, how many field types? Diversity in contrast includes a measure of abundance or relative abundance which emphasizes not only how many different types, but which of these types are common versus rare. There is also a growing interest in measures of functional diversity, which rather than considering the taxonomic or evolutionary relationship between species, considers the functional role that they play such as nitrogen fixation, pollination, or pest consumption (Wood et al., 2015), or in providing for human nutrition (DeClerck et al., 2011; Remans et al., 2011).

## *What use of diversity: sampling versus complementary effects*

The late 1990s was marked by an important debate in biodiversity and ecosystem service research. Several studies were showing that increased diversity, particularly in a series of grassland experiments, had greater productivity than species poor mixtures (Tilman et al., 1996; Hector et al., 1999; Loreau and Hector, 2001; Tilman et al., 2001). Debate was centred on whether this increased productivity was due to a sampling effect, that increasing diversity had simply improved the odds of including a productive species, or if it involved a complementary effect due to niche differentiation and synergistic interactions between species. For example, the nitrogen fixed by a legume and made available to an adjacent grass species, or two species with different root lengths acquiring water and nutrient from different soil depths, are two simple examples of complementarity.

The notion of increasing the use of agricultural biodiversity often implies making use of the complementary effect and increasing the number of species at the plot level. However, the sampling effect is just as important in agroecology and is the basis of global efforts to conserve agricultural biodiversity both *in situ* and *ex situ* (in fields and in gene banks, as described in Part 6 of this Handbook). Ensuring that this diversity is conserved, documented, and available is an important manifestation of the sampling effect. Thereby, enabling farmers, breeders, and agronomists to find the best varieties, landraces, or species for a specific function and increasing productivity or the provision of other agroecological services through the targeted use of that species is an appropriate use of biodiversity in agriculture. In light of increasing environmental, economic, and social conditions, ensuring that our library of species and varieties, both in field and out, is available, documented, and curated is fundamental.

## *Systems-based approaches: TEEBAgriFood*

Recognizing, valuing, and managing these multiple domains of diversity, and their contribution to agroecological functions, quickly becomes an exercise in complexity. Gliessman and colleagues noted many years ago, 'Understanding the ecological foundation of how diversity functions, and taking advantage of this complexity, rather than eliminating it, has been argued to be the *only* strategy that will lead to sustainability' (Gliessman et al., 1998). Frameworks are helpful tools for organizing and categorizing the information behind complex systems. Here we present TEEB's framework which is valuable for contextualizing the multiple dimensions of biodiversity's interactions within production systems.

In 2014, The Economics of Ecosystems and Biodiversity (TEEB) launched an effort to develop a specific TEEB framework for food and agriculture. The resulting framework (**Figure 16.1**

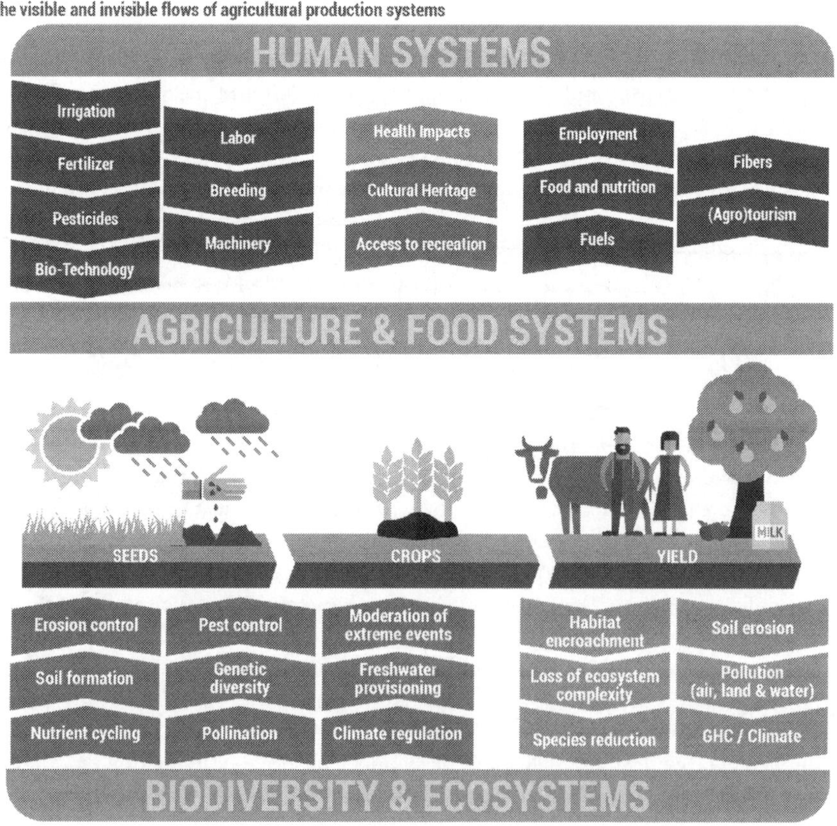


*Figure 16.1* Framework for eco-agri-food systems developed by The Economics of Ecosystems and Biodiversity for Food and Agriculture representing the interaction between human systems, agricultural systems, and ecosystems

*Source*: From The Economics of Ecosystems and Biodiversity (TEEBAgriFood) (2015).

*Framework for eco-agri-food systems*) provides a particularly clear way to consider the role of biodiversity in agriculture and food systems. The TEEBAgriFood framework identifies three systems that interact to create food systems: (1) human systems, (2) agricultural systems, and (3) ecosystems. Naturally, agricultural systems are located between the human and ecosystems and represent human interaction with nature for the production of food. While the intent of the framework is to capture key interactions linking these to human and environmental health, its particular strength is in describing the impacts and interactions on the ground – the fields, farms, and landscapes, where food is grown. Considering **Figure 16.1**, the top two rows describe major interactions between human systems and agricultural systems. These are recognizable to anyone working in agronomy and agriculture and describe the inputs needed to transform seeds to crops, and hence to crop yield. They also describe the outputs, particularly in terms of employment, food and nutrition, fuels, and fibres. From an ecosystem service point of view, these are traditionally classified as provisioning services. In the Millennium Ecosystem Assessment (MEA), these were the only ecosystem services that were observed to be increasing (MEA, 2005).

Adding the biodiversity and ecosystem row makes an important step in highlighting the invisible positive (and negative) flows of biodiversity and ecosystems to and from agricultural systems. Increasingly, there is a recognition of the negative externalities in terms of biodiversity and habitat loss, and contributions to greenhouse gases, pollution, land degradation, and public health. There are a growing number of programs and projects that aim to decrease the environmental impacts of agriculture. These are often counted in conservation or sustainable agriculture programs. We consider them in the next section, 'A safe space for wild biodiversity'.

More interesting perhaps are the 'invisible' benefits to agriculture and food systems which describe in the broadest terms biodiversity's contribution to agriculture. These include ecosystem services such as erosion control, soil nutrient cycling and fertility, pollination, and pest control services. As an interesting sidebar, my post-doc reminds me that these are invisible only in modern systems, but quite often very visible in traditional systems – that is, that visibility or value is a social value determined by the user rather than an ecological value. Each of these services can be provided by managing biodiversity in agricultural systems, or can be managed through the addition of external inputs such as fertilizers, pesticides, and herbicides. Without prejudging which input is more sustainable, productive, or resilient, the TEEBAgriFood framework ensures that biodiversity and ecosystems are included and tallied both on the input and output side of the agri-food system equation. We discuss biodiversity's contribution to agricultural systems in the section 'Agricultural biodiversity: agriculture's invisible workhorse'.

A non-intuitive point that TEEBAgriFood makes regarding biodiversity and ecosystem services in agricultural systems is that the notion of provisioning services as described in many ecosystem service frameworks may, in effect, be of little utility outside of subsistence and hunter/gatherer systems (forests and fisheries). It begs the question of classifying food production as an ecosystem service when comparing, for example, the yield of conventional versus organic maize as provisioning services. One system produces food with important ecosystem disservices, while the latter produces food with important ecosystem services: the environmental dependencies and externalities of the provisioning services of both are completely different. It thus suggests that of the three ecosystem service types, regulating services might be the most important focal topic in agroecosystem service research. Cultural services are extremely important in food systems, but have proven particularly difficult to define and to associate with measures of sustainability. While we recognize cultural services as an important motivational force, we have not, however, discussed them further in this chapter.

The third dimension that relates to the TEEBAgriFood conceptual frameworks is that while services to agriculture are well captured, as are impacts of agriculture, each of the 'invisible negative flows' can hypothetically be made positive. While this would not permit us to change the direction of the arrows in the figure – it would change their colour to 'invisible' positive benefits. This is one of the underlying assumptions of landscape multifunctionality: that decisions we make regarding the management of agricultural systems determine whether the systems become net sinks or net sources of services (Tilman and Clark, 2014). It also recognizes that while agriculture can be a tremendous driver of these major externalities, it also has the greatest potential to be the single most important solution for reversing these trends (Foley et al., 2011).

## A safe space for wild biodiversity

The biosphere integrity planetary boundary confirms what many biodiversity scientists have been claiming all along: the current loss of biodiversity globally is of unprecedented proportions with extinction rates that are on the order of 100–1,000 times background rates. Agricultural expansion and invasive species are primary drivers with some estimates suggesting that agriculture accounts for 31% of biodiversity loss (Brook et al., 2008). Solutions to halting or reducing this biodiversity loss are highly controversial; some argue having divided conservation biology into two distinct camps focusing on the intrinsic and instrumental values of biodiversity. Amongst the intrinsic values, for example, are proposals such as E. O. Wilson's recent 'Half Earth' (2016) which calls for protecting half of the global landmass for biodiversity. This is supported by conservation biologists such as Soule (2014) who call for a continued focus on the role of protected areas. This branch of conservation biology often argues that biodiversity should be conserved for its own sake and is concerned that conservation efforts that focus on biodiversity's instrumental value risk communicating that some biodiversity does not need to be conserved. Conservation biologists that focus on intrinsic values often fall into the land sparing world view – suggesting that agriculture and conservation should occur in distinct locations with the most productive lands for either food production, or biodiversity conservation clearly delineated and set aside for those specific functions.

Much of the focus on conservation for its intrinsic value entails biodiversity conservation in protected areas where human influence is minimal, and where conservation objectives are the primary goal. Classic examples are the National Parks and Wilderness areas that were founding actions of the U.S. conservation effort supported by iconic conservationists John Muir and Theodore Roosevelt. However, agricultural lands can also provide important conservation space for wild biodiversity. Much research on biodiversity conservation in agriculture has been conducted, including under the auspices of 'countryside biogeography' (Daily et al., 2001; Ricketts et al., 2001; Hughes et al., 2002; Daily et al., 2003; Horner-Devine et al., 2003; Luck and Daily, 2003; Mayfield and Daily, 2005; Ranganathan et al., 2007; Sekercioglu et al., 2007). Studies under this theme have highlighted the conservation value of mosaic landscapes where natural vegetation is embedded in agricultural matrices with evidence that the land use diversification of agricultural landscapes increases diversity by creating novel and more diversified habitats (Fahrig et al., 2011). Many of these studies have likewise demonstrated that agricultural land uses that are analogs to natural vegetation of a region have greater conservation value than agricultural land uses that differ from background vegetation structure and composition. This has driven significant research on the conservation value of shaded coffee-based (Caudill et al., 2015), cacao-based (Deheuvels et al., 2014) and livestock-based (Harvey et al., 2005, 2006) agroforests. In these examples, efforts are made to understand the contribution of agriculture to providing habitat for wild biodiversity.

While agricultural systems can be managed to increase conservation values, and indeed many species of conservation interest can be found in agricultural systems of different types, they often struggle to protect species of greatest conservation concern. Conservation values are often limited to production systems that are amenable to conservation interventions – particularly shade-tolerant perennial crops such as coffee and cacao. The conservation value of annual or horticultural crops is generally much lower and much more challenging requiring more research and novel ideas.

Increasing the habitat value of agricultural land uses primarily entails changing the vegetation structure and configuration of that land use, or changing the type and timing of management actions. For the former, agroforestry systems provide some of the best examples of vegetation management in agricultural systems, increasing tree density and diversity as a means of increasing habitat value. Management practices have centred on the type and timing of agricultural management activities with numerous studies focusing on the value of organic agriculture on conservation values. Timing of these activities can also be important, for example our own work recommending that pruning of coffee plants in Central America not be undertaken between March and June when birds are nesting and particularly vulnerable (Martinez-Salinas and DeClerck, 2010). Similar recommendations have been made for grassland management, for example, to avoid harvesting actions when young are fledging. In other cases, farmers can take specific actions to increase the conservation values of their agricultural lands. In addition to the habitat value provided by management of agricultural landscapes and mosaics, the arrangement of agricultural land uses within a landscape plays an important role in facilitating the movement of species between patches of habitat. This can occur at multiple scales. In Costa Rican landscapes, we have, for example, found evidence that strategically placed agroforestry systems can provide important dispersal routes between forest patches, and that these are used by forest-dependent species in both individual and inter-generational movements.

Some conservation biologists who have recognized this important contribution of agricultural systems to connectivity have argued that in an age of climate change, the land sparing/land sharing debate is a moot point: conservation is fully dependent on land sharing to facilitate the migration of wild biodiversity to core habitat with climate shifts (**Figure 16.2** *Land-sparing versus land-sharing*).

*Figure 16.2* Land-sparing versus land-sharing

*Note*: This is a fascinating debate in agriculture and conservation, however the lack of scale definition in the debate causes important problems. Some consider land-sharing to mean full integration of agriculture from the field scale up, whereas others discuss the debate using entire landscapes as the based unit. We expect that like the Escher image on the left, the best strategy is maintaining the entire gradient across all scales as in the image on the right so that they become completely distinguishable, yet completely indistinguishable.

*Source*: Credit: inspired by a keynote given by Tony Simons, director of ICRAF at a Landscapes for People, Food and Nature meeting, Nairobi, Kenya, 2012.

## Agricultural biodiversity: agriculture's invisible workhorse

Agriculture is fully dependent on biodiversity. This is often a point that is missing from the land-sparing/land-sharing debate. The exclusion of biodiversity from agriculture would lead to the development of an agriculture whose negative externalities and dependencies would be wholly unsustainable, and unacceptable.

That biodiversity provides services to agriculture is not a novel concept. In fact, it is the fundamental basis of agroecology and agroforestry, each of which manipulates agricultural biodiversity to provide specific agroecological functions. Classic examples include increasing plant diversity in field margins as a habitat for pest predators, agroforestry systems that increase field tree diversity to provide pest control and moisture management functions, or crop rotations as a means of both pest and soil fertility management (Rapidel et al., 2011). Agroecological functions that make use of biodiversity aim to address key agricultural production functions, namely: soil quality and conservation, diversity of planting material, weed management, pest reduction, and pollination, amongst others. Management options that permit the integration of agricultural biodiversity are not limited to different polycultures, but can include the management of field scale monocultures in space (diversified landscape composition), and time (e.g. crop rotation).

Considering biodiversity's contribution to ecosystem services of importance to agriculture requires careful consideration of the ecological mechanisms by which agroecosystem services arise. These are well covered in the agroecological and agroforestry literature amongst others (**Table 16.1** *Examples of how changes in agricultural biodiversity influence agroecologial services*).

Managing diversity in agriculture systems is knowledge intensive and complex, but it is not impossible. While **Table 16.1** provides a snapshot of the ecological levels and mechanisms that provide services to agriculture by considering each service and scale independently (following the sort of reductionist approach favoured by researchers), in reality, the management of these services requires an integrative approach that considers the management of multiple services at multiple spatial scales. It should also act over the course of at least one full cropping cycle, with some services requiring multi-year considerations. While farmers have utilized a systems approach for millennia, it is only more recently that systems-based approaches are gaining greater focus in agriculture and conservation.

Systems that utilize diversity are varied. They extend from rustic or traditional production systems rich in farmer observations and interactions with the land, to modern systems incorporating precision agriculture techniques that rely on careful environmental monitoring and measurements to guide the application of agriculture inputs and reduce externalities (Garbach et al., 2017). There is no 'one size fits all' approach – one of the advantages of integrating diversity into production systems is that the only steadfast rule is that one should maintain diversity because of the functions it provides, and because it maintains important space available for future use by society – today's, and tomorrow's.

Scale is a critical issue in the use of diversity in production systems. Rather than assuming that biodiversity should be maintained at any single scale, such as mixed cropping systems or polycultures, it is important to let the management objective determine the scale at which diversification should be managed and the form of diversification that best matches these objectives. Field scale genetic and species diversification is often possible from both an ecological as well as an economic point of view for horticultural crops – mixed fields of fresh produce supplying the diversified baskets of many Community Supported Agricultural systems is a good example of a farming system built around diversification. However, species diversification can be much more challenging with grain crops which require large expanses of land, and simultaneous yield maturation for mechanized harvesting. In these systems, increasing genetic diversity is an option – so

Table 16.1 Examples of how changes in agricultural biodiversity influence agroecological services

| *Increasing this diversity. . .* | *. . .provides this service. . .* | *by. . . .* |
|---|---|---|
| Genetic | Soil fertility | N/A |
| Species | | • Including nitrogen fixing species can be an important source of soil N and organic matter.<br>• Differing plant materials provide a more diversified food source for soil communities and > regular nutrient availability. |
| Fields | | N/A |
| Landscape | | N/A |
| Genetic | Pest and disease regulation | • Increasing chance of resistant strain or variety. |
| Species | | • Increasing the odds of a resistant species.<br>• Creating an inhospitable habitat for target pest. |
| Fields | | • Decrease pest movement pest between fields. |
| Landscape | | • Decrease pest movement, and/or increase predator movement. |
| Genetic | Pollination | • Increases pollinator resistance to disturbance and resilience of pollination service. |
| Species | | |
| Fields | | • If staggered, flowering periods can provide continuous nectar source to pollinators. |
| Landscape | | • Increase connectivity and access to crop by pollinators. |
| Genetic | Moderation of extreme events | • Increased odds of unaffected variety. |
| Species | | • Increased odds of unaffected species.<br>• Creates a environmental buffer to extremes. |
| Fields | | • Increased odds unaffected fields. |
| Landscape | | • Increased odds of unaffected farm. |
| Genetic | Soil conservation | N/A |
| Species | | • Combined perennial and annual crops or different phenologies and rooting depths maintains ground cover year round. |
| Fields | | • Low erosivity fields in vulnerable sites. |
| Landscape | | N/A |

long as maturation times do not vary. Within these systems, diversification in time in the form of crop rotations or in space in the form of maintaining diversity in field margins, riparian buffers, or adjacent fields may provide some of the diversification benefits sought (Ricketts et al., 2004).

In certain cases, large expanses of monocultures can actually benefit diversity in agricultural landscapes. This is evident in our analysis of California rice systems. While many associate California with an arid desert-like environment where flooded rice would be inappropriate, the state is hyperdiverse with ecosystems ranging from the Mojave desert to temperate rainforest cloaked in coastal redwoods. Possibly the state's most undervalued ecosystem from a conservation point of view is the Central Valley, though second only to 'Silicon Valley' from an economic perspective. The Central Valley historically was one of the world's largest wetlands covering 18,000 $km^2$ of the valley, forming a core element of the Pacific migratory flyway. This coverage has been reduced to just 600 $km^2$ today. Most agricultural land uses of the valley are highly productive, producing a large variety of fruits, nuts, and vegetables, but most of these land uses are inhospitable to migratory waterfowl. A relatively recent (1996) shift to winter flooding of 200,000 ha of rice fields has changed this by recreating a large expanse of wetland habitat that effectively doubles the area of winter habitat for migratory waterfowl, adding 800 km$^2$ when it is most needed (Elphick and Oring, 2003). In this particular case, a large expanse of monocultural rice favours the conservation of hundreds of species of migratory waterfowl because of fallow season flooding. Partnerships with conservation and state organizations vary water depths during the fallow to favour a diversity of shorebirds and waders. While an atypical example, the California rice case encourages considering which diversity outcomes are sought, and carefully understanding the mechanisms and scale at which diversity should be managed.

## Agriculture as the final battleground for sustainability

The third dimension of biodiversity in agricultural landscapes considers the services or disservices provided by agriculture that are transferred off-farm – or ecosystem services *from* agriculture. There appears to be an inherent assumption that agricultural systems are about provisioning services, whereas forest systems are the chief providers of regulating services. This assumption drives debates on land-sparing versus land-sharing. This is an inherently false assumption, however, as agriculture ecosystems may be our best option for securing regulating, cultural, and habitat services as well. In contrast to protected areas, we have a greater history of managing agricultural landscapes, and options for combining built and green infrastructure to secure service to and from agriculture are limited only by our creativity and ingenuity. In protected areas, by contrast – environmental ethics would dictate that we should limit human interventions as much as possible. Thus, while protected areas have incredible value and must remain a critical global priority, we are limited to the services that these areas would provide with minimal human intervention.

## Conclusions: a diversity of examples for diversification

Diversity is a complex topic. Mentioning agricultural biodiversity or agrobiodiversity in conversation does not conjure any single image. Many scientists and practitioners who specialize in genetic diversity think of crop wild relatives and the importance of protecting centres of origins of these crops, or of maintaining genetic diversity in fields either as a conservation tool (Hajjar et al., 2008; Jarvis et al., 2011), or as a means of reducing the incidence of pests and diseases (Mulumba et al., 2012). To others who work on agroecological approaches, agrobiodiversity conjures images of polycultures and species mixtures at field and farm scales (Ponisio et al., 2015). Here the interactions between different crops are an important management tool for supporting production systems such as in many organic farms, or agroforestry systems. There is also a growing community of agroecologists interested in the contribution of wild biodiversity to providing specific functions to agriculture. Best known here are the numerous studies on pollination by bees and wild pollinators (Kremen et al., 2007; Ricketts et al., 2008; Lebuhn et al., 2013) and the role of birds (Philpott et al., 2009; Karp et al., 2013; Frishkoff et al., 2014) and predatory insects in pest management including studies that might be more traditionally classified as Integrated Pest Management (Cheatham et al., 2009). More recently, agroecologists are coming to consider how landscape diversity contributes to both conservation and production functions (Fahrig et al., 2011). Conservation biologists, who as recently as ten years ago shunned agricultural lands as overly influenced by human interventions, now commonly collaborate with farming communities in securing the conservation value of these landscapes (Mace, 2014). Largely missing still is a deeper understanding of the literally invisible contributions made by soil biodiversity, which is likely the single most important and undermanaged form of diversity in agriculture – despite its contribution to agroecological metabolism (Beed et al., Chapter 8 of this Handbook).

The multiple functions, dependencies, impacts, and contributions made by agricultural landscapes to human well-being and biodiversity conservation have increasingly made them places of both conceptual and practical integration. It is, therefore, not surprising that agricultural systems and landscapes provide as many examples as they do, and that there continues to be interest in landscape multifunctionality. While environmental sustainability has driven much of the change in how agriculture is conducted, there is growing evidence that health dimensions as mediated by diversity and quality of food produced, and impacts of agricultural practices on human health are increasingly becoming influential drivers of agricultural management options. We suspect that social issues, particularly around employment quantity and quality, will become more important. This evolution of agricultural systems research, following similar trends in conservation biology (Mace, 2014), calls for more interdisciplinary approaches that better integrate the social and the ecological sciences and metrics that articulate the impacts of human interventions on agroecological resilience, adaptability, and environmental change.

## References

AQUASTAT (2014) *Infographics on Water Resources and Uses*, FAO, Rome, Italy.

Avelino, J., Romero-Guridan, A., Cruz-Cuellar, H. and DeClerck, F. A. J. (2012) 'Landscape context and scale differentially impact coffee leaf rust, coffee berry borer and coffee root-knot nematodes', *Ecological Applications*, vol. 22, pp. 584–596.

Brook, B. W., Sodhi, N. S. and Bradshaw, C. J. A. (2008) 'Synergies among extinction drivers under global change', *Trends in Ecology & Evolution*, vol. 23, pp. 453–460.

Butchart, S. H. M., Walpole, M., Collen, B., van Strien, A., Scharlemann, J. P. W., Almond, R. E. A., Baillie, J. E. M., Bomhard, B., Brown, C., Bruno, J., Carpenter, K. E., Carr, G. M., Chanson, J., Chenery, A. M., Csirke, J., Davidson, N. C., Dentener, F., Foster, M., Galli, A., Galloway, J. N., Genovesi, P., Gregory, R. D., Hockings, M., Kapos, V., Lamarque, J. F., Leverington, F., Loh, J., McGeoch, M. A., McRae, L., Minasyan, A., Morcillo, M. H., Oldfield, T. E. E., Pauly, D., Quader, S., Revenga, C., Sauer, J. R., Skolnik, B. S., Spear, D., Stanwell-Smith, D., Stuart, S. N., Symes, A., Tierney, M., Tyrrell, T. D., Vie, J. C. and Watson, R. (2010) 'Global biodiversity: Indicators of recent declines', *Science*, vol. 328, pp. 1164–1168.

Carpenter, S. R. and Bennett, E. M. (2011) 'Reconsideration of the planetary boundary for phosphorus', *Environmental Research Letters*, vol. 6, pp. 1–12.

Caudill, S. A., DeClerck, F. J. A. and Husband, T. P. (2015) 'Connecting sustainable agriculture and wildlife conservation: Does shade coffee provide habitat for mammals?', *Agriculture Ecosystems & Environment*, vol. 199, pp. 85–93.

Cheatham, M. R. M., Rouse, N., Esker, P. D., Ignacio, S., Pradel, W., Raymundo, R., Sparks, P. D., Forbes, G. A., Gordon, T. R. and Garrett, K. A. (2009) 'Beyond yield: Plant disease in the context of ecosystem services', *Phytopathology*, vol. 99, pp. 1228–1236.

Daily, G. C. (1997) *Nature's Services: Societal Dependence on Natural Ecosystems*, Island Press, Washington, DC, USA.

Daily, G. C., Ceballos, G., Pacheco, J., Suzan, G. and Sanchez-Azofeifa, A. (2003) 'Countryside biogeography of neotropical mammals: Conservation opportunities in agricultural landscapes of Costa Rica', *Conservation Biology*, vol. 17, pp. 1814–1826.

Daily, G. C., Ehrlich, P. R. and Sanchez-Azofeifa, G. A. (2001) 'Countryside biogeography: Use of human-dominated habitats by the avifauna of southern Costa Rica', *Ecological Applications*, vol. 11, pp. 1–13.

DeClerck, F. A. J. (2016) 'Biodiversity central to food security', *Nature*, vol. 531, p. 305.

DeClerck, F. A. J., Chazdon, R., Holl, K. D., Milder, J. C., Finegan, B., Martinez-Salinas, A., Imbach, P., Canet, L. and Ramos, Z. (2010) 'Biodiversity conservation in human-modified landscapes of Mesoamerica: Past, present and future', *Biological Conservation*, vol. 143, pp. 2301–2313.

DeClerck, F. A. J., Fanzo, J., Palm, C. and Remans, R. (2011) 'Ecological approaches to human nutrition', *Food and Nutrition Bulletin*, vol. 32, pp. S41–S50.

Deheuvels, O., Rousseau, G. X., Quiroga, G. S., Franco, M. D., Cerda, R., Mendoza, S. J. V. and Somarriba, E. (2014) 'Biodiversity is affected by changes in management intensity of cocoa-based agroforests', *Agroforestry Systems*, vol. 88, pp. 1081–1099.

Diaz, S. and Cabido, M. (2001) 'Vive la difference: Plant functional diversity matters to ecosystem processes', *Trends in Ecology & Evolution*, vol. 16, pp. 646–655.

Díaz, S., Demissew, S., Carabias, J., Joly, C., Lonsdale, M., Ash, N., Larigauderie, A., Adhikari, J. R., Arico, S., Báldi, A., Bartuska, A. Baste, I. A., Bilgin, A., Brondizio, E., Chan, K. M. A., Figueroa, V. E., Duraiappah, A., Fischer, M., Hill, R., Koetz, T., Leadley, P., Lyver, P., Mace, G. M., Martin-Lopez, B., Okumura, M., Pacheco, D., Pascual, U., Pérez, E. S., Reyers, B., Roth, E., Saito, O., Scholes, R. J., Sharma, N., Tallis, H., Thaman, R., Watson, R., Yahara, T., Hamid, Z. A., Akosim, C., Al-Hafedh, Y., Allahverdiyev, R., Amankwah, E., Asah, S. T., Asfaw, Z., Bartus, G., Brooks, L. A., Caillaux, J., Dalle, G., Darnaedi, D., Driver, A., Erpul, G., Escobar-Eyzaguirre, P., Failler, P., Fouda, A. M. M., Fu, B., Gundimeda, H., Hashimoto, S., Homer, F., Lavorel, S., Lichtenstein, G., Mala, W. A., Mandivenyi, W., Matczak, P., Mbizvo, C., Mehrdadi, M., Metzger, J. P., Mikissa, J. B., Moller, H., Mooney, H. A., Mumby, P., Nagendra, H., Nesshover, C., Oteng-Yeboah, A. A., Pataki, G., Roué, M., Rubis, J., Schultz, M., Smith, P., Sumaila, R., Takeuchi, K., Thomas, S., Verma, M., Yeo-Chang, Y. and Zlatanova, D. (2015) 'The IPBES conceptual framework – connecting nature and people', *Current Opinion in Environmental Sustainabilty*, vol. 14, pp. 1–16.

The Economics of Ecosystems and Biodiversity (TEEBAgriFood) (2015) *TEEB for Agriculture & Food: An Interim Report*, United Nations Environment Programme, Geneva, Switzerland.

Elphick, C. S. and Oring, L. W. (2003) 'Conservation implications of flooding rice fields on winter waterbird communities', *Agriculture Ecosystems & Environment*, vol. 94, pp. 17–29.

Estrada-Carmona, N., Hart, A. K., DeClerck, F., Harvey, C. A. and Milder, J. C. (2014) 'Integrated landscape management for agriculture, rural livelihoods, and ecosystem conservation: An assessment of experience from Latin America and the Caribbean', *Landscape and Urban Planning*, vol. 129, pp. 1–11.

Fahrig, L., Baudry, J., Brotons, L., Burel, F. G., Crist, T. O., Fuller, R. J., Sirami, C., Siriwardena, G. M. and Martin, J. L. (2011) 'Functional landscape heterogeneity and animal biodiversity in agricultural landscapes', *Ecology Letters*, vol. 14, pp. 101–112.

Flynn, D. F. B., Gogol-Prokurat, M., Nogeire, T., Molinari, N., Richers, B. T., Lin, B. B., Simpson, N., Mayfield, M. M. and DeClerck, F. (2009) 'Loss of functional diversity under land use intensification across multiple taxa', *Ecology Letters*, vol. 12, pp. 22–33.

Foley, J. A., Ramankutty, N., Brauman, K. A., Cassidy, E. S., Gerber, J. S., Johnston, M., Mueller, N. D., O'Connell, C., Ray, D. K., West, P. C., Balzer, C., Bennett, E. M., Carpenter, S. R., Hill, J., Monfreda, C., Polasky, S., Rockstrom, J., Sheehan, J., Siebert, S., Tilman, D. and Zaks, D. P. M. (2011) 'Solutions for a cultivated planet', *Nature*, vol. 478, pp. 337–342.

Frishkoff, L. O., Karp, D. S., M'Gonigle, L. K., Mendenhall, C. D., Zook, J., Kremen, C., Hadly, E. A. and Daily, G. C. (2014) 'Loss of avian phylogenetic diversity in neotropical agricultural systems', *Science*, vol. 345, pp. 1343–1346.

Garbach, K., Milder, J. C., DeClerck, F. A. J., Driscoll, L., Montenegro de Wit, M. and Gemmill-Herren, B. (2017) 'Examining multi-functionality for crop yield and ecosystem services in five systems of agroecological intensification', *International Journal of Agricultural Sustainability*, vol. 15, pp. 11–28

Gliessman, S. R., Engels, E. and Krieger, R. (1998) *Agroecology: Ecological Processes in Sustainable Agriculture*, Ann Arbor Press, Ann Arbor, MI, USA.

Hajjar, R., Jarvis, D. I. and Gemmill-Herren, B. (2008) 'The utility of crop genetic diversity in maintaining ecosystem services', *Agriculture Ecosystems & Environment*, vol. 123, pp. 261–270.

Harvey, C. A., Medina, A., Sanchez, D. M., Vilchez, S., Hernandez, B., Saenz, J. C., Maes, J. M., Casanoves, F. and Sinclair, F. L. (2006) 'Patterns of animal diversity in different forms of tree cover in agricultural landscapes', *Ecological Applications*, vol. 16, pp. 1986–1999.

Harvey, C. A., Villanueva, C., Villacis, J., Chacon, M., Munoz, D., Lopez, M., Ibrahim, M., Gomez, R., Taylor, R., Martinez, J., Navas, A., Saenz, J., Sanchez, D., Medina, A., Vilchez, S., Hernandez, B., Perez, A., Ruiz, E., Lopez, F., Lang, I. and Sinclair, F. L. (2005) 'Contribution of live fences to the ecological integrity of agricultural landscapes', *Agriculture Ecosystems & Environment*, vol. 111, pp. 200–230.

Hector, A., Schmid, B., Beierkuhnlein, C., Caldeira, M. C., Diemer, M., Dimitrakopoulos, P. G., Finn, J. A., Freitas, H., Giller, P. S., Good, J., Harris, R., Hogberg, P., Huss-Danell, K., Joshi, J., Jumpponen, A., Korner, C., Leadley, P. W., Loreau, M., Minns, A., Mulder, C. P. H., O'Donovan, G., Otway, S. J., Pereira, J. S., Prinz, A., Read, D. J., Scherer-Lorenzen, M., Schulze, E. D., Siamantziouras, A. S. D., Spehn, E. M., Terry, A. C., Troumbis, A. Y., Woodward, F. I., Yachi, S. and Lawton, J. H. (1999) 'Plant diversity and productivity experiments in European grasslands', *Science*, vol. 286, pp. 1123–1127.

Horner-Devine, M. C., Daily, G. C., Ehrlich, P. R. and Boggs, C. L. (2003) 'Countryside biogeography of tropical butterflies', *Conservation Biology*, vol. 17, pp. 168–177.

Hughes, J. B., Daily, G. C. and Ehrlich, P. R. (2002) 'Conservation of tropical forest birds in countryside habitats', *Ecology Letters*, vol. 5, pp. 121–129.

IPES-Food (2016) *From Uniformity to Diversity: A Paradigm Shift from Industrial Agriculture to Diversified Agro-ecological Systems*, International Panel of Experts on Sustainable Food Systems.

Jarvis, D. I., Hodgkin, T., Sthapit, B. R., Fadda, C. and Lopez-Noriega, I. (2011) 'An heuristic framework for identifying multiple ways of supporting the conservation and use of traditional crop varieties within the agricultural production system', *Critical Reviews in Plant Sciences*, vol. 30, pp. 125–176.

Karp, D. S., Mendenhall, C. D., Sandi, R. F., Chaumont, N., Ehrlich, P. R., Hadly, E. A. and Daily, G. C. (2013) 'Forest bolsters bird abundance, pest control and coffee yield', *Ecology Letters*, vol. 16, pp. 1339–1347.

Kremen, C., Williams, N. M., Aizen, M. A., Gemmill-Herren, B., LeBuhn, G., Minckley, R., Packer, L., Potts, S. G., Roulston, T. R., Steffan-Dewenter, I., Vazquez, D. P., Winfree, R. W., Adams, L., Crone, E. E., Greenleaf, S. S., Keitt, T. H., Klein, A. M., Regetz, J. and Ricketts, T. H. (2007) 'Pollination and other ecosystem services produced by mobile organisms: A conceptual framework for the effects of land-use change', *Ecology Letters*, vol. 10, pp. 299–314.

Lebuhn, G., Droege, S., Connor, E. F., Gemmill-Herren, B., Potts, S. G., Minckley, R. L., Griswold, T., Jean, R., Kula, E., Roubik, D. W., Cane, J., Wright, K. W., Frankie, G. and Parker, F. (2013) 'Detecting insect pollinator declines on regional and global scales', *Conservation Biology*, vol. 27, pp. 113–120.

Loreau, M. and Hector, A. (2001) 'Partitioning selection and complementarity in biodiversity experiments', *Nature*, vol. 412, pp. 72–76.

Loreau, M., Naeem, S. and Inchausti, P. (eds.) (2002) *Biodiversity and Ecosystem Functioning, Synthesis and Perspectives*, Oxford Biology, Oxford University Press, Oxford, UK.

Luck, G. W. and Daily, G. C. (2003) 'Tropical countryside bird assemblages: Richness, composition, and foraging differ by landscape context', *Ecological Applications*, vol. 13, pp. 235–247.

Ludwig, J. A. and Reynolds, J. F. (1988) *Statistical Ecology: A Primer on Methods and Computing*, Wiley and Sons, New York, NY, USA.

Mace, G. M. (2014) 'Whose conservation?', *Science*, vol. 345, pp. 1558–1560.

Martinez-Salinas, A. and DeClerck, F. (2010) 'The role of agroecoystems and forests in the conservation of birds within biological corridors', *Mesoamericana*, vol. 14, pp. 35–50.

Mayfield, M. M. and Daily, G. C. (2005) 'Countryside biogeography of neotropical herbaceous and shrubby plants', *Ecological Applications*, vol. 15, pp. 423–439.

Millennium Ecosystem Assessment (MEA) (2005) *Ecosystems and Human Well-Being: Current State and Trends*, Island Press, Washington, DC, USA.

Mulumba, J. W., Nankya, R., Adokorach, J., Kiwuka, C., Fadda, C., De Santis, P. and Jarvis, D. I. (2012) 'A risk-minimizing argument for traditional crop varietal diversity use to reduce pest and disease damage in agricultural ecosystems of Uganda', *Agriculture Ecosystems & Environment*, vol. 157, pp. 70–86.

Naeem, S. (2002) 'Ecosystem consequences of biodiversity loss: The evolution of a paradigm', *Ecology*, vol. 83, pp. 1537–1552.

Naeem, S., Bunker, D. E., Hector, A., Loreau, M. and Perrings, C. (2009) *Biodiversity, Ecosystem Functioning, and Human Well-Being: An Ecological and Economic Perspective*, Oxford Biology, Oxford University Press, Oxford, UK.

Naeem, S., Duffy, J. E. and Zavaleta, E. (2012) 'The functions of biological diversity in an age of extinction', *Science*, vol. 336, pp. 1401–1406.

Ostergard, H., Finckh, M. R., Fontaine, L., Goldringer, I., Hoad, S. P., Kristensen, K., van Bueren, E. T. L., Mascher, F., Munk, L. and Wolfe, M. S. (2009) 'Time for a shift in crop production: Embracing complexity through diversity at all levels', *Journal of the Science of Food and Agriculture*, vol. 89, pp. 1439–1445.

Philpott, S. M., Soong, O., Lowenstein, J. H., Pulido, A. L., Lopez, D. T., Flynn, D. F. B. and DeClerck, F. (2009) 'Functional richness and ecosystem services: Bird predation on arthropods in tropical agroecosystems', *Ecological Applications*, vol. 19, pp. 1858–1867.

Ponisio, L. C., M'Gonigle, L. K., Mace, K. C., Palomino, J., de Valpine, P. and Kremen, C. (2015) 'Diversification practices reduce organic to conventional yield gap', *Proceedings of the Royal Society B-Biological Sciences*, vol. 282, p. 20141396.

Ramankutty, N., Evan, A. T., Monfreda, C. and Foley, J. A. (2008) 'Farming the planet: 1. Geographic distribution of global agricultural lands in the year 2000' *Global Geochemical Cycles*, vol. 22, p. GB1003.

Ranganathan, J., Chan, K. M. A. and Daily, G. C. (2007) 'Satellite detection of bird communities in tropical countryside', *Ecological Applications*, vol. 17, pp. 1499–1510.

Rapidel, B., DeClerck, F. A. J., Le Coq, J. and Beer, J. (2011) *Ecosystem Services from Agriculture and Agroforestry: Measurement and Payment*, Earthscan for Routledge, Abingdon, UK.

Remans, R., Flynn, D. F. B., DeClerck, F., Diru, W., Fanzo, J., Gaynor, K., Lambrecht, I., Mudiope, J., Mutuo, P., Nkhoma, P., Siriri, D., Sullivan, C. and Palm, C. (2011) 'Assessing nutritional diversity of cropping systems in African villages', *PLoS One*, vol. 6, pp. 1–11.

Ricketts, T. H., Daily, G. C., Ehrlich, P. R. and Fay, J. P. (2001) 'Countryside biogeography of moths in a fragmented landscape: Biodiversity in native and agricultural habitats', *Conservation Biology*, vol. 15, pp. 378–388.

Ricketts, T. H., Daily, G. C., Ehrlich, P. R. and Michener, C. D. (2004) 'Economic value of tropical forest to coffee production', *Proceedings of the National Academy of Sciences USA*, vol. 101, pp. 12579–12582.

Ricketts, T. H., Regetz, J., Steffan-Dewenter, I., Cunningham, S. A., Kremen, C., Bogdanski, A., Gemmill-Herren, B., Greenleaf, S. S., Klein, A. M., Mayfield, M. M., Morandin, L. A., Ochieng, A., Potts, S. G. and Viana, B. F. (2008) 'Landscape effects on crop pollination services: Are there general patterns? (vol. 11, pg 499, 2008)', *Ecology Letters*, vol. 11, pp. 1121–1121.

Rockstrom, J., Steffen, W., Noone, K., Persson, A., Chapin, F. S., Lambin, E. F., Lenton, T. M., Scheffer, M., Folke, C., Schellnhuber, H. J., Nykvist, B., de Wit, C. A., Hughes, T., van der Leeuw, S., Rodhe, H., Sorlin, S., Snyder, P. K., Costanza, R., Svedin, U. S., Falkenmark, M., Karlberg, L., Corell, R. W., Fabry, V. J., Hansen, J., Walker, B., Liverman, D., Richardson, K., Crutzen, P. and Foley, J. A. (2009) 'A safe operating space for humanity', *Nature*, vol. 461, pp. 472–475.

Scholes, R. J. and Biggs, R. (2005) 'A biodiversity intactness index', *Nature*, vol. 434, pp. 45–49.

Sekercioglu, C. H., Loarie, S. R., Brenes, F. O., Ehrlich, P. R. and Daily, G. C. (2007) 'Persistence of forest birds in the Costa Rican agricultural countryside', *Conservation Biology*, vol. 21, pp. 482–494.

Soule, M. (2014) 'The "new conservation" (vol. 27, pg 895, 2013)', *Conservation Biology*, vol. 28, pp. 1135–1135.

Steffen, W., Broadgate, W., Deutsch, L., Gaffney, O. and Ludwig, C. (2015a) 'The trajectory of the Anthropocene: The great acceleration', *The Anthropocene Review*, vol. 2, pp. 81–98.

Steffen, W., Crutzen, P. J. and McNeill, J. R. (2007) 'The Anthropocene: Are humans now overwhelming the great forces of nature?', *Ambio*, vol. 36, pp. 614–621.

Steffen, W., Richardson, K., Rockstrom, J., Cornell, S. E., Fetzer, I., Bennett, E. M., Biggs, R., Carpenter, S. R., de Vries, W., de Wit, C. A., Folke, C., Gerten, D., Heinke, J., Mace, G. M., Persson, L. M., Ramanathan, V., Reyers, B. and Sorlin, S. (2015b) 'Planetary boundaries: Guiding human development on a changing planet', *Science*, vol. 347, p. 736.

Tilman, D. and Clark, M. (2014) 'Global diets link environmental sustainability and human health', *Nature*, vol. 515, p. 518.

Tilman, D., Reich, P. B., Knops, J., Wedin, D., Mielke, T. and Lehman, C. (2001) 'Diversity and productivity in a long-term grassland experiment', *Science*, vol. 294, pp. 843–845.

Tilman, D., Wedin, D. and Knops, J. (1996) 'Productivity and sustainability influenced by biodiversity in grassland ecosystems', *Nature*, vol. 379, pp. 718–720.

US Environmental Protection Agency (US EPA) (2011) *Global Anthropogenic Non-CO2 Greenhouse Gas Emissions: 1990–2030,* US EPA, Washington DC, USA.

Vermeulen, S. J., Campbell, B. M. and Ingram, J. S. I. (2012) 'Climate change and food systems', *Annual Review of Environment and Resources*, vol. 37, pp. 195–222.

Wilson, E. O. (2016) *Half Earth: Our Planet's Fight for Life*, Liveright Publishing Corporation, New York, NY, USA.

Wood, S. A., Karp, D. S., DeClerck, F., Kremen, C. K., Naeem, S. and Palm, C. A. (2015) 'Functional traits in agriculture: Agrobiodiversity and ecosystem services', *Trends in Ecology & Evolution*, vol. 30, pp. 531–539.

# 17

# LEVERAGING AGRICULTURAL BIODIVERSITY FOR CROP IMPROVEMENT AND FOOD SECURITY

*Rodomiro Ortiz*

## Introduction

To avoid a net expansion of harvested cropland, it is proposed that crop yields must grow by at least a third more in the next 45 years than they did in the previous half century (Searchinger et al., 2014). Furthermore, land sparing strategies will be needed to minimize the negative impacts of food production on biodiversity (Phalan et al., 2011) by maximizing agricultural outputs to allow land to be set aside for conservation. To achieve this, plant breeding programmes should use the power of selection to develop phenotypically and genetically diverse high-yielding populations.

High crop yields can be achieved either by increasing 'yield potential' through plant breeding, or by reducing 'yield gaps' by developing cultivars with improved adaptation to stressful environments. This might include environments affected by adverse climate, poor or saline soils, or biotic stresses such as pests or diseases, among other factors (Wang et al., 2015). Breeding gains are believed to be feasible due to the existence of genetic variation for most agronomic traits, including variation in crop wild relatives, landraces, or other available bred-germplasm (Bernardo and Bohn, 2008). Improved knowledge of how genetic diversity of crops is distributed within resources of these kinds will facilitate the selection of suitably diverse parents in breeding crosses while advances in automated plant phenotyping and phenomics will allow rapid screening of traits in the resulting offspring. The use of high-throughput DNA marker tools, and associated bioinformatic analyses, is also facilitating the search for useful sources of variation for cross-breeding. This chapter provides an overview of the use of genetic diversity in plant breeding, including what can be learned from studies of crop domestication and evolution. The chapter concludes that it will be necessary to embrace a knowledge-led plant breeding approach to leverage agricultural biodiversity as effectively as possible.

## Plant breeding: an overview

The systematic genetic enhancement of crops depends on the introduction of useful variation into breeding programmes and subsequent selection of promising individuals displaying traits of interest (Baenziger and Al-Otayk, 2007). The concept of cross-breeding emphasizes the use of diversity from landraces and crop wild relatives (i.e. the primary and secondary gene pools), followed by efficient selection methods based on both Mendelian and quantitative genetics (Prohens, 2011). Hybridization between plants with desirable traits remains the main source for increasing genetic variation, although transgenic and cisgenic approaches now also provide a means of accessing sources of variation beyond the crop gene pool as traditionally understood (Ortiz, 2015). Selection of progeny generally depends on performance trials carried out over multiple generations across sites and years, making crop improvement slow. I will describe how selection may benefit from the use of DNA markers, while advances in statistics (combined with sound experimental design) may allow more effective testing strategies to be developed (Knight, 2003). Despite this, many concerns remain regarding the low rate of breeding progress in various crops in recent years, particularly in self-pollinating cereals (Stamp and Visser, 2012).

Stress adaptation, diverse quality attributes (for food, feed, fibre, fuel, feedstock), efficiency of input uses (nutrients, water), and high yields of edible parts are among the main goals of plant breeding. Plant breeding programmes often primarily aim to develop cultivars with high yield potential, together with resistance to pathogens and pests or adaptation to stress. Safety and quality of human food and animal feed are also targets for plant breeding, whose objectives may also aim to reduce toxic molecules from crops (e.g. cassava), and to develop cultivars with potential as nutritionally enhanced food.

If plant breeding is to be practiced sustainably, it must be productive and competitive without leading to loss of genetic diversity in the elite breeding populations (Cowling, 2013). Migration, mutation, selection, random genetic drift, and non-random mating can all affect the frequency of alleles within a population. Migration and mutation are used in sustainable plant breeding to increase diversity in the elite cultigen pool, although crossing outside this elite breeding pool may lead to negative impacts in quantitative trait performance. Nevertheless, germplasm enhancement methods that facilitate allele introgression while minimizing the negative impacts of linkage drag, that is fitness reduction due to deleterious genes introduced along with the desired trait(s), have been developed. Incorporation of rare donor alleles for quantitative traits into the elite breeding pool (Cowling et al., 2009) and retention of rare positive mutations (Walsh and Lynch, 2015) can be achieved by using large population sizes and short generation intervals along with moderate selection intensity. This can be further facilitated by pursuing an omics-led breeding approach, as I will describe. As noted recently by Ceccarelli (2015), decentralized selection in early stages at the target environment(s) along with participatory plant breeding can further increase efficiency as measured by the ratio between the number of cultivars adopted and the number of crosses made, the response to selection, and the benefit/cost ratio (see Ríos Labrada and Ceballos-Müller, Chapter 40 of this Handbook, for a full description of a participatory plant breeding case study).

## Agricultural biodiversity: from conservation to sustainable use

Plant genetic resources are considered to be one of the main pillars of plant breeding. This genetic endowment provides the means to foster adaptability and resilience in agro-ecosystems. The 20th century saw the rise of attempts to preserve agricultural biodiversity, mostly through collecting and *ex situ* storage of plant genetic resources in genebanks (Lusty et al., 2014). Evaluation and use of genetic resources has received less attention and the focus of the former has typically been on discarding or culling materials (Mackay et al., 2005). The characterization for enhanced utilization of genetic diversity includes the systematic evaluation of large numbers of genebank accessions, nowadays with the aid of molecular biology and biometrics. Nevertheless, the effective and efficient identification of useful genetic variation in genebanks for further use by plant breeders remains difficult.

Elite bred germplasm show the highest loss in genetic diversity, while the lowest levels have been recorded in crop wild relatives, although a meta-analysis revealed a lack of significant reduction of regional diversity in released cultivars (van de Wouw et al., 2010). It has been noted, however, that genetic diversity loss related to plant breeding follows spatial and temporal trends and can be affected by the methods used (Rauf et al., 2010), for example during domestication or the pre-systematic plant breeding era, or after the use of pedigree selection in the systematic plant breeding era. Sometimes, after a severe diversity loss, plant breeding has been able to release cultivars that actually increased genetic diversity (Christiansen et al., 2002). Introduction of plant genetic resources increases genetic diversity in local germplasm, while high yielding hybrids lead to losing genetic diversity when replacing landraces or indigenous germplasm. Participatory plant breeding seems to be an effective approach for developing allelic-rich broad-based germplasm, while recurrent, mass, or bulk selection are less detrimental to genetic diversity than pedigree selection.

## Genebanks: searching for useful diversity

There are about 1,750 genebanks worldwide that currently store 7.4 million accessions of plant, of which approximately a quarter may be regarded as unique or genetically distinct (see Chapters 36–37 of this Handbook for examples of the uses of such *ex situ* approaches). The use of genebank accessions in public research has increased considerably in recent years (Dulloo et al., 2013), particularly as a means of studying genetic diversity, morphological or quality trait variation, and host plant resistance, and to allow the mapping of quantitative trait loci (QTL). Perhaps because of this, crop wild relatives were the subject of 20% of research articles between 1996 and 2006. *Ex situ* germplasm preservation research also includes comparing plants derived from stored seed in genebanks with those collected on recent trips, which can provide a means for detecting and understanding adaptive evolution (Pennisi, 2011), for example how plant species adapt to climate change, invasive species, or altered land use, among others. This evolutionary research requires collecting adequate sample sizes within and across populations throughout the geographic spread of a species, which can be challenging.

Finding the desired trait in a genebank sometimes seems to resemble the proverbial 'needle in a haystack' approach. For example, a single accession of the wild rice *Oryza nivara* provided the resistance to grassy stunt virus (McCouch, 2013). Small subsets of genebanks accessions using adequate sampling may be able to capture variation for specific traits, thus making more rational and efficient the search for useful variation. A core collection includes a limited set of genebank accessions that represent – with minimum repetitiveness – the available genetic diversity of a crop species and its wild relatives. A genetic distance-based criterion allows simultaneous evaluation of all traits that describe the genebank accessions, provide intuitive and interpretable criteria for the evaluation of a core collection, and relate it to its genetic diversity (Odong et al., 2013). The quality criterion of the core collection sampling depends on the objectives and subset type and should be based on data not used for selecting its genebank accessions.

Genebank accessions are mostly collected from the sites in which they evolved. Hence, they are expected to have adaptive traits that have been shaped by the selection pressures acting at these sites. Population genomics scores large numbers of DNA markers in individuals from different environments with the aim of identifying those showing unusual patterns of variation, which can be inferred to be due to selection (Stinchcombe and Hoekstra, 2008). For example, the population structure of sorghum accessions worldwide was characterized with a genome-wide map based on single nucleotide polymorphisms (SNPs) (Morris et al., 2013) and identified patterns of ancient crop diffusion in diverse agro-climatic regions across Africa and Asia. This research shows that agro-climatic constraints and geographic isolation shaped the diffusion process. Coupling population genomics and quantitative genetics provided a powerful approach for further uncovering the mechanisms underlying adaptation. For example, branch length appears to be an agro-climatic trait in sorghum because dense panicles lead to high yields, while open panicles reduce loss under humidity. Moreover, if association between SNPs and the geographical ranges of landraces reflects adaptation, then it will become feasible to predict phenotypic variation for adaptive traits. In this regard, Lasky et al. (2015) demonstrated that the environment accounts for significant SNP variation irrespective of geographical distance, and that SNPs predicted genotype × environment interactions under both drought and aluminum toxicity. Such genomic signatures of adaptation have the potential to facilitate germplasm enhancement and marker-aided breeding. Local adaptation patterns and co-evolution have also been noted between barley and the fungus which causes net blotch in this crop (Rau et al., 2015). Distinct co-evolutionary outcomes in the same hosts ensued even when the pathogen strains were considered to have very similar niche specializations and lifestyles. This research was also able to identify latitudinal clines of host plant resistance and differential selective pressures at different sites which were associated with their respective ecological conditions. Such knowledge may allow deploying efficiently host plant resistance by plant breeding programs. These findings also support the use of an evolutionary plant breeding approach, in which highly genetically diverse crop populations are left to the forces of natural selection (Döring et al., 2011). In this way, individual plants favored by the environment will contribute more seed to the next generation than plants showing low fitness, thus adapting their resulting population for their local environment, that is, breeding for locally-adapted resilience.

The Focused Identification of Germplasm Strategy (FIGS) assumes that germplasm does indeed reflect the selection pressures of the site in which it evolved. FIGS uses *a priori* information related to the quantification of the trait-environment relationship – itself based on geographical information systems along with statistical and modeling techniques – to define a 'best bet' subset of genebank accessions with a high probability of possessing the desired trait. FIGS has been used to discover genes for drought adaptation in faba bean (Khazaei et al., 2013), and resistance to Russian wheat aphid (El Bouhssini et al., 2011) and wheat stem rust (Bari et al., 2012; Endresen et al., 2012), among others.

Bioinformatics tools are also assisting the analysis of germplasm collections available at genebanks (Davenport et al., 2004), and sampling genetic resources and selecting core subsets (Thachuk et al., 2009). Screening of genebank accessions depends on greenhouse testing or field trials and, increasingly, on the use of DNA marker technology. However, morphological traits do not always provide a fair measurement of genetic values and may not reveal the true variation in a genebank (Tanksley and McCouch, 1997). In either case, the association of high-density DNA markers with phenotypic data is the most relevant for crop germplasm enhancement (Jansky et al., 2015). Ongoing projects such as *Seeds of Discovery* for maize and wheat (Prasanna, 2012) or the *3000 Rice Genome Project* (Li et al., 2014) are currently characterizing germplasm, unraveling their genetic architecture – particularly for multi-genic traits – and providing a means to molecularly dissect genotype × environment interactions. (Genetic architecture refers in this case to the number and location of genes affecting a trait, the magnitude of their effects, and the relative contributions of additive, dominant, and epistatic gene effects; Holland, 2007). This ensuing knowledge may lead to tapping more precisely the available trait variation in genebanks, and to identifying useful allelic combinations for target quantitative traits. DNA sequencing is filling genetic gaps in genebanks, thus ensuring that crop related diversity is preserved. Likewise, genome resequencing allows genes that may have been lost during domestication to be identified and used in the development of new breeding lines, including genes restricted to exotic germplasm. The genomic estimated breeding value (GEBV) is an important measure in this respect (Login and Reif, 2014) and is expected to accelerate the incorporation of traits from genebank accessions into elite breeding pools.

## Towards an effective conservation for use of agricultural biodiversity

A comprehensive understanding of genome organization and its evolutionary relationships is another important tool to enhance the transfer of alleles from crop wild relatives and landraces to breeding populations (Budak, 2010). Landraces are increasingly being replaced by bred-cultivars, leading to a loss of germplasm that could be a valuable source of genes or gene combinations – due, for example, to their rich ancestry, and to variation resulting from their exposure to a wide range of stress responses (Newton et al., 2010). In this regard, it will be essential to gather knowledge on the extent and distribution of landrace genetic diversity in agricultural systems and how it is maintained therein (Jarvis et al., 2011), as well as how seed replacement of landraces and cultivars by farmers occurs (Zeven, 1999). As noted by Dwivedi et al. (2016), landraces are heterogeneous, local adaptations of domesticated plant species that are sources of traits for efficient input uptake and utilization, or for adaptation to stressful environments. They propose a systematic landrace evaluation to establish diversity patterns in order to facilitate the search for genes that enhance edible yield or abiotic stress adaptation.

The rate at which cultivars containing genes from crop wild relatives have been released has increased over the last 30–40 years (Hajjar and Hodgkin, 2007). Crop wild relatives often provide sources of host-plant resistance to new (or more virulent) pathogen races or adaptation to stressful environments affected by abiotic factors (Dwivedi et al., 2008). Furthermore, novel genetic variation can be introduced to the modern cultigen pool by re-synthesis of crops from ancestral relatives derived from the analysis of multiple layers of variation in *ex situ* germplasm collections (Jones et al., 2013). Cytology, gene expression, and DNA marker-aided trait dissecting research could also facilitate alien introgression into the cultigen pool (Gill et al., 2011). Hence, a systematic conservation programme of global crop wild relative diversity should be sought, particularly at this time of changing climate and growing world population (Maxted et al., 2012; Cobben et al., 2013; Castañeda-Álvarez et al., 2016). To this end, a prioritized crop wild relative inventory has been developed, including 1,667 taxa divided between 37 families, 108 genera, 1,392 species and 299 sub-specific taxa (Vincent et al., 2013). Asia with 262 taxa, China with 222 taxa, and southern Europe with 181 taxa are the regions with the greatest number of priority crop wild relatives. This inventory facilitates *in situ* and *ex situ* conservation at various levels. *In situ* dynamic conservation of wild populations in genetic reserves maintains the evolution of crop wild relatives in their natural ecosystems. This conservation strategy should show complementarity to standard *ex situ* conservation in genebanks. For example, quantifying genetic changes between *ex situ* and *in situ* accessions validates *ex situ* collecting and maintenance protocols, defines appropriate recollection intervals, and allows an early detection mechanism to avoid any further decline in vulnerable *in situ* populations (Greene et al., 2014). Furthermore, a systematic strategy to evaluate traits of crop wild relatives held in genebanks for traits should be pursued to continue providing sources of variation for plant breeding (Jansky et al., 2013). This evaluation needs to continue during introgression and incorporation of crop wild relatives germplasm into the cultigen pool due to unexpected outcomes according to the genetic background, for example due to genes that may enhance cultivar performance being hidden in low-yielding wild ancestral forms (McCouch, 2004). The range of phenotypic variation can then be broadened by crossing these genetically divergent parents.

Allard (1966) acknowledges that plant breeding is domesticating crop wild relatives when introgressing their genes into the cultigen pool. Hence, germplasm enhancement or pre-breeding can be defined as 'any manipulation of germplasm leading to domestication' (Smith, 1993, p. 190). Some of the resulting offspring may show unexpected phenotypes based on the parents' attributes, including transgressive variation that can ensue from positive interactions between the genotypes of the parents (Ortiz, 2015). Despite the benefits of exploiting allele and genotypic frequency differences and distinct favorable multi-allelic epistatic interactions between exotic germplasm and the cultigen pools (Allard, 1997), this approach also involves challenges related to the direct transfer of genetic variation between lines. Pre-breeding products with enhanced genetic value are incorporated as sources of variation into the breeding population(s) following a process known as parent building. Hence, pre-breeding is the first step for using plant genetic resources after collecting, identifying, conserving, characterizing, and evaluating their diversity, thus linking genebanks with plant breeding programs. It can be also defined as the first stage of a plant breeding program that uses exotic germplasm. Its impacts, therefore, will be measured in the mid- to long-term, which calls for public funding or public-private partnerships to sustain genetic gains; that is, the predicted change in the mean value of a trait within a breeding population.

Pre-breeding germplasm includes composites, recurrent selection population(s), introgression lines, and isogenic lines ensuing from advanced backcrossing. Pre-breeding may take five to eight years and begins with evaluation of genebank accessions to identify promising trait(s) donors. The next step is hybridization using diverse donor accessions and adapted germplasm (e.g. cultivars) as recipients, which produces a large segregating population that combines the desired trait(s) with an agronomically suitable genetic background. Selected pre-breeding germplasm will be evaluated in target environments to identify promising introgression germplasm, to enrich variability in the cultigen pool, and to breed new cultivars. DNA markers can also be used at this stage, and can provide a means for identifying, tracking, and incorporating favorable alleles that are present in the pre-breeding population. Likewise, molecular markers allow reliable estimates of genetic diversity, and of the genetic architecture of quantitative traits.

## Knowledge-led conservation through use of agricultural biodiversity

The plant breeding paradigm changed from selecting phenotypes to selecting genes in the 21st century (Koornneef and Stam, 2001). The interactions between genes, organs, and environmental factors and how genetic variation translates into phenotypic performance in the field remain, however, a challenge (Bevan and Uauy, 2013), particularly when breeding objectives involve multiple traits that need to be weighted according to their relative importance (Sölkner et al., 2008). The analysis of complex quantitative traits with the aid of dense DNA markers is increasing knowledge about their genetic architecture, while prediction methods regarding the merits of breeding populations are becoming more powerful as a result of increasing genomic information (Hill, 2010). For example, best linear unbiased predictors (BLUPs) allow breeding values to be estimated with great accuracy, thus increasing genetic gains from selection (Ramalho et al., 2013). BLUPs can also be useful in selecting pre-breeding germplasm in order to introgress beneficial loci into the cultigen pool. GEBV – based on simultaneously fitting very dense high throughput DNA markers with phenotypic data – will further facilitate the use of variants with low minor allele frequency (Hill, 2012), which are difficult to detect, though each individually contributes a small amount of trait variation.

High-throughput genotyping enables the screening of large germplasm collections, thus aiding the identification of novel alleles from various sources, and thereby expanding the agricultural biodiversity available for plant breeding (Langridge and Fleury, 2011). SNPs revolutionized the pace and precision of plant genetic analysis and have facilitated marker-aided breeding due to their abundance and their amenability for high-throughput detection (Mammadov et al., 2012). These factors also lead to lower costs per data point due to an economy of scale (Bernardo, 2008). Genomic advances permit direct study of the relationship between genotype and phenotype, and of variants in genes of interest (Prohens et al., 2011). Moreover, 'omics' tools allow screening germplasm for allelic variants in target genes, discovery and mapping of new genes and regulatory sequences, and also provide a means for understanding the molecular basis of complex traits (Pérez de Castro et al., 2012). Furthermore, marker-assisted breeding techniques – including facilitated backcrossing and gene pyramiding, assisted indirect selection and GEBV – offer an efficient way of using as much available genetic diversity as possible. In summary, omics-led breeding can accelerate the rate of genetic gain, the measure of expected genetic improvement. Genetic gain is considered to depend on the population's phenotypic variation, the probability of transmitting a trait phenotype from parent to offspring or heritability, the selection intensity of the percentage of the population that will be used as parents of the next generation, and the time to complete a selection cycle or how many generations per year (Moose and Munn, 2008). Hence, increasing phenotypic variation, heritability, or selection intensity, or decreasing time, enhances genetic gain. A genomics-led plant breeding approach impacts genetic gains positively because it expands genetic diversity, increases favorable gene action, and boosts selection efficiency. However, as pointed out by Bernardo (2008), gain per unit of cost and time rather than gain per cycle should be considered when using DNA marker-aided breeding – particularly when the phenotyping for the desired trait(s) is time-consuming, expensive, or unreliable DNA markers may reduce the selection cycle time or increase cycles of selection per year, for example by allowing multiple selection cycles of DNA marker-aided breeding in a greenhouse or by using an off-season nursery. DNA marker-based selection seems to be most efficient vis-à-vis phenotypic selection if environments of high heritability for the trait of interest are used to identify DNA markers for use in selection. This indirect selection approach can subsequently be implemented in environments where heritability is low for the target trait.

Over the last decade, the number of sequenced crop genomes has increased steadily year on year, principally due to improvements in the cost and speed of DNA sequencing technology (Bolger et al., 2014). The availability of reference crop genome sequences – although sometimes incomplete – and high throughput re-sequencing has been used to improve our understanding of plant domestication, the characterization of agricultural biodiversity, and the ease of its use in plant breeding (Morrell et al., 2012). Furthermore, sequence data allows the origin of genes and gene families to be studied, and the rates of sequence divergence and signatures of selection to be tracked over time (Hancock, 2005). For example, low-coverage sequencing data of 1,479 rice accessions (including landraces and modern cultivars) from 73 countries detected 200 regions spanning 7.8% of the rice genome that had been differentially selected between two sub-populations (Xie et al., 2015). These two putative heterotic groups result from different breeding histories and can be considered breeding signatures; interestingly, the numbers present in a cultivar are positively correlated with its grain yield and may be useful to predict agronomic potential. Moreover, comparative evolutionary analysis at the genomic and transcriptomic levels may allow the synthetic reconstruction of traits and identification of candidate genes controlling them. This was demonstrated by Denton et al. (2013), who determined a mechanistic understanding of $C_4$ photosynthesis after comparing $C_3$ and $C_4$ species of the grass genus *Alloteropsis* (Panicoideae, Poaccae). Phylogenetic analyses of nuclear genes and leaf transcriptomes in the *Alloteropsis* $C_3$ taxon were compared with five $C_4$ species with varying anatomy and biochemistry and showed that fundamental elements of the $C_4$ pathway were acquired via a minimum of four independent lateral gene transfers from $C_4$ taxa that diverged from this group more than

20 million years ago (Christin et al., 2012). Molecular genetics of crop domestication also reveals diverse plant developmental pathways that were the targets of 'genetic tinkering' by Neolithic populations (Doebley et al., 2006). In this regard, it seems that transcriptional regulators were key in domestication because they are the dominant class of genes regulating plant morphological development. Likewise, intense selection results in significant linkage drag by accumulating deleterious alleles and losing favorable alleles (Walsh, 2008), thus crop wild relatives which have undergone weaker selection pressures during domestication may show greater variation, allowing their further use in plant breeding.

A genome-wide association study (GWAS) aims to unlock the 'secrets' of heritable complex traits by mapping QTL with high resolution in unstructured populations, and is a resource for gene discovery at a genome-wide scale (George and Cavanagh, 2015). This linkage-disequilibrium mapping approach uses the non-random associations of loci in haplotypes as a powerful tool for dissecting complex quantitative traits after the minimization of spurious associations due to population structure (Abdurakhmonov and Abdukarimov, 2008). Population-based association studies depend on sampling individuals from germplasm collections or natural populations, and also require the availability of DNA markers distributed at sufficient density throughout the genome. Mixed linear models analyze genotype × environment interaction effects when using association mapping designs (Saïdou et al., 2014). The genetic model underlying quantitative trait variation determines the use of marker-aided selection in plant breeding (Morgante and Salamini, 2003). Large sample sizes ensure selection of the most appropriate model, the power of which may be affected by low allele frequency or heritability due to the effects of rare alleles or alleles with small effects, respectively. Nonetheless, as indicated by Collard and Mackill (2008), genomic-led plant breeding will accelerate the genetic gains that are possible in breeding programmes by allowing a precision approach towards the development of new cultivars with improved traits, including those accessed from landrace material.

A whole-genome strategy that takes account of full genome sequencing efforts, the availability of genome-wide DNA markers, well-characterized environmental factors, and representative or complete sets of genetic resources and breeding materials can facilitate marker-aided breeding (Yu et al., 2012). Such an ideal strategy would include seed DNA-based genotyping to simplify marker assisted selection (MAS), thus reducing breeding costs and increasing scale and efficiency; selective genotyping and phenotyping combined with pooled DNA analysis to capture the most important contributory factors; a flexible genotyping system refined for the selection method being used; marker-trait association analysis using joint linkage and linkage disequilibrium mapping; and a sequence-based approach for DNA marker development, allele mining, gene discovery and marker-aided breeding. This kind of approach would also require the use of appropriate technology: genotype-by-sequencing platforms, high-throughput precision phenotyping, environmental assays for environment-typing in managed environments or multi-site trials, and breeding informatics along with advanced biometrics and modeling. Computer simulations could also provide a means of validating theoretical models and guiding empirical experimental design (Li et al., 2012). Taken further, *in silico* plant breeding has been suggested as a way of identifying optimal candidate parents for various scenarios (e.g. crossing schemes, selection and propagation methods, population size, selection intensity) that should follow empirical validation to decide on the breeding strategy that leads to the highest possible genetic gains.

Breeding by design ideally requires precise genetic mapping, high-resolution chromosome haplotyping, and extensive phenotyping to control all allelic variation at all loci of agronomic importance (Peleman and van der Voort, 2003), thus providing means to combine the most favorable alleles at all of these. However, association analysis estimation may ignore genes with small effects that trigger underpinning quantitative traits, while GEBV, on the other hand, estimates marker effects across the whole genome on the target population based on a prediction model developed in the training population, thus capturing these small effect QTL (Abera Desta and Ortiz, 2014). GEBV estimates marker effects across the whole genome of the breeding population – which only needs to be genotyped, not phenotyped – based on prediction models developed in a training population, whose individuals are both phenotyped and genotyped. It requires, therefore, a suitable genotyping strategy and a sound data recording system for its proper exploitation. GEBV is thus an attractive, potent, and valuable approach and has been suggested as a possible replacement for both phenotypic selection and MAS protocols (Nakaya and Isobe, 2012). GEBV accelerates the breeding cycle while also using DNA marker information to maintain genetic diversity and prolong genetic gains in traits of interest vis-à-vis phenotypic selection (Lorenz et al., 2011). This genomic selection approach also provides a promising avenue for predicting hybrid performance, particularly when established heterotic pools are lacking (Zhao et al., 2015). Relatedness, genotype × environment interaction, and experimental design, however, affect the prediction accuracy.

## Epigenetics: the new frontier?

The environmental biologist C. H. Waddington (1952) used the term 'epigenetics' for what changing patterns of gene expression that underlie development, often triggered by signals sent from other cells (Ptashne, 2013; McKeown and Spillane, 2014). For example, heritable changes in plant flowering time and other traits in *Arabidopsis* are due to epigenetics alone rather than by any DNA sequence changes (Pennisi, 2013). An epigenetic mechanism such as DNA methylation does not alter the sequence of bases but influences a trait by suppressing or promoting a gene's activity, and such modification can on rare occasions persist through multiple generations. Epigenetic components also contribute to differences in fertility, growth, and yield in plants (Duszynska et al., 2014; Fort et al., 2016). Hauben et al. (2010) demonstrated increased seed yield potential by selecting populations with particular epigenomic states in rapeseed or canola. The DNA methylation patterns plus both agronomical and physiological characteristics of the selected lines were heritable. More recently, Ong-Abdullah et al. (2015) described a tissue culture-induced epigenetic defect known as 'mantle' that significantly reduced yield in oil palms arising from the specific loss of a number of methyl groups in a particular region of their DNA. Their genome-wide methylation mapping was able to identify precisely 'spots' in oil palm genome responsible for the origin of mantled abnormality. This finding may allow worthless individuals to be identified and discarded at the plantlet stage, enabling their timely replacement in plantations and optimizing land resource use.

## References


Abdurakhmonov, I. Y. and Abdukarimov, A. (2008) 'Application of association mapping to understanding the genetic diversity of plant germplasm resources', *International Journal of Plant Genomics*, vol. 2008, Article 574927, doi: 10.1155/2008/574927

Abera Desta, Z. and Ortiz, R. (2014) 'Genomic selection: Genome-wide prediction in plant improvement', *Trends in Plant Science*, vol. 19, pp. 592–601.

Allard, R. W. (1966) *Principles of Plant Breeding*, John Wiley and Sons, New York, NY.

Allard, R. W. (1997) 'Genetic basis of the evolution of adaptedness', *Euphytica*, vol. 92, pp. 1–11.

Baenziger, S. and Al-Otayk, S. M. (2007) 'Plant breeding in the 21st century', *African Crop Science Proceedings*, vol. 8, pp. 1–3.

Bari, A., Street, K., Mackay, M., Endresen, D. T. F., De Pauw, E. and Amri, A. (2012) 'Focused identification of germplasm strategy (FIGS) detects wheat stem rust resistance linked to environmental variables', *Genetic Resources and Crop Evolution*, vol. 59, pp. 1465–1481.

Bernardo, R. (2008) 'Molecular markers and selection for complex traits in plants: Learning from the last 20 years', *Crop Science*, vol. 48, pp. 1649–1664.

Bernardo, R. and Bohn, M. (2008) 'Plant breeding in times of change', *Crop Science*, vol. 48, pp. S1–S2.

Bevan, M. W. and Uauy, C. (2013) 'Genomics reveals new landscapes for crop improvement', *Genome Biology*, vol. 14, p. 206.

Bolger, M. E., Weisshaar, B., Scholz, U., Stein, N., Usadel, B. and Mayer, K. F. X. (2014) 'Plant genome sequencing – applications for crop improvement', *Current Opinion in Biotechnology*, vol. 26, pp. 31–37.

Budak, H. (2010) 'Plant genetic resources: Effective utilization', *Encyclopedia of Biotechnology in Agriculture and Food*, vol. 1, pp. 504–508.

Castañeda-Álvarez, N., Khoury, C. K., Achicanoy, H. A., Bernau, V., Dempewolf, H., Eastwood, R. J., Guarino, L., Harker, R. H., Jarvis, A., Maxted, N., Müller, J. V., Ramirez-Villegas, J., Sosa, C. C., Struik, P. C., Vincent, H. and Toll, J. (2016) 'Global conservation priorities for crop wild relatives', *Nature Plants*, vol. 2, p. 16022.

Ceccarelli, S. (2015) 'Efficiency of plant breeding', *Crop Science*, vol. 55, pp. 87–97.

Christiansen, M. J., Andersen, S. B. and Ortiz, R. (2002) 'Diversity changes in an intensively bred wheat germplasm during the 20th century', *Molecular Breeding*, vol. 9, pp. 1–11.

Christin, P. A., Edwards, E. J., Besnard, G., Boxall, S. F., Gregory, R., Kellog, E. A., Hartwell, J. and Osborne, C. P. (2012) 'Adaptive evolution of $C_4$ photosynthesis through recurrent lateral gene transfer', *Current Biology*, vol. 22, pp. 445–449.

Cobben, M. M., van Treuren, R. and van Hintum, Th. J. L. (2013) 'Climate change and crop wild relatives: Can species track their suitable environment, and what do they lose in the process?', *Plant Genetic Resources: Characterization and Utilization*, vol. 11, pp. 234–237.

Collard, B. C. Y. and Mackill, D. J. (2008) 'Marker-assisted selection: An approach for precision plant breeding', *Philosophical Transactions of the Royal Society B – Biological Sciences*, vol. 363, pp. 557–572.

Cowling, W. A. (2013) 'Sustainable plant breeding', *Plant Breeding*, vol. 132, pp. 1–9.

Cowling, W. A., Buirchell, B. J. and Falk, D. E. (2009) 'A model for incorporating novel alleles from the primary gene pool into elite crop breeding programs while reselecting major genes for domestication or adaptation', *Crop Pasture Science*, vol. 60, pp. 1009–1015.

Davenport, G., Ellis, N., Ambrose, M. and Dicks, J. (2004) 'Using bioinformatics to analyse germplasm collections', *Euphytica*, vol. 137, pp. 39–54.

Denton, A. K., Simon, R. and Weber, A. P. M. (2013) '$C_4$ photosynthesis: From evolutionary analyses to strategies for synthetic reconstruction of the trait', *Current Opinion in Plant Biology*, vol. 16, pp. 315–321.

Doebley, J. F., Gaut, B. S. and Smith, B. D. (2006) 'The molecular genetics of crop domestication', *Cell*, vol. 127, pp. 1309–1321.

Döring, T. F., Knapp, S., Kovacs, G., Murphy, K. and Wolfe, M. S. (2011) 'Evolutionary plant breeding in cereals – into a new era', *Sustainability*, vol. 3, pp. 1944–1971.

Dulloo, M. E., Thormann, I., Fiorino, E., De Felice, S., Rao, V. R. and Snook, L. (2013) 'Trends in research using plant genetic resources from germplasm collections: From 1996 to 2006', *Crop Science*, vol. 53, pp. 1–11.

Duszynska, D., McKeown, P. C., Juenger, T. E., Pietraszewska-Bogiel, A., Geelen, D. and Spillane, C. (2014) 'Gamete fertility and ovule number variation in selfed reciprocal $F_1$ hybrid triploid plants are heritable and display epigenetic parent-of-origin effects', *New Phytologist*, vol. 198, pp. 71–81.

Dwivedi, S. L., Cecarelli, S., Blair, M., Upadhyaya, H., Are, A. K. and Ortiz, R. (2016) 'Landrace germplasm: A useful resource for improving yield and abiotic stress adaptation', *Trends in Plant Science*, vol. 21, pp. 31–42.

Dwivedi, S. L., Stalker, H. T., Blair, M. W., Bertioli, D., Upadhyaya, H. D., Nielen, S. and Ortiz, R. (2008) 'Enhancing crop gene pools with beneficial traits using wild relatives', *Plant Breeding Reviews*, vol. 30, pp. 179–230.

El Bouhssini, M., Street, K., Amri, A., Mackay, M., Ogbonnaya, F. C., Omran, A., Abdalla, O., Baum, M., Dabbous, A., and Rihawi, F. (2011) 'Sources of resistance in bread wheat to Russian wheat aphid (*Diuraphis noxia*) in Syria identified using the Focused Identification of Germplasm Strategy (FIGS)', *Plant Breeding*, vol. 130, pp. 96–97.

Endresen, D. T. F., Street, K., Mackay, M., Bari, A., Amri, A., De Pauw, E., Nazari, K. and Yahyaoui, A. (2012) 'Sources of resistance to stem rust (Ug99) in bread wheat and durum wheat identified using Focused Identification of Germplasm Strategy', *Crop Science*, vol. 52, pp. 764–773.

Fort, A., Ryder, P., McKeown, P. C., Wijnen, C., Aarts, M. G., Sulpice, R. and Spillane, C. (2016) 'Disaggregating polyploidy, parental genome dosage and hybridity contributions to heterosis in *Arabidopsis thaliana*', *New Phytologist*, vol. 209, pp. 590–599.

George, A. W. and Cavanagh, C. (2015) 'Genome-wide association mapping in plants', *Theoretical and Applied Genetics*, vol. 128, pp. 1163–1174.

Gill, B. S., Friebe, B. R. and White, F. F. (2011) 'Alien introgressions represent a rich source of genes for crop improvement', *Proceedings National Academy of Sciences USA*, vol. 108, pp. 7657–7658.

Greene, S. L., Kisha, T. J., Yu, L.-X. and Parra-Quijano, M. (2014) 'Conserving plants in gene banks and nature: Investigating complementarity with *Trifolium thompsonii* Morton', *PLoS One*, vol. 9, p. e105145.

Hajjar, R. and Hodgkin, T. (2007) 'The use of wild relatives in crop improvement: A survey of developments over the last 20 years', *Euphytica*, vol. 156, pp. 1–13.

Hancock, J. F. (2005) 'Contributions of domesticated plant studies to our understanding of plant evolution', *Annals of Botany*, vol. 96, pp. 953–963.

Hauben, M., Haesendonckx, B., Standaert, E., Van Der Kelen, K., Azmi, A., Akpo, H., Van Breusegem, F., Guisez, Y., Bots, M., Lambert, B., Laga, B. and De Block, M. (2010) 'Energy use efficiency is characterized by an epigenetic component that can be directed through artificial selection to increase yield', *Proceedings National Academy of Sciences USA*, vol. 106, pp. 20109–20114.

Hill, W. G. (2010) 'Understanding and using quantitative genetic variation', *Philosophical Transactions of the Royal Society B – Biological Sciences*, vol. 365, pp. 73–85.

Hill, W. G. (2012) 'Quantitative genetics in the genomics era', *Current Genomics*, vol. 13, pp. 196–206.

Holland, J. B. (2007) 'Genetic architecture of complex traits in plants', *Current Opinion in Plant Biology*, vol. 10, pp. 156–161.

Jansky, S. H., Dawson, J. and Spooner, D. M. (2015) 'How do we address the disconnect between genetic and morphological diversity in germplasm collections?', *American Journal of Botany*, vol. 102, pp. 1213–1215.

Jansky, S. H., Dempewolf, H., Camadro, E. L., Simon, R., Zimnoch-Guzowska, E., Bisognin, D. A. and Bonierbale, M. (2013) 'A case for crop wild relative preservation and use in potato', *Crop Science*, vol. 53, pp. 746–754.

Jarvis, D. I., Hodgkin, T., Sthapit, B. R., Fadda, C. and Lopez-Noriega, I. (2011) 'An heuristic framework for identifying multiple ways of supporting the conservation and use of traditional crop varieties within the agricultural production system', *Critical Reviews in Plant Sciences*, vol. 30, pp. 125–176.

Jones, H., Gosman, N., Horsnell, R., Rose, G. A., Everest, L. A., Bentley, A. R., Tha, S., Uauy, C., Kowalski, A., Novoselovic, D., Simek, R., Kobiljski, B., Kondic-Spika, A., Brbaklic, L., Mitrofanova, O., Chesnokov, Y., Bonnett, D. and Greenland, A. (2013) 'Strategy for exploiting exotic germplasm using genetic, morphological, and environmental diversity: The *Aegilops tauschii* Coss. example', *Theoretical and Applied Genetics*, vol. 126, pp. 1793–1808.

Khazaei, H., Street, K., Bari, A., Mackay, M. and Stoddard, F. L. (2013) 'The FIGS (Focused Identification of Germplasm Strategy) approach identifies traits related to drought adaptation in *Vicia faba* genetic resources', *PLoS One*, vol. 8, p. e63107.

Knight, J. (2003) 'A dying breed', *Nature*, vol. 421, pp. 568–570.

Koornneef, M. and Stam, P. (2001) 'Changing paradigms in plant breeding', *Plant Physiology*, vol. 125, pp. 156–159.

Langridge, P. and Fleury, D. (2011) 'Making the most of "omics" for crop breeding', *Trends in Biotechnology*, vol. 29, pp. 33–40.

Lasky, J. R., Upadhyaya, H. D., Ramu, P., Deshpande, S., Hash, C. T., Bonnette, J., Juenger, T. E., Hyma, K., Acharya, C., Mitchell, S. E., Buckler, E. S., Brenton, Z., Kresovich, S. and Morris, G. P. (2015) 'Genome-environment associations in sorghum landraces predict adaptive traits', *Science Advances*, vol. 1, p. e1400218.

Li, J.-Y., Wang, J. and Zeigler, R. S. (2014) 'The 3,000 rice genomes project: New opportunities and challenges for future rice research', *GigaScience*, vol. 3, p. 8.

Li, Y., Zhu, C., Wang, J. and Yu, J. (2012) 'Computer simulation in plant breeding', *Advances in Agronomy*, vol. 116, pp. 219–264.

Login, C. F. and Reif, J. C. (2014) 'Redesigning the exploitation of wheat genetic resources', *Trends in Plant Science*, vol. 19, pp. 631–636.

Lorenz, A. J., Chao, S., Asoro, F. G., Heffner, E. L., Hayashi, T., Iwata, H., Smith, K. P., Sorrells, M. E. and Jannink, J.-L. (2011) 'Genomic selection in plant breeding: Knowledge and prospects', *Advances in Agronomy*, vol. 110, pp. 77–123.

Lusty, C., Guarino, L., Toll, J. and Lainoff, B. (2014) 'Genebanks: Past, present, and optimistic future', pp. 417–432 in N. K. Van Alfen (ed.), *Encyclopedia of Agriculture and Food Systems*, Vol. 3, Elsevier, San Diego, CA, USA.

Mackay, M., von Bothmer, R. and Skovmand, B. (2005) 'Conservation and utilization of plant genetic resources – future directions', *Czech Journal of Genetics and Plant Breeding*, vol. 41, pp. 335–344.

Mammadov, J., Aggarwal, R., Buyyarapu, R. and Kumpatla, S. (2012) 'SNP markers and their impact on plant breeding', *International Journal of Plant Genomics*, vol. 2012, article728398.

Maxted, N., Kell, S., Ford-Lloyd, B., Dulloo, E. and Toledo, A. (2012) 'Toward the systematic conservation of global crop wild relative diversity', *Crop Science*, vol. 52, pp. 774–785.

McCouch, S. (2004) 'Diversifying selection in plant breeding', *PLoS Biology*, vol. 2, pp. 1507–1512.

McCouch, S. (2013) 'Feeding the future', *Nature*, vol. 499, pp. 23–24.

McKeown, P. C. and Spillane, C. (2014) 'Landscaping plant epigenetics', *Methods in Molecular Biology*, vol. 1112, pp. 1–24.

Moose, S. P. and Munn, R. H. (2008) 'Molecular plant breeding as the foundation for 21st century crop improvement', *Plant Physiology*, vol. 147, pp. 969–977.

Morgante, M. and Salamini, F. (2003) 'From plant genomics to breeding practice', *Current Opinion in Biotechnology*, vol. 14, pp. 214–219.

Morrell, P. L., Buckler, E. S. and Ross-Ibarra, J. (2012) 'Crop genomics: Advances and applications', *Nature Genetics*, vol. 13, pp. 85–96.

Morris, G. P., Ramu, P., Deshpande, S. P., Hash, C. T., Shah, T., Upadhyaya, H. D., Riera-Lizarazu, O., Brown, P. J., Acharya, C. B., Mitchell, S. E., Harriman, J., Glaubitz, J. C., Buckler, E. S. and Kresovich, S. (2013) 'Population genomic and genome-wide association studies of agroclimatic traits in sorghum', *Proceedings National Academy of Sciences USA*, vol. 110, pp. 453–458.

Nakaya, A. and Isobe, S. N. (2012) 'Will genomic selection be a practical method for plant breeding?', *Annals of Botany*, vol. 110, pp. 1303–1316.

Newton, A. C., Akar, T., Baresel, J. P., Bebeli, P. J., Bettencourt, E., Bladenopoulos, K. V., Czembor, J. H., Fasoula, D. A., Katsiotis, A., Koutis, K., Koutsika-Sotiriou, M., Kovacs, G., Larsson, H., Pinheiro de Carvalho, M. A. A., Rubiales, D., Russell, J., Dos Santos, T. M. M. and Vaz Patto, M. C. (2010) 'Cereal landraces for sustainable agriculture: A review', *Agronomy for Sustainable Development*, vol. 30, pp. 237–269.

Odong, T. L., Jansen, J., van Eeuwijk, F. A. and van Hintum, T. J. L. (2013) 'Quality of core collections for effective utilisation of genetic resources, review, discussion and interpretation', *Theoretical and Applied Genetics*, vol. 126, pp. 289–305.

Ong-Abdullah, M., Ordway, J. M., Jiang, N., Ooi, S.-E., Kok, S.-Y., Sarpan, N., Azimi, N., Hashim, A. T., Ishak, Z., Rosli, S. K., Malike, F. A., Abu Bakar, N. A., Marjuni, M., Abdullah, N., Yaakub, Z., Amiruddin, M. D., Nookiah, R., Singh, R., Low, T. L., Chan, K.-L., Azizi, N., Smith, S. W., Bacher, B., Budiman, M. A., Van Brunt, A., Wischmeyer, C., Beil, M., Hogan, M., Lakey, N., Lim, C.-C., Arulandoo, X., Wong, C.-K., Choo, C.-N., Wong, W.-C., Kwan, Y.-Y., Alwee, S. S. R. S., Sambanthamurthi, R. and Martienssen, R. A. (2015) 'Loss of *Karma* transposon methylation underlies the mantled somaclonal variant of oil palm', *Nature*, vol. 525, pp. 533–537.

Ortiz, R. (2015) *Plant Breeding in the Omics Era*, Springer International Publishing, Cham, Switzerland.

Peleman, J. D. and van der Voort, J. R. (2003) 'Breeding by design', *Trends in Plant Science*, vol. 8, pp. 330–334.

Pennisi, E. (2011) 'Banking seeds for future evolutionary scientist', *Science*, vol. 333, p. 1693.

Pennisi, E. (2013) 'Evolution heresy? Epigenetics underlies heritable plant traits', *Science*, vol. 341, p. 1055.

Pérez de Castro, A. M., Vilanova, S., Cañizares, J., Pascual, L., Blanca, J. M., Díez, M. J., Prohens, J. and Picó, B. (2012) 'Application of genomic tools in plant breeding', *Current Genomics*, vol. 13, pp. 179–195.

Phalan, B., Onial, M., Balmford, A. and Green, R. Y. (2011) 'Reconciling food production and biodiversity conservation: Land sharing and land sparing compared', *Science*, vol. 333, pp. 1289–1291.

Prasanna, B. M. (2012) 'Diversity in global maize germplasm: Characterization and utilization', *Journal of Biosciences*, vol. 37, pp. 843–855.

Prohens, J. (2011) 'Plant breeding: A success story to be continued thanks to the advances in genomics', *Frontiers in Plant Science*, vol. 2, p. 51.

Prohens, J., Fita, A. M., Rodríguez-Burruezo, A., Raigón, M. D., Plazas, M. and Vilanova, S. (2011) 'Breeding for the present and the future: Achievements and constraints of conventional plant breeding and contributions of genomics to a new Green Revolution', *Bulletin UASVM Horticulture*, vol. 68, pp. 26–33.

Ptashne, M. (2013) 'Epigenetics: Core misconcept', *Proceedings National Academy of Sciences USA*, vol. 110 (18), pp. 7101–7103.

Ramalho, M. A. P., Carvalho, B. L. and Rodrigues Nunes, J. A. (2013) 'Perspectives for the use of quantitative genetics in breeding of autogamous plants', *ISRN Genetics*, vol. 2013, article 718127.

Rau, D., Rodriguez, M., Murgia, M. L., Balmas, V., Bitocchi, E., Bellucci, E., Nanni, L., Attene, G. and Papa, R. (2015) 'Co-evolution in a landrace meta-population: Two closely related pathogens interacting with the same host can lead to different adaptive outcomes', *Scientific Reports*, vol. 5, p. 12834.

Rauf, S., Texeira da Silva, J. A., Khan, A. A. and Naveed, A. (2010) 'Consequences of plant breeding on genetic diversity', *International Journal of Plant Breeding*, vol. 4, pp. 1–21.

Saïdou, A.-A., Thuillet, A.-C., Couderc, M., Mariac, C. and Vigouroux, Y. (2014) 'Association studies including genotype by environment interactions: Prospects and limits', *BMC Genetics*, vol. 15, p. 3.

Searchinger, T., Hanson, C. and Lacape, J.-M. (2014) 'Crop Breeding: Renewing the Global Commitment', Working Paper, Installment 7 of Creating a Sustainable Food Future, World Resources Institute, Washington, DC, USA.

Smith, G. A. (1993) 'The theory of pre-breeding', *Journal of Sugar Beet Research*, vol. 30, pp. 189–195.

Sölkner, J., Grausgruber, H., Okeyo, A. M., Ruckenbauer, P. and Wurzinger, M. (2008) 'Breeding objectives and the relative importance of traits in plant and animal breeding: A comparative review', *Euphytica*, vol. 161, pp. 273–282.

Stamp, P. and Visser, R. (2012) 'The twenty-first century, the century of plant breeding', *Euphytica*, vol. 186, pp. 585–591.

Stinchcombe, J. R. and Hoekstra, H. E. (2008) 'Combining population genomics and quantitative genetics: Finding the genes underlying ecologically important traits', *Heredity*, vol. 100, pp. 158–170.

Tanksley, S. D. and McCouch, S. D. (1997) 'Seed banks and molecular maps: Unlocking genetic potential from the wild', *Science*, vol. 277, pp. 1063–1066.

Thachuk, C., Crossa, J., Franco, J., Dreisigacker, S., Warburton, S. and Davenport, G. F. (2009) 'Core Hunter: An algorithm for sampling genetic resources based on multiple genetic measures', *BMC Bioinformatics*, vol. 10, p. 243.

van de Wouw, M., van Hintum, Th., Kik, C., van Treuren, R. and Visser, B. (2010) 'Genetic diversity trends in twentieth-century crop cultivars: A meta analysis', *Theoretical and Applied Genetics*, vol. 120, pp. 1241–1252.

Vincent, H., Wiersema, J., Kell, S., Fielder, H., Dobbie, S., Castañeda-Álvarez, N. P., Guarino, L., Eastwood, R., León, B. and Maxted, N. (2013) 'A prioritized crop wild relative inventory to help underpin global food security', *Biological Conservation*, vol. 167, pp. 265–275.

Waddington, C. H. (1952) *The Epigenetics of Birds*, Cambridge University Press, Cambridge, UK.

Walsh, B. (2008) 'Using molecular markers for detecting domestication, improvement and adaptation genes', *Euphytica*, vol. 161, pp. 1–17.

Walsh, B. and Lynch, M. (2015) *Evolution and Selection of Quantitative Traits*, Vol. 1, Foundations, http://nitro.biosci.arizona.edu/zbook/NewVolume_2/newvol2.html, accessed 29 December 2015.

Wang, J., Araus, J. L. and Wan, J. (2015) 'Breeding to optimize agriculture in a changing world', *The Crop Journal*, vol. 3, pp. 169–173.

Xie, W., Wang, G., Yuan, M., Yao, W., Lyu, L., Zhao, H., Yang, M., Li, P., Zhang, X., Yuan, J., Wang, Q., Liu, F., Dong, H., Zhang, L., Li, X., Meng, X., Zhang, W., Xiong, L., He, Y., Wang, S., Yu, S., Xu, C., Luo, J., Li, X., Xiao, J., Lian, X. and Zhang, Q. (2015) 'Breeding signatures of rice improvement revealed by a genomic variation map from a large germplasm collection', *Proceedings of the National Academy of Sciences USA*, vol. 112, pp. E5411–E5419.

Yu, Y., Lu, Y., Xie, C., Gao, S., Wan, J. and Prasanna, B. M. (2012) 'Whole-genome strategies for marker-assisted plant breeding', *Molecular Breeding*, vol. 29, pp. 833–854.

Zeven, A. C. (1999) 'The traditional inexplicable replacement of seed and seed ware of landraces and cultivars: A review', *Euphytica*, vol. 110, pp. 181–191.

Zhao, Y., Mette, M. F. and Reif, J. C. (2015) 'Genomic selection in hybrid breeding', *Plant Breeding*, vol. 134, pp. 1–10.

# 18

# NEGLECTED NO MORE

## Leveraging underutilized crops to address global challenges

*Gennifer Meldrum and Stefano Padulosi*

### Introduction

Crop biodiversity is a key resource to foster more sustainable, productive, and nutritious agriculture, but it is largely underexploited. Farmers' fields around the world have become more similar over the past 50 years, increasingly based on a small selection of global commodities (Khoury et al., 2014). Just 18 crops cover 85% of arable land, among which only three – rice, maize and wheat – cover more than 40% (Leff et al, 2004; Stamp et al., 2012). The homogeneity of production systems is reflected in human diets, for which the `big three' make up more than 50% of caloric intake and just 94 species provide 90% of calories, protein, fat, and weight (Stamp et al., 2012; Khoury et al, 2014).

There is a vast reserve of edible plants that currently do not make a major contribution to diets and production systems at the global scale. 7,000 plants are known to have been used as food by humans throughout history (Myers, 1983; Wilson, 1992; Henry, Chapter 1 of this Handbook). *Mansfeld's Encyclopedia* documents 6,040 crops, among which the families with the most species are Poaceae (725), Leguminosae (653), Compositae (284), Rosaceae (263), Euphorbiaceae (172), Lamiaceae (169), Solanaceae (130), and Apiaceae (108) (Khoshbakht and Hammer, 2008). There are even more plants that could be better exploited for the benefit of humankind, as it is estimated that 75,000 higher plant species have edible parts out of (Wilson, 1992; Khoshbakht and Hammer, 2008), and there are also numerous edible algae species (e.g. Dawczynski et al., 2007).

Many plants are important in the traditional food systems of specific localities, but their use is declining for a variety of historic, social, political, and agronomic reasons. These crops are known as neglected and underutilized species, also called orphan crops, minor crops, development opportunity crops, and Cinderella species (IPGRI, 2002; Leakey, 2012; Ebert, 2014). 'Neglected' refers to the lack of attention that these crops have received from research and development, while 'underutilized' refers to their potential to be used and marketed in local and global markets (Padulosi and Hoeschle-Zeledon, 2004; Gruère et al, 2008). The declining use of these species is not necessarily because they have low value. Instead, it relates to priorities in research and development, which have focused on rice, wheat, and maize with a calorie centred approach to improving food security, as well as commoditization and globalization of agricultural produce largely driven by Western priorities and the interests of private seed companies (Stamp et al., 2012; Jacobsen et al., 2013; Ebert, 2014). It also relates to European colonization which led to a dramatic exchange of plant material between the continents and associated policies such as forbidding cultivation of local species that contributed to displace native crops (Hernandez Bermejo and Leon, 1994; Clement, 1999; Small, 2013; Williams, Chapter 11 of this Handbook). Volumes on *The Lost Crops of the Incas* (1989) and *The Lost Crops of Africa* (1996, 2006, 2008) highlight many plants that were important in indigenous food cultures that were left behind in the process of colonization and modern agricultural development. Similar lists of plants can be found for Asia (e.g. Arora, 2014) and by examination of the ethnobotanical literature that shows extraordinary diversity in traditional farming systems and indigenous diets around the globe (e.g. Joshi et al., 2015, Sujarwo et al., 2016; Ursoa et al., 2016).

Neglected and underutilized species remain an important resource for many rural communities living in marginal areas such as hills and drylands where the Green Revolution has been less successful due to difficult growing conditions and poor access to irrigation and inputs. So-called 'minor' crop species are relied on as staple foods throughout the developing world, where 27 minor grains, pulses, tubers, and oil crops occupy around 250 million hectares and make a significant contribution to diets (Naylor et al., 2004). Improving the yields and marketability of these neglected crops would enhance their contribution to the food security and livelihoods of resource-poor farmers that depend on them for subsistence. Revitalizing, scaling up, and expanding production and use of these crops could also support adaptation of agriculture to climate change and improve nutrition beyond their current ranges (Ortiz, Chapter 17 of this Handbook).

Neglected species have often received scant attention from breeding and seed commercialization efforts, have poor representation in national and global germplasm collections, and limited documentation of their distribution and production (Galluzzi and Noriega, 2014). Not all edible plants can become global commodities, but they could contribute to better nutrition and more resilient production in specific regions. Some species, such as cassava *(Manihot esculenta)*, sorghum *(Sorghum bicolor)*, and pearl millet *(Pennisetum glaucum)* are major staples in some regions and should not be considered underutilized in those contexts. Yet they could be considered underutilized from the perspective of global markets and production systems, which are not currently realizing their benefits for nutrition (e.g. Stefoska-Needham et al., 2015), or regions where their use is recommended to adapt to increasing drought risk (Githunguri et al., 2015).

This chapter explores the strategic roles that this broad portfolio of crops can have in supporting climate change adaptation and improving nutrition. It then explores how value chain development can be used as an approach to realize their benefits for humankind.

## Critical roles of NUS in sustainable agriculture under climate change

Many neglected and underutilized species (NUS) are associated with marginal rainfed lands and are hardy to abiotic stresses (e.g. drought, frost, and heat) that challenge global crops. For example, on the Andean Altiplano, native pseudocereals – quinoa *(Chenopodium quinoa)* and cañahua *(Chenopodium pallidicaule)* – and native tubers – potato (*Solanum* spp.), oca *(Oxalis tuberosa)*, isaño *(Tropaeolum tuberosum)*, and papalisa *(Ullucus tuberosus)* – are essentially the only crops that can produce a harvest with the poor soils and high risk of drought and frost that characterize this high altitude plain (>3500 masl; García et al., 2007). Millets adapted to dryland conditions are the major staples across the semi-arid tropics where the major cereals cannot thrive: sorghum and pearl millet are widely grown, while minor millets such as foxtail millet *(Setaria italica)*, finger millet *(Eleusine coracana)*, proso millet *(Panicum miliaceum)*, little millet *(Panicum sumatrense)*, barnyard millet *(Echinochloa crus-galli* and *E. colona)*, kodo millet *(Paspalum scrobiculatum)*, fonio (*Digitaria* spp.), and teff *(Eragrostis tef)* are important in more restricted regions (McDonough et al., 2000; Bala Ravi, 2004).

Due to their adaptation to marginal and risky environments, underutilized crops can play significant roles in reducing the sensitivity of farming systems to climate change and maintaining and improving yields with more efficient use of water and inputs (Mayes et al., 2011; Padulosi et al., 2011; Ebert, 2014; Chivenge et al., 2015). Hardy underutilized species can improve harvest security by diversifying production systems and even replacing cultivations that become maladapted to emerging conditions. Lin (2011) identified seven types of crop diversification to support climate change adaptation, among which neglected and underutilized species could contribute to: crop rotation, polycultures (including intercropping and relay cropping), agroforestry, and mixed landscapes. For example, drought-tolerant legumes such as Bambara groundnut *(Vigna unguiculata)*, pigeon pea *(Cajanus cajan)*, grass pea *(Lathyrus sativus)*, and tepary bean *(Phaseolus acutifolius)* can be integrated into crop rotation and polyculture systems to diversify production and benefit soil quality through nitrogen fixation. Underutilized tree species, including leguminous and multipurpose species, can feature in agroforestry systems and diversified landscapes to mitigate and build resilience to climate change and variability (Mbow et al., 2014) by improving soil quality, mitigating water and temperature stress, and providing food, fodder, fuel, medicine and other products (Kaushik and Kumar, 2003; Mbow et al, 2014).

The fact that underutilized species are in the hands of the poor means they are an accessible means of adaptation. These crops are often used in traditional risk management strategies that farmers have relied on for generations. For example, indigenous farmers on the Andean Altiplano are known to plant quinoa in mixture with more frost-tolerant cañahua to ensure they secure a harvest and similarly to plant frost-hardy bitter potatoes *(Solanum juzepczukii)* in addition to tastier frost-susceptible potatoes *(Solanum tuberosum)* (Aguilar and Jacobsen, 2003; Condori et al., 2014). In the drylands of Rajasthan, India, minor millets with short growth cycles – proso millet and foxtail millet – are used as contingency crops when insufficient rains mean the main crop – pearl millet – will have low yields (Saxena, 1991). Teff is used in a similar way in Ethiopia to replace failed crops in mid-season because it can deliver a harvest in a short time (Small, 2015).

## Nutritional benefits of NUS

In addition to providing reliable food sources under challenging climate conditions, the neglected and underutilized species can have several roles in more nutrition-sensitive agriculture. Many underutilized grains have high levels of important micronutrients and more optimally balanced nutrition profiles compared with major staples. For example, quinoa and teff are high in fibre, calcium, and iron and, compared with maize and rice, have higher protein and a more favourable fatty acid composition (Hager et al., 2012). Substituting dominant staples or fortifying flours with these underutilized grains can bring important nutrition value. For example, adding amaranth *(Amaranthus cruentus)* flour to bread increases protein, lipid, fibre, and mineral content, although research is needed to determine the most effective ratios for this mix (Sanz-Penella et al., 2013). There are also many neglected and underutilized fruits, vegetables, and pulses that have comparable or higher nutrient values than global crops (Keatinge et al., 2011). Among the indigenous vegetables of Africa, the leaves from cowpea *(Vigna unguiculata)*, baobab (*Adansonia* spp.), amaranth, spider plant *(Cleome gynandra)*, jute mallow *(Corchorus olitorius)*, moringa *(Moringa oleifera)*, African nightshade (*Solanum* spp.), cassava *(Manihot esculenta)*, pumpkin (*Cucurbita* spp.), and sweet potato (*Ipomea* spp.) stand out for their high in β-carotene and iron and can contribute to improving these nutrient deficiencies in local populations by integrating them in balanced diets (Yang and Keding, 2009). The indigenous gac fruit *(Momordica cochinchinensis)* in Vietnam has exceptional β-carotene content and high acceptability among children but production and consumption has been declining (Vuong, 2000).

Increasing consumption of such nutrient-dense underutilized fruits, vegetables, and pulses could bring important nutrition gains.

Some underutilized species have been recognized as 'superfoods' because of their high nutrient value but also for their qualities in promoting well-being beyond nutrition. Such 'nutraceutical' properties are often recognized and valued in traditional food and medicine of indigenous communities (e.g. Singh et al., 2015; Tribess et al., 2015; Zhang et al., 2015). Some species are recognized for having strong antioxidant properties, such as edible seaweeds (Yuan and Walsh, 2006) and fruits in the genera *Pometia, Averrhoa, Syzygium, Salacca, Phyllanthus, Garcinia, Sandoricum,* and *Maipighia* (Ikram et al., 2009). Alternative grains like quinoa, amaranth (*Amaranthus* spp.) and buckwheat *(Fagopyrum esculentum)* have gained appeal for being gluten-free and having a low glycemic index and there is increasing attention to promote these grains to reduce the burden of type 2 diabetes and cardiovascular disease (e.g. Dixit et al., 2011). Several other underutilized species can also produce nutritious gluten-free flours that are suitable for coeliacs, including tigernut *(Cyperus esculentus)*, lupin *(Lupinus albus)*, carob *(Ceratonia siliqua)*,and chestnut *(Castanea)* (O'Shea et al., 2014).

## Promoting NUS through value chain development

Neglected and underutilized species can provide numerous benefits for producers and consumers but, by definition, their full value is not currently being realized. The underutilization of these species is a result of market imperfections that lead to weak demand and/or inefficient supply (Gruère et al., 2008). Value chain development can stimulate a more effective use of these species, enabling them to reach a new market equilibrium that better reflects their value and improves the flow of benefits between producers and consumers (Gruère et al., 2008). Enhancing commercial potential and income opportunities for these hardy crops can motivate farmers to increase their production and enhance their supply in the food system, while marketing and awareness campaigns can promote greater consumption of their nutritious products. Common constraints and approaches for developing the value chains underutilized species are discussed in the following paragraphs.

Consumer demand is essential for the successful commercialization of underutilized plant species. Often, consumers are not aware of these crops and their positive attributes, while, in other cases, people may be interested in them but they are not available in an accessible location, with acceptable quality, or at a competitive price or convenience compared with other products (Gruère et al., 2008). A market analysis is an important step to identify potential buyers and the best strategy for preparing, packaging, and labelling to attract consumers (Will, 2008). High nutrient and nutraceutical values are a strong entry point for promoting the use of these species, as evidenced by the recent rise in popularity of 'superfoods' like açai berry *(Euterpe oleracea)*, goji berry *(Lycium barbarum)*, chia seeds *(Salvia hispanica)*, quinoa, and maca *(Lepidium meyenii)* to name a few examples (Herman, 2013; Spiegel, 2014). Another marketing opportunity for underutilized crops is emerging with growing urban populations and the diasporae of migrants who desire to eat familiar foods in their new contexts. Increasing interest among consumers for natural and traditional foods, as well exotic and novel culinary experiences, provide openings to commercialize underutilized crops using labels and promotional campaigns to educate consumers about their attributes linked to good nutrition, sustainability, and cultural traditions (Gruère et al., 2008).

Strong marketing can be important to reverse perceptions of 'food of the poor' that underutilized crops sometimes carry in their native ranges, which have developed through the process of their marginalization. Long and drudgerous processing requirements are often a factor why these crops are falling out of favour as more convenient foods are increasingly available. Providing access to processing facilities and marketing processed products with attractive recipes can help maintain and put these crops back on the plates of consumers. For example, packages of fonio prepared by artisanal processors are popular in markets in the capitals of Mali and Burkina Faso, which save women's time to de-husk, wash, and cook this tasty traditional grain, although the high cost is a barrier for many to access the product (Konkobo-Yaméogo et al., 2004).

Even with high demand, commercialization of underutilized crops can be hindered by inefficiencies in the supply chain. Farmers may have low incentive to produce and sell underutilized crops due to high transaction costs (e.g. for transportation or processing) or low competitiveness compared with crops with more established market channels (Gruère et al., 2008). Poor coordination and transparency between value chain actors, low access to credit, and lack of physical infrastructure are other factors that constrain the quantity, quanitity, and consistency of supply for underutilized crops. Networking between farmers and other value chain actors (e.g. multi-stakeholder platforms) can help organize the value chain, orient it to market opportunities, and build trust and transparency between actors (e.g. Polar et al., 2010). Collective action among small scale farmers (e.g. cooperatives, associations, farmers' clubs, or self-help groups) can help them gain bargaining power, enable them to share capital investments, and achieve a larger scale and consistency of production (Gruère et al., 2008). For example, organizing collectives among Pioroa farmers in Venezuela allowed them to reach a scale of production that made transportation of their agroforestry products by boat from their remote Amazonian community to the market a profitable venture (Van Looy et al., 2008). Training farmers to build their business skills and capacity to deliver high quality products supports this process. Facilitating access to market information, micro-credit, and other government-led financing schemes can also be key to upgrade the value chains of underutilized crops for the benefit of the poor. For example, gaining access to micro-finance enabled producers of African nut *(Ricinodendron heudelotii)* in Cameroon to secure higher prices because they could wait to sell when prices were higher, while acting collectively improved their understanding of market opportunities and their bargaining power (Pye-Smith, 2010).

Lack of improved germplasm for underutilized species can be an additional hindrance for their supply and competitiveness. These crops have received limited breeding attention and often have low yields and other intrinsic features that constrain their use (such as high seed shattering or toxins) that could be improved with research attention. Aside from poor investment, breeding for underutilized species can be challenged by strong outcrossing, gene by environment interactions, poor availability of germplasm, and long generation times in the case of trees. For example, breeding efforts have shown promise for developing grasspea *(Lathyrus sativus)* varieties that are low in β-ODAP, a neurotoxin which is harmful when the crop is consumed in large quantities, but strong environmental interactions and cross-pollination present challenges to ensure the safety of this hardy and nutritious crop (Kumar et al., 2011; Girma and Korbu, 2012). There is optimism that domestication and breeding for underutilized species will be facilitated by emerging advanced breeding techniques, such as marker assisted selection, micro-propagation, and genetic transformation (Naylor et al., 2004; Ochatt and Jain, 2007; Mayes et al., 2011; Stamp et al., 2012; Tadele and Assefa, 2012; Jain and Gupta, 2013). Rapid breeding gains have been made for several crops in the last century, especially when necessity demanded an influx of research attention (Stamp et al., 2012). The development and promotion of short-duration lines of mungbean *(Vigna radiata)* in the last 30 years contributed to an increase in production and consumption of this nutritious pulse in Asia, with 1.5 million farmers adopting improved varieties and consumption increasing by 22–66% (Ebert, 2014). A century ago, kiwifruit *(Actinidia chinensis)* was a wild fruit collected in China, but the selection and promotion of a highly palatable and storable variety from seeds brought to New Zealand in 1904 led to the rise of this fruit to global commodity with an industry worth USD 1.9 billion in 2012 (Ferguso, 2012; Ward and Courtney, 2013). Similar gains could be made for other crops with investment in targeted breeding programs (Stamp et al., 2012).

In addition to crop improvement, research attention is often needed to develop practices and technologies to enhance the effectiveness and efficiency in the value chains of underutilized species. Such attention, which has largely escaped these crops, can readily provide solutions to overcome constraints to their production, consumption, and marketing. For example, a major constraint for the promotion of underutilized fruits and vegetables is high perishability. The development of hermetic packages that safeguard and prolong the shelf life of rocket (*Eruca sativa* and *Diplotaxis* spp.) up to three to four days were key in boosting the marketing of this vegetable and other similar delicate leafy greens that are susceptible to fast wilting and enzymatic browning (Del'Innocenti et al., 2007; Nicola et al., 2010). Prior to the application of this technology in the early 1990s, rocket was harvested mainly in the wild in southern Europe and sold on a small scale in bundles in local markets (Padulosi and Pignone, 1997), while today more than 3,600 ha of greenhouse cultivations are estimated to occur in Italy with a total export value of EUR 40 million (Quadretti, 2012). Juice blends, jams, and dehydrated products are other value-adding strategies that can enable commercialization of underutilized fruits and vegetables which are limited by their short shelf life and high seasonality to help bring their nutrition benefits to consumers year-round (Van Looy et al., 2008; Bhardwaja and Pandey, 2011; Joshi and Mathur, 2015).

Addressing just one bottleneck is not sufficient in most cases to promote underutilized crops which usually face many constraints at different points along their value chains. The various issues should be dealt with simultaneously, enhancing supply and demand together in order to successfully upgrade the value chain. A 'holistic approach' was successfully applied to promote minor millets in South Asia and Andean grains in Latin America that involved inter-disciplinary and inter-sectoral initiatives along each segment of the value chain (Padulosi et al., 2014, 2015). Improved lines of quinoa, cañahua, and finger millet were developed through participatory variety selection trials that matched the preferences of farmers and consumers. Improved agronomic practices suitable to marginal conditions were developed and instructed to farmers which, along with high quality seed of selected varieties, contributed to yield increases (between 39% and 172% in India). Technology suitable to cottage industry scales was developed and introduced to communities to increase efficiency and reduce drudgery in processing, while farmer collectives were mobilized for commercialization of the grains. In India, the introduction of mills was associated with an increase in household consumption of millets by 7–13%. Increased production (45% in Peru and 140% in Bolivia) and consumption of Andean grains (44% in Peru and 13% in Bolivia) showed a similar success of the approach in South America (Bioversity International, 2015).

## Risks and best practices for value chain development of NUS

The recent boom of quinoa is an example of the enormous success that a formerly underutilized species can build worldwide in a short time. Until the mid-1980s, quinoa was consumed only by indigenous farmers in the Andean highlands, where the crop is an integral feature of traditional subsistence agriculture. Due to its low prestige, markets for quinoa were almost absent or highly localized until recognition of its nutritional values in the 1980s led to a growing demand in the United States and Europe (Small, 2013; Avitabile, 2015). An export market developed and as popularity of quinoa rose, its production skyrocketed from 10,000–20,000 metric tons in the 1990s to nearly 100,000 metric tons in 2012, almost exclusively from Peru and Bolivia (Avitabile, 2015). Exports grew to encompass around half of Bolivia's production and a quarter of Peru's production in 2012 (Krivonos, 2013). The market price of quinoa increased with the soaring demand, and farm gate prices also rose from USD 435/ton in 1991 to USD 1,332/ton in 2010 in Bolivia (Avitabile, 2015). The high price encouraged migrants to return to their villages to cultivate quinoa, re-populating rural areas that had been abandoned in the 1980s with liberalization of the economy, closure of national mines, and intense drought (Kerssen, 2015).

The rise of quinoa has diversified the global food basket and brought income to resource-poor farmers on the Andean Altiplano, which sets an example for what other underutilized crops can achieve. However, this case also revealed some challenges to ensure that the benefits of crop development are realized by the communities that have been custodians of their seed for generations. Some issues that emerged with the quinoa case are discussed in the following paragraphs, which are hotly debated (e.g. Jacobsen, 2011; 2012; Winkel et al., 2012), but represent issues that could arise in the development of other underutilized crops. Some best ways forward to avoid these pitfalls while realizing the benefits of underutilized species are suggested.

Controversy emerged with the quinoa boom as its high price was barring Bolivians from consuming their traditional and highly nutritious crop, which they would instead sell to purchase cheaper and less nutritious products like noodles and rice (Jacobsen, 2011). This analysis has been contested by others, who maintain that the shift in diet occurred before the quinoa boom and that producer communities continue to eat quinoa, while the income gained from its marketing has enabled them to purchase other nutritious foods, such as meat, fruits, and vegetables (Laguna, 2011; Winkel et al., 2012). This case reveals a caveat in developing global value chains for underutilized species that the nutritious product is largely exported for the benefit of wealthy health-conscious consumers in the Global North. While not discounting the contribution that underutilized crops like quinoa can make to enhancing food security and nutrition around the globe, it is clear that in order for nutrition benefits of these crops to be realized by the poor in their native regions, a focus on domestic markets development is most strategic. Promoting production of nutritious local species in home gardens, sharing traditional and novel recipes for their preparation, and increasing awareness of their value (e.g. through traditional food fairs) are actions that can encourage increased consumption in rural communities. Linking nutritious crops to policy schemes that promote their consumption is another viable approach to bring their nutrition benefits to local people, while stimulating their production in publically-supported value chains. For example, inclusion of amaranth in school feeding programs in Bolivia gave children opportunity to consume this nutritious traditional food while also stimulating production and generating income for producers and other value chain actors throughout the region (Padulosi et al., 2014). Another example is the inclusion of millets ('coarse grains') in the Public Distribution System in India with an amendment to the Food Security Bill in 2013. This policy change is poised to give a major boost to cultivation and use of these nutritious, climate-hardy cereals and will ensure their benefits reach the most needy, as public procurement programmes purchase millet from farmers at a minimum support price and poor households gain access to the grains at subsidized rates.

Aside from the consequences for nutrition, another major concern with the boom of quinoa was the erosion of the genetic base through the promotion of just a few varieties (del Castillo et al., 2007; Skarbø, 2015). More than 100 varieties of quinoa have been recorded in the Southern Altiplano but the export market has focused on just a handful of varieties (Avitabile, 2015). Conscious of the dramatic erosion of crop diversity that occurred with the Green Revolution, care must be exercised when promoting underutilized species to prevent the loss of intra-specific genetic diversity that is vital to enable adaptation to changes in the environment and social preferences over time. In the holistic value chain approach used by Padulosi et al. (2014), the conservation of crop genetic resources was a central component involving integrated *ex situ* and on-farm conservation approaches (see Dulloo et al., Chapter 36 of this Handbook). An assortment of landraces of quinoa were promoted in local markets, highlighting the unique values in each variety. Promoting variety mixtures is a similar approach, which has been successful in marketing diversity in Andean potatoes (Devaux et al., 2011). Agritourism was another approach explored by Padulosi and colleagues (2014) to market Andean grains while supporting their conservation. The village of Santiago de Okola on the shores of Lake Titicaca in the centre of genetic diversity of quinoa developed a resort where tourists can taste their traditional foods and witness the unique diversity of quinoa and other Andean crops (Taranto and Padulosi, 2009). Applying such good practices that recognize and promote diversity can reduce the risks of eroding genetic resources with the development of underutilized crops.

A further criticism of the quinoa boom was that high prices inspired unsustainable production practices. The massive increase in quinoa production in Peru and Bolivia was achieved primarily by expanding production area – shifting from cultivation on hillsides to mechanized farming in flatter areas that were previously used for communal grazing (Winkel et al., 2012; Kerssen, 2015). Traditional fallow lengths of six to ten years were cut short to nearly continuous cultivation and the ratio of llamas to cultivated area declined below adequate levels to rejuvenate soil quality with manure fertilization (Small, 2013; Kerssen, 2015). Together these changes contributed to soil degradation and declining productivity (Herman, 2013; Small, 2013, although also contested by Winkel et al., 2012). The fragile Altiplano ecosystem is challenged to meet the demands of a global market, which is a concern that could also arise with the development of other species grown in sensitive or marginal ecosystems. A related concern is that a surge in market demand can lead to overexploitation of wild gathered species. Sustainability issues in production of underutilized species could be managed with better regulation and consumer indications. Almost all production of quinoa has been organic due to the dominant consumer base but the regulations of organic production are not specific to the precise agroecological requirements of the Altiplano (Herman, 2013). Participatory guarantee systems are one approach that could ensure production adheres to more sustainable and site-specific practices.

Certification and labelling is also a promising way forward to manage the challenge of intellectual property rights that can arise with development of underutilized species. Other countries have also become interested in quinoa, and it has been successfully cultivated in several places outside its centre of origin, including the United States, Canada, Egypt, Kenya, India, and several northern European countries (Small, 2013; Bazile et al, 2016). This crop could have an important role in improving nutrition worldwide, but there is also a threat that the knowledge and custodianship of Andean farmers will be undervalued with its commoditization. Gruère et al. (2008) recognized the threat of commoditization in value chain development where rising price can attract big investments. They recommend to use a form of supply control to ensure that small producers retain their margins over time. Territorial indications are one form of supply control that could be important in securing market share for Bolivian and Peruvian producers as quinoa production expands worldwide. Such labels could emphasize the unique value of the varieties produced in the centre of crop origin by the indigenous peoples who domesticated and tended it through generations. A new form of certification that recognizes rare and locally-specific crops and varieties could be a similar means to draw consumer attention to products produced by small farmers and help maintain their market share (Padulosi et al. 2015).

## Conclusions

Crop diversification is increasingly called for to strengthen the resilience of agriculture in an uncertain climate, as well to support the development of more nutrition-sensitive agriculture (Frison et al., 2011; Lin, 2011; Jaenicke and Vichow, 2013). Neglected and underutilized species can play a central role in diversification strategies as they include many species tolerant of marginal, risky, and harsh environments and many species which are highly nutritious compared with globalized crops (Keatinge et al., 2011; Padulosi et al., 2011; Kahane et al., 2013; Chivenge et al., 2015). In the pursuit to feed an estimated 9 billion people by 2050 while maintaining critical environmental services and biodiversity, neglected and underutilized species are further recognized to have important values that can support more sustainable and equitable agriculture on marginal croplands, where many of the world's smallholder farmers are situated (Mayes et al., 2011; Padulosi et al., 2011; Ebert, 2014). These crops are of unique value to the poor, who are their primary cultivators, and they are thus highly strategic assets to help alleviate poverty and hunger among the most vulnerable. For these reasons, neglected and underutilized species are major assets in holistic, multi-pronged, and context-specific approaches to agricultural development which are increasingly called for by scientists (e.g. Foley et al., 2011; Hanspach et al., 2013; Godfray et al., 2014) and may be most relevant to achieving multifaceted world development targets, such as the sustainable development goals.

The challenge remains to realize the potentials in these crops in the face of many constraints that exist for their mainstreaming. Value chain development is one strategy to promote neglected and underutilized species by stimulating consumption and generating income incentives for farmers to upscale or adopt their cultivation (Gruère et al., 2008; Will, 2008; Padulosi et al., 2014, 2015). However, increasing demand and price for a crop does not guarantee that the income and nutrition benefits of the development reach the resource poor producers that have been their custodians for generations, nor that the crop will be produced sustainably. Strategies and approaches are needed to avoid these pitfalls so that value chain development of underutilized species is constructive towards addressing global challenges. Promoting local value chains, linking the crops with public programs, taking active action to conserve their genetic diversity, and using certifications and labelling to promote sustainable practices and retain niche markets for small producers are promising strategies going forward.

## References


Aguilar, P. C. and Jacobsen, S. E. (2003) 'Cultivation of quinoa on the Peruvian Altiplano', *Food Reviews International*, vol. 19, pp. 31–41.

Arora, R. K. (2014) *Diversity in Underutilized Plant Species: An Asia-Pacific Perspective*, Bioversity International, New Delhi, India.

Avitabile, E. (2015) *Value Chain Analysis, Social Impact and Food Security: The Case of Quinoa in Bolivia*, PhD Thesis, Roma Tre University, Rome, Italy.

Bala Ravi, S. (2004) 'Neglected millets that save the poor from starvation', *Leisa India*, March, pp. 34–36.

Bazile, D., Pulvento, C., Verniau, A., Al-Nusairi, M., Ba, D., Breidy, J., Hassan, L., Mohammed, M.I., Mambetov, O., Otambekova, M., Sepahvand, N., Shams, A., Souici, D., Miri, K., and Padulosi, S. (2016) 'Worldwide evaluations of quinoa: preliminary results from post international year of Quinoa FAO projects in nine countries' *Frontiers in Plant Science*, vol 7, pp 1–18.

Bhardwaja, R. L. and Pandey, S. (2011) 'Juice blends – a way of utilization of under-utilized fruits, vegetables, and spices: A review', *Critical Reviews in Food Science and Nutrition*, vol. 51, pp. 563–570.

Bioversity International (2015) *Andean Lost Grains in Bolivia and Peru*, Bioversity International, Maccarese, Rome, Italy.

Chivenge, P., Mabhaudhi, T., Modi, A. T. and Mafongoya, P. (2015) 'The potential role of neglected and underutilised crop species as future crops under water scarce conditions in Sub-Saharan Africa', *International Journal of Environmental Research and Public Health*, vol. 12, pp. 5685–5711.

Clement, C. R. (1999) '1492 and the loss of Amazonian crop genetic resources', *Economic Botany*, vol. 53, pp. 188–202.

Condori, B., Hijmans, R. J., Ledent, J. F. and Quiroz, R. (2014) 'Managing potato biodiversity to cope with frost risk in the High Andes: A modelling perspective', *PLoS One*, vol. 9, p. e81510.

Dawczynski, C., Schubert, R. and Jahreis, G. (2007) 'Amino acids, fatty acids, and dietary fibre in edible seaweed products', *Food Chemistry*, vol. 103, pp. 891–899.

del Castillo, C., Winkel, T., Mahy, G. and Bizoux, J. P. (2007) 'Genetic structure of quinoa (*Chenopodium quinoa* Willd.) from the Bolivian Altiplano as revealed by RAPD markers', *Genetic Resources and Crop Evolution*, vol. 54, pp. 897–905.

Del'Innocenti, E., Pardossi, A., Tognoni, F. and Guidi, L. (2007) 'Physiological basis of sensitivity to enzymatic browning in "lettuce", "escarole" and "rocket" salad when stored as fresh-cut products', *Food Chemistry*, vol. 104, pp. 209–215.

Devaux, A., Ordinola, M. and Horton, D. (eds.) (2011) *Innovation for Development: The Papa Andina Experience*, International Potato Center, Lima, Peru.

Dixit, A. A., Azar, K. M. J., Gardner, C. D. and Palaniappan, L. P. (2011) 'Incorporation of whole, ancient grains into a modern Asian Indian diet to reduce the burden of chronic disease', *Nutrition Reviews*, vol. 69, pp. 479–488.

Ebert, A. W. (2014) 'Potential of underutilized traditional vegetables and legume crops to contribute to food and nutritional security, income and more sustainable production systems', *Sustainability*, vol. 6, pp. 319–335.

Ferguson, A. R. (2012) 'Kiwifruit: the wild and the cultivated plants', *Advances in Food and Nutrition Research*, vol 68, pp. 15–32.

Foley, J. A., Ramankutty, N. and Brauman, K. A. (2011) 'Solutions for a cultivated planet', *Nature*, vol. 478, pp. 337–342.

Frison, E. A., Cherfas, J. and Hodgkin, T. (2011) 'Agricultural biodiversity is essential for a sustainable improvement in food and nutrition security', *Sustainability*, vol. 3, pp. 238–253.

Galluzzi, G. and López Noriega, I. (2014) 'Conservation and use of genetic resources of underutilized crops in the Americas – a continental analysis', *Sustainability*, vol. 6, pp. 980–1017.

García, M., Raes, D., Jacobsen, S. E. and Michel, T. (2007) 'Agroclimatic constraints for rainfed agriculture in the Bolivian Altiplano', *Journal of Arid Environments*, vol. 71, pp. 109–121.

Girma, D. and Korbu, L. (2012) 'Genetic improvement of grass pea (*Lathyrus sativus*) in Ethiopia: An unfulfilled promise', *Plant Breeding*, vol. 131, pp. 231–236.

Godfray, H., Charles, J. and Garnett, T. (2014) 'Food security and sustainable intensification', *Philosophical Transactions of the Royal Society B – Biological Sciences*, vol. 369, p. 20120273.

Gruère, G. P., Giuliani, A. and Smale, M. (2008) 'Marketing underutilized plant species for the benefit of the poor: A conceptual framework', pp. 73–87 in A. Kontoleon, U. Pasqual and M. Smale (eds.), *Agrobiodiversity Conservation and Economic Development*, Routledge, Abington, Oxon, UK.

Hager, A. S., Wolter, A., Jacob, F., Zannini, E. and Arendt, E. K. (2012) 'Nutritional properties and ultra-structure of commercial gluten-free flours from different botanical sources compared to wheat flours', *Journal of Cereal Science*, vol. 56, pp. 239–247.

Hanspach, J., Abson, D. J., Loos, J., Tichit, M., Chappell, M. J. and Fischer, J. (2013) 'Develop, then intensify', *Science*, vol. 341, p. 713.

Herman, M. (2013) 'Successes and pitfalls of linking nutritionally promising Andean crops to markets', pp. 164–185 in J. Fanzo, D. Hunter, T. Borelli and F. Mattei (eds.), *Diversifying Food and Diets: Using Agricultural Biodiversity to Improve Nutrition and Health*, Routledge, Abington, Oxon, UK.

Hernandez Bermejo, J. and Leon, J. (1994) *Neglected Crops: 1492 from a Different Perspective*, FAO, Rome, Italy.

Ikram, E. H. K., Eng, K. H., Jalil, A. M. M., Ismail, A., Idris, S., Azlan, A., Nazri, H. S. M., Diton, N. A. M. and Mokhtar, R. A. M. (2009) 'Antioxidant capacity and total phenolic content of Malaysian underutilized fruits', *Journal of Food Composition and Analysis*, vol. 22, pp. 388–393.

IPGRI (2002) *Neglected and Underutilized Plant Species: Strategic Action Plan of the International Plant Genetic Resources Institute*, IPGRI, Rome, Italy.

Jacobsen, S.-E. (2011) 'The situation for quinoa and its production in southern Bolivia: From economic success to environmental disaster', *Journal of Agronomy and Crop Science*, vol. 197, pp. 390–399.

Jacobsen, S.-E. (2012) 'What is wrong with the sustainability of quinoa production in southern Bolivia – a reply to Winkel et al (2012)', *Journal of Agronomy and Crop Science*, vol. 198, pp. 320–323.

Jacobsen, S.-E., Sørensen, M., Pedersen, S. M. and Weiner, J. (2013) 'Feeding the world: Genetically modified crops versus agricultural biodiversity', *Agronomy for Sustainable Development*, vol. 33, pp. 651–662.

Jaenicke, H. and Vichow, D. (2013) 'Entry points into a nutrition-sensitive agriculture', *Food Security*, vol. 5, pp. 679–692.

Jain, S. M. and Gupta, S. D. (eds.) (2013) *Biotechnology of Neglected and Underutilized Crops*, Springer, Berlin, Germany.

Joshi, N., Siwakoti, M. and Kehlenbeck, K. (2015) 'Wild vegetable species in Makawanpur District, Central Nepal: Developing a priority setting approach for domestication to improve food security', *Economic Botany*, vol. 69, pp. 161–170.

Joshi, P. and Mathur, B. (2015) 'Development of value added products from the leaf powders of dehydrated less utilized green leafy vegetables', *Nutrition & Food Science*, vol. 45, pp. 302–309.

Kahane, R., Hodgkin, T., Jaenicke, H., Hoogendoorn, C., Hermann, M., Keatinge, J. D. H., d'Arros Hughes, J., Padulosi, S. and Looney, N. (2013) 'Agrobiodiversity for food security, health and income', *Agronomy for Sustainable Development*, vol. 3, pp. 671–693.

Kaushik, N. and Kumar, V. (2003) 'Khejri (*Prosopis cineraria*)-based agroforestry system for arid Haryana, India', *Journal of Arid Environments*, vol. 55, pp. 433–440.

Keatinge, J. D. H., Yang, R. Y., Hughes, J., Easdown, W. J. and Holmer, R. (2011) 'The importance of vegetables in ensuring both food and nutritional security in attainment of the Millennium Development Goals', *Food Security*, vol. 3, pp. 491–501.

Kerssen, T. M. (2015) 'Food sovereignty and the quinoa boom: Challenges to sustainable re-peasantisation in the southern Altiplano of Bolivia', *Third World Quarterly*, vol. 36, pp. 489–507.

Khoshbakht, K. and Hammer, K. (2008) 'Species richness in relation to the presence of crop plants in families of higher plants', *Journal of Agriculture and Rural Development in the Tropics and Subtropics*, vol. 109, pp. 181–190.

Khoury, C., Bjorkman, A. D., Dempewolf, H., Ramirez-Villegas, J., Guarino, L., Jarvis, A., Rieseberg, L. H. and Struik, P. C. (2014) 'Increasing homogeneity in global food supplies and the implications for food security', *Proceedings of the National Academy of Sciences USA*, vol. 111, pp. 4001–4006.

Konkobo-Yaméogo, C., Chaloub, Y., Kergna, A., Bricas, N., Karimou, R. and Ndiaye, J. L. (2004) 'La consommation urbaine d'une céréale traditionnelle en Afrique de l'Ouest: le foni', *Cahiers Agricultures*, vol. 13, pp. 125–128.

Krivonos, E. (2013) *Food Outlook: Biannual Report on Global Food Markets*, FAO Trade and Markets Division, Rome, Italy.

Kumar, S., Bejiga, G., Ahmed, S., Nakkoul, H. and Sarker, A. (2011) 'Genetic improvement of grass pea for low neurotoxin (β-ODAP) content', *Food and Chemical Toxicology*, vol. 49, pp. 589–600.

Laguna, P. (2011) *Mallas y Flujos: Acción Colectiva, Cambio Social, Quinua y Desarrollo Regional Indígena en los Andes Bolivianos*, PhD Thesis, Wageningen UR, The Netherlands.

Leakey, R. R. B. (2012) 'Participatory domestication of Indigenous Fruit and Nut trees: New crops for sustainable agriculture in developing countries', pp. 479–501 in P. Gepts, T. R. Famula, R. L. Bettinger, S. B. Brush, A. B. Damiana, P. E. McGuire and C. O. Qualset (eds.), *Biodiversity in Food and Agriculture: Domestication, Evolution and Sustainability*, Cambridge University Press, Cambridge, UK.

Leff, B., Ramankutty, N. and Foley, J. A. (2004) 'Geographic distribution of major crops across the world', *Global Biogeochemical Cycles*, vol. 18, p. GB1009.

Lin, B. B. (2011) 'Resilience in agriculture through crop diversification: Adaptive management for environmental change', *BioScience*, vol. 61, pp. 183–193.

Mayes, S., Massawe, F. J., Alderson, P. G., Roberts, J. A., Azam-Ali, S. N. and Herman, M. (2011) 'The potential for underutilized crops to improve security of food production', *Journal of Experimental Botany*, vol. 63, pp. 1075–1079.

Mbow, C., Smith, P., Skole, D., Duguma, L. and Bustamante, M. (2014) 'Achieving mitigation and adaptation to climate change through sustainable agroforestry practices in Africa', *Current Opinion in Environmental Sustainability*, vol. 6, pp. 8–14.

McDonough, C. M., Rooney, L. W. and Serna-Saldivar, S. O. (2000) 'The millets', pp. 271–300 in K. Kulp and J. G. Ponte (eds.), *Handbook of Cereal Science and Technology*, 2nd ed., CRC Press, Boca Raton, FL, USA.

Myers, N. (1983) *A Wealth of Wild Species: Storehouse for Human Welfare*, Westview Press, Boulder, CO, USA.

Naylor, R. L., Falcon, W. P., Goodman, R. M., Jahn, M. M., Sengooba, T., Tefera, H. and Nelson, R. J. (2004) 'Biotechnology in the developing world: A case for increased investments in orphan crops', *Food Policy*, vol. 29, pp. 15–44.

Nicola, S., Fontana, E., Tibaldi, G. and Zhau, L. (2010) 'Qualitative and physiological response of minimally processed rocket (*Eruca sativa* Mill.) to package filling amount and shelf life temperature', *Acta Horticulturae*, vol. 877, pp. 611–618.

Ochatt, S. and Jain, S. M. (2007) *Breeding of Neglected and Under-Utilized Crops, Spices and Herbs*, Science Publishers Inc., Enfield, NH, USA.

O'Shea, N., Arendt, E. and Gallagher, E. (2014) 'State of the Art in gluten-free research', *Journal of Food Science*, vol. 79, pp. R1067–R1076.

Padulosi, S., Amaya, K., Jager, M., Gotor, E., Rojas, W. and Valdivia, R. (2014) 'A holistic approach to enhance the use of neglected and underutilized species: The case of Andean grains in Bolivia and Peru', *Sustainability*, vol. 6, pp. 1283–1312.

Padulosi, S., Heywood, V., Hunter, D. and Jarvis, A. (2011) 'Underutilized species and climate change', pp. 507–521 in S. S. Yadav, R. J. Redden, J. L. Hatfield, H. Lotze-Campen and A. E. Hall (eds.), *Crop Adaptation to Climate Change*, Wiley-Blackwell, Hoboken, NJ, USA.

Padulosi, S., Hodgkin, T., Williams, J. T. and Haq, N. (2002) 'Underutilised crops: Trends, challenges and opportunities in the 21st Century', pp. 323–338 in J. Engels, V. R. Rao and M. Jackson (eds.), *Managing Plant Genetic Diversity*, CAB International, Wallingford, UK.

Padulosi, S., Mal, B., King, O. I. and Gotor, E. (2015) 'Minor millets as a central element for sustainably enhanced incomes, empowerment, and nutrition in rural India', *Sustainability*, vol. 7, pp. 8904–8933.

Padulosi, S. and Pignone, D. (1997) *Rocket: An Old Mediterranean Crop for the World, Report of the II International Workshop on Rocket 13 December 1996, Padova, Italy*, IPGRI, Rome, Italy.

Padulosi, S. and Hoeschle-Zeledon, I. (2004) 'Underutilized plant species: What are they?', *LEISA India*, vol 20, pp 5–6.

Padulosi, S., Maccari, M., Meldrum, G., Gullotta, G. and the Conference Participants (2016) 'Certification for the conservation of agricultural biodiversity', in S. Padulosi, G. Meldrum and G. Gullotta (eds.), *Agricultural Biodiversity to Manage the Risks and Empower the poor. Proceedings of the International Conference 27–29 April 2015, Rome, Italy*, Bioversity International, Maccarese, Italy.

Polar, V., Rojas, W., Jäger, M. and Padulosi, S. (2010) *Taller de análisis multiactoral para la promoción del uso sostenible del amaranto: memorias del taller realizado en Sucre, Bolivia, 19–20 de noviembre de 2009*, Fundación PROINPA y Bioversity International, Sucre, Bolivia.

Pye-Smith, C. (2010) *The Fruits of Success: A Programme to Domesticate West and Central Africa's Wild Fruit Trees Is Raising Incomes, Improving Health and Stimulating the Rural Economy*, World Agroforestry Centre, Nairobi, Kenya.

Quadretti, R. (2012) 'Il valore del settore della rucola in Italia e' stimato in 30–40 milioni di euro solo per l'export', *Fresh Plaza*, www.freshplaza.it/article/44942/Il-valore-del-settore-della-rucola-in-Italia-e-stimato-in-30-40-milioni-di-euro-solo-per-lexport

Sanz-Penella, J. M., Wronkowska, M., Soral-Smietana, M. and Haros, M. (2013) 'Effect of whole amaranth flour on bread properties and nutritive value', *LWT-Food Science and Technology*, vol. 50, pp. 679–685.

Saxena, M. B. L. (1991) 'Efforts to mitigate effects of drought on agricultural production', in S. Kumar Lal and U. R. Nahar (eds.), *Development of Underdeveloped Regions: A Case of Arid Regions*, Mittal Publications, Delhi, India.

Singh, N. P., Gejurel, P. R. and Rethy, P. (2015) 'Ethnomedicinal value of traditional food plants used by the Zeliang tribe of Nagaland', *Indian Journal of Traditional Knowledge*, vol. 14, pp. 298–305.

Skarbø, K. (2015) 'From lost crop to lucrative commodity: Conservation implications of the quinoa rennaissance', *Human Organization*, vol. 74, pp. 86–99.

Small, E. (2013) 'Quinoa – is the United Nations' featured crop of 2013 bad for biodiversity?', *Biodiversity*, vol. 14, pp. 169–179.

Small, E. (2015) 'Blossoming treasures of biodiversity – 47. Teff & Fonio – Africa's sustainable cereals', *Biodiversity*, vol. 16, pp. 27–41.

Spiegel, A. (2014) 'According to Google, the other superfoods have got nothing on quinoa', *Huffpost Taste*, www.huffingtonpost.com/2014/07/24/superfoods_n_5613758.html, accessed 25 February 2016.

Stamp, P., Messmer, R. and Walter, C. (2012) 'Competitive underutilized crops will depend on the state funding of breeding programmes: An opinion on the example of Europe', *Plant Breeding*, vol. 131, pp. 461–464.

Sujarwo, W., Arinasa, I. B. K., Caneva, G. and Guarrera, P. M. (2016) 'Traditional knowledge of wild and semi-wild edible plants used in Bali (Indonesia) to maintain biological and cultural diversity', *Plant Biosystems*, vol. 150, pp. 971–976.

Tadele, A. and Assefa, K. (2012) 'Increasing food production in Africa by boosting the productivity of understudied crops', *Agronomy*, vol. 2, pp. 240–283.

Taranto, S. and Padulosi, S. (2009) 'Tasting the results of a joint effort', *Leisa Magazine*, vol. 25, pp. 32–33.

Tribess, B., Pintarelli, G. M., Bini, L. A., Camargo, A., Funez, L. A., de Gasper, A. L. and Zeni, A. L. (2015) 'Ethnobotanical study of plants used for therapeutic purposes in the Atlantic Forest region, Southern Brazil', *Journal of Ethnopharmacology*, vol. 164, pp. 136–146.

Ursoa, V., Signorinib, M. A., Toninic, M. and Bruschia, P. (2016) 'Wild medicinal and food plants used by communities living in Mopane woodlands of southern Angola: Results of an ethnobotanical field investigation', *Journal of Ethnopharmacology*, vol. 177, pp. 126–139.

Van Looy, T., Carrero, G. O., Mathijs, E. and Tollens, E. F. (2008) 'Underutilized agroforestry food products in Amazonas (Venezuela): A market chain analysis', *Agroforestry Systems*, vol. 74, pp. 127–141.

Vuong, L. (2000) 'Underutilized β-carotene – rich crops of Vietnam', *Food & Nutrition Bulletin*, vol. 21, pp. 173–181.

Ward, C. and Courtney, D. (2013) 'Kiwifruit: Taking its place in the global fruit bowl', *Advances in Food and Nutrition Research*, vol. 68, pp. 1–14.

Will, M. (2008) *Promoting Value Chains of Neglected and Underutilized Species for Pro-Poor Growth and Biodiversity Conservation: Guidelines and Good Practices*, Global Facilitation for Underutilized Species, Rome, Italy.

Wilson, E. O. (1992) *The Diversity of Life*, Harvard University Press, Cambridge, MA, USA.

Winkel, T., Bertero, H. D., Bommel, P., Bourliaud, J., Chevarría Lazo, M., Cortes, G., Gasselin, P., Geerts, S., Joffre, R., Léger, F., Martinez Avisa, B., Rambal, S., Rivière, G., Tichit, M., Tourrand, J. F., Vassas Toral, A., Vacher, J. J. and Vieira Pak, M. (2012) 'The sustainability of quinoa production in southern Bolivia: From misrepresentations to questionable solutions. Comments on Jacobsen (2011, J. Agron. Crop Sci. 197: 390–399)', *Journal of Agronomy and Crop Science*, vol. 198, pp. 314–319.

Yang, R.-Y. and Keding, G. B. (2009) 'Nutritional contributions of important African indigenous vegetables', in C. M. Shackleton, M. W. Pasquini and A. W. Dresche (eds.), *African Indigenous Vegetables in Urban Agriculture*, Earthscan, Sterling, VA, USA.

Yuan, Y. A. and Walsh, N. A. (2006) 'Antioxidant and antiproliferative activities of extracts from a variety of edible seaweeds', *Food and Chemical Toxicology*, vol. 44, pp. 1144–1150.

Zhang, L., Zhang, Y., Pei, S., Geng, Y., Wang, C. and Yuhua, W. (2015) 'Ethnobotanical survey of medicinal dietary plants used by the Naxi People in Lijiang Area, Northwest Yunnan, China', *Ethnobiology and Ethnomedicine*, vol. 11, p. 40.

# 19

# AGROBIODIVERSITY, RESILIENCE, ADAPTATION AND CLIMATE CHANGE

*Brenda B. Lin*

## Introduction

Resilience in agriculture is essential for the long-term sustainability of crop production. Ecologically, agricultural resilience leads to a more stable, functioning agricultural system that ensures production, food security, and environmental cycling (Matson et al., 1997, Altieri, 1999). Socially, agricultural resilience leads to stable production levels that protect social structures and economic systems at various scales (Adger, 2000; Marshall, 2010). The combination of these two factors elevate the need to create and maintain environmental and social agricultural structures that can withstand and recover from unwanted shocks that threaten the long-term sustainability of agriculture.

Global environmental changes, such as land use changes, economic pressures, and shifting dietary patterns are affecting many of the parameters in which agriculture has been managed. However, one of the most influential changes to the agricultural system is that of climate change. Continuing changes in the mean values and variability of current climate and projected future climate scenarios are causing great concern over agricultural sustainability, food production, and the livelihoods of farmers (Izumi et al., 2013). Reports from the IPCC AR5 show that each of the last three decades has been successively warmer than any preceding decade since 1850; in the Northern Hemisphere, the period from 1983 to 2012 was probably the warmest 30-year period during the past 1,400 years (IPCC, 2013). The number of warm days and nights has increased globally, and the frequency of heatwaves across Europe, Asia, and Australia has also increased. Extreme precipitation events over most mid-latitude land masses and wet tropical regions are likely to become increasingly intense and frequent by 2100, as global mean surface temperature increases (IPCC, 2013).

Such changes in climate patterns will have significant ramifications for food production and food security (Deryng et al., 2014), affecting food prices of key commodities, impacting on human health, and increasing the number of people in poverty (Nellemann et al., 2009). Climate change studies highlight the urgent need to develop adaptive agroecosystems because many rural farmers depend on rain-fed subsistence agriculture for their livelihoods (Haile, 2005). Many communities depend greatly on the ecosystem services provided by agricultural systems (food, fodder, fuel) for their livelihoods and have few other livelihood strategies (Altieri, 1999). Additionally, many smallholder farms have little capital to invest in expensive adaptation strategies, increasing the vulnerability of rural agricultural communities to environmental change. All such factors point to a growing need to build and increase resilience within current agricultural systems in order to help farmers and agricultural systems transition into new environmental regimes.

## What is resilience?

Many managed ecosystems, including agriculture, often fail to respond smoothly to external changes and pressures, leading to greater research on ecological regime shifts, thresholds, and resilience (Folke et al., 2004). Understanding how agricultural systems can respond more smoothly to external changes and pressures is imperative to maintain food production and farmer livelihoods.

Resilience is defined as the propensity of a system to retain its organizational structure and productivity following a perturbation (Holling, 1973). Thus, a resilient agroecosystem will continue to provide a vital service such as crop production if challenged by a heatwave or by a large reduction in rainfall. In agricultural systems, crop biodiversity may provide the link between stress and ecological resilience because a diversity of organisms is required for ecosystems to function and provide services (Heal, 2000). Removing whole functional groups of species or removing entire trophic levels can cause ecosystems to shift from a desired to less-desired state, affecting their capacity to generate ecosystem services (Folke et al., 2004). This effect highlights the possibility that agricultural systems already may be in a less-desired state for the continued delivery of ecosystem services in a changing environment.

Social resilience is another type of resilience important to the agricultural system, and it represents the ability of a community to withstand external shocks and stresses without significant upheaval (Adger et al., 2002). Resource-dependent industries are particularly vulnerable to climate change, as they are highly dependent on a particular natural system (Marshall, 2010). When communities are resilient, they may be able to absorb these shocks, and even respond positively to them. However, when communities are less resilient, or when external changes are rapid and far-reaching, communities may be unable to react and respond (Adger et al., 2002). Changes in economic resources or a loss of institutional capacity can all lead to less resilient communities (Marshall, 2010). The challenge for the research community is to develop resilient agricultural systems using rational, affordable strategies such that ecosystem functions and services can be maintained and livelihoods can be protected.

## The importance of agrobiodiversity for ecosystem function and resilience

Questions of increasing resilience in agricultural systems may depend heavily on the biodiversity and ecosystem functioning of the system. Biodiversity – which allows for the coexistence of multiple species, fulfilling similar functions, but with different responses to human landscape modification – enhances the resilience of ecosystems (Loreau and Mazancourt, 2013). This concept is linked to the insurance hypothesis (Yachi and Loreau, 1999), which proposes that biodiversity provides an insurance, or buffer, against environmental fluctuations because different species respond differently to change, leading to more predictable aggregate community or ecosystem properties. Such diversity insures the maintenance of a system's functional capacity against potential human management failure that may result from an incomplete understanding of the effects of environmental change (Elmqvist et al., 2003).

Vandermeer et al. (1998) elucidated the main issues linking the role of diversity in agroecosystems to functional capacity and resilience. First, biodiversity enhances ecosystem function because different species or genotypes perform slightly different roles and therefore occupy different niches. Second, biodiversity is neutral or negative in that there are many more species than there are functions; thus, redundancy is built into the system. Third, biodiversity enhances ecosystem function because those components that appear redundant at one point in time may become important when some environmental change occurs. The key here is that when environmental change occurs, the redundancies of the system allow for continued ecosystem functioning and provisioning of services. These three hypotheses are not mutually exclusive and change over time and space; therefore, all linkages between diversity and function may be useful for the long-term maintenance of sustainable agricultural systems.

The recognition that biodiversity is integral to the maintenance of ecosystem functioning points to the utility of crop diversification as an important resilience strategy for agroecosystems. Traditional agricultural communities manage biodiversity at various scales, creating dynamic landscape mosaics of fields, gardens, orchards, pastures, and ecosystem patches (Hodgkin et al., 2013). Diversification can occur in many forms (genetic variety, species, structural), giving farmers a wide variety of options and combinations for the implementation of this strategy (**Figure 19.1** *Different forms of diversification*). A review of 172 case studies and project reports from around the world shows that agricultural biodiversity contributes to resilience through a number of, often combined, strategies: the protection and restoration of ecosystems, the sustainable use of soil and water resources, agro-forestry, diversification of farming systems, various adjustments in cultivation practices, and the use of stress-tolerant crops and crop improvement

*Figure 19.1* Different forms of diversification including (a) mixed species grasses in a pasture field, (b) taro crops with mixed cover cropping and trees, (c) cropped field alongside a eucalyptus plantation, and (d) canola and wheat cropped across a landscape

*Source*: Photos a and b by Brenda Lin; Photo c by CSIRO Science Images; Photo d by Carl Davies.

(Hodgkin et al., 2013). Diversification at the within-crop scale may refer to changes in crop structural diversity; for example, using a mixture of crop varieties that have different plant heights. Diversification at the within-field scale may be represented by areas between and around fields where trap crops or natural enemy habitat can be planted. At the landscape scale, diversification may be achieved by integrating multiple production systems, such as mixing agroforestry management with cropping, livestock, and fallow to create a highly diverse piece of agricultural land (Altieri, 1999; Gurr et al., 2003). It is important to recognize that diversity can be created temporally as well as spatially, adding even greater functional diversity and resilience to systems with sensitivity to temporal fluctuations in climate.

## Examples of climate challenges and agrobiodiversity pathways towards increasing resilience

Climate change will affect both biotic (pest, pathogens, pollinators) and abiotic (solar radiation, water, temperature) factors in crop systems, threatening crop sustainability and production. A substantial amount of evidence is now showing how diverse agroecosystems, with a broader range of traits and functions, can perform better under changing environmental conditions. The following are a few of the major example showing how the greater functional capacity of agrobiodiverse agroecosystems can protect crop productivity against increasing environmental stressors. This includes shifts in pest patterns, shifts in disease spread, and challenges of dealing with crop production under climate extremes.

### *Shifts in the distribution and abundance of pest species*

In agricultural systems, as in natural ecosystems, herbivorous insects can have significant impacts on plant productivity. The challenges of pest suppression may intensify in the future as changes in climate affect pest ranges and potentially bring new pests into agricultural systems. For example, La Niña events caused by oceanic cooling are often associated with increased prevalence of the brown planthopper *(Nilaparvata lugens)*, a major pest of rice (ADB, 2009). It is expected that insect pests will generally become more abundant as temperatures rise as a result of range extensions and phonological changes. This abundance will be accompanied by higher rates of population development, growth, migration, and overwintering (Cannon, 1998; Bale et al., 2002). Migrant pests are expected to respond more quickly to climate change than plants, and they may be able to colonize newly available crops and habitats (Cannon, 1998; Bale et al., 2002).

However, there are a variety of barriers to range expansions, and promoting such barriers to range expansion and pest viability may have immediate negative impacts on pest outbreaks. Increasing the agrobiodiversity of on-farm vegetation that promotes natural enemy abundance may be one way to create a biotic barrier against new pests. The composition of the plant community, also known as the planned diversity of the system, can be an important determinant of the total biodiversity in the system (Matson et al., 1997). With greater plant species richness and diversity in spatial and temporal distribution of crops, diversified agroecosystems mimic more natural systems and are therefore able to maintain a greater diversity of animal species, many of which are natural enemies of crop pests (Altieri, 1999). Many examples of pest suppression have been shown within agricultural systems possessing greater diversity and complexity, especially in comparison with less-complex systems (Cannon, 1998). For example, in willow systems, insect pest outbreaks of the leaf beetle *Phratora vulgatissima* are greater in willow monocultures than in natural willow habitats (Dalin et al., 2009). However, a review of specialist and generalist natural enemy responses to agricultural diversification showed that diversification may reduce natural enemy searching efficiency, and pest control by specialist enemies may be less effective in a more diverse agroecosystems because a lower concentration of host plants may reduce attraction or retention of these specialist enemies (Sheehan, 1986).

Habitat management is one method used within agricultural systems to alter habitats to improve the availability of the resources natural enemies require for optimal performance (Landis et al., 2000). Such management techniques have been developed for use at within-crop, within-farm, or landscape scales, and some have been proven to be very economical for farmers. In one review examining pest management in agriculture (Gurr et al., 2003), the authors found that many degrees of complexity exist in increasing biodiversity for pest management. Simply diversifying the plant age structure of a monoculture or strip-cutting fields such that natural enemies have a temporal refuge can improve in-field habitats for natural enemies. Larger-scale changes, such as integrating annual and perennial non-crop vegetation; increasing crop diversity within the field; or increasing farm-wide diversification with silviculture, agroforestry, and livestock may also provide a variety of other functions to the system (Gurr et al., 2003 and Chapter 6 of this Handbook).

In an example from a meta-analysis of the density response of natural enemies (invertebrate predators and parasitoids) to experimental changes in structural complexity, Langellotto and Denno (2004) found that increasing structural complexity led to a significant rise in natural enemy abundance at habitat and within-plant scales. Hunting and web-building spiders showed the strongest response to structural complexity, followed by hemipterans, mites, and parasitoids. Evidence of greater spider abundance in response to diversification has also been shown by Sunderland and Samu (2000), who found in a meta-analysis that abundance increased with structural complexity in 63% of the studies they examined. The central conclusion of this review was that spiders tend to concentrate in diversified patches, and greater diversification throughout the whole crop would offer the best prospect of improving pest control (Sunderland and Samu, 2000).

One example of a perennial system that exhibits a rich range of natural enemy pest control is the coffee agroforestry system, where there is a wide variety of spatial and temporal diversity determined by the shade trees planted within the cropping system. Greater natural enemy presence has been observed in the more diverse and shaded agroforestry systems, and increased bird diversity and density have been shown to reduce herbivore plant damage through greater insectivorous bird predation (Perfecto et al., 2004). It has also been observed that predatory ground-dwelling ants are attracted to and prey upon the coffee berry borer, a major pest of coffee production, with greater efficiency in diversified coffee systems when compared with unshaded monocultures (Armbrecht and Gallego, 2007).

## *Changes in disease distribution and viability*

Losses caused by pathogens can contribute significantly to declines in crop production, and changes in climate potentially could affect plant disease distribution and viability in new agricultural regions. From 2001 to 2003, 10% of the global crop losses in wheat, rice, and maize were shown to be a result of pathogens, and despite a clear increase in pesticide use, crop losses have not significantly decreased during the last 40 years (Oerke, 2006). Already observed climate warming appears to have been associated with shifts in plant hosts for some fungi (Gange et al., 2011). In forests of Canada and the western United States, warmer temperatures have been associated with large-scale outbreaks of bark beetles (Bentz et al., 2010; Woods et al., 2010; Woods, 2011), and an increasing severity of phoma stem canker has been observed and modelled on winter oilseed rape in the United Kingdom under climate change (Barnes et al., 2010).

The diversity of crop species in an agroecosystem has a much less predictable effect on microbial pathogens compared with crop pests, as microclimatic conditions play an important role in the development and severity of a disease (Matson et al., 1997; Fuhrer, 2003). The effect of climate change on disease prevalence is therefore much less certain. Climate change could have a positive, a negative, or no impact on individual plant diseases (Chakraborty et al., 2000), but it is suspected that milder winters may favor many crop diseases, such as powdery mildew, brown leaf rust, and stripe rust, whereas warmer summers may provide optimal conditions for other diseases, such as Cercosporea lead spot disease (Patterson et al., 1999). Global change is also predicted to alter the distribution and abundance of arthropod vectors that distribute viruses, thereby affecting the rates of and chances for crop transmission (Anderson et al., 2004). Trends of soil-borne pathogens shows increasing growth with climate change with larger rates of increase in modelled data shown from 2020 to 2030 compared with that of 2000 to 2020 (Manici et al., 2014).

A central tenet of epidemiology is that both the number of diseases and the incidence of disease should increase proportionally to host abundance (Tilman et al., 2002). In one grassland study, in which grassland plant species richness and composition were manipulated, the pathogen load was almost three times greater in the monoculture plots, where host abundance was at a maximum, than in the polyculture plots planted with 24 grassland species. Additionally, the loss of genetic diversity in crop production has led to a hypothesized increase in crop disease susceptibility as a result of higher rates of disease transmission. Many mechanisms reduce the spread of disease in agricultural systems with greater varietal and species richness. Barrier and frequency effects occur when other disease-resistant varieties or species block the ability of a disease or virus to transmit and infect a susceptible host (Finckh et al., 2000). These effects increase with greater spatial and temporal diversity in the agricultural system, and intentional crop system diversity with greater barrier effects can significantly reduce pathogen impacts on crop production. Multiline cultivars and varietal mixtures have been used to effectively retard the spread and evolution of fungal pathogens in small grains and to control some plant viruses (Matson et al., 1997). In Uganda, planting susceptible varieties of common bean with at least 50% of a resistant variety in the same plot, significantly decreased bean fly damage, and in Ecuador, banana trials confirmed that planting resistant and susceptible varieties together can reduce the Sigatoka infection affecting bananas by 40% (Jarvis et al., 2016).

One well-known example of barrier effects in rice production showed that genetic variation within species and within populations can increase the ability of an agricultural system to respond to pathogen diseases. Zhu et al. (2000) demonstrated that in-field genetic crop heterogeneity suppresses disease in rice crops suffering from rice blast. Disease-susceptible rice varieties, when planted in mixtures with resistant varieties over large tracts of land, had 89% greater yield and 94% reduced fungal blast occurrence than when planted in monoculture. Because of this experiment's success, fungicidal sprays were no longer applied to these fields after the trial. Rather, farmers grew rice in mixtures in order to improve the resilience of the systems while reducing economic costs (**Figure 19.2** *The main disease of rice spreads more slowly in mixtures of rice varieties than in monocultures*). There have been few such large-scale experiments to study the efficacy of genetic heterogeneity to increase production, reduce chemical use, and potentially stabilize or even reduce food prices for a region, but these results do provide evidence that intraspecific crop diversification has the potential to effectively control fungal disease spread and protect against crop loss.

Increasing diversification of cereal cropping systems by alternating crops, such as oilseed, pulse, and forage crops, is another option for managing plant disease risk (Krupinsky et al., 2002). Disease cycles can be interrupted through crop rotation by interchanging cereal crops with broadleaf crops that are not susceptible to the same diseases. Reduced tillage could enhance

*Figure 19.2* The main disease of rice

*Note*: Rice blast (pictured inset) spreads more slowly in mixtures of rice varieties than in monocultures, as Zhu et al. (2000) discovered in their large-scale experiments in China.

*Source*: Large photo: Serajulhaque; Inset Photo: Donald Groth, Louisiana State University AgCenter, Bugwood.org

soil biodiversity, leading to greater disease suppression, and stand densities could be adjusted to allow for better microclimatic adjustments to disease growth. These examples show that farmers can take advantage of greater crop diversification to reduce disease susceptibility in agricultural systems, thereby limiting the amount of production loss as a result of crop diseases. Although changes in disease spread and severity are uncertain under climate change, greater genetic variation across space and time could potentially reduce adverse disease transmission impacts that may accompany climate change.

## Changes in climate means and extremes

Agricultural vulnerabilities have been found in a number of important crop species. Observations of rice production in the Philippines during an El Niño drought season showed reductions in seed weight and overall production (Lansigan et al., 2000). Studies of wheat have demonstrated that heat pulses applied to wheat during anthesis reduced both grain number and weight, highlighting the effect of temperature spikes on grain fill (Wollenweber et al., 2003). In maize, researchers observed reduced pollen viability at temperatures above 36 °C, a threshold similar to those in a number of other crops (Porter and Semenov, 2005). Such crops require the development of resilient systems that can buffer against increasing climate variability and extreme events, especially during highly important development periods such as anthesis. There are a variety of ways that diversified agricultural systems which are more structurally complex are able to mitigate the effects of climate change on crop production.

Diversified agroecosystems have become more important for agriculture as climate fluctuations have increased. Research has shown that crop yields are quite sensitive to changes in temperature and precipitation, especially during flower and fruit development stages. Temperature maximums and minimums, as well as seasonal shifts, can have large effects on crop growth and production. Greater variability of precipitation, including flooding, drought, and more extreme rainfall events, has affected food security in many parts of the world (Parry et al., 2005). In a comparative study of farming systems in Sweden and Tanzania, two locations where agriculture has suffered from climate variation and extreme events, it was found that agricultural diversity increased the resilience of the production systems. Sweden suffered from cold-tolerance issues, whereas Tanzania suffered from problems of heat tolerance and irregular El Niño cycles. Both locations experienced greater seasonal drought. In these cases, research showed that successful management practices able to buffer systems from climate variation and protect production were those that were generally more ecologically complex, incorporating wild species into the agricultural system and increasing the temporal and spatial diversity of crops (Tengö and Belfrage, 2004).

Increased tree density within agricultural systems can also protect crops from climate fluctuations and storm events and create a buffer to reduce the impact of floods and droughts on farming systems. In New Zealand, widely-spaced poplar trees reduced pasture production losses caused by landslides during cyclonic storms by 13.8% with, on average, with each tree saving 8.4 m$^2$ of agricultural surface area from production loss (Hawley and Dymond, 1988). If the trees had been planted in a 10 m grid with 100% establishment, storm damage would have been reduced by at least 70% compared with areas without tree cover.

Trees in the landscape also provide the important service of reducing damaging wind speeds associated with extreme storm events to protect crop production. Windbreaks located perpendicular to prevailing winds can increase farm production simply by reducing wind and modifying microclimate. In citrus and vegetable systems in Florida, windbreaks reduced wind speed by up to 31 times windbreak height on their leeward side, although there was great variability in this reduction depending on the height and porosity of the windbreak and wind direction relative to the windbreak (Tamang et al., 2010). In rice systems, trees within agroecosystems have been shown to provide a protective role, for example, through the creation of windbreaks to prevent damage from excessive wind speeds (Umrani and Jain, 2010). Combined with more resistant rice varieties, the increased diversity of agroecosystems will be a critical buffer against extreme weather events and increase the resilience of farmers to cope with climate change. Higher air and soil temperatures on the leeward side of shelterbelts can also extend the growing season by allowing earlier germination and more rapid initial growth (Brandle et al., 2004).

Diverse, complex systems such as agroforestry systems have shown that they are able to buffer crops from large fluctuations in temperature (Lin, 2007), thereby keeping crops in closer-to-optimal conditions. The more shaded systems have also been shown to protect crops from lower precipitation and reduced soil water availability (Lin et al., 2008) because the overstory tree cover reduces soil evaporation and improves soil water infiltration. The ability of increased complexity in agroforestry systems associated with the roots, trunks, and capture of organic matter by trees reduces surface water run-off and increases infiltration and soil water holding capacity. These processes also reduce the risk of flash floods during heavy rainfall and storms (Smith et al., 2012). In one example from Mexico, greater farming intensity of coffee agroforestry systems was correlated with the percentage of farm area lost to landslides and the amount of coffee production lost to premature fruit drop (Philpott et al., 2008).

## Encouraging the adoption of agrobiodiversity to create resilient farm systems

The dependence of social resilience on ecological resilience indicates that agrobiodiversity can have a large role increasing not only ecological stability, but social stability as well (Adger et al., 2002). Highly diverse farm systems that can increase ecosystem functions and protect crops from a range of potential environmental pressures will be increasingly necessary as climate variables push crops outside their thresholds. Although there are substantial benefits when structural and temporal diversity is maintained, farmers are still primarily concerned with productivity and yield. Changes in management must ensure that production stability is maintained in order to support and increase the social-ecological resilience of the system.

### *Evidence that biodiverse systems can maintain and increase economic stability*

Farmers and agricultural managers must consider the variety of ways that diversification can occur within the system and develop methods that best meet their specific needs of crop production and resilience. Of course, as climate change variability increases, the value of resilience will also increase, especially in production systems sensitive to climate variation. However, a farmer's decision to move towards diversified agricultural systems will be highly influenced by the ability of the diversification strategy to support the economic resilience of farms.

A variety of research has shown that high plant diversity within agricultural plots can yield higher production levels than systems with low plant diversity. Grassland experiments have shown that greater plant species diversity is correlated with greater temporal stability in annual aboveground plant production, demonstrating that a more efficient and sustainable supply of food, such as fodder, can be enhanced by increasing biodiversity (Cadotte et al., 2012). In a study examining the effect of species diversity on crop and weed biomass in perennial herbaceous polycultures, biomass increased log linearly with species richness and polycultures outyielded monocultures by an average of 73% (Picasso et al., 2008). A growth in production has also been seen in field experiments manipulating diversity in crop rotations (crops, cover crops, and chemical inputs), showing significantly greater corn grain yields with increased diversification over time (Smith et al., 2008). Such results demonstrate that diverse polycultures can have higher and more stable yields that lead to increased economic benefits for farmers.

However, not all studies have shown that greater diversity leads to increased production yield. In one study, biodiverse rotational systems of three to six species produced 25% lower yield versus integrated monocropped grain systems, although the grain was of higher protein quality. The high-quality grain from the more biodiverse system must be of greater value to overcome the economic benefit of higher production in the lower-quality monoculture (Snapp et al., 2010).

Cost-cutting may present another viable way for farmers to see the possible economic benefits of greater biodiversity. For example, one financially beneficial type of habitat management that has been widely adopted at the within-field scale is the beetle bank, where native grasslands and refugia are maintained at the field margins to protect carabid beetle populations. In one analysis of the costs and benefits associated with pest suppression, the cost of establishing a beetle bank in a 20-hectare (ha) wheat field, combined with yield loss resulting from land removed from production, was calculated at USD 130 for the first year with subsequent costs and yield losses of USD 45 per year. However, the ability to keep aphid populations below a spray threshold through natural enemy suppression saved about USD 450 per year in labour and pesticide costs, and the prevention of aphid induced yield loss saved about USD 1,000 per year for the 20-ha field. These figures show that the loss in productive land for the establishment of the beetle banks was more than offset by the money saved from reduced pesticide use and aphid induced yield loss (Thomas et al., 1991).

Additionally, many biodiverse systems can provide diversified economic income streams for farmers. For example, agroforestry systems offer additional income from both timber and non-timber products provided by shade trees (Somarriba et al., 2004; see also Ingram et al., Chapter 4 of this Handbook). Escalante et al. (1987) reported that fruit and timber from the shade canopy contributed 55–60% of income, respectively. Reviewing a 10-year research study in Central America, Méndez and colleagues (2010) concluded that coffee smallholders managed four types of plant agrodiversity: shade trees, agricultural crops, medicinal plants, and epiphytes and used the plants for food (fruit), firewood, medicine, shade, timber, and ornamental purposes (see also Leakey, Chapter 14 of this Handbook). Farmers reported that agrobiodiversity contributed to household livelihoods by generating products for consumption and sale, reducing vulnerability to market fluctuations and household dependence on outside products, and increasing local commerce. In Nicaragua and El Salvador, the productive value of associated agrobiodiversity goods produced by coffee-growing households accounts for at least 50% of household income (Méndez et al., 2010). The alternative products and income protect farmers when extreme fluctuations when coffee prices occur.

## *Development of tools and decision support systems*

Development of larger-scale diversified landscapes that support and improve ecological resilience in agricultural systems requires a more in-depth analysis of the farm business and landscape-level scenario modelling for on-farm diversity possibilities. For example, Boody et al. (2009) examined how two watersheds in Minnesota would fare under a variety of future land-use scenarios including (a) a continuation of current trends, (b) the application of best management practices (BMPs) over the landscape, (c) a mixture of agricultural uses that maximize diversity and profitability, and (d) a scenario increasing vegetative cover over the landscape (Boody et al., 2009). The scenario that maximized on-farm diversity and profitability moved beyond BMPs alone and included organic cropland, five-year crop rotations, and intensive managed grazing. This diverse system increased profits and biodiversity while reducing environmental externalities (e.g. water quality, greenhouse gases, sedimentation, and flooding), thereby creating a win-win solution. Such scenario modelling of landscapes could be very useful for farmers making decisions about large tracts of land or in systems where there is a cooperative structure in land management. These types of modelling scenarios may also assist decision-makers in long-term planning of landscapes.

Economic models that can predict threshold prices at which farmers begin to adopt environmental land-use practices or payments for ecosystem services can also be highly effective in encouraging farmer adoption of diversified agricultural systems. In one model of the potential of farmers to participate in carbon sequestration contracts and increase sequestration potential through agroforestry and terracing of fields, analysis showed that at prices higher than $50 per metric ton of carbon, adoption would increase substantially, and at prices of $100 per metric ton of carbon, terrace and agroforestry adoption for carbon sequestration would have the potential to raise per capita incomes by up to 15% (Antle et al., 2007). Such economic models are also helpful for understanding whether price incentives are effective for a particular goal. In a study by Wu et al. (2004) of price incentives for agriculture conservation practices in order to reduce nutrient and soil pollution of the Mississippi River, an economic model showed that payments of $50 per acre for conservation tillage and crop rotation increased the adoption of these conservation practices but were limited in their potential to reduce hypoxia, the ultimate goal. Such results allowed policy-makers to concentrate on alternate conservation options and incentives that would have a larger impact on the ultimate goal of reducing hypoxia (Wu et al., 2004).

Another option is to provide direct support to farmers through outreach and on-the-ground assistance. More than ever, resource-users will need to anticipate and prepare for each climate-related challenge, and institutions will need to be particularly supportive if resource industries and the extended social systems dependent on them are to be sustained (Marshall, 2010). When farmers are active participants in developing adaptation solutions, such as the modelling scenarios of on-farm crop mixtures and rotations, solutions can be developed that are more readily adopted onto their farms. For example, researchers worked with cattle-graziers in Australia to cope and adapt to climate variability by facilitating collaborative learning amongst graziers and other stakeholders to develop strategic skills, increasing climate awareness, developing financial security, and adopting climate tools such as seasonal climate forecasts (Marshall, 2010). In communities with fewer resources, community-based adaptation (CBA) is often used for agricultural adaptation because it emphasized the social, political, and economic drivers of vulnerability and highlights the needs of vulnerable people within a local context (Forsyth, 2013). Stakeholder involvement and participatory research are often very useful tools in developing adaptation options that will be adopted by a local community because these methods recognize that knowledge often lies with the farmers in the field, and that local considerations should be integrated into long-term planning (Rivington et al., 2007).

## Conclusions

It is abundantly clear that farmers are facing growing stress from climate change, and that the greater implementation of diversified agricultural systems may be a productive way to build resilience into agricultural systems. Although climate change may produce a shift in pests, diseases, and production thresholds, agricultural systems with greater plant biodiversity improves the system's resilience by insuring that many valuable ecosystem functions are maintained through unpredictable climate transitions and outcomes. Although a diverse system may seem functionally redundant at the present, they may no longer prove redundant as future changes occur. The diversity of plant species within the agroecosystem therefore provides long-term sustainability options for agricultural systems by building up a bank of ecological strategies to employ in the future and are an important asset for farmers and communities to manage risk.

Globally, diversified agriculture can play a large role in safeguarding food security and production in regions where farmers have little access to chemical, structural, or technological resources. Diversified farming strategies are supported by international research efforts, including the International Assessment of Agricultural Knowledge, Science and Technology for Development (IAASTD, 2009), a global report of more than 400 scientists that concluded that locally adapted seed and ecological farming methods better addressed the complexities of climate change, hunger, poverty, and production demands on agriculture in the developing world. The report also showed that the ecological processes of these more complex systems could be used to protect farmers from climatic change and improve food security.

Understanding the potential of increasing diversity within farm systems is essential to helping farmers adapt to greater climate variability of the future. The adoption of diversified agricultural systems could be bolstered if farmers have a better idea of how to optimize a diversified structure to maximize production and profits. Crop and landscape simulation models that can model a range of climate scenarios and landscape modelling with farm profitability scenarios would help farmers find optimal strategies for maintaining production and profit. Stakeholder-based and community-based participatory research would also be highly beneficial, as researchers could model strategies that seem plausible to farmers. By adopting farm systems that promote ecosystem services for pest and disease control and resilience to climate change variability, farmers are less at risk to production loss and are more generally resilient to environmental change.

## References


ADB (Asian Development Bank) (2009) *The Economics of Climate Change in Southeast Asia: A Regional Review*, Manila, The Philippines.

Adger, W. N. (2000) 'Social and ecological resilience: Are they related?', *Progress in Human Geography*, vol. 24, pp. 347–364.

Adger, W. N., Kelly, P. M., Winkels, A., Huy, L. Q. and Locke, C. (2002) 'Migration, remittances, livelihood trajectories, and social resilience', *AMBIO: A Journal of the Human Environment*, vol. 31, pp. 358–366.

Altieri, M. A. (1999) 'The ecological role of biodiversity in agroecosystems', *Agriculture, Ecosystems & Environment*, vol. 74, pp. 19–31.

Anderson, P. K., Cunningham, A. A., Patel, N. G., Morales, F. J., Epstein, P. R. and Daszak, P. (2004) 'Emerging infectious diseases of plants: Pathogen pollution, climate change and agrotechnology drivers', *Trends in Ecology & Evolution*, vol. 19, pp. 535–544.

Antle, J. M., Stoorvogel, J. J. and Valdivia, R. O. (2007) 'Assessing the economic impacts of agricultural carbon sequestration: Terraces and agroforestry in the Peruvian Andes', *Agriculture, Ecosystems & Environment*, vol. 122, pp. 435–445.

Armbrecht, I. and Gallego, M. C. (2007) 'Testing ant predation on the coffee berry borer in shaded and sun coffee plantations in Colombia', *Entomologia Experimentalis et Applicata*, vol. 124, pp. 261–267.

Bale, J. S., Masters, G. J., Hodkinson, I. D., Awmack, C., Bezemer, T. M., Brown, V. K., Butterfield, J., Buse, A., Coulson, J. C., Farrar, J., Good, J. E. G., Harrington, R., Hartley, S., Jones, T. H., Lindroth, R. L., Press, M. C., Symrnioudis, I., Watt, A. D. and Whittaker, J. B. (2002) 'Herbivory in global climate change research: Direct effects of rising temperature on insect herbivores', *Global Change Biology*, vol. 8, pp. 1–16.

Barnes, A. P., Wreford, A., Butterworth, M. H., Semenov, M. A., Moran, D., Evans, N. and Fitt, B. D. L. (2010) Adaptation to increasing severity of phoma stem canker on winter oilseed rape in the UK under climate change. *Journal of Agricultural Science*, vol. 148, pp. 683–694.

Bentz, B. J., Régnière, J., Fettig, C. J., Hansen, E. M., Hayes, J. L., Hicke, J. A., Kelsey, R. G., Negron, J. F. and Seybold, S. J.; (2010) Climate change and bark beetles of the Western United States and Canada: Direct and indirect effects, *BioScience*, vol. 60, pp. 602–613.

Boody, G., Vondracek, B., Andow, D. A., Krinke, M., Westra, J., Zimmerman, J. and Welle, P. (2009) 'Multifunctional agriculture in the United States', *BioScience*, vol. 55, pp. 27–38.

Brandle, J. R., Hodges, L. and Zhou, X. H. (2004) 'Windbreaks in North American agricultural systems', *Agroforestry Systems*, vol. 61–62, pp. 65–78.

Cadotte, M. W., Dinnage, R. and Tilman, D. (2012) 'Phylogenetic diversity promotes ecosystem stability', *Ecology*, vol. 93, pp. S223–S233.

Cannon, R. J. C. (1998) 'The implications of predicted climate change for insect pests in the UK, with emphasis on non-indigenous species', *Global Change Biology*, vol. 4, pp. 785–796.

Chakraborty, S., Tiedemann, A. V. and Teng, P. S. (2000) 'Climate change: Potential impact on plant diseases', *Environmental Pollution*, vol. 108, pp. 317–326.

Dalin, P., Kindvall, O. and Björkman, C. (2009) 'Reduced population control of an insect pest in managed willow monocultures', *PLoS One*, vol. 4, p. e5487.

Deryng, D., Conway, D., Ramankutty, N., Price, J. and Warren, R. (2014) 'Global crop yield response to extreme heat stress under multiple climate change futures', *Environmental Research Letters*, vol. 9, p. 034011.

Elmqvist, T., Folke, C., Nystrom, M., Peterson, G., Bengtsson, J., Walker, B. and Norberg, J. (2003) 'Response diversity, ecosystem change, and resilience', *Frontiers in Ecology and the Environment*, vol. 1, pp. 488–494.

Escalante, E., Aguilar, A. and Lugo, R. (1987) 'Identificacion, evaluacion y distribucion espacial de especies utilizados como sombra en sistemas tradicionales de cafe (*Coffea arabica*) en dos zonas del estado de Trujillo, Venezuela', *Venezuela Forestal*, vol. 3, pp. 50–62.

Finckh, M. R., Gacek, E., Goyeau, H., Lannou, C., Merz, U., Mundt, C., Munk, L., Nadziak, J., Newton, A., De Vallavieille-Pope, D. and Wolfe, M. (2000) 'Cereal variety and species mixtures in practice, with emphasis on disease resistance', *Agronomie*, vol. 20, pp. 813–837.

Folke, C., Carpenter, S., Walker, B., Scheffer, M., Elmqvist, T., Gunderson, L. and Holling, C. S. (2004) 'Regime shifts, resilience, and biodiversity in ecosystem management', *Annual Review of Ecology, Evolution, and Systematics*, vol. 35, pp. 557–581.

Forsyth, T. (2013) 'Community-based adaptation: A review of past and future challenges', *Wiley Interdisciplinary Reviews: Climate Change*, vol. 4, pp. 439–446.

Fuhrer, J. (2003) 'Agroecosystem responses to combinations of elevated $CO_2$, ozone, and global climate change', *Agriculture, Ecosystems & Environment*, vol. 97, pp. 1–20.

Gange, A. C., Gange, E. G., Mohammad, A. B., and Boddy, L. (2011) 'Host shifts in fungi caused by climate change?', *Fungal Ecology*, vol. 4, pp. 184–190.

Gurr, G. M., Wratten, S. D. and Luna, J. M. (2003) 'Multi-function agricultural biodiversity: Pest management and other benefits', *Basic and Applied Ecology*, vol. 4, pp. 107–116.

Haile, M. (2005) 'Weather patterns, food security and humanitarian response in sub-Saharan Africa', *Philosophical Transactions of the Royal Society B – Biological Sciences*, vol. 360, pp. 2169–2182.

Hawley, J. G. and Dymond, J. R. (1988) 'How much do trees reduce landsliding?', *Journal of Soil and Water Conservation*, vol. 43, pp. 495–498.

Heal, G. (2000) *Nature and the Marketplace: Capturing the Value of Ecosystem Services*, Island Press, Washington, DC, USA.

Hodgkin, T., Eyzaguirre, P., Mijatovic, D. and van Oudenhoven, F. (2013) *The Role of Agricultural Biodiversity in Strengthening Resilience to Climate Change: Towards an Analytical Framework*, FAO, Rome, Italy.

Holling, C. S. (1973) 'Resilience and stability of ecological systems', *Annual Review of Ecology and Systematics*, vol. 4, pp. 1–23.

International Assessment of Agricultural Knowledge, Science and Technology for Development (IAASTD) (2009) *Agriculture at a Crossroads. Global Report*, B. D. McIntyre, H. R. Herren, J. Wakhungu and R. T. Watson (eds.), Island Press, Washington, DC, USA.

IPCC (2013) 'Summary for policymakers', pp. 3–29 in *Climate Change 2013: The Physical Science Basis. Contribution of Working Group I to the Fifth Assessment Report of the Intergovernmental Panel on Climate Change*, T. F. Stocker, D. Qin, G.-K. Plattner, M. Tignor, S. K. Allen, J. Boschung, A. Nauels, Y. Xia, V. Bex and P. M. Midgley (eds.), Cambridge University Press, Cambridge, UK and New York, NY, USA.

Izumi, T., Sakuma, H., Yokozawa, M., Luo, J., Challinor, A. J., Brown, M. E., Sakurai, G. and Yamagata, T. (2013) 'Prediction of seasonal climate-induced variations in global food production', *Nature Climate Change*, vol. 3, pp. 904–908.

Jarvis, D. I., Hodgkin, T., Brown, A. H., Tuxill, J., Noriega, I. L., Smale, M. and Sthapit, B. (2016) *Crop Genetic Diversity in the Field and on the Farm: Principles and Applications in Research Practices*, Yale University Press, New Haven, CT, USA.

Krupinsky, J. M., Bailey, K. L., McMullen, M. P., Gossen, B. D. and Turkington, T. K. (2002) 'Managing plant disease risk in diversified cropping systems', *Agronomy Journal*, vol. 94, pp. 198–209.

Landis, D. A., Wratten, S. D. and Gurr, G. M. (2000) 'Habitat management to conserve natural enemies of arthropod pests in agriculture', *Annual Review of Entomology*, vol. 45, pp. 175–201.

Langellotto, G. and Denno, R. (2004) 'Responses of invertebrate natural enemies to complex-structured habitats: A meta-analytical synthesis', *Oecologia*, vol. 139, pp. 1–10.

Lansigan, F. P., de los Santos, W. L. and Coladilla, J. O. (2000) 'Agronomic impacts of climate variability on rice production in the Philippines', *Agriculture, Ecosystems & Environment*, vol. 82, pp. 129–137.

Lin, B. B. (2007) 'Agroforestry management as an adaptive strategy against potential microclimate extremes in coffee agriculture', *Agricultural and Forest Meteorology*, vol. 144, pp. 85–94.

Lin, B. B., Perfecto, I. and Vandermeer, J. (2008) 'Synergies between agricultural intensification and climate change could create surprising vulnerabilities for crops', *BioScience*, vol. 58, pp. 847–854.

Loreau, M. and Mazancourt, C. (2013) 'Biodiversity and ecosystem stability: A synthesis of underlying mechanisms', *Ecology Letters*, vol. 16, pp. 106–115.

Manici, L. M., Bregaglio, S., Fumagalli, D. and Donatelli, M. (2014) 'Modelling soil borne fungal pathogens of arable crops under climate change', *International Journal of Biometeorology*, vol. 58, pp. 2071–2083.

Marshall, N. A. (2010) 'Understanding social resilience to climate variability in primary enterprises and industries', *Global Environmental Change*, vol. 20, pp. 36–43.

Matson, P. A., Parton, W. J., Power, A. G. and Swift, M. J. (1997) 'Agricultural intensification and ecosystem properties', *Science*, vol. 277, pp. 504–509.

Méndez, V. E., Bacon, C. M., Olson, M., Morris, K. S. and Shattuck, A. K. (2010) 'Agrobiodiversity and shade coffee smallholder livelihoods: A review and synthesis of ten years of research in Central America: Special focus section on geographic contributions to agrobiodiversity research', *Professional Geographer*, vol. 62, pp. 357–376.

Mijatovic, D., van Oudenhoven, F., Eyzaguirre, P. and Hodgkin, T. (2013) 'The role of agricultural biodiversity in strengthening resilience to climate change: Towards an analytical framework', *International Journal of Agricultural Sustainability*, vol. 11, pp. 95–107.

Nellemann, C., MacDevette, M., Manders, T., Eickhout, B., Svihus, B., Prins, A. G. and Kaltenborn, B. P. (eds.) (2009) *The Environmental Food Crisis – The Environment's Role in Averting Future Food Crises: A UNEP Rapid Response Assessment*, United Nations Environment Programme, GRID-Arendal, www.grida.no

Oerke, E.-C. (2006) 'Crop losses to pests', *The Journal of Agricultural Science*, vol. 144, pp. 31–43.

Parry, M., Rosenzweig, C. and Livermore, M. (2005) 'Climate change, global food supply and risk of hunger', *Philosophical Transactions of the Royal Society B – Biological Sciences*, vol. 360, pp. 2125–2138.

Patterson, D. T., Westbrook, J. K., Joyce, R.J.V., Lingren, P. D. and Rogasik, J. (1999) 'Weeds, insects, and diseases', *Climatic Change*, vol. 43, pp. 711–727.

Perfecto, I., Vandermeer, J. H., Bautista, G. L., Nuñez, G. I., Greenberg, R., Bichier, P. and Langridge, S. (2004) 'Greater predation in shaded coffee farms: The role of resident Neotropical birds', *Ecology*, vol. 85, pp. 2677–2681.

Philpott, S. M., Lin, B. B., Jha, S. and Brines, S. J. (2008) 'A multi-scale assessment of hurricane impacts on agricultural landscapes based on land use and topographic features', *Agriculture, Ecosystems & Environment*, vol. 128, pp. 12–20.

Picasso, V. D., Brummer, E. C., Liebman, M., Dixon, P. M. and Wilsey, B. J. (2008) 'Crop species diversity affects productivity and weed suppression in perennial polycultures under two management strategies', *Crop Science*, vol. 48, pp. 331–342.

Porter, J. R. and Semenov, M. A. (2005) 'Crop responses to climatic variation', *Philosophical Transactions of the Royal Society B – Biological Sciences*, vol. 360, pp. 2021–2035.

Rivington, M., Matthews, K. B., Bellocchi, G., Buchan, K., Stöckle, C. O. and Donatelli, M. (2007) 'An integrated assessment approach to conduct analyses of climate change impacts on whole-farm systems', *Environmental Modelling & Software*, vol. 22, pp. 202–210.

Sheehan, W. (1986) 'Response by specialist and generalist natural enemies to agroecosystem diversification: A selective review', *Environmental Entomology*, vol. 15, pp. 456–461.

Smith, R., Gross, K. and Robertson, G. (2008) 'Effects of crop diversity on agroecosystem function: Crop yield response', *Ecosystems*, vol. 11, pp. 355–366.

Smith, J., Pearce, B. D. and Wolfe, M. S. (2012) 'A European perspective for developing modern multifunctional agroforestry systems for sustainable intensification', *Renewable Agriculture and Food Systems*, vol. 27, pp. 323–332.

Snapp, S. S., Gentry, L. E. and Harwood, R. (2010) 'Management intensity – not biodiversity – the driver of ecosystem services in a long-term row crop experiment', *Agriculture, Ecosystems & Environment*, vol. 138, pp. 242–248.

Somarriba, E., Harvey, C., Samper, M., Anthony, F., González, J., Staver, C. and Rice, R. (2004) 'Biodiversity conservation in neotropical coffee (*Coffea arabica*) plantations', pp. 198–226 in G. Schroth, G. da Fonseca, C. Harvey, C. Gascon, H. Vasoncelos and A. Izac (eds.), *Agroforestry and Biodiversity Conservation in Tropical Landscapes*, Island Press, Washington, DC, USA.

Sunderland, K. and Samu, F. (2000) 'Effects of agricultural diversification on the abundance, distribution, and pest control potential of spiders: A review', *Entomologia Experimentalis et Applicata*, vol. 95, pp. 1–13.

Tamang, B., Andreu, M. and Rockwood, D. (2010) 'Microclimate patterns on the leeside of single-row tree windbreaks during different weather conditions in Florida farms: Implications for improved crop production', *Agroforestry Systems*, vol. 79, pp. 111–122.

Tengö, M. and Belfrage, K. (2004) 'Local management practices for dealing with change and uncertainty: A cross-scale comparison of cases in Sweden and Tanzania', *Ecology and Society*, vol. 9, p. 4.

Thomas, M. B., Wratten, S. D. and Sotherton, N. W. (1991) 'Creation of "island" habitats in farmland to manipulate populations of beneficial arthropods: Predator densities and emigration', *Journal of Applied Ecology*, vol. 28, pp. 906–917.

Tilman, D., Cassman, K. G., Matson, P. A., Naylor, R., and Polasky, S. (2002) 'Agricultural sustainability and intensive production practices', *Nature*, vol. 418, pp. 671–677.

Umrani, R. and Jain, C. K. (2010) *Agroforestry Systems and Practices*, Global Media, Jaipur, India.

Vandermeer, J., van Noordwijk, M., Anderson, J., Ong, C. and Perfecto, I. (1998) 'Global change and multi-species agroecosystems: Concepts and issues', *Agriculture, Ecosystems & Environment*, vol. 67, pp. 1–22.

Wollenweber, B., Porter, J. R. and Schellberg, J. (2003) 'Lack of interaction between extreme high-temperature events at vegetative and reproductive growth stages in wheat', *Journal of Agronomy and Crop Science*, vol. 189, pp. 142–150.

Woods, A. J. (2011) 'Is the health of British Columbia's forests being influenced by climate change? If so, was this predictable?', *Canadian Journal of Plant Pathology*, vol. 33, pp. 117–126.

Woods, A. J., Heppner, D., Kope, H. H., Burleigh, J. and Maclauchlan, L. (2010) 'Forest health and climate change: A British Columbia perspective', *The Forestry Chronicle*, vol. 86, pp. 412–422.

Wu, J., Adams, R. M., Kling, C. L. and Tanaka, K. (2004) 'From microlevel decisions to landscape changes: An assessment of agricultural conservation policies', *American Journal of Agricultural Economics*, vol. 86, pp. 26–41.

Yachi, S. and Loreau, M. (1999) 'Biodiversity and ecosystem productivity in a fluctuating environment: The insurance hypothesis', *Proceedings of the National Academy of Sciences USA*, vol. 96, pp. 1463–1468.

Zhu, Y., Chen, H., Fan, J., Wang, Y., Li, Y., Chen, J., Fan, J., Yang, S, Hu, L., Leung, H., Mew, T. W., Teng, P. S., Wang, Z. and Mundt, C. C. (2000) 'Genetic diversity and disease control in rice', *Nature*, vol. 406, pp. 718–722.

# 20

# AN ARGUMENT FOR INTEGRATING WILD AND AGRICULTURAL BIODIVERSITY CONSERVATION

*Simon J. Attwood, Sarah E. Park, Paul Marshall, John H. Fanshawe and Hannes Gaisberger*

*'The last word in ignorance is the man who says of an animal or plant, "What good is it?" If the land mechanism as a whole is good, then every part is good, whether we understand it or not.'*

– Aldo Leopold, *Round River: From the Journals of Aldo Leopold*

## Wild biodiversity conservation

A fundamental postulate of conservation biology is that 'Biotic diversity has intrinsic value,[1] irrespective of its instrumental or utilitarian value' (Soulé, 1985). Much of the rationale for WBD conservation was originally constructed around intrinsic values of nature, ideas of wilderness, and the protection of sites of outstanding beauty. A notable example is the designation of Yellowstone National Park in 1872. Here the combined efforts of the geologist Ferdinand Hayden, landscape artist Thomas Moran and photographer William Jackson were instrumental in bringing the beauty of the area to the attention of the U.S. Congress (Ross-Bryant, 2013). Even today, this National Park bases its conservation ethos on 'highlight[ing] the park's amazing wildlife, geothermal areas, rich history and awe-inspiring wilderness' (Yellowstone Association, 2016).

As early as the 1930s, however, a different conservation paradigm started to surface (Peterson, 2010). This is based upon the premise that WBD has utilitarian and instrumental values for humanity. Using this perspective, conservation is justified only to the extent that it benefits human society. It follows that conservation efforts can be evaluated in terms of their costs and benefits to society. Utilitarian perspectives of ecological function started to truly gain traction in the late 1960s and 1970s. Westman (1977) reported on several early attempts to evaluate and quantify the benefits derived from various ecosystems and their processes. In doing so, he notes the 'inexorable quest' of Western policy makers to quantify the monetary value of that which had formerly been regarded as 'priceless' and 'public goods' (*sensu* Mitchell and Carson, 1989), such as clean air and water, and wilderness. These had generally been considered only in terms of their intrinsic or aesthetic values. As the application of a utilitarian perspective has grown, the natural world has increasingly come under the quantitative eye of economists and policy makers.

However, as Westman stated, and as others later came to demonstrate, the benefits of nature in an undeveloped, compared with a developed, state could be more objectively demonstrated using a utilitarian approach, thus leading to (in theory, at least) more informed decision-making (Peh et al., 2013).

Utilitarian perspectives of ecological function and biodiversity have informed and underpinned the concept of 'ecosystem services' (first termed by Ehrlich and Ehrlich, 1981). Ecosystem services describe the direct and indirect contributions of ecosystems and biodiversity to human well-being (TEEB Foundations, 2010). Subsequent description and categorisation of ecosystem services has evolved; for instance, the Millennium Ecosystem Assessment (MEA) used the following categories: supporting (e.g. nutrient cycling), provisioning (e.g. food), regulating (e.g. climate regulation) and cultural (e.g. recreational) (MEA, 2005). Similarly, TEEB (The Economics of Ecosystems and Biodiversity) has more recently developed a list of 22 broad ecosystem services divided into four categories (provisioning, regulating, habitat and supporting, cultural and amenity) (De Groot et al., 2010).

Over the last couple of decades, ecosystem service concepts and frameworks have been used to produce increasingly impressive and influential estimates of the economic 'value' of biodiversity to humanity (e.g. Costanza et al., 1997). They have also described in detail the extent to which ecosystem services underpin human well-being (MEA, 2005), and in doing so, galvanised the creation and application of a wide range of tools and approaches for assessing and valuing ecosystem services in a range of contexts (e.g. Peh et al., 2013). Many advocates of ecosystem services argue that the act of putting a financial value on biodiversity provides the means for achieving its conservation (Juniper, 2013); others disagree, stressing the intrinsic (McAuley, 2006; Monbiot, 2013). With vociferous advocates on both sides, the 'utilitarian versus intrinsic' debate remains one of the most hotly contested areas in biodiversity conservation (Justus et al., 2009; Schröter et al., 2014).

Regardless of issues around utilitarian and intrinsic approaches to conservation, a substantial body of evidence shows that WBD makes enormous contributions to a wide range of ecosystem services that benefit humans (**Table 20.1** *Ecosystem service generation from wild biodiversity and agricultural biodiversity*). Consequently, there is a considerable push to both institutionalise and create incentives for the conservation of ecosystem services. Payments for Ecosystem Services (PES) is a collective term used to describe a wide range of policy and institutional mechanisms used to incentivise WBD and ecosystem service conservation and deliver them to a wide range of stakeholders in numerous countries around the world.

Payments for Ecosystem Services (PES) are incentives (e.g. monetary payments, tax levies) provided to owners or managers of land and other natural resources in exchange for maintaining a supply of ecosystem services. PES programs can involve contracts between consumers of ecosystem services and those who supply them (private deals), trading in formal markets (regulatory ecosystem services markets) or direct payments by governments or public institutions to landowners and/or managers (public payment schemes).

One of the largest and original PES programs is the United States Conservation Reserve Program. This public payment PES scheme paid $19.5 billion to 'rent' a combined 33.9 million acres of land through 239,000 contracts with farmers and landowners, who agreed to manage the land so as to reduce soil erosion, improve water quality and foster wildlife habitat (Young and Osborn, 1990). A local government authority-facilitated PES scheme run in Honduras offers an example of a private PES approach. Here the scheme was aimed at restoring water quality in the Cumes River. The villagers downstream who relied on clean river water made monthly payments as incentives to coffee producers upstream to improve land management and reduce the impacts of their farming practices on water quality (Porras and Neves, 2006). In contrast, regulatory PES schemes are characterised by open trading, with one of the best known examples

*Table 20.1* Ecosystem service generation from wild biodiversity and agricultural biodiversity using the TEEB ecosystem service classification (www.teebweb.org/resources/ecosystem-services/) and with selected supporting references for each example

| *Ecosystem service (ES)* | *How wild biodiversity contributes to ES* | *Selected key references* | *How agricultural biodiversity contributes to ES* | *Selected key references* |
|---|---|---|---|---|
| Provisioning: Food | Wild caught and farmed fish and other aquatic organisms;<br>Harvested wild plants;<br>Other wild animals (e.g. mammals, birds, insects). | De Groot et al., 2012;<br>Nicholson et al., 2009;<br>Worm et al., 2006;<br>Reuter et al., 2016. | Crop provisioning;<br>Livestock provisioning;<br>Nutritional and dietary diversity; increased number of functional traits leads to more resistant and resilient crops. | Thrupp, 2000;<br>Johns and Sthapit, 2004;<br>Kremen and Miles, 2012;<br>Hajjar et al., 2008;<br>Malézieux et al., 2009. |
| Provisioning: Raw materials | Wood (e.g. for building, boats, fuel), biochemical compounds (e.g. gums, oils), fibres, animal feed (e.g. grasses). | De Groot et al., 2012;<br>De Groot et al., 2002;<br>Schwenk et al., 2012. | Fibre, oils, biochemical compounds, animal feeds (e.g. grasses), timber, fertiliser, fuel. | Calvet-Mir et al., 2012 |
| Provisioning: Fresh water | Native vegetation influencing local to global rainfall patterns; roles in global hydrological cycle; localised water purification. | Porras et al., 2008;<br>Sheil 2014;<br>Brauman et al., 2007. | Reduced need for pesticides due to agrobiodiversity-based pest and disease control; complex vegetation structure as filtration. | Hajjar et al., 2008;<br>Knowler and Bradshaw, 2007;<br>Reganold, 1995. |
| Provisioning: Medicinal resources | Plants and animal parts used as traditional medicines; raw materials for pharmaceuticals. | Khan et al., 2013 | Plants used as traditional medicines; raw materials for pharmaceuticals. | Khan et al., 2013. |
| Regulating: Local climate and air quality | Provision of shade by trees; forests influence rainfall and water availability at multiple scales; plants regulating air quality by removing pollutants from atmosphere. | Jim and Chen, 2009;<br>Lawrence and Vandecar, 2015. | Increased trait diversity and varieties adapted to local and future conditions (increased capacity for adaptation to climate change). | Bellon et al., 2011. |

| | | | | |
|---|---|---|---|---|
|  Regulating: Carbon sequestration and storage | Ecosystems storing and sequestering greenhouse gases (thus regulating climate); biodiversity improving capacity of ecosystems to adapt to effects of climate change. | Alongi, 2012; Rajab et al., 2016. | Increased carbon sequestration through more continuous biomass; increased soil function and carbon sequestration; increased use of legumes reduces need for NPK use. | Hajjar et al., 2008; Chianu et al., 2011; Rajab et al., 2016. |
|  Regulating: Moderation of extreme events | Ecosystems and living organisms create buffers against natural disasters, thereby preventing/reducing possible damage. e.g. wetlands absorbing flood water, tree and grass roots stabilising soil on slopes, coral reefs and mangroves protecting coastlines from storm surges and damage. | Nedkov et al., 2012; Brauman et al., 2007; Zedler and Kercher, 2005; Barbier et al., 2011. | Soil erosion reduction due to more continuous ground cover (e.g. cover crops, mulch); improved soil structure and condition through local crop variety use. | Kassam et al., 2009; Altieri, 2002; Hajjar et al., 2008; Bellon and Taylor, 1993. |
|  Regulating: Waste-water treatment | Wetlands filter both human and animal waste and agricultural run-off, acting as a natural buffer to the surrounding environment. Soil microorganisms metabolise and break down waste and pollutants. Pathogen elimination/ reduction. | Zedler et al., 2005; Brander et al., 2013; Blumenfeld et al., 2009. | Land use practices that ensure perennial ground cover, favour deep-rooted crops and protect or restore riparian vegetation contribute to better quality of water flowing out of agricultural areas. | Ayers and Westcot, 1985; Osborne and Kovacic, 1993. |
|  Regulating: Erosion prevention and maintenance of soil fertility | Vegetation cover prevents/reduces soil erosion (e.g. through reduced water impact, soil stabilisation of root systems, increased organic matter in soil, increased porosity). Soil fertility is maintained through complex interactions and functions of soil biota including bacteria, fungi and arthropods. | Mohammad and Adam, 2010; Barrow, 1991. | Soil erosion reduction due to more continuous ground cover (e.g. cover crops, mulch); improved soil structure and condition through local crop variety use. | Kassam et al., 2009; Altieri, 2002; Hajjar et al., 2008; Bellon and Taylor, 1993; Snapp et al., 2010. |

*(Continued)*

*Table 20.1* (Continued)

| *Ecosystem service (ES)* | *How wild biodiversity contributes to ES* | *Selected key references* | *How agricultural biodiversity contributes to ES* | *Selected key references* |
|---|---|---|---|---|
| Regulating: Pollination | Animal-driven pollination is provided mainly by insects, but also by some species of birds and bats. It is essential for the pollination of many fruit and vegetable crops. | Hoehn et al., 2008; Albrecht et al., 2012; Nicholls and Altieri, 2013. | Greater crop diversity attracting greater abundance and diversity/richness of pollinating species. | Brooker et al., 2015; Nicholls and Altieri, 2013. |
| Regulating: Biological control | Ecosystems regulate pests and diseases through the activities of predators and parasitoids. Birds, bats, insects and other arthropods (e.g. wasps, spiders), frogs and fungi all act as natural controls on a wide range of pests and diseases. | Letourneau et al., 2011; Karp et al., 2013. | Inter-cropping and inter-specific crop diversity providing habitat and resources for natural enemies. Intra-specific diversity suppressing pests and diseases. | Hajjar et al., 2008; Jarvis et al., 2007; Flint and Roberts, 2008; Noman et al., 2013. |
| Habitat/supporting: Habitats for species | Habitats provide everything that individual organisms or communities or organism needs to survive: food, water and shelter. Each ecosystem provides different habitats that can be essential for a species' life cycle. | Fiedler et al., 2008. | Inter-cropping and inter-specific crop diversity providing habitat. Low external input agricultural systems supporting greater wild biodiversity. | Wright et al.,2012; Perfecto and Vandermeer, 2008; Laube et al., 2008. |
| Habitat/supporting: Maintenance of genetic diversity | Genetic diversity is the variety of genes between and within species populations. Genetic diversity provides the basis for species to adapt to changing environmental conditions (e.g. climatic change) . | Barrett and Schluter, 2008. | Genetic diversity distinguishes different breeds or races from each other thus providing the basis for locally well-adapted cultivars and a gene pool for further developing commercial crops and livestock. | Lin, 2011. |
| Cultural: Recreation and mental and physical health | Recreational pursuits in green space have positive physical and mental health benefits. The positive impact of green space on mental health is increasingly becoming recognised. | Díaz et al., 2006; Fuller et al., 2007; Sandifer et al., 2015. | Agricultural landscapes, like grasslands and forests, offer space for recreation, including horse-riding and mountain-biking, while well-managed aquatic systems, including lakes and rivers, offer recreational fishing. | van Berkel and Verberg (2012). |

| | | | | |
|---|---|---|---|---|
|  Cultural: Tourism | Ecosystems and biodiversity play an important role for many kinds of tourism which in turn provides considerable economic benefits for many countries. Cultural and eco-tourism can also educate people about the importance of biological diversity. | Glowinski, 2008; US Fish and Wildlife, 2014; Balmford et al., 2015. | Increasingly, farms land farmed landscapes attract tourists, so-called agri-tourism, notably from urban areas. Forests and marine habitats are also critical, including coral reefs, and areas recreational fishing, including sports sea fishing. | Carpio et al., 2008; Phelan and Sharpley, 2010. |
|  Cultural: Aesthetic appreciation and inspiration for culture, art and design | Biodiversity, ecosystems and natural landscapes have been the source of inspiration for much of our art, culture and increasingly for science. | Oswald, 2005; Buckland, 2006; Armitage and Dee, 2009; Weintraub, 2012; Nature's Toolbox, 2012. | Landscapes, such as Globally Important Agricultural Heritage Sites (GIAHS), have significant cultural value, and regular feature in the work of a wide range of artists, from painters to writers to photographers.<br>Inspiration to artists from Renaissance paintings to food sculptures of Lernet and Sander. | Lu and Li (2006); Nahuelhual (2013); Lernet and Sander; Ackroyd & Harvey, 2016. |
|  Cultural: Spiritual experience and sense of place | Nature is a common element of all major religions and traditional knowledge, and associated customs are important for creating a sense of belonging. | Tucker and Grim,1997–2004; Kala and Sharma, 2010; Cardelús et al., 2013. | The existence, maintenance and use of traditional foods, drinks and flavourings, is a commonplace component of many faith-based practices, including in terms of fasting, and restrictions. Domestic animals also play a critical role many cultural traditions. | Lindgreen and Hingley, 2009; Schut, 2012; Nath et al., 2013; Weldon and Campbell, 2014. |

*Source*: Reproduced from Attwood et al. (in preparation).

being the carbon market established by the Kyoto Protocol. Managing the growth of forests is a prominent mechanism for sequestering carbon and generating carbon dioxide emission reduction certificates. These are sold through the market to entities required to offset their emissions in order to meet sectoral or national commitments.

While PES can apply to any type of ecosystem service valued by a potential purchaser, the majority of operational programs focus predominantly on climate change mitigation, watershed services and biodiversity conservation. PES schemes require specific conditions to operate effectively. These include a clear demand for ecosystem services that are financially valuable, threats to the supply of ecosystem services, specific actions to address supply constraints, and dependable institutions for implementing and enforcing contract arrangements (Forest Trends/The Katoomba Group/UNEP, 2008).

## Ecosystem service research trends

Along with the development and expansion of PES schemes, research on ecosystem services has grown rapidly over the last 20 years. The number of academic papers focused on ecosystem services has increased from just two publications in 1995 to almost 800 in 2015. There has also been an increase in the diversity of disciplines to which the concept is applied. Having been initially nurtured in forest and woodland conservation arenas in its early years (nearly a quarter of all papers published before the year 2000 related to forests or woodlands), the concept has evolved rapidly and has been incorporated into disciplines as diverse as marine or ocean science, business and education. With almost a third of all ecosystem service journal papers published in 2015 focusing on policy related issues, research investment is set to support the apparent wave of enthusiasm by economists, businesses, politicians and policy makers to put a price on nature and stoke a nascent market of buyers and sellers of the services it provides.

Arguably the most notable trend in research on ecosystem services over the past two decades has been in the agriculture and farming domains. The relationship between biodiversity and agriculture and farming has dominated the scientific literature on ecosystem services over the past ten years (representing 28% of publications between 2006 and 2015). The relationship between biodiversity and agriculture is complex and highly interdependent. For instance, agriculture is dependent upon biological diversity for ecosystem service delivery (e.g. pollination, nutritional diversity). Agricultural systems and landscapes can also support very high levels of biodiversity (Tscharntke et al., 2012), including threatened species (Wright et al., 2012). Yet agricultural expansion and intensification are a great threat to many ecosystems, habitats and species (Laurance et al., 2014), many of which are functionally significant for human society (Attwood et al., 2008). This has led to an increasing use of an ecosystem services lens in locations where land-use and natural resource decisions attempt to reflect and negotiate complex societal, economic and ecological trade-offs.

Ecosystem services are also being used within the nexus between agriculture, poverty and food security. Here, many global development institutions, researchers and practitioners are adopting a utilitarian lens in viewing the conservation of biodiversity as a central tenet of human development. Approximately 5% of ecosystem publications over the past decade have related to poverty and food security. Over the same period, a number of high-profile global development and research-for-development initiatives have made notable shifts in their strategies to reflect the ecosystem services mantra. For example, the Millennium Development Goals, instigated in 2000, did not contain any explicit mention of ecosystem services. However, Goal 7, 'To ensure environmental sustainability', contains targets that seek to 'reduce biodiversity loss', and 'reverse loss of environmental resources' (Way, 2015). These are closely related to ecosystem services but, crucially, the predominantly utilitarian and market-based language is absent. In contrast, the recently agreed Sustainable Development Goals (SDG) refer or allude to ecosystem services several times, notably in Goal 15. Here the targets are to 'sustainably manage forests, combat desertification, halt and reverse land degradation, halt biodiversity loss', including: 'by 2020, integrate ecosystem and biodiversity values into national and local planning, development processes, poverty reduction strategies and accounts' (United Nations, 2015). Whilst the transition in language between these evolving global targets is subtle, it is significant. The Convention on Biological Diversity's (CBD) Aichi Biodiversity Targets (2011–2020) goes further still, with Strategic Goal D being to 'enhance the benefits to all from biodiversity and ecosystem services' (CBD, 2011). The targets for the goals take into account multiple types of services and also include the need for equitable benefit distribution among end users.

## Agricultural biodiversity conservation

The agriculture-biodiversity interface spans an enormous range of locations and issues, yet much of the focus of research, policy and practice has concentrated on how WBD utilises agricultural land or is impacted (often negatively) by agricultural practices (Wood and Lenne, 1997). Although presently less prominent, there also exists a growing and parallel stream of discourse, research and action focused on the conservation and use of inter- and infra-specific crop diversity and crop wild relatives (Jackson et al., 2007). Research and practice on agricultural biodiversity (ABD) is centred most prominently on food security, sustainable intensification, pest and disease control, climate adaptation and human well-being outcomes (e.g. Castañeda-Álvarez et al., 2016). The rationale for conserving ABD is largely based on its utilitarian value, with advocates citing the proven linkages between diversified food production and societal requirements for food and nutrition (Jackson et al., 2007). Mirroring the evolution of a utilitarian perspective of WBD and the capture of values through PES market mechanisms, recent attempts have been made to develop and implement analogous payment schemes for ABD (Narloch et al., 2011).

Much like the conservation of WBD, there is a parallel and burgeoning emphasis on the conservation of ABD such as crops and livestock in global conservation and development frameworks. For instance, Aichi Biodiversity Target 13 is aimed at conserving the genetic diversity of cultivated plants, domesticated farm animals and crop wild relatives (CBD, 2011), and SDG target 2.5 focuses on maintaining genetic diversity of seeds, cultivated plants, farmed and domesticated animals and their related wild species (United Nations, 2015). Accordingly, there is a growing interest in incentivising *in situ* ABD conservation through Payments for Agrobiodiversity Conservation Services (PACS) which are analogous to PES. There is a considerable need for PACS due in part to market failures to recognise the public good of ABD conservation and the eroding of ABD through economic incentives for commercial, high-yielding crops (Narloch et al., 2011). The few instances of their use, to date, focus on ABD-dependent poor smallholder farmers in the developing world. These farmers play a pivotal role in conserving ABD but cannot easily afford the opportunity costs between maintaining ABD and adopting improved crops and varieties (Krishna et al., 2013). As examples of PACS, Narloch et al. (2013) described a reverse-auction process (i.e. sealed bids from applicants) operating in Bolivia and Peru aimed at conserving crop diversity of quinoa *(Chenopodium quinoa)*. This scheme has been developed to address a narrowing in the number of quinoa varieties being grown (due to commercial pressures) and the need to conserve particular landraces and maintain traditions of farmer cooperation and equitability. A further example used a modelling approach to examine payment for minor millet landraces in India. This study indicated that farmer willingness to participate and levels of compensation required were strongly linked to crop and variety consumption value (Krishna et al., 2013).

As research in this area grows, a range of potential obstacles to successful PACS implementation are becoming apparent. These include the creation of institutions capable of delivering PACS, resolution of context-specific land tenure arrangements and issues and the need for effective baselining and monitoring (Narloch et al., 2011). These are all issues that are shared by PES, and indicate that the development of PACS has the opportunity to be informed by the greater (current) level of WBD PES development and deployment.

## Integrating wild and agricultural biodiversity

Today, we witness an ecosystem services lens applied to both WBD and ABD, with conservation efforts in the two arenas focused on biodiversity in agricultural systems and the maintenance of biodiversity on farms and in farmed landscapes (FAO, 1997). Despite this convergence, there remain few examples in the research, policy development or practitioner communities where WBD and ABD are dealt with as an integrated ecological system and conservation challenge. Yet there exists a high degree of spatial congruence between areas of high crop diversity and wild biodiversity (**Figure 20.1**), implying the existence of areas with simultaneously high conservation priorities for both wild and agricultural biodiversity. As a consequence, actions, interventions and policies need to reflect an integrated perspective if they are to ensure trade-offs and synergies between target species for conservation are not overlooked.

Evidence suggests that multiple elements of both WBD and ABD in these geographic areas of overlap generate an extremely wide range of ecosystem services (**Table 20.1**). It is hardly surprising that ABD generates a considerable number and diversity of provisioning services (e.g. food, raw materials), species and varietal diversity of agricultural crops at various scales and can also provide regulating ecosystem services including reduced soil erosion, increased rates of pollination and increased pest and disease control through biological mechanisms (Jackson et al., 2007; Mulumba et al., 2012). However, increased diversity of cropping systems can also result in greater habitat

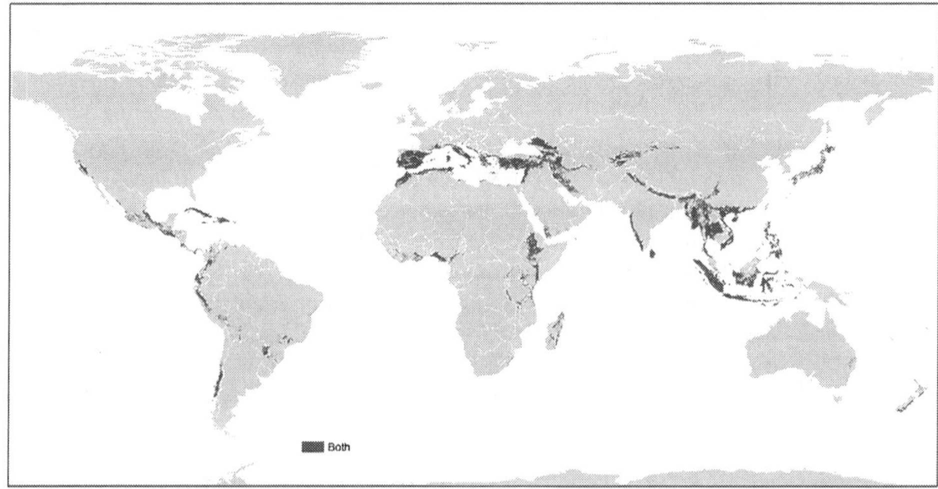


*Figure 20.1* Spatial overlap of areas of high crop diversity (>15 spp. crop harvested, from Monfreda et al., 2008) and biodiversity hotspots (Mittermeier et al., 2011) globally

complexity, both structurally and compositionally, which in turn supports a greater diversity of wild species at the field scale and in adjacent land uses and habitats, many of which may also be beneficial for production and provide their own ecosystem services, such as predatory arthropods (Letourneau et al., 2011; see also Beed et al., Chapter 8 of this Handbook). Agrobiodiversity-based management approaches to production not only have food security benefits (Rusinamhodzi et al., 2012; Bommarco et al., 2013), but can also lead to agricultural systems that support greater wild biodiversity (Bengtsson et al., 2005) and improve landscape permeability between native vegetation remnants (Melo et al., 2013). Such positive ecosystem services can have further beneficial effects in terms of the reduced need for expensive and potentially environmentally damaging external inputs, such as synthetic pesticides. Given that both WBD and ABD contribute to delivering a suite of similar ecosystem services, in some cases potentially being inter-dependent, mechanisms need to be explored and implemented that consider and enable the simultaneous conservation of both types of biodiversity. Importantly, such mechanisms need to explicitly consider the synergies and trade-offs occurring between ABD and WBD conservation efforts.

The evolution of PES has made considerable ground in galvanising markets for ecosystem services for WBD, though it is only relatively recently that PACS has started to explore the potential to value ABD (Pascual and Perrings, 2007; Narloch et al., 2011, 2013). With the increased emphasis on the conservation of ABD, not least through global development agendas such as the Aichi Biodiversity Target 13 and SDG target 2.5, it is likely that mechanisms such as PACS will receive increased focus. This presents an opportunity for the many lessons from PES design, implementation and monitoring, to be incorporated into efforts to incentivise ABD conservation:

- Environmental and social change can take a great deal of time to occur, and therefore schemes and incentive programs should be conducted over long time periods (Attwood et al., 2009). This also provides surety for applicants and participants in schemes.

  *(Zammit et al., 2010)*

- Management actions need to be underpinned by scientific evidence (Sutherland et al., 2013). For instance, systematic review approaches can be used to determine which management actions are likely to deliver a particular response (Dicks et al., 2014), and target taxa can be grouped into 'guilds' of response to particular management interventions.

  *(Dolman et al., 2012)*

- Payment options should be carefully appraised and considered in relation to the context of the objectives – for example, fixed rate payments versus conservation options, direct payments versus tax relief, individual actions versus collective actions.
- Monitoring of scheme effectiveness is essential in order to indicate success (or otherwise) of management interventions and value for money in terms of investment, and provide a basis upon which to refine and improve the scheme (Lindenmayer et al., 2012). Failure to effectively monitor outcomes has been a major source of criticism of many European agri-environment schemes.

  *(Kleijn and Sutherland, 2003)*

## An over-reliance on utilitarian perspectives?

The rush to embrace a utilitarian perspective on both the wild and agricultural biodiversity associated with agricultural systems and landscapes, to develop methods to value it, and to build mechanisms to promote incentives for its conservation, has been accompanied by a growing body of disquiet and criticism of these approaches. McAuley (2006) examined a number of compelling arguments against the commodification of nature (and in favour of intrinsic arguments for conservation), proposing where an ecosystem services argument is limited and may even damage conservation efforts. This might happen, for example, due to highly ephemeral and volatile markets, cost-effective technological surrogates and opposing stances of biodiversity conservation and economic benefits.

Other criticisms have also been expressed. The relationship between biodiversity, ecological function and ecosystem services has been argued to be too poorly understood to allow effective management interventions to be prescribed or implemented (Hails and Ormerod, 2013). Provisioning ecosystem services are generally more readily valued and easily utilised than other less tangible or marketable classes of ecosystem services (Hails and Ormerod, 2013), and increasing provisioning services can often result in a decline in other ecosystem services (Benayas et al., 2009). Whilst ecosystem service valuations are continuously being refined and tested, the wide range of approaches, coupled with the inherent difficulty in measuring all services and values for all potential recipients, means that nature is frequently likely to be mis-valued (Jackson et al., 2007; Stoeckl et al., 2011, 2014).

Ecosystem service arguments aim to provide a rationale for improved decision-making that takes into account the benefits that nature provides to humanity. However, ecosystem service perception, use and valuation (monetary or otherwise) are highly subjective and user-specific (Daw et al., 2011). Unless there are more equitable power balances in how nature is managed, then the ecosystem service benefits of the most powerful are likely to hold sway (Scheffer et al., 2014). This creates an important role for public policy in ensuring that the multiple perspectives on ecosystem service values are fully and more accurately integrated into decision-making.

## Conclusions

In this chapter, we chart the seemingly inexorable rise of the ecosystem services concept and the utilitarian framing it offers for valuing both wild and agricultural biodiversity as an incentive for conservation. Acknowledging the present philosophical debate around intrinsic versus utilitarian perspectives of nature and the many reasons to be wary of uncritically applying and relying upon ecosystem service approaches for biodiversity conservation, the natural world continues to decline. Wild and agricultural biodiversity loss is accelerating, multiple planetary boundaries are further transgressed and critical environmental issues receive declining media attention (Andrews et al., 2016). In reflecting on the evolution of the ecosystem services concept as it has been applied to WBD and ABD, and the development of PES and, more recently, PACS, we highlight important observations on the spatial proximity of WBD and ABD, their intricate connection through myriad ecological processes and the vast array of ecosystem services that they collectively provide to underpin global agricultural production. What is also clear from this reflection is that WBD and ABD conservation attempts have been largely pursued separately in terms of research, policy and incentive schemes. We argue that there is value in taking a more integrated perspective of biodiversity conservation that acknowledges and acts on the synergies between WBD and ABD in valuing and conserving biodiversity. The challenge lies before researchers, economists, policy makers and practitioners to develop theories, tools and mechanisms to take a more integrated perspective of biodiversity conservation in ways that deliver effective conservation, food security and poverty reduction outcomes. PES and PACS will undoubtedly continue to play an important role in operationalising wild and agricultural biodiversity conservation through the utilitarian concept of ecosystem services. The challenge will be to design and deploy schemes that integrate multiple ecosystem services from both wild and agricultural biodiversity and, importantly, identify and manage trade-offs and synergies. When wielded judiciously, such schemes can contribute much to the development of a pathway towards integrating funding and the conservation of biodiversity across multiple ecosystems and land uses.

## Note

1 Intrinsic values of biodiversity are difficult to define (Justus et al., 2009), but an illustrative example could be that nature has a fundamental right to exist and humans do not have the right to eradicate other species (Wilshusen et al., 2002).

## References


Ackroyd and Harvey (2016) www.conflictedseeds.com/into-the-blue/

Albrecht, M., Schmid, B., Hautier, Y. and Müller, C. B. (2012) 'Diverse pollinator communities enhance plant reproductive success', *Proceedings of the Royal Society of London B–Biological Sciences*, vol. 279, pp. 4845–4852.

Alongi, D. M. (2012) 'Carbon sequestration in mangrove forests', *Carbon Management*, vol. 3, pp. 313–322.

Altieri, M. A. (2002) 'Agroecology: The science of natural resource management for poor farmers in marginal environments', *Agriculture, Ecosystems & Environment*, vol. 93, pp. 1–24.

Andrews, K., Boykoff, M., Daly, M., Gifford, L., Luedecke, G., McAllister, L. and Nacu-Schmidt, A. (2016) *United States Coverage of Climate Change or Global Warming, 2004–2016*, Center for Science and Technology Policy Research, Cooperative Institute for Research in Environmental Sciences, University of Colorado, CO, USA http://sciencepolicy.colorado.edu/icecaps/research/media_coverage/usa/index.html, accessed 21 April 2016.

Armitage, S. and Dee, T. (eds.) (2009) *The Poetry of Birds*, Allen Unwin, London, UK.

Attwood, S. J., Maron, M., House, A. P. N. and Zammit, C. (2008) 'Do arthropod assemblages display globally consistent responses to intensified agricultural land use and management?', *Global Ecology and Biogeography*, vol. 17, pp. 585–599.

Attwood, S. J., Park, S. E., Maron, M., Collard, S. J., Robinson, D., Reardon-Smith, K. M. and Cockfield, G. (2009) 'Declining birds in Australian agricultural landscapes may benefit from aspects of the European agri-environment model', *Biological Conservation*, vol. 142, pp. 1981–1991.

Attwood, S. J., Park, S. E., Marshall, P., Fanshawe, J., DeClerck, F., Jarvis, D., Drucker, A. and Fadda, C. (in preparation) 'Ecosystem service conservation should integrate both wild and agricultural biodiversity'.

Ayers, R. S. and Westcot, D. W. (1985) *Water Quality for Agriculture. FAO Irrigation and Drainage Paper 29 Rev. 1*, FAO, Rome, Italy.

Balmford, A., Green, J. M. H., Anderson, M., Beresford, J., Huang, C., Naidoo, R., Walpole, M. and Manica, A. (2015) 'Walk on the wild side: Estimating the global magnitude of visits to protected areas', *PLoS Biology*, vol. 13, p. e1002074.

Barbier, E. B., Hacker, S. D., Kennedy, C., Koch, E. W., Stier, A. C. and Silliman, B. R. (2011) 'The value of estuarine and coastal ecosystem services', *Ecological Monographs*, vol. 81, pp. 169–193.

Barrett, R. D. and Schluter, D. (2008) 'Adaptation from standing genetic variation', *Trends in Ecology & Evolution*, vol. 23, pp. 38–44.

Barrow, C. J. (1991) *Land Degradation: Development and Breakdown of Terrestrial Environments*, Cambridge University Press, Cambridge, UK.

Bellon, M. R. and Taylor, J. E. (1993) '"Folk" soil taxonomy and the partial adoption of new seed varieties', *Economic Development and Cultural Change*, vol. 41, pp. 763–786.

Bellon, M. R., Hodson, D. and Hellin, J. (2011) 'Assessing the vulnerability of traditional maize seed systems in Mexico to climate change', *Proceedings of the National Academy of Sciences USA*, vol. 108, pp. 13432–13437.

Benayas, J. M. R., Newton, A. C., Diaz, A. and Bullock, J. M. (2009) 'Enhancement of biodiversity and ecosystem services by ecological restoration: A meta-analysis', *Science*, vol. 325, pp. 1121–1124.

Bengtsson, J., Ahnström, J. and Weibull, A. C. (2005) 'The effects of organic agriculture on biodiversity and abundance: A meta-analysis', *Journal of Applied Ecology*, vol. 42, pp. 261–269.

Blumenfeld, S., Lu, C., Christophersen, T. and Coates, D. (2009) 'Water, wetlands and forests. A review of ecological, economic and policy linkages', no. 47 in (eds.), *CBD Technical Series*, Secretariat of the

Convention on Biological Diversity and Secretariat of the Ramsar Convention on Wetlands, Montreal, Canada and Gland, Switzerland.

Bommarco, R., Kleijn, D. and Potts, S. G. (2013) 'Ecological intensification: Harnessing ecosystem services for food security', *Trends in Ecology and Evolution*, vol. 28, pp. 230–238.

Brander, L., Brouwer, R. and Wagtendonk, A. (2013) 'Economic valuation of regulating services provided by wetlands in agricultural landscapes: A meta-analysis', *Ecological Engineering*, vol. 56, pp. 89–96.

Brauman, K. A., Daily, G. C., Duarte, T. K. and Mooney, H. A. (2007) 'The nature and value of ecosystem services: An overview highlighting hydrologic services', *Annual Reviews of Environment and Resources*, vol. 32, pp. 67–98.

Brooker, R. W., Bennett, A. E., Cong, W. F., Daniell, T. J., George, T. S., Hallett, P. D., Hawes, C., Iannetta, P. P., Jones, H. G., Karley, A. J. and Li, L. (2015) 'Improving intercropping: A synthesis of research in agronomy, plant physiology and ecology', *New Phytologist*, vol. 206, pp. 107–117.

Buckland, D. (2006) *Burning Ice: Art & Climate Change*, Cape Farewell, London, UK.

Calvet-Mir, L., Gómez-Baggethun, E. and Reyes-García, V. (2012) 'Beyond food production: Ecosystem services provided by home gardens. A case study in Vall Fosca, Catalan Pyrenees, Northeastern Spain', *Ecological Economics*, vol. 74, pp. 153–160.

Cardelús, C. L., Scull, P., Hair, J., Baimas-George, M., Lowman, M. D. and Eshet, A. W. (2013) 'A preliminary assessment of Ethiopian sacred grove status at the landscape and ecosystem scales', *Diversity*, vol. 5, pp. 320–334.

Carpio, C. E., Wohlgenant, M. K. and Boonsaeng, T. (2008) 'The demand for agritourism in the United States', *Journal of Agricultural and Resource Economics*, vol. 2008, pp. 254–269.

Castañeda-Álvarez, N. P., Khoury, C. K., Achicanoy, H. A., Bernau, V., Dempewolf, H., Eastwood, R. J., Guarino, L., Harker, R. H., Jarvis, A., Maxted, N. and Müller, J. V. (2016) 'Global conservation priorities for crop wild relatives', *Nature Plants*, vol. 2, p. 16022.

CBD (2011) *Aichi Biodiversity Targets*. www.cbd.int/sp/targets/, accessed 21 April 2016.

Chianu, J. N., Nkonya, E. M., Mairura, F. S., Chianu, J. N. and Akinnifesi, F. K. (2011) 'Biological nitrogen fixation and socioeconomic factors for legume production in sub-Saharan Africa: A review', *Agronomy for Sustainable Development*, vol. 31, p. 139.

Costanza, R., d'Arge, R., De Groot, R. S., Farber, S., Grasso, M., Hannon, B., Limburg, K., Naeem, S., O'Neil, R. V., Paruelo, J., Raskin, R. G., Sutton, P. and van den Belt, M. (1997) 'The value of the world's ecosystem services and natural capital', *Nature*, vol. 387, pp. 253–260.

Daw, T., Brown, K., Rosendo, S. and Pomeroy, R. (2011) 'Applying the ecosystem services concept to poverty alleviation: The need to disaggregate human well-being', *Environmental Conservation*, vol. 38, pp. 370–379.

De Groot, R. S., Wilson, M. A. and Boumans, R. M. J. (2002) 'A typology for the classification, description and valuation of ecosystem functions, goods and services', *Ecological Economics*, vol. 41, pp 393–408.

De Groot, R. S., Fisher, B., Christie, M., Aronson, J., Braat, L., Haines-Young, R., Gowdy, J., Maltby, E., Neuville, A., Polasky, S., Portela, R. and Ring, I. (2010) 'Integrating the ecological and economic dimensions in biodiversity and ecosystem service valuation', pp. 9–40 in P. Kumar (ed.), *The Economics of Ecosystems and Biodiversity (TEEB): Ecological and Economic Foundations*, Earthscan for Routledge, Abingdon, UK.

De Groot, R., Brander, L., Van Der Ploeg, S., Costanza, R., Bernard, F., Braat, L., Christie, M., Crossman, N., Ghermandi, A., Hein, L. and Hussain, S. (2012) 'Global estimates of the value of ecosystems and their services in monetary units', *Ecosystem Services*, vol. 1, pp. 50–61.

Díaz, S., Fargione, J., Chapin, F. S., III, and Tilman, D. (2006) 'Biodiversity loss threatens human well-being', *PLoS Biology*, vol. 4, p. e277.

Dicks, L. V., Walsh, J. C. and Sutherland, W. J. (2014) 'Organising evidence for environmental management decisions: A "4S" hierarchy', *Trends in Ecology and Evolution*, vol. 29, pp. 607–613.

Dolman, P. M., Panter, C. J. and Mossman, H. L. (2012) 'The biodiversity audit approach challenges regional priorities and identifies a mismatch in conservation', *Journal of Applied Ecology*, vol. 49, pp. 986–997.

Ehrlich, P. and Ehrlich, A. (1981) *Extinction: The Causes and Consequences of the Disappearance of Species*, Random House, New York, NY, USA.

Fiedler, A. K., Landis, D. A. and Wratten, S. D. (2008) 'Maximizing ecosystem services from conservation biological control: the role of habitat management', *Biological Control*, vol. 45, pp. 254–271.

Flint, M. L. and Roberts, P. A. (1988) 'Using crop diversity to manage pest problems. Some California examples', *American Journal of Alternative Agriculture*, vol. 3, pp. 163–167.

Food and Agriculture Organization of the United Nations (FAO) (1997) *The State of the World's Plant Genetic Resources for Food and Agriculture*, FAO, Rome, Italy, www.fao.org/fileadmin/templates/agphome/documents/PGR/SoW1/SoWfullE.pdf, accessed 21 April 2016.

Forest Trends/The Katoomba Group/UNEP (2008) *Payments for Ecosystem Services Getting Started: A Primer: Forest Trends and the Katoomba Group*, www.unep.org/pdf/PaymentsForEcosystemServices_en.pdf, accessed 21 April 2016.

Fuller, R. A., Irvine, K. N., Devine-Wright, P., Warren, P. H. and Gaston, K. J. (2007) 'Psychological benefits of greenspace increase with biodiversity', *Biology Letters*, vol. 3, pp. 390–394.

Glowinski, S. L. (2008) 'Bird-watching, ecotourism, and economic development: A review of the evidence', *Applied Research in Economic Development*, vol. 5, pp. 67–68.

Hails, R. S. and Ormerod, S. J. (2013) 'Editorial: Ecological science for ecosystem services and the stewardship of natural capital', *Journal of Applied Ecology*, vol. 50, pp. 807–810.

Hajjar, R., Jarvis, D. I. and Gemmill-Herren, B. (2008) 'The utility of crop genetic diversity in maintaining ecosystem services', *Agriculture, Ecosystems & Environment*, vol. 123, pp. 261–270.

Hoehn, P., Tscharntke, T., Tylianakis, J. M. and Steffan-Dewenter, I. (2008) 'Functional group diversity of bee pollinators increases crop yield', *Proceedings of the Royal Society of London B–Biological Sciences*, vol. 275, pp. 2283–2291.

Jackson, L. E., Pascual, U. and Hodgkin, T. (2007) 'Utilizing and conserving agrobiodiversity in agricultural landscapes', *Agriculture, Ecosystems and Environment*, vol. 121, pp. 196–210.

Jarvis, D. I., Brown, A. H. D., Imbruce, V., Ochoa, J., Sadiki, M., Karamura, E., Trutmann, P. and Finckh, M. R. (2007) 'Managing crop disease in traditional agroecosystems. Benefits and hazards of genetic diversity', pp. 292–319 in D. I. Jarvis, C. Padoch and H. D. Cooper (eds.), *Managing Biodiversity in Agricultural Ecosystems*, Bioversity International, Columbia University Press, New York, NY, USA.

Jim, C. Y. and Chen, W. Y. (2009) 'Ecosystem services and valuation of urban forests in China', *Cities*, vol. 26, pp. 187–194.

Johns, T. and Sthapit, B. R. (2004) 'Biocultural diversity in the sustainability of developing-country food systems', *Food and Nutrition Bulletin*, vol. 25, pp. 143–155.

Juniper, T. (2013) *What Has Nature Ever Done for Us? How Money Really Does Grow on Trees*, Profile Books, London, UK.

Justus, J., Colyvan, M., Regan, H. and Maguire, L. (2009) 'Buying into conservation: Intrinsic versus instrumental value', *Trends in Ecology and Evolution*, vol. 24, pp. 187–191.

Kala, M. and Sharma, A. (2010) 'Traditional Indian beliefs: A key towards sustainable living', *Environmentalist*, vol. 30, pp. 85–89.

Karp, D. S., Mendenhall, C. D., Sandí, R. F., Chaumont, N., Ehrlich, P. R., Hadly, E. A. and Daily, G. C. (2013) 'Forest bolsters bird abundance, pest control and coffee yield', *Ecology Letters*, vol. 16, pp. 1339–1347.

Kassam, A., Friedrich, T., Shaxson, F. and Pretty, J. (2009) 'The spread of conservation agriculture: Justification, sustainability and uptake', *International Journal of Agricultural Sustainability*, vol. 7, pp. 292–320.

Khan, S. M., Page, S., Ahmad, H., Shaheen, H., Ullah, Z., Ahmad, M. and Harper, D. M. (2013) 'Medicinal flora and ethnoecological knowledge in the Naran Valley, Western Himalaya, Pakistan', *Journal of Ethnobiology and Ethnomedicine*, vol. 9, p. 4.

Kleijn, D. and Sutherland, W. J. (2003) 'How effective are European agri-environment schemes in conserving and promoting biodiversity?', *Journal of Applied Ecology*, vol. 40, pp. 947–969.

Knowler, D. and Bradshaw, B. (2007) 'Farmers' adoption of conservation agriculture: A review and synthesis of recent research', *Food Policy*, vol. 32, pp. 25–48.

Kremen, C. and Miles, A. (2012) 'Ecosystem services in biologically diversified versus conventional farming systems: Benefits, externalities, and trade-offs', *Ecology and Society*, vol. 17, p. 4.

Krishna, V. V., Drucker, A. G., Pascual, U., Raghu, P. T. and King, E. I. O. (2013) 'Estimating compensation payments for on-farm conservation of agricultural biodiversity in developing countries', *Ecological Economics*, vol. 87, pp. 110–123.

Laube, I., Breitbach, N. and Böhning-Gaese, K. (2008) 'Avian diversity in a Kenyan agroecosystem: Effects of habitat structure and proximity to forest', *Journal of Ornithology*, vol. 149, pp. 181–191.

Laurance, W. F., Sayer, J. and Cassman, K. G. (2014) 'Agricultural expansion and its impacts on tropical nature', *Trends in Ecology and Evolution*, vol. 29, pp. 107–116.

Lawrence, D. and Vandecar, K. (2015) 'Effects of tropical deforestation on climate and agriculture', *Nature Climate Change*, vol. 5, pp. 27–36.

Lernet and Sander. http://lernertandsander.com/cubes/

Letourneau, D. K., Armbrecht, I., Rivera, B. S., Lerma, J. M., Carmona, E. J., Daza, M. C., Escobar, S., Galindo, V., Gutiérrez, C., López, S. D. and Mejía, J. L. (2011) 'Does plant diversity benefit agroecosystems? A synthetic review', *Ecological Applications*, vol. 21, pp. 9–21.

Lin, B. B. (2011) 'Resilience in agriculture through crop diversification: Adaptive management for environmental change', *BioScience*, vol. 61, pp. 183–193.

Lindenmayer, D. B., Zammit, C., Attwood, S. J., Burns, E., Shepherd, C. L., Kay, G. and Wood, J. (2012) 'A novel and cost-effective monitoring approach for outcomes in an Australian biodiversity conservation incentive program', *PloS One*, vol. 7, p. e50872.

Lindgreen, A. and Hingley, M. K. (2009) *The New Cultures of Food: Marketing Opportunities from Ethnic, Religious and Cultural Diversity*, Gower Publishing Limited, Farnham, UK.

Lu, J. and Li, X. (2006) 'Review of rice–fish-farming systems in China – one of the globally important ingenious agricultural heritage systems (GIAHS)', *Aquaculture*, vol. 260, pp. 106–113.

Malézieux, E., Crozat, Y., Dupraz, C., Laurans, M., Makowski, D., Ozier-Lafontaine, H., Rapidel, B., De Tourdonnet, S. and Valantin-Morison, M. (2009) 'Mixing plant species in cropping systems: Concepts, tools and models: a review', pp. 329–353 in E. Lichtfouse, M. Navarrete, P. Debaeke, S. Véronique and C. Alberola (eds.). *Sustainable Agriculture*, Springer Netherlands, Dordrecht, the Netherlands.

McAuley, D. J. (2006) 'Selling out nature', *Nature*, vol. 443, pp. 27–28.

Melo, F. P., Arroyo-Rodríguez, V., Fahrig, L., Martínez-Ramos, M. and Tabarelli, M. (2013) 'On the hope for biodiversity-friendly tropical landscapes', *Trends in Ecology and Evolution*, vol. 28, pp. 462–468.

Millennium Ecosystem Assessment [MEA] (2005) *Ecosystems and Human Well-being*, World Resources Institute, Washington, DC, USA, www.millenniumassessment.org/documents/document.356.aspx.pdf, accessed 21 April 2016.

Mitchell, R. and Carson, R. (1989) *Using Surveys to Value Public Goods: The Contingent Valuation Method*, RFF Press, Washington, DC, USA.

Mittermeier, R. A., Turner, W. R., Larsen, F. W., Brooks, T. M. and Gascon, C. (2011) 'Global biodiversity conservation: The critical role of hotspots', pp. 3–22 in F. E. Zachos and J. C. Habel (eds.), *Biodiversity Hotspots*, Springer Berlin, Heidelberg, Germany.

Mohammad, A. G. and Adam, M. A. (2010) 'The impact of vegetative cover type on runoff and soil erosion under different land uses', *Catena*, vol. 81, pp. 97–103.

Monbiot, G. (2013) *Feral: Searching for Enchantment on the Frontiers of Rewilding*, Penguin, London, UK.

Monfreda, C., Ramankutty, N. and Foley, J. A. (2008) 'Farming the planet: 2. Geographic distribution of crop areas, yields, physiological types, and net primary production in the year 2000', *Global Biogeochemical Cycles*, vol. 22, pp. 337–342.

Mulumba, J. W., Nankya, R., Adokorach, J., Kiwuka, C., Fadda, C., De Santis, P. and Jarvis, D. I. (2012) 'A risk-minimizing argument for traditional crop varietal diversity use to reduce pest and disease damage in agricultural ecosystems of Uganda', *Agriculture, Ecosystems and Environment*, vol. 157, pp. 70–86.

Nahuelhual, L., Carmona, A., Laterra, P., Barrena, J. and Aguayo, M. (2014) 'A mapping approach to assess intangible cultural ecosystem services: The case of agriculture heritage in Southern Chile', *Ecological Indicators*, vol. 40, pp. 90–101.

Narloch, U., Drucker, A. G. and Pascual, U. (2011) 'Payments for agrobiodiversity conservation services for sustained on-farm utilization of plant and animal genetic resources', *Ecological Economics*, vol. 70, pp. 1837–1845.

Narloch, U., Pascual, U. and Drucker, A. G. (2013) 'How to achieve fairness in payments for ecosystem services? Insights from agrobiodiversity conservation auctions', *Land Use Policy*, vol. 35, pp. 107–118.

Nath, J., Henderson, J. Coveney, J. and Ward, P. (2013) 'Consumer faith: An exploration of trust in food and the impact of religious dietary norms and certification', *Food, Culture and Society*, vol. 16, pp. 421–436.

Nature's Toolbox (2012) www.artworksforchange.org.

Nedkov, S. and Burkhard, B. (2012) 'Flood regulating ecosystem services – mapping supply and demand, in the Etropole municipality, Bulgaria', *Ecological Indicators*, vol. 21, pp. 67–79.

Nicholls, C. I. and Altieri, M. A. (2013) 'Plant biodiversity enhances bees and other insect pollinators in agroecosystems: A review', *Agronomy for Sustainable Development*, vol. 33, pp. 257–274.

Nicholson, E., Mace, G. M., Armsworth, P. R., Atkinson, G., Buckle, S., Clements, T., Ewers, R. M., Fa, J. E., Gardner, T. A., Gibbons, J. and Grenyer, R. (2009) Priority research areas for ecosystem services in a changing world. *Journal of Applied Ecology*, vol. 46, pp. 1139–1144.

Noman, M. S., Maleque, M. A., Alam, M. Z., Afroz, S. and Ishii, H. T. (2013) 'Intercropping mustard with four spice crops suppresses mustard aphid abundance, and increases both crop yield and farm profitability in central Bangladesh', *International Journal of Pest Management*, vol. 59, pp. 306–313.

Osborne, L. L. and Kovacic, D. A. (1993) 'Riparian vegetated buffer strips in water-quality restoration and stream management', *Freshwater Biology*, vol. 29, pp. 243–258.

Oswald, A. (2005) *The Thunder Matters: 101 Poems for the Planet*, Faber, London, UK.

Pascual, U. and Perrings, C. (2007) 'Developing incentives and economic mechanisms for in situ biodiversity conservation in agricultural landscapes', *Agriculture, Ecosystems and Environment*, vol. 121, pp. 256–268.

Peh, K. S. H., Balmford, A., Bradbury, R. B., Brown, C., Butchart, S. H., Hughes, F. M., Stattersfield, A., Thomas, D. H., Walpole, M., Bayliss, J. and Gowing, D. (2013) 'TESSA: A toolkit for rapid assessment of ecosystem services at sites of biodiversity conservation importance', *Ecosystem Services*, vol. 5, pp. 51–57.

Perfecto, I. and Vandermeer, J. (2008) 'Biodiversity conservation in tropical agroecosystems', *Annals of the New York Academy of Sciences*, vol. 1134, pp. 173–200.

Peterson, G. (2010) 'Growth of ecosystem services concept', *Resilience Science*, vol. 21, http://rs.resalliance.org/2010/01/21/growth-of-ecosystem-services-concept/

Phelan, C. and Sharpley, R. (2011) 'Exploring agritourism entrepreneurship in the UK', *Tourism Planning & Development*, vol. 8, pp. 121–136.

Porras, I. T., Grieg-Gran, M. and Neves, N. (2008) *All That Glitters: A Review of Payments for Watershed Services in Developing Countries* (No. 11), IIED, London, UK.

Porras, I. and Neves, N. (2006) *Markets for Watershed Services-Country Profile: Honduras – Jesus de Otoro PASOCAC Initiative*, watershedmarkets.org, www.watershedmarkets.org/documents/Honduras_Jesus_de_Otoro.pdf, accessed 21 April 2016.

Rajab, Y. A., Leuschner, C., Barus, H., Tjoa, A. and Hertel, D. (2016) 'Cacao cultivation under diverse shade tree cover allows high carbon storage and sequestration without yield losses', *PLoS ONE*, vol. 11, p. e0149949.

Reganold, J. P. (1995) 'Soil quality and profitability of biodynamic and conventional farming systems: A review', *American Journal of Alternative Agriculture*, vol. 10, pp. 36–45.

Reuter, K. E., Randell, H., Wills, A. R., Janvier, T. E., Belalahy, T. R. and Sewall, B. J. (2016) 'Capture, movement, trade, and consumption of mammals in Madagascar', *PLoS ONE*, vol. 11, p.e0150305.

Ross-Bryant, L. (2013) *Pilgrimage to the National Parks: Religion and Nature in the United States*, Routledge, New York, NY, USA.

Rusinamhodzi, L., Corbeels, M., Nyamangara, J. and Giller, K. E. (2012) 'Maize – grain legume intercropping is an attractive option for ecological intensification that reduces climatic risk for smallholder farmers in central Mozambique', *Field Crops Research*, vol. 136, pp. 12–22.

Sandifer, P. A., Sutton-Grier, A. E. and Ward, B. P. (2015) 'Exploring connections among nature, biodiversity, ecosystem services, and human health and well-being: Opportunities to enhance health and biodiversity conservation', *Ecosystem Services*, vol. 12, pp. 1–15.

Scheffer, M., Folke, C., Schellnhuber, H., Nykvist, B., De Wit, C. A., Hughes, T., van der Leeuw, S., Rodhe, H., Sörlin, S., Snyder, P. K., Costanza, R., Svedin, U., Falkenmark, M., Karlberg, L. and Corell, R. W. (2014) 'Ecosystem services and capitalism: A valuation or de-valuation of "nature"?', *Journal of Human Rights and the Environment*, vol. 5, pp. 107–111.

Schröter, M., Zanden, E. H., Oudenhoven, A. P., Remme, R. P., Serna-Chavez, H. M., Groot, R. S. and Opdam, P. (2014) 'Ecosystem services as a contested concept: A synthesis of critique and counter-arguments', *Conservation Letters*, vol. 7, pp. 514–523.

Schut, M. (ed.) (2010) *Food & Faith: Justice, Joy, and Daily Bread*, Morehouse Publishing, New York, NY, USA.

Schwenk, W. S., Donovan, T. M., Keeton, W. S. and Nunery, J. S. (2012) 'Carbon storage, timber production, and biodiversity: Comparing ecosystem services with multi-criteria decision analysis', *Ecological Applications*, vol. 22, pp. 1612–1627.

Sheil, D. (2014) 'How plants water our planet: Advances and imperatives', *Trends in Plant Science*, vol. 19, pp. 209–211.

Snapp, S. S., Blackie, M. J., Gilbert, R. A., Bezner-Kerr, R. and Kanyama-Phiri, G. Y. (2010) 'Biodiversity can support a greener revolution in Africa', *Proceedings of the National Academy of Sciences USA*, vol. 107, pp. 20840–20845.

Soulé, M. E. (1985) 'What is conservation biology? A new synthetic discipline addresses the dynamics and problems of perturbed species, communities, and ecosystems', *BioScience*, vol. 35, pp. 727–734.

Stoeckl, N., Farr, M., Larson, S., Adams, V. M., Kubiszewski, I., Esparon, M. and Costanza, R. (2014) 'A new approach to the problem of overlapping values: A case study in Australia's Great Barrier Reef', *Ecosystem Services*, vol. 10, pp. 61–78.

Stoeckl, N., Hicks, C. C., Mills, M., Fabricius, K. and Esparon, M. (2011) 'The economic value of ecosystem services in the Great Barrier Reef: Our state of knowledge', *Ecological Economics Reviews*, vol. 1219, pp. 113–133.

Sutherland, W. J., Mitchell, R., Walsh, J., Amano, T., Ausden, M., Beebee, T. J., Bullock, D., Daniels, M., Deutsch, J., Griffiths, R. A. and Prior, S. V. (2013) 'Conservation practice could benefit from routine testing and publication of management outcomes', *Conservation Evidence*, vol. 10, pp. 1–3.

TEEB (2010), *The Economics of Ecosystems and Biodiversity Ecological and Economic Foundations*, P. Kumar (ed.), Earthscan for Routledge, London, UK and Washington, DC, USA.

Thrupp, L. A. (2000) 'Linking agricultural biodiversity and food security: the valuable role of agrobiodiversity for sustainable agriculture', *International Affairs*, vol. 76, pp. 283–297.

Tscharntke, T., Clough, Y., Wanger, T. C., Jackson, L., Motzke, I., Perfecto, I., Vandermeer, J. and Whitbread, A. (2012) 'Global food security, biodiversity conservation and the future of agricultural intensification', *Biological Conservation*, vol. 151, pp. 53–59.

Tucker, M. E. and Grim, J. (eds.) (2004) *Religions of the World and Ecology: Buddhism, Christianity, Confucianism, Daoism, Hinduism, Indigenous Traditions, Islam, Jainism, Judaism*, Harvard University Press, Cambridge, MA, USA.

United Nations (2015) *Sustainable Development Knowledge Platform: Goal 15*, United Nations, New York, NY, USA, https://sustainabledevelopment.un.org/sdg15, accessed 21 April 2016.

US Fish and Wildlife (2014) *2011 National Survey of Fishing, Hunting, and Wildlife-Associated Recreation. Revised February 2014*, US Census Bureau, Suitland, MD, USA.

Van Berkel, D. B. and Verburg, P. H. (2014) 'Spatial quantification and valuation of cultural ecosystem services in an agricultural landscape', *Ecological Indicators*, vol. 37, pp. 163–174.

Way, C. (2015) *The Millennium Development Goals Report 2015*, United Nations, New York, NY, USA.

Weintraub, L. (2012) *To Life! Eco Art in Pursuit of a Sustainable Planet*, University of California Press, Berkeley, CA, USA.

Weldon, S. and Campbell, S. (2014) *Faith in Food: Changing the World One Meal at a Time*, Bene-Factum, London, UK.

Westman, W. E. (1977) 'How much are nature's services worth?', *Science*, vol. 197, pp. 960–964.

Wilshusen, P. R., Brechin, S. R., Fortwangler, C. L. and West, P. C. (2002) 'Reinventing a square wheel: Critique of a resurgent "protection paradigm" in international biodiversity conservation', *Society and Natural Resources*, vol. 15, pp. 17–40.

Wood, D. and Lenne, J. M. (1997) 'The conservation of agrobiodiversity on-farm: Questioning the emerging paradigm', *Biodiversity and Conservation*, vol. 6, pp. 109–129.

Worm, B., Barbier, E. B., Beaumont, N., Duffy, J. E., Folke, C., Halpern, B. S., Jackson, J. B., Lotze, H. K., Micheli, F., Palumbi, S. R. and Sala, E. (2006) 'Impacts of biodiversity loss on ocean ecosystem services', *Science*, vol. 314, pp. 787–790.

Wright, H. L., Lake, I. R. and Dolman, P. M. (2012) 'Agriculture – a key element for conservation in the developing world', *Conservation Letters*, vol. 5, pp. 11–19.

Yellowstone Association (2016) www.yellowstoneassociation.org/about, accessed 8 April 2016.

Young, C. E. and Osborn, C. T. (1990) 'Costs and benefits of the conservation reserve program', *Journal of Soil and Water Conservation*, vol. 45, pp. 370–373.

Zammit, C., Attwood, S. and Burns, E. (2010) 'Using markets for woodland conservation on private land: Lessons from the policy-research interface', pp. 297–307 in D. B. Lindenmayer, A. F. Bennett and R. J. Hobbs (eds.), *Temperate Woodland Conservation and Management*, CSIRO Publishing, Melbourne, Australia.

Zedler, J. B. and Kercher, S. (2005) 'Wetland resources: status, trends, ecosystem services, and restorability', *Annual Review of Environment and Resources*, vol. 30, pp. 39–74.

# PART 4

# Agricultural biodiversity

## Human health and well-being

# 21

# HARVESTING COMMON GROUND

## Maximizing the co-benefits of agrobiodiversity and human health

*Cristina Romanelli and Cristina Tirado*

### Introduction

Agricultural biodiversity is a cornerstone of food security and essential for human, animal, plant, microbial, and environmental health. Yet, few concrete efforts have been made to holistically examine either the common drivers of biodiversity loss in agroecosystems and human ill health, or their implications for the science-policy interface. Despite their significant contributions to calorie production, modern agroecosystems, reliant on monocultures, high input levels, and intensification, have not substantially contributed to reducing chronic hunger or malnutrition (FAO, 2015a). Millions of people remain hungry, over 800 million still suffer from chronic or acute malnutrition (FAO, IFAD and WFP, 2014; FAO, 2015a), and ecosystems are increasingly imperiled.

Agrobiodiversity not only serves utilitarian purposes, but it also sustains critical ecosystem functions (e.g. nutrient cycling and pest, disease, pollution, and sediment regulation) and cultural ecosystem services (e.g. socio-cultural fulfillment, sense of place, community cohesion) that are integral to human health and well-being, particularly in traditional communities (Milcu et al., 2013).

The biotic and abiotic interactions of agroecosystems modulate health outcomes at multiple scales, from the individual to planetary (Romanelli et al., 2015; Whitmee et al., 2015). At the individual scale, agroecosystems can sustain microbial diversity in our microbiota, contribute to human nutrition, and improve immunoregulation and inflammatory responses (Pudasaini et al., 2013; Rook, 2013). At the community level, they sustain production and contribute to human and ecosystem resilience (Jarvis et al., 2007). Within the broader landscape, agroecosystems affect the delivery of essential ecosystem services including the productivity of crops and availability and safety of wild foods, livestock, agroforestry products, and fish, and they contribute to erosion control as well as the regulation of water quality and availability.

Within this complex mix of biotic and abiotic interactions, new opportunities for disease and ill health also emerge. These have included malnutrition, malaria, HIV/AIDS, diet-related diseases, and a host of food-, water-, vector-borne, zoonotic, and other diseases (Romanelli et al., 2015). When health gains have been achieved, these are often inequitably distributed, disproportionately exposing vulnerable populations – including women, children, and the poor – to its unintended consequences.

The human-environment interactions at the heart of agroecosystem management are indivisible from the notion of sustainable development (Zimmerer and Vanek, 2016). This chapter reviews key considerations regarding the intersection of agrobiodiversity and human health for policy and practice. It summarizes common drivers of agrobiodiversity loss and ill health, explores health benefits of agroecosystems, and discusses some sustainable pathways towards common solutions, particularly at the local or community level. It argues that agrobiodiversity can not only attenuate critical drivers of biodiversity loss and the incremental impacts of climate change, it can contribute to improved health outcomes while bolstering ecosystem and human resilience.

## Common drivers of agrobiodiversity loss and ill health

### *Land use change and intensification*

Land use change is a defining feature of agricultural production and a leading driver of disease emergence in humans and wildlife (Karesh et al., 2012). Modern agricultural practices can alter vegetation patterns, habitats, and species composition, creating conditions that may more favourably support disease vectors, and thereby contributing to pathogen dispersion, prevalence and, sometimes, persistence (e.g. Pulliam et al., 2011). The introduction and consumption of domesticated and farmed species also offer new types of interactions among species and novel opportunities for disease transmission (WHO and CBD, 2015). Irrigated systems can also serve as breeding sites for vectors of human and domesticated animal diseases (Fernando and Halwart, 2000).

In Africa, Asia, and elsewhere, deforestation is increasing contact between humans and the natural reservoirs of diseases, for example in Malaysia, where deforestation and intensive agriculture enabled the emergence of Nipah virus (Pulliam et al., 2011; Daszak et al., 2013). Conversion of forested areas to paddyfields and irrigation can also create new habitats for the breeding of vectors of malaria (*Anopheles culicifacies* and other *Anopheles* vectors), Japanese encephalitis *(Culex tritaeniorhynchus, C. gelidus*, and *C. fuscocephala)*, dengue *(Aedes albopictus)* and lymphatic phylariasis (Amerasinghe et al., 1991; Ijumba and Lindsay, 2001; Bambaradeniya and Amerasinghe, 2004; Erlanger et al., 2005; Morand et al., 2014). For example, it has been estimated that 220 million people with Japanese encephalitis live in proximity to rice-irrigation schemes (Keiser et al., 2005). Such risks may be reduced through more sustainable management of aquatic agroecosystems by incorporating a diverse aquatic fauna: larvivorous fish have long been used as a form of vector control in irrigated systems (Howard et al., 2007). Reviving these traditional practices, and integrating fish farming in irrigation systems, may improve control of insect vectors, reduce plant pests, and decrease the need for insecticides, while increasing yields (Fernando and Halwart, 2000).

The conversion of mangrove ecosystems into monoculture, aquaculture, and rice production systems also contributes to loss of aquatic agrobiodiversity (Das and Vincent, 2009). Mangroves support important wetland communities of plants and animals and are natural sources of food, fuel, medicines, and protection against wind, waves, and water currents. In addition to protecting coral reefs and sea-grass beds and providing spawning grounds for many aquatic species (FAO, 2007), they can also act as natural bioshields that protect shorelines and human communities from the impacts of climate-related events. Yet population pressure and competition for land and resources has led to the conversion of mangroves to other uses, including infrastructure, aquaculture, oil drilling, and rice and salt production. More than 20% of mangrove area, 3.6 million hectares, was lost between 1980–2005 (FAO, 2007).

Under the right conditions, climate adaptation and disaster risk management strategies focused on mangrove conservation and repopulation can contribute to livelihoods, protect customary use and cultural identity, and guard against the impacts of biodiversity loss, disaster risk, and the corrosion of ecosystem services. For example, aqua-silviculture systems that integrate mangrove protection with low-density pond culture of fish, shrimp, and crab have long been used in Southeast Asia (Primavera, 2004). Integrated aquaculture systems in the Asia-Pacific region have also successfully restored deteriorating wild fish populations, contributed to the sustainability of marine ecosystems, and contributed to food security and nutrition (NACA, 2010). Such efforts remain challenging, particularly where traditional customs and values are inadequately preserved. For example, in Andra Pradesh, India, the extensive plantation of the non-native tree, *Casuarina equisetifolia* L., has hindered conservation efforts and contributed to the infringement of indigenous land rights and poor management of plantations (Shanker et al., 2008; Feagin et al., 2010). Conversely, community-based aquaculture practices that combine polyculture, agriculture, and mangroves, and responsible self-regulation with holistic Integrated Coastal Zone management, offer considerable potential to maximize socio-environmental co-benefits (Primavera, 2006).

## *Livestock intensification and consumption*

The shift towards increased meat consumption as countries become more affluent accelerates pressures on agroecosystems (Tilman et al., 2002; Jackson et al., 2007). The use of antibiotics in livestock intensification also contributes to the global surge in antimicrobial resistance, posing major threats to public and animal health (Byarugaba, 2004; Zhu et al., 2013) including the emergence of infectious diseases (Levy and Marshall, 2004). The causes of antimicrobial resistance are complex, and although genes for antibiotic resistance occur widely in nature, their inappropriate use and overuse, including non-therapeutic use of antibiotics as growth promoters, is a major cause of resistance (WHO, 2013). Hence, limiting the reintegration of contaminated manure into cropping systems and reducing contamination of water supplies is essential. Conversely, coupled waste management and cropping systems can promote more effective wastewater management, improve sanitation, and reduce the risk of contamination (Tomich et al., 2011).

## *Invasive species*

Invasive alien species pose considerable threats to ecosystems, biodiversity, agriculture, health, and livelihoods, and may be causative agents of algal blooms (Hallegraeff, 1998; Pyšek and Richardson, 2010; Coetzee and Hill, 2012). Invasive species may also threaten the availability of clean water supplies. For example, the introduction of the water hyacinth *(Eichhornia crassipes)* in Lake Victoria had deleterious impacts on small-scale freshwater fishing, food security, and nutrition for local communities, and contributed to the spread of water-borne diseases (Pejchar and Mooney, 2009). Invasive species can also be harmful to the well-being of communities whose sense of place may be disrupted (McNeely, 2001). Efforts to eradicate invasives can also be hazardous to ecosystem and human health by contaminating water supplies (Romanelli et al., 2015). However, agrobiodiversity can contribute to the suppression of some invasive species; for example, ecological weed management using locally available resources (primarily at the gene or species level of agrobiodiversity) can suppress weeds without resorting to synthetic herbicides (FAO and CBD, 2016).

### *Chemicals and pollution*

Pollution from agricultural production and other industrial uses poses direct threats to agroecosystems and human health. Pollution also plays a potentially significant role in the development of respiratory and water-borne diseases, including acute respiratory infections and chronic obstructive pulmonary diseases (Pimentel et al., 2007; Pruss-Ustun et al., 2016). Some pollutants also accumulate, persist, and are absorbed by soils and plants used for human consumption, further compounding associated health risks and associated loss of income and livelihoods (Pimentel, 1995; Beccaloni et al., 2010; Russo and Verdiani, 2012). Conversely, biodiversity – especially plant biodiversity – has been shown to play an instrumental role in the regulation and provision of water and air quality (Quijas et al., 2012). More broadly, agrobiodiversity can help to maximize agronomic, environmental, and economic benefits while reducing or mitigating the impacts of chemical inputs and pollution commonly associated with modern agriculture. It can also help farmers increase yields and optimize health outcomes using methods such as mixed farming systems, by replacing chemical inputs, and harnessing holistic strategies that support long-term fertility (Bos and Van de Ven, 1999; IPES-Food, 2016).

### *Climate change impacts*

Changes in climate combine with other environmental threats to traditional food systems, medicinal plants, and ethnopharmacological discovery (Cavaliere, 2009; Heywood, 2011). For example, diversity in the production of secondary chemical products is an important source of existing and new metabolites of pharmacologic interest in medicinal plants which may be affected by climate change (Ziska et al., 2009). Pharmacologic compounds might respond to recent or projected changes in $CO_2$ and/or temperature, affecting the production and concentration of atropine and scopolamine in jimson weed (*Datura stramonium*; Ziska et al., 2005), or morphine production in wild poppy (*Papaver setigerum*; Ziska et al., 2008). While many interactions between $CO_2$, plant toxicology, and pest pathology remain largely unknown, over 700 plant species are poisonous to humans; longer growing seasons could increase their abundance (Ziska and McConnell, 2015).

## The value of agroecosystems to health and well-being

### *Medicinal plants*

Across communities worldwide, traditional medicine plays crucial roles in linking health-related knowledge to affordable healthcare delivery. In some countries, up to 80% of the population rely on traditional medicine derived from biological resources for primary healthcare (Farnsworth and Soejarto, 1991; WHO, 2002). Traditional medicine also provides income and sustains livelihoods and holds immeasurable ethno- and biocultural value (Golden et al., 2012). Furthermore, ~75% of compounds isolated from higher plants with common biomedical uses are rooted in traditional medicine (Unnikrishnan and Suneetha, 2012). The trade in medicinal plants is also of enormous economic value, estimated at USD 60 million per year in South Africa alone (Roe et al., 2002). Yet wild plant populations are in sharp decline: 1 in 5 species is estimated to be threatened with extinction in the wild. Animals used for food and medicine are also more threatened than those which are not (WHO and CBD, 2015). Biological resources used as medicine are also threatened by the erosion of traditional knowledge, conflicts over intellectual property rights, biopiracy, destructive practices such as overharvesting, and poorly controlled international trade (Sheng-Ji, 2011; Payyappallimana et al., 2015).

The loss of medicinal plant species and associated loss of knowledge of its properties can hamper access of some communities to treatment (Ji et al., 2004), inhibit the dissemination of traditional knowledge, and hinder the potential for new treatments (Unnikrishnan and Suneetha, 2012). Northwest Yunnan China alone is home to over 2,000 species of medicinal plants, including one-third of the world's medicinal *Paris* species, and many are used for traditional Chinese and Tibetan medicine as well as the ethnopharmaceutical industry, though several species are under threat of extinction (Long et al., 2003). In India, approximately 300 plants of medicinal value, and some faunal species, are categorized as threatened and their cultivation is not economically viable given the lower costs of wild sourcing. This is compounded by a general misunderstanding of relevant agro-sourcing techniques (Hamilton, 2004). Conserving medicinal plants while preserving agrobiodiversity provides invaluable opportunities to safeguard scientific and traditional knowledge (or ethnobiological knowledge), conserve ecosystems, and safeguard human health. Several initiatives, supported by botanical gardens, are aimed at the conservation, education, and promotion of sustainable harvesting and use of medicinal plants (Waylen, 2006).

## *Genetic diversity in agroecosystems, ecosystem services, and human health*

The steady decline of genetic diversity in agroecosystems resulting from intense selection has been dramatic, affecting not only cultivated plant varieties but also their wild relatives (FAO, 1998).[1] As staple crops increase in abundance, their nutritional value is decreasing, contributing to the transition away from traditional, nutrient-rich diets, towards more energy intensive diets. This trend is often accompanied by increased meat consumption and reduced physical activity, culminating in a perfect storm of (agro)biodiversity loss and rising burden of non-communicable diseases (Tilman and Clark, 2014; Clonan et al., 2016). Diverse animal and plant breeds also support cultural ecosystem services that are embedded in the socio-cultural fabrics of communities and are integral to their well-being (Huffman, 2003; Alves and Rosa, 2007; Unnikrishnan and Suneetha, 2012). Selective specialization in a smaller number of crops and genotypes also increases vulnerability to infestation as exemplified by black Sigatoka infestations (*Mycosphaerella fijiensis* Morelet) of banana plantations (Altieri, 2002). In addition to providing reservoirs for crop genetic diversity, agrobiodiversity can maximize the health benefits of underutilized and neglected crops, sustain livelihoods, and promote food security among smallholder farmers and communities while increasing local availability of products rich in micronutrients (Johns and Eyzaguirre, 2006; Kahane et al., 2013). Examples of increasing micronutrient contents through the introduction of genes from neglected or underutilized species through classical breeding methods abound (Kappas et al., 2012; Pudasaini et al., 2013). The peach palm *(Bactris gasipaes)*, traditionally grown by Amazonian Amerindians, reportedly very rich in protein, carotenoids, vitamin E monounsaturated oleic acids, and potassium, provides one of many examples of health benefits provided by traditional crops, with added benefits of supporting traditional food cultures (Graefe et al., 2013; Kahane et al., 2013).

## *Soil, crops, and human health*

We are only beginning to understand the range of potential health benefits derived from improved soil management (DeClerck et al., 2011). The biological management of soil in agroecosystems provides critical opportunities to reduce the prevalence of soil-borne pathogens and pests that affect humans (e.g. toxoplasmosis, salmonellosis, ascariasis), plants (e.g. potato blight, root knot) and wildlife (e.g. anthrax) (Wall et al., 2015). Soil-transmitted intestinal parasitism alone affects approximately 2 billion people annually, an estimated 50% of which are in China (de Silva et al., 2003). Recent findings suggest that, together with improved sanitation measures, maintaining or restoring soil biodiversity and ecological complexity can be effective in reducing human and wildlife diseases (Wall et al., 2015). In Cambodia, *S. stercoralis* has been found to affect ~45% of the population, and infection risk was positively correlated with lower soil organic carbon content and the conversion of land from forests to cropland (Khieu et al., 2014; Wall et al., 2015). These findings are in line with others, demonstrating that diversifying land use practices to support soil diversity and ecological complexity can enhance ecosystem functions and related ecosystem services, including hydrological and nutrient cycling (Swift and Anderson, 1993; Ferris and Tuomisto, 2015). Soil biodiversity also plays a key role in terrestrial crop production and productivity, plant biomass and metabolism, nutrient supply, pollination and the regulation of crop pests, pathogens and parasites (Bronick and Lal, 2005; de Vries et al., 2013; Bardgett and van der Putten, 2014) with inevitable implications for human health (DeClerck et al., 2011; Brevik and Sauer, 2015).

Soil organisms are also consumed as sources of protein or medicines in some communities. For example, in the Amazon basin over 30 Amerindian communities use terrestrial invertebrates as sources of animal protein (Paoletti et al., 2000). Beyond dietary value, the rapidly emerging field of research examining the links between microbial diversity and immunology provides promising evidence of potential psychological, physiological, and endocrinological health benefits of exposure to microbial biodiversity in soils and the broader environment to regulate gut microbiota (Amaranthus and Allyn, 2013). Other potential health benefits of exposure to microbial diversity may include reduction of dysbiosis (e.g. West et al., 2015; Logan et al., 2016) and improved immunoregulatory function and inflammatory responses (Hertzen and Haahtela, 2006; Hanski et al., 2012; Rook, 2013; Hertzen et al., 2015; Rook and Knight, 2015). While we are rapidly gaining invaluable insights on the links between soil microbial diversity and human health, more interdisciplinary and integrative forms of scientific research are needed to better understand the full breadth of interactions and opportunities for more sustainable management of agroecosystems (Brevik and Sauer, 2015).

## Pollinators

The importance of insect pollination for agriculture is unequivocal; unfortunately, global pollinator species are steadily declining with negative consequences for pollination-dependent crops, food security, health, well-being, and livelihoods (Kremen et al., 2002; Potts et al., 2010; Bauer and Sue Wing, 2016; see also Gemmill-Herren, Chapter 7 of this Handbook). The harmful impacts of modern agricultural practices, including the use of chemical fertilizers and pesticides, monocropping, habitat loss, and other factors, have contributed to this alarming and costly decline (Bauer and Sue Wing, 2016).

From a health perspective, pollinators are not only critical to nutritional status (Ellis et al., 2015; Smith et al., 2015) but also an important source of income and livelihoods. In a comprehensive modeling study examining 224 food types across 156 countries, it was found that a 50% loss of pollination services could lead to 700,000 additional deaths yearly, while the complete removal of pollinators could result in up to 71 million people becoming vitamin A deficient in low income countries (Smith et al., 2015). The resulting declines in fruits, vegetables, nuts, and seeds, could increase global annual deaths from non-communicable and malnutrition-related diseases by 2.7% to exceed 1.42 million annual deaths. Disability-adjusted life-years (DALYs) would also increase by 2.7%, potentially affecting an estimated 27 million (Smith et al., 2015).

Traditional agroecosystem practices can make a significant contribution to the preservation of birds, bats, and insect pollinator species and reduce reliance on pesticides and insecticides. Planting pollinizer trees and restoring nesting habitats for honeybees can be excellent strategies for supporting pollination services. Measures such as preserving and exchanging traditional, locally-adapted open pollinated seeds and landraces can also strengthen food security and community-based sovereignty while supporting cultural cohesion, biocultural heritage, and collective connections to place (Pautasso et al., 2013; Campbell and Veteto, 2015).

## Pest and disease control

Agricultural intensification and the shift away from agrobiodiversity to monoculture have led to a steady rise in the use of pesticides to minimize costly crop losses. Crop losses due to insect pests could be sufficient to feed an additional 1 billion people (Birch et al., 2011). Global pesticide consumption in 2006–2007 alone was estimated at 5.2 billion pounds, with global expenditures for pesticides in excess of USD 39 billion (Grube et al., 2011). Despite this pervasive use, crop losses have not declined correspondingly: data for 19 regions on potential and actual losses for wheat, rice, maize, potatoes, soybeans, and cotton between 2001 and 2003 concluded that 'total global potential loss due to pests varied from about 50% in wheat to more than 80% in cotton production' (Oerke, 2006, p. 31). As climate change proceeds, migratory ranges and behaviours of pests are expected to become less predictable, further compounding the potential for crop losses (Birch et al., 2011). Conversely, maintaining crop variety diversity can decrease vulnerability, reduce crop losses, and improve yields, providing diversification of foods and maximizing the natural regulation of pests, with related health benefits (e.g. Wolfe, 2000; Bambaradeniya and Amerasinghe, 2004; Tomich et al., 2011).

The ubiquitous presence of pesticides in the environment has also been linked to pollinator declines, compromised immune function in some marine species, and pesticide resistance in target species, including at least 273 plant species (Horrigan et al., 2002). Their use can also lead to the widespread decline of beneficial insect and bird species, disruption of predator/prey interactions, and the pollution of surface and groundwater as a result of agricultural pesticide runoff and airborne pesticide contamination (Horrigan et al., 2002). Among the health problems arising from pesticide residues are increased risks for some cancers and reproductive and endocrine system disorders (Horrigan et al., 2002). Moreover, several developing countries lack adequate programs to control exposure to pesticides, as a result of which an estimated 25 million agricultural workers worldwide are subject to unintended pesticide poisonings every year (Alavanja, 2009).

Human exposure to chemical pesticides (including through residues of neurotoxic pesticides in food) can have detrimental health impacts on all segments of the population (Grandjean and Landrigan, 2006). Fetuses, infants, and young children are particularly vulnerable to exposure to pesticides even at low levels of exposure (Grandjean and Landrigan, 2014). This is in part attributable to higher doses per body weight in young children, rapid growth and development of their organ systems, and their decreased ability to detoxify (Landrigan et al., 1999; Sheffield and Landrigan, 2010). Amongst reported neurotoxic effects, pesticide exposure (in utero, infancy, and early childhood) has been linked to birth defects, developmental delays including to psychomotor development, respiratory diseases, cognitive disorders, neurobehavioural development disorders, attention deficit hyperactivity disorder, and autism spectrum disorder (Eskenazi et al., 1999; Rauh et al., 2006; Bjørling-Poulsen et al., 2008; Grandjean and Landrigan, 2014).

Conversely, the loss of agrobiodiversity means that there is a vast underutilized potential to reduce crop losses from insect pests and vector-borne crop viruses, given their typically lower incidence in polycultures (Matson, 1997; Thrupp et al., 2003; Jacobsen et al., 2013). Genetic diversity in particular has been found to 'significantly reduce pathogen impacts on crop productivity' (Matson, 1997, p. 505). Agrobiodiversity has not only been identified as an effective way to reduce the need for pesticides, it can also contribute to climate resilience (Jacobsen et al., 2015).

## Finding common ground

### *Maximizing agricultural biodiversity to improve health outcomes*

Agrobiodiversity loss and ill health share many drivers, and there is considerable scope to find common ground to maximize co-benefits for agroecosystems and the farmers and communities whose lives, health, and well-being depend on them. Recognizing the value of traditional farming systems for (domestic and wild) biodiversity conservation, adopting integrative approaches, combining traditional and science-based knowledge, and supporting subsidiarity are a solid first step (GEF, 2005; DeLind and Howard, 2008; Johns et al., 2013). It is equally important to jointly support community-based *in situ* and *ex situ* conservation initiatives; maintain wild habitats within production landscapes; and promote measures to jointly safeguard traditional knowledge, biodiversity, and ethno and biocultural diversity (Pimbert, 2006; Pollan, 2008; Barthel et al., 2013). Further co-benefits can be attained by recognizing the property rights of traditional farmers and indigenous peoples for genetic resources and land rights, adopting regulatory instruments that jointly support agrobiodiversity and health, establishing traditional seed exchange networks, supporting integrated vector and pest management, and other complementary measures (GEF, 2005; Pautasso et al., 2013; Edelman, 2014; Fernandez-Wulff, 2014). The following examples are provided.

#### *Traditional farming systems: the value of home gardens*

Traditional home and community gardens are important reservoirs of plant genetic resources offering significant potential for addressing micronutrient deficiencies (Fanzo et al., 2013) and can also serve as repositories for beneficial species used as medicines. For example, wormseed *(Dysphania ambrosioides)*, an herb native to Latin America, not only acts as a biopesticide, but is also used for various culinary and medicinal purposes (Leiva et al., 2002). Home and community gardens also support mental health and promote well-being through contact with nature in urban environments (Yotti' Kingsley et al., 2009), and afford coping strategies (e.g. as a source of income, community mobilization, nutrition, physical activity) in households affected by illness (Unruh, 2002; Mubvami and Manyati, 2007; Kirshbaum, 2007; Pushpakumara et al., 2012). Maximizing the use of medicinal plants in herbal home gardens can also support access to healthcare and the revival of traditional knowledge (Payyappallimana, 2010). It is estimated that ~200,000 home gardens spanning ten Indian states are used as a source of primary healthcare among economically disadvantaged households (Payyappallimana, 2010). Studies report substantial cost savings as a result of their integration with healthcare (Hariramamurthi, 2007).

#### *Conserving agro- and ethnobiodiversity through in situ and ex situ conservation*

Innovative approaches combining *in situ* and *ex situ* conservation of agrobiodiversity can deliver joint benefits to agrobiodiversity and human health. For example, the Foundation for Revitalization of Local Health Traditions (FRLHT) instituted the largest global *in situ* conservation network in India through the establishment, between 1993 and 2014, of 110 Medicinal Plant

Conservation Areas across 12 states in India. Its aim is to conserve and study medicinal plants in their natural environments while preserving their genetic diversity, and devising strategies for the sustainable management of rare, endangered, and vulnerable species through unique Public-Private Partnerships (Payyappallimana et al., 2015).

Related FRLHT initiatives have also made it possible to overcome traditional barriers to *ex situ* conservation, including the tendency for centralized institutions to perpetuate simplified industrial production systems, thereby eroding the very genetic diversity they purportedly intend to preserve. It has been argued that *ex situ* institutions, which tend to privilege corporate and academic plant breeders, should serve to complement farmer-led, agroecology *in situ* approaches which can support a wider web of diversity (Montenegro de Wit, 2015). Mutually supportive policies can then ensure that when seeds are returned to the land from seed banks they do not 'summarily encounter monoculture fields, or landscapes scarce in farmers and their knowledge' (Montenegro de Wit, 2015, p. 637).

The FRLHT's Medicinal Plant Conservation Parks aims to address this challenge through a community-based *ex situ* conservation initiative aimed at the sustainable use of medicinal plants and safeguarding associated knowledge. Pilot projects were initiated to integrate these practices in the formal primary health care centres and promote them through community health programs. Through these initiatives, communities have initiated the creation of ethno-medicinal forests and resource centres, local pharmacopoeia databases drawing on traditional knowledge, community and home gardens and seed banks, outreach nurseries for the promotion of cultivation and sustainable wild collection of medicinal plants, and measures to contribute to income generation. A Medicinal Plant Conservation Network working with different rural communities was also established. Within this scope, traditional healers associations were created and have collaborated with various organizations and government departments to support medicinal plant conservation programmes in various states. The Network is also working in related areas of health research and promotion, and facilitating community exchanges across healer associations in India and in Asian, South Asian, and African countries (Payyappallimana et al., 2015).

## The need for integrative approaches

Throughout history, the ecological, social, political, and economic impacts of unsustainable consumption and production practices associated with the management of agroecosystems have frequently been addressed within the siloed confines of specific disciplines, sectors, and practices (Romanelli et al., 2014). Sectoral policies in this area have typically provided a partial picture of the interrelated nature of these contexts with equally limited policy responses to address them. Cross-sectoral and interdisciplinary collaboration are needed to ensure the coherence of policies, standardization of metrics and indicators, and more integrated interpretation of data across disciplines (WHO and CBD, 2015). This need for interdisciplinarity has given rise to holistic approaches such as EcoHealth and One Health, which share the aim of bridging human health with the health of other species and ecosystems to address a set of complex challenges within their related ecological, social, political, and economic contexts (Webb et al., 2010; Parkes, 2011).

A growing number of examples are emerging in the context of agroecosystem management. For example, in Carchi, Ecuador, the *Ecosalud* project held across three small communities jointly addressed the impacts of hazardous pesticides on the health of agroecosystems and the neurotoxic burden on the health of farmers. It successfully contributed to building community capacity through knowledge production, education, and promoting alternative crop management technologies and practices. The pilot was later scaled up to other provinces with larger indigenous populations and different production systems (Cole et al., 2007; Orozco et al., 2011; Charron, 2012).

Integrative approaches to fisheries and aquaculture also offer significant potential for overcoming sectoral and governmental fragmentation, contributing to the development of public-private partnerships and developing institutional capacity (Soto et al., 2012). As a part of the Pacific Adaptation to Climate Change Project, the Palau Food Security pilot project adopted a comprehensive, community-based, 'ridge to reef' approach that successfully combined agroforestry, wetland, and mariculture components focused on sustainable ecosystem management, strengthening food security, and livelihoods and cultural identity, with the added aims of reducing dependence on imported foods, improving nutrition, and reducing the high burden of non-communicable diseases (McGregor et al., 2012).

## *Integrating biocultural, traditional, and scientific knowledge*

Approaches that combine the co-production of knowledge, community-based participatory research and management, and education provide novel opportunities to identify, mitigate, and monitor ecological and health risks within agroecosystems. A small, but growing, body of literature examining the added value of new forms of knowledge generation and dissemination is emerging at this nexus (Unnikrishnan and Suneetha, 2012; WHO and CBD, 2015). The added value of combining scientific knowledge (e.g. agroecology, biomedicine, epidemiology) and local knowledge (e.g. farmers or traditional healers) for the sustainable management of agroecological landscapes spans various dimensions of health, ranging from food security, nutrition, and associated non-communicable diseases to infectious diseases, poverty alleviation, and cultural heritage.

Leptospirosis, identified as the world's most widespread zoonotic diseases (Bharti et al., 2003), is exemplary of the common challenges and opportunities at this interface. Some outbreaks of leptospirosis in rural settings are associated with crops such as rice and taro which are grown in flooded or semi-flooded areas (VWB, 2010). While information about its pathogenesis is incomplete, it has been established that leptospirosis can be transmitted to humans from direct contact with the urine of infected wild or domesticated animals or contaminated water and soil (Bharti et al., 2003; Adler and de la Peña Moctezuma, 2010). In 2005, an integrative research programme was established to examine the human-environment dynamics of leptospirosis emergence in Hawaii's 'ahupua'a' region, where taro farming and wild pig hunting practices are potentially significant risk factors (VWB, 2010). Taro (*Colocasia esculenta* (L.) Schott), a staple crop used as food and medicine in Asia, the Pacific, and elsewhere, is rich in dietary fibre, antioxidants, vitamins, and minerals, and possesses vast cultural and spiritual significance for many Pacific islanders (Ramanatha Rao et al., 2010). Potential measures to mitigate disease risk, for example excluding taro cultivation, would not only be socially unacceptable but also could further erode traditional knowledge and undermine nutritional and medicinal benefits from its harvesting. By convening different stakeholders, including taro farmers and scientific experts, the programme enabled more targeted identification of opportunities and challenges in the management of agroecosystems and leptospirosis outbreaks[2] (VWB, 2010).

Such approaches are also useful for identifying of government policies that may provide perverse incentives contributing to disease outbreaks. In Peru, for example, farmers received domesticated livestock

> as an incentive for clearing tropical rain forest, including pigs, cattle, and imported Asian water buffalo. These animals not only are vectors for transmitting leptospires to the environment, but activities that lead to land clearance inevitably will lead to other unanticipated consequences, such as facilitating tropical viral emergence and reemergence, as has occurred with sylvatic yellow fever, alphaviruses, arenaviruses, etc.
>
> *(Vinetz et al., 2005, p. 303)*

## *Integrated pest and vector management*

Pesticides are toxic by design with well-documented impacts on biodiversity, ecosystems, and human health (Zhou et al., 2011). Biological control methods such as integrated pest management (IPM) in agroecosystems can be combined with education, public mobilization, community empowerment, and other forms of epidemiological control to minimize the unintended consequences of chemical pesticides while supporting livelihoods. Within rice agroecosystems, IPM makes it possible to preserve multiple habitats that can sustain animals including predators and parasitoids of crop pests, with added health benefits (Bambaradeniya and Amerasinghe, 2004).

In Sri Lanka, the risks of irrigated agriculture to agroecosystems and human health prompted large-scale collaboration between the health, agriculture, and environment sectors targeting rice irrigation systems to target education and build capacity targeting local farmer field schools through the implementation of a project on integrated pest and vector management, to reduce the risk of malaria and other health risks (Van Den Berg et al., 2007). Collaboration was prompted by finding a shared objective of augmenting the role of rural communities in sustainable ecosystem management. In addition to addressing the growing burden of malaria vector resistance to insecticides, it also sought to increase food safety and reduce health hazards of direct exposure to pesticides by promoting sustainable agroecology practices, harnessing knowledge on vector ecology, and encouraging sustainable agroecosystem management. Cross-sectoral community-based interventions were supported by relevant government ministries and UN agencies (FAO, WHO, UNEP) to promote community awareness, training, and education on integrated pest and vector management in irrigation agriculture to improve health outcomes. Over five years, an 82% reduction in insecticide application and a 23% reduction in yields was reported, with resulting health and social benefits to communities (Van Den Berg et al., 2007).

## *Integrative approaches in aquaculture and fisheries*

Capture fisheries and aquaculture supply an estimated 3 billion people with almost 20% of their average intake of animal protein, and an additional 1.3 billion with approximately 15% (Béné et al., 2015). Aquaculture accounts for almost half of all fish consumed by humans, and its share is expected to exceed 60% by 2030 (FAO, 2014), attracting increased analytic attention to the potentially protective health benefits of fish consumption (WHO, 2011; HLPE, 2014; Kassam, 2014). Risks of contamination and toxicity to both human populations and aquacultured species (Sapkota et al., 2008) and threats to biodiversity (Diana, 2009) persist. Maximizing co-benefits to agroecosystems and well-being will require better integration with other sectors, including capture fisheries. However, it will also require supporting agroecology, promoting diversity and knowledge exchange, and integrating health concerns. *Menidia estor*, a species long used in artisanal fisheries in Lake Pátzcuaro, Mexico, is one of several examples of how small-scale aquaculture, together with community development, participative rural appraisal, education and technology and knowledge sharing, can combine to achieve this end, while contributing to community cohesion, supporting livelihoods and well-being (Ross et al., 2008).

Beyond aquaculture, a broader approach to the sustainable conservation of fisheries resources is urgently needed. Strong connections between fisheries and public health outcomes are evident (e.g. nutrition, stroke, cardiovascular disease, early cognitive development; Kawarazuka, 2010; Golden et al., 2016) and the co-benefits that can be achieved by working across sectors and scales in the management of aquatic and other ecosystems need to be promoted (Bayles et al., 2016; Blasiak et al., 2016).

## Conclusions

Conserving healthy agroecosystems and human populations while rising to the challenge of increasingly complex and interconnected global environmental changes demands transformative changes to food production systems. Technological innovation will be important, and perhaps essential, but almost certainly insufficient on its own to achieve this aim. Sustainable alternatives to intensively-managed landscapes will require profound changes in the management of agroecosystems, ranging from dedicated investments to integrative solutions capable of ensuring that growth in productivity does not further encroach on the health of socio-ecological and human systems.

Mutually supportive policies, adequate institutional and incentive frameworks, and more proactive governance are needed to jointly support agrobiodiversity and health. Awareness-raising and extension are critical steps towards the adoption of more effective and efficient technologies and practices. These also demand sound scientific knowledge, and the meaningful inclusion and engagement of smallholder farmers, fisherfolk, and other knowledge holders. New, diverse, and sustainable paradigms of ecological intensification in smallholder farming (e.g. Caron et al., 2014; IPES-Food, 2016) can help to leverage agrobiodiversity for sustainable production, sustain cross-sectoral partnerships, maximize the value of scientific knowledge and other knowledge systems, and support research on underlying biological mechanisms to maximize human health outcomes. As we embark on new global commitments for sustainable development, these imperatives are not only relevant, they are necessary.

## Notes

1 The loss of varieties is often, but not always, synonymous with the loss of genetic diversity, as genes may be present in other varieties each with a unique combination of genes and value for humans and the surrounding ecosystems upon which they depend for food security.

2 For example, more culturally appropriate prevention and treatment methods, ecological factors that may favour emergence and spread such as stagnant water, cattle proximity to water bodies, presence of rodents (VWB, 2010).

## Acknowledgments

The authors thank Dr. Peter Stoett and Dr. Unnikrishnan Payyappallimana for their valuable insights during the development of this chapter.

## References

Adler, B. and de la Peña Moctezuma, A. (2010) 'Leptospira and leptospirosis', *Veterinary Microbiology*, vol. 140, pp. 287–296.

Alavanja, M. C. R. (2009) 'Pesticides use and exposure, extensive worldwide', *Reviews on Environmental Health*, vol. 24, pp. 303–309.

Altieri, P. (2002) 'Fatal harvest: Old and new dimensions of the ecological tragedy of modern agriculture', *Journal of Business Administration and Policy Analysis*, vol. 30–31, pp. 1–26.

Alves, R. R. N. and Rosa, I. M. L. (2007) 'Biodiversity, traditional medicine and public health: Where do they meet?', vol. 3, p. 14.

Amaranthus, M. and Allyn, B. (2013) *Healthy Soil Microbes, Healthy People*, www.theatlantic.com/health/archive/2013/06/healthy-soil-microbes-healthy-people/276710/, accessed 24 July 2016.

Amerasinghe, F. P., Amerasinghe, P. H. and Peiris, J. (1991) 'Anopheline ecology and malaria infection during the irrigation development of an area of the Mahaweli Project, Sri Lanka', *American Journal of Tropical Medicine and Hygiene*, vol. 45, pp. 226–235.

Bambaradeniya, C. N. B. and Amerasinghe, F. P. (2004) 'Biodiversity associated with the rice field agroecosystem in Asian countries: A brief review,' International Water Management Institute, Working Paper 63.

Bardgett, R. D. and van der Putten, W. H. (2014) 'Belowground biodiversity and ecosystem functioning', *Nature*, vol. 515, pp. 505–511.

Barthel, S., Crumley, C. and Svedin, U. (2013) 'Bio-cultural refugia – safeguarding diversity of practices for food security and biodiversity', *Global Environmental Change*, vol. 23, pp. 1142–1152.

Bauer, D. M. and Sue Wing, I. (2016) 'The macroeconomic cost of catastrophic pollinator declines', *Ecological Economics*, vol. 126, pp. 1–13.

Bayles, B. R., Brauman, K. A., Adkins, J. N., Allan, B. F., Ellis, A. M., Goldberg, T. L., Golden, C. D., Grigsby-Toussaint, D. S., Myers, S. S., Osofsky, S. A., Ricketts, T. H. and Ristaino, J. B. (2016) 'Ecosystem services connect environmental change to human health outcomes', *EcoHealth*, vol. 13, pp. 443–449.

Beccaloni, E., Vanni, F. and Giovannangeli, S. (2010) 'Agricultural soils potentially contaminated: Risk assessment procedure case studies', *Annali dell'Istituto Superiore di Sanità*, vol. 46, pp. 303–308.

Béné, C., Barange, M., Subasinghe, R., Pinstrup-Andersen, P., Merino, G., Hemre, G-I. and Williams, M. (2015) 'Feeding 9 billion by 2050 – putting fish back on the menu', *Food Security*, vol. 7, pp. 261–274.

Bharti, A. R., Nally, J. E., Ricaldi, J. N., Matthias, M. A., Diaz, M. M., Lovett, M. A., Levett, P. N., Gilman, R. H., Willig, M. R., Gotuzzo, E., Vinetz, J. M. and the Peru-United States Leptospirosis Consortium (2003) 'Leptospirosis: A zoonotic disease of global importance', *The Lancet Infectious Diseases*, vol. 3, pp. 757–771.

Birch, A. N. E., Begg, G. S. and Squire, G. R. (2011) 'How agro-ecological research helps to address food security issues under new IPM and pesticide reduction policies for global crop production systems', *Journal of Experimental Botany*, vol. 62, pp. 3251–3261.

Bjørling-Poulsen, M., Andersen, H. R. and Grandjean, P. (2008) 'Potential developmental neurotoxicity of pesticides used in Europe', *Environmental Health*, vol. 7, p. 1.

Blasiak, R., Pacheco, E., Furuya, K., Golden, C. D., Jauharee, A. R., Natori, Y., Saito, H., Sinan, H., Tanaka, T., Yagi, N. and Yiu, E. (2016) 'Local and regional experiences with assessing and fostering ocean health', *Marine Policy*, vol. 71, pp. 54–59.

Bos, J. F. F. P. and Van de Ven, G. W. J. (1999) 'Mixing specialized farming systems in Flevoland (The Netherlands): Agronomic, environmental and socio-economic effects', *Netherlands Journal of Agricultural Science*, vol. 47, pp. 185–200.

Brevik, E. C. and Sauer, T. J. (2015) 'The past, present, and future of soils and human health studies', *Soil*, vol. 1, pp. 35–46.

Bronick, C. J. and Lal, R. (2005) 'Soil structure and management: A review', *Geoderma*, vol. 124, pp. 3–22.

Byarugaba, D. K. (2004) 'A view on antimicrobial resistance in developing countries and responsible risk factors', *International Journal of Antimicrobial Agents*, vol. 24, pp. 105–110.

Campbell, B. C. and Veteto, J. R. (2015) 'Free seeds and food sovereignty: Anthropology and grassroots agrobiodiversity conservation strategies in the US South', *Journal of Political Ecology*, vol. 22, pp. 445–465.

Caron, P., Biénabe, E. and Hainzelin, E. (2014) 'Making transition towards ecological intensification of agriculture a reality: The gaps in and the role of scientific knowledge', *Current Opinion in Environmental Sustainability*, vol. 8, pp. 44–52.

Cavaliere, C. (2009) 'The effects of climate change on medicinal and aromatic plants', *HerbalGram: The Journal of the American Botanical Council*, vol. 81, pp. 44–57.

Charron, D. F. (2012) 'Ecohealth: Origins and approach', pp. 1–3 in D. F. Charron (ed.), *Ecohealth Research in Practice*, Springer New York, New York, NY, USA.

Clonan, A., Roberts, K. E. and Holdsworth, M. (2016) 'Socioeconomic and demographic drivers of red and processed meat consumption: Implications for health and environmental sustainability', *Proceedings of the Nutrition Society*, vol. 75, pp. 367–373.

Coetzee, J. A. and Hill, M. P. (2012) 'The role of eutrophication in the biological control of water hyacinth, *Eichhornia crassipes*, in South Africa', *BioControl*, vol. 57, p. 247.

Cole, D. C., Sherwood, S., Paredes, M., Sanin, L. H., Crissman, C., Espinosa, P. and Munoz, F. (2007) 'Reducing pesticide exposure and associated neurotoxic burden in an Ecuadorian small farm population', *International Journal of Occupational and Environmental Health*, vol. 13, pp. 281–289.

Das, S. and Vincent, J. R. (2009) 'Mangroves protected villages and reduced death toll during Indian super cyclone', *Proceedings of the National Academy of Sciences USA*, vol. 106, pp. 7357–7360.

Daszak, P., Zambrana-Torrelio, C., Bogich, T. L., Fernandez, M., Epstein, J. H., Murray, K. A. and Hamilton, H. (2013) 'Interdisciplinary approaches to understanding disease emergence: The past, present, and future drivers of Nipah virus emergence', *Proceedings of the National Academy of Sciences USA*, vol. 110, pp. 3681–3688.

DeClerck, F. A. J., Fanzo, J., Palm, C. and Remans, R. (2011) 'Ecological approaches to human nutrition', *Food and Nutrition Bulletin*, vol. 32, pp. S41–S50.

DeLind, L. B. and Howard, P. H. (2008) 'Safe at any scale? Food scares, food regulation, and scaled alternatives', *Agriculture and Human Values*, vol. 25, pp. 301–317.

de Silva, N. R., Brooker, S., Hotez, P. J., Montresor, A., Engels, D. and Savioli, L. (2003) 'Soil-transmitted helminth infections: Updating the global picture', *Trends in Parasitology*, vol. 19, pp. 547–551.

de Vries, F. T., Thébault, E., Liiri, M., Birkhofer, K., Tsiafouli, M. A., Bjørnlund, L., Bracht Jørgensen, H., Brady, M. V., Christensen, S., de Ruiter, P. C., d'Hertefeldt, T., Frouz, J., Hedlund, K., Hemerik, L., Hol, W. H., Hotes, S., Mortimer, S. R., Setälä, H., Sgardelis, S. P., Uteseny, K., van der Putten, W. H., Wolters, V. and Bardgett, R. D. (2013) 'Soil food web properties explain ecosystem services across European land use systems', *Proceedings of the National Academy of Sciences USA*, vol. 110, pp. 14296–14301.

Diana, J. S. (2009) 'Aquaculture production and biodiversity conservation', *BioScience*, vol. 59, pp. 27–38.

Edelman, M. (2014) 'Food sovereignty: Forgotten genealogies and future regulatory challenges', *The Journal of Peasant Studies*, vol. 41, pp. 959–978.

Ellis, A. M., Myers, S. S. and Ricketts, T. H. (2015) 'Do pollinators contribute to nutritional health?', *PLoS ONE*, vol. 10, p. e114805.

Erlanger, T. E., Keiser, J., Caldas De Castro, M., Bos, R., Singer, B. H., Tanner, M. and Utzinger, J. (2005) 'Effect of water resource development and management on lymphatic filariasis, and estimates of populations at risk', *The American Journal of Tropical Medicine and Hygiene*, vol. 73, pp. 523–533.

Eskenazi, B., Bradman, A. and Castorina, R. (1999) 'Exposures of children to organophosphate pesticides and their potential adverse health effects', *Environmental Health Perspectives*, vol. 107, pp. 409–419.

Fanzo, J., Hunter, D., Borelli, T. and Mattei, D. (eds.) (2013) *Diversifying Food and Diets: Using Agricultural Biodiversity to Improve Nutrition and Health*, Earthscan for Routledge, Abingdon, UK.

Food and Agriculture Organization of the United Nations (FAO) (1998) *The State of the World's Plant Genetic Resources for Food and Agriculture*, FAO, Rome, Italy.

FAO (2007) *The World's Mangroves 1980–2005*, FAO Forestry Paper 153, FAO, Rome, Italy.

FAO (2014) *The State of World Fisheries and Aquaculture 2014*, FAO, Rome, Italy.

FAO (2015a) *The State of Food Insecurity in the World 2015*, FAO, Rome, Italy.

FAO (2015b) '*Second Report on the State of the World's Animal Genetic Resources for Food and Agriculture*. B. D. Scherf and D. Pilling (eds.), FAO Commission on Genetic Resources for Food and Agriculture Assessments', Rome, Italy.

FAO and CBD Secretariat (2016) *Mainstreaming Ecosystem Services and Biodiversity into Agricultural Production and Management in East Africa*, FAO, Rome, Italy.

FAO, IFAD and WFP (2014) *The State of Food Insecurity in the World 2014*, FAO, Rome, Italy.

Farnsworth, N. R. and Soejarto, D. D. (1991) 'Global importance of medicinal plants', pp. 35–51 in O. Akerele and V. Heywood (eds.), *Conservation of Medicinal Plants*, Cambridge University Press, Cambridge, UK.

Feagin, R. A., Mukherjee, N., Shanker, K., Baird, A. H., Cinner, J., Kerr, A. M., Koedam, N., Sridhar, A., Arthur, R., Jayatissa, L. P., Seen, D. L., Menon, M., Rodriguez, S., Shamsuddoha, Md. and Dahdouh-Guebas, F. (2010) 'Shelter from the storm? Use and misuse of coastal vegetation bioshields for managing natural disasters', *Conservation Letters*, vol. 3, pp. 1–11.

Fernandez-Wulff, P. (2014) 'Securing sovereignties: Implications of institutional food governance frameworks for agrobiodiversity protection in urban and peri-urban landscapes in Mexico and Ecuador', *Revista de la Escuela Jacobea de Posgrado*, vol. 6, pp. 1–68.

Fernando, C. H. and Halwart, M. (2000) 'Possibilities for the integration of fish farming into irrigation systems', *Fisheries Management and Ecology*, vol. 7, pp. 45–54.

Ferris, H. and Tuomisto, H. (2015) 'Unearthing the role of biological diversity in soil health', *Soil Biology and Biochemistry*, vol. 85, pp. 101–109.

GEF (2005) *Mainstreaming Biodiversity in Production Landscapes*, C. Petersen and B. Huntley (eds.), GEF, Washington, DC, USA.

Golden, C. D., Allison, E. H., Cheung, W. W., Dey, M. M., Halpern, B. S., McCauley, D. J., Smith, M., Vaitla, B., Zeller, D. and Myers, S. S. (2016) 'Fall in fish catch threatens human health', *Nature*, vol. 534, pp. 317–320.

Golden, C. D., Rasolofoniaina, B. J., Anjaranirina, E. J., Nicolas, L., Ravaoliny, L. and Kremen, C. (2012) 'Rainforest pharmacopeia in Madagascar provides high value for current local and prospective global uses', *PLoS ONE*, vol. 7, p. e41221.

Graefe, S., Dufour, D., van Zonneveld, M., Rodriguez, F. and Gonzalez, A. (2013) 'Peach palm (*Bactris gasipaes*) in tropical Latin America: Implications for biodiversity conservation, natural resource management and human nutrition', *Biodiversity and Conservation*, vol. 22, pp. 269–300.

Grandjean, P. and Landrigan, P. J. (2006) 'Developmental neurotoxicity of industrial chemicals', *The Lancet*, vol. 368, pp. 2167–2178.

Grandjean, P. and Landrigan, P. J. (2014) 'Neurobehavioural effects of developmental toxicity', *The Lancet Neurology*, vol. 13, pp. 330–338.

Grube, A., Donaldson, D., Kiely, T. and Wu, L. (2011) *Pesticides Industry Sales and Usage*, Environmental Protection Agency of the USA, Washington, DC, USA.

Hallegraeff, G. M. (1998) 'Transport of toxic dinoflagellates via ships ballast water: Bioeconomic risk assessment and efficacy of possible ballast water management strategies', *Marine Ecology Progress Series*, vol. 168, pp. 297–309.

Hamilton, A. C. (2004) 'Medicinal plants, conservation and livelihoods', *Biodiversity and Conversation*, vol. 13, pp. 1477–1517.

Hanski, I., von Hertzen, L., Fyhrquist, N., Koskinen, K., Torppa, K., Laatikainen, T., Karisola, P., Auvinen, P., Paulin, L., Mäkelä, M. J., Vartiainen, E., Kosunen, T. U., Alenius, H. and Haahtela, T. (2012) 'Environmental biodiversity, human microbiota, and allergy are interrelated', *Proceedings of the Academy of Sciences USA*, vol. 109, pp. 8334–8339.

Hariramamurthi, G. (2007) 'Home herbal gardens – a novel health security strategy based on local knowledge and resources', pp. 167–184 in G. Bodeker and G. Burford (eds.), *Traditional, Complementary and Alternative Medicine Policy and Public Health Perspectives*, World Scientific, London, UK.

Hertzen, von L., Beutler, B., Bienenstock, J., Blaser, M., Cani, P. D., Eriksson, J., Färkkilä, M., Haahtela, T., Hanski, I., Jenmalm, M. C., Kere, J., Knip, M., Kontula, K., Koskenvuo, M., Ling, C., Mandrup-Poulsen, T., von Mutius, E., Mäkelä, M. J., Paunio, T., Pershagen, G., Renz, H., Rook, G., Saarela, M., Vaarala, O., Veldhoen, M. and de Vos, W. M. (2015) 'Helsinki alert of biodiversity and health', *Annals of Medicine*, vol. 47, pp. 218–225.

Hertzen, von L. and Haahtela, T. (2006) 'Disconnection of man and the soil: Reason for the asthma and atopy epidemic?'. *Journal of Allergy and Clinical Immunology*, vol. 117, pp. 334–344.

Heywood, V. H. (2011) 'Ethnopharmacology, food production, nutrition and biodiversity conservation: Towards a sustainable future for indigenous peoples', *Journal of Ethnopharmacology*, vol. 137, pp. 1–15.

HLPE (2014) *Sustainable Fisheries and Aquaculture for Food Security and Nutrition*, FAO, Rome, Italy.

Horrigan, L., Lawrence, R. S. and Walker, P. (2002) 'How sustainable agriculture can address the environmental and human health harms of industrial agriculture', *Environmental Health Perspectives*, vol. 110, pp. 445–456.

Howard, A., Zhou, G. and Omlin, F. X. (2007) 'Malaria mosquito control using edible fish in western Kenya: Preliminary findings of a controlled study', *BMC Public Health*, vol. 7, p. e199.

Huffman, M. A. (2003) 'Animal self-medication and ethno-medicine: Exploration and exploitation of the medicinal properties of plants', *Proceedings of the Nutrition Society*, vol. 62, pp. 371–381.

Ijumba, J. N. and Lindsay, S. W. (2001) 'Impact of irrigation on malaria in Africa: Paddies paradox', *Medical and Veterinary Entomology*, vol. 15, pp. 1–11.

IPES-Food (2016) *From Uniformity to Diversity: A paradigm shift from industrial agriculture to diversified agroecological systems*, E. A. Frison (ed.), International Panel of Experts on Sustainable Food Systems.

Jackson, L. E., Pascual, U. and Hodgkin, T. (2007) 'Utilizing and conserving agrobiodiversity in agricultural landscapes', *Agriculture, Ecosystems & Environment*, vol. 121, pp. 196–210.

Jacobsen, S. E., Sørensen, M. and Pedersen, S. M. (2013) 'Feeding the world: Genetically modified crops versus agricultural biodiversity', *Agronomy for Sustainable Development*, vol. 33 p. 651.

Jacobsen, S-E., Sørensen, M., Pedersen, S. M. and Weiner, J. (2015) 'Using our agrobiodiversity: Plant-based solutions to feed the world', *Agronomy for Sustainable Development*, vol. 35, p. 1217.

Jarvis, D. I., Padoch, C. and Cooper, H. D. (eds.) (2007) *Managing Biodiversity in Agricultural Ecosystems*, Columbia University Press, New York, NY, USA.

Ji, H., Shengji, P. and Chunlin, L. (2004) 'An ethnobotanical study of medicinal plants used by the Lisu People in Nujiang, Northwest Yunnan, China', *Economic Botany*, 58, pp. S253–S264.

Johns, T. and Eyzaguirre, P. B. (2006) 'Linking biodiversity, diet and health in policy and practice', *Proceedings of the Nutrition Society*, vol. 65, pp. 182–189.

Johns, T., Powell, B., Maundu, P. and Eyzaguirre, P. B. (2013) 'Agricultural biodiversity as a link between traditional food systems and contemporary development, social integrity and ecological health', *Journal of the Science of Food and Agriculture*, vol. 93, pp. 3433–3442.

Kahane, R., Hodgkin, T., Jaenicke, H., Hoogendoorn, C., Hermann, M., Keatinge, J. D. H., Hughes, J. d'A., Padulosi, S. and Looney, N. (2013) 'Agrobiodiversity for food security, health and income', *Agronomy for Sustainable Development*, vol. 33, pp. 671–693.

Kappas, M., Gross, U. and Kelleher, D. (2012) *Global Health*, Universitätsverlag Göttingen, Germany.

Karesh, W. B., Dobson, A., Lloyd-Smith, J. O., Lubroth, J., Dixon, M. A., Bennett, M., Aldrich, S., Harrington, T., Formenty, P., Loh, E. H., Machalaba, C. C., Thomas, M. J. and Heymann, D. L. (2012) 'Ecology of zoonoses: Natural and unnatural histories', *The Lancet*, vol. 380, pp. 1936–1945.

Kassam, L. (2014) *Aquaculture and Food Security, Poverty Alleviation and Nutrition in Ghana*, WorldFish, Penang, Malaysia.

Kawarazuka, N. (2010) 'The contribution of fish intake, aquaculture, and small-scale fisheries to improving nutrition: A literature review', *The WorldFish Center Working Papers*, No. 2016, WorldFish, Penang, Malaysia.

Keiser, J., Maltese, M. F., Erlanger, T. E., Bos, R., Tanner, M., Singer, B. H. and Utzinger, J. (2005) 'Effect of irrigated rice agriculture on Japanese encephalitis, including challenges and opportunities for integrated vector management', *Acta Tropica*, vol. 95, pp. 40–57.

Khieu, V., Schär, F., Forrer, A., Hattendorf, J., Marti, H., Duong, S., Vounatsou, P., Muth, S. and Odermatt, P. (2014) 'High prevalence and spatial distribution of *Strongyloides stercoralis* in rural Cambodia', *PLoS Neglected Tropical Diseases*, vol. 8, p. e2854.

Kirshbaum, M. N. (2007) 'A review of the benefits of whole body exercise during and after treatment for breast cancer', *Journal of Clinical Nursing*, vol. 16, pp. 104–121.

Kremen, C., Williams, N. M. and Thorp, R. W. (2002) 'Crop pollination from native bees at risk from agricultural intensification', *Proceedings of the National Academy of Sciences USA*, vol. 99, pp. 16812–16816.

Landrigan, P. J., Claudio, L., Markowitz, S. B., Berkowitz, G. S., Brenner, B. L., Romero, H., Wetmur, J. G., Matte, T. D., Gore, A. C., Godbold, J. H. and Wolff, M. S. (1999) 'Pesticides and inner-city children: Exposures, risks, and prevention', *Environmental Health Perspectives*, vol. 107, pp. 431–437.

Leiva, J. M., Azurdia, C., Ovando, W., López, E. and Ayala, H. (2002) 'Contributions of home gardens to *in situ* conservation in traditional farming systems – Guatemalan component', pp. 56–72 in J. Watson and P. Eyzaguirre (eds.), *Home Gardens and* In Situ *Conservation of Plant Genetic Resources in Farming Systems*, Proceedings of the Second International Home Gardens Workshop, 17–19 July 2001, Witzenhausen. IPGRI, Rome, Italy.

Levy, S. B. and Marshall, B. (2004) 'Antibacterial resistance worldwide: Causes, challenges and responses', *Nature Medicine*, vol. 10, pp. S122–S129.

Logan, A. C., Jacka, F. N. and Prescott, S. L. (2016) 'Immune-microbiota interactions: Dysbiosis as a global health issue', *Current Allergy and Asthma Reports*, vol. 16, p. 13.

Long, C. L., Li, H., Ouyang, Z., Yang, X., Li, Q. and Trangmar, B. (2003) 'Strategies for agrobiodiversity conservation and promotion: A case from Yunnan, China', *Biodiversity and Conservation*, vol. 12, pp. 1145–1156.

Matson, P. A. (1997) 'Agricultural intensification and ecosystem properties', *Science*, vol. 277, pp. 504–509.

McGregor, A., Basilius, L. and Taro, T. (2012) *The Palau PACC Food Security Project: A Benefit-Cost Analysis*, www.adaptation-undp.org/sites/default/files/downloads/palau_pacc_cba_final_report.pdf

McNeely, J. A. (ed.) (2001) *The Great Reshuffling: Human Dimensions of Invasive Alien Species*, IUCN, Gland, Switzerland and Cambridge, UK.

Milcu, A. I., Hanspach, J., Abson, D. and Fischer, J. (2013) 'Cultural ecosystem services: A literature review and prospects for future research', *Ecology and Society*, vol. 18, p. 44.

Montenegro de Wit, M. (2015) 'Are we losing diversity? Navigating ecological, political, and epistemic dimensions of agrobiodiversity conservation', *Agriculture and Human Values*, vol. 33, pp. 625–640.

Morand, S., Jittapalapong, S., Suputtamongkol, Y., Abdullah, M. T. and Huan, T. B. (2014) 'Infectious diseases and their outbreaks in Asia-Pacific: Biodiversity and its regulation loss matter', *PLoS ONE*, vol. 9, p. e90032.

Mubvami, T. and Manyati, M. (2007) 'HIV/AIDS, urban agriculture and community mobilisation: Cases from Zimbabwe', *Urban Agriculture*. www.syrialearning.org/resource/7787

NACA (2010) *Success Stories in Asian Aquaculture*, S. S. De Silva and F. B. Davy (eds.), International Development Research Centre, Dordrecht, the Netherlands.

Oerke, E. C. (2006) 'Crop losses to pests', *The Journal of Agricultural Science*, vol. 144, pp. 31–43.

Orozco, F. A., Cole, D. C., Ibrahim, S. and Wanigaratne, S. (2011) 'Health promotion outcomes associated with a community-based program to reduce pesticide-related risks among small farm households', *Health Promotion International*, vol. 26, pp. 432–446.

Paoletti, M. G., Dufour, D. L., Cerda, H., Torres, F., Pizzoferrato, L. and Pimentel, D. (2000) 'The importance of leaf- and litter-feeding invertebrates as sources of animal protein for the Amazonian Amerindians', *Proceedings of the Royal Society of London B – Biological Sciences*, vol. 267, pp. 2247–2252.

Parkes, M. W. (2011) 'Diversity, emergence, resilience: Guides for a new generation of ecohealth research and practice', *EcoHealth*, vol. 8, pp. 137–139.

Pautasso, M., Aistara, G., Barnaud, A., Caillon, S., Clouvel, P., Coomes, O. T., Delêtre, M., Demeulenaere, E., De Santis, P., Döring, T., Eloy, L., Emperaire, L., Garine, E., Goldringer, I., Jarvis, D., Joly, H., Leclerc, C., Louafi, S., Martin, P., Massol, F., McGuire, S., McKey, D. B., Padoch, C., Soler, C., Thomas, M. and Tramontini, S. (2013) 'Seed exchange networks for agrobiodiversity conservation: A review', *Agronomy for Sustainable Development*, vol. 33, pp. 151–175.

Payyappallimana, U. (2010) 'Role of traditional medicine in primary health care', *Yokohama Journal of Social Sciences*, vol. 14, pp. 57–77.

Payyappallimana, U., Suneetha, M. S., Timoshyna, A., Graz, B., Leaman, D., Bussman, R. W., Hariramamurthi, G., Shankar, D., van't Klooster, C. I. E. A., Bodeker, G., Sekagya, Y., Hemstra, W., Gomez, F., Verschuuren, B., de Ravin, E., Ligare, J., Reid, A. M. and Petersen, L. M. (2015) 'Traditional medicine', in C. Romanelli, D. Cooper, D. Campbell-Lendrum, M. Maiero, W. B. Karesh, D. Hunter and C. D. Golden (eds.), *Connecting Global Priorities: Biodiversity and Human Health*, World Health Organization, Geneva, Switzerland.

Pejchar, L. and Mooney, H. A. (2009) 'Invasive species, ecosystem services and human well-being', *Trends in Ecology & Evolution*, vol. 24, pp. 497–504.

Pimbert, M. (2006) *Transforming Knowledge and Ways of Knowing for Food Sovereignty*, International Institute for Environment and Development, London, UK.

Pimentel, D. (1995) 'Amounts of pesticides reaching target pests: Environmental impacts and ethics', *Journal of Agricultural and Environmental Ethics*, vol. 8, p. 17.

Pimentel, D., Cooperstein, S., Randell, H., Filiberto, D., Sorrentino, S., Kaye, B., Nicklin, C., Yagi, J., Brian, J., O'Hern, J., Habas, A. and Weinstein, C. (2007) 'Ecology of increasing diseases: Population growth and environmental degradation', *Human Ecology*, vol. 35, pp. 653–668.

Pollan, M. (2008) 'Farmer in chief', *New York Times Magazine*. www.nytimes.com/2008/10/12/magazine/12policy-t.html

Potts, S. G., Biesmeijer, J. C., Kremen, C., Neumann, P., Schweiger, O. and Kunin, W. E. (2010) 'Global pollinator declines: Trends, impacts and drivers', *Trends in Ecology & Evolution*, vol. 25, pp. 345–353.

Primavera, J. H. (2004) 'Retaining our mangrove greenbelt: Integrating mangroves and aquaculture', *Fish for the People*, vol. 2, pp. 20–26.

Primavera, J. H. (2006) 'Overcoming the impacts of aquaculture on the coastal zone', *Ocean & Coastal Management*, vol. 49, pp. 531–545.

Pruss-Ustun, A., Wolf, J., Corvalán, C., Bos, R. and Neira, M. (2016) *Preventing Disease Through Healthy Environments*, World Health Organization, Geneva, Switzerland.

Pudasaini, R., Sthapit, S. and Suwal, S. (2013) 'The role of integrated home gardens and local, neglected and underutilized plant species in food security in Nepal and meeting the Millennium Development Goal 1', pp. 242–256 in J. Fanzo, D. Hunter, T. Borelli and D. Mattei (eds.), *Diversifying Food and Diets: Using Agricultural Biodiversity to Improve Nutrition and Health*, Earthscan for Routledge, Abingdon, UK.

Pulliam, J. R. C., Epstein, J. H., Dushoff, J., Rahman, S. A., Bunning, M., Jamaluddin, A. A., Hyatt, A. D., Field, H. E., Dobson, A. P., Daszak, P. and the Henipavirus Ecology Research Group (HERG) (2011) 'Agricultural intensification, priming for persistence and the emergence of Nipah virus: A lethal bat-borne zoonosis', *Journal of the Royal Society Interface*, vol. 9, pp. 89–101.

Pushpakumara, D., Marambe, B. and Silva, G. (2012) 'A review of research on homegardens in Sri Lanka: The status, importance and future perspective', *Tropical Agriculturist*, vol. 160, pp. 55–125.

Pyšek, P. and Richardson, D. M. (2010) 'Invasive species, environmental change and management, and health', *Annual Review of Environment and Resources*, vol. 35, pp. 25–55.

Quijas, S., Jackson, L. E., Maass, M., Schmid, B., Raffaelli, D. and Balvanera, P. (2012) 'Plant diversity and generation of ecosystem services at the landscape scale: Expert knowledge assessment', *Journal of Applied Ecology*, vol. 49, pp. 929–940.

Ramanatha Rao, V., Matthews, P. J., Eyzaguirre, P. B. and Hunter, D. (eds.) (2010) *The Global Diversity of Taro: Ethnobotany and Conservation*, Bioversity International, Maccarese, Italy.

Rauh, V. A., Garfinkel, R., Perera, F. P., Andrews, H. F., Hoepner, L., Barr, D. B., Whitehead, R., Tang, D. and Whyatt, R. W. (2006) 'Impact of prenatal chlorpyrifos exposure on neurodevelopment in the first three years of life among inner-city children', *Pediatrics*, vol. 118, pp. e1845–e1859.

Roe, D., Mulliken, T., Milledge, S., Mremi, J., Mosha, S. and Greig-Gran, M. (2002) *Making a Living or Making a Killing*, Biodiversity and Livelihoods Issue Papers 06, TRAFFIC/IIED, London, UK.

Romanelli, C., Buss, D., Coates, D., Hodgkin, T., Stoett, P. and Boischio, A. (2015) 'Freshwater, wetlands, biodiversity and human health', pp. 46–62 in C. Romanelli, D. Cooper, D. Campbell-Lendrum, M. Maiero, W. B. Karesh, D. Hunter and C. D. Golden (eds.), *Connecting Global Priorities: Biodiversity and Human Health*, World Health Organization, Geneva, Switzerland.

Romanelli, C., Cooper, H. D. and de Souza Dias, B. F. (2014) 'The integration of biodiversity into One Health', *Reviews in Science and Technology*, vol. 33, pp. 487–496.

Rook, G. A. (2013) 'Regulation of the immune system by biodiversity from the natural environment: An ecosystem service essential to health', *Proceedings of the National Academy of Sciences USA*, vol. 110, pp. 18360–18367.

Rook, G. A. and Knight, R. (2015) 'Environmental microbial diversity and noncommunicable diseases', pp. 150–163 in C. Romanelli, D. Cooper, D. Campbell-Lendrum, M. Maiero, W. B. Karesh, D. Hunter and C. D. Golden (eds.), *Connecting Global Priorities: Biodiversity and Human Health*, World Health Organization, Geneva, Switzerland.

Ross, L. G., Martinez Palacios, C. A. and Morales, E. J. (2008) 'Developing native fish species for aquaculture: The interacting demands of biodiversity, sustainable aquaculture and livelihoods', *Aquaculture Research*, vol. 39, pp. 675–683.

Russo, G. and Verdiani, G. (2012) 'The health risk of the agricultural production in potentially contaminated sites: An environmental-health risk analysis', *Journal of Agricultural Engineering*, vol. 43, p. e15.

Sapkota, A., Sapkota, A. R., Kucharski, M., Burke, J., McKenzie, S., Walker, P. and Lawrence, R. (2008) 'Aquaculture practices and potential human health risks: Current knowledge and future priorities', *Environment International*, vol. 34, pp. 1215–1226.

Shanker, K., Namboothri, N., Rodriguez, S. and Sridhar, A. (eds.) (2008) *Beyond the Tsunami: Social, Ecological and Policy Analyses of Coastal and Marine Systems on the Mainland Coast of India*, Post-tsunami environment initiative report submitted to the United Nations Development Programme, UNDP/UNTRS, Chennai and ATREE, Bangalore, India.

Sheffield, P. E. and Landrigan, P. J. (2010) 'Global climate change and children's health: Threats and strategies for prevention', *Environmental Health Perspectives*, vol. 119, pp. 291–298.

Sheng-Ji, P. (2011) 'Ethnobotanical approaches of traditional medicine studies: Some experiences from Asia', *Pharmaceutical Biology*, vol. 39, pp. 74–79.

Smith, M. R., Singh, G. M., Mozaffarian, D. and Myers, S. S. (2015) 'Effects of decreases of animal pollinators on human nutrition and global health: A modelling analysis', *The Lancet*, vol. 386, pp. 1964–1972.

Soto, D., White, P., Dempster, T., De Silva, S., Flores, A., Karakassis, Y., Knapp, G., Martinez, J., Miao, W., Sadovy, Y., Thorstad, E. and Wiefels, R. (2012) 'Addressing aquaculture-fisheries interactions through the implementation of the ecosystem approach to aquaculture (EAA)', pp. 385–436 in R. P. Subasinghe, J. R. Arthur, D. M. Bartley, S. S. De Silva, M. Halwart, N. Hishamunda, C. V. Mohan and P. Sorgeloos (eds.), *Farming the Waters for People and Food*, Proceedings of the Global Conference on Aquaculture 2010, Phuket, Thailand. 22–25 September 2010. FAO, Rome, Italy and NACA, Bangkok, Thailand.

Swift, M. J. and Anderson, J. M. (1993) 'Biodiversity and ecosystem function in agricultural systems', pp. 15–41 in E. D. Schultz and H. Mooney (eds.), *Biodiversity and Ecosystem Function*, Springer, Berlin, Germany.

Thrupp, L. A. (2003) 'Agricultural biodiversity: A key element of ecosystem health and sustainable food security', pp. 317–331 in D. J. Rapport, W. L. Lasley, D. E. Rolston, N. O. Nielsen, C. O. Qualset and A. B. Damania (eds.), *Managing for Healthy Ecosystems*, CRC Press Inc, Boca Raton, FL, USA.

Tilman, D., Cassman, K. G., Matson, P. A., Naylor, R. and Polasky, S. (2002) 'Agricultural sustainability and intensive production practices', *Nature*, vol. 418, pp. 671–677.

Tilman, D. and Clark, M. (2014) 'Global diets link environmental sustainability and human health', *Nature*, vol. 515, pp. 518–522.

Tomich, T. P., Brodt, S., Ferris, H., Galt, R., Horwath, W. R., Kebreab, E., Leveau, J. H. J., Liptzin, D., Lubell, M., Merel, P., Michelmore, R., Rosenstock, T., Scow, K., Six, J., Williams, N. and Yang, L. (2011) 'Agroecology: A review from a global-change perspective', *Annual Review of Environment and Resources*, vol. 36, pp. 193–222.

Unnikrishnan, P. M. and Suneetha, M. S. (2012) *Biodiversity, Traditional Knowledge and Community Health: Strengthening Linkages*, UNU-IAS Policy Report, United Nations University-Institute of Advanced Studies, Yokohama, Japan.

Unruh, A. M. (2002) 'The meaning of gardens and gardening in daily life: A comparison between gardeners with serious health problems and healthy participants', *Acta Horticultura*, vol. 639, pp. 67–73.

Van Den Berg, H., Von Hildebrand, A., Ragunathan, V. and Das, P. K. (2007) 'Reducing vector-borne disease by empowering farmers in integrated vector management', *Bulletin of the World Health Organization*, vol. 85, pp. 501–568.

Vinetz, J. M., Wilcox, B. A., Aguirre, A., Gollin, L. X., Katz, A. R., Fujioka, R. S., Maly, K., Horwitz, P. and Chang, H. (2005) 'Beyond disciplinary boundaries: Leptospirosis as a model of incorporating transdisciplinary approaches to understand infectious disease emergence', *EcoHealth*, vol. 2, pp. 291–306.

VWB (2010) *One Health for One World: Compendium Case Studies*, Veterinarians without Borders/Vétérinaires sans Frontières, Ottawa, Canada.

Wall, D. H., Nielsen, U. N. and Six, J. (2015) 'Soil biodiversity and human health', *Nature*, vol. 528, pp. 69–76.

Waylen, K. (2006) *Botanic Gardens: Using Biodiversity to Improve Well-being*, Botanic Gardens Conservation International, Richmond, UK.

Webb, J. C., Mergler, D., Parkes, M. W., Saint-Charles, J., Spiegel, J., Waltner-Toews, D., Yassi, A. and Woollard, R. F. (2010) 'Tools for thoughtful action: The role of ecosystem approaches to health in enhancing public health', *Canadian Journal of Public Health/Revue Canadienne de Sante Publique*, vol. 101, pp. 439–441.

West, C. E., Renz, H., Jenmalm, M. C., Kozyrskyj, A. L., Allen, K. J., Vuillermin, P., Prescott, S. L. and the in-FLAME Microbiome Interest Group (2015) 'The gut microbiota and inflammatory noncommunicable diseases: Associations and potentials for gut microbiota therapies', *Journal of Allergy and Clinical Immunology*, vol. 135, pp. 3–13.

Whitmee, S., Haines, A., Beyrer, C., Boltz, F., Capon, A. G., de Souza Dias, B. F., Ezeh, A., Frumkin, H., Gong, P., Head, P., Horton, R., Mace, G. M., Marten, R., Myers, S. S., Nishtar, S., Osofsky, S. A., Pattanayak, S. K., Pongsiri, M. J., Romanelli, C., Soucat, A., Vega, J. and Yach, D. (2015) 'Safeguarding human health in the Anthropocene epoch: Report of the Rockefeller Foundation–Lancet Commission on planetary health', *The Lancet*, vol. 386, pp. 1973–2028.

WHO (2002) *WHO Traditional Medicine Strategy 2002–2005*, WHO, Geneva, Switzerland.

WHO (2011) *Report of the Joint FAO/WHO Expert Consultation on the Risks and Benefits of Fish Consumption*, FAO, Rome, Italy.

WHO (2013) *The Evolving Threat of Antimicrobial Resistance: Options for Action*, WHO, Geneva, Switzerland.

WHO and CBD (2015) *Connecting Global Priorities: Biodiversity And Human Health: A State Of Knowledge Review*, WHO, Geneva, Switzerland.

Wolfe, M. S. (2000) 'Crop strength through diversity', *Nature*, vol. 406, pp. 681–682.

Yotti' Kingsley, J., Townsend, M. and Wilson, C. H. (2009) 'Cultivating health and wellbeing: Members' perceptions of the health benefits of a Port Melbourne community garden', *Leisure Studies*, vol. 28, pp. 207–219.

Zhou, P., Wu, Y., Yin, S., Li, J., Zhao, Y., Zhang, L., Chen, H., Liu, Y., Yang, X. and Li, X. (2011) 'National survey of the levels of persistent organochlorine pesticides in the breast milk of mothers in China', *Environmental Pollution*, vol. 159, pp. 524–531.

Zhu, Y. G., Johnson, T. A., Su, J. Q., Qiao, M., Guo, G. X., Stedtfeld, R. D., Hashsham, S. A. and Tiedje, J. M. (2013) 'Diverse and abundant antibiotic resistance genes in Chinese swine farms', *Proceedings of the National Academy of Sciences USA*, vol. 110, pp. 3435–3440.

Zimmerer, K. S. and Vanek, S. J. (2016) 'Toward the integrated framework analysis of linkages among agrobiodiversity, livelihood diversification, ecological systems, and sustainability amid global change', *Land*, vol. 5, pp. 1–24.

Ziska, L. H., Emche, S. D., Johnson, E. L., George, K., Reed, D. R. and Sicher, R. C. (2005) 'Alterations in the production and concentration of selected alkaloids as a function of rising atmospheric carbon dioxide and air temperature: Implications for ethno-pharmacology', *Global Change Biology*, vol. 11, pp. 1798–1807.

Ziska, L. H., Epstein, P. R. and Schlesinger, W. H. (2009) 'Rising $CO_2$, climate change, and public health: Exploring the links to plant biology', *Environmental Health Perspectives*, vol. 117, pp. 155–158.

Ziska, L. H. and McConnell, L. L. (2015) 'Climate change, carbon dioxide, and pest biology: Monitor, mitigate, manage', *Journal of Agricultural and Food Chemistry*, vol. 64, pp. 6–12.

Ziska, L. H., Panicker, S. and Wojno, H. L. (2008) 'Recent and projected increases in atmospheric carbon dioxide and the potential impacts on growth and alkaloid production in wild poppy (*Papaver setigerum* DC.)', *Climatic Change*, vol. 91, pp. 395–403.

# 22

# EDIBLE INSECT DIVERSITY FOR FOOD AND NUTRITION

*Wendy Lu McGill, Komi K. M. Fiaboe, Sunday Ekesi and Sevgan Subramanian*

## Introduction

Insects constitute a large part of the earth's terrestrial biomass, with an estimated 10 quintillion (10,000,000,000,000,000,000) individual insects alive at any given time (van Huis et al., 2013). Insects play intrinsically important roles in all terrestrial ecosystems and contribute to essential ecosystem services as plant pollinators and by disposing of plant and animal waste (see Gemmill-Herren, Chapter 7 of this Handbook). Among their contributions to ecosystem services, some insect species also offer potential as a nutrient-rich food for humans, and as a feed additive (Vantomme et al., 2012). The consumption of insects provides many benefits, including providing a nutritious source of micronutrients and protein with far lower environmental impact as compared with traditional livestock (van Huis et al., 2013). In fact, edible insects, or insects that are safe for humans to eat, are already used as an important food source for humans in many parts of the world and are considered a frequently-consumed food source for an estimated 2 billion people. The majority of these consumers live in Asia, sub-Saharan Africa and Latin America, many in areas which are facing increasing climate-change pressures (Kelemu et al., 2015). Hence, eating insects is more the norm than the exception at the global scale, despite Western societal biases against this food source. In this chapter, we review the status of insects as a critical component of agricultural biodiversity, and future prospects for their exploitation as sustainable food sources.

## Insects as a human food source

Insects make up approximately 1 million of the 1.5 million species of organisms currently catalogued and an estimated 2,000 species have been identified as edible to date (**Figure 22.1** *Number of insect species recorded to be used for human consumption*). Although this is a small proportion of the total diversity of insects, it still far exceeds the number of species of conventional livestock consumed by humans, and is comparable to the number of plant species consumed (see Chapters 1–5 of this Handbook). The quantity and quality of edible insects useable as a food source can therefore be considered a significant additional source of agricultural biodiversity. This diversity is increasingly regarded as an untapped resource for a world struggling to feed a growing population with shrinking resources and mounting climate change effects on agriculture yields (van Huis et al., 2013). Insects are usually eaten when they are at their largest life stage and with the smallest amount of exoskeleton, which leads to the larvae and pupae being highly prized in many species, although insects such as crickets may also be consumed at the adult stage. In contrast to most reared vertebrate livestock, an estimated 92% of the known edible insect species consumed are caught from the wild, although cultivated or semi-cultivated approaches are gaining increasing popularity (Yen, 2015, and see section 'Insects as semi-cultivated food').

## *Global picture of edible insect prevalence by region*

Insect species reported as edible are not uniformly distributed across all geographic locations, with the majority of species reported from South America, Asia and sub-Saharan Africa (**Figure 22.2** *Recorded numbers of insect spcies consumed by country*). This distribution may be partly influenced by

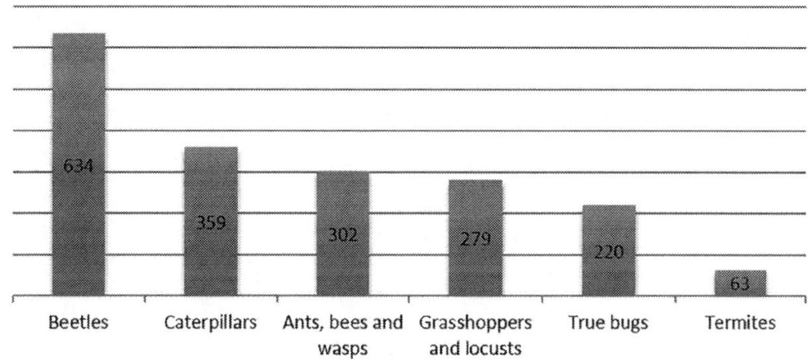


*Figure 22.1* Number of insect species recorded to be used for human consumption

*Source*: Adapted from Jongema (2015).

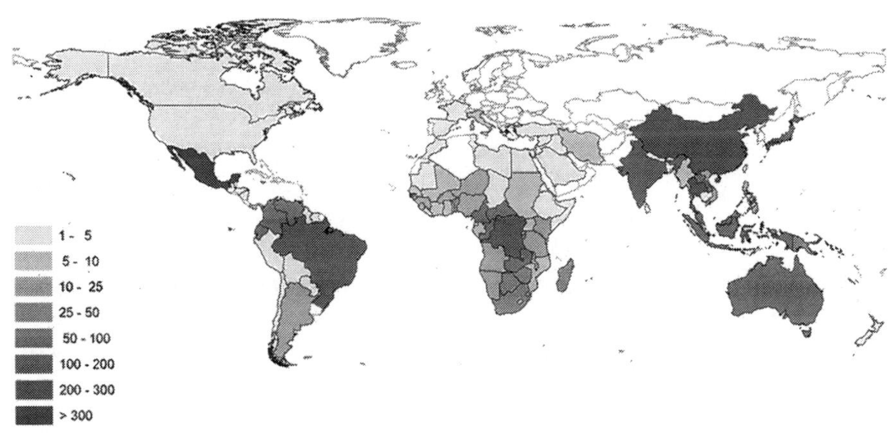


*Figure 22.2* Recorded numbers of insect species consumed by country

*Source*: Centre of Geo Information, van Lammeren, after Jongema, 2015.

total available insect diversity (with tropical regions and rainforests being centres of biodiversity for most insect groups), but also likely reflects the areas of the developing world in which insect consumption is widely practiced. The practice of entomophagy is far from universal across all geographic locations (**Table 22.1** *Edible species consumed by country*), and insects constitute varying proportions of diets in the areas where they are consumed. For example, in parts of Central Africa, over 50% of total protein consumed is derived from insects, but this value is typically much lower in societies where insect consumption is less usual, or where they are regarded as a seasonal delicacy (Melo et al., 2011; Kelemu et al., 2015). Generally, the practice is more common in the developing world (although even here it can be largely restricted to rural communities), while the 'Global North' is an outlier in the sense of making very little use of edible insect species, despite the presence of many species which are could be suitable as food sources. Cultural attitudes towards entomophagy may also vary widely, even in areas in which insects are consumed. In some cases, they may only be eaten as 'famine food' in times of hardship, or by the poor; in other cases, they may be considered delicacies (Durst et al., 2010). Traditional contributions of insects to food supplies in the three best-studied areas (Latin America, South and Southeast Asia and sub-Saharan Africa) are summarized in the following sections.

*Table 22.1* Edible species consumed by country

| *Region/country* | *Number of edible species* | *Source* |
|---|---|---|
| *Africa* | 524 | Ramos-Elorduy (1997) |
| | 246 | Van Huis (2003) |
| Angola | 4 | Ramos-Elorduy (1997) |
| Central African | 185 | " |
| Republic | 26 | " |
| | 41 | " |
| Congo | 30 | DeFoliart (1997) |
| Madagascar | 22 | " |
| South Africa | 15 | Ramos-Elorduy (1997) |
| | 36 | DeFoliart (1997) |
| Zaire/D.R.Congo | 35 | Ramos-Elorduy (1997) |
| | 4 | " |
| | 31 | " |
| | 51 | " |
| | 19 | Ramos-Elorduy (1997), Ramos-Elorduy et al. (1997) |
| | 62 | DeFoliart (1997) |
| Zambia | 33 | Ramos-Elorduy (1997) |
| Zimbabwe | 16 | " |
| | 32 | DeFoliart (1997) |
| *Americas* | | |
| Brazil | 23 | DeFoliart (1997) |
| Colombia | 48 | " |
| Ecuador | 83 | Onore (1997) |
| Oaxaca, Mexico | 78 | Ramos-Elorduy et al. (1997) |

| *Region/country* | *Number of edible species* | *Source* |
|---|---|---|
| Mexico | 545 | Ramos-Elorduy (2008) |
| USA | 69 | DeFoliart (1997) |
| *Asia* | | |
| Burma | 17 | " |
| China | 46 | " |
| India | 24 | " |
| Irian Jaya, New Guinea, Indonesia | >39 | Ponzetta and Paoletti (1997) |
| Java, Indonesia | 8 | Lukiwati (2010) |
| Indonesia | 48 | Ramos-Elorduy (1997) |
| | 25 | DeFoliart (1997) |
| Japan | 119 | Ramos-Elorduy (1997) |
| | 27 | DeFoliart (1997) |
| Laos | 21 (not counting insect-derived structures e.g. honeycomb, wasp nests) | Boulidam (2010) |
| Sabah, Borneo (Malaysia) | >60 | Chung (2010) |
| Sarawak (Malaysia) | >25 | " |
| Northeast India | 81 | Chakravorty et al. (2011) |
| Philippines | 11 | Adalla and Cervancia (2010) |
| | 21 | DeFoliart (1997) |
| Sri Lanka | 33 | Nandasena et al. (2010) |
| Thailand | 15 (forest insects only) | Leksawasdi (2010) |
| | 36 | Ramos-Elorduy (1997) |
| | 80 | DeFoliart (1997) |
| | Up to 194 | Sirimungkararat et al. (2010) |
| Vietnam | 24 | DeFoliart (1997) |
| *Oceania* | | |
| Australia | 40 | Ramos-Elorduy (1997) |
| | 21 | Meyer-Rochow and Changkija (1997) |
| | 49 | DeFoliart (1997) |
| Papua New Guinea | 39 | Meyer-Rochow (1973) |
| | 34 | DeFoliart (1997) |
| New Zealand | 4 | Meyer-Rochow and Changkija (1997) |
| *Europe* | | |
| Friuli- Venezia Giulia, Italy | 5 | Dreon and Paoletti (2009) |
| **World** | >2,000 | Jongema (2015) |

*Note*: Potential and challenges of insects as an innovative source for food and feed production.

*Source*: Adapted from Rumpold and Schlüter (2013).

### Latin America

Latin America is considered to have the highest recorded number of edible insect species, and the practice of entomophagy is widespread in both Central and South American countries, particularly in areas with tropical ecosystems. 679 species have been recorded as eaten in 23 countries, with many variations in the choice of insect (van Huis et al., 2013). For example, the most commonly-consumed insects in Mexico include maguey moth caterpillars, various species of ant, and grasshoppers, or *chapulines* (Ramos-Elorduy, 1997). Unlike some other countries, in Mexico, insects are also eaten by high-income consumers and are available at high-end restaurants even in urban areas: *chapulines* in particular are highly prized and are also exported (Melo et al., 2011). Anthropological research has suggested that the practice of gathering and eating these species has survived since prehistoric times and largely survived colonization and other cultural shifts within the local populations, including the Spanish colonization and the more modern globalization of diets (Melo et al., 2011).

### Eastern and Southeastern Asia

Asian countries also consume a wide range of insect diversity, with 170 species recorded in China and 164 species in Laos, Myanmar, Thailand and Vietnam. In Japan, wasps are harvested as a delicacy, and in South Korea, silk worm larvae are used as a food by-product of the silk industry. In northern Thailand, honeybees are utilized as a food source as well as for honey production. Yen (2009) noted that entomophagy in this country seems to be on the increase, as Thais from the northeast migrate to other parts of the country, introducing the practice as they go. The weaver ant (*Oecophylla* spp.) is also consumed across subtropical southeast China, Bangladesh, India, Malaysia and Sri Lanka. Interestingly, weaver ants serve a dual purpose as both a biological control agent for local crops such as mangoes, while the larvae and pupae, which are called 'ant eggs', are consumed (van Huis et al., 2013). This suggests the possibility of using edible insect biodiversity to provide additional ecosystem services (see also Gurr et al., Chapter 6 of this Handbook).

### Sub-Saharan Africa

In Africa, 470 species of insect have been recorded to be consumed (Kelemu et al., 2015). While these species vary widely and include caterpillars, termites, crickets, grasshoppers and locusts, a particularly significant species is the palm weevil larva, which is consumed in several countries, especially around the Congo Basin region (van Huis et al., 2013). While numbers of recorded edible insect species are no higher than in other regions, the number of people and households who frequently consume insects seems to be particularly high here, as in some other parts of sub-Saharan Africa. For example, 72% of households in southern South Africa report eating insects regularly (Dzerefos et al., 2013), and in Zimbabwe, a sample survey found that fewer than 10% of households did not eat insects on a regular basis (Dube et al., 2013).

## Contribution of biodiversity to insect consumption

Among edible insects, not all kinds are used for food to the same extent (**Figure 22.1**). Overall, 80% of edible insect species belong to just four orders, which are, in order of prominence:

- Coleoptera (beetles, most often eaten during the larvae stage, when there is no or little exoskeleton and fat content is higher);

- Lepidoptera (e.g. butterflies and moths, also commonly eaten as larvae [caterpillars]);
- Hymenoptera (e.g. bees, wasps, ants);
- Orthoptera (e.g. grasshoppers, crickets).

In most parts of the world, beetles are the insects most commonly consumed, together with butterfly or moth larvae (caterpillars). All of these have good fat and protein profiles relative to human nutritional needs.

## *Insects as a seasonal, wild-caught food*

As mentioned previously, over 90% of edible insects are collected in the wild, although a growing number of insects are farmed for human consumption. Until now, almost all of this harvesting has been unregulated, and in some areas may have led to unsustainable practices: harvesting in the wild has been linked to over collecting, forest destruction, and extinction of species (Yen, 2009; Schabel, 2010), so ensuring sustainable use and conservation of the associated habitats is essential. On the other hand, the harvesting of insects can be associated with improved conservation strategies when properly regulated, especially their conservation by traditional communities (Meyer-Rochow and Chakravorty, 2013). It can also relieve the pressure to farm other livestock which may have even worse effects on the local habitat (Yen, 2009).

Most commonly, the habitats concerned are forests, although grasslands and wetlands are also important sources. Examples of insect diversity largely exploited through harvesting directly from the wild includes members of the following species and groups:

- Flying termites (sub-Saharan Africa and South Asia)
- Lake flies (Lake Victoria);
- Nsenene grasshoppers (Uganda);
- Chapuline grasshoppers (Mexico);
- Saturniid caterpillars (e.g. mopane caterpillar, Southern Africa (Stack et al., 2003), and other species in Central and East Africa);
- Shea butter caterpillar (West and Central Africa);
- Tree locust (Central and East Africa);
- Bamboo caterpillar (Laos).

## Insects as 'semi-cultivated' food

In this section, we consider current knowledge of insects which are raised for consumption by semi-cultivated approaches, that is, by manipulating natural environment to enhance quality and quantity of insects gathered (Van Itterbeeck and van Huis, 2012; Anankware et al., 2015). While the majority of edible insects are still collected from the wild, knowledge of specific insect species' biology and interaction with the ecosystems where they live allows the people gathering them to manipulate insect habitats to improve the quality and quantity of wild populations of harvested insects. Considered to be an ancient practice used by early humans until the present day (Van Itterbeeck and van Huis, 2012), the following three examples of this practice will also illustrate the ability for so-called 'semi-cultivation' to reduce negative environmental impact of collection practices on edible insect biodiversity.

### *Example 1: palm weevil larvae*

Several species of palm weevil larvae are edible, providing a soft-bodied and high fat source of nutrition. Many indigenous groups in Asia, Africa and South America practice semi-cultivation of the larvae, generally by felling palm trees and opening the trunks to facilitate more ovipositing by adult females of their eggs, which grow into the larvae that is collected. By using selected fallen or intentionally cut down trees, fewer trees are actually cut down, while a larger number of larvae can be harvested more easily in one to three months after the eggs have been laid (Van Itterbeeck and van Huis, 2012). Additionally, indigenous groups in Venezuela have used a specific species of palm trees over others because the protein and nutrition content of the harvested larvae is much higher than when using other species (van Huis et al., 2013).

### *Example 2: mopane caterpillars*

Mopane caterpillars are collected in the wild and consumed throughout Africa (van Huis et al., 2013). Harvest quantity and quality of the harvest can be achieved by refraining from cutting down trees where the mopane caterpillars live, as well as local practices or rules around collection that ensure habitat is protected. Other methods of semi-cultivation include shade cloths or shade houses put over trees to protect caterpillars. Fire management as a forestry tool is also employed to avoid harming caterpillar populations, by burning early in the caterpillar life cycle, which has been shown to increase insect harvest. Clearing the forest canopy, sometimes called 'slash and burn' agriculture, is a strategy used by farmers to improve soil, and for mopane caterpillar collection has been shown to improve harvest yields, with promising results from selective cutting that remove selected trees instead of all trees (Stack et al., 2003; van Huis et al., 2013).

### *Example 3: termites*

Termites can be collected via semi-cultivation by replicating the conditions found inside termite mounds, using a large water receptacle that is filled with wetted cardboard, paper or other cellulose materials. The receptacle is held in place over a termite mound entrance and termites can be harvested in about one month (Dossey et al., 2016).

## Edible insects as a farmed food

Given the risks of allowing harvesting of insects directly from the wild, farming them (as 'micro-livestock') is an attractive alternative. As many insects have a rapid life cycle and can be grown under controlled conditions, this can be done in efficiently where the know-how is available.

### *History of insects in agriculture*

Human beings have, in fact, farmed insects for thousands of years: honeybees (subspecies of *Apis melifera* and silk worms (the larvae of the moth, *Bombyx mori*) are likely the ones with the longest farmed histories. Silk worms were recorded to be farmed as early as 2700 BCE and continue to be cultivated widely today, especially in South Korea, China and India, where the 'worms' are raised on leaves of the white mulberry bush *(Morus alba)* and eventually boiled to remove the silk. *B. mori* is considered to be a completely domesticated species, being derived from Chinese populations of the wild progenitor, *B. mandarina*. In China, cockroaches are also raised for medicinal and cosmetic applications, with a smaller emphasis on raising them for food, although the two main varieties of cockroaches are considered edible. *Periplaneta americana*, or the so-called American Cockroach, is the most commonly raised cockroach in China and *Blattella germanica*, the German Cockroach, is the other commonly raised type of edible cockroach (Yi et al., 2010).

### *Farming insects for food*

The majority of insect farms worldwide currently consist of pet feed (primarily for reptiles and amphibians), fish food, zoos, pest control companies (particularly for biocontrol), research labs and a handful of aquaculture companies. There are examples of medium- to large-scale farms in Thailand and China that produce insects for human food and medicinal applications, respectively, but these remain specific to, and isolated within, their regions.

In the United States and Europe, an increasing number of companies are growing edible insect species for human food and animal feed (Dossey et al., 2016). In places where insects are regularly consumed as a food, farming is generally rare, with the notable exceptions the previously mentioned cases of Thailand and China, which both have significant numbers of insect farms. In Thailand, for example, an estimated 20,000 small to medium farms raise house crickets *(Acheta domesticus)* for human consumption (Schabel, 2010).

Despite the fact that eating insects is not a common practice in North America and Europe, the majority of insect farms are in these places. An estimated 30 edible insect farms for food and feed are operational in North America and Europe, almost all of which raise house crickets *(Acheta domesticus)* and/or mealworms *(Tenebrio molitor)*. There are almost double that number of consumer product companies making food with insect ingredients, notably powders made from pulverized insects added to value added products for example granola bars or biscuits and other baked goods (Dossey et al., 2016).

## The importance of edible insects in the human diet

### *Contribution of insects to nutritional value of diets*

Edible insect species are widely regarded as a high quality food source, providing a rich source of micronutrients, protein and varying levels of fat and essential fatty acids – in some cases, equal to those found in poultry and fish (Womeni, 2009). Amounts of micronutrients, protein and fat vary by species and life stage during which the insect is eaten; however, a significant number of edible insect species also provide complete amino acids needed for human nutrition (van Huis et al., 2013). Similarly, edible insect chitinous exoskeletons can provide high carbohydrate levels similar to that found in whole grains (Raubenheimer and Rothman, 2013). While more research is clearly needed, existing data show that some edible insect species have more iron and calcium than in beef and that many insects have significant levels of B vitamins and vitamin E, lack of which cause significant global health problems, including anaemia, eye sight loss and other public health issues, respectively.

The most comprehensive published survey of insect nutrition is from a 2013 compilation (Rumpold and Schlüter, 2013) for 236 edible insects' nutritional profiles. **Tables 22.2** and **22.3** indicate the nutritional profiles and protein content of some of the most commonly eaten insect orders, respectively. It is clear from this there is significant variation in the nutritional profiles of these species with, in some cases, orders of magnitude of variation within the species. The interacting genetic and environmental factors that determine these values represent an important focus for future research.

*Table 22.2* Nutritional profiles of edible insects by class

| | Coleoptera (beetles) *Rhynchophorus phoenicis* (larvae) | Lepidoptera (butterflies, moths) *Bombyx mori* (pupae) | *Cirina forda* (Westwood) (*larvae*) | Orthoptera (crickets, grasshoppers, locusts) *Acheta domesticus* (adults) | *Ruspolia differens* (brown form; adult) |
|---|---|---|---|---|---|
| **Nutrient composition** | | | | | |
| Protein (%) | 10.33–41.69 | 48.70–58.00 | 20.20–74.35 | 64.38–70.75 | 44.30 |
| Fat (%) | 19.50–69.78 | 30.10–35.00 | 5.25–14.30 | 18.55–22.80 | 46.20 |
| Fibre [%] | 2.82–25.14 | 2.00 | 1.80–9.40 | | 4.90 |
| Nitrogen-free extract (i.e. carbohydrates) [%] | 5.49–48.60 | 1.00 | 2.36–66.60 | 2.60 | |
| Ash [%] | 2.54–5.70 | 4.00–8.60 | 1.50–11.51 | 3.57–5.10 | 2.60 |
| Energy [kJ/kg] | 20,038–20,060.63 | 23,236.74 | 15,030.61 | 19,057.89 | 2.60 |
| **% Fatty acids** | | | | | |
| Palmitic acid (C16:0) | 32.40–36.00 | 22.77–26.20 | 13.00 | | 32.10 |
| Staeric acid (C18:0) | 0.30–3.10 | 4.50–7.00 | 16.00 | | 5.90 |
| Saturated fatty acids (SFA) total | 38.90–40.90 | 28.80–33.20 | 31.60 | | 39.10 |
| Palmitoleic acid (C16:1n7) | 3.30–36.00 | 0.60–1.70 | 0.20 | | 1.40 |
| Oleic acid (18:1n9) | 30.00–41.50 | 26.00–36.90 | 13.90 | | 24.90 |
| Monounsaturated fatty acids (MUFA) total | 43.40–66.60 | 26.61–36.90 | 14.90 | | 26.30 |
| Linoleic acid (18:2n6) | 13.00–26.00 | 4.20–7.30 | 8.10 | | 29.50 |
| Linoleic acid (18:3 n3/6) | 2.00–3.50 | 27.70–38.02 | 45.50 | | 4.20 |
| Polyunsaturated fatty acids (PUFA) total | 17.70–28.00 | 29.90–43.92 | 53.80 | | 33.80 |
| SFA/(MUFA+PUFA) | 0.43–0.64 | 0.40–0.50 | 0.46 | 0.56 | 0.65 |
| **Minerals [mg/100 g]** | | | | | |
| Calcium | 54.10–208.00 | 158.00 | 7.00–37.20 | 132.14–210.00 | 24.50 |
| Potassium | 1,025.00–2,206.00 | | 47.60–2,130.00 | 1,126.62 | 259.70 |
| Magnesium | 33.60–131.80 | 207.00 | 1.87–69.89 | 80.00–109.42 | 33.10 |
| Phosphorous | 352.00–685.00 | 474.00 | 45.90–1.090.00 | 780.00–957.79 | |
| Sodium | 44.80–52.00 | | 44.40–210.00 | 435.06 | 121.00 |
| Iron | 14.70–30.80 | 26.00 | 1.30–64.00 | 6.27–11.23 | 229.70 |
| Zinc | 26.50–15.80 | 23.00 | 4.27–24.20 | 18.64–21.79 | 13.00 |
| Manganese | 0.80–3.50 | 0.71 | 7.00–10,163.10 | 2.97–3.73 | 12.40 |
| Copper | 1.60 | 0.15 | | 0.85–2.01 | 2.50 |
| Selenium | 1.60 | 0.15 | | 0.60 | 0.50 |
| **Vitamins** | | | | | |
| Retinol [μg/100 g] | 11.25 | | 2.99 | 24.33 | 2.80 |
| α-Tocopherol [IU/kg] | | | | 63.96–81.00 | 22.64 |

| | Coleoptera (beetles) *Rhynchophorus phoenicis* (larvae) | Lepidoptera (butterflies, moths) *Bombyx mori* (pupae) | *Cirina forda* (Westwood) (*larvae*) | Orthoptera (crickets, grasshoppers, locusts) *Acheta domesticus* (adults) | *Ruspolia differens* (brown form; adult) |
|---|---|---|---|---|---|
| Ascorbic acid [mg/100 g] | 4.25 | | 1.95 | 9.74 | 0.1 |
| Thiamin [mg/100 g] | 3.38 | | | 0.13 | n.d. |
| Riboflavin [mg/100 g] | 2.21–2.51 | | 2.21 | 11.07 | 1.4 |
| Niacin [mg/100 g] | 3.36 | 0.95 | | 12.59 | 2.4 |
| Pantothenic acid [mg/100 g] | | | | 7.47 | |
| Biotin [μg/100 g] | | | | 55.19 | |
| Folic acid [mg/100 g] | | | | 0.49 | 0.9 |

*Source*: Adapted from Rumpold and Schlüter (2013).

*Table 22.3* Comparative protein range for insect orders by life stage

| *Insect Order* | *Stage* | *Range (% protein)* |
|---|---|---|
| Coleoptera | Adults and larvae | 23–66 |
| Lepidoptera | Pupae and larvae | 14–68 |
| Hemiptera | Adults and larvae | 42–74 |
| Homoptera | Adults, larvae and eggs | 45–57 |
| Hymenoptera | Adults, pupae, larvae and eggs | 13–77 |
| Odonata | Adults and naiad | 46–65 |
| Orthoptera | Adults and nymphs | 23–65 |

*Source*: Adapted from Rumpold and Schlüter (2013).

The nutritional content of different insect species (and insects at different stages of their life cycle) can differ widely when compared with conventional livestock (**Tables 22.2, 22.3;** Xiaoming et al., 2010). The usefulness of insects therefore depends upon the choice of insect used, the preparation method and the nutritional needs of the consumer (Payne et al., 2016). However, some common trends can be identified, which are discussed in the following sections.

## *Insect content of proteins and micronutrients*

Many edible insect species are considered to be good sources of lipids, including polyunsaturated and other fatty acids such as ω-3 and ω-6 fatty acids (Womeni, 2009; Xiaoming et al., 2010), which are particularly important for childhood development. Levels vary by species and method of preparation or cooking, and by insect diet. Like with meat products, these levels of fats also lead to rapid spoilage in insect food products, a problem particularly in areas where refrigeration is uncommon (van Huis et al., 2013). Many edible insects also contain high amounts of iron. Increased consumption of insects could be a powerful remedy for iron deficiency, defined by the World Health Organization (WHO) as the world's most common health problem caused by malnutrition, affecting an estimated nearly half of pregnant women and children in developing countries, also contributing to approximately 20% of all maternal death. Zinc deficiency is similarly a large-scale public health issue in developing countries facing food and nutrition insecurity. Edible insect species in general have significant levels of zinc, sometimes higher even than the levels observed in beef. Hence, they represent a good prospect for alleviating zinc deficiency.

## *Edible insects as feed*

Feed for livestock is an expanding industry worth an estimated USD 350 billion globally and the Food and Agriculture Organization of the United Nations (FAO) estimates it will need to expand 70% by 2050 in order to satisfy demand for meat. Rising costs of livestock feed inputs, particularly corn, soy and fishmeal, combined with the environmental impacts of cultivating or harvesting these sources, are creating a strong push factor in the search for alternate livestock feed resources (van Huis et al., 2013).

Given this background, insects have a strong potential as a lower-cost replacement for fishmeal in livestock feed with similar nutritional qualities, particularly for many kinds of poultry and fish. Both poultry and fish eat insects when they are available, which makes it even more appropriate to consider for feed. Hogs or pigs can eat insects as well, and while it is not part of a ruminant's natural diet, insects as a protein source could be included in cattle feed. Insects have also been proposed as a means of reusing animal waste (manure) – a growing environmental challenge as the number of livestock being reared increase to meet the greater demand for meat.

A variety of insects have historically been used in poultry food, including grasshoppers, crickets, cicadas, beetles, ants and bees or wasps. Commercially, the larvae of the black soldier fly has been tested by companies in North America and South Africa to create a high-protein and high-fat feed, as well as for the black soldier fly's ability to reduce house flies and pathogens found in manure, making it useful for both feed production and manure management. This insect species is also able to thrive on food waste (van Huis, et al., 2013).

Companies/projects currently using insects for animal feed include AgriProtein (www.agriprotein.com), PROteINSECT (www.proteinsect.eu) and EnviroFlight (www.enviroflight.net).

## Conclusions

From the overview provided in this chapter, it is clear that while the harvesting of wild insects, and rearing insects in cultivated and semi-cultivated settings, is an important source of income, nutrition and food security for billions of people worldwide, the agrobiodiversity of insect consumption has been little considered: in fact, research on the subject still seems quite narrow. For example, historical commentaries on insect consumption are well-established; in the past few years, broader reports on the global prevalence of insect cultivation and semi-cultivation have also appeared. However, the magnitude of the roles of insects in food security, food sovereignty, livelihoods and social structure is less well understood. In particular, there is a need to understand the factors involved in domesticating and breeding insects in order to facilitate their future sustainable use under cultivation or semi-cultivation. Insect breeding programmes will need an appreciation of the genetic diversity of wild edible insects, which has not so far been attempted. As insect consumption and farming have significant potential to provide animal protein without the same level of environmental costs of 'traditional' livestock, understanding and deploying edible insect genetic diversity will become ever more necessary in the future, and research programmes will need to be developed to address this.

## References

Adalla, C. B. and Cervancia, C. R. (2010) 'Philippine edible insects: A new opportunity to bridge the protein gap of resource-poor families and to manage pests', pp. 151–160 in P. B. Durst, R. N. Leslie and K. Shono (eds.), *Forest Insects as Food: Humans Bite Back*, FAO, Regional Office for Asia and the Pacific, Chiang Mai, Thailand.

Anankware, P., Fening, K. O., Osekre, E. and Obeng-Ofori, D. (2015) 'Insects as food and feed: A review', *International Journal of Agricultural Research and Reviews*, vol. 3, pp. 143–151.

Boulidam, S. (2010) 'Edible insects in a Lao market economy', pp. 131–140 in P. B. Durst, R. N. Leslie and K. Shono (eds.), *Forest Insects as Food: Humans Bite Back*, FAO, Regional Office for Asia and the Pacific, Chiang Mai, Thailand.

Chakravorty, J., Ghosh, S. and Meyer-Rochow, V. B. (2011) 'Practices of entomophagy and entomotherapy by members of the Nyishi and Galo tribes, two ethnic groups of the state of Arunachal Pradesh (North-East India)', *Journal of Ethnobiology and Ethnomedicine*, vol. 7, p. 5.

Chung, A. Y. C. (2010) 'Edible insects and entomophagy in Borneo', pp. 141–150 in P. B. Durst, R. N. Leslie and K. Shono (eds.), *Forest Insects as Food: Humans Bite Back*, FAO, Regional Office for Asia and the Pacific, Chiang Mai, Thailand.

DeFoliart, G. R. (1997) 'An overview of the role of edible insects in preserving biodiversity', *Ecology of Food and Nutrition*, vol. 36, pp. 109–132.

Dossey, A. T., Morales-Ramos, J. A. and Rojas, G. M. (eds.) (2016) *Insects as Sustainable Food Ingredients: Production, Processing and Food Applications*, Academic Press, USA.

Dreon, A. L. and Paoletti, M. G. (2009) 'Edible wild plants and insects in Western Friuli local Knowledge (Friuli Venezia Giulia, Italy)', Konrad Thaler Memorial book', *Contributions to Natural History*, vol. 12, pp. 461–488.

Dube, S., Dlamini, N. R., Mafunga, A., Mukai, M. and Dhlamini, Z. (2013) 'A survey on entomophagy prevalence in Zimbabwe', *African Journal of Food, Agriculture, Nutrition and Development*, vol. 13, pp. 7242–7253.

Durst, P. B., Leslie, R. N. and Shono, K. (eds.) (2010) *Forest Insects as Food: Humans Bite Back*, FAO, Regional Office for Asia and the Pacific, Chiang Mai, Thailand.

Dzerefos, C. M., Witkowsi, E. T. F. and Toms, R. (2013) 'Comparative ethnoentomology of edible stinkbugs in southern Africa and sustainable management considerations', *Journal of Ethnobiology and Ethnomedicine*, vol. 9, p. 20.

FAO (2015) *Edible Insects Stakeholder Directory*, FAO, Rome, Italy, www.fao.org/forestry/edibleinsects/stakeholder-directory/en/, accessed 6 December 2016.

Jongema, Y. (2015) *World List of Edible Insects*, Wageningen U.R., the Netherlands, www.wur.nl/upload_mm/7/4/1/ca8baa25-b035-4bd2-9fdc-a7df1405519a_WORLD%20LIST%20EDIBLE%20INSECTS%202015.pdf

Kelemu, S., Niassy, S., Torto, K., Fiaboe, K., Affognon, H. and Tonnang, N. (2015) 'African edible insects for food and feed: Inventory, diversity, commonalities and contribution to food security', *Journal of Insects as Food and Feed*, vol. 1, pp. 103–119.

Leksawasdi, P. (2010) 'Compendium of research on selected edible insects in northern Thailand', pp. 183–188 in P. B. Durst, R. N. Leslie and K. Shono (eds.), *Forest Insects as Food: Humans Bite Back*, FAO, Regional Office for Asia and the Pacific, Chiang Mai, Thailand.

Lukiwati, D. R. (2010) 'Teak caterpillars and other edible insects in Java', pp. 91–14 in P. B. Durst, R. N. Leslie and K. Shono (eds.), *Forest Insects as Food: Humans Bite Back*, FAO, Regional Office for Asia and the Pacific, Chiang Mai, Thailand.

Melo, V., Garcia, M., Sandoval, H., Jiménez, H. D. and Calvo, C. (2011) 'Quality proteins from edible indigenous insect food of Latin America and Asia', *Emirates Journal of Food and Agriculture*, vol. 23, pp. 283–289.

Meyer-Rochow, V. B. (1973) 'Edible insects in three different ethnic groups of Papua and New Guinea', *American Journal of Clinical Nutrition*, vol. 26, pp. 673–677.

Meyer-Rochow, V. B. and Changkija, S. (1997) 'Uses of insects as human food in Papua New Guinea, Australia, and North-East India: Cross-cultural considerations and cautious conclusions', *Ecology of Food and Nutrition*, vol. 36, pp. 159–185.

Meyer-Rochow, V. B. and Chakravorty, J. (2013) 'Notes on entomophagy and entomotherapy generally and information on the situation in India in particular', *Applied Entomology and Zoology*, vol. 48, pp. 105–112.

Nandasena, M. R. M. P., Disanayake, D. M. S. K. and Weeratunga, L. (2010) 'Sri Lanka as a potential gene pool of edible insects', pp. 161–165 in P. B. Durst, R. N. Leslie and K. Shono (eds.), *Forest Insects as Food: Humans Bite Back*, FAO, Regional Office for Asia and the Pacific, Chiang Mai, Thailand.

Onore, J. (1997) 'A brief note on edible insects in Ecuador', *Ecology of Food and Nutrition*, vol. 36, pp. 277–285.

Payne, C. L. R., Scarborough, P., Rayner, M. and Nonaka, K. (2016) 'Are edible insects more or less 'healthy' than commonly consumed meats? A comparison using two nutrient profiling models developed to combat over- and undernutrition', *European Journal of Clinical Nutrition*, vol. 70, pp. 285–291.

Ponzetta, M. T. and Paoletti, M. G. (1997) 'Insects as food of the Irian Jaya populations', *Ecology of Food and Nutrition*, vol. 36, pp. 321–346.

Ramos-Elorduy, J. (1997) 'Insects: A sustainable source of food?', *Ecology of Food and Nutrition*, vol. 36, pp. 247–276.

Ramos-Elorduy, J. (2008) 'Energy supplied by edible insects from Mexico and their nutritional and ecological importance', *Ecology of Food and Nutrition*, vol. 47. pp. 280–297.

Ramos-Elorduy, J., Pino Moreno, J. M., Escamilla Prado, E., Perez, M. A., Lagunez Otero, J. and Ladron de Guevara, O. (1997) 'Nutritional value of edible insects from the state of Oaxaca, Mexico', *Journal of Food Composition and Analysis*, vol. 10, pp. 142–157.

Raubenheimer, D. and Rothman, J. M. (2013) 'Nutritional ecology of entomophagy in humans and other primates', *Annual Review of Entomology*, vol. 58, pp. 141–160.

Rumpold, B. A. and Schlüter, O. K. (2013) 'Potential and challenges of insects as an innovative source for food and feed production', *Innovative Food Science and Emerging Technologies*, vol. 17, pp. 1–11.

Schabel, H. G. (2010) 'Forest insects as food: A global review', pp. 37–64 in P. B. Durst, D. V. Johnson, R. N. Leslie and K. Shono (eds.), *Forest Insects as Food: Humans Bite Back*, FAO, Regional Office for Asia and the Pacific, Chiang Mai, Thailand.

Sirimungkararat, S., Saksirirat, W., Nopparat, T. and Natongkham, A. (2010) 'Edible products from eri silkworm (*Samia ricini* D.) and mulberry silkworm (*Bombyx mori* L.) in Thailand', pp. 189–200 in P. B. Durst, R. N. Leslie and K. Shono (eds.), *Forest Insects as Food: Humans Bite Back*, FAO, Regional Office for Asia and the Pacific, Chiang Mai, Thailand.

Stack, J., Dorward, A., Gondo, T., Frost, P., Taylor, F. and Kuebgaseka, N. (2003) *Mopane Worm Utilisation and Rural Livelihoods in Southern Africa*, paper presented at the International Conference on Rural Livelihoods, Forests and Biodiversity, 19–23 May 2003, Bonn, Germany.

van Huis, A. (2003) 'Insects as food in sub-Saharan Africa', *Insect Science and Its Application*, vol. 23, pp. 163–185.

van Huis, A., Van Itterbeeck, J., Klunder, H., Mertens, E., Halloran, A., Muir, G. and Vantomme, P. (2013) *Edible Insects: Future Prospects for Food and Feed Security*, FAO, Rome, Italy.

Van Itterbeeck, J. and van Huis, A. (2012) 'Environmental manipulation for edible insect procurement: A historical perspective', *Journal of Ethnobiology and Ethnomedicine*, vol. 8, p. 3.

Vantomme, P., Mertens, E., van Huis, A. and Klunder, H. (2012) *Assessing the Potential of Insects as Food and Feed in Assuring Food Security*, FAO, Rome, Italy.

Womeni, H. L. (2009) 'Oils of insects and larvae consumed in Africa: Potential sources of polyunsaturated fatty acids', *Oléagineux, Corps Gras, Lipides*, vol. 16, pp. 230–235.

Xiaoming, C., Ying, F., Hong, Z. and Zhiyong, C. (2010) 'Review of the nuritive value of edible insects', in P. B. Durst, D. V. Johnson, R. L. Leslie and K. Shono (eds.), *Forest Insects as Food: Humans Bite Back*, Proceedings of a Workshop on Asia-Pacific Resources and Their Potential for Development. FAO Regional Office for Asia and the Pacific, Bangkok.

Yen, A. L. (2009) 'Entomophagy and insect conservation: Some thoughts for digestion', *Journal of Insect Conservation*, vol. 13, p. 667.

Yen, A. L. (2015) 'Insects as food and feed in the Asia Pacific region: Current perspectives and future directions', *Journal of Insects as Food and Feed*, vol. 1, pp. 33–35.

Yi, C., He, Q., Wang, L. and Kuang, R. (2010) 'The utilization of insect-resources in Chinese rural area', *Journal of Agricul Science*, vol. 2, pp. 146–154.

# 23

# AGRICULTURAL BIODIVERSITY AND CULTURAL HERITAGE

*Juliana Santilli*

## Introduction

Culture and agriculture are intimately related, even at the level of the term 'agri-culture' (Sauer, 1986; Santilli, 2013). This chapter will analyze how legal instruments aimed at safeguarding cultural heritage can be used to promote every element of a biodiversity-rich agricultural system, whether tangible (agroecosystems, cultivated plants) or intangible (agricultural techniques, practices and knowledge). I will argue that safeguarding traditional food ways and dietary diversity is also an important way to promote agrobiodiversity and food security (see also Chapter 24 by Kuhnlein and Chapter 25 by Raneri and Kennedy of this Handbook; Röessler, 2005; Santilli, 2011). The UNESCO Convention for the Protection of the World Cultural and Natural Heritage and the Convention for the Safeguarding of the Intangible Cultural Heritage are both examples of instruments that can be (and, in some cases, have been) used to promote agrobiodiversity and food diversity in different, innovative ways and will be explored from this perspective in this chapter. Brazilian and Peruvian cultural heritage national instruments and their roles in promoting traditional agricultural ecosystems will also be discussed.

## The UNESCO Convention for the Safeguarding of Intangible Cultural Heritage: interfaces with agrobiodiversity and food diversity

The Convention for the Safeguarding of Intangible Cultural Heritage was adopted in 2003 and entered into force in 2006. It represents the first binding multilateral instrument for the safeguarding of the world's intangible cultural heritage, which is defined by the Convention as

> the practices, representations, expressions, knowledge and skills – as well as the instruments, objects, artifacts and cultural spaces associated therewith – that communities, groups and, in some cases, individuals recognize as part of their cultural heritage. This intangible cultural heritage, transmitted from generation to generation, is constantly recreated by communities in response to their environment, their interaction with nature and their history, and provides them with a sense of identity and continuity.
>
> *(UNESCO, 2003; see also Chapter 37 and Chapter 38 of this Handbook by Vernooy et al. and Taylor, respectively)*

According to the Convention, intangible cultural heritage is manifested *inter alia* in the following domains: oral traditions and expressions, including language as a vehicle of the intangible cultural heritage, performing arts, social practices, rituals and festive events, knowledge and practices concerning nature and the universe and traditional craftsmanship (this is an inclusive, rather than exclusive, list, which means that it is not complete, and that member States may include other domains). According to the definition of UNESCO, 'Safeguarding' refers to any measure aimed at ensuring 'the viability of the intangible cultural heritage, including the identification, documentation, research, preservation, protection, promotion, enhancement, transmission, particularly through formal and non-formal education, as well as the revitalization of the various aspects of such heritage' (UNESCO, 2003).

The UNESCO Convention's main message is that cultural heritage does not end at monuments and collections of objects. It also includes traditions or living expressions inherited from our ancestors and passed on to our descendants, which are important in maintaining cultural diversity in the face of growing globalization and cultural homogenization (Phillips, 2005; Amoêda et al., 2010; Santilli, 2011; Petrillo, 2012). Intangible cultural heritage is traditional, contemporary and living at the same time, and it does not represent inherited traditions from the past only, but also contemporary rural and urban practices in which diverse cultural groups take part, and will presumably also apply to new forms of knowledge that integrate scientific approaches with these. Just like culture in general, intangible heritage is constantly changing and evolving, and being enriched by each new generation. Intangible cultural heritage can be recognized as such only by the communities that create, maintain and transmit it – without their recognition, nobody else can decide for them that a given expression or practice is their heritage. Some examples of intangible cultural heritage included in UNESCO's Representative List of Intangible Cultural Heritage are the chant of the Sybil on Majorca (Spain), which marks the annual Christmas Vigil; Huaconada, a ritual dance performed in the village of Mito, in the Peruvian Andes; and the Marimba music and traditional chants of Colombia's South Pacific region.

Historically, UNESCO's Representative List of Intangible Cultural Heritage has focused primarily on performing arts and crafts. More recently, however, traditional agricultural practices have also been recognized as intangible cultural heritage. They were recognized as cultural expressions as fundamental to identity and worthy of recognition as dance, theatre or music. Three such examples were inscribed in UNESCO's Representative List of Intangible Cultural Heritage of Humanity in 2014. The first was the traditional cultivation of '*vite ad alberello*' (head-trained bush vines) within the *commune* of the Italian Mediterranean island of Pantelleria (Petrillo, 2012). A second was know-how related to the production of mastic from the mastic tree *(Pistacia lentiscus)* on the Greek island of Chios, sometimes called the 'tears of Chios'. The final example is the know-how related to seed-oil extraction and other traditional uses of the argan, *Argania spinosa* (L.) Skeels, a small tree endemic to southwest Morocco. The oil is used for culinary purposes but has also attracted attention for its medical and cosmetic properties, and has been exported as a luxury product. UNESCO considers that safeguarding of intangible heritage should focus on the processes involved in its *transmission* between generations, rather than on the outputs that are produced from this heritage (e.g. the traditional methods used to extract and use argan oil are systematically transmitted by 'argan women', who pass on this knowledge to their daughters from a young age (www.unesco.org/culture/ich/en/RL/argan-practices-and-know-how-concerning-the-argan-tree-00955), and it is this system of traditional knowledge, rather than the argan oil itself, which is inscribed in the Representative List.

Since food heritage is directly associated with crop genetic diversity, it is also worth mentioning some culinary systems that have been included in UNESCO's Representative List of Intangible Cultural Heritage of Humanity – these are summarized in **Boxes 23.1–23.3** (*Traditional Mexican cuisine, the Mediterranean diet and the gastronomic meal of the French*, respectively).

## Box 23.1 Traditional Mexican cuisine

'Traditional Mexican cuisine – ancestral, ongoing community culture, the Michoacán paradigm' was inscribed in UNESCO's list in 2010. According to UNESCO, traditional Mexican cuisine is a comprehensive cultural model comprising farming, ritual practices, age-old skills, culinary techniques and ancestral community customs. It is made possible by collective participation in the entire traditional food chain: from planting and harvesting to cooking and eating. The basis of the system is founded on corn, beans and chili grown with the use of unique farming methods such as milpas (rotating swidden fields of corn and rotation crops) and chinampas (man-made farming islets in lakes); cooking processes such as nixtamalization (lime-hulling maize, to increase its nutritional value); and unique utensils such as local varieties of grinding stones and mortars. The use of landraces of other crops such as tomatoes, avocados, squashes, vanilla and cocoa is also noted. Mexico's application to UNESCO stressed the presence not only of foods, recipes and food-related customs, but also of 'a complex cultural system of agricultural practices, traditions and symbolisms imbued with religious meaning and steeped in ritual'. UNESCO's designation should contribute not only to foster national cultural identity and promote traditional cuisine, but also to the preservation of native plant species, varieties and agroecosystems.

## Box 23.2 The Mediterranean diet

The 'Mediterranean diet of Spain, Greece, Italy, Morocco, Portugal, Cyprus and Croatia' was also inscribed in UNESCO's list in 2013. It is consider to constitute a 'set of skills, knowledge, practices and traditions ranging from the landscape to the table, including the crops, harvesting practices, fishing, conservation, processing, preparation and, particularly, consumption of food'. It is stated to be a cultural system rooted in respect for the territory and biodiversity, and which ensures the conservation of traditional activities and crafts linked to fishing and farming within communities of the countries concerned (Tilman and Clark, 2014).

## Box 23.3 The gastronomic meal of the French

The gastronomic meal of the French is another expression of intangible cultural heritage which has, since 2010, been inscribed in UNESCO's list. UNESCO defines the gastronomic meal of the French as 'a customary social practice for celebrating important moments in the lives of individuals and groups, such as weddings, birthdays, achievements and reunions. It is a festive meal bringing people together for an occasion to enjoy the art of good eating and drinking. The gastronomic meal emphasizes togetherness, the pleasure of taste, and the balance between human beings and the products of nature' (UNESCO, 2010).

Other inscriptions include washoku (the traditional dietary cultures of the Japanese, notably for the celebration of New Year), Turkish coffee culture and tradition, Kimjang, the collective practice of making and sharing kimchi (preserved vegetables seasoned with spices and fermented seafood, which is an integral parts of meals in Republic of Korea), among others. For additional details on biodiversity and nutrition, see also Chapter 6 of the CBD/WHO report, *Connecting Global Health Priorities*.

## Registry of Intangible Cultural Heritage and agrobiodiversity-rich systems in the Brazilian Amazon: a new perspective for the safeguarding of traditional agricultural systems

In 1988, the Brazilian Constitution approved expanded the concept of cultural heritage and explicitly recognized its dual nature – tangible and intangible. According to the Constitution, Brazilian cultural heritage consists of goods, of a material and immaterial nature, taken individually or as a whole, which bear reference to the identity and memory of the various groups that form the Brazilian society, including forms of expression; ways of creating, making and living; scientific, artistic and technological creations; works, objects, documents, buildings and other spaces intended for artistic and cultural expressions; and urban complexes and sites of historical, natural, artistic, archaeological, paleontological, ecological and scientific value. Thus, cultural heritage includes not only properties but also oral traditions and expressions; innovative ways of creating, making and living; social practices; and knowledge concerning nature, among others. The concept adopted by the Brazilian Constitution was that it is not possible to understand cultural heritage without taking into consideration the values invested in it and what it stands for – its immaterial or intangible dimension – and, likewise, the dynamics of intangible heritage cannot be understood without knowledge of the material culture which supports it. The constitutional definition comprehends cultural expressions which are not objects, but dynamic processes, and it values 'living' heritage, rooted in the daily lives of communities. According to the Constitution, the Brazilian government must, in cooperation with society, promote and protect the Brazilian cultural heritage by means of inventories, registries, vigilance, protection decrees, expropriation and other forms of precaution and safeguarding (Londres Fonseca, 2003; Ribeiro, 2007).

On 4 April 2000, a presidential decree (no. 3551) created an intangible cultural heritage registry, which is divided into four different books (Registries of Knowledge, Cultural Expressions, Celebrations and Cultural Spaces). The main objective of the registry is to gather and systematize thoroughly all knowledge and documentation related to the cultural expression or practice for which recognition is sought, to enable its widespread diffusion and social recognition. The registry has a declaratory nature (i.e. it only declares or recognizes something that already exists as a cultural expression or practice), and it must always be supported by the local communities involved in its production and transmission. Cultural heritage safeguarded by the registry does not necessarily generate goods and services with an economic value, despite their high cultural, symbolic, political and social value.

When an intangible cultural heritage is registered, it receives the title of 'cultural heritage of Brazil', and its registry creates the legal obligation for governmental agencies (at federal and state levels) to develop safeguarding actions and plans, aimed at supporting the continuity of its existence and transmission and at providing the necessary social and material conditions for its continuity. The registry also takes into consideration the dynamic and evolving nature of intangible cultural heritage, and IPHAN (the Brazilian federal agency in charge of safeguarding cultural heritage) must re-evaluate all registered heritage at least once every ten years, in order to decide whether to re-validate the title of 'cultural heritage of Brazil' of Brazil (IPHAN, 2003).

On 8 November 2010, IPHAN provided the first recognition of an agrobiodiversity-rich traditional agricultural system as part of the 'intangible cultural heritage of Brazil', specifically the Traditional Agricultural System of the Negro River region in the northwestern region of the Brazilian Amazon (Santilli, 2013). The request for recognition was filed by the Association of Indigenous Communities of the Middle Negro River (ACIMRN) in July 2007, with the support of two interdisciplinary research programs on agrobiodiversity and associated traditional knowledge developed in the Brazilian Amazon (**Box 23.4** *Interdisciplinary approaches to understanding agrobiodiversity know-how in the Amazon*).

It has further been argued that the cultural heritage of the Negro River for which recognition was sought from IPHAN can be linked to a much wider and more sophisticated set of social-ecological relationships and so provides the opportunity to seek registration for broader elements of Brazilian cultural heritage (Emperaire et al., 2008). These might include the registry of traditional agricultural systems such as that of the Negro River, as characterized by a set of interdependent elements rather than any single object or specific good. Emperaire et al. (2008) also added that the traditional agricultural system of Negro River is very rich in agrobiodiversity: studies carried out in two communities of the Middle Negro River – Tapereira and Espírito Santo – and in the city of Santa Isabel do Rio Negro, identified 243 cultivated crops including 73 varieties of cassava. Each family cultivates between 17 and 97 different species and from 6 to 20 cassava varieties. In addition to the cassava genetic diversity, the studies also found a high diversity of peppers, pineapples, yams and bananas, which confirms the regional importance of the Negro River in terms of conservation of agricultural diversity. In Brazil, as in most developing countries, most native plant genetic resources are conserved on farms, regardless of being located within or outside the limits of protected areas, and these resources are not well represented in *ex situ* collections (Sauer, 1986). Of the 250,000 accessions conserved in the genebanks of Embrapa (Brazil's main agricultural research institution), for example, approximately 76% are exotic species, and only the remaining 24% represent native species (Goedert, 2007, p. 33). On-farm conservation focuses attention on agricultural crops of interest to farmers and, as Charles Clement et al. (2007, p. 515) explained, 'so many people are involved with on-farm conservation because it is intrinsic to their social and economic organizations; knowing and conserving biological

## Box 23.4 Interdisciplinary approaches to understanding agrobiodiversity know-how in the Amazon

The two programs are (1) 'Traditional Management of Cassava in the Brazilian Amazon,' 1998–2000, which was developed through a partnership between CNPq (Brazilian National Council for Scientific and Technological Development), Instituto Socioambiental (a Brazilian non-governmental organization) and Institut de Recherche pour le Développement (IRD), with financial support from Bureau des Ressources Génétiques (BRG), CNPq and IRD and (2) 'Local Populations, Agrobiodiversity and Associated Traditional Knowledge in the Brazilian Amazon' (PACTA) 2005–2009, which was developed through a partnership between CNPq, Unicamp (State University of Campinas, in São Paulo State) and IRD, with the participation of the Association of Indigenous Communities of the Middle Negro River (ACIMRN), with financial support from: IRD, CNPq, Agence Nationale de la Recherche, Biodivalloc and BRG (Heckenberger et al., 2007).

diversity over time and space is one of the main factors in their social reproduction' (see also Chapter 35 of this Handbook by Sthapit et al.).

Intangible cultural heritage includes not only songs, tales and dances, but also agricultural knowledge innovations and practices held by traditional and local farmers, encompassing many different forms of cultivation (home gardens, swidden, agroforestry systems; Lira and Amoêda, 2010). Such innovations and practices include biological control of pests and diseases and genetic improvement of local plant varieties through farmer selection and breeding. Traditional and local knowledge associated with agrobiodiversity has been recognized as part of the Brazilian intangible cultural heritage and, therefore, must be safeguarded (Nogueira, 2006; Ribeiro, 2007). Both aspects of this cultural heritage – material/tangible (agroecosystems and cultivated plants) and immaterial/intangible (agricultural knowledge and practices) – are protected by the Brazilian Constitution (article 216), and therefore, safeguarding measures must contemplate both of them, which are intrinsically linked.

## Recognition of traditional knowledge associated with maize diversity and of local foods as intangible cultural heritage in Peru, and the creation of the 'Parque de la Papa'

Like Brazil, Peru has also edited National Directorial Resolution (*Resolución Directoral Nacional*) no. 1986/INC, of 23 December 2009, declaring, as 'national cultural heritage', the knowledge, practices and technologies associated to the traditional cultivation of maize in the Sacred Valley of Incas, in the Andes of Peru. It represents the first time that an agricultural system has been recognized as cultural heritage in Peru (Ruiz Muller, 2009).

According to the aforementioned Resolution, maize (or *Sara* in Quechua) has been cultivated in the Peruvian Andes for millennia, despite being of Mesoamerican origin, with 55 maize varieties found in the region. In the region of Ayacucho in the south-central Andes, maize remains have been dated to 4,300 BCE and to 2,500–1,800 BCE in coastal areas (Tapia, 1999). Maize, furthermore, had great symbolic and cultural value for pre-Hispanic peoples. During the Inca Empire, maize was so important that holidays, calendars, land divisions and social relationships were all established around its sowing and harvesting cycles. Inca society developed sophisticated practices and technologies to produce maize and develop new varieties of maize adapted to different geographic and climatic regions, as well as develop complex irrigation and storage systems. The Sacred Valley of the Incas is located at an altitude between 2,600 and 3,050 meters above sea level, and its temperate climate is favourable to maize cultivation. Eight native varieties are currently cultivated, of which the best known is the so-called 'giant white corn' *(maíz blanco gigante)*. Each maize variety has its particular characteristics, and is used in a specific ceremony, for magical or medicinal purposes or for the worship of deities. Maize harvesting is done in a collective manner, through reciprocal and communal work (called *ayni*), and ritual elements are also present in maize harvesting, such as the offering of a traditional drink *(challasqa)* to the first cut stems. Practices and technologies associated with the cultivation of maize are important because of both their symbolic and economic dimensions, according to the Resolution, which was enacted in accordance with Peruvian Law no. 28296, of 2004, and its regulation, approved through Supreme Decree no. 011–2006-ED. Peru ratified, in 2004, UNESCO's Convention for the Safeguarding of Intangible Cultural Heritage.

According to Peruvian Law no. 28296 *(Ley General del Patrimonio Cultural de la Nación)*, the intangible/immaterial cultural heritage of the Peruvian nation is constituted of:

> creations of a cultural community based on tradition, which are expressed by its members individually or in a collective manner, and which are recognized by the community

> as expressions of its cultural and social identity, including orally transmitted values, such as indigenous languages and dialects and traditional knowledge, whether artistic, culinary, medicinal, technological, folklore or religious, and the collective knowledge of peoples and other cultural expressions or manifestations, which together constitute our cultural diversity.

This law also affirms that intangible cultural heritage belongs to the Peruvian nation, and that no natural or legal person can claim ownership over it, and that the communities that maintain and preserve intangible cultural heritage are their direct possessors. This law created the National Registry of Folklore and Popular Culture *(Registro Nacional de Folclore y Culturas Populares)*, where all tangible and intangible cultural heritage, belonging to folklore and popular culture, are registered. Safeguarding actions and policies are aimed at identifying, documenting, registering, inventorying, preserving, promoting, valorizing, transmitting and revitalizing intangible cultural heritage. The official agency responsible for safeguarding intangible cultural heritage is *Instituto Nacional de Cultura*, and its *Dirección de Registro y Estudio de la Cultura del Perú Contemporáneo* (DREPC).

Maize, as a food, had already been included in the declaration of the Peruvian traditional food as cultural heritage. Peruvian traditional food is based on several millennia of cultural development by diverse ethnic groups, and is one of oldest in the world. Agricultural technologies, as well as the management of water, were highly-developed by the Incas, which led to the domestication of a huge variety of plants and to the use of a large variety of fauna species. Peruvian food is a result of the country's rich biodiversity and cultural diversity. Other traditional foods recognized as cultural heritage of Peru include: *pisco*, a grape brandy produced in Peru. Grapes used for manufacture of *pisco* result from a mild weather and from the tectonic formation of the soil in the province of Pisco, extending to the valleys of Lima, Ica, Arequipa, Moquegua and some valleys of Tacna with similar conditions; *pisco sour*, a cocktail containing *pisco*, lemon or lime juice, egg whites, syrup and bitters; *ceviche*, which is a dish made of cubed raw fish, lime or lemon juice, onion, and traditional Andean spices which include salt and chili. A result of the mixture between Muslim and native Andean cuisines, ceviche is consumed in all parts of Peru; *pachamanca*, which is a unique and ancient way of cooking certain foods (lamb, chicken, guinea pig, marinated in spices, as well as sweet potato, chili, beans etc.), which are distributed within a hole in the ground and covered with rocks at high temperatures (the earthen oven is known as a *huatia*). *Pachamanca* is used mainly in the central Peruvian Andes, and has existed since the time of the Inca Empire. Peru has already recognized, as part of its cultural heritage, traditional knowledge relating to the medicinal and religious uses of the plant-based brew ayahuasca, especially in the Amazon. In addition, 144 native varieties of potato have been described in the 'Catalog of Native Potato Varieties of Huancavelica, Peru,' published by the International Potato Center (CIP) and the Federación Departamental de Comunidades Campesinas (FEDECH) in 2006 (see also Argumedo, 2008; Nazarea, Chapter 39 of this Handbook).

## The UNESCO Convention for the Protection of the World Cultural and Natural Heritage and the concept of cultural landscapes

The UNESCO Convention concerning the Protection of the World Cultural and Natural Heritage (known as the World Heritage Convention) was adopted in 1972, with the purpose of ensuring the identification, protection, conservation, presentation and transmission to future generations of cultural and natural heritage of 'outstanding universal value' from the point of view of history, art, science, aesthetics, ethnology or anthropology. It has been ratified by 187 States Parties. Among the 911 properties (sites) inscribed on the World Heritage List, 704 are cultural (of which 66 are cultural landscapes), 180 natural and 27 mixed (natural/cultural) properties, located in 151 States Parties (as of June 2010).

The World Heritage Convention was developed from the merging of two separate movements: the first focusing on the preservation of cultural sites, and the second dealing with the conservation of nature. Reflecting an (almost) antagonistic perception of nature and culture, the convention originally divided World Heritage sites into two categories: natural and cultural heritage. According to Peter Fowler (2003), when the Convention was adopted, nature conservationists' thinking was along the lines that the less human interference there had been with an area, the 'better' it was. Similarly, the cultural movement embraced mainly monuments, buildings and ruins as isolated phenomena largely in the minds of architects, with little thought of context and the landscape itself. Most cultural heritage sites on the list were monuments and buildings, recognized as masterpieces of human creativity. On the other hand, natural heritage sites inscribed on the World Heritage List were mainly pristine and wilderness areas, with little human interference. Later, a 'mixed' (cultural and natural) category of site was created, to enable the inscription of properties (sites) which could have their recognition justified under both natural and cultural criteria. However, this category also did not explore much the interfaces between biological and cultural diversity.

It was only in 1992 that the World Heritage Committee established a new and innovative category of site: the 'cultural landscape', within the Operational Guidelines for the Implementation of the World Heritage Convention. This happened in the same year (1992) that the United Nations Conference on Environment and Development was held, in Rio de Janeiro, and which led to the adoption of the Convention on Biological Diversity.

Two years later, in 1994, IUCN (The World Conservation Union, which is the advisory body of the World Heritage Committee for natural sites) recognized 'protected landscapes/seascapes' on an equal footing with other categories of protected areas. These areas are designated 'Category V' in IUCN's system for categorizing protected areas, and they are defined, as 'areas of land, with coast and sea as appropriate, where the interaction of people and nature over time has produced an area of distinct character with significant aesthetic, ecological and/or cultural value, and often with high biological diversity'. There are similarities between UNESCO's World Heritage 'cultural landscape' category and IUCN Category V of protected areas (protected landscapes/seascapes), especially on the emphasis placed on human/nature interaction (Philips, 2005). However, in the latter, the emphasis is on biodiversity conservation and ecosystem integrity, whereas on UNESCO's cultural landscapes, the emphasis is on human history, continuity of cultural traditions and social values and aspirations. Besides, the fundamental criterion for recognition of a World Heritage Cultural Landscape is that of 'outstanding universal value', whereas there is less stress placed on outstanding qualities in the case of IUCN Category V protected landscapes/seascapes (Phillips, 2005).

Cultural landscapes are justified for inclusion in the UNESCO World Heritage List when interactions between people and their environment are evaluated as being of 'outstanding universal value'. According to the Operational Guidelines for the Implementation of the World Heritage Convention:

- Cultural landscapes are cultural properties which represent 'the combined works of nature and of man'. They are illustrative of the evolution of human society and settlement over time, under the influence of the physical constraints and/or opportunities presented by their natural environment and of successive social, economic and cultural forces, both external and internal.

- Cultural landscapes should be selected on the basis of both their outstanding universal value and their representation in terms of a clearly defined geo-cultural region and also for their capacity to illustrate the essential and distinct cultural elements of such regions.
- The term 'cultural landscape' embraces a diversity of manifestations of the interaction between humankind and its natural environment.
- Cultural landscapes often reflect specific techniques of sustainable land-use, considering the characteristics and limits of the natural environment they are established in, and a specific spiritual relation to nature. Protection of cultural landscapes can contribute to modern techniques of sustainable land-use and can maintain or enhance natural values in the landscape and help conserve agrobiodiversity. The continued existence of traditional forms of land-use supports biological diversity in many regions of the world. The protection of traditional cultural landscapes is therefore helpful in maintaining biological diversity.

## Future safeguarding of agrobiodiversity within cultural landscapes

The World Heritage Committee's decision to designate a 'cultural landscape' category was an important development in linking conservation of natural and cultural heritage. According to Mechtild Röessler, cultural landscapes are at the interface between nature and culture, tangible and intangible heritage, biological and cultural diversity, and they represent 'a tightly woven net of relationships that are the essence of culture and people's identity' (Röessler, 2005, p. 37). He pointed out that the recognition of cultural landscapes gave value to land-use systems that represent the continuity of people working the land over centuries and sometimes millennia to adapt the natural environment and retain or enhance biological diversity. According to Röessler (2005, p. 40), the key world crops were developed in the spectacular agricultural systems in the High Andes, terraced rice paddies in Asia or oasis systems in the Sahara, and the global importance of these systems and the genetic diversity of these cultural landscapes were recognized (as a result of their inscription as cultural landscapes).

The 'continuing' form of 'organically evolved landscapes' represents the category of cultural landscape that is most adequate for safeguarding biodiversity-rich agricultural systems. Some examples of agricultural landscapes inscribed under the World Heritage List are (a) Rice Terraces of the Philippine Cordilleras, which were the first site to be included on the World Heritage Cultural Landscape list under the continuing organically evolved category, in 1995 (Nozawa et al., 2008). In 2001, they were included in the World Heritage in Danger List, since uncontrolled tourism and the introduction of open-market economy threatened both the natural heritage of the province and the traditional practices of its inhabitants; (b) Archaeological Landscape of the First Coffee Plantations in the southeast of Cuba; (c) Agricultural Landscape of Southern Öland, in Sweden; (d) Tokaj Wine Region Historic Cultural Landscape, in Hungary; (e) Puszta Pastoral Landscape of Hortobagy National Park, in Hungary. All these examples show the potential for using the 'cultural landscape' category to promote and safeguard sites which are important for agrobiodiversity heritage, including the genetic diversity of the plants and animals essential for their functions and the know-how of the local communities which preserve them (Singh and Varaprasad, 2008; Santilli, 2013).

## References

Amoêda, R., Lira, S. and Pinheiro, C. (2010) *Heritage 2010 – World Heritage and Sustainable Development*, Green Lines Institute for Sustainable Development, Barcelos, Portugal.

Argumedo, A. (2008) 'The Potato Park, Peru: Conserving agrobiodiversity in an andean indigenous biocultural heritage area', pp. 45–58 in T. Amend, J. Brown, A. Kothari, A., Phillips and S. Stolton (eds.), *Protected Landscapes and Agrobiodiversity Vales*, IUCN and GTZ, Kasparek Verlag, Heidelberg, Germany.

Clement, C., Rocha, S., Cole, D. and Vivan, J. (2007) 'Conservação on farm', pp. 513–544 in L. Nass (ed.), *Recursos genéticos vegetais*, Embrapa Recursos Genéticos e Biotecnologia, Brasília, Brazil.

Emperaire, L. and Peroni, N. (2007) 'Traditional management of agrobiodiversity in Brazil: A case study of manioc', *Human Ecology*, vol. 35, pp. 761–768.

Emperaire, L., Velthem, L. H. V. and Oliveira, A. G. (2008) *Patrimônio cultural imaterial e sistema agrícola: o manejo da diversidade agrícola no médio Rio Negro (AM)*, study presented at the 26th Meeting of the Brazilian Anthropology Association, held between 1 and 4 June, 2008, in Porto Seguro, Bahia, Brazil.

Fowler, P. J. (2003) *World Heritage Cultural Landscapes: 1992–2002*, UNESCO World Heritage Series, no. 6, UNESCO, Paris, France.

Goedert, C. (2007) 'Histórico e avanços em recursos genéticos no Brasil', pp. 25–60 in L. Nass (ed.), *Recursos genéticos vegetais*, Embrapa Recursos Genéticos e Biotecnologia, Brasília, Brazil.

Heckenberger, M., Russell, J. C., Toney, M. R. and Schmidt, M. J. (2007) 'The legacy of cultural landscapes in the Brazilian Amazon: Implications for biodiversity', *Philosophical Transactions of the Royal Society B – Biological Sciences*, vol. 362, pp. 197–207.

Instituto do Patrimônio Histórico e Artístico Nacional (Iphan); Fundação Nacional de Arte (Funarte) (2003) *O Registro do Patrimônio Imaterial: Dossiê Final das Atividades da Comissão e do Grupo de Trabalho Patrimônio Imaterial*, IPHAN, Brasília, Brazil.

Lira, S. and Amoêda, R. (2010) *Constructing Intangible Heritage*, Green Lines Institute for Sustainable Development, Barcelos, Portugal.

Londres Fonseca, M. C. (2003) 'Para além da pedra e cal: por uma concepção ampla de patrimônio cultural', pp. 56–75 in R. Abreu and M. Chagas (eds.), *Memória e patrimônio: ensaios contemporâneos*, DP & A, Rio de Janeiro, Brazil.

Nogueira, M. D. (2006) 'Mandioca e farinha: identidade cultural e patrimônio nacional,' pp. 25–27 in *Agrobiodiversidade e Diversidade Cultural*, Ministério do Meio Ambiente, Brasília, Brazil.

Nozawa, C., Malingan, M., Plantilla, A. and Ong, J. (2008) 'Evolving culture, evolving landscapes: The Philippine rice terraces', pp. 71–93 in T. Amend, J. Brown, A. Kothari, A. Philipps and S. Stolton (eds.), *Protected Landscapes and Agrobiodiversity Values*, IUCN (Values of Protected Landscapes and Seascapes, a series published by the Protected Landscapes Task Force of IUCN´s World Commission on Protected Areas), Gland, Switzerland.

Petrillo, P-L. (2012) 'La dimensione culturale del patrimonio agro-alimentare italiano in ambito UNESCO. Strumenti e procedure', pp. 41–59 in T. Scovazzi, B. Ubertazzi and L. Zagato (a cura di) *Il Patrimonio Culturale Intangibile nelle sue Diverse Dimensioni*, Giuffré, Milano, Italy.

Phillips, A. (2005) 'Landscape as a meeting ground: Category V protected landscapes/seascapes and world heritage cultural landscapes', pp. 19–35 in J. Brown, N. Mitchell and M. Beresford (eds.), *The Protected Landscape Approach: Linking Nature, Culture and Community*, IUCN, Gland, Switzerland and Cambridge, UK.

Ribeiro, R. (2007) *Paisagem cultural e patrimônio*, Iphan, Rio de Janeiro, Brazil.

Röessler, M. (2005) 'World heritage cultural landscapes: A global perspective', pp. 37–46 in J. Brown, N. Mitchell and M. Beresford (eds.), *The Protected Landscape Approach: Linking Nature, Culture and Community*, IUCN, Gland, Switzerland and Cambridge, UK.

Ruiz Muller, M. (2009) *Las Zonas de Agrobiodiversidad y el Registro de Cultivos Nativos en el Perú: Aprendiendo de Nosotros Mismos*, Sociedad Peruana de Derecho Ambiental, Bioversity International, Lima, Peru.

Santilli, J. (2011) *Agrobiodiversity and the Law: Regulating Genetic Resources, Food Security and Cultural Diversity*, Routledge, Abingdon, UK.

Santilli, J. (2013) 'Agrobiodiversity: Towards inovating legal systems', pp. 167–184 in E. Coudel, H. Devautour, C. T. Soulard, G. Faure and B. Hubert (eds.), *Renewing Innovation Systems in Agriculture and Food: How To Go Towards More Sustainability?* Wageningen Academic Publishers, Wageningen, the Netherlands.

Sauer, C. (1986) 'As plantas cultivadas na América do Sul tropical', pp. 59–90 in B. Ribeiro (ed.), *Suma etnológica brasileira: etnobiologia*, 3rd ed., Vozes, Finep, Petrópolis, Brazi.

Singh, A. K. and Varaprasad, K. S. (2008) 'Criteria for identification and assessment of agro-biodiversity heritage sites: evolving sustainable agriculture', *Current Science*, vol. 94, pp. 1131–1138.

Tapia, M. (1999) *Agrobiodiversidad en los Andes*, Fundacion Friedrich Ebert, Lima, Peru.
Tilman, D. and Clark, M. (2014) 'Global diets link environmental sustainability and human health', *Nature*, vol. 515, p. 518.
UNESCO (2003) *Convention for the Safeguarding of the Intangible Cultural Heritage 2003*, http://portal.unesco.org/en/ev.php-URL_ID=17716&URL_DO=DO_TOPIC&URL_SECTION=201.html
UNESCO Intergovernmental Committee for the Safeguarding of the Intangible Cultural Heritage (2010) *Convention for the Safeguarding of the Intangible Cultural Heritage, Fifth Session*, UNESCO, Nairobi, Kenya. www.unesco.it/_filesPATRIMONIOimmateriale/DecisioniImmateriale.pdf
UNESCO, World Heritage Centre (2003) *Cultural Landscapes: The Challenges of Conservation*, World Heritage Paper, no. 7, http://unesdoc.UNESCO.org/images/0013/001329/132988e.pdf, accessed 20 January 2011.

# 24

# HOLDING ON TO AGROBIODIVERSITY

## Human nutrition and health of Indigenous Peoples

*Harriet V. Kuhnlein*

### Introduction: why this chapter is relevant to maintaining agrobiodiversity

Food is obviously important for human health. It is a major consideration of virtually all national development agencies and several United Nations agencies: how to prevent malnutrition and ensure food security for the world's populations, and how to accomplish this goal while protecting human rights, food sovereignty, and environmental sustainability. Agricultural production on this planet is able to provide enough energy (calories) for all people, yet we are told that roughly half of the world's people suffer from malnutrition in one or more of its complex forms (undernutrition, overnutrition, or micronutrient deficiencies) (International Food Policy Research Institute, 2015).

Globally, more than 790 million people are undernourished in energy alone (Food and Agriculture Organization of the United Nations (FAO), 2015), more than 2 billion suffer from anemia (WHO, 2015a), and more than 1.9 billion adults and 42 million children under five years of age are overweight or obese (WHO, 2015b). It appears there does not exist a country (or even a subpopulation of a country) without some form of malnutrition in many of its people as reported in the 2015 Global Nutrition Report (International Food Policy Research Institute, 2015). This is ironic, when there are enough resources and enough food produced for all within the many diverse ecosystems and cultures that we know. Our thinkers, sociologists, economists, agronomists, educators, and political leaders must solve the problem of unequal distribution of food and food security, particularly for vulnerable women and children. This is a multidisciplinary problem that will require multidisciplinary actions for sustainable solutions, based on a daily food supply that ensures good health and well-being and contributes to peace for all the world's peoples. Considering food systems of Indigenous Peoples through a *multidisciplinary lens is one way to move forward.*

The food systems of cultures of Indigenous Peoples hold vast collective knowledge rooted in historical continuity within their local territories. In several cultures, knowledge of local food resources has been documented to include up to 390 plant and animal species, many of them uncultivated foods harvested from the wild within an ecosystem that may be only a few square kilometres in area (Kuhnlein et al., 2009).

This knowledge of diversity and food use should be considered in the context of the world's food crops today. An estimated total of 300,000 plant species are known on the earth; about 10,000 of them have been used as food since the historical origins of agriculture (see Henry, Chapter 1 of this Handbook). Our global food system has made about 150–200 of these commercially available, but today, only four of these (rice, wheat, maize, and potatoes) provide more than 50% of the world's food energy (usually in highly refined forms), and 30 crops supply an estimated 90% (FAO, 2010).

Indigenous and Tribal Peoples everywhere experience disparities in contrast to their national mainstream population, often resulting from colonization and assimilation. Irrespective of geography, their land and resources have been assaulted, threatening access to their own food. They are often marginalized and disenfranchised, live in extreme poverty, have disparities in wellness (greater chronic and infectious diseases and poorer life-expectancy), and suffer lack of health resources and/or recognition of their traditional foods and medicines (UNPFII, 2009; WHO/UNEP/CBD, 2015).

In any region, Indigenous Peoples are among the billions suffering malnutrition of one form or another. Nevertheless, Indigenous Peoples living in their rural homelands still possess rich and diverse knowledge, values, and traditions related to their natural resources, including their food resources. The wisdom inherent in indigenous ways of knoing and doing connect the land and food to physical and mental health and spirituality. There is a tremendous potential for indigenous cultures to express their human right to self-determination and have a positive influence on the food-system development of any region or country. They have a great deal to share concerning the world's food bounty, not only among themselves, but also with all humankind (Kuhnlein et al., 2013).

This chapter provides a structure for research on vastly diverse food systems of indigenous cultures. Such study includes learning how food is accessed, processed, and used; its sociocultural impact; and documentation of its nutritional qualities (Kuhnlein and Receveur, 1996).

## Biodiversity in Indigenous Peoples' food systems

The United Nations has documented the presence of more than 400 million Indigenous Peoples in about 70 countries. They compose about 5% of the world's population, but 15% of the global poor (FAO, n.d.; www.fao.org/indigenous-peoples/en). The vast knowledge of food biodiversity rests with Indigenous Peoples still living in their rural homelands – roughly 50% – with the rest having migrated to urban and other areas. Food biodiversity is found in the rural areas where cultural activities are still practiced and agriculture is often performed with unique species or varieties of crops, or where wild foods are harvested from adjacent uncultivated lands (see examples in Kuhnlein et al., 2009; Termote et al., 2010; Powell et al., 2013).

**Table 24.1** *Percent of energy derived from traditional sources* shows the number of species of animals and plants, and their contribution to dietary energy, from several local indigenous food systems recently studied (data from Kuhnlein et al., 2009; Kuhnlein and Humphries, 2013). While dietary energy is obtained from both traditional local food and food purchased from markets, this analysis focused only on traditional food sources. This table demonstrates the portion of dietary energy attained only from local food sources, with a separate tally made of the numbers of local animal foods, both domesticated and wildlife.

Greater agricultural industrialization has created very large farms that are linked to large food processing industries. These farms use chemical fertilizers and equipment requiring extensive fossil fuels, and lead to a profit-driven economic base. Industrialized agriculture food systems contribute to food biodiversity loss and heavily impact the environment, particularly climate

*Table 24.1* Percent of energy derived from traditional sources; numbers of traditional species/varieties; number of domesticated and wild animals

| *Culture* | *% Dietary energy* | *No. species/ varieties* | *No. domesticated animals* | *No. species wildlife* |
|---|---|---|---|---|
| Awajún, Peru | 93 | 223 | 0 | 110 |
| Bhil, India | 59 | 95 | 3 | 20 |
| Dalit, India | 43 | 329 | 15 | 25 |
| Gwich'in, Canada | 33 | 50 | 0 | 35 |
| Igbo, Nigeria | 96 | 220 | 9 | 31 |
| Ingano, Colombia | 47 | 160 | 2 | 91 |
| Inuit, Canada | 41 | 79 | 0 | 66 |
| Karen, Thailand | 85 | 387 | 5 | 56 |
| Maasai, Kenya | 6 | 35 | 17 | 2 |
| Nuxalk, Canada | 30 | 67 | 0 | 39 |
| Pohnpei, Micronesia | 27 | 381 | 5 | 157 |

change (WHO/UNEP/CBD, 2015). As the impact of climate change affects us all, it is essential that we reconsider and support food systems, such as those of Indigenous Peoples, which are known to have sustained populations through time. In today's world, we must give special attention to our food systems' environmental sustainability, and especially to limiting industrial production of red meat animals. Red meat is in demand by the wealthy, but is resource-intensive and gas (methane) polluting (CGRFA, 2013; Johnston et al., 2014). As noted earlier, agricultural industrial systems contain few species/varieties/subspecies of crops in comparison to the biodiverse food systems of Indigenous Peoples.

## *The traditional food systems of Indigenous Peoples*

*Hunter-gatherer* (or foraging) food systems are found in ecological areas unsuitable for agriculture, such as dense forests and the Arctic. Populations of Dene and Inuit cultures in the Canadian Arctic access broad territories with many wildlife animal species. The Dene have access to 17 land mammals, 16 birds, 20 fish and other seafood, and 48 plants (mostly berries and herbs); the Inuit, 14 sea mammals, 14 land mammals, 70 birds, 48 fish and other seafood, and 48 plants (here taken to include several species or varieties of seaweed) (Kuhnlein and Receveur, 2007). In contrast, the Awajún in tropical northwest Peru use 94 plants (tubers, fruits, and vegetables) and 113 species of fish, birds, and other animals (Creed-Kanashiro et al., 2009).

*Pastoralist* food systems use domesticated animals (such as cattle, camels, sheep, horses, and reindeer, depending on the culture) that graze on lands unsuitable for cultivation. They can be fully or partly nomadic, depending on grazing seasons and water availability. Wild plants provide minor dietary energy in contrast to the animal food sources. Climate change and drought seriously affect pastoralists, and many depend on food aid (usually of donated grains) or end up migrating to urban areas (Oiye et al., 2009).

Indigenous Peoples are often *peasant farmers* with horticultural food systems that do not use mechanization, and who produce agriculture in village units, usually not dependent on commercialization. They may keep small animals (chickens, guinea pigs, etc.) and a few larger animals for the household, but the main diet is local grains, roots, and wild plants and animals. Swidden (land cleared for cultivation by slashing and burning vegetation) agriculture and forested areas can yield a vast diversity of species and varieties of wild foods. The Karen villages in Kanchanaburi district in Western Thailand practice swidden cultivation of more than 25 varieties of rice, and harvest about 355 species of other grains, seeds, fish, insects, tubers, fruits, and vegetables (Chotiboriboon et al., 2009).

Where continuous crops can be grown and harvested year round, *smallholder farmer* food systems use intensive human labor, along with animal and limited mechanical labor. They often use terracing along with animal or other fertilizer. Here, diversity in food species can also be extensive. For example, Dalit farmers in Zaheerabad district in India harvest more than 320 species of plants, both cultivated and uncultivated 'weeds' (Salomeyesudas and Satheesh, 2009). Another notable example is the terraced and flooded rice ecosystems of Asia, which provide biodiverse aquatic animal food species (Halwart and Bartley, 2007).

Smallholder farmers and peasant farmers may choose to grow crops for sale in markets for cash, or for sharing in their communities. Cash-cropping is routinely practiced in areas adjacent to towns or cities where transportation is available, and if practiced, can lead to purchases of food for family use in markets where their own crops are sold. Cash-cropping usually leads to biodiversity loss in family diets, as land is converted to agriculture for production (CGRFA, 2013).

All societies today use foods distributed from industrial agriculture and the global economy, but the food systems of rural Indigenous Peoples retain a mix of local indigenous food and food purchased from markets. Understanding and documenting the complexity of these mixed-food systems, and especially the biodiversity in local indigenous food resources, can be accomplished with systematic, interdisciplinary effort. This information is critical to building health-promotion activities for the Indigenous Peoples involved.

## Documenting Indigenous Peoples' food systems

The research process to document a particular food system with the intention of building the knowledge base to create successful health promotion activities can be thought of as a five-step process (Kuhnlein et al., 2006):

1 Prepare the research team;
2 Gather the cultural food list data;
3 Compile the scientific parameters of foods in the food list;
4 Understand the food use and nutrient intake patterns, and their cultural and health contexts; and
5 Plan for use of the food system data.

### *Step 1: Prepare the research team*

This begins with collecting and reviewing existing data on the culture and region, as well as information that may be available on the known species used for food, such as scientific identifications, nutrient composition and patterns of use. Establishing the interdisciplinary team to complete the food system documentation early on helps. To make best use of the food system documentation, in addition to background and understanding in nutrition, the team requires expertise from:

- the leadership of the local culture;
- a social scientist who can provide background on community history and understanding the contextual features of the local ecosystem and culture;

- a food analysis specialist with access to taxonomists and nutrient laboratories;
- a food and dietary database specialist; and
- a specialist in data translation and intervention planning.

It is also useful to invite involved policy makers at local, state, and/or national levels, if it is agreeable to the community leadership, so that they can become apprised of the local food system and situation of the local culture. Capacity building on several levels can take place; not only are team members learning from the community, but also community members are learning from experts in the social and natural sciences. All team members should be apprised of the contextual factors of the ecosystems and cultures under review in the documentation process. This is especially important when the ultimate goals are to use local food-system data to create, implement, and evaluate a health-promotion intervention program that uses the local food system (Pelto et al., 2013).

### *Create local partnerships*

A key procedure is establishing cooperative and supportive relationships with the responsible members of local authority, and with population subgroups, in an ethically-appropriate manner for the culture. For most Indigenous Peoples, this involves contacting the Tribal management center, as well as local chiefs who are pivotal to community engagement. Local, state and, perhaps, even national government authorities must be involved in facilitating arrangements. This critical step sets the stage for forming partnerships to create priorities, research agreements, budgets, management structure and processes for successful community interaction and data collection. Examples of agreements and forms for obtaining informed consent are given in Sims and Kuhnlein (2003).

### *The contributions of social science*

Important topics for the social science team member include understanding the food identities of the culture and region, the factors that shape local dietary patterns, and the biodiversity within those patterns. The foods that are acceptable and desirable through habit and custom must be known to influence food preferences and practices for growing, harvesting, preserving, processing, and preparing food for the family table. Also, the food system species/varieties/cultivars and their properties must be known in order to set the stage for education and awareness-building. Interviews within the culture can glean information on local knowledge, practices, and technologies for each species, and will guide how and which samples are profitably taken for analysis. The big-picture influences on food accessibility (land access, climate events, political stability, food aid, etc.), as well as the local intrahousehold factors influencing food preparation (food purchasing, water, cooking utensils, etc.) must be understood. Income, religious practices, and social identities are important, as are the general cultural taste preferences and appreciation of locally available foods (CGRFA, 2013).

## *Step 2: Gather the cultural food list data*

The food list data can be quite extensive, depending on the type of food system (see previous section, 'The traditional food systems of Indigenous Peoples') and how intact the ecosystem is for agriculture or for providing wild foods. This important step sets the stage for interviews on the characteristics of each food species, and prioritizing for sample collection for herbarium or zoological identifications and laboratory analysis. At this stage, information can be collected from a focus group of four to six members; perhaps one group of women and a second of men.

Guidelines on conducting these interviews are given in Kuhnlein et al. (2006), along with sample data collection forms. Once seasonality has been determined, the team may develop a short (5-point) quantitative scale for availability. Other scales might investigate taste appreciation for women in pregnancy, for children, for men of different ages, or for ease of cultivation or harvest. This information may inform decisions for sampling, which may be taken for foods known to be effective for infant and young child feeding, for expected richness in nutrient content, and so forth.

## *Step 3: Compile the scientific parameters of foods in the food list*

Using food knowledge as a platform for developing health promotion interventions is a viable concept with Indigenous Peoples. Food is the natural connection from the land to the health of people, and it is understood that health incorporates physical, mental, emotional, and spiritual dimensions of individuals and communities. Food touches all of these dimensions. Therefore, for scientists whose ultimate goal is to improve the health of Indigenous Peoples, documenting food systems with as much detail and quality as possible is crucial at this stage.

In building Indigenous Peoples' nutrition programs, there is no greater need for scientific information than for the nutrient composition of available and accessible foods. The food taxonomy and food analysis specialists need contemporary procedures for effective work, which begins with completion of the food list (Kuhnlein et al., 2006). Guidelines on developing data on food composition and food consumption as indicators for food biodiversity are available from FAO (FAO, 2008, 2010a). The INFOODS network at FAO is a source for identification of national laboratories that can advise on selection of qualified analytical laboratories (FAO, 2016). It could be that a particular nutrient of concern can be a priority, such as zinc, vitamin A, or foods which provide a rich diversity of micronutrients.

Food composition data are essential for understanding the health properties of foods. To do this properly, the scientific identification of the species must first be made beyond the 'aggregate' level (fruit) to the defined genus, species and, if identified, subspecies level. This is important because vast differences can exist not only among fruits (e.g. common market banana and common market orange are vastly different in vitamin C content) but also within particular species. Sometimes the variation in content of a particular nutrient within a variety can exceed the variation between species. A 200 g portion of rice might provide 25% or more than 65% of protein need, depending on the variety (Kennedy and Burlingame, 2003). Banana varieties/cultivars within the Pacific Islands of Micronesia have a tremendous variation in pro-vitamin carotenoids, from 25 μg per 100 g to 8000 μg per 100 g (Englberger et al., 2003). Other examples of food diversity with vastly different nutrient quantities within species and varieties are found elsewhere (FAO/INFOODS, 2013), and point to the need to establish nutrient composition databases for understanding and using the values of biodiversity. This information can help to build successful health promotion programs using specific foods from the local food system (examples are given in Kuhnlein et al., 2013).

It is very clear that obtaining accurate information on food species and variety/cultivar identifications are needed *before* the samples are taken for expensive nutrient analyses. Guidelines for recording and taking samples for botanical or zoological taxonomic identifications are outlined in Kuhnlein et al. (2006).

Ideally, all foods in the food system are catalogued as presented in **Figure 24.1** *Sample page of food catalogue* , with taxonomic name, seasonality, patterns of use, taste appreciation, nutrient

**COMMUNITY FOOD SYSTEM DATA TABLE # 18**

**Food category:** Leafy Vegetables
**Scientific identification:**
*Amaranthus gangeticus*
**Local name & other common names:**
thota koora, Amaranth tender (English)
**Part(s) used:** Leaves
**Preparation:** As a curry with pulses or other greens.

| Nutrient | Nutrient Composition/100g (edible portion) |
|---|---|
| | Leaves |
| Moisture,g | 85.7 |
| Energy, Kcal | 45 |
| Protein, g | 4.0 |
| Fat, g | 0.5 |
| Carbohydrate, g | 6.1 |
| Fiber, g | 1.0 |
| Ash, g | 2.7 |
| Vitamin A, RE-μg | 2339 |
| Vitamin A, RAE-μg | 1170 |
| Beta carotene, μg | 7400* |
| Total carotene, μg | 20,670* |
| Vitamin C, mg | 99 |
| Thiamin, mg | 0.03 |
| Riboflavin, mg | 0.30 |
| Niacin, mg | 1.2 |
| Folate, μg | 149 |
| Calcium, mg | 397 |
| Iron, mg | 3.5 |
| Phosphorus, mg | 83 |
| Zinc, mg | - |

- not analyzed

**Wild or cultivated:** Wild
**Home harvested, collected or purchased:** Collected in the fields.
**Cost of production (if known):** Nil
**Importance value to the community by age/gender:** Unknown
**Reference:** Nutritive value of Indian foods, 2002. S no 49 (ref #2). Values with * see ref #1.
**Code:** n/a

**Seasonality and use**†

| | Winter | Summer | Rainy |
|---|---|---|---|
| **Season available** | • | | • |
| **Season of use and frequency *-rarely *-occasionally ***-frequently** | ••• | ••• | ••• |

†Winter = November-February, Summer = March-May, Rainy (South-West monsoon season) = June-October

*Figure 24.1* Sample page of food catalogue

*Source*: Centre for Indigenous Peoples' Nutrition and Environment (2009).

contents, and so forth. This information can be used to create a food system book for the community: one page per food, with photographs and seasonality and scientific information.

### *Step 4: Understand the food use and nutrient intake patterns, and their cultural and health contexts*

This stage builds on the information from Step 3. With nutrient data of the local foods along with national nutrient data tables, dietary intake interviews can be conducted and analyzed. Usually, food frequency instruments and 24-hour recalls are used for this data process.

At the same time, food security interviews can be conducted, using the FAO international assessment scale (FAO, 2016b), and qualitative interviews can determine other aspects of dietary adequacy. It is during this step that anthropometric or other health measures can also be taken from members of the interviewees' families to establish nutritional status. These procedures are standard methodology to the nutritionist in the team.

With these data, the team understands how foods are used in the food system (both traditional and market foods) and determines the food security and nutrient needs in the community. All these data, together with key health indicators, help prioritize the developing intervention strategy.

### *Step 5: Plan for use of the food system data*

How will the team use the information garnered in steps 1–4? Returning the results to the communities that contributed the information and provided the samples is critical for continued success to the project. Community leaders can guide the researchers to do this in meaningful ways, such as media presentations (radio, local TV), workshop presentations, providing school and library documents, and sharing data with local health care providers. Workshop discussions can be held on cultural attributes and ecosystem threats to elements of the food system, and how community members perceive positive change might take place. The presence of elders is especially important to give context to the discussions. From here, the possibility of interventions to improve nutrition and health can be discussed, and plans for interventions made (see following sections).

## Cultural advantages and ecosystem threats to the food systems of Indigenous Peoples

Indigenous Peoples are very aware of the cultural advantages and ecosystem threats to their local food resources. Indigenous Peoples appreciate their cultural food because it is an essential component of their identity and culture (see **Table 24.2** *Key cultural attributes of harvest and use*

*Table 24.2* Key cultural attributes of harvest and use of Indigenous Peoples' food

- Essential part of identity and culture;
- Tasty and fresh (no preservatives);
- Provides good nutrition;
- People can be 'in tune with nature';
- Saves money;
- Favors sharing;
- Brings respect, builds pride and confidence; and
- Educates children: survival skills, food preparation, spirituality, patience.

*Source*: Kuhnlein et al. (2001).

*of Indigenous Peoples' food*); particular species are often iconic to the culture (e.g. the Karat banana in Pohnpei, Micronesia, or dried caribou meat for the Arctic Dene people). Not only does the harvest and use of traditional food bring a close relationship to the natural environment, but also it provides opportunities for fitness and recreation during harvest. Indigenous Peoples recognize that natural food from the local environment is healthy, without food additives and the contaminants of industrialization. Indigenous families with food to spare take pride in sharing within their communities, so that many people can benefit from the food and share in financial savings. Being able to successfully harvest wild animals and plants brings pride and confidence in the culture and ecosystem. Importantly, the education of children in indigenous communities would not be complete without teaching them how to prepare these food, from its natural state to offering it to the family table. Children must learn the benefits of harvesting local food for their survival skills, spiritual values, and cultural preservation (Kuhnlein et al., 2001).

In light of all the cultural and health benefits of using their local foods, it's not surprising that Indigenous Peoples are dismayed by ecosystem changes that detract from these valued food resources. While change is always occurring in all food environments, there can be serious impacts from unexpected change from natural disasters or political instability. The effects of industrial development have secondary effects on local food systems (e.g. see Gaydos et al., 2015). These include change related to deforestation; resource extraction (oil, gas, coal, minerals) and their resulting pollution; dams; and urban sprawl. These insults result in further habitat destruction and loss of wild animals and plants (in both numbers of species as well as individuals within species) as well as loss of agricultural varieties. The impact of climate change and global warming further exacerbates these effects.

Added to these challenges to food species in natural ecosystems are people's migration away from the homeland to urban areas for employment, and the encroachment of outsiders into the territories with intention of bioprospecting as well as resource extraction. In fact, Indigenous Peoples are often pushed out of their home ecosystems by settlers and colonists who proceed with industrial agriculture pursuits and cash-cropping, destroying the ecosystem in the process, and imposing trespassing restrictions. Once Indigenous Peoples leave their home territory for urban areas, not only do they have less access to their traditional food base, but also the foods that can be accessed must be purchased and are often of poor nutritional quality. With sustained presence away from their rural home territories, dietary patterns risk becoming permanently imbalanced, with health consequences leading to chronic disease (see, e.g. Kuhnlein, 1992; Golden et al., 2011).

## Building health promotion activities for better use of Indigenous Peoples' food systems

In view of these daunting challenges, health promotion activities for Indigenous Peoples in their rural home settings require efforts to stabilize ecosystem deterioration with conservation and restoration efforts that use indigenous values. In forest regions, efforts should contribute to species protection and maintenance; in agricultural areas, traditional farmers should be encouraged to retain and share their seeds and seedlings within their communities. These activities begin with the information from Steps 1–5 in the preceding section, 'Documenting Indigenous Peoples' food systems'. It's essential to review and share this knowledge with the local community, and encourage them to use their cultural and ecosystem knowledge to maintain their food systems as best they can to ensure access to the diversity of foods they know and want.

The team of experts visits the community to showcase results of the food system documentation and to express the value found in local foods and practices. At the same time, the realities of the market food system can be presented, with education on health risks and consequences of shifting too much to foods of poor nutritional value in contrast to local foods.

Next, the team helps the community brainstorm the many possible activities that can be undertaken, and how to acquire the resources needed. Community and research teams who have worked for years to build interventions with Indigenous Peoples agree that the documentation of the food systems is the first step, but that the efforts cannot stop with the documentation (Kuhnlein et al., 2013). In fact, the research teams are obliged to use the extensive food systems information for the health benefit of the community in as many ways as possible.

Setting overall objectives for health promotion activities is the first order of collaboration. Then, the question of how to involve active community participation and support must be considered. State-of-the-art participatory process engenders mutual listening and learning, with community leaders and research colleagues contributing equally. Every indigenous community has unique cultural, social, and ecosystem characteristics, so every program has different social capital, singular options for capacity building, and distinct logistical constraints (Fanzo et al., 2011; Kuhnlein et al., 2013).

Improving health of Indigenous Peoples in rural settings anywhere in the world requires thought to the current state of the 'nutrition transition' from diet and lifestyle based entirely in the local ecosystem to the contemporary setting. Behavior change in that transition usually means the inclusion of purchased, often highly processed, food; less physical activity; and more obesity, with its propensity to increasing chronic disease (Popkin et al., 2012).

Bringing the indigenous perspectives on health to include the social, mental, and spiritual aspects, as well as physical aspects, is important to contextualize meaningful intervention planning for communities of Indigenous Peoples. By focusing on the local food system, and the cultural foods in it, food insecurity and malnutrition are addressed from a multi-nutrient perspective. Activities based in agrobiodiversity require attention to both agriculture and harvest of wild foods to address improved and sustainable food availability, access, and use.

The best evaluation indicators for health improvement based in the local food system:

- are based in improving food availability and use;
- involve the interdisciplinary partners using both qualitative and quantitative methods dependent on the priorities; and
- track community engagement.

Depending on information already in hand, the team may decide to expand, using a baseline health assessment to augment food system data, such as that described by Englberger et al. (2013).

## *Typical intervention themes*

The CINE-FAO Indigenous Peoples' food systems program (Kuhnlein et al., 2013) identified several intervention themes from nine case studies from diverse ecosystems:

- Working with youth and the schools;
- Engagement with elders to share knowledge with the community;
- Sharing information on the many positive qualities and wholesomeness of the local food resources;
- Capacity building and empowerment, particularly of women;
- Networking and media within the region of communities with similar culture;
- Developing partnerships with NGOs and other stakeholders; and
- Engagement with government offices.

> **Box 24.1 Community engagement**
>
> The essence of community engagement for behavior change is to build awareness and pride that the local foods, technologies, and dietary patterns can be enhanced to contribute to better health.

Community enthusiasm and support for interventions need reinforcement with resources so that the 'bottom up' thinking and action is supported from the 'top down', as well as throughout the infrastructure (**Box 24.1** *Community engagement*). It is also very helpful if the program can develop some measureable livelihood activity as a result of engagement with local foods and their technologies. Another point of reinforced support for the community program was continuing recognition and encouragement from the network of NGO, government, and inter-community leaders into the community (Kuhnlein et al., 2013). In addition to promoting market-based approaches, national strategies and action plans targeted to Indigenous Peoples should promote sustainable solutions by effectively mainstreaming, resourcing, and supporting revitalization of cultural knowledge and use of local foods known by Indigenous Peoples in their homelands as well as in other areas where they may have relocated.

Indigenous Peoples in their rural home territory intrinsically know how to connect with nature in intimate ways that ensured their survival over millennia. Their food systems and diets worldwide contain diversity suited to their local environments, and need to be recognized for their values to counter malnutrition and disease and their ability to mitigate the worsening effects of environmental degradation and the introduction of industrially-processed foods that are nutrient-poor and calorie-rich. It is essential to document these food systems so that policies can be created to protect ecosystems and the health of the Indigenous Peoples who know and use their long-evolved cultures and patterns of living. These treasures of human knowledge benefit the entire planet and humankind.

Many national and international policies are in place to protect the rights of Indigenous Peoples, and to showcase traditions that are part of national heritages. Most countries have a branch of government specifically for matters of their Indigenous Peoples. At the international level several United Nations agencies promote issues of Indigenous Peoples' food systems, nutrition, and health, which work with the United Nations Permanent Forum on Indigenous Issues. It is important to recognize disparities faced by Indigenous Peoples by ensuring that national data are disaggregated for indigeneity for indicators of social and economic life, as well as for food security, health, and other measures of well-being. This recognition sets the stage for building platforms and policies for capacity-building and self-determination that are the cornerstones of successful interventions. This is especially true for interventions that promote the many positive qualities of traditional knowledge about the agrobiodiversity within local food systems of Indigenous Peoples to improve nutrition and health.

## Acknowledgements

This chapter is a brief synthesis of an extensive body of work involving CINE and FAO, and countless other partners. Over many years, Indigenous Peoples in 12 diverse rural ecosystems and more than 40 interdisciplinary collaborators created traditional food system documentations and health promotion activities for communities using local food systems. Sentinel publications of this work are cited here. Once again, a special thank you to Bill Erasmus, National Chief of the Dene Nation and Regional Chief of the Assembly of First Nations (Canada), and the CINE Governing Board for initiating CINE in 1993 and for continuing inspiration, guidance, and support.

## References

Centre for Indigenous Peoples' Nutrition and Environment (2009) *Global Health Case Studies – Dalit*, www.mcgill.ca/cine/files/cine/Dalit_Datatables_leafyvegs_Jn06.pdf, accessed 25 January 2016.

Chotiboriboon, S., Tamachotipong, S., Sirisai, S., Dhanamitta, S., Smitasiri, S., Sappasuwan, C., Tantivatanasathien, P. and Eg-Kantrong, P. (2009) 'Thailand: Food system and nutritional status of indigenous children in a Karen community', pp. 59–81 in H. V. Kuhnlein, B. Erasmus and D. Spigelski (eds.), *Indigenous Peoples' Food Systems: The Many Dimensions of Culture, Diversity and Environment for Nutrition and Health*, FAO, Rome, Italy.

Commission on Genetic Resources for Food and Agriculture (CGRFA) (2013) 'Characterization of different food systems, including traditional food systems in relation to biodiversity and nutrition', 14th Regular Session, Item 2.5 of the Provisional Agenda, FAO, Rome, Italy www.fao.org/docrep/meeting/027/mg270e.pdf, accessed 25 January 2016.

Creed-Kanashiro, H., Roche, M., Cerrón, I. T. and Kuhnlein, H. V. (2009) 'Traditional food system of an Awajun community in Peru', pp. 59–81 in H. V. Kuhnlein, B. Erasmus and D. Spigelski (eds.), *Indigenous Peoples' Food Systems: The Many Dimensions of Culture, Diversity and Environment for Nutrition and Health.* FAO, Rome, Italy.

Englberger, L. A., Lorens, A., Albert, K., Pedrus, P., Levendusky, A., Hagilmai, W., Paul, Y., Moses, P., Jim, R., Jose, S., Nelber, D., Santos, G., Laufer, K., Kaufer, L., Larsen, K., Pretrick, M. and Kuhnlein, H. V. (2013) 'Let's go local! Pohnpei promotes local food production and nutrition for health', pp. 191–220 in H. V. Kuhnlein, B. Erasmus, D. Spigelski and B. Burlingame (eds.), *Indigenous Peoples' Food Systems and Wellbeing: Interventions and Policies for Healthy Communities*, FAO, Rome, Italy.

Englberger, L., Schierle, J., Marks, G. C. and Fitzgerald, M. H. (2003) 'Micronesian banana, taro and other foods: Newly recognized sources of provitamin A and other carotenoids', *Journal of Food Composition and Analysis*, vol. 16, pp. 3–19.

Fanzo, J., Holmes, M., Junega, P., Musinguzi, E., Smith, I. F., Ekesa, B. and Bergamini, N. (2011) *Improving Nutrition with Agricultural Biodiversity*, Bioversity International, Maccarese, Italy.

FAO (2008) *Expert Consultation on Nutrition Indicators for Biodiversity 1: Food Composition*, FAO, Rome, Italy.

FAO (2010a) *Expert Consultation on Nutrition Indicators for Biodiversity 2: Food Consumption*, FAO, Rome, Italy.

FAO (2010b) *The State of Food Insecurity in the World*, FAO, Rome, Italy, www.fao.org/docrep/013/i1683e/i1683e.pdf, accessed 25 January 2016.

FAO (2015) *The State of Food Insecurity in the World*, FAO, Rome, Italy, www.fao.org/3/a-i4646e/index.html, accessed 25 January 2016.

FAO (2016a) *International Network of Food Data Systems, Standards and Guidelines*, FAO, Rome, Italy, www.fao.org/infoods/infoods/standards-guidelines/en/, accessed 25 January 2016.

FAO (2016b) *The Food Insecurity Experience Scale*, FAO, Rome, Italy, www.fao.org/economic/ess/ess-fs/voices/fiesscale/en/, accessed 25 January 2016.

FAO (n.d.) *Indigenous Peoples*, FAO, Rome, Italy, www.fao.org/indigenous-peoples/en/, accessed 25 January 2016.

FAO/INFOODS (2013) *Report on the Nutrition Indicator for Biodiversity – Food Composition. Global Progress Report 2012.* FAO, Rome, Italy.

Gaydos, J. K., Thixton, S. and Donatuto, J. (2015) 'Evaluating threats in multinational marine ecosystems: A coast Salish First Nations and tribal perspective', *PLoS ONE*, vol. 10, p. e0144861.

Golden, C. D., Fernald, L. C. H., Brashares, J. S., Rasolofoniaina, B. J. R. and Kremen, C. (2011) 'Benefits of wildlife consumption to child nutrition in a biodiversity hotspot', *Proceedings of the National Academy of Sciences USA*, vol. 108, pp. 19653–19656.

Halwart, M. and Bartley, D. (2007) 'Aquatic biodiversity in rice-based ecosystems', pp. 181–199 in D. I. Jarvis, D. Padoch and H. D. Cooper (eds.), *Managing Biodiversity in Agricultural Ecosystems*, Columbia University Press, Columbia, NY, USA.

International Food Policy Research Institute [IFPRI] (2015) *Global Nutrition Report 2015: Actions and Accountability to Advance Nutrition and Sustainable Development*, IFPRI, Washington DC, USA.

Johnston, J. L., Fanzo, J. C. and Cogill, B. (2014) 'Understanding sustainable diets: A descriptive analysis of the determinants and processes that influence diets and their impact on health, food security and environmental sustainability', *Advances in Nutrition*, no 5, pp. 418–429.

Kennedy, G. and Burlingame, B. (2003) 'Analysis of food composition data on rice from a plant genetic resources perspective', *Food Chemistry*, vol. 80, pp. 589–596.

Kuhnlein, H. V. (1992) 'Change in the use of traditional foods by the Nuxalk Native people of British Columbia', *Ecology of Food and Nutrition*, vol. 27, pp. 259–282.

Kuhnlein, H. V., Erasmus, B. and Spigelski, D. (2009) *Indigenous Peoples' Food Systems: The Many Dimensions of Culture, Diversity and Environment for Nutrition and Health*, FAO, Rome, Italy www.fao.org/docrep/012/i0370e/i0370e00.htm, accessed 25 January 2016.

Kuhnlein, H. V., Erasmus, B., Spigelski, D. and Burlingame, B. (2013) *Indigenous Peoples' Food Systems and Wellbeing: Interventions and Policies for Healthy Communities*, FAO, Rome, Italy, www.fao.org/docrep/018/i3144e/i3144e00.htm, accessed 25 January 2016.

Kuhnlein, H. V. and Humphries, M. M. (2013) *Animal Food Diversity in Indigenous Peoples' Food Systems*', Proceedings: Asia and Pacific Symposium on Sustainable Diets: Human Nutrition and Livestock, FAO, Rome, Italy and Ministry of Industry and Agriculture of Mongolia, Ulaanbaatar, Mongolia.

Kuhnlein, H. V. and Receveur, O. (1996) 'Dietary change and traditional food systems of Indigenous Peoples', *Annual Review of Nutrition*, vol. 16, pp. 417–442.

Kuhnlein, H. V. and Receveur, O. (2007) 'Local cultural animal food contributes high levels of nutrients for Arctic Canadian indigenous adults and children', *Journal of Nutrition*, vol. 137, pp. 1110–1114.

Kuhnlein, H. V., Receveur, O. and Chan, H. M. (2001) 'Traditional food systems research with Canadian Indigenous Peoples', *International Journal of Circumpolar Health*, vol. 60, pp. 112–122.

Kuhnlein, H. V., Smitasiri, S., Yesudas, L., Bhattacharjee, L. Dan and Ahmed, S. (2006) *Documenting Traditional Food Systems of Indigenous Peoples: International Case Studies: Guidelines for Procedures*, Centre for Indigenous Peoples' Nutrition and Environment, McGill University, Montreal, Canada, www.mcgill.ca/cine/sites/mcgill.ca.cine/files/manual.pdf, accessed 25 January 2016.

Oiye, S., Ole Simel, J., Oniang'o, R. and Johns, T. (2009) 'The Maasai food system and food and nutrition security', pp. 59–81 in H. V. Kuhnlein, B. Erasmus and D. Spigelski (eds.), *Indigenous Peoples' Food Systems: The Many Dimensions of Culture, Diversity and Environment for Nutrition and Health*, FAO, Rome, Italy.

Pelto, G. H., Armar-Klemesu, M., Siekmann, J. and Schofield, D. (2013) 'The focused ethnographic study: Assessing the behavioural and local market environment for improving the diets of infants and young children 6–23 months old and its use in three countries', *Maternal and Child Nutrition*, vol. 9, supplement 1, pp. 35–46.

Popkin, B. M., Adair, L. S. and Ng, S. W. (2012) 'Global nutrition transition and the pandemic of obesity in developing countries', *Nutrition Reviews*, vol. 70, pp. 3–21.

Powell, B., Maundu, P., Kuhnlein, H. V. and Johns, T. (2013) 'Wild foods from farm and forest in the East Usambara Mountains, Tanzania', *Ecology of Food and Nutrition*, vol. 52, pp. 451–478.

Salomeyesudas, B. and Satheesh, P. V. (2009) 'Traditional food system of Dalit in Zaheerabad Region, Medak District, Andhra Pradesh, India', pp. 59–81 in H. V. Kuhnlein, B. Erasmus and D. Spigelski (eds.), *Indigenous Peoples' Food Systems: The Many Dimensions of Culture, Diversity and Environment for Nutrition and Health*, FAO, Rome, Italy.

Sims, J. and Kuhnlein, H. V. (2003) *Indigenous Peoples and Participatory Health Research. Planning and Management: Preparing Research Agreements*, World Health Organization (WHO), Geneva, Switzerland, www.who.int/ethics/indigenous_peoples/en/index3.html, accessed 25 January 2016.

Termote, C., Van Damme, P. and Djailo, B. D. (2010) 'Eating from the wild: Turumbu indigenous knowledge on non-cultivated edible plants, Tshopo District, DR Congo', *Ecology of Food and Nutrition*, vol. 49, pp. 173–207.

United Nations Secretariat of the Permanent Forum on Indigenous Issues [UNPFII] (2009) *State of the World's Indigenous Peoples*, Department of Economic and Social Affairs, ST/ESA/328, United Nations, New York, NY, USA.

WHO (2015a) *Micronutrient Deficiencies*, WHO, Geneva, Switzerland, www.who.int/nutrition/topics/ida/en/, accessed 25 January 2016.

WHO (2015b) *Obesity and Overweight*, WHO, Geneva, Switzerland, www.who.int/mediacentre/factsheets/fs311/en/, accessed 25 January 2016.

WHO and Secretariat of the Convention on Biological Diversity (2015) *Connecting Global Priorities: Biodiversity and Human Health: A State of Knowledge Review*, Geneva, Switzerland and Montreal, Canada.

# 25

# AGRICULTURAL BIODIVERSITY FOR HEALTHY DIETS AND HEALTHY FOOD SYSTEMS

*Jessica E. Raneri and Gina Kennedy*

## Introduction

Despite progress in global development, malnutrition remains a serious challenge with 1 in 3 people malnourished, 2 billion suffering from micronutrient deficiencies and 795 million suffering from hunger (IFPRI, 2015). At the same time, there is rising concern over the sustainability of food systems (IPES-Food, 2016) as well as the health of ecosystems and natural resources underpinning our food systems and ultimately our diets (Bereuter and Glickman, 2015; Steffen et al., 2015). The most biodiverse regions are found in developing countries where most of the world's poor and malnourished reside. These populations rely on local biodiversity across multiple dimensions of their livelihoods including for income, food production, household nutrition, medicine, cultural and social practices. However, biodiversity is being eroded and the global agriculture and food system is a significant driver of this, with farming practices shifting away from diverse small scale systems towards larger scale systems based on monoculture (Khoury et al., 2014; IPES-Food, 2016). Poor diet quality and unsustainable food production practices (coupled with increasing population-driven demand) will require the development of systems that are more sustainable, resilient and equitable. Promoting and mainstreaming the use of biodiversity in food systems will be an important component of this. Importantly, empowering local communities to produce and consume biodiverse foods could improve accessibility to a more diversified and nutritionally balanced diet, which at the same time is more environmentally sustainable, especially when enabling policies are in place. This chapter will review the role of agrobiodiversity in the diet and in local food systems, and propose approaches to better use local biodiversity.

## Definitions of agrobiodiversity and food systems

**Box 25.1** provides definitions for the terms biodiversity, agricultural biodiversity and biodiverse foods.

## Food systems

Food systems are the complex of environmental, agricultural and human resources, processes, interactions and externalities linked to what and how we eat from farming, distribution, retailing and consumption (including waste) (Pinstrup-Andersen, 2010). They exist at multiple scales

### Box 25.1 Definition of the terms biodiversity, agricultural biodiversity and biodiverse foods

Biodiversity includes the variety of plants, terrestrial animals and marine and other aquatic resources (species diversity), along with the variety of genes contained in all individual organisms (genetic diversity) and the variety of habitats and biological communities (ecosystem diversity) (Bioversity International, 2011).

Agricultural biodiversity includes ecosystems, animals, plants and microorganisms related to food and agriculture (see the chapters in Section 1 of this Handbook). Every plant, animal and micro-organism plays its part in the regulation of essential ecosystem services, such as water conservation, decomposition of waste, nutrient cycling, pollination, pest and disease control, climate regulation, erosion control, flood prevention, carbon sequestration and many other ecosystem-oriented factors (WHO, UNEP and CBD, 2015).

Biodiverse food is an even more specific term, and is defined as the diversity of plants, animals and other organisms used for food, including the genetic resources within and between species, and provided by ecosystems (FAO-PAR, 2011). This term has a more narrow definition than 'biodiversity' or 'agricultural biodiversity'.

from local to regional to global, and interact with (i.e. influence and are influenced by) other overlapping systems such as climate and agricultural systems. Numerous actors are involved in food systems that influence what we eat, including those directly involved in production, processing or food transformation, distribution, retailing, cooking and vending or sale of food. In recent decades, massive transformations have occurred in the way food systems function, resulting in more capital-intensive farming, decreased crop diversity and longer, more complex supply chains (Hawkes et al., 2012).

## *Local food systems*

Many of the examples used to highlight the relationship between biodiversity and healthy diets operate at the local scale. A local food system provides a more direct interaction between producer, marketer and consumer, and often assumes the consumption of foods that are produced nearby (Feagan, 2007). However, the concept of 'local' is relative, and can have many different definitions, from foods produced in the same village or community, province or even country (Hinrichs, 2003) to foods produced within a specified distance, such as a 400-mile radius from the point of production (Johnson et al., 2013). For the purpose of this chapter, we will refer to local food systems at the community and in-country regional scale, as opposed to national or international scales. Regardless of the geographical radius used to define a 'local' food system, these systems are generally assumed to have several common characteristics and potential benefits, including a shortened food chain, heightened community-level food security, improved sustainability/increased resource efficiency and often a perception of better quality (Hinrichs, 2000; Feagan, 2007). However, due to the unique and context dependent nature of local food systems, each needs to be evaluated as to what the specific outcomes of such a system actually are (Born and Purcell, 2006). There are many different elements involved in any food system, with the three major components being those related to production, marketing and consumption, each of which includes an array of complex factors and issues including individuals, economy and environment. The role of biodiversity in each of these food system components is under-studied, but examples can be used to highlight the potential of biodiversity to contribute to improved and healthier diets from more sustainable food systems.

## Overview of diet quality and measures of biodiverse foods in diets

The definition of diet quality includes aspects of adequacy in terms of meeting energy and nutrient needs, balance or dietary variety and moderation in terms of limiting or avoiding unhealthy dietary components such as salt or trans-fat. A good quality diet is one that meets all vitamin and mineral requirements within the recommended proportions of fat, protein and carbohydrate and also with limited intake of certain dietary components that have been linked to chronic disease (Mozaffarian and Ludwig, 2010). People consume a combination of foods and not simply individual nutrients in isolation. Approaches that consider the synergy between dietary components and diversity within the diet, not just their standalone individual nutrient value, are important (Mozaffarian and Ludwig, 2010).

Different dietary diversity indicators have been developed that capture different levels of diversity: food group diversity, intra-food group diversity and intra-species diversity (**Table 25.1** *Common dietary diversity indicators*).

Inter-food group level indicators are the most commonly collected of all dietary diversity measures and are calculated based on the number of different food groups consumed (e.g. staples, legumes or dairy). Dietary diversity indicators reflect one aspect, but not all important aspects, of diet quality. Studies have shown nutritional quality of diets improves as a higher diversity of

*Table 25.1* Common dietary diversity indicators

| *Level of diet diversity measured* | *Typical measurements* | *Definition* | *References* |
|---|---|---|---|
| Inter-food group diversity | Individual and household dietary diversity scores | The number of food groups consumed by a target individual or household over a standardized reference period | (WHO, 2008; FAO, 2011b; FAO and FHI 360, 2016) |
| | Minimum dietary diversity | The proportion of a target age group consuming a minimum number of food groups over a standardized reference period | (WHO, 2008; FAO and FHI 360, 2016) |
| Intra-food group diversity (potential for species/cultivar/breed/variety level diversity to be captured) | Within food group diversity | The number of different food items consumed within a food group | (Foote et al., 2004) |
| Inter- and intra-species (species/cultivar/breed/variety level) diversity | Across and within species diversity | Count of foods reported in food consumption surveys described at the level of genus, species, subspecies and variety/cultivar/breed. Exceptions are wild and underutilized foods, which are acceptable when described at genus/species level and/or with local name. | (FAO, 2010) |

food items or food groups is consumed (Kennedy et al., 2009; Arimond et al., 2010). Most food-based dietary guidelines include key messages related to the importance of an inter-food group diversified diet, and both WHO and FAO recommend a predominately plant-based diet rich in a variety of vegetables, fruits and pulses (WHO and FAO, 2004).

A drawback of the data collection methods used to construct the most commonly used indicators of dietary diversity (inter-food group based diversity scores) is the lack of information on biodiversity. For example, one can typically understand the percentage of the target population that consumed 'fruit' in the previous 24 hours, but one does not necessarily know the inter-food group diversity consumed (i.e. which fruits?). It is even more difficult to obtain intra-species information on the breeds, varieties or cultivars consumed.

The greatest potential for measuring and understanding the contribution of food biodiversity lies in intra-food group and intra-species diet diversity measures, both of which are not commonly recorded. Foote et al. (2004) showed that intra-food group diversity presented strong associations with nutrient adequacy for some food groups. Intra-dairy food diversity (the number of different foods within that food group) was strongly associated with higher calcium and vitamin A adequacy; intra-grain variety with better folate and magnesium adequacy; intra-fruit diversity with higher probability of adequacy for vitamins C and A; and intra-vegetable diversity showed similar results as fruit diversity, but with weaker associations. However, it is still necessary to consider the role biodiversity does or could have when thinking about the diversity component of these indices. For example, the intra-food group diversity indicator by Foote et al. (2004) would deliver a count of three for dairy diversity when cow milk, cow cheese and cow yoghurt are consumed (one species). At the same time, it would also deliver a count of three when cow milk, goat cheese and sheep yoghurt (three species) were consumed, therefore not necessarily capturing species diversity in the indicator.

Few diet quality studies have explicitly explored or included data below the species level, that is, varietal or breed information. When varietal or breed food diversity is considered, it is often specific to a single or small number of species (Blair et al., 2010). Challenges in collecting dietary intakes of biodiverse foods are often attributed to the lack of skills and knowledge of both researcher and study participants in correctly recalling and identifying varietal level detail; however, additional challenges include often limited scope of research or projects to capture data beyond food group present/absence, lack of suitable tools or methods to collect such data, missing or incomplete nutrient composition data and limited awareness of possible differences in nutrient composition between different species or varieties (Nesbitt et al., 2010). Despite these challenges, FAO has published recommendations for an indicator for biodiversity and food consumption (as defined in **Table 25.1**) (FAO, 2010). Efforts need to be taken to develop assessment tools incorporating such indicators.

## Biodiverse food and diet quality pathways

Households that diversify their production systems are able to influence their diets beyond simply diversifying the foods and nutrients directly available for their consumption. For populations living in urban and/or developed country settings, purchasing foods is the primary, and often only, possibility (although see also the possible contribution of urban agricultural systems; Keding et al., Chapter 32 of this Handbook). However, even the rural poor, who rely to some extent on household production for their diets, often still need markets to access food (Baiphethi and Jacobs, 2009).

There are two key agrobiodiversity production-to-consumption impact pathways that can be marshalled to achieve improvements in diet quality:

1 Increased availability of diverse and nutrient-dense foods for direct consumption by households through own production of both plants and animals, as well as wild harvest/catch.
2 Increased income through the sale and marketing of agricultural biodiversity. This also allows improved household resilience through diversifying livelihood options and improving farm level ecosystem services, which can feed back to supporting total farm productivity. The second pathway can also feed into the first, as excess foods initially planned for a household's own consumption can be sold on the local market.

Nutrition is complex, and it cannot be assumed that the outcomes of improved diet and nutrition will result from the right incentives being in place to implement these pathways without also considering improved targeting, environmental influences such as water and sanitation, education on nutritional issues and women's empowerment (Ruel and Alderman, 2013). Several reviews have shown that income increases alone are often insufficient to bring about positive changes in diet and nutrition (Masset et al., 2012; Webb and Kennedy, 2014; World Bank, 2013). Key features to enable increases in income to be transformed into positive nutrition outcomes include empowering individuals with nutrition knowledge and awareness of the importance of a diverse and healthy diet, inclusive economic or pro-poor growth, income in the hands of women and behaviour change communication (World Bank, 2007, 2013; McNulty, 2013; **Figure 25.1** *Impact pathways for agrobiodiversity for improved diets and nutrition*).

## Biodiversity and improved diets: plant genetic resources and nutrition

The importance of biodiverse foods for improving diets and nutrition has been best documented in food composition science, the study of the amount of macro and micronutrients per 100 g of edible food. The differences in nutrient composition between species, varieties and breeds of cultivated and wild foods are often significant (Charrondière et al., 2013). Ultimately, this could mean the difference between a diet being adequate or inadequate in certain micronutrients and highlights the importance in capturing biodiversity level information in dietary intake assessments (Islam et al., 2016). The nutrient composition of a single variety can differ when cultivated in a different season, different ecosystem/habitat conditions and when different production methods or inputs are used (Bates, 1971). There is a strong evidence base documenting the difference in micronutrient content of different varieties of a single species (Kennedy and Burlingame, 2003; Islam et al., 2016). A recent comparison between millet varieties showed significant differences in iron and calcium contents with ranges between 1.7–18.6 mg and 8–350 mg per 100 g, respectively (Saleh et al., 2013). A similar comparison between different sweet potato varieties showed beta-carotene content (a precursor to vitamin A) varied from 0.2 μg-226 μg/100 g between white, yellow, purple and orange-fleshed varieties (Teow et al., 2007). The nutrient composition of a given variety can also differ when cultivated in a different seasons, different ecosystem/habitat conditions and when different production methods or inputs are used (Bates, 1971).

The shift from traditional to more modern production systems, leading to the introduction of improved varieties and species, has been highlighted as a significant cause of genetic erosion, particularly of local and indigenous species and varieties (FAO, 1997). The shift has been accompanied by changing dietary patterns from traditional to more Westernized diets, with some evidence of an increase in poorer quality diets, with decreasing biodiversity and micronutrients, particularly for rural poor populations (Gómez and Ricketts, 2013), and increasing consumption of processed and energy-dense foods, linked to increases in the prevalence of non-communicable diseases (Popkin, 2006).

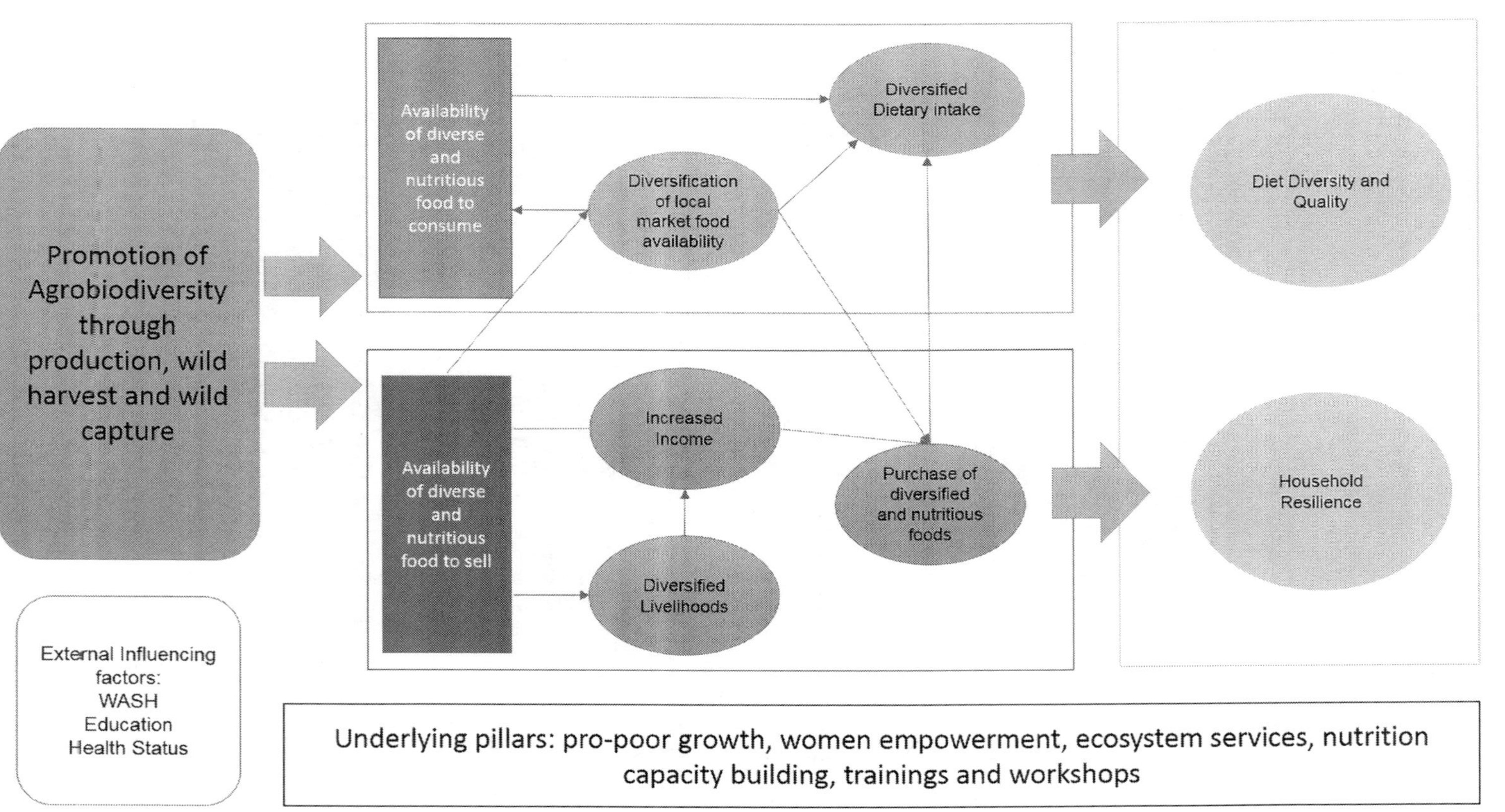


*Figure 25.1* Impact pathways for agrobiodiversity for improved diets and nutrition

*Note*: Pathways are not automatic nor can they be assumed.

*Source*: Authors.

## Biodiversity and improved diets: animal genetic resources and nutrition

Animal source foods (ASF) include meat, fish, insects and the products that are produced from animals including dairy and eggs, and are rich sources of protein, iron, zinc, calcium and vitamin B12. In populations with these specific micronutrient deficiencies, modest increases in consumption of ASF can help bridge nutrient gaps (Murphy and Allen, 2003). Livestock production has a key role to play in ensuring the consumption of ASF, either through direct consumption, and/or through increased income pathways from the sale of their products (Jin et al., 2014).

Similar to the global trend of larger-scale crop production systems, large-scale livestock production has had negative effects on the diversity of livestock genetic resources, although its extent is poorly understood. Up to 70% of the world's livestock genetic resources are managed by the rural poor and directly contribute to their livelihoods. These local breeds often provide multiple ecosystem services and tend to be easier to care for than industrialised large-scale breeds as they are low-input, better able to utilize low-quality fodder and offer multiple services to farming households beyond the consumption or sale of their products (FAO, 2015b).

The nutritional value of local breeds is not well understood. As with plants, however, nutrient composition, and in particular essential fatty acid composition, can vary drastically depending not just on species and breed, but also on rearing practices and conditions (Kim et al., 2009). For example, Medhammar et al. (2012) documented significant differences between vitamin A content of cow (46 µg/100 g – 12% of recommended daily intake [RDI]) and Bactrian camel (96 µg/100 g 24% of RDI) milk. Considerable variation in micronutrient content was also observed among different breeds of the same species: for example, the range of calcium content per 100 g of buffalo milk was 147–220 mg (average 191 mg, S.D 38), and for yak milk it was 119–134 mg/100 g was (average 129 mg, S.D 7), and even this depended on the breed. Variation is also documented between iron content for iron content for eggs of different species: marine turtle (0.9 mg), chicken (1.75 mg), quail (3.65 mg) and duck (3.85 mg) (FAO, 2015a; USDA, 2016).

Not only do different fish and aquatic species provide a range of different nutrients, but the ways in which they are traditionally prepared and consumed can determine the final nutrient content (Uran and Gokoglu, 2014, reviewed also by Halwart and Bartley, Chapter 5 of this Handbook). Small indigenous fish species that poor rural populations rely on for their diets are often consumed whole, meaning that the flesh, bones, internal organs (offal) and eyes are all eaten, resulting in the consumption of important nutrients, including protein, vitamin A, B12, D, calcium, zinc and essential fatty acids (EFAs) including ω-3 (Kongsbak et al., 2008). Larger fish are instead often utilized for their flesh alone, meaning that while protein is provided, many other key nutrients like vitamin A and calcium are not, as these are present in the non-flesh components that are discarded (Roos et al., 2003). Larger wild fish also tend to contain higher amounts of heavy metals, which can have negative effects on health when consumed in large quantities over time (Ouédraogo and Amyot, 2011). Wild fish and aquatic species are, however, an important source of food, especially for the global poor, although overfishing has caused critical decreases in some species population (Zhou et al., 2015). Aquaculture (or fish farming) is part of the solution to ensuring aquatic species diversity is sustained and wild populations not over-exploited, yet has been met with mixed responses. Many consumers perceive farmed fish to be of inferior nutritional quality, particularly in regards to EFAs (Claret et al., 2014). Some studies have shown that while wild fish can have higher concentrations of EFAs, these levels fluctuate seasonally, whereas farmed fish have more constant and higher total fatty acid concentrations, which often results in larger amounts of EFAs being present in farmed fish per portion size (González, 2006).

An ASF alternative to high-resource and carbon-intensive livestock production lies with insects. Insects have long been used in traditional food systems and provide a more sustainable source of energy, EFAs, protein and micronutrients (Mlcek et al., 2014; see also McGill et al., Chapter 22 of this Handbook). As with crops, livestock and fish, there is a large variance in micronutrient composition among different insect species and orders. Like small fish, the consumption of the entire insect body increases the micronutrient content through the ingestion of shells, eyes and internal organs, and generally provide sources of vitamin A, B, C and D (Mlcek et al., 2014). Silkworm pupae have nearly twice as much zinc as chicken (Belluco et al., 2013) and over 4 and 7 times more iron and 3.6 and 3 times more calcium than beef and pork, respectively. Variation in micronutrient content between wild and farmed insects has been attributed to differences in the insect's diets, particularly for carotenoids: farmed insects were found to contain little to none, whereas wild species contained a rich variety (Mlcek et al., 2014). There is increasing interest and curiosity about the potential of insects as a sustainable source of ASF (Mlcek et al., 2014), and in populations where insect consumption has been a traditional part of the diet, there are fewer cultural and social barriers to increasing their consumption. However, the promotion of insects as food has been met with consumer hesitation and even fear, particularly in Western populations or those undergoing Westernization transformation of diets (Rumpold and Schlüter, 2013).

## Biodiversity and improved diets through increased yield, income and resilience

This section will outline how local biodiversity within a landscape can improve diets through increases in yield (and therefore income) via supporting ecosystem service functions, decreasing barriers to accessing nutritious foods and improving household resilience.

### *Landscape biodiversity to support productivity for nutrition*

Utilization of biodiversity in production systems can provide poor rural households the possibility of higher productivity and yields – both for individual species and the farm as a whole – by improving pest management, soil quality, space and light management and capture of above- and below-ground resources (Altieri et al., 2012). In addition to leading to larger quantities and better quality of foods available for direct consumption, increased productivity, resulting in net farming revenue increases, can lead to improved food adequacy (Tibesigwa et al., 2015), most likely through the extra income being used to purchase additional, nutritious foods (Ruel and Alderman, 2013).

The quality of agricultural soil, and the diversity of animals, fungi and microbes it contains can ultimately influence human nutrition (Wall et al., 2015). There is limited evidence that suggests that biodiversity in soil can also influence the effectiveness of agronomic biofortification of crops, with positive correlations of microbial populations in soils with zinc, magnesium, iron and copper uptake and bioavailability in some cereals; the exact mechanisms are not well understood, however (Schulin et al., 2009; Pii et al., 2015; see also Beed et al., Chapter 8 of this Handbook). Soil biodiversity can certainly improve the efficiency of a crop's nutrient uptake from the soil, leading to improved yields and making more food directly available for consumption (Bender and van der Heijden, 2015).

Rich animal pollinator diversity can influence nutrient availability through a decrease of up to 31% in yield gaps on small-scale farms (Garibaldi et al., 2016). Pollinators are estimated to contribute up to 35% of total global food, with staples, fruits and vegetables most vulnerable to yield decreases when confronted with decreased pollinator diversity (Klein et al., 2007; Gemmill-Herren, Chapter 7 of this Handbook). Animal pollinators are critical in the supply of dietary micronutrients, with nearly 100% of vitamin C, over 70% of carotenoids and 55% of folate consumed globally being sourced from animal-pollinated plants (Eilers et al., 2011). Smith et al. (2015) suggested that a 100% loss of pollinators would result in 2.27 billion and 1.4 billion people with reduced vitamin A and folate intake, respectively, due to reduced availability of fruit, vegetables, nuts and seeds.

Honeybees are the dominant pollinator used in large-scale agriculture (Klein et al., 2007). However, decreasing population trends for both domesticated and wild bees worldwide have been documented, often associated with agriculture intensification and the increased use of pesticides and associated habitat loss, as lands are converted for agricultural purposes (Goulson et al., 2015). This high dependence on a single pollinator species highlights a critical vulnerability in the current food system. Wild non-bee pollinators including ants, flies, wasps and beetles are often neglected but have the potential to be almost as effective as honeybees for crop pollination, and respond less negatively to land use changes (Rader et al., 2016). The utilization of wild pollinator diversity can also be financially cheaper and less labour intensive than assisted or hand-pollination (Westerkamp and Gottsberger, 2000). Biodiversity in complex landscapes provides an opportunity to increase pollinator diversity and population sizes by increasing the levels of pollinator-friendly flowering plants in and around farms (Saunders, 2016).

## *Wild and forest genetic resources and nutrition*

Wild and semi-wild foods can be collected or hunted from forests, around villages and even on farms and can be a critical coping strategy for poor rural households, particularly during shocks such as crop failure, drought or loss of off-farm income (Hunter et al., 2016). Wild foods have the potential to play an important role in the diet, specifically by contributing to key micronutrients, in particular for iron, zinc, calcium, vitamin A and iron (Powell et al., 2015; Fungo et al., 2016). For example, wild baobab seed contains more protein than sorghum or millet (Murray et al., 2001) and wild amaranth provides up to six times more β-carotene than savoy cabbage (Achigan-Dako et al., 2014; USDA, 2016). Crop wild relatives may have more desirable micronutrient profiles as well as being more resilient to climate changes than their cultivated counterparts (see also Henry, Chapter 1 of this Handbook), so they can be used in crop improvement programmes that aim to improve nutritional quality (Iizumi and Ramankutty, 2015).

Studies have documented the positive relationship between canopy cover of forests, dietary diversity and the consumption of ASF (Ickowitz et al., 2014). While the exact mechanism of how canopy cover is linked with diet quality is unclear, plausible pathways include the unique production systems implemented in forest areas and the rich biodiversity present in forests supporting ecosystem services such as animal pollination (Powell et al., 2015). However, the importance of wild foods in the diet is not necessarily dependent on their availability. Boedecker et al. (2014) documented low consumption of wild edible plants despite a richly biodiverse environment. While the enabling or determining factors as to how, why and when available wild and forest foods are utilized in different landscapes are not well documented, cultural preferences, tradition and economic status are likely to play a part.

Forests can contribute to nutrition beyond acting as landscapes for the supply of wild foods. Products including timber, seeds and leaves can be utilized for various other purposes, including fuel, fodder, construction materials and medicine, and whether or not used directly by the collecting household, they are often an important source of income. Wild animal and plant products can provide nutrient-dense foods at no immediate financial cost, essentially improving access to healthy and diverse diets by decreasing the cost barrier to purchasing nutrient-rich foods (Termote et al., 2014). Despite the apparent free financial cost of accessing these foods, it is important to consider what negative externalities might be incurred, including over-harvesting and the time-cost burden associated with harvesting (particularly for women). Interestingly, in more traditional local food systems, wild genetic resources tend to be sustainably managed by communities (see also Boshier et al. and Ingram et al., Chapter 3 and Chapter 4 of this Handbook, respectively).

## *Biodiversity for nutrition resilience in the face of changing climates*

With increasing pressure from climate change, including more extreme weather events, researchers and farmers are searching for production solutions to diversify their risks, and adapt their systems. Such changes can cause longer lean seasons, increased incidence of pests or disease and delayed or even destroyed harvests, with the potential to result in serious problems for food and nutrition security (Bebber and Gurr, 2015; Lesk et al., 2016). Climate change is expected to reduce the nutrient composition and availability of foods that can significantly affect the global population's diet (Myers et al., 2014). Identifying which animal breeds or crop varieties are better able to cope with future climates has the potential to ensure continued productivity under changing climatic conditions, which could enable local food systems to adapt to climate change, and continue to make important nutrients available both locally and globally. Intra-species diversity is not the only way to reduce climate change vulnerability, however. Inter-species (and even food group) diversification systems such as mixed crop-livestock-tree farming systems can also help poor households to be more resilient to the effects of climate change (Tibesigwa et al., 2015).

## Biodiversity and improve diets: a Vietnamese case study

A multi-stakeholder effort is being developed by the CGIAR to better understand local food systems and the role of biodiversity at different scales from individuals, households (and their farms), villages and the wider landscapes through participatory research (see example in **Box 25.2** *Vietnam – Thai ethnic groups diversify their gardens and their meals*). The approach is designed to understand and minimize trade-offs between promoting ecosystem service functioning and improving nutrition.

### Box 25.2 Vietnam – Thai ethnic groups diversify their gardens and their meals

A sample of 416 households was randomly selected in the Mai Son district of Northwest Vietnam. Three surveys were administered to capture information on the levels of biodiversity in agricultural production (including capture of wild foods), in the diet and in the market. In total, 398 different species were produced on-farm or collected from the wild. A 24-hour dietary recall study showed that food groups with low consumption (26% of women or children) included legumes, nuts and seeds, dairy, dark green leafy vegetables and vitamin A-rich vegetables and fruit. These food groups also represented a small proportion of the diversity available in the local production (13%) and market (8%) systems. The proportion of women and children reaching Minimum Dietary Diversity (MDD) was 59% and 58%, respectively, and only 18% of women reported that diet diversity was important to prevent undernutrition. Those who reached MDD included a higher percentage of consumers of these food groups compared with those who did not reach it (up to 44%).

A community-based intervention is underway, where locally available but underutilized species or varieties from the most under-consumed crop food groups were selected for promotion. The process included participatory workshops with women to identify and overcome barriers as to why these foods were not produced and consumed more frequently or abundantly (**Figure 25.2** *Women*

*Figure 25.2* Women farmers prioritizing which crops to select from under-consumed food groups to form the basis of intervention

*farmers prioritizing which crops to select from under-consumed food groups to form the basis of intervention*). One example used pumpkin. The two main barriers to production were (a) preference for varieties that remained greener for longer (the flavour was preferred over the sweetness of orange varieties) and (b) unreliable fruit quantity.

Exploring further, participants stated that they did not know that orange pumpkin was more nutritious, and stated that they would try to grow more of it, but did not know appropriate recipes. Further discussions identified that one reason pumpkin plants tended to not produce many fruits was because flowers and leaves were often picked to consume as vegetables. Together with the research team, participants identified solutions to overcome these barriers to develop learning modules: (a) participatory cooking lessons to experiment with orange pumpkin in local recipes and (b) management practices on how to maximize pumpkin fruit formation, including having two plants, one for fruit production and the other for leaf and flower harvest.

Each village then formed a 'diversity club' lead by the village health worker, who delivered basic nutrition education, together with the learning modules focusing on the target crops, and directly linking nutrition with agriculture through seasonal planting and availability calendars.

## Limitations and barriers to understanding the role of biodiversity for improved diets

There are very few national policies specifically targeted at improving conservation and use of biodiversity in local food systems as a means of achieving improved nutrition. In trying to understand the role local biodiversity has in healthy food systems and diets, approaches that look at different aspects of the food system need to be utilized. An understanding of what a current landscape and its production system can offer in terms of supplying nutrients through local biodiversity is one such approach that is relatively easy to implement, but not applied widely, often due to methodological limitations including time, expert knowledge and appropriate validated tools and indicators. The lack of tools, metrics and approaches has inevitably led to a small, disjointed evidence base. Innovative methods and approaches that can support the correct identification and nomenclature of biodiversity during both production and dietary intake assessments is one of many critical factors that hinders efforts from different disciplines to collaborate and link data sets (Auestad and Fulgoni, 2015).

The lack of detailed food composition data, including at the infra-specific level, is often a serious limitation to understanding what potential contribution local foods could have in bridging nutrient gaps. FAO INFOODS advocates for the documentation and sharing of these data, as well as providing training to researchers and other stakeholders; however, this area of research is underfunded. Preferences tend towards funding research on crops and animals that already contribute to current diets substantially, in an attempt to obtain a large, immediate impact. Increased awareness of the critical roles that many biodiverse foods could play in providing solutions to some of the world's current large-scale problems, including climate change, system fragility and malnutrition, is needed to facilitate international cooperation to include biodiversity in global programmes and agendas (Hunter et al., 2016).

Another approach is identifying what are the current barriers to encouraging better utilization of local biodiversity by households and individuals to achieve more diverse and better quality diets. To build the case and understand the comparative advantage that biodiversity has for improving diets, studies are needed that seek to understand what coping strategies different populations will organically adopt in situations where food biodiversity is low (or will decrease), and where certain species or varieties are no longer viable sources of foods or nutrients due to climate change, over-exploitation and decreasing productivity. As regions most vulnerable to climate change are also those that experience high prevalence of malnutrition, these questions are urgent and critical.

Currently, production and diet datasets are difficult to combine. The development of biodiversity nutrition indicators to capture and compare the contribution of biodiversity in production systems, landscapes and diets will facilitate a better understanding of the relationship between these complementary dimensions, and help build the stronger evidence base required to better inform national and global agriculture, nutrition, health and environment policies and strategies.

## Conclusions

The assumption is that biodiversity has a critical role to play in ensuring the sustained supply of diverse and nutritious foods in local food systems. However, the multiple levels and complexity of biodiversity, including its interactions at different scales, can make it difficult to correctly measure and monitor its role in food systems, and in particular diets, in the absence of validated methods and indicators, and clear definitions. The consequence is we do not fully understand the extent of how the current global trend of decreasing biodiversity will quantifiably negatively impact nutrition.

Biodiversity has a critical role to play in ensuring the sustained supply of diverse and nutritious foods in local food systems, from diversity in the soil to increased resilience during climate change and increased micronutrient contents of crops and diets. The role of biodiversity for nutrition is complex, as the relationships between biodiversity at the different landscape scales have a synergistic and often interdependent relationship on each other. Developing specific tools and methods that capture information on biodiversity at different scales, and in particular in the diet, will help a more robust evidence base to be generated. A more complete and extensive evidence base is the key component needed to facilitate the development of national and global policies that promote the conservation of biodiversity through local food system, with the objective of improving diets and nutrition.

## References


Achigan-Dako, E. G., Sogbohossou, O. E. and Maundu, P. (2014) 'Current knowledge on *Amaranthus* spp.: Research avenues for improved nutritional value and yield in leafy amaranths in sub-Saharan Africa', *Euphytica*, vol. 197, pp. 303–317.

Altieri, M. A., Ponti, L. and Nicholls, C. I. (2012) 'Soil fertility, biodiversity and pest management', pp. 72–84 in G. M. Gurr, S. D. Wratten, W. E. Snyder and D. M. Y. Read (eds.), *Biodiversity and Insect Pests: Key Issues for Sustainable Management*, John Wiley and Sons, UK.

Arimond, M., Wiesmann, D., Becquey, E., Carriquiry, A., Daniels, M., Deitchler, M., Fanou-Fogny, N., Joseph, M., Kennedy, G., Martin-Prevel, Y. and Brouwer, I. (2010) 'Simple food group diversity indicators predict micronutrient adequacy of women's diets in five diverse, resource poor settings', *Journal of Nutrition*, vol. 140, pp. 2059S–2069S.

Auestad, N. and Fulgoni, V. L. (2015) 'What current literature tells us about sustainable diets: Emerging research linking dietary patterns, environmental sustainability, and economics', *Advances in Nutrition*, vol. 6, pp. 19–36.

Baiphethi, M. N. and Jacobs, P. T. (2009) 'The contribution of subsistence farming to food security in South Africa', *Agrekon*, vol. 48, pp. 459–482.

Bates, T. E. (1971) 'Factors affecting critical nutrient concentrations in plants and their evaluation: A review', *Soil Science*, vol. 112, pp. 116–130.

Bebber, D. P. and Gurr, S. J. (2015) 'Crop-destroying fungal and oomycete pathogens challenge food security', *Fungal Genetics and Biology*, vol. 74, pp. 62–64.

Belluco, S., Losasso, C., Maggioletti, M., Alonzi, C. C., Paoletti, M. G. and Ricci, A. (2013) 'Edible insects in a food safety and nutritional perspective: A critical review', *Comprehensive Reviews in Food Science and Food Safety*, vol. 12, pp. 296–313.

Bender, S. F. and van der Heijden, M. G. A. (2015) 'Soil biota enhance agricultural sustainability by improving crop yield, nutrient uptake and reducing nitrogen leaching losses', *Journal of Applied Ecology*, vol. 52, pp. 228–239.

Bereuter, D. and Glickman, D. (2015) 'Healthy food for a healthy world: Leveraging agriculture and food to improve global nutrition', *Chicago Council on Global Affairs*, Chicago, IL, USA www.thechicagocouncil.org/sites/default/files/GlobalAg-HealthyFood_FINAL.pdf

Bioversity International (2011) *Bioversity International Nutrition Strategy 2011–2021: Resilient Food and Nutrition Systems: Analyzing the Role of Agricultural Biodiversity in Enhancing Human Nutrition and Health*, Bioversity International, Maccarese, Italy.

Blair, M. W., González, L. F., Kimani, P. M. and Butare, L. (2010) 'Genetic diversity, inter-gene pool introgression and nutritional quality of common beans (*Phaseolus vulgaris* L.) from Central Africa', *Theoretical and Applied Genetics*, vol. 121, pp. 237–248.

Boedecker, J., Termote, C., Assogbadjo, A. E., Van Damme, P. and Lachat, C. (2014) 'Dietary contribution of Wild Edible Plants to women's diets in the buffer zone around the Lama forest, Benin – an underutilized potential', *Food Security*, vol. 6, pp. 833–849.

Born, B. and Purcell, M. (2006) 'Avoiding the local trap scale and food systems in planning research', *Journal of Planning Education and Research*, vol. 26, pp. 195–207.

Charrondière, U. R., Stadlmayr, B., Rittenschober, D., Mouille, B., Nilsson, E., Medhammar, E., Olango, T., Eisenwagen, S., Persijn, D., Ebanks, K. and Nowak, V. (2013) 'FAO/INFOODS food composition database for biodiversity', *Food Chemistry*, vol. 140, pp. 408–412.

Claret, A., Guerrero, L., Ginés, R., Grau, A., Hernández, M. D., Aguirre, E., Peleteiro, J. B., Fernández-Pato, C. and Rodríguez-Rodríguez, C. (2014) 'Consumer beliefs regarding farmed versus wild fish', *Appetite*, vol. 79, pp. 25–31.

Eilers, E. J., Kremen, C., Greenleaf, S. S., Garber, A. K. and Klein, A. M. (2011) 'Contribution of pollinator-mediated crops to nutrients in the human food supply', *PLoS ONE*, vol. 6 p. e21363.

Food and Agriculture Organization of the United States (FAO) (1997) *The State of the World's Plant Genetic Resources for Food and Agriculture*, FAO, Rome, Italy.

FAO (2010) *Expert Consultation on Nutrition Indicators for Biodiversity 2: Food Consumption*, FAO, Rome, Italy.

FAO (2011a) *World Livestock 2011 – Livestock in Food Security*, FAO, Rome, Italy.

FAO (2011b) *Guidelines for Measuring Household and Individual Dietary Diversity*, FAO, Rome, Italy.

FAO (2015a) *FAO/INFOODS Food Composition Database for Biodiversity Version 3.0 – BioFoodComp3.0*, FAO, Rome, Italy.

FAO (2015b) *The Second Report on the State of the World's Animal Genetic Resources for Food and Agriculture*, B. D. Scherf and D. Pilling (eds.), FAO Commission on Genetic Resources for Food and Agriculture Assessments, Rome, Italy, www.fao.org/3/a-i4787e/index.html

FAO and FHI 360 (2016) *Minimum Dietary Diversity for Women: A Guide for Measurement*, FAO, Rome, Italy.

FAO-PAR (2011) *Biodiversity for Food and Agriculture*, FAO, Rome, Italy.

Feagan, R. (2007) 'The place of food: Mapping out the "local" in local food systems', *Progress in Human Geography*, vol. 31, pp. 23–42.

Foote, J. A., Murphy, S. P., Wilkens, L. R., Basiotis, P. P. and Carlson, A. (2004) 'Dietary variety increases the probability of nutrient adequacy among adults', *The Journal of Nutrition*, vol. 134, pp. 1779–1785.

Fungo, R., Muyonga, J., Kabahenda, M., Kaaya, A., Okia, C. A., Donn, P., Mathurin, T., Tchingsabe, O., Tiegehungo, J. C., Loo, J. and Snook, L. (2016) 'Contribution of forest foods to dietary intake and their association with household food insecurity: A cross-sectional study in women from rural Cameroon', *Public Health Nutrition*, vol. 2016, pp. 1–12.

Garibaldi, L. A., Carvalheiro, L. G., Vaissière, B. E., Gemmill-Herren, B., Hipólito, J., Freitas, B. M., Ngo, H. T., Azzu, N., Sáez, A., Åström, J. and An, J. (2016) 'Mutually beneficial pollinator diversity and crop yield outcomes in small and large farms', *Science*, vol. 351, pp. 388–391.

Gómez, M. I. and Ricketts, K. D. (2013) 'Food value chain transformations in developing countries: Selected hypotheses on nutritional implications', *Food Policy*, vol. 42, pp. 139–150.

González, S., Flick, G. J., O'Keefe, S. F., Duncan, S. E., McLean, E. and Craig, S. R. (2006) 'Composition of farmed and wild yellow perch (*Perca flavescens*)', *Journal of Food Composition and Analysis*, vol. 19, pp. 720–726.

Goulson, D., Nicholls, E., Botías, C. and Rotheray, E. L. (2015) 'Bee declines driven by combined stress from parasites, pesticides, and lack of flowers', *Science*, vol. 347, p. 1255957.

Hawkes, C., Friel, S. Lobstein, T. and Lang, T. (2012) 'Linking agricultural policies with obesity and non-communicable diseases: A new perspective for a globalizing world', *Food Policy*, vol. 37, pp. 343–353.

Hinrichs, C. C. (2000) 'Embeddedness and local food systems: Notes on two types of direct agricultural market', *Journal of Rural Studies*, vol. 16, pp. 295–303.

Hinrichs, C. C. (2003) 'The practice and politics of food system localization', *Journal of Rural Studies*, vol. 19, pp. 33–45.

Hunter, D., Özkan, I., Moura de Oliveira Beltrame, D., Samarasinghe, W. L. G., Wasike, V. W., Charrondière, U. R., Borelli, T. and Sokolow, J. (2016) 'Enabled or disabled: Is the environment right for using biodiversity to improve nutrition?', *Frontiers in Nutrition*, vol. 3, p. 14.

Ickowitz, A., Powell, B., Salim, M. A. and Sunderland, T. C. (2014) 'Dietary quality and tree cover in Africa', *Global Environmental Change*, vol. 24, pp. 287–294.

Iizumi, T. and Ramankutty, N. (2015) 'How do weather and climate influence cropping area and intensity?', *Global Food Security*, vol. 4, pp. 46–50.

International Food Policy Research Institute (IFPRI) (2015) *Global Nutrition Report 2015: Actions and Accountability to Advance Nutrition and Sustainable Development*, Washington, DC, USA, www.ifpri.org/publication/global-nutrition-report-2015

IPES-Food (2016) *From Uniformity to Diversity: A Paradigm Shift from Industrial Agriculture to Diversified Agro Ecological Systems*, International Panel of Experts on Sustainable Food Systems, www.ipes-food.org/images/Reports/UniformityToDiversity_FullReport.pdf

Islam, S. N., Nusrat, T., Begum, P. and Ahsan, M. (2016) 'Carotenoids and β-carotene in orange fleshed sweet potato: A possible solution to vitamin A deficiency', *Food Chemistry*, vol. 199, pp. 628–631.

Jin, M. and Iannotti, L. L. (2014) 'Livestock production, animal source food intake, and young child growth: The role of gender for ensuring nutrition impacts', *Social Science & Medicine*, vol. 105, pp. 16–21.

Johnson, R., Aussenberg, A. R. and Cowan, T. (2013) *The Role of Local Food Systems in U.S. Farm Policy*, Congressional Research Service, Washington, DC, USA.

Kennedy, G. and Burlingame, B. (2003) 'Analysis of food composition data on rice from a plant genetic resources perspective', *Food Chemistry*, vol. 80, pp. 589–596.

Kennedy, G., Fanou, N., Seghieri, C. and Brouwer, I. D. (2009) *Dietary Diversity as a Measure of the Micronutrient Adequacy of Women's Diets: Results from Bamako, Mali Site*, Food and Nutrition Technical Assistance II Project, Academy for Educational Development, Washington, DC, USA.

Khoury, C. K., Bjorkman, A. D., Dempewolf, H., Ramirez-Villegas, J., Guarino, L., Jarvis, A. and Struik, P. C. (2014) 'Increasing homogeneity in global food supplies and the implications for food security', *Proceedings of the National Academy of Sciences USA*, vol. 111, pp. 4001–4006.

Kim, D. H., Seong, P. N., Cho, S. H., Kim, J. H., Lee, J. M., Jo, C. and Lim, D. G. (2009) 'Fatty acid composition and meat quality traits of organically reared Korean native black pigs', *Livestock Science*, vol. 120, pp. 96–102.

Klein, A. M., Vaissiere, B. E., Cane, J. H., Steffan-Dewenter, I., Cunningham, S. A., Kremen, C. and Tscharntke, T. (2007) 'Importance of pollinators in changing landscapes for world crops', *Proceedings of the Royal Society of London B – Biological Sciences*, vol. 274, pp. 303–313.

Kongsbak, K., Thilsted, S. H. and Wahed, M. A. (2008) 'Effect of consumption of the nutrient-dense, freshwater small fish *Amblypharyngodon mola* on biochemical indicators of vitamin A status in Bangladeshi children: A randomised, controlled study of efficacy', *The British Journal of Nutrition*, vol. 99, pp. 581–597.

Lesk, C., Rowhani, P. and Ramankutty, N. (2016) 'Influence of extreme weather disasters on global crop production', *Nature*, vol. 529, pp. 84–87.

Masset, E., Haddad, L., Cornelius, A. and Isaza-Castro, J. (2012) 'Effectiveness of agricultural interventions that aim to improve nutritional status of children: Systematic review', *British Medical Journal*, vol. 344, p. d8222.

McNulty, J. (2013) *Challenges and Issues in Nutrition Education*, Nutrition Education and Consumer Awareness Group, FAO, Rome, Italy.

Medhammar, E., Wijesinha-Bettoni, R., Stadlmayr, B., Nilsson, E., Charrondiere, U. R. and Burlingame, B. (2012) 'Composition of milk from minor dairy animals and buffalo breeds: A biodiversity perspective', *Journal of the Science of Food and Agriculture*, vol. 92, pp. 445–474.

Mlcek, J., Rop, O., Borkovcova, M. and Bednarova, M. (2014) 'A comprehensive look at the possibilities of edible insects as food in Europe: A review', *Polish Journal of Food and Nutrition Sciences*, vol. 64, pp. 147–157.

Mozaffarian, D. and Ludwig, D. S. (2010) 'Dietary guidelines in the 21st Century – a time for food', *Journal of the American Medical Association*, vol. 304, pp. 681–682.

Murphy, S. P. and Allen, L. H. (2003) 'Nutritional importance of animal source foods', *The Journal of Nutrition*, vol. 133, pp. 3932S–3935S.

Murray, S. S., Schoeninger, M. J., Bunn, H. T., Pickering, T. R. and Marlett, J. A. (2001) 'Nutritional composition of some wild plant foods and honey used by Hadza foragers of Tanzania', *Journal of Food Composition and Analysis*, vol. 14, pp. 3–13.

Myers, S. S., Zanobetti, A., Kloog, I., Huybers, P., Leakey, A. D., Bloom, A., Carlisle, E., Dietterich, L. H., Fitzgerald, G., Hasegawa, T. and Holbrook, N. M. (2014) 'Rising $CO_2$ threatens human nutrition', *Nature*, vol. 510, p. 139.

Nesbitt, M., McBurney, R. P., Broin, M. and Beentje, H. J. (2010) 'Linking biodiversity, food and nutrition: The importance of plant identification and nomenclature', *Journal of Food Composition and Analysis*, vol. 23, pp. 486–498.

Ouédraogo, O. and Amyot, M. (2011) 'Effects of various cooking methods and food components on bioaccessibility of mercury from fish', *Environmental Research*, vol. 111, pp. 1064–1069.

Pii, Y., Mimmo, T., Tomasi, N., Terzano, R., Cesco, S. and Crecchio, C. (2015) 'Microbial interactions in the rhizosphere: Beneficial influences of plant growth-promoting rhizobacteria on nutrient acquisition process: A review', *Biology and Fertility of Soils*, vol. 51, pp. 403–415.

Pinstrup-Andersen, P. (2010) *The African Food System and Its Interaction with Human Health and Nutrition*, Cornell University Press, Ithaca, NY, USA.

Popkin, B. M. (2006) 'Global nutrition dynamics: The world is shifting rapidly toward a diet linked with non-communicable diseases', *American Journal of Clinical Nutrition*, vol. 84, pp. 289–298.

Powell, B., Thilsted, S. H., Ickowitz, A., Termote, C., Sunderland, T. and Herforth, A. (2015) 'Improving diets with wild and cultivated biodiversity from across the landscape', *Food Security*, vol. 7, pp. 535–554.

Rader, R., Bartomeus, I., Garibaldi, L. A., Garratt, M. P., Howlett, B. G., Winfree, R., Cunningham, S. A., Mayfield, M. M., Arthur, A. D., Andersson, G. K. and Bommarco, R. (2016) 'Non-bee insects are important contributors to global crop pollination', *Proceedings of the National Academy of Sciences USA*, vol. 113, pp. 146–151.

Romanelli, C., Cooper, D., Campbell-Lendrum, D., Maiero, M., Karesh, W. B., Hunter, D. and Golden, C. D. (2015) *Connecting Global Priorities: Biodiversity and Human Health: A State of Knowledge Review*, WHO/CBD, Rome, Italy.

Roos, N., Islam, M. M. and Thilsted, S. H. (2003) 'Small indigenous fish species in Bangladesh: Contribution to vitamin A, calcium and iron intakes', *The Journal of Nutrition*, vol. 133, pp. 4021S–4026S.

Ruel, M. T. and Alderman, H. (2013) 'Nutrition-sensitive interventions and programmes: How can they help to accelerate progress in improving maternal and child nutrition?', *The Lancet*, vol. 382, pp. 536–551.

Rumpold, B. A. and Schlüter, O. K. (2013) 'Potential and challenges of insects as an innovative source for food and feed production', *Innovative Food Science and Emerging Technologies*, vol. 17, pp. 1–11.

Saleh, A. S., Zhang, Q., Chen, J. and Shen, Q. (2013) 'Millet grains: Nutritional quality, processing, and potential health benefits', *Comprehensive Reviews in Food Science and Food Safety*, vol. 12, pp. 281–295.

Saunders, M. E. (2016) 'Resource connectivity for beneficial insects in landscapes dominated by monoculture tree crop plantations', *International Journal of Agricultural Sustainability*, vol. 14, pp. 82–99.

Schulin, R., Khoshgoftarmanesh, A., Afyuni, M., Nowack, B. and Frossard, E. (2009) 'Effects of soil management on zinc uptake and its bioavailability in plants', pp. 95–114 in G. S. Banuelos and Z-Q. Lin (eds.), *Development and Use of Biofortified Agricultural Products*, CRC Press, Boca Raton, FL, USA.

Smith, M. R., Singh, G. M., Mozaffarian, D. and Myers, S. S. (2015) 'Effects of decreases of animal pollinators on human nutrition and global health: A modelling analysis', *The Lancet*, vol. 386, pp. 1964–1972.

Steffen, W., Richardson, K., Rockström, J., Cornell, S. E., Fetzer, I., Bennett, E. M. and Sörlin, S. (2015) 'Planetary boundaries: Guiding human development on a changing planet', *Science*, vol. 347, p. 1259855.

Teow, C. C., Truong, V. D., McFeeters, R. F., Thompson, R. L., Pecota, K. V. and Yencho, G. C. (2007) 'Antioxidant activities, phenolic and β-carotene contents of sweet potato genotypes with varying flesh colours', *Food Chemistry*, vol. 103, pp. 829–838.

Termote, C., Raneri, J., Deptford, A. and Cogill, B. (2014) 'Assessing the potential of wild foods to reduce the cost of a nutritionally adequate diet: An example from eastern Baringo District, Kenya', *Food and Nutrition Bulletin*, vol. 35, pp. 458–479.

Tibesigwa, B., Visser, M. and Turpie, J. (2015) 'The impact of climate change on net revenue and food adequacy of subsistence farming households in South Africa', *Environment and Development Economics*, vol. 20, pp. 327–353.

United States Department of Agriculture (USDA) (2016) *National Nutrient Database for Standard Reference Version 2.6.1*, USDA, Washington, DC, USA.

Uran, H. and Gokoglu, N. (2014) 'Effects of cooking methods and temperatures on nutritional and quality characteristics of anchovy (*Engraulis encrasicholus*)', *Journal of Food Science and Technology*, vol. 51, pp. 722–778.

Wall, D. H., Nielsen, U. N. and Six, J. (2015) 'Soil biodiversity and human health', *Nature*, vol. 528, pp. 69–76.

Webb, P. and Kennedy, E. (2014) 'Impacts of agriculture on nutrition: Nature of the evidence and research gaps', *Food and Nutrition Bulletin*, vol. 35, pp. 126–132.

Westerkamp, C. and Gottsberger, G. (2000) 'Diversity pays in crop pollination', *Crop Science*, vol. 40, pp. 1209–1222.

World Bank (2007) *From Agriculture to Nutrition: Pathways, Synergies and Outcomes*, The World Bank Agriculture and Rural Development Department, Washington DC, USA.

World Bank (2013) *Improving Nutrition through Multisectoral Approaches*, The World Bank, Washington, DC, USA.

World Health Organization (WHO) and FAO (2004) *Vitamin and Mineral Requirements in Human Nutrition*, 2nd ed., Geneva, Switzerland.

WHO (2008) *Indicators for Assessing Infant and Young Child Feeding Practices, Part 1: Definitions*, Conclusions of a Consensus Meeting Held 6–8 November 2007, in Washington, DC, USA.

WHO, UNEP and Convention on Biological Diversity [CBD] (2015) *Connecting Global Priorities: Biodiversity and Human Health: A State of Knowledge Review*, www.cbd.int/en/health/stateofknowledge\nhttp://apps.who.int/iris/bitstream/10665/174012/1/9789241508537_eng.pdf

Zhou, S., Smith, A. D. and Knudsen, E. E. (2015) 'Ending overfishing while catching more fish', *Fish and Fisheries*, vol. 16, pp. 716–722.

# PART 5

# The drivers of agricultural biodiversity

# 26

# LAW, POLICY AND AGRICULTURAL BIODIVERSITY

*Juliana Santilli*

## Introduction

The Convention on Biological Diversity (CBD) is considered to be the first legal instrument to attempt to comprehensively regulate the conservation and use of biological diversity at a global scale. It entered into force on 29 December 1993 after being signed by 157 countries in the course of the 2nd Conference of the United Nations on Environment and Development (UNCED), which had taken place in Rio de Janeiro the previous year. The CBD has three principal objectives: the conservation of biological diversity, the sustainable use of the *components* of biological diversity, and the 'fair and equitable sharing' of the benefits arising from their utilization. The CBD is one of the mostly widely ratified international instruments: 192 countries are now parties to the CBD, in addition to the European Union. The members include every country that is a member of the UN with the exception of the United States, Andorra and South Sudan. The aspects of the CBD relating to the sharing of the benefits of the use of genetic resources have been supplemented by Nagoya Protocol (NP) on Access to Genetic Resources and the Fair and Equitable Sharing of Benefits Arising from their Utilization in a new international agreement, which was adopted at the 10th meeting of the Conference of the Parties (COP) to the CBD in Nagoya, Japan, on 29 October 2010. The NP entered into force on 12 October 2014, and aims to ensure that the benefits arising from the utilization of genetic resources are shared fairly and equitably (Santilli, 2011).

The CBD and NP brought about a profound change to the way in which genetic resources of relevance to agriculture are viewed as 'common heritage of humankind'. Under the CBD, such genetic resources are understood to be subject to sovereign rights of nation states. The regulation of how – and by whom – they are accessed, is therefore subject to national law of the countries concerned (for an interpretation of the possible consequences of this, see also Mulvany, Chapter 43 of this Handbook). The CBD also states that access to genetic resources must be subject to Prior Informed Consent (PIC) and granted in 'mutually agreed upon terms', and to fair and equitable sharing of any benefits which might derive from their use (Santilli, 2013a; Engels and Rudebjer, Chapter 41 of this Handbook).

According to the CBD, the conditions under which genetic resources, including those of relevance to food and agriculture, are accessed, or under which benefits arising from their use are shared, need to be regulated under bilateral agreements between the country which provides the genetic resources, and that which is making use of them. This also applies to traditional knowledge which is associated with genetic resources or their use, and must be agreed on a case-by-case basis (Santilli, 2013a; see also Villanueva et al., Chapter 27 of this Handbook). Parties of the CBD must also agree to 'respect, preserve and maintain knowledge, innovations and practices of indigenous and local communities'. This system was principally developed to regulate access to wild genetic resources for pharmaceutical or chemical purposes, or other non-food- or agriculture-related uses.

Following the adoption of the CBD, it came to be recognized that plant genetic resources (including crops, landraces, wild relatives; see Henry, Chapter 1 of this Handbook) were subject to special requirements distinct from those relating to other genetic resources (Moore and Tymowski, 2005; Halewood and Nnadozie, 2008; Frison et al., 2011). The recognition of this 'special nature' of plant genetic resources led to the development of the first international instrument concerned specifically with their conservation and sustainable use, the International Treaty on Plant Genetic Resources for Food and Agriculture (ITPGRFA; **Box 26.1** *Summary of the key features of the PGRFA*; and Andersen, Chapter 28 of this Handbook). The ITPGRFA is a legally-binding instrument which also mandates the 'fair and equitable' sharing of any benefits arising from the use of plant-related genetic resources. The ITPGRFA also created a global common pool of plant genetic resources for food and agriculture (currently limited to a list of 64 crops and forages conserved in public domain *ex situ* collections) – these crops are categorized under Annex I of the Treaty and their usage is governed under a multilateral system (MLS). The ITPGRFA was adopted on 3 November 3 2001, and came into effect on 29 June 2004. Notably, the ITPGRFA operates in concordance with the CBD, that is, the laws regulating the 'fair and equitable' sharing of benefits are vested in the national law of the countries to whom the genetic resources 'belong' but differs with regard to the status of those crops designated under Annex I and governed under the MLS rather than the bilateral regime of the CBD (**Table 26.1** *Main differences between the CBD bilateral regime and the multilateral system [FAO Treaty]*).

According to the preamble of the ITPGRFA, parties are 'convinced of the special nature of PGRFA, their distinctive features and problems needing distinctive solutions'. Some of the distinctive features of PGRFA are summarized in **Box 26.1**.

*Table 26. 1* Main differences between the CBD bilateral regime and the multilateral system (FAO Treaty)[1]

| | *CBD* | *FAO Treaty (Multilateral System)* |
|---|---|---|
| Scope | All forms of biodiversity, including both wild and domesticated species. | The Treaty covers all plant genetic resources for food and agriculture, but the multilateral system includes only those that are listed in Annex I, *and* which are under management and control of the contracting parties and in public domain. |
| Objectives | Conservation of biological diversity, sustainable use of the components of biological diversity and fair and equitable sharing of the benefits arising out of the utilization of genetic resources. | Conservation and sustainable use of plant genetic resources for food and agriculture and the fair and equitable sharing of the benefits arising out of their use, in harmony with CBD, for sustainable agriculture and food security. |

| | CBD | FAO Treaty (Multilateral System) |
|---|---|---|
| Access purposes | Conservation and sustainable use for any purposes, in principle, but CBD was conceived mainly for chemical, pharmaceutical, and/or other non-food/feed uses. | Utilization and conservation for research, breeding and training for food and agriculture, and as long as it does not include chemical, pharmaceutical and/or other non-food/feed industrial uses. |
| Access and benefit-sharing | CBD recognizes sovereign rights of states over their natural resources, and the authority to determine access to genetic resources rests with national governments and is subject to national access and benefit-sharing laws.<br><br>Access depends on 'mutually agreed upon terms", established through bilateral contracts between providers and users, on a case by case basis. Access is subject to prior informed consent of the country of origin of resources, and to fair and equitable sharing of benefits deriving from their use.<br><br>Access to associated traditional knowledge depends also on prior informed consent of Indigenous peoples and local communities. | Contracting parties (of the FAO Treaty) agree to establish a multilateral system of access and benefit sharing (which applies only to 35 food crops and 29 forages listed in Annex I of the Treaty, under the management and control of the contracting parties and in the public domain). A Standard Material Transfer Agreement (SMTA) establishes access and benefit-sharing conditions, and access is facilitated and expeditious. Benefit-sharing is mandatory only when commercialized products (that incorporate material accessed from the multilateral system) are *not* available without restriction to others for further research and breeding (ex: patented genetic materials). The equitable share corresponds to 1.1% of gross product sales minus 30%, which represents 0.77% *or* 0.5% of all product sales resulting from the same crop.<br><br>Other benefit-sharing mechanisms are: exchange of information, access to and transfer of technology and capacity-building. |
| Forms of conservation | *Ex situ* conservation is considered as complementary to *in situ* conservation, and must preferably take place in the country of origin of genetic resources. | Articles 5 and 6 of the FAO treaty establishes principles and guidelines for *in situ*, on-farm and *ex situ* conservation of all plant genetic resources for food and agriculture.<br><br>The multilateral system of access and benefit-sharing (articles 12 and 13) apply only to plant genetic resources listed in Annex I and under management and control of the contracting parties and in public domain.<br><br>Access to plant genetic resources for food and agriculture found in *in situ* conditions must be provided according to national laws. |

*Sources*: CBD, articles 1, 8, 9 and 15 (www.cbd.int/convention/text/, accessed 10 August 2015) and FAO Treaty, articles 1, 5,6, 10, 11, 12 and 13 (www.planttreaty.org/texts_en.htm).

## Box 26.1 Summary of the key features of the PGRFA

- Migrations and exchanges among different countries have led to the development of plant varieties whose composition is based on genetic materials from many geographical origins, which can often make it difficult to attribute a single geographical origin to a given plant variety. In such cases, it may not even be possible to accurately identify all the progenitor germplasm involved in the development of the new variety and even where they are known it is challenging to evaluate the relative importance of each variety. For example, the spring bread wheat variety known as Veery, developed by the International Maize and Wheat Improvement Center (CIMMYT), was the product of 3,170 different crosses involving some 51 parental varieties, from at least 26 different countries (Moore and Tymowski, 2005, p. 24).
- All countries are dependent, to a greater or lesser extent, on PGRFA originating from other parts of the world. There is no self-sufficient country in terms of PGRFA and all are inter-dependent, with an average of 50% dependence on other countries (Palacios, 1997). This inter-dependence among countries is greater in regard to PGRFA than regarding other genetic resources. Therefore, countries frequently need to access and use PGRFA originating from other countries for research and breeding purposes, as well as for direct use in their agricultural and food systems. Maintaining the flow and exchange of PGRFA is essential to breeders, farmers and consumers, especially in the face of climate change-related breeding challenges (Fujisaka et al., 2009).
- According to the ITPGRFA, parties are obliged to promote and support the conservation of their PGRFA. This includes both *in situ* and *ex situ* conservation approaches, but also specifies the obligation to support the efforts of farmers and local communities to manage and conserve plant genetic resources on-farm. The ITPGRFA is, therefore, the first legally-binding international treaty that has acknowledged the role of local farmers (and farming communities) in the conservation of agrobiodiversity. The ITPGRFA does not specify exactly kinds of measures should be taken in this regard, but does suggest certain legal actions (**Table 26.2** *Measures for safeguarding genetic resources under the ITPGRFA*).
- In the exercise of their sovereign rights, the Treaty's parties agreed to establish a multilateral system (MLS) of access and benefit sharing, both to facilitate access to PGRFA, and to share, in a fair and equitable way, the benefits arising from the utilization of these resources (Chiarolla and Jungcurt, 2011). The MLS applies only to 35 food crops and 29 forage species (including legumes and grasses) that are listed in Annex I of the Treaty (see **Table 26.3** *List of crops covered under the multilateral system (Annex I of the Treaty): food crops*; and **Table 26.4** *List of crops covered under the multilateral system (Annex I of the Treaty): forages*) and that are under the management and control of parties and in the public domain. Forages were included because they are mainly destined for animal feed, which are then consumed by humans. This access is provided freely (or for a minimal charge), provided that this access is solely for purposes of conservation, and of utilization and research, breeding and training, and may not include chemical, pharmaceutical and/or other industrial uses (e.g. drug discovery by pharmaceutical concerns, or production of bioethanol or other biofuels). Annex I plant genetic resources are considered global commons (Hermitte and Kahn, 2004).

*Source*: Adapted from Santilli (2013a).

*Table 26.2* Measures for safeguarding genetic resources under the ITPGRFA

| *Category* | *Aims* |
|---|---|
| Agricultural policy frameworks | – To promote the development and maintenance of diverse farming systems that enhance the sustainable use of agricultural biological diversity and other natural resources.<br>– To review and adjust breeding strategies and regulations concerning variety release and seed distribution. |
| Research frameworks | – To strengthen research which enhances and conserves biological diversity by maximizing intra- and interspecific variation for the benefit of farmers, especially those who generate and use their own varieties and apply ecological principles in maintaining soil fertility and in combating diseases, weeds and pests. |
| Plant breeding programmes | – To promote breeding efforts which strengthen the capacity to develop varieties best adapted to social, economic and ecological conditions, including in marginal areas.<br>– To promote the inclusion of farmer participation, especially in the developing world.<br>– To create strong links between plant breeding and agricultural development in order to reduce crop vulnerability and genetic erosion, and promote increased world food production compatible with sustainable development. |
| Germplasm availability | – To broaden the genetic base of crops and increasing the range of genetic diversity available to farmers.<br>– To promote greater use of local and locally adapted crops, varieties and underutilized species.<br>– To support the wider use of diversity of varieties and species in on-farm management. |

*Source*: Adapted from Santilli (2013a).Used with permission.

*Table 26.3* List of crops covered under the multilateral system (Annex I of the Treaty): food crops

| *Crop* | *Genus* | *Observations* |
|---|---|---|
| Breadfruit | *Artocarpus* | Breadfruit only |
| Asparagus | *Asparagus* | |
| Oat | *Avena* | |
| Beet | *Beta* | |
| Brassica complex | *Brassica* et al. | Genera included are *Brassica*, *Armoracia*, *Barbarea*, *Camelina*, *Crambe*, *Diplotaxis*, *Eruca*, *Isatis*, *Lepidium*, *Raphanobrassica*, *Raphanus*, *Rorippa*, *Sinapis*, comprising oilseed and vegetable crops such as cabbage, rapeseed, mustard, cress, rocket, radish, and turnip; *Lepidium meyenii* (maca) is excluded |
| Pigeon Pea | *Cajanus* | |
| Chickpea | *Cicer* | |
| Citrus | *Citrus* | Genera *Poncirus* and *Fortunella* are included as root stock |
| Coconut | *Cocos* | |
| Major aroids | *Colocasia*, *Xanthosoma* | Major aroids include taro, cocoyam, dasheen and tannia |
| Carrot | *Daucus* | |
| Yams | *Dioscorea* | |
| Finger Millet | *Eleusine* | |

(*Continued*)

*Table 26.3* (Continued)

| *Crop* | *Genus* | *Observations* |
|---|---|---|
| Strawberry | *Fragaria* | |
| Sunflower | *Helianthus* | |
| Barley | *Hordeum* | |
| Sweet Potato | *Ipomoea* | |
| Grass pea | *Lathyrus* | |
| Lentil | *Lens* | |
| Apple | *Malus* | |
| Cassava | *Manihot* | *Manihot esculenta* only |
| Banana/ Plantain | *Musa* | Except *Musa textilis* |
| Rice | *Oryza* | |
| Pearl Millet | *Pennisetum* | |
| Beans | *Phaseolus* | Except *Phaseolus polyanthus* |
| Pea | *Pisum* | |
| Rye | *Secale* | |
| Potato | *Solanum* | Section tuberose included, except *Solanum phureja* |
| Eggplant | *Solanum* | Section melongena included |
| Sorghum | *Sorghum* | |
| Triticale | *Triticosecale* | |
| Wheat | *Triticum et al.* | Including *Agropyron*, *Elymus* and *Secale* |
| Fava Bean/ Vetch | *Vicia* | |
| Cowpea et al. | *Vigna* | |
| Maize | *Zea* | Except *Z. perennis*, *Z. diploperennis* and *Z. luxurians* |

*Table 26.4* List of crops covered under the multilateral system (Annex I of the Treaty): forages

| *Genera* | *Species* |
|---|---|
| LEGUME FORAGES | |
| *Astragalus* | *chinensis, cicer, arenarius* |
| *Canavalia* | *ensiformis* |
| *Coronilla* | *varia* |
| *Hedysarum* | *coronarium* |
| *Lathyrus* | *cicera, ciliolatus, hirsutus, ochrus, odoratus, sativus* |
| *Lespedeza* | *cuneata, striata, stipulacea* |
| *Lotus* | *corniculatus, subbiflorus, uliginosus* |
| *Lupinus* | *albus, angustifolius, luteus* |
| *Medicago* | *arborea, falcata, sativa, scutellata, rigidula, truncatula* |
| *Melilotus* | *albus, officinalis* |
| *Onobrychis* | *viciifolia* |

| *Genera* | *Species* |
|---|---|
| *Ornithopus* | *sativus* |
| *Prosopis* | *affinis, alba, chilensis, nigra, pallid* |
| *Pueraria* | *phaseoloides* |
| *Trifolium* | *alexandrinum, alpestre, ambiguum, angustifolium, arvense, agrocicerum, hybridum, incarnatum, pratense, repens, resupinatum, rueppellianum, semipilosum, subterraneum, vesiculosum* |
| GRASS FORAGES | |
| *Andropogon* | *gayanus* |
| *Agropyron* | *cristatum, desertorum* |
| *Agrostis* | *stolonifera, tenuis* |
| *Alopecurus* | *pratensis* |
| *Arrhenatherum* | *elatius* |
| *Dactylis* | *glomerata* |
| *Festuca* | *arundinacea, gigantea, heterophylla, ovina, pratensis, rubra* |
| *Lolium* | *hybridum, multiflorum, perenne, rigidum, temulentum* |
| *Phalaris* | *aquatica, arundinacea* |
| *Phleum* | *pratense* |
| *Poa* | *alpina, annua, pratensis* |
| *Tripsacum* | *laxum* |
| OTHER FORAGES | |
| *Atriplex* | *halimus, nummularia* |
| *Salsola* | *vermiculata* |

## Accessing plant genetic resources included in the MLS of the ITPGRFA

As described in **Box 26.1**, the MLS of the ITPGRFA makes 64 Annex I crops available for free (or for a token payment), provided they are being sought for food production purposes (including feed and forage, but excluding industrial applications). Key features of the MLS are as follows (summarized from Santilli, 2013a):

- Each country which is party to the ITPGRFA has equal access to the genetic resources available under the MLS, regardless of how many such resources that country has submitted to it.
- Access must be facilitated pursuant to the agreement of a Standard Material Transfer Agreement (SMTA) between the provider and the recipient.
- Persons or institutions that receive plant genetic resources through the MLS cannot prevent third parties from receiving the same resources through the system by establishing intellectual property (IP) rights over them.
- The MLS provides for two different benefit-sharing frameworks: the first includes the exchange of information, access and transfer of technology and capacity-building and is not connected with any specific access or transfer while the second relates to the sharing of monetary and other benefits of commercialization and is specific to a given access or transfer agreement, among other conditions (**Box 26.2** *Commercialization of products incorporating MLS material*).

### Box 26.2 Commercialization of products incorporating MLS material

The ITPGRFA stipulates that any recipient of PGRFA who then commercializes a product that incorporates material accessed from the MLS must make a payment into the Treaty's Benefit Sharing Fund. The amount to be paid should represent an 'equitable share' of the benefits, except whenever such a product is *available without restriction to others for further research and breeding*, in which case the recipient is 'encouraged' to make such a payment on a voluntary basis. Note that, in either case, the potential monetary benefit does *not* return to the country in which the PGRFA originated or to the providing institution which provided the plant genetic resources. This is an important difference in relation to CBD's bilateral system, where the country of origin of the genetic resources receives all the benefit-sharing derived from its use and/or commercialization.

*Source*: Santilli (2013a).

## The CBD, the Nagoya Protocol and the ITPGRFA

In order to oversee the implementation of access and benefit-sharing provisions under the CBD, a further instrument, the Nagoya Protocol (NP), was developed (CBD, 2013). By definition, the NP applies only to genetic resources (and the traditional knowledge associated with this) that are already subject to regulation under the CBD. It does not apply to genetic resources which are regulated by other, more specialized international access and benefit-sharing instruments. If access to a plant genetic resource, whether listed in Annex I of the ITPGRFA or otherwise, is aimed at 'chemical, pharmaceutical, and/or other industrial uses', then these resources remain subject to the sovereignty of their countries of origin, and to the bilateral regime established by the CBD and the NP. As noted earlier, the ITPGRFA is currently the only international agreement to establish a multilateral instrument to oversee access and benefit-sharing provisions, but FAO's Commission on Genetic Resources for Food and Agriculture (CGRFA) is discussing the possibility of developing other specialized ABS instruments to regulate the use and exchange of genetic resources in the main sub-sectors of the food and agriculture sector (animal, aquatic, forest and microbial genetic resources for food and agriculture).

## The UPOV system and the Agreement on Trade-Related Aspects of Intellectual Property Rights (TRIPS)

The International Convention for the Protection of New Varieties of Plants was adopted in 1961, and it established the so-called Plant Breeders' Rights (PBRs) or Plant Variety Rights (PVRs). UPOV is the French acronym for Union for the Protection of New Varieties of Plants, which is the name of the organization that the International Convention (called the UPOV Convention) established. Such intellectual property rights (IPRs) for plant varieties were developed when plant breeding became an economically promising activity and started to attract the investments of private companies, who pushed for proprietary rights over plant varieties. Such an IPR regime gives breeders exclusive (monopolistic) rights over the production and selling of newly developed plant varieties, for a certain period of time.

Plant breeders have always argued that, because seeds are self-replicable, farmers can reproduce them easily, and do not need to buy seeds of newly created plant varieties. The establishment of IPRs over newly developed varieties aimed to ensure breeders' exclusivity in the production and sales of such plant varieties.

When European breeders conceived the UPOV system (an alternative or *sui generis* system), they wanted to keep plant breeding out of the plant patent system established in the United States, because they considered it to be inadequate for plant variety protection. Thus, they developed a *sui generis* IPR system, whose main principles were established during the International Convention for Protection of New Plant Varieties, held in Paris, in 1957. Until then, the United States was the only country to grant patents for plant varieties, by means of the Plant Patents Act of 1930, which was especially designed to protect vegetatively reproduced ornamentals and fruit varieties. Later, Japan, Australia and New Zealand also allowed plant varieties to be patented, but most countries adopt a *sui generis* system of plant variety protection, based on the UPOV system. In most countries (Europe, Canada and Latin American countries), patents are granted neither to plant and animal varieties, nor to essential biological processes for the production of plants and animals.[2] They are, however, granted to genetically modified organisms (GMOs) and non-biological processes.

In their original conception, PBRs should grant free access to genetic resources while, at the same time, protect breeders' innovations. To develop new plant varieties, breeders need to have access to the widest genetic diversity possible. Therefore, PBRs should allow free access to new plant varieties, not for reproduction and marketing (which would violate breeders' rights), but for being used as an initial source of variation for the purpose of creating other varieties.

PBRs maintain the so-called 'breeders' exemption' (or 'privilege'), which means that IPRs over plant varieties do not prevent breeders from using any genetic material as an initial source of variation in the development of new plant varieties. The authorization from the initial breeder (holder of IPRs) is not required for such purposes. Besides, the right to freely use protected varieties is not limited to the stage of research aimed at creating new varieties, but extends to sales of the newly developed variety. When a breeder creates a new plant variety (even if he accessed protected varieties as a source of genetic variation), and this new variety becomes distinguishable from others by at least one important trait, its production and sales do not need the prior consent of the original plant breeder. The same is not true for patent law: any new invention which incorporates a patented invention depends on the authorization from the original inventor, since research exemptions in patent law are usually much narrower.

The UPOV Convention was signed in 1961, but came into force in 1968. It was initially signed by five developed countries (France, the Netherlands, West Germany, Belgium and Italy). See **Box 26.3** *Key features of the UPOV convention.*

The UPOV Convention remained as an instrument adopted mainly by developed countries until the Trade-Related Aspects of Intellectual Property Rights (TRIPS) Agreement was signed in 1994, and became one of the main pillars of the World Trade Organization (WTO). The TRIPS Agreement was an important landmark for IPRs, since its adoption became a necessary condition for countries to become members of WTO. Member countries must accept all agreements in the WTO 'package', with no exceptions. Some of the main differences brought by TRIPS are discussed in **Box 26.4** *Key features of Trade-Related Aspects of Intellectual Property Rights (TRIPS), 1994.*

Before TRIPS, countries could establish the duration of patents in their territories, but after TRIPS, the duration of patents cannot be under 20 years, and member countries can exclude patentability only in the exceptional cases listed in Article 27. Article 27.3 (b) contains the provisions that are more directly related to PGRFA:

### Box 26.3 Key features of the UPOV convention

- The breeders' right is, as all IPRs, exclusive and temporary. Exclusivity extends to production for commercial purposes, offering for sales and marketing of the (reproductive or vegetative) propagating material of the plant variety.
- The breeders' authorization is not necessary for use of the plant variety as a source of variation in plant breeding (the so-called breeders' exemption).
- To be protected, a plant variety must be sufficiently homogenous (or uniform), considering the particular features of its sexual reproduction or vegetative propagation. It must also be stable in its essential characteristics, that is, it must maintain these characteristics throughout repeated successive cycles of propagation or, when the breeder has defined a particular cycle of reproduction or multiplication, at the end of each cycle.
- To be protected, a plant variety must be clearly distinguishable, by one or several important traits, from any other variety whose existence is well-known at the time of the filing of the application for protection, that is, what is essential for protection is the difference in relation to what is already known.
- Protection is granted to the breeders' right independently of the origin (artificial or natural) of the initial variation from which the variety has resulted. In other words, protection reaches not only new plant varieties created through classical plant breeding, but also varieties whose improvement was based on the discovery and selection of mutants or variants found in a population of cultivated plants. According to the UPOV Convention (1991 Act), the 'breeder' is 'the person who bred, or discovered and a developed, a variety'.[3]
- To be protected, a plant variety must be new (novel) within the territory of the State where the application (for a breeder's right) has been filed. Nor may have been marketed in the territory of any other state for longer than six years in the case of vines, forest trees, fruit trees and ornamental trees, nor for longer than four years in the case of any other plant (Munyi, 2015).

### Box 26.4 Key features of Trade-Related Aspects of Intellectual Property Rights (TRIPS), 1994

- According to TRIPS, patents must be granted to inventions, whether products or processes, in all fields of technology, as long as they are new, involve an inventive step and are capable of industrial application. Before the TRIPS Agreement had been signed, countries were allowed to exclude certain industrial or technological sectors from patentability, according to their own national development strategies. Pharmaceutical, food and chemical products, for instance, were excluded from patentability by many countries.
- After TRIPS, WTO principles for multilateral prevention and settlement of disputes between member countries also became applicable to IPRs. This includes the possibility of commercial retaliation, including 'cross-retaliation'. In other words, in the event of non-compliance by members of their obligations under TRIPS, a retaliation may be adopted by a complaining party in a different sector from that in which the infraction was made: goods, services or IPRs. A violation

of IPRs by one country can lead another country to retaliate in a different sector, such as goods or services.

- According to TRIPS, member countries do not have the obligation to implement, in their national legislation, more extensive protection than is required in the Agreement. They may, however, extend protection for IPRs above the minimum standards established in TRIPS, and this has occurred through several bilateral and regional free trade agreements signed between the United States and European Union and developing countries. Known as 'TRIPS-plus', these agreements impose obligations not included in TRIPS, such as mandatory adoption of the 1991 Act of the UPOV Convention and the obligation to patent plants, animals and biotechnological inventions.

> Article 27.3 Members may also exclude from patentability
>
> (b) plants and animals other than microorganisms, and essentially biological processes for the production of plants and animals, other than non-biological and microbiological processes. However, Members shall provide for the protection of plant varieties either by patents or by an efficient *sui generis* system, or by any combination thereof.

Member countries may exclude from patentability plant and animals, as well as essentially biological processes for the production of plants and animals, but they have to allow patenting of microorganisms and non-biological and microbiological processes (such as transgenic plants and genetic engineering processes). They are obliged to protect plant varieties, and have to choose between a patent system, a *sui generis* system (which the TRIPS Agreement does not define, but it is understood as a special, of-its-own-kind system), or a combination of both. UPOV has always argued that the adoption of its Convention was the most efficient form of protecting plant varieties.

The UPOV Convention has undergone successive revisions (in 1972, 1978 and 1991). Such revisions have granted stricter protection for breeders' rights, and brought PBRs closer to the patent system. Up until 1998, it was still possible to become a UPOV member adopting the 1978 UPOV Act. Since then, countries wishing to become members of this organization must adopt the 1991 UPOV Act (see **Box 26.5** *Breeders' rights as provided under the UPOV Act, 1991*).

The UPOV 1978 and 1991 Acts differ in several important aspects (**Table 26.5** *Main differences between the 1978 and 1991 UPOV Acts and the patent system*). For example, they differ significantly in relation to their approach to farmers' rights (Santilli, 2013b). Under the 1978 UPOV Act, farmers could save seeds of protected varieties for use in coming harvests, without the breeder's authorization. Under the 1991 Act, the right of farmers to use saved seeds to replant his fields is subjected to recognition by national laws, which can only establish such an exception to the breeder's right 'within reasonable limits and as long as the legitimate interests of the breeder are safeguarded, protected,' and as long as farmers use saved seeds only on their own holdings. The exchange of seeds among farmers is not allowed because farmers must multiply seeds on their own lands, to be used also on their own lands only, and not in someone else's holdings. Sales of seeds of protected varieties to other farmers are not permitted either. Under the 1991 Act, national laws may decide that farmers can no longer re-utilize stored seeds in future harvests, or that only some farmers (e.g. small-scale farmers) have this right, or that royalties must be paid to the breeders for farmers to be allowed to maintain this tradition.

### Box 26.5 Breeders' rights as provided under the UPOV Act, 1991

The duration of breeders' rights is extended, from a minimum of 15 years, for most plant species (and 18 years for grapevines and trees), in the 1978 Act, to at least 20 years (and 25 years for grapevines and trees) in the 1991 Act. The scope of protection for the breeder's right is also expanded: in the 1978 Act, it covers production for commercial purposes, offering for sale and marketing of propagating material of the plant variety. In the 1991 Act, it covers production or reproduction (multiplication) of the propagating material of the protected variety, conditioning, offering for sale, selling, exporting, importing or stocking for any of the aforementioned purposes.

The object of protection has also expanded: in the 1978 Act, it covered only the reproductive or vegetative propagating material, as such, of the plant variety, while in the 1991 Act, it covers not only the reproductive or vegetative propagating material, but also the harvested material (including entire plants and parts of plants) – when obtained through the unauthorized use of propagating material of the protected variety, if the breeder has not had 'reasonable opportunity' to exercise his right in relation to the propagating material. Furthermore, the 1991 Act also establishes that countries can extend protection to products made directly from harvested material of the protected variety (e.g. soya oil, soya flour).

The concept of plant variety was not defined in the original version of the UPOV Convention, but according to the 1991 Act, 'variety' means a plant grouping within a single botanical taxon of the lowest known rank, which grouping, irrespective of whether the conditions for the grant of a breeder's right are fully met, can be defined by the expression of the characteristics resulting from a given genotype or combination of genotypes, distinguished from any other plant grouping by the expression of at least one of the said characteristics and considered as a unit with regard to its suitability for being propagated unchanged.

*Table 26.5* Main differences between the 1978 and 1991 UPOV Acts and the patent system

| | *1978 UPOV Act* | *1991 UPOV Act* | *Patent system (TRIPS Agreement)* |
|---|---|---|---|
| Protection coverage | Plant varieties of nationally defined genera or species. (Member countries may limit botanical genera and species covered by protection[7]) | Plant varieties of all genera and species must be protected. | Any invention, be it a product or a process, in all technological sectors (exceptions are listed on Article 27), must be protected. |
| Conditions for protection | Novelty, Distinctness, Homogeneity, Stability, Variety Denomination. | Novelty, Distinctness, Uniformity, Stability, Variety Denomination. | Novelty, inventive step (or non-obviousness) activity and industrial application. |
| Protection duration | At least 15 years (18 years for vines and trees) | At least 20 years (25 years for vines and trees). | No less than 20 years. |

| | *1978 UPOV Act* | *1991 UPOV Act* | *Patent system (TRIPS Agreement)* |
|---|---|---|---|
| Protection scope | Production for purposes of commercial marketing, offering for sale and marketing of the propagating material of the plant variety. Protection covers vegetative or reproductive propagating material, as such, of the variety. | Production, conditioning, offering for sale, selling, exporting, importing or stocking for aforementioned purposes of propagating materials of the variety. Protection may also cover the harvested product, if obtained through an unauthorized use of propagating material, and if the breeder has had no 'reasonable opportunity' to exercise his right in relation to the propagating material. Protection may also be extended to products made directly from harvested material of the protected variety. | In respect of a product: making, using, offering for sale, selling or importing, stocking for purposes of offering for sale, etc. In respect of a process: using the process, doing any of the aforementioned acts in respect of a product obtained directly by means of the process. |
| Breeders' exemption | Yes, the breeders' exemption is recognized. However, when the repeated use of the variety is necessary for the commercial production of another variety, the breeder's authorization is required. | Yes, the breeders' exemption is recognized. However, 'essentially derived' varieties and varieties that are not distinguishable from the protected variety are not included in the breeder's exemption. When the repeated use of the variety is necessary for the commercial production of another variety, the breeder's authorization is also required. | Depends on the laws in each country, but exemptions are usually to research/ experimental use. |
| Farmers' 'privilege' | There is no explicit mention, but since the breeder's authorization is required only for production with commercial purposes, farmers can use saved seeds (of protected varieties) for replanting on their own lands, as well as exchange seeds among themselves. Sales of protected seeds depend on exceptions to the breeder's right established in national laws. | Each country may decide whether to allow (or not) 'within reasonable limits and as long as the legitimate interests of the breeders are safeguarded' that farmers use, for propagation purposes only, and on their own lands, the product of the harvest of protected varieties. Exchanges among farmers are not allowed. | Generally no provision is made, but national laws may establish it. |
| Double protection (under patents and plant breeders' right) | Is not allowed. Only one form of protection (patent or breeder's right) is allowed for the same botanical genus or species. | Is allowed | Up to national laws |

National laws can also limit the size of the lands, the quantity of seeds and the plant species to which the farmers' right to save seed are applicable. According to the European Council Regulation 2100/94, on Community Plant Variety Rights, farmers' rights are governed by the following rules: the farmers' right to save seeds is restricted to approximately 20 species (including fodder plants, cereals, potatoes, oils and fibre plants) and requires that they pay an 'equitable remuneration' to the holder, which must be 'sensibly lower than the amount charged for the licensed production of propagating material of the same variety in the same area'. Small-scale farmers (who do not grow plants on an area bigger than the area which would be needed to produce 92 tonnes of cereals) are exempt from the payment of royalties.

Another difference between the 1978 and the 1991 Acts is that the first one explicitly prohibits double protection (by breeder's right and patent) for a single variety, and countries which allow both forms of protection must allow only one form in relation to a single botanical genus or species. The prohibition of double protection was removed from the 1991 Act. The UPOV system thus ceased to be an alternative to the patent system, in its original form, since the 1991 Act permits the breeder's right to be used as an additional protection for patents. The UPOV system is actually becoming increasingly similar to the patent system, especially for countries which adopted the 1991 Act.

## The future of seed laws

The final aspect of the legal status of PGRFA relates to the existence of seed laws (where 'seed' can indicate any plant propagule, including cuttings and tubers). Seed laws are distinct from IPR or PBR, both of which grant ownership rights over new plant varieties, with the express aim of stimulating innovations in plant breeding. Rather, seed laws represent a 'legal support' for the 'modernization' of agriculture, and especially for the use of seed produced by professional breeders or breeding companies as opposed to those developed within farming communities (Santilli, 2013b). Because of this, seed laws do not typically recognize the existence of diversified local seed systems of the kind which predominate in most developing countries (Louwaars, Chapter 34 of this Handbook).

Farm-produced seeds are by far the most important source for small-scale farmers in low-input agriculture in developing countries, especially for crops such as indigenous vegetables, manioc, yam, sweet potato and many pulses, important for home consumption and the local market (Louwaars, 2007). Developing countries have been increasingly adopting seed laws aimed at promoting formal seed systems, which leave little (if any) legal space for farmers' seed systems. These laws usually establish mandatory seed registration and certification requirements that can be met only by the large seed industry. With a few exceptions, farmers' seed exchanges and local seed sales are outlawed, and strong penalties are imposed upon those who violate seed laws (Coomes et al., 2015).

The main justification for a strict control over production and trading of seeds has been the risk of diseases – especially dissemination across different regions, and the need to insure the genetic purity and capacity for germination and vigor of seeds. This is an important argument, and it certainly must be taken into consideration. However, local seed systems use mainly locally adapted varieties that are distributed and sold at the local level, and generally do not involve distribution over large distances nor across different geographical regions. It will be important to evaluate what benefits such strict controls really bring to farmers, and compare them with the difficulties that they create for them.

Ideally, seed laws would take account the particular requirements of farming systems in the developing world also, with due regard for the roles of farmers in the use of PGRFA. It may be necessary to review and, where necessary, revise the existing seed laws (regarding point of variety release, evaluation and registration, seed quality control, production, storage and distribution) to ensure that they meet these requirements if, originally, the intent of seed laws was to avoid the dissemination of poor-quality seeds, this original purposes has typically been overstepped (Santilli, 2013b). New priorities, such as agrobiodiversity conservation and use, must be taken into consideration and determine the revision of many seed laws.

## Notes

1 To learn more about the Treaty and its member countries, see www.planttreaty.org

2 On 9 December 2010, the European Patent Office's Enlarged Board of Appeal rendered its decision to exclude classical plant breeding processes from patentability (EPC, article 53b). According to the Board's decision, while technical devices or means, such as genetic markers, may themselves be patentable inventions, their use does not make an essentially biological process patentable. The Board also held that processes for producing plants by inserting or modifying a trait in the genome by using genetic engineering (which produce Genetically Modified Organisms – GMOs) do not rely on sexual crossing of whole genomes and may therefore be patentable. The legal questions referred to the Enlarged Board of Appeal arose in two plant breeding patent cases: (a) Case G2/07: Plant Bioscience (a British private company) claimed a patent on a method of producing broccoli *(Brassica oleracea)* with elevated levels of glucosinolates (organic compounds which are thought to prevent cancer). The patent owned by Plant Bioscience was opposed by Syngenta and by Limagrain. The Board decided that the claimed broccoli breeding process is an 'essentially biological process', and is therefore excluded from patentability, and (b) Case G1/08: The Ministry of Agriculture of Israel claimed a patent on a method for breeding tomato plants that produce tomatoes with reduced fruit water content, but the Board also decided that the claimed tomato breeding process is an 'essentially biological process', and is therefore excluded from patentability (for source, see www.ipeg.eu/blog/wp-content/uploads/Plant-Breeding-Method_EPO_G1_08_en.pdf, accessed 20 January 2013.

3 A common mistake regarding the 1991 UPOV Act is to assume that it forbids farmers from using saved seeds for use in coming harvests in any circumstance. The UPOV Convention and any legislation based on it are applicable only to protected varieties (by means of IPRs). Varieties in the public domain do not have these restrictions (although many seed laws also impose restrictions on farm-saved seed).

## References


Chiarolla, C. and Jungcurt, S. (2011) 'Outstanding issues on access and benefit sharing under the multilateral system of the International Treaty on Plant Genetic Resources for Food and Agriculture', a background study paper by the Berne Declaration and the Development Fund.

Convention on Biological Diversity [CBD] (2013) *Nagoya Protocol on Access to Genetic Resources and the Fair and Equitable Sharing of Benefits Arising from their Utilization: Background and Analysis*, Berne Declaration, Bread for the World, Ecoropa, Tebtebba, Third World Network.

Coomes, O. T., McGuire, S. J., Garine, E., Caillon, S., McKey, D., Demeulenaere, E., Jarvis, D., Aistara, G., Barnaud, A., Clouvel, P., Emperaire, L., Louafi, S., Martin, P., Massol, F., Pautasso, M., Violon, C. and Wencélius, J. (2015) 'Farmer seed networks make a limited contribution to agriculture? Four common misconceptions', *Food Policy*, vol. 56, pp. 41–50.

Frison, C., López, F. and Esquinas-Alcázar, J. T. (eds.) (2011) *Plant Genetic Resources and Food Security: Stakeholder Perspectives on the International Treaty on Plant Genetic Resources for Food and Agriculture*, Food and Agriculture Organization of the United Nations (FAO), Rome, Italy, Bioversity International, Maccarese, Italy and Earthscan for Routledge, Abingdon, UK.

Fujisaka, S., Williams, D. and Halewood, M. (eds.) (2009) *The Impact of Climate Change on Countries' Interdependence on Genetic Resources for Food and Agriculture*, FAO, Commission on Genetic Resources for Food and Agriculture, Background Study Paper no. 48, FAO, Rome, Italy.

Halewood, M. and Nnadozie, K. (2008) 'Giving priority to Commons: The International Treaty on Plant Genetic Resources for Food and Agriculture (ITPGRFA), pp. 115–140 in G. Tansey and T. Rajotte (eds.), *The Future Control of Food: A Guide to International Negotiations and Rules on Intellectual Property, Biodiversity and Food Security,* Earthscan, London, UK.

Hermitte, M. A. and Kahn, P. (eds.) (2004) *Les Ressources Génétiques Végétales et le Droit dans les Rapports Nord-Sud*, Bruylant, Bruxelles, Belgium (Travaux du Centre René-Jean Dupuy pour le Droit et le Développement et du Centre de Recherche sur le Droit des Sciences et Techniques, v. II).

Louwaars, N. (2007) *Seeds of Confusion: The Impact of Policies on Seed Systems*, PhD dissertation, Wageningen, the Netherlands.

Moore, G. and Tymowski, W. (eds.) (2005) Explanatory Guide to the International Treaty on Plant Genetic Resources for Food and Agriculture. IUCN, Gland, Switzerland.

Munyi, P. (2015) 'Plant variety protection regime in relation to relevant international obligations: Implications for smallholder farmers in Kenya', *The Journal of World Intellectual Property*, vol. 18, pp. 65–85.

Palacios, X. F. (1997) *Contribution to the Estimation of the Interdependence of Countries in the Field of Plant Genetic Resources*, Commission on Genetic Resources for Food and Agriculture, Background Study Paper no. 7, Rev. 1, FAO, Rome, Italy, ftp://ftp.fao.org/docrep/fao/meeting/015/j0747e.pdf, accessed 4/15/2013.

Santilli, J. (2011) *Agrobiodiversity and the Law: Regulating Genetic Resources, Food Security and Cultural Diversity*, Earthscan for Routeldge, Abingdon, UK.

Santilli, J. (2013a) 'Local varieties, informal seed systems and the Seed Law: Reflections from Brazil', pp. 338–344 in W. De Boef, A. Subedi, N. Peroni, M. Thijssen and E. O'Keeffe (eds.), *Community Biodiversity Management: Promoting Resilience and the Conservation of Plant Genetic Resources*, Earthscan for Routledge, Abingdon, UK.

Santilli, J. (2013b) 'Agrobiodiversity: Towards innovating legal systems', pp. 167–184 in E. Coudel, H. Devautour, C. T. Soulard, G. Faure and B. Hubert (eds.), *Renewing Innovation Systems in Agriculture and Food*, Wageningen Academic Publishers, Wageningen, the Netherlands.

# 27

# USING ACCESS AND BENEFIT-SHARING POLICIES TO SUPPORT CLIMATE CHANGE ADAPTATION

*Ana Bedmar Villanueva, Isabel López Noriega, Michael Halewood, Gloria Otieno and Ronnie Vernooy*

## Introduction

According to the Intergovernmental Panel on Climate Change (IPCC), the earth's surface has become progressively warmer during the last three decades, with temperatures in each decade exceeding those in the preceding decade since 1850. Changes in temperature and precipitation, and increased atmospheric $CO_2$, have already led shifts in the production of food and non-food crops around the world, affecting agricultural incomes and food security. Climate projections depend on the chosen scenario and the assumptions made, but overall it is predicted that by mid-21st century the global temperature will increase about 4°C above late 20th century levels, with highly irregular changes in precipitation around the globe (IPCC, 2014).

Agriculture has been identified as one of the sectors most vulnerable to climate change. Researchers estimate that climate change has already reduced the production of globally important crops. For instance, for the period 1980–2008, higher temperatures have led to a decrease of global maize and wheat production of 3.8% and 5.5%, respectively, though global soybean and rice yields have, so far, remained relatively unaffected (Lobell et al., 2011). According to the IPCC (2014), climate change will increase further the inter-annual variability of crop yields in many regions. Studies predict that climate change will continue to cause shifts in areas suitable for cultivation of a wide range of crops (e.g. Lane and Jarvis, 2007) and crop yields are predicted to decrease markedly by 2050 (Lobell et al., 2007, 2008). It is also expected that climate change will impact agricultural biodiversity and increase the genetic erosion of landraces (Mercer and Perales, 2010). These changes will have implications for agricultural production and eventually food security (e.g. Lobell and Gourdji, 2012; IPCC, 2014).

To deal with these climate-related impacts, researchers have identified a range of potential coping strategies. One of the most important is to take advantage of the diversity of plant genetic resources for food and agriculture (PGRFA) to identify and develop crops, forages and trees that are adapted to the new climate conditions (Lipper and Cooper, 2009; Ortiz, 2011). This is not entirely new, of course. In the past, smallholder farmers responded to environmental changes by selecting adapted species and cultivars, and combining crop, trees and livestock production to reduce risks of crop failures (e.g. Altieri, 1999; Sthapit et al., 2010; Ortiz, 2011; Lasco et al., 2014). Similarly, plant breeders have also purposely bred materials that are adapted to different climate-related stresses, relying on traits derived from the genetic diversity of their crops (Lipper and Cooper, 2009; Ortiz, 2011). What is new, however, is that climate change is increasing the urgency of these efforts, requiring an acceleration in the 'turn-around' time for acquiring or developing new crop varieties, animal breeds and tree populations that are adapted to the new conditions. This urgency is likely to provoke an increase in the demand for PGRFA worldwide, both in terms of volume and diversity (e.g. Jarvis et al., 2010; Ramirez-Villegas et al., 2012).

Up-scaled use of PGRFA requires an enhancement of the collective technical capacities of farmers, breeders and researchers to identify and acquire potentially adapted species and varieties. It also depends upon the existence of a supportive policy environment to develop and nurture the formation of the requisite partnerships among actors at local, national and international levels, and to encourage the exchange and sharing of genetic diversity. Over the years, the international community has adopted a number of multilateral environmental agreements that have the potential to contribute to the availability of the requisite funds to support capacity strengthening for key actors, enhanced networking, technology pooling and transparent access to genetic resources and equitable sharing of benefits arising from their use. These agreements include the International Treaty on Plant Genetic Resources for Food and Agriculture (Plant Treaty), the Convention on Biological Diversity (CBD) and its Nagoya Protocol (NP) on access and benefit sharing (ABS), the International Convention to Combat Desertification and the United Nations Framework Convention on Climate Change (UNFCCC). All four agreements broadly support the sustainable management and use of biological resources for improved human well-being. They should eventually contribute to farmers' improved access to the necessary diversity for their crops, animals and trees to adapt to changing climates, ensuring agricultural production and food security (Vernooy et al., 2015).

Facilitating the exchange and use of PGRFA for climate change adaptation has been one of the main objectives of the 'Genetic Resources Policy Initiative' (known as GRPI). This initiative, which started in 2012, has involved partners from Bhutan, Nepal, Uganda, Rwanda, Côte d'Ivoire, Burkina Faso, Guatemala and Costa Rica and has been coordinated by Bioversity International with funds from the Government of the Netherlands. GRPI's work on climate change has focused on (a) developing new or strengthening existing partnerships among a range of stakeholders in each country, (b) measuring possible impacts of climate change on target crops in each country, (c) identifying sources of PGRFA with potentially useful traits for climate change adaptation from local, national and international sources, and (d) developing policies to support the exchange of PGRFA for climate change adaptation.

This chapter describes the approaches and methods that were adopted by GRPI in these four areas of work, and some of the most salient results and lessons learned throughout the project. The following section presents the tools and methods that the project partners used to identify climate change impacts and identify potentially adapted genetic materials; it provides a general overview of the results of those exercises, with highlights from a few national case studies. Thereafter, the chapter presents the progress in all eight countries to develop supportive policies, with a particular focus on those addressing ABS-related issues. To conclude, we reflect upon the lessons learned from project experiences and results across the eight countries. We compare our own experiences and findings with the existing literature on issues such as the impacts of climate change on cropping systems, international interdependence on PGRFA, impediments to germplasm exchange and factors affecting national policy development. We conclude with recommendations for potential future policy initiatives to enhance the ability of countries (and their farmers, plant breeders, researchers, etc.) to take advantage of PGRFA diversity for climate change adaptation.

## Documenting climate change impacts and finding potentially adapted germplasm

The approach we used for conducting this work differed somewhat in each country, with each country's research teams adapting and improving methods and tools as they learned how to use them. The experiences of the eight countries were further enriched by the integration of a few additional components developed in Zambia and Zimbabwe, also supported by GRPI (we will refer to the work in these two countries later in this chapter). What we describe here is, therefore, a generic version of a method that we developed over time.

In each country, national partners identified two sites where the impact of climate change was becoming evident on crops grown by farmers and where farmers would potentially be willing to participate in an experimental process to bring in more diversity. A range of tools and methods is available for different actors to assess the extent to which climate change is affecting, or is predicted to affect, crops production. In GRPI, participatory assessments with farmers, extension agents and other local actors were combined with the use of geographic information systems and climate modeling tools. Where resources were available and time permitted, multi-stakeholder teams of researchers (including combinations of local farmers, extension agents, researchers from national agricultural research organizations, including breeders and genebank staff, and scientists from Bioversity International) joined forces at the reference sites to analyze climate changes, adaptation options and germplasm needs with the farmers. Farmers shared information and their perspectives on the changes in climate they were experiencing, the impacts on their crops and some of the coping strategies that they were implementing. In some of the reference sites, the farmers identified local and/or improved varieties that stood out as performing better than others under the present climate-related stresses. In these cases, farmers agreed to include those varieties in local experimental trials. These interactions allowed scientists working on PGRFA conservation and plant breeding to focus on priority crops and traits and to begin looking for potentially useful materials from elsewhere.

The steps supported by the project included working with national teams to identify potentially adapted germplasm from various sources, including their own national genebanks, collections held in other countries and international collections hosted by the International Agricultural Research Centres supported by the CGIAR. A number of digital tools are available to combine agronomic data of crop species and varieties with past, current and future climate data to show the suitability of species and varieties to the climatic conditions of a given place. These tools include DIVA-GIS, which maps the distribution of biological diversity and links this distribution to climate data such as that provided by WorldClim; MaxEnt, which models the climatic range within which a particular crop or variety can occur; and Climate Analogues, which is used to identify future climate conditions at a particular location, the sites that currently resemble these conditions and locations that have or will have similar climate conditions. All these tools can guide plant scientists in a number of tasks, including planning the collection of PGRFA in areas where target crops may present promising climate adaptation traits, studying and facilitating possible changes in cropping partners (both geographically and time-wise) in response to temperature and rainfall changes, and comparing current and future environmental constraints for target crops, and defining breeding priorities accordingly. Another set of digital resources that can be very useful in identifying sources of promising climate adaptation traits are those that contain georeferenced data of crop species and varieties found in *in situ* conditions and in *ex situ* collections. Good examples of these tools are the web portal of the Global Biodiversity Information Facility (GBIF), which provides access to biodiversity data held by hundreds of institutions, and Genesys, an online database that provides access to the information about the accessions held in the international genebanks maintained by the CGIAR centers, the collections of the United States Department of Agriculture (USDA) and the genebanks of 40 European countries.

Although many of these tools and datasets are freely available, plant scientists in developing countries are not always aware of their existence, or do not have the knowledge to use them. The GRPI team organized a number of training workshops to strengthen the capacities of genebank managers, plant breeders, plant pathologists, extension agents and other experts working on PGRFA. The multidisciplinary setting of these workshops allowed participants to learn from each other about climate change and agricultural production, and to revisit their own perceptions from alternative angles proposed by other disciplines. Over the course of the workshops, it became evident that one of the greatest limitations that stakeholders face is the limited availability of comprehensive data sets about the PGRFA conserved on farm and in *ex situ* collections. Limited passport data and lack of phenotypic characterization of available germplasm make it difficult to evaluate their potential suitability for any given environmental conditions. (For a full description of the requirements of digitized archives for recording genetic resources, see Endresen, Chapter 42 of this Handbook).

Another limitation that was also recognized during the workshops refers to breeders' general propensity to use limited sources of germplasm. The most common sources of genetic materials for crop improvement efforts in the countries appear to have been breeders' own working collections, their national genebanks, regionally organized characterization networks, the international genebanks hosted by the CGIAR and CGIAR breeders. Other national and international genebanks whose collections can be consulted and accessed through online systems appeared to have been largely ignored, or simply not used because of breeders' lack of familiarity with these genebanks' databases and ordering systems. In this regard, the workshops were useful for the participants to become familiar with DIVA-GIS and MaxEnt, and to learn how to interrogate the Genesys portal.

Over the course of several months, scientists from national research organizations and Bioversity International applied the participatory methods and the digital resources described previously to first understand climate-related stresses in selected sites in each country, and to then identify PGRFA potentially adapted to such stresses. Climate change scenario analysis was used for the identification of present and future (2050s) climate-related stresses at the selected study sites. Three possible sources of PGRFA were considered: varieties in farmers' hands found and conserved *in situ* through farmer-managed systems; accessions in national genebank collections; and accessions in international genebanks, for which the Genesys database was consulted. Some of the research teams involved in the project did not use their own national collections because they did not have enough data on such collections or because the data was not in an appropriate format. This limitation also extended to national collections of other countries, which could not be included in the searches for adapted materials because appropriate accession level information is not available online. As a result, potentially useful germplasm held in a country's collections, and in surrounding countries, did not appear in the searches for potentially suitable PGRFA. Ultimately, only accessions held in the collections that are included in the Genesys portal were included in the exercises. Clearly, one could improve the potential efficacy of this process by widening access to data on collections of countries that share similar climate change-related challenges in contiguous or comparable agro-ecologies.

To illustrate the results of applying these tools, selected findings obtained for some of the project countries are presented in the following paragraphs. Our results provide evidence of the need for countries to look for PGRFA outside their own territories in order to introduce the traits that will allow their agricultural production systems to adapt to the new climatic conditions and to the biotic and abiotic stresses associated with these new conditions. Our studies demonstrate that local farmers and national genebanks conserve a diversity of materials that are adapted to the new conditions. These materials can be used by farmers 'as they are'; they could also be considered for use by breeders as sources of genetic traits to integrate into their crop improvement programmes. In addition, the results show that a small and decreasing proportion of the diversity that is currently conserved in national genebanks may meet the needs for adaptive traits of the target crops in the future.

The results of the exercises described in the previous paragraphs in a selected site in Burkina Faso led to the identification of suitable analogue sites for millet, that is, those places around the world where millet is currently cultivated and where current temperature and precipitation patterns are similar to those expected in a millet-growing site in Burkina Faso in the 2050s. It is also possible to compare these points with the origins of millet accessions which have been collected in the areas that present most similarities (using records from Genesys). According to this analysis, there seems to be a good representation of materials of potential interest for adapting Burkina's millet production to the climatic conditions ahead in an international genebank of the CGIAR. However, it is likely that additional or more promising PGRFA from sites with analogue climates are stored in national genebanks or other collections within countries that have not yet shared data on Genesys.

In Uganda, national partners applied the tools described previously, taking Hoima as the reference community. Hoima farmers ranked three varieties of common bean being used at present for climate related challenges. Of these, two consisted of improved varieties that have been in the farming system for over 20 years and qualified as landraces. The other was a farmer variety. Potentially suitable accessions for present and future conditions were identified from Ethiopia and Tanzania in the regional collections held by CIAT. Additional accessions were identified from other parts of Uganda, Tanzania, Kenya, the Democratic Republic of Congo and Ethiopia (**Figure 27.1** *Potentially adaptable bean accessions for current and 2050's climatic conditions in Hoima, Uganda*). Results for Hoima revealed that the number of accessions potentially adapted to 2050's climate from the international genebank will increase compared with the present, mainly because even though temperatures will increase, a rise in precipitation will favor accessions found in hot humid areas of East and Central Africa, such as the Democratic Republic of Congo.

In Zimbabwe, national research partners and grassroots organizations working with farmers in rural areas identified Tsholotsho as a good study site for the purpose of our study. **Figure 27.2** shows the sites of collection of the sorghum accessions conserved in the national genebank in Zimbabwe and the sites from which potentially adopted sorghum accessions for present and 2050's predicted climate conditions in Tsholotsho, based on the 1.5–2°C increase of temperatures predicted for Zimbabwe, could be obtained. Thirty-one sorghum accessions (out of the 178 sorghum accessions available in the national genebank) were identified as being potentially adapted to the present climate conditions in the study site. This was reduced to 20 for the predicted climate conditions of the 2050s (**Figure 27.2**). We also assessed the number of potentially adapted sorghum accessions for present climate conditions available from international sources, and found that the 514 accessions suitable and available for present conditions would also be reduced to 242 if the climate conditions predicted for the 2050s were to come about (**Figure 27.3**).

National partners used the tools described here for other purposes, including to map the geographical coverage of existing national collections and to identify areas for further collection of germplasm of bean, maize, amaranth, different species of *Capsicum*, cassava and other tubers (in Guatemala), and to identify promising varieties of common bean and millet from local, national

| Species | Accession number | Type of material | Country of origin/occurrence | Holding institute |
|---|---|---|---|---|
| *Pennisetum glaucum (L.) R. Br. americanum* | IP 12412 | Traditional cultivar/Landrace | Republic of South Africa | ICRISAT |
| *Pennisetum glaucum (L.) R. Br. americanum* | IP 13343 | Traditional cultivar/Landrace | Sudan | ICRISAT |
| *Pennisetum glaucum (L.) R. Br. americanum* | IP 15833 | Traditional cultivar/Landrace | Tanzania | ICRISAT |
| *Pennisetum glaucum (L.) R. Br. americanum* | IP 18969 | Traditional cultivar/Landrace | Namibia | ICRISAT |
| *Pennisetum glaucum (L.) R. Br. americanum* | IP 5635 | Traditional cultivar/Landrace | Niger | ICRISAT |
| *Pennisetum glaucum (L.) R. Br. americanum* | IP 6383 | Traditional cultivar/Landrace | Mali | ICRISAT |
| *Pennisetum glaucum (L.) R. Br. americanum* | IP 8791 | Traditional cultivar/Landrace | Botswana | ICRISAT |
| *Pennisetum glaucum (L.) R. Br. americanum* | IP 9936 | Traditional cultivar/Landrace | Sudan | ICRISAT |
| | | | | |
| *Pennisetum glaucum (L.) R. Br. americanum* | IP 15319 | Traditional cultivar/Landrace | India | ICRISAT |
| *Pennisetum glaucum (L.) R. Br. americanum* | IP 17913 | Traditional cultivar/Landrace | India | ICRISAT |
| *Pennisetum glaucum (L.) R. Br. americanum* | IP 18143 | Traditional cultivar/Landrace | Pakistan | ICRISAT |
| *Pennisetum glaucum (L.) R. Br. americanum* | IP 3230 | Traditional cultivar/Landrace | India | ICRISAT |
| *Pennisetum glaucum (L.) R. Br. americanum* | IP 3954 | Traditional cultivar/Landrace | India | ICRISAT |
| *Pennisetum glaucum (L.) R. Br. americanum* | IP 4342 | Traditional cultivar/Landrace | India | ICRISAT |

*Figure 27.1* Potentially adapted bean accessions for current and 2050's climatic conditions in Hoima (1°25′55″N, 31°21′9″E) Uganda

*Source*: Image produced by the authors.

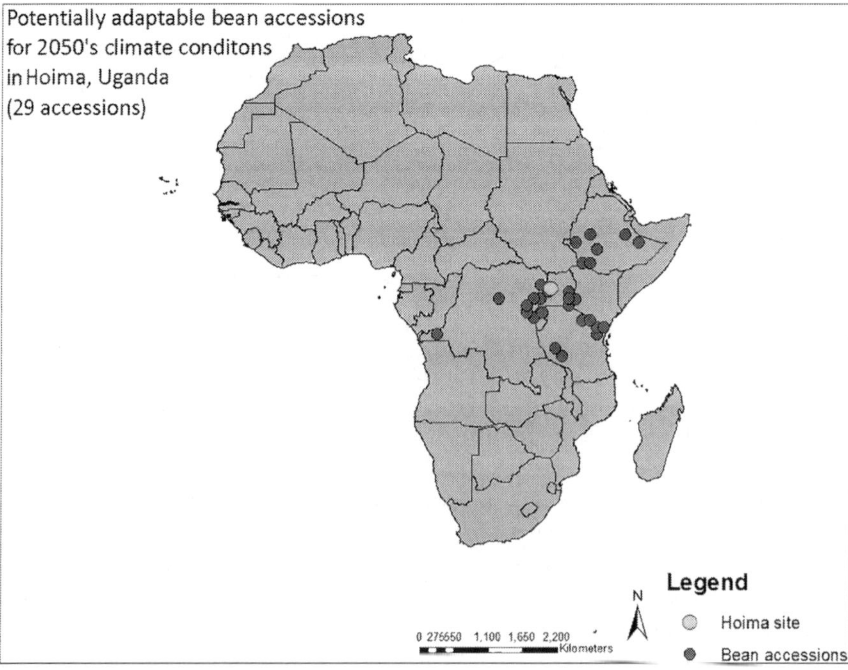


*Figure 27.2* From left to right: geographic sites of collection of sorghum in the national genebank in Zimbabwe and sites of collection of the potentially adapted sorghum accessions in the national genebank for present and for 2050's climate conditions in Tsholotsho (located in Matebeleland at 19° 46′ 0″ South, 27° 45′ 0″ East, in the North of the country), Zimbabwe

*Source*: Image produced by the authors.

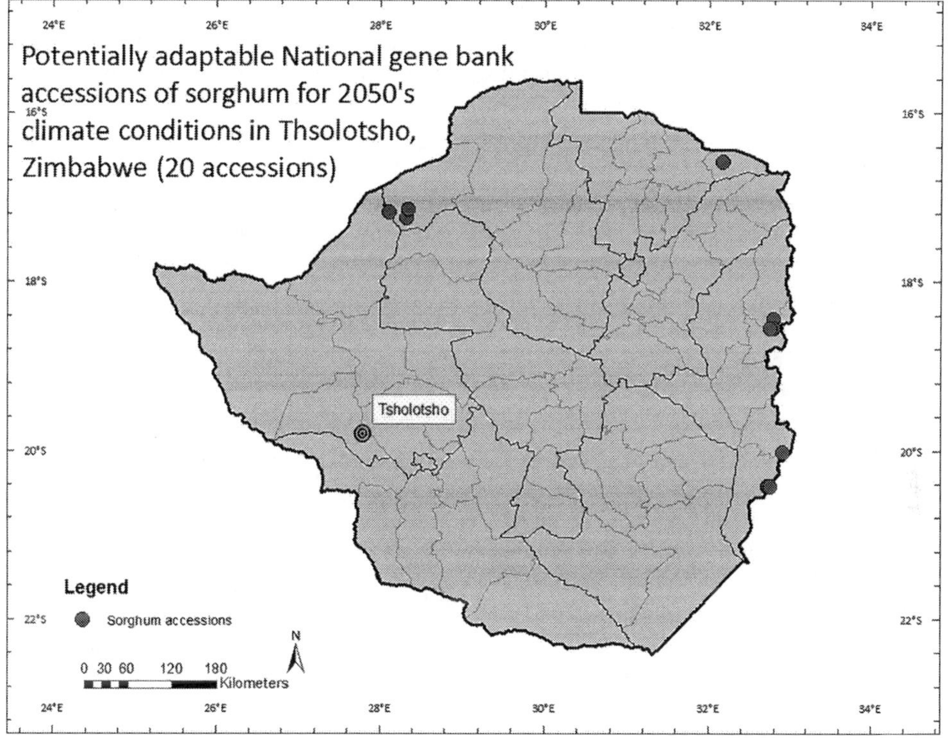


*Figure 27.3* From left to right: geographic distribution of the collections of sorghum around the world and distribution of the potentially adapted sorghum accessions from international sources for present and for 2050's climate conditions in Tsholotsho, Zimbabwe

*Source*: Image produced by the authors.

and international collections whose adaptation potential is currently being tested in the field (in Uganda and Burkina Faso; see Bougma et al., 2015).

Based on their experiences, we can conclude that these tools and resources are very useful for putting together a portfolio of promising genetic resources coming from local, national and foreign sources for a given place. It is important to bear in mind that these tools are based on mean temperature and precipitation data, and that they do not take into consideration soil characteristics. In addition to climate relevant traits (i.e. temperature and rainfall), other important environmental aspects, such as soil composition and presence of pests and diseases, must be taken into consideration. In addition, palatability features, cooking properties and other basic characteristics of the varieties, such as the colour and shape of the grain, and consumers' gastronomic preferences, are important for assessing the actual usefulness of the material in the environmental and socio-economic conditions of the target sites.

## Developing ABS policies: implementing the Plant Treaty's multilateral system of ABS

While plant breeders and other scientists can count on a range of tools to identify sources of germplasm with promising adaptation traits that they can incorporate in their crop improvement programmes, access to this germplasm continues to be constrained by a number of challenges.

They include poor information and information systems on the diversity available (as already mentioned), weak conservation capacities and reduced germplasm viability, insufficient numbers of seeds per accession and limited resources for multiplication. Policy and legal challenges represent another important obstacle to the flow of PGRFA for climate change adaptation. In 2001, the countries of the Food and Agricultural Organization of the United Nations (FAO) adopted the Plant Treaty, whose core component is the multilateral system (MLS) of ABS. Through the MLS, countries create an international pool of PGRFA for 64 priority crops and forages of global importance to be used for research, training and breeding purposes. In exchange of putting their own PGRFA in the pool, countries obtain access to PGRFA of all other countries, along with those in the collections held by international organizations that have signed agreements with the Governing Body of the Plant Treaty. The MLS sets out mandatory benefit-sharing requirements: when recipients commercialize new PGRFA products that incorporate material from the MLS, and do not allow others to use those products for research and breeding, they must pay 1.1% of gross sales to an international benefit sharing fund created under the Plant Treaty's framework. Those funds are used to support research and capacity building in developing countries, through projects selected through a competitive bidding scheme.

The fact that countries are highly interdependent on the genetic resources of food security crops and forages is the main reason that for creating the MLS. An appreciation of the extent to which any country depends on resources from other countries for its agricultural development, and the extent to which this dependence is likely to increase as a result of climate change, is an important element to fully understand why participation in the Plant Treaty's MLS is so relevant.

The number of countries that are parties to the Plant Treaty has increased continuously since its adoption. However, only a few countries have taken measures to ensure the full implementation of the MLS. The immediate consequence of this situation is a lack of practical mechanisms for researchers, plant breeders and other PGRFA users to easily acquire promising germplasm from other countries, though access to the international collections is more straightforward.

As well as increasing national actors' capacities to make use of PGRFA for climate change adaptation purposes, the GRPI team worked with national teams to put in place mechanisms for the countries to operate in accordance with the MLS of the Plant Treaty. In the early planning stages of the project, representatives from the eight countries came together with specialists from the Plant Treaty and Bioversity International to develop a common implementation methodology, including a wide diversity of interventions and multiple steps. In practice, the country teams dedicated most of their time and efforts to a limited number of activities, which we will briefly describe in this section.

In order to prepare countries for regulatory frameworks that could help make ABS work in practice, the country teams analyzed whether there was sufficient legal space for the implementation of the MLS, and identified options for the revision of the relevant policies, laws and/ or other instruments when this was not the case. Existing policies and laws were reviewed, multi-stakeholder meetings were organized to seek inputs from a wide range of government and non-government agencies, the research community and, where possible, farmers and their organizations. In cases where shortcomings or gaps were identified, the country teams developed draft amendments to existing instruments that were subsequently introduced into the formal policy-making processes of the relevant organizations and political bodies in each country. This work led to concrete policy changes, such as a revision of the 2003 Biodiversity Act in Bhutan, new ABS laws in Burkina Faso, Costa Rica, Côte d'Ivoire, Guatemala and Rwanda, a revised Agrobiodiversity Policy and Act in Nepal and a new National Environment (Access to Genetic Resources and Benefit Sharing) Regulations and Temporary Procedure for Accessing PGRFA (Statutory instrument) in Uganda (see the following case studies for more details).

Country teams clarified who in the country has authority to consider requests for access to materials in the MLS, and what kind of procedures should be used. They then identified the PGRFA in the country that are 'under the management and control of the Contracting Party and in the public domain' (as stated in the Plant Treaty), which is a requisite to inform potential users about the germplasm included in the MLS. By December 2015, Bhutan, Burkina Faso, Costa Rica, Guatemala, Nepal, Rwanda and Uganda had prepared lists of accessions to be included in the MLS, and notifications were sent or were being prepared to be sent to the Secretary of the Plant Treaty.

National country teams encountered a number of challenges during this process. They included the general lack of awareness among national stakeholders about the importance and the operations of the Plant Treaty in general, and the MLS in particular. In some countries, functionaries were reluctant to exercise their discretion to provide PGRFA in the absence of a formal policy document confirming their duty and mandate to do so. The connections and coordination among agencies responsible for and involved in implementing the Plant Treaty, usually the Ministry of Agriculture and the Ministry of Environment, respectively, were relatively weak. In addition, linking implementation of the Plant Treaty/MLS with other policies, programmes and strategies (e.g. dealing with climate change adaptation or biodiversity conservation and their financing) emerged as an important issue that was not properly considered in most of the countries. Another challenge (addressed largely through the research described in the first part of this chapter) was that many stakeholders and national policymakers were not aware of the usefulness of being able to access PGRFA from other countries, rather than focusing narrowly on their obligations as providers.

The following three case studies (**Boxes 27.1–27.3**) provide insights into how some of the country teams addressed some of these challenges.[1]

## Box 27.1 Case study 1: Nepalese government adopts two policies increasing availability and use of crop diversity for climate resilience

Nepal acceded to the Plant Treaty in 2009, after it had approved the Nepal Biodiversity Strategy and Action Plan 2002 (NBSAP) and Agrobiodiversity Policy (2007). The NBSAP sets national priorities regarding the use and conservation of biological resources and benefit sharing; the Agrobiodiversity Policy addresses conservation and use of agrobiodiversity in particular. Since both instruments predate Nepal's accession to the Plant Treaty, their treatment of ABS is oriented to implementing the CBD, putting systems in place whose primary focus are to prevent unauthorized access to genetic resources, and to negotiate ABS agreements. For Nepalese organizations and individuals to be able to pool and share crop genetic resources through the MLS, it was considered necessary to revise the NBSAP and the Agrobiodiversity Policy to make policy space and provide direction to implement the Plant Treaty in harmony with the CBD.

In 2012, the national GRPI team, including staff from the Nepal Agricultural Research Council (NARC), the Ministry of Agricultural Development (MoAD) and Local Initiatives for Biodiversity, Research and Development (LIBIRD), received approval from the MoAD Secretary,to coordinate a process to revise the 2007 Agrobiodiversity Policy, including a series of consultations with seed companies, community seedbanks, farmers organizations, other ministries, research organizations and the CBD, the UNFCCC, the National Plant Treaty Focal Point and the National Agriculture

Biodiversity Conservation Committee. As part of those consultations, the national team shared information about how access to PGRFA from other countries will become increasingly important for Nepal to adapt to changing climatic conditions. The first draft was considered by the National Agrobiodiversity Conservation Committee, which is chaired by the MoAD Secretary. The national team then made revisions following the committee's recommendations, and the revised draft was submitted by the Secretary to the Council of Ministers, which approved the policy. The approved revisions also promote community-based agrobiodiversity management, *in situ* and on farm conservation and the function of the newly formed national genebank. The country team also made substantial contributions to revising the NBSAP 2014–2020, reflecting the same priorities as the Agrobiodiversity Policy and the need to integrate biodiversity into climate change strategies. The revised version was approved by Cabinet

*Source*: Based on the blog by Michael Halewood, Madan Bhatta, Bal K. Joshi, Chiranjibi Bhattarai and Devendra Gauchan 'Securing crop diversity for climate change adaptation: creating policy space for Nepal to participate in the multilateral system of access and benefit sharing'.

## Box 27.2 Case study 2: ensuring facilitated exchange of PGRFA in Costa Rica

A national research team consisting of the Plant Treaty National Focal Point and researchers from various organizations conducted research, awareness-raising and capacity-building activities to identify and discuss options for the implementation of the Plant Treaty in Costa Rica, paying particular attention to its potential in supporting national efforts for agriculture adaptation to climate change. During the process, they conducted research on past levels of reliance on 'foreign germplasm', and investigated case studies of potentially increased dependence upon other countries' PGRFA in the light of climate change. Legal and policy analyses of different implementation options were conducted and consultations held with relevant governmental organizations to agree on the most efficient and feasible ways to implement the MLS in harmony with other related conventions, like the CBD and its NP. Likewise, the National Institute of Agricultural Technology (INTA) was supported in identifying the national collections included in the MLS. INTA notified the Plant Treaty Secretariat about the inclusion of those collections, now shared with all potential PGRFA users worldwide (notice to the Plant Treaty Secretariat regarding materials included in the MLS, 14 October 2015).

In parallel, in 2015, national governmental agencies signed an agreement with key measures that facilitate the effective implementation of the MLS providing access to Costa Rica's PGRFA through the MLS in harmony with other international conventions (in Spanish, the memorandum of understanding has the name of *Carta de Entendimiento para la implementación del Sistema Multilateral de Acceso y Distribución de Beneficios del Tratado Internacional de Recursos Fitogenéticos para la Agricultura y la Alimentación y su relación con el régimen legal nacional de acceso y distribución de beneficios con miras a lograr una implementación sinérgica de ambos régimen*). This agreement is a milestone in the country's efforts to make the Plant Treaty/MLS work.

### Box 27.3 Case study 3: Uganda adopts two policies to increase availability and use of PGRFA for climate change adaptation

In Uganda, the national research team consisted of the Plant Treaty National Focal Point, genebank staff and researchers from government and non-government organizations. As in the case of the other two case studies presented previously, the research team conducted research, awareness-raising and capacity-building activities to identify options for Uganda to implement the Plant Treaty putting special emphasis on how to use it to address climate change related-challenges. They assessed past levels of dependence upon 'foreign germplasm', and investigated the potential increase of this interdependence based on predicted climate change scenarios. They coordinated country-wide consultations with organizations holding PGRFA collections, to identify those which are automatically, or could voluntarily be, included in the MLS. As a result, the national team prepared Uganda's first list of crop accessions to be made available through the MLS and notified it to the Plant Treaty Secretariat accordingly, creating the opportunity for users in Uganda and around the world to access germplasm conserved in the country. The national team negotiated an agreement between lead agencies across three sectors to define responsibilities and coordinate actions for regulating access to PGRFA and benefit sharing. This agreement was developed establishing (a) that the National Council for Science and Technology is ultimately responsible for implementing both Plant Treaty and the CBD/NP in Uganda, but that it delegates responsibility (b) to the Uganda National genebank for regulating access to PGRFA under the Plant Treaty and (c) to the National Environmental Management Agency for regulating access under the CBD/NP. This overcomes a policy bottleneck that had existed for many years, whereby no organization was clearly recognized to have authority to provide access to PGRFA.

## Reflections and options for future action

The results of our country-level work have underscored that climate changes, particularly those which involve shifting and unpredictable rainfall patterns, but also rising minimum temperatures, often have negative impacts on a number of crops in the countries concerned. The research has also demonstrated (where relevant data was available, which was certainly not always the case) that a smaller and smaller proportion of materials currently held in the national genebanks of the partnering countries has the potential to be well-adapted to the predicted climate changes of the next 30 years. They also demonstrated that there are many potentially adapted materials originally collected from other countries and continents currently in *ex situ* collections around the world that are potentially adapted (or at least possess important adaptive traits) to those conditions. These findings are consistent with the literature stating that climate change will increase countries' interdependence for germplasm; they will increasingly need access to diversity originally evolved or developed outside each other's borders to adapt to climate changes (Fujisaka et al., 2011; Ramirez-Villegas et al., 2012; Jarvis et al., 2015).

At the same time, participatory research with farmers and others in the reference sites has also revealed that there can be potentially adapted populations or varieties among the range of materials being used by farmers in those areas, but which are overlooked or underutilized. This may occur due to a number of possible factors, including lack of awareness of those materials, lack of availability of quality seed of those varieties and government incentives to use other materials. National teams generally expressed interest in pursuing a combination of strategies for using genetic diversity for adapting to climate changes at the reference sites, including identifying and making optimum use of existing, better performing materials and introducing materials from 'outside', be they from other communities, national or international genebanks or public and private sector breeders and seed providers.

The Plant Treaty and its MLS in particular are well suited to supporting the exchange of information and PGRFA for climate change adaptation. However, they are not self-executing: that is to say, it is not enough to simply ratify the Plant Treaty for stakeholders in the countries concerned to be able to take advantage of the extraordinary array of genetic diversity that is available through the MLS. Considerable additional resources need to be dedicated to building the capacity of stakeholders within countries to be able to do so. For example, the ability to make better use of PGRFA for climate change adaption through the kinds of exercises GRPI sponsored in the eight countries depends on access to information about potentially adapted materials. The partners' searches for potentially adapted materials usually do not include genebanks from surrounding countries, where one might expect potentially adapted materials to have evolved or been developed, because those countries do not have information about their collections available online (and in many cases, do not have the information systematically collated offline either).

Many of the stakeholders who could potentially make use of PGRFA diversity through the MLS neither know it exists, nor would know how to use the tools and methods necessary to identify potentially useful materials through it. Investment in building new coalitions of actors and novel partnerships between local, national and global actors are necessary to make best use of the information and materials available. As part of this, there needs to be increased recognition of farmers as active participants in these efforts, and not just beneficiaries of research and development conducted by others. As a consequence, we believe that countries would clearly benefit from boosting the capacity of national and local level organizations to provide technical backup for potential users. In particular, countries should be supported to identify and request materials located in collections around the world; introduce them into their production systems and evaluate their performance while strengthening linkages between local communities, and national genebanks, breeders, formal sector breeders and international organizations. Of course, in addition to needing increased capacity to use the system to access materials, there is the bigger challenge of building capacity to actually use those materials in breeding. Some countries have very few or no breeders, and can provide very little support for farmers to experiment with new materials.

Policy implementation projects that do not include capacity building to help countries take advantage of the MLS as recipients and users of PGRFA (and instead focus entirely on putting systems in place for them to supply PGRFA) are less likely to make progress, because they do not 'speak to' the sense policymakers, scientists and farmers have of their country's immediate needs. By the same token, policy development and implementation efforts need to be accompanied by well-funded, wide-reaching communication campaigns to raise awareness among stakeholders generally, and to place indirect (but strategic) pressure on policymakers to take action. MLS policy development projects should engage and provide training for national juridical scientists and lawyers (from Ministries of Justice if possible) from the beginning and support their participation throughout the project. Most countries do not have lawyers with specialization in this field who can take a lead role in drafting formal policy and legal documents on short notice without having been involved in thinking through options from the beginning of the policy development process.

Implementation of the MLS also needs to be 'linked up' with, and supported by, other related policy development efforts at national level. Project experiences have demonstrated that progress implementing the MLS can be either slowed down or accelerated depending upon the quality of links it has to national level efforts to implement the NP on ABS. In most countries, the Ministry of Agriculture ultimately has responsibility for implementing the Plant Treaty and the Ministry of Environment has responsibility for implementing the NP. In many countries, simultaneous, mutually supportive implementation of both has required key actors from both sectors to overcome long settled patterns of competitiveness and mutual disregard of these agencies. Some project partners have engaged in complex, but highly successful, efforts to find the requisite common ground and shared purpose (and implementing mechanisms) for implementing these agreements together, for example the memorandums of understanding formally establishing mandates and operational areas of the lead agencies. In the longer term, it is also important to embed the MLS in other national plans and strategies, as a means of raising awareness, as well as to build political momentum and encourage support from public finances. The MLS does not appear in many countries' National Adaptation Programmes of Action (NAPAs) (Bedmar Villanueva et al., 2015) where one would hope to see its potential contributions underscored. Nepal has provided a model for integrating the Plant Treaty, the MLS, agricultural biological diversity and their combined contribution to climate change adaptation, in their NBSAP and National Agrobiodiversity Policy. Ultimately, it would make sense for the Plant Treaty to figure in national economic and agricultural development plans, rural develop strategies and policies to promote the status of indigenous and local peoples.

## Note

1 The case study was prepared by Gloria Otieno, John Wasswa Mulumba and Francis Ogwal. The full version of it was first published online as a blog, https://grpi2.wordpress.com/2016/03/02/climate-change-adaptation-and-mutually-supportive-implementation-of-access-and-benefit-sharing-policies-in-uganda/

## References

Altieri, M. A. (1999) 'The ecological role of biodiversity in agroecosystems', *Agriculture, Ecosystems and Environment*, vol. 74, pp. 19–31.

Bedmar Villanueva, A., Halewood, M. and López Noriega, I. (2015) Agricultural Biodiversity in Climate Change Adaptation Planning: An Analysis of the National Adaptation Programmes of Action, CCAFS Working Paper no. 95, CGIAR Research Program on Climate Change, Agriculture and Food Security (CCAFS), Copenhagen, Denmark.

Bougma, A., Galluzzi, G. and Sawadogo, M. (2015) *The Importance of International Exchanges of Plant Genetic Resources for National Crop Improvement in Burkina Faso*, CCAFS Working Paper no. 152, CCAFS, Copenhagen, Denmark.

Fujisaka, S., Williams, D. and Halewood, M. (eds.) (2011) The Impact of Climate Change on Countries' Interdependence on Genetic Resources for Food and Agriculture, Background Study No 48, Food and Agriculture Organization of the United Nations (FAO), Rome, Italy.

IPCC (2014) *Climate Change 2014: Synthesis Report*, Contribution of Working Groups I, II and III to the Fifth Assessment Report of the Intergovernmental Panel on Climate Change (Core Writing Team, R. K. Pachauri and L. A. Meyer [eds.]), IPCC, Geneva, Switzerland.

Jarvis, A., Upadhyaya, H., Gowda, C. L. L., Aggarwal, P. K., Fujisaka, S. and Anderson, B. (2010) *Climate Change and its Effect on Conservation and Use of Plant Genetic Resources for Food and Agriculture and Associated Biodiversity for Food Security. FAO Thematic Background Study*, FAO, Rome, Italy.

Jarvis, A., Upadhyaya, H., Gowda, C. L. L., Aggarwal, P. K., Fujisaka, S. and Anderson, B. (2015) 'Plant genetic resources for food and agriculture and climate change', pp. 9–22 in *Coping With Climate Change: The Roles of Genetic Resources for Food and Agriculture*, FAO, Rome, Italy.

Lane, A. and Jarvis, A. (2007) 'Changes in climate will modify the geography of crop suitability: Agricultural biodiversity can help with adaptation', *SAT -Journal*, vol. 4, pp. 1–12.

Lasco, R. D, Delfino, R. J. P., Catacutan, D. C., Simelton, E. S. and Wilson, D. M. (2014) 'Climate risk adaptation by smallholder farmers: The roles of trees and agroforestry', *Current Opinion in Environmental Sustainability*, vol. 6, pp. 83–88.

Lipper, L. and Cooper, D. (2009) 'Managing plant genetic resources for sustainable use in food and agriculture', pp. 27–39 in A. Kontoleon, U. Pascual and M. Smale (eds.), *Agrobiodiversity Conservation and Economic Development*, Routledge, Abingdon, UK and New York, NY, USA.

Lobell, D. B., Burke, M. B., Tebaldi, C., Mastrandrea, M. D., Falcon, W. P. and Naylo, R. L. (2008) 'Prioritizing climate change adaptation needs for food security in 2030', *Science*, vol. 319, pp. 607–610.

Lobell, D. B. and Christopher, B. F. (2007) 'Global scale climate – crop yield relationships and the impacts of recent warming', *Environmental Research Letters*, vol. 2, p. 014002.

Lobell, D. B. and Gourdji, S. M. (2012) 'The influence of climate change on global crop productivity', *Plant Physiology*, vol. 160, pp. 1686–1697.

Lobell, D. B., Schlenker, W. and Costa-Roberts, J. (2011) 'Climate trends and global crop production since 1980', *Science*, vol. 333, pp. 616–620.

Mercer, K. L. and Perales, H. R. (2010) 'Evolutionary response of landraces to climate change in centers of crop diversity', *Evolutionary Applications*, vol. 3, pp. 480–493.

Ortiz, R. (2011) 'Agrobiodiversity management for climate change', pp. 189–211 in J. M. Lenné and D. Wood (eds.), *Agrobiodiversity Management for Food Security: A Critical Review*, CAB International, Wallingford, UK.

Ramirez-Villegas, J., Jarvis, A., Fujisaka, S., Hanson, J. and Leibing, C. (2012) 'Crop and forage genetic resources: International interdependence in the face of climate change', pp. 78–98 in M. Halewood, I. López Noriega and S. Louafi (eds.), *Crop Genetic Resources as a Global Commons: Challenges in International Law and Governance*, Routledge, Abgindon, UK.

Sthapit, B., Padulosi, S. and Mal, B. (2010) 'Role of on-farm/*in situ* conservation and underutilized crops in the wake of climate change', *Indian Journal of Plant Genetic Resources*, vol. 23, pp. 145–156.

Vernooy, R., Bessette, G. and Rudebjer, P. (eds.) (2016) *Resource Box for Resilient Seed Systems: Handbook*, Bioversity International, Maccarese, Italy, www.bioversityinternational.org/e-library/publications/detail/resource-box-for-resilient-seed-systems-handbook/

# 28

# 'STEWARDSHIP' OR 'OWNERSHIP'

## How to realize farmers' rights?

*Regine Andersen*

### Introduction

Over the last ten millennia, farmers from all cultivated regions of the world have contributed to developing the enormous diversity of crop genetic diversity that is available today. This has been recognized in the International Treaty on Plant Genetic Resources for Food and Agriculture (ITPGRFA) as the basis for food and agriculture production throughout the world (Article 9). During the last hundred years, division of labour within the agricultural sector has increased, leading to the professionalization of plant breeding and the development of high yielding varieties. These varieties have boosted agricultural production while simultaneously time wiping out untold other varieties. Breeders' innovations have been protected and promoted with intellectual property rights, whereas the legal space for farmers to continue their contributions to the conservation and sustainable use of crop genetic resources has been reduced, and mechanisms to promote their contribution are lacking. The ITPGRFA was meant to balance this situation with its Multilateral System of Access and Benefit-Sharing and its provisions on farmers' rights. However, the benefit-sharing mechanism is hardly functioning, and farmers' rights are only vaguely addressed in the Treaty. This reflects the great controversies that have surrounded these issues over the years of negotiation and implementation. As an international regime, the Treaty provides an arena for developing international norms on the management of plant genetic diversity for food and agriculture. This is an ongoing process and depends on interests and power, as well as our capabilities of framing the issues and the challenges at stake. In this chapter, I provide a historical overview of the process related to Farmers' Rights under the Treaty and present a model for understanding these developments through a 'stewardship' and an 'ownership' approach. I suggest that a clear grasp of these approaches and their potential consequences is important to develop international norms and regulations that really contribute the realization of Farmers' Rights.

### The historical development of farmers' rights

The enormous diversity of food crops available today has developed through careful selection of seeds and propagating material and exchange over short and long distances, in close interaction with nature. At the core of this fabulous innovation are the farmers of the last ten millennia and more, the custodians of crop genetic diversity (Andersen, 2016). An estimated 7,000 species are now used as crops worldwide (Wilson, 1992; Meldrum and Padulosi, Chapter 18 of this Handbook), with great diversity within species. The continuous growth of crop diversity was, however, brought to a halt in the last century, when modern plant breeding introduced genetically homogenous high-yielding varieties. Given the great value of crop genetic resources for food security, this caused international concern: plant genetic diversity has been argued to be more important for farming than any other environmental factor because it enables farmers to adapt to changing environmental conditions, including climate change (Andersen, 2008; Fujisaka et al., 2009; United Nations, 2009).

In response to the rapid erosion of crop genetic resources, the International Board for Plant Genetic Resources (IBPGR) was founded in 1974 under the auspices of the Consultative Group on International Agricultural Research (CGIAR).[1] Located at the FAO headquarters in Rome, it drew on staff designated for the FAO program on genetic resources conservation. Collecting missions were accelerated, and gene banks were constructed and expanded at national, regional and international levels. (FAO, 1986, 1998). Only 15% of the samples collected were designated for storage in developing countries, whereas 85% were stored in industrialized countries and in the gene banks of the international agricultural research centres (IARCs) of the CGIAR (Fowler, 1994), most of which were then located in the developed world. The IBPGR and the IARCs did invaluable work in saving fast-eroding plant varieties from extinction – but in the process, developing countries lost control over their own genetic resources. This led to the FAO Conference deciding in 1981 to draft the elements of a legal convention for the establishment of an international gene bank. This was reported back to the FAO Conference two years later (Fowler, 1994).

During the negotiations, a major conflict lay between those in favouring plant breeders' rights over improved plant varieties and those in favour of unrestricted access to all varieties (Fowler, 1994, pp. 187–191). The United States and representatives of the seed industry were the leading proponents of the former stance, while developing countries made up the latter position. This point is worth noting since most developing countries were later to change their position on access in order to provide for control over their genetic resources and benefits from their use, which required a stricter regulation of access. (This position was voiced a decade later under the Convention on Biological Diversity [CBD] and in response to the emerging Agreement on Trade-Related Aspects of Intellectual Property Rights [TRIPS Agreement], which was then being negotiated in the Uruguay Round leading to the establishment of the World Trade Organization [WTO]. This is an important background for understanding the access and benefit sharing arrangements which eventually emerged under the CBD and its Nagoya Protocol.)

When the International Undertaking on Plant Genetic Resources was adopted in 1983 by the 22nd session of the FAO Conference, it was adhered to by 113 countries. The adoption of the International Undertaking can be seen as a partial victory for developing countries because it was achieved despite the opposition of major industrialized countries led by the United States. The victory was only partial, however, because the new agreement ended up as a legally non-binding undertaking, without the adherence of industrialized countries that were important to the international management of PGRFA.

The objectives of the International Undertaking were to ensure that PGRFA would be explored, preserved, evaluated, and made available for plant breeding and scientific purposes. The International Undertaking was based on 'the universally accepted principle that plant genetic resources are a heritage of mankind and consequently should be available without restriction'. The two pronged goal was clear: conservation and access.

Along with the International Undertaking, the Commission on Plant Genetic Resources (CPGR) was also established.[2] The CPGR was an intergovernmental body charged with ensuring the implementation of the International Undertaking and monitoring it, especially the operation of international arrangements for the management of PGRFA.

The main reason that developed countries did not adhere to the International Undertaking[3] was its statement that genetic resources should be available without restriction, which was seen to be in conflict with plant breeders' rights. Therefore, countries could adhere to the International Undertaking only if the text was modified in some way (Andersen, 2005). It was in this context that the concept of farmers' rights was taken up in the FAO for the first time. The first documented use of the concept was at a meeting of the working group in 1986 (FAO, 1986) and arose as a response to the increased demand for plant breeders' by drawing attention towards the unremunerated innovations of farmers that were seen as the foundation of all modern plant breeding. The working group produced a report on how to deal with the reservations towards the International Undertaking and on how to attract greater adherence (FAO, 1986, para. 8), the third chapter of which is devoted to farmers' rights. It not only linked the issue to the question of access to genetic resources but also revealed substantial uncertainties as to the understanding of the concept, and called for further elucidation. At the second meeting of the working group in 1987, farmers' rights were hence addressed in greater detail, with particular attention to the need to reward farmers for their contribution to PGRFA. The rights holders were not to be single farmers or communities but, rather, entire peoples – that is, a form of a collective right. This concept can be regarded as the foundation for the stewardship approach to farmers' rights that is discussed later in this chapter.

The idea of developing farmers' and plant breeders' rights simultaneously in order to balance the two also emerged:

> The Working Group concurred that Breeders' Rights and Farmers' Rights were parallel and complementary rather than opposed and that the simultaneous recognition and international legitimization of both these rights could help to boost and speed up the development of the people of the world.
>
> *(FAO, 1986, para. 12)*

At the second session of the CPGR in 1987, the contact group agreed that, 'while the so-called "farmers' rights" could not yet be given a precise definition, some sort of compensation for their most valuable contribution to the enrichment of the plant genetic resources of the world was well-founded and legitimate'. It was pointed out that one way of giving practical recognition to this right could be via a form of multifaceted international cooperation that included freer exchange of plant genetic resources, information and research findings, and training. Another way could be through monetary contributions for programmes furthering the objectives of the International Undertaking (FAO, 1986, Appendix G).

Thus, the contact group did not arrive at a definition of 'farmers' rights' but outlined some means of according them practical recognition within the framework of the International Understanding.

Nevertheless, deep controversies over these issues remained between the countries of the Organisation for Economic Development and Co-operation (OECD), on the one hand, and the group of developing countries and their NGO supporters, on the other. These controversies were also fuelled by the Uruguay Round of the General Agreement on Tariffs and Trade (GATT), which ultimately led to the WTO, where intellectual property rights (IPR) were brought into the negotiations by the United States.[4] During the first years of the Uruguay Round, which started in 1986, an agreement on IPRs was strongly opposed by several developing countries. Indeed, by the 1988 mid-term review of the Round, it was determined that such an agreement would be impossible (Evans and Walsh, 1994). During 1989, however, those developing countries that were in opposition changed their positions and dropped their earlier resistance to an agreement on IPRs. This radical shift clearly resulted from their recognized need to make concessions within the negotiations, since a consensus on all of the agreements would be needed before the package could be adopted (Yusuf, 1998). Thus, the resulting Agreement on Trade-Related Aspects of Intellectual Property Rights (TRIPS Agreement) excluded from patentability plants and animals (other than micro-organisms) and essential biological processes for the production of plants and animals (other than non-biological and microbiological processes), but it did oblige members to provide for the protection of plant varieties either by patents or an effective *sui generis* system, or a combination of these (Article 27.3.b). Even though several different *sui generis* systems are in operation, the term has most often been used with respect to the International Union for the Protection of New Varieties of Plant (UPOV) (Andersen, 2008, pp. 164–168).

The developments at the FAO Conference in 1989 should be seen in the light of the Uruguay Round, as what was sacrificed there was taken up again at the FAO in other ways. Two resolutions were adopted by this Conference: Resolution 4/89 on the Agreed Interpretation of the International Undertaking and Resolution 5/89 on Farmers' Rights (both Resolutions annexed to the International Undertaking). These Resolutions were adopted by consensus, but arose only as a result of tense negotiations: there had again been fierce resistance to the idea of plant breeders' rights among developing countries, and the interpretations that provided for the acceptance of these rights could only be adopted with the simultaneous recognition of farmers' rights (Andersen, 2005).

Resolution 4/89 stated that 'Plant Breeders' Rights as provided for under UPOV . . . are not incompatible with the International Undertaking' (para. 1) and that

> states adhering to the Undertaking recognize the enormous contribution that farmers of all regions have made to the conservation and development of plant genetic resources, which constitute the basis of plant production throughout the world, and which form the basis for the concept of Farmers' Rights.
>
> *(para. 3)*

Resolution 5/89 represented a milestone as the first recognition by the FAO Conference of farmers' contributions to the global pool of genetic diversity, and indeed outlined the contents and implications of the concept itself (**Box 28.1** *Extract from Resolution 5/89, Farmers' Rights*).

In 1991, a new annex to the International Undertaking was adopted as Resolution 3/91 (FAO, 1991). This time, the Conference stated that the concept of genetic resources as the heritage of mankind, as applied in the International Undertaking, was subject to the sovereignty of states.[5] This interpretation might be seen to have been heavily influenced by the ongoing negotiations for a Convention on Biological Diversity (CBD), which was adopted only six months later and which also incorporated the principle of national sovereignty in Article 3. As a result of the CBD negotiations (and in response to the emerging intellectual property regime), negotiators from developing countries demanded control over access to their genetic resources as well as the fair and equitable sharing of the benefits arising from their use. In many circles, this demand brought about a shift in thinking on genetic resources, from a perspective based on the common heritage of mankind to a bilateral approach to benefit sharing, which was in turn a response to the IPR regime emerging from the Uruguay Round (Andersen, 2008). This shift can be seen as the beginning of the 'ownership approach' to farmers' rights, as set out later in this chapter.

After Resolution 3/91, FAO members stated that the conditions for access to plant genetic resources required further clarification (FAO, 1991, para. d). The original purpose of the International

## Box 28.1 Extract from Resolution 5/89, Farmers' Rights

The FAO Conference . . . [e]ndorses the concept of Farmers' Rights (Farmers' Rights mean rights arising from the past, present and future contributions of farmers in conserving, improving, and making available plant genetic resources, particularly those in the centres of origin/diversity. These rights are vested in the International Community, as trustee for present and future generations of farmers, for the purpose of ensuring full benefits to farmers, and supporting the continuation of their contributions, as well as the attainment of the overall purposes of the International Undertaking) in order to:

- ensure that the need for conservation is globally recognized and that sufficient funds for these purposes will be available;
- assist farmers and farming communities, in all regions of the world, but especially in the areas of origin/diversity of plant genetic resources, in the protection and conservation of their plant genetic resources, and of the natural biosphere;
- allow farmers, their communities, and countries in all regions, to participate fully in the benefits derived, at present and in the future, from the improved use of plant genetic resources, through plant breeding and other scientific methods.

*(FAO, 1989)*

Undertaking – which was to ensure unrestricted access to genetic resources – was no longer clear, and the principles of 'the common heritage of mankind' that had controlled these resources were blurred.

The adoption of the Convention on Biological Diversity (CBD) in 1992 was a decisive event for the development of the International Undertaking regime. The CBD became the first legally binding international agreement to address the sustainable management of biological diversity worldwide[6] and was developed as a stand-alone convention as well as a framework convention (Andersen, 2008).

At the Conference for the Adoption of the Agreed Text of the Convention on Biological Diversity in May 1992, the Nairobi Final Act was adopted (UNEP, 1992), including a resolution on the inter-relationship between the CBD and the promotion of sustainable agriculture (Resolution 3). This resolution recommended that ways and means be explored to develop complementarity and cooperation between the CBD and the Global System for the Conservation and Sustainable Use of Plant Genetic Resources for Food and Sustainable Agriculture (UNEP, 1992, para. 2), which had been established under the FAO with the International Undertaking acting as a central component. Finally, the resolution recognized the need to seek solutions to two outstanding matters concerning PGRFA: (a) access to *ex situ* collections that had not been acquired in accordance with the CBD and (b) the question of farmers' rights.

At its 27th session in 1993, the FAO Conference accordingly requested the FAO director-general to provide a forum for negotiations for harmonizing the International Undertaking with the CBD (Resolution 7/93): this was the point of departure for the lengthy negotiations that finally resulted in the adoption of the ITPGRFA in 2001.

Revising the International Undertaking in harmony with the CBD was a challenging task. The specific features, uses, and management needs of PGRFA had to be considered.[7] PGRFA constitute the basis of farming and are, except for their wild relatives, domesticated resources.

Since access to PGRFA is a condition for the further domestication, and thus continued existence, of these resources, expeditious facilitation of access was a major concern to the negotiators. To ensure access, it was also important that transferred PGRFA should remain in the public domain and not be made subject to exclusive IPRs. A means of benefit sharing other than that envisaged under the CBD had to be found, focussed on those who conserve and sustainably use the resources, rather than on the specific providers. This was because (a) for most crops, it is difficult to identify the countries of origin (the countries entitled to provide access under the CBD; Andersen, 2001; Fowler, 2001); (b) all countries are interdependent on PGRFA, so a complicated system of transfers between providers and recipients would hamper expeditious access (Palacios, 1998); (c) rewarding only the current providers of genetic resources would not be fair to farmers who maintain or develop genetic diversity that will benefit future generations.

Throughout the negotiations, farmers' rights were one of the most contested issues. Most developing countries, as well as some industrialized countries (e.g. Norway) had advocated comprehensive and internationally binding recognition of farmers' rights, a stance opposed by countries such as the United States and Australia. The controversies were complex and a breakthrough seemed unlikely when, in 1999, negotiators from the North decided to meet some of the demands from the South – and this compromise led to the long-awaited breakthrough. What resulted was the final text of the ITPGRFA on farmers' rights as we know it today.[8]

When the ITPGRFA was finally adopted in November 2001, many observers had almost given up on ever reaching a consensus. Indeed, full consensus proved impossible, and the Treaty had to be put to the vote: 116 countries voted in favour of the Treaty and two countries abstained (Japan and the United States). The ITPGRFA was the first legally binding agreement to deal exclusively with PGRFA, and it was also incidentally the first international treaty of the new millennium.[9] Since then, both the United States and Japan have revised their policies and also ratified.[10] The ITPGRFA entered into force on 29 June 2004,[11] and as of October 2016, it has been ratified by 141 states.

The objectives of the ITPGRFA are the conservation and sustainable use of PGRFA as well as the fair and equitable sharing of benefits arising from their use – in harmony with the CBD – for sustainable agriculture and food security (Article 1). The Treaty sets out that the contracting parties shall promote an integrated approach to the exploration, conservation, and sustainable use of PGRFA (Article 5): suggested measures include improving *ex situ* conservation of plant varieties and wild crop species and providing farmers with support for on-farm management and conservation of PGRFA – the latter being particularly relevant for farmers' seed systems and farmers' rights.

The ITPGRFA stipulates that contracting parties shall develop and maintain appropriate policies and legal measures that promote sustainable use of PGRFA (Article 6). This provision is an obligation for all contracting parties and may include such measures as promoting diverse farming systems; encouraging research that enhances and conserves biological diversity; developing plant breeding with the participation of farmers in developing countries; broadening the genetic bases of crops; increasing the range of genetic diversity available to farmers; expanding the use of local and locally adopted crops and underutilized species; making wider use of a diversity of varieties and species in on-farm management, conservation, and sustainable use; and adjusting the breeding strategies and regulations on variety release and seed distribution.

The ITPGRFA also sets out a Multilateral System of Access and Benefit Sharing (MLS) (in Articles 10–13[12]) which covers 35 food crops and 29 forage plants that are in the public domain and under the management and control of the contracting parties (the Annex I crops), see Engels and Rudebjer, Chapter 41 of this Handbook.[13]

In the preamble to the ITPGRFA, the contracting parties affirm that the past, present, and future contributions of farmers in all regions of the world – particularly those in the centres of origin and diversity – in conserving, improving, and making available these resources, constitute the basis of farmers' rights. They also affirm that the rights recognized in the ITPGRFA to save, use, exchange, and sell farm-saved seed and other propagating material, to participate in relevant decision making, and to encourage fair and equitable benefit sharing are fundamental to the realization of farmers' rights. Article 9 of the ITPGRFA recognizes the enormous contribution of farmers in the conservation and development of PGRFA and that this contribution constitutes the basis of food and agriculture production throughout the world. It explicitly states that responsibility for the implementation of farmers' rights, as they relate to the management of PGRFA, rests with national governments. Certain measures to protect and promote farmers' rights are suggested, for example the protection of traditional knowledge, the right to participate in equitable benefit sharing, and the right to participate in decision making at the national level. Also the rights that farmers have to save, use, exchange, and sell farm-saved seeds and propagating materials are addressed, but without any particular direction. As these provisions are vague, contracting parties, in particular developing countries, have sought guidance and assistance for the implementation of Farmers' Rights since the entry into force of the Treaty, without much effect so far. There have, however, been consultation processes between the sessions of the Governing Body and negotiations related to the resolutions from the Governing Body that contribute to shaping a common ground of understanding of what it takes to realize farmers' rights. In order to make progress in this regard, it may be useful to analyze the negotiations and discussions along the lines of a 'stewardship' and an 'ownership' approach to realizing farmers' rights.

## Two approaches to the realization of farmers' rights under the Treaty

As described earlier, farmers' rights constitute a cornerstone of the ITPGRFA.[14] Achieving the conservation and sustainable use of crop genetic resources as set out in Article 1 depends decisively on farmers and their ability to maintain these resources *in situ* on-farm, which in turn depends on farmers' rights. The provisions on access and benefit sharing under the Treaty are vital to the realization of farmers' rights but as the aforementioned historical account outlines, the topic of Farmers' Rights has been discussed in the contexts of different rationales, resulting in different perceptions on their main contents. Two basic ways of approaching the concept of Farmers' Rights have been advanced previously (Andersen, 2006, 2016) and are further developed here.

### *The 'stewardship approach'*

The stewardship approach describes the idea that agro-biodiversity as a principle belongs to the common heritage of mankind and that it should be shared for the common good as part of the public domain. As such, the stewardship approach can be said to have been the dominant rationale throughout the history of agriculture until the advent of intellectual property rights. In terms of farmers' rights, a stewardship approach would refer to the rights that farmers must be granted collectively in order to enable them to continue as stewards and innovators of agro-biodiversity and reward them for this contribution. A core idea is to uphold and enhance the 'legal space' required for farmers to continue this role. Another core idea is that farmers involved in the maintenance of agro-biodiversity – on behalf of their generation and for the benefit of all mankind – should be rewarded and supported for their contributions, and that this principle should constitute the basis of a benefit-sharing system.

## The 'ownership approach'

The ownership approach evolved when the interests in the commercial use of genetic resources increased along with the growing economic stakes of biotechnologies in the second half of the last century, followed by demands for intellectual property rights to protect and promote inventions. As intellectual property systems are costly institutions, the capacity of developing countries, rich in genetic resources, to develop and effectively use such systems was limited (Andersen, 2008). These emerging power asymmetries were met with much protest against intellectual property rights to genetic resources from the 'Global South', along with the demands of securing control over their resources through systems regulating access on mutually agreed terms and prior informed consent between purported owners and users of these resources. There should be fair and equitable sharing of the benefits arising from the use of genetic resources between purported owners and users of these resources. This is the basis of the ownership approach, which describes the idea that establishing individual or collective ownership to genetic resources provide important incentives to promote breeding as well as the conservation and sustainable use of agro-biodiversity. Furthermore, it enables control over the genetic resources that are covered with ownership rights for the holders of such rights, the purported owners, and makes it possible to trade with them as well as to attract benefit sharing. In terms of farmers' rights, an ownership approach would establish the right of farmers to be rewarded on an individual or collective basis for genetic material that has been obtained from their fields and used in commercial varieties and/or protected with intellectual property rights. The idea is that such a reward system is necessary to enable the equitable sharing of benefits arising from the use of agro-biodiversity and to establish an incentive structure for the continued maintenance of this diversity. Access and benefit-sharing legislation and farmers' intellectual property rights would be central instruments.

The distinctions between the two approaches are not clear-cut. An evolving ownership approach to the management of crop genetic resources will enable different actors to exclude each other from the access to, and use of, these vital resources, and thereby reduce the legal space for all to contribute to the conservation and sustainable use of crop genetic diversity (Andersen, 2008). A stewardship approach would maintain and enhance the legal space and possibilities to contribute to the conservation and sustainable use of crop genetic resources. The paradox is, however, that without sufficient measures to avoid it, the stewardship approach might result in genetic resources and information from the public domain being privatized and thus becoming subject to the ownership approach. Whereas the stewardship approach may result in misappropriation of crop genetic resources by third parties, the ownership approach may result in disincentives to share crop genetic resources among farmers and thus reduce the millennia-old traditions of seed exchange and distributions that have contributed to the agro-biodiversity we have today. It is important to understand not only the different rationales behind the two approaches, but also how they can be combined to achieve the conservation and sustainable use of genetic resources, the sharing of benefits arising from the use of these resources, and the realization of farmers' rights.

The next section will examine in detail the four elements of farmers' rights – namely, protection of traditional knowledge, benefit sharing, participation in decision making, and the rights to save, use, exchange, and sell farm-saved seed – and how they can be interpreted under the stewardship and ownership approaches. It will also discuss how the two approaches can be combined to achieve the goals of the International Treaty.

## Protecting farmers' traditional knowledge

Understanding traditional knowledge related to plant genetic resources for food and agriculture requires a holistic understanding of the dynamic nature of this knowledge, including factors such as livelihoods, cultures, and landscapes. Traditional knowledge is vital to understanding the properties of plants, their uses, and how they are cultivated. It includes knowledge on how to select seeds and propagating material, how to store them, and how to use them for the next harvest. Thus, it also comprises the basic necessities for farmers to be able to maintain crop genetic diversity in the fields. Article 9.2(a) is the only provision on traditional knowledge in the ITPGRFA, and provides for 'the protection of traditional knowledge relevant to plant genetic resources for food and agriculture'. The Treaty provides no further guidance on how this article can be interpreted and operationalized. However, since the objectives of the ITPGRFA are to be implemented in harmony with the CBD (Article 1), Article 8j of the CBD is also relevant in this context. According to this article, each contracting party shall – as far as possible and as appropriate and pursuant to national legislation – respect, maintain, and preserve traditional knowledge, innovation, and practices and promote their wider application, with the approval of the holders of such knowledge, innovations, and practices. The equitable sharing of benefits from its use should be encouraged.

Understanding the challenges related to the protection of traditional knowledge has significantly influenced current views about how Article 9.2(a) can be implemented. Examining the contents of this right from the stewardship and an ownership approaches suggests rather different possibilities:

1 *Protection against extinction* means ensuring that traditional knowledge is kept alive and can further develop among farmers. Under a stewardship approach, the best way to protect traditional knowledge from the threat of extinction is to share it – a widespread approach in the North – and, thus, the motto: 'protection by sharing'. Measures for the sharing of traditional knowledge include:

   - Seminars and gatherings among farmers to share knowledge;
   - Seed fairs for the exchange of propagating material and associated knowledge;
   - Documentation of knowledge in seed catalogues and registries;
   - Documentation of knowledge in books, magazines, and on websites; and
   - Documentation of knowledge in gene banks and making such knowledge accessible.

2 *Protection against misappropriation* is a different approach. It is based on the anticipation that farmers' varieties, and associated knowledge, could be appropriated by commercial actors without prior informed consent from the holders of this knowledge and benefit-sharing on mutually agreed terms. Thus, the sharing of knowledge should not take place unless measures are in place to avoid this. This view is often accompanied by a widespread regret that the fear of misappropriation has made it necessary to be cautious. An ownership approach to protecting traditional knowledge would mean providing farmers with the right to act against misappropriation of their knowledge and to decide over the use of this knowledge and related plant genetic resources.

In order to consider the two approaches, it is important to assess the threat of misappropriation of crop genetic resources. To what extent is such misappropriation taking place? According to existing documentation, it seems that, in developing new varieties, commercial plant breeders tend to use already improved varieties from their own stocks or from other plant breeders. Farmers' varieties are generally regarded as being difficult to work with due to their genetic heterogeneity. Only when particular traits are sought – those not found in their own stocks or other improved varieties – are farmers' varieties deemed necessary. When they are sought, they are normally obtained from gene banks and not from farmers' fields or markets. In gene banks, little traditional knowledge is typically included in the passport data. Thus, traditional knowledge related to crop genetic resources is still rarely used in commercial breeding. Generally, the genetic foundation for commercial plant breeding appears to be narrowing (Esquinas-Alcázar, 2005, p. 948). This situation, together with the effects of climate change, may well change demand for landraces and farmers' varieties – together with their associated knowledge – in the future (Esquinas-Alcázar, 2005).

In any case, based on the ownership approach, protection of traditional knowledge would mean offering ownership status to farmers with the right to act against misappropriation and to decide over the use of their knowledge and related plant genetic resources. In Norway, farmers stress that their traditional knowledge is about to disappear. Therefore, protection, as they understand it, must ensure that such knowledge does not die out (Andersen, 2011). To achieve this, knowledge must be shared in the broadest manner possible. Norwegian farmers are thus prone to a stewardship approach. They fear that an ownership approach to protection could provide disincentives to sharing knowledge between and among farmers. Proponents of the stewardship approach insist that ownership in this context has been an alien idea among farmers and that it represents a profound break with traditional perceptions.

Ultimately, the measures that are chosen should reflect the situation. What is most important today, with the rapid erosion of traditional knowledge, is to protect traditional knowledge related to crop genetic resources from becoming extinct. Nevertheless, avoiding misappropriation is important, and considered a condition in many communities for sharing knowledge. For this purpose, we need to take a closer look at what misappropriation of traditional knowledge may be about in the context of the ITPGRFA and the multilateral system on access and benefit sharing.

Basically, there are three forms of action that farmers tend to regard as misappropriation: (a) if farmers' varieties and related knowledge are used in commercial plant breeding without recognizing the farmers in question; (b) if plant breeders obtain IPR to farmers' varieties, thereby removing the varieties from the public domain and the traditional uses of farmers; and (c) if plant breeders profit from the use of farmers' varieties and related knowledge without sharing the benefits with the farmers in question.

Measures to avoid such misappropriation could include:

- *Certifying recognition*: Recognition is very important to many farmers, particularly in the South. Ways of showing recognition include naming varieties after the farmers or communities in question, providing information about the farmers on the wrapping of products, and/or rewarding farmers for their contribution in terms of benefit sharing (see discussion later in this chapter) or with awards. With respect to the first measures, it may be difficult to identify the individual farmers in question since several farmers/communities/regions may have maintained a crop variety or contributed to its development. Awards are different in this regard since they can often be awarded for the maintenance of diversity and related knowledge, as such, and not necessarily for specific varieties.
- *Avoiding breeders' claims to intellectual property rights on farmers' varieties*: Documenting plant varieties and their related knowledge is normally a useful way to establish prior art. It means that no one can claim intellectual property rights over those varieties in the form in which they are documented. This measure is, to date, the most promising means of ensuring protection against the misappropriation of genetic resources and associated traditional

knowledge while, at the same time, promoting the sharing of knowledge. Plant variety registries have been established locally in many countries – for example, in the Philippines and in Nepal (Andersen and Winge, 2008). The formulation of legal clauses in catalogues of genetic material and associated material is also a measure to avoid misappropriation, as has been done with great success in Peru (see following paragraphs).

- *Ensuring benefit sharing*: Under the ITPGRFA, benefit sharing is to take place according to the Standard Material Transfer Agreement in the multilateral system. The benefits should be shared with farmers in developing countries and in countries with economies in transition who conserve and sustainably use crop genetic diversity and related knowledge (not between specific providers of genetic resources and the users of these specific resources). It should be noted, however, that there are many questions related to benefit sharing, which will be addressed in the following paragraphs.

Other measures for protection against misappropriation, as provided under the Convention on Biological Diversity and its Nagoya Protocol in access and benefit-sharing could include regulating access to genetic resources and associated traditional knowledge with measures on prior informed consent and mutually agreed terms, and could introduce 'user country measures' such as conditions for intellectual property rights and certificates of origin for genetic resources and following the appropriate legal procedures for access to genetic resources in provider countries.

There exist many useful and inspiring databases and catalogues on crop genetic resources and associated traditional knowledge around the world. These sources also establish prior art with regard to farmers' varieties and contribute to benefit sharing by making the knowledge accessible. Some of them also give explicit recognition to farmers. An impressive example is the potato catalogue from Huancavelica, Peru (Centro Internacional de la Papa and Federación Departamental de Comunidades Campesinas, 2006; see also Scurrah et al., 2008). Other success stories include *in situ* conservation in Switzerland, which has combined on-farm conservation of a huge number of crop varieties with a range of measures for the dissemination of information regarding the varieties and the associated traditional knowledge (Andersen and Winge, 2008); the community registry at Bohol, the Philippines, which is helping to keep traditional knowledge alive and accessible (Andersen and Winge, 2013); and information and seminar activities in Norway that are helping to disseminate traditional knowledge (Andersen and Winge, 2008).

These models have succeeded in implementing farmers' rights with respect to traditional knowledge that is associated with crop genetic resources. However, they are only a beginning. Much more is needed to keep such knowledge alive among farmers and to promote its further development. In many countries, it would appear to be necessary to raise awareness about the importance of traditional knowledge related to crop genetic resources and to develop strategies on how to maintain and disseminate traditional knowledge in a systematic way before such knowledge is lost completely.

Finally, whether a stewardship approach, an ownership approach, or a combination of the two is chosen, it is important to ensure that it does not provide any disincentives to the sharing of knowledge and genetic resources among farmers and that it does not contribute to genetic erosion or the loss of traditional knowledge.

## Ensuring equitable benefit sharing

Article 9.2(b) of the ITPGRFA concerns a farmer's right to participate equitably in the sharing of benefits arising from the utilization of plant genetic resources for food and agriculture. To interpret this provision, some guidance can be found in Article 13 on benefit sharing in the multilateral system. This article lists the most important benefits as: (a) facilitated access to plant genetic resources for food and agriculture; (b) the exchange of information; (c) access to, and transfer of, technology; (d) capacity building, and (e) the sharing of monetary and other benefits arising from commercialization. Moreover, it specifies that benefits arising from the use of plant genetic resources for food and agriculture that are shared under the multilateral system should flow primarily, directly, and indirectly to farmers in all countries – especially in developing countries and countries with economies in transition – who conserve and sustainably utilize plant genetic resources for food and agriculture.

Whereas these provisions all relate to the multilateral system and not directly to the provisions on farmers' rights in the ITPGRFA, they reflect a line of thought on benefit sharing that is relevant for interpreting Article 9.2(b) as a measure to protect and promote farmers' rights. First, it is clear that there are many forms of benefit sharing, of which monetary benefits compose only one part. Second, the benefits are not only to be shared with those few farmers who happen to have plant varieties that are utilized by commercial breeding companies but also with farmers in all countries that are engaged in the conservation and sustainable use of agro-biodiversity.

Measures to ensure the equitable sharing of benefits arising from the use of genetic resources can be designed in many ways. Under an ownership approach, these measures would mandate the development of direct benefit sharing in which the benefits would be shared directly between the purported 'owners' and 'buyers' of genetic resources – based on a prior informed consent on mutually agreed terms (as set out in the CBD).[15]

In the South, policies on benefit sharing – if any – are normally present in the laws and regulations on access to biological resources, which are sometimes found in the national legislation on the protection of biological diversity. Countries with legislation on indigenous peoples' rights often include provisions on benefit sharing in these laws, which then also cover indigenous farmers. Most of these regulations compose forms of direct benefit sharing between the 'owners' and the 'buyers' of genetic resources, often based upon prior informed consent on mutually agreed terms, as set out in the CBD. However, despite all of these efforts, so far there have hardly been any examples of direct monetary benefit sharing between the providers and recipients of plant genetic resources for food and agriculture as a result of such legislation.

There are, however, other ways of sharing benefits, which are often referred to as indirect approaches to benefit sharing. These approaches are in line with FAO's mandate in the early days of negotiations on farmers' rights, inspired by a stewardship approach. A basic principle was that benefits should be shared among 'entire peoples', the stewards of plant genetic resources in agriculture and society at large (FAO, 1987, Appendix F, section 8). This principle is based on the idea that it is farmers' legitimate right to be rewarded for their contributions to the global genetic pool from which we all benefit, and it is an obligation of the international community to ensure that such recognition and reward is provided.

Where should the funds come from to enable such benefit sharing? First of all, as already noted, the benefit-sharing mechanism under the multilateral system specifies that the benefits from the system should flow primarily to farmers in all countries, especially in developing countries and countries with economies in transition, who conserve and sustainably use crop genetic resources (Article 13.3). The basic principles of the multilateral system is that the countries that are parties to the ITPGRFA include all the genetic material of their Annex I crops that are in the public domain and under their control in the multilateral system. This material is freely accessible upon signing a standard material transfer agreement. In order for this material to remain in the public domain, it is not allowed to seek intellectual property rights on the material in the form it is received. If recipients develop it further and then patent it, then a mandatory fixed payment is to be paid to the benefit-sharing fund under the multilateral system. If the developed material is commercialized, but without patenting, then a contribution is voluntary. Other voluntary payments may also be paid to the benefit-sharing fund, and most of the funds received so far belong to this latter category. However, it is uncertain how much funding can be generated by this mechanism and even whether this mechanism will be successful and make a substantial difference to the farmers it is supposed to be helping.

The funding strategy of the ITPGRFA (as set out in Article 18) is another important source insofar as it supports the implementation of conservation (Article 5), sustainable use (Article 6), and farmers' rights (Article 9), which would all greatly benefit diversity farmers. However, since there are to date no fixed mandatory contributions, it is uncertain how much money the fund can generate. Thus, for the time being, Article 7 on international cooperation and Article 8 on technical assistance are important provisions on benefit sharing. In these articles, the contracting parties agree to promote the provision of technical assistance to developing countries and countries with economies in transition, with the objective of facilitating the implementation of the ITPGRFA. The third source of benefit sharing, and the most successful at the present time, is official development assistance (Brush, 2005; Andersen, 2008). Official development assistance can be channelled through bilateral or multilateral cooperation or through NGOs. There are many examples of NGO-channelled support, which have greatly supported diversity farmers in the South and thus contributed to benefit sharing in many developing countries.

In an international stakeholder survey carried out in 2005, the most frequently mentioned non-monetary benefits were (Andersen, 2005):

- access to seeds and propagating material and related information;
- participation in the definition of breeding goals;
- participatory plant breeding with farmers and scientists collaborating;
- stronger and more effective farmers' seed systems;
- conservation activities, including local gene banks; and
- enhanced utilization of farmers' varieties, including market access.

*(Andersen, 2005)*

This 2005 survey showed that – for many reasons – benefit sharing is more promising when the primary target for funding is the farming community that actually contributes to the maintenance of plant genetic diversity rather than the providers of genetic resources to commercial plant breeders. Since then, many organizations have engaged in such forms of benefit sharing, as documented in Andersen and Winge (2013) and Vernooy et al. (2015), for example.

Still, the dominant view on benefit sharing in many countries, particularly in the South, is the ownership approach, whereby direct benefit sharing between purported 'owners' and 'buyers' is the preferred mode. While such an ownership approach might seem to be fair and equitable as a point of departure, there are many difficulties with it. These difficulties include the facts that:

- it is difficult to identify exactly who should be rewarded;
- the demand for farmers' varieties among commercial breeders is limited, so relatively few farmers would benefit and most of the contributors to the global pool of genetic resources would remain unrewarded;
- the approach could lead to disincentives to share seeds and propagating material among farmers because of the expectations of personal benefit or the benefit to a community;
- although several countries in the South have enacted legislation on direct benefit sharing, no instances of such benefit sharing have been reported so far with regard to agro-biodiversity; and
- in many countries, the transaction costs of establishing access and benefit-sharing legislation have been considerable.

Thus, the ownership approach has not proven to be especially promising so far, and these concerns must be taken into account when measures are designed to ensure benefit sharing that is in line with the intentions of the ITPGRFA.[16]

According to the findings of the Farmers' Rights Project, three categories of measures appear to be particularly important when seeking to operationalize the concept of benefit sharing with regard to farmers' rights (Andersen, 2009). The first category ensures that *incentive structures* in agriculture favour farmers who conserve and sustainably use plant genetic resources for food and agriculture. Such incentive structures might include extension services to support particularly the farmers of the first group, loans on favourable conditions for the purchase of farm animals and other necessary input factors, the facilitation of marketing products from diverse varieties, and other infrastructure measures. A strategy for such incentive structures would substantially support farmers who conserve and sustainably use agro-biodiversity. This has not been done systematically in any country so far. In fact, existing incentive structures have generally proven to be detrimental to farmers' customary practices. However, there are also many local-level initiatives that can provide good models of how incentive structures could be designed on a larger scale.

The second category would create *reward and support systems* that would enable farmers to benefit significantly from their contributions to the global genetic pool, through added value to the crops they grow and through improved livelihoods and increased income. There currently exist many small-scale programs and projects that demonstrate the enormous potential in this regard – such as community seed banks, seed fairs, and registries (to ensure access); dynamic conservation programs coupled with participatory plant breeding; plant breeding and farmers' field schools; capacity building; and various marketing activities. Today, however, the benefit of these programs reaches a limited number of farmers. A major challenge is to scale up these activities so that all farmers engaged in the maintenance of agro-biodiversity can share in these benefits. Examples of successful upscaling of such programmes has, however, been possible, as has happened in Nepal (Vernooy et al., 2015), for example. NGOs and IGOs are central in such efforts, and there are also examples of state entities engaging in the work.

The third category would ensure the *recognition of farmers' contributions* to the global genetic pool in order to show that their contributions are valued by society. One form of recognition that is often discussed is the procurement of intellectual property rights for farmers, under an ownership approach. There are strong views for and against such rights. Proponents claim that farmers should be granted intellectual property rights on an equal footing with breeders as a matter of fairness. Opponents stress that such a system would create disincentives for farmers to share their seeds because of the expectations that the seeds could prove to be economically valuable. Such a development could be harmful to traditional seed systems and could negatively affect farmers' rights to save, use, exchange, and sell their own seeds. A more usual way of granting recognition to farmers and farming communities is through awards for innovative practices, as has been done in several countries. Yet this is not to say that farmers are not entitled to intellectual property rights. Rather, it indicates where the greatest potential for benefit sharing may lie and what dangers should be avoided if countries are seeking to establish intellectual property rights for farmers.

There are many good examples of indirect forms of benefit sharing, including incentive structures in the Philippines; community seed fairs in Zimbabwe; community gene banks and on-farm conservation in India; dynamic conservation and participatory plant breeding in France; participatory plant breeding in Nepal, which is adding value to farmers' varieties; capacity building for seed potato selection in Kenya; the development of a Peruvian Potato Park; and the reward for best farming practices in Norway (Andersen and Winge, 2008, 2013; Vernooy et al., 2015). These are all examples of programs and developments that provide models for the further implementation of farmers' rights. The major challenge today is to find ways and means to scale up such activities – for example, through the national agricultural extension service systems and other ways of linking up with government policies, as exemplified in Nepal (Vernooy et al., 2015). However, such initiatives are heavily dependent on political will, which is often lacking. In order to increase the political will, it is necessary to raise awareness in society in general on the vital importance of agro-biodiversity and farmers' rights.

## Participation in decision making

Article 9.2(c) deals with the right of farmers to participate in decision making at the national level on matters related to the conservation and sustainable use of plant genetic resources for food and agriculture. However, no further guidance is provided in the ITPGRFA as to how such decision making can be implemented in practice. To operationalize this measure, it will be necessary to specify the 'relevant matters' in which farmers can have the right to participate as well as the way in which they can participate.

The development of laws and regulations related to the management of plant genetic diversity in agriculture is clearly relevant for farmers' participation. At the current time, there are numerous examples of such laws and regulations, including seed acts, seed certification regulations, other regulations regarding seed distribution and trade, plant variety protection laws, patent laws, bio-prospecting laws or regulations, laws on the conservation and sustainable use of biodiversity in general or crop genetic resources in particular (as well as on several specific crops), and legislation on the rights of indigenous peoples and traditional knowledge. In addition, it is also important to consider any legislation that regulates mainstream agriculture since such legislation tends to produce incentive structures that are often detrimental to farmers' rights without providing any compensation. The extensive use of hearings at various stages in the decision process is an important measure to ensure participation. It is particularly important to ensure that farmers that are engaged in the management of plant genetic diversity are aware of the processes and are explicitly invited to participate through their organizations.

The implementation of laws and regulations is also relevant to farmers' participation. The way in which these regulations are interpreted and implemented often has an enormous influence on a farmer's management of these resources and also on his or her livelihood. Normally, such acts and regulations establish boards and institutions to oversee and/or administer implementation. Farmers' representation and participation in these bodies is therefore integral, and the means by which farmers are selected for membership is of crucial importance. If they are appointed by a government official, for example, they can hardly be said to represent the farmers of the country. If, however, they are appointed by farmers through their own organizations, it is more likely that they will be regarded as true representatives of the farming community – depending on the number of farmers that they represent and the process by which they were appointed. Again, it is essential to ensure that farmers are actually represented and engaged in agro-biodiversity conservation – there are too few success stories in this regard. In addition, the development of policies and programs in agriculture, particularly in relation to the management of plant genetic resources for food and agriculture, also requires farmer participation. In order to create policies and programs that are valuable for farmers, they have to be targeted specifically at the situations that farmers are in, taking farmers' perspectives as points of departure.

Ultimately, then, the implementation of farmers' rights requires farmers' participation. This is not only because of their unquestioned right in this regard, according to the ITPGRFA, but also because they are the ones who can best define the needs and priorities of farmers in the context of farmers' rights and they are also the central actors in the implementation process. Comprehensive consultative processes of various kinds are relevant – the better represented farmers are, the greater legitimacy the results will have and the more likely it is that they will constitute effective measures for the realization of farmers' rights. In particular, it is important for farmers to actually be involved in the management of plant genetic diversity in order to participate in such processes since they constitute the main target group of the ITPGRFA.

There are two major preconditions for the increased participation of farmers in decision making. First, decision makers need to be aware of the role that is played by farmers in conserving and developing plant genetic resources for food and agriculture, and thus in contributing to national food security, in order to understand why their participation is so important. Second, without prior capacity building, many of the world's farmers would not be in a position to participate effectively in complicated decision-making processes. Hence, it is essential to raise awareness among decision makers on the role of farmers in agro-biodiversity management and to build the capacity of farmers' organizations. While there is not much evidence of the former to date, there has been much more activity with regard to the latter goal.

In general, we find few examples of legislation on farmers' participation, although some countries in the South have extensive legislation on farmers' participation in decision making (Andersen, 2005). All the same, the actual participation of farmers in decision-making processes seems marginal and is often limited to large-scale farmers who are normally not engaged in the maintenance of plant genetic diversity. In the North, the participation of farmers in decision-making processes is more common, even if diversity farmers are rarely represented, but such participation does not usually involve specific laws or policies. It should be noted that some farmers in the North claim that their influence is decreasing, due to their countries' commitments to regional and international organizations and agreements such as the World Trade Organization (WTO) and the European Union (EU) (Andersen, 2005).

While the process of implementing participation has been slow, there have been a few success stories. The most comprehensive consultative process on the implementation of farmers' rights to date was carried out in Peru in 2008, and it involved 180 farmers from many different regions as well as numerous central decision makers (Scurrah et al., 2008).[17] Other success stories include capacity-building measures to prepare farmers for participating in decision making in Malawi, Zimbabwe, the Philippines, and Peru, and several successful advocacy campaigns regarding the implementation of elements of farmers' rights, where farmers have been directly involved, as for example in India, Norway, and Nepal (Andersen and Winge, 2008, 2013).

Under both the stewardship and ownership approaches, participation in relevant decision making is important but for different reasons. Under a stewardship approach, the most important objectives would be to ensure legal space for farmers to continue their practices as custodians and innovators of plant genetic resources and to establish reward mechanisms for farmers' contributions to the global genetic pool. Under the ownership approach, the goals would be to ensure appropriate legislation on access and benefit sharing as well as to safeguard farmers' intellectual property rights to the genetic resources in their fields and related knowledge. It is clear that these two sets of objectives could be conflicting. However, the overall objectives of the ITPGRFA to conserve, sustainably use, and share benefits from crop genetic resources for sustainable agriculture and food security may serve as guiding principles. Measures that limit a farmer's ability to take part in these activities would go against the intentions of the Treaty.

## Farmers' rights to save, use, exchange, and sell farm-saved seed

Farmers' customary use of propagating material – to save, use, exchange, and sell farm-saved seed and propagating material – is a pivotal element of farmers' rights and rooted as a 10,000-year-old tradition that enabled mankind to develop today's rich agro-biodiversity. However, the ITPGRFA is vague on farmers' rights to save, use, exchange, and sell farm-saved seed. Section 9.3 of the Treaty states that nothing in the relevant article (Article 9 on farmers' rights) 'shall be interpreted to limit any rights that farmers have to save, use, exchange and sell farm-saved seed, subject to national law and as appropriate', but this article does not really offer much direction, except for labelling these practices as 'rights'. Despite this lack of precision, the general line of thought would seem clear. It is important to grant their rights to save, use, exchange, and sell farm-saved seed, but individual countries are free to define the legal space that they deem to be sufficient.

The freedom to define such legal space for farmers is restricted by other international commitments. Most countries in the world are members of the WTO and are thus obliged to implement the WTO Agreement on Trade-Related Aspects of Intellectual Property Rights (TRIPS Agreement).[18] According to the TRIPS Agreement, all WTO member countries must protect plant varieties either by patents, by an effective *sui generis* system (a system of its own kind), or a combination of both (Article 27.3.b). The limits to a *sui generis* system and the meaning of an 'effective' *sui generis* system are not explicitly defined in the text. In other words, countries have to introduce some sort of plant breeders' rights.

The Union for the Protection of New Varieties of Plants (UPOV) explains that the most effective way to comply with the provision concerning an effective *sui generis* system is to follow the model of the International Convention for the Protection of New Varieties of Plants (UPOV Convention).[19] There are several versions of the UPOV model. The most recent (the 1991 Act of the UPOV Convention) provides that plant breeders are to be granted comprehensive rights – to the detriment of farmers' customary rights to save, re-use, exchange, and sell seeds. It is possible to make exceptions for small-scale farmers but only within strict limits. Exchange and sales of seeds among farmers are prohibited. It should be noted, however, that these regulations apply only to seeds protected by plant breeders' rights and not to traditional varieties.

The UPOV model has met resistance from some countries and many organizations that fear that ratification of the Convention would be detrimental to the rights of farmers to save and share propagating material. The TRIPS Agreement provides only minimum standards, leaving enough scope for the development of other solutions that are more compatible with the demand for farmers' rights. The challenge in the context of the ITPGRFA is thus for WTO member countries to meet their TRIPS obligations regarding plant breeders' rights, while also maintaining the necessary legal space to realize farmers' rights to propagating material.

A further constraint to farmers' rights in many countries is the introduction of seed laws that affect all propagating material, whether it is protected with intellectual property rights or not. The most important factor is that these laws also affect traditional varieties and farmers' varieties. They require that all varieties be officially approved for release and that seed and propagating material be certified before they are offered on the market. The original reason for these regulations was to ensure plant health and seed quality. However, in many countries, the regulations have gone so far that they now hinder the maintenance of crop genetic resources in the fields in two ways. First, since traditional varieties are normally not genetically homogeneous enough to meet the requirements for approval and certification, these varieties are excluded from the market and gradually disappear from active use when those farmers who currently use them begin to give them up. Second, many seed laws also stipulate that only authorized seed shops are allowed to sell seeds, and they prohibit all other seed exchange (with rare exceptions).

This is the case in most of Europe. The EU has tried to solve these hurdles with a specific directive on conservation varieties. However, EC Directive 62/2008 (EU Conservation Varieties Directive) is not adequate with regard to farmers' rights, because (a) seed exchange and sale are still prohibited among farmers; (b) only varieties deemed interesting by certain authorities can be covered by the system, which limits diversity; (c) the variety release and certification criteria are still too strict to allow for the release of many traditional and farmers' varieties; (d) the marketing and use of the varieties are limited to the regions of origin; (e) only limited quantities may be used; and (f) the conservation varieties may not be further developed by farmers. A comprehensive evaluation was carried out by the EU Commission to provide a foundation for revisions of the EU directives on seeds and propagating material. The evaluation led to a proposal to simplify the whole structure of relevant directives and solve many of the constraints highlighted previously. The proposal was approved by the EU Parliament, but eventually turned down by the EU Commission, thus further prolonging these issues.

When combined, these two processes – restrictions on plant variety release and seed marketing laws – may constitute serious obstacles to the implementation of the ITPGRFA in terms of *in situ* on-farm conservation and sustainable use as well as to farmers' rights. It is a paradox that rules originally intended to protect plant health have, in fact, contributed to removing the very basis for ensuring plant health in future – namely, the diversity of genetic resources.

What possibilities are there to make such laws more compatible with the customary rights of farmers, which are so crucial to the maintenance of agro-biodiversity for food security, today and in the future?

Under a stewardship approach, the goal would be to grant the rights to save, use, exchange, and sell farm-saved seed, whether from protected or non-protected varieties. Due to the present constrains of existing legislation, however, the challenge seems rather to uphold or re-establish sufficient legal space for farmers to continue their crucial role as custodians and innovators within the existing legal framework on plant breeders' rights, variety release, and seed distribution.

Under an ownership approach, on the other hand, the goal would be to provide farmers with intellectual property rights on the varieties in their fields on equal footing with breeders' rights. Arguments related to this objective have been discussed earlier in this chapter.

There are several pertinent stories on how legal space for farmers' rights can be established and maintained in order to allow farmers to maintain their traditional practices and innovation in agriculture (see, e.g. Andersen and Winge, 2008, 2013). These include India's 2001 *Protection of Plant Varieties and Farmers' Rights Act*;[20] Norway's 'no' to stricter plant breeders' rights in order to maintain the balance with farmers' rights, and the ways in which farmers are circumventing the law in the Basque Country in Spain. Nevertheless, establishing and maintaining legal space for farmers' rights to save, use, exchange, and sell farm-saved seed constitutes the main barrier to implementing the ITPGRFA in terms of the conservation and sustainable use of crop genetic diversity and of the realization of farmers' rights. Solutions are urgently needed.

Undoubtedly, there are many other means of combining the stewardship and ownership approaches in order to realize farmers' rights to seed and propagating material. What matters in this context is that the approach that is chosen must not conflict with the principles of the stewardship approach, which has been the primary goal of the FAO since the issue was first taken up as well as the rationale behind the ITPGRFA.

## Future directions: how can Farmers' Rights be realized?

Whereas the implementation of Farmers' Rights under the ITPGRFA is a national responsibility, the Governing Body of the ITPGRFA is responsible for promoting the full implementation of the Treaty, including the provision of policy direction and guidance, and monitoring of implementation (Article 19). According the Article 21, the Governing Body is to ensure compliance with all provisions of the ITPGRFA, and the Preamble of the Treaty highlights the necessity of promoting farmers' rights at the national as well as international levels. In this final section, I will consider how the Governing Body has carried out its responsibilities, with a view to national implementation.

In the first session of the Governing Body in 2006, the issue of farmers' rights was on the working agenda. Since then, the topic has been discussed at each session of the Governing Body, resulting in resolutions from the decisions made (see Resolutions 2/2007, 6/2009, 6/2011, 8/2013, and 5/2015 of the Governing Body of the International Treaty). There has been extensive consultation processes prior to each of the sessions of the Governing Body, most notably the Informal International Consultation on Farmers' Rights in Lusaka, Zambia, in 2007; the Global Consultation on Farmers' Rights in Addis Ababa, Ethiopia, in 2010; and the Global Consultation on Farmers' Rights in Bali, Indonesia, in 2016. Each of the first consultations resulted in comprehensive reports and summarizing input papers which were presented at the Governing Body at its sessions in 2007 (by Norway and Zambia) and 2011 (by Ethiopia). The consultation in 2016 had just been finalized when this chapter was submitted.

The resolutions to date call for:

- information gathering and knowledge exchange;
- the formulation of national action plans;
- the reviewing and adjusting national measures;
- engagement with farmers' organizations and relevant stakeholders in decision making;
- the enhancement of interactions and coordinations between institutions;
- regional workshops and other consultations;
- preparation of a study on lessons learned, to be presented to the Governing Body;
- a consideration of success stories and how they can be used to promote farmers' rights;
- the launch and implementation of a joint capacity development programme;
- the finalization of an educational module on Farmers' Rights;
- the identification of the interrelations between UPOV/WIPO and the Treaty with regard to Farmers' Rights;
- a report on any discussions related to farmers' rights in other FAO fora;
- an invitation to farmers' organizations to participate in sessions of the Governing Body;
- an invitation for contracting parties and development cooperation organizations to provide support;
- the conducting of active outreach activities on Farmers' Rights to stakeholders; and
- support for the implementation of these decisions and reporting back to the Governing Body.

The list is comprehensive and, at first sight, promising, and some of the decisions can be regarded as a breakthrough for the negotiations. Since the entry into force of the Treaty, much has been achieved in terms of establishing a joint understanding of important issues related to the realization of farmers' rights. However, little is happening from the side of Contracting Parties as well as the Secretariat in terms of implementation. Many of the provisions are made subject to the availability of funding, which is mostly scarce. Some NGOs and IGOs are doing substantial work to realize farmers' rights in many countries, but national efforts are lagging behind. To strengthen the work on farmers' rights much more attention to the topic and its pivotal importance for the implementation of the Treaty is required.

Since 2007, developing countries, along with some developed ones, have demanded that voluntary guidelines be prepared to guide and assist countries in the implementation of Farmers' Rights. There was strong resistance against that from several developed countries. Nevertheless, the demand is being repeated with greater strength for each session of the Governing Body. It is demanded that the guidelines be developed through a participative, inclusive, and transparent manner. Not only would such guidelines provide necessary guidance and assistance for contracting parties and other stakeholders, it would also provide an important arena for establishing a common ground of understanding with regard to why farmers' rights are important for the implementation of the Treaty and what it takes to realize these rights.

## Conclusions

The International Treaty on Plant Genetic Resources for Food and Agriculture is the single most important international instrument that currently exists to ensure the sustainable management of crop genetic resources. After ten years of implementation, it is evident that progress has so far been slow. Developing countries are demanding a functioning benefit-sharing mechanism and greater emphasis on the realization of farmers' rights in order to support the Treaty, for example by placing their genetic resources in the multilateral system. Action in this regard is urgently required. By understanding the different rationales behind the discussion in the Governing Body, that is, the stewardship and the ownership approaches, it might become clearer how they affect the conservation and sustainable use of crop genetic resources for food and agriculture. The consequences of the ownership approach might be detrimental to the on-farm conservation and sustainable use of crop genetic resources, as shown in this chapter. The stewardship approach could, seen in isolation, provide a solid basis for the on-farm conservation and sustainable use of crop genetic resources. The paradox is, however, that the resources from the public domain can be made subject to private ownership and thus be turned into a part of the ownership approach. Thus, the stewardship approach could not be the sole approach under the treaty, but may need to be complemented by elements of the ownership approach.

Much has been achieved with regard to developing a joint understanding of farmers' rights, their importance, and the steps required for their realization – and there are many success stories, mainly at a local level. Much still remains to be done to ensure that these rights are realized on a scale that is required to enable farmers to continue to maintain and further develop the crop genetic diversity. This is a contribution to ensuring the basis of local and global food security and to recognize and reward these farmers for their contributions to the global genetic pool. Awareness of the challenges, political priority, and international cooperation are required to make farmers' rights a reality.

## Notes

1 In 1974, the International Board for Plant Genetic Resources (IBPGR) was transformed into the IPGRI, which is now Bioversity International, a part of the Consultative Group on International Agricultural Research (CGIAR). The CGIAR was founded in 1971 on the initiative of the Ford and Rockefeller Foundations to unite privately funded international agricultural research centres (IARCs) into one network. As an informal association of public and private donors that support the IARCs, it is a donor-led group that has provided a forum for discussion of research priorities and coordination of funding (FAO, 1998, p. 248). As divisions of the network, the IARCs have their own governing bodies. The United Nations Environment Programme (UNEP), the FAO, the United Nations Development Programme, and the World Bank co-sponsor the system, and the CGIAR is headquartered at the premises of the World Bank in Washington, DC (FAO, 1998).

2 It was established by FAO Conference Resolution 9/83. It was later renamed the Commission on Genetic Resources for Food and Agriculture (CGRFA), as its mandate was broadened (as discussed later in this chapter).

3 At that time, there were still only 74 signatories.

4 General Agreement on Tariffs and Trade, 30 October 1947, 55 UNTS 194.

5 This principle was first voiced at the 1972 United Nations Conference on the Human Environment in Stockholm in the form that states have sovereign rights to exploit their natural resources in accordance

with their own environmental priorities (Stockholm Declaration on the Human Environment, 16 June 1972, 11 ILM 1416 (1972), Principle 21).

6 According to the Treaty Reference Guide of the United Nations Office of Legal Affairs, the term 'agreement' can be used for legally binding as well as non-binding agreements (see http://untreaty.un.org/ola-internet/Assistance/Guide.htm#agreements [last accessed 15 June 2012]).

7 This section is based on Andersen et al. (2010).

8 A thorough analysis of the recognition of farmers' rights in the ITPGRFA is found in Bjørnstad (2004). Further analyses of the ITPGRFA provisions on farmers' rights are provided by the Farmers' Rights Project, online: www.farmersrights.org (last accessed 15 June 2012); see also Moore and Tymowski (2005).

9 The Cartagena Protocol on Biosafety to the Convention on Biological Diversity, 29 January 2000, online: http://sedac.ciesin.org/pidb/texts-menu.html. It is not dealt with in this chapter, but, as a protocol to the CBD, it is a part of an already established regime.

10 The United States has also signed the CBD but has not ratified it.

11 An interesting analysis of the contents and prospects of the ITPGRFA is found in Fowler (2004). Explanations on the background and contents of the ITPGRFA are presented in Moore and Tymowski (2005).

12 This section is based on Andersen (2008) and Andersen et al. (2010).

13 For example, rice, wheat, maize, rye, potatoes, beans, cassava, and bananas. Not included are other important crops, including soybeans, tomatoes, cotton, sugarcane, cocoa, and groundnuts, as well as many vegetables and important tropical forage plants.

14 This chapter is based on the results of the Farmers' Rights Project of the Fridtjof Nansen Institute, an international project designed to support the implementation of farmers' rights, as they are addressed in the ITPGRFA. Started in 2005, it is a long-term project with many different components, comprising research and surveys as well as policy guidance, facilitation of consultations, information, and capacity building. For an overview of the research reports and activities, see www.farmersrights.org. International Treaty on Plant Genetic Resources for Food and Agriculture [ITPGRFA], 29 June 2004, online: www.planttreaty.org/texts_en.htm (last accessed 15 June 2012).

15 Convention on Biological Diversity, 31 ILM 818 (1992).

16 An agreement on access to teff genetic resources in Ethiopia, and the fair and equitable sharing of benefits derived from their use, has been hailed as one of the most advanced of its time. A thorough study of this agreement between a Dutch company and Ethiopian authorities shows, however, that the implementation failed. As a result of several circumstances, Ethiopia was left with fewer possibilities for generating and sharing the benefits from the use of teff genetic resources than before (Andersen and Winge, 2012).

17 Progress is slow, however, due to a lack of resources and political attention.

18 Agreement on Trade-Related Aspects of Intellectual Property Rights, Annex 1C of the Marrakech Agreement Establishing the World Trade Organization, 15 April 1994, 33 ILM 15 (1994).

19 International Convention for the Protection of New Varieties of Plants, 2 December 1961, online: www.upov.int/en/publications/conventions/index.html (last accessed 15 June 2012).

20 *Protection of Plant Varieties and Farmers' Rights Act*, 2001, online: http://agricoop.nic.in/seeds/farmersact2001.htm (last accessed 15 June 2012).

## References

Andersen, R. (2001) 'Conceptualizing the convention on biological diversity: Why is it difficult to determine the "country of origin" of agricultural plant varieties?', FNI Report no. 7/2001, Fridtjof Nansen Institute (FNI), Lysaker, Norway.

Andersen, R. (2005) 'The farmers' rights project – background study 2: Results from an international stakeholder survey on farmers' rights', FNI Report no. 9/2005, FNI, Lysaker, Norway.

Andersen, R. (2006) 'Realising farmers' rights under the International treaty on plant genetic resources for food and agriculture, summary of findings from the farmers' rights project (phase 1)', FNI Report no. 11/2006, FNI, Lysaker, Norway.

Andersen, R. (2008) *Governing Agrobiodiversity: Plant Genetics and Developing Countries*, Ashgate, Aldershot, UK.

Andersen, R. (2009) 'Information paper on farmers' rights submitted by the Fridtjof Nansen Institute, Norway, based on the farmers', Rights Project, input paper submitted to the Secretariat of the ITPGRFA, 19 May 2009, Doc. IT/GB-3/09/Inf, Rome, Italy.

Andersen, R. (2011) 'Farmers' rights in Norway: A case study', FNI Report no. 11/2011 (Norwegian edition) and FNI Report no. 17/2012 (English edition), FNI, Lysaker, Norway.

Andersen, R. (2016) 'Realising farmers rights to crop genetic resources', chapter 7 in M. Halewood (ed.), *Farmers' Crop Varieties and Farmers' Rights: Challenges in Taxonomy and Law*, Earthscan for Routledge, Abingdon, UK.

Andersen, R., Tvedt, M. W., Fauchald, O. K., Winge, T., Rosendal., K. and Schei, P. J. (2010) *International Agreements and Processes Affecting an International Regime on Access and Benefit Sharing under the Convention on Biological Diversity Implications for its Scope and Possibilities of a Sectoral Approach*. FNI, Lysaker, Norway.

Andersen, R. and Winge, T. (2008) 'The farmers' rights project – background study 7: Success stories from the realization of farmers' rights related to plant genetic resources for food and agriculture', FNI Report 4/2008, FNI, Lysaker, Norway.

Andersen, R. and Winge, T. (2012) 'The access and benefit sharing agreement on teff genetic resources: Facts and lessons', FNI Report 6/2012, FNI, Lysaker, Norway.

Andersen, R. and Winge, T. (2013) *Realising Farmers' Rights to Crop Genetic Resources: Success Stories and Best Practices*, Routledge, Abingdon, UK.

Bjørnstad, B. S-I. (2004) 'Breakthrough for "the South"? FNI Report 13/2004, FNI, Lysaker, Norway.

Brush, S. B. (2005) 'Protecting traditional agricultural knowledge', *Washington University Journal of Law and Policy*, vol. 17, pp. 59–109.

Centro Internacional de la Papa and Federación Departemental de Comunidades Campesinas (2006) *Catálogo de Variedades de Papa Nativa de Huancavelica, Peru*, Centro Internacional de la Papa and Federación Departemental de Comunidades Campesinas, Lima, Peru.

Esquinas-Alcázar, J. (2005) 'Protecting crop genetic diversity for food security: Political, ethical and technical challenges', *Nature Reviews Genetics*, vol. 6, pp. 946–953.

Evans, P. and Walsh, J. (1994) *The EIU guide to the New GATT.* Inter-American Institute for Cooperation on Agriculture, San José, Costa Rica.

Food and Agriculture Organization of the United Nations (FAO) (1986) FAO, Rome, Italy.

FAO (1987) *Report of the Second Session of the Commission on Plant Genetic Resources*, Doc. CL 91/14, FAO, Rome, Italy.

FAO (1989) *FAO C 1989/REP, Conference Resolution 5/89, Farmer's Rights*, Report of the Conference of FAO, 25th session, Rome, Italy.

FAO (1991) *FAO C 1991/REP, Conference Resolution 3/91*, Report of the Conference of FAO, 26th session, Rome, Italy.

FAO (1998) *State of the World's Plant Genetic Resources for Food and Agriculture*, FAO, Rome, Italy.

Fowler, C. (1994) *Unnatural Selection: Technology, Politics and Plant Evolution*, Gordon and Breach, Yverdon, Switzerland.

Fowler, C. (2001) 'Protecting famer innovation: The convention on biological diversity and the question of origin', *Jurimetrics*, vol. 41, pp. 477–488.

Fowler, C. (2004) 'Diversity and protectionism – use of genebanks: Trends and interpretations', pp. 49–51 in *Food Security and Biodiversity: Sharing the Benefits of Plant Genetic Resources*, Presentation made at the World Food Day, Basel, Switzerland.

Fujisaka, S., Williams, D. and Halewood, M. (eds.) (2009) *The Impact of Climate Change on Countries' Interdependence on Genetic Resources for Food and Agriculture*, Background Paper No. 48, FAO, Rome, Italy.

Moore, G. and Tymowski, W. (2005) *Explanatory Guide to the International Treaty on Plant Genetic Resources for Food and Agriculture*, IUCN Environmental Policy and Law Paper no. 57, International Union on the Conservation of Nature, Gland, Switzerland and Cambridge, UK.

Palacios, X. F. (1998) *Contribution to the Estimation of Countries' Interdependence in the Area of Plant Genetic Resources*, Background Study Paper no. 7, Commission on Genetic Resources for Food and Agriculture, FAO, Rome, Italy.

Scurrah, M., Andersen, R. and Winge, T. (2008) *Farmers' rights in Peru: Farmers' perspectives*, FNI Report no. 16/2008, FNI, Lysaker, Norway.

United Nations (2009) *Seed Policies and the Right to Food: Enhancing Agrobiodiversity and Encouraging Innovation*, Interim report of the UN Special Rapporteur on the Right to Food, transmitted by the Secretary General to the members of the General Assembly of the UN for its sixty-fourth session, UN, New York, NY, USA.

United Nations Environment Programme (UNEP) (1992) *Nairobi Final Act of the Conference for the Adoption of the Agreed Text of the Convention on Biological Diversity*, UNEP, Nairobi, Kenya.

Vernooy, R., Shrestha, P. and Sthapit, B. (eds.) (2015) *Community Seed Banks: Origins, Evolution and Prospects*, Earthscan for Routledge, Abingdon, UK.

Wilson, E. O. (1992) *The Diversity of Life*, Penguin, London, UK.

Yusuf, A. A. (1998) 'TRIPS: Background, principles and general provisions', pp. 3–21 in C. M. Correa and A. A. Yusuf (eds.), *Intellectual Property and International Trade: TRIPS Agreement*, 2nd ed., Kluwer Law International, Alphen aan den Rij, the Netherlands.

# 29

# LAND-USE RETENTION AND CHANGE TO IMPROVE AGRICULTURAL BIODIVERSITY

*Craig J. Pearson*

## Biodiversity is a part of public value

Biodiversity is the genetic diversity of soil organisms, plants and animals. It is valuable in its own right, essential in that it confers functional consequences: direct, essential benefits such as maintaining nutrient cycling, and contributions to outcomes such as mitigation of climate change and human mental and physical health. These outcomes have, with creative accounting, been ascribed astronomical financial value: Costanza et al. (1997) and Pascual and Muradian (2010, p. 205) provide examples of various attempts to put a monetary value on biodiversity and ecosystem services more generally. International examples of this kind include TEEB (The Economics of Ecosystems and Biodiversity, 2015), a United Nations initiative that aims to 'make nature's values visible', which is an ongoing program that seeks to quantify the value of agriculture and biodiversity.

However, when we enumerate the ecosystem goods and services that are part of, or flowing from, biodiversity, it invites evaluation: are birds, for example, more or less important than food security? I once asked a village elder in a remote, drought-prone area of Ethiopia what was the benefit he most valued from a program to introduce leguminous trees into village farming systems: was it the high-quality feed the trees provided for livestock, or cash obtained from sale of seed? His response: no, the biggest benefit was that the trees had brought the birds back.

It is widely recognized that the industrialization of commercial agriculture has had major impacts of providing relatively safe and low-cost nutritious food for our growing global population and reducing biodiversity: TEEB assert that 'agriculture is thought to cause around 70% of the projected loss of terrestrial biodiversity' (TEEB, 2015, p. 12). While acknowledging past mistakes, a constructive approach is to recognize that agricultural land management provides our best opportunity to conserve and, indeed, increase biodiversity, with mutual benefits: to both eat and have our cake.

We need biodiversity *and* food, and if we consider them as separate entities then each of us will weight differently the balance between them.

Viewing land-use policy and management in an holistic way, to achieve multiple outcomes, may be termed the 'landscape' approach: to take account of food, biodiversity and environment to allocate and manage land to achieve genuine sustainability. A key principle in this approach (one of ten principles set out by Sayer et al., 2013) is to recognize the multifunctionality of land, the need for assessment and management based on multiple, complex and sometimes conflicting perspectives.

There are many good examples where taking a multifunctional 'landscape' perspective has improved the design of agriculture, and the allocation of land to various aspects of it, giving rise to direct biodiversity benefits (e.g. Sayer et al., 2013, and later in this chapter). However, the majority of these have, to date, been driven by concern with one, or a relatively small number, of issues, such as water or soil erosion. For example, the grassing of swales has reduced soil erosion through localized waterways in the U.S. Midwest, through fields of corn and soybeans. These permanently-grassed swales improve biodiversity through creating and maintaining contiguous perennial habitats adjacent to the crop fields. Minimum or zero tillage, which was introduced to maximize soil water storage and minimize soil structural degradation and erosion, is an example of a relatively recent global practice that has likely improved on-farm invertebrate and vertebrate biodiversity.

More often, though, direct intervention to improve ecosystem services, for example, by payment to retain areas of remnant forest or wetland, results in these areas being isolated from, and seen as competitors to, adjacent food production. Similarly, as urbanism becomes our predominant living style, accommodation, not food or biodiversity, becomes a single-issue priority: 'much urban space continues to be designed and planned . . . with a consumptive attitude to non-urban landscape' (Knight and Riggs, 2010, p. 120).

Tackling specific outcomes from, or components of, biodiversity usually does not create an holistic view of land-use. So, as a prelude to discussing how to change land-use to improve agricultural biodiversity, and as a proposal to reduce the confrontation associated with an either/or perspective on biodiversity and agriculture, a more holistic view is to see biodiversity and agriculture as components of land-use that contribute to 'public value'.

The idea of public value arose about 25 years ago and has been publicized by Moore (1995), for example. It posits that public servants' (and, by inference, politicians') purpose should be to create public 'value', not necessarily aim to maximize financially-measured wealth. This gives rise to three tests for public action, or political intervention (Alford and O'Flynn, 2009):

- Aim to create something valuable;
- Be legitimate and sustainable, that is, attract support and resources; and
- Be do-able with the available organizational capabilities.

Creating 'something valuable' means something substantial, but not necessarily monetary. 'Attract support' means, to me, that land-managers – mostly farmers, and urban dwellers in the case of urban agriculture – have to commit to action, otherwise (irrespective of who is paying) the adopted practices will not be sustainable.

Seeing landscapes or regions as whole systems that provide food, fibre, shelter, transport and biodiversity and maintain emergent ecosystem services such as clean water and air, within the context of optimizing public value, provides a basis for sensible, non-confrontational action. It is consistent with the 'landscape' approach. It contrasts with, and doubtless will run parallel with, conservationists' (and certain agriculturists') perspective of alienating land *from* agriculture to enhance biodiversity. The Gondwana Link project, proposing an arc of what is presently high value farmland to be replaced by joined-up 'native' revegetation from the western woodland north of Esperance to the coastal Karri forests in Western Australia, is an example of the latter, either/or approach (Munro and Lindenmayer, 2011).

Privately-powered urban agriculture, legislated urban and peri-urban greenways in Boston, London, Canberra, Ottawa, Barcelona and many other cities, and many (but still a minority of) broad-scale farmers provide examples of how agriculture and biodiversity conservation can be mutually beneficial.

## Land-related actions to preserve or improve biodiversity

Biodiversity may be preserved and improved by:

- maintaining heterogeneity of quality habitats, that is, those rich in species biodiversity;
- preserving patch-size and contiguity of non-cultivated habitats;
- reducing the contrast between edges of disturbed, for example cultivated agricultural areas and others;
- maintaining vegetated ground cover through growing perennial crops or minimum or zero tillage for annual crops;
- multi-storied agricultural communities, where trees may serve as sources of food, fibre, shelter and shade (for livestock or humans); and
- localized cycling of organic waste through grazing animals or recycling of urban waste to peri-urban cropland.

These actions are most applicable, but not necessarily restricted, to enhancing biodiversity in extensive non-urban landscapes. In urban areas, the first two (habitat quality and patch-size) may be addressed by planning for preservation or re-introduction of parkland and urban agriculture. Further, parkland and urban agriculture in private allotments and community food gardens may be either a scattering of isolated patches, as has predominated historically, or it might be joined-up into contiguous networks, for example of collectively managed backyards.

Whereas 20th-century agricultural science championed monocultures and relatively simple food webs, at the expense of biodiversity, in this century, there is the growing realization that high species diversity confers advantages which, perhaps only after a few years, outperform monocultures in productivity and carbon storage (e.g. Tilman et al., 2001). It is fashionable to advocate re-integration of crop and livestock systems, with buffer strips to catch waste and grass swales to channel water and minimize erosion (Naylor et al., 2005).

There is thus a biological underpinning for the idea of seeing biodiversity preservation and food production as integrated and complementary, or concurrent goals of land-use, rather than the traditional perspective that protected areas, for example urban green spaces and national parks, are distinct and agricultural areas exist to maximize productivity by ignoring or minimizing biodiversity. Practical manifestations of this holism include (a) widespread advocacy and adoption of urban agroecology in the Global South by civil society and NGOs; (b) a rise in organic-certified farming (although it remains less than 10% of value in all countries except Germany); (c) calls to place higher value on agricultural perennials including priority for their breeding, to 'blur the distinction between working lands and protected areas' (Atwell et al., 2010, p. 1089); (d) government-sponsored recreational easements through farmland; and (e) conservation easements: farmland held in perpetuity, usually by an NGO land trust but sometimes by farmers themselves, to maintain biodiversity within agriculture (Byers and Ponte, 2005).

Practical examples of the potential holism of agriculture and biodiversity include some traditional farming systems. In the Global South from sub-Saharan Africa to tropical Indonesia, there are continuums of food garden and farm size, biodiversity and commercialism from subsistence garden to smallholder farm to more extensive farms that employ mechanization and grow monocultures. A study of 51 gardens in Niamey, Niger, grouped these into five categories (Bernholt et al., 2009):

- Small subsistence, mostly peri-urban, managed by women;
- Small, species-poor urban gardens without an upper tree canopy;
- Relatively small, mostly stratified urban gardens with intermediate plant diversity;
- Intermediate-sized commercial gardens, mostly tenant-farmed by families; and
- Large commercial peri-urban gardens, managed by men with off-farm income.

*Table 29.1* Categorization of food gardens and urban farms showing average size and biodiversity in Niamey, Niger

| *Small subsistence (mostly peri-urban)* | *Small species-poor without upper canopy* | *Relatively small stratified urban* | *Intermediate commercial mostly rented* | *Large commercial with off-farm income* |
|---|---|---|---|---|
| Size 737 m2 | 438 m2 | 591 m2 | 1089 m2 | 4355 m2 |
| Total 11.4 spp | 9.9 spp | 13.6 spp | 31.7 spp | 41.7 spp |
| 1.6 local spp | 1.9 | 2.4 | 6.3 | 13.0 |
| 2.8 perennial spp | 4.0 | 6.9 | 16.3 | 26.0 |

*Source*: From Bernholt et al. (2009).

The gardens with highest species richness and diversity, particularly of local and perennial species, were the large, peri-urban commercial gardens. Ornamental species occurred only in these gardens. On the other hand, vegetables were most important in the smaller, less biodiverse categories (**Table 29.1** *Categorization of food gardens and urban farms*).

A message that may be derived from extrapolating these data is that resource-poor households won't necessarily maintain biodiversity any better than commercially-oriented mechanized farmers.

Throughout these categories (and other food/garden typologies in use elsewhere in the world) there is an emphasis on encouraging multilayered plantings and biodiversity. At the large non-urban end of the landscape continuum, in east Africa grain yields have not consistently responded to the 'Green Revolution' of crop monocultures and higher rates of inorganic fertilizers. Instead, now, multi-storey systems are being advocated, whereby maize is grown under woodlands of indigenous, leguminous trees.

Agricultural conservation of biodiversity is most easily seen within and adjacent to cities: diversity of food plants, ornamentals and 'weeds', butterflies, birds and worms is prominent in household and community gardens surrounded by hard infrastructure, whereas it is easier to overlook as we drive through extensive farmland. A component of this conservation of biodiversity is the maintenance of, and access to, indigenous or 'wild' species. This is a relatively small and diminishing percentage of food or medicinal consumption; to cite one example, in which 1,158 households were interviewed in six medium-sized cities (of 72,000 to about 400,000 people) across Africa (Sclesinger et al., 2015), about 15% of urban households and 15–20% of peri-urban households collected wild fruits and vegetables. Not surprisingly, a high percentage (about 90%) of households who consumed wild plants and animals believed that their availability was declining. In developed economies, access to wild species is lower and likely to be non-existent other than through local farmers' markets judging from an example of Melbourne, Australia (Donati et al., 2013): of more than 90 species of food plants that were found in farmers markets, only five or six were sourced from wild, not cultivated. Paradoxically though, concern by gardeners' clubs may increase the cultivation of landraces and 'wild' material.

In developed economies, when fewer members of families worked for wages, it was common for most household gardens to be, at least seasonally, self-sufficient in vegetables and eggs, as in the Global South. Nowadays, with both adults usually working full-time away from the home, lot sizes smaller, fresh food more available through supermarkets and fast-food more popular and locally accessible, home gardens are less likely to provide food. In these economies, city-regions are typically not food self-sufficient within their boundaries, relying instead on networks/chains to be sustainable (food secure) and resilient (flexible). By contrast, cities in the Global South more commonly rely on local production, importing staples in a lean, for example dry, season when gardens are not productive (Pearson and Dyball, 2014). The contribution of cities to food and biodiversity preservation is discussed in Keding et al., Chapter 32 of this Handbook. In developed economies, urban refuges for food production and biodiversity include using 'waste' spaces held by governments, for example adjacent to railways and highways which, if communally managed, are called community gardens, and if let to individuals, allotments; under-used land, often owned by local governments, for example abandoned tennis courts, food patches adjacent to footpaths, 'remnant' private land and vacant lots. Food gardens may be sanctioned or 'guerrilla' and sometimes in planter (raised) beds to avoid contaminated soil on brown-field sites or near traffic. These food gardens serve multiple functions, social as well as generating fresh food and form networks to share information and advocate on behalf of urban food producers (e.g. Pearson et al., 2010, Australian community gardens, http://communitygarden.org.au).

Governments, NGOs and civil society encourage urban and peri-urban gardens in both the Global South and developed economies where poor diets and poor access to food are increasingly common, driven by affluence and rising societal inequalities. There are many programs at local, regional and global scales that have addressed, and are addressing, hunger and poor diets through better and more diverse nutrition, based on encouraging more biodiversity. That is, food *and* biodiversity. McEwan et al. (2013) described contemporary global programs; Baker and de Zeeuw (2015) described more regional and local. Approaches range from government's direct financial intervention, such as price incentives to local producers and price regulation by the Municipal Secretariat of Belo Horizontale, Brazil, to supporting community food gardens and markets, which is most common in developed economies, exemplified by the Toronto Food Policy Council, Canada, and local government provision of vacant land (in Toronto, Cape Town, Baltimore and others). Less common is the embedding of urban agriculture in land-use plans (Baker and de Zeeuw give an example of Dar es Salaam, Tanzania) and policies that encourage actions to promote outcomes, for example reducing greenhouse gasses and increasing nutrient recycling, that will encourage urban agriculture, in Bulawayo, Zimbabwe, and Ghent, Belgium. Building regulations that make green walls or roofs financially attractive are widespread, particularly in highly urbanized developed economies, for example Seattle, United States, and Munich, Germany. Arguably the most effective programs, however, are those initiated by NGOs and community activists. Global programs such as the Helen Keller International (www.hki.org) that was developed in Bangladesh and later expanded to Cambodia, Nepal and the Philippines and now employs more than 700 people globally, and programs that are locally focused like Incredible Edible Todmorden (www.incredible-edible-todmorden.co.uk) that has created 40 public fruit and vegetable gardens in Yorkshire in the United Kingdom. In June 2015, the journal *Farming Matters* provided descriptions of community-initiated successes in China, South Africa, Egypt and Japan (http://issuu.com/agricultures/docs/farming_matters_31). In the long term, urban agriculture might be promoted most for its capacity to deal cost-effectively with waste: 'What is now needed are urban sanitation strategies that recognize the role of urban agriculture . . . particularly in those developing countries where conventional sanitation remains a grave challenge' (Lydecker and Drechsel, 2010, p. 102).

IIASTD (2008) concluded that

> Current assessments indicate that new research investments could improve multifunctional performance significantly and rapidly in all parts of the world. This requires that (1) existing systems of multifunctional merit be upscaled and their underlying principles

> brought into mainstream practice; (2) empirically tested designs for new approaches and systems be more widely promoted in small-scale and industrial systems; (3) data and information be available in key areas of concern; and (4) policies and institutions that facilitate multifunctional agriculture be strengthened.
>
> *(IAASTD, 2008, p. 6)*

Success – that is, sustainability – of biodiverse urban and peri-urban food production depends first on multi-stakeholder commitment (top-down and bottom-up education, empowerment, resources and financial reward; see for example Seymoar et al., 2010 for a four-directional participatory framework for change, developed by the International Center for Sustainable Cities). Success, beyond those that are purely subsistence, depends also on their marketing. While some, perhaps the majority in most cities, provide food only for the gardeners and for sharing or exchanging with friends and neighbors, commercially-viable gardens develop a suite of clients:

- Contract selling to community-supported agriculture (CSA) groups;
- Direct selling at farm gate;
- Retail through farmers' markets and for example to restaurants; and
- Wholesale, usually specialty foods.

Urban food gardens and markets can maintain great biodiversity. One example, from Melbourne, Australia, identified about 90 species of food plants in gardens and local farmers' markets (Donati et al., 2013). The number is driven by a combination of the motives of the growers, economics and, of course, site and climatic suitability. As a consequence, there is strong seasonality in food on offer, and some species are not grown in proportion to dietary demand because it is easier and cheaper to obtain them through commercial food chains. Fairview Farms, Los Angeles (www.fairviewgardens.org/), illustrates the diversity and seasonality of species that can be commercially viable. This farm, a remnant lot which was once a weekend retreat but is now surrounded by suburbia, offers:

- Winter: Brussels sprouts, garlic, cherimoyas, radicchio, endive, bokchoy, peas, beans, snap peas, faba beans and greens;
- Spring: squash, garlic, basil, potatoes, berries, snap peas, faba beans and greens;
- Summer: tomatoes, basil, avocado, corn, aubergine, stone fruits, for example peaches, capsicum, melons, beans, cucumbers, berries, squash, figs; and
- Autumn: tomatoes, basil, pomegranates, apples, lima beans, capsicum, cucumbers, corn, berries, snap peas, lima beans, green beans, aubergine, figs, apples.

As mentioned earlier, the relatively close connection between producer and client/consumer allows food gardens such as Fairview in California to produce a range of varieties and maintain diverse, and sometimes threatened 'heirloom' germplasm. Their intensive production also supports the production practices identified earlier, such as minimum tillage, composting and local return of nutrients which maintains invertebrate and vertebrate diversity.

Urban location, as well as allowing for intensive, biodiverse farming methods, exemplifying what is needed more generally (Pearson, 2007), also provides opportunities for value-adding to their clients' food experiences. Fairview Farms, for example, runs farm tours, children's gardens linked with schools, adult education programs and volunteer days. Many other examples are provided by the RUAF Foundation (Resource Centres on Urban Agriculture & Food Security, www.ruaf.org/urban-agriculture-and-biodiversity). Schemes of this kind serve as supplementary sources of income that address the need for urban communities to become reconnected with their food.

## Options to change land-use

**Figure 29.1**, *Land-use and bioversity* attempts to describe how land-use changes or evolves. It also gives a framework to assist us in thinking how we might develop an integrated approach to land-use that values biodiversity and other things such as food and space for active recreation as parts of a connected whole. At the top of the figure, 'natural capital' encompasses biodiversity (and ecosystem attributes such as climate, soils and water) as capitals, or stocks, that can be maintained or eroded, and which set constraints on what is possible for any space. The earliest settlers made their decisions about whether to farm, and what type of farming, or whether to build a town, based on their assessment

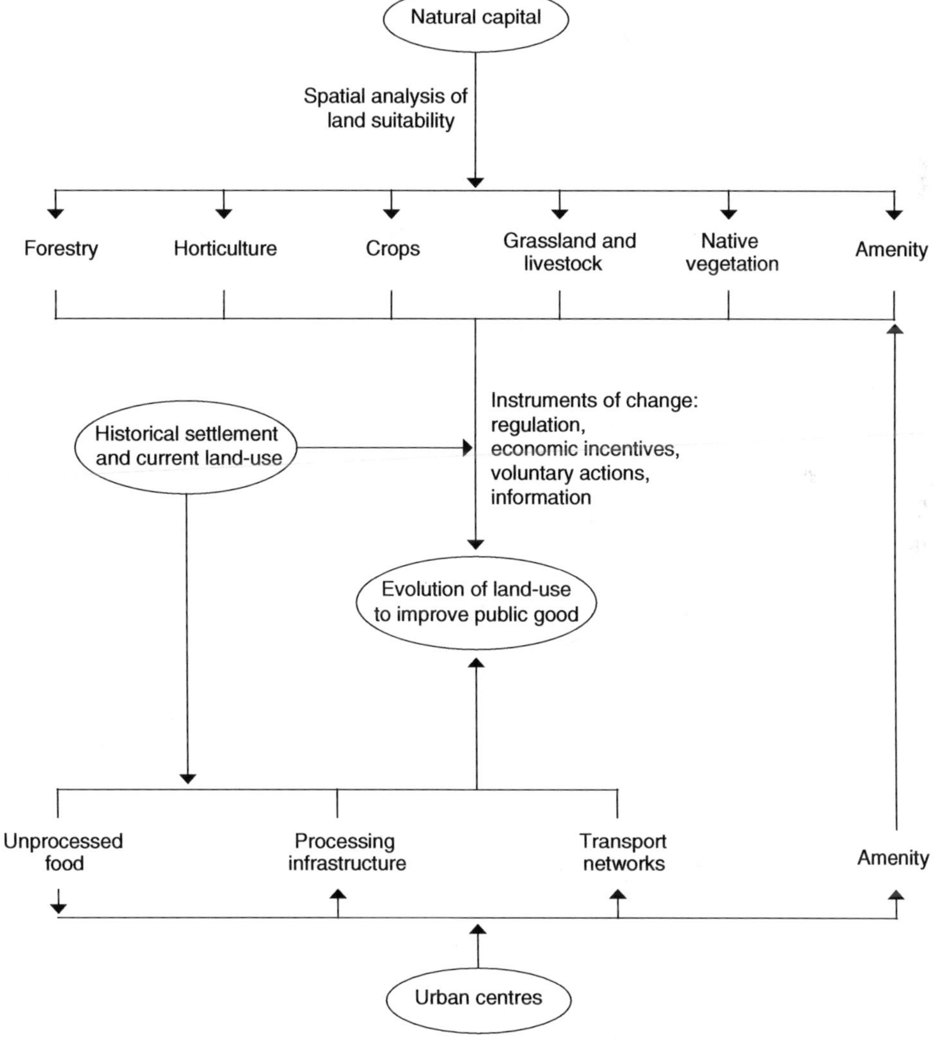


*Figure 29.1* Land-use and biodiversity

*Note*: A schema to illustrate the issues associated with retaining, or changing, land-use to maintain or improve biodiversity, as a key element of 'natural capital'; within each of the possible land-uses for example horticulture, there are broad principles that, if followed, should maximize diversity of species of soil organisms, plants and animals.

*Source*: Author.

of natural capital, followed by trial and error. The figure also shows the primacy of history and current land use – the lozenge at the left of the figure. As we know in relation to contentious changes in urban land use, historical land use establishes powerful rights; these may be changed voluntarily or overridden by a range of instruments. Today, to provide guidance for planning or policy, the optimal distribution of various land-based products including those arising from biodiversity can be modelled through scenarios driven by plant suitability to soils, climate and so forth, just as urban and peri-urban land use that takes account of siting of factories, houses, infrastructure, playing fields and parks can be modelled using mixes of citizen priorities and preferences and computerized land suitability mapping. Finally, **Figure 29.1** attempts to also remind us that, as global population and urbanization increases, it will increasingly be urban centres – their people and their perceived needs – that consume unprocessed food from rural lands, and choose where to site transport infrastructure and processing capacity that are so important in driving changes in agricultural land use. The figure also acknowledges that alienation of land for amenity and recreation – gardens, urban parks, greenbelts, regional and national nature reserves – has almost always been driven directly by urban politics.

These perspectives and processes for alienating land for food and biodiversity are important: while some urban land is identified early in the settlement process for parks and gardens, rarely is there consideration, much less protection, of urban agriculture. This is despite public interest in local food production, increasing demand for food production and use to be taught in schools, and the observation that some parcels of land within urban conurbations – such as floodways and otherwise-unused land next to arterial roads and railways – is suited to agriculture and unsuited to housing. By contrast, market forces and common sense encourage agricultural specialization in the most appropriate locations in non-urban settings.

There are numerous tools for identifying which land would be best suited to various purposes or to maintain or re-establish particular vegetation types. These can be grouped into those that are based on heuristics or models of plant growth or invertebrate or vertebrate population dynamics; multi-criteria models using assigned, subjective valuations of suitability or desirability; scenarios based on collective judgments, for example focus groups, that may employ models to inform participants of biological fit; and financial market-driven models.

As Benke et al. (2011) pointed out, any model seeking to develop scenarios or posit an optimum mix of land-uses, needs to recognize scale – an optimum for a farm may differ from that for a region and purpose. For example, is the purpose of a land-use scenario to suggest an optimum allocation for food security, or to maximize regional revenue? If it is the latter, as Benke et al. again illustrate, our models will likely predict fewer, rather than more, agricultural enterprises. Analyses are presently coalescing on regional, rather than local or national, scales; Hinrichs (2013) termed our current increased focus on the regional scale, 're-regionalizing'.

Once we – this collective term refers to 'society' whether through expert judgment (public servants seeking to improve 'public good'), political decision or grass-roots activism – have identified desirable land-uses, the question arises: how can we influence land-use change? The process is usually to plan regionally and implement incrementally, locally. Broadly, the levers are:

- legislation: regulation;
- economic incentives such as differential land-taxes and factors such as government provision of infrastructure;
- market responses, such as prices and distance to market which confer advantages of some products (e.g. perishables), over others;
- non-economic incentives, such as land-swapping;
- voluntary actions: motivated by community, peer actions and personal values; and
- information and moral suasion.

These levers are described further in relation to urban agriculture in Pearson et al. (2010). Examples have been given earlier in this chapter. In five of the previous six levers, market prices directly or indirectly drive most farmer action. This (re)action is often irrational, such as by planting more wheat in response to a decline in prices.

However, there is also much evidence that what farmers or, in the cities, householders, grow, and how they grow it, depends also on non-market motives and values (e.g. Brenner et al., 2013). Further, actions are influenced by perceptions – what things look like and what we think they mean, irrespective of whether this is an accurate reading of the landscape or not. Ives and Kendall (2013) provided an analysis of the importance of beliefs and values, as distinct to knowledge, in making judgments about the desirability of certain types of peri-urban landscape, while Schirmer et al. (2013) gave examples of farmers' perceptions. For example, farmers felt scattered trees provide less community or ecological benefits compared with clumps or strips of trees, likely giving rise to them placing less value on the preservation or regeneration of individual trees and woodlands.

Price motivation plus awareness that beliefs and values drive change has led to proposals to target revegetation taking account of the profitability of current farm enterprises or gross 'opportunity costs or benefit' arising from enhancing biodiversity (e.g. Crossman and Bryan, 2009) or sequestering carbon (Longmire et al., 2015 and references therein).

It is my guess that the aforementioned instruments work best, in reverse order: household gardeners and farmers provide outstanding examples of coupling food production and biodiversity through creating multi-storeyed, diverse 'fields', most likely motivated by an un-knowable combination of desire to improve biodiversity, aesthetics and profit. Celebrating and promoting these provides the best advocacy for change to biodiverse agriculture that is both sustainable and profitable. The gradual shift to regenerative agriculture (see e.g. Pearson, 2007) which is more biodiverse, is likely occurring because farmers are noticing that those who convert do, after a few years, have lower input costs and experience less volatility in farm profitability.

At the other end of the spectrum, there are some examples of successful legislation, such as the Toronto greenbelt (legislated for in 2004) which put a halt to conversion of highest-quality agricultural land into urban areas, golf courses and quarries; the Ottawa greenbelt (1956); Boston (1952); Barcelona (no date available); Seoul (1971); Melbourne's 12 'green wedges' (somewhat protected since 1960s, legislated 1971); and the Washington State Mountains to Sound Greenway (MTSG, legislated 1991). However, unless the land within the greenbelt is government-owned, as in the case of Ottawa, it remains problematic whether these areas are used for agriculture: with the exception of vegetable cultivation on highly fertile peat soils, in Toronto, Boston and Melbourne, there is increasing displacement of food production by affluent rural residences. Not necessarily bad for biodiversity (relative to the monocultural extensive agriculture that the estates may have replaced) or the recreational horse industry, but not contributing to biodiverse food security. The Vienna greenbelt (which has evolved since 1872) may provide a more diverse, and balanced, scenario for maintaining food production and biodiversity. Within it, over 2,000 indigenous plant species are found to grow (Breiling and Ruland, 2008). The Vienna greenbelt has supported the development of protected forests in some areas, while reducing the protection for agricultural biodiversity in habitat-field, habitat-vineyard and habitat-hedge programs, or of small food allotments (Kleingartens) and intensive (presumably low-biodiversity) greenhouse production of tomatoes and cucumbers in others (Breiling and Ruland, 2008).

It remains to be seen whether community motivation or government action will preserve urban agriculture with its benefits for local ecosystem – and food genetic – biodiversity. Collective community action (e.g. community gardens) and community engagement with food production (through CSAs and farmers' markets) are increasing, but urban and peri-urban land is inexorably being taken out of food for housing and urban infrastructure. It is often, perhaps generally, accepted that governments have the right to legislate against this trend, and deny windfall profits to speculators through legislation or land-swaps, or less effectively, to encourage retention of urban agriculture by differential taxes. Throughout our urbanizing world the question is, will they?

## References


Alford, J. and O'Flynn, J. (2009) 'Making sense of public value: Concepts, critiques and emergent meanings', *International Journal of Public Administration*, vol. 32, pp. 171–91.

Atwell, R. C., Schulte, L. A. and Westphal, L. M. (2010) 'How to build multifunctional agricultural landscapes in the U.S. Corn Belt: Add perennials and partnerships', *Land Use Policy*, vol. 27, pp. 1082–1090.

Baker, L. and de Zeeuw, H. (2015) 'Urban food policies and programs', pp. 26–55 in H. de Zeeuw and P. Drechsel (eds.), *Cities and Agriculture: Developing Resilient Urban Food Systems*, Routledge, New York, NY, USA.

Benke, K. K., Wyatt, R. G. and Sposito, V. A. (2011) 'A discrete simulation approach to spatial allocation of commodity production for revenue optimization over a local region', *Journal of Spatial Science*, vol. 56, pp. 89–101.

Bernholt, H., Kehlenbeck, K., Gebauer, J., and Buerkert, A. (2009) 'Plant species richness and diversity in urban and peri-urban gardens of Niamey, Niger', *Agroforestry Systems*, vol. 77, pp. 159–179.

Breiling, M. and Ruland, G. (2008) 'The Vienna green belt: From localized protection to a regional concept', pp. 167–183 in M. Amati (ed.), *Urban Green Belts in the Twenty-First Century*, Ashgate, Aldershot, UK.

Brenner, J. C., Lavallato, S., Cherry, M. and Hileman, E. (2013) 'Land use determines interest in conservation easements among private landowners', *Land Use Policy*, vol. 35, pp. 24–32.

Byers, E. and Ponte, K. M. (2005) *The Conservation Easement Handbook*, Land Trust Alliance, Washington, DC, USA.

Costanza, R., d'Arge, R., de Groot, R., Faber, S., Grasso, M., Hannon, B., Limburg, K., Naeem, S., O'Neill, R. V., Paruelo, J., Raskin, R. G., Sutton, P. and van den Belt, M. (1997) 'The value of the world's ecosystem services and natural capital', *Nature*, vol. 387, pp. 253–60.

Crossman, N. D. and Bryan, B. A. (2009) 'Identifying cost-effective hotspots for restoring natural capital and enhancing landscape multifunctionality', *Ecological Economics*, vol. 68, pp. 654–68.

Donati, K., Taylor, C. and Pearson, C. J. (2013) 'Local food and dietary diversity: Farmers' markets and community gardens in Melbourne, Australia', pp. 326–335 in J. Fanzo, D. Hunter, T. Borelli and F. Mattei (eds.), *Diversifying Food and Diets*, Routledge, Abingdon, UK.

Hinrichs, C. C. (2013) 'Regionalizing food security: Imperatives, intersections and contestations in a post-9/11 world', *Journal of Rural Studies*, vol. 29, pp. 7–18.

IIASTD (International Assessment of Agricultural Knowledge, Science and Technology for Development) (2008) *Towards Multifunctional Agriculture for Social, Environmental and Economic Sustainability*, www.unep.org/dewa/Assessments/Ecosystems/IAASTD/tabid/105853/

Ives, C. D. and Kendall, D. (2013) 'Values and attitudes of the urban public towards peri-urban agricultural land', *Land Use Policy*, vol. 34, pp. 80–90.

Knight, L. and Riggs, W. (2010) 'Nourishing urbanism: A case for a new paradigm', *International Journal of Agricultural Sustainability*, vol. 8, pp. 116–126.

Longmire, A., Taylor, C. and Pearson, C. J. (2015) 'An open-access method for targeting revegetation based on potential for emissions reduction, carbon sequestration and opportunity cost', *Land Use Policy*, vol. 42, pp. 578–585.

Lydecker, M. and Drechsel, P. (2010) 'Urban agriculture and sanitation services in Accra, Ghana: The overlooked contribution', *International Journal of Agricultural Sustainability*, vol. 8, pp. 94–103.

McEwan, M., Prain, G. and Hunter, D. (2013) 'Opening a can of mopane worms: Can cross-sectoral partnerships leverage agricultural biodiversity for better quality diets?', pp. 207–228 in J. Fanzo, D. Hunter, T. Borelli and F. Mattei (eds.), *Diversifying Food and Diets*, Routledge, Abingdon, UK.

Moore, M. (1995) *Creating Public Value: Strategic Management in Government*, Harvard University Press, Cambridge, MA, USA.

Munro, N. and Lindenmayer, D. (2011) *Planting for Wildlife*, CSIRO, Melbourne, Australia.

Naylor, R., Steinfeld, H., Walter Falcon, W., Galloway, J., Smil, V., Bradford, E., Alder, J. and Mooney, H. (2005) 'Losing the links between livestock and land', *Science*, vol. 310, pp. 1621–1622.

Pascual, U. and Muradian, R. (2010) 'The economics of valuing ecosystem services and biodiversity', pp. 183–256 in P. Kumar (ed.), *The Economics of Ecosystems and Biodiversity: Ecological and Economic Foundations*, Earthscan for Routledge, Abingdon, UK.

Pearson, C. J. (2007) 'Regenerative, semi-closed systems: A priority for twenty-first century agriculture', *BioScience*, vol. 57, pp. 409–418.

Pearson, C. J., and Dyball, R. (2014) 'City food security', pp. 113–122 in L. Pearson, P. Roberts and P. Newton (eds.), *Resilient and Sustainable Cities: A Future*, Earthscan, New York, NY, USA.

Pearson, L. J., Pearson, L. and Pearson, C. J. (2010) 'Sustainable urban agriculture: Stocktake and opportunities', *International Journal of Agricultural Sustainability*, vol. 8, pp. 7–19.

Sayer, J., Sunderland, T., Ghazoul, J., Pfund, J-L., Shell, D., Meijaard, E., Venter, M., Boedhihartono, A. K., Day, M., Garcia, C., van Oosten, C. and Buck, L. E. (2013) 'Ten principles for a landscape approach to reconciling agriculture, conservation, and other competing land uses', *Proceedings of the National Academy of Sciences USA*, vol. 110, pp. 8349–8356.

Schirmer, J., Clayton, H. and Sherren, K. (2013) 'Reversing scattered tree decline on farms: Implications of landholder perceptions and practice in the Lachlan catchment, New South Wales', *Australasian Journal of Environmental Management*, vol. 19, pp. 91–107.

Sclesinger, J., Drescher, A. and Shackleton, C. M. (2015) 'Socio-spatial dynamics in the use of wild natural resources: Evidence from six rapidly growing medium-sized cities in Africa', *Applied Geography*, vol. 56, pp. 107–115.

Seymoar, N-K., Ballantyne, E. and Pearson, C. J. (2010) 'Empowering residents and improving governance in low income communities through urban greening', *International Journal of. Agricultural Sustainability*, vol. 8, pp. 26–39.

TEEB (The Economics of Ecosystems and Biodiversity) (2015) *Agrifood Interim Report*, pp. 1–24, www.teebweb.org/publication/teebagfood-interim-report/

Tilman, D., Reich, P. B., Knop, J., Wedin, D., Mielke, T. and Lehman, C. (2001) 'Diversity and productivity in a long-term grassland experiment', *Science*, vol. 294, pp. 843–845.

# 30

# MARKETS, CONSUMER DEMAND AND AGRICULTURAL BIODIVERSITY

*Matthias Jaeger, Alessandra Giuliani and Irene van Loosen*

## Introduction

This chapter focuses on the marketability of agricultural biodiversity, henceforth called 'agrobiodiversity', by examining the relations between markets, agrobiodiversity products and consumer demand, choices and drivers of consumer behaviour. The first subsection gives an introduction to contemporary shifts in agrobiodiversity conservation and related markets trends, and underlines the potential of agrobiodiversity products to enhance livelihood security and agrobiodiversity conservation. Throughout the chapter, it will be demonstrated that there can be opportunities and obstructions at both the demand and the supply side of markets for agrobiodiversity products. To this end, the next subsection focuses on the supply side, and on linking supply and demand, while the third subsection offers an overview of consumer trends and market opportunities for agrobiodiversity products. Selected case studies from different regions of the world are presented to provide insights on the potential of market-based approaches to stimulate agrobiodiversity conservation and use while simultaneously enhancing livelihoods.

## Agrobiodiversity as a source of commercially valuable traits

### *The societal value of agrobiodiversity*

Agrobiodiversity is a key public good that delivers crucial services for human well-being. It is considered to contribute substantially to poverty reduction, food security, health improvement, income generation and resilience (Koziell and McNeill, 2003; Roe and Elliot, 2004; FAO, 2005; see also Altieri et al., Chapter 13 of this Handbook). The main societal benefits stemming from the conservation of agrobiodiversity are tangible in the form of agro-ecosystems that are capable of producing highly diverse natural products (Pascual et al., 2011) and of ensuring future food provision (Smale et al., 2004). Subsistence farmers are inclined to conserve agrobiodiversity because crop diversification acts as a natural insurance against plant diseases, climate variability and market fluctuations, thereby strengthening sustainable livelihood strategies (Smale et al., 2004). Furthermore, in some cases, the specific crop traits preferred by local farmers cannot be obtained through commercial seed markets and have to be obtained locally (Smale et al., 2004; Galluzzi et al., 2015). However, as farmers become increasingly commercially oriented, they tend to grow crops with reduced genetic diversity.

### *Contemporary shifts in agrobiodiversity conservation*

Since the start of scientific plant breeding, the breeding and production of seed has shifted from being the sole preserve of farmers (GIZ, 2005) to an activity that is increasingly defined by large-scale commercial actors promoting high-yield crops varieties, while globalization and trade liberalization have led many developed and developing countries to focus on producing a limited number of cash crops for export (German Federal Ministry of Food, Agriculture and Consumer Protection, 2010). Agrobiodiversity loss is driven by variety replacement, land use changes, environmental degradation and a general shift in food and farming systems that has been taking place since the Green Revolution (Camacho-Henriquez et al., 2015).

Consequently, some agro-ecosystems are increasingly characterized by rising levels of intensification and corresponding falling levels of agrobiodiversity (GIZ, 2007a; Pascual et al., 2011). This contributes to many problems related to ecosystem sustainability, food and nutrition security, and climate change adaptation, amplified by a worldwide overdependence on a limited number of economically important plant species (Khoury et al., 2014).

It is often perceived that once farmers become increasingly involved in the market, they become more specialized, also contributing to reduced agrobiodiversity (Kruijssen et al., 2009). Current market systems fail to adequately value agrobiodiversity and ecosystem services (Van Dusen and Taylor, 2005). Therefore, conservation of biodiversity becomes problematic unless local people involved in the production, processing and marketing of resources related to biodiversity perceive a tangible benefit. Establishing market chains for specialized products based on agrobiodiversity traits that enhance agrobiodiversity maintained on farms and livelihoods of those involved is one solution to this problem (FAO, 2005). One way to improve the livelihood security of farmers while simultaneously stimulating biodiversity conservation is to identify new opportunities for marketing 'agrobiodiversity products' and in particular products derived from those crops and species that are considered neglected and underutilized (Giuliani, 2007; see also Meldrum and Padulosi, Chapter 18 of this Handbook). This is helped by emerging trends in demand for local, diverse, healthy, high-value and 'exclusive' food products, especially in developed countries and where there is an emerging middle-class in developing nations (GIZ, 2007a). We define agrobiodiversity products as 'products originating from local useful plants and animals that are very well adapted to local conditions, reflect traditional knowledge in terms of their development or processing, and are part of the local culture' (GIZ, 2007a, p. 1).

## Agrobiodiversity products: matching supply and demand

### *Value chains for agrobiodiversity products*

To understand the marketing potential of an agrobiodiversity product and its suitability for niche markets, information is needed on both the product and the value chain through which it will be marketed. (We define the value chain as 'the sequence of processes from the provision of specific inputs to primary production, transformation, marketing and to final consumption', as well as 'the linkages and coordination between the producers, processors, traders and distributors of a particular product' [Will, 2008, p. 16]). Generally, products with a high degree of genetic diversity will be produced by short value chains with many small, non-specialized suppliers, as these tend to use more species and varieties than large-scale producers (GIZ, 2007a). For a successful value chain approach, an adequate level of supply and purchasing power of the consumer segment should be guaranteed (GIZ, 2007a). Farmers will frequently need assistance to access markets and improve their cultivation practices and post-harvesting technologies, while consumers should be provided with evidence of the nutritional and societal benefits of agrobiodiversity products (Padulosi et al., 2013; Camacho-Henriquez et al., 2015).

## *Drivers of NUS as high value agrobiodiversity product*

Drivers that can foster or hamper market development of neglected and underutilized species (NUS) have been identified (Will, 2008) (**Table 30.1** *Opportunities and challenges for market development of NUS*). Opportunities can change into threats where inappropriate promotion strategies or market incentives that are not embedded in sustainability strategies override the balance of social, environmental and economic benefits (Meldrum and Padulosi, Chapter 18 of this Handbook). Vice versa, threats to biodiversity and pro-poor growth may transform into opportunities, provided that realistic supply, and especially market potentials, can be identified and realized in a sustainable way (Kruijssen and Sudha, 2008; Will, 2008).

*Table 30.1* Opportunities and challenges for market development of NUS

| *Drivers* | *Opportunities* | *Challenges* |
|---|---|---|
| Globalization (trade) | Access to new export markets | Increased competition |
| Globalization (culture) | Exposure to global diet diversity | Decreasing variety/homogenization of diets |
| International agreements | Promotion of conversation/ utilization of NUS | Increased market access requirements |
| Urbanization | Rising incomes and increasing demand for convenience foods | Disappearance of indigenous knowledge on NUS uses and recipes |
| Consumer trends | Changing consumer attitudes towards health and environment | Increasing demand for global brands |
| Climate change | Increasing need for climate-tolerant species | Increasing risk of crop failures because of extreme weather events |
| Commoditization of NUS | Growing shares of NUS in local, regional and global markets | Risk of commoditization of NUS could result in: |
| Poverty alleviation | Alternative sources of income for smallholder farmers | • biodiversity reduction in smallholder farmer systems; |
| Food security/ improved nutrition | Access to food and enriched diets for the rural and urban poor | • unsustainable collection and production practices;<br>• marginalization of smallholder farmers. |

*Source*: Adapted from Will (2008).

### Limitations in the marketing of agrobiodiversity products

The marketing of agrobiodiversity products is hampered for a number of reasons. Agrobiodiversity is prone to market failure because of its characteristics as an impure public good with intergenerational and interregional dimensions, that is, agrobiodiversity has both public and private economic attributes, and farmers as a group tend to generate less diversity than is desirable in contemporary and future society (Smale et al., 2004; Gruère et al., 2009). While the societal benefits of agrobiodiversity conservation are high, individual farmers producing for the market have little private incentive to preserve genetic diversity, as conservation costs are also high and there is insufficient reward in the marketplace (Pascual et al., 2011). Consumers benefit directly from agrobiodiversity conservation in the form of an abundance of crop varieties, animal breeds and food products. Nonetheless, the costs of *in situ* conservation are borne directly by farmers, while the costs of *ex situ* conservation are largely paid for by public funds (Smale et al., 2004). Besides this economic mismatch, in many countries, agrobiodiversity conservation by farmers is impeded by governmental subsidizing of intensive agriculture, signalling a portentous policy failure in creating incentives to conserve the majority of NUS (Pascual et al., 2011). In a perfectly functioning market, no plant species would be considered underutilized (Gruère et al., 2009). The potential value of any NUS is higher than its observed (current) value, while the total value of a NUS can be divided into public and private assets (**Figure 30.1** *The value of NUS*). Although NUS could have high public and private value, they suffer from missing output markets,[1,2] suboptimal market equilibria[3] and market failure.[4] To secure and stimulate agrobiodiversity conservation, it is necessary to demonstrate and capture both its public and private values.

Furthermore, although the marketing of NUS could provide numerous opportunities for private industry, there is a lack of knowledge regarding the commercially valuable traits and qualities of these crop species to adequately address current consumer preferences. It is assumed that better information would lead to a more complete market valuation of agrobiodiversity products (Gruère et al., 2009).

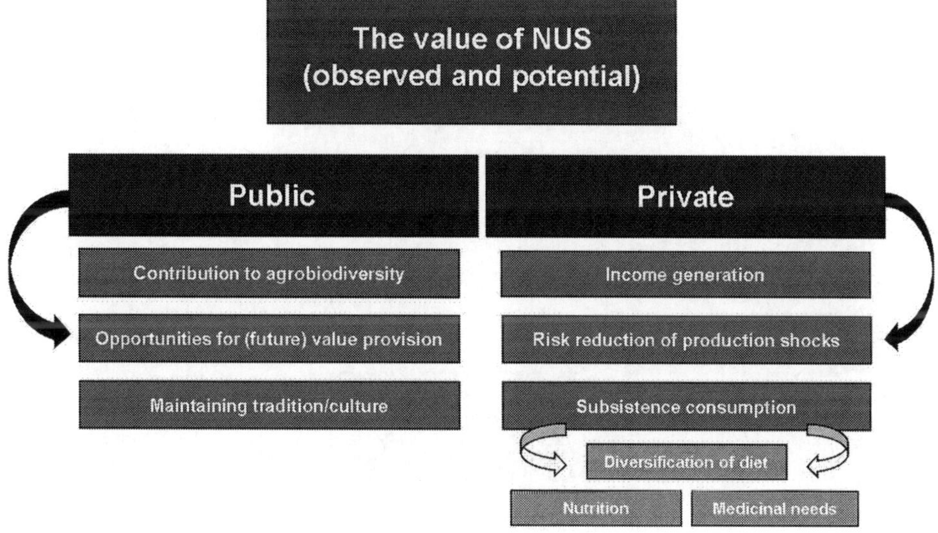


*Figure 30.1* The value of NUS

*Sources*: Adapted from Gruère et al. (2009) and Will (2008).

## Interventions to increase the value of NUS

In those cases where missing output markets and suboptimal market equilibria are caused by weak demand, inefficient supply or both, market development is likely to improve the situation. On the other hand, when the problem is market failure, public intervention is necessary to reach the socially optimum market level, capture the public value of agrobiodiversity products and ensure the availability of agrobiodiversity to users (Gruère et al., 2009). International policy efforts that aim to translate the value of agrobiodiversity conservation into economic values could promote more equitable, effective and efficient conservation practices (Smale et al., 2004). However, it is difficult to fully capture all the value components of agrobiodiversity conservation in quantitative valuations (Smale et al., 2004). Policy interventions that could contribute to this aim can be grouped into two approaches: (a) *in situ* and *ex situ* conservation strategies to increase the observed value of NUS, and (b) policies aimed at lowering transaction costs by overcoming market barriers and imperfections (Gruère et al., 2009).

A European example of a marketing and conservation strategy to increase the demand of a NUS and support production by mountain-based smallholder farmers in Italy is the case of emmer *(Triticum dicoccon)*, a hulled wheat with high-value nutritional properties. This demonstrates that proper interventions, integrated at different societal levels, can stimulate agrobiodiversity conservation and use and bring substantial economic benefits to smallholder farmers (Giuliani et al., 2009; see **Figure 30.2** *Strategy to increase the demand for emmer in Italy*.)

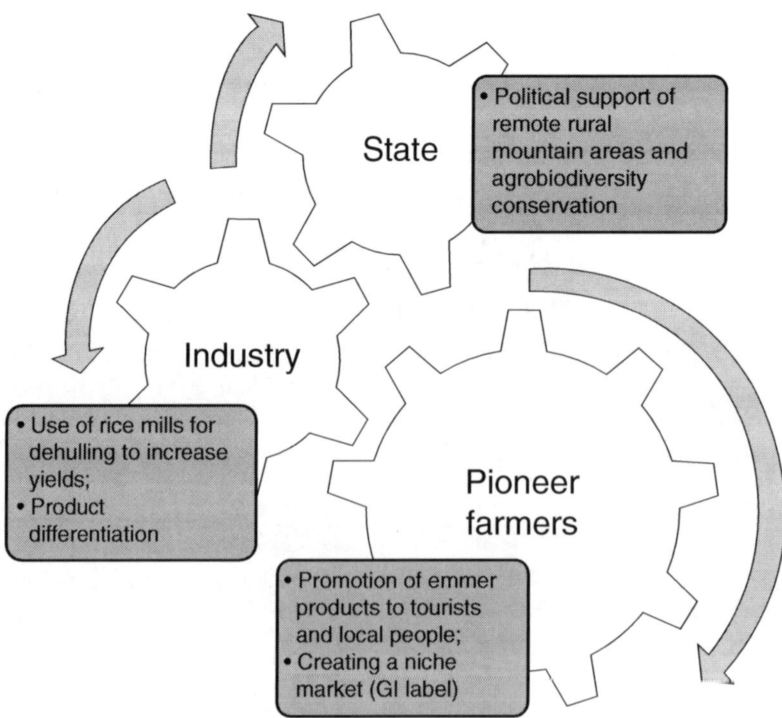


*Figure 30.2* Strategy to increase the demand for emmer in Italy

*Source*: Adapted from Giuliani et al. (2009).

## *Overcoming market barriers and imperfections*

According to Smale et al. (2004, p. 123), 'institutional structures are needed to compensate for the inability of markets to provide sufficient incentives for farmers to allocate their resources in ways that are consistent with the needs of society', for example by introducing policy measures to prompt cost-effective *in situ* conservation of NUS. These measures tend to be most successful in areas with limited access to commercial markets, heterogeneity in agro-ecological conditions and low population density (Van Dusen, 2000; Smale et al., 2004) and are particularly useful for NUS with limited potential private value but large potential public value (Gruère et al., 2009).

Demand-related policies to stimulate the conservation and use of NUS have to consider the concerns, preferences and cultural identities of the local farmers that grow a NUS, as they currently constitute its principal consumer group. Production and conservation could for instance be enhanced by improving the genetic traits of NUS in participation with the farmers themselves (Smale et al., 2004). On the other hand, supply-related policies at the local and regional levels could focus on the establishment of community seed banks (Vernooy et al., 2015; see also Taylor, Chapter 38 of this Handbook) to improve farmers' access to higher quality seed.

Strengthening farmers' links with markets and institutions and improving infrastructure is an approach that could be particularly effective for agrobiodiversity products and in particular for NUS with missing output markets (Smale et al., 2004). Gruère et al. (2009) suggested three requirements for the successful commercialization of NUS: (a) expansion of demand, (b) improved efficiency of production and marketing channels, and (c) supply control through product differentiation and quality certification as a mechanism to ensure suitable profits for the producers, thereby stimulating pro-poor economic growth.

In recent years, value chain development (VCD) has gained recognition as a tool for linking the supply capacities of the rural poor to market opportunities. VCD is a participatory, business-oriented approach that aims to capture the best value at all stages of production, processing and trading, from farmers through traders, processors and retailers, to the final consumer (Will, 2008). A successful marketing chain brings a product of satisfactory quality onto the market at a reasonable price (Gruère et al., 2009), thereby increasing the public and private value of the good. While the potential of VCD for NUS remains largely unlocked, it could serve as an effective instrument for facilitating market access for farmers producing NUS and agrobiodiversity products (Horna et al., 2007).

It is important to assess the potential benefits, economic viability and sustainability of VCD for each individual case, as the public and private investments of building structures and developing the capacities necessary for the integration of NUS producers into the value chain must be able to overcome restrictions such as farmers' lack of resources or capacities, their risk adversity or their inability to conform with market standards (Will, 2008). Any value chain for NUS must have realistic potential for agrobiodiversity conservation and livelihood improvement. At the same time, it is crucial to create sufficient demand for the agrobiodiversity products that originate from underutilized species by implementing a range of measures to market the products (**Figure 30.3** *Possible measures to create demand for NUS*).

## *The marketing of NUS: two case studies*

Two examples of the successful marketing of NUS are the case of Andean grains in Bolivia and Peru (**Box 30.1**, *Marketing Andean grains in Bolivia and Peru*) and the case of minor millets in India (**Box 30.2**, *Marketing minor millets in India*).

*Figure 30.3* Possible measures to create demand for NUS

*Source*: Adapted from Will (2008).

## Box 30.1 Marketing Andean grains in Bolivia and Peru

Through a UN-supported project aimed at the genetic improvement and improved marketing of highly nutritious traditional grains such as quinoa and amaranth, it proved possible to improve food security, nutrition, farmers' incomes and livelihoods in poor communities in Bolivia and Peru. While traditional grains are increasingly being replaced by global cereal crops (which leads to the erosion of local food cultures), the project led to production, sales and consumption of Andean grains drastically increasing. This project applied a holistic, participatory value chain approach through which farmers benefitted from improved plant varieties, capacity development, technological innovations and new market opportunities. Besides economic benefits, cultural, gender and nutrition aspects were taken into account. Multi-stakeholder platforms actively engaged relevant organizations and actors in the newly found Andean grain value chains and facilitated access to national and international markets. By stimulating the cultivation of highly divergent, endangered plant species, the project contributed to the preservation of agricultural biodiversity and indigenous knowledge in the region. In conclusion, the project demonstrated that NUS can become valid instruments of development in marginal areas.

*Sources*: Padulosi et al. (2014) and Bioversity International (2015).

### Box 30.2 Marketing minor millets in India.

In recent years, the production and consumption of minor millets in India has declined, despite their high nutritious value and adaptability to marginal environments. Their wider use is also impeded by perceptions on minor millets as crops of the poor, neglect by policy makers and inefficient production, processing and marketing methods. To improve the cultivation and consumption of this NUS, a multidisciplinary, holistic approach to mainstream several millet species into value chains was used, thereby improving incomes, food security and nutrition in poor communities. Farmers were trained in cultivation and processing practices, innovative recipes for millet varieties were gathered and 15 community gene banks were established. Findings revealed that raising the production, marketing and consumption of minor millets in India has the potential to contribute to the food and nutrition security of the urban and rural poor, while at the same time promoting economic development, the empowerment of vulnerable groups such as women and the conservation of agrobiodiversity.

*Source*: Padulosi et al. (2015).

## Consumer trends and market opportunities for agrobiodiversity products

Before, during and after developing value chains for NUS, it is essential to assess the consumer side of marketing agrobiodiversity products. This section looks at current consumer trends and market opportunities for these products, provides an overview of existing marketing concepts, strategies and tools to capture their private value, considers institutional arrangements necessary to build successful markets for agrobiodiversity products and presents case studies of geographical areas where such markets have been developed.

### *Current and emerging consumer demand for agrobiodiversity products*

Agrobiodiversity products could be successfully marketed in several ways to spur consumer demand. In particular, agrobiodiversity products have the potential to respond to the emerging consumer trend of preferring healthy, fresh, locally-produced, 'exotic' food of known origin and assured, ethical production methods over the reigning culture of mass consumption that is characterized by processed foods, convenience products and resulting agrobiodiversity loss (German Federal Ministry of Food, Agriculture and Consumer Protection, 2010). Although many consumers around the world are still unaware of the close-knit relation between their food cultures and biodiversity conservation, and the valuable attributes biodiversity products may have for a healthy lifestyle, there is an increasing global consumption trend towards food and natural beauty products that are made with traditional methods and that are geographically linked to an area's cultural assets (Will, 2008; Gruère et al., 2009; Pallante and Drucker, 2014).

Consumers' preferences and purchasing decisions could contribute greatly to the conservation of agrobiodiversity. An increasing segment of this market group has come to realize the haziness surrounding the origin, production process and quality of food stuffs they consume (Pistorius et al., 2000), as well as the effect their consumption patterns may have on the environment, society and future generations (German Federal Ministry of Food, Agriculture and Consumer

Protection, 2010). These reflective drivers of consumption behaviour (Perry and Grace, 2015) and the current and emerging trend of increasing consumer demand for agrobiodiversity products are stimulated by public awareness campaigns organized by NGOs, education institutes, grassroots organizations and international organizations, aiming to raise awareness and increase public knowledge on agrobiodiversity value, and thence indirectly raising the public and private value of NUS and agrobiodiversity products (Gruère et al., 2009; German Federal Ministry of Food, Agriculture and Consumer Protection, 2010). Marketing agrobiodiversity products allows companies to reach a new customer segment and establish a socially responsible and eco-friendly reputation, while local producers are motivated to continue the conservation of agrobiodiversity and in particular NUS and have the opportunity to improve income (Pistorius et al., 2000; Gruère et al., 2009).

## *Agrobiodiversity products and consumer behaviour*

As VCD will only be profitable when consumers buy the final product, it is crucial to create demand by educating consumers and employing a successful branding strategy to enhance consumer perception of the agrobiodiversity product (Pistorius et al., 2000; Will, 2008). As market opportunities for agrobiodiversity products tend to increase when consumer income rises, both in industrialized and developing countries (Gruère et al., 2009), marketers of agrobiodiversity products tend to focus on higher-income societal groups for their niche markets. Higher incomes and the development of commercial markets lead to the continuation of NUS conservation if there is consumer demand for a unique attribute of the NUS that cannot be produced or delivered by modern crop varieties (Smale et al., 2004).

Pallante and Drucker (2014) in their study on finger millet markets among Nepalese urban consumers demonstrated that niche product market development can be a successful instrument to ensure the conservation of NUS in developing countries. They found that consumers with certain socioeconomic characteristics displayed a willingness to pay for the unique characteristics of locally produced finger millet that would allow farmers to obtain a price premium, thereby demonstrating that preferred quality of food products increases some consumers' willingness to pay higher prices. Instead of switching from the production of finger millet to a modern crop variety, the price premium would then incentivize farmers to maintain the conservation of finger millet, creating a situation where market-based incentives are resulting in the *in situ* conservation of NUS. Although the markets for NUS tend to be small (Smale et al., 2004), creating a successful niche market for a line of agrobiodiversity products may attract public and private investment to conserve NUS on a larger scale (Pallante and Drucker, 2014).

## *Marketing concepts, strategies and tools for agrobiodiversity products*

### *Labels and certification schemes*

In a context of increasing international trade and product uniformity, calls for market transparency, sustainable consumption and the conservation of agrobiodiversity have led to the development of a range of private labels and certification schemes for food products that could facilitate the development of niche markets for NUS. These allow consumers to make informed decisions with regard to their consumption patterns and have the potential to enhance sustainable food production and processing (Bérard and Marchenay, 2006; German Federal Ministry of Food, Agriculture and Consumer Protection, 2010).

Examples include eco-labels (e.g. sustainable forest management or environmentally sustainable fisheries) and fair trade labels, as well as products that are specifically linked to regional markets, cultural knowledge, traditional processing methods or a specific region of origin (Gruère et al., 2009; German Federal Ministry of Food, Agriculture and Consumer Protection, 2010). Several attributes of NUS that could contribute to their marketability and branding strategies include a striking name, an association with traditional knowledge and utilization and the geographical origin or the history of a product (Will, 2008). Geographical indications (GIs), labels with international reputation that protect and link a product to a locality with its particular history, reputation, traditional values, functional traits, characteristics and qualities, are also useful for product promotion (Bérard and Marchenay, 2006; Will, 2008). The identity of GI products as distinguished origin-linked products mirrors the distinctive mixture of local natural resources (local animal breeds and plant species, climate and soil, traditional tools, etc.) and cultural capital (traditional know-how and skills) in a particular territory. Such products can contribute to biocultural diversity conservation, socio-cultural development and poverty reduction (Vandecandelaere et al., 2009; Thevenod-Mottet, 2010). Two case studies on the use of geographical indications to market biodiversity products are provided in **Box 30.3** *Using GI to market biodiversity products in Kodagu, India* and **Box 30.4** *Using GI to increase the profitability of the* Chivito Criollo del Norte Neuquino*, a local goat breed from Patagonia, Argentina.*

It is likely that value chain development will benefit from integrated systems of good practices that are stimulated by private labelling and quality assurance schemes (Will, 2008). Hence, it is in the commercial interest of value chain operators to develop standards and quality assurance systems along the value chain. In the case of agrobiodiversity products, these marketing tools may allow local producers to continue small-scale production based on traditional processes and methods, thereby protecting local cultural attributes, knowledge and practices (Bérard and Marchenay, 2006). If the profit margin of marketing agrobiodiversity products through these channels is high enough, producers are incentivized to refrain from conforming to globalized production processes or switching to other livelihood strategies, thereby contributing to *in situ* conservation of agrobiodiversity.

## Box 30.3 Using GI to market biodiversity products in Kodagu, India

In this case study, Garcia et al. (2007) studied the ability of GIs to serve as a tool for rural development by assessing the impact of an existing GI for Coorg orange on biodiversity conservation in Kodagu province, India. Kodagu's reputation as an area with exceptional biodiversity could be used to valorize Coorg orange, a NUS that has gradually been replaced by more lucrative cash crops. In 2004, an application for a Coorg orange GI was filed by a regional government agency in a top-down approach to support local producers. However, the government's strategy to transfer the ownership of the GI to the farmers failed for several reasons. The farmers did not understand the GI's meaning and never agreed with plans included in the agreement to preserve the planting area's biodiversity and introduce organic practices. Additionally, poor relations between them and the regional state agency existed. Consequently, the farmers have never used the GI to market their oranges, and it is unlikely that this GI will have a positive impact on the landscape of Kodagu. Garcia et al. (2007) concluded that a successful GI needs to be appropriated by producers and has to secure their income, as otherwise they have no incentives to protect the locality's biodiversity and landscape as part of the GI agreement.

**Box 30.4 Using GI to increase the profitability of the *Chivito Criollo del Norte Neuquino*, a local goat breed from Patagonia, Argentina**

Neuquén criollo goats are the main source of income and animal protein for many households in the north of Neuquén province in Patagonia, Argentina. The goats are well adapted to the transhumant movements which have traditionally shaped the lives of the goat keepers or *crianceros*. However, the sustainability of the system is threatened by changes restricting livestock movements, notably the fencing of traditional grazing areas. A programme for the conservation and improvement of the Neuquén criollo goat was started 15 years ago. Further developments included measures to increase the value of goat products by developing Codes of Practices indicating the breed and the importance of nomadic grazing, as well as the kid age and the slaughter seasons, which gives the meat its special flavour (specific quality linked to its geographical origin). Kid meat is now sold under a distinct GI. This commercial-legal innovation enhanced the profitability of the traditional product of the system and improved the livelihoods of the local producers (Vandecandelaere et al., 2009).

For consumers, established private quality schemes and labels confirm and guarantee the quality of the agrobiodiversity products on offer (GIZ, 2007b), thereby increasing their loyalty and stabilizing demand and profits (Will, 2008). In some regions around the world, labels that ensure the quality and authenticity of food products have been functioning for centuries. However, private labelling will be marketable only if consumers are willing to pay price premiums that are high enough to cover the costs along the production and processing side of the value chain, which may result in highly priced products. Furthermore, a functioning value chain based on a well-known brand is a prerequisite for successful private labelling. For these reasons, the use of these marketing tools is still less common in developing countries (Smale et al., 2004).

## *Agritourism*

An alternative measure to promote the *in situ* conservation of NUS as well as rare useful animal breeds is agritourism: a form of tourism which capitalizes on rural culture as a tourist attraction (GIZ, 2007b; see also Nazarea, Chapter 39 of this Handbook). Through agritourism, typical regional breeds and varieties may be kept in use to exhibit a landscape with cultural, historical and natural attractions to tourists, who in turn provide additional income to local farmers and foster regional development through schemes of equitable profit-sharing. Currently, this type of consumer involvement in agrobiodiversity conservation is chiefly applied in developed regions, but this is changing (GIZ, 2007b). For example, 'Santiago de Okola', a Bolivian village where local capacity building and infrastructure improvement resulted in the establishment of a local tourism organization, a website, a community museum on agrobiodiversity, and annual events to celebrate indigenous crops and food culture, demonstrates an innovative agritourism approach. These activities are now self-sustainable and contribute to livelihood improvement and the conservation of NUS in the community (Padulosi et al., 2014).

### *Institutional arrangements and strategies for the successful marketing of agrobiodiversity products*

As highlighted, agrobiodiversity conservation is prone to market failure because of its characteristics as an impure public good. In order to achieve supply control and ensure the workability of private labels and quality schemes for agrobiodiversity products, the support of well-developed institutions is often indispensable (see **Box 30.5** *Direct sales and agrobiodiversity conservation in Toscana, Italy*). These include multi-stakeholder platforms, cooperative agreements, joint ventures, legal requirements for distinctness, legal frameworks to ensure access to resources and property rights, grading schemes and quality standards (Gruère et al., 2009; German Federal Ministry of Food, Agriculture and Consumer Protection, 2010).

Broadly speaking, we can divide interventions in markets for agrobiodiversity products as legislative or market-based approaches. Here, legislative measures comprise technical regulations for products and processing methods, while market-based models use price and quantity control to internalize externalities (German Federal Ministry of Food, Agriculture and Consumer Protection, 2010).

While public and private institutional arrangements for supply control and quality certification are now present in most industrialized countries, they are still rare in developing nations. In those cases where quality standards and infrastructure are absent, it can be very costly and difficult to implement these arrangements (Gruère et al., 2009). Exceptions are the Participatory Guarantee Schemes (PGS), locally focused quality assurance systems which certify producers based on active participation of stakeholders and are built on a foundation of trust, social networks and knowledge exchange. To cite one of a number of successful cases, Pacific Islanders have started to reach high-level niche markets across the oceans with their own certified organic fruit specialty products (IFOAM, 2015). An example of successfully linking agricultural biodiversity to public procurement programs in a developing country is the school feeding program that has been implemented in Sucre, Bolivia, as part of the Andean grains project described in **Box 30.1** (Padulosi et al., 2014). By providing nationally produced amaranth energy bars to school children,

#### Box 30.5 Direct sales and agrobiodiversity conservation in Toscana, Italy

Bocci and Chiari (2009) investigated the impacts of direct sales initiatives on farming systems in Toscana, an Italian region where short supply chains from farmers to consumers are still common. To meet consumer demand for fresh, local produce, with the support of regional funding, the 'Filiera Corta' project was started: an initiative to set up local sales points where farmers can sell their produce directly to consumers. It was found that all participating farms examined in the study reported a higher number of cultivated species as a result of the direct sales project. As they also contributed to the conservation of agrobiodiversity by cultivating traditional, local varieties, Bocci and Chiari (2009) concluded that the case study provides evidence that direct sales is a useful tool to promote diversification of farm production, both in species and varieties. However, transferring to a farming system with a direct sales policy may cause problems for farmers, for example technical and organizational difficulties, lack of manpower in the countryside, higher personnel costs, unstable demand and the need for additional investments related to direct sales. Therefore, so far only a limited number of producers has adopted direct sales as their primary marketing strategy.

public procurement is used as a powerful complementary tool to market-based approaches that links agrobiodiversity products to high value markets. However, in many other cases, the inability to comply with international standards and access markets may prevent regions of origin reaping benefits from participating in markets for agrobiodiversity products (Will, 2008). Consequently, there is a need for international institutional cooperation and joint action to stimulate the preservation of global public goods such as agrobiodiversity (Will, 2008; German Federal Ministry of Food, Agriculture and Consumer Protection, 2010). A good example is the mechanism of the UN International Year, targeting for example quinoa (2013) and pulses (2016), where a multi-stakeholder approach has been used to stimulate both supply and demand in an holistic way by addressing bottlenecks and constraints along the entire value chain from farm to fork.

## Conclusions

Agrobiodiversity products and NUS have great potential for high value agrobiodiversity-based product differentiation by functioning as instruments for agrobiodiversity conservation and farmers' livelihood improvement as well as meeting consumers' emerging demand for healthy and functional food products from known, local origins. However, value chain development for agrobiodiversity products is hindered by missing markets, market failure and imperfections, constraints that could be addressed by introducing market development policies, policy interventions and institutional arrangements. Labelling and quality assurance schemes are useful tools to capture the public and private value of agrobiodiversity products by linking locally-bound products to commercial markets while ensuring quality for consumers. While progress has been made in the marketing and commercialization of agrobiodiversity products, there are still ample opportunities around the world where market-based approaches could be implemented to prompt agrobiodiversity conservation and enhance livelihoods simultaneously. However, value chain development for agrobiodiversity products needs to be complemented by international strategies for joint agrobiodiversity conservation.

## Notes

1 A wide range of terms are used for underutilized plant species, including 'minor', 'neglected', 'local', 'traditional', 'underexploited', 'underdeveloped', 'orphan', 'lost', 'new', 'niche', 'promising 'and 'alternative' (Padulosi et al., 2002; Giuliani, 2007).

2 When primary producers do not or cannot access a market for their products due to exogenous constraints (i.e. high transaction costs) or endogenous constraints (i.e. the community is able to access a local market but there is a lack of economic incentive for each household to sell or buy the NUS) (Gruère et al., 2009).

3 It can be due to different market imperfections: a weak market demand, an inefficient supply or both conditions. One consequence is a price that does not encompass the full value of the product (Gruère et al., 2009).

4 In these cases, the limited use of NUS fails to reveal their public value (Gruère et al., 2009).

## References

Bérard, L. and Marchenay, P. (2006) 'Local products and geographical indications: Taking account of local knowledge and biodiversity', *International Social Science Journal*, vol. 58, pp. 109–116.

Bioversity International (2015) *Andean 'Lost Grains' in Bolivia and Peru*, Bioversity International, Maccarese, Italy.

Bocci, R. and Chiari, T. (2009) *The Sustainable Use of Agrobiodiversity in Italy: Report on Case Studies on Article 6 of the International Treaty on Plant Genetic Resources for Food and Agriculture*, Instituto Agronomico per l'Oltremare (IAO), Florence, Italy.

Camacho-Henriquez, A., Kraemer, F., Galluzzi, G., de Haan, S., Jäger, M. and Christinck, A. (2015) 'Decentralized collaborative plant breeding for utilization and conservation of neglected and underutilized crop genetic resources', pp. 25–61 in J. Al-Khayri, S. Mohan Jain and D. Johnson (eds.), *Advances in Plant Breeding Strategies: Breeding, Biotechnology and Molecular Tools*, Springer International Publishing, Cham, Switzerland.

FAO [Food and Agriculture Organization of the United Nations] (2005) *Building on Gender, Agrobiodiversity and Local Knowledge, A Training Manual*, FAO, Rome, Italy.

Galluzzi, G., Estrada, R., Apaza, V., Gamarra, M., Pérez, Á., Gamarra, G., Altamirano, A., Cáceres, G., Gonza, V., Sevilla, R., López Noriega, I. and Jäger, M. (2015) 'Participatory breeding in the Peruvian highlands: Opportunities and challenges for promoting conservation and sustainable use of underutilized crops', *Renewable Agriculture and Food Systems*, vol. 30, pp. 408–417.

Garcia, C., Marie-Vivien, D., Kushalappa, C. G., Chengappa, P. G. and Nanaya, K. M. (2007) 'Geographical indications and biodiversity in the Western Ghats, India: Can labeling benefit producers and the environment in a mountain agroforestry landscape?', *Mountain Research and Development*, vol. 27, pp. 206–210.

German Federal Ministry of Food, Agriculture and Consumer Protection (2010) *Conservation of Agricultural Biodiversity, Development and Sustainable Use of Its Potentials in Agriculture, Forestry and Fisheries*, A Strategy of the German Federal Ministry of Food, Agriculture and Consumer Protection on Conservation and Sustainable Use of Biodiversity for Food, Agriculture, Forestry and Fisheries', BMELV, Bonn, Germany.

Giuliani, A. (2007) *Developing Markets for Agrobiodiversity: Securing Livelihoods in Dryland Areas*, Earthscan Publications, London and Sterling, UK.

Giuliani, A., Karagöz, A. and Zencirci, N. (2009) 'Emmer (*Triticum dicoccon*) production and market potential in marginal mountainous areas of Turkey', *Mountain Research and Development*, vol. 29, pp. 220–229.

GIZ (2005) 'Farmers as bankers – community seed banks', People and Diversity Issue Paper Series, Sector Project "People and Biodiversity in Rural Areas", GIZ, Eschborn, Germany.

GIZ (2007a) 'Value chains and the conservation of biodiversity', Issue Papers: People, Food and Biodiversity, Sector project "Global Food Security and Agrobiodiversity", GIZ, Bonn, Germany.

GIZ (2007b) 'Maintaining and promoting agricultural diversity through tourism', Issue Papers: People, Food and Biodiversity, Sector project "Global Food Security and Agrobiodiversity", GIZ, Bonn, Germany.

Gruère, G., Giuliani, A. and Smale, M. (2009) 'Marketing underutilized plant species for the poor: A conceptual framework', pp. 62–81 in A. Kontoleon, U. Pascual and M. Smale (eds.), *Agrobiodiversity, Conservation and Economic Development*, Routledge for Earthscan, Abingdon, UK and New York, NY, USA.

Horna, D., Timpo, S. and Gruère, G. (2007) *Marketing Underutilized Crops: The Case of the African Garden Egg* (Solanum aethiopicum) *in Ghana*, Report of the Global Facilitation Unit for Underutilized Species, Bioversity International, Maccarese, Italy.

IFOAM (2015) *The Global PGS Newsletter*, IFOAM – Organics International, March–April, vol. 5 (4).

Khoury, C. K., Bjorkman, A. D., Dempewolf, H., Ramirez-Villegas, J., Guarino, L., Jarvis, A., Rieseberg, L. H. and Struik, P. C. (2014) 'Increasing homogeneity in global food supplies and implications for food security', *Proceedings of the National Academy of Sciences USA*, vol. 111, pp. 4001–4006.

Koziell, I. and McNeill, C. I. (2003) 'Reducing poverty by using biodiversity sustainably', *Development Policy Journal*, vol. 3, pp. 71–80.

Kruijssen, F., Giuliani, A. and Sudha, M. (2009) 'Marketing underutilized crops to sustain agrobiodiversity and improve livelihoods', *Acta Horticulturae* (ISHS), vol. 806, pp. 415–422.

Kruijssen, F. and Sudha, M. (2008) 'Enhancing biodiversity management and utilization to improve livelihoods – a case study of "kokum" in India', *Acta Horticulturae* (ISHS), vol. 794, pp. 165–171.

Padulosi, S., Amaya, K., Jäger, M., Gotor, E., Rojas, W. and Valdivia, R. (2014) 'A holistic approach to enhance the use of neglected and underutilized species: The case of Andean grains in Bolivia and Peru', *Sustainability*, vol. 6, pp. 1283–1312.

Padulosi, S., Hodgkin, T., Williams, J. T. and Haq, N. (2002) 'Underutilized crops: Trends, challenges and opportunities in the 21st century', pp. 323–338 in J. M. M. Engels, V. Ramanatha Rao, A. H. D. Brown and M. T. Jackson (eds.), *Managing Plant Genetic Resources*, CABI Publishing, Wallingford, UK and International Plant Genetic Resources Institute (IPGR), Rome, Italy.

Padulosi, S., Mal, B., King, O. I. and Gotor, E. (2015) 'Minor millets as a central element for sustainably enhanced incomes, empowerment, and nutrition in rural India', *Sustainability*, vol. 7, pp. 8904–8933.

Padulosi, S., Thompson, J. and Rudebjer, P. (2013) *Fighting Poverty, Hunger and Malnutrition with Neglected and Underutilized Species (NUS): Needs, Challenges and the Way Forward*, Bioversity International, Maccarese, Italy.

Pallante, G. and Drucker, A. (2014) *Niche Markets for Agrobiodiversity Conservation: Preference and Scale Heterogeneity Effects on Nepalese Consumers' WTP for Finger Millet Products* (no. 1414), Sustainability Environmental Economics and Dynamics Studies, Ferrara, Italy.

Pascual, U., Narloch, U., Nordhagen, S. and Drucker, A. (2011) 'The economics of agrobiodiversity conservation for food security under climate change', *Economía Agraria y Recursos Naturales*, vol. 11, pp. 191–220.

Perry, B. D. and Grace, D. C. (2015) 'How growing complexity of consumer choices and drivers of consumption behaviour affect demand for animal source foods', *EcoHealth*, vol. 12, pp. 703–712.

Pistorius, R., Röling, N. G. and Visser, B. (2000) 'Making agrobiodiversity work: Results of an on-line stakeholder dialogue (OSD) in the Netherlands', *NJAS-Wageningen Journal of Life Sciences*, vol. 48, pp. 319–340.

Roe, D. and Elliot, J. (2004) 'Poverty reduction and biodiversity conservation: Rebuilding the bridges', *Oryx*, vol. 38, pp. 137–139.

Smale, M., Bellon, M. R., Jarvis, D. and Sthapit, B. (2004) 'Economic concepts for designing policies to conserve crop genetic resources on farms', *Genetic Resources and Crop Evolution*, vol. 51, pp. 121–135.

Thevenod-Mottet, E. (2010) 'Geographical indications and biodiversity' pp. 201–212 in S. Lockie and D. Carpenter (eds.), *Agriculture, Biodiversity and Markets: Livelihoods and Agroecology in Comparative Perspective*, Earthscan, London, UK.

Vandecandelaere, E., Arfini, F., Belletti, G. and Marescotti, A. (eds.) (2009) *Linking People, Places and Products: A Guide for Promoting Quality Linked to Geographical Origin and Sustainable Geographical Indications*, FAO and SINER-GI, Rome.

Van Dusen, M. E. (2000) '*In situ* conservation of crop genetic resources in the Mexican milpa system', Doctoral dissertation, University of California Davis, CA, USA.

Van Dusen, M. E. and Taylor, J. E. (2005) 'Missing markets and crop diversity: Evidence from Mexico', *Environment and Development Economics*, vol. 10, pp. 513–531.

Vernooy, R., Shrestha, P., and Sthapit, B. (eds.) (2015) *Community Seed Banks: Origins, Evolution and Prospects*, Routledge, Abingdon, UK.

Will, M. (2008) *Promoting Value Chains of Neglected and Underutilized Species for Pro-Poor Growth and Biodiversity Conservation: Guidelines and Good Practices*, Global Facilitation Unit for Underutilized Species (GFU), Rome, Italy.

# 31
# COMMUNITY BIODIVERSITY MANAGEMENT

*Walter Simon de Boef and Abishkar Subedi*

## Introduction

*Ex situ* and *in situ* conservation are distinguished as separate conservation strategies by the Convention on Biological Diversity (CBD). *In situ* conservation is defined as

> the conservation of ecosystems and natural habitats and the maintenance and recovery of viable populations of species in their natural surroundings and, in the case of domesticated and cultivated species, in the surroundings where they have developed their distinctive properties.
>
> *(CBD, 1992, p. 4)*

When applied in the field of plant genetic resources (PGR), *in situ* conservation is translated into practices that address conservation in the context of the livelihoods of small-scale, and often poor, farmers (Jarvis et al., 2011). Since the early 1990s, organizations with widely dissimilar backgrounds have been associating their conservation actions with small-scale, poor farmers for whom the maintenance and use of local varieties was, and continues to be, an option to meet their livelihood needs (Keleman et al., 2009). They have thus entered into the field of, and the debate on the linkage between, biodiversity conservation and poverty reduction, more specifically the area of (agro-) biodiversity conservation and livelihood development (Fisher et al., 2008).

It has become clear that the dynamic nature of farmers' management and utilization of local crops and varieties did not match the expectations of conservationists for the design of *in situ* and on-farm conservation strategies (Hardon and de Boef, 1993; De Boef, 2000). While the term 'conservation' can imply the halting of change, or the maintenance of something in its present state, active on-farm management, implemented by farming communities, is needed to achieve conservation of PGR. 'On-farm management', the dynamic process that promotes and sustains conservation, recognizes the importance of the farmers and communities who cultivate agrobiodiversity and incorporates its use into strategies that aim to improve the livelihood of farming communities (Jarvis et al., 2011). The fact that conservation efforts can contribute to development processes allows us to move beyond discussion of how to implement *in situ* conservation and contribute to farming communities managing agrobiodiversity for better livelihoods (De Boef et al., 2013a).

## On-farm management and community biodiversity management

### *Limitations of* in situ *conservation approaches*

Agrobiodiversity is increasingly approached by conservation and development organizations in the context of sustainable livelihood development, rather than as a means to solely achieve conservation. Jarvis et al. (2011) pointed out that most initiatives are small, with modest aims and a limited area for implementation and application. These initiatives have been developed to solve problems associated with the use and maintenance of agrobiodiversity by farmers and their communities; moreover, most take place outside the domain of direct influence of national Plant Genetic Resources for Food and Agriculture (PGRFA) programmes. Only to a limited extent do stakeholders benefit from or have formal linkages with such programmes (Borgen Nilsen et al., 2013). This situation is a reflection of the way in which professional PGRFA programmes approach on-farm management, detached from livelihood development and primarily focusing on conservation (De Boef et al., 2013a, 2013c). They target a multitude of crops, in dissimilar locations and situations. Each individual experience, albeit modest in itself, contributes to a comprehensive body of knowledge and experiences on how to associate conservation, or rather diversity-oriented practices, with farmers' livelihood development.

In this chapter, we introduce a methodology and share experiences of organizations in Brazil, France, Nepal and Mesoamerica that support farmers in what is referred to as community biodiversity management (CBM). Based on these experiences, we first provide some background on the evolution of the methodology, particularly in Nepal, and describe how CBM relates to the realization of on-farm management as conservation strategy. We share a range of actions and process-oriented practices that contribute to farming communities engaging in a collective and purposeful manner in the management of agrobiodiversity. In conclusion, the relation between CBM, *in situ* conservation and the empowerment of farming communities in the agrobiodiversity management is disentangled.

## Strengthening community institutions

CBM is a methodology whereby conservation and development organizations, through a participatory process, help to build community-based organizations and strengthen their capabilities to achieve the conservation and sustainable use of agrobioversity. This contributes to the empowerment of farmers and their organizations, which ultimately results in a situation where the community purposely and collectively manages its biodiversity in a sustainable manner. No longer is conservation in the hands of a few farmer households; rather, it is embedded in a collective, community-wide approach. Organizations using the CBM methodology to reach that goal require knowledge, skills and expertise for building social institutions at community levels. The methodology is thereby built upon several strategies for self-organization and self-governance in a context of common property management and community-based natural resource and biodiversity management (Borrini-Feyerabend et al., 2008; Fisher et al., 2008).

### *Emergence of a methodology in Nepal*

CBM evolved only gradually from practice to a methodology. A key reference point is the work of the NGO Local Initiatives for Biodiversity, Research and Development (LI-BIRD) and its partners in Nepal. Subedi et al. (2013a) provided the details of the step-wise process by which CBM developed in the practice of this research and development NGO in response to a rather negative reaction of partner communities to a scientific agrobiodiversity project which was perceived as extractive. The methodology and its practices evolved in the early 2000s in a few rural communities in Nepal, and LI-BIRD with its national partners has engaged in further out- and up-scaling; with several international partners, and has engaged in further mainstreaming of the methodology in other South Asian countries and beyond (De Boef et al., 2013b).

## *CBM and conservation strategies*

'*In situ* conservation' can be considered an emergent property (De Boef, 2000) of the process whereby communities purposely manage agrobiodiversity. Conservation and development organizations can play only an external role as facilitator or service provider; they strengthen the enabling environment in which farmers manage in a dynamic manner agrobiodiversity, and thereby realize *in situ* conservation. The CBM methodology becomes the means by which such dynamic processes are continued, strengthened or revitalized (Shrestha et al., 2013a).

CBM can be achieved only when from the onset of any intervention communities and their organizations are recognized as key actor (Shrestha et al., 2013a). It is crucial to institutionalize local level decision-making on agrobiodiversity conservation and use, but also create sustainable, community-based, structures. Embedded within a livelihood approach, CBM bridges conservation and development objectives that were for a long time considered conflicting. It ensures that communities have the capacity to manage the biological and genetic resources that they depend upon, both now and in the future.

## Practices contributing to CBM

CBM includes many practices that are used both by community-based organizations (CBOs) concerned with conservation and use, and by external stakeholders that aim to strengthen communities in conservation and livelihood development. Practices can be single actions that are geared towards the following:

- Enhancing awareness on conservation and diversity;
- Increasing an understanding of diversity, associated social structure and institutions;
- Strengthening capabilities within CBOs; and
- Encouraging communities to make informed decisions over their agrobiodiversity.

Such single-action practices include diversity fairs, diversity kits, diversity blocks, diversity poetry and drama. Practices can also aim towards the development of community institutions, such as community seed banks (CSBs) and the community biodiversity registers (CBR), requiring a process of capacity development and the establishment and consolidation of institutional and working modalities. These are not single-action practices; they constitute complex, multi-year learning processes.

Other, similar multiple-action practices address more entrepreneurial aspects of agrobiodiversity management, such as the value addition of products of local crops and varieties (De Boef et al., 2013b). Such practices also include methods for farmer and community participation in crop improvement, such as grassroots breeding, participatory genetic enhancement of local varieties and participatory varietal selection (De Boef et al., 2013b). Finally, there are practices that target seed production and seed marketing of local varieties, thereby contributing to strengthening informal seed systems (De Boef et al., 2010). We briefly describe a number of these practices in the following sections. For description of multiple-action practices such as those related to value addition, participatory crop improvement and seed production, we refer the reader to chapters in Part 6 of this Handbook.

## *The 'diversity fair'*

The diversity fair is a very popular practice. Its origin is in the Andean countries (Tapia and Rosa, 1993), and since the early 1990s, it has spread globally. Organizations employ it to sensitize communities on the value and importance of biodiversity and traditional knowledge (Rijal et al., 2000). Experiences in Ecuador (Tapia and Carrera, 2013) and Brazil (Dias et al., 2013) illustrate that diversity fairs raise awareness, and document and monitor agrobiodiversity, in a process that contributes to strengthening communities in their biodiversity management. In Nepal, LI-BIRD and local partners have approached the diversity fair as a collective process during which farmers collect and display plant parts, seed, fruit samples and traditional food items. They share biodiversity-related information and associated traditional knowledge (ATK) either orally, through illustrations or through displays in their stalls.

The diversity fair addresses a range of objectives (Shrestha et al., 2013b):

- Enhancing the understanding of the richness of diversity;
- Identifying traditional knowledge and custodians;
- Locating valuable plant genetic resources and traditional knowledge;
- Enhancing social interactions among community members;
- Promoting exchange of knowledge among and between farmers, and with researchers and conservation professionals;
- Facilitating farmers to obtain new seed and planting materials, thus increasing the biodiversity in their home garden, farms and in the village; and
- Generating inputs that are vital to the development of a plan vital for the community to engage in biodiversity management.

A food fair may also accompany the diversity fair, facilitating the exchange of recipes, and as such it is likely to acknowledge the role of women in the culture and their responsibilities in the preparation of food. The diversity fair provides a good resource for assessing the quality of farm-saved and informally exchanged seed, defining in what manner informal seed systems can be strengthened. Finally, the diversity fair also offers an easy way for professionals to collect seed of local varieties for genebanks, which may serve for *ex situ* conservation or for further crop improvement (Shrestha et al., 2013b).

The diversity fair can be considered as a stepping stone to CBM since farmers, farmers' groups, students, teachers, researchers and development workers obtain insights into local agrobiodiversity in the community; the community and CBOs start to develop a local agrobiodiversity database when documenting the biodiversity displayed by fair participants; and the community and CBO begin to assume responsibility in managing its agrobiodiversity.

## *Rural poetry and drama*

Rural poetry and drama are innovative practices of creating awareness on the value of biodiversity, and of documenting traditional knowledge and information. When LI-BIRD applied such practices in Nepal, local poets (both male and female), and/or theatre companies were invited to participate. LI-BIRD first shared with the artists the objectives and the different steps involved.

The artists visited different households and discussed many aspects of agrobiodiversity with experienced farmers, both young and elderly, male and female, addressing the following topics:

- Agrobiodiversity use and value;
- Agrobiodiversity extent and distribution;
- Associated traditional knowledge and associated information;
- Food culture; and
- Proverbs, myths and sayings.

Directly after these discussions, the artists converted the local information that has been gathered into poems or drama, emphasizing the value of conservation and the importance of local PGR. Community members were invited to participate and listen to the poems or join in the presentation of the drama. The poets documented, enriched and returned the information provided by the community in the form of melodious poems and songs. The theatre company presented a theme-based play. In these artistic ways, community members felt and internalized the importance of biodiversity in their daily life and they could better imagine the consequences should such a valuable biodiversity be lost. Following the poetry readings or drama presentations, during a short discussion the audience engaged in a reflection to summarize the key messages and lessons (Shrestha et al., 2013b).

## *Diversity block*

The diversity block is a non-replicated experimental plot of farmers' varieties that is established and managed by a farmers' group under their own management conditions. The plot size depends on the type of crop, availability of land, management capacity of the farmers' group, and the amount of seed they want to produce. Dias et al. (2013) described ways in which public gene banks in Brazil engage with farming communities in the (re-) introduction of germplasm through diversity blocks. Kendall and Gras (2013) provided insight how AgroBio Périgord in France installs a diversity block with multiple functions:

- *Introductory blocks* that are used to evaluate varieties that have been newly introduced under common production and management conditions; the varieties are compared with material that is well adapted, are included in demonstration blocks and are further multiplied;
- *Multiplication blocks* that are used to maintain varieties under controlled pollination;
- *Breeding blocks* for the involvement of farmers in participatory breeding;
- *Variety demonstration blocks* that are used to compare selected local varieties; during regular field days, farmers evaluate the varieties, thereby contributing to awareness raising and enhancing farmers' skills; and
- *Crop diversity demonstration blocks*, which aim to raise awareness among visitors on new crops that may be interesting to include in their production system.

LI-BIRD and local partners in Nepal also used the diversity block in its CBM activities. Additional goals are to test consistency in naming farmers' varieties and to identify suitable parents for participatory plant breeding. LI-BIRD establishes diversity blocks deliberately near roads or public places, with signboards for each plot, which encourages community members to stop and see the differences between the varieties, thereby raising awareness and promoting the use of local agrobiodiversity (Shrestha et al., 2013b).

## The diversity kit

A set of small quantities of seed of different crops and varieties that is made available to farmers for informal research and development is referred to as the diversity kit (Sthapit et al., 2008; Canci et al., 2013). The basic idea of the diversity kit is:

- to deploy a diversity of crops and varieties, giving priority to neglected, underutilized, rare and unique varieties and species;
- to increase community access to seed and knowledge; and
- to promote biodiversity conservation through use.

Deploying a diversity kit involves the following steps:

- Identification and selection of varieties favoured by farmers through a diversity fair;
- Identification of crops and varieties on the verge of disappearing;
- Selection of varieties from community seed banks and community biodiversity registers, or inventories of biodiversity;
- Establishment of diversity blocks;
- Production of quality seed of selected varieties;
- Development of information sheets for each variety containing varietal characteristics as well as the methods of cultivation and use; and
- Packaging and distribution of seed to farming households in the community.

In the municipality of Guaraciaba, in the state of Santa Catarina, Brazil, the diversity kit has evolved from the original CBM practice from Nepal (Sthapit et al., 2008) to a practice whose goals reach beyond agrobiodiversity conservation and use (Canci et al., 2013). Small-scale farming communities in Guaraciaba decided to use diversity kits to restore food security and revive the habit of growing their crops for household food security. Community members received a kit containing the seed of several maize, rice, legume and vegetable varieties. The diversity kit became an instrument for restoring farmers' autonomy in food, seed and varietal security; it revitalized the farmers' informal exchange of seed and associated information.

In Nepal, LI-BIRD and local partners have used the diversity kit to promote the broader use of homegarden species, resulting in an increase in dietary diversity and better income of participating families. In a wide range of situations, the diversity kit has proven very useful practice in a larger CBM process since it is easy to implement, requires few resources and takes little time, but can be very effective in building a firm basis in awareness and social organization for CBM.

### *Community seed banks*

When farmers lose their seed or varieties, they depend either on quality seed of improved varieties that has been commercialized through agro-dealers, or on the seed of improved varieties that is distributed by governments. However, those accessible varieties are not necessarily adapted to local agro-ecological conditions or specific demands. Consequently, limitations of farm-saved seed and the informal seed systems led to the establishment of community seed banks (CSBs) for increasing seed and food security. CSBs ensure sufficient seed of the right (local) varieties is available at the right time and for an affordable price, thus enhancing seed security (De Boef et al., 2010). CSBs serve as backup to the informal seed sector, and they motivate farming communities to rely on their own institutions and remain autonomous in their food and seed security.

The success of CSBs reaches beyond strengthening informal seed supply. The Seeds of Passion network is a well-known, extensive and sophisticated network of community seed banks in the state of Paraiba, Brazil. It includes more than 240 community seed banks, involving more than 800 families in 63 municipalities. It has been able to rescue nearly 300 crop varieties. Small-scale famers, with their traditional knowledge and local varieties, have assumed both individual and collective responsibility for maintaining agricultural biodiversity (Dias da Silva, 2013).

Another CSB example is the Collaborative Programme on Participatory Plant Breeding (CP-PPB) in Mesoamerica. Set up in 2000, it works through participatory plant breeding with small-scale farmers to maintain, characterize and improve varieties of maize, beans, sorghum and other crops. In response to several natural catastrophes, the network has supported the establishment of CSBs, which have been set up to enhance local seed and varietal security during the emergency periods that often follow floods, droughts and hurricanes. The CSBs have been established in accessible areas of the communities; a local committee is responsible for custodianship. CSBs can be immediately accessed and utilized in times of emergency, while in normal conditions they are used strategically as seed stock for supporting production. In addition, the efforts of the network in Mesoamerica has enhanced community resilience (Fuentes and Alonzo, 2013).

CSBs are older than the CBM methodology itself, with their application dating back to the early 1990s (Cooper et al., 1992). Today, CSBs are a common component in CBM programmes and are used in every corner of the world. The CSB is instrumental to the CBM components of setting up institutional modalities, consolidating community roles in planning and implementation and community monitoring and evaluation. Shrestha et al. (2013c), in an analysis of experiences, indicated that the establishment of CSBs has led to significant investment by conservation and development organizations in CBM components such as awareness-raising, the creation of social networks and institutions and the capacity-building of community organizations. Most experiences illustrated that CSBs are sustained by the motivation of communities for seed security and sovereignty. Shrestha et al. (2013c) concluded that by linking conservation with access to seed and varieties, CSBs can be considered a driving force for the CBM process and for enhancing community capacity contributing to conservation of agrobiodiversity and promoting resilience.

## *Community biodiversity register (CBR)*

A CBR is basically a farmers' information database which documents and monitors (agro-) biodiversity and associated traditional knowledge (ATK), thereby protecting them from biopiracy (Rijal et al., 2003; Subedi et al., 2005). Through this practice, communities gain a better understanding of their own biological assets and values, and are better able to use those assets for livelihood development while appreciating and sustaining them for future generations.

The experience of LI-BIRD and partners with CBRs can be summarized as a series of interlinked steps. These steps may vary and can be adapted depending upon the context of any given community and type of biodiversity being addressed:

- *Selecting the area and community*: in choosing an area, criteria are used that address availability and richness of biodiversity and/or PGR. The community and engaged stakeholders must recognize that diversity is an important asset of their livelihood, and must be interested in addressing agrobiodiversity conservation and use. A participatory diagnostic survey verifies key characteristics and sets a basis for the establishment of the CBR.

- *Informing the community on CBR rationale and objectives*: during a series of village workshops, a common understanding is reached of the rationale behind the CBR's establishment and way that it will operate, and the design of an action plan.
- *Strengthening institutional capacity*: several participatory appraisal tools provide inputs to the CBR's institutional set up. Local institutions are identified that the community considers interested, skilful and legitimate for coordinating or facilitating their CBR. The appraisal defines who will be a member of the committee that will provide strategic support, facilitate collective decision-making, engage in capacity-building and ensure overall monitoring.
- *Defining a specific focus and initial requirements for data collection*: actual implementation of the CBR starts with the development of the register's format, for which a minimum set of data is required on species, variety or other biological resources; utilization; status; need for conservation; curators or holders of ATK and means of transfer from one generation to another; decision makers (men and women, young and elderly) concerning the management of the resource; and degree and way which the resources are shared within and outside the community or beyond. With this knowledge basis, the community starts to collect an initial set of data on the resources identified.
- *Documenting, compiling and validating CBR information*: the institution and/or CBR committee strengthen the capacity of each specific group, to ensure that they are capable of assuming the responsibility to document their PGR and ATK. They explore how the CBR can be associated to other practices that are part of the community's CBM plan. These include the use of a diversity fair, during which the information recorded in the CBR can be verified, and additional, relevant information can be collected, which may lead to follow-up CBM practices, such as diversity blocks and diversity kits. This step is crucial but also resource-demanding for the supporting organization and the community itself.
- *Analyzing and sharing information*: a regular series of village level stakeholder workshops to discuss and analyze the status and trends of biological resources that can be detected from the CBR. Through the use of four-cell analysis (Subedi et al., 2005), the community learns about how many households cultivate certain crops or varieties in large or small areas. The outcome of this discussion is crucial in identifying follow-up CBM practices. Various communication tools, such as posters, pamphlets or radio programmes, as well as other CBM practices, can be used to share the outcomes of this analysis with an audience beyond those households directly engaged in the CBR.
- *Designing and implementing conservation and development plans*: committee members facilitate a participatory process to identify priorities for conservation and livelihood improvement. It is crucial that the priorities are based on evidence in the CBR and are endorsed through a participatory and transparent process of decision-making. The committee needs to take on a role beyond that of managing the CBR. Their role gradually evolves into one of leadership, where they take a responsibility for facilitating the CBM process and practices; for guiding the community towards collective action; and for ensuring partnerships and collaboration with stakeholders, including local government. Once the institutional responsibilities and social organization have been defined, the successive component is the establishment of the CBM fund.

In Begnas, Nepal, one of LI-BIRD's CBM sites, CBR proved an effective tool for locating unique and rich PGR at both household and community level. The community was able to identify a single household that maintains more than 20 rice landraces, in a community where over 40 rice landraces could be found. When the CBR committee members shared this information in their village, it had an immediate impact. Custodian farmers and farmers' groups that had been conserving unique or abundant diversity were publicly recognized and were awarded with grants from the CBM fund. Farmers realized that material in few hands was highly vulnerable to genetic erosion. Upon recognizing this situation, the leadership in the community encouraged 22 farmers' groups to form a CBO, which in turn established a community seed bank. The CBOs were able to access funds from both local government and other developmental organizations for the construction of their CSBs, using information from the CBR as evidence (Singh et al., 2006). In addition, the community identified unique traits in several species from the CBR, sharing this information with relevant stakeholders. The information was used in participatory crop improvement, value-addition and market linkage programmes as a means to create incentives for farmers to continue cultivating these species and varieties (Subedi et al., 2013b).

## CBM and empowerment

It is assumed that organized communities of small-scale farmers become better able to respond to those common uncertainties that kept them poor. Through collective organization and the implementation of CBM practices, farming communities become better able to maintain their diversity of local varieties. Organizations such as Seeds of Passion in Brazil and the CP-PPB in Mesoamerica refer in their strategies to the empowerment of farming communities. In order to obtain a common understanding on the relationship between CBM, *in situ* conservation and empowerment, four assumptions can be formulated that are also illustrated in **Figure 31.1** *CBM as methodology and result*:

1. The CBM methodology contributes to *in situ* conservation of agrobiodiversity;
2. The CBM methodology contributes to the empowerment of farming communities and their local institutions;
3. Empowerment leads to a situation where communities manage agrobiodiversity in a collective and purposeful manner; and
4. Farming communities collectively and purposefully manage agrobiodiversity in a way that is sustainable contributes to the implementation of *in situ* conservation.

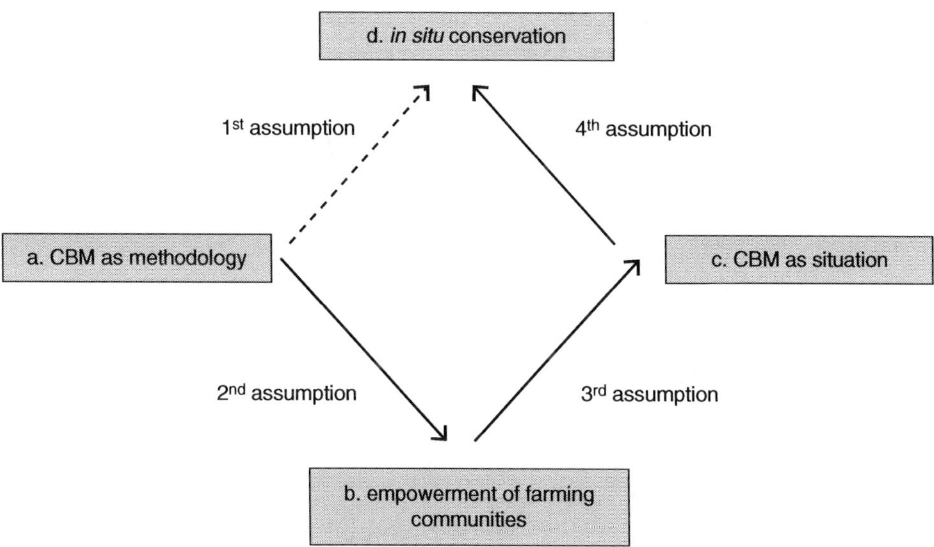


*Figure 31.1* CBM as methodology and result

*Source*: De Boef et al. (2013c). Used with permission.

Chambers (1993) defined empowerment as a process of transformation that involves enhancing the awareness of poorer people of imbalances in power relations; only then can these people make effective choices to transform those imbalances and put these choices into practice. Empowerment is reached when those people conclude such a transformation, are capable of reflecting upon the effectiveness of the choices and thereby further engage themselves in the process of empowerment. The concepts of 'agency' and 'structure' help to understand that in CBM it is crucial to find the right balance between strengthening community-based capabilities and organizations, and addressing relevant policy and legal frameworks, as well as traditional and informal institutions, norms and values.

The term 'agency' is based on Paulo Freire's (1976) 'agents of change', in which people take greater control over their lives through conscious action. In a context of changing imbalances in power, agency is about what Bartlett (2008) called lasting changes in perceptions and relationships. Long (2001, pp. 112–113) emphasized that collective rather than individual agency results in empowerment. He stated,

> Agency is only manifested, and can only become effective, when individuals interact . . . agency entails a complex set of social relationships . . . that include individuals, organizations, relevant technologies, financial and material resources. . . . How they are cemented together is what counts in the end.

Agency reaches consolidation when perceptions and relationships are transformed. Then empowerment is achieved, that is, self-determination emerges as the outcomes of the transformation processes are determined by the collective and purposeful actions of farmers or farming communities, for example in their management of agrobiodiversity, rather than by development professionals. An example could be where a farming community with a CSB is faced with changes in rainfall patterns, and seeks support from the genebank to either restore or introduce adapted materials in their collection. Consequently, the community develops the capacity to approach a formal institution, and through this relationship and its conscious action, it increases its ability to cope with changing conditions, which we can understand as an expression of agency.

In Barra, Nepal, LI-BIRD, together with the local CBM committee, explored ways to sustain the CSB. A solution was found to link it with a community-based trust fund. Farming households who access the fund multiply the less popular varieties maintained in the CSB. This allows the continuous regeneration of even the most unpopular materials of the CSB, while the micro-credit contributes to social inclusion through value addition. This mechanism contributes to the empowerment of a community in organizing itself (agency), and assists it in providing access to financial services to poorer farming households. It illustrates the importance of agency for contributing to empowerment in a CBM process (Subedi et al., 2013a).

'Structure' is defined in the context of empowerment as the formal and informal context within which actors operate, covering rules, social forces or institutions such as social class, religion, gender, ethnicity, and customs (Alsop and Heinsohn, 2005). It defines the rules of the game that limit or influence the opportunities that determine actions of individuals and groups of individuals.

In the context of informal seed supply, several formal and informal rules emerge concerning practical PGR management. In many countries, plant variety protection and seed laws limit farmers' room for manoeuvre in informal seed supply, which is a vital component of their management of local crops and varieties. AgroBio Périgord in France has been able to develop a mechanism for facilitating the exchange of seed of local varieties among farmers (agency). Farmers are supported in coping with the limitations that variety and seed laws impose on small-scale farmers (Kastler et al., 2013). In Brazil, farmers associated with the Seeds of Passion Network have become engaged in commercial seed production of local varieties. They do meet regulatory barriers in their promotion and commercial seed production of local varieties, which are addressed together with NGOs and agricultural researchers. Where structure poses limitations on the farmers' groups for achieving their aims (such as the commercial seed production of local varieties), through innovative arrangements or transformations as expressions of agency, they may be able find their own solutions, which in the end may in turn contribute to transformation at a more structural level.

Many CBM processes primarily focus on strengthening the capabilities of local organizations or CBOs. However, many conservation and development organizations, such as LI-BIRD, but also the networks described from Brazil, France and Mesoamerica, link grassroots action with advocacy, contributing to policy processes. In this way, these NGOs show that they consciously balance agency and structure in their operations to contribute to empowerment.

'Empowerment means that people, especially poorer people, are enabled to take more control over their lives' (Chambers, 1993, p. 12). As professionals, we need to understand that, together with farming communities, we engage ourselves in processes of such transformation, in our case with the aim that farming communities take more control in agrobiodiversity management. The voice of the professional in relation to empowerment is emphasized by Bartlett (2008). If we take the matter of agency seriously, then the distinction between professionals and those they are trying to empower no longer holds; we as professionals become subject to the development or empowerment processes ourselves. We cannot promote transformations in relationships of rural people, between rich and poor, between CBOs and NGOs, gene banks or governments, and between farming communities and professionals, without also being open to changes in our own relationships with the people we are motivating to take control over their own development and actions in the conservation and use of agrobiodiversity. As professionals, we cannot escape from this transformation if we, and our organizations, claim to contribute to the empowerment of communities in their agrobiodiversity management.

## References


Alsop, R. and Heinsohn, N. (2005) *Measuring Empowerment in Practice: Structuring Analysis and Framing Indicators*', Policy Research Working Paper 3510, World Bank, Washington, DC, USA.

Bartlett, A. (2008) 'No more adoption rates! Looking for empowerment in agricultural development programmes', *Development in Practice*, vol. 18, pp. 524–538.

Borgen Nilsen, L., Subedi, A., Ehsan, M. D., Ghosh, K., Chavez-Tafur, J., Blundo Canto, G. M. and de Boef, W. S. (2013) 'The relationship between national plant genetic resources programmes and practitioners promoting on-farm management: Results from a global survey', *Plant Genetic Resources: Characterization and Utilization*, vol. 13, pp. 36–44.

Borrini-Feyerabend, G., Pimbert, M., Taghi Farvar, M., Kothari, A. and Renard, Y. (2008) *Sharing Power: A Global Guide to Collaborative Management of Natural Resources*, Earthscan for Routledge, Abingdon, UK.

Canci, A., Guadagnin, C. A., Henke, J. P. and Lazzari, L. (2013) 'The diversity kit: Restoring farmers' sovereignty over food, seed and genetic resourcesin Guaraciaba, Brazil', pp. 32–36 in W. S. de Boef, N. Peroni, A. Subedi, M. Thijssen and E. O'Keeffe (eds.), *Community Biodiversity Management: Promoting Resilience and the Conservation of Plant Genetic Resources*, Earthscan for Routledge, Abingdon, UK.

CBD (1992) *Convention on Biological Diversity*, Secretariat of the Convention on Biological Diversity, Montreal, Canada, www.cbd.int/doc/legal/cbd-en.pdf, accessed 16 February 2012.

Chambers, R. (1993) *Challenging the Professions: Frontiers for Rural Development*, Intermediate Technology Publications, London, UK.

Cooper, D., Vellvé, R. and Hobbelink, H. (1992) *Growing Diversity: Genetic Resources and Local Food Security*, Intermediate Technology, London, UK.

De Boef, W. S. (2000) *Tales of the Unpredictable: Learning about Institutional Frameworks That Support Farmer Management of Agro-Biodiversity*, PhD thesis, Wageningen University, The Netherlands.

De Boef, W. S., Dempewolf, H., Byakweli, J. M. and Engels, J. M. M. (2010) 'Integrating genetic resource conservation and sustainable development into strategies to increase the robustness of seed systems', *Journal of Sustainable Agriculture*, vol. 34, pp. 504–531.

De Boef, W. S., Peroni, N., Subedi, A., Thijssen, M. and O'Keeffe, E. (eds.) (2013b) *Community Biodiversity Management: Promoting Resilience and the Conservation of Plant Genetic Resources*, Earthscan for Routledge, Abingdon, UK.

De Boef, W. S., Thijssen, M. H., Shrestha, P., Subedi, A., Feyissa, R., Gezu, G., Canci, C., De Fonseca Ferreira, M. A. J., Dias, T., Swain, S. and Sthapit, B. R. (2013a) 'Moving beyond the dilemma: Practices that contribute to the on-farm management of agrobiodiversity', *Journal of Sustainable Agriculture*, vol. 36, pp. 788–809.

De Boef, W. S., Verhoosel, K. and Thijssen, M. (2013c) 'Community biodiversity management and empowerment', pp. 365–377 in W. S. de Boef, N. Peroni, A. Subedi, M. Thijssen and E. O'Keeffe (eds.), *Community Biodiversity Management: Promoting Resilience and the Conservation of Plant Genetic Resources*, Earthscan for Routledge, Abingdon, UK.

Dias, T., da Fonseca Ferreira, M. A. J., Barbieri, R. L., Teixeira, F. F. and de Azevedo, S. G. (2013) 'Gene banks that promote on-farm management through the reintroduction of local varieties in Brazil', pp. 91–95 in W. S. de Boef, N. Peroni, A. Subedi, M. Thijssen and E. O'Keeffe (eds.), *Community Biodiversity Management: Promoting Resilience and the Conservation of Plant Genetic Resources*, Earthscan for Routledge, Abingdon, UK.

Dias da Silva, E. (2013) 'Community seed banks in the semi-arid region of Paraiba, Brazil', pp. 102–108 in W. S. de Boef, N. Peroni, A. Subedi, M. Thijssen and E. O'Keeffe (eds.), *Community Biodiversity Management: Promoting Resilience and the Conservation of Plant Genetic Resources*, Earthscan for Routledge, Abingdon, UK.

Fisher, R. J., Maginnis, S., Jackson, W., Barrow, E., and Jeanrenaud, S. (eds.) (2008) *Linking Conservation and Poverty Reduction: Landscapes, People and Power*, Earthscan for Routledge, Abingdon, UK.

Freire, P. (1976) *Education: The Practice of Freedom*, Writers and Readers Publishing Cooperative, London, UK.

Fuentes, M. R. and Alonzo, R. S. (2013) 'Community seed reserves: Enhancing sovereignty and resilience in Central America', pp. 96–101 in W. S. de Boef, N. Peroni, A. Subedi, M. Thijssen and E. O'Keeffe (eds.), *Community Biodiversity Management: Promoting Resilience and the Conservation of Plant Genetic Resources*, Earthscan for Routledge, Abingdon, UK.

Hardon, J. J. and de Boef, W. S. (1993) 'Linking farmers and plant breeders in local crop development', pp. 64–171 in W. S. de Boef, K. Amanor, K. Wellard and A. Bebbington (eds.), *Cultivating Knowledge: Genetic Diversity, Farmers Experimentation and Crop Research*, Intermediate Technology, London, UK.

Jarvis, D. I., Hodgkin, T., Sthapit, B. R., Fadda, C. and Lopez-Noriega, I. (2011) 'An heuristic framework for identifying multiple ways of supporting the conservation and use of traditional crop varieties within the agricultural production system', *Critical Reviews in Plant Science*, vol. 30, pp. 125–176.

Kastler, G., Onorati, A. and Brac, B. (2013) 'Seeds and peasant autonomy', pp. 47–53 in *Right to Food and Nutrition Watch. Alternatives and Resistance to Policies that Generate Hunger*, Global Network for the Right to Food and Nutrition.

Keleman, A., Raño, H. G. and Helling, J. (2009) 'Maize diversity, poverty, and market access: Lessons from Mexico', *Development in Practice*, vol. 19, pp. 187–199.

Kendall, J. and Gras, E. (2013) 'The maison de la semence paysanne and diversity platform: Promoting agrobiodiversity in France', pp. 43–50 in W. S. de Boef, N. Peroni, A. Subedi, M. Thijssen and E. O'Keeffe (eds.), *Community Biodiversity Management: Promoting Resilience and the Conservation of Plant Genetic Resources*, Earthscan for Routledge, Abingdon, UK.

Long, N. (2001) *Development Sociology: Actor Perspectives*, Routledge, Abingdon, UK.

Rijal, D. K., Rana, R. B., Subedi, A. and Sthapit, B. R. (2000) 'Adding value to landraces: Community-based approaches for in-situ conservation of plant genetic resources in Nepal', pp. 166–172 in E. Friis-Hansen and B. R. Sthapit (eds.), *Participatory Approaches to the Conservation and Use of Plant Genetic Resources*, International Plant Genetic Resources Institute (IPGRI), Rome, Italy.

Rijal, D. K., Subedi, A., Upadhyay, M. P., Rana, R. B., Chaudhary, P., Tiwari, R. K., Sthapit, B. R. and Gauchan, D. (2003) 'Community biodiversity register: Developing community based database for genetic resources and local knowledge of Nepal', pp. 28–40 in B. R. Sthapit, M. P. Upadhyay, B. K. Baniya, A. Subedi and B. K. Joshi (eds.), *On Farm Management of Agricultural Biodiversity in Nepal, Proceedings of a National Workshop, 24–26 April 2001, Lumle, Nepal*, IPGRI, LI-BIRD and NARC, Kathmandu, Nepal.

Shrestha, P., Gezu, G., Swain, S., Lassaigne, B., Subedi, A. and de Boef, W. S. (2013c) 'The community seed bank: A common driver for community biodiversity management', pp. 109–117 in W. S. de Boef,

N. Peroni, A. Subedi, M. Thijssen and E. O'Keeffe (eds.), *Community Biodiversity Management: Promoting Resilience and the Conservation of Plant Genetic Resources*, Earthscan for Routledge, Abingdon, UK.

Shrestha, P., Shrestha, P., Subedi, A., Peroni, N. and de Boef, W. S. (2013b) 'Community biodiversity management: Defined and contextualized', pp. 19–25 in W. S. de Boef, N. Peroni, A. Subedi, M. Thijssen and E. O'Keeffe (eds.), *Community Biodiversity Management: Promoting Resilience and the Conservation of Plant Genetic Resources*, Earthscan for Routledge, Abingdon, UK.

Shrestha, P., Subedi, A. and Sthapit, B. (2013a) 'Enhancing awareness on the value of local biodiversity in Nepal', pp. 72–75 in W. S. de Boef, N. Peroni, A. Subedi, M. Thijssen and E. O'Keeffe (eds.), *Community Biodiversity Management: Promoting Resilience and the Conservation of Plant Genetic Resources*, Earthscan for Rouledge, Abingdon, UK.

Singh, D., Subedi, A. and Shrestha, P. (2006) 'Enhancing local seed security and on-farm conservation through a community seed bank in Bara district of Nepal', pp. 99–128 in R. Vernooy (ed.), *Social and Gender Analysis In Natural Resource Management: Learning Studies and Lessons from Asia*, Sage, New Delhi, India.

Sthapit, B. R., Shrestha, P. K. and Upadhyay, M. P. (eds.) (2008) *Good Practices: On-Farm Management of Agricultural Biodiversity in Nepal*, NARC, LI-BIRD, IPGRI and IDRC, Kathmandu, Nepal.

Subedi, A., Devkota, R., Poudel, I. and Subedi, S. (2013b) 'Community biodiversity registers in Nepal: Enhancing the capabilities of communities to document, monitor and take control over their genetic resources', pp. 83–90 in W. S. de Boef, N. Peroni, A. Subedi, M. Thijssen and E. O'Keeffe (eds.), *Community Biodiversity Management: Promoting Resilience and the Conservation of Plant Genetic Resources*, Earthscan for Routledge, Abingdon, UK.

Subedi, A., Poudel, I., Regmi, B., Baral, K., Suwal, R., Rijal, D., Sthapit, B. R. and Shrestha, P. K. (2005) 'Strengthening the community biodiversity registers for agriculture, forest and wetland biodiversity management: Users and livelihood perspectives', pp. 41–54 in A. Subedi, B. R. Sthapit, M. P. Upadhay and D. Gauchan (eds.), *Learning from Community Biodiversity Register in Nepal, Proceedings of National Workshop, 27–28 October 2005, Kathmandu, Nepal*, LI-BIRD, Kathmandu, Nepal.

Subedi, A., Shrestha, P., Upadhyay, M. and Sthapit, B. (2013a) 'The evolution of community biodiversity management as a methodology for implementing *in situ* conservation of agrobiodiversity in Nepal', pp. 11–18 in W. S. de Boef, N. Peroni, A. Subedi, M. Thijssen and E. O'Keeffe (eds.), *Community Biodiversity Management: Promoting Resilience and the Conservation of Plant Genetic Resources*, Earthscan for Routledge, Abingdon, UK.

Tapia, C. and Carrera, H. (2013) 'Practices that contribute to promoting and appreciating Andean crops and identity in Cotacachi, Ecuador', pp. 77–82 in W. S. de Boef, N. Peroni, A. Subedi, M. Thijssen and E. O'Keeffe (eds.), *Community Biodiversity Management: Promoting Resilience and the Conservation of Plant Genetic Resources*, Earthscan for Routledge, Abingdon, UK.

Tapia, M. E. and Rosa, A. (1993) 'Seed fairs in the Andes: A strategy for local conservation of plant genetic resources', pp. 111–118 in de W. S. Boef, K. Amanor, K. Wellard and A. Bebbington (eds.), *Cultivating Knowledge: Genetic Diversity, Farmer Experimentation and Crop Research*, Intermediate Technology, London, UK.

# 32

# THE ROLE AND IMPORTANCE OF AGRICULTURAL BIODIVERSITY IN URBAN AGRICULTURE

*Gudrun B. Keding, Céline Termote and Katja Kehlenbeck*

## Introduction

While in 1950, 30% of the world's population lived in urban areas, in 2014, more than half (>54%) of the world's population is urban, and the urban population is projected to reach 66% by 2050. However, this projected growth is not evenly distributed: rather, 90% of the increase will take place in Africa and Asia (UN/DESA, 2014). Worldwide, about 25–30% of the urban population is involved in the agro-food sector (Orsini et al., 2013) while in developing countries, the number of urban dwellers who engage in some form of agriculture can be much higher such as 45% in Lusaka, Zambia, 68% in the five biggest cities of Tanzania and even 80% in Brazzaville, Congo (Shackleton et al., 2009). The figure is 42% in Guatemalan cities and 68% in Nicaragua, while in Asian countries, it varies from 11% in Indonesia to 70% in Vietnam (Zezza and Tasciotti, 2010). Urban agriculture, being defined as the production of agricultural products (crops or livestock) in a homestead or plot in an urban or peri-urban area, is in most cases an informal activity and therefore rather challenging to describe with accurate figures and trends (Orsini et al., 2013). In fact, most research studies on private gardens have so far taken place in developed countries and only recently have studies on the biodiversity of urban gardens in tropical developing cities begun to arise (Goddard et al., 2009). Following a review of urban agriculture in developed countries (Mok et al., 2014), the study of Hamilton et al. (2014) attempted to estimate the number of households engaged in urban crop production in developing countries in 2010, both as a total and also per region. In total, 266 million households were assessed, including 29 million in Africa, 182 million in Asia, 39 million in Latin America and 15 million in Eastern Europe (Hamilton et al., 2014).

In both the developed and developing world, plant production, especially of horticultural crops such as fruits, vegetables and herbs, is more common in urban areas than rearing livestock (Orsini et al., 2013), although livestock can also be important at a local scale (**Box 32.1** *Importance of livestock in urban agriculture*). The presence of plants in urban environments has several advantages (Smith et al., 2006; Goddard et al., 2009; Orsini et al., 2013), such as:

- the provision of food, which can contribute to food and nutritional security as well as the provision of plants with uses in traditional medicinal practices;
- contribution to the development of local economies engaged in production, processing and trading of the agricultural products;

## Box 32.1 Importance of livestock in urban agriculture

The keeping of livestock in cities is not new and also not restricted to the tropics but occurs worldwide – and like urban gardening – with opportunities and challenges. Next to the production of food, animals often have an important role in terms of social aspects, provide transport services, recycle organic waste and produce manure for improving soil fertility of urban gardens, but at the same time, livestock can cause pollution and transmit diseases. Still, it highly depends on stakeholders' experience whether urban livestock is seen as positive or negative and more research is needed on the role of urban livestock for example for nutrition and livelihoods of women or poorer sections of a community (Schierer et al., 2000). In addition to livestock, wild animals can also contribute to urban biodiversity, but these are typically insects and birds rather than wild mammals. For example, the diversity of animals was found to be maintained in urban gardens through various management practices that promote plant diversity as well as through increased landscape structure and landscape diversity. These animals were either pollinators (bees or bumblebees), or seed dispersers or insectivores (birds) (Taylor and Lovell, 2014) and thus contributed only indirectly to food diversity and security. The importance of social aspects is demonstrated by the use of domestic animals such as horses, donkeys and ducks on urban farms for children in cities such as Berlin, Germany. These are meant less for food production but to combine with the gardens as a means of education and recreation within densely populated built-up areas (Rosol, 2010).

- ecological and environmental impacts such as the modification of microclimates and production of oxygen as well as absorption of pollutants;
- social and cultural aspects such as the social inclusion of disadvantaged people or social groups and education especially of children; and
- the provision of breeding sites, migration corridors and shelter for beneficial and/or threatened wild fauna such as birds and insects.

*(Goddard et al., 2009)*

Biodiversity in general is crucial in urban food systems in the fight against hunger and diet-related diseases as well as in generating resilient food systems. At the same time, the rapid growth of urban areas, globalisation of food production and consumption and the growing industrialisation of agricultural systems threatens the biodiversity of food systems (Secretariat of the Convention on Biological Diversity, 2012).

Urban agriculture itself also poses some risks to humans, for example pollution through excessive use of fertilisers and pesticides in crop production and animal wastes in livestock production, contamination of produced food due to use of sewage and waste-water for irrigation of crops, exposure to zoonoses such as avian influenza (in the case of livestock production) and the provision of breeding sites for mosquitoes and other pests in water holes and irrigated agricultural plots (Ahmed et al., 2015).

While environmental and ecological aspects, both positive and negative, are in general of high importance in urban agriculture and are well documented as such (see **Box 32.2** *Case study: trees in urban agriculture*), maintenance of biodiversity specifically for food and agriculture is only one aspect of this and is generally under-researched (Orsini et al., 2013). In particular, research on community gardens in cities is mostly focussed on assessing their social impacts while fewer studies concentrate on natural sciences, for example the potential of community gardens in agrobiodiversity conservation and associated gardening practices (Guitart et al., 2012; see **Box 32.3** *Case study: the rising popularity of traditional leafy vegetables in major towns of Kenya*). This chapter will therefore examine the current literature and selected case studies to understand what role agrobiodiversity (ABD) can play in urban agriculture. We will highlight the opportunities and constraints that urban farmers face and that characterise urban production systems and consequently frame the scope for ABD in these systems – and the other way around, how ABD can contribute to overcome some of the challenges or obstacles of urban farming.

## Box 32.2 Case study: trees in urban agriculture

Trees add several benefits to urban agriculture and provide both production and service functions. Integration of trees into urban gardens helps using resources such as space, sunlight, water and soil nutrients more efficiently. For example, tree roots can reach deeper soil layers than annual crops, take up water and nutrients from these soil layers and release nutrients via fallen leaves back to the top soil, thus making nutrients available for shallow-rooted annual crops. Trees can provide high-value products of high market demand such as fruits, leaves for vegetable or plant parts used as medicine. In a study of 51 urban and peri-urban gardens in Niamey, Niger, as many as 54 woody species (including 29 fruit tree and shrub species) were documented, and vegetable trees such as *Moringa oleifera* and *Adansonia digitata* (baobab) were found in 55% and 45% of the surveyed gardens, respectively (Bernholt et al., 2009). In urban vegetable gardens of Bamako, Mali, high-value fruit trees such as mango, pawpaw, banana, lime and guava were cultivated together with indigenous fruit species including *Tamarindus indica* and *Ziziphus mauritiana* (K. Kehlenbeck, personal observation). Other commonly grown woody species in urban gardens of Niamey and Bamako included medicinal (e.g. neem; *Azadirachta indica*) and fodder (e.g. *Gliricidia sepium*) trees. Side products of urban trees include fuel wood and timber, often of short supply in many cities of sub-Saharan Africa. Trees in urban gardens of Niamey and Bamako also provide service functions for example diverse *Cassia*, *Albizia* and *Acacia* species grown for improving soil fertility. Additional service functions of trees in urban agriculture include providing shade, reducing soil erosion, improving microclimate, providing habitat for beneficial insects and birds and indicating plot borders. However, trees are less commonly planted if land tenure of the urban gardens is not secured (Bernholt et al., 2009), as they are rather a long-term investment that provides first economic profit only some months or even years after planting.

## Box 32.3 Case study: the rising popularity of traditional leafy vegetables in major towns of Kenya

In Kenya, traditional leafy vegetables were long considered food for the poor, and were often replaced by introduced vegetables such as kales and collard greens. However, since the 1990s, more attention in research and development was given to these foods, and since 1997, the production, marketing and consumption of traditional leafy vegetables in Kenya has again increased. The vegetables became particularly popular in towns conquering even large urban supermarkets and demand soon outstripped supply. Interestingly, it was found that 'women still dominated most of the ALVs activities, and those households that marketed ALVs were relatively better off than those that did not' (Gotor and Irungu, 2012, p. 41). Yet with increasing popularity, there is also a risk of less popular varieties being lost and diversity again decreasing. Even intra-specific variety is, however, important as for example different populations/ethnic groups favour different varieties of the same vegetable (Cernansky, 2015).

This chapter will briefly define what urban agriculture is, and provide an overview of the extent of urban farming worldwide using examples from different continents. New trends in urban agriculture, including possible roles for ABD, will also be discussed. We will describe the opportunities and constraints that farmers face in urban production systems, including limited space, close proximity to markets, environmental sustainability (and waste handling), high land value and uncertain land tenure. The social and cultural importance of urban gardens will also be emphasised. Various farming practices will be presented, including micro-gardening, community gardening and the farming of common land for both crops and livestock. These practices define the nature of urban production sites and the associated constraints such as little and expensive space automatically limit the choice of the diversity of urban crops, fish and livestock (DeNeergaard et al., 2009). Home gardens – both rural and urban – are in general known for being places where high levels of inter- and intra-specific plant genetic diversity is preserved (Galluzzi et al., 2010). To address food insecurity both in developing but also in developed countries, different types of urban agriculture are suggested to contribute to food security while simultaneously enhancing environmental quality (Bhatt and Farah, 2010). The importance of ABD in this context can sometimes be overlooked, and so will be discussed in particular detail.

## Opportunities for urban farmers – and ABD in urban agriculture

### *Close proximity to markets*

One advantage of producing agricultural goods, particularly of fresh, highly perishable vegetables, herbs and fruits, directly in town or in peri-urban areas close to buyers and consumers, is the proximity to markets for the produce (AVRDC 2013; Orsini et al., 2013). A strong market orientation of crop production can lead to specialisation in a few common crops, thus resulting in poor agrobiodiversity, yet a high species diversity is also possible, for example by growing different species and varieties of vegetables (Orsini et al., 2013) or mixed vegetable, herb and fruit gardens (Bernholt et al., 2009). Even specific varieties to serve certain market niches and cultural preferences of parts of the urban communities can be cultivated by growers if the demand of consumers is well known.

In Vietnam, for example, the diversity available in city markets is dictated by predominant cultural tastes, while rural people eat a greater variety of foods (Trinh et al., 2003). Thus, the diversity in urban farmers' fields is also influenced by the predominant cultural demand as urban produce will be sold most likely within the urban area itself. If good market channels are available for certain foods, this can lead to mono-cropping close to these markets and decreasing diversity in urban farmers' fields. However, improved market opportunities and structures for more diverse foods can also have a positive effect on increasing ABD in urban agriculture. A precondition is that demand for a variety of species and maybe even different cultivars is available. Consumers need to be aware and informed if this knowledge does not traditionally exist. In addition, to increase the market potential of agricultural products and thus support the conservation of

*Figure 32.1* Commercial production of vegetables and herbs in urban gardens of Niamey, Niger (left) and Bamako, Mali (right)

*Sources*: H. Bernholt (left), K. Kehlenbeck (right).

certain species on farm, capacity building of producers might be necessary, for example for cultivation practices under the local conditions and on matching marketing strategies, as well as on improving or reorganising market relationships (Giuliani, 2007; see also Jager, Giuliani and van Loosen, Chapter 30 of this Handbook).

Commercial production may also, however, lead to the dominance of exotic species and the loss of indigenous, traditional ones. Exotic species such as lettuce in Niamey (**Figure 32.1**, *Commercial production of vegetables and herbs in urban gardens*, left) or white cabbage and swiss chard in Nairobi (K. Kehlenbeck, personal observation) have a ready market, seeds of improved varieties are easily available and NGOs and extension service officers often promote them. In a study of urban and peri-urban gardens of Niamey, Niger, it was found that the highest species richness, particularly of indigenous species, was found in gardens managed by households who were not completely dependent on the generation of cash income through their gardens (Bernholt et al., 2009).

## Environmental sustainability

Even when some food is produced in urban areas, additional food is required, and this must be imported into cities leading to a nutrient surplus. Disposing of the resulting waste often poses a challenge for waste handling facilities, yet at the same time waste can also be an opportunity for urban farmers (Deneergaard et al., 2009). In fact, in urban farming, organic wastes can be used as compost while even inorganic wastes can be useful, for example plastic containers or tanks as planting pots or for soilless cultivation (Orsini et al., 2009; **Figure 32.2** *Use of waste as planting containers for seedlings and vegetables*). When organic waste is applied this can contribute to a sustainable environment (FAO, 201), but only if practiced well since poor agricultural practices in urban areas can have detrimental effects for both environment and humans. Next to waste recycling, food production in towns also reduces emission that would otherwise arise through transport, storage and partly packaging (de Zeeuw, 2010).

For a smallholder system to be sustainable, diversification in general and especially with greater use of highly valuable but presently less considered or underutilised species can be a crucial element. Next to environmental services and resilience in farming systems through higher ABD, the latter can directly contribute to health and nutrition of the farming family as well as providing a

*Figure 32.2* Use of waste such as egg shells and broken gum boots as planting containers for seedlings and vegetables in an urban garden in Kampala, Uganda

*Source*: K. Kehlenbeck

source of income and risk management tools for smallholders (Kahane et al., 2013). Risk management strategies would be similar to those used in rural areas such as growing species with different susceptibilities to pests, diseases or water stress, as well as mixing early and late maturing cultivars of a given species to extend the harvesting season.

A special challenge for cities is the absence of pollinators such as bees in many urban areas, which can prevent pollination and consequently fruit setting of many crops and trees. As with rural agriculture, it can be expected that higher ABD (including the cultivation of 'bee plants') will contribute to the resettlement of pollinators (Gliessman, 2007; see also Gemmill-Herren, Chapter 7 of this Handbook, and **Box 32.4** *Case study: minority crops in urban gardens increase flower*

## Box 32.4 Case study: minority crops in urban gardens increase flower visitors in hyper-arid South Sinai, Egypt

The urban gardens supported an abundant and diverse community of spontaneously occurring wild flora, with abundances matching those found in surrounding unmanaged plots. Interestingly, it was the minor, but culturally significant, vegetables and herbs such as fennel, oregano, mint and rosemary that played an important role in attracting common and regionally endemic pollinators as they provided a succession of floral resources over a longer period while abundance of wild flowering plants became scarcer during the months of June/July. Meanwhile, wild as well as cultivated plants benefited from the increased presence of pollinators. It is thus striking to think that a change in cultural eating habits could have serious consequences on the pollination networks in this region. Cultivated flora supplemented wild floral resources elongating the flowering season for pollinators. The study, furthermore, emphasised the positive link between cultural practices and biodiversity conservation. The inclusion of plants and flowers of cultural importance alongside food crops seems to have both social and ecological benefits that likely apply in other home garden systems (Norfolk et al., 2014).

*visitors in hyper-arid South Sinai, Egypt*). Another environmental issue is the occurrence of invasive species and the flora of urban gardens (whether food plants or ornamentals) is considered the most likely source of potentially invasive alien plants (Smith et al., 2006).

While one would expect a decline of ABD from rural via semi-rural to peri-urban home gardens, this seems to be not the case in general. Differences between the three conditions occur, yet biodiversity partly even increases in cities regarding herbaceous, mainly ornamental species. This increased 'global flow of exotic plants' was already established for the Global North, and for example in Mexico, it was discovered that while the number of herbaceous species being exclusive to a certain home garden increases from rural (22) via semi-rural (24) to peri-urban (75), it is the other way around for tree and shrub species whose number decreases from rural (18) via semi-rural (13) to peri-urban (eight) home gardens (Poot-Pool et al., 2015).

## Social and cultural importance of urban gardens

Fast-growing urban populations do not only require food but also seek opportunities to improve their incomes, while also retaining aspects of their pre-migration traditions and cultures. This includes eating and dietary habits which are connected to certain foods which, if not available in the urban markets, are brought into or produced in the urban areas when possible. Through these processes, urban ABD is enriched with 'new' varieties. In general, it is known that growing native species and conserving their traditional cultivation and consumption practices is relevant for people to maintain their culture and traditions (Astudillo and Aroni, 2012). Provision of well-structured, species-rich green spaces through urban agriculture could also contribute to mental and physical well-being of urban communities, for example through the reduction of stress or improved social cohesion within neighbourhoods (Horwitz et al., 2015; see also **Box 32.5** *Case study: 'International Gardens' in Göttingen, Germany*).

Another social aspect of urban gardening is education. Agriculture in the city is an ideal opportunity for urban children to learn about the origins of the foods they are consuming. Many modern

### Box 32.5 Case study: 'International Gardens' in Göttingen, Germany

In 1996, an international garden pilot project was established by immigrants in Göttingen, a small town in central Germany. They founded the association '*Internationale Gärten*' where nowadays families from about 20 countries all over the world do gardening together and can engage in intercultural exchanges (Müller, 2002). Meanwhile, using the gardens in Göttingen as a model, more international gardens have been established all over Germany which can be classified as a social movement and is named the 'Intercultural Gardens Network' coordinated by the *Stiftung Interkultur* (Intercultural Foundation) (Müller, 2007). In mid-2016, nearly 240 intercultural garden projects existed in Germany while more are in a planning stage (Stiftungsgemeinschaft anstiftung & ertomis, 2016). The main aim and focus of these garden projects are the social and cultural aspects. Thereby, diversity of crops in these urban gardens was seldom a topic. For example, in a study on community gardens in Berlin, the topic of 'diversity' is mentioned only in regard of the users of the gardens which reflect the diversity of the neighbourhood. This included people with different political attitudes, different religions, various nationalities and ages (Rosol, 2010). It is likely that immigrants moving in from other countries will either bring their own seeds or get seeds from family and friends back in their countries and through this increase ABD in these urban gardens.

city children grow up without knowing where the milk they are drinking daily actually comes from. They have no idea what happens beyond the face of the supermarket. Having urban farmers close by that can be visited or even fostering school gardens where children can experiment planting seeds and follow how small seeds grow up till producing fruits, like in the example of community gardens in Berlin (Rosol, 2010), will help to create awareness of the origins of food. Garden classes can also contribute to increase the willingness of children to try new food and might even influence healthy eating behaviour (Gibbs et al., 2012). In addition, in urban gardens, different varieties and cultivars of one species can be used to display the richness of ABD. Not only children but also adults can learn the benefits of ABD in terms of the different tastes available, or regarding prolonged seasons for fresh produce through early and late maturing varieties. Next to the importance of ABD, learning about sustainable food systems in general will be possible in urban gardens including the maintenance of local knowledge of the garden plants (Esa and Jiwa, 2015). Consequently, an important aspect of ABD conservation is a successful transformation of science into practice and in general the integration of capacity building and knowledge sharing in all projects.

## Constraints for urban farmers – and ABD in urban agriculture

### *Space limitations*

As in urban areas, there is usually a high competition for land; a major constraint for urban agriculture is limited space (Orsini et al., 2013). Home gardens, including those in urban areas, were found to have greater species richness the larger they are (Sunwar et al., 2006); however, the relationship is not linear. In the United Kingdom, for example, through doubling garden size species richness increased by only 25% (Smith et al., 2006). As land availability in urban areas is limited, the intensification of agriculture and a market-oriented production is typical. High value horticultural crops with several harvests per year such as herbs and leafy vegetables are often favoured if enough labour is available (Orsini et al., 2013).

Different solutions for using the little space available as best as possible are applied in urban farming. 'Spatial' or 'vertical farming' uses the vertical space above-ground through climbing plants or growing herbal crops in additional containers on shelves, walls or structures hanging from the roof (**Figure 32.3a** *Use of limited space in urban homegardens of Kampala, Uganda*). Urban

*Figure 32.3* Use of limited space in urban homegardens of Kampala, Uganda

*Note*: From left to right: (a) onion garden in a structure hanging from the roof; (b) sack garden with onions, seedlings of Chinese cabbage and mint; (c) multiple layers of fruit trees such as mango and banana plants as top layer; maize, cassava and okra in the intermediate layer; and small herbs, medicinal plants and cocoyam in the lower layer, mixed with climbers such as pumpkin and Indian spinach.

*Source*: K. Kehlenbeck.

vertical farming also refers to cultivating plants in a skyscraper greenhouse or on inclined surfaces which is discussed as a solution for growing more food in cities to address global food insecurity and especially marginalised urban populations (Besthorn, 2013). 'Micro-gardening' is a related approach and refers to production of vegetables, herbs and tubers on rooftops, patios or balconies, in plastic containers, milk cartons or even in old tires and gunny bags (FAO, 2010; **Figure 32.3b** and **Box 32.6** *Case study: the example of micro-gardens in Dakar, Senegal, and rooftop gardens in Bologna, Italy*). Multilayer farming, which is typical for homegardens, refers to the combination of trees, shrubs and herbal crops in one plot to use the available space efficiently (**Figure 32.3c**). Sequential farming (growing four or more crops on the same plot per year to use the space as efficiently as possible), is also a typical feature of urban agriculture. In order to manage these intensive cropping systems sustainably, higher crop diversity should be applied, as a balanced crop mixture will use resources such as water, nutrients and light more efficiently than single crops (Gliessman, 2007).

Organoponic systems where crops are grown in containers filled with organic matter or compost are a possibility to optimise cultivation in limited spaces but also where soil fertility and water availability is low (Orsini et al., 2013). Where organic matter or any kind of local substrate for growing crops is not available, growing vegetables in water with a soluble fertiliser (hydroponic systems) is also a possibility (FAO, 2010).

## *Environmental sustainability*

Urban farming has impacts on the urban environment and is affected by it, yet this depends to a large extent on the typology of the urban agricultural system. In general, in many urban areas air, water and soil pollution is a major threat to public health and urban agriculture can theoretically contribute positively in all areas (Orsini et al., 2013). On the other hand, when poor practices are

### Box 32.6 Case study: the example of micro-gardens in Dakar, Senegal, and rooftop gardens in Bologna, Italy

Micro-gardens provide solutions for the constraints of urban farmers such as limited space, yet they provide also better opportunities to produce crops of higher quality as demanded by the urban population. Training is highly important, as was reported in the case of Dakar, Senegal, where new knowledge was gained and spread on plant nutrients and the application of solid substrates to replace the soil. For the latter, agricultural waste was used, namely groundnut shells and rice husks, and so costs for farmers minimised (Ba and Ba, 2007). This also contributed to waste recycling at the same time. Soilless crop production systems can be also established on rooftops, which not only provides a solution to space limitations, but is also a new strategy to ensure food supply and food security for the growing number of urban dwellers (Orsini et al., 2014). For the city of Bologna, Italy, it was estimated that an area of 82 ha on urban flat roofs could potentially be available, and that up to 12,500 tonnes of vegetables could be produced from this each year. This would provide 77% of the current requirements of the urban population of Bologna. In addition, these rooftop gardens would be able to capture about 624 tonnes of $CO_2$ per annum and would even allow the interconnection of centres of biodiversity in town. A network of 'green corridors' with a total length of an estimated 94 km would thus be created, and would provide an important living space for beneficial insects such as pollinators (Orsini et al., 2014).

applied, urban agriculture can also have negative effects on both human health and the environment (**Box 32.7** *Case study: waste-water management and aquaponics in urban environments*). The use of solid waste and waste-water, which is often used for irrigating urban crops, can cause various problems and challenges. Possible hazardous substances in the water or waste can include toxic chemical compounds or medicines, pathogens and heavy metals, all of which bear a risk for farmers who handle them, and for the consumer (DeNeergaard et al., 2009). Also, if pesticides are used inappropriately, that is, at times shortly before harvest, on inappropriate parts of the plants or at the wrong concentration, this can be harmful for consumers (Lock and van Veenhuizen, 2001).

In fact, several different studies in Asia have found that the intensification of urban agriculture caused environmental risks to significantly increase, largely due to the pollution of surface and groundwater with nitrate due to excessive application of fertilisers (Huang et al., 2006; Khai et al., 2007). Agrochemicals are also widely used in urban agriculture nowadays (Brock and Foeken, 2006) and misapplication can easily happen (**Figure 32.4** *Urban gardener applying pesticides on his leafy vegetables in an urban garden in Niamey, Niger*) when there is a lack of knowledge or farmers try to maximise production in response to a promising market (DeNeergaard et al., 2009). Food safety is in general a serious risk in urban agricultural production and concerns not only pesticide residues such as organochlorine insecticides, as in an example from Australia where, even years after they were deregistered and banned from usage, unacceptable levels of the pesticides were still found, for example in eggs of backyard poultry because these insecticides accumulate in fat

## Box 32.7 Case study: waste-water management and aquaponics in urban environments

The use of waste-water is informal but widespread in some parts of Asia and it has shown potential, for example in Bangladesh and India. A major issue is the treatment of the waste-water, which cannot be too costly for farmers, and at the same time, produce fish that is safe for human consumption (Edwards, 2005). One solution could be the combination of fish and crop production in the same system such as aquaponics.

Aquaponics is an environmentally sustainable food producing technology that is very adaptable and amenable to both urban contexts and community-led development and capacity building (Laidlow, 2013). Aquaponics is the combination of aquaculture and hydroponics. In aquaponics, the nutrient-rich water that results from fish excrement provides a source of natural fertiliser for the growing plants. A small pump brings the nutrient-rich water from the fish container to the plant growing beds (can be as simple as half a barrel filled with gravel). As the plants consume the nutrients, they purify the water and the 'clean' water that is flowing back in the fish container brings additional oxygen for the fish. A natural microbial process keeps both the fish and plants healthy. Low-cost systems, using locally available materials such as barrels, gravel, and so forth have been built by NGOs, communities and/or private farmers in rural as well as urban Kenya (Okimah and Taub, 2013; Irungu et al., 2015; amshaafrica.org; aquaponicskenya.com). The systems require very little space and are thus ideal for rooftops, patios, yards or small farms, and can easily be scaled up according to space and/or need. A young farmer in the study from Irungu et al. (2015) was earning approximately KES 300,000 (USD 3,300) per month using aquaponics technology to rear fish and grow strawberries. The technology is resourceful because ammonia produced by the fish is filtered out of the ponds through stone-filled towers, providing free nutrients and water for the strawberry plants.

*Figure 32.4* Urban gardener applying pesticides on his leafy vegetables in an urban garden in Niamey, Niger
*Note*: Note the inappropriate application tool and the total lack of any protective equipment.
*Source*: H. Bernholt.

(Gaynor, 2001). Yet another serious challenge is posed by microbial contamination, for example with pathogenic strains of *E. coli* or other coliform bacteria (Gueye and Sy, 2001) or zoonotic diseases transmitted either indirectly through the consumption of contaminated food or through direct contacts between livestock and humans (Muchaal, 2001).

As in mono-cropping systems, farmers might see themselves as being forced to apply pesticides, whereas increasing ABD can reduce the need for pesticides even in small plots, for example through intercropping. Certain combinations of species can be particularly helpful and can be adapted to the particular situations and environments involved in urban agriculture (Gliessman, 2007), just as in rural agricultural systems.

## High land value and uncertainty of land tenure

Land for agriculture in urban areas is not only scarce but also valuable. Often, it does not belong to the person who cultivates it, so land tenure is uncertain. This uncertainty influences the choice of crops to be cultivated, and consequently, short-cycle crops such as leafy vegetables are often planted as well as less perennial crops such as (fruit) shrubs or trees. In addition, practices for restoring soil fertility are also selected according to fast, short-term results at the expense of more sustainable medium- or long-term strategies (Orsini et al., 2013). Common land in urban areas, for example at roadsides, is also often used for crop cultivation as well as animal grazing, either by herders or simply through staking animals to trees or the like in developing countries. With this approach, farmers risk theft and vandalism, yet theft of animals or mature crops also happens in rural areas and is not an exclusive urban problem. In developed countries, farming on land without having the legal right to use is also called guerilla gardening, yet often the lands are abandoned sites and not cared for anyway (Paull, 2013; **Box 32.8** *Case study: farming common land for open source food and agricultural biodiversity in Todmorden, England*).

### Box 32.8 Case study: farming common land for open source food and agricultural biodiversity in Todmorden, England

While not being food insecure, an impulse for starting to farm common land in the city of Todmorden in England was regular reports on the challenges of dysfunctional eating and increasing obesity rates in Britain in general (the study is discussed in more depth in the following chapter by Jiggins, Chapter 33 of this Handbook). At the same time, studies showed that children had increasingly lost any natural relation to and knowledge about where food comes from, how it is produced and how to prepare it. The question of self-sufficiency for Todmorden was raised because policy makers had focussed for many years on feeding Britain cheaply instead of locally or seasonally (Paull, 2013). In the course of the 'Incredible Edible Todmorden' project, permission gardens and guerilla gardens were established in and around the town and functioned as 'propaganda gardens' in order to bring food issues back into public awareness. Boards next to the gardens invited the public to pick the crops grown in the gardens and showed pictures and names of the crops, listed times when ready to pick and suggested recipes for preparation. Thereby, the diversity of crops in each plot was meant to contribute to 'mixed picking' and consequently encouraged the testing of unfamiliar crops next to familiar ones. While the promotion and conservation of ABD was one aspect of the project, the main aim was to remind urban dwellers that 'food doesn't grow on supermarket shelves' and to promote local fresh and quality food (Paull, 2013).

## Conclusions and outlook: contribution of ABD to improve food security and environmental quality in urban areas

The opportunities and challenges for urban farmers and ABD in urban agriculture described in this chapter are all addressed in the recommended actions in the Milan Urban Food Policy Pact which was signed on 15 October 2015 by 100 mayors and representatives of local governments around the world (Milan Urban Food Policy Pact, 2015). To conserve biodiversity is mentioned among the 37 recommended actions on food production, namely to 'Apply an ecosystem approach to guide holistic and integrated land use planning and management' including to enhance opportunities for conservation of biodiversity. Here, a better collaboration between urban and rural authorities is highlighted which would be a prerequisite to effectively manage natural resources and for example establish green corridors not only in cities, like in the example of Bologna, but among urban, peri-urban and rural areas. The recommended actions on food production in the Milan Urban Food Policy Pact also stress the importance of securing access and tenure to land as well as environmental sustainability including short food chains, improved waste-water management and food safety.

Next to the part on food production, biodiversity is indirectly also mentioned in the recommended actions on sustainable diets and nutrition where the promotion of sustainable diets, including among others environmental friendliness, is emphasised. In addition, the increased consumption of fresh, nutrient-rich produce such as fruits and vegetables is suggested in order to address non-communicable diseases associated with poor diets and obesity, as in the example of Incredible Edible Todmorden in England which, however, concerns not only developed but increasingly also developing countries.

Much emphasis is given to education and training in regard to all facets of urban agriculture in general and ABD in particular. Taking into account that the children of today are the consumers of tomorrow as well as the increasing evidence that year-round diverse diets based on nutritious foods are crucial in reaching good nutrition and health, one cannot start early enough to teach our next generation consumers. Agriculture in the cities can contribute to that while at the same time, organised school visits can provide extra incentives to innovatively diversify and intensify urban farms. In the Milan Pact, the development of sustainable dietary guidelines is suggested, however, not only for consumers but also to inform city planners, producers and processors, food service providers and retailers. In addition, technical training for producers is proposed as well as raising awareness of the problem of food loss and waste (Milan Urban Food Policy Pact, 2015).

For the future of ABD in urban agriculture, a holistic and multi-sectoral approach is inevitable to connect 'environmental quality and food security through innovative urban design enhancing food production in the city' (Bhatt and Farah, 2010, p. 79). ABD, on the one hand getting the opportunity to be actively used and conserved through urban agriculture, provides on the other hand the potential for more diverse and sustainable food systems including better rural-urban linkages and sustainable, healthy diets for a growing urban future generation.

## References


Ahmed, S., Simiyu, E., Githiri, G., Sverdlik, A. and Mbaka, S. (2015) *Cooking Up a Storm: Community-Led Mapping and Advocacy with Food Vendors in Nairobi's Informal Settlements*, IIED Working Paper, International Institute for Environment and Development, London, UK.

Astudillo, D. and Aroni, G. (2012) 'Livelihoods of quinoa producers in southern Bolivia', pp. 78–145 in A. Giuliani, F. Hintermann, W. Rojas and S. Padulosi (eds.), *Biodiversity of Andean Grains: Balancing Market Potential and Sustainable Livelihoods*, Bioversity International, Maccarese, Italy.

AVRDC (2013) *Peri-Urban Vegetable Production Promising for Young People in Africa*, Fresh – News from AVRDC – The World Vegetable Center, Tainan, Taiwan, http://203.64.245.61/web_docs/media/newsletter/2013/009_Aug-15-2013.pdf, accessed May 2016.

Ba, A. and Ba, N. (2007) 'Micro-gardens in Dakar', *Urban Agriculture Magazine*, vol. 19, pp. 30–31.

Bernholt, H., Kehlenbeck, K., Gebauer, J. and Buerkert, A. (2009) 'Plant species richness and diversity in urban and peri-urban gardens of Niamey, Niger', *Agroforestry Systems*, vol. 77, pp. 159–179.

Besthorn, F. H. (2013) 'Vertical farming: Social work and sustainable urban agriculture in an age of global food crises', *Australian Social Work*, vol. 66, pp. 187–203.

Bhatt, V. and Farah, L. M. (2010) 'Urban design for food-security: Thinking globally designing locally', *Acta Horticulturae*, vol. 881, pp. 79–84.

Brock, B. and Foeken, D. (2006) 'Urban horticulture for a better environment: A case study of Cotonou, Benin', *Habitat International*, vol. 30, pp. 558–578.

Cernansky, R. (2015) 'Super vegetables: Long overlooked in parts of Africa, indigenous greens are now capturing attention for their nutritional and environmental benefits', *Nature*, vol. 522, pp. 146–148.

Deneergaard, A., Drescher, A. W. and Kouame, C. (2009) 'Urban and peri-urban agriculture in African cities', pp. 35–64 in C. M. Shackleton, M. W. Pasquini and A. W. Drescher (eds.), *African Indigenous Vegetables in Urban Agriculture*, Earthscan, London, UK.

De Zeeuw, H. (2010) 'Cities farming for the future – multi-stakeholder policy formulation and action planning on urban agriculture in developing countries', *Acta Horticulturae*, vol. 88, pp. 97–109.

Edwards, P. (2005) 'Development status of, and prospects for, wastewater-fed aquaculture in urban environments', pp. 45–59 in A. Desbonnet, P. Edwards and D. Baker (eds.), *Urban Aquaculture*, CABI International, Wallingford, UK.

Esa, N. and Jiwa, R. A. M. (2015) 'Enhancing students' local knowledge through themed garden project', *SHS Web of Conferences*, vol. 18, http://dx.doi.org/10.1051/shsconf/20151804004

FAO (2010) *Urban and Peri-Urban Horticulture: With Micro-Gardens, Urban Poor 'Grow Their Own'*, Food and Agriculture Organization of the United Nations, Rome, Italy.

Galluzzi, G., Eyzaguirre, P. and Negri, V. (2010) 'Home gardens: Neglected hotspots of agro-biodiversity and cultural diversity', *Biodiversity and Conservation*, vol. 19, pp. 3635–3654.

Gaynor, A. (2001) 'Pesticide soil contamination: A case study from Perth, Western-Australia', *Urban Agriculture Magazine*, vol. 1 (3), www.ruaf.org/sites/default/files/Pesticide%20Soil%20Contamination.pdf, accessed May 2016.

Gibbs, L., Staiger, P. K., Johnson, B., Block, K., Macfarlane, S., Gold, L., Kulas, J., Townsend, M., Long, C. and Ukoumunne, O. (2012) 'Expanding children's food experiences: The impact of a school-based kitchen garden program', *Journal of Nutrition Education and Behaviour*, vol. 45, pp. 137–146.

Giuliani, A. (2007) *Developing Markets for Agrobiodiversity: Securing Livelihoods in Dryland Areas*, Earthscan, London, UK.

Gliessman, S. R. (2007) *Agroecology: The Ecology of Sustainable Food Systems*, CRC Press, Boca Raton, FL, USA.

Goddard, M. A., Dougill, A. J. and Benton, T. G. (2009) 'Scaling up from gardens: Biodiversity conservation in urban environments', *Trends in Ecology and Evolution*, vol. 25, pp. 90–97.

Gotor, E. and Irungu, C. (2012) 'The impact of Bioversity International's African leafy vegetables programme in Kenya', *Impact Assessment and Project Appraisal*, vol. 28, pp. 41–55.

Gueye, N. F. D. and Sy, M. (2001) 'The use of wastewater for urban agriculture – the example of Dakar, Nouakchott and Ouagadougou', *Urban Agriculture Magazine*, vol. 1 (3), www.ruaf.org/sites/default/files/The%20Use%20of%20Wastewater%20for%20Urban%20Agriculture.pdf, accessed May 2016.

Guitart, D., Pickering, C. and Byrne, J. (2012) 'Past results and future directions in urban community gardens research', *Urban Forestry & Urban Greening*, vol. 11, pp. 364–373.

Hamilton, A. J., Burry, K., Mok, H.-F., Barker, S. F., Grove, J. R. and Williamson, V. G. (2014) 'Give peas a chance? Urban agriculture in developing countries: A review', *Agronomy for Sustainable Development*, vol. 34, pp. 45–73.

Horwitz, P., Kretsch, C., Jenkins, A., Rahim bin Abdul Hamid, A., Burls, A., Campbell, K., Carter, M., Henwood, W., Lovell, R., Malone-Lee, L. C., McCreanor, T., Moewaka-Barnes, H., Montenegro, R. A., Parkes, M., Patz, J., Roe, J. J., Romanelli, C., Sitthisuntikul, K., Stephens, C., Townsend, M. and Wright, P. (2015) 'Contribution of biodiversity and green spaces to mental and physical fitness, and cultural dimensions of health', pp. 200–220 in World Health Organization and Secretariat of the Convention on Biological Diversity (ed.), *Connecting Global Priorities: Biodiversity and Human Health: A State of Knowledge Review*, WHO Press, Geneva, Switzerland.

Huang, B., Shi, X., Yu, D., Öborn, I., Blombäck, K., Pagella, T. F., Wang, H., Sun, W. and Sinclair, F. L. (2006) 'Environmental assessment of small-scale vegetable farming systems in peri-urban areas of the Yangtze river delta region, China', *Agriculture, Ecosystems & Environment*, vol. 112, pp. 391–402.

Irungu, K. R. G., Mbugua, D. and Muia, J. (2015) 'Information and communication technologies (ICTs) attract youth into profitable agriculture in Kenya', *East African Agricultural and Forestry Journal*, vol. 81, pp. 24–33.

Kahane, R., Hodgkin, T., Jaenicke, H., Hoogendoorn, C., Hermann, M., Keatinge, J. D. H., Hughes, J. D., Padulosi, S. and Looney, N. (2013) 'Agrobiodiversity for food security, health and income', *Agronomy for Sustainable Development*, vol. 33, pp. 671–693.

Khai, N. M., Ha, P. Q. and Öborn, I. (2007) 'Nutrient flows in small-scale peri-urban vegetable farming systems in southeast Asia: A case study in Hanoi', *Agriculture, Ecosystems & Environment*, vol. 122, pp. 192–202.

Laidlow, J. (2013) *A Comparative Case Study Analysis of Two Urban Aquaponics Social Enterprises in the Cities of Melbourne, Australia and Milwaukee, USA*, Submitted in Part Requirement for the Degree of Bachelor of Social Science (Honours), School of Global, Urban and Social Studies, RMIT University, Melbourne, Australia.

Lock, K. and van Veenhuizen, R. (2001) 'Balancing the positive and negative health impacts', *Urban Agriculture Magazine*, vol. 1 (3), www.ruaf.org/sites/default/files/Balancing%20the%20Positive%20and%20Negative%20Health%20Impacts.pdf, accessed May 2016.

Milan Urban Food Policy Pact (2015) www.foodpolicymilano.org/wp-content/uploads/2015/10/Milan-Urban-Food-Policy-Pact-EN.pdf, accessed May 2015.

Mok, H.-F., Williamson, V. G., Grove, J. R., Burry, K., Barker, S. F. and Hamilton, A. J. (2014) 'Strawberry fields forever? Urban agriculture in developed countries: A review', *Agronomy for Sustainable Development*, vol. 34, pp. 21–43.

Muchaal, P. (2001) 'Zoonoses of dairy cattle with reference to Africa', *Urban Agriculture Magazine*, vol. 1 (3), www.ruaf.org/sites/default/files/Zoonoses%20of%20Dairy%20Cattle%2C%20with%20Reference%20to%20Africa.pdf, accessed May 2016.

Müller, C. (2002) *Wurzeln schlagen in der Fremde. Die Internationalen Gärten und ihre Bedeutung für Integrationsprozesse*, ökom Verlag, München, Germany.

Müller, C. (2007) 'Intercultural gardens: Urban places for subsistence production and diversity', *German Journal of Urban Studies*, vol. 46 (1), www.difu.de/node/5963, accessed May 2016.

Norfolk, O., Eichhorn, M. P. and Gilbert, F. (2014) 'Culturally valuable minority crops provide a succession of floral resources for flower visitors in traditional orchard gardens', *Biodiversity Conservation*, vol. 23, pp. 3199–3217.

Okimah, O. and Taub, M. (2013) *SEED Certification: A Framework for Addressing Triple Bottom Line Sustainability*, FLEA 2013–29th Conference, Sustainable Architecture for a Renewable Future, Munich, Germany, 10th–12th September 2013.

Orsini, F., Gasperi, D., Marchetti, L., Piovene, C., Draghetti, S., Ramazzotti, S., Bazzocchi, G. and Gianquito, G. (2014) 'Exploring the production capacity of rooftop gardens (RTGs) in urban agriculture: The potential impact on food and nutrition security, biodiversity and other ecosystem services in the city of Bologna', *Food Security*, vol. 6, pp. 781–792.

Orsini, F., Kahane, R., Nono-Womdim, R. and Gianquinto, G. (2013) 'Urban agriculture in the developing world: A review', *Agronomy for Sustainable Development*, vol. 33, pp. 695–720.

Orsini, F., Michelon, N., Scocozza, F. and Gianquinto, G. (2009) 'Farmers-to-consumers: An example of sustainable soilless horticulture in urban and peri-urban areas', *Acta Horticulturae*, vol. 809, pp. 209–220.

Paull, J. (2013) '"Please pick me": How Incredible Edible Todmorden is repurposing the commons for open source food and agricultural biodiversity', pp. 336–345 in J. Fanzo, D. Hunter, T. Borelli and F. Mattei (eds.), *Diversifying Food and Diets: Using Agricultural Biodiversity to Improve Nutrition and Health*, Earthscan from Routledge, Abingdon, UK.

Poot-Pool, W. S., van der Wal, H., Flores-Guido, S., Pat-Fernandez, J. M. and Esparza-Olguin, L. (2015) 'Home garden agrobiodiversity differentiates along a rural-peri-urban gradient in Campeche, Mexico', *Economic Botany*, vol. 69, pp. 203–217.

Rosol, M. (2010) 'Public participation in post-fordist urban green space governance: The case of community gardens in Berlin', *International Journal of Urban and Regional Research*, vol. 34 (3), pp. 548–563.

Schierer, H., Tegegne, A. and van Veenhuizen, R. (2000) 'Livestock in and around cities', *Urban Agriculture Magazine*, vol. 1 (3), www.ruaf.org/sites/default/files/Livestock%20in%20and%20around%20cities%20%28editorial%29.pdf, accessed May 2016.

Secretariat of the Convention on Biological Diversity (2012) *Cities and Biodiversity Outlook*, CBD, Montreal, Canada.

Shackleton, C. M., Pasquini, M. W. and Drescher, A. W. (2009) *African Indigenous Vegetables in Urban Agriculture*, Earthscan for Routledge, Abingdon, UK.

Smith, R. M., Thompson, K., Hodgson, J. G., Warren, P. H. and Gaston, K. J. (2006) 'Urban domestic gardens (ix): Composition and richness of the vascular plant flora, and implications for native biodiversity', *Biological Conservation*, vol. 129, pp. 312–322.

Stiftungsgemeinschaft anstiftung & ertomis (2016) *Interkulturelle Gärten – StadtLandschaften der Migrationsgesellschaft*, http://anstiftung.de/urbane-gaerten/interkulturelle-gaerten-ig, accessed May 2016.

Sunwar, S., Thornstrom, C. G., Subedi, A. and Bystrom, M. (2006) 'Home gardens in western Nepal: Opportunities and challenges for on-farm management of agrobiodiversity', *Biodiversity and Conservation*, vol. 15, pp. 4211–4238.

Taylor, J. R. and Lovell, S. T. (2014) 'Urban home food gardens in the Global North: Research traditions and future directions', *Agriculture and Human Values*, vol. 31, pp. 285–305.

Trinh, L. N., Watson, J. W., Hue, N. N., De, N. N., Minh, N. V., Chu, P., Sthapit, B. R. and Eyzaguirre, P. B. (2003) 'Agrobiodiversity conservation and development in Vietnamese home gardens', *Agriculture, Ecosystems & Environment*, vol. 97, pp. 317–344.

UN/DESA (2014) *World Urbanization Prospects: The 2014 Revision, Highlights*, United Nations, Department of Economic and Social Affairs, Population Division, New York, NY, USA.

Zezza, A. and Tasciotti, L. (2010) 'Urban agriculture, poverty, and food security: Empirical evidence from a sample of developing countries', *Food Policy*, vol. 35, pp. 265–273.

# 33

# GENDER AND AGRICULTURAL BIODIVERSITY

*Janice Jiggins*

## Introduction

Many researchers since the mid-20th century have sought to document and explain trends over time and space in the human use – and abuse – of biodiversity in agriculture. Their work connects two key concepts: *gender*, which stands for the socially-defined relationship between men and women; and *agro-biodiversity*, which stands for the relationship between ecological functioning and the biological diversity of plant genetic resources, on farm and in farm landscapes. Both concepts take three forms: as research informed by scientific disciplines, as agricultural practices and as social movements. We might note that all these forms of human endeavour have 'fuzzy' temporal and spatial characteristics that are further inflected by the specific contexts and histories of households, communities and societies in their relationship to natural and agricultural biodiversity. Thus, we might also note that both concepts, and their various applications, are heavily laden with pre-analytic values. Although researchers, development funding agencies and field practitioners should, in theory, state up front their own normative preferences concerning the desirability of any set of relationships, and the outcomes of these, it seems evident that undeclared values and assumptions often do influence both what is researched on this topic and how matters are interpreted.

*Women* in rural areas are positioned in relation to the two concepts as co-creators, managers and users of agro-biodiversity and almost everywhere as the main household managers of the food products that flow from its exploitation. Where ecological functioning and biodiversity are deteriorating, it is women, because of their social positioning, who are often found to be the most disadvantaged (e.g. Abdelali-Martini et al., 2008; Goodrich, 2012). The livelihoods of women who are directly dependent on access to and the right to use healthy agro-ecosystems rich in biodiversity are especially threatened by the loss or impairment of resources, both in traditional forms of agriculture (e.g. Agarwal, 1986) and consequently on the industrialisation of agriculture and the consolidation of land rights under a single (usually male) owner (FAO, 2005).

An associated concept is that of *social justice*. Social justice is usually taken to encompass fairness in nutritional and livelihood outcomes, equity of opportunity and the integrity of food system governance (Food Ethics Council, 2010). Interpretation of these norms in terms of gender relations is highly dependent on local contexts and histories. However, *gender equity* is commonly seen as integral to social justice (Gallié, 2013).

Some citizens, field workers and researchers go further, identifying something essential in the relationship between women's nurturing roles in the family and community and their contributions to agro-biodiversity conservation and development (Howard [2003] discusses this point). The empirical evidence does not allow firm conclusions. One study in the Gambia of men's and women's expertise in the selection of the seed of locally-grown rice varieties indicates, for instance, that socially-ascribed gender roles (gender identities) are more determinant of skill differences than the innate capabilities of men and women (Nuijten, 2010; Delêtre et al., 2011).

## The evidential foundations

In terms of academic and policy research, we can identify a number of trends in the literature from the mid-20th century onward. As women in an increasing number of countries became recognised in their own right as legal persons, gained the vote and access to formal schooling, and thus also access to academic careers, female researchers took the lead in the increasing number of studies on 'women in agriculture and natural resource management' throughout the world (Feldstein and Poats, 1989; Paris, 1992; Agarwal, 1994; Tapia and de la Torre, 1998; Agarwal, 2002). Their efforts rapidly diversified and diffused into farming systems research, and to women in agro-forestry, fishing, livestock, soil and water management and natural and farm biodiversity studies. They also expanded further into the design and impacts of related development projects: for example, several recent studies offer compelling examples from the world of agro-forestry (Kiptot and Franzel, 2012; Leakey, 2012); others offer design guidelines for fisheries and aquaculture (Spliethoff, 1994; Catacutan et al., 2014). Examples have also been developed of gender impact research related to crop-livestock interactions (Paris, 2002). See also Lilja et al. (2001) for a more general treatment of the challenges of gender impact research. The concept of 'gender' in this area emerged from studies such as these, as researchers began to understand the dynamic and relational nature of the inter-actions that shape outcomes, and the complex ways in which they interplay with household composition and structure and with other socio-economic markers such as age and class (for guidance on how to document and analyse these, see FAO, 2005).

The concerted international effort to raise the productivity of smallholder farming in the tropics and improve natural resource management and conservation at the same time was led by, but not confined to, the international centres of agricultural research (the CGIAR family of institutes), the United Nations family of development organisations (notably, the Food and Agricultural Organization [FAO]), and the World Bank, as well as by innumerable development projects; local, national and international non-government organisations; national extension services; and women's organisations and community-based groups. The degree to which any of these organisations, either formally or in practice, has been able and willing to deal with gender and agro-biodiversity issues has been highly variable. However, by the early years of the new millennium, there was overwhelming evidence from research and practice (assessed in detail in McIntyre et al., 2009) that might be crudely summarised as follows:

- Gender analysis in research offers a great deal of insight and efficiency for little additional effort;
- Women as well as men play substantial roles across all forms of agriculture and biodiversity management in many countries, as well as in processing and marketing the products, and in seed system management;
- Gender equity, as a matter of social justice as well as pragmatically in terms of the effectiveness and efficiency of sustainable agricultural modernisation, is a goal worth striving for;

- The outcomes of so-called 'gender blind' and 'gender neutral' agricultural technology and socio-economic development efforts have tended to disadvantage women disproportionately, by reducing or further conditioning their access to resources and control over the benefits that flow from the use of agro-biodiversity;
- The simplification of farm landscapes and food cultures consequent on the promotion of industrialised mono-cropping have had seriously negative impacts on specific categories of women, and particularly those directly dependent for their livelihoods on land and agro-biodiversity; and
- The nutritional consequences of the shift to industrially-processed foods, where associated with erosion of agro-biodiversity, have been negative for both men and women.

*(see also the chapters in Part 4 of this Handbook)*

There are two further trends that need to be considered before turning to case studies. The dynamic of gender relationships in relation to agro-biodiversity unfolds in the wider context of two unprecedented societal shifts never before encountered in human history: 'peak population' and urbanisation. Their importance to this chapter is twofold: they indicate that predictions of future patterns and trends in gender/agro-biodiversity relationships are highly sensitive to other forces of change, and they suggest that the outcomes are much more than a matter of highly localised projects that create 'islands of success'.

## Demography

Demographic analysis shows that the rate of increase in human populations peaked around the 1980s, led by downward shifts in birth rates in highly populous countries that include China, Indonesia and Bangladesh (Tomlinson [2013] analyses the implications for food security). For many rural women and men, this has begun to open up new livelihoods outside drudgery on small family farms and as labourers, and to instead offer possibilities for making their own life choices in ways never before envisaged. Their choices are thought likely to relieve pressures on agro-biodiversity in some areas. At the same time, gender relations have become more problematic in countries where there is a strong preference for sons (including large parts of India, China, Pakistan and Central Asia). This has given rise to new tensions in the search for marriage partners, family formation and household structures. Rather than increasing the value of women, the rising imbalance between the sexes in such areas seems to be motivating increasing violence in the effort to secure the sexual, labour and domestic services of women. However, if we step back and look at the larger picture up to the end of the current century, we might take hope from demographic trends that could give rise to significant reduction of the current (and rising) pressures on agro-biodiversity as 'peak global population' (currently estimated at around 9 billion by mid-century) flattens and the total size of populations that are already shrinking in an increasing number of countries, begin to fall throughout most areas of the world.

## Urbanisation

At the same time, both women and men are leaving the land and moving into cities at a rising rate and unprecedented numbers, leaving some rural areas considerably less populated. The 'food security' challenge is increasingly an urban challenge, with over half of the world's people already urban-based (RUAF, 2010). Researchers already detect concomitant erosion of age-old knowledge and experience and re-conceptualisations of what is considered food (e.g. fewer urban children are able to identify the source of or to name 'raw' food; households that are almost entirely dependent on processed food), cooking (e.g. re-defined as heating pre-packaged meals, opening tins, re-constituting pre-processed foods), farming (e.g. urban agriculture) and the biodiversity of cities (e.g. urban foxes living off food waste and small household pets). On the other hand, entirely new agro-biodiversity potentials are opening up, including vertical vegetable, herb and salad greenhouses combined with apartment blocks and supermarkets, but also farmers' markets, community gardens and other citizen-led initiatives and insectories (see McGill et al., Chapter 22 of this Handbook) feeding off supermarket waste, and producing the feedstock for urban fish, pig and poultry production as well as raw materials for (processed) food products.

The implications of demographic change and urbanisation for gender relations and biodiversity are as yet poorly studied. We can observe they seem to be pushing significant change in the relation between production and consumption (Carolan, 2012). For instance, in the Netherlands, some 3,300 farmers (out of a total of 67,000) are selling directly to consumers via on-farm shops or farmers' markets, direct deliveries that they organise themselves and direct deliveries organised by farmer cooperatives. These efforts typically are associated with the values of agro-biodiversity conservation. Nonetheless, we might also note that such actions appear insignificant in the face of the juggernaut of 'business as usual'. These causes and effects were first signalled at the global level by the Millennium Ecosystem Assessment (2003) and elaborated in the International Assessment of Agricultural Science and Technology for Development (McIntyre et al., 2009), the Global Ecological Footprint Index (Wackenagel and Rees, 1996), the WWF's Living Planet Index; and the proposed Food and Human Security Index (Carolan, 2012), among others. These schemes attempt to integrate data across a range of human and bio-physical variables while the FAO's (2013) 2nd Global Plan of Action for Plant Genetic Resources for Food and Agriculture proposed a standard set of indicators specifically for agro-biodiversity. Increasing use of these indicators will allow integration of information that is inclusive of both men's and women's interactions with agro-biodiversity.

Yet effort is not motivated by despair, so what are the options for building on the lessons of development experience summarised earlier and that offer hope? We present in brief three cases, from Peru, China and Europe, of well-documented efforts that succeeded in making a difference. They allow some key generic points to be made yet also serve to illustrate the importance of embedding initiatives in the context in which they occur.

## *Peru: the Quechua community-based Potato Park*

At the turn of the millennium, five Quechua communities formed an association to establish a Potato Park on some 9,600 ha, lying 3,500–5,100 m above sea level (IIED, 2011). The aim was to safeguard the bio-cultural heritage of Quechua peoples through conservation of their staple crop, the potato, and innovation in the management of agro-biodiversity, under a form of community self-organisation based on customary law and the Inca notion of *Ayllu*. *Ayllu* conceptualises 'community' as comprising three inter-linked and inter-dependent life-worlds – the domesticated, the wild and the spiritual. The knowledge needed for conservation and innovation is seen as arising from the flow between all three. Women are honoured as mothers and potato farmers who connect the life worlds through the principle of nurturing. They have special responsibility for the varieties needed for culturally-valued foods, and for using processing residues in feeding livestock (llama and sheep). The communities are actively engaged in developing a range of 'own label' commercial products from selected varieties and opening a restaurant to present their potato-based recipes to a wider public.

In 2000, 623 named potato varieties were cultivated within the Park; the living collection today totals 1,460, with around 4,000 varieties conserved *ex situ*. In a unique legal agreement with the International Potato Center (CIP), numerous varieties originally acquired by CIP from the region have been repatriated, and a close working relationship has been established between the communities and CIP to co-create knowledge and experience about genetic enrichment, and for cleaning and maintaining the accessions free from viruses. The accessions are conserved in poly-tunnels and greenhouses as well as *in situ* in community-managed Gene Reserves. The ancient Quechua form of communicating and storing information, *Quipu* (knotted strings), has been adapted to store complex chromosomal and molecular information in a form retrievable by community members, complemented by increasing use of smart phones, and web and Internet technologies. In 2000, the communities also established an Indigenous Biocultural Heritage Area as a legal innovation in order to preserve and promote native varieties, protect the environment and establish legal recognition of their biocultural heritage's role in maintaining potato diversity.

Higher temperatures and increased temperature fluctuations over the last decades have intensified pest and disease pressures. In the past, the communities responded by shifting production to higher altitudes, but potato growing has now reached the upper limits of cultivable land, which has also increased competition between the land for potatoes and other high altitude crops. The communities, CIP and the University of Wisconsin are together developing new cultivars suitable for growing at lower elevations and higher temperatures, based on Participatory Plant Breeding procedures with groups of men and women farmers (personal communication).

In order to protect both old and new varieties as unique bio-cultural products when brought to market (whether as part of traditional or novel products), the communities have developed an informal Collective Trademark. The trademark is associated with an inter-communal agreement that establishes equitable arrangements for sharing the benefits derived from market returns. Under this agreement, women are recognised both as individuals and as members of households and communities.

### *Southwest China: agro-biodiversity conservation and development through novel arrangements for Plant Breeding, Access and Benefit-Sharing and urban consumer markets*

A study carried out in the mid-1990s of the impact of maize hybrids in southwest China showed that more than 80% of the maize seed was supplied by local farmers, who refreshed and maintained named varieties by breeding from local landraces and officially released seeds (Song, 1998; Song and Jiggins, 2003). A subsequent study (Li, 2012) showed that by the mid-1990s, hybrids had taken over throughout Guangxi, Yunnan and Guizhou except in the mountainous areas where some 25 million people live, most of whom are poor small farmers from minority ethnic groups. Public sector breeders became alarmed at the loss of maize genetic diversity in farmers' fields – an essential 'raw material' for professional seed breeding – and the narrow genetic base of the hybrids distributed through the public system (by the late 1990s, the parentage of 91.6% of the available hybrids consisted of approximately 20 elite inbred lines). After visiting the fields of experienced 'farmer breeders' and observing the rich landrace diversity maintained by communities, the maize breeders at the Guangxi Maize Research station agreed to collaborate with farmers and community groups (initially in three villages), municipal extension services, and researchers from the Chinese Academy of Agricultural Sciences in a Participatory Plant Breeding (PPB) project supported by the International Development Research Centre, Canada. Between 2000 and 2011, four open pollinated varieties (OPVs) and one hybrid were bred through the project and approved for local release. However, only the hybrid (Guino, released in 2006) passed the official regional seed performance testing procedures. By agreement among the parties, the other seeds are being produced and sold locally by a women's seed producers group. In 2010 – for the first time in China – a contract-based Access and Benefit Sharing (ABS) agreement was negotiated that fixes the financial and genetic resource returns to each party involved in the PPB effort (Song and Vernooy, 2010). The public sector breeders, researchers, municipalities and farmer groups have subsequently extended the PPB effort to other crops and to an increasing number of villages throughout the mountainous parts of southwest China. PPB procedures based on evolutionary population-based decentralised breeding have led to high adoption rates of improved seed in the 'difficult' environments of the southwest. This experience, among others from around the world (Harwood, 2012; Heinemann et al., 2013; Phillips, 2013; Ceccarelli, 2015), demonstrates that there is no biological justification for the worldwide standard seed testing criteria that is, that a new seed should be distinctive, uniform and stable. Policy effort is instead on-going to devise a *sui generis* regulatory, seed performance testing, breeders' rights and intellectual property rights regime suited to China's needs under rapid agricultural modernisation and the commercialisation of seed breeding in a context in which millions of poor people in the southwest and other parts of China continue to seek livelihoods through farming for the foreseeable future.

At the same time, those involved began to realise that it was unrealistic for farmers to continue to maintain landraces and PPB varieties if these activities were not linked to new income opportunities beyond the ABS contract. They began to develop new links between women's and men's producer groups and urban consumer groups, and an urban entrepreneur interested in opening a restaurant selling organic and traditional foods and products. The restaurant as a form of 'community-supported agriculture' took off, and the producer groups now supply an expanding chain of restaurants. These activities are further promoted through Farmer and Seed Biodiversity Fairs and specialised urban market promotions.

## *A European case: an inclusive urban-based citizen initiative*

Todmorden is a former Victorian mill town in West Yorkshire, United Kingdom, situated in the Upper Calder Valley some 17 miles from the large city of Manchester. There are some 17,000 residents, of mixed socio-economic and ethnic background. One day in 2008, Pam Warhurst, inspired by a talk by Professor Tim Lang, a renowned food system researcher, sat talking with her friend Mary Clear about the prevailing 'gloom and doom' (for the history and development of this case, see Warhurst and Dobson, 2014). They noted how blame for nutritional, health and environmental problems was always directed to someone else. They decided to 'just do something, take action, right here and now'. They called an open meeting – 'if you eat, this is for you'. Some 60 people turned up, and together they decided to begin growing fruit, vegetables and herbs on any bits and pieces of uncultivated land around the town: by the police, fire and railway stations, along the river side, on roundabouts and so on. They put up signs inviting anyone to join in and to share seeds and the produce for free – what became known as 'propaganda gardens'. From the beginning, they emphasised the importance of bringing together concern for access to quality food, the environment, biodiversity, health and social justice at local scale, under the slogan 'community, education and business'. They claimed authority under the European Union's Aarhus Convention that enables citizens to act as legally recognised persons in matters of the environment and natural resource management.

An increasing number of volunteers were drawn into exploring and developing their own initiatives. A collective ambition emerged to grow sufficient fruit, vegetables and herbs to meet local demand by 2018. The local council, the major social housing agency (Pennine Housing) and every local school have since joined in. The Todmorden High School, for instance, has set up a 'food hub' to increase poorer residents' access to fresh produce. The local technical college has, since 2013, been offering a new qualification in agro-ecological horticulture in response to demand. Others have created neighbourhood maps to indicate suitable sites (over 500 by end of 2012) to expand production. Members of the movement are routinely consulted on major land developments and natural resource management in the area. Two green-field sites have been donated to allow expanded production, at Walsden and Gorpley. At Gorpley, Todmorden residents are developing agro-ecological approaches to small-scale hilltop farming and aim to supply small enterprises that have been established to process and sell local potato favourites such as crisps, soups and baked goods. Local history groups, meanwhile, are recording older residents' memories of and knowledge about wild life, fruit, herb and field crop varieties, production techniques and recipes. A successful bid for National Lottery funding enabled a Sustainable Environmental Technology Centre to be built as a community facility for sharing ideas, experience, information and education with residents and other communities and visitors. Numerous other citizen-led enterprises have spun off, such as an 'incredible edible' farm, an aqua garden and an urban bee project. Similar movements have begun in Spain, Ireland, Canada and other U.K. towns and villages, and visitors from France have set up an agro-ecological beef and social justice project *(Nourriture à partager)* in the village of Colroy-la-Roche.

## Reflection on lessons learned

Concerned scholars and practitioners point to six key components of experience and research-based analysis of efforts such as those sketched earlier:

1 Agro-biodiversity conservation and development is not merely or even essentially a technical and bio-physical matter: it is a matter of the deliberate choice of actors to create novel social-technical networks of inter-action at territorial (rather than only plot or farm) scales.
2 Agro-biodiversity conservation and innovation require effort to bring into existence novel seed systems and seed system regulation and governance, as well as novel food systems and markets.
3 Successful effort creates territorial spaces that challenge the dominant framing of property and bio-cultural value. This also implies that gender relations recognise and reward women for the contributions they make, and their aspiration to be treated with justice as human beings, as legal persons and as citizens.
4 Further amendment is required to the laws, regulations, protocols and conventions that govern plant genetic resources, seed improvement, official release and sale. Recognition of women's and men's essential and continuing roles in conserving, managing and developing the biodiversity of farm seed, genetic resources and the natural resources of territorial landscapes is essential.
5 Cognitive capacity is a universal human constant and its exercise is a necessity for individual and social existence. By challenging dominant claims to what is considered knowledge and who is considered knowledgeable, new pathways for applying diverse capacities for smart and flexible adaptive co-learning can be opened up.
6 Sustainable futures rest on the 'positive deviance' of those who are trying to make a difference.

In terms of technology and farm system design the key, as Altieri (1999) emphasised, 'is to identify the type of biodiversity that is desirable to maintain and/or enhance . . . ecological services' (p. 22) and then to determine the best practices that will encourage the productivity of the biodiversity components. From a gender perspective, the essential questions that then arise include (a) *who* helps identify what is desirable? (b) what is included in the valuation of *desirability*? (c) *which services* are taken into account? and (d) who helps determine *best practices*? The scientific literature suggests that agro-biodiversity research driven by the agricultural science community typically avoids asking such questions. The poor adoption rates of the specific technologies and farm designs that emerge from 'agro-biodiversity research as business as usual' suggest that truly transformative change will emerge elsewhere, with the support of science rather than driven by science.

Levidow et al. (2013), working with the Transform network, suggested that in the context of the European Union the potential to re-shape agro-food markets in association with agro-biodiverse farming systems builds on three principles and practices: the power of collective action at territorial scales; innovative arrangements for participatory research and governance among farmers, citizens and local governments; and the co-creation of transdisciplinary knowledge that includes the practical experience of men and women in food and agriculture.

This is a large agenda, but the increasing number of publications presenting evidence-based instances of such transformative action (e.g. De Boef et al., 2013; Fondazione ACRA-CCS, 2013; ILEIA, 2016) suggests there is hope for timely changes that are making a difference.

## Conclusions

The trend data related to agro-biodiversity are evidence of widespread, systemic failure to conserve and manage the resources on which human existence depends. Women and children are typically among the worst affected by the consequences. The growing number of instances of transformative action taken by women and men around the world, in both rural and urban settings, offers some hope that innovative ways forward, with some degree of gender equity and social justice, can become the dominant way of doing business.

## References


Abdelali-Martini, M., Amri, A., Ajlonni, M., Assi, R., Sbieh, Y. and Khnifes, A. (2008) 'Gender dimensions in the conservation and sustainable use of agro-biodiversity in West Asia', *Journal of Socio-Economics*, vol. 37, pp. 355–363.

Agarwal, B. (1986) *Cold Hearths and Barren Slopes: The Woodfuel Crisis in the Third World*, Allied Publishers Pvt. Ltd., New Delhi, India.

Agarwal, B. (1994) 'Gender and command over property: A critical gap in economic analysis and policy in South Asia', *World Development*, vol. 22, pp. 1455–1478.

Agarwal, B. (2002) 'Are we not peasants too? Land rights and women's claims in India', *Seeds*, vol. 21, p. 30.

Altieri, M. (1999) 'The ecological role of biodiversity in agroecosystems', *Agriculture, Ecosystems & Environment*, vol. 74, pp. 19–31.

Carolan, M. (2012) 'The Food and Human Security Index: Rethinking food security and "growth"', *International Journal of the Sociology of Agriculture and Food*, vol. 19, pp. 176–200.

Catacutan, D., McGaw, E. and Llanza, M. A. (eds.) (2014) *In Equal Measure. A User Guide to Gender Analysis in Agroforestry*, ICRAF, The Philippines.

Ceccarelli, S. (2015) 'Efficiency of plant breeding', *Crop Science*, vol. 55, pp. 87–97.

De Boef, W. S., Subedi, A., Peroni, N., Thijssen, J. M. and O'Keeffe, E. O. (2013) *Community Biodiversity Management: Promoting Resilience and Their Conservation of Plant Genetic Resources*, Routledge, Abingdon, UK.

Delêtre, M., McKay, D. B. and Hodkinson, T. R. (2011) 'Managing exchange: Seed exchanges and dynamics of manioc diversity', *Proceedings of the National Academy of Sciences USA*, vol. 108, pp. 18249–18254.

FAO (2005) *Building on Gender, Agrobiodiversity and Local Knowledge: A Training Manual*, Food and Agriculture Organization of the United Nations (FAO), Rome, Italy, www.fao.org/sd/links/documents_download/manual.pdf/

FAO (2013) *2nd Global Plan of Action for Plant Genetic Resources for Food and Agriculture*, GRFA-14/13/Report, FAO, Rome, Italy.

Feldstein, H. and Poats, S. (eds.) (1989) *Working Together: Gender Analysis in Agriculture*, Kumarian Press, West Hartford, CT, USA.

Fondazione ACRA-CCS (2013) *Farmers' Rights in Practice: Synthesis of the Case Studies on Sustainable Use of Agrobiodiversity*, issuu.com/fondazioneacra/docs/farmers_rights/55

Food Ethics Council (2010) *Food Justice: The Report of the Food and Fairness Inquiry*, FEC, Brighton, UK.

Gallié, A. (2013) 'Governance of seed and food security through Participatory Plant Breeding: Empirical evidence and gender analysis from Syria', *Natural Resources Forum*, vol. 37, pp. 31–42.

Goodrich, C. (2012) *Gender Dynamics in Agro-Biodiversity Conservation in Sikkim and Nagaland*, ICRISAT, Routledge India, New Delhi, India.

Harwood, J. (2012) *Europe's Green Revolution and Others Since the Rise and Fall of Peasant-Friendly Plant Breeding*, Routledge, Abingdon, UK.

Heinemann, J., Massaro, J. M., Coray, D. S., Agapito-Tenfen, S. Z. and Wen, J. B. (2013) 'Sustainability and innovation in staple crop production in the US Midwest', *International Journal of Agricultural Sustainability*, vol. 12, pp. 71–88.

Howard, P. (ed.) (2003) *Women and Plant Genetic Relations in Biodiversity Management and Conservation*, ZED Books, London, UK.

IIED (2011) *Community Biocultural Protocols; Building Mechanisms for Access and Benefit-Sharing among the Communities of the Potato Park Based on Customary Quechua Norms*, IIED, London, UK, www.bioculturalheritage.org

ILEIA (2016) 'Access and Benefit Sharing of Genetic Resources', Special issue *Farming Matters*, April, Bioversity International, Maccarese, Italy, and ILEIA, Wageningen, The Netherlands.

Kiptot, E. and Franzel, S. (2012) 'Gender and agroforestry in Africa: A review of women's participation', *Agroforestry Systems*, vol. 84, pp. 35–58.

Leakey, R. R. B. (2012) *Living with the Trees of Life: Towards the Transformation of Tropical Agriculture*, CABI, Wallingford, UK.

Levidow, L., Pimbert, M., Stassart, P. and Vanloqueren, G. (2013) *Agroecology in Europe: Conforming or Transforming the Dominant Agro-Food Regime?*, Paper presented at Agroecology for Sustainable Food Systems in Europe: A Transformative Agenda, 26–27 June, Brussels, Belgium, European Network of Scientists for Social and Environmental Responsibility.

Li, J. (2012) *Inducing Multi-Level Institutional Change Through Participatory Plant Breeding in Southwest China.* PhD thesis, Wageningen University, The Netherlands.

Lilja, N., Ashby, J. A., Sperling, L. and Jones, A. L. (eds.) (2001) *Assessing the Impact of Participatory Research and Gender Analysis*, CGIAR Programme for Participatory Research and Gender Analysis, International Center for Tropical Agriculture (CIAT), Cali, Colombia.

McIntyre, B. D., Herren, H. R., Wakhungu, J. W. and Watson, R. I. (eds.) (2009) *Agriculture at a Crossroads: International Assessment of Agricultural Knowledge, Science and Technology*, Island Press, Washington, DC, USA.

Millennium Ecosystem Assessment (2003) United Nations Environment Programme (UNEP), Nairobi, Kenya.

Nuijten, E. (2010) 'Gender and the management of crop diversity in the Gambia', *Journal of Political Ecology*, vol. 17, pp. 42–58.

Paris, T. R. (1992) 'Socio-economic issues concerning women in animal production', pp. 247–270 in P. Bunyavejchewin, S. Sangdid and K. Hangsanet (eds.), *Animal Production and Rural Development. Proceedings of the Sixth AAAP Animal Science Congress 1*, The Animal Husbandry Association of Thailand, Bangkok, Thailand.

Paris, T. R. (2002) 'Crop–animal systems in Asia: Socio-economic benefits and impacts on rural livelihoods', *Agricultural Systems*, vol. 71, pp. 147–168.

Phillips, C. (2013) *Saving More Than Seeds: Practices and Policies of Seed Saving*, Ashgate, Farnham, UK.

RUAF (2010) 'The role of urban agriculture in sustainable urban nutrient management', *Urban Agriculture*, vol. 23, pp. 1–56.

Song, Y. (1998) *'New' Seed in 'Old' China; Impact of CIMMYT Collaborative Programme on Maize Breeding in Southwest China*, PhD Thesis, Wageningen University, The Netherlands.

Song, Y. and Jiggins, J. (2003) 'Women and maize breeding: The development of new seed systems in a marginal area of southwest China', pp. 273–288 in P. L. Howard (ed.), *Women and Plant – Gender Relations in Biodiversity Management And Conservation*, Zed Books, London & New York.

Song, Y. and Vernooy, R. (eds.) (2010) *Seeds and Synergies: Innovating Rural Development in China*, Practical Action Publishing, Burton on Dunsmore, U.K. and International Development Research Centre, Ottawa, Canada.

Spliethoff, P. C. (1994) *Fisheries and Aquaculture: Operational Guidelines for the Incorporation of Gender in Project/ Programme Preparation and Design*, The European Commission, Brussels, Belgium.

Tapia, M. E. and De la Torre, A. (1998) *Women Farmers and Andean Seeds*, Bioversity International, Maccarese, Italy.

Tomlinson, I. (2013) 'Doubling food production to feed the 9 billion: A critical perspective on a key discourse of food security in the U.K.', *Journal of Rural Studies*, vol. 29, pp. 81–90.

Wackenagel, M. and Rees, W. (1996) *Our Ecological Footprint: Reducing Human Impact on the Earth*, New Society Publishers, Vancouver, Canada.

Warhurst, P. and Dobson, J. (2014) *Incredible! Plant Vegetables, Grow a Revolution*, www.incredible-edible-todmorden.co.uk

## Web resources

Centre for Agroecology and Food Security: www.coventry.ac.uk/cafs
FAO-GRFA [GRA-14/13/Report]: www.fao.org/docrep/meeting/028/mg538e.pdf/
Global Ecological Footprint: www.footprintnetwork.org
IAASTD: www.agassessment/org
Incredible Edible: www.incredible-edible-todmorden.co.uk/
Living Planet Index: www.panda.org; www.unep-wcmc.org
Landesa Cetner forWomen's Land Rights: www.landesa.org/women-and-land/

# 34

# SEED SYSTEMS

## Managing, using and creating crop genetic resources

*Niels P. Louwaars*

### Introduction

Within the broad term 'agrobiodiversity', the genetic diversity that exists within crops is a component of special importance for humankind, as it is the basis of all our food, feed, fibres and more. Current levels of agrobiodiversity have developed through a combination of natural selection and both intentional and unintentional selection by farmers over millennia – and more recently by professional plant breeders working towards various goals. Seeds and other plant reproductive materials (hereafter included in the word 'seed') are the basis of all crop production and genetic resources provide the building blocks of all seed. Seed systems therefore play an important role in determining which types of genetic diversity are used by farmers. Seed systems have been defined as 'the total of . . . seed production, selection and exchange activities' (after Almekinders, 2000, p. 1). This chapter takes a seed systems perspective to analyse the ways that farmers deal with seeds in relation to their maintenance of, use of and contribution to crop genetic diversity. It also analyses how the most important regulatory frameworks influence different seed systems.

### Roles of diversity in agricultural systems

Diversity plays an important role in farming, especially as a source of material for selection. Farmers in many cultures are known to experiment, and are often keen on 'things to try' and evaluating new seeds in order to see whether they fit in their farming system. Similarly, professional breeders need to access diversity and create further diversity through crossing or other techniques in order to have a population from which to select. Recent concerns about reduction of crop genetic diversity from the 1970s onward led to the development of conservation and management strategies in three complementary areas: *ex situ*, on-farm and *in situ*. The first two are closely linked to particular seed systems. Diversity can also be analysed in terms of its agronomical value: where the agro-ecology of an area is diverse or unpredictable, it may be wise not to grow one uniform variety or even one crop (Hodgekin et al., 2007). Diversity provides yield stability, especially at low yield levels. When drought hits a crop, more drought-tolerant individuals may survive and give some yield; when the season has ample rainfall, the higher-yielding types in the same population are likely to prevail. The same is true for crop responses to pests and diseases: if a uniform variety is susceptible to (for example) a fungus, an epidemic may quickly develop, whereas a genetically diverse crop may slow down the spread of the disease. In severely risky conditions, crop mixtures are important for yield stability (Sthapit et al., 2008); for other farming systems, diversity in rotation (Gaudin et al., 2015) or selectable stability factors may suffice (Mickelbart et al., 2015). However, in systems where the environment is more predictable, or can be kept under control, the importance of diversity in the field is minimal. Hydroponic horticulture under LED-lighting is an extreme of case of such a controlled environment.

## Formal and farmers' seed systems

Farmers access seed for their next crop in a variety of ways. Broadly speaking, a distinction can be made between formal and farmers' seed systems (Louwaars et al., 2013). The former commonly consist of components such as 'genetic resources management', 'breeding', and 'multiplication' and 'distribution' in a strictly organised fashion, often including formal variety release and seed certification. Formal seed systems take place among specialised actors. These seed chains are subject to some kind of regulation in most countries, hence the word 'formal'.

Informal or farmers' seed systems are based on farmers' selection and reproduction practices, and involve the sharing of seeds among farmers through different mechanisms. These are often closely connected to the culture of the farming community (Coulibaly et al., 2014; Coomes et al., 2015; see also the case study of Cuba presented by Ríos Labrada and Ceballos-Müller, Chapter 40 of this Handbook). Since seeds are the carriers of DNA and therefore of diversity in genetic makeup, seed systems simultaneously use, conserve and contribute to genetic diversity.

The distinction between formal and farmers' seed systems is becoming a little academic as linkages are increasingly developed between the two, and intermediate systems may be identified. Louwaars (1994) introduced the term 'integrated seed systems', pointing to various ways where formal and farmers' systems can contribute to each other. This can happen in any link of the seed chain. Genebanks have started to re-introduce diversity, breeders from the formal sector have joined farmers in various forms of participatory plant breeding (Jiggins and DeZeeuw,1992; Bishaw and Turner, 2008) and farmer-groups have become more specialised in seed production, thus forming various intermediaries between local and formally regulated forms of seed supply. This diversity of seed systems led to a framework for integrated seed sector development (Louwaars and de Boef, 2012), requiring an approach to seed policies and laws that provide the necessary policy space for *all* seed systems to operate side by side (Louwaars et al., 2013). For the purpose of this chapter, the distinction between formal and farmers' seed systems will be observed, but the possibility of increasing intermediate forms should always be borne in mind.

## Farmers' seed systems: using and maintaining diversity

### *Farmers' seed systems as an origin of diversity*

Farmers' seed systems have domesticated wild plant species to become crops, and have in turn developed a wide array of selections in response to the agro-ecology and human preferences during that domestication (Pautasso, 2014). While domestication is connected with a significant reduction of diversity, subsequent growing and selection processes over the 10,000 years of agriculture in different parts of the world have increased diversity, along with natural evolutionary processes, that is, through recombination and mutation, and changing preferences of farmers. Locally adapted landraces were developed, and when conditions change, they adapt to the new conditions given enough time to do so. Farmer selection and regular or even occasional exchange contribute to such adaptation. It must be borne in mind though that natural selection and farmer selection are sometimes complementary and sometimes antagonistic. For example, when a new strain of a plant disease appears, plants that show a genetic resistance or tolerance will produce more seeds, and farmers are likely to discard affected plants. Natural and farmers' selection thus reinforce each other. However, natural selection may favour more but smaller seeds that shed and spread easily, whereas a farmer may want plump seeds that remain on the plant until harvest.

When a farmer has selected a better seed, this quickly becomes known in the community and requests for a sample can normally not be denied – the selection thus spreads within the community through the farmers' seed system. Crossing borders to other communities, or to other valleys or regions, may not be so easy, hence the use of the term 'local seed system' (Almekinders et al., 1994). Farmers' seed systems thus create diversity and maintain it through their use in farmers' fields. However, in a strict sense this is not conservation, as the diversity is by definition 'mobile': specific traits can also easily get lost through genetic drift, as a result of an emergency such as severe drought or displacement of communities as a result of war, but even where specific genes may be lost, diversity remains to be used (Ferguson et al., 2012).

Two trends are important in judging the role of farmers' seed systems in relation to genetic resource conservation and use: ecological change and the availability of modern varieties, both of which I now discuss.

## *Ecological and socio-economic changes and crop genetic diversity*

Where one of the key features of landraces is that they can adapt to changing conditions, there are also limits to that resilience. When changes occur too quickly, the available genetic diversity within that locality may not be enough to cope with the changes, and adaptation may not be able to keep up. The introduction of chemical fertilisers or irrigation are examples of such sudden changes, and in many parts of the world these changes triggered the widespread use of modern, uniform varieties as a logical consequence (see following section). Also, markets often demand features that may not be easily met by the varieties bred by farmers without risks of severely reducing resilience, such as uniform seed colour of beans. Currently there are questions about the ability of local varieties to respond to climate change, especially more frequent and severe droughts.

## *Modern varieties in farmers' seed systems*

Local seed systems are currently not only dealing with the traditional farmers' varieties. Through local selection and exchange mechanisms, modern varieties can also find their way to remote and resource-poor farmers who do not have access to formal seed markets. Lipper et al. (2012) identified that many smallholders purchase grain from markets, and that this may well be of modern varieties. McGuire and Sperling (2016) suggested that novel ways of reaching farmers with improved germplasm may be found outside of formal seed systems, and modern varieties can be adopted or mixed with local ones in this way (Sperling and Scheidegger, 1995). If they are mixed with local varieties, this use of improved germplasm may enrich local diversity, but it may also push out some components from the existing population. Such improvement of the local variety through the introduction of materials from formal breeding happens simply because the latter are available and farmers like 'things to try', but it can also be a deliberate action in participatory plant breeding (PPB) (Almekinders and Hardon, 2006; Ceccarelli et al., 2009). PPB combines local and scientific knowledge and local and outside genetic resources. It aims at developing better varieties for local conditions, at least partly as a result of the poor adoption of seeds breed for uniform conditions as opposed to the complex, diverse and risk-prone environments smallholders farm. It typically involves the selection by farmers of a wide range of diversity brought in from different sources, and/or the crossing of local materials with plants from a research station with specific complementary traits. By doing that, it may deter farmers from choosing modern varieties and thus maintain a higher level of genetic diversity on-farm: PPB may enrich diverse landraces, or it may maintain diversity because farmers in different localities may select different components of the diversity offered or created (Coomes et al., 2015). Farmers' seed systems are therefore the most common way to multiply and distribute the products of PPB. Such programmes also may strengthen the capacity of farmers to breed and perform selection even without further involvement of the scientific partners in the programme, thus contributing to empowerment and sustainability (de Boef et al., 2013; see also Taylor, Chapter 38 of this Handbook). Farmers may also select uniform varieties from formal breeding programmes in such participatory programmes, especially when their ecological conditions are quite predictable.

### *Maintaining, creating and using genetic resources*

Farmers' seed systems commonly harbour a wide range of genetic resources, especially when the ecology is diverse and versatile. However, both natural and anthropogenic disasters can disrupt genetic diversity. It is therefore not fully correct to speak of on-farm 'conservation' of genetic resources; rather, it would be better to speak of on-farm management.

To cope with some of the hazards of losing valuable diversity, farmer groups in various countries have organised community genebanks or seed banks (Berg and Abay, 2008; Vernooy et al., 2014). These may have two distinct functions: (1) to store enough seed of the locally-adapted varieties for farmers who for whatever reason have nothing to plant, and (2) to preserve the diversity of varieties for multiplication should problems arise with the modern varieties that have entered the farming system. Community seed banks are explored in more depth in Vernooy et al., Chapter 37 of this Handbook.

With respect to use, farmers' seed systems maintain diversity through use, which means that they allow for the development of new diversity through natural processes or by the inclusion of foreign materials – either from other communities or from formal sources. The latter is more and more common. When it is done consciously, for example through PPB, a wide range of diversity is commonly brought in to provide a choice for farmers to choose from. PPB also needs access to a wide range of genetic resources (see Ortiz, Chapter 17 and Ríos Labrada and Ceballos-Müller, Chapter 40, both in this Handbook).

New diversity in farmers' seed systems are created mainly through natural mechanisms of evolution: introgression and mutation (Koonin, 2009). There is a difference in this respect between farmers' seed systems in the centres of diversity of the crop, where some introgression with the wild populations may occur, and in areas where the crop appears only in cultivated fields. In the latter, enrichment of the population depends more on the introduction of materials from other communities, and more recently, from research stations through demonstration fields, commercial introductions and indeed through PPB programmes. Mutation is a more untargeted way of creating diversity. The vast majority of mutations are known to be negative with regard to fitness, but important new traits may also emerge in this way.

## 'Formal' seed systems using and maintaining diversity

### *The emergence of formal systems*

Formal seed systems have emerged with the professionalisation of the components of the seed chain. The historic trend in most of Europe is that traders picked up seed from areas suitable for the production of healthy (seed) crops, and farmers in these regions tended to concentrate on seed rather than crop production. An example is the emergence of multiple vegetable seed companies in and around the village of Andijk in the Netherlands. The area had deep soils suitable for the production of vegetables such as cabbage and carrot and was also in the vicinity of a major market – the city of Amsterdam. Its vicinity to the sea also made it a region with a low disease pressure and the cool summers and mild winters of the maritime climate allowed good seed set. By the early 1800s, specific varieties had been selected and seed was already being produced for sale to other regions in the Netherlands and neighbouring Germany; 200 years later, it still harbours a group of companies who collectively supply much of the global vegetable seed market. In these companies, genetic resource management, laboratory research, plant breeding, testing varieties, seed production, seed conditioning, seed treatment, seed quality control and seed marketing are some of the specialised functions. The previous case describes a formal seed system that evolved through specialisation from farmers' seed systems where the farmers basically performed selection, production and exchange.

Formal systems in other regions have their roots in the emergence of scientific plant breeding in the public sector, which had to develop ways to get the new varieties to the farmers. Both plant breeding in the 19th century in the United States and the Green Revolution from the 1950s (see Pingali, Chapter 12 of this Handbook) are typical examples of this development of – largely public – formal seed systems. Formal seed chains are commonly public-private collaborations where education and fundamental research are organised primarily by the government, whereas seed multiplication and marketing are private. Whether plant breeding is done in the public or private domains depends on the history of seed sector development, on government policies and the type of crop (Louwaars and Burgaud, 2016). For example, plant breeding of most crops in the United States is still done by universities, whereas private investment goes mainly to a few commercial crops. In the Netherlands, only breeding of fruit trees and 'new crops' like quinoa or elephant grass is carried out at the public research institute Wageningen UR, whereas all other breeding is strictly private. In emerging countries, most of the breeding is public, supported by international institutes.

## Maintaining diversity in formal seed systems

Formal seed systems are commonly based on uniform varieties. The rationale is that breeders select the preferred combination of positive traits in a plant and maximise performance of the crop by multiplication of that genotype. The second argument for uniform crops is mechanisation: if all plants perform the same way, crop management – especially harvesting – is much easier. Possible risks of uniformity, such as susceptibility to diseases, may be tackled by stacking resistance genes or breeding for horizontal as opposed to vertical resistances. When leaf blight attacked almost all maize hybrids in the United States in the early 1970s, because they were all based on a particular parenthood, the breeding industry was able to come up with alternative hybrids within a very short time (Ullstrup, 1972).

Still, when the same uniform varieties are used over large areas, such as the famous IR8 rice, which was popular from Pakistan to Indonesia, challenges to sustainability are inevitable. Since formal seed systems are not by themselves ideally suited to maintain diversity in the field, mechanisms to overcome resultant failures at the level of plant breeding are important (see also **Box 34.1** *Breeding for varietal diversity in wheat*). Breeders have always been keen to collect diversity that they consider interesting and their working collections initially contained many existing varieties collected from the market and from other regions. Farmers' varieties became less and less interesting to formal breeders, as their genetic distance from advanced commercial materials became larger and more tedious to introgress into elite materials. There were however always

### Box 34.1 Breeding for varietal diversity in wheat

Several efforts have been made to actually breed for varietal diversity. A famous example is the wheat multi-line 'Tumult' which consisted of several near-isogenic lines, each with a different resistance gene to yellow rust. It has not been a success since the additional time required to develop this variety meant that the yield levels of the uniform varieties had bypassed Tumult already by the time of release and farmers did not adopt Tumult widely. Furthermore, additional costs in seed production contributed further to the lack of popularity (Groenewegen, 1977; Zeven and Waninge, 1985).

breeders who took the effort to use less related materials. An example is the small Dutch cereal breeding company Zelder that made – through the personal interest of its senior breeder L. Groenewegen in the 1980s – large numbers of wide crosses that their successors, Wiersum Plant Breeding, relies on today. With time, the term 'pre-breeding' was adopted to define the process of making distant materials suitable for use in plant breeding programmes, and is commonly considered a public task (Alston and Gray, 2013) even though companies may also consider it a strategic investment to create unique basic starting materials for their breeding programmes.

Next to the working collections, specialised genebanks were created following widespread concern at the loss of genetic resources when farmers who had hitherto planted local varieties adopted the modern uniform varieties developed by breeders instead (Damania, 2008). The collection, conservation, description and documentation of the crop diversity in genebanks have all become specialised roles while crop diversity has become fixed – or even frozen! – in genebanks (reviewed in Dulloo et al. and Vernooy et al., Chapters 36–37 of this Handbook, respectively). The evolution of collected materials can be halted at the genebank level, but it continues when the materials are used by (pre-) breeders. Promoting the use of materials through accurate description and documentation is therefore very important (van Hintum and Knüpfler, 2010; Endresen, Chapter 42 of this Handbook). Genebanks also need more secure long-term funding, need to be in a secure place and collections need to be duplicated. Concerns about this led to the development of the Global Crop Diversity Trust and the Global Seed Vault in permafrost conditions of Svalbard, Norway.

## *Creating and using diversity in formal seed systems*

Plant breeders use all the diversity that they can access and that they consider potentially useful for their various breeding goals. Breeders have to balance the cost in time and effort with the expected benefits when using particular materials in their programmes. Promoting the use of genebank materials thus involves proper description, which may involve research on particular traits that may be identified in the collection, and subsequent documentation in an accessible form (van Hintum et al., 2011). Such work is increasingly carried out via public-private partnerships. For example, vegetable breeding companies in the Netherlands support the national genebank in describing large numbers of genebank materials in their own premises.

Technological developments are important in promoting the use of genebank materials in breeding. Market assisted selection allows for an increasingly efficient backcrossing in order to transfer a trait into commercial materials. This saves both time and trial field space, and greatly supports diversity in plant breeding. However, a gradual change of focus is emerging in breeding.

Where crossing and selection have always been a black box, where next to the target traits a lot of other traits travelled along in crossing and selection programmes, the more and more precise breeding methods lead to less and less linkage drag (Peng et al., 2014). This contributes to the predictability of breeding, but at the same time reduces the chance of haphazard recombination, which might be – unexpectedly – positive.

In addition to this, Van de Wouw et al. (2013) showed that the diversity among new varieties of some crops in the Netherlands and France has actually been increasing since the 1990s, a trend that the researchers contribute to the more frequent use of genebank materials as a result of the advantages of molecular selection methods. Plant breeding, even though it is largely focussed on selection, can thus contribute to the enhancement of diversity in the field.

Whereas in farmers' seed systems enhancing diversity depends on sharing materials among communities, formal seed systems can facilitate much easier exchange of materials and introduce new diversity for farmers that can afford to purchase such seeds. The international research institutes of the CGIAR (Consultative Group on International Agricultural Research) exchange millions samples among dozens of countries every year, and commercial breeders do the same as part of their ongoing business. Enhancing diversity at the level of the crop is also common in formal plant breeding. Interspecific crosses may be possible, albeit often with considerable effort, introducing traits that hitherto were unknown in a crop. An example is clubroot resistance in cabbage, which required several bridges to be crossed between the various species in the *Brassica-Raphanus* complex of species (Chiang et al., 1980; Gowers, 1982). Genetic transformation is of course another way to bring traits into a crop from another species, increasing diversity within a crop. However, this is currently done in few crops and with few traits, given the cost of the technology and especially the extensive regulation procedures and public/societal resistance. Newer breeding methods provide yet additional ways to enhance diversity in a crop (Kumar and Jain, 2015; Sauer et al., 2016). Various targeted mutagenesis techniques are being developed that might create novel alleles of an existing trait much more efficiently than conventional mutation methods. These developments in the formal seed system provide exciting new opportunities from the viewpoint of crop diversity.

## Regulating seeds and its effects on diversity

The ability of seed systems to maintain, use and contribute to diversity is affected by national and international policy and regulatory frameworks, notably seed laws and laws that create rights over seeds, particularly intellectual property rights, rights derived from national sovereign rights to genetic resources and rights on traditional knowledge.

### *Seed laws*

Seed laws are regulating the formal seed systems. They intend to support agricultural production and protect farmers from using poor quality seed. They commonly regulate the identity, purity and quality of the seed in the market and regulate the release of varieties at least of certain major crops. There are some – often unintended – negative effects with regard to diversity, particularly when the seed laws are formulated in too broad terms. A common phrase is 'all seed has to be certified' (see examples in Louwaars, 2005). In order to guarantee the variety name on a seed bag, which is very important for farmers who buy seeds, the variety has to be described, and it has to be stable in its main characteristics over the years. Stability over years is best attained with uniformity, which is also the basis of the DUS-testing for the grant of plant breeders' rights (Van Wijk and Louwaars, 2014). It is guaranteed by a detailed description and a strict certification system that assures the identity throughout the multiplication system over all generations that it takes to produce marketable quantities from the small amounts of breeders' seed.

Genetically diverse varieties that evolve with time cannot fit in such regulated system with obligatory variety lists and certification systems. One solution is to make that voluntary, such as in the United States, where farmers can choose between certified seed with its official guarantees, and seed where the farmer has to trust the supplier. India has recently changed its seed laws from voluntary to obligatory seed quality controls to avoid misrepresentation. Realising that the seed laws may create a system that is too strict with regard to diversity, some countries have created openings in their laws for diverse varieties (Louwaars, 2005). The first is the concept of 'commercial seed' in certification schemes, where only the seed quality and not the varietal identity are guaranteed. This is particularly important in horticulture where the follow-up of new varieties is more dynamic than in field crops, and in situations of emergency seed provision, requiring quick bulking of locally-adapted seeds (Sperling and McGuire, 2010). The European Union has introduced the concept of 'conservation varieties' in order for traditional farmers' varieties to be allowed in the seed market. That rule does however not seem to have stimulated the creation of new, diverse varieties. The reason for this may be that it would also create opportunities for less scrupulous seed producers to sell sub-standard seed as a 'diverse variety'. In other countries, the local sales and exchange of seed is explicitly permitted. The national seed quality control agencies in some of these even support farmers' seed systems by offering seed testing facilities also to non-certified seeds so that at least germination and purity may be assured.

Strict variety release systems based on official grow-out tests for the value for cultivation and use (VCU) of new varieties can be very restrictive to the diversity in the seed market (Tripp, 1997). Few varieties are commonly released, and when the trials do not mimic farmers' conditions, potentially inappropriate varieties may be selected by the variety release committee; varieties with specific adaptations to a particular region may on the other hand be overlooked (Tripp and Louwaars, 1997). The formulation of seed laws should therefore carefully take into account the dual objectives of providing guarantees to farmers and creating a level playing field for seed producers, and of maintaining diversity in the field.

## *Intellectual property rights*

The second regulatory area is intellectual property laws. Plant breeders' rights and patents apply to well-described varieties and inventions, respectively. These rights are meant to support innovation by providing a temporary exclusive right on the commercialisation of the variety or invention. This means that in plant breeders' rights, varieties are tested for their distinctiveness, uniformity and stability. Since it promises advantages in commercial exploitation, intellectual property rights are clearly linked to the formal seed systems.

Intellectual property rights do not affect farmers' seed systems, except when the protected inventions enter these systems or when farmer-varieties fall within the scope of one or more claims of a patent. As indicated earlier, modern varieties are frequently reproduced and exchanged among farmers. This could impair the rights of the breeder. However, as intellectual property rights deal with commercial exploitation, plant breeders' rights allow for the private and non-commercial use of protected varieties. The International Union for the Protection of New Varieties of Plants (UPOV) published an interpretation in 2014 that this exemption also applies to the exchange of protected variety seeds of basic food crops among smallholder farmers (www.upov.int/about/en/faq.html#Q30). This means that the rights apply only to commercial farming. The situation with patents is slightly different when a patented trait enters the informal seed systems by natural cross-pollination. In most cases, this would lead to what is called innocent infringement on the right of the patent holder.

These intellectual property rights do not exclude farmers from applying for these rights if their varieties or inventions comply with the criteria for protection. In practice, however, this rarely happens, both because the development of new plants and varieties in farmers' seed systems is a collective effort, records are not kept about the details of such inventions and access to the complex and expensive protection procedures is absent in practice. Partly as a result of the spread of intellectual property rights, alternative rights have been created in international agreements on biodiversity, with the aim to balance rights: national sovereign rights over genetic resources established by the Convention on Biological Diversity (www.CBD.int) and farmers' rights, established in Article 9 of the International Treaty on Plant Genetic Resources for Food and Agriculture (ITPGRFA – www.planttreaty.org). (The broader impact of these frameworks are discussed in Engels and Rudebjer, Chapter 41 of this Handbook).

With regard to the use of genetic resources, there is a significant difference between plant breeders' rights and patents. The former has a 'breeders' exemption' which allows all breeders to freely use protected materials for further breeding. The patent system has a 'research exemption' which in most countries allows research done on the invention, but which does not allow the development of a new commercial product – a new variety – with the protected plant. This makes plant breeders' rights an open innovation system. In various countries, proposals are launched to introduce a breeder's exemption in patent law to correct this. Depending on the scope of such exemption, that could facilitate breeding for both the formal and farmers' seed systems through participatory breeding.

## *Biodiversity rights*

In 1992, the Convention on Biological Diversity introduced national sovereign rights over genetic resources. It obliges signatory countries to conserve and to promote sustainable use of the country's genetic resources. It also allows countries to make access to their genetic resources subject to prior informed consent and mutually agreed terms. It also includes an article, 8j, which suggests countries should provide certain rights to their local and indigenous communities.

In theory, these rules should not affect farmers' seed systems using their own genetic resources, but they can create restrictions for communities to access materials from other communities or from abroad. In such cases, the farmers concerned would have to negotiate access, which is likely to be alien to their normal management of plant materials. These rules do however affect formal seed systems. After the Convention on Biological Diversity came into force, the collection of genetic resources and the sharing among genebanks became much more complex. Recent implementation of the user-compliance rules in the Nagoya Protocol may severely restrict the use of genetic resources. Proposals in Europe are that detailed pedigree information has to be maintained in order for governments to check on adherence to prior informed consent and mutually agreed terms. That could be a challenge, especially for smaller breeders, but it would be totally impossible in PPB, which is by definition unable to trace the various components in the farmers' seed systems.

Mainly because of the shared view that access to plant genetic resources for food and agriculture (PGRFA) is necessary for global food security, debates in the 1990s resulted in the International Treaty on PGRFA, providing multilateral agreements for both access and benefit sharing for a list of major food and feed crops. This facilitates access to important genetic resources both for the formal and farmers' seed systems. The use of the Standard Material Transfer Agreement (SMTA) has reduced the need for negotiation for every transfer.

However, many genebank collections have not been introduced to the multilateral system, and the pledges to the multilateral benefit sharing fund has not yet met expectations. The Treaty also introduced the concept of Farmers' Rights based on the contributions that farmers have made on the development and maintenance of PGRFA. The concept provides for rights on traditional knowledge, to the sharing of benefits and to participate in policy making related to PGRFA. In addition, it provides for the right of farmers to save, use and exchange seeds, a right which is made 'subject to national law and as appropriate'. This clearly aims to protect farmers' seed systems but allows countries to limit those rights, for example through seed laws or intellectual property rights. India has done that by limiting sales to non-commercial types of seed, meaning sales from unlabelled bags in markets.

Whether the implementation of rights on traditional knowledge may limit the exchange of seeds among communities and with formal seed systems remains to be seen.

## Conclusions

Seeds are the carriers of crop genetic diversity. Seed systems provide the mechanisms for conservation, the use and distribution and the creation and loss of diversity. Various seed systems have emerged, broadly defined as formal and farmers' seed systems. Diversity can have an agronomic function, contributing to yield stability, and it has an important function to allow adaptation to changing conditions and needs through various types of breeding. Both contribute to the sustainability of agriculture. Farmers' seed systems are able to maintain diversity in farmers' fields as long as such diversity has a benefit for farmers. That function is under pressure in many areas when scientifically bred varieties become available for more particular areas, needs and farming systems. Modern varieties already form an important part of the seeds that are maintained and shared in farmers' seed systems. The advantage of on-farm management of genetic diversity is that it is dynamic; the disadvantage is that it cannot claim to conserve specific diversity, and the diversity is not readily available for breeders outside the community. Supporting the further development of local varieties and enrichment of the local gene pool through PPB requires a broad genetic resource base to be available without any restrictions. Farmers' seed systems create new diversity mainly through evolutionary processes: introgression and mutation, the former especially in the centres of diversity where the crop can cross with wild populations.

Formal seed systems create almost exclusively uniform varieties. They have been the cause of disappearance of many farmers' varieties, especially in benign ecologies, such as irrigated farming and large 'recommendation domains' (Perrin et al., 1976). Diversity is, however, present in terms of diversity among varieties, which tends to increase after the initial years of the Green Revolution, and diversity in time. Modern plant breeding methods are contributing to enhanced levels of use of more distant materials in breeding programmes, hence potentially broadening the genetic base for farmers. Formal seed systems contribute to diversity both by their ability to combine materials from widely different geographical areas, and through new breeding methods to actually create allelic diversity.

Formal and farmers' seed systems are differentially affected by different regulatory frameworks. Implementing such frameworks should take into account genetic resource management and the differences between the needs of different seed systems in addition to their primary objectives such as farmer protection (seed laws), innovation (intellectual property rights) and national sovereignty (biodiversity laws). The seed system perspective provides a useful framework for such analysis.

## References


Almekinders, C. J. M. (2000) *The Importance of Informal Seed Sector and Its Relation with the Legislative Framework*. Paper presented at GTZ-Eschborn, July 4–5, 2000, http://citeseerx.ist.psu.edu/viewdoc/download?doi=10.1.1.195.468&rep=rep1&type=pdf, accessed September 2015.

Almekinders, C. J. M. and Hardon, J. (eds.) (2006) *Bringing Farmers Back into Breeding. Experiences with Participatory Plant Breeding and Challenges for Institutionalisation*, Agromisa Special 5, Agromisa, Wageningen, The Netherlands.

Almekinders, C. J. M., Louwaars, N. P. and de Bruijn, G. H. (1994) 'Local seed systems and their importance for improved seed supply in developing countries', *Euphytica*, vol. 78, pp. 207–216.

Alston, J. M. and Gray, R. S. (2013) 'Wheat research funding in Australia: The rise of public – private – producer partnerships', *EuroChoices Special Issue: Innovation in Agri-food*, vol. 12, pp. 30–35.

Berg, T. and Abay, F. (2008) 'Community seed banks: Experiences from Tigray in Ethiopia', pp. 100–103 in M. H. Thijssen, Z. Bishaw, A. Beshir and W. S. de Boef (eds.), *Farmers' Seeds and Varieties: Supporting Informal Seed Supply in Ethiopia*, Wageningen International, Wageningen, the Netherlands.

Bishaw, Z. and Turner, M. (2008) 'Linking participatory plant breeding to the seed supply system', *Euphytica*, vol. 163, pp. 31–44.

Ceccarelli, S., Guimarães, E. P. and Weltizien, E. (eds.) (2009) *Plant Breedingand Farmer Participation*, Food and Agriculture Organization of the United Nations (FAO), Rome, Italy.

Chiang, B., Chiang, M., Grant, W. and Crete, R. (1980) 'Transfer of resistance to race 2 of *Plasmodiophora brassicae* from *Brassica napus* to cabbage (*B. oleracea* spp. *capitata*). IV. A resistant 18-chromosome B 1 plant and its B 2 progenies', *Euphytica*, vol. 29, pp. 47–55.

Coomes, O., Mcguire, S., Garine, E., Caillon, S., Mckey, D., Demeulenaere, E., Jarvis, D., Aistara, G., Barnaud, A., Clouvel, P., Emperaire, L., Louafi, S., Martin, P., Massol, F., Pautasso, M., Violon, C. and Wencélius, J. (2015) 'Farmer seed networks make a limited contribution to agriculture? Four common misconceptions', *Food Policy*, vol. 56, p. 41.

Coulibaly, H., Bazile, D. and Sidibé, A. (2014) 'Modelling seed system networks in Mali to improve farmers seed supply', *Sustainable Agriculture Research*, vol. 3, pp. 18–32.

Damania, A. B. (2008) 'History, achievements, and current status of genetic resources conservation', *Agronomy Journal*, vol. 100, pp. 9–21.

de Boef, W. S., Subedi, A., Peroni, N., Thijssen, M. and O'Keeffe, E. (2013) *Community Biodiversity Management: Promoting Resilience and the Conservation of Plant Genetic Resources*, Issues in Agricultural Biodiversity Series, Bioversity International, Maccarese, Italy.

Ferguson, M. E., Jones, R. B., Bramel, P. J., Domínguez, C., Torre Do Vale, C. and Han, J. (2012) 'Post-flooding disaster crop diversity recovery: A case study of cowpea in Mozambique', *Disasters*, vol. 36, pp. 83–100.

Gaudin, A. C. M., Tolhurst, T. N., Ker, A. P., Janovicek, K., Tortora, C. and Martin, R. C. (2015) 'Increasing crop diversity mitigates weather variations and improves yield stability', *PLoS One*, vol. 10, p. e0113261.

Gowers, S. (1982) 'The transfer of characters from *Brassica campestris* L. to *Brassica napus* L.: Production of clubroot-resistant oil-seed rape (*B. napus* ssp *oleifera*)', *Euphytica*, vol. 31, pp. 971–976.

Groenewegen, L. J. M. (1977) 'Multilines as a tool in breeding for reliable yields', *Cereal Research Communications*, vol. 5, pp. 12–132.

Hodgekin, T., Rana, R., Tuxill, J., Balma, D., Subedi, A., Mar, I., Karamura, D., Valdivia, R., Collando, L., Latournerie, L., Sadiki, M., Sawandogo, M., Brown, A. H. D. and Jarvis, D. J. (2007) 'Seed systems and crop genetic diversity in agroecosystems', pp. 77–116 in D. I. Jarvis, C. Padoch and H. D. Cooper (eds.), *Managing Biodiversity in Agricultural Ecosystems*, Columbia University Press, New York, NY, USA.

Jiggins, J. and de Zeeuw, H. (1992) 'Participatory technology development in practice: Processes and methods', pp. 135–162 in C. Reijntjes, B. Haverkort and A. Waters-Bayer (eds.), *Farming for the Future*, Macmillan, London, UK.

Koonin, E. V. (2009) 'Evolution of genome architecture', *International Journal of Biochemistry and Cell Biology*, vol. 41, pp. 298–306.

Kumar, V. and Jain, M. (2015) 'The CRISPR – Cas system for plant genome editing: Advances and opportunities', *Journal of Experimental Botany*, vol. 66, pp. 47–57.

Lipper, L., Cavatassi, R. and Winters, P. (2012) 'Seed supply in local markets: Supporting sustainable use of crop genetic resources', *Environment and Development Economics*, vol. 17, pp. 507–521.

Louwaars, N. P. (1994) 'Integrated seed supply: Institutional linkages in relation to system efficiency, biodiversity and gender', pp. 7–15 in S. David (ed.), *Alternative Approaches to Bean Seed Production and*

*Distribution in Eastern and Southern Africa: Proceedings of a Working Group Meeting, Kampala, Uganda, 10–13 October 1994*, Network on Bean Research in Africa, Workshop Series No. 32, CIAT, Kampala, Uganda.

Louwaars, N. P. (2005) 'Seed laws: Biases and bottlenecks', *Seedling*, p. e437, GRAIN, www.grain.org/seedling_files/seed-05-07-2.pdf

Louwaars, N. P. and Burgaud, F. (2016) 'Variety registration: The evolution of registration systems with a special emphasis on agrobiodiversity conservation', pp. 184–211 in M. Halewood (ed.), *Farmers' Crop Varieties and Farmers' Rights – Challenges in Taxonomy and Law*, Earthscan, London, UK.

Louwaars, N. P. and de Boef, W. S. (2012) 'Integrated seed sector development in Africa: A conceptual framework for creating coherence between practices, programs and policies', *International Journal for Crop Improvement*, vol. 26, pp. 29–59.

Louwaars, N. P., de Boef, W. S. and Edeme, J. (2013) 'Integrated seed sector development: A basis for seed policy and law', *Journal for Crop Improvement*, vol. 27, pp. 186–214.

McGuire, S. and Sperling, L. (2016) 'Seed systems smallholder farmers use', *Food Security*, vol. 8, pp. 179–195.

Mickelbart, M. V., Hasegawa, H. M. and Bailey-Serres, J. (2015) 'Genetic mechanisms of abiotic stress tolerance that translate to crop yield stability', *Nature Reviews Genetics*, vol. 16, pp. 237–251.

Pautasso, M. (2014) 'Network simulations to study seed exchange for agrobiodiversity conservation', *Agronomy for Sustainable Development*, vol. 35, pp. 145–150.

Peng, T., Sun, X. and Mumm, R. (2014) 'Optimized breeding strategies for multiple trait integration: I. Minimizing linkage drag in single event introgression', *Molecular Breeding*, vol. 33, pp. 89–104.

Perrin, R., Winkelmann, D., Moscardi, E. and Anderson, J. (1976) *From Agronomic Data to Farmer Recommendations, and Economics Training Manual*, CIMMYT, Mexico DF, Mexico.

Sauer, N. J., Mozoruk, J., Miller, R. B., Warburg, Z. J., Walker, K. A., Beetham, P. R., Schöpke, C. R. and Gocal, G. F. W. (2016) 'Oligonucleotide-directed mutagenesis for precision gene editing', *Plant Biotechnology Journal*, vol. 14, pp. 496–502.

Sperling, L. and McGuire, S. (2010) 'Persistent myths about emergency seed aid', *Food Policy*, vol. 3, pp. 195–201.

Sperling, L. and Scheidegger, U. (1995) *Participatory Selection of Beans in Rwanda: Results, Methods and Institutional Issues*, Gatekeeper Series No 51. IIED, London, UK, http://pubs.iied.org/pdfs/6065IIED.pdf

Sthapit, B., Rana, R., Eyzaguirre, P. and Jarvis, D. (2008) 'The value of plant genetic diversity to resource-poor farmers in Nepal and Vietnam', *International Journal of Agricultural Sustainability*, vol. 6, pp. 148–166.

Tripp, R. (ed.) (1997) *New Seed and Old Laws: Regulatory Reform and the Diversification of National Seed Systems*, Intermediate Technology Publications, London, UK.

Tripp, R. and Louwaars, N. P. (1997) 'The conduct and reform of crop variety regulation', pp. 88–120 in R. Tripp (ed.), *New Seed and Old Laws: Regulatory Reform and the Diversification of National Seed Systems*, Intermediate Technology Publications, London, UK.

Ullstrup, A. J. (1972) 'The impacts of the southern corn leaf blight epidemics of 1970–1971', *Annual Review of Phytopathology*, vol. 101, pp. 37–50.

Van de Wouw, M., Van Treuren, R. and Van Hintum, T. (2013) 'A historical analysis of diversity trends in French and Dutch lettuce cultivars', *Euphytica*, vol. 190, pp. 229–239.

Van Hintum, T. and Knüpfler, H. (2010) 'Current taxonomic composition of European genebank material documented in EURISCO', *Plant Genetic Resources*, vol. 8, pp. 182–188.

Van Hintum, T., Menting, F. and Van Strien, E. (2011) 'Quality indicators for passport data in ex situ genebanks', *Plant Genetic Resources*, vol. 9, pp. 478–485.

Van Wijk, A. J. P. and Louwaars, N. P. (2014) *Framework for the Introduction of Plant Breeder's Rights: Guidance for Practical Implementation*, Roelofarendsveen, Naktuinbouw, The Netherlands, ISBN 978-90-815169-0-7

Vernooy, R., Sthapit, B., Galluzzi, G. and Shrestha, P. (2014) 'The multiple functions and services of community seedbanks', *Resources*, vol. 3, pp. 636–656.

Zeven, A. C. and Waninge, J. (1985) 'The yielding capacity of the winter wheat multiline Tunult, its components and recurrent parent Tadorna', *Cereal Research Communications*, vol. 13, pp. 85–87.

# PART 6

# Safeguarding agricultural biodiversity

# 35

# UNCOVERING THE ROLE OF CUSTODIAN FARMERS IN THE ON-FARM CONSERVATION OF AGRICULTURAL BIODIVERSITY

*Bhuwon Sthapit, Ramanatha V. Rao, Hugo Lamers and Sajal Sthapit*

## Context

On-farm management of agricultural biodiversity is a complementary strategy to *ex situ* conservation of genetic resources in genebanks. It is especially important for two roles: (1) the conservation of species whose seed cannot be maintained in genebanks (such as fruit tree species with recalcitrant seeds); and (2) the continuation of the evolutionary processes affecting local crop diversity through natural and human selection, which is essential for building local adaptation and resilience into production systems. Furthermore, on-farm management maintains associated traditional knowledge and practices which contribute to the appreciation of crop genetic diversity, and to its cultivation and use in ways that can be transmitted by farmers to future generations. Agricultural biodiversity contributes to reducing malnutrition and hidden hunger, alleviating poverty and combating climate change challenges, but this diversity is in danger of disappearing. The global economy's heavy reliance on small numbers of crop species, and to the narrow genetic diversity of these, puts future food and nutrition security at risk. While on-farm approaches can be appropriate for the conservation of many forms of agricultural biodiversity (livestock, pollinator, soil microfauna) our discussion in this chapter will focus around the conservation of plant genetic resource diversity.

While there is growing consensus that agricultural biodiversity is being lost from production systems around the world, estimates of the extent of this loss remain crude. Often the simplest and most accessible measure is the change in the number of landraces and varieties that has occurred over time. Yet the number of landraces and varieties is only a reliable proxy for allelic or phenotypic diversity in some cases (Sadiki et al., 2007). We do know for a fact that at least the number of landraces and varieties being grown by farmers is declining across the world (e.g. Hammer et al., 1996; Chaudhary et al., 2004; Hammer and Laghetti, 2005; FAO, 2010). Even if the number of landraces and varieties are a good proxy for genetic diversity in just a fraction of crops and system, the ubiquity of declines in varietal richness is a reliable indicator that agricultural biodiversity is being threatened.

Despite the advances of modern plant breeding and molecular techniques, most of the crop varieties planted in developing countries are the products of farmers' selection and innovation

(Zeven, 1998; Thiele, 1999; Tripp, 2001). At the same time as this important resource is vanishing, there are some farmers who continue to actively maintain and employ agricultural biodiversity on their farms, and who possess specialized knowledge about its use and cultivation. This is particularly true with regards to neglected and underutilized crops, and to perennial fruit trees. We recognize them as the 'custodian farmers' of diverse crop species and varieties (Sthapit et al., 2013a). Their role has been systematically researched only in recent years. In this chapter we discuss who custodian farmers are, how to recognize them and how to strengthen their many potential roles in on-farm conservation and continued evolution of agricultural biodiversity.

## Definition

Not all farmers are equally involved in the conservation of agricultural biodiversity, and nor should that be the goal of on-farm conservation programs. While all farmers are users of agricultural biodiversity, only a few of them play prominent and active roles in the different tasks and roles related to the availability and conservation of diverse genetic resources of agricultural crops. The term 'custodian' literally means a guardian, caretaker, protector or warden. A custodian is usually defined as someone who is responsible for looking after something important or valuable. Custodian farmers are defined herein as men and women farmers who actively maintain, adapt and disseminate agricultural biodiversity and related knowledge over time and space at farm and community levels and are recognized by their community members for their efforts (Sthapit et al., 2013a). They are the champions of *in situ* and on-farm conservation of agricultural biodiversity. Custodian farmers are often actively supported in their efforts by household members and family traditions. Although concept such as 'leader farmer', 'progressive farmer', 'farmer researcher' and 'nodal farmer' have been around for decades (Collins, 1914; Boster, 1985; Nabhan, 1989; Juma, 1989; Brush, 1991; van der Heide et al., 1996), custodian farmers seem to have been largely neglected by science and policymakers until recent years, when a number of researchers have begun to pay more attention and tribute to them (Negri, 2003; Gruberg et al., 2013; Sthapit et al., 2013a, 2015b). In the book *The Custodians of Biodiversity*, Ruiz and Vernooy (2012) refer to the inclusive category of farmers as custodians of biodiversity recognizing their role in passing on and utilizing the traditional knowledge associated with agrobiodiversity. They lament that policy debates have not adequately involved farmers in the formulation of policies related to access to and benefit sharing. However, the custodian farmers we refer to here are a quite specific group composing the small number of farmers who are uncommonly motivated in maintaining diversity in their farms and communities.

## The characteristics of custodian farmers

Both the term and concept of 'custodian farmer' are relatively new in the field of *in situ* and on-farm conservation of agricultural biodiversity (Negri, 2003). Subedi et al. (2003) originally called them 'nodal farmers' in their studies of social seed networks. These individuals, who play a significant role in the flow of genetic materials and crop genetic diversity, tend to be educated, have both farming and off-farm employment opportunities and greater socio-economic status. Paudel et al. (2015) identified key network members, constituted either as nodal farmer or bridging (connector) farmers, occupying a central position in the network, who promote seed flow of local crop diversity, thus strengthening crop genetic resources on farm. They also found that the nodal farmers in a network may change from year to year, and that new nodal farmers may also appear. This fluctuating characteristic of nodal farmers makes it difficult to use the concept for targeting farmers for conservation activities. The term custodian farmer could be seen as an elaboration of the term nodal farmer by taking into account additional roles and functions besides the physical role of being a nodal point in seed exchange. Custodian farmers tend to be more stable in their existence in the network over a period of time and space as one of their roles is to safeguard and provide continuity of specific varieties, seeds or planting materials for the next generation. They are thus more conservation-oriented individuals (Sthapit et al., 2015a) who are interested in the genetic diversity of clonally propagated crops, perennial fruit trees or livestock breeds.

The general characteristics of custodian farmers are as follows:

- Driven by conservation ideology (out of interest or concern);
- Knowledge holder on agricultural biodiversity (ability to distinguish high value, rare and unique traits);
- Recognized by the community as source of interesting genetic resources and knowledge;
- Highly motivated and self-directed; and
- Consistent commitment.

A custodian farmer should not be seen as the antagonist of a progressive, innovative or entrepreneurial farmer; concepts which have been widely used and discussed in agricultural literature (Röling, 1988; McElwee, 2006; Díaz-Pichardo et al., 2012). Case studies in India, Indonesia, Malaysia and Thailand (Sthapit et al., 2013a), in Bolivia (Gruberg et al., 2013) and in Nepal (Sthapit et al., 2015b) suggest that custodian farmers may not be progressive or innovative farmers in the context of modern agriculture, but they are an important component of rural agricultural development and typically command the respect of people in the region for their role in the informal seed system and the conservation of genetic resources. Custodian farmers can often be classified as progressive and innovative farmers, but they applied the new practices, knowledge or entrepreneurial skill sets associated with progressive or innovative farmers within a traditional crop or farm system. Additionally, recent studies by Gajanana et al. (2015) and Lamers et al. (2015) have reported that it is not only economic factors that motivate farmers to conserve crop diversity but also that personal, ecological, social and cultural/religious factors influence their choices of what to conserve and experiment with. Interest in specific biological traits and uniqueness of varieties also play an important role in decision making by the custodian farmer.

## Functions

Based on case studies from several countries, custodian farmers have been identified as falling into one of four broad types based on a combination of three main functions (see **Figure 35.1** *Typology of custodian farmers*):

1. Farmers who *maintain* a rich and unique portfolio of species and varieties;
2. Farmers who *maintain* and *promote* a portfolio of species and varieties;
3. Farmers who *maintain* and *adapt* a portfolio of species and varieties; and
4. Farmers who actively *maintain*, *adapt* and *promote* their portfolio of species and varieties.

'Maintain' refers to the number of species or varieties a custodian farmer has. 'Promote' refers to the sharing of material (seeds, saplings) and related knowledge about specific crops, varieties and traits. 'Adapt' refers to simple selection, breeding involving crossing or experiments such as trait identification or adaptation to local or particular conditions. Discussions and case studies suggest that the boundaries distinguishing the different types of custodian farmer may be blurred or difficult to determine as they depend on factors such as crop type, local culture, exposure to

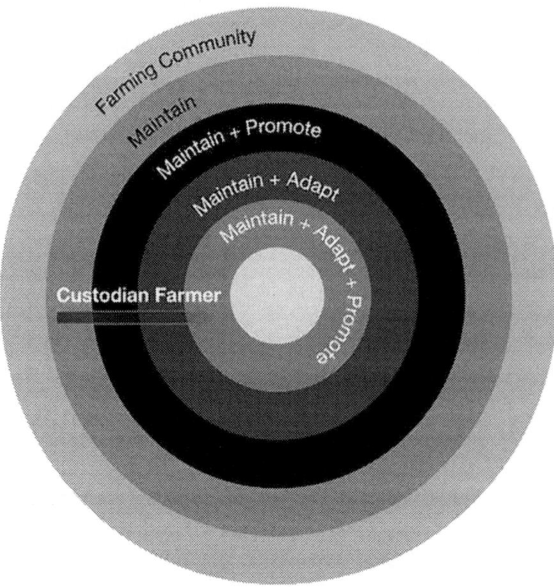


*Figure 35.1* Typology of custodian farmers (Sthapit et al., 2013a)

*Note*: The arrow illustrates that, with increased awareness and capability, custodian farmers are able to take on additional functions, which make them increasingly proactive agents of change for on-farm conservation of agricultural biodiversity.

new knowledge and settings and environmental conditions. Therefore, the purpose of this categorization is simply to shed light on the diversity of custodian farmer types one may expect to encounter in the field based on the key functions they perform. The role of custodian farmer is dynamic; as farmers acquire more knowledge, skills, social connections and recognition, they may choose to take on more functions and may assume a leadership role in the community or village.

## Methodology: how to identify custodian farmers

The method of identification of custodian farmers are evolving and new perspectives are emerging. Two major workshops were held in February and July/August 2013, respectively, and the case studies conducted by Gruberg et al. (2013) helped to establish a common understanding about the best methods and approach to be used to identify a custodian farmer. One workshop was held in the context of a project on tropical fruit tree diversity[1] and the second in the context of neglected and underutilized crops[2] which both had the goals of developing a methodology of documenting custodian farmers, understanding of characteristics and motivations of custodian farmers and exploring policy options to consolidate roles of such farmers in *in situ* and on-farm conservation of agricultural biodiversity.

The workshop held in February 2013 entitled 'Custodian farmers of agricultural biodiversity: policy support for their roles in use and conservation' was organized to bring together global experts on agricultural biodiversity conservation and 20 custodian farmers from South and Southeast Asia to share expertise and experiences. The key steps used to identify custodian farmers are illustrated **Figure 35.2** *Key steps to identify custodian farmers.* A checklist was used in steps 2 to 4 to help practitioners to identify and document such custodian farmers in a systematic

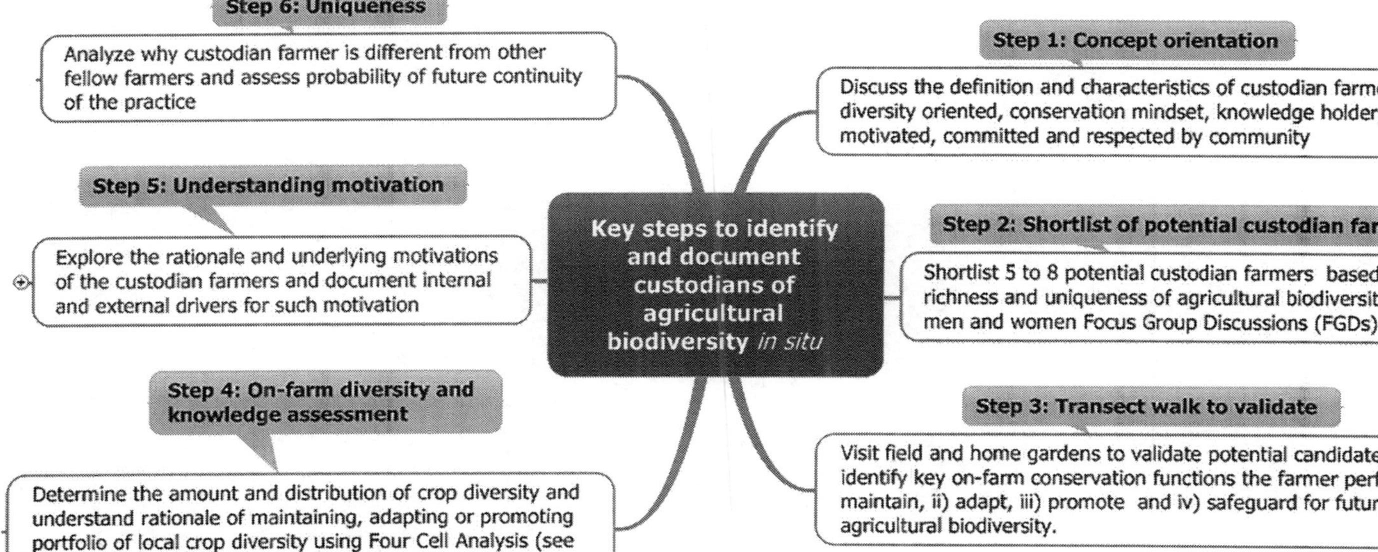


*Figure 35.2* Key steps to identify custodian farmers

*Table 35.1* Key checklist questions to identify custodian farmers of on-farm conservation of agricultural biodiversity

| *Functions* | *Key questions/checklist* |
|---|---|
| Context | What is the agroecosystem of the subject?<br>Note characteristics of household, farm, forestry and landscapes, livelihood activities |
| Maintain | Which crops and landraces are maintained by the farmer? How many crops/landraces are maintained?<br>Do they maintain specific crop or varieties for specific/unique trait? |
| Adapt | Does the farmer only grow or also try to improve, evaluate the species/varieties grown and/or select particular seeds? If yes, which species/varieties, and how these are done? |
| Promote | Do they share seeds and knowledge – which and how?<br>Do they share with just relatives and neighbours or common people? |
| Continuation | How will unique crops and trees continue to grow in the future?<br>What efforts have they made to transfer knowledge and practices? |
| Motivations | Anecdotal stories showcasing why they maintain |
| Unique features | Why is this custodian special or different from the others? |
| Support | What kinds of support is received from external agencies?<br>What are drivers of such practice? |

manner (**Table 35.1** *Key checklist questions to identify custodian farmers of on-farm conservation of agricultural biodiversity*). As part of the workshop, 20 case studies of farmers in India, Indonesia, Malaysia, Thailand and Nepal were collected and described to understand what motivates custodian farmers to conserve, innovate and disseminate tropical fruit tree diversity, find ways to formally recognize such farmers and create mechanisms to support and expand their role in the management of local crop biodiversity *in situ* and on farm. In our first attempts to identify custodian farmers, we found that the concept was not always obvious to villagers, researchers or genetic resource specialists in on-farm conservation. Often it was confused with the more widely known terms such as 'progressive farmer', 'innovative farmer' or 'leader farmer'. There was a tendency to identify a village leader or progressive farmer who uses modern varieties and technologies, or to pinpoint a wealthier largeholder farmer with strong institutional connections rather than identifying custodian farmers on the basis of their key functions, such as maintenance, selection and promotion of local crop diversity. After gaining in-depth knowledge of such custodian farmers, we found that they have rich traditional knowledge, seek diverse sources of knowledge and skills from various sources and have capacity to innovate in their own context. These farmers are often well connected with formal and informal institutions as sources of information and materials. Interviewing these farmers and understanding their practices helped us identify certain practices closely associated with on-farm conservation which were defined as good practices for diversity (GPDs) management and use.

The second workshop held in Pokhara, Nepal, from 31 July to 2 August 2013 focused particularly on the link between custodian farmers and seed exchange systems for traditional crops. Sthapit et al. (2015b) were interested in why some farmers were keen to grow, select and save seeds of a number of crops and varieties, whereas other farmers were either uninterested or opted to engage in specialized commercial farming using a limited number of varieties. A key lesson was that specialized commercial farmers and custodian farmers are not mutually exclusive or antagonistic concepts. In fact, custodian farmers are also involved in progressive commercial farming and there can be a positive synergy between the two. The in-depth knowledge of the genetic resources they have can be applied to the benefit of the commercial farming they are doing and also tap into niche markets for their varieties. On the other hand, the income from commercial farming can help them financially sustain their custodian roles. After some local preparation workshops and the larger regional meeting in Pokhara, several of the identified participating custodian farmers have shown a more active and confident role. A short video documentary on the custodian farmers in Nepal (https://www.youtube.com/watch?v=-pDVJMmQIAk) was also developed and in the process the important role played by the wives of the presumed male custodian farmers was also recognized. Hence, the concepts of 'custodian couples' or even 'custodian families' were proposed by participants. These individuals have increasingly started to expedite the exchange of germplasm and knowledge among fellow farmers and also to experiment with newer seed material. We observed active communication and seed-sharing actions when a participatory seed exchange and learning process was facilitated for a whole morning during the custodian farmer workshop held in Nepal (Sthapit et al., 2015b).

One can define the method for identifying custodian farmers which was adopted after both workshops and the case studies in Bolivia reported by Gruberg et al. (2013) as a 'positive deviant' approach[3] exploring why some farmers in similar contexts were able to maintain rich biodiversity with better management and production practices, whereas other neighbouring farmers were not. This led us to identification of custodian households as positive deviants. Custodians of on-farm conservation are those farmers who, for various reasons, can be distinguished from others by their contribution to conserving and promoting crop genetic diversity. This concept of positive deviance applies especially when employing steps 4 to 6 (**Figure 35.2**) with the purpose of triangulation of information.

## How to strengthen the roles of custodian farmers

Recently a few countries such as India, Indonesia and Nepal have recognized custodian farmers by facilitating awards for outstanding custodians. For example, in India, the Protection of Plant Varieties and Farmers' Rights Act (PPV & FRA) issues a Plant Genome Saviour award for outstanding farmers (since 2012) and farming communities (since 2008) who safeguard plant genetic resources (see http://plantauthority.gov.in/PGSFR.htm). Efforts to conceptualize custodian farmers involved in on-farm conservation of tropical fruit tree diversity were initiated in India, Indonesia, Malaysia, Nepal and Thailand as reported by Sthapit et al. (2013b). Currently there is an increasing trend of documenting custodians of agricultural biodiversity in several countries, including in Bolivia (Gruberg et al., 2013), India (Bernhart, 2015) and Nepal (Sthapit et al., 2015a). Our work indicates that custodian farmers can be created if information on agrobiodiversity conservation, principles of plant breeding, varietal development, seed production, forums for interaction with other like-minded farmers and so forth are provided.

The concept is evolving, and academic research has been initiated (Bernhart, 2015). In India, ICAR Government of India has mainstreamed custodian farmers as an entry point for implementing on-farm and *in situ* conservation of agricultural biodiversity. They decided to identify and organize custodian farmer workshops in four geographic regions in India. Although the concept of custodian farmers and methods to identify are not adequately documented, **Table 35.1** provides a checklist of key questions and steps for identification of custodian farmers are illustrated in **Figure 35.2**. The results of identified custodian farmers that support the process of evolutionary on-farm conservation of agricultural biodiversity are summarized in **Table 35.2** *Comparative characteristics of custodian farmers reported from six countries*. The challenge is finding ways to consolidate roles of such farmers in on-farm conservation efforts at the large scale.

*Table 35.2* Comparative characteristics of custodian farmers reported from six countries

| *Country* | *Custodian farmer* | *Crop diversity* | *Why she or he is different?* | *Reference* |
|---|---|---|---|---|
| Bolivia | Doña Viviana Herrera (woman) | 120 crop species including 90 potatoes, 12 quinoa, 12 beans, two canahua, two oats, and two wheat varieties | She is a single mother in her 40s from La Paz and has shown natural leadership in collecting and safeguarding 105 unique potato varieties but also continuing to maintain 30 varieties inherited from her grandfather. | Gruberg et al. (2013) |
| India | Datatreya Hedge (man) | 52 mango varieties including appemedi types and four varieties of *Garcinia indica* | His main source of livelihood is from commercial orchards of arecanut, banana, cardamom and pepper, but he has a passion for local mango diversity. He has a multi-species orchard in Sirsi, Western Ghat, India, and is the custodian of 12 unique appemedi mangoes and one rare, pale yellow Kokum which is considered to have ayurveda medicinal value. | Sthapit et al. (2013b) |
| Indonesia | Ahmad Kusasi (man) | Six species of mango species including Rawa-rawa and Kuini as unique species, rice and rubber crops | He lives in Telaga Langsat of South Kalimantan and is custodian of six species of mango: *M. casturi, griffithii, odorata, applanata, foetida* and *indica.* He domesticated Tandui, a mango relative from the forest as the root and bark are used for medicinal purpose in the treatment of diabetes. | Sthapit et al. (2013b) |
| Malaysia | Palin Along (man) | 16 species of tropical fruits and two varieties of Aroi-aroi *(G. forbesii)* | He is a full time farmer with five children in mixed home gardens and rice farm in Papar, Sabah. His aroi-aroi variety has thick skin and is valued for its medical properties. | Sthapit et al. (2013b) |
| Nepal | Til Bahadur Rawal (man) | 70 varieties of 30 species of cereals, fruits, vegetables, legumes, oilseeds and medicinal plants | He is a curious, diversity minded and conservation oriented farmer from Talium, Jumla, who is custodian of 20 bean varieties, developed own red rice from natural Jumli Marsi population and has own household seed bank for safeguarding local seed. | Sthapit et al. (2015a) |
| Thailand | Suradech Tapuan (man) | 21 mango varieties including four wild relatives | He lives in Chiang Mai and is the custodian of unique mango varieties but also a champion of side grafting techniques suitable for rainfed conditions. He serves as a local resource person to other farmers. | Sthapit et al. (2013b) |

## Potential roles of custodian farmers

A major area of future research should focus on how to strengthen the role of custodian farmers in the conservation domain and as part of the wider agriculture and food sector. In this chapter, we will provide with the major roles that custodian farmers often have within their farming communities with suggestions which skills that are associated with these roles could be strengthened.

### *Conserver*

By definition, custodian farmers tend to maintain a number of crop species and varieties, rich in diversity, compared with fellow farmers in the same community. They also maintain very rare and unique type of crops and varieties to showcase their pride and hobby. Sthapit et al. (2015b) reported that custodian farmers are often active members of community seedbanks or are involved in other local efforts to conserve agricultural biodiversity (see also Vernooy et al., Chapter 37 of this Handbook). Local conservation efforts can be greatly boosted by identifying custodian farmers and observing their methods of engagement with the wider community. How best to do this remains a challenge; a sound method is still under development. Understanding the motivation of such farmers and promoting a network of such custodians will assist development of a conservation strategy. Sripinta et al. (2016) and Vasudeva et al. (2016) cited some examples of grafting techniques that support conservation efforts.

### *Farmer breeder and innovator*

We observed that most custodian farmers have special appreciation of genetic diversity and have the ability to identify specific traits and carry out selection of specific materials for future cultivation. With better exposure of custodian farmers to breeding skills and knowledge, these farmers could play a key role in participatory plant breeding and in strengthening local seed systems. This enhanced knowledge enables farmers to produce, select, save and acquire farmer-preferred quality seeds or planting materials. There will never be enough trained plant breeders and public sector resources to carry out plant breeding in all neglected and underutilized crops, vegetable, fruits and fodder trees. In such a context and to meet the new demands created by climate change for new and adapted crops and varieties, the roles of custodian farmers as innovator and promoter of agrobiodiversity should be systematically identified and understood. Their plant breeding skills and knowledge of how to distinguish high value traits, along with their leadership qualities, should be used to strengthen local seed systems and secure local food security. Instead of relying on the few trained professionals from the formal sector to develop solutions, we should empower farmers with key principles, examples and networks to then explore on their own and devise customized solutions. In developing countries like Nepal, farmers have limited literacy and even more limited access to knowledge resources. Hence, the catalytic effect that knowledge and information could have to allow them to transform their own lives is lacking.

### *As a focus for local resources*

Farmers have imperfect access to information[4] about varieties and genetic diversity. Access to unique and locally adapted traditional local varieties is often poor within the community, even when a sufficient quantity of seed is available (Badstue, 2006), because of poor access to information (Tripp, 2001), weak social networks (Subedi et al., 2003), social exclusion (Sthapit and Joshi, 1996) and weak institutional mechanisms (Shrestha et al., 2012). Traditionally custodian farmers play the role of providers of information about local crop diversity at the community level. With increased social connection with research, NGO and extension agencies and enhanced capacity building on principles of plant breeding and seed selection by these custodian farmers, they can play a greater role as local resource people. Sthapit (2013a) and Sthapit et al. (2015b) documented some such custodian farmers.

### *Roles as agents of change and in farmer-to-farmer extension*

One potential role of custodian farmer could be as change agents within the community once the government agencies or projects start to recognize him or her publicly. This has happened in Bolivia (e.g. Doña Viviana Herrera), India (e.g. Hedge), Indonesia (e.g. Ahmad Kusasi), Thailand (e.g. Suradech Tapuan) and Nepal (e.g. Til Bahadur Rawal) in a short period of time (Gruberg et al., 2013; Sthapit et al., 2015b; summarized in **Table 35.2**). Such change agents could play an important role in developing teams of local leaders to mobilize social capital and bring about behavioural change. Such agents can play key roles in establishing legitimate governing structures and mechanisms for seed production and distribution. Exchange visits by such custodian farmers between communities and countries can also inspire spontaneous sharing, learning and exchange of knowledge, practices and germplasm. We also found that these farmers assist in farmer-to-farmer extension of knowledge and technologies in very simple and practical ways.

### *Roles as local seed suppliers*

Despite all past public and private efforts in seed sector development, informal seed systems continue to dominate in most developing countries, supplying more than 90% of the total seed used by farmers, which include farmer-saved seed, farmer-to-farmer exchange, community-based seed systems and informal grain (seed) markets (Tripp, 2001; GIZ, 2014; McGuire and Sperling, 2016). Seed is usually saved by farmers from their own harvest or obtained from their social networks of family, friends or neighbours. McGuire and Sperling (2016), using comprehensive datasets of 9,660 households across six countries and covering 40 crops, showed that farmers access 90% of their seed from informal seed systems with 51% of that deriving from local markets. Traditional varieties dominate (over 95%) the farming system, and most farmers obtain traditional and underutilized crops locally, because they trust the people they get seed from and obtaining the seed is a simple, low-cost transaction (Lipper et al., 2009). Custodian farmers have been found to be main sources and seed suppliers of local crop diversity and, therefore, contribute to local food security and livelihood.

### *Shared custodianship and networking*

There is a physical limit to how an individual custodian farmer can maintain diversity and share seed, which is dependent upon their landholding and the resource base of the family. Greater amounts of crop diversity are maintained at the community level than by a single household through the actions of different farmers maintaining different varieties (Dyer and Taylor, 2008). Farmers also rely on one another for seed (germplasm) exchange, through which the most adapted varieties migrate (seed flow), colonize (increase area) and re-populate.[5] Custodian farmer Khem Chand from Nepal mentioned that he shares his varieties with other farmers as a safety back-up mechanism for his varieties. During a bad year, if he loses a variety, he can contact the farmers he had given the seed to before to re-populate his fields. The process of social seed networks often serves the purpose of meta-population dynamics under human and natural selection pressure

(Subedi et al., 2003, Paudel et al., 2015). Community seedbanks can provide an institutional platform to consolidate the roles of custodian farmers and link with the farming community as local crop diversity is declining at local level because of increasing dependence on seed companies and weak social seed networks (Sthapit, 2013b; Vernooy et al., 2014). Shrestha et al. (2013) demonstrated that community seed bank could serve shared custodianship of local crop diversity without undermining the roles of custodian farmers as conservers, innovators, and promoters.

## How can we support and strengthen custodian farmers?

Meldrum (2015) put forward that one means of supporting and consolidating the roles of custodian farmers in on-farm conservation would be through establishment of a custodian farmer network that would reflect and bolster shared custodianship at the community level. Such a network could foster connections between farmers to leverage complementarities in maintaining, adapting and promoting crop diversity and facilitate flows of material and knowledge. This seems to be an attractive option for scaling up and mainstreaming shared custodianship of agricultural biodiversity. However, such a network will require external intervention and resource support to thrive in the long run. Alternatively, existing community seedbanks can be a platform for such network members to congregate and engage in community actions for maintaining, adapting and promoting crop diversity at community and formal levels. Such an initiative could be supported by a variety of local government interventions, for example by using a Community Biodiversity Management fund in Nepal (Shrestha et al., 2013). Experiences in Nepal show that visits to and interactions with the scientists at the National Genebank can be a great motivator for community seedbanks and custodian farmers, often giving them a sense of belonging as a part of national and global efforts on conservation of agricultural biodiversity. National genebanks can provide periodic training and small financial support to community seedbanks or custodian farmer networks for characterization and evaluation of varieties. In return, the genebanks can mobilize these network to regenerate germplasm in their target environments. Custodian farmers can also play a crucial role in conducting pre-breeding or grassroots breeding work in their communities that will improve the population of the local landraces while also setting strong foundations for future plant breeding work. The transformative change in the roles of custodian farmers will occur if they have the opportunity to build social capital for collective action and develop leadership that foresees benefits to all community members.

## Conclusions

The important role that custodian farmers play in conservation, innovation and development is often underestimated, undervalued and unrecognized. It is a challenge to redress this situation and recognize the contribution by custodian farmers, which is exacerbated by their lack of links to mainstream research and development institutes or networks. Surprisingly, there has been no attempt by any national plant genetic resources programme or conservation agency to systematically identify or locate custodians. Mechanisms that establish connections between custodian farmers, the wider network of regional farmers and national and international genetic resource systems would help to address this challenge. Considering this as a new concept, a simple process by which custodian farmers' unique, rare or elite varieties could be formally registered and thus enter the commercial multiplication and distribution system would add value for policymakers and development workers alike. The custodians are potential farmer breeders and basic seed producers for further seed multiplication for community seedbanks or private seed companies. The decision to facilitate the process of mainstreaming the efforts by custodian farmers into national

R&D systems should be taken up by the responsible authorities in the countries, who should provide a platform that support and strengthen leadership capacity of custodian farmers.

## Acknowledgements

We gratefully acknowledge all the farming communities who provide conceptual insights into custodian farmers and Arwen Bailey for language editing. Financial support of GEF UNEP is gratefully appreciated.

## Notes

1 The GEF Project, 'Conservation and Sustainable Use of Wild and Cultivated Tropical Fruit Tree Diversity: Promoting Sustainable Livelihoods, Food Security and Ecosystem Services', was financed by GEF and implemented by UNEP, and technically executed by Bioversity International in India, Indonesia, Malaysia and Thailand.

2 With the support from the IFAD-NUS3 project, GEF UNEP funded Local Crops Project and SDC funded Diversifying Availability of Diverse Seeds, all contracted by Bioversity International with scope of working in neglected and underutilized species (NUS) related crops.

3 Positive deviance (PD) is an approach to behavioural and social change based on the observation that in any community there are people whose uncommon but successful behaviours or strategies enable them to find better solutions to a problem than their peers, despite facing similar challenges and having no extra resources or knowledge than their peers. These individuals are referred to as positive deviants (Tuhus-Dubrow, 2009).

4 Access to diversity refers to people having adequate land (natural capital), income (financial capital) or connections (social capital) to purchase or barter for variety (Sperling et al., 2006).

5 This is also recognized as the meta-population theory in ecological science (Alvarez et al., 2005).

## References

Alvarez, N., Garine, R., Khasah, C., Dounias, E., Hossaert-McKey, M. and McKey, D. (2005) 'Farmers' practices, meta-population dynamics and conservation of agricultural biodiversity on-farm: A case study of sorghum among the Duupa in sub-Sahelian Cameroon', *Biological Conservation*, vol. 121, pp. 533–543.

Badstue, L. B. (2006) *Smallholder Seed Practices. Maize Seed Management in the Central Valleys of Oaxaca, Mexico*, Doctoral Thesis, Wageningen University, Wageningen, the Netherlands.

Bernhart, A. (2015) *Cultivating Values: Perception and Decision Making amongst Swidden Subsistence Farmers in Meghalaya, Northeast India*, MSc thesis in Biodiversity, Conservation and Management, Oxford University Centre for the Environment, UK.

Boster, J. S. (1985) 'Selection for perceptual distinctiveness: Evidences from Aguaruna cultivars of *Manihot esculenta*', *Economic Botany*, vol. 39, pp. 310–325.

Brush, S. B. (1991) 'A farmer-based approach to conserving crop germplasm', *Economic Botany*, vol. 45, pp. 153–165.

Chaudhary, P., Gauchan, D., Rana, R. B., Sthapit, B. R. and Jarvis, D. I. (2004) 'Potential loss of rice landraces from a Terai community in Nepal: A case study from Kachorwa, Bara', *Plant Genetic Resources Newsletter*, vol. 137, pp. 1–8.

Collins, G. N. (1914) 'Pueblo Indian maize breeding: Varieties specially adapted to regions developed by Hapis and Navajos-their work not sufficiently appreciated-probably much yet to be learned from them', *Journal of Heredity*, vol. 5, pp. 255–268.

Díaz-Pichardo, R., Cantú-González, C., López-Hernández, P. and McElwee, G. (2012) 'From farmers-to-entrepreneurs: The importance of collaborative behaviour', *Journal of Entrepreneurship*, vol. 21, pp. 91–116.

Dyer, G. A. and Taylor, J. E. (2008) 'A crop population perspective on maize seed systems in Mexico', *Proceedings of the National Academy of Sciences USA*, vol. 105, pp. 470–475.

FAO (2011) *Save and Grow: A Policymaker's Guide to the Sustainable Intensification of Smallholder Crop Production*, FAO, Rome, Italy.

Food and Agriculture Organisation of the United Nations (FAO) (2010) *The Second Report on the State of the World's Plant Genetic Resources for Food and Agriculture*, FAO, Rome, Italy.

Gajanana, T. M., Dinesh, M. R., Rajan, S., Vasudeva, R., Singh, S. K., Lamers, H. A. H., Parthasarathy, P. A., Sthapit, B. R. and Ramanatha Rao, V. (2015) 'Motivation for on-farm conservation of mango (*Mangifera indica*) diversity in India – a case study', *Indian Journal of Plant Genetic Resources*, vol. 28, pp. 1–6.

Gautam, R. K., Sankaran, M., Zamir Ahmed, S. K., Sunder, J., Ram, N. and Dam Roy, S. (2014) *Custodian Farmers and Communities of Biodiversity Conservation and Utilization in Andaman and Nicobar Islands, India*, CIARI, Port Blair.

GIZ (2014) *Farmer Seed Systems: The Challenges in Linking Formal and Informal Seed Sectors*, Documentation of the Expert Talk, 4th June 2014, Bonn, Germany.

Gruberg, H., Meldrum, G., Padulosi, S., Rojas, W., Pinto, M. and Crane, T. (2013) *Towards a Better Understanding of Custodian Farmers and Their Roles: Insights from a Case Study in Cachilaya, Bolivia*, Bioversity International, PRONIPA, Wageningen UR, CCAFS and IFAD, Maccarese, Italy.

Hammer, K., Knupffer, H., Xhuveli, L. and Perrino, P. (1996) 'Estimating genetic erosion in landraces – two case studies', *Genetic Resources and Crop Evolution*, vol. 43, pp. 329–336.

Hammer, K. and Laghetti, G. (2005) 'Genetic erosion – examples from Italy', *Genetic Resources and Crop Evolution*, vol. 52, pp. 629–634.

Juma, C. (1989) 'Local initiatives in maintaining for biological diversity', *ILEIA Newsletter*, vol. 5, pp. 10–11.

Lamers, H. A. H., King, E. D. I. O., Sthapit, S., Bernhart, A., Rafieq, A., Boga Andri, K., Gajanana, T. M., Shafie Md. Sah, M., Umar, S., Brooke, P., Rajan, S., Sripinta, P., Nimkingrat, T., Singh, S. K., Singh, T. and Sthapit, B. R. (2015) 'Characteristics and motivations of custodian farmers in South and South East Asia: A preliminary reflection', pp. 15–20 in S. Sthapit, G. Meldrum, S. Padulosi and N. Bergamini (eds.) *Strengthening the Role of Custodian Farmers in the National Conservation Programme of Nepal*, Proceedings of the National Workshop 31 July to 2 August 2013, Pokhara, Nepal, Bioversity International, Rome Italy and LI-BIRD, Pokhara, Nepal.

Lipper, L., Anderson, C. L., and Dalton, T. J. (2009) *Seed Trade in Rural Markets Implications for Crop Diversity and Agricultural Development*, Earthscan and FAO, London, UK.

Meldrum, G. (2015) 'Connecting custodian farmers through collective institutions to strengthen on-farm conservation: Maintaining, adapting and promoting crop diversity at individual and community scales', pp. 97–104 in S. Sthapit, G. Meldrum, S. Padulosi and N. Bergamini (eds.), *Strengthening the Role of Custodian Farmers in the National Conservation Programme of Nepal*, Proceedings of the National Workshop 31 July to 2 August 2013, Pokhara, Nepal, Bioversity International, Maccarese, Italy and LI-BIRD, Pokhara, Nepal.

McElwee, G. (2006) 'Farmers as entrepreneurs: Developing competitive skills', *Journal of Developmental Entrepreneurship*, vol. 11, pp. 187–206.

McGuire, S. J. and Sperling, L. (2016) 'Seed systems smallholder farmers use', *Food Security*, vol. 8, pp. 179–195.

Nabhan, G. P. (1989) *Enduring Seeds: Native American Agriculture and Wild Plant Conservation*, North Point Press, San Francisco, CA, USA.

Negri, V. (2003) 'Landraces in central Italy: Where and why they are conserved and perspectives for their on-farm conservation', *Genetic Resources and Crop Evolution*, vol. 50, pp. 871–885.

Paudel, D., Sthapit, B. R. and Shrestha, P. K. (2015) 'An analysis of social seed network and its contribution to on-farm conservation of crop genetic diversity in Nepal', *International Journal of Biodiversity*, vol. 2015, p. 13.

Rajan, M. R., Dinesh, K. V., Ravishankar Singh, A., Singh, S. K., Singh, I. P., Vasudeva, R., Reddy, B. M. C., Parthasarathy, V. A. and Sthapit, B. R. (2014) *Heirloom Varieties of Important Tropical Fruits: A Community Initiative to Conservation*, ICAR/GEF UNEP/Bioversity International, India.

Röling, N. (1988) *Extension Science, Information Systems in Agricultural Development*, Cambridge University Press, Cambridge, UK.

Ruiz, M. and Vernooy, R. (2012) *The custodians of Biodiversity: Sharing access to and Benefits of Genetic Resources*, Earthscan from Routledge, Abingdon, UK.

Sadiki, M., Jarvis, D. I., Rijal, D., Bajracharya, J., Hue, N. N., Camachi, T. C., Bugos-May, L. A., Sawadogo, M., Balma, D., Lope, D., Arias, L., Karamura, D., Williams, D., Chavez-Servia, J. L., Sthapit, B. and Rao, V. R. (2007) 'Variety names: An entry point to crop genetic diversity and distribution in agroecosystems?', pp. 34–76 in D. I. Jarvis, C. Padoch and H. D. Cooper (eds.), *Managing Biodiversity in Agricultural Ecosystems*, Bioversity International, Maccarese, Italy and Columbia University Press, NY, USA.

Shrestha, P., Sthapit, S., Devkota, R. and Vernooy, R. (2012) 'Workshop summary report', *National workshop on community seed banks, 14-15 June 2012, Pokhara, Nepal.* LI-BIRD/USC Canada Asia/OXFAM Nepal/ Bioversity International.LI-BIRD, Pokhara, Nepal.

Shrestha, P., Sthapit, S., Subedi, A. and Sthapit, B. (2013) 'Community biodiversity management fund: Promoting conservation through livelihood development in Nepal', pp. 118–122 in W. S. de Boef,

A. Subedi, N. Peroni and M. Thijssen (eds.), *Community Biodiversity Management: Promoting Resilience and the Conservation of Plant Genetic Resources*, Earthscan from Routledge, Abingdon, UK.

Sperling, L., Cooper, H. D. and Remingto, T. (2006) 'Moving towards more effective seed aid', *Journal of Development Studies*, vol. 44, pp. 573–600.

Sripinta, P., Posawang, S., Noppornphan, C., Somsri, S. and Sthapit, B. (2016) 'Combination of side-grafting technique and informal germplasm exchange system in non-irrigated mango orchards in Thailand', pp. 199–204 in B. R. Sthapit, H. A. H. Lamers, V. R. Rao and A. Bailey (eds.), *Good Practices of* In Situ *and On-Farm Conservation of Tropical Fruit Tree Diversity*, Earthscan from Routledge, Abingdon, UK.

Sthapit, B. R. (2013b) 'Emerging theory and practice: Community Seed Banks, seed system resilience and food security', in P. Shrestha, R. Vernooy and P. Chaudhary (eds.), *Community Seed Bank is Nepal*, Proceedings of the National Workshop, Pokhara, Nepal.

Sthapit, B .R. and Joshi, K. D. (1996) 'Methodological issues for seed systems of crop varieties developed through participatory plant breeding', pp. 155–164 in *New Frontiers in Participatory Research and Gender Analysis*. Proc. of the International Seminar on Participatory Research and Gender Analysis for Technology Development (September 9–14, 1996), CGIAR System wide Program on PRGA for Technology Development and Institutional Innovation, Cali, Columbia.

Sthapit, B. R., Lamers, H. A. H. and Ramanatha Rao, V. (2013a) *Custodian Farmers of Agricultural Biodiversity: Selected Profiles from South and South East Asia*, Proceedings of the Workshop on Custodian Farmers of Agricultural Biodiversity, 11–12 February 2013, New Delhi, India.

Sthapit, B. R., Lamers, H. A. H., Ramanatha Rao, V. and Bailey, A. (eds.) (2016) *Good Practices of* In Situ *and On-Farm Conservation of Tropical Fruit Tree Diversity*, Earthscan from Routledge, Abingdon, UK.

Sthapit, B. R. and Ramanatha Rao, V. (2009) 'Consolidating community's role in local crop development by promoting farmer innovation to maximise the use of local crop diversity for the well-being of people', *Acta Horticulturae*, vol. 806, pp. 659–676.

Sthapit, B. R., Rana, R. B., Subedi, A., Gyawali, S., Bajracharya, J., Chaudhary, P., Joshi, B. K., Sthapit, S., Joshi, K. D. and Upadhyay, M. P. (2006) 'Participatory four cell analysis (FCA) for local crop diversity', pp. 13–16 in B. R. Sthapit, P. K. Shrestha and M. P. Upadhyay (eds.), *Good Practices: On-farm Management of Agricultural Biodiversity in Nepal*, NARC, LI-BIRD, IPGRI and IDRC, Pokhara, Nepal.

Sthapit, B. R., Shrestha, P. K. and Upadhyaya, M. P. (2006) *Good Practices: On-Farm Management of Agricultural Biodiversity in Nepal*, NARC, LI-BIRD, IPGRI and IDRC, Pokhara, Nepal.

Sthapit, B. R., Vasudeva, R., Rajan, S., Sripinta, P., Reddy, B. M. C., Idha Widi Arsanti, Idris, S., Lamers, H. and Ramanatha Rao, V. (2015a) 'On-farm conservation of tropical fruit tree diversity: Roles and motivations of custodian farmers and emerging threats and challenges', *Acta Horticulturae 1101. ISHS 2015.* doi: 10.17660/ActaHortic.2015.1101.11 *Proc. XXIX IHC – IV Intl. Symp. on Plant Genetic Resources (eds H. Jaenicke et al.).*

Sthapit, S., Meldrum, G., Padulosi, S. and Bergamini, N. (eds.) (2015b) *Strengthening the Role of Custodian Farmers in the National Conservation Programme of Nepal*, Proceedings of the National Workshop 31 July to 2 August 2013, Pokhara, Nepal, Bioversity International, Maccarese, Italy and LI-BIRD, Pokhara, Nepal.

Subedi, A., Chaudhary, P., Baniya, B., Rana, R., Tiwari, R. K., Rijal, D., Jarvis, D. and Sthapit, B. R. (2003) 'Who maintains crop genetic diversity and how: Implications for on-farm conservation and utilization', *Culture and Agriculture*, vol. 25, pp. 41–50.

Thiele, G. (1999) 'Informal potato seed systems in the Andes: Why are they important and should we do with them?', *World Development*, vol. 27, pp. 83–99.

Tripp, R. (2001) *Seed Provision and Agricultural Development*, The Institution of Rural Change, ODI, London, UK.

Tuhus-Dubrow, R. (2009) *The Power of Positive Deviants: A Promising New Tactic for Changing Communities from the Inside*, Globe, Boston, November 29, 2009.

Van der Heide, W. M., Tripp, R. and de Boef, W. S. (1996) *Local Crop Development: An Annotated Bibliography*, IPGRI, Rome, Italy/CPRO-DLO, Wageningen, The Netherlands/ODI, London, UK.

Vasudeva, R., Hegde, N., Reddy, B. M. C. and Sthapit, B. (2016, in press) 'An informal network of grafting experts to help communities conserve and use wild pickle mango (*Mangifera indica*) diversity in the central Western Ghats region of Karnataka', pp. 165–171 in B. R. Sthapit, H. A. H. Lamers, V. R. Rao and A. Bailey (eds.), *Good Practices of In Situ and On-Farm Conservation of Tropical Fruit Tree Diversity*, Earthscan from Routledge, London, UK.

Vernooy, R., Sthapit, B., Galluzzi, G. and Shrestha, P. (2014) 'The multiple functions and services of community seed banks', *Resources*, vol. 3, pp. 636–656.

Zeven, A. C. (1998) 'Landraces: A review of definitions and classification', *Euphytica*, vol. 104, pp. 127–139.

# 36

# AGRICULTURAL BIODIVERSITY CONSERVATION AND MANAGEMENT – THE ROLE OF *EX SITU* APPROACHES

*Ehsan Dulloo, Jean Hanson and Bhuwon Sthapit*

## Introduction

The conservation and management of agricultural biodiversity is critical to ensure food and nutritional security and to provide humanity with food, fibre, fodder and fuels (Porter et al., 2014; see also Part 1 of this Handbook). Conservation of agricultural biodiversity is also essential for providing novel genetic combinations required for the development of plant varieties and animal breeds to meet the challenges of climate change: in a *Science* editorial, Swaminathan (2009) noted that the loss of every gene, population or species limits our options to cope with future challenges. Yet it is widely recognised that the diversity of plants, animals and micro-organisms which constitute agricultural biodiversity are under severe threat (FAO, 2010), leading to global calls for action to safeguard them. The State of the World Reports on plants, animals and forest genetic resources (FAO, 1998, 2010, 2009, 2012) and their respective Global Plans of Action, the International Treaty on Plant Genetic Resources for Food and Agriculture and Convention on Biological Diversity (CBD), all call on member states to take measures to ensure the *ex situ* and *in situ* conservation and sustainable use of these resources (CBD, 2014).

Different approaches are available for the conservation of agricultural biodiversity, which can be broadly divided into *ex situ*, *in situ*, on farm and *circa situ* conservation (Heywood and Dulloo, 2005; **Box 36.1** *Definitions of* in situ, ex situ *and* circa situ *conservation*). For plant genetic resources, *ex situ* conservation has traditionally been the method of choice because it allows ready access to the genetic material. For animal and forest genetic resources, *in situ* conservation has instead been preferred, as live animals must be maintained in populations on farm while many species of tree are difficult to conserve *ex situ*. These approaches and methods have their strengths and weaknesses (see **Table 36.1**). It will be important to adopt complementary conservation approaches, both for conserving genetic diversity and to support the climate change adaptation needed for future agroecological resilience.

### Box 36.1 *Definitions of* in situ, ex situ *and* circa situ *conservation*

- *In situ* conservation refers to the conservation of ecosystem and natural habitats and the maintenance and recovery of viable populations of species in their natural surroundings and in the case of domesticated or cultivated species, in the surroundings where they have developed their distinctive properties.
- *Ex situ* conservation refers to the conservation outside the area where it grows naturally, in facilities such as seed banks, *in vitro* and cryopreservation, DNA banks, botanic gardens, field genebanks, arboreta, orchards and so forth.
- *Circa situ* refers to a type of conservation that emphasises the role of regenerating saplings in remnants vegetation in heavily modified or fragmented landscape.

*Table 36.1* Relative advantages and disadvantages of complementary conservation strategies (modified from Maxted et al., 1997)

| *Conservation strategy* | *Advantages* | *Disadvantages* |
|---|---|---|
| *Ex situ* | Feasible for medium- and long-term secure storage species | Problems storing seeds of 'recalcitrant' species |
| | Greater diversity of each target taxon conserved | Practical limitation on storing the diversity of 'recalcitrant' species in field genebanks |
| | Easy access for characterization and evaluation | Freezes evolutionary development, especially that which is related to pest and disease resistance |
| | Little maintenance once material is collected (except for field genebanks and conserved botanic gardens) | Genetic diversity is potentially lost with each regeneration cycle |
| | | Commonly restricted to a single target taxon |
| *In situ* | Dynamic conservation in relation to environmental changes and utilisation | Materials not easily available for utilisation |
| | Permits species/pathogens interactions, so continuing dynamic evolution possible disasters, especially concerning resistance to pest and diseases | Vulnerable to natural and man-made disasters, for example fire, cyclones, vandalism, changes in land use, deforestation and so forth |
| | Provides easy evolutionary and genetic study | Require active supervision and monitoring |
| | Best for 'recalcitrant' species | Appropriate management regimes poorly understood |
| | Possibility of multiple target taxa reserves | Require active supervision and monitoring |
| | | Limited genetic diversity can be conserved in any one reserve |

*Source*: Modified from Maxted et al. (1997).

*Ex situ* conservation of agricultural biodiversity involves a number of different approaches ranging from seed banks to *in vitro* conservation, cryopreservation, field genebanks, botanic gardens, pollen banks and DNA conservation. The form of *ex situ* conservation used is largely determined by the method of reproduction of the species in question, as well as the purpose of the conservation and the intended use of the material. There are currently about 7.4 million plant genetic resources accessions conserved in over 1,750 genebanks with more than 2,500 botanical gardens growing over 80,000 plant species (FAO, 2010).

Crop genebanks were established as a response to the problem of genetic erosion to conserve landraces that were being replaced by new, high-yielding varieties during the Green Revolution. They also to support current and future use through continued selection and breeding. Genebanks may be considered as archives of genetic diversity that make the past accessible as future sources of diversity for scientists and breeders (Peres, 2016). Through conserving valuable resources, much like an archive, the potential value of genetic resources can be accumulated for future generations and selected using contemporary technology based on the actual and perceived usefulness of the germplasm for the future.

This chapter provides an overview of in *ex situ* conservation methods of plant agricultural biodiversity, both from a perspective of providing general principles and practical guidelines on the different *ex situ* methods. We focus principally on plant genetic resources for food and agriculture.

## Seed genebank management

For those species that have orthodox seeds, seed storage is the most efficient and low cost method for conservation for long periods. Seed storage is based on the principle that dry seeds can be stored in cold conditions for long periods without a major decline in viability. The longevity of seeds during storage depends on many factors, the most important being species and genotype, quality and condition of seeds at harvest, initial seed viability, seed moisture content and temperature during storage (Roberts, 1972). The longevity of most crop species has already been determined and specific longevity can be modelled based on viability equations if the initial viability and storage conditions are known (Ellis and Roberts, 1980). This is not the case for forages, trees and crop wild relatives where there is generally a lack of information on seed storage behaviour during *ex situ* conservation resulting in differences in conservation and management (Hay and Probert, 2013). Seed storage behaviour and longevity may also vary between accessions within a species. Hence, longevity and storage conditions must often be determined empirically for any given sample and greater research is needed to determine the optimum monitoring intervals, germination protocols and storage conditions for species of conservation importance.

### *Seed quality at harvest*

Quality seeds are those with high viability and vigour, free from seed-borne pests and diseases and true to type for the genotype and species. Seed quality is established during seed development while on the mother plant in the field and is influenced by many factors, including isolation distance, soil fertility, water availability and temperature and disease and insect infestation during the growing season (George, 1987; Kameswara Rao et al., 2016). Following appropriate multiplication or regeneration guidelines is key to the production of high quality seeds for storage in genebanks.

## *Seed drying and moisture content during storage*

It has been accepted for many years that seed moisture content during storage has a major effect on seed longevity with even small decreases in seed moisture resulting in significant increases in longevity for orthodox seeds (Harrington, 1970; Ellis, 1998). Seeds have a critical moisture level that supports maximum longevity for the storage temperature and drying below this does not increase seed longevity further. The critical moisture level varies by species, and although a wide range of drying conditions can be used to achieve critical moisture levels, the norm is to equilibrate seeds in an environment of about 15%+3% RH at the storage temperature. This may be difficult to achieve at low temperatures due to the physics of water holding capacity of air at lower temperatures. Recommendations have focussed on drying seeds under cool conditions and low relative humidity, but recent work with rice has challenged those recommendations. In rice, use of hot air drying at 45°C actually improved longevity for seeds with moisture contents greater than 16.2% and did not reduce longevity for seeds of lower moisture content when compared with seeds dried using recommended drying conditions (Whitehouse et al., 2015).

However, despite the determination of critical moisture contents, there remains much debate about optimum moisture contents for storage, especially the effects of ultra-low moisture contents on viability (Vertucci and Roos, 1993). Rapid or over drying to ultra-low moisture contents may cause physical damage and cracking of the seed coat in a few species such as groundnut and soybean, which are oily seeds with low critical moisture contents of 2% and 3.3%, respectively. Current recommendations for seed moisture levels during storage are typically conservative and do not include ultra-low moisture content storage.

## *Seed packaging*

After drying, seeds should be stored in moisture proof packages to avoid increases in moisture content that can affect longevity if humidity in the store is not controlled. Most genebanks use hermetic packaging for storage. There are a range of packaging materials and types that meet moisture proof requirements (Gómez Campo, 2002, 2006; Manger et al., 2003; Walters, 2007), including jars and cans with sealed lids, sealed cans and laminated aluminum foil pouches. Vacuum sealing of dry seeds is practised in many genebanks on the principle that respiration and seed deterioration can be reduced by reduction of oxygen around the seeds. While there is no data on its effects on longevity over the long term, it does allows rapid visual inspection and detection of faulty seals or damaged bags which allow moisture to enter packaging. As long as the containers are moisture proof, the choice of packaging is often determined by practical issues such as cost, seed size, shelf dimensions and ease of access and options for resealing.

## *Seed storage*

Seed storage temperature is the other important factor for retaining seed longevity in the long term. The general rule that longevity is doubled for each 5°C reduction of storage temperature led to recommendations for genebank storage using cold conditions (Harrington, 1970). Dry seeds are able to withstand very low temperatures, but freezing moist seeds can result in membrane damage and seed death from ice crystals forming inside the cells. Some species have recalcitrant seeds that cannot be dried and stored under traditional cold storage, but new methods for cryopreservation have been developed to handle them (Walters et al., 2013). Storage temperatures depend on the species and the desired length of storage period, with sub-zero temperatures ranging from -20°C to cryopreservation in liquid nitrogen at -196°C commonly being used for long-term storage (Walters et al., 2004; Li and Pritchard, 2009).

Genebanks must ensure that seeds are kept viable for as long as possible. While many seeds are long-lived and can withstand dry and cold storage for many years, it is important to monitor viability at intervals during the storage period, especially for wild species where there is a lack of information on longevity during long-term storage. Most monitoring intervals have been based on predictions of seed longevity in the absence of substantive evidence of actual longevity and many genebanks monitor viability every five to ten years. Since monitoring depletes seed number, a method called sequential testing that uses fewer seeds and gives a good estimate of viability was developed and has been recommended for use in genebanks (Ellis et al., 1980).

### *Regeneration and multiplication*

Genebanks make small quantities of seeds available, usually for research, selection and breeding for development of new varieties and for demonstration and training in order to promote use of the germplasm. All germplasm should be provided with information, including passport, germination and characterization data, if available. Distribution depletes the seed stocks, and seed multiplication is necessary to restock. Seeds also deteriorate with time and lose viability and need to be regenerated.

Germplasm regeneration/multiplication is one of the most critical operations, with a high risk of loss of material, or of change in the genetic integrity of accessions. This occurs while materials are in the field due to selection pressure, out-crossing and mechanical mixtures. Risks can be mitigated by always using a sample size sufficient to capture diversity, by selecting an environment where the crop grows well and produces seeds and by planting out-crossing species in isolation (Engels and Rao, 1995; Dulloo et al., 2008). Pests and diseases can also be managed by agrochemicals and roguing during the planting cycle to ensure disease-free seeds are produced for storage.

### *Genebank standards for orthodox seeds*

Following acceptable international standards for the collection, conservation and management of genebanks collections is important to ensure genetic integrity, seed quality and availability of germplasm. The Genebank Standards for Plant Genetic Resources for Food and Agriculture (FAO, 2013) covers voluntary procedures that can be applied universally to safeguard and enhance the conservation of plant genetic resources. They are based on strong scientific principles and are also forward looking, taking account of recommended changes in seed management and techniques based on a better understanding of population structure and diversity coming from research and advances in molecular biology. They set the benchmark for scientific and technical best practices, based on current research findings and scientific knowledge, and reflect the international policy environment for the conservation and use of plant genetic resources.

## Field genebank management

Field genebanks are used for plants species that produce seeds which cannot be dried and/or stored at low temperatures. They are conserved as live plants in the field or in pots or trays in greenhouses or shade houses. Field genebank is also used for plants that produce very few seeds, are vegetatively propagated and/or plants that require a long life cycle to generate breeding and/or planting materials (FAO, 2013). It must be pointed that the maintenance of a living collection in the field has many constraints in terms of requiring large areas of lands, large inputs of labour and time, the fact that the planting material is not readily available for distribution, as well as problems with pest and diseases, vulnerability to adverse weather conditions, the risk of policy changes in land tenure, vandalism and thefts, to mention a few (Dulloo et al., 2010). Also, compared with other forms of *ex situ* conservation such as seeds and cryopreservation, field genebanks are expensive to maintain (Dulloo et al., 2009). For the aforementioned reasons, it is recommended to use field genebank only as a last resort, when the plant species cannot be conserved by any alternative method. FAO (2013) provided standards for the establishment and management of field genebanks. We provide hereunder a brief summary of the key steps in establishing and maintaining a field genebank.

## *Site selection*

Depending on the crop type, appropriate planting sites should be selected to suit the agro-ecological needs of all accessions which are envisaged to be included in the field genebank. The FAO key standards for site selection of field genebank considered the following key points:

- Similarity of the agro-ecological conditions (climate, elevation, soil, drainage) to the environment of origin of the accessions;
- Risks from natural and man-made disasters and hazards such as pests, diseases, animal damage, floods, droughts, fires, snow and freeze damage, volcanoes, hail, thefts or vandals;
- Risks of geneflow and contamination from crops or wild populations of the same species as a risk to genetic integrity;
- Secured land tenure and sufficient space to allow for future expansion of the collection;
- Easy and reliable access to staff, supplies, deliveries and water; and
- Adequate facilities for propagation and quarantine.

The establishment of field genebank is costly and it is important that aforementioned factors are well thought out before a site is selected: for full details, see Reed et al. (2004) and recommended FAO standards (FAO, 2013).

## *Acquisition*

Acquisition is the process of collecting or requesting materials for inclusion in the field genebank, together with the relevant supporting data (FAO, 2013). During the acquisition process, it is important that planting materials are:

- acquired legally with relevant technical documentation;
- accompanied by at least a minimum of associated data as detailed in the FAO/Bioversity multi-crop passport descriptors (Alercia et al., 2015);
- collected from healthy, growing plants;
- transported as quickly as possible to the field genebank to prevent loss and deterioration of the material; and
- acquired from other countries or regions within the country should pass through the relevant quarantine process and meet the associated requirements before being incorporated into the field collection.

It is important to emphasise here the need to adequately document the materials that are being acquired and to follow correct legal procedures. All too often information about accessions in a genebank is not available, and this reduces the value of the accession and field genebank and limits its use.

## *Field establishment*

This step involves the planting out of the acquired accessions in the field, which should be done so as to ensure that the location of each accession is properly labelled and documented to allow relocation if needed. There are three key factors that need attention when setting out the collection:

1. A sufficient number of plants should be maintained to capture the genetic diversity within the accession and to ensure the safety of the accession and limit genetic erosion. The aim of genetic resource collection is to conserve the maximum level of genetic diversity in the species. As mentioned before, field genebanks are very vulnerable and accessions can easily be lost for various reasons. It is thus important that adequate numbers of plants of each genotype are planted. The precise number of plants will often depend on the species itself for example whether it is propagated vegetatively or through seed and whether annual or perennial, and also on the size of the plants (space considerations). There is no recommended number of plants that should be planted but in general three to five individuals are maintained per genotype.
2. A field genebank should have a clear map showing the exact location of each accession in the plot. Each accession should be clearly labelled, georeferenced on the field and documented. The layout of accessions in the field genebank should consider factors such as plot size, spacing, the risk of geneflow between accessions and the heterogeneity of the micro-environment across the genebank. An important point is that many plants (especially annuals) are regenerated frequently and may be replanted in different parts of the field genebank. Thus, the layout of a genebank is not fixed and may change according to the planting schedule which makes proper labelling particularly important.
3. For the successful establishment of plants, appropriate cultivation practices should be followed, taking into account micro-environment, soil, planting time, rootstock, watering regime, pest, disease and weed control. Different plants may need different space and support consideration – shade trees, stakes, raised beds and so forth. Facilities for irrigation, fertiliser and pesticide application to control pest and diseases and weeding regimes should be well established for the field genebank at the establishment stage.

## *Management*

The day-to-day curation of the field collection is critical to avoid any loss of genetic diversity from the collection. It involves many different activities including pest and disease control, proper nutrition of the plants, watering, weeding, pruning and monitoring of accessions to ensure that the genetic integrity of the collections is maintained.

According to the FAO standard (2013), plants and soil should be regularly monitored for pests and diseases. Appropriate cultivation practices such as fertilisation, irrigation, pruning, trellising, rootstock and weeding should be performed to ensure satisfactory plant growth. The genetic identity of each accession should be monitored by ensuring proper isolation of accessions wherever appropriate, avoiding inter-growth of accessions, proper labelling and field maps and periodic assessment of identity using morphological or molecular techniques.

## *Regeneration and propagation*

Regeneration and propagation refers to the re-establishment of germplasm samples which are genetically similar to the original collection when vigour or plant numbers are low (Dulloo et al., 2008). This is a particularly challenging and costly activity for field genebank curators.

As only a few plants can be maintained in field genebank, the death of a plant represents a significant loss of genetic diversity. In practice, when one or more of the plant within an accession dies, it is important to replace it using the original stock. The reasons for the death of the plant(s) should be established and measures taken to secure the surviving plants of the accession and any new regenerated materials. Often the causes may be due to pest and diseases, either air- or soil-borne, and this may require changing the site in which the accession is grown. To regenerate the plants, it is recommended not to use seeds from the accession itself, as this may lead to genetic drift and will not represent true-to-type plant material. Instead surviving planting materials from the accessions should be propagated for replacing gaps in the accession. When a plant has been regenerated in the field collection, it is important to document the procedures that were used to do this, including the date, the authenticity of the accession, labels and location maps in the genebank information system.

Additional information for the management of germplasm collections held in field genebanks are available in a number of technical guidelines and training manuals (e.g. Crop Genebank Knowledge Base; Engelmann, 1999; Said Saad and Ramanatha Rao, 2001; Reed et al., 2004; Geburek and Turok, 2005; Bioversity International et al., 2011).

## *In vitro* conservation and cryopreservation

Conservation methods for non-orthodox and vegetatively propagated plants are also needed. Storage behaviour is particularly critical for handling and preparing non-orthodox seeds or other plant materials for preservation. Options for short-, medium- and long-term storage include hydrated storage, *in vitro*/slow growth and cryopreservation of non-orthodox seeds.

### *Seed storage behaviour*

As a first step to preservation, it is important to ascertain the response of seed or other propagules to desiccation. Seeds of different species respond differently to drying. The so-called 'orthodox seeds' are desiccation tolerant and can be dried to very low moisture content and are conventionally conserved in seeds banks (see 'Genebank standards for orthodox seeds') while non-orthodox seeds are desiccation and cold sensitive. There is a high variability in storage behaviour between and within species as well as from localities where they are collected and from year to year (Berjak and Pammenter, 2004), thus the need to perform seed behaviour desiccation test prior to preservation. There are three recommended protocols for determining seed storage behaviour, depending on amount of seeds available. A full protocol is provided by Hong and Ellis (1996) that discriminates between orthodox and non-orthodox seeds. Pritchard (2004) designed a protocol for cases when seeds are limiting. It is also considered important to assess axis water content rather than the whole seeds (Berjak, personal communication, 2011). Because of the variability in desiccation responses it is recommended to determine a drying time course assessing loss of viability with declining water content for each accession.

### *Hydrated storage of recalcitrant seeds*

For species whose seeds exhibits non-orthodox behaviour, it is often necessary to maintain them under short- to medium-term storage before they can be prepared for longer-term conservation. The basic principle maximising the storage life span of non-orthodox seeds is that water content should be retained at essentially the same level at collection (FAO, 2013). Care should thus be taken to ensure that seeds do not lose moisture during transportation and short-term storage and kept at the lowest temperature that are not detrimental to the seeds. This can be achieved by keeping them in closed conditions under saturated relative humidity, as for example in polythene bag with an inner paper bag inside at appropriate temperature (Pasquini et al., 2011). Any dehydration can stimulate germination or cause deleterious changes leading to loss of vigour and viability. Under hydrated storage, conditions are favourable for the proliferation of fungi, bacteria and viruses which may be detrimental to the seeds and also may restrict the transfer of germplasm across countries. In principle such materials cannot be exchanged, unless they are transported to countries where such organisms will not be a problem. Prior to packing them, seeds should be disinfected, dried of excess liquid and a broad spectrum fungicide applied. Appropriate phytosanitary measures needs to be taken to eliminate surface and internal contaminants on seeds.

## *In vitro* conservation/slow growth

The *in vitro*/slow-growth conservation method aims to introduce explants, that is, small tissue pieces, from the donor plants into sterile culture and maintain them in a pathogen-free and controlled environment in a synthetic medium (Thormann et al., 2006). The cultures can be stored under conditions of either slow or suspended growth. Despite the problems of somaclonal variation associated with *in vitro* conservation, it still provides a medium-term solution for conservation of many vegetatively propagated plants. For example four international centres (Bioversity, CIAT, CIP and IITA) of the CGIAR holds over 28,000 accessions of banana, plantain, potatoes, sweet potatoes and yam *in vitro* and in cryopreservation (Benson et al., 2011). *In vitro* cultures also serve as disease-free materials for distribution or multiplication, and as a source of explants for cryopreservation. *In vitro*/slow growth requires the determination of the optimal conditions with regard to light-regime, temperature and medium composition for specific species. While standard protocols exist (George, 1993; Chandel et al., 1995; Hartmann et al., 2002), it is often necessary to refine the protocols for *in vitro* conservation of particular crops empirically and sometimes even to do so for different accessions of the same crop (van den Houwe, personal communication, 2016). Modifications are often necessary to adapt for culture medium, temperature, the condition of the culture vessels and rooms. Optimal storage temperatures for cold-tolerant species may be from 0–5°C or somewhat higher; for material of tropical provenance, the lowest temperatures tolerated may be in the range from 15–20°C, depending on the species (cited in FAO, 2013).

## *Cryopreservation*

Cryopreservation refers to the conservation of explants (cell suspensions, calluses, shoot tips, embryos and seeds) at −196°C in liquid nitrogen under which conditions cell division is arrested and this guarantees long-term preservation of tissues in a genetically unaltered state (Engelmann, 2000). One of the challenges with cryopreservation is that explants can suffer from freezing injury when immersed in liquid nitrogen (i.e. crystallisation of intracellular water into ice). The explants contain high levels of water and must be dehydrated: FAO (2013) provides globally accepted standards for cryopreservation. To address this problem, two main approaches have been developed to reduce the cryopreservation damage, namely conventional slow freezing, based upon freeze-induced dehydration, and flash-freezing (vitrification), which involves dehydration prior to cooling (Engelmann, 2011). Cryopreservation involves a number of steps including (1) selection, (2) preculture, (3) cryopreservation techniques, (4) retrieval from storage, and (5) seedling or plantlet establishment.

The best explants for cryopreservation depends on the plant type. In general they can be produced from embryonic axes, shoot tips, meristematic and embryogenic tissues. Excised embryos/

axes are the explants of choice for cryopreservation of recalcitrant seeds, while for vegetatively propagated species, buds and shoot tips, meristematic and embryogenic tissues are preferred. Whole anthers or isolated pollen grains can be used for cryopreservation as well (see Ganeshan et al., 2008, for a review).

The choice of the cryopreservation protocol depends on the response of the explant to desiccation. Whatever methods are used, the water content should lie within the range that prevents intracellular ice-crystal formation on cooling and warming, but also avoids desiccation damage to subcellular structure (FAO, 2013). It is recommended that a drying time-course of excised embryos/axes be conducted to identify the drying time required to reduce material to appropriate water content for subsequent cryopreservation (FAO, 2013). Most plant vitrification protocols use cryoprotectants such as dimethyl sulfoxide (DMSO), glycerol and other Plant Vitrification Solutions (PVS) which helps reduce freezing injury. The tissues are desiccated with a cocktail of vitrification solutions, followed by rapid freezing. The vitrified material is thawed in 40°C water and the cryoprotectants then removed (Thormann et al., 2006). Other techniques (encapsulation-dehydration) involves the encapsulation of explants in alginate beads, pre-grown in liquid medium enriched with sucrose for one to seven days, partially desiccated in the air current of a laminar airflow cabinet or with silica gel down to a water content around 20% (fresh weight basis), and then frozen rapidly. A combination of encapsulation-dehydration and vitrification techniques can also be used, in which samples are encapsulated in alginate beads and then subjected to freezing by vitrification (Thormann et al., 2006).

The final step is to generate and establish a seedling or plantlet. It first involves the retrieval of the germplasm from cryostorage (see Benson and Harding, 2012 for a review). The recovered material is then introduced to a recovery medium initially in the dark. The success of the cryopreservation is measured as the resultant seedlings each producing both a root and a shoot or when shoots are obtained in case of vegetatively propagated material (see Thormann et al., 2006 for details).

## DNA banking and bioinformatics

DNA banking is an efficient, simple and long-term method to conserve diversity using either whole DNA or segments of DNA with specific genes or alleles that confer specific traits of interest. DNA is relatively stable and can be conserved in cool temperatures for long periods. The concept of DNA storage to reconstitute diversity has been considered for the last decade (de Vicente and Andersson, 2006), and has become a viable option for conservation of biodiversity with the development of the clustered regularly interspaced short palindromic repeats (CRISPR-CAS) system which together with specific endonuclease enzymes can be used for breaking DNA and subsequent DNA recombination or gene editing (Belhaj et al., 2013; Puchta and Fauser, 2013). DNA banks can now be considered as a means of complementary conservation, providing a low cost storage method. However, the use of DNA banks remains limited, as gene editing is still an experimental and expensive process and has been established only for major crops such as rice and wheat (Shan et al., 2014), requiring a large amount of time and effort to develop the protocols.

DNA storage is particularly useful for difficult species that cannot be conserved in seed or field genebanks and need to be conserved *ex situ* because of high risk of genetic erosion or extinction in their natural environments (de Vicente and Andersson, 2006). The potential for DNA storage is promising due to the small sample size containing a large amount of genetic information, the stable nature of DNA in cold storage and the rapidly evolving field of gene editing. Plant recovery is expensive because whole plants cannot be directly reconstituted from DNA, which is usually inserted back into somatic cells or embryos that can then be grown into whole plants in *in vitro* culture.

DNA barcoding is already being used in genebanks for fingerprinting and accession identification (Jarret, 2008). Advances in plant genomics and bioinformatics will undoubtedly change the future of genebanking away from seeds and tissues to storage of gene sequences in '*in silico*' genebanks. These will rely on the ability to produce DNA with specific sequences that can be reinserted into cells from available plants through gene editing to produce ideal plants with specific traits rather than using the natural diversity available in the seed genebank collections. *In silico* evaluation is already commonplace for genes or genotypes of interest for breeders and it is not a question of 'if' but of 'when' *in silico* genebanks will be established as another approach for conservation and use of biodiversity.

## Community genebanks

Globally over about 85% of smallholder farmers in developing nations depend upon local seed system for their livelihoods and food security (Tripp, 2001). Smallholder family farms constitute 98% of all farms and at least 53% of agricultural land, thus producing at least 53% of the world's food (Graeub et al., 2016). However, farmer seed system is currently under stress (Coomes et al., 2015) for many diverse reasons:

- weakening social seed networks and poor exchange of seed;
- continued push towards monoculture;
- consolidation of seed supply into few and large seed companies;
- poor investment in strengthening multifunctionality of farmer seed system and productivity;
- lack of community-based institutional support;
- climate-induced adversity including new diseases and pests; and
- widespread disengagement of youth from agriculture.

Community seed banks have evolved in various circumstances to address the aforementioned challenges and strengthen multiple functions of farmers' seed system. Community seed banks have been around for about 30 years but have only recently been systematically reviewed (Sthapit, 2013; Vernooy et al., 2014, 2015) to analyse their strengths, weaknesses/gaps and opportunities. They have been designed and implemented to conserve, restore, revitalise, strengthen and improve resilient local seed systems to address the challenges of food insecurity, malnutrition, poverty, and climate change. Vernooy et al. (2015) reviewed the history, evolution, experiences, successes and failures, challenges and prospects of 35 community seed banks from 25 countries (also refer to Vernooy et al., Chapter 37 of this Handbook). The results categorised the functions and services of community seedbanks into three core areas: conservation, access and availability of planting materials and food and seed sovereignty.

The community seed banks are collections of locally important seed that are maintained and governed by a local community via locally developed rules and regulations in a central location using storage structures that are shared among community members. First, a community seed bank aims to safeguard locally adapted varieties, landraces and heirloom varieties. Second, it is considered to be a local solution to increase access and availability of quality of portfolio of seeds and planting materials as well as sourcing new genetic diversity for selection. Finally, it is a community platform to empower women, youth and community members to regain, maintain and increase their control over seeds and facilitate them for clear expression of farmers' rights. A community seed bank is defined as a community driven and community-owned effort to conserve and use both local and improved varieties for food security and to improve the livelihoods of farmers.

Community seed banks tend to be small-scale local institutions, which store seed on a short-term basis, serving individual communities or several communities in surrounding villages. These community seed banks are relatively inexpensive, usually employing relatively simple low cost storage technologies. They carry out assembly (deposit), replication, storage, distribution, germination quality testing and variety selection. In contrast to other forms of *ex situ* conservation, community seed banks are controlled and governed by local community at local level.

The concept of the community seed bank stimulates scientists, breeders and development workers to find new ways of collaborating with farmers and vice versa in the different functions of farmer seed system. Farmers' seed systems can be substantially improved through the introduction of scientific knowledge and practices developed by the formal seed system. Participatory crop improvement using local crop diversity can enhance knowledge and technical competencies of community seed bank and address community needs for diverse set of crops and varieties (see for example the case study provided in Ríos Labrada and Ceballos-Müller, Chapter 40 of this Handbook). In the wake of climate change and market vulnerability, community seed banks can provide immediate access to locally adapted diverse portfolio of crops and genetic diversity. This will in turn develop community resilience to cope with vulnerability caused by climate change and market forces. Furthermore, community seed banks, as platforms of community-based management of agricultural biodiversity, will ensure the effective implementation of Farmers' Rights (in terms of recognition, participation in decision making, benefit sharing and supportive policy and seed regulatory framework; see also Taylor, Chapter 38 of this Handbook). A well-managed community seed bank also provides an opportunity to (a) integrate informal and formal seed systems for addressing local problems, (b) promote *in situ* and *ex situ* linkages to back up genetic resources locally for use as building blocks of crop improvement and food security, and (c) ensure community development in a sustainable way. There are many challenges in using community seed banks, but there is also scope to use them as an open source seed network in order to (a) strengthen multifunctionality of farmer seed system; (b) conserve and/or revive traditional crop varieties; (c) strengthen farmer capacity in selection of functional traits, plant breeding and seed production; (d) generate data of value for cultivation; and (e) improve access and availability of local crop diversity.

Sustainability, the longer-term organizational viability, is the most challenging aspect of community seedbanks. Vernooy et al. (2015) suggested that for a community seedbank to be sustainable, a number of conditions need to be met: having legal recognition and protection, options for financial viability, members with adequate technical knowledge, effective operational mechanisms and empowering community from outset. In contrast to international and national genebanks, community seed banks have not yet benefited from the support of international bodies such as the CBD, ITPGRFA and Global Crop Diversity Trust.

## Documentation systems for *ex situ* genebanks

Optimum genebank management relies on having a well-documented system that can be used to track and relate data on all genebank activities for each accession (Konopka and Hanson, 1985; National Academy of Sciences, 1993). Genebank operations generate a large amount of management data that are used for decision making for monitoring, regeneration, multiplication and distribution timing and methods. These data are internal and not usually of interest to others outside the genebank. Other types of information on the collections is of interest to external users because it greatly enhances the selection of accessions and use of the germplasm. Collection site and environmental data give a good indication of adaptation and where the materials can be used and, together with characterisation and evaluation data, allow users to make better informed requests for germplasm.

Internal documentation differs between genebanks but has some common principles. It should be accession specific, well organised, searchable, accurate and sufficiently detailed to facilitate management decisions. Genebank data management systems can be developed on paper for smaller collections or as a computerised system for larger or more complex managed systems (Painting et al., 1995). The software used is less important than having a well-structured and ordered data management system that fits the needs of the genebank staff and is quick and easy to search. Generic database software systems such as Microsoft Access, SQL and MySQL are successfully used in many genebanks (Agrawal et al., 2007), while GRINGlobal (www.grin-global.org/index.php/Main_Page), a new specialist publicly available open source genebank management system based on MySQL and developed by USDA is now being adopted in several genebanks. Barcoding is also being introduced into many genebanks to allow scanning and rapid linking to databases for data search and entry.

Passport, characterisation and evaluation data are usually made publicly available to users, and accession related information is usually provided to users along with seed samples to facilitate use. A common set of descriptors are used to support a comparable understanding of the diversity within collections of major crops (Alercia et al., 2015). Much of this data is being made available on line through Genesys (www.genesys-pgr.org/), which is a free online global portal which allows the exploration of the world's crop diversity through a single website. Genesys provides a gateway to information on plant genetic resources for food and agriculture allowing users to search and order germplasm from 447 national and international genebanks. It holds information on more than 2.8 million samples of crop, forage and tree diversity held in their germplasm collections. Genesys makes it easy for anyone with a collection of crop diversity to share their data. Partner institutions upload information about their crop accessions to the portal. Users can then explore this vast resource searching for germplasm of interest and request seeds and other planting materials from many of the genebanks holding them.

Phenoytping and genotyping of genebank accessions are also generating a lot of bioinformatics data of genetic sequences related to specific traits or accession identity. These data are large, and in 2015, a new big data partnership called Divseek (www.divseek.org) was launched to foster the genomic characterisation of the 7 million crop accessions currently being stored at genebanks. Divseek will support efforts to characterise crop diversity and developed a unified and coordinated information management platform to provide easy access to genotypic and phenotypic data associated with genebank accessions.

## Enhancing the use of *ex situ* materials: characterisation and evaluation

The usefulness of the germplasm is determined by its traits but in order to make full use of it, information must be available as to which accessions show which traits. A set of standard morphological descriptors covering plant, stem, leaf, flower, pod and seed traits can be used to describe the phenotype depending on the species (Bioversity International, 2007). All can be scored or measured and expressed in numeric values to facilitate data analysis. Other traits such as biomass, disease and pest tolerance, and drought tolerance are usually assessed in the field or, if genetic markers are available for the trait, large numbers of accessions can be screened in the laboratory (de Vicente et al., 2004).

Using modern methods of phenotyping and genotyping it is now more possible to accurately identify and group accessions with similar traits (these recent developments are reviewed by

Ortiz, Chapter 17 of this Handbook). Grouping or making subsets of similar accessions based on this data helps users to locate traits of interest in small sets of samples. Grouping accessions to select a core set that include members that encompass maximum diversity in core collections helps users to evaluate diversity within a species using a smaller number of accessions than using entire large collections (Johnson and Hodgkin, 1999; van Hintum et al., 2000). Specific accessions can be selected, and users can then look at others in the same group that probably have similar characteristics. It has also been clearly demonstrated that materials from the same area often share traits that confer adaptation to that specific environment. This principle underlies the development of the Focused Identification of Germplasm Strategy (FIGS), which is a new technique using cutting-edge applied Bayesian mathematics and geographical information data for searching genebanks to pinpoint specific accessions with traits of interest (ICARDA, 2013). Building on the foundation of the FIGS approach, other studies such as ecogeographical filtering and calibration method have been developed and tested (Thormann et al., 2014). These methods combine spatial distribution of the target taxon on ecogeographical land characterisation map with the ecological characterisation of those environment that are likely to impose selection pressure for the adaptive trait investigated (see Thormann et al., 2014 for guidelines on the predictive characterisation).

Studies of diversity also provide information on the coverage of the collection and helps with identification of gaps in collections resulting in better insight about the composition of the collection and its genetic diversity. Gap analysis methodology using geographic information systems (Jarvis et al., 2005) or sampling, geographic and information gaps (Ramírez-Villegas et al., 2010). This information can be matched with user demands for specific traits to determine where to acquire or collect additional materials to fill those gaps and better respond to users.

## References


Agrawal, R. C., Behera, D. and Saxena, S. (2007) 'Genebank information management systems (GBIMS)', *Computers and Electronics in Agriculture*, vol. 59, pp. 90–96.

Alercia, A., Diulgheroff, S. and Mackay, M. (2015) *FAO/Bioversity Multi-Crop Passport Descriptors (MCPD V.2.1)*, Food and Agriculture Organization of the United Nations (FAO), Rome/Bioversity International, Maccarese, Italy, www.bioversityinternational.org/e-library/publications/detail/faobioversity-multi-crop-passport-descriptors-v21-mcpd-v21/

Belhaj, K., Chaparro-Garcia, A., Kamoun, S. and Nekrasov, V. (2013) 'Plant genome editing made easy: Targeted mutagenesis in model and crop plants using the CRISPR/Cas system', *Plant Methods*, vol. 9, pp. 1–10.

Benson, E. E., Harding, K., Debouck, D., Dumet, D., Escobar, R., Mafla, G., Panis, B., Panta, A., Tay, D., Van den houwe, I. and Roux, N. (2011) *Refinement and Standardization of Storage Procedures for Clonal Crops - Global Public Goods Phase 2: Part II. Status of* In Vitro *Conservation Technologies For: Andean Root And Tuber Crops, Cassava, Musa, Potato, Sweetpotato and Yam*, System-wide Genetic Resources Programme, Rome, Italy.

Benson, E. E. and Harding, K. (2012) 'Cryopreservation of shoot tips and meristems: an overview of contemporary methodologies', *Plant Cell Culture Reports*, vol. 877, pp. 191–226.

Berjak, P. and Pammenter, N. W. (2004) 'Recalcitrant seeds', pp. 305–345 in R. L. Benech-Arnold and R. A. Sánchez (eds.). *Handbook of Seed Physiology: Applications to Agriculture*, Haworth Press, New York, NY, USA.

Bioversity International (2007) *Guidelines for the Development of Crop Descriptor Lists*, Bioversity Technical Bulletin Series, Bioversity International, Maccarese, Italy.

Bioversity International, Food and Fertilizer Technology Center, Taiwan Agricultural Research Institute-Council of Agriculture (2011) *A Training Module for the International Course on the Management and Utilisation of Field Genebanks and* In Vitro *Collections*, TARI, Fengshan, Taiwan.

Chandel, K. P. S., Chaudhury, R., Radhamani, J. and Malik, S. K. (1995) 'Desiccation and freezing sensitivity in recalcitrant seeds of tea, cocoa and jackfruit', *Annals of Botany*, vol. 76, pp. 443–450.

Convention on Biological Diversity (CBD) (2014) *Global Biodiversity Outlook 4*, Convention on Biological Diversity, Montréal, Canada.

Coomes, T., McGuire, S. J., Garine, E., Caillon, S., McKey, D., Demeulenaere, E., Jarvis, D., Aistara, G., Bearnaud, A., Clouvel, P., Emperaire, L., Louafi, S., Martin, P., Massol, F., Pautasso, M., Violon, C. and Wencelius, J. (2015) 'Farmer seed networks make a limited contribution to agriculture? Four common misconceptions', *Food Policy*, vol. 56, pp. 41–50.

de Vicente, M. C. and Andersson, M. S. (eds.) (2006) *DNA Banks – Providing Novel Options for Genebanks? Topical Reviews in Agricultural Biodiversity*, International Plant Genetic Resources Institute, Rome, Italy.

de Vicente, M. C., Metz, T. and Alercia, A. (2004) *Descriptors for Genetic Markers Technologies*, International Plant Genetic Resources Institute, Rome, Italy.

Dulloo, M. E., Ebert, A. W., Dussert, S., Gotor, E., Astorga, C., Vasquez, N., Rakotomalala, J. J., Rabemiafara, A., Eira, M., Bellachew, B., Omondi, C., Engelmann, F., Anthony, F., Watts, J., Qamar, Z. and Snook, L. (2009) 'Cost efficiency of cryopreservation as a long term conservation method for coffee genetic resources', *Crop Science*, vol. 49, pp. 2123–2138.

Dulloo, M. E., Hanson, J., Jorge, M. A. and Thormann, I. (2008) 'Regeneration guidelines: General guiding principles', pp. 1–6 in M. E. Dulloo, I. Thormann, M. A. Jorge and J. Hanson (eds.), *Crop Specific Regeneration Guidelines*, [CD-ROM], CGIAR System-wide Genetic Resource Programme (SGRP), Rome, Italy.

Dulloo, M. E., Hunter, D. and Borelli, T. (2010) *Ex situ* and *in situ* conservation of agricultural biodiversity: Major advances and research needs', *Notulae Botanicae Horti Agrobotanici Cluj*, vol. 38, pp. S123–S135.

Ellis, R. H. (1998) 'Longevity of seeds stored hermitically at low moisture contents', *Seed Science Research*, vol. 8, pp. S9–S10.

Ellis, R. H. and Roberts, E. H. (1980) 'Improved equations for the prediction of seed longevity', *Annals of Botany*, vol. 45, pp. 13–30.

Ellis, R. H., Roberts, E. H. and Whitehead, J. (1980) 'A new, more economic and accurate approach to monitoring the viability of accessions during storage in seed banks', *Plant Genetic Resources Newsletter*, vol. 41, pp. 3–18.

Engelmann, F. (ed.) (1999) *Management of Field and* In Vitro *Germplasm Collections*, Proceedings of a Consultation Meeting, CIAT, 15–20 January 1996, Cali, Colombia, and IPGRI, Rome, Italy.

Engelmann, F. (2000) 'Importance of crypreservation for the conservation of plant genetic resources', pp. 8–20 in F. Engelmann and H. Tagaki (eds.), *Cryopreservation Techniques for* Ex Situ *Plant Conservation of Tropical Plant Germplasm: Current Research Progress and Application*, Japan International Research Center for Agricultural Sciences, Tsukuba, Japan/International Plant Genetic Resources Institute, Rome, Italy.

Engelmann, F. (2011) 'Germplasm collection, storage and preservation', pp. 255–268 in A. Altman and P. M. Hazegawa (eds.), *Plant Biotechnology and Agriculture – Prospects for the 21st Century*, Academic Press, Oxford, UK.

Engels, J. M. M. and Rao, R. R. (eds.) (1995) *Regeneration of Seed Crops and Their Wild Relatives*, Proceedings of a Consultation Meeting, ICRISAT, 4–7 December 1995, Hyderabad, India and IPGRI, Rome, Italy.

FAO (1998) *The State of the World's Plant Genetic Resources For Food and Agriculture*, FAO, Rome, Italy.

FAO (2009) *The State of Food and Agriculture. Livestock in the Balance.* FAO, Rome, Italy.

FAO (2010) *The Second Report on the State of the World's Plant Genetic Resources for Food and Agriculture*, FAO, Rome, Italy.

FAO (2012) *The State of the World's Forest Genetic Resources*, FAO, Rome, Italy.

FAO (2013) *Genebank Standards for Plant Genetic Resources for Food and Agriculture*, FAO, Rome, Italy.

Ganeshan, S., Rajasekharan, P. E., Shashikumar, S. and Decruze, W. (2008) 'Cryopreservation of pollen', pp. 443–464 in B. M. Reed (ed.), *Plant Cryopreservation: A Practical Guide*, Springer, New York, NY, USA.

Geburek, T. and Turok, J. (eds.) (2005) *Conservation and Management of Forest Genetic Resources in Europe*, Arbora Publishers, Zvolen, Slovakia.

George, E. F. (1993) *Plant Propagation by Tissue Culture: Part 1: The Technology*, 2nd ed., Exegenics Limited, Whitchurch, Shropshire, UK.

George, R. A. T. (1987) 'Review of the factors affecting seed yield and quality', *Acta Horticulturae*, vol. 215, pp. 15–16.

Gómez-Campo, C. (2002) 'Long term seed preservation: The risk of using inadequate containers is very high', *Monographs ETSIA*, vol. 163, pp. 1–10.

Gómez-Campo, C. (2006) 'Erosion of genetic resources within seed genebanks: The role of seed containers', *Seed Science Research*, vol. 16, pp. 291–294.

Graeub, B. E., Chappell, M. J., Wittmann, H., Ledermann, S., Bezner Kerr, R. and Gemmill-Herren, B. (2016) 'The state of family farms in the world', *World Development*, vol. 87, pp. 1–15.

Harrington, J. F. (1970) 'Seed and pollen storage for conservation of plant gene resources', pp. 501–521 in O. H. Frankel and E. Bennett (eds.), *Genetic Resources in Plants: Their Exploration and Conservation*, Blackwell Scientific Publications, Oxford, UK.

Hartmann, H. T., Kesler, D. E., Davies, F. T. and Geneve, R. L. (2002) *Plant Propagation – Principles and Practices*, 7th ed., Prentice Hall, Upper Saddle River, NJ, USA.

Hay, F. R. and Probert, R. J. (2013) 'Advances in seed conservation of wild plant species: A review of recent research', *Conservation Physiology*, vol. 1, doi: 10.1093/conphys/cot030

Heywood, V. H. H. and Dulloo, M. E. (2005) *In Situ Conservation of Wild Plant Species – a Critical Global Review of Good Practices*, Technical Bulletin No 11, IPGRI, Rome, Italy.

Hong, T. D. and Ellis, R. H. (1996) 'A protocol to determine seed storage behaviour', *IPGRI Technical Bulletin No. 1* (J. M. M. Engels and J. Toll, vol. eds.), International Plant Genetic Resources Institute, Rome, Italy.

ICARDA (2013) *A New Approach to Mining Agricultural Gene Banks – to Speed the Pace of Research Innovation for Food Security, 'FIGS' – the Focused Identification of Germplasm Strategy: Research to Action 3*,. International Center for Agricultural Research in the Dry Areas, Box 114/5055, Beirut, Lebanon.

Jarret, R. L. (2008) 'DNA barcoding in a crop genebank: The *Capsicum annuum* species complex', *The Open Biology Journal*, vol. 1, pp. 35–42.

Jarvis, A., Yeaman, S., Guarino, L. and Tohme, J. (2005) 'The role of geographic analysis in locating, understanding, and using plant genetic diversity', pp. 279–298 in E. Zimmer (ed.), *Molecular Evolution: Producing the Biochemical Data, Part B*, Elsevier, New York, NY, USA.

Johnson, R. C. and Hodgkin, T. (1999) *Core Collections for Today and Tomorrow*, IPGRI, Rome, Italy.

Kameswara Rao, N., Dulloo, M. E. and Engels, J. M. M. (2016) 'A review of the factors that influence the production of quality seeds for long-term conservation in genebanks', *Genetic Resources and Crop Evolution*, vol. 64, pp. 1061–1074.

Konopka, J. and Hanson, J. (1985) *Documentation of Genetic Resources Information Handling System for Genebank Management*, IPGRI, Rome, Italy.

Li, D. Z. and Pritchard, H. W. (2009) 'The science and economics of *ex situ* plant conservation', *Trends in Plant Science*, vol. 14, pp. 614–621.

Manger, K. R., Adams, J. and Probert, R. J. (2003) 'Selecting seed containers for the Millennium Seed Bank Project: A technical review and survey', pp. 637–652 in R. D. Smith, J. B. Dickie, S. H. Linington, H. W. Pritchard and R. J. Probert (eds.), *Seed Conservation: Turning Science Into Practice*, Royal Botanic Gardens, Kew, UK.

Maxted, N., Ford-Lloyd, B. V. and Hawkes, J. G. (eds.) (1997) *Plant Genetic Conservation: The In Situ Approach*, Chapman & Hall, London, UK.

National Academy of Sciences (1993) 'Documentation of genetic resources', pp. 205–218 in National Research Council (eds.), *Managing Global Genetic Resources: Agricultural Crop Issues and Policies*, The National Academies Press, Washington, DC, USA.

Painting, K. A., Perry, M. C., Denning, R. A. and Ayad, W. G. (1995) *Guidebook for Genetic Resources Documentation*, IPGRI, Rome, Italy.

Pasquini, S., Braidot, S., Petrussa, E. and Vianello, A. (2011) 'Effect of different storage conditions in recalcitrant seeds of holm oak (*Quercus ilex* L.) during germination', *Seed Science and Technology*, vol. 39, pp. 165–177.

Peres, S. (2016) 'Saving the gene pool for the future: Seed banks as archives', *Studies in History and Philosophy of Science Part C: Studies in History and Philosophy of Biological and Biomedical Sciences*, vol. 55, pp. 96–104.

Porter, J. R., Xie, L., Challinor, A. J., Cochrane, K., Howden, S. M., Iqbal, M. M., Lobell, D. B. and Travasso, M. I. = (2014) 'Food security and food production systems', pp. 485–533 in C. B. Field, V. R. Barros, D. J. Dokken, K. J. Mach, M. D. Mastrandrea, T. E. Bilir, M. Chatterjee, K. L. Ebi, Y. O. Estrada, R. C. Genova, B. Girma, E. S. Kissel, A. N. Levy, S. MacCracken, P. R. Mastrandrea and L. L. White,. (eds.), *Climate Change 2014: Impacts, Adaptation, and Vulnerability: Part A: Global and Sectoral Aspects*, Contribution of Working Group II to the Fifth Assessment Report of the Intergovernmental Panel on Climate Change, Cambridge University Press, Cambridge, UK and New York, NY, USA.

Pritchard, H. W. (2004) 'Classification of seed storage 'types' for ex situ conservation in relation to temperature and moisture', pp. 139–161 in E. O. Guerrant, K. Havens and M. Maunder (eds.), *Ex Situ Plant Conservation: Supporting Species Survival In The Wild*, Island Press, Washington DC, USA.

Puchta, H. and Fauser, F. (2013) 'Gene targeting in plants: 25 years later', *International Journal of Developmental Biology*, vol. 57, pp. 629–637.

Ramírez-Villegas, J., Khoury, C., Jarvis, A., Debouck, D. G. and Guarino, L. (2010) 'A gap analysis methodology for collecting crop genepools: A case study with *Phaseolus* beans', *PLoS One*, 5, p. e13497.

Reed, B., Engelmann, F., Dulloo, M. E. and Engels, J. M. M. (2004) *Technical Guidelines on Management of Field and In Vitro Germplasm Collections. Handbook for Genebanks No.* 7, IPGRI, Rome, Italy.

Roberts, E. H. (1972) 'Storage environment and the control of viability', pp. 14–58 in E. H. Roberts (ed.), *Viability of Seeds*, Chapman and Hall, London, UK.

Said Saad, M. and Ramanatha Rao, V. (2001) *Establishment and Management of Field Genebank: A Training Manual*, IPGR-APO, Serdang, Indonesia.

Shan, Q., Wang, Y., Li, J. and Gao, C. (2014) 'Genome editing in rice and wheat using the CRISPR/Cas system', *Nature Protocols*, vol. 9, pp. 2395–2410.

Sthapit, B. (2013) 'Emerging theory and practice: Community seed banks, seed system resilience and food security', pp. 16–40 in P. Shrestha, R. Vernooy and P. Chaudhary (eds.), *Community Seedbanks in Nepal: Past, Present, Future*, Proceedings of a National Workshop, 14–15 June 2012, Pokhara, Nepal. Local Initiatives for Biodiversity, Research and Development, Pokhara, Nepal, and Bioversity International, Maccarese, Italy.

Swaminathan, M. S. (2009) 'Genebanks for a warming planet', *Science*, vol. 325, p. 531.

Thormann, I., Dulloo, M. E. and Engels, J. M. M. (2006) 'Techniques of *ex situ* plant conservation', pp. 7–36 in R. Henry (ed.), *Plant Conservation Genetics*, Centre for Plant Conservation Genetics, Southern Cross University, The Haworth Press, Lismore, Australia.

Thormann, I., Parra-Quijano, M., Endresen, D. T. F., Rubio-Teso, M. L., Iriondo, L. J. and Maxted, N. (2014) *Predictive Characterization of Crop Wild Relatives and Landraces: Technical Guidelines Version 1*. Bioversity International, Maccarese, Italy.

Tripp, R. (2001) *Seed Provision and Agricultural Development*, The Institutions of Rural Change, ODI, London, UK.

van Hintum, Th. J. L., Brown, A. H. D., Spillane, C. and Hodgkin, T. (2000) *Core Collections of Plant Genetic Resources. IPGRI Technical Bulletin No. 3*, IPGRI, Rome, Italy.

Vernooy, R., Shrestha, P. and Sthapit, B. (eds.) (2015) *Community Seed Banks. Origins, Evolution and Prospects*, Routledge, Milton Park and New York, NY, USA.

Vernooy, R., Sthapit, B., Galluzzi, G. and Shrestha, P. (2014) 'The multiple functions and services of community seed banks', *Resources*, vol. 3, pp. 636–656.

Vertucci, C. W. and Roos, E. E. (1993) 'Theoretical basis of protocols for seed storage II: The influence of temperature on optimal moisture levels', *Seed Science Research*, vol. 3, pp. 201–213.

Walters, C. (2007) 'Materials used for seed storage containers: Response to Gómez-Campo [Seed Science Research 16, 291–294 (2006)]', *Seed Science Research*, vol. 17, pp. 233–242.

Walters, C., Berjak, P., Pammenter, N., Kennedy, K. and Raven, P. (2013) 'Preservation of recalcitrant seeds', *Science*, vol. 339, pp. 915–916.

Walters, C., Wheeler, L. J. and Stanwood, P. C. (2004) 'Longevity of cryogenically-stored seeds', *Cryobiology*, vol. 48, pp. 229–244.

Whitehouse, K. J., Hay, F. and Ellis, R. H. (2015) 'Increases in the longevity of desiccation-phase developing rice seeds: Response to high-temperature drying depends on harvest moisture content', *Annals of Botany*, vol. 116, pp. 247–259.

# 37

# SEEDS TO KEEP AND SEEDS TO SHARE

## The multiple roles of community seed banks

*Ronnie Vernooy, Pitambar Shrestha and Bhuwon Sthapit*

### Introduction

Community seed banks – locally governed and managed, mostly informal, institutions whose core function is to maintain seeds for local use (Development Fund, 2011; Shrestha et al., 2012; Sthapit, 2013) – have been around for about 30 years. They have been designed and implemented to conserve, restore, revitalize, strengthen and improve local seed systems, and most are especially, but not solely, focused on local crop varieties. They handle major crops, minor crops and so-called neglected and underutilized species. Community seed banks seek to regain, maintain and increase the control of farmers and local communities over seeds and to strengthen or establish dynamic forms of cooperation among farmers, and between farmers and others involved in the conservation and sustainable use of agricultural biodiversity (Vernooy, 2013; see also Taylor, Chapter 38 of this Handbook).

The drivers underlying their establishment, evolution and sustainability over time vary considerably. Some were set up following a famine, drought or flood and the loss of local seed supplies (e.g. in Bangladesh, Ethiopia, Guatemala, Zimbabwe).[1] Others were initiated following participatory crop improvement efforts that resulted in the availability of new cultivars and new skills to locally maintain healthy and genetically pure seed (for example, in Bolivia, Honduras, Nicaragua). Still others were established because farmers were far removed from a reliable source of quality seed (e.g. in Burkina Faso, India, Nepal, Mali). In developed countries, community seed banks often arose when hobby farmers and gardeners started to conserve and exchange their seeds in their neighbourhoods (e.g. in Australia, Canada, United States). Depending on management capabilities, governance modality and type, and level and duration of external support, community seed banks have experienced variable fortunes, as some rapidly withered while others endured and prospered.

Surprisingly, despite 30 years of existence and growth, very few scientific publications can be found that review the history, evolution, experiences, successes, challenges and prospects of community seed banks. This seems illustrative of the general neglect of both the actual achievements of community seed banks and of the potential they have as key rural organizations led by farmers themselves dedicated to seed and food security and sovereignty. Based on a global review of the literature and a large number of in-depth case studies (Vernooy et al., 2015), this chapter summarizes the main findings of a comprehensive comparative analysis of key operational aspects of community seed banks: functions and services, governance and management, technical aspects, support and networking, policy and legal environment, and sustainability. Assessing the achievements, there is much to celebrate. There are, however, also some common weaknesses and challenges. The chapter concludes with three broad possible scenarios for the future development of community seed banks.

## Functions and services

Community seed banks perform multiple functions. Depending on the objectives set by its members, these can include awareness-raising and education about the need to conserve agricultural biodiversity; documentation of traditional knowledge and information; the collection, production, distribution and exchange of seeds; sharing of knowledge and experience; promotion of ecological agriculture; participatory crop improvement experiments; income-generating activities for members; networking and policy advocacy; and the development of other community enterprises. Apart from the concrete results that these activities produce, farmers' involvement can contribute to their empowerment as individuals and groups. Based on our global review of community seed banks, we can conclude that some are highly focused on conservation of agricultural biodiversity (including reviving lost local varieties), while others give priority to both conservation and to access and availability of diverse types of seeds and planting materials suitable to various agro-ecological domains, primarily for local farmers. In addition to these two main functions, promoting seed and food sovereignty is another core element of some community seed banks (Vernooy et al., 2014).

A community seed bank is based on the principle of conserving local varieties 'on farm', that is, in farmers' fields or home gardens. However, most community seed banks include a seed storage facility collectively managed by the farming community. This represents a community-level *ex situ* facility, similar to that of a national or international gene bank (see Dulloo et al., Chapter 36 of this Handbook). In practice, except in a few cases, community seed banks store seeds only for one season and regenerate seeds each year through various mechanisms. For example, the community seed bank in Bara, Nepal, establishes a diversity block of more than 80 local rice varieties in an appropriate area each year to characterize and multiply seeds for the next season. At the same time, they also distribute seeds of each local variety to one or more members on a loan basis, so that the bank has two sources of new seeds each year. Such on-farm conservation efforts allow continued evolution through both natural and human selection. A recently established community seed bank in Bhutan is putting efforts into maintaining existing varieties of buckwheat *(Fagopyrum esculentum)* and restoring lost ones to enhance genetic diversity in the area, thereby strengthening farmers' capacity to adapt to changing climatic conditions. Community seed banks in Mexico were established as part of a national strategy for *in situ* and on-farm conservation. There, 25 community seed banks have formed a network that has been integrated into a National System of Plant Genetic Resources for Food and Agriculture. These community seed banks have focused on conserving a large number of local varieties of maize, beans, squash and chili.

Access to and availability of a large quantity of farmer-preferred varieties, local or improved or both, are the core business of some community seed banks. Depending on rules and regulations set by the farmers' organization operating the community seed bank, they provide seed on a cash or loan basis. When community seed banks sell seeds, they will almost always set a competitive price based on a service motive rather than to make a profit. In the case of seed loans, the borrower must return 50–100% more than the borrowed amount after harvesting his or her crop. For example, each year, the Kiziba community seed bank in Uganda provides common bean seeds to more than 200 farmers. Here, the borrowers have to return twice the amount they borrowed. The community seed bank in Bara, Nepal, in collaboration with a local research organization, has developed a new rice variety named Kachorwa 4 using a participatory plant breeding method. This community seed bank now produces and sells 5,000–10,000 kg of seeds of Kachorwa 4 each year and generates income to support the seed bank. Three community seed banks in Zimbabwe, supported by the Community Technology Development Trust, have maintained, over time, 31–57 local varieties, mostly of sorghum, pearl millet and cowpea *(Vigna unguiculata)*. Farmers associated with these community seed banks have developed links with seed companies and produce and sell more than 350,000 kg of improved varieties of sorghum, cowpea and pearl millet seeds each year.

Some community seed banks function beyond the scope of conservation of agricultural biodiversity and making seeds available to farmer communities. Members of community seed banks are often working on issues such as empowerment of farming communities, promotion of ecological agriculture, implementation of participatory plant breeding and grassroots breeding activities, establishing farmers' rights over seeds, and development of fair community-level benefit-sharing mechanisms that may arise from the use of genetic resources (De Boef and Subedi, 2013). Although primarily facilitated by civil society organizations, this kind of community seed bank has developed seed autonomy to some extent. For example, in Bangladesh, the Nayakrishi seed huts and community seed wealth centres, which are supported by the NGO UBINIG (www.ubinig.org; Policy Research for Development Alternative), have been able to promote ecological agricultural among 300,000 farming households in the country. In the state of Minas Gerais, Brazil, community seed banks are known as 'regional seed houses' and represent an important conservation strategy. In this way, they complement other strategies and actions used by networks of peasant farmers, organizations and social movements in the field of agro-ecology, as well as federal teaching and research institutions. The objective of the regional seed houses is to strengthen agricultural biodiversity as managed by communities, identifying the diversity, species density and varieties resistant to climate change; diversifying local diets; ensuring both local and regional food security (and sovereignty); and conserving traditional native seeds as well as the biodiversity of the region's agricultural systems.

## Governance and management

Governance of a community seed bank is a process whereby a group of individuals works as a collective to ensure the health of the organization. It usually includes moral, legal, political and financial aspects. The way in which accountability is dealt with is central to governance. The issue of accountability, apart from proper management of infrastructure and finances, is most clearly expressed through the rules and regulations concerning the use of seeds maintained in community seed banks. All community seed banks need to adopt clear principles regarding such issues.

Management refers to the day-to-day coordination, execution and monitoring of key tasks required to maintain a community seed bank in the short and long term. It usually involves human resources, as well as technical, administrative, organizational and financial elements. In most countries, community seed banks are characterized by a high degree of voluntary effort, and this has a direct impact on the way management is organized. Of all the community seed banks reviewed, only a small number have all the basic elements of governance and management structures. Some have detailed formalized rules and regulations; some have only general working principles; and many have mostly informal ways of organizing both governance and day-to-day management. A typology of five categories of governance and management systems has been

*Table 37.1* Governance and management structures of community seed banks

| *Type* | *Basic elements of governance and management* |
|---|---|
| Basic stage of implementation without key formal elements of governance | Run by external stakeholders, usually project managers, often NGO or donor staff.<br>Custodian farmers are encouraged to take a leadership role as they have an affinity with local crop diversity. |
| Under strong control of a public-sector agency and managed as a kind of decentralized national gene bank | Operated by public-sector agency.<br>Phytosanitary regulations in place.<br>Technically driven operational plans for ensuring quality and genetic purity. |
| Governed by a board of volunteers and managed as a seed network based on formal membership | Managed by small committees with both conservation and commercial arms.<br>Support from private companies, membership fees and income from seed sales. |
| Governed by elected committee (of men and women farmers) with transparent operational plans and guided by locally developed rules and regulatory framework | Executive committee (usually with balanced representation of women and men) has overall responsibility for collecting, cleaning, drying, storing, distributing and regenerating seed.<br>Locally developed operation plans match technical requirements.<br>Identified roles and responsibilities of committee members.<br>Sometimes include an ex *situ* backup system.<br>Sometimes include a community biodiversity fund.<br>Sometimes include social auditing. |
| Governed by ideology of free access, open source and seed sovereignty | Volunteer based (with varying degrees of formal management) or network of seed saver groups.<br>Some cases prefer the concept of seed library over seed bank as seed should not be privatized. |

*Source*: Adapted from Sthapit et al. (2012, p. 27).

developed (**Table 37.1** *Governance and management structures of community seed banks*). In many community seed banks, no matter which type, women play key roles, sometimes facilitated by outside intervention, but often because of women's strong interest and leading role in seed management in the household and community (see also Jiggins, Chapter 33 of this Handbook).

This typology is static by nature, while most community seed banks have evolved and continue to evolve through a 'learning by doing' approach. Over time, a clearer distinction between what is governance and what is management might emerge, rules and regulations will become more elaborate and formalized and, overall, the activities related to governance and management will become more complex. For example, in Mali, community seed banks have been formally registered as cooperative societies whose governance and management follow internal regulations. Each community seed bank has a general assembly, a board of directors and an oversight committee. The general assembly is the decision-making body and meets at least once a year, with additional meetings held on special occasions. The board of directors is in charge of implementing the decisions made by the general assembly while the oversight committee ensures that these decisions are applied correctly.

## Technical aspects

Community seed banks that are set up without proper understanding of the complexities of seed management may have a short lifespan. The basic requirements for seed management are the seed should be physically and genetically pure, it should be free from pest and disease, it should germinate and establish quickly and it should be accompanied by useful information and knowledge. Our global review revealed there are a wide variety of ways in which community seed banks deal with technical issues. The technology used ranges from simple to complex. Some rely on local knowledge and expertise, while others involve expertise from outside the community (e.g. agronomists, plant breeders, gene bank managers, organizational experts). Costs vary considerably, and planning ranges from *ad hoc* to detailed.

The number of local varieties collected and conserved in each community seed bank varies, depending on many factors: the number of crop species grown locally and their availability; human and technical capacity, resources and strategies chosen to identify and collect in the community and surrounding areas; the level of awareness of the value of local genetic resources and their role in conservation; the motivation to promote community seed banking efforts; and the nature of the policy and legal environment in which a community seed bank operates. The actual selection of crop species and varieties for conservation and management by a community seed bank is usually a matter of discussion among the farmers in charge, in a number of cases informed by interaction with outsiders, such as NGO or government research or extension staff. What matters is that there is a clear rationale for the crops selected based on an informed discussion among community members. Many community seed banks focus on local varieties of crop species that are of global significance and local importance and of which there is mainly traditional seed available locally (e.g. in Bangladesh, India and Nepal). Some specialize in a few crops native to the area, such as maize and beans in Guatemala; maize, beans, squash and chili in Mexico and the southwestern United States; potatoes in Bolivia; and sorghum, pearl millet and cowpeas in Zimbabwe. Some community seed banks have given priority to reviving traditional crops associated with local culture. For example, buckwheat in Bhutan used to be the staple crop, but because of government intervention, its diverse varieties were completely replaced by potato in the late 1970s. Another example is the recovery of 'lost' crop varieties in Ethiopia where, after repeated severe droughts and the complete failure of improved varieties of wheat, local wheat varieties that were still maintained by the National Gene Bank were restored to use through the community seed bank.

Our global review suggests that the steps after selection of seeds are not always carried out with the rigour one expects. The steps include information management, internal quarantine (to safeguard against seed-borne disease) and monitoring of seed germination, viability and vigour. Capacity development and stronger technical support could make these operations more robust, both in the short and long term.

Depending on the crop species, community seed banks usually follow traditional methods for storing seeds and planting material, not only to make management simple, but also because farmers are well acquainted with the traditional system, and thus, there are fewer chances of making mistakes in construction. Mud, bamboo, straw, dried bottle gourds and so forth are used to make structures and equipment. Sun drying seeds is common before cooling for storage in mud-sealed containers. In Bangladesh, the community seed bank consists of a storage area and a meeting room constructed using locally available materials; seeds are stored in traditional containers, such as earthen pots. In most cases, community seed banks consist of just one room for everything, but some (e.g. in Zimbabwe and Nepal) have separate rooms for local germplasm and bulk seed storage as well as office and meeting space. To keep stored seeds healthy and viable, community seed banks are gradually replacing traditional storage structures with modern equipment, such as airtight, transparent plastic or glass jars, metal bins and even SuperGrain bags (multilayer plastic bags that provide a gas and moisture barrier). These practices are becoming common in Nepal, Mexico, Guatemala and China. In Nepal, zeolites (aluminosilicate-based absorbents) have been introduced to control moisture levels.

To ensure good-quality seed (free from disease, insects, weeds and inert materials and not 'contaminated' by other varieties), community seed banks employ various measures. Some establish a technical committees for this purpose (e.g. Bangladesh, Costa Rica and Uganda), while in others, the bank's executive committee is responsible for seed quality in the field and in storage (e.g. Nepal). In Nepal, a local person is hired by the community to be in charge of materials and quality assurance in the seed bank (Sthapit et al., 2012). In Bangladesh, community seed banks supported by UBINIG have a Specialized Women's Seed Network responsible for day-to-day management and the annual regeneration of seeds. However, not all community seed banks have well-defined practices in this regard.

Many community seed banks have documented information and traditional knowledge associated with their genetic resources in various forms, for example, in a biodiversity registry (a kind of catalogue). Description can include invaluable traits, such as tolerance to drought, flooding, diseases and insects; eating qualities; market-related information traits; fruiting period; and religious and cultural importance. Such documentation may provide the basis for further development of valuable traits through breeding and promotional activities. However, very few community seed banks have characterized their accessions in detail using standard descriptors or published a diversity catalogue. They may need to collaborate closely with research organizations to carry out this type of work. Apart from traditional knowledge, the nutritional and medicinal properties of local varieties conserved in community seed banks are largely lacking.

## Support and networking

Community seed banks mobilize a range of actors in conservation, plant breeding and rural development to find new ways of collaborating with farmers and strengthening the multifunctionality of farmers' seed systems. Some community seed banks have excelled in building relationships but, overall, the networks that our case studies describe differ considerably. Some are stable, but remain limited in scope with few connections. Others span a large geographic area, include many social actors from various fields and have a large number of connections. The latter are part of, or becoming part of, a more-or-less formal group, network, association or federation of community seed banks along with other rural development organizations, such as NGOs, cooperatives, farmers' enterprises and farmers' unions. Such connections increase the chances of accessing new materials and information. Currently, one such network operating at the state level in Brazil includes more than 240 community seed banks. Likewise, the Spanish seed network, 'Resembrando e Intercambiando', is an informal federation that brings together 26 local seed networks that are distributed throughout the country.

Some community seed banks interact regularly with researchers (e.g. Brazil, Costa Rica, Guatemala, Mali, Malaysia and Uganda cases) or with extension agents (e.g. Bhutan, China and Zimbabwe cases). Others however have little or no contact with these professionals or prefer not to interact with them, for example, because of very different views on the value of traditional varieties/modern varieties or the perceived risk of becoming dependent on external organizations (e.g. some examples from India). Some community seed banks cooperate with national gene banks or national-level agencies in charge of plant genetic resources (e.g. Bhutan, Ethiopia, Mexico and Zimbabwe), while some have started to explore working together (e.g. India and Nepal) or envision doing so (e.g. South Africa). National guidelines for such cooperation that spell out roles, rights and duties are still lacking.

In some countries, community seed banks are part of a dynamic network alongside the formal research system, jointly conducting participatory plant breeding and participatory variety selection and exchanging knowledge and experiences. Some community seed banks have evolved into more than just seed-oriented organizations and serve as platforms for social learning, mobilization and community development more broadly (e.g. Nepal).

The most common relations found among our case studies are between community seed banks and international or national NGOs (e.g. the Community Technology Development Trust, the Norwegian Development Fund, LI-BIRD, USC Canada and Welthungerhilfe, all of which are described in greater detail in Chapter 35 of this Handbook (Sthapit et al.), as well as ActionAid and OXFAM-NOVIB). In some cases, national and international research organizations (notably Bioversity International) provide technical and financial support. Through these support organizations, some community seed banks have started to interact with national government agencies that set policies on plant genetic resources (e.g. Honduras). However, even when long-term relations exist, they are seldom stable because of their often highly personal nature, and they will most likely never be stable, given the financial uncertainty that affects these organizations. Relationships with the secretariats of international agreements such as the Convention on Biological Diversity (CBD) and the International Treaty on Plant Genetic Resources for Food and Agriculture (ITPGRFA) have not been established.

Sometimes, community seed bank leaders take the lead in establishing and maintaining a network; sometimes, there is much greater participation by members. In some cases, women farmers play a strong role in almost all operations of community seed banks; in other cases, women and men share roles and activities. Sometimes, the government initiates networking. The Bhutan government is developing a national strategy to establish and support community seed banks. This represents an institutional model that could guide solid operations, good governance and management and sustainability. Networking in developed countries (e.g. Australia, Canada, European countries and the United States) appears to function well with strongly committed members, focused objectives and sound self-financing mechanisms. In developing countries, most networking is facilitated, at least initially, by donors or national or international NGOs, and local buy-in takes time and is sometimes hindered by distrust.

The Zimbabwean community seed banks have developed close working relations with the national gene bank, which provides training and back-up storage of seed samples collected by the community banks and participates in seed fairs. The national extension service has provided technical support from the beginning. The Community Technology Development Trust, the NGO supporting the community seed banks, has signed a Memorandum of Understanding with the Zimbabwe farmers' union to facilitate scaling up of seed banks and networking among farmers at the national level.

## Policy and legal environment

Across the world, community seed banks operate in countries with diverse political regimes and policy and legal contexts. To date, very little attention has been paid to analyzing the policy and legal environment in which community seed banks operate. Our global review suggests that currently a variety of policies and laws affect community seed banks, both positively and negatively.

National seed policies and related laws normally address seed production (multiplication), standardization, certification and commercialization; variety improvement, registration and release procedures; protection of intellectual property (often mostly concerning breeders' rights); technical support to the seed sector (research and extension services); and farmers' organizations (as discussed in the chapters in Part 5 of this Handbook). As such, they have an immediate impact on the operations of many community seed banks, particularly those that focus on providing access to and availability of seeds. Specific measures spelled out in policies and laws can offer concrete support to community seed banks but, to date, more often than not, they have the opposite effect. In Zimbabwe, farmers are not allowed to sell farm-saved seed. In Mexico, legislation to protect farmers' genetic resources is still lacking, although community seed banks do receive technical and financial support from the government. In Nicaragua, various civil society organizations are campaigning for enactment of a legal framework to promote and protect seeds of local varieties.

On the positive side, in recent years promising changes have been taking place in a number of countries. Our assessment is that this positive trend will likely continue and expand, given the potential of community seed banks as well as increasing awareness of this potential among key decision-makers and their interest in integrating community seed banks into the broader framework of policies, strategies and programs.

For example, in Mexico, community seed banks receive financial and technical support from the federal government; this scheme seems unique in terms of its size and scope. In Nepal, the national policy environment has become more favourable for community seed banks. The Department of Agriculture has mainstreamed community seed banks in its plans and programs as a strategy to increase access to quality improved seeds and to conserve local crops. The recently amended national seed regulation has relaxed its requirements for registering local crop varieties, making it possible for individual and organized farmers to register their locally bred varieties. In 2014, Bhutan's National Biodiversity Centre drafted a guide for community seed banks (in English). The guide has six chapters that include definitions, objectives, functions, organizers and collaborators, scope and establishment and management guidelines. Wider dissemination of such guides might be of help to other governments interested in promoting seed banks.

In South Africa, the Department of Agriculture, Forestry and Fisheries (DAFF) considers community seed banks to be a means to strengthen informal seed systems, support conservation of traditional farmer varieties and maintain seed security at the district and community levels. The 'Departmental Strategy on Conservation and Sustainable Use of Genetic Resources for Food and Agriculture' proposes, among other focus areas, both *ex situ* and *in situ* conservation of plant genetic resources for food and agriculture. DAFF is in the process of setting up the first community seed banks in the country in selected regions of mainly smallholder farms.

Brazil is the country with the most supportive policies and laws in relation to community seed banks. Over the last few years, three Brazilian states (Paraíba, Alagoas and Minas Gerais) have approved laws aimed at providing a legal framework for existing community seed banks created and maintained by small-scale farmers' associations with the support of NGOs and sometimes local governments. In four other states (Bahia, Pernambuco, Santa Catarina and São Paulo), similar bills are being discussed in their legislative assemblies. A special community seed bank program allows Paraíba's state government to buy seeds of local varieties for distribution among farmers and community seed banks. Previously, only certified seeds of improved varieties had been used for this purpose. This law has also allowed farmers to use seeds of local varieties to produce food and sell it to public schools and hospitals (through contracts with state government agencies). The state of Minas Gerais approved its first community seed bank law in 2009. It established, for the first time, a legal definition of a community seed bank and offered some protection to farmers in terms of access and availability: 'a germplasm collection of local, traditional and creole plant varieties and, landraces, administered locally by family farmers, who are responsible for the multiplication of seeds or seedlings for distribution, exchange, or trade among themselves.'

Sometimes, national policies and laws contradict each other. In Rwanda, for example, the government has started to support the establishment of community seed banks in selected areas. However, the policy of land consolidation and growing a single priority crop has a negative impact on community seed bank activities, because the local varieties of different crops cannot be grown freely by farmers. This is also hindered by the government's distribution of improved varieties of seeds and fertilizers to farmers under the crop intensification program. A number of countries make it difficult to establish and operate community seed banks for political reasons. Some governments consider them 'competitors' of the government-controlled conservation and/or seed systems. Others are worried about community-based organizations at large.

In countries such as China, the policy and legal environment do not favour conservation by farmers and their communities, although in recent years, some opportunities for local initiatives including the establishment of a small number of community seed banks have been created with the support of international organizations, among them Bioversity International. In Nicaragua, where there are a good number of community seed banks, the lack of supportive conservation policies on native genetic resources combined with the promotion of a few improved varieties of staple grains by research and extension agencies has resulted in the loss of local varieties in recent decades.

## Sustainability

Sustainability, or long-term organizational viability, is the greatest challenge facing community seed banks. There are considerable differences in performance of community seed banks in terms of technical and operational capacities, such as adherence to phytosanitary standards, quality seed production, technical rigour in monitoring germination and ensuring viability of stored seed, management of information about stored varieties and growing conditions and governance and operational management. Technical and operational challenges are compounded by lack of legal recognition (although, as we have noted, improvements are underway in this regard in some countries) and scarce financial resources. Past experience has shown that community seed bank initiatives are usually quite effective during their initial years. For those that depend heavily on external support, a reduction in external funding and technical support might create serious problems. What capacities must community seed banks have to be and to remain effective in the long run? Our global review suggests that a number of conditions must be met: legal recognition and protection, options for financial viability, members with adequate technical knowledge and effective operational mechanisms. Combining these four dimensions of sustainability is a major challenge for community seed banks.

Without legal recognition, community seed banks are less likely to be sustainable in the long run. Most community seed banks have been established with support from NGOs through project funds, usually of short duration. Unfortunately, community seed banks have not yet benefited from the support of international bodies such as the CBD and ITPGRFA. For seed banks to find their own funding, they require legal recognition and registration in most countries; many funding agencies also often hesitate to provide support to an organization that is not a legal entity. On the positive side, obtaining legal recognition contributes to building confidence among community seed bank members by requiring them to speak on equal terms with public, private and civil society organizations.

Community seed banks usually follow traditional knowledge-based practices that are relatively simple and low cost, but some use modern equipment and the latest technologies. In addition to the physical facilities of the banks, the technical knowledge acquired and used by members plays a significant role in maintaining the quality of seeds. When members are fully equipped with the technical knowledge they need to conserve and produce genetically and physically pure seed, chances of long-term functioning of the seed bank are good. Depending on the types of seeds and volume of annual transactions, proper seed management requires regular involvement of one or more people throughout the year to ensure that day-to-day functions are carried out smoothly. To be financially viable and not completely dependent on voluntary labour, a community seed bank should be designed in such a way that it generates economic incentives at two levels: for its members (in particular those playing key roles) and for the organization as a whole. One important reason why community seed banks become less functional when external support is finished is the lack of economic incentives to support the livelihoods of member families.

Many community seed banks have difficulties to develop a sound 'business' plan in terms of economic empowerment and financial sustainability. The exceptions are those seed banks that are evolving to the production and marketing of farmer-preferred varieties of local and improved seeds. In cases where this strategy is successful, it has generated economic benefits at both levels: seed producer members and the seed bank. It has also gone hand in hand with making seeds available to members and others, usually at a lower price than other sources. Community seed banks in Nepal, Zimbabwe and Costa Rica are producing and selling seeds in large volumes and doing well financially. Some are in the process of developing community seed banks as seed enterprises, for example Uganda.

The operational dimension is important in terms of sustainability, because it is through the practices related to seed circulation among members and non-members that a community seed bank comes to life and remains active. Clear roles and responsibilities of the management team are features of well-governed community seed banks. In Bangladesh, for example, the Mamudpur Nayakrishi Seed Hut (community seed bank) has two committees. The seven members of the Natural Resource Audit Committee are responsible for regenerating seeds, and for recording and maintaining data. The 11 members of the Specialized Women Seed Network carry out the tasks of seed handling, safe storage, distribution and exchange. Similarly, the Kiziba community gene bank in Uganda has divided major tasks among a general manager, a records manager, a distribution manager, a quality control manager and mobilizers.

## Prospects

What does the future for community seed banks look like? We present three scenarios as 'seedlings for reflection' to conclude this chapter. The first scenario consists of 'business as usual'. In this scenario, community seed banks would continue to come and go, perhaps increase in number in countries where they have made a recent start, but decrease in countries where strong growth occurred earlier. Support from external agencies would remain an important driver, although dwindling international development funds would most likely put the brakes on current levels of support. Perhaps a few 'new' countries would develop a strategy for institutional support through a specific policy clause or a national conservation strategy. In a few countries, existing or emerging networks would be consolidated. Other such initiatives would be difficult because of lack of recognition, weak financial and technical support and difficulties in establishing effective collaboration with other actors, such as research agencies and national gene banks. Community seed banks around the world would remain largely disconnected from each other.

The second scenario is one of increasing institutionalization. Community-based frameworks for the conservation of agricultural biodiversity would gain ground in many countries and internationally. Building on these processes, community seed banks, with the technical support of external agencies, would pursue interactions with national and even international gene banks to set up robust, dynamic and well-funded national systems that are well connected to the international level. Through this system, community seed banks would become part of a global system of conservation and exchange, receive institutional recognition and benefit from adequate, long-term technical and financial support. Community seed banks could form an international 'confederation' to share knowledge and experience and speak with a common voice. The system at large would operate in an enabling policy and legal environment at national levels and under international agreements, such as the International Treaty on Plant Genetic Resources for Food and Agriculture and the Convention on Biological Diversity's Nagoya Protocol. Community seed banks would embody the concrete practices that would make local access and benefit sharing a reality, as intended by international agreement.

The third scenario is the establishment and expansion of open-source seed systems around the world. These systems, inspired by the experiences of creating free and open-source software development and distribution systems, are systems that allow the pooling of genetic resources to ensure they are freely available for all to use, share, save, replant and improve (Kloppenburg, 2010; www.opensourceseedinitiative.org/about/). For a global open-source seed system to become a reality, well-functioning connectivity of community seed banks with each other and with other seed actors would be required. Another condition would be the creation of a supportive, or at least non-obstructive, policy and legal environment. An open-source seed system would be based on the principle that benefits can be maximized if no access and use restrictions exist based, in particular, on (private) monopolistic property rights. The underlying logic is that farmers are both users and innovators of technology, that is, seeds in this case. Such a system would aim to promote experimentation, innovation, sharing, exchanging, using or reusing seeds. To implement a model of this kind, community seed banks would have to be empowered to enable them to serve as nodal agencies for bringing together farmers, plant breeders, gene bank managers and others in the following areas:

- Legitimization of community seed banks as local organizations for the conservation of agricultural biodiversity, the organization of seed fairs, participatory seed exchanges and community seed production and distribution;
- Conservation and revival of existing varieties by providing access to and availability of rare and unique local varieties;
- Participatory varietal selection to generate added value for cultivation and use of existing varieties; and
- Participatory plant breeding to develop newer varieties and provide options for access to new diversity to cope with adversity and strengthen farmers' skills in selection.

This scenario would be supported by significant local resource mobilization because of increased levels of awareness of and concerns about the need to safeguard agricultural biodiversity. International benefit-sharing funds would be strong supporters of community seed banks, and this might further influence government policies in support of community seed banks.

## Note

1 Detailed case studies of community seed banks in most of the countries mentioned in this chapter can be found in Vernooy et al. (2015).

## References

de Boef, W. S. and Subedi, A. (2013) 'Practices contributing to community biodiversity management', pp. 65–72 in W. S. de Boef, A. Subedi, N. Peroni, M. Thijssen and E. O'Keeffe (eds.), *Community Biodiversity Management: Promoting Resilience and the Conservation of Plant Genetic Resources*, Routledge, Milton Park and New York.

Development Fund (2011) *Banking for the Future: Savings, Security and Seeds*, Development Fund, Oslo, Norway, www.planttreaty.org/sites/default/files/banking_future.pdf, accessed 1 October 2015.

Kloppenburg, J. (2010) 'Seed sovereignty: The promise of open source biology', pp. 152–167 in H. Wittman, A. A. Desmarais and A. Wiebe (eds.), *Food Sovereignty: Reconnecting Food, Nature and Community*, Fernwood, Halifax, Canada.

Shrestha, P., Sthapit, S., Devkota, R. and Vernooy, R. (2012) 'Workshop summary report', *National workshop on community seed banks, 14-15 June 2012, Pokhara, Nepal.* LI-BIRD/USC Canada Asia/OXFAM Nepal/ Bioversity International.LI-BIRD, Pokhara, Nepal.

Sthapit, B. (2013) 'Emerging theory and practice: Community seed banks, seed system resilience and food security', pp. 16–40 in P. Shrestha, R. Vernooy and P. Chaudhary (eds.), *Community Seedbanks in Nepal: Past, Present, Future: Proceedings of a National Workshop, 14–15 June 2012, Pokhara, Nepal.* Local Initiatives for Biodiversity, Research and Development, Pokhara, Nepal and Bioversity International, Maccarese, Italy.

Sthapit, B., Shrestha, P. and Upadhyay, M. (eds.) (2012) *On-Farm Management of Agricultural Biodiversity in Nepal: Good Practices*, revised ed., Bioversity International, Rome, Italy; Local Initiatives for Biodiversity, Research and Development, Pokhara, Nepal and Nepal Agricultural Research Council, Khumaltar, Nepal.

Vernooy, R. (2013) 'In the hands of many: A review of community gene and seedbanks around the world', pp. 3–15 in P. Shrestha, R. Vernooy and P. Chaudhary (eds.), *Community Seedbanks in Nepal: Past, Present, Future: Proceedings of a National Workshop, 14–15 June 2012, Pokhara, Nepal.* Local Initiatives for Biodiversity, Research and Development, Pokhara, Nepal and Bioversity International, Maccarese, Italy.

Vernooy, R., Shrestha, P. and Sthapit, B. (eds.) (2015) *Community Seed Banks: Origins, Evolution and Prospects*, Routledge, Milton Park and New York, www.bioversityinternational.org/e-library/publications/detail/community-seed-banks-origins-evolution-and-prospects/, accessed 25 February 2016.

Vernooy, R., Sthapit, B., Galluzzi, G. and Shrestha, P. (2014) 'The multiple functions and services of community seed banks', *Resources*, vol. 3, pp. 636–656, doi:10.3390/resources3040636, accessed 1 October 2015.

# 38

# 'BECAUSE IT IS OURS'

## Farmers' knowledge, innovation and identity in the making of agricultural biodiversity

*Dan Taylor*

'Because it is ours' is an assertion of farmers' custodianship of their agricultural biodiversity, the knowledge and innovation that underpins it and an expression of their identity. Hence, to be a farmer is a statement of practice and place that is both relational and contextual in which seeds are embodied with cultural meaning as well as being instrumental in food and farming outcomes – seeds that are the direct product of farmers' actions. In referring to these as 'seeds of the people', farmers reaffirm their collective ownership of their agricultural biodiversity and the inter-subjective meaning that is its accompaniment. Yet farmers are eclectic in their choice of seeds, for example: replacing one crop with another due to labour availability, the likelihood of drought or market opportunities, or indeed choosing an off-farm opportunity rather than an agricultural one. This eclecticism reveals farmers' innovation and improvisational capacities in which agricultural biodiversity is utilised in agricultural ecosystems which mimic the ecosystems they have replaced. In this process, nature is socially constructed while culture is naturalised. In this chapter, I discuss how agricultural biodiversity is situated in the interstices of these two trends as farmers reinvent their identities in the process of seed conservation, and in the creation of crop diversity.

### Introduction

Current attempts to modernise agriculture by African governments underplay the importance of agricultural biodiversity to farming and the local or traditional knowledge that underpins it. While some studies concerning indigenous agriculture make no distinction between knowledge and practice, others are dismissive.

The pressures for resource-poor famers to disregard local agricultural practices is increasing, with the promotion of high yielding varieties or 'new' seeds for Africa's farmers (New Alliance for Food Security and Nutrition, 2013; AGRA, 2015). This constitutes an attempt by governments to address deficits in national food production and promote markets (Government of Malawi, 2011) through techno-economic change – putatively a combination of new technologies and formal markets. This narrow focus reduces a complex array of historical, political, social, cultural and economic factors to a monocausal explanation – a failure to modernise with its all attendant implications. Modernisation in this sense implies the increasing commodification of agriculture as governments subscribe to modes of rationality or normative reason inscribed in neoliberal expansionism (Brown, 2015). This provides the enabling mechanism for market penetration by the private sector into the rural hinterlands. The aim is to populate rural areas with the hallmarks of industrial agriculture: technologies that are assumedly scale neutral and predicated on a package of farming inputs – fertiliser, pesticides and 'new' seeds particularly higher yielding 'modern' varieties (Lipton and Longhurst, 1989). One crop dominates – maize – a cross-pollinator well-suited to a wide range of environments but also to the techniques of crop hybridisation and its concomitant proprietary protection. At the expense of other staple crops better adapted to a continent with considerable climatic unpredictability (Purseglove, 1968), maize in southern Africa has become most governments' and many farmers' crop of choice for food security but also as a signifier of modernity in contrast to crops that are traditional. (I use the terms 'local', 'traditional' or 'landrace' interchangeably to refer to resource-poor farmers' own seeds.)

This process of commodification has been enabled by depicting African agriculture as unproductive and futile, as exemplified in the discourse of politicians, administrators and agricultural personnel throughout settler history and resonates with contemporary discourses by African governments in justifying their involvement in new expansionist initiatives (New Alliance for Food Security and Nutrition, 2013; AGRA, 2015) of development and modernisation – and supported by epistemic communities of agronomists and other agricultural scientists (Sumberg and Thompson, 2012).

In all three countries to which I will refer – Malawi, South Africa and Zimbabwe, where I have worked in various capacities with farmers from the 1980s until now – I have observed the economic interests of powerful external agencies elide farmers' role as creators of biodiversity in the process of varietal selection. Reducing choice through legal instruments, governments wish to replace seed recycling with the purchase of modern seed varieties by invoking legislation that supports private sector initiatives (New Alliance for Food Security and Nutrition, 2013). In this respect, governments are obscurantist: resource-poor farmers are made invisible in an approach that devalues their everyday lived experience as social agents of change (Castro et al., 2012).

In this chapter, I narrow my discussion to farmers' knowledge of soils and seeds and how this knowledge and related practices – whether old, new or, for want of a better word, 'hybridised' – leads to the reinvention of the local identities in which context agricultural biodiversity is created.

## Seeds are ours

'Because it is ours' is an assertion of farmers' ownership and custodianship of their agricultural biodiversity, the knowledge and innovation that underpins it and an expression of their identity. Hence, to be a farmer is a statement of practice and place that is both relational and contextual in which seeds are embodied with cultural meaning as well as being instrumental in food and farming outcomes. This situates farming both temporally and spatially – nothing is fixed, and new knowledge displaces old as it is borrowed, adopted, adapted and appropriated. Indeed this leads sometimes to re-identifying the exogenous as endogenous as the new itself becomes old with the passage of time. In this sense, agricultural knowledge and its associated practices are both socially and historically situated.

Geertz (1983) wrote that knowledge has two propositions (p. 218): it is always 'local knowledge rather than placeless principle' and it is 'constructive of social life not reflective'. Neither is local knowledge just about spatial location but it is 'primarily relational and contextual' (Appadurai, 1995, p. 204).

Agriculture, in referring both to the cultivation of the land (the act of farming) and the culture of the people (farmers who undertake this task), is also both constituent and reflective of that social change. Just as local judgements of 'good' and 'bad' farming change with the availability of new knowledge which overrides the old, so the availability of options influences the relative importance of agriculture relative to people's access to other economic opportunities. Similarly, social relations change, and with them the customs and practices on which they were predicated. A weighting is attached to agriculture's contribution to local well-being recalibrating farmers' calculus of risk and return in selecting livelihood options. The outcome, in doing so, redefines the role and importance of farming in everyday life.

Knowledge as it relates to agriculture is about doing and knowing, and knowing about doing (Hobart, 1995), for it is through work that agricultural knowledge is embodied in practices that are both cultural and instrumental. This knowledge is found in the conservation of seeds and an understanding of soils that conflates people's association with their land as place and belonging and conferring a sense of personhood. Thus, land has both symbolic and practical values.

## Seed varieties

The usage of indigenous varieties or landraces is not arbitrary; rather, they are chosen with particular characteristics in mind. They are farmer selected and manipulated and so in defining a landrace, human selection remains the determining feature (Longley and Richards, 1993). A landrace is a variety created or developed by farmers.

Farmers are acutely aware of the seeds they use and the crops they plant, differentiating one variety from another, their characteristics and planting niches. Where farmers fail to name a variety, it is usually due to its 'hybrid' nature; in other words, cross-pollination or varietal 'mixing' makes classification an onerous and pointless task. There is no aspiration to know names for their own sake but rather for the properties they contain. As farmers admit, names are not necessarily important (Taylor, 1999a).

It is indisputable that farmers pay considerable attention to the attributes of different varieties, travelling long distances to acquire suitable types and breeding into existing varieties, the characteristics they feel are important – in all cases there is unspoken recognition of the value of local varieties. Indeed there are numerous reasons why local varieties are retained. While farmers recognise the yield potential of modern varieties, they also understand the bioclimatic limitations of their immediate farming environment: choices are made following careful consideration that includes the gender specific preferences of women (for which see Jiggins, Chapter 33 of this Handbook).

Local varieties of staples are preferred for their drought resistance, drought recovery abilities, disease and insect resistance, storability, taste, texture (especially when ground by 'traditional' methods), cheapness and accessibility and cultural implications ('because they are ours') (see Taylor, 1988, 1999a).

These varieties tend to be well adapted to the local environment. Grown continuously for years under the same sorts of stresses and subject to the pressures of farmers' selection for specific characteristics, local varieties express the desirable traits needed for food security under marginal conditions; in particular, drought resistance and storability though taste preferences are often mentioned. Farmers have noted that traditional varieties (of maize, in this case) recover after a drought spell, an attribute normally associated with sorghum which enters a dormancy phase under adverse growing conditions (Purseglove, 1968). Combined with greater pest and disease resistance, local varieties have a considerable advantage over newer cultivars which fall prey to pests and diseases. Furthermore traditional varieties are not susceptible to premature germination that occurs in local storage silos which are not moisture proof (Taylor, 1999a).

Local varieties are also preferred not only for their taste but also their texture, a point frequently overlooked by plant breeders in their pursuit of yield maximisation. Van Oosterhout (1993) demonstrated for sorghum how gastronomic criteria are prioritised in varietal selection.

Taste and texture relates to food preparation as well as eating. Suitability for pounding or grinding remains important where the 'traditional' mortar and pestle type systems prevail.

Certain seeds are important for ritual purposes, as there is a strong association between seeds, ownership and identity. Thus, traditional varieties are articulated as our seed, the people's seed, mother's seed or grandmother's seed.

Seeds belong to all, but the gendered nature of seed is revealed. The linkage between seeds and women is indicative of the primary role women play in seed identification, choice and selection. Thus, in attributing functional reasons for the conservation of landraces, there is the mistake to overlook an important, additional reason for their maintenance: that they embody meaning and identity, or to use the specific words used by farmers: 'because they are ours'.

In stating that the 'seed is ours', farmers acknowledge both their instrumental value and cultural significance, but recognise their more intrinsic value, in that they have served 'us' – as a community, group or nation – in the past, present and potentially in the future. Seeds encompass local understandings, inter-subjective meaning and processes of self-identification within them. The seed becomes a cultural artefact and a signifier of difference. This is neither primordialist nor essentialist, for there is always a temporality in this identification, as 'local' seeds are modified through farmers' actions in the process of creating new varieties.

Such is the case of maize, the dominant staple in southern Africa for not much more than 150 years (McCann, 2005; Taylor, 2012). Maize has not been the main staple crop for long in southern Africa, considering the centuries of human presence on the continent. It has superseded both sorghum and millet, previously the predominant crops. Millets and sorghums, unlike maize, are both indigenous African crops, and would have both been grown for their taste, drought resistance and, especially in the case of finger millet, their storability (Taylor, 1999a).

Plant breeding by farmers is innovation borne out of farmers' knowledge and need, and embedded in their practices as seed is selected for different characteristics including a degree of genetic heterogeneity which spreads risk. Failure to breed true to type is likened to a refusal to modernise. Whereas although the formal seed sector is promoted and the informal denigrated (Chaves Posada, 2015), the truth is somewhat different, as Saunders (1930) explained in the case of maize:

> It follows, therefore, that seed from a variety grown in a specific locality for a number of years may yield a crop not at all identical with that from the same original seed grown in a different area. Moreover, each grower has *his own preferences as to type and may shift the average of any individual property by selection according to his fancies.*
>
> *(p. 147, emphasis added)*

Farmers in this sense become the creators of agricultural biodiversity.

## Soils

Farmers consider soils of equal importance, as was made immediately clear to me when I asked a farmer how he selects seed and his reply was, 'The soil selects the seed'. This implies that the farmer manages not only the crop itself but also the overall context in which plant growth takes place, enabled by a fertile soil. But a fertile soil is not simply a soil that contains nutrients. For example, the peaty bog soils of the swamp forests that are found on the northeastern coastal region of South Africa are perceived as providing both fertility for the crops and wealth for the farmer, providing a dual meaning for a single term (Taylor, 1999b). However, they are very low in nutrient content (Taylor, 1988). A fertile soil in this sense is not synonymous with fertility in terms of its soil nutrient content as can be deduced from these peaty bog soils but provides a reliable means for ensuring wealth and well-being – food security and income. Farmers use a number of evocative words to refer to soil fertility which further demonstrates conceptual differences in understanding. Fertility is described as fertile and wealthy; rotten and rich; fat and rich.

Thus, fertility is not a property possessed by a soil, but the context in which a crop is ensured. For the low resource farmer, a good soil is then the embodiment of prosperity, access to which offers the best guarantee – weather permitting – of a successful agricultural outcome. But words such as 'wealthy', 'rotten', 'rich' and 'fat' connote abundance and excess, and specifically in the case of 'rotten', surplus, putrefaction and renewal. In summary, a fertile soil is soft, moist, friable, contains organic matter and is dark/black in colour.

Soil fertility also has an association with plants of a certain type. It is plant indicators such as the blackjack (*Bidens* spp.) and amaranth (*Amaranthus* spp.) that reveal a fertile soil. On the other hand, the presence of witchweed (*Striga* spp., a parasitic weed which attacks grasses) particularly in maize and sorghum fields, indicates that the soil is 'tired'. Where fertility is related to plant pioneers, it is management related, and in this sense, the farmer's role is custodianship – to ensure that agriculture takes place in the context which best guarantees the desired result. It is therefore incumbent on the farmer to rest a soil that is 'tired', or to allow the soil to 'replenish its hunger' in order that it may once again be 'satisfied', or 'rich' in terms of the above explanation. In *isiZulu*, the opposite of hunger is not to be full but to be satisfied (Taylor, 1999a).

Thus, the emphasis on a soil-crop match is essential for successful low input agriculture. From this, it can be seen that local agricultural knowledge is not an abstract knowledge (Hobart, 1995) about the soil, the presence or uses of plants or different varieties of seed. It is the applied knowledge of what soil is good for what crop, what plant can be used for what purpose and what seed variety will be planted depending on a reading of the weather anticipated for a given season and the selection criteria involved. It is all about knowing how to practise agriculture gained through working the land, that either confirms or rejects past experience.

## Case studies

The four case studies that follow (all abridged), which I documented over the years, exemplify what I have presented thus far, but I offer this caveat: I have witnessed the gradual aging of farmers and the alienation of youth from the land. Farming is both more, and less, important depending on individual and collective circumstances. At the same time, migratory labour has been part of rural life for a long time and has been accompanied by greater urbanisation. Increasingly, farming has become either a part-time activity due to economic hardship, low returns and low expectations and/or a last resort. This is because farmers are subject to constraints (related to both climate and policy) that impinge on their choices and limit their ability to respond to these pressures. These are the result of an invariant set of policies that make it so. These trends are stronger in South Africa, where historically a more industrialised economy and racial segregation have disadvantaged resource-poor farmers, but, elsewhere too, aspirations exceed what farming has to offer.

The four farmers in my case studies are exceptional in their capacity to farm successfully and in their demonstrable agricultural knowledge and in their practical innovations, but also in their role as custodians of agricultural biodiversity (as explored by Sthapit et al., Chapter 35 of this Handbook) –

while not forgetting the importance of cultural values. While they are all men, either they or their wives pointed out that wives worked alongside husbands, were custodians of knowledge in their own right and made a critical contribution to the farming effort.

The first farmer lives in northern Malawi and regards the conservation of landraces as a priority, and this is revealed in the case study that follows (see **Box 38.1** *Conserving seeds in Malawi*).

## Box 38.1 Conserving seeds in Malawi

EM, from the Northern Region of Malawi, conserves traditional seeds.

He works with his wife and maintains separate plots for these traditional varieties, which include finger millet (accessed through the extension worker), pearl millet (accessed through neighbouring Zambia), sorghum, sweet sorghum, cowpea, green gram, sesame, Bambara groundnut, yams, traditional maize (Kafula a small, [red] early maturing variety; and a late maturing variety), okra, beans, (*Vigna* spp. and *Phaseolus* spp.) and indigenous African leafy vegetables (such as *Amaranthus*, *Cleome*, *Chenopodium* and *Solanum* spp.).

He sources his seed from a variety of people and places. He protects his crops using the sweet and bitter properties of plants to make up the pesticides. He says that seeds must be conserved to ensure cultural continuity – otherwise they will be forgotten – but he recognises their usefulness in ensuring stable yields across widespread fluctuations in weather patterns experienced of late.

Acutely aware of the drought-resistant properties of the more traditional crops such as sorghum and millet and the particular characteristics of the local maize varieties he cultivates, he plants a diversified mix of crops to mitigate risk and to provide him with nutritious food. He says: '*a farmer must be active, constantly seeking ways to improve his practices, because it is only in this way that he can have a better life.*'

(Field Notes: Dan Taylor, 2012; see also Find Your Feet, 2012)

The second farmer is an innovator in his construction of terraces as a response to a problem of water loss and soil erosion. His improved management led to successful agricultural outcomes and a diversification in the number of crops planted (**Box 38.2** *Conserving soil and water in Zimbabwe*).

## Box 38.2 Conserving soil and water in Zimbabwe

MM is a successful farmer in the dry lowlands of Zimbabwe. His farm is sandy with low water holding capacity but affords access to a perennial water supply. He was able to gravitate water to his fields but found that he was wasting a lot of water through runoff and was also losing soil as it was washed away. He decided to terrace his land to stabilise the soil and conserve water. He used locally available rocks to create a series of 'walled' terraces that allowed the flow of water from one terrace to the next in sequence or via furrows to the next level of terraces.

The terraces follow the contour which he pegged by eye. He undertook most of the construction work himself but with some help from his children. Black polythene pipes carry the water directly to the field or feed a large pond stocked with fish and from there is taken to the fields using a sprinkler or flood irrigation. MM has compost pits where he puts crop residues which he mixes with manure from his cattle, goats and poultry which is applied to his lands. He has three compost pits, one very large and two smaller. Animals are also important for him, not only for the food they supply but also for the manure that is essential for his farming practices.

MM grows for home consumption and stores excess production from one year to the next. Due to the drought-prone area in which he lives, a harvest cannot be guaranteed in any year, necessitating that a food reserve be maintained in the event of a serious drought. He started off growing vegetables, but now in a single season he grows maize, sorghum and millet, as well as groundnuts, sweet potatoes and leafy green vegetables, both indigenous (such as *Amaranthus*, *Cleome* and *Solanum* spp.) and modern.

(Field Notes: Dan Taylor, 2011)

The third farmer is a successful innovator who maintains his own crop varieties, works collaboratively with his wife and has a deep knowledge of culture and custom (**Box 38.3** *Gendered knowledge and the division of labour in South Africa*).

## Box 38.3 Gendered knowledge and the division of labour in South Africa

Agriculture is primarily PZ's responsibility. He states that his wife is too busy maintaining the homestead. Nevertheless, many agricultural tasks are shared. The main portion of his farm is situated on fairly steep topography. He ploughs with oxen and rotates crops and areas under cultivation. He uses his own maize seed variety due to its drought-resistant attributes. It is an early maturing 'traditional' variety. Cross-pollination from other maize planted in the area has occurred.

His sorghum is a dwarf variety. He claims that although it is not a bird-resistant variety, he is successful because he plants at a time so that it reaches the vulnerable 'soft dough' stage when the preferred Guinea grass is flowering and the Red ivory tree is fruiting, leaving his sorghum to 'harden'. Seed selection is mainly the preoccupation of his wife, who selects maize in the field according to cob size.

Maize is hung in the kitchen until planting time. It is blackened by the cooking fire and thus protected from insect damage by the smoke. Sorghum is selected in the field according to the size of head (inflorescence), size of seed and whether seed appears true-to-type. Groundnuts and Bambara groundnut are normally selected in the field according to the size of the pod. Cowpeas are selected from stored sacks of unshelled pods. At the time of planting, the seeds are shelled and winnowed in a basket. The smaller seeds fall to the bottom, leaving the large seeds on the top where they can easily be removed (the same procedure can be followed for other pulses).

He clearly articulates the relationship between agriculture and migratory labour as he knew it. He states that the timing of job seeking was critical both for the welfare of the job seeker and his family. Sons intending to work elsewhere would assist with planting prior to their departure. If they were successful in finding work, they would be absent for the full duration of their employment. However, if they failed, then they could return home where they would be entitled to share in a harvest, to which they had already contributed labour.

The fourth farmer is an excellent manager of crops and vegetables and has created a 'mosaic' of plants, matching plants to soil moisture regimes. He generally manages his crops without the need for irrigation by making use of micro-climates. He is a craftsman with a strong affiliation to custom and culture (**Box 38.4** *Using agroecological niches in South Africa*).

## Box 38.4 Using agroecological niches in South Africa

DM is married with two wives. Adjacent to his house is his homestead garden which is planted to a variety of fruit trees and crops, creating a mixed mosaic of staple and vegetable crops, with individual plots marked by fruit trees. This garden is strategically placed to make optimal use of an advancing/retreating wetland. The garden slopes gently, becoming wetter as it descends to a permanent wetland. This changing topography with its differing soil moisture regimes offers a wide range of agroecological niches for a number of crops both spatially and temporally.

A high water table means that irrigation water is unnecessary or available within a metre of the soil surface. Most of the garden however requires only supplementary irrigation, and shallow wells are dug at various locations. Areas are carefully selected to match plant requirements. Towards the wetland, he plants water-tolerant crops like (African and Asian) rice, taro and bananas; in the middle, vegetables such as aubergines, beans, cabbages, capsicums (including chillies), carrots, onions and maize; and then towards the top, groundnuts, potatoes, pumpkins and sweet potatoes, avocado, mango, lemon, pineapple and pawpaw. A rotation of crops and, to a limited extent, areas is followed, but due to the application of kraal manure, there is little need to rest an area for more than a full season, if at all.

'Traditional' maize seed is selected from his own harvest. Agriculture is a shared homestead activity, with DM responsible for the swamp and homestead gardens and his wives for dryland fields, where they grow maize, groundnuts and other crops. He has considerable respect for his wives and consults with them when decisions have to be made. One of his wives is a herbalist whom he respects for her knowledge. He has bought seed from as far away as 500 km. His knowledge of cultural matters is extensive, explaining to me systems of past reciprocity *(ilima and isenenene)*, and he is a fine craftsman. He is apparently one of only two surviving people still able to make a particular kind of basket *(isihundu)* – made from a local sedge – used for carrying various items in an area devoid of clay for pottery.

(Field Notes: Dan Taylor: see also 1999a)

These four case studies illustrate the link between farmers' knowledge, practices, innovations and their identity and the use, conservation and creation of agricultural biodiversity and, indeed, cultural diversity. The intertwining of agriculture and culture is maintained by knowing about past beliefs and current practices. All four demonstrate diverse repertoire of agricultural practices which encourages the fostering of agricultural biodiversity, diversity that has allowed them to utilise existing micro-climates or agroecological niches, and at the same time to create several more.

It is their extraordinary attention to detail and the confidence to improvise that distinguishes these from most other farmers. This suggests that it is the management of knowledge rather than the simple application of inputs that is required for an agricultural future characterised by increased climatic unpredictability and the vagaries of climate change – as well as imposed regulation. This requires the aptitude to foresee agricultural opportunities and mitigate constraints. The need to experiment and make logical deductions from their observations is what these farmers are adept at doing, but this takes place in a non-conducive policy environment.

This calls for a re-examination of ways farmers' agency can provide the catalyst for agricultural innovation in which the (latent) improvisational capacities of farmers are unlocked. Working largely alone, incremental changes are made, observed and evaluated, prior to major changes being introduced. This technical competence is matched by knowledge of custom and culture. That husbands and wives work closely together is essential for successful farming outcomes; that husbands respect their wives and their knowledge is not unsurprising given the difficulties of succeeding in such difficult conditions. But it would appear that the mutual dependence this signifies is also an indication of women's role as central to household cohesiveness: in this sense, the household is the site of social and physical reproduction providing a nexus for all else.

However, the general failure of farmer support agencies be they state, private sector or civil society, to respect farmers' knowledge as the basis for action, as depicted by De Schlippe writing in 1956, remains as relevant today as it was then. This imposition of technologies either overt or covert, through 'agronomy's persuasive powers' (see Taylor, 2016) continues as *modus operandi* with participation a justificatory rhetorical device (Msukwa and Taylor, 2011). This power relationship undermines farmers' agency and the potential for social transformation.

## Change and continuity

The cultivation of polycultures (a wide range of crops with different growth habits and times to harvest) offers considerable food security options when juxtaposed with the cultivation of single crops or monocultures (see also Altieri et al., Chapter 13 of this Handbook). Agricultural ecosystems mimic the ecosystem they have replaced, substituting a human-created and managed landscape in place of a natural one (cf. Guyer and Richards, 1996), which incidentally is seldom pristine. The notion of mimicry in agriculture assumes the cultivation of an array of plants with different morphological and physiological requirements – plants with different times to harvest, indeterminate or determinate growth habits, variation in heights, adaptability to soil moisture availability, as well as photoperiod requirements – are managed to counter climatic variability and optimise yields. While inter-species competition impacts on neighbouring crop yield, the assumption is that the cumulative total yield of all crops in the field offers a greater yield, expressed as land equivalent ratio, and therefore food security, in contrast to the cultivation of monocultures.

The idea of polycultures – complex mixes of crops – that reduce risk and ensure a yield from some crops, if not all others, suggest farming systems that are inherently robust and resilient

(Altieri, 1987). As risk reducing strategies, they illustrate a closeness of match between crop requirements and immediate environment. The intentional combination of annual crops and perennial trees – wild or cultivated – constitutes a form of agroforestry (further examples are given by Leakey, Chapter 14 of this Handbook). Indigenous moisture-tolerant trees are maintained as a part of converted wetlands, whereas other trees may be left in fields as nutrient providers (legumes), as sources of wild fruit, or for shade. While at first sight, the planting appears to be completely random, areas will be matched to plant requirements (Taylor, 1999b). But agriculture changes over time and with it the crops planted, which may, at a given time, have a positive or negative impact on agricultural biodiversity.

The changing methods of agricultural production and associated use of agricultural biodiversity can either be cause or effect in the changes to the social organisation of agriculture itself. Thus, traditional knowledge implies not social continuity as such, but a sense of continuity in that the present is made authentic through the social imaginary or, by manipulating – consciously or unconsciously – memories of the past (cf. Williams, 1981; see also Nazarea, Chapter 39 of this Handbook). Thus, tradition itself denotes a cultural appropriation in which social change is manifest in the changing social relationships by which tradition is redefined and, particularly in the case of agriculture, in the increasing or decreasing use, and importance, of different techno-cultural artefacts.

For example, the prevalence of new technologies such as the plough involved men in agricultural activities to a far greater extent and changed the division of labour (Taylor, 2012). Also the increasing cultivation of maize – and its subsequent displacement of sorghum and millet – meant that crop production required neither a common date of planting nor the need to guard the crop against bird damage. Labour-time was freed, and the importance of reciprocal relationships, required in the planting and guarding of the crop, was reduced. At the same time, it diminished control by local chiefs over planting dates and therefore the agricultural production cycle. Similarly, the cash economy changed not only social relationships in the countryside by substituting money for reciprocal labour, but also cash offered an additional means to wealth creation and a store of wealth. Cattle no longer provided the only or main means of holding assets that could be liquidated on demand. Change is inexorable: the question is not whether tradition changes, but the degree to which its trajectory is deflected to maintain or alter existing patterns of control. Tradition becomes the dialectic of continuity and discontinuity in mutual antithesis, incorporating both local choice and imposed transformation.

The conservation of agricultural biodiversity is the manifestation of a dynamic process of continuity and change. The planting of seeds is an activity that farmers have undertaken for millennia; however, seeds can either continue as the outcome of farmers' action, choices and concomitant innovation that may apply, or fall prey to corporate concentration under the control of a deceasing number of large transnational companies whose proprietary motivations reduce biodiversity to a question of economic return. Perhaps we are destined to live with seeds as focal points subjected to ongoing contestation about use and meaning but without denouement; it is a struggle between farmers' rights to seeds as cultural and technical artefacts and corporate objectification for which seeds are mere inputs in an industrial production process (ETC, 2015).

## Conclusions

The conservation and utilisation of agricultural biodiversity is a basic right falling within the broader ambit of farmers' rights (Chaves Posada, 2015), the physical manifestation of which are seeds. If the right to plant, recycle, exchange or simply keep such seeds forms part of an inalienable bundle of rights, then the unfettered right for farmers to continue innovating in the development of traditional seeds is fundamental and a priority. This implies that, whether such seeds are stored in community seed banks, kept in homes, exchanged with kinfolk, bought by strangers or sold to vendors, the universal recognition of farmers' rights in the present should continue seamlessly with centuries of seed selection from the past through to the future. Our obligation to conserve seeds is mediated by our commitment to posterity not to foreclose options.

The conservation of agricultural biodiversity should not be reduced to a teleological viewpoint, but better understood as a response to change and opportunity. Thus, it is not a case of biodiversity extant, but as biological and social work in progress. This suggests that agricultural biodiversity does not exist outside of the creative actions of famers who, in planting seeds and then harvesting their crops, plan to, choose to or, serendipitously, conserve an existing variety or create a new one. If then farmers are the active agents of change in which agricultural biodiversity is the manifestation, it implies that agricultural biodiversity is a construct which does not exist outside of the social relations of its production. Hence, agricultural and biological diversity is conserved, used and modified by deliberation, chance or need, but it is subject to the 'guiding hands' of farmers in the development of seeds that have the resilience to accommodate new and unanticipated challenges. At the same time, the tendency to objectify and essentialise culture suggests that it exists in perpetuity within an unchanging social landscape. This constitutes a failure to interrogate its shared meanings (or situate its 'webs of meaning') as the cumulative product of social organisation, human interaction, conflicting needs, contested values and historical change shaped by the contours of power and domination. Thus, in adopting a synchronic rather than diachronic perspective, we miscomprehend the multiple trajectories of change in which local and global are ineluctably interwoven and the limits to, and possibilities of, farmers' agency. Here, where little is immutable, we address one contradiction with another: nature is acculturated and culture is naturalised.

Thus, it follows that at the interstices of nature and culture where nature is socially constructed while culture is naturalised, a space exists for farmers to reaffirm, reconstruct local or reinvent identities; hence in the liminalities of knowledge and practice farmers reinvent their identities in the process of seed conservation, and in the creation of crop diversity. For to be a farmer is to be inextricably of the land and seeds are, or can be, cultural artefacts and a means of change through which this is expressed: to borrow from Appadurai (1989), seeds – like things – have social lives.

If we are to follows Richards in treating agriculture as 'performance' in which the outcome can be known only with hindsight – rather than a predetermined series of steps or systems (Richards, 1993) – then the seed is the outcome of a permutation of possibilities for which no *a priori* position can be taken (Taylor, 1999a). Yet the threats to agricultural biodiversity are not simply related to environmental factors such as those impacted by climate change (Castro et al., 2012). Rather, it is the marginalisation of the resource-poor farmers that situates them as 'falling outside of history'. As neoliberalism's logic seeks to commodify the seeds of poor famers, 'the seed is ours' has the potential to mobilise farmers as a global force for change.

## References


Alliance for Green Revolution for Africa (AGRA) (2015) *Improved Seed Varieties Wet [sic] Appetite for Farming*, www.agra.org/what-we-do/program-for-africas-seed-systems/, accessed 24 August 2015.

Altieri, M. A. (1987) *Agroecology: The Scientific Basis of Alternative Agriculture*, Intermediate Technology Publications, London, UK.

Appadurai, A. (1989) *The Social Life of Things: Commodities in Cultural Perspective*, Cambridge University Press, Cambridge, UK.

Appadurai, A. (1995) 'The production of locality', pp. 204–225 in R. Fardon (ed.), *Counterworks: Managing the Diversity of Knowledge*, Routledge, London, UK.

Brown, W. (2015) *Undoing the Demos: Neoliberalism's Stealth Revolution*, Massachusetts Institute of Technology, Cambridge, MA, USA.

Castro, A. P., Taylor, D. and Brokensha, D. (2012) *Climate Change and Threatened Communities: Vulnerability, Capacity and Action*, Practical Action Publications, London, UK.

Chaves Posada, J. (2015) *Farmers' Rights Related to Plant Genetic Resources for Food and Agriculture in Malawi*, Global Forum on Agricultural Research, Development Fund of Norway and Centre for Environmental Policy and Advocacy, Grøset, Oslo, Norway.

De Schlippe, P. (1956) *Shifting Agriculture in Africa: The Zande System of Agriculture*, Routledge and Kegen Paul, London, UK.

ETC Group (2015) *Corporate Monopolies*, www.etcgroup.org/issues/corporatemonopolies, accessed 28 August 2015.

Find Your Feet (2012) *Recognising the Unrecognised: Farmer Innovation in Northern Malawi, A Report by Find Your Feet*, Find Your Feet, London, UK.

Geertz, C. (1983) *Local Knowledge*, Fontana Press, London, UK.

Government of Malawi (2011) *Malawi Agricultural Sectorwide Approach: A Prioritised and Harmonised Agricultural Development Agenda: 2011–2015*, Ministry of Agriculture and Food Security, Lilongwe, Malawi.

Guyer, J. and Richards, P. (1996) 'The social shaping of biodiversity: Perspectives on the management of biological variety in Africa', *Africa: Journal of the International African Institute*, vol. 66, pp. 1–13.

Hobart, M. (1995) 'As I lay laughing: Encountering global knowledge in Bali', pp. 49–72 in R. Fardon (ed.), *Counterworks: Managing the Diversity of Knowledge*, Routledge, London, UK.

Lipton, M. and Longhurst, R. (1989) *New Seeds and Poor People*, Unwin, London, UK.

Longley, K. and Richards, P. (1993) 'Selection strategies of rice farmers in Sierra Leone', pp. 51–57 in W. de Boef, K. Amanor and K. Wellard, with A. Bebbington (eds.), *Cultivating Knowledge: Genetic Diversity, Farmer Experimentation and Crop Research*, Intermediate Technology Publications, London, UK.

McCann, J. C. (2005) *Maize and Grace: Africa's Encounter with a New World Crop 1500–2000*, Harvard University Press, Cambridge, MA, USA.

Msukwa, C. A. P. S. and Taylor, D. (2011) 'Why can't development be managed more like a funeral? Challenging participatory practices', *Development in Practice*, vol. 21, pp. 59–72.

New Alliance for Food Security and Nutrition (2013) *Country Cooperation Framework to support the New Alliance for Food Security & Nutrition in Malawi*, https://new-alliance.org/progress, accessed 24 August 2015.

Purseglove, J. W. (1968) *Tropical Crops: Monocotyledons*, Longman, London, UK.

Richards, P. (1993) 'Cultivation: Knowledge or performance', pp. 61–78 in M. Hobart (ed.), *An Anthropological Critique of Development: The Growth of Ignorance*, Routledge, London, UK.

Saunders, A. R. (1930) *Maize in South Africa*, Central News Agency, Johannesburg, South Africa.

Sumberg, J. and Thompson, J. (2012) *Contested Agronomy: Agricultural Research in a Changing World*, Routledge, London, UK.

Taylor, D. (1988) 'Agricultural practices in Eastern Maputaland', *Development Southern Africa*, vol. 5, pp. 465–481.

Taylor, D. (1999a) *Fields of Futility or Hidden Hope? Agricultural Knowledge and Practice of Low Resource Farmers in the KwaZulu-Natal Province of South Africa*, PhD Thesis, University College London, UK.

Taylor, D. (1999b) '*Umnotho Wethu Amadobo*: The clash between indigenous agricultural knowledge and a western conservation ethic in Maputaland, South Africa', pp. 172–183 in G. Prain, S. Fujisaka and M. D. Warren (eds.), *Biological and Cultural Diversity: The Role of Indigenous Agricultural Experimentation in Development*, CABI, Wallingford, UK.

Taylor, D. (2012) 'Risk and abandonment and the meta-narrative of climate change', chapter 5 in A. P. Castro, D. Taylor and D. Brokensha (eds.), *Climate Change and Threatened Communities: Vulnerability, Capacity and Action*, Practical Action Publications, London, UK.

Taylor, D. (2016) *Contours of Domination: Agronomy's Powers of Persuasion*, Paper presented at the conference, Contested Agronomy: Whose Agronomy Counts? 23–25 February, Institute of Development Studies, Brighton, UK.

Van Oosterhout, S. (1993) 'Sorghum genetic resources of small-scale farmers in Zimbabwe', pp. 95–98 in W. de Boef, K. Amanor and K. Wellard, with A. Bebbington (eds.), *Cultivating Knowledge: Genetic Diversity, Farmer Experimentation and Crop Research*, Intermediate Technology Publications, London, UK.

Williams, R. (1981) *Culture*, Fontana Paperbacks, Glasgow, UK.

# 39

# LANDSCAPES OF LOSS AND REMEMBRANCE IN AGROBIODIVERSITY CONSERVATION

*Virginia D. Nazarea*

In the remote archipelago of Svalbard in Norway, only 810 miles short of the North Pole, in a cavern dug 390 feet inside a sandstone mountain, stands a terrestrial, frigid Noah's Ark for plants. It houses 'spare copies' of seeds held in gene banks worldwide, thus serving as the ultimate refuge for biodiversity. The seeds are packed in multi-ply foil bags that are sealed in 'black boxes' whose contents are known only to the scientists who deposited them there. By design, everything is going for it in terms of long-term conservation – the icy bedrock that keeps the collection in permafrost, the ideal elevation that protects it from tectonic activity, and the impressive governmental and multilateral funding that the futuristic set-up attracts

Thousands of miles away, close to the sacred valley of the Incas in Pisaq, in the *Departamiento* of Cusco, Peru, where Quechua farmers have dug the soil, made offerings, and cultivated potatoes and other Andean crops for centuries, a conversation is unfolding among the women as warm reminiscences flow around the topic of food:

> Before, we ate potatoes, fava, quinoa, wheat, barley. With fava we cooked *phuspu*. Barley and wheat were used to make *sankhu*. We ground the toasted barley in large *batanes* (grinding stones). My father ground the flour with *mate* (medicinal herb) and the peels he used for soups. My mother brought *llullucha* (sweet algae) in baskets. We ate only what the *chacra* (farm) produced; now we eat noodles and rice.
>
> In our grandparents' time, there was tarwi, wheat, potatoes, corn. We made *moraya* and *chuño* (two types of freeze-dried potatoes). We also ate *linli* which is olluco dried and soaked before eating. My father cultivated a lot of olluco so that even the pigs could eat it. Today we don't see olluco often. Even if we find them, they are small.

Many local communities have lost part of their native crop diversity due to a host of confounding factors, including agricultural development, market integration, and agrarian unrest. In the 1960s and 1970s, international agricultural research centers were established to avert famine by promoting the Green Revolution, among them the International Potato Center (CIP) in Lima, Peru. The gene banks associated with these centers conserve the reproductive material or germplasm of different crops *ex situ*, away from the cultural and biophysical forces that shaped them. These resources are exchanged for scientific inquiry, plant breeding, and genetic engineering and many of their desirable traits have been incorporated into 'improved' varieties (as described in Ortiz, Chapter 17 of this Handbook). Located in centres of domestication and diversity in the Global South and linked with seed repositories and plant breeding and biotechnology laboratories in the Global North, gene banks have been the focus of acrimonious debates over rights and access to germplasm (Kloppenburg, 1988; Fowler and Mooney, 1990).

Returning germplasm from gene bank collections to communities can be considered as backflow from what some critics have characterized as in appropriative incursions by the Global North into the rich genetic and cultural heritage of the Global South (Mgbeoji, 2006). Negotiations for the return of native potatoes between Quechua communities and CIP, brokered by an NGO – the Association for Nature and Sustainable Development (ANDES) – led to the establishment of the Potato Park in Cusco, Peru in 2003 (www.parquedelapapa.org/). The Repatriation Agreement was signed on 17 December 2014, a much-lauded first in biodiversity conservation that unequivocally recognized the rights of indigenous farmers to their landraces and acknowledged the benefits developed countries have derived from their use. The repatriation of potatoes from the CIP gene bank to the six communities composing the Park also effectively reinforced the paradigm of complementing *ex situ* conservation with more accessible *in situ* conservation in farmers' fields.

Repatriation seeks to re-integrate into farming systems 'lost' crops or varieties of crops from germplasm accessions that have been collected over time and deposited in gene banks. Yet in a visit to the community gene bank in the Potato Park in 2009, I noted over 400 varieties that had been repatriated from the CIP gene bank while, at the same time, over 700 that had been collected from the communities and packaged for cleaning and conservation at the gene bank. In a further development that received international coverage, 1,500 native potatoes from the Potato Park in Cusco were shipped to the Svalbard Seed Vault in Norway for storage and safekeeping because, according to Alejandro Argumedo of ANDES, 'Peruvian potato culture is under threat' (Native Village Youth and Education News, 2011).

Meanwhile, in the past decade, a groundswell of culinary revival has put Peru on the international gastronomic map. With Lima as its epicentre, a social movement based around food has been cresting in Peru, one that is affective – drawing on emotional attachment, and in relation to meaning, comfort, and pride in their heritage – and inclusive. Every Saturday, young chefs influenced by the renowned and influential chef, Gaston Acurio, would explore the Andes in search of local ingredients that they can re-incorporate into their cuisine, principal among them the native potato varieties. These once-lowly, twisted, and bumpy potatoes have acquired the 'heirloom/gourmet' status, promoted by Peru's largest supermarket chain, Wong's. A cookbook dedicated to the use of traditional potato varieties was released by Wong's around 2006. Annually, in September, Peru holds the *Mistura* (mixture), a popular food festival wherein people from the highlands, the jungle, the desert, and the coast bring a wide variety of their products to Lima. A whole range of food stalls from high-end cuisine to street food, traditional to fusion, presents an extraordinary opportunity to see, feel, smell, and taste agrobiodiversity. Since it was first organized by the *Sociedad Peruana de Gastronomia* in 2008 – the same year the Svalbard Seed Vault was established – the Mistura has matured from its charismatic origin to a broader social movement and continues to distill new directions in re-valuing and re-crafting Peruvian cuisine.

From plant exploration worldwide to conservation in botanic gardens and gene banks, the science and technology of crop biodiversity conservation has been dominated by *landscapes of loss* that promote the principle of containment. As the argument goes, agricultural modernization, globalization, political upheavals, and climate change have all but banished traditional varieties of crops, introducing unprecedented uniformity and vulnerability to our food systems. To counter genetic erosion – the loss of much-needed diversity on which the viability of our food production depends – the global plant genetic resources system, of which the CIP gene bank and the Svalbard Seed Vault are a part, is charged with the conservation of 'irreplaceable' resources *ex situ* – in cold storage, in trust, and into perpetuity for humankind. Gene banks are encased in concrete buildings comprising adjoining rooms maintained in different degrees of coldness corresponding to the intended length of storage of seeds and other reproductive material. Systematic passport data characterize the source of these germplasm materials and well-defined transfer agreements and rules of exchange govern access by different users. To prevent loss and contamination, seed accessions are held in short-term or long-term storage under highly-controlled conditions and grown out in a no less rigorous fashion (see also Dulloo et al., Chapter 36 of this Handbook). For ultimate long-term storage, back-up copies of national and global collections are stored in black boxes in the arctic vault in Svalbard.

By 'landscapes of remembrance', I wish to emphasize the everyday practices and sensory memory – the aesthetics, aromas, tastes, and textures – that crops and other culturally significant plants inhabit and evoke. These compelling and enduring practices, sensations, and sentiments have as much if not more relevance to the conservation of biodiversity as discourses and programs emanating from high and low. Sensory memory, in turn, can sustain and enliven alternatives that might have been abandoned or suppressed, including culinary preferences and rituals that require that a wide variety of plants remain *in memory* and *in place* (Nazarea and Rhoades, 2013). Instead of concentrating on landscapes of loss, the interplay between landscapes of loss and landscapes of memory or remembrance in biodiversity conservation needs further examination. In relation to repatriation initiatives, for example, the containment of wild, cultivated, and improved varieties in gene banks, the return of native varieties to counter genetic erosion in centres of origin as exemplified by the repatriation project, and the fueling of social movements drawing on a contagion of emotion like the Mistura present a multifaceted puzzle: beyond formal systems based on landscapes of loss, what moves conservation of biodiversity and defense of cultural heritage?

## Agrobiodiversity conservation: spanning the *ex* and the *in*

A selective and disjointed focus on gene banks for *ex situ* conservation and on biocultural heritage areas such as the Potato Park for *in situ* conservation tempts us, first, to polarize what is really a continuum of conservation strategies and, second, to privilege landscapes of loss over landscapes of remembrance. I suggest that an interesting location for the study of recovery and resilience is that transformative space between loss and memory. By covering (or uncovering) the range, or gradient, of biodiversity conservation measures, and dallying on this transformative space, I seek to explore how and to what extent Pierre Nora's (1997) injunction – 'If we can live in memory, we would not have to consecrate sites of memory to its name' – applies to potatoes, palates, and parks. Although 'loss' of traditional varieties and local knowledge brought on by agricultural commercialization cannot be ignored, this concept becomes problematic when we consider the irony of local loss in the context of global conservation as well as linear, programmatic repatriation vis-à-vis the more complex cultural conceptions of loss and return. The sombre discourse of loss is often used to justify projects that seek to recover and restore, but it tends to privilege vulnerability over resilience and dependence over agency. The broader significance of this chapter resides in its exploration of different expressions, dimensions, and measures of legitimacy and 'heft,' aside from historical force and social status. This angle is particularly relevant in the realm of plant genetic resources, because crops are 'good to think and talk about' but they are also incorporated into the body as food or embodied in ritual. The intensity and variety of human responses to these resources tends to be more of a sensual rather than discursive nature.

Beyond strengthening the complementation between *ex situ* and *in situ* conservation, repatriation of plant genetic resources conserved in gene banks to their original custodians, as is happening in the Andes, can be considered as a much-needed restorative measure. What has been collected will be returned and reintegrated into farmer systems from which they have been taken or lost. However, the situation may not be straightforward, or tractable. For many scientists at CIP, potatoes are 'accessions' in gene banks – to be characterized, evaluated, conserved, exchanged, and bred. But to the Quechua farmers in Cusco, potatoes are their *wawas* or 'infants' – bundled, sung to, passed on, and celebrated in myth and ritual, and in everyday life. We shall see how these divergent perspectives became entangled when Quechua communities, with the help of ANDES, demanded that potatoes previously collected by CIP from their land be returned.

Quechua farmers have been keeping and indeed enhancing their crop genetic resources over time. This brings into serious question the taken for granted discourse of loss. For the indigenous, particularly elderly, *paperos* (potato growers), the source of germplasm had always been communities higher up on the Andean slope, particularly Chawaytire and Paucartambo (see also Zimmerer, 1996). To further complicate matters, not all scientists regard potatoes as mere 'accessions' and, even for those who do, not all of the time. Here, I attempt to examine biodiversity conservation as scientific mandate, a popular call to arms in the local and global arena, and as a mad pursuit of muses. I draw from life histories collected over a period of more than ten years, beginning with the establishment of the Potato Park.

## Conservation as a many-splendoured thing

On one hand, the diverse homegardens and familiar trails where Quechua women continue to cultivate mixed varieties of potatoes and gather edible greens represent not only successful instances of *in situ* conservation but also 'milieus of memory' (Nora, 1989). On the other hand, the Svalbard Seed Vault conserves germplasm accessions under permafrost in the remote island of Spitsbergen. These two extremes provide counterpoints, forming a conceptual arc from warm, throbbing repositories to frigid black boxes. Between the memory and the exile is the Potato Park in Cusco, Peru. To put a face (or multiple faces) to this arc, I foreground the life histories of one legendary potato collector in Cusco, one founder-administrator and one collector-breeder at CIP, two brothers who co-founded ANDES, and two Quechua farmers who live in the communities of the Potato Park, one affiliated with ANDES and the Park and one not.

In the 1940s, preceding the Repatriation Agreement by a lifetime, a near-mythical character dubbed by the locals as 'Yabar Loco' was a figure of great mystery and intrigue in Paucartambo. According to his nephew (from his first cousin, by marriage) who had spent summers of his youth with his uncle, Abel Yabar, who lived close by, Yabar Loco owned an *hacienda* of close to 300 hectares in the higher zone called *cullo calla*, or 'the place of the fog'. He lived alone in a house that people referred to as *Manicomio Azul* – 'the blue insane asylum'. The reason for his notoriety was his solitary life coupled with his obsession with collecting potatoes. Yabar cultivated potatoes but never sold them to make a profit. In his *finca* (farm), he had hundreds of varieties labeled in pots or planted in terraces. These were collected across the valley and brought to his hacienda by his laborers who lived there with their families. Despite living an 'enclosed life', as described by his nephew, Yabar's fame spread beyond the valley, attracting the attention of the Russians who sent a 'spy' from the Vavilov Center. The *Ruso* (Russian man) – as he was popularly called – 'came in working clothes' ostensibly seeking work. Eventually, he befriended Yabar. They would be seen walking the land, trawling for potatoes. At some point, oral history has it that the Ruso shipped potato samples back to Russia without Yabar's knowledge. The nephew heard about this growing up although he did not actually witness it. But there may be some truth to this as Alejandro Argumedo, co-founder and co-director of ANDES, is initiating efforts to seek the repatriation of native potatoes from the Vavilov Center.

In the late 1960s, Dr. Richard Sawyer was appointed by North Carolina State University to coordinate its Potato Program in Peru. His vision was grander than his mandate, however, for he wanted to establish an international centre for potatoes. By 1970, he had a board in place, and by 1972, the new institute was well on its way. He recalled that entering the doctoral program at Cornell, where 'they decided that since I was from Maine, I had to have a potato assistantship,' was formative. Coming out of the program with a specialization in postharvest technology and growth regulators for potatoes and onions, he worked first in the industry until he realized that it was not for him. Thus, he spearheaded what came to be known as the North Carolina Agricultural Mission with renewed passion. Rather than investing in infrastructure, he used local facilities and built the staff, recruiting specialists in different fields nationally and internationally. He recognized the value of approaching the problem with 'different eyes' and found 'mavericks who were good at what they did'. He hired social scientists because he believed production is a multifaceted problem and saw the role of CIP in Third World countries as supporting, not competing with, the National Research System (NARS). When I asked what he thought about the repatriation initiative, his response was that it was only right for CIP to repatriate because it alone has collected and maintained the accessions of native potatoes in its gene bank and is capable of cleaning the potatoes of virus before distribution.

One of the scientists recruited by Dr. Sawyer was a Peruvian national, Carlos Ochoa. Before joining CIP, Dr. Ochoa worked at the Mantaro Valley Experiment Station as a wheat breeder. But after working there for some time, he thought, 'Wheat never really did a good thing for this country, this is stupid. . . . It's a country for potatoes, and I started to do the first work in potato breeding.' He bred two successful varieties in the 1950s, one he named *Mantaro*, after his research site, and the other *Renacimiento*, meaning 'rebirth'. He moved to the Agrarian University at La Molina, where he founded the National Potato Program. It gained strong, widespread support around the country. However, CIP was established around this time with funding from the Rockefeller Foundation and, with offers of superior working conditions and research support, he moved to CIP. He was tasked with establishing the world's first germplasm bank for potatoes, a daunting assignment that precluded breeding. He put his energy into collecting wild potatoes throughout the Andean region. Exploring every possible niche, he discovered more than 80 species, close to half of all wild potatoes known to science. Clandestinely, he continued breeding potatoes, starting from varieties farmers 'had feelings for'. Using native potatoes or *papas rusticas* as progenitors instead of official breeding lines, he bred a variety that he named *Micaela Bastidas* after the wife of the Incan rebel, Túpac Amaru, and one that he named *Tomasa* after the Incan lieutenant who died tragically in what later became his family's farm. All of his varieties were named to honor places, events, and traditions. Ironically, Dr. Ochoa's varieties – bred to address particularities of locality and matters of the heart – were the ones accepted throughout the nation and the world.

In the 1990s, the brothers Argumedo – Alejandro and Cesar – came to Cusco from Ayacucho and started organizing Quechua farmers around the idea of a biocultural heritage reserve. They aspired to knit development and conservation around the idea of *Incary* or 're-membering' the Incan body that was dismembered with colonial conquest. They founded ANDES, the non-government organization that brokered the Repatriation Agreement between the Quechua communities and CIP. From the 'communities of the Potato Park' they recruited local people to serve as ANDES *tecnicos*, among them Orestes Castaneda. For Orestes, well-being or *kausayniykuy* encompasses all the necessities and comforts in life, including the rocks, the lakes, the animals, and the trees. When he was growing up, they used only manure and other organic matter to grow potatoes. His father's *chacras* (fields) yielded abundant food. He recalled that when improved potatoes appeared and fertilizers were introduced, they started producing 'potatoes that are neither good nor tasty', those that end up small, contaminated, and green (poisonous). Slowly, they are 'beginning to value the teachings of our forefathers and just now we are noticing how important it is to maintain our knowledge'. Proud for having 'the only park that has different varieties of potatoes in the world', he admonished his neighbors to be vigilant about their unique heritage.

In Cuyo Grande, one of the communities of the Potato Park, Luisa Huaman lived by herself and still walked to her potato fields in spite of her advanced age. She recalled that in her youth 'everything was silent'; there were no cars, not even trees, just grasses and spiny bushes like *kantu kiswar*, *quena*, and *chachacomo*. They gathered spines and used these as fuel for cooking. She also remembered cooking only in clay pots that made their food taste rich and kept it warm. Now, they cook in whatever vessel is available, including metallic ones. She still insisted, however, on preparing hearty soups and fortifying drinks for herself and her loved ones. When she was a younger, they planted potatoes in *puqos*, where they would put guano droppings, three or four small potatoes and, in the middle of the plate, three coca leaves as an offering. According to her, 'before planting the potato one must make a payment and then you can blow some alcohol or *chicha* (a fermented drink from corn) to the *apus* (gods)'. Before, there were no eucalyptus trees, and rain fell regularly and gently on their crops. They planted legumes like fava, grains like wheat and barley, and tubers like *olluco*, *oca*, and *anu*. They had a lot of chickens and cows and also raised pigs, so there was a lot of lard. They used lard to flavor their dishes along with *yuyu* or wild greens that they would collect. In her memory,

> The potatoes were big and there were varieties like *pasnacha*, *peruntus*, *serqa*, *qompis*, *puka nawi*, *churos*, *puka churos*, and *chillico*. The *pasnacha* potato was pretty, rich-tasting, and yellow. . . . When you ran in the *chacras* the potatoes would come out of the soil and it would not be necessary to dig.

## Sensuous conservation in a landscape of remembrance

The trope of loss in the science and politics of plant genetic resources conservation foregrounds the abandonment of native varieties and attrition of local knowledge in favor of Green Revolution cultivars and high-input technologies. This somber discourse of loss is used to justify projects that seek to recover and restore but, in rendering affective attachment moot and divesting germplasm of memory and meaning, it privileges vulnerability over resilience. In reality, CIP did not repatriate the native potatoes from its gene bank on empty land, or in fields uniformly planted to modern varieties. Many Quechua farmers had persevered in feeding their children 'foods that make them strong' and keeping the variety that 'makes daughter in law cry', the one 'whose skin bursts when cooked', and the one 'that's shaped like pig's droppings' (www.culturalsurvival.org/publications/cultural-survival-quarterly/quechua-guardians-potato) among many, many others. For centuries, they have sustained practices that necessitated keeping bitter, dense, and bumpy potatoes for consumption, ritual, and whimsy. In contrast to the linear conception of loss and return that undergirds repatriation, Quechua farmers have traditionally regenerated their seeds by 'walking' them. They recognize nodes for recuperation in their landscape, call out the spirit of lost seeds, and 'scold' prodigal potatoes before taking them back.

Rural landscapes in the Andes have been aptly characterized as being 'in filigree' (Valladolid and Apfel-Marglin, 2001), even 'kaleidoscopic' (Brush, 2005). Intricate and complex, Andean cosmology is animated by plants, animals, humans, rocks, wind, soil, and streams that are co-equal, mutually responsive, and on their way to completion (Gonzales, 2000, 2013). Humans are not normally regarded as stewards of nature, and the idea of conservation is alien since it implies a hierarchical separation that is difficult to imagine in a nested and transformative world. Over centuries, Quechua farmers have domesticated the potato, nurtured its diversity, shaped it to a myriad uses, and integrated it into the *ayllu*, the central collectivity of nature, humans, and gods. Landscapes are places with deep emotional and cognitive resonance and ambivalence. In some cultures such as those in the Andes, the landscape *moves* and *speaks* for it is populated with sentient beings and inscribed with lessons for those who understand (Basso, 1996; Nazarea and Guitarra, 2004).

Re-embodiment countering trauma and loss can come in the form of 'concrete utopias', where interior or 'wish landscapes' are mapped onto constrained exterior landscapes through objects that enliven senses and emotions (Bloch, 1995). This is where the Andes' vision of 're-membering' and initiatives at the Potato Park towards the complementation of repatriation of potatoes with the recuperation of customary laws and revitalization of culinary traditions become very important. Cultural memory re-awakens alternatives, including a wide array of plants and other living things that may have been buried or purged. It has the potential to impart a different, largely neglected, dimension to biodiversity conservation that hinges on synaesthetic appreciation and emotional attachment to plants and other sentient beings. For conservation to tap into this sensuous realm, it has to be rooted more deeply, to include the pleasure and the dignity, the wholeness and the rightness, emanating from the availability and accessibility of a diversity of plants and the complex lifeworlds that they help imagine and congeal. Any movement that promotes cultural memory and synaesthesia will counter the rendering and de-animation that programmatic conservation can unwittingly instigate.

The idea of repatriation of germplasm from gene banks for *in situ* conservation in centers of origin and diversity like the Andes revolves around the relocalization of the supposedly disappeared and the delocalized. However, if varieties, practices, and knowledge are not lost but instead continue to be loved and lived – if they persist in crevices of production and 'pockets of memory' (Nazarea, 1998) – we need to seriously re-think the loss-dominated paradigm of conservation. What Bernard Herman (2013, p. 120) wrote in reference to the history of materiality applies equally well to potatoes of various origins and seed banks of varying scales: 'things possess the aura of heft, of manifesting themselves not as abstractions, but as tangible and real. Their paradox resides in what things are and what things mean'. In many conservation programs, *heft* is invested automatically in what is official and organized, such as gene banks, germplasm accessions, and biodiversity conservation treaties. Whatever falls outside this purview is then rendered meaningless, ineffectual. Surprisingly, tenacious 'asides', though lightweight, remain vibrant with emotion and significance.

## References

Basso, K. (1996) 'Wisdom sits in place: Notes on a Western Apache landscape', pp. 53–90 in S. Feld and K. H. Basso (eds.), *Senses of Place*, School of Americas Research, Santa Fe, NM, USA.

Bloch, E. (1995) *The Principle of Hope*, [trans. N. Plaice, S. Plaice and P. Knight], MIT University Press, Cambridge, MA, USA.

Brush, S. B. (2005) *Farmers' Bounty: Locating Crop Diversity in the Contemporary World*, Yale University Press, New Haven, CT, USA and London, UK.

Fowler, C. and Mooney, P. R. (1990) *Shattering: Food, Politics, and the Loss of Genetic Diversity*, University of Arizona Press, Tucson, AZ, USA.

Gonzales, T. (2000) 'The cultures of the seed in the Peruvian Andes', pp. 193–216 in S. B. Brush (ed.), *Genes in the Field: On-Farm Conservation of Crop Diversity*, IPGRI, Rome, Italy, IDRC, Ottawa, Canada and Lewis, Boca Raton, FL, USA.

Gonzales, T. (2013) 'Sense of place and indigenous people's biodiversity conservation in the Americas', p. 85 in V. Nazarea, R. Rhoades and J. Andrews-Swann (eds.), *Seeds of Resistance, Seeds of Hope: Place and Agency in the Conservation of Biodiversity*, University of Arizona Press, Tucson, AZ, USA.

Herman, B. (2013) 'Swelling toads, translation, and the paradox of the concrete', pp. 119–133 in P. N. Miller, (ed.), *Cultural Histories of the Material World*, University of Michigan Press, Ann Arbor, MI, USA.

Kloppenburg, J. R. (1988) *Seeds and Sovereignty: The Use and Control of Plant Genetic Resources*, Duke University Press, Durham, NC, USA.

Mgbeoji, I. (2006) *Global Biopiracy: Patents, Plants, and Indigenous Knowledge*, Cornell University Press, New York, NY, USA.

Native Village Youth and Education News (2011), vol. 3. www.nativevillage.org/Archives/2011%20Archives/SEPT%202011%20News/V3%20Sept%202011%20%20Native%20Village%20News.htm

Nazarea, V. (1998) *Cultural Memory and Biodiversity*, University of Arizona Press, Tucson, AZ, USA.

Nazarea, V. and Guitarra, R. (eds.) (2004) *Stories of Creation and Resistance*, Ediciones Abya-Yala, Quito, Ecuador.

Nazarea, V. and Rhoades, R. (2013) 'Conservation beyond design', pp. 3–18 in V. Nazarea, R. Rhoades and J. Andrews-Swann (eds.), *Seeds of Resistance, Seeds of Hope: Place and Agency in the Conservation of Biodiversity*, University of Arizona Press, Tucson, AZ, USA.

Nora, P. (1989) 'Between history and memory', *Representations*, vol. 26, pp. 7–23.

Valladolid, J. and Apfel-Marglin, F. (2001) 'Andean cosmovision and the nurturing of biodiversity', pp. 639–670 in J. Grim (ed.), *Interbeing of Cosmology and Community*, Harvard University Press, Cambridge, MA, USA.

Zimmerer, K. (1996) *Changing Fortunes: Biodiversity and Peasant Livelihood in the Peruvian Andes'*, University of California Press, Berkeley and Los Angeles, CA, USA.

# 40

# FROM PARTICIPATORY PLANT BREEDING TO LOCAL INNOVATION NETWORKS IN CUBA

*Humberto Ríos Labrada and Juan Ceballos-Müller*

## Introduction

At the beginning of the last century, plant breeding gradually began to be removed from farmers' hands, with the result that what had been done by many people in many diverse places began to be done by fewer and fewer people in relatively few places (Ceccarelli et al., 2012). Today, participatory plant breeding has brought farmers back into breeding (Almekinders and Hardon, 2006; Conny and Hardon, 2006). At the moment, farmers are participating in research activities in the field of seed conservation, plant/animal breeding, seeds selection, varieties/crops diffusion, farming system improvements and business management, opening multiple windows to maximise positive effects initiated with participatory plant breeding. Participatory plant breeding emerged as an alternative to reach better impact in heterogeneous environments. The heterogeneity of farming systems and farming itself forced scientists to go beyond their own discipline and work and interact with others, including the farmers, to improve their livelihoods. In practice, farmers and scientist from fields as diverse as sociology, economy, anthropology, agronomy and business management have been inspiring plant breeding, thus becoming a modern science field producing new knowledge and practices based on collective action. This chapter provides an example of how participatory plant breeding led to strengthening local innovation systems in order to improve food security in a centralised socioeconomic system, using Cuba as an example.

## The 'Golden Age' of conventional plant breeding in Cuba

During the 'golden years' of the eastern socialist countries, a centralised plant breeding model was a standard component of the high-input agriculture practised in Cuba, and particularly for the country's cash crops. Wide geographical adaptation characteristics were encouraged by policy makers, with most Cuban governmental organisations providing incentives to scientists involved in releasing a variety to State Enterprises characterised by large areas of land in monoculture (between 1,000 and 100,000 hectares). This was accompanied by intensive mechanisation, high agrochemical inputs and the construction of enormous artificial irrigation systems.

In the 1980s, ambitious plant breeding programmes were developed for sugar cane, root and tuber crops, rice, tobacco, coffee, horticultural crops, pastures, grains, fibres and some fruit trees, undertaken by 15 research institutes and their corresponding governmental networks of experimental stations that spread over the island. Heterogeneous, disease resistant and low input varieties were only accessible only to professional plant breeders, and farmers were not involved in these breeding programmes.

Before new varieties were released, they went through a rigorous scientific evaluation, and the research institutes had to send their results to the National Scientific Forum *(Consejo Científico)*, which checked the scientific results and, if approved, in turn sent them to a so-called Expert Group *(Grupo Expertos)*, consisting of researchers, lecturers and production directors of the big state enterprises. If this group also approved the results, they were forwarded to the Vice-Minister for Mixed Crops *(Vice-Ministro Cultivos Varios)* who, in turn, would send the results to the provincial delegations, which would incorporate them into their provincial production plans, and the state enterprises were then obliged to use the selected varieties in their production system, a rather top-down approach without consultation of local state producers.

Following the collapse of the Eastern Block in 1989, the Cuban agricultural sector had to cope with a drastic reduction in inputs and trade support, shifting gradually towards more self-sufficient forms of production.

Many remarkable technical and social transformations occurred as a response to this challenge. In the 1980s, Cuba had carried out 87% of its external trade under preferential price agreements, imported 95% of its fertiliser and herbicide requirements, and owned one tractor for every 125 hectares of farm land. After the collapse, foreign purchase capacity was reduced from USD 8.1 billion in 1989 to USD 1.7 billion in 1993. This greatly affected the country's ability to buy agricultural inputs (Funes, 1997). The collapse generated a deficit of energy, supplies and chemicals, and forced significant changes in the ways in which food was produced and distributed in Cuba. Due to these deficits, in the 1990s, Cuba moved from being the largest consumer of agrochemicals in Latin America to one with vast experience in organic agriculture in the world.

This transition period went hand in hand with a severe economic depression, and the income of scientists, lecturers, technicians, government employees and the public sector in general became so low that many professionals emigrated to look for better opportunities elsewhere. In this process of change, state enterprises gradually lost importance in the production and supply of food for local consumption, and low-input family farming emerged, to supply local markets instead.

The new low-input agriculture in Cuba and the diversity of crops now produced by these farmers led to significant differentiation of production systems, and hence specific seed demand. The public plant breeding sector was uncertain about how to deal with the diversity of seeds now demanded by small farmers. In the remainder of this chapter, we discuss how this led to the development of plant breeding programmes of a participatory nature.

## The emergence of participatory plant breeding in Cuba

At the beginning of the 1990s, an Optical Neuritis outbreak quickly spread across Cuba due to widespread vitamin A deficit. In 1992, the Central government of Cuba asked the National Institute for Agricultural Sciences (INCA) to breed pumpkin (*Cucurbita moschata* Duch). At that time, the government seed company had available only one pumpkin variety which covered 40,000 hectares of the country, representing effectively 100% of the total area covered of this crop. Due to the new 'silver leaf' disease combined with limited irrigation (not enough oil available for pumping water) and limited chemical disease control, the yields of pumpkin diminished nationwide from 2–3 ton/hectare to less than 0.5 ton/hectare.

Two approaches were taken to seek improved pumpkin genetic material. The first was to explore the possibility of purchasing modern seed varieties (MV) from international seed companies. The government acquired different varieties from such companies for testing under Cuba's new, low-input conditions. The second approach was to test, under low-input conditions, a sample of landraces from the national gene bank managed by the Institute for Fundamental Research in Tropical Agriculture (INIFAT), in charge of *ex situ* conservation.

Overall, the 20 MVs tested had very low yields, high pest and disease infestations and poor culinary quality (Ríos et al., 1996).

In contrast, within the pool of 33 landraces evaluated, favourable variation was found for some characteristics important for the new breeding programme. During the 1993 summer season, two veteran farmers from Batabanó District (58 and 70 years old, respectively) were involved in the selection process and they chose among 13 *half sib* families according to yield and fruit shape and selected individual fruits within those chosen families. Afterwards, the chosen families (represented by selected individual fruits) were sown at the same time by the two farmers on-farm and at the INCA experimental station under low-input conditions during the cool and dry season and after four breeding cycle two new pumpkin varieties were released. **Table 40.1** *Comparison of input use and results of pumpkin breeding strategies in Habana Province* shows a comparison of plant breeding practices under high-input agriculture and those described here, carried out under low-input conditions. The comparison is made in terms of energy consumption, inputs used on farm and farmers' participation.

*Table 40.1* Comparison of input use and results of pumpkin breeding strategies in Habana Province

| *Indicators* | *Pumpkin breeding before the special period (1980s)* | *Pumpkin breeding under conditions of the special period (1990s)* |
|---|---|---|
| Mineral fertilisation (kg ha$^{-1}$) | Nitrogen: 42<br>Phosphorus: 39<br>Potassium: 62 | 0 |
| Organic soil amendments | Rarely applied | Typically 6–7 tons ha$^{-1}$ |
| Frequency and amount of artificial irrigation (summer season) | 9–11 times season$^{-1}$, 2000 m$^3$ ha$^{-1}$ | 2–4 times season$^{-1}$, 200 m$^3$ ha$^{-1}$ |
| Number of varieties released in 10 years | 1 | 2 |
| Varietal maintenance and seed multiplication | Isolation | Cross pollination |
| Pest and disease control | Agrochemical intensive | Biological |
| Use of honeybees | Sporadically | Frequently |
| Yield | 6–8 tons ha$^{-1}$ | 6–8 tons ha$^{-1}$ |
| Farmer participation | Contracted seed production | On farm selection of *half sib* families |
| Researcher participation | Screening germplasm and varietal evaluation and selection, and cross pollination control | Screening germplasm, facilitating availability of new germplasm, evaluation of variety with farmers |
| Energy requirements (kcal ha$^{-1}$)[a] | Fertilisation: 679,000<br>Irrigation: 10,160,000<br>Pesticides: 6,160,000<br>Total: 16,999,000 | Fertilisation: 42,000<br>Irrigation: 3,697,200<br>Pesticides: 88,000<br>Total: 3,827,200 |

*Source*: Ríos (1999).

*Table 40.2* Economic impact of pumpkin breeding under low input conditions

| *Indicators (calculated as averages)* | *Varieties bred under high input conditions sown in low input conditions (top-down approach)* | *Varieties bred and sown under low input conditions (on farm, with farmers participation)* |
|---|---|---|
| Cost $ha^{-1}$ under low input condition (Cuban pesos) | 702.3 | 708.3 |
| Fruit yield (tons $ha^{-1}$) | 1.5 | 6.7 |
| Total income (0.16 Cuban pesos $kg^{-1}$) | 240 | 1,080 |
| Net income $ha^{-1}$ (Cuban pesos) | –462* *average net loss | 372 |
| Benefit/cost ratio | 0.34:1 | 1.5:1 |

*Source*: Ríos (1999).

The crop improvement programmes performed under low-input conditions were more efficient in terms of energy use. Notably, the yield obtained under the low-input conditions was also comparable to yields achieved under the conventional, high-input technological package. The economic impact of varieties selected under high – as compared to low – input conditions was evaluated by growing the most popular variety disseminated in Cuba, which was named *RG*, under low-input conditions, as well as two varieties selected collaboratively with farmers under those low-input condition (**Table 40.2** *Economic impact of pumpkin breeding under low input conditions*).

This first experience of working on-farm, with farmers and Cuban pumpkin landraces provided to INCA plant breeders four important insights:

1. Wide phenotypic variability of useful traits exists among Cuban landraces grown under low-input conditions. It is possible to increase production by selecting directly for fruit yield under low-input conditions.
2. Genetic advance was higher on farmers' field.
3. Farmers had the capacity to choose varieties locally adaptive. They understood better than professional plant breeders which types of varieties local farmers preferred.
4. INCA plant breeders realised: 'Farmers can be plant breeders like us, they just need to have access to diversity of seeds'.

## Widening the scope towards participatory plant breeding

Inspired by the first impact on participatory pumpkin breeding and other international experiences on participatory plant breeding, INCA plant breeders felt the necessity to involve other disciplines, crops and consider new locations to involve farmers as plant breeders.

A first multidisciplinary team was formed, including representatives of INCA, the Agrarian University of Havana and the Centre for Psychological and Sociological Research. This team developed a Participatory Seed Diffusion (PSD) process that was implemented between 2000 and 2007. Initially, PSD promoted maize and improved beans varieties and landraces in 'seed diversity fairs' as an approach where plant breeders, farmers and extension agents had access to diversity in one or more crops over La Palma, Batabanó and San Antonio de Los Baños districts. Varieties from formal and informal seed sources were sown under the usual cultural practices of the target environment and farmers had the possibility to choose 4/6 varieties per crop in the field.

In the diversity seed fairs (**Figure 40.1** *Farmers choosing varieties in diversity seed fairs*), participants did not know the seed sources in the plot during the selection exercise and only afterwards was the varieties' identity revealed. Subsequently, the farmers organised trials with selected seeds on their own farms and discussions on varietal performance took place within the communities between farmers and researchers. Around 35–100 maize, beans and rice varieties were displayed and farmers were invited to select five to seven varieties for each crop. After selection, the researcher provided between 20–200 seeds of each chosen variety to the farmers to take back home for testing.

In this period, as never before, culinary aspects were considered, and women organized cooking evaluations as a new criteria in varietal selection (**Figure 40.2** *Sweet potato culinary test organized by women of La Tunas province*).

Male farmers mostly voted for varieties with high yield and associated characteristics. Female participants voted for varieties related to culinary properties. In the cooking test, men noted that more than 80% of the varieties tested were of good quality, whereas women were more rigorous (see broader discussions of the importance of gender in the conservation and sustainable use of agricultural biodiversity in Jiggins, Chapter 33 of this Handbook). This is not surprising given that Cuban women do most of the cooking, but in conventional breeding, culinary aspects had seldom been considered (Ríos et al., 2012).

INCA scientists had to reconsider their conventional belief that farmers could manage no more than six varieties and few crops and that diversity had to be gradually released otherwise 'crop diversity would make farmers uneasy'.

*Figure 40.1* Farmers choosing varieties in diversity seed fairs in the Northeast 'Las Caobas' village, Holguin Province

*Source*: H. Ríos.

*Figure 40.2* Sweet potato culinary test organized by women of La Tunas province

*Source*: Photo: H. Ríos.

*Table 40.3* Crop yield and number of varieties in La Palma, District, and Pinar del Rio province over four years of PSD

| | *Crop yield (t/ha)* | | *Number of varieties* | |
|---|---|---|---|---|
| | *Before PSD* | *After four years of PSD* | *Before PSD* | *After four years of PSD* |
| Tomato | 8.0 | 12.0 | 3 | 42 |
| Maize | 1.4 | 2.4 | 4 | 52 |
| Bean | 0.4 | 1.4 | 5 | 200 |
| Rice | 1.9 | 3.8 | 6 | 45 |

*Source*: Ríos (1999).

One of the main impacts of farmers participation was the increasing number of crops handled over time. The approach began with maize and beans, but six years later, more than 20 crops were in the hands of the farmers' experimental network and crop yield and number of varieties managed by farmers increased significantly (**Table 40.3** *Crop yield and number of varieties in La Palma, District, and Pinar del Rio province over four years of PSD*).

By the end of 2007, 7,000 farmers from 49 communities, 850 research and extension workers and 258 policy makers of five provinces were participating in the PSD (Ríos, 2007). Due to increased yield, crop diversity and the mobilisation of small farmers around seed diversity, an increasing interest emerged by new villages, local universities, government and NGOs to be part of the process. Over the coming seven years, the multidisciplinary team engaged with local district government staff and gradually managed to have them embrace PSD, and they participated in the organisation of new seed diversity fairs with more crops and then a chain reaction process took place in different regions of Cuba (Ríos, 2009). The farmers' fields turned into a potential small experimental station, with fellow farmers selecting varieties and receiving small amounts of the seed varieties they had selected, with the farm turning into a 'diversity nucleus' of its own right. Then more farmers copied the process, creating new diversity seed nucleus and expanding seed diversity (Ríos, 2009).

A strong farmer led experimental network emerged that initially considered only maize, beans and rice seeds, but gradually moved to other crops and agro-ecological practices (Ríos, 2009). Today, this innovation network (five universities, five research stations and two NGOs) plays a crucial role in disseminating good agricultural practices to over 50,000 farmers in currently 45 districts (INCA-PIAL, 2016).

The multidisciplinary team realised that the PSD process had evolved from a technological into a social learning process. Through PSD, 95 community seed banks managed by farmers were created (Ortiz and Acosta, 2013) and diversity seed flows strongly intensified within and between communities as well as with conventional seed banks.

Farmers reinforced their experimentation capacity by testing, adopting and diffusing seeds from formal and informal seed systems; researchers learnt how to facilitate seed diversity and knowledge exchange among farmers, research organisations and NGOs. In short, PSD created a learning community of farmers, NGO representatives and researchers, believing that only together they could transform the Cuban rural reality.

It was extremely important that ownership of the PSD process had been transferred to farmers and 'champions' at district level (see Taylor, Chapter 38 of this Handbook). Reflecting, one may say that the multidisciplinary team from INCA, the Agrarian University of Havana and the Centre for Psychological and Sociological Research brokered the emergence of PSD in Cuba.

## Expanding participatory approaches in Cuba

The promising results achieved during the first seven years of PSD prompted the team and partners to amplify the pilot experience. They were eager to find out how PSD could be adapted to others parts of the country with different biophysical and socioeconomic features.

How is PSD to be scaled up while maintaining a dynamic, open process based on the collective actions of various stakeholders? In terms of what to scale, the team decided on the following:

- Keeping the practice of seed diversity fairs, farmer experimentation and local seed multiplication with various crops, but this time organized by district stakeholders and providing also benefits to the participating farmers.
- Local stakeholders should look into specific local challenges, and should be supported in also becoming owners of the solutions, not just of their problems.
- Encouraging 'conventional' research organisations and universities to work directly with farmers, facilitating access to genetic diversity and agro-ecological practices.
- Building up capacity to broker innovations at two levels, at the district level where farmers and local organisation generated new evaluation of the performance of PSD in the field, and at the national level where public policies are decided.

This new expansion wave beyond PSD focused on a bottom-up approach, involving farmers and key local stakeholders in the search for best agricultural practices, giving birth to the 'Local Agricultural innovation Programme' *(PIAL-Programa de Innovación Agropecuaria Local)*. PIAL has been using the action learning approach promoted by ICRA[1] geared towards stimulating experiential learning (learning by doing) and purposeful interaction to adapt and coordinate activities, taking 'learners' through facilitated on-the-job learning cycles (**Figure 40.3** *Interactive learning cycles*).

The 'interactive learning cycle' engages all relevant actors, that is, those actors and stakeholders who really faced a common innovation challenge and stand out to profit from joint learning and action (**Figure 40.4** *Event organised by a learning group to share drafting technique*). Actors reflect on

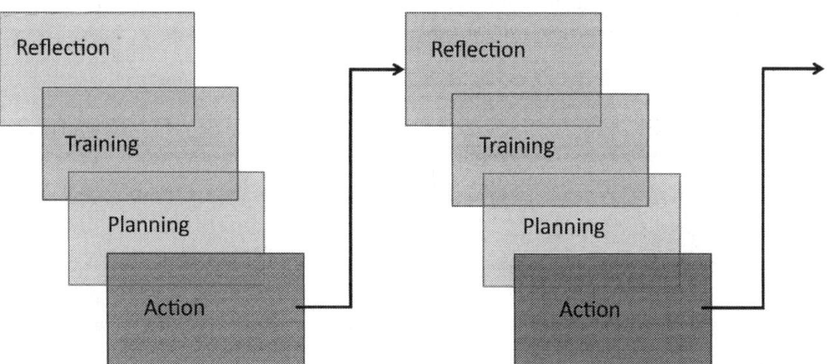


*Figure 40.3* Interactive learning cycles

*Source*: ICRA training material, 2012.

*Figure 40.4* Event organised by a learning group to share drafting technique

*Note*: The workshop was led by a champion farmer in Madruga District, Mayabeque Province.

*Source*: Photo: E. Calves.

the challenges they face, learn how to deal with them, plan how to apply the lessons learnt and then apply them in their own working environment. However, for an action learning cycles to be successful, it requires someone to bring all actors together and keep them geared in the jointly agreed direction (Ríos and Ceballos-Müller, 2016). PIAL identified 'champions' who had excelled in the previous years and, with the support of a professional facilitator, trained them on the job as innovation brokers or facilitators.

Over the course of eight years, five learning cycles were conducted at district level in different regions of Cuba, applying in each cycle a two-track interactive and experiential learning approach. 'District champions' were identified from different organisations (including university lecturers, researchers, technicians and farmers) and trained on the job as innovation facilitators/ brokers. As a key component of the training, the 'District Champions' facilitated a learning cycle with a group of actors and stakeholders coming together to address a specific challenge at their working places.

For instance, in Guisa District, a specific challenge was access to food at reasonable prices. As in most of the country, the national government supplies food to local consumers through a ration card which is good for only ten days of the monthly family food intake. Consumers are forced to access the rest of their food either at free market shops downtown, which are open only during normal working office hours, or access through vendors at far higher prices. In particular, public workers are unable to be at the market shops in time, nor can they to afford the high prices of the vendors.

A representative of the local government of Guisa championed and facilitated a learning cycle to come up with a solution (**Figure 40.5** *Learning cycle to promote the 'Green Baskets' as an alternative to local food supply*). A group of local actors (farmers, local radio, and education workers union, consumers) came up with the idea of organising a food delivery service for local consumers, called 'The Green Baskets', which could deliver food outside working hours and at better prices than those of the vendors.

By the end of 2011, more than 19,500 farmers had access to seed diversity as well as agro-ecological practices promoted by PIAL and a significant impact on family farming was demonstrated

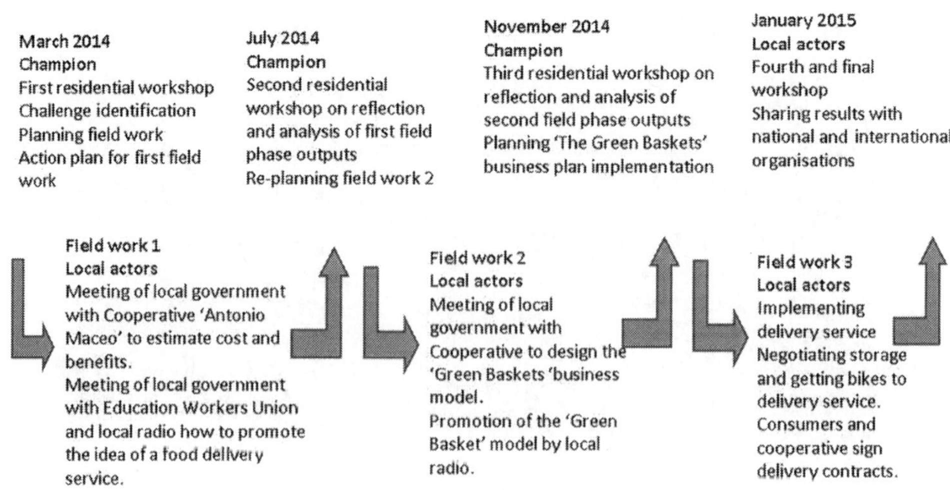


*Figure 40.5* Learning cycle to promote the 'Green Baskets' as an alternative to local food supply, Guisa District, Granma Province

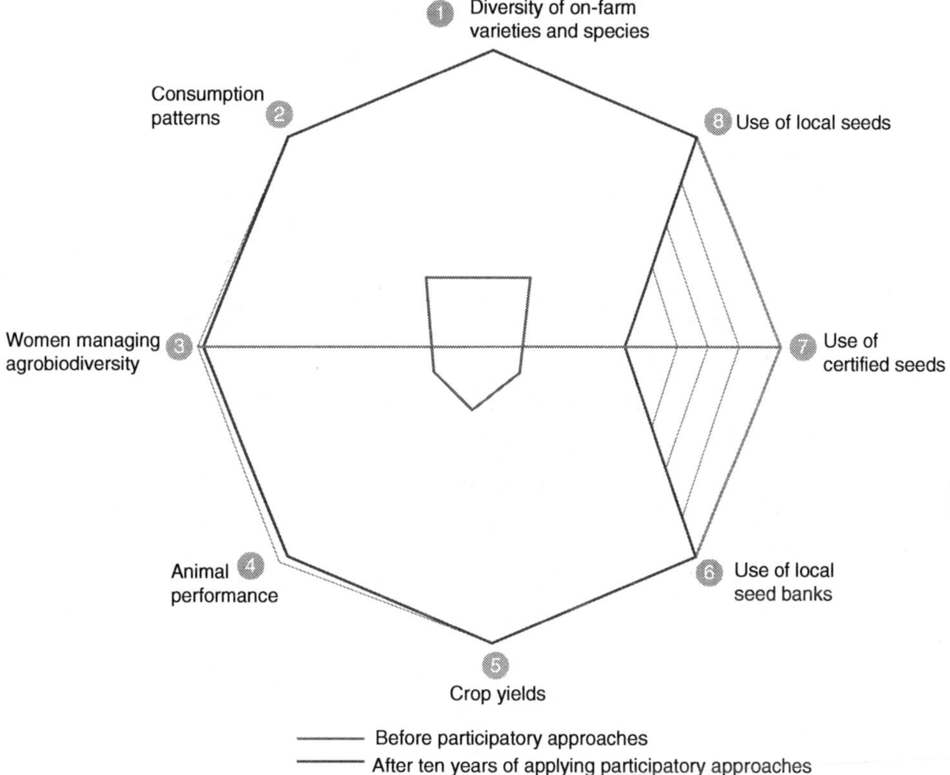


*Figure 40.6* Impact of interactive learning cycle to enhance livelihood improvement

*Note*: Farmer survey.

*Source*: Ortiz and De la Fé (2013).

before and after the introduction of participatory approaches in Cuba (**Figure 40.6** *Impact of interactive learning cycle to enhance livelihood improvement*). Ortiz and De la Fé (2013) demonstrated that community seed bank management by farmers had had a significant impact in improving their farming systems, but that the availability of certified seeds had not, because these seeds had limited local adaptation and poor germination percentage (below 70%).

## The Cuban government announces political changes

Taking advantage of the fact that by 2014 the Cuban government had started promoting self-employment *(por cuenta propia)*, PIAL also started exploring alternative approaches to make farming more sustainable and economically viable. In two further learning cycles (2014–2015), an interactive learning approach was developed to catalysing business ideas. Again, learning groups were formed with key local actors, and joined by farmers who had previously shown themselves to be business minded. The groups jointly started identifying business ideas, the feasibility of which was then tested in the field. Between March 2014 and January 2015, some 13 business ideas were brought forward, analysed and validated by the learning groups using the CANVAS business model.[2] Two business ideas are exemplified in **Box 40.1** *The market garden* and **Box 40.2** *An*

*Figure 40.7* Gina, a farmer participant of an action learning cycle explaining her cooperative business model to commercialise local seeds in Jesus Menendez District, Las Tunas Province

*Source*: Photo: H. Ríos.

*entrepreneur couple*, and in **Figure 40.7** *Gina, a farmer participant of an action learning cycle explaining her cooperative business model.*

Because most Cuban farmers still have relatively little access to agro-chemical inputs, they are typically agro-ecologically oriented by default. It was therefore natural to emphasise this and start referring to them as 'green' (agro-ecological) entrepreneurs in the aforementioned process of turning farming into a business as well. Farmers and other participants of the learning cycle were extremely motivated by the newly introduced entrepreneurial perspective and eager to follow the CANVAS model, visualising their value proposition, clients, commercialisation channels, strategy to keep relationships with clients, business partners and investments. In short, farmers could actually think and act as small business people, even using the PIAL logo as a market brand for their local products (see Jaeger et al., Chapter 30 of this Handbook, for a broader discussion of the importance of marketing of agro-biodiverse products).

## Box 40.1 The market garden

*'I used to farm using monocultures and chemicals. It is harder work to farm ecologically, but I notice the difference in the soil and in the taste of the food.'*

(Statement from Roberto Ochoa, 2015)

**Entrepreneurs:** Roberto Ochoa and Dania Roja, Cooperative Frank Pais, Gibara District
**Selling Product:** Community market garden
**Background:** They have 1,600 families in their community.
**Business Description:** The idea came from the university and the community working together: farmers wanted a place to buy vegetables, a community market garden. Roberto had a *finca (farm)*, so they thought it would be a good idea to situate the garden there, and he and his wife both participated in the business model workshops. In an arid zone and with problems with accessing water, they are constructing a well, at a cost of 7,000 pesos (USD 290). There is also a micro dam and a turbine, and plans to establish a *Punta de Venta (selling point)* on the Cooperative. They will employ five women who will earn approximately 300 pesos/month each (USD 13).
**Future Plans:** To undertake schools education on the market garden.

*Source*: Wright and Vargas (2016).

## Box 40.2 An entrepreneur couple

*'Before we made the business plan with the project, we thought that 'business' was illegal, and we knew nothing about obtaining bank loans.'*

(Statement from Miguel Leyva, 2015)

**Entrepreneurs:** Juan Miguel Leyva Fidalgo y Mayte, Finca el Renacer, CCS Jose Manuel Rodriguez
**Selling Products:** Farm machinery and pigs
**Background:** Juan is a mechanical engineer and also produces biofertiliser and sells this product and trains other farmers to make it. Mayte is an agronomist.
**Business Description:** Both Juan and Mayte made business plans with the project. Mayte went on the business training course. She started her business in January with ten pigs, and spent 10,000 pesos on feed, supplemented with sweet potato, cassava and forage plants, as well as with the biofertiliser. The feed is milled in order to obtain a better conversion rate. The pigs are sold whole, between 85 kg and 120 kg. She decides what to do with the profit.

Juan's first business idea was to make biogas; then he changed this to an idea to help local women make some income. The women are in an Art and Agroforestry group, making artisanal trinkets from local materials such as shells and wood. The trinkets sell at ten pesos (USD 42 cents) for larger ones and take one day to produce ten. At the same time, he developed another idea, as he'd read that equipment is a limiting factor for agro-ecology, so he obtained funds from the project for some basic tools and lends his services to producers to undertake soldering and making agricultural equipment. He developed a seed planter that took three days to make, and he hires this out and makes a profit. To undertake the planting takes one man and one ox or horse for one day; without the machine, takes two oxen and two men for one day for the same job. He could produce a lot more equipment, but the CCS is not organised to make a contract with him so he couldn't be paid. Every month he advertises his services in the Cooperative meetings, but finds he gets more interest from elsewhere.
**Future Plans:** He is currently applying for a 50,000 peso (~USD 2,083) bank loan for an agri-tourism project, and plans to develop a large ranch and offer food and women's handicrafts, with women attending to the tourists. He is also now pursuing the biogas idea again.

*Source*: Wright and Vargas (2016).

## Some final reflections

Cuba was forced to change from an industrial agricultural model into a more agro-ecological one. Under low inputs conditions of the sort encountered in many developing countries, farmers were nevertheless able to improve yield crops.

Access to agrobiodiversity, experimentation and seed multiplication by farmers, choosing seeds according to their own criteria, has made plant breeding processes both more participatory and demand driven.

Moving from a participatory plant breeding initiative towards local innovation networks, family farmers became key players in this process. Important for this was a bottom-up approach, which started at local (district) level and gradually extended to include other actors at provincial and even national levels. One major factor contributing to the success of this scheme was the fact that the learning groups focused on real challenges farmers were facing, and that facilitators were available and well trained to move the groups to action, and collectively work towards solutions.

This 'action-based learning approach' (**Figure 40.8** *ICRA's Action Learning Approach*) is a valuable method to promote change in the rural institutional landscape. The approach helps in achieving a common understanding among a group of people as diverse as local government (representing the state doctrine), other public organisations (still rather conventional oriented) and emerging, more business-minded farmers.

Forming brokers who themselves formed learning groups (i.e. a two-track approach) was a successful technique for generating innovations appropriate for use in the local agricultural system. Many local 'champions' became catalysers of innovations and learnt to link different public stakeholders and farmers in a joint collective effort to introduce changes at local level.

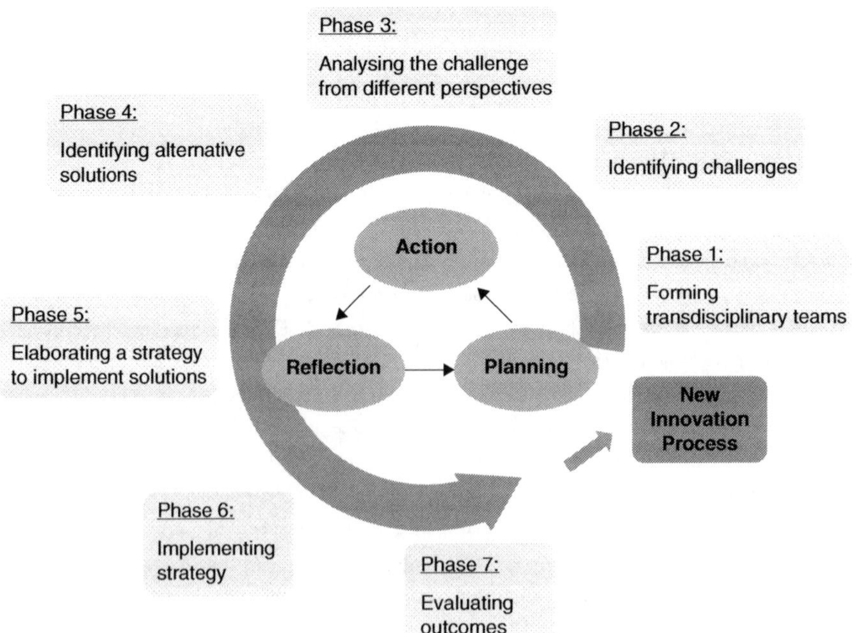


*Figure 40.8* ICRA's Action Learning Approach

*Source*: ICRA training materials, 2014.

Even so, in the last few years, the brokerage efforts have increasingly concentrated on incorporating entrepreneurial perspectives in farming and supporting the emerging business ideas of small farmers. A future threat for these small farmers might be competition from big agribusiness that may develop in the wake of improving relations with other countries, especially the United States, which could bring an influx of agricultural products and agribusinesses in the future. It will therefore be important to continue the development of farmers' business skills and ability to identify market niches.

In 2015, after 25 years of innovation brokerage and action learning, over 50,000 farmers have been reached in all ten Provinces of Cuba and have benefitted from action learning through the PIAL network (**Figure 40.9** *Evolution of action learning and innovation brokerage in Cuba*).

In the process of moving from a participatory plant breeding initiative towards local innovation networks, the role of professional plant breeders and farmers has changed. Farmers, on the one hand, have shown the capacity to improve cash crops like pumpkin, maize and beans, have successfully integrated many crops into their farming systems and finally have begun to introduce an entrepreneurial perspective to their interactions with communities, and with public and private actors. On the other hand, professional plant breeders are now working together with farmers to achieve seed diversity and convincing district, provincial and national policy makers to jointly develop plant breeding and agro-ecological practices diffusion programmes with farmers, thus joining forces to improve farming system and benefit also from national and international solutions.

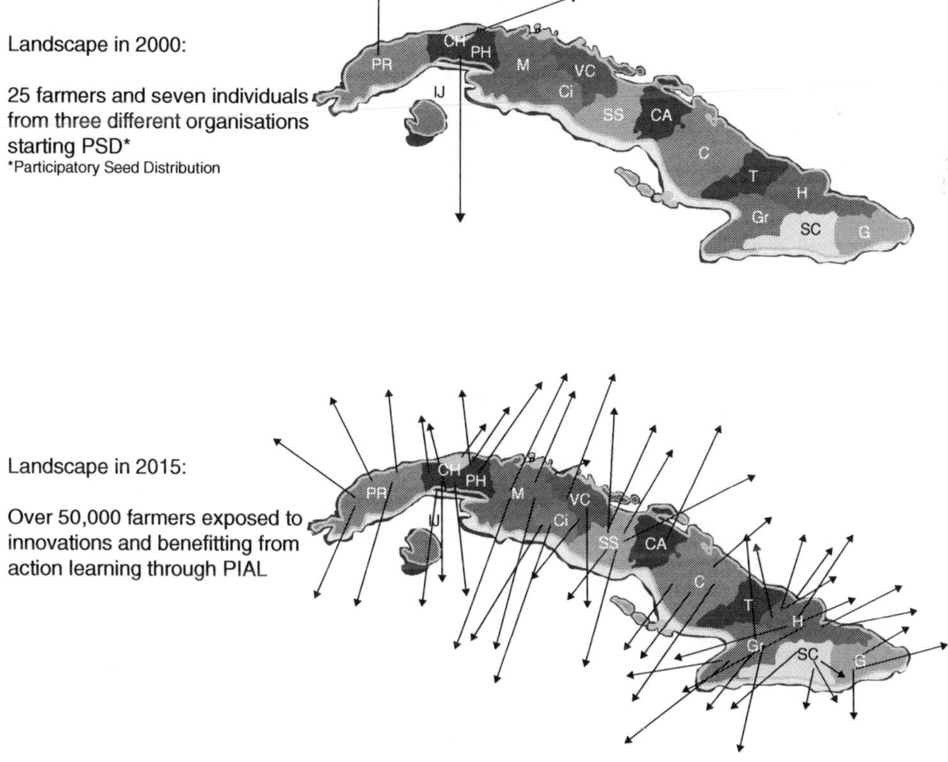


*Figure 40.9* Evolution of action learning and innovation brokerage in Cuba

*Source*: Ríos and Ceballos-Müller (2016).

## Notes

1 *Stichting* ICRA (based in the Netherlands) aims to support leadership and to develop critical mass in facilitating learning and action for agricultural and rural innovation.
2 The CANVAS business model is a strategic management and entrepreneurial tool. It allows one to describe, design, challenge, invent, and pivot a business model. www.businessmodelgeneration.com/downloads/businessmodelgeneration_preview.pdf).

## References


Almekinders, C. J. M. and Hardon, J. (eds.) (2006) *Bringing Farmers Back into Breeding. Experiences with Participatory Plant Breeding and Challenges for Institutionalisation*, Agromisa Special 5, Agromisa, Wageningen, The Netherlands.

Ceccarelli, S., Galié, A., Mustafa, Y. and Grando, S. (2012) 'Participatory barley breeding farmers' inputs become everyone gain', pp. 53–66 in M. Ruiz and R. Vernooy (eds.), *The Custodians of Biodiversity*, Earthscan for Routledge, London, UK.

Conny, A. and Hardon, J. (2006) 'Bringing farmers back into breeding: Experiences with participatory plant breeding and challenges for institutionalisation', in *Agromisa Special 5*, Agromisa, Wageningen, the Netherlands.

Funes, F. (1997) 'Experiencias cubanas en agroecología', pp. 3–7 in *Revista Agricultura Orgánica*, Agosto-Diciembre.

ICRA training materials 2012, www.icra-edu.org/

ICRA training materials 2014, www.icra-edu.org/

INCA-PIAL 2016, https://inca.edu.cu/wordpress/index.php/redes/pial/

Ortiz, R. and Acosta, R. (2013) 'Los Centros de Diseminación de la biodiversidad Agrícola en el contexto del Programa de Innovación Agropecuaria Local', in R. Ortiz, R. Acosta and C. De La Fé (eds.), *La Biodiversidad en Manos del Campesinado Cubano*, Instituto Nacional de Ciencias Agrícolas, Cuba.

Ortiz, R. and De La Fé, C. (2013) 'Herramientas más utilizadas por el programa de Innovación Agropecuaria Local para Diseminar la Diversidad Agrícola', in R. Ortiz , R. Acosta and C. De La Fé (eds.), *La Biodiversidad en Manos del Campesinado Cubano*, Instituto Nacional de Ciencias Agrícolas, Cuba.

Ríos, H. (1999) *Mejoramiento de cultivares de Calabaza (Cucurbita moschta Duch) para condiciones de bajos insumos*, PhD Thesis, Havana Agricultural University, La Havana, Cuba.

Ríos, H. (2007) 'The origins of participatory plant breeding and "Local Innovation"', *Seeds of Survival Newsletter*, November 2007, pp. 4–5, www.cbd.int/doc/external/cop-09/usc-sosnewsletter-en.pdf

Ríos, H. (2009) 'Participatory seed diffusion: Experiences from the field', pp. 589–612 in S. Ceccarelli and E. P. Guimarães (eds.), *Plant Breeding and Farmer Participation*, Food and Agriculture Organization of the UN, Rome, Italy.

Ríos, H., Batista, O. and Fernandez, A. (1996). 'Characteristics and potentialities of Cuban pumpkin (Cucurbita moschata Duch) germplasm', *Cultivos Tropicales*, vol. 1996, pp. 88–91.

Ríos, H. and Ceballos-Müller, J. (2016) 'Brokering innovation and fostering action learning – Towards promoting "agro-ecological entrepreneurship" in the new Cuban economic model', *Action Research for Food Systems Transformation*, Centre for Agroecology and Water and Resilience, Coventry University, Coventry, UK.

Wright, J. and Vargas, D. (2016) *Green Entrepreneurs in Cuba*, Evaluation Report, March 2016, Coventry University, Coventry, UK.

# 41

# STRENGTHENING INSTITUTIONS AND ORGANIZATIONS, AND BUILDING CAPACITY FOR THE CONSERVATION AND USE OF AGRICULTURAL BIODIVERSITY

*Johannes Engels and Per Rudebjer*

## Introduction

Agricultural biodiversity, comprising plant, livestock, aquatic and forest genetic diversity, as well as micro-organisms and invertebrates, spans the genetic, species and ecosystems levels. Many interacting biological, environmental, social and economic processes determine how agricultural biodiversity changes over time. Hence, a broad range of organizations and institutions, in multiple sectors, are involved in, or influence, the conservation and use of this diversity locally, nationally and internationally. However, only a few organizations, in particular genebanks and to some extent botanic gardens, have the conservation and use of this diversity as their primary mandate. Therefore, building capacity for the conservation and use of agricultural biodiversity necessarily involves many organizations and institutions that have core missions *other* than the conservation and use of agricultural biodiversity, usually across multiple sectors (described in **Box 41.1** *Three levels of capacity*). This raises two challenges: the need to operate across multiple sectors in integrated landscapes, and to integrate agricultural biodiversity into research and development agendas within each sector, be it agriculture, forestry, biodiversity conservation, nutrition and so on.

### Box 41.1 Three levels of capacity

Within any particular area, including the conservation and use of agricultural biodiversity, the overall capacity to perform and deliver over time depends on three inter-related levels:

1 The capacity of the individual to perform (knowledge, skills and attitudes);
2 The capacity of organizations to deliver (facilities, financial resources, leadership, strategy, external relations, among others);

3 The capacity at the institutional level to provide an enabling environment (the 'rules of the game', policies and laws, good governance, etc.).

Successful capacity development efforts need to consider all three levels, as well as the connections between them. However, it is common for these levels to be blurred when capacity development is discussed in global policy instruments, perhaps because the text is not written by capacity development specialists. Such is the case in the Global Plans of Action discussed in this chapter. For example, a statement such as 'develop institutional capacity' seems to refer to not only the institutional environment for agricultural biodiversity but also the organizations involved, such as agricultural research organizations, universities and genebanks. The reader is alerted that 'institutions' is not a well-defined term in many of the documents discussed here.

It is not only agriculture that depends on agricultural biodiversity: many other activity areas partly or entirely build on, or make use of it, including tourism, urban planning, pharmaceutical discovery and so forth (see, for example, Santilli and Kuhnlein, Chapters 23 and 24 of this Handbook, respectively). Although some of these activities have existed for hundreds or even thousands of years, only recently have we realized that these natural resources are eroding and need urgent protection. Thus, integrating agricultural biodiversity into broader agendas is both a national and institutional priority. However, no national institutional framework for guiding and doing this and which could be copied or adjusted from one country to another currently exists. Consequently, this chapter intends to provide suggestions, ideas and elements on how to develop a national institutional framework that fits the needs of the country in question.

The legal and policy area is an important component of the institutional framework for conserving and using agricultural biodiversity. In recent years, the global community has developed a number of international policy instruments and global plans of action (GPA) to conserve agricultural biodiversity and to support and regulate its sustainable use. These action plans are based on national and thematic reports on the state of the world's aquatic, forest, plant and animal genetic resources, respectively. All the GPAs make clear that strengthening of policies and institutional capacities are essential steps towards the sustainable conservation and use of agricultural biodiversity, and for the fair and equitable sharing of benefits deriving from their use (FAO, 2007, 2011a, 2014b). With respect to the use of agricultural biodiversity, the Sustainable Development Goals (SDGs), agreed in 2015, deserve particular attention. Several of the 17 goals depend on well-managed agricultural biodiversity, such as Goal 2: *End hunger, achieve food security and improved nutrition and promote sustainable agriculture*; and Goal 15: *Sustainably manage forests, combat desertification, halt and reverse land degradation, halt biodiversity loss.*

The institutional 'landscape' for agricultural biodiversity is complex, involving stakeholders in multiple sectors. Unfamiliarity with the concept of agricultural biodiversity itself, and weak multi-sectoral collaboration, are two key challenges in many of the organizations involved. For example, many countries have separate governmental entities for biodiversity conservation (usually part of the ministry of environment), and for the use of biodiversity for food and agriculture (typically the ministry of agriculture, forestry and/or fisheries). This divide complicates planning and implementation, in particular with respect to overlapping legal and policy instruments, multiple reporting lines and opportunities for synergies and collaboration.

This chapter will first focus on the human and institutional capacity needed to implement the two most important global legal instruments related to agricultural biodiversity, the Convention on Biological Diversity (CBD) and the International Treaty on Plant Genetic Resources for Food and Agriculture (the Treaty, for short). We present an institutional framework for how these legal instruments are connected with the organizations and processes, at international and national levels, through which they are being implemented.

Second, we discuss a possible national implementation framework for the conservation and use of agricultural biodiversity (see **Figure 41.1**, *Institutional framework for agricultural biodiversity*. We describe the diversity of institutions involved in the preparation and implementation of biodiversity strategies and action plans, within which agricultural biodiversity falls. Two case studies, from Germany and Uganda, give more detailed insights into how such processes are being handled in practice. We close the chapter with some remarks on the way forward.

Two important legal instruments of relevance to agricultural biodiversity (CBD, and the Treaty) have been negotiated and agreed upon among states and subsequently signed and ratified by most countries of the world. A third intergovernmental agreement on the SDGs provides a broader development agenda to which agricultural biodiversity can make important contributions.

## *The Convention on Biological Diversity*

When the **Convention on Biological Diversity (CBD)** entered into force in 1993, agricultural biodiversity played a very minor role, as it was only marginally treated during the negotiation process. This omission was addressed in the 1996 Conference of Parties' decision to establish a multi-year programme of activities on agricultural biodiversity, and to request that this be managed by FAO (CBD, 1996). The objectives of the CBD are presented in **Box 41.2** *Objectives of the CBD.*

### Box 41.2 Objectives of the CBD

The **Convention on Biological Diversity (CBD)** entered into force on 29 December 1993. It has three main objectives:

1. The conservation of biological diversity;
2. The sustainable use of the components of biological diversity; and
3. The fair and equitable sharing of the benefits arising out of the utilization of genetic resources.

A **National Biodiversity Strategy and Action Plan (NBSAP)** is the principal instrument for implementing the CBD at the national level (CBD, undated-a). The Convention requires countries to prepare a NBSAP and to ensure that this is mainstreamed into the planning and activities of all sectors that can have an impact (positive and negative) on biodiversity. As of December 2015, 184 of 196 Parties (94%) had developed NBSAPs in line with Article 6 of the CBD (CBD, undated-b). The NBSAP is also a logical starting point for the planning and implementation of agricultural biodiversity actions at the national level.

The CBD has designed a useful capacity building package to facilitate the NBSAP development process. Nine capacity building modules are available online, including, among others, how to prepare and update an NBSAP; mainstreaming biodiversity into sectoral and cross-sectoral strategies, plans and programmes; setting national biodiversity targets; ensuring inclusive societal engagement, obtaining political and financial support; and developing an NBSAP communication strategy (CBD, undated-c).

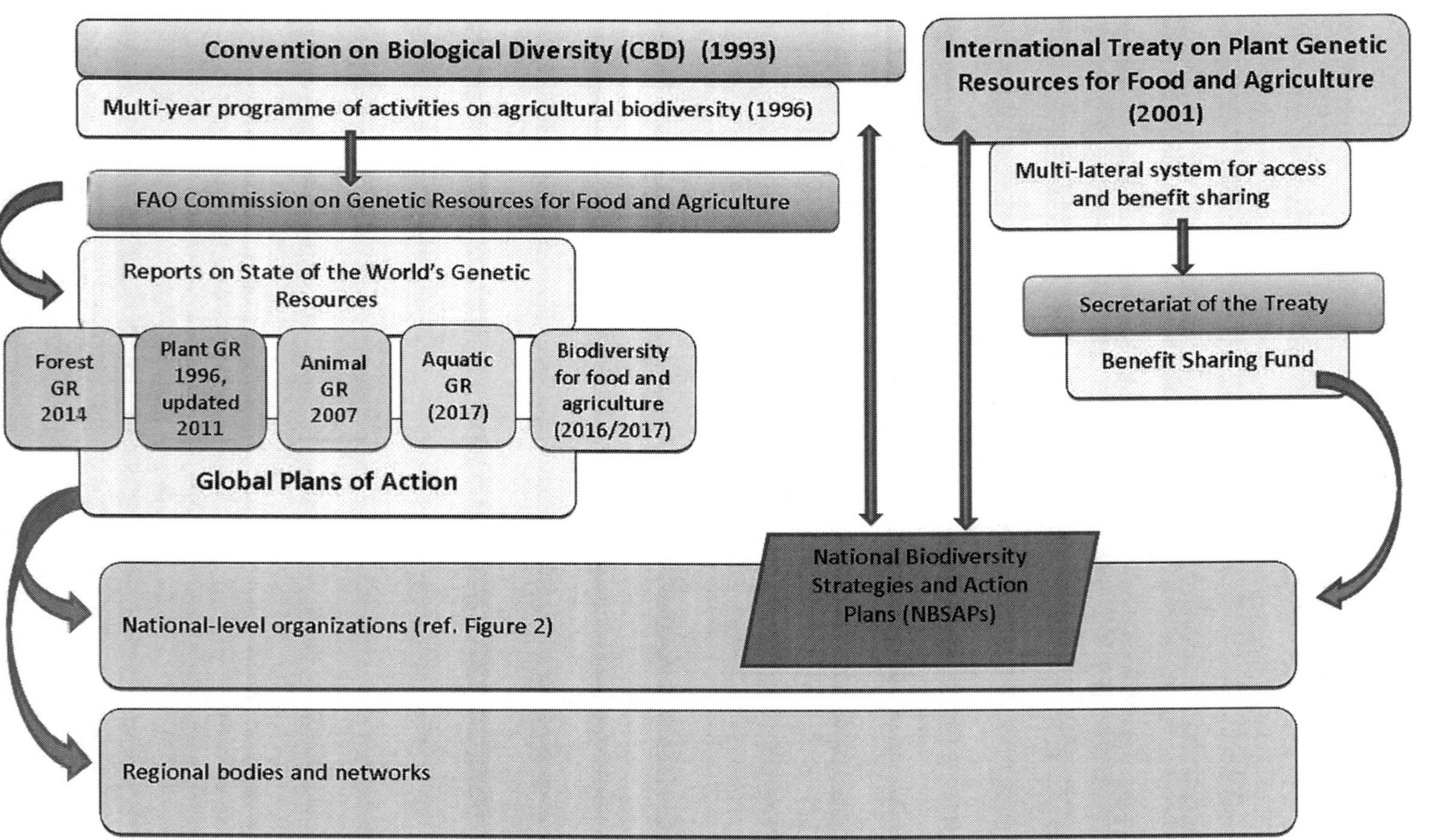


*Figure 41.1* Institutional framework for agricultural biodiversity

*Note*: Figure illustrates how these legal instruments are connected with the organizations and processes at international and national levels, through which they are being implemented.

*Source*: Authors.

National Focal Points of the CBD are therefore key persons in mainstreaming agricultural biodiversity issues into the NBSAPs within each country. The National Focal Points are responsible for receiving and disseminating information related to the CBD; ensuring adequate representation of the country in meetings; identifying experts to participate in technical expert groups; responding to requests for inputs by parties and by the secretariat; collaborating with national focal points in other countries to facilitate implementation of the CBD; and to monitor, promote and facilitate the national implementation of the CBD (CBD, 2009). The model of national focal points is an important instrument at the national level as it facilitates the identification of the national office, headed by the focal point within the country, with clear responsibilities and authority – an important condition for effective coordination.

The Commission on Genetic Resources for Food and Agriculture was set up by the Food and Agriculture Organization of the United Nations (FAO) in 1983 to deal with issues related to plant genetic resources. It was granted an expanded mandate in 1995 to also serve countries in implementing the CBD in the area of agricultural biological diversity, that is, not only plants but also animal, forest and aquatic genetic resources. A key mechanism for this task is overseeing and guiding the global assessments of the state of the world's forest, plant and animal genetic resources for food and agriculture. The Commission has also negotiated other international instruments, including the International Treaty on Plant Genetic Resources for Food and Agriculture (see next section).

Working closely with member states, each of which prepares national reports, and international experts who prepare thematic studies, the Commission has published ground-breaking reports on the 'state of the world's genetic resources' for food and agriculture for plants (FAO, 1997, 2011a), animals (FAO, 2007; FAO, 2011b), and forests (FAO, 2014a). Reports on aquatic genetic resources, on biodiversity for food and agriculture and a third, updated, report on plants are in preparation. The Commission is addressing micro-organism and invertebrate genetic resources, and cross-cutting areas, such as the application of biotechnology in conservation and use, access and benefit sharing, targeted indicators and ecosystems approaches to biodiversity management.

Each 'State of the World' report provides the basis for, and is accompanied by, a Global Plan of Action, endorsed by FAO member countries. These address identified gaps and challenges reported in the country reports as well as in the state of the world reports. They outline what countries, as well as regional and international organizations, should do to strengthen the conservation and use of genetic resources for food and agriculture. The following Global Plans of Action are available:

- Second Global Plan of Action for Plant Genetic Resources for Food and Agriculture *(FAO, 2011a)*
- Global Plan of Action for Animal Genetic Resources *(FAO, 2007)*
- Global Plan of Action for the Conservation, Sustainable Use and Development of Forest Genetic Resources *(FAO, 2014b)*

The Global Plans of Action seek to create an efficient system for the conservation and sustainable use of genetic resources for food and agriculture. They are intended as comprehensive frameworks to guide and catalyze action at community, national, regional and international levels through better cooperation, coordination and planning, and by strengthening capacities. They contain sets of recommendations and priority activities that respond to the needs and priorities identified in the global assessments. Notably, the development of human and institutional capacity features strongly. However, these reports give little information on *how* to enact the required change and implementation process. Countries need to figure this out for themselves, in light of their own unique agricultural and environmental setting, the organizations involved and their capacities and the enabling institutional environments in which they operate (Baur et al., 2002). They need to build on their own strengths and particularities.

## *The International Treaty on Plant Genetic Resources for Food and Agriculture*

The International Treaty on Plant Genetic Resources for Food and Agriculture (the Treaty), ratified in 2004, is a legally binding instrument that covers all plant genetic resources relevant for food and agriculture. It is in harmony with the Convention on Biological Diversity. Its aims are indicated in **Box 41.3** *Aims of the Treaty*. No such instrument exists (yet) for genetic resources for food and agriculture other than plants.

No country is self-sufficient in plant genetic resources, and international cooperation and exchange of genetic resources are therefore of pivotal importance for food security. Through the Treaty, countries have agreed to establish a Multilateral System to facilitate access to key plant genetic resources for food and agriculture, and to share the benefits derived from that access in a fair and equitable way. The Multilateral System includes at present 64 of our most important food and feed crop gene pools, including their wild relatives.

In recognition of the enormous contribution that farmers and their communities have made and continue to make to the conservation and development of plant genetic resources, the Treaty established the principle of Farmers' Rights, which include the protection of traditional knowledge, and the right to participate equitably in benefit-sharing and in national decision-making about plant genetic resources (see also Andersen, Chapter 28 of this Handbook). It has given governments the responsibility for implementing these rights. Besides Farmers' Rights and the Multilateral System, the programme of the Treaty also includes the Benefit-sharing Fund, the Global Information System and provisions on sustainable use. The Commission and the Treaty's Governing Body contribute in different, but mutually supportive, ways to ensure the conservation and sustainable use of plant genetic resources. They cooperate to monitor threats and identify priority actions for the future.

### Box 41.3 Aims of the Treaty

**The International Treaty for Plant Genetic Resources for Food and Agriculture** entered into force on 29 June 2004 and aims at:

1 Recognizing the enormous contribution of farmers to the diversity of crops that feed the world;
2 Establishing a global system to provide farmers, plant breeders and scientists with access to plant genetic materials; and
3 Ensuring that recipients share benefits they derive from the use of these genetic materials with the countries where they have been originated.

Countries that have ratified the Treaty agree to make genetic diversity – and related information – of crops and related species listed in Annex I, that are under control and management of the government, available to all signatories through the Multilateral System. A Standard Material Transfer Agreement (MTA) is available for this process. The development the human and institutional capacity for implementing the Treaty is ongoing, to address a significant lack of awareness and understanding of this instrument.

### *The Sustainable Development Goals*

As not all aspects of agricultural biodiversity management at the national level are explicitly addressed by international instruments such as the CBD and the Treaty, the framework provided by the Sustainable Development Goals (SDGs) could prove a useful alternative. The scope of the SDGs explicitly calls for the inclusion of socio-economic aspects when considering the conservation and use of agricultural biodiversity, an approach which could facilitate a holistic approach towards the planning and implementation of national agricultural biodiversity strategies. Specifically, the 2030 Agenda for Sustainable Development, adopted on 25 September 2015, outlines 17 SDGs and their associated 169 targets. To achieve many of the goals, agricultural biodiversity can and/or should play an important role, particularly:

- Goal 1: End poverty in all its forms everywhere;
- Goal 2: End hunger, achieve food security and improved nutrition and promote sustainable agriculture;
- Goal 3: Ensure healthy lives and promote well-being for all at all ages;
- Goal 4: Ensure inclusive and equitable quality education and promote lifelong learning opportunities for all; and
- Goal 15: Sustainably manage forests, combat desertification, halt and reverse land degradation, halt biodiversity loss.

Dialogue and engagement with the national SDG processes will be very important. Organizations and institutions implementing and monitoring the SDG will need awareness of how the conservation and use of agricultural biodiversity relates to poverty reduction, food and nutrition security, and sustainable agriculture, among others. This is an important entry point for mainstreaming agricultural biodiversity into national programmes, including in education and research programmes.

## National implementation of conservation and use of agricultural biodiversity

### *Multiple sectors and organizations*

At the national level, a wide range of organizations in multiple sectors plays a role in implementing the global institutional framework for the conservation and use of agricultural biodiversity. **Figure 41.2** *National level ABD actors* outlines a typical set of organizations involved in, or having an impact on, the conservation and use of agricultural biodiversity at the national level:

- Government institutions at national, district and local level;
- Academic institutions responsible for research and higher education;
- The private sector, including small and medium agro-enterprises; and
- Civil society, from agricultural producers to consumers, including NGOs.

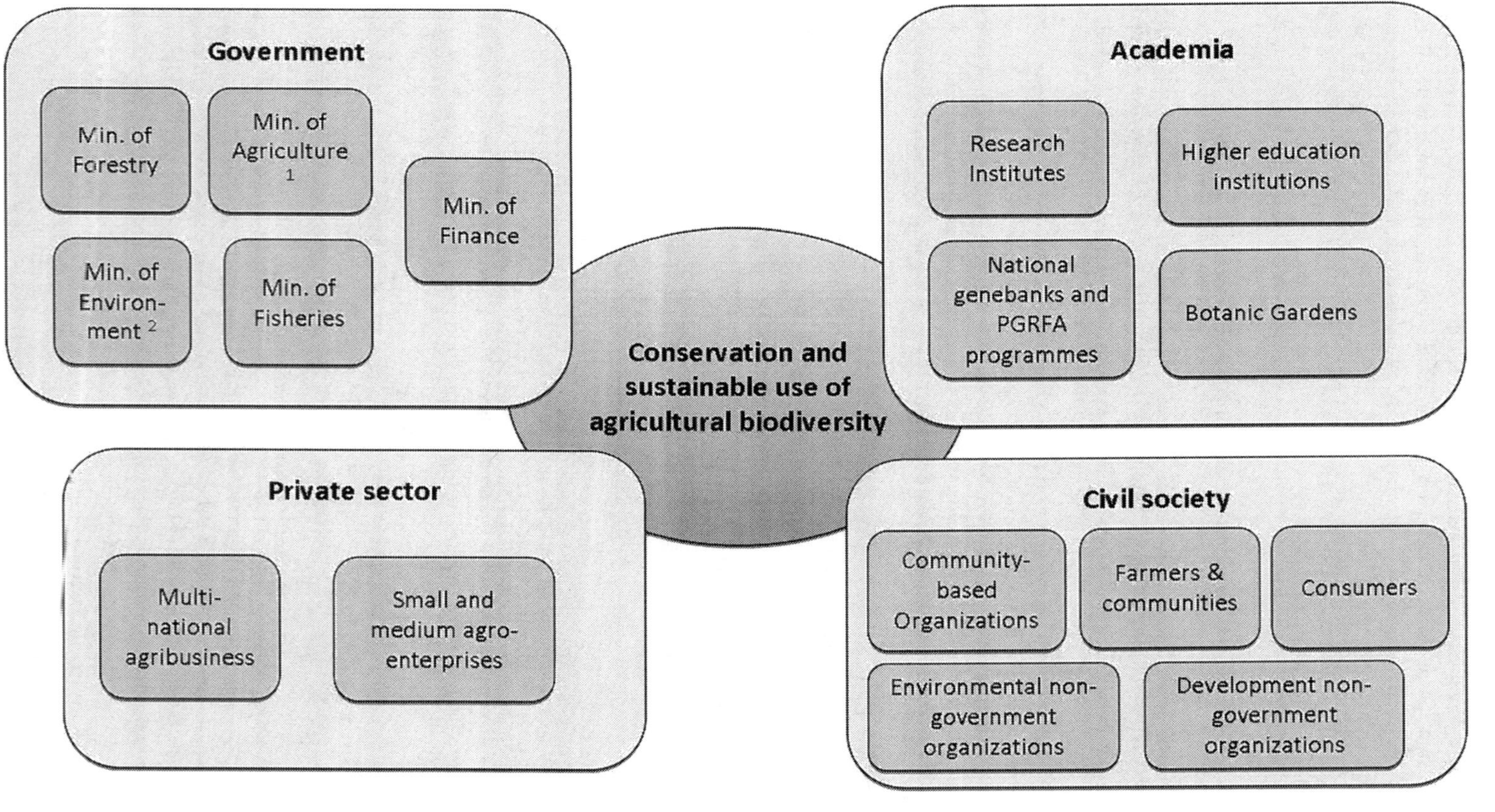


*Figure 41.2 National level ABD actors.*

*Notes*: [1]Typically a country's focal point for FAO's Commission on Genetic Resources for Food and Agriculture and for the Treaty. [2]Typically a country's focal point for the Convention on Biological Diversity.

*Source*: Authors.

Each country is unique and needs to analyze its own organizational set-up and enabling institutional environment to find out where and how new agricultural biodiversity components and processes would best 'fit' (Spillane et al., 1999; Engels et al., 2001). Often, this means integrating agricultural biodiversity aspects into existing processes, rather than starting new, dedicated ones afresh. One example of this is the integration of agricultural biodiversity into a country's NBSAPs – the principal instrument for implementing CBD at the national level. This is currently an area where progress is urgently needed. In particular, awareness of intra-specific diversity (the genetic diversity within species) is weak in most NBSAPs (**Figure 41.2**).

Government organizations are the key actors for implementing and reporting on CBD and the Treaty, as they are the legal parties to such international agreements. As every country may have its own unique organizational structure, it would be difficult to describe a typical national set-up for these functions. However, the responsibility for overseeing the implementation of the CBD typically lies with the ministry of environment, whereas the ministry of agriculture is the body responsible in most countries for overseeing the implementation of the Treaty. The responsible ministries have nominated national focal points that play a key role in the coordination of the implementation of these instruments at national level.

Individual countries have created (or are still in the process of creating) their own unique solutions for an efficient coordination between these two sectors. For example, in Germany, the Ministry for Food and Agriculture has formed a multi-stakeholder scientific advisory committee for biodiversity and genetic resources that actively engages representatives of other ministries, research institutions and others in their deliberations and report writing.

Academic institutions play an important role in initiating, preparing and implementing governmental policies and responsibilities. Through research, they help generate evidence-based solutions to societies' problems. Universities and other tertiary education institutions build human capacity through formal education and informal training. As such, this stakeholder group is important in terms of awareness creation, but also as a direct partner in the actual activities of conserving and using agricultural biodiversity. The mainstreaming of agricultural biodiversity issues into the programmes of academic institutions is thus a priority.

The private sector plays an important role in the use of agricultural biodiversity, both at international and local scales. In recent years, some companies started to develop increasingly important Corporate Social Responsibility, for example IKEA has a policy that 100% of its raw materials should be certified or recycled by 2020. However, due to the obvious need to be profitable, not all important tasks related to the conservation and use of agricultural biodiversity can and will be addressed by commercial companies. For instance, seed producers tend to focus on a somewhat limited set of commercially interesting food crops, with the consequence that hundreds of neglected and underutilized species have to rely on traditional and informal seed and knowledge systems, including seed networks, custodian farmers and community genebanks, sometimes with the support from the national genebank, but mostly left largely to themselves. Traditional varieties and landraces may not be officially allowed for sale due to national seed legislation, thus hampering the exchange of diversity between (local) farmers. Small and medium enterprises are important actors in the (seed) value chain of products stemming from agricultural biodiversity (Louwaars et al., 2013), and hence contribute to creating income and to 'conservation through use' (De Boef and Thijssen, 2007). Consumers, obviously, play a central role, as their increasing demand for 'novel food', 'whole food', 'organic' products, Fair Trade produce and geographic indicators can all trigger a change in what farmers produce.

Civil society benefits directly and indirectly from products and services derived from agricultural biodiversity. It can also strongly influence what is grown, traded and consumed. Decisions on what crops or varieties to eat, how and where to buy food, whether to pay a premium for organic or fair trade products and so forth can have important consequences. As such, this stakeholder group is an important target of awareness campaigns and they can be instrumental in influencing policy-makers, bottom-up. Non-governmental organizations (NGOs) of different kinds are also important actors from the local to the international levels. Whether they come from an environmental or a development angle, they can help create awareness, develop capacity and play an important role in development and empowerment related to agricultural biodiversity.

## Data management

Data management is key to the planning, implementation, monitoring and coordination of agricultural biodiversity conservation and use. Disparate information is needed to monitor the status and trends of the biodiversity in a given country, and to report back to the CBD and the Treaty, as well as for decision-making and priority setting in general. International organizations such as the Secretariats of the aforementioned legal instruments and their hosting institutions (UNEP and FAO) as well as other governmental and non-governmental organizations are active in this field to offer guidance and assistance.

The Governing Body of the Treaty recently adopted the vision and the first Programme of Work on the Global Information System (GLIS). The Vision states that GLIS 'integrates and augments existing systems to create the global entry point to information and knowledge for strengthening the capacity for PGRFA conservation, management and utilization'. The Governing Body also translated the vision into seven objectives and a programme of work with concrete activities for the period 2016–2022 (FAO, 2015).

## Implementation of global plans of action at national and regional level

The sectoral GPAs provide a unique agreed global framework for action; the logical next step would be to consider how countries individually (or jointly) can go about their implementation (Engels, 2002). The main responsibility for implementing a GPA lies with national governments. When analyzing the GPAs for AnGR, PGRFA and Forest GR, a striking similarity can be concluded for priority action points at the national level. The salient priorities of the existing GPAs have been summarized in **Box 41.4** *Common priority action points of the GPAs.*

### Box 41.4 Common priority action points of the GPAs on plants, animals and forests

- Develop national strategies for *in situ* and *ex situ* conservation of plants, animals and forests, and their sustainable use.
- Update conservation and management needs and integrate them into wider policies, programmes and frameworks of action at national, regional and global levels.
- Establish or strengthen national institutions.
- Establish or strengthen national educational and research facilities.
- Strengthen national human capacity for characterization, inventory and monitoring of trends and associated risks, for sustainable use and development, and for conservation.
- Establish or strengthen national/international information sharing, research and education.
- Strengthen international cooperation to build capacities in developing countries and countries with economies in transition.

- Establish regional focal points and strengthen national/international networks.
- Raise national awareness of the roles and values of genetic resources.
- Review and develop national policies and legal frameworks for genetic resources.
- Strengthen efforts to mobilize resources, including financial resources, for the conservation, sustainable use and development of genetic resources.

To illustrate the relevance of GPAs as 'tools' for the planning and implementing actions at the national and regional level, we provide some examples and extracts in Boxes 41.5 *Selected priorities of Priority Area 4* and 41.6 *Identified strategic regional and international priorities*, respectively. This is particularly relevant at the regional level, as planning and coordination of activities is more complex, and should be driven by biological and strategic considerations. The strategic priorities for the implementation of the GPA for AnGR at the national level in the strategic priority area 'Policies, institutions and capacity-building' are included in **Box 41.5**, as an example.

For the details on the corresponding rationale and actions under each of these strategic priorities, see the GPA document (FAO, 2007). Considering the fact that most of the genetic resources at the species level are distributed across multiple countries, there is a strong argument in favor of collaborating at the sub/regional level to achieve more effectiveness and efficiency with the implementation at the national level. The corresponding identified priorities at the regional and international level are listed in **Box 41.6**, as an example.

### Box 41.5 Selected priorities of Priority Area 4 'Policies, Institutions and Capacity-building' of the GPA on AnGR for the implementation at the national level

SP (Strategy Priority) 12: Establish or strengthen national institutions, including national focal points, for planning and implementing AnGR measures, for livestock sector developments.

SP 13: Establish or strengthen national educational and research facilities.

SP 14: Strengthen national human capacity for characterization, inventory and monitoring of trends and associated risks, for sustainable use and development, and for conservations.

SP 18: Raise national awareness of the roles and values of AnGR.

SP 20: Review and develop national policies and legal frameworks for AnGR.

Examples of regional and global activities that have been identified by the animal genetic resources community while preparing the GPA for AnGR are provided in **Box 41.6**. For example, in Strategic Priority 17, networks have been identified as important mechanisms to pursue regional activities and contribute to global ones. Obviously, information management and the development of legal frameworks as well as building capacity are other key activities to be implemented at those levels.

### Box 41.6 Identified strategic regional and international priorities for the implementation of the GPA on AnGR

SP 15: Establish or strengthen international information sharing, research and education.

SP 16: Strengthen international cooperation to build capacities in developing countries and countries with economies in transition.

SP 17: Establish regional focal points and strengthen international networks.

SP 19: Raise regional and international awareness of the roles and values of AnGR.

SP 21: Review and develop international policies and regulatory frameworks relevant to AnGR.

SP 22: Coordinate the Commission's efforts on AnGR policy with other international fora.

SP 23: Strengthen efforts to mobilize resources, including financial resources, for the conservation, sustainable use and development of AnGR.

The Commission on Genetic Resources for Food and Agriculture oversees, monitors and evaluates the implementation of the GPAs. It also adopts separate funding strategies (www.fao.org/docrep/012/i1674e/i1674e00.htm) which aim to enhance the availability, transparency, efficiency and effectiveness of the provision of substantial and additional financial resources, and to strengthen international cooperation to support and complement the efforts of developing countries and countries with economies in transition in the implementation of the GPA.

Furthermore, FAO supports the implementation of the GPAs by facilitating global and regional collaboration and networks, supporting the convening of intergovernmental meetings, maintaining and updating information systems for some of the sectors, developing communication products and coordinating the preparation of global status and trends reports. Furthermore, FAO has developed a set of technical guidelines (FAO, 2011b), and provides technical assistance and training to support capacity-building and action at country level (FAO, 2016).

## National strategies for plant genetic resources

In the case of PGRFA, the 'Draft Guidelines for Developing a National Strategy for Plant Genetic Resources for Food and Agriculture: Translating the Second Global Plan of Action for Plant Genetic Resources for Food and Agriculture into National Action' provide a very useful basis for countries to develop a national strategy for PGRFA (www.fao.org/3/a-ml472e.pdf). Such a strategy will facilitate the integration of specific national conditions and requirements with responsibilities that stem from international instruments such as the Treaty, the GPA on PGRFA and other obligations related to PGRFA, and thus, to take the greatest advantage of international obligations. The current draft contains a useful, albeit somewhat generic, checklist for the development process (see **Box 41.7** *Checklist for the development of national strategies for PGRFA*).

### Box 41.7 Checklist for the development of national strategies for PGRFA

Checklist for the establishment, maintenance or strengthening of a national framework for PGRFA (noting that each question in the checklist refers to a particular step in elaborating a National Strategy for PGRFA, based on the idealized model presented in this document).

**Checklist for establishing the foundations for a National Strategy for PGRFA:**

- Has the National Focal Point for PGRFA been identified?
- Is there an active PGRFA Programme in the country?
- Is there a suitable committee in place to drive the preparation of the National Strategy for PGRFA?
- Have the PGRFA stakeholders in the country been identified?
- Are there active linkages and partnerships between stakeholders at national level?
- Is there engagement with regional and sub-regional PGRFA collaborations?
- Are means in place to convene ad hoc working groups and enlist expertise?
- Has a country assessment on the state of PGRFA been conducted or updated?
- Has the vision statement been drafted and agreed?
- Have goals and objectives been formulated?
- Has an action plan been formulated?
- Is a budget in place for the strategy-development activities?
- Has a monitoring plan been formulated?
- Has a communication plan been formulated?

**Checklist for finalizing and presenting the National Strategy for PGRFA:**

- Has a consultation document been prepared?
- Have stakeholder consultations been initiated . . .
    - via common stakeholder consultations/meetings?
    - via electronic consultations?
    - via one-to-one meetings?
- Have stakeholder concerns been incorporated into a revised Strategy?
- Have costs been budgeted and financial resources mobilized?
- Are monitoring capacities identified and in place?
- Has the draft National Strategy for PGRFA been validated?

**Checklist for implementing the National Strategy for PGRFA:**

- Are enabling capacities in place?
- Has the National Strategy for PGRFA been widely disseminated?
- Have efforts to raise awareness of the strategy been planned and carried out?
- Have the steps for implementing the strategy been initiated?
- Have the steps for monitoring and evaluating the plan been agreed?
- Have the national information systems been established or updated with information generated from implementation and monitoring of the strategy?

*Source*: FAO (2014c).

Whenever possible, it seems that the development of strategies for PGRFA, and obviously also for any of the other sectors of agricultural biodiversity, should be closely linked to and based upon existing National Biodiversity Strategic Action Plans. The processes of preparing and/or updating any of these strategies should be done in close consultation with the respective focal points and, where relevant, the respective key stakeholders.

## Case studies: examples of institutional strengthening at the national level

### Case study 1: coordination of agricultural biodiversity activities in Germany (text provided by Frank Begemann)

In addition to the National Strategy on Biological Diversity in Germany, the Federal Ministry of Food and Agriculture (BMEL) published a Strategy for Biodiversity for Food, Agriculture, Forestry and Fisheries. This so-called agrobiodiversity strategy provides the general framework for the four national programmes for plant, animal, forest and aquatic genetic resources for food and agriculture. A programme for genetic resources of microbes and invertebrates is under development, covering *inter alia* pollination, soil diversity, human nutrition, animal nutrition, animal health, plant breeding, plant health and renewable resources.

Due to the federal constitution of Germany, responsibilities for conservation and use of agricultural biodiversity are shared among the Federal and 16 *Länder* governments. A wide range of stakeholders is involved, including research, administration, farmers, breeders and interested civil society. The national programmes are implemented under the guidance of four respective national committees consisting of representatives of these stakeholder groups. For advice on cross-cutting issues, BMEL has established a Scientific Advisory Board for Biodiversity and Genetic Resources for Food and Agriculture.

The national programmes have no single dedicated budget line. They are rather funded via the contributions in kind by all different stakeholders within their own financial means. The Federal Government, the *Länder*, and the various state and private institutions and other stakeholders implement the national programmes through their joint efforts and individual contributions.

While the different national programmes, their related activities, stakeholder groups and infrastructures are different by nature, it is important to keep a coherent policy and consistent organization of the work. Therefore, an Information and Coordination Centre for Biological Diversity (IBV) was created in 1991. The IBV, a part of the Federal Office for Agriculture and Food (BLE), supports the development and execution of the national programmes and acts as the secretariat of the respective advisory and national coordination committees. To offer well-informed advice, IBV maintains a knowledge base that includes *inter alia* national inventories for plant, animal, forest and aquatic genetic resources. These national databases facilitate an overview of the genetic diversity available in Germany and are valuable planning tools for monitoring and assessment of agricultural biodiversity trends in Germany.

These national inventories also provide the German data for the respective European databases: EURISCO (plants), EFABIS (animals) and EUFGIS (forestry) and the global databases WIEWS and Genesys (plants), DADIS (animals) and REFORGEN (forestry). By nature of its competence, the IBV is also involved as a national knowledge hub for nation-wide and international affairs. It therefore supports international cooperation, for example in the FAO matters of the Commission on Genetic Resources for Food and Agriculture and the CBD activities related to agricultural biodiversity.

An online Information System Genetic Resources (GENRES, www.genres.de) is maintained by IBV to provide an overview of the most relevant activities and stakeholders in Germany.

### Case study 2: mainstreaming agricultural biodiversity at both national and local levels in Uganda (text provided by John Mulumba)

In Uganda, the National Biodiversity Strategy and Action Plan brings together all aspects of biodiversity management, including agricultural biodiversity. It outlines strategies to be undertaken and identifies lead agencies. However, the lack of a centrally allocated budget impacts negatively on its implementation, coordination, monitoring and reporting of achievements. Resource mobilization for the activities is undertaken at different national, sectoral, programme and project levels.

The National Environment Statute has established a technical committee on biodiversity to advise on matters of biodiversity conservation in the broad sense, and consequently, there is no specific focus to agricultural biodiversity. The Agricultural Sector Development Strategy and Investment Plan (DSIP 2010–2015) focuses heavily on deriving economic returns from agricultural biodiversity at the expense of its sustainable management for longer-term utilization.

The National Development Plan 2015–2020 sets targets towards ending hunger and achieving food security and improved nutrition and promoting sustainable agriculture. The targets include maintaining ecosystems (including rangelands) that strengthening the capacity for adaptation to climate change; maintaining genetic diversity in seed and plant genebanks; and ensuring benefit sharing. This is yet to be reflected in the investment plans, especially those of the Ministry of Agriculture. The complex national planning processes and resource allocation, and the complicated assignment of institutional roles and responsibilities for agricultural biodiversity management, are a hitch to well-coordinated agricultural biodiversity management and capacity building in Uganda.

The National Agricultural Research Organization (NARO) coordinates agricultural biodiversity-related research within its different institutes, but its strategic plan 2008–2018 does not explicitly bring out strategic interventions for agricultural biodiversity management and capacity building. The pressure to have products and results for the consumer/market overrides allocation of sufficient resources for agricultural biodiversity coordination and institutional strengthening.

The new Biodiversity and Biotechnology Program (BBP) under NARO's National Agricultural Research Laboratories (NARL) comprises (1) Plant Genetic Resources Centre (PGRC), (2) Biological Control Unit and (3) Biotechnology Centre. The existence of these three units under one agricultural research programme creates a great opportunity for agricultural biodiversity deliverables. However, for being a programme within an institute it might not give the programme sufficient muscle, visibility and capacity to attract adequate resources and infrastructure to handle the wider agricultural biodiversity scope so as to bring out the larger national image. The programme, in addition to the *ex situ* collections at the PGRC, is currently rolling out a community-based system of conservation through community seed banks which is being managed by the communities themselves.

The decentralized governance system moved powers from the central government to lower-level government units, to enable districts and sub-counties to initiate, plan, budget and implement development programmes, based on community priorities. However, local governments remain constrained by financial resources and availability of technical skills to effectively perform their responsibilities. Technical support on agricultural biodiversity is predominantly sought from the Ministry of Agriculture. But the Ministry also has very limited technical staff deployed at district level.

A wide range of NGOs is engaged in different aspects of agricultural biodiversity management, working particularly at the community level. However, the absence of platforms that enhance synergies and complementarity among government agencies and NGOs at the national and lower levels is an issue. Streamlining coordination and capacity building require more attention.

Lack of a specific policy on agricultural biodiversity is yet another limitation. If the draft national policies on PGRFA and seed are passed, they will provide remedies to many of the challenges, and consequently, the coordination of and institutional strengthening in agricultural biodiversity shall be improved.

**Lessons from the case studies**

The previous case studies show very different approaches to the management of agricultural biodiversity. In both countries, governments aim at building, whenever possible, on existing structures. Resource allocation has been handled very differently, however. Whereas in Germany, the mandates and budgets of existing institutions seem to be sufficient to implement a national programme under the strong leadership of IBV, in Uganda, the lack of sufficient funds is a hindrance for adequate coordination and implementation. Possibly the most important lessons we can learn from these two cases are to provide due authority to the coordinating body, the need to make clear arrangements for budgetary allocations and to manage expectations, that taking a sectoral approach seems to fit best with existing structures and that the NBSAP seems to be a logical starting point.

## Emerging issues on capacity development

Some general conclusions for strengthening the institutional framework for handling agricultural biodiversity at the national level seem to emerge:

- *Involving multiple sectors*: country's ministries are by definition sector oriented: the ministry of environment is typically responsible for CBD-related matters, while the ministry of agriculture is usually responsible for agricultural biodiversity, that is, matters that fall under the FAO Commission and the Treaty. Fisheries and forestry may be handled by yet other ministries, or be part of the ministry of agriculture. Food production and safety aspects might be either dealt with by the ministry of agriculture or assigned to the ministry of health, for example. Navigating this complexity is one of the challenges in establishing and implementing a cross-cutting agenda such as that of agricultural biodiversity. This will require investment in the institutional framework of the country in question by creating and assigning responsibilities and authority to an entity that coordinates, facilitates, communicates and shares information and knowledge as well as pro-actively engages ministries and other organizations concerned with specific responsibilities and activities that are of importance for the development and implementation of a broadly based and comprehensive agricultural biodiversity agenda.
- *Integrating agricultural biodiversity into organizations that have quite different core mandates*: Few organizations are fully dedicated to agricultural biodiversity only. In most countries, national genebanks and, to a lesser extent, botanic gardens play a key role in conserving and using these resources and coordinating the national PGRFA programme. However, this means that many issues regarding agricultural biodiversity will be handled by organizations that are not specialized in this field.
- *Strengthening higher education*: Higher educational institutions rarely teach agricultural biodiversity as a stand-alone programme, or even as a course (Rudebjer et al., 2011). This means that in general, graduates of agricultural and forestry programmes have limited background in, and knowledge of, issues such as crop wild relatives, neglected and underutilized species, informal seed systems or regarding the existence and/or function of the Treaty's MLS and so forth.

- *Facilitating participatory multi-sector, multi-stakeholder processes*: Complex and multifaceted issues such as an ecosystem-level approach to the management of biodiversity, and pollinators and micro-organisms provide particular challenges since they are managed at landscape level, involving multiple stakeholders. Often, the local private benefits of using agricultural biodiversity and the external costs, such as loss of environmental services, clash. Thus, managing cross-cutting issues demand a broad portfolio of skills, in particular for multi-stakeholder analysis and negotiating agreed solutions.
- *Influencing policies*: The fact that many different stakeholders are involved in agricultural biodiversity management, use and conservation; that the specific knowledge on these resources is multifaceted and widely spread; and that the interests are diverse and sometimes leading to conflicts, all this requires that well-defined policies and laws are needed in order to guide states and its people conserving and utilizing these resources sustainably. Such legal frameworks can function only if they are developed in close consultation with the stakeholders and address the issues in a logical and practical way.

*(Engels et al., 2002)*

## Concluding remarks on the way forward

As countries have agreed on legal frameworks for the implementation of the necessary activities at the national and regional level, this chapter has analyzed these frameworks and summarized the key features and mechanisms that have been developed to assist countries with their implementation. Two case studies have been included to illustrate the different ways countries are using to cope with their responsibilities.

As with other complex processes and responsibilities, multiple factors need to be considered when implementing the agreed frameworks of the CBD and the Treaty. We identify these most important factors as:

- *Establishment and operation of an effective institutional framework with adequate and steady funding*: A functional institutional framework provides the opportunity for people and organizations to interact with authorities that have the knowledge and authority to advise and direct stakeholders, to provide a platform for debate, to facilitate coordination, to provide funding for agreed activities and so forth.
- *Adequate coordination of activities with all relevant stakeholders*: The complexity and multifaceted nature of agricultural biodiversity and the need for involving relevant stakeholders in its conservation and use are two important arguments for coordinating the planning and implementation of agricultural biodiversity actions.
- *Paying attention to the needs for developing capacity at all levels*: individual, organizational and institutional; by doing so, it will be possible to effectively engage and/or build on them, to share implementation responsibilities more widely and so forth.
- *Providing a conducive policy framework for the agricultural biodiversity activities*: A supportive policy framework for the conservation and use of agricultural biodiversity is a necessity, as it provides for transparent, convincing and conducive conditions to all stakeholders involved.
- *Engaging actively into regional operational agricultural biodiversity networks*: The nature and distribution of agricultural biodiversity requires collaboration between countries that have such resources in common for efficient and effective conservation approaches. Regional fora, in particular specialized regional networks addressing one or more specific sectors of agricultural biodiversity, should be used to establish or strengthen such collaboration.

- *Whenever possible, link conservation activities with development opportunities*: As conservation usually does require funding (rather than providing revenues) and frequently requires (in kind) contributions from those stakeholders involved, it is argued that linking conservation with other economic activities in a region, that is, development projects and so forth, would provide the possibility to integrate the conservation philosophy with activities that are aimed at creating earnings.
- *Generating awareness among the broader public, school children, students, consumers and so forth on the importance and potential of agricultural biodiversity*: The need for conservation of agricultural biodiversity to keep options open for future generations and the potential for using it in breeding and business, among others, are compelling arguments for raising awareness of agricultural biodiversity in society at large.

## References

Baur, H., Watts, J. and Engels, J. (2002) 'The importance of stakeholder involvement in the implementation of the Global Plan of Action', pp. 14–24 in J. M. M. Engels, D. Kiambi, J. Watts and I. Zoungrana, (eds.) *Proceedings of International Workshop 'Strengthening Policy and Institutional Frameworks for Conservation and Sustainable Use of Plant Genetic Resources (PGR): National Programmes and Networks as Strategic Tools'.* October 2002, Zschortau, Germany. IPGRI, Rome and DSE/ZEL, Zschortau.

Boef, de W. S. and Thijssen, M. (2007) *Participatory Tools Working with Crops, Varieties and Seeds, Guide Book for Professionals Working Agrobiodiversity Conservation, Participatory Plant Breeding and Informal Seed Sector Development*, Wageningen International, Wageningen, the Netherlands.

CBD (1996) *COP 3 Decision III/11. Conservation and Sustainable Use of Agricultural Biological Diversity*, www.cbd.int/decision/cop/default.shtml?id=7107, accessed 2 February 2016.

CBD (2009) *Role of the CBD National Focal Point.* Module A-2, Version 2 – February 2009 www.cbd.int/doc/training/nbsap/a2-train-role-nfp-v2-2009-02-en.pdf.

CBD (undated-a) *National Biodiversity Strategies and Action Plans (NBSAPs)*, www.cbd.int/nbsap/, accessed 20 January 2016.

CBD (undated-b). *Latest NBSAPs*, www.cbd.int/nbsap/about/latest/, accessed 31 January 2016.

CBD (undated-c). *NBSAP Capacity Building Modules*, www.cbd.int/nbsap/training/default.shtml, accessed 20 January 2016.

Commission on Genetic Resources for Food and Agriculture (2015) www.fao.org/nr/cgrfa/cgrfa-about/cgrfa-history/en/, accessed 15 September 2015.

Engels, J. M. M. (2002) 'The International Treaty, the Global Plan of Action and the State of the World's PGRFA Report', pp. 90–97 in *Proceedings of International Workshop 'Strengthening Policy and Institutional Frameworks for Conservation and Sustainable Use of Plant Genetic Resources (PGR): National Programmes and Networks as Strategic Tools'.* October 2002, Zschortau, Germany. IPGRI, Rome and DSE/ZEL, Zschortau.

Engels, J. M. M., Kiambi, D., Watts, J. and Zoungrana, I. (eds.) (2002) *Strengthening Policy and Institutional Frameworks for Conservation and Sustainable Use of Plant Genetic Resources (PGR): National Programmes and Networks as Strategic Tools.* Proceedings of an International Workshop. Pages 111. October 2002, Zschortau, Germany. IPGRI, Rome and DSE/ZEL, Zschortau.

Engels, J. M. M., Withers, L., Raymond, R. and Fassil, H. (2001) 'The importance of PGR and strong national programmes', in J. M. M. Engels, R. Vodouhe, J. Thompson, A. Zannou, E. Hehne and M. Grum (eds.), *Towards Sustainable National Plant Genetic Resources Programmes: Policy, Planning and Coordination Issues*, 01/2001; International Plant Genetic Resources Institute, Nairobi, Kenya.

FAO (2007) *Global Plan of Action for Animal Genetic Resources and the Interlaken Declaration*, Commission on Genetic Resources for Food and Agriculture, FAO, Rome, Italy, ftp://ftp.fao.org/docrep/fao/010/a1404e/a1404e00.pdf

FAO (2009) *International Treaty on Plant Genetic Resources for Food and Agriculture*, FAO, Rome, Italy.

FAO (2011a) *Second Global Plan of Action for Plant Genetic Resources for Food and Agriculture*, FAO, Rome, Italy.

FAO (2011b) 'Developing the Institutional Framework for the Management of Animal Genetic Resources. *FAO Animal Production and Health Guidelines, No. 6*, FAO, Rome, Italy.

FAO (2014a) *State of the World's Forest Genetic Resources*, Commission on Genetic Resources for Food and Agriculture, FAO, Rome, Italy.

FAO (1997) *State of the World's Plant Genetic Resources for Food and Agriculture*, FAO, Rome, Italy.

FAO (2014b) *Global Plan of Action for the Conservation, Sustainable Use and Development of Forest Genetic Resources*, FAO, Rome, Italy, www.fao.org/3/a-i3849e.pdf

FAO (2014c) *Draft Guidelines for Developing a National Strategy for Plant Genetic Resources for Food and Agriculture: Translating the Second Global Plan of Action for Plant Genetic Resources for Food and Agriculture into National Action*, CGRFA/WG-PGR-7/14/Inf.1, FAO, Rome, Italy.

FAO (2015) *Vision Paper on the Development of the Global Information System* (IT/GB 6/15/7), Item 10 of the Provisional Agenda of the Sixth Session of the Governing Body of the Treaty, FAO, Rome, Italy, www.planttreaty.org/sites/default/files/gb6w07e.pdf, accessed 2 February 2016.

FAO (2016) *Implementing the Global Plan of Action for Animal Genetic Resources: Agriculture and Consumer Protection Department*, FAO, Rome, Italy, www.fao.org/ag/againfo/programmes/en/A5.html, accessed 1 February 2016.

Louwaars, N. P., de Boef, W. S. and Edeme, J. (2013) 'Integrated seed sector development in africa: A basis for seed policy and law', *Journal of Crop Improvement*, vol. 27, pp. 186–214.

Rudebjer, P., Chakeredza, S., Njoroge, K., van Schagen, B., Kamau, H. and Baena, M. (2011) *Teaching Agrobiodiversity for Food and agriculture: A Curriculum Guide for Higher Education*, Bioversity International, Maccarese, Italy.

Spillane, C., Engels, J., Fassil, H., Withers, L. and Cooper, D. (1999) 'Strengthening national programmes for plant genetic resources for food and agriculture: Planning and coordination', pp. 1–51 in J. M. M. Engels (ed.), *Issues in Genetic Resources No. 8*, IPGRI, Rome, Italy.

United Nations (2015) *United Nations General Assembly Draft Outcome Document of the United Nations Summit for the Adoption of the Post-2015 Development Agenda*. UN, accessed 14 December 2015.

## List of acronyms

AnGR: Animal Genetic Resources
BLE: Federal Office for Agriculture and Food (Germany)
BMEL: Federal Ministry of Food and Agriculture (Germany)
CBD: Convention on Biological Diversity
FAO: Food and Agricultural Organization of the United Nations
FGR: Forest Genetic Resources
GENRES: Information System Genetic Resources (Germany)
GLIS: Global Information System (FAO) GPA: Global Plan of Action
IBV: Information and Coordination Centre for Biological Diversity (Germany)
MLS: Multilateral System of the International Treaty
NARO: National Agricultural Research Organization (Uganda)
NBSAP: National Biodiversity Strategy and Action Plan
PGRFA: Plant Genetic Resources for Food and Agriculture
SDGs: Sustainable Development Goals SMTA: Standard Material Transfer Agreement

### European genetic resources databases

EURISCO (plants – IPK, Germany, www.ipk-gatersleben.de/en/genebank/genebank-documentation/eurisco/)
EFABIS (animals – efabis-regional.iasrj.eu)
EUFGIS (forestry – Bioversity International, http://www.eufgis.org/)

### Global genetic resources databases

WIEWS (plants – FAO)
GENESYS (plants – The Global Crop Diversity Trust)
DADIS (animals – FAO)
REFORGEN (forestry – FAO)

# 42

# INFORMATION, KNOWLEDGE AND AGRICULTURAL BIODIVERSITY

*Dag Endresen*

## Introduction

Plant genetic resources for food and agriculture include an estimated 7.4 million *ex situ* accessions conserved in genebank collections. An estimated 40% of these accessions are both electronically documented and freely available from online genebank data platforms such as Genesys (Alercia and Mackay, 2013; www.genesys-pgr.org/) and EURISCO (FAO, 2010; Dias et al., 2011; http://eurisco.ipk-gatersleben.de/). Approximately 21% of the world's flora is classified as a crop wild relative and as such a potential gene donor for crops (Maxted and Kell, 2009). The Global Biodiversity Information Facility (GBIF) (Telenius, 2011) integrates and provides extensive occurrence information about collection data, including genebank accessions *ex situ* and wild plants *in situ*, including many crop wild relatives. However, neither GBIF nor the genebank data portals focus on providing data on the molecular genetic diversity or conservation status of the collections. Some *ex situ* genebank accessions do provide associated measurement data from characterization and evaluation trials. However, the lack of easy access to experimental trait information online continues to be reported as a major limitation to the efficient use of plant genetic resources (FAO, 2010). Data on *ex situ* genebank collections, crop wild relative *in situ* populations, genetic data, and trait measurements are generally created and made available by different sub-groups of practitioners, and each sub-group has shown a tendency to develop its own documentation practices and data standards. This chapter will describe how knowledge organization principles can be used to create a more unified data landscape for agricultural biodiversity. It is concluded that the introduction of persistent and globally unique digital identifiers, resolvable to machine-readable information, and based on a standardized and formally declared data domain model is one of the fundamental first steps for an effective integration of agricultural biodiversity information (FAO, 2014).

## What is genetic diversity?

The food crops and farm animals we depend upon for our livelihood are exposed to many stresses, such as evolving plant diseases, pests, and climate change. Plant breeding programs require access to novel genetic diversity to maintain and improve food crops to keep pace with these challenges (see Ortiz, Chapter 17 of this Handbook). To select the appropriate genetic diversity to do this, plant breeders and crop scientists need access to relevant information from a wide range of distributed information sources. Heterogeneous data formats such as non-standardized table header labels and database access interfaces makes data integration challenging. In contrast, standardization of data formats and communication protocols makes data acquisition and processing easier. Data interoperability principles describe how heterogeneous systems can exchange data with each other and interpret that data in a manner that is meaningful to the end-user. To make optimal use of the emerging large amounts of information about genetic diversity, we will also need novel approaches and tools for data analysis.

The loss of suitable habitat for the wild relatives of the cultivated plants has raised concerns regarding their survival *in situ* (Iriondo et al., 2008). There are also indications of a gradual replacement of more genetically diverse landraces and traditional cultivars with genetically more uniform modern cultivars (Tanksley and McCouch, 1997; Zeven, 1998). *In situ* and on-farm conservation of plant genetic resources in their natural habitat are generally considered the optimal strategies for maintaining of valuable genetic diversity (Maxted et al., 1997; Brush, 2000). When maintained in their natural environment, plant populations are better able to adapt and respond to changing conditions (Dulloo et al., Chapter 36 of this Handbook). However, *ex situ* backup for *in situ* populations of crop wild relatives and landraces maintained on farm will also be needed, in particular for two reasons: (1) many of the *in situ* populations and on farm landraces are threatened and can be lost forever without safety-backup *ex situ* and (2) the systems established by genebanks for distribution of cultivated genetic diversity for utilization in breeding and research would be an efficient approach for increased mobilization of wild genetic resources also.

The genetic diversity available in the breeders' material has already been intensively explored, and there is an emerging need to start looking into traditional landraces (farmers varieties) and crop wild relatives as new sources of genetic materials (Tanksley and McCouch, 1997; Porch et al., 2013). The wider, more general biodiversity community manages much of the relevant information on crop wild relatives. Much of the information on plant biodiversity, including crop wild relatives, is made open and freely available on the Internet by networks such as the Global Biodiversity Information Facility (GBIF; www.gbif.org). The data models and data exchange solutions standardized by the Biodiversity Information Standards (TDWG; www.tdwg.org) society for the Natural History Museums and Botanical Gardens are largely directly compatible with the corresponding solutions for documentation of genetic diversity and genebank collections. Collaborative development of knowledge organization principles and solutions between natural history museums and genebank institutions will not only pool efforts, but also ensure improved and easier access to a larger amount of relevant and useful information within both communities.

## Big data solutions

The amount of data being produced and made available in the modern world has already reached enormous volumes, and the rate of new data creation does not seem to be slowing down (Marz and Warren, 2015). Data on biological diversity and genetic resources is no exception. In particular, access to unprecedented volumes of molecular genetic data is increasing rapidly. The wide variation of data formats and data models in use makes for substantial challenges when attempting to integrate and analyze these voluminous and dispersed data reservoirs. Attempts to centralize datasets into large central data portals have a tendency to create duplicate sets of data when the links to the source data are broken (Belbin et al., 2013; Mesibov, 2013). The 'tidal wave' of large volumes of data requires completely new strategies for approaching data analysis. The proposed approach is to seek solutions to allow new ways for data to be shared, found, and combined with other data to be reused by people or services without the originator ever needing to directly interact with them. These approaches should include technologies to document the context and meaning of data, with resolvable identifiers always provided, and should develop models and serializations to allow different sets of data to be combined more easily.

## Linked open data

Tim Berners-Lee is globally famous as the inventor of the Internet (Berners-Lee and Fischetti, 2000). He is also a founding member and administrative director of the World Wide Web Consortium (W3C), where he has contributed to the description of a deployment scheme and best practice guide for publishing linked open data (LOD) on the Internet with the goal to establish a 'Web of Data' (Berners-Lee, 2006; Bizer et al., 2009). According to the best practice guidelines (http://5stardata.info/en/), one star (★) is awarded for simply publishing data on the Web under an open license. If data is published as structured data, for example as a MS Excel spreadsheet table, two stars (★★) are awarded. Using a non-propriety and open format such as tab-delimited text, comma-separated text (CSV), extensible markup language (XML) or the increasingly popular JavaScript object notation (JSON), will give one more star, to a total of three stars (★★★). Four stars (★★★★) require the use of URIs (uniform resource identifiers; Berners-Lee et al., 2005) to denote things so that other people can point to them not only by linking to your complete dataset, but also by linking all the way to the actual data entity or set of information inside the dataset. The top, five-star ranking (★★★★★) is awarded for adding links to external data. The best practice for five-star linked data is to use a structured data model such as RDF (resource description framework).

Semantic web technologies have generated positive expectations in the biodiversity informatics community (Hardisty et al., 2013). However, widely adapted examples of using these technologies for biodiversity data are yet to be completed. The EU INSPIRE directive provides guidelines and examples of environmental and biodiversity data expressed using RDF and Linked Open Data principles (Tarasova et al., 2015). Baskauf et al (2015, 2016) provided guidelines and examples of how to express and publish biodiversity data using Darwin Core and RDF. For example, the identification of locations where a specimen was collected (dwc:locationID) with persistent identifiers from GeoNames (www.geonames.org) allows the user to discover additional related information about this location by following and resolving a chain of linked identifiers. Persistent identifiers can be used in this manner to build a so-called 'Knowledge Graph' (Singhal, 2012), with decentralized information structured around identified real-world entities based on a relationship graph. The five-star schema is a useful guideline for moving towards a 'Web of Data' (www.w3.org/2013/data/), with a vision of allowing the user to interact directly with information distributed across the Internet without a central coordinator, in a similar manner as if the data were stored in a local database system. **Box 42.1** *Semantic web technologies* provides an introduction to some of these semantic web technologies (Allemang and Hendler, 2011; Wood et al., 2014).

### Box 42.1 Semantic web technologies

The Resource Description Framework (RDF; www.w3.org/RDF/) is a standard data model recommended from the W3C for interchange of data on the Web designed to allow for easier data merging even if data is documented using different schema. The RDF data model describe all data as 'triples':

subject, predicate, and object, or entity-attribute-value, for example 'this germplasm' 'is part of' 'this collection'. RDF Schema (RDFS; www.w3.org/TR/rdf-schema/), Web Ontology Language (OWL; www.w3.org/TR/owl-primer) and Simple Knowledge Organization System (SKOS; www.w3.org/TR/skos-primer) are based on RDF and provide languages to express RDF vocabularies. RDFS is a more basic and general-purpose language. OWL is designed to be more expressive with support for more formalized and computable semantics when building ontologies. SKOS is designed for representation of structured controlled vocabularies. SKOS can be used for building a bridge between different types of knowledge representation systems and can also be a suitable and user-friendly technology for exposing and promote the reuse of terminology formally declared using other vocabulary and ontology languages.

## Biodiversity information architecture

The Biodiversity Information Standards (TDWG) (formerly the Taxonomic Databases Working Group) is a non-profit association for development and promotion of biodiversity informatics standards. The technical architecture group (TDWG-TAG) of the Biodiversity Information Standards has described three fundamental principles of biodiversity informatics using the metaphor of a three-legged stool (**Figure 42.1** *Biodiversity information architecture illustrated by a three-legged stool*). The first leg (1) represents the ontologies and standardized vocabularies that provide a semantic layer to ensure a common understanding of the data types, data attributes, and controlled data values used to describe them. The second leg (2) illustrates the collaborative development of data exchange technology and standardized protocols for how to publish information. The third leg (3) represents persistent identification technology. Information about physical entities such as biological specimens, events such as material collecting and measurement experiments, ontology and vocabulary terminology, and so forth are generally described and documented across distributed data sources. Persistent identifiers will allow data users to connect distributed information about the same things when data publishers reuse the very same identifier names. Identifiers can alternatively be explicitly linked together (e.g. using

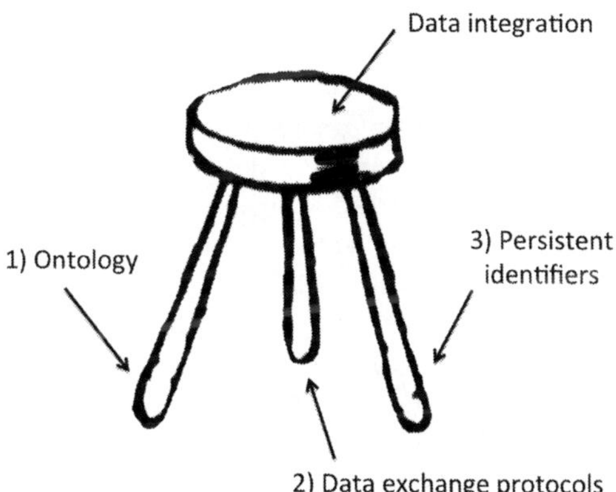


*Figure 42.1* Biodiversity information architecture illustrated by a three-legged stool

*Source*: TDWG, (2006). Image: www.clipartbest.com/clipart-MTLM9q6Ta.

relationship properties; see **Box 42.2** *Definitions of some relationship properties*). Development of new and cross-dataset, multiple purpose annotation services could also be a good tool for linking identifiers.

## Box 42.2 Definitions of some relationship properties

*owl:sameAs*: the property that determines that two given individuals are equal.

*rdfs:seeAlso*: further information about the subject resource.

*skos:closeMatch* is used to link two concepts that are sufficiently similar to be able to be used interchangeably in some information retrieval applications. In order to avoid the possibility of 'compound errors' when combining mappings across more than two concept schemes, skos:closeMatch is not declared to be a transitive property.

*skos:exactMatch* is used to link two concepts, indicating a high degree of confidence that the concepts can be used interchangeably across a wide range of information retrieval applications. skos:exactMatch is a transitive property, and is a sub-property of skos:closeMatch.

*skos:broadMatch* is used to state a hierarchical mapping link between two conceptual resources in different concept schemes.

*skos:narrowMatch* is used to state a hierarchical mapping link between two conceptual resources in different concept schemes.

## Ontologies and controlled vocabularies

Ontologies and controlled vocabularies are tools for the development of a shared and agreed standard terminology to organize information and support knowledge representation and management. Ontologies can be developed to organize and categorize physical things such as specimens, genebank accessions, genetic properties, alleles, institutions, and people; or events such as the collecting of seed material, trait measurements, and seed distribution (see also **Table 42.1**). Such things and events are here classified as 'classes' (rdfs:Class or owl:Class) in a formal ontology. Ontologies can also include formal descriptions of information attributes such as the scientific name, catalog- or accession-number, or who collected a specimen or genebank accession. When using RDF and ontologies, such information attributes are classified as 'properties' (rdf:Property). When, for example, presenting information in a spreadsheet, the actual physical things or events represented by the information in a record or in a horizontal line is the 'class' and the column headers are 'properties'. Properties are organized into two main types. So-called 'object properties' (owl:ObjectProperty) link individuals to other individuals using URIs, and 'datatype properties' (owl:DataTypeProperty) that link individuals to data values given as literals (www.w3.org/TR/owl-ref/#Property).

The genetic resources and crop genebank communities have achieved wide agreement on using the Multi-Crop Passport Descriptor list (MCPD) (Alercia et al., 2015) as a preferred standard data exchange format. The first version of the MCPD was initially introduced in 1997 (Hazekamp et al., 1997) and released in 2001 (Alercia et al., 2001) by the Food and Agriculture Organization of the United Nations (hereafter FAO) and Bioversity International (formerly IBPGR 1974–1991; IPGRI 1991–2006). The MCPD established a standard set of minimum descriptors for genebank accessions (specimens) of any agricultural crop based on the prior and

*Table 42.1* Mapping between MCPD, Darwin Core, and ABCD 2.06

| *Term* | *MCPD (2015)* | *Darwin Core (DwC) and Darwin Core germplasm extension (g)* | *ABCD 2.06 ** |
|---|---|---|---|
| NA | (not applicable) | dwc:datasetID | DataSet/DatasetGUID |
| 0 | PUID | dwc:occurrenceID | Unit/UnitGUID |
| 1 | INSTCODE | dwc:institutionCode | Unit/SourceInstitutionID |
| 2 | ACCENUMB | dwc:catalogNumber | Unit/UnitID |
| 3 | COLLNUMB | dwc:recordNumber | Unit/CollectorsFieldNumber |
| 4 | COLLCODE | g:collectingInstituteID | Unit/Gathering/Agent/Organisation/Name/Abbreviation |
| 4.1 | COLLNAME | dwc:recordedBy | Unit/Gathering//GatheringAgent/AgentText |
| 4.1.1 | COLLINSTADDRESS | dwc:recordedBy | Unit/Gathering/Agent/Organisation/Name/Text |
| 4.2 | COLLMISSID | dwc:collectionCode | Unit/Gathering/Project/ProjectTitle |
| 5 | GENUS | dwc:genus | ScientificName/NameAtomised/Botanical/GenusOrMonomial |
| 6 | SPECIES | dwc:specificEpithet | ScientificName/NameAtomised/Botanical/FirstEpithet |
| 7 | SPAUTHOR | dwc:scientificNameAuthorship (if SUBTAXA is empty) | ScientificName/NameAtomised/Botanical/AuthorTeamParenthesis + ScientificName/NameAtomised/Botanical/AuthorTeam (if SUBTAXA is empty) |
| 8 | SUBTAXA | dwc:infraspecificEpithet | ScientificName/NameAtomised/Botanical/Rank + ScientificName/NameAtomised/Botanical/SecondEpithet |
| 9 | SUBTAUTHOR | dwc:scientificNameAuthorship | ScientificName/NameAtomised/Botanical/AuthorTeamParenthesis + ScientificName/NameAtomised/Botanical/AuthorTeam |
| 10 | CROPNAME | dwc:vernacularName | TaxonIdentified/InformalNameString |
| 11 | ACCENAME | g:breedingIdentifier | ScientificName/NameAtomised/Botanical/CultivarGroupName + ';' + ScientificName/NameAtomised/Botanical/CultivarName + ';' + ScientificName/NameAtomised/Botanical/TradeDesignationName(s) |
| 12 | ACQDATE | g:acquisitionDate | Unit/SpecimenUnit/Acquisition/AcquisitionDate |
| 13 | ORIGCTY | dwc:countryCode | Unit/Gathering/Country/ISO3166Code |

(*Continued*)

*Table 42.1* (Continued)

| *Term* | *MCPD (2015)* | *Darwin Core (DwC) and Darwin Core germplasm extension (g)* | *ABCD 2.06* * |
|---|---|---|---|
| 14 | COLLSITE | dwc:locality | Unit/Gathering/LocalityText |
| 15.1 | DECLATITUDE | dwc:decimalLatitude | Unit/Gathering/SiteCoordinateSets/SiteCoordinates/ CoordinatesLatLon/LatitudeDecimal |
| 15.2 | LATITUDE | dwc:verbatimLatitude | Unit/Gathering/SiteCoordinateSets/SiteCoordinates/ CoordinatesLatLon/VerbatimLatitude |
| 15.3 | DECLONGITUDE | dwc:decimalLongitude | Unit/Gathering/SiteCoordinateSets/SiteCoordinates/ CoordinatesLatLon/LongitudeDecimal |
| 15.4 | LONGITUDE | dwc:verbatimLongitude | Unit/Gathering/SiteCoordinateSets/SiteCoordinates/ CoordinatesLatLon/VerbatimLongitude |
| 15.5 | COORDUNCERT | dwc:coordinateUncertaintyInMeters | Unit/Gathering/SiteCoordinateSets/SiteCoordinates/ CoordinatesLatLon/CoordinateErrorDistanceInMeters |
| 15.6 | COORDDATUM | dwc:geodetic.Datum | Unit/Gathering/SiteCoordinateSets/SiteCoordinates/ CoordinatesLatLon/SpatialDatum |
| 15.7 | GEOREFMETH | dwc:georeferenceSources | Unit/Gathering/SiteCoordinateSets/SiteCoordinates/ GeoreferenceSources |
| 16 | ELEVATION | dwc:minimumElevationInMeters | Unit/Gathering/Altitude/MeasurementAtomised/ MeasurementLowerValue + Unit/Gathering/Altitude/ MeasurementAtomised/ MeasurementScale set to 'm' |
| 17 | COLLDATE | dwc:eventDate | Unit/Gathering/DateTime/ISODateTimeBegin |
| 18 | BREDCODE | g:breedingInstituteID | Unit/PlantGeneticResourcesUnit/BreedingInstitutionCode |
| 18.1 | BREDNAME | g:breedingInstitute | Unit/PlantGeneticResourcesUnit/DecodedBreedingInstitute |
| 19 | SAMPSTAT | g:biologicalStatus | Unit/PlantGeneticResourcesUnit/BiologicalStatus |
| 20 | ANCEST | g:ancestralData, g:purdyPedigree | Unit/PlantGeneticResourcesUnit/AncestralData |
| 21 | COLLSRC | g:acquisitionSource | Unit/PlantGeneticResourcesUnit/CollectingAcquisitionSource |

| | | | |
|---|---|---|---|
| 22 | DONORCODE | g:donorInstituteID | Unit/SpecimenUnit/History/PreviousUnit(s)/PreviousSourceInstitutionID |
| 22.1 | DONORNAME | g:donorInstitute | Unit/PlantGeneticResourcesUnit/DecodedDonorInstitute |
| 23 | DONORNUMB | g:donorsIdentifier | Unit/SpecimenUnit/History/PreviousUnit(s)/PreviousUnitID |
| 24 | OTHERNUMB | dwc:otherCatalogNumbers | Unit/PlantGeneticResourcesUnit/OtherIdentification |
| 25 | DUPLSITE | g:safetyDuplicationInstituteID | Unit/PlantGeneticResourcesUnit/LocationSafetyDuplicates |
| 25.1 | DUPLINSTNAME | g:safetyDuplicationInstitute | Unit/PlantGeneticResourcesUnit/DecodedSafetyDuplicationLocation |
| 26 | STORAGE | g:storageCondition | Unit/PlantGeneticResourcesUnit/TypeGermplasmStorage |
| 27 | MLSSTAT | g:mlsStatus | (missing) |
| 28 | REMARKS | dwc:occurrenceRemarks | Unit/Notes |

⋆ 'Unit/' = 'Datasets/Dataset/Units/Unit/'; 'ScientificName/' = 'Unit/Identifications/Identification/Result/TaxonIdentified/ScientificName/'. Table generated by the author based on mapping between MCPD and ABCD made in collaboration with Javier de la Torres (Bioversity International) at the BioCASE Wiki; and mapping between MCPD/EURISCO and ABCD presented by Walter Berendsohn and Helmut Knüpffer (2006). This mapping process is described in Endresen and Knüpffer (2012).

crop-specific descriptors developed and released by Bioversity International (Bioversity International, 2007; Gotor et al., 2008; Faberova, 2010).

The Biodiversity Information Standards (TDWG) has ratified and released two different controlled vocabularies for the description of specimens and species occurrences with a similar coverage as the MCPD has for genebank accessions. The Access to Biological Collections Data (ABCD) standard was ratified by TDWG in September 2005 (the current version 2.06 was released in 2007) (TDWG, 2007; Holetschek et al., 2012). The Darwin Core standard (DwC) was ratified in October 2009 and is regularly updated with proposed minor and major revisions to individual terms after consensus is reached during an open peer review period of 30 days announced within the TDWG community (TDWG, 2009; Wieczorek et al., 2012).

Both the ABCD and the Darwin Core standards have been mapped to the MCPD (**Table 42.1** *Mapping between MCPD, Darwin Core, and ABCD 2.06*) and extended with all the missing unmapped MCPD descriptors (Berendsohn and Knüpffer, 2006; Knüpffer et al., 2007; Endresen and Knüpffer, 2012). The mapping of terms and descriptors between the ABCD, Darwin Core, and MCPD is important not least to achieve integration between agrobiodiversity data (including genebank collections) and other large sources of biodiversity information, such as the museum and biodiversity monitoring datasets published within the Global Biodiversity Information Facility (GBIF). The GBIF portal is based on the Darwin Core standard and provides a particularly important source for information on crop wild relatives, where expertise and species occurrence data are often found outside of the agrobiodiversity community and agrobiodiversity data portals such as Genesys and EURISCO.

The Dublin Core metadata terms were developed by the Dublin Core Metadata Initiative (DCMI; http://dublincore.org/documents/dcmi-terms/) and provide a vocabulary of properties, classes, and controlled values for use in resource descriptions (Weibel et al., 1998; Kunze and Baker 2007). The current version of the Dublin Core terms was revised and released in 2008 as the so-called 'terms namespace' (dct = http://purl.org/dc/terms/). This revision was a refinement of the element terms for the purpose of harmonization with RDF technology. Darwin Core is based on the Dublin Core standard and should be viewed as an extension of the Dublin Core for biodiversity information (Wieczorek et al., 2012). Both Dublin Core and Darwin Core are declared using RDF. Darwin Core is itself designed to accommodate extensions to expand the core set of terms to meet requirements from sub-communities such as the agrobiodiversity community. The missing and un-mapped descriptors from the MCPD were declared as SKOS and released as the Darwin Core germplasm extension for genebanks (Endresen and Knüpffer, 2012; http://terms.tdwg.org/wiki/Germplasm). The germplasm vocabulary thus provides a bridge between the MCPD and Darwin Core.

The Darwin Core vocabulary was initially developed as a pragmatic solution to facilitate standardized biodiversity data exchange using flat text files or XML. To facilitate and promote the use of Darwin Core terms to describe and publish biodiversity collections data as RDF, Baskauf and Webb (2015) developed a Darwin Core ontology extension, Darwin Core Semantic Web (Darwin-SW or DSW). The DSW influenced some major revisions of the Darwin Core standard and established a more explicit domain model for example to separate collection specimens from observations on living organisms in the wild, and the distinction between real-world species occurrences and different types of evidence for species occurrences. This allows the use to, for example, introduce a data model that explicitly allows for more than one set of evidence for the same real-world species occurrence.

Further ontology refinements to the term listing of vocabularies such as the Darwin Core and MCPD have been developed. The Crop Ontology (CO) (Shrestha et al., 2010) includes an RDF representation in the OWL language for the long-standing Bioversity crop descriptor lists and includes OWL representations for the MCPD terms. The CO could be seen as an emerging bridge to the Open Biological and Biomedical Ontologies (OBO) Foundry (Smith et al., 2007; www.obofoundry.org/) including ontologies such as the Plant Ontology (PO) (Cooper et al., 2013) and the Plant Trait Ontology (TO) (Jaiswal et al., 2002; Arnaud et al., 2012). The OBO Foundry establishes a set of principles for building semantic interoperability between ontologies. The Biological Collections Ontology (BCO) (Walls et al., 2014) established a bridge between the traditional specimen-based museum collections described using Darwin Core and the genomic information resources described using Gene Ontology (GO) (Ashburner et al., 2000) and the Minimum Information for any (x) Sequence (MIxS) ontology (Yilmaz et al., 2011). The GO and BCO ontologies were also developed within the OBO Foundry system.

FAO had already initiated a multilingual agricultural thesaurus (AGROVOC) in the early 1980s (FAO, 2016). AGROVOC was published online around 2000 and today includes more than 32,000 concepts presented online as Linked Open Data using the SKOS language (Caracciolo et al., 2013).

## Data exchange protocols

Even when data attributes and types are standardized using Darwin Core or other vocabularies and ontologies, a user wanting to access and integrate dispersed data published by other people will typically find a number of different access types and file formats. The five-star Linked Open Data guideline promotes RDF as a data exchange model (Berners-Lee, 2006). Baskauf et al. (2015, 2016) developed best practice guidelines for publishing specimen collection data with the RDF model. However, at the present time, very little biodiversity data, including genebank accession data, are published as RDF. A typical solution to facilitate a more homogenous data interface has been to develop and implement standardized data publishing software. When the EURISCO genebank data portal for Europe was developed, the data publishing procedure was dependent on a manual procedure where each national focal point would collect the genebank accession inventory from each genebank in the respective country, harmonize and combine datasets before the national inventory was uploaded to EURISCO (Faberova, 2010). Other agrobiodiversity data portals, including Genesys, have typically followed very similar data publication routines dependent on manual data updates.

When the GBIF data portal was created and released around 2003, it was based on two of the existing data publishing software packages, DiGIR and BioCASe. The Distributed Generic Information Retrieval (DiGIR) open source software package was initiated at the TDWG conference in Frankfurt in 2000 to publish natural history collections datasets standardized using Darwin Core online as XML (extensible markup language) (Stein and Wieczorek, 2004). The BioCASe (Biological Collection Access Service) (Holetschek et al., 2012) is typically used for biodiversity data, using the ABCD standard online as XML. Typically, this data-publishing approach will require the user of the data service to page through XML responses of for example 1,000 records at a time until all records have been downloaded. For large datasets and filter conditions matching many data records, retrieving the search results through paging can be time-consuming and might also be vulnerable to page loss. The GBIF Integrated Publishing Toolkit (IPT) (Robertson et al., 2014) therefore introduced the Darwin Core Archive exchange format. The Darwin Core Archive is a compressed zip archive including one or more data files (CSV), a single document to describe the relationship between data files (meta.xml) and one document containing metadata that actually describes the dataset (generally expressed using the ecological metadata language, EML). IPT version 1.0 was released in February 2009, with an improved version 2.0 officially released in February 2011. The current version of the IPT will generate globally unique and resolvable Digital Object Identifier (DOI) for each published dataset to support easier data citation and data usage tracking.

Formats such as the JSON-LD (JavaScript Object Notation for Linked Data) (Sporny et al., 2014) for publishing RDF data on the Web is currently gaining popularity and supporting software implementations. RDF data models using serializations such as the JSON-LD could become the preferred data exchange format also for agrobiodiversity datasets. The *Web of Data* using RDF or similar models will depend on the successful implementation of globally unique and resolvable identifiers to be described further in the next section.

## Globally unique identifiers

Accession numbers are human-readable identifiers that have long-standing and proven utility. However, when combining many genebank collections in large, integrated information systems, it is very soon discovered that the same alphanumerical string might often be used as the accession number identifier for more than one genebank, often to represent entirely different species. The Genesys portal provides a total of 56 different genebank accessions (from 39 different species and 40 different genebank institutes), all of which have been assigned an identical accession number '123' (www.genesys-pgr.org/explore?filter={%22acceNumb%22:[%22123%22]}). When combining genebank accession information with information sources from the larger biodiversity community, such as occurs in GBIF, the problem of non-unique accession number alphanumeric name strings is even further amplified. The GBIF portal provides a total of 1,362 occurrence records with catalog number '123' (GBIF, 2016; www.gbif.org/occurrence/search?CATALOG_NUMBER=123; **Figure 42.2** *Two of the 1,362 specimens published in GBIF with catalog number = 123*)

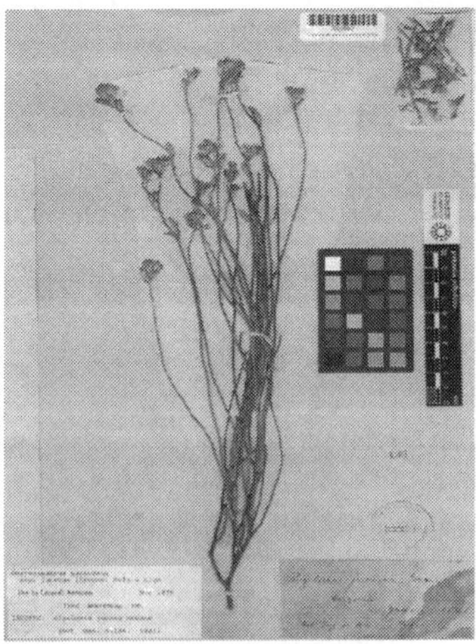

b) *Mercurialis ovata*

*Figure 42.2* Two of the 1,362 specimens published in GBIF with catalog number = 123

*Note*: (a) *Bigelowia juncea* Greene, catalogNumber = 123, occurrenceID = urn:catalog:CAS:BOT:123, data publisher = Department of Botany, California Academy of Sciences, accessed at [www.gbif.org/occurrence/543392241] (CAS Botany, 2016; doi:10.15468/7gudyo). (b) *Mercurialis ovata* Sternb. & Hoppe, catalog number = 123, data publisher = Herbarium der Regensburgischen Botanischen Gesellschaft

*Source*: © H. Gigglberger, Universität Regensburg, Germany, accessed at [www.gbif.org/occurrence/283363] (Herbarium der Regensburgischen Botanischen Gesellschaft, 2016; doi:10.15468/dnmpiw).

Globally unique and resolvable *persistent identifiers* for genebank accessions would enable information about the same physical accession to be published without central coordination on an open platform such as the World Wide Web and to be linked together through the principles of Linked Open Data (http://linkeddata.org/). Persistent identifier names must be (a) globally unique, (b) resolvable (machine actionable on the World Wide Web), and (c) demonstrate a long-term commitment on providing or enabling persistent access to data and associated metadata. Many different approaches and identifier syntax-schema have already been developed, for an overview of selected identifier schemes (FAO, 2014). Guidelines for deployment in biodiversity informatics and specimen databases are in progress (Page, 2008, 2009; Richards et al., 2011; Hagedorn et al., 2013; Guralnick et al., 2015). The good news is that starting to use almost any of these identifier technologies will immediately provide major benefits and new opportunities for data management and data exchange. Different types of identifier names and resolution services could be mapped, new resolution protocols and formats can be added later to be discovered and used for example through (HTTP-) content negotiation, and initial resolution services could be redirected to other emerging resolution services.

The W3C promotes the use of HTTP (hypertext transfer protocol)-URIs (Universal Resource Identifiers) as a general principle for identifier technologies. HTTP-URIs are a good and pragmatic solution and can easily be resolved directly using the Internet. However, embedding the method for identifier resolution directly inside the identifier name string might lead to undesired limitations during the expected lifetime of the identifiers. Persistent identifier solutions must be designed to last for a very long time. Even long after the physical genebank accessions themselves might be lost, information about them and derived genetic resources and cultivars might reference previous accessions. A good strategy would be to think of the HTTP-URI identifier name string as being composed of two parts, a http-resolver-authority and another part that is persistent and globally unique by itself, irrespective of the prefixed resolver part (http://resolver-authority + globally-unique-persistent-identifier).

The Life Science Identifier (LSID) scheme (Clark et al., 2004) was specifically designed to identify biological specimens and enabled the reuse of locally unique names such as accession numbers and specimen catalog number as the 'objectID' of the identifier name string (urn:lsid:[authority]:[namespace]:[objectID]). LSIDs are a special form of URNs and thus compatible with RDF data models. However, the LSID resolution system is not compatible with the HTTP-URI recommended by the W3C (because LSID is proposed as a new Internet transfer protocol at the same hierarchical level as the HTTP protocol).

The Digital Object Identifier (DOI) system (DOI Foundation, 2016; www.doi.org) is based on the Handle system (http://handle.net/) and was originally developed and introduced in 2000 by the publishing industry for digital content on the Internet. The centralized DOI system guarantees that DOI name strings are globally unique within the context of the DOI system. Official DOI registration agencies such as DataCite or CrossRef operate services to request and register new DOI names together with descriptive metadata on the object. As of the time of writing (January 2016), more than 120 million DOI names have been registered and the annual growth rate is 18%. The DOI system operates a global DOI resolver service at 'http://doi.org'. DOI names '<doi>' are generally presented either with a simple prefix: 'doi:<doi>', or as the HTTP-URI form by prefixing with the resolver address: 'http://doi.org/<doi>'. DOI names have been suggested (FAO, 2014) as the preferred object identifier system for the development of the Global Information System (GLIS) on Plant Genetic Resources for Food and Agriculture (PGRFA) referred to in Article 17 of the International Treaty (FAO, 2009).

A Universally Unique Identifier (UUID) (Leach et al., 2005) is a 128-bit (16 byte) number typically displayed using the canonical format of 32 hexadecimal digits displayed in five character groups separated by four hyphens. UUIDs can be generated by anybody in a distributed network without central coordination with a very high probability that the number generated is globally unique and will not be unintentionally created again. UUIDs are widely used, and tools to generate them are very common across different computer platforms. Uniform Resource Names (URNs) are a type or subset of Uniform Resource Identifiers (URIs) that use the 'urn' scheme and '*are intended to serve as persistent, location-independent, resource identifiers*' (Moats, 1997, p. 1). UUID is formally registered as an URN namespace (Leach et al., 2005) and already widely used as object identifiers across many different domains including biodiversity informatics (Hagedorn et al., 2013). The Genesys portal introduced in April 2015 (Genesys, 2015) PURL prefixed UUIDs to persistently identify all genebank accessions included in the portal. Note that the PURL prefixed UUID creates only a complementary machine-readable identifier for the genebank accession and that the UUID is not intended to *replace* the genebank accession number as the preferred human-readable identifier.

## Conclusions

A key step towards implementing semantic web technologies for genebank data is to establish and use persistent identifiers for your own collections, and to reuse persistent identifiers from external systems as often as possible (Guralnick et al., 2015). Widespread implementation and use of semantic web technologies for biodiversity information have so far been slow to happen. However, the rapidly growing volumes of data produced and made available will demand new data management practices where storing locally cached copies of external data will rapidly become less attractive (Marz and Warren, 2015). Further harmonization and common standardized solutions for data exchange in the larger biodiversity informatics community, including information on genetic resources, is needed because researchers and other users of these data are anticipated to require seamless access to increasingly larger volumes of data maintained and accessed directly from an heterogeneous network of data sources (Hardisty et al., 2013).

## References


Alercia, A., Diulgheroff, S. and Mackay, M. (2015) 'FAO/Bioversity multi-crop passport descriptors V.2.1 [MCPD V.2.1]', FAO/Bioversity International, Rome, Italy, www.bioversityinternational.org/e-library/publications/detail/faobioversity-multi-crop-passport-descriptors-v21-mcpd-v21/, accessed 8 January 2016, doi: 10.13140/RG.2.1.4280.2001

Alercia, A., Diulgheroff, S. and Metz, T. (2001) *FAO/IPGRI Multi-Crop Passport Descriptors, December 2001*, International Plant Genetic Resources Institute (IPGRI) and Food and Agriculture Organization of the United Nations (FAO), Rome, Italy, www.bioversityinternational.org/e-library/publications/detail/faoipgri-multi-crop-passport-descriptors-mcpd/, accessed 8 January 2016.

Alercia, A. and Mackay, M. (2013) 'A gateway to plant genetic resources utilization', *Acta Horticulturae*, vol. 983, pp. 25–30.

Allemang, D. and Hendler, J. (2011) *Semantic Web for the Working Ontologist, Second Edition: Effective Modeling in RDFS and OWL*, Morgan Kaufmann, MA, USA.

Arnaud, E., Cooper, L., Shrestha, R., Menda, N., Nelson, R. T., Matteis, L., Skofic, M., Bastow, R., Jaiswal, P., Mueller, L. and McLaren, G. (2012) 'Towards a reference plant trait ontology for modeling knowledge of plant traits and phenotypes', pp. 220–225 in *KEOD 2012: Proceedings of the International Conference on Knowledge Engineering and Ontology Development*, http://wrap.warwick.ac.uk/id/eprint/59831, accessed 8 January 2016.

Ashburner, M., Ball, C., Blake, J., Botstein, D., Butler, H., Cherry, J. M., Davis, A. P., Dolinski, K., Dwight, S. S., Eppig, J. T., Harris, M. A., Hill, D. P., Issel-Tarver, L., Kasarskis, A., Lewis, S., Matese, J. C., Richardson, J. E., Ringwald, M., Rubin, G. M. and Sherlock, G. (2000) 'Gene Ontology: Tool for the unification of biology', *Nature Genetics*, vol. 25, pp. 25–29.

Baskauf, S. J. and Webb, C. O. (2015) 'Darwin-SW: Darwin Core-based terms for expressing biodiversity data as RDF', *Semantic Web*, pre-print, pp. 1–15, doi: 10.3233/SW-150203

Baskauf, S. J., Wieczorek, J., Deck, J. and Webb, C. O. (2015) 'Lessons learned from adapting the Darwin Core vocabulary standard for use in RDF', *Semantic Web*, pre-print, pp. 1–11, doi: 10.3233/SW-150199

Baskauf, S. J., Wieczorek, J., Deck, J., Webb, C. O., Morris, P. J. and Schildhauer, M. (2016) *Darwin Core RDF Guide*, Biodiversity Information Standards (TDWG), http://rs.tdwg.org/dwc/terms/guides/rdf/, accessed 8 January 2016.

Belbin, L., Daly, J., Hirsch, T., Hobern, D. and La Salle, J. (2013) 'A specialist's audit of aggregated occurrence records: An "aggregator's" perspective', *Zookeys*, vol. 305, pp. 67–76.

Berendsohn, W. and Knüpffer, H. (2006) *Draft Mapping of Eurisco Descriptors to ABCD 2.06*, www.bgbm.org/tdwg/codata/Schema/Mappings/EURISCO-2-ABCD.pdf, accessed 8 January 2016.

Berners-Lee, T. (2006) *Linked Data*, www.w3.org/DesignIssues/LinkedData.html, accessed 8 January 2016.

Berners-Lee, T., Fielding, R. and Masinter, L. (2005) '*Uniform Resource Identifiers (URI): Generic Syntax*, Internet Engineering Task Force (IETF), Freemont, CA, USA, http://tools.ietf.org/html/rfc3986, accessed 8 January 2016, doi: 10.17487/RFC3986

Berners-Lee, T. and Fischetti, M. (2000) *Weaving the Web: The Original Design and Ultimate Destiny of the World Wide Web by Its Inventor*, HarperBusiness, New York, USA.

Bioversity International (2007) *Development of Crop Descriptor Lists: Guidelines for Developers*, Bioversity International, Maccarese, Italy, ISBN: 978-92-9043-792-1, www.bioversityinternational.org/e-library/publications/detail/developing-crop-descriptor-lists/, accessed 8 January 2016.

Bizer, C., Heath, T. and Berners-Lee, T. (2009) 'Linked data: The story so far', *International Journal on Semantic Web and Information Systems (IJSWIS)*, vol. 5, pp. 1–22.

Brush, S. B. (ed.) (2000) *Genes in the Field: On-Farm Conservation of Crop Diversity*, Lewis Publishers, CRC Press, Boca Raton, FL, USA.

Caracciolo, C., Stellato, A., Morshed, A., Johannsen, G., Rajbahndari, S., Jaques, Y. and Keizer, J. (2013) 'The AGROVOC linked dataset', *Semantic Web*, vol. 4, pp. 341–348.

CAS Botany (2016) California Academy of Sciences: CAS Botany (BOT), CA, USA, www.gbif.org/occurrence/543392241, accessed 21 January 2016, doi: 10.15468/7gudyo

Clark, T., Martin, S. and Liefeld, T. (2004) 'Globally distributed object identification for biological knowledge bases', *Briefings in Bioinformatics*, vol. 5, pp. 59–70.

Cooper, L., Walls, R. L., Elser, J., Gandolfo, M. A., Stevenson, D. W., Smith, B., Preece, J., Athreya, B., Mungall, C. J., Rensing, S., Hiss, M., Lang, D., Reski, R., Berardini, T. Z., Li, D., Huala, E., Schaeffer, M., Menda, N., Arnaud, E., Shrestha, R., Yamazaki, Y. and Jaiswal, P. (2013) 'The Plant Ontology as a tool for comparative plant anatomy and genomic analyses', *Plant and Cell Physiology*, vol. 54, pp. 1–23.

Dias, S., Dulloo, M. E. and Arnaud, E. (2011) 'The role of EURISCO in promoting use of agricultural biodiversity', pp. 270–277 in N. Maxted, M. E. Dulloo, B. V. Ford-Lloyd, L. Frese, J. Iriondo and M. A. A. P. de Carvalho (eds.), *Agrobiodiversity Conservation: Securing the Diversity of Crop Wild Relatives and Landraces*, CABI, Wallingford, UK.

DOI Foundation (2016) *DOI Handbook*, International DOI Foundation, UK, www.doi.org/hb.html, accessed 21 February 2016, doi: 10.1000/182

Endresen, D. T. F. and Knüpffer, H. (2012) 'The Darwin Core extension for genebanks opens up new opportunities for sharing genebank data sets', *Biodiversity Informatics*, vol. 8, pp. 11–29.

Faberova, I. (2010) 'Standard descriptors and EURISCO development', *Czech Journal of Genetics and Plant Breeding*, vol. 46, S106–S109.

FAO (2009) *International Treaty on Plant Genetic Resources for Food and Agriculture*, FAO, Rome, Italy, www.fao.org/docrep/011/i0510e/i0510e00.htm, accessed 8 January 2016.

FAO (2010) *The Second Report on the State of the World's Plant Genetic Resources for Food and Agriculture*, Commission on Genetic Resources for Food and Agriculture (CGRFA), FAO, Rome, Italy, ISBN: 978-92-5-106534-1, www.fao.org/docrep/013/i1500e/i1500e00.htm, accessed 8 January 2016.

FAO (2014) *Technical Options to Facilitate the Establishment of Data Links in the Field of Plant Genetic Resources for Food and Agriculture: Permanent Unique Identifiers, IT/COGIS-1/15/3, November 2014*, International Treaty on Plant Genetic Resources for Food and Agriculture (ITPGRFA), FAO, Rome, Italy, www.planttreaty.org/sites/default/files/cogis1w3.pdf, accessed 8 January 2016.

FAO (2016) *AGROVOC Multilingual Agricultural Thesaurus*, Agricultural Information Management Standards (AIMS), FAO, Rome, Italy, http://aims.fao.org/vest-registry/vocabularies/agrovoc-multilingual-agricultural-thesaurus, accessed 21 February 2016.

GBIF (2016) *GBIF Occurrence Download: CATALOG_NUMBER=123, Search Results*, http://doi.org/10.15468/dl.cccmwb, accessed 21 February 2016.

Genesys (2015) *Database Upgrade Completed*, www.genesys-pgr.org/content/news/38/database-upgrade-completed, last updated 16 April 2015, accessed 18 February 2016.

Gotor, E., Alercia, A., Rao, V. R., Watts, J. and Caracciolo, F. (2008) 'The scientific information activity of Bioversity International: The descriptor lists', *Genetic Resources and Crop Evolution*, vol. 55, pp. 757–772.

Guralnick, R. P., Cellinese, N., Deck, J., Pyle, R. L., Kunze, J., Penev, L., Walls, R., Hagedorn, G., Agosti, D., Wieczorek, J., Catapano, T. and Page, R. D. M. (2015) 'Community next steps for making globally unique identifiers work for biocollections data', *ZooKeys*, vol. 494, pp. 133–154.

Hagedorn, G., Catapano, T., Güntsch, A., Mietchen, D., Endresen, D., Sierra, S., Groom, Q., Biserkov, J., Glöckler, F. and Morris, R. (2013) *Best Practices for Stable URIs*, http://wiki.pro-ibiosphere.eu/wiki/Best_practices_for_stable_URIs, accessed 8 January 2016.

Hardisty, A., Roberts, D. and The Biodiversity Informatics Community (2013) 'A decadal view of biodiversity informatics: Challenges and priorities', *BMC Ecology*, vol. 13, pp. 1–23.

Hazekamp, T., Serwinski, J. and Alercia, A. (1997) 'Appendix II: Multicrop passport descriptors (final version)', Appendix II of E. Lipma, M. W. M. Jongen, T. J. L. van Hintum, T. Grass and L. Maggioni (eds.), *Central Crop Databases: Tools for Plant Genetic Resources Management*, International Plant Genetic Resources Institute (IPGRI), Rome, Italy and WUR Centre for Genetic Resources (CGN), Wageningen, the Netherlands.

Holetschek, J., Dröge, G., Güntsch, A. and Berendsohn, W. G. (2012) 'The ABCD of primary biodiversity data access', *Plant Biosystems*, vol. 146, pp. 771–779.

Iriondo, J. M., Maxted, N. and Dulloo, M. E. (2008) *Conserving Plant Genetic Diversity in Protected Areas*, CABI, Wallingford, UK.

Jaiswal, P., Ware, D., Ni, J., Chang, K., Zhao, W., Schmidt, S., Pan, X., Clark, K., Teytelman, L., Cartinhour, S., Stein, L. and McCouch, S. (2002) 'Gramene: Development and integration of trait and gene ontologies for rice', *Comparative and Functional Genomics*, vol. 3, pp. 132–136.

Knüpffer, H., Endresen, D. T. F., Faberova, I. and Gaiji, S. (2007) 'Integrating genebanks into biodiversity information networks', pp. 34–35 in *Proceedings of the 18th EUCARPIA Conference, Genetic Resources Section, Plant Genetic Resources and Their Exploitation in the Plant Breeding for Food and Agriculture*, Piešt'any, Slovak Republic, ISBN: 9788088872634, doi: 10.13140/2.1.4172.8960.

Kunze, J. and Baker, T. (2007) *The Dublin Core Metadata Element Set, RFC 5013*, Internet Engineering Task Force (IETF), Freemont, CA, USA, http://tools.ietf.org/html/rfc5013, accessed 8 January 2016, doi: 10.17487/RFC5013

Leach, P., Mealling, M. and Salz, R. (2005) *A Universally Unique Identifier (UUID) URN Namespace, RFC 4122*, Internet Engineering Task Force (IETF), Freemont, CA, USA, http://tools.ietf.org/html/rfc4122, accessed 8 January 2016, doi: 10.17487/RFC4122

Marz, N. and Warren, J. (2015) *Big Data: Principles and Best Practices of Scalable Real-Time Data Systems*, Manning Publications Co., Shelter Island, NY, USA.

Maxted, N., Ford-Lloyd, B. V. and Hawkes, J. G. (eds.) (1997) *Plant Genetic Conservation: The In Situ Approach*, Chapman & Hall, London, UK.

Maxted, N. and Kell, S. (2009) *Establishment of a Global Network for the In Situ Conservation of Crop Wild Relatives: Status and Needs*, FAO, Rome, Italy, www.fao.org/docrep/013/i1500e/i1500e18a.pdf, accessed 8 January 2016.

Mesibov, R. (2013) 'A specialist's audit of aggregated occurrence records', *ZooKeys*, vol. 293, pp. 1–18.

Moats, R. (1997) *URN Syntax: RFC 2141*, Internet Engineering Task Force (IETF), Freemont, CA, USA, http://tools.ietf.org/html/rfc2141, accessed 8 January 2016, doi: 10.17487/RFC2141

Page, R. D. M. (2008) 'Biodiversity informatics: The challenge of linking data and the role of shared identifiers', *Briefings in Bioinformatics*, vol. 9, pp. 345–354.

Page, R. D. M. (2009) 'bioGUID: Resolving, discovering, and minting identifiers for biodiversity informatics', *BMC Bioinformatics*, vol. 10, S5, doi: 10.1186/1471–2105–10–s14–s5

Porch, T. G., Beaver, J. S., Debouck, D. G., Jackson, S. A., Kelly, J. D. and Dempewolf, H. (2013) 'Use of wild relatives and closely related species to adapt common bean to climate change', *Agronomy*, vol. 3, pp. 433–461.

Richards, K., White, R., Nicolson, N. and Pyle, R. (2011) *Beginners' Guide to Persistent Identifiers: Version 1.0*, Global Biodiversity Information Facility (GBIF), Copenhagen, Denmark, www.gbif.org/resource/80575, accessed 8 January 2016, ISBN: 87-92020-14-3

Robertson, T., Döring, M., Guralnick, R., Bloom, D., Braak, K., Otegui, J., Russell, L. and Desmet, P. (2014) 'The GBIF integrated publishing toolkit: Facilitating the efficient publishing of biodiversity data on the Internet', *PLoS ONE*, vol. 9, p. e102623.

Shrestha, R., Arnaud, E., Mauleon, R., Senger, M., Davenport, G. F., Hancock, D., Morrison, N., Bruskiewich, R. and McLaren, G. (2010) 'Multifunctional crop trait ontology for breeders' data: Field book, annotation, data discovery and semantic enrichment of the literature', *AoB PLANTS*, vol. 2010, pp. plq008.

Singhal, A. (2012) *Introducing the Knowledge Graph: Things, Not Strings*, GoogleBlog, Google Inc., Mountain View, CA, USA, http://googleblog.blogspot.co.uk/2012/05/introducing-knowledge-graph-things-not.html, accessed 20 February 2016.

Smith, B., Ashburner, M., Rosse, C., Bard, J., Bug, W., Ceusters, W., Goldberg, L. J., Eilbeck, K., Ireland, A., Mungall, C., The OBI Consortium, Leontis, N., Rocca-Serra, P., Ruttenber, A., Sansone, S. A., Scheuermann, R. H., Shah, N., Whetzel, P. L. and Lewis, S. (2007) 'The OBO Foundry: Coordinated evolution of ontologies to support biomedical data integration', *Nature Biotechnology*, vol. 25, pp. 1251–1255.

Sporny, M., Longley, D., Kellogg, G., Lanthaler, M. and Lindström, N. (2014) *JSON-LD 1.0: A JSON-Based Serialization for Linked Data*, World Wide Web Consortium (W3C), Cambridge, MA, USA, www.w3.org/TR/json-ld/, accessed 8 January 2016.

Stein, B. R. and Wieczorek, J. (2004) 'Mammals of the world: MaNIS as an example of data integration in a distributed network environment', *Biodiversity Informatics*, vol. 1, pp. 14–22.

Tanksley, S. D. and McCouch, S. R. (1997) 'Seed banks and molecular maps: Unlocking genetic potential from the wild', *Science*, vol. 277, pp. 1063–1066.

Tarasova, T., Mynarz, J. and Archer, P. (2015) 'SmOD INSPIRE Vocabularies', World Wide Web Consortium (W3C), Cambridge, MA, USA, www.w3.org/2015/03/inspire/, accessed 8 January 2016.

TDWG (2006) *Technical Roadmap 2006*, Technical Architecture Group (TAG), Biodiversity Information Standards (TDWG), www.tdwg.org/activities/tag/documents/, accessed 8 January 2016.

TDWG (2007) *Access to Biological Collection Data (ABCD), Version 2.06*, Access to Biological Collection Data Task Group, Biodiversity Information Standards (TDWG), www.tdwg.org/standards/115, accessed 21 February 2016.

TDWG (2009) *Darwin Core*, Darwin Core Task Group, Biodiversity Information Standards (TDWG), www.tdwg.org/standards/450, http://rs.tdwg.org/dwc/, accessed 21 February 2016.

Telenius, A. (2011) 'Biodiversity information goes public: GBIF at your service', *Nordic Journal of Botany*, vol. 29, pp. 378–381.

Walls, R., Deck, J., Guralnick, R., Baskauf, S., Beaman, R., Blum, S., Bowers, S., Buttigieg, P. L., Davies, N., Endresen, D., Gandolfo, M. A., Hanner, R., Janning, A., Krishtalka, L., Matsunaga, A., Midford, P., Morrison, N., O Tuama, E., Schildhauer, M., Smith, B., Stucky, B. J., Thomer, A., Wieczorek, J., Whitacre, J. and Wooley, J. (2014) 'Semantics in support of biodiversity knowledge discovery: An introduction to the biological collections ontology and related ontologies', *PLoS ONE*, vol. 9, p. e89606.

Weibel, S., Kunze, J., Lagoze, C. and Wolf, M. (1998) 'Dublin core metadata for resource discovery', *RFC2143*, www.rfc-editor.org/info/rfc2413.

Wieczorek, J., Bloom, D., Guralnick, R., Blum, S., Döring, M., Giovanni, R., Robertson, T. and Vieglais, D. (2012) 'Darwin Core: An evolving community-developed biodiversity data standard', *PLoS ONE*, vol. 7, p. e29715.

Wood, D., Zaidman, M., Ruth, L. and Hausenblas, M. (2014) *Linked Data*, Manning Publications, New York, NY, USA.

Yilmaz, P., Kottmann, R., Field, D., Knight, R., Cole, J. R., Amaral-Zettler, L., Gilbert, J. A., Karsch-Mizrachi, I., Johnston, A., Cochrane, G., Vaughan, R., Hunter, C., Park, J., Morrison, N., Rocca-Serra, P., Sterk, P., Arumugam, M., Bailey, M., Baumgartner, L., Birren, B. W., Blaser, M. J., Bonazzi, V., Booth, T., Bork, P., Bushman, F. D., Buttigieg, P.nL., Chain, P. S. G., Charlson, E., Costello, E. K., Huot-Creasy, H., Dawyndt, P., DeSantis, T., Fierer, N., Fuhrman, J. A., Gallery, R. E., Gevers, D., Gibbs, R. A., Gil, I. S., Gonzalez, A., Gordon, J. I., Guralnick, R., Hankeln, W., Highlander, S., Hugenholtz, P., Jansson, J., Kau, A. L., Kelley, S. T., Kennedy, J., Knights, D., Koren, O., Kuczynski, J., Kyrpides, N., Larsen, R., Lauber, C. L., Legg, T., Ley, R. E., Lozupone, C. A., Ludwig, W., Lyons, D., Maguire, E., Methé, B. A., Meyer, F., Muegge, B., Nakielny, S., Nelson, K. E., Nemergut, D., Neufeld, J. D., Newbold, L. K., Oliver, A. E., Pace, N. R., Palanisamy, G., Peplies, J., Petrosino, J., Proctor, L., Pruesse, E., Quast, C., Raes, J., Ratnasingham, S., Ravel, J., Relman, D. A., Assunta-Sansone, S., Schloss, P. D., Schriml, L., Sinha, R., Smith, M. I., Sodergren, E., Spor, A., Stombaugh, J., Tiedje, J. M., Ward, D. V., Weinstock, G. M., Wendel, D., White, O., Whiteley, A., Wilke, A., Wortman, J. R., Yatsunenko, T. and Glöckner, F. O. (2011) 'Minimum information about a marker gene sequence (MIMARKS) and minimum information about any (x) sequence (MIxS) specifications', *Nature Biotechnology*, vol. 29, pp. 415–420.

Zeven, A. C. (1998) 'Landraces: A review of definitions and classifications', *Euphytica*, vol. 104, pp. 127–139.

# 43

# BIODIVERSITY IS GIVEN LIFE BY SMALL-SCALE FOOD PROVIDERS

## Defending agricultural biodiversity and ecological food provision in the framework of food sovereignty

*Patrick Mulvany*

> 'What are we fighting for? A world where . . . we are able to conserve and rehabilitate rural environments, fish populations, landscapes and food traditions based on ecologically sustainable management of land, soils, water, seas, seeds, livestock and all other[agricultural] biodiversity.'
>
> *Declaration of Nyéléni, Nyéléni 2007: forum for food sovereignty, Sélingué, Mali, 2007 (Nyeleni, 2007a)*

### Introduction

Agricultural biodiversity is the basis of all food, fibre and other products of ecosystems used by people, their livestock and other farmed, fished and harvested species (Platform for Agrobiodiversity Research (PAR) and FAO, 2011). Agricultural biodiversity is dependent on, and is the product of, ecological food provision: they are inter-dependent, but agricultural biodiversity will be sustained and used equitably only in the framework of food sovereignty.

Agricultural biodiversity includes not only the species of direct use to humans but also all the species which support the necessary ecosystem functions above and below ground and in waters. It also has critical, but often under-recognised, linkages with culture, spirituality and livelihoods (Pimbert, 2006). It is a creation of humankind whose food and livelihood security and food sovereignty depend on the sustained management of the biodiversity that is important for food and agriculture, the origins of which lie in the careful selection and inventive developments of female and male small-scale food providers over more than ten millennia (ITDG, 1996; Mulvany, 2001).

Agricultural biodiversity is one of the last 'resources' that continues to be developed and utilised by small-scale food providers within their own biodiverse, ecological food production systems, and which have not been completely removed from the 'commons' or from local control by means of privatisation, commodification, financialisation or commerce (Shiva et al., 2002).

Although varieties of some, mainly industrial, commodity crops have been enclosed through plant variety rights and patents, most agricultural biodiversity is not. Within this category are the more than 30,000 edible plant species (FAO, 1997a), as well as other useful plant, animal, insect, fungal and microbial species, and innumerable species that perform essential ecosystem functions. There are however increasing numbers of legal and other instruments that could hasten the enclosure of these resources and which risk 'criminalising' the biodiverse and ecological peasant production processes which both depend on and sustain agricultural biodiversity (Tansey and Rajotte, 2008; Halewood et al., 2013; Via Campesina, 2013b).

This dynamic subset of biodiversity is developed and maintained in ecological production systems by mainly small-scale food providers to secure livelihoods, food and a resilient production environment. Yet, along with much of earth's biodiversity, it is being lost at alarming rates due the ravages of industrial food and fibre production and related changes in consumption patterns (Secretariat of the Convention on Biological Diversity (SCBD/GBO-4), 2014). Its loss threatens global food supplies.

**Box 43.1 'Food sovereignty ensures that the rights to use and manage lands, territories, waters, seeds, livestock, and biodiversity are in the hands of those of us who produce food'**

Declaration of Nyéléni, 2007.

Food sovereignty (**Box 43.1**), with its clarity about building upon local knowledge and skills, eschewing the privatisation of the commons and working with 'nature', has been argued to be the best framework within which agricultural biodiversity, and the systems of ecological food provision with which it has mutual interdependence, can be sustained (ETC Group, GRAIN and ITDG, 2002; Windfuhr and Jonsén, 2005; Nyeleni, 2007b; see also **Table 43.1** *Nyéléni 2007: Forum for Food Sovereignty Definition of Food Sovereignty*).

*Table 43.1* Nyéléni 2007: Forum for food sovereignty definition of food sovereignty (from the Declaration of Nyéléni [Nyeleni 2007a])

| *Nyéléni 2007: Forum for food sovereignty*<br>*Definition of food sovereignty (from the Declaration of Nyéléni [Nyélén 2007a])* |
| --- |
| Food sovereignty is the right of peoples to healthy and culturally appropriate food produced through ecologically sound and sustainable methods, and their right to define their own food and agriculture systems. It puts the aspirations and needs of those who produce, distribute and consume food at the heart of food systems and policies rather than the demands of markets and corporations. It defends the interests and inclusion of the next generation. It offers a strategy to resist and dismantle the current corporate trade and food regime, and directions for food, farming, pastoral and fisheries systems determined by local producers and users. Food sovereignty prioritises local and national economies and markets and empowers peasant and family farmer-driven agriculture, artisanal – fishing, pastoralist-led grazing, and food production, distribution and consumption based on environmental, social and economic sustainability. Food sovereignty promotes transparent trade that guarantees just incomes to all peoples as well as the rights of consumers to control their food and nutrition. It ensures that the rights to use and manage lands, territories, waters, seeds, livestock and biodiversity are in the hands of those of us who produce food. Food sovereignty implies new social relations free of oppression and inequality between men and women, peoples, racial groups, social and economic classes and generations. |

(*Continued*)

*Table 43.1* (Continued)

*Six principles of food sovereignty**
*(from Nyéléni 2007 Synthesis Report [Nyéléni 2007b], p. 76)*

| *Food sovereignty:* | *is FOR* | *is AGAINST* |
|---|---|---|
| **1. Focuses on food for people:** | Food sovereignty puts the right to sufficient, healthy and culturally appropriate food for all individuals, peoples and communities, including those who are hungry, under occupation, in conflict zones and marginalised, at the centre of food, agriculture, livestock and fisheries policies; | and *rejects* the proposition that food is just another commodity or component for international agri-business. |
| **2. Values food providers:** | Food sovereignty values and supports the contributions, and respects the rights, of women and men, peasants and small scale family farmers, pastoralists, artisanal fisherfolk, forest dwellers, indigenous peoples and agricultural and fisheries workers, including migrants, who cultivate, grow, harvest and process food; | and *rejects* those policies, actions and programmes that undervalue them, threaten their livelihoods and eliminate them. |
| **3. Localises food systems:** | Food sovereignty brings food providers and consumers closer together; puts providers and consumers at the centre of decision-making on food issues; protects food providers from the dumping of food and food aid in local markets; protects consumers from poor quality and unhealthy food, inappropriate food aid and food tainted with genetically modified organisms; | and *rejects* governance structures, agreements and practices that depend on and promote unsustainable and inequitable international trade and give power to remote and unaccountable corporations. |
| **4. Puts control locally:** | Food sovereignty places control over territory, land, grazing, water, seeds, livestock and fish populations on local food providers and respects their rights. They can use and share them in socially and environmentally sustainable ways which conserve diversity; it recognizes that local territories often cross geopolitical borders and ensures the right of local communities to inhabit and use their territories; it promotes positive interaction between food providers in different regions and territories and from different sectors that helps resolve internal conflicts or conflicts with local and national authorities; | and *rejects* the privatisation of natural resources through laws, commercial contracts and intellectual property rights regimes. |
| **5. Builds knowledge and skills:** | Food sovereignty builds on the skills and local knowledge of food providers and their local organisations that conserve, develop and manage localised food production and harvesting systems, developing appropriate research systems to support this and passing on this wisdom to future generations; | and *rejects* technologies that undermine, threaten or contaminate these, e.g. genetic engineering. |
| **6. Works with nature:** | Food sovereignty uses the contributions of nature in diverse, low external input agroecological production and harvesting methods that maximise the contribution of ecosystems and improve resilience and adaptation, especially in the face of climate change; it seeks to "heal the planet so that the planet may heal us"; | and *rejects* methods that harm beneficial ecosystem functions, that depend on energy intensive monocultures and livestock factories, destructive fishing practices and other industrialised production methods, which damage the environment and contribute to global warming. |

** These six principles are interlinked and inseparable: in implementing the food sovereignty policy framework all should be applied.*

## Resilient, biodiverse and ecological food provision

Biodiversity means

> the acceptance that we are different and that all peoples and each individual has the freedom to think and to be. Seen in this way, biodiversity is not only flora, fauna, earth, water and ecosystems; it is also cultures, systems of production, human and economic relations, forms of governance; in essence it is freedom.
>
> *(Via Campesina III International Conference, 2006)*

In the report *Biodiverse Agriculture for a Changing Climate*, Ensor (2009) noted: 'Biodiverse agroecological approaches bring multiple benefits, simultaneously building resilience in ecosystems and farming communities, while reducing greenhouse gas emissions from food production and drawing carbon from the atmosphere' (p. 1). He further elaborates on the 'productivity-enhancing, purifying, regulating and recycling functions provided to agroecosystems by their embedded agricultural biodiversity . . . [which] improve ecosystem functioning, photosynthesis and nutrient capture' (Ensor, 2009, p. 10). This is achieved by having a sufficient (and large) number of 'target' and 'associated' species in a productive ecosystem that can collectively make optimal use of available energy and nutrients from light, air, soil and water (Finke and Snyder, 2008). Sustainability is enhanced through homeostasis[1] that improves ecosystem resilience and, as numbers of species in the ecosystem increase so does, productivity (Egziabher, 2002).

Ecological food production can also sustain and improve livelihoods through improved productivity per unit area and unit of water. In the negotiated 'Findings' of the International Assessment of Agricultural Knowledge, Science, and Technology for Development (IAASTD) it was concluded that 'an increase and strengthening of agricultural knowledge, science and technology [AKST] towards agro-ecological sciences will contribute to addressing environmental issues while maintaining and increasing productivity'.[2] (IAASTD, 2008). The productivity of biodiverse agroecology, in terms of food and other outputs from the whole production system, not just the yield of a commodity from a monoculture, can be as high if not greater than from a 'conventional' industrial crop.[3]

In addition to ecosystem and livelihoods benefits, the nutritional benefits of biodiverse food systems are significant and seriously under-emphasised in policy and practice (Mulvany and Ensor, 2011; World Health Organization and Secretariat of the Convention on Biological Diversity, 2015). As Denis Lairon, the President, Federation of European Nutrition Societies, said, it is 'very urgent to profoundly change our food strategy and to promote fair, culturally-appropriated, biodiversity-based, sustainable diets' (Lairon, 2010, p. 35). The benefits of biodiverse, agroecological approaches, in terms of realising the Right to Food, have also been highlighted by the UN Special Rapporteur on the Right to Food in his communications on seeds and agroecology to the UN (De Schutter, 2009, 2011).

In conclusion, the more biodiverse and ecological approaches to production practiced by small-scale food providers have the potential to be more productive and resilient, and to be better for people and the environment (Altieri, 1995; Elfstrand et al., 2011; FAO, 2012; europAfrica, 2013; UNCTAD, 2013). Indeed, it is these biodiverse and complex food webs that provide food to more than 70% of the world's peoples (ETC Group, 2013).

## Enclosure of agricultural biodiversity

Agricultural biodiversity is threatened by the spread of 'uniform' industrial production systems in monocultures, livestock factories and aquaculture and by legal instruments which allow enclosure of the commons including agricultural biodiversity (ETC Group, GRAIN and ITDG, 2002). In the landmark publication *The Threatened Gene*, Cary Fowler and Pat Mooney charted the politics surrounding the loss of genetic diversity (Fowler and Mooney, 1990). This seminal work awakened people across the globe to the threats and laid the basis for collective action to resist enclosure.

While peasant, pastoral and artisanal production and harvesting uses and develops varieties and breeds of many thousands of species, this diversity is being replaced by industrial production systems which focus on relatively few crop, livestock, tree and aquatic species. Fewer than 150 plant species are commercially produced, with just four – rice, wheat, maize/corn and potatoes – dominating the industrial commodity chain, which has also focused livestock production on only five types of livestock species – bovines, chickens, pigs, sheep and goats (Wint and Robinson, 2007). Relatively few tree species are used in plantations for, for example producing oils, cellulose/fibre/wood products. Most global consumption of 'wild' fish (the industrial catch) comes from only five groups of species: three groups of finfish – Salmonidae, Cyprinidae and Cichlidae – marine crustaceans and the bivalve molluscs (mussels, clams, scallops and oysters), many of which are over-exploited. Farmed fish and aquaculture are similarly dominated by limited groups of species (ETC Group, 2009; see also Bartley and Halwart, Chapter 5 of this Handbook).

Using financial, legal, corporate, market and governance systems and structures, which privilege power, those who control industrial production, harvesting, processing, distribution and retail are concentrating resources under their control, including the agricultural biodiversity commons (Tansey and Rajotte, 2008).

Seed laws, originally designed to protect farmers and gardeners, are now designed, with the help of Plant Variety Protection measures and IPRs, to benefit the seed industry[4] (Mulvany, 2005).

Acquisitions and mergers also allow concentration of businesses into larger conglomerates and trans-national corporations which control industrial agricultural input supplies. For example, the seed industry is dominated by just three companies, which are also among the leading manufacturers of agrochemicals (EcoNexus and Berne Declaration, 2013; ETC Group, 2011). This leads to domination in the market by varieties of seeds that are compliant to an industry's chemicals, for example glyphosate-tolerant crop varieties.

Since the landmark *Diamond v. Chakrabarty* case in the United States in 1980, it has been increasingly permissible to patent living beings and genes, conferring ownership of whole organisms and their products that contain proprietary genes (Commission on Intellectual Property Rights (CIPR, 2002). This encourages science and technology development mainly to serve the interests of capital. Scientists and corporations or 'legal persons' are rewarded by monopoly privileges (patents and other restrictive intellectual property rights) on their products and processes. These manipulate and modify the living organisms and genetic resources in ways that improve benefits for the powerful (Tansey and Rajotte, 2008).

Of particular interest to capital are varieties and breeds that contain proprietary modified genes; genetically-modified varieties containing patented genes allow control of markets and production by the patent holder. This control can spread to include crops grown in adjacent fields that have been contaminated by the GM genes, further extending the reach of the patent holder, usually a biotech corporation or client scientist.[5]

Land and water 'grabs' reduce the territories available for biodiverse peasant, pastoral and artisanal fisheries production and harvesting (GRAIN, 2012). Food chains lock in producers to serve industrial retail interests using production processes that grow few, often protected, non-reproducible, hybrid or genetically-modified, varieties of crops, industrial breeds of livestock or harvest or cultivate limited species of fish and aquatic organisms (ETC Group, 2013).

Further enclosures are imminent or planned, aided by the spread of patentable New Plant Breeding Technologies (NPBTs). From Terminator to NanoBio to SynBio to Gene Drives,[6] life (not as we know it!) will be privatised and in the hands of patent holders; the basis of the production of food, other 'natural' goods and many materials will be in corporate hands. The Economics of Ecosystems and Biodiversity (TEEB) will provide the data that could inadvertently hasten the commodification of nature, although that is not their stated aim. Soil carbon trading will facilitate enclosure of territories. Water, already privatised in many parts of the world, will become an increasingly important portfolio in hedge, offshore and sovereign funds, managed far from those who need and use it. Indeed, as Pat Mooney of the ETC group has said: 'in 2012 at the Earth Summit Rio+20, the world gave itself permission to privatise everything'.[7]

In summary, trade and intellectual property agreements, commercial contracts, seed laws and restrictive technologies are developed, by the systems and structures which serve the powerful, into potent instruments. These can undermine and enclose the agricultural biodiversity 'commons' and 'criminalise' biodiverse and ecological peasant production processes and their components, which depend on and sustain agricultural biodiversity.

## The erosion of agricultural biodiversity

Beyond the impacts of 'variety displacement' resulting from the spread of 'uniform' production systems, such as monocultures and livestock factories, aided by the structures and processes outlined earlier, agricultural biodiversity is further threatened by changes in climate, patterns of land and water use and consumption patterns, which are accelerated by industrialised societies (SCBD, 2014).

These pressures have led to losses of crop varieties on-farm, estimated to be as high as 90% on-farm (FAO, 1997a), and even a significant proportion of seeds in the 6.5 million samples stored in 1,400 genebanks across the world are in urgent need of regeneration if not already dying (Fowler, 2008). One livestock breed is lost every month (FAO, 2007). Most commercial fishing grounds are over-fished, with threats to the viability of sub-species. And with the loss of territories from locally-controlled food provision to industrial production and harvesting, and with the impacts of climate change, inevitably this will result in further losses of agricultural biodiversity.

There are few data recorded about the diversity of species used in local production. Much of the information is anecdotal, provided by local people. The fate of the diversity of the many thousands of species, cultivated, farmed or fished, which are important in the diets of many people but are not commercially exploited is under-recorded, except for relatively few case studies. And there are even fewer data about all the species that support the ecosystem functions essential for the production and harvesting of the species humans use, most of which, perhaps with the exception of pollinators, are rarely surveyed.

This 'hidden' agricultural biodiversity is, however, still mainly in the control of peasant farmers, pastoralists, forest dwellers and artisanal fishers, Indigenous Peoples and other small-scale food providers. Much of this is agricultural biodiversity is still a part of the 'commons'. It currently provides food for the majority of people in the world using a wide range of species (ETC Group, 2009, 2013; **Box 43.2**).

**Box 43.2 'If conservation priorities are guided by the mistaken assumption that humanity depends on a handful of commodity crops, then we run the risk of undermining food security' Hope Shand, *Human Nature* (Shand, 1997, p. 19).**

The 'headline' losses of seed diversity are, however, mainly focused on the losses of varieties of a limited number of commercial crop species, especially staple cereals such as rice, maize and wheat. It can be argued that, by accepting this dominant narrative in industrialised societies, in which few species and varieties and breeds used in industrial commodity production feed the world, it may conveniently obscure the existence of the vast majority of agricultural biodiversity that still remains in, the potentially more important, biodiverse and ecological food production systems, which use and are supported by many tens of thousands of species (ETC Group, 2009, 2013).

Even though agricultural biodiversity provides the resilience that is the bulwark against potential failures of large-scale commercial, industrial production, there is a systemic dysfunctionality in the industrial food regime. It requires 'diversity' in competitive markets, and vigorously exploits market niches for diversely packaged processed foods, but eschews diversity in production. Industrial foods are made from a limited range of uniform ingredients grown monoculturally, which exacerbates the reduction of biodiversity and complexity in production systems, undermining its own sustainability (adapted from Ensor, 2009).

In *Biodiverse Agriculture for a Changing Climate*, Jonathon Ensor stated:

> Diversity is the enemy of these large scale processes: diversity creates a complex landscape that prevents the homogenisation of methods and the uniformity of product demanded by the commodity supply chain. This simplification and the associated deterioration of the agroecosystems is compensated for through the introduction of chemical inputs – fertilisers, pesticides and herbicides and the increasing using of antibiotics in livestock. Thus, fossil fuel dependent industrial processes are required to provide agricultural inputs and sustain productivity. Yet while yields may be supported in the short term, these highly simplified agroecosystems cannot achieve homeostasis and remain in long term decline . . . though intensive inputs may make agricultural production in a given season high, sustained high productivity over years is not possible.
>
> *(Ensor, 2009, p. 2)*

It may be convenient to minimize discussion about the wide range of agricultural biodiversity used in the majority food system. This enables proponents of the minority industrial food regime to assert that as there is an accepted 'huge erosion of agricultural biodiversity' (**Box 43.3** *Biodiversity is in peril*), there is no alternative but to consume their industrial foods, made from their limited range of proprietary seeds, if a growing world population is to be fed. It could become a self-fulfilling assertion.

### Box 43.3 Biodiversity is in peril

*'Plant [varieties] are being lost due to modern practices. Women traditionally held knowledge, we are losing part of ourselves as women when we lose our seeds and the knowledge they contain. Loss of biodiversity is connected to loss of identity and loss of knowledge.'* Nyéléni 2007b: Forum for Food Sovereignty, Synthesis Report.

- **The industrial model of production and consumption** is rapidly destroying rural societies that manage biodiversity for food and agriculture.
- It uses **genetically uniform monocultures** of crops, livestock and fish, increasingly genetically modified, while **locking up diversity in gene banks**.
- **Land grabs and ocean/water grabs** extend the area under this model of production. Likewise, the spread of agrofuel and cellulose plantations, mining and large dams occupy our biodiverse territories.
- Intensive use of **pesticides, herbicides and chemical fertilisers** further reduce biodiversity and ecosystem functions.
- **Climate change**, exacerbated by this model, is putting new pressures on the local diversity of crops and livestock as weather patterns change, and new pests and diseases proliferate.
- **Industrial research systems** for this model, de-value and erode peasant and indigenous knowledge, local research capacities and the multitude of local innovation systems which foster biodiversity.
- **Monopolies** control industrial seed, agrochemical and industrial commodity markets, which jeopardise freedom for peasants to access and use biodiversity.
- **Industrial Property Rights** and other laws which protect monopolies **criminalise peasant producers** who challenge the industrial model of production and its effects.

*Source*: From the Brochure 'Peasants Give Life to Biodiversity' (IPC, 2016).

## Peasants give life to biodiversity

Confronting these onslaughts on agricultural biodiversity, and defending biodiverse, ecological food provision are arguably among the most significant challenges for those, especially small-scale peasant food providers, who wish to realise food sovereignty and defend future food provision. As explained earlier, not all agricultural biodiversity has been enclosed: it is being sustained when peasant production systems, pastoralism and artisanal fisheries are protected. A summary of the challenges and responses can be found in the brochure 'Peasants Give Life to Biodiversity' (IPC for Food Sovereignty, 2016).

During the Leipzig process in 1990s,[8] although it dealt exclusively with crop plant diversity, *in situ* conservation, development and sustainable use of genetic resources for food and agriculture (and, by implication, all agricultural biodiversity) became mainstream. It moved to being a recognised activity worthy of official scientific support from being simply something that good food producers did as a routine. *In situ* conservation, development and sustainable use is practiced on-farm, on the range and in productive waters by farmers, gardeners, herders and fisherfolk. It includes activities such as multi-variety cropping (Rahmanian, 2013), seed saving (Stickland, 2001), community seed banks (Lewis and Mulvany, 1997), community seed systems (Jarvis et al., 2003), participatory plant breeding (PPB) (Ceccarelli et al., 2009), maintaining breeds of livestock (Gura et al., 2002) and selective fishing (ICSF, 2005), as well as protecting pollinators (Gemmill-Herren and Ngo, 2013), maintaining productive landscapes (GIAHS, 2013) and restoring mangroves, the breeding grounds for many aquatic organisms (Bosire et al., 2008).

Ecological food provision,[9] especially when practiced in the framework of Food Sovereignty, depends on and develops agricultural biodiversity (UKFG, 2010). Agroecology (*sensu* Altieri, 1995) is the most well known term for this, but it is not always recognised by pastoralists and fishers as descriptive of their production and harvesting systems. Where local, biodiverse and ecological food provision is practiced, agricultural biodiversity is sustained. Protection of these production systems, the commons upon which they depend and the communities of peasants, pastoralists, forest dwellers or fishers is a *sine qua non* for conservation and development of agricultural biodiversity.

Since the work of Vavilov in the early 20th century, identifying the centres of origin and diversity of crop plants used by humans, international attention has been increasingly drawn to defending the diversity of crops both on-farm and in *ex situ* collections. As work developed, it was recognised that effective international governance structures were required to protect these resources and facilitate their continued and sustainable use for the benefit of all humankind. In the 21st century, there are now many institutions that govern agricultural biodiversity or components of it, sometimes competitively and lacking effective harmony. Internationally FAO, especially its Commission on Genetic Resources for Food and Agriculture (CGRFA), and the Convention on Biological Diversity (CBD) have overall governance of agricultural biodiversity.[10] There are others that cover aspects of agricultural biodiversity. The International Seed Treaty (ITPGRFA) focuses on 35 genera of seeds and 29 species of forages and has legally-binding clauses on Farmers' Rights, sustainable use and conservation of PGRFA; the Cartagena Protocol on Biosafety (CBP) governs the transboundary movement of genetically engineered species/living modified organisms (GMOs/LMOs); the World Trade Organization (WTO) has an agreement on intellectual property rights that deals with plant varieties and microbial processes (TRIPS); the World Intellectual Property Organization (WIPO) has agreements on the use of genetic resources and traditional knowledge and it also houses the Union for the protection of new varieties of plant (UPOV) now with some 74 members, mostly signed up to UPOV 91.

At regional levels in most parts of the world, there are similar institutions that control and govern aspects of agricultural biodiversity and have charge of making and enforcing laws; for example in the European Union (EU), there are regulations that govern intellectual property, GMOs, seed licensing, cloning and so forth. Governance bodies are most often dominated by lawyers, corporate interests and those seeking to preserve genetic resources *ex situ* that is, away from the place where they were developed for example in gene banks. There is a thin legal line that distinguishes between *ex situ* preservation and BioPiracy.

Female and male peasant farmers and gardeners, herders, fishers, forest dwellers, Indigenous Peoples and other small-scale food providers, who sustain biodiversity, need to be central in governance and decision making about the conservation, development and sustainable use of agricultural biodiversity and its governance, at local national, regional and international levels. However, there are many legal, commercial and technological measures, agreed by those with power, that exclude these developers and custodians of agricultural biodiversity from any meaningful participation. Participation is too often relegated to belated, and usually ignored, contributions to government and secretariat-led governance processes.

In democratic forums, peasants can challenge and start to redress imbalances in power that have served monopoly interests and which threaten biodiversity and peasant livelihoods. They participate in many international forums which deal with aspects of genetic resources and biodiversity governance but only as observers despite being those who give life to biodiversity. The UN Committee on World Food Security (CFS) is more democratic and provides a good example. It is mandated to provide global governance on food security. Since its renewal in 2009, peasant organisations and social movements have equal voice with governments in the CFS. The Civil Society Mechanism of the CFS, dominated by social movements of small-scale food providers, contributes to agenda setting. A challenge for the CFS is to address biodiversity and agroecology issues and to assess the contributions to food security by UN and other forums concerned with the governance of genetic resources, biodiversity and related issues.

**Box 43.4**

We want local food producers to be at the heart of a participatory, inclusive decision-making process. We must defend collective rights; change laws and discriminatory policies, and develop new legal frameworks that respect and protect Farmers' Rights to use, save, exchange and sell seeds and livestock breeds, putting the control of biodiversity and knowledge back in the hands of peasants. Policies need to value local knowledge, and give us the opportunity to share our knowledge.

*(Report of the International Forum for Agroecology, Nyéléni, 2015)*

There are many programmes of work, guided by governance structures and based on analyses of 'States of the World' of particular types of species – plants, livestock, fisheries, forests and so forth – which outline global programmes that could help sustain agricultural biodiversity, if they were to support biodiverse and ecological food provision. The global programmes depend, ultimately, on the contribution of work by the originators and custodians of agricultural biodiversity (**Box 43.4**).

The most challenging, and potentially interesting, assessment is currently underway, organised by the CGRFA. It is the State of the World's Biodiversity for Food and Agriculture (see **Box 43.5**).

**Box 43.5 State of the World's Biodiversity for Food and Agriculture (SoW-BFA)[11]**

This cross-sectoral assessment, using the ecosystem approach, covers plants, animals, aquatic and soil organisms, pollinators as well as other associated species and the ecosystem functions they provide. It also includes social, legal and institutional issues. Data was being collected in 2014, analysis was carried out in 2015, the draft was published in 2016 with the final version presented in 2017 as a landmark contribution to the International Decade on Biodiversity.

If the assessment were to encompass and reinforce the views of small-scale food providers and develop an action plan to support their biodiverse and ecological production systems it could help to:

- contribute to changes in policy and practice that will enhance agricultural biodiversity and related ecosystem functions in all production systems and at all scales;
- identify ways in which the developers and conservers of agricultural biodiversity and its related ecosystem functions – the (especially small-scale) food providers – farmers, gardeners, livestock keepers, fishers, forest dwellers, Indigenous Peoples and so forth – can be protected and supported so that they can continue producing food as well as other multiple benefits in their biodiverse, resilient and ecological systems, thereby contributing to food provision, well-being and the conservation, development and sustainable use of agricultural biodiversity and its related ecosystem functions;
- increase recognition of the overriding contribution of the knowledge, skills, innovations and practices of the (especially small-scale) food providers to the conservation, development and sustainable use of agricultural biodiversity and its related ecosystem functions;
- increase recognition of the contribution of the food sovereignty framework, developed by the social movements of (especially small-scale) food providers, to improving the policy environment for the conservation, development and sustainable use of agricultural biodiversity and its related ecosystem functions;
- identify the principal drivers causing the loss of agricultural biodiversity, its related ecosystem functions and biodiverse food production systems and suggest mitigation measures (e.g. ref IAASTD);
- provide a framework for the analysis of policy, production systems, research and practice which helps policy makers, academics, change agents and others to assess impacts on the conservation, development and sustainable use of agricultural biodiversity and its related ecosystem functions;
- identify the key enablers/stressors, policies and actors which impact positively and negatively on the conservation, development and sustainable use of agricultural biodiversity and its related ecosystem functions and suggest governance structures at all levels which best contribute to an improved environment and better outcomes;
- provide stimuli for the inter and intra community and intergenerational transfer of knowledge and skills that enable continued conservation, development and sustainable use of agricultural biodiversity and its related ecosystem functions; and
- mitigate the negative impacts of externally controlled markets (inputs and outputs) on the conservation, development and sustainable use of agricultural biodiversity and its related ecosystem functions.

## Resistance is fertile

Even though enclosures of agricultural biodiversity and related knowledge are increasing, most people in most countries are unbowed. They are resisting through actions and activities and even contesting monopoly power of corporations in the courts (Mullin, 2013; **Box 43.6**).

**Box 43.6 'We need to put the control of seeds, biodiversity, land and territories, waters, knowledge, culture and the commons in the hands of the peoples who feed the world.' Declaration of the Forum for Agroecology, Nyéléni, Mali, 2015**

Though the threat is to all agricultural biodiversity, the most iconic campaigns focus on seeds. For more than 30 years, there have been campaigns to protect seeds and reverse decisions that undermine seed diversity on-farm. In the past few years, food sovereignty campaigns have re-energised as populations are faced with increasingly bad policies and actions by states, intergovernmental bodies and corporations restricting access to seeds, contaminating the environment with GMOs and passing laws and agreements that favour industry (**Box 43.7** *Declaration of Via Campesina*).

**Box 43.7 As Via Campesina declare:**

'Peasant and farmers' seeds are under threat of extinction. If we do not change the course history is taking, our children will not be able to produce their own food. If the know-how of farmers and peasants in selecting and conserving seeds disappears as older people pass away, our children will be left at the mercy of multinationals. If small-scale practitioners do not, starting today, go and retrieve from still accessible refrigerated banks the seeds of their parents which are required for new selections, then these seeds will no longer be available tomorrow. This is why La Via Campesina is developing its seed campaign along two axes:

1. by exchanging know-how from farmer to farmer, and organizing collectively to produce and conserve locally our own seeds intended for small-scale farming and organic farming; and
2. by fighting against the 'Monsanto' Laws, and enshrining in the laws of each country and at the global level the recognition of the inalienable rights of peasants and family farmers to conserve, use, exchange, sell and protect their seeds.'

*(Via Campesina, 2013a)*

A way of contesting the industry-led attack on seeds campaigns is to present the impacts of their technologies and processes on all agricultural biodiversity, at genetic, species and ecosystem levels, and on the food system. Presenting biodiverse, ecological food provision as the norm in most parts of the world, and the most efficient system of providing wholesome, healthy, nutritious food, can unsettle their worldview. In industrialised societies, the growing resistance is equally fertile: guerrilla and propaganda gardening, community supported agriculture schemes, food collectives, local farmers' markets, seed fairs, permaculture/organic/low input food production and many other actions by civil society are operating despite and outwith any laws or other biodiversity-destroying measures.

## Agricultural biodiversity and food sovereignty

The inter-dependence of agricultural biodiversity and ecological food provision as well as with environmental and social (health) sustainability is clear. But benefits to people and planet can be properly realised only if its development and the resultant food provision is in the framework of food sovereignty.

The contested discussion about 'sustainable agriculture' is examined in a paper prepared for the Irish development NGO, Trócaire – 'Food security, poverty reduction, climate change: placing Trócaire's livelihoods work in context' (Coupe et al., 2011). In this paper, a comparative table is presented (see **Appendix 43.1** *Comparison of ecological, sustainable intensification and industrialised production models*) which, under three domains of 'sustainable agriculture' – Ecological Small-scale Food Production (in framework of Food Sovereignty; see **Box 43.8** *Small-scale food providers*), Sustainable Intensification and 'Slightly Green' High External Input Industrialised Commodity Production – compares their performance based on criteria derived from the six pillars of food sovereignty (Nyeleni, 2007b). The analysis shows clear and lasting benefits to people and the planet from biodiverse approaches that are within the framework of food sovereignty. It shows, as well, that there are opportunities in the contested 'middle ground' of 'sustainable intensification'; social movements are also trying to occupy this space with production systems based on their definition of agroecology, while simultaneously challenging and calling for increased regulation and dismantling of production using industrial technologies, at all scales (*Declaration of the Forum for Agroecology*, Nyéléni, Mali, 2015). It is worth reflecting on this struggle: for as much as social movements defend biodiverse food sovereignty, seek to occupy the middle ground and campaign against industrial production, well-funded, corporate agribusinesses and their lobbies and compliant scientists are doing the opposite. In this struggle, the co-option by the agribusiness lobby of civil society organisations, as opinion-formers and legitimisers of their approach, is something that social movements are aware of, and hence are cautious in their alliances.

### Box 43.8 Small-scale food providers

Small-scale food providers live in a multitude of diverse societies in nearly every ecosystem on earth. Using their own methods, tools and customary practices, in approaches embracing collective rights, their dynamic management of biodiversity, above and below ground and in waters, has developed production systems that have co-evolved with them over millennia.

Working with nature, in the framework of food sovereignty and their **intertwined actions of production, innovation, resistance and protest**, they continue to give life to biodiversity for food and agriculture. They are doing this by using their biodiverse and ecological model of production, producing and processing locally for local markets. By connecting those who grow with those who eat, they also are reclaiming their territories and ensuring they have access to our seeds, livestock breeds, fish seed and wider biodiversity. Their innovative research, co-creating knowledge with specialists, enhances biodiversity. And they are actively promoting our approach in policy forums.

> Peasant systems for rediscovering, re-valuing, conserving and exchanging seeds, together with local adaptation due to the local selection and reproduction in farmers' fields, maintain and increase the genetic biodiversity that underlies our world food systems and gives us the required capacity and flexibility to address diverse environments, a changing climate and hunger in the world.
>
> *(Bali Seed Declaration, 2011)*[12]

## Conclusion

Despite the accumulated evidence of the failures of industrialised approaches and the contrasting positive practices of small-scale food providers supported by the findings of IAASTD (2008) that chart a different, sustainable and equitable way forward, institutions and governments continue to invest in and roll out industrialised approaches, at all scales, promoting the proprietary technologies they depend on. The scientific challenge now is to move away from this reductionist approach and towards ecological food provision, one that embraces complexity and diversity, sustainably using technologies that are freely available for the majority of food providers. The political challenge is for governments to regulate and reduce the negative impacts of industrial food systems and defend, support and promote ecological food provision, using natural wealth that may not be commodified though there are increasing attempts to privatise it, and adopting policies within the food sovereignty framework in order to safeguard the world's food supply. Such an approach depends on and favours agricultural biodiversity and the biodiverse, ecological model of food provision. (UKFG, 2010)

This biodiverse, ecological model of food provision, developed in the framework of food sovereignty, is more resilient and can produce more food over time per unit area, or per volume of water, than industrial monocultures. This model of 'peasant' production is dependent on, and also regenerates, and develops, agricultural biodiversity above- and below-ground, on-farm, on the range and in productive waters (**Box 43.9** *Peasants enhance biodiversity in the framework of food sovereignty*).

Given the interdependencies described earlier of agricultural biodiversity and ecological food provision developed in the framework of food sovereignty, it is argued that the food sovereignty movement needs to give as high a priority to defending access to and control over all agricultural biodiversity's conservation, sustainable use and development as it does currently to defending peasant seeds.

### Box 43.9 Peasants enhance biodiversity in the framework of food sovereignty

**Respecting the collective rights of the women and men who use, maintain and enhance peasant biodiversity for food and agriculture, we will strive to:**

**Strengthen and promote** our dynamic management of biodiversity, based on ecological principles and collective rights over knowledge, resources and territories.

**Transform research** so that it is reframed by peasants for the co-creation of diverse knowledges, which shall not be patented.

**Realise actions** that guarantee the collective rights of peasants and Indigenous Peoples to use, exchange, breed, select and sell their seeds, livestock breeds, fish seed.

**Reinforce** our interconnecting and collective rural-urban food webs and local markets in ways that sustain biodiversity in our territories and feed the majority.

*Source*: From the Brochure 'Peasants Give Life to Biodiversity' (IPC, 2016).

## Notes

1 Homeostasis is achieved when an ecosystem maintains a biological equilibrium between its different components.

2 IAASTD, Finding #7 (IAASTD, 2008).

3 This is examined in Ensor (2009) and summarised in UKFG (2010), building on the findings of Pimentel et al. (2005).

4 For an account of this process of exclusion in the United States, see Chapter 6 'Traditional knowledge and intellectual property: seeking alternatives' in Debora J. Halbert's book *Resisting Intellectual Property* (Halbert, 2005).
5 For more opinions on the possible risks of GM technologies see *The GMO Emperor Has No Clothes: A Global Citizens' Report on the State of GMOs – False Promises, Failed Technologies* (Shiva et al., 2011).
6 New Plant Breeding Technologies (NPBTs) include a wide range of technologies beyond first generation genetic modification. These include transformations that prevent the germination of harvested seeds, broadly classed as Genetic Use Restriction Technologies (GURTs) and dubbed 'Terminator Technologies' by campaigners; biotechnologies operating at nano-scale, so-called nanobiotechnologies, result from the merging of the living and non-living realms at the nano-scale to make hybrid materials and organisms; Synthetic Biology (SynBio) brings together engineering and the life sciences in order to design and construct new biological parts, devices and systems that do not currently exist in the natural world or to tweak the designs of existing biological systems. The mostly patentable technologies being developed in this way include the technologies to create so-called Gene Drives, which is the practice of stimulating biased inheritance of particular genes to alter entire populations.
7 More on the privatisation of nature in *Who Will Control the Green Economy?* (ETC Group, 2011).
8 The FAO 'Leipzig' conference on plant genetic resources for food and agriculture in 1996 was a landmark event for all who had an interest in conserving agricultural biodiversity. For an introduction to this and the other events that surrounded this process, and what was achieved, see *The Year of Agricultural Biodiversity Revisited* (GRAIN, 1997).
9 Ecological food provision can include many types of food production when these are practiced ecologically, for example peasant production, pastoralism, artisanal fishing, agroecology, organic agriculture and gardening, permaculture, Low-External Input Agriculture, natural farming and ecoagriculture.
10 Much of this section is derived from discussions held by the IPC for Food Sovereignty in 2012.
11 For more on SoW-BFA, see www.fao.org/nr/cgrfa/biodiversity/sowbfa/en/.
12 For a link to the text, visit http://climateandcapitalism.com/2011/03/20/la-via-campesina-the-bali-seed-declaration/.

## References


Altieri, M. (1995) *Agroecology: The Science of Sustainable Agriculture*, Intermediate Technology Publications, London, UK.

Bosire, J. O., Dahdouh-Guebas, F., Walton, M., Crona, B. I., Lewis, R. R., Field, C., Kairo, J. G. and Koedam, N. (2008) 'Functionality of restored mangroves: A review', *Aquatic Botany*, vol. 89, pp. 251–259.

Ceccarelli, S., Guimarães, E. P. and Weltizien, E. (eds.) (2009) *Plant Breeding and Farmer Participation*, Food and Agriculture Organization of the United Nations (FAO), Rome, Italy, ftp://ftp.fao.org/docrep/fao/012/i1070e/i1070e.pdf

Commission on Intellectual Property Rights (CIPR) (2002) *Integrating Intellectual Property Rights and Development Policy*, London, UK, www.iprcommission.org/papers/pdfs/final_report/ciprfullfinal.pdf

Convention on Biological Diversity (CBD) (1992) *Text of the Convention on Biological Diversity*, CBD Secretariat, www.cbd.int/convention/text/default.shtml, accessed January 2014.

Coupe, S., Ensor, J. and Mulvany, P. M. (2011) *Food Security, Poverty Reduction, Climate Change: Placing Trócaire's Livelihoods Work in Context*, (Practical Action Internal Report That Provided the Basis for a 2012 Trócaire Discussion Paper, www.manosunidasonline.org/redes/documentos_publicos/AgriculturaySeg.Alimentaria/Nexus_Final_Trocaire.pdf

De Schutter, O. (2009) Seed Policies and the Right to Food: Enhancing Agrobiodiversity, Encouraging Innovation, presented at the 64th Session of the UN General Assembly (A/64/170), www.srfood.org/images/stories/pdf/otherdocuments/20091021_background-doc_seed-policies-and-the-right-to-food_en.pdf

De Schutter, O. (2011) *Agroecology and the Right to Food*. Report presented at the 16th Session of the United Nations Human Rights Council [A/HRC/16/49], www.srfood.org/en/agroecology

EcoNexus and Berne Declaration (2013) *AGROPOLY: A Handful of Corporations Control World Food Production*, EcoNexus, UK and Berne Declaration, Switzerland, http://econexus.info/publication/agropoly-handful-corporations-control-world-food-production

Egziabher, T. B. G. (2002) 'The human individual and community in the conservation and sustainable use of biological resources', Darwin Lecture *op cit*. Egziabher's discussion of homeostasis relies on V. H. Heywood and R. T. Watson (1995) *Global Biodiversity Assessment*, UNEP and Cambridge University Press, Cambridge, UK, www.nyeleni.org/IMG/pdf/Tewolde_Darwin_Lecture2002.pdf

Elfstrand, S., Malmer, P. and Skagerfält, B. (2011) *Strengthening Agricultural Biodiversity for Smallholder Livelihoods: What Knowledge Is Needed to Overcome Constraints and Release Potentials*. Report for Oxfam Novib and HIVOS. The Resilience and Development Programme (SwedBio). Stockholm Resilience Centre, Stockholm, Sweden, www.stockholmresilience.org/download/18.5ea7abe0139d0dada524d0/Mapping+report+111114+final+PDF+layout.pdf

Ensor, J. (2009) *Biodiverse Agriculture for a Changing Climate*, Practical Action, Rugby, UK. www.practicalaction.org/media/download/5807, accessed January 2014

ETC Group (2009, 2013) *Who Will Feed Us? The Industrial Food Chain or Peasant Food Webs?*, www.etcgroup.org/content/poster-who-will-feed-us-industrial-food-chain-or-peasant-food-webs and www.etcgroup.org/files/ETC_Who_Will_Feed_Us.pdf

ETC Group (2011) *Who Will Control the Green Economy?* etcGroup, Ottawa, Canada. www.etcgroup.org/content/who-will-control-green-economy-0

ETC Group, GRAIN and ITDG (2002) *Sustaining Agricultural Biodiversity and the Integrity and Free Flow of Genetic Resources for Food for Agriculture*, Forum for Food Sovereignty, Rome, Italy, www.ukabc.org/accessgenres.pdf, accessed January 2014

europAfrica (2013) *Family Farmers for Sustainable Food Systems*, www.europafrica.info/en/publications/family-farmers-for-sustainable-food-systems

FAO (1997a) *First Report of the State of the World's Plant Genetic Resources for Food and Agriculture*, FAO, Rome, Italy, http://apps3.fao.org/wiews/docs/SWRFULL2.PDF

FAO (1997b) *Technical Workshop on Farming Systems Approaches for the Sustainable Use and Conservation of Agricultural Biodiversity and Agro-Ecosystems*, FAO, Rome, Italy. www.fao.org/sd/epdirect/EPre0037.htm, accessed January 2014.

FAO (1999) *Sustaining Agricultural Biodiversity and Agro-Ecosystem Functions*, Workshop Report, FAO, Rome, Italy (also provided as an information document for CBD and CGRFA meetings), www.fao.org/sd/epdirect/EPre0080.htm, accessed January 2014.

FAO (2007) *The State of the World's Animal Genetics Resources for Food and Agriculture*, FAO, Rome, Italy.

FAO (2008) *Agricultural Biodiversity in FAO*, FAO, Rome, Italy, www.fao.org/docrep/010/i0112e/i0112e00.htm, accessed January 2014

FAO (2012) *Save and Grow: A Policymaker's Guide to the Sustainable Intensification of Smallholder Crop Production*, FAO, Rome, Italy, www.fao.org/ag/save-and-grow/

FAO (2013) *Biodiversity for a World without Hunger*, FAO, Rome, Italy, www.fao.org/biodiversity/en/

Finke, D. and Snyder, W. (2008) 'Niche partitioning increases resource exploitation by diverse communities', *Science*, vol. 321, pp. 1488–1490.

Fowler, C. (2008) *The Svalbard Global Seed Vault: Securing the Future of Agriculture*, Global Crop Diversity Trust, c/o FAO, Rome, Italy.

Fowler, C. and Mooney, P. (1990) *The Threatened Gene: Food, Politics, and the Loss of Genetic Diversity*, Lutterworth Press, Cambridge, UK, www.docshut.com/iyhunm/the-threatened-gene-food-politics-and-the-loss-of-genetic-diversity.html, accessed January 2014.

Gemmill-Herren, B. and Ngo, H. (2013) *Give Bees a Chance*, International Pollinators Initiative (www.internationalpollinatorsinitiative.org/), http://wle.cgiar.org/blogs/2013/08/22/give-bees-a-chance/ accessed January 2014.

GIAHS (2013) *Globally Important Agricultural Heritage Systems (GIAHS)*, FAO, Rome, Italy. www.fao.org/giahs/giahs/en/

GRAIN (1997) *The Year of Agricultural Biodiversity Revisited*, GRAIN, Barcelona, Spain, www.grain.org/es/article/entries/209-the-year-of-agricultural-biodiversity-revisited

GRAIN (2012) *Squeezing Africa Dry: Behind Every Land Grab Is a Water Grab*, GRAIN, Barcelona, Spain. www.grain.org/article/entries/4516-squeezing-africa-dry-behind-every-land-grab-is-a-water-grab.pdf

Gura, S., Köhler-Rollefson, I., Mathias, E. and Anderson, S. (2002) *Livestock Diversity: Keepers' Rights, Shared Benefits and Pro-Poor Policies*, Documentation of a Workshop with NGOs, Herders, Scientists, and FAO at the NGO/CSO Forum for Food Sovereignty Rome, 13 June 2002. German NGO Forum on Environment & Development, Bonn, Germany, ftp://ftp.fao.org/docrep/nonfao/lead/x6104E/x6104E00.pdf

Halbert, D. J. (2005) *Resisting Intellectual Property*, Routledge, Abingdon, UK, www.e-reading.co.uk/bookreader.php/135963/Halbert__Resisting_Intellectual_Property_Law.pdf

Halewood, M., Noriega, I. L. and Louafi, S. (eds.) (2013) *Crop Genetic Resources as a Global Commons: Challenges in International Law and Governance*, Routledge and Bioversity International, Abingdon, UK and Maccarese, Italy, www.bioversityinternational.org/uploads/tx_news/Crop_GR_as_a_global_commons_Book_01.pdf

IAASTD (2008) *Reports of the International Assessment of Agricultural Knowledge, Science, and Technology for Development, including: Global Summary for Decision Makers; Synthesis Report*, Sub-Global Reports, Island Press, Washington DC, USA, www.unep.org/dewa/assessments/ecosystems/iaastd/tabid/105853/default.aspx

ICSF (2005) *The Ideal Model*, The text of ICSF's presentation to the Sixth Meeting of the UN Open-ended Informal Consultative Process on Oceans and the Law of the Sea, International Collective in Support of Fishworkers, Chennai, India, http://community.icsf.net/en/samudra/detail/EN/923-The-ideal-model.html

International Planning Committee (IPC) for Food Sovereignty (2016) *Peasants Give Life to Biodiversity*, Agricultural Biodiversity Working Group of the IPC for Food Sovereignty, Rome, Italy, www.foodsovereignty.org/biodiversity

ITDG (1996) *Dynamic Diversity: Farmers, Herders and Fisherfolk Safeguarding Biodiversity*, three booklets covering crops, livestock and fisheries, prepared for the 1996 World Food Summit, ITDG, Rugby, UK.

Jarvis, D., Sevilla-Panizo, R., Chávez-Servia, J. L. and Hodgkin, T. (eds.) (2003) *Seed Systems and Crop Genetic Diversity On-Farm*, Workshop Proceedings, Pucallpa, Peru, IPGRI, Rome.

Lairon, D. (2010) 'Biodiversity and sustainable nutrition with a food-based approach', in B. Burlingame et al. (eds.), *Sustainable Diets and Biodiversity: Directions and Solutions for Policy Research and Action*, Proceedings of the International Scientific Symposium, 5 November 2010, FAO, Rome, Italy, www.fao.org/docrep/016/i3022e/i3022e.pdf

Lewis, V. and Mulvany, P. M. (1997) *A Typology of Community Seed Banks*, ITDG, Rugby, UK, www.ukabc.org/communityseedbanks.pdf

Mullin, J. (2013) *Organic Farmers Can't Fight Monsanto Patents in Court: But Monsanto Won't Be Able to Sue over "Incidental Infringement" of GMO Crops*, http://arstechnica.com/tech-policy/2013/06/organic-farmers-cant-fight-monsanto-patents-in-court/

Mulvany, P. M. (2001) 'Knowing agricultural biodiversity', in B. Gemmill (ed.), *Managing Agricultural Resources for Biodiversity Conservation*, National Biodiversity Planning Tools, ELCI/UNEP-GEF, www.ukabc.org/knowagbiod.pdf, accessed January 2014.

Mulvany, P. M. (2005) 'Corporate control over seeds: Limiting access and farmers' rights', *IDS Bulletin*, vol. 36 (2), www.future-agricultures.org/pdf%20files/9559%20IDS%20P68-73.pdf

Mulvany, P. M. (2009) 'Agriculture at a crossroads: A summary of the IAASTD findings', *Agriculture for Development*, Autumn, 2008, www.ukfg.org.uk/docs/IAASTD_Ag4DevAutumn2008Final.pdf

Mulvany, P. M. and Ensor, J. (2011) 'Changing a dysfunctional food system: Towards ecological food provision in the framework of food sovereignty', *Food Chain*, vol. 1, pp. 34–51.

Nyeleni (2007a) *Declaration of Nyéléni, Nyéléni 2007: Forum for Food Sovereignty*, Sélingué, Mali, www.nyeleni.org/IMG/pdf/DeclNyeleni-en.pdf

Nyeleni (2007b) *Synthesis Report, Nyéléni 2007: Forum for Food Sovereignty*, Sélingué, Mali, www.nyeleni.org/IMG/pdf/31Mar2007NyeleniSynthesisReport-en.pdf

Nyéléni (2015) www.foodsovereignty.org/forum-agroecology-nyeleni-2015/

Pimbert, M. (2006) *Transforming Knowledge and Ways of Knowing for Food Sovereignty and Bio-Cultural Diversity*, IIED, http://pubs.iied.org/pdfs/G01098.pdf

Pimentel, D., Hepperly, P., Hanson, J., Douds, D. and Seidel, R. (2005) 'Environmental, energetic, and economic comparisons of organic and conventional farming systems', *Bioscience*, vol. 55, pp. 573–582.

Platform for Agrobiodiversity Research (PAR) and FAO (2011) *Biodiversity for Food and Agriculture: Contributing to Food Security and Sustainability in a Changing World*, FAO, Rome, Italy, www.fao.org/fileadmin/templates/biodiversity_paia/PAR-FAO-book_lr.pdf, accessed January 2014.

Rahmanian, M. (2013) *Biodiversity and Livelihoods: From Single Varieties to "Mega-Populations"*, CENESTA, Iran, www.fao.org/fileadmin/templates/nr/documents/CGRFA/SIS_BFA_Biodiversity_and_livelihood.pdf

Secretariat of the Convention on Biological Diversity (SCBD) (2014) *Global Biodiversity Outlook 4 (GBO-4)*, SCBD, Montréal, Canada.

Shand, H. (1997). *Human Nature: Agricultural Biodiversity and Farm-Based Food Security*, RAFI/FAO, Rome, Italy, www.etcgroup.org/content/human-nature-agricultural-biodiversity-and-farm-based-food-security

Shiva, S., Barker, D. and Lockhart, C. (2011) *The GMO Emperor Has No Clothes: A Global Citizens' Report on the State of GMOs: False Promises, Failed Technologies*, Navdanya International, Florence, Italy.

Shiva, V., Bhar, R. H. and Jafri, A. H. (2002) *Corporate Hijack of Biodiversity: How WTO-TRIPs Rules Promote Corporate Hijack of People's Biodiversity and knowledge*, Biodiversity and Seed Sovereignty, Navdanya, India, http://navdanya.org/attachments/Biodiversity_and_Seed_Sovereignty4.pdf

Stickland, S. (2001) *Back Garden Seed Saving: Keeping Our Vegetable Heritage Alive*, HDRA, Eco-logic Books, Bath, UK.

Tansey, G. and Rajotte, T. (eds.) (2008) *The Future Control Of Food: A Guide to International Negotiations and Rules on Intellectual Property, Biodiversity, and Food Security*, Earthscan for Routledge/IDRC, Abingdon, UK.

UK Food Group (UKFG) (2010) *Securing Future Food: Towards Ecological Food Provision*, UKFG, London, UK, www.ukfg.org.uk/securing_future_food_publication/

United Nations Conference on Trade and Development (UNCTAD) (2013) *Wake Up before It Is Too Late: Make Agriculture Truly Sustainable Now for Food Security in a Changing Climate*, UNCTAD, Trade and Environment Review 2013, http://unctad.org/en/PublicationsLibrary/ditcted2012d3_en.pdf

Via Campesina (2013a) *Our Seeds, Our Future: Notebook #6*, La Via Campesina, Jakarta, Indonesia, http://viacampesina.org/downloads/pdf/en/EN-notebook6.pdf

Via Campesina (2013b) *African Declaration on Peasant Seeds*, La Via Campesina, Harare, Pakistan, http://viacampesina.org/en/index.php/main-issues-mainmenu-27/biodiversity-and-genetic-resources-mainmenu-37/1519-defending-peasant-seeds-is-fighting-for-our-right-to-life

Windfuhr, M. and Jonsén, J. (2005) *Food Sovereignty: Towards Democracy in Localised Food Systems*, ITDG, FIAN-International, www.ukabc.org/foodsovpaper.htm.

Wint, W. and Robinson, T. (2007) *Gridded Livestock of the World 2007*, FAO, Rome, Italy.

World Health Organization and Secretariat of the Convention on Biological Diversity (2015). *Connecting Global Priorities: 'Biodiversity and Human Health: A State of Knowledge Review*, WHO/SCBD.

# INDEX

Note: Page numbers in italic indicate a figure and page numbers in bold indicate a table on the corresponding page.